Allianz
The Power On Your Side

GW00801735

MEMBER
General Insurance
STANDARDS COUNCIL

NORTHERN IRELAND YEARBOOK 2004

A Comprehensive Reference Guide to the Political, Economic and Social Life of Northern Ireland

Written and Produced by Lagan Consulting 028 9261 3216
Editor: Michael McKernan
Public Affairs Editor: Owen McQuade
Research Manager: Sandra Dane
Design: Gareth Duffy

Published by bmf Publishing
76 Main Street
Moira
Co. Down, BT67 0LQ
028 9261 9933

Distribution and Marketing by tSO Ireland
16 Arthur Street
Belfast, BT1 4GD
028 9023 5401

Print Management by The Northern Whig, Belfast

ISBN: 0-9537672-9-9

A Comprehensive Guide to Northern Ireland

Foreword

Welcome to the third edition of the Northern Ireland Yearbook - a comprehensive guide to the social economic and political life of Northern Ireland. It remains the only substantial book published that draws together all strands of public life in Northern Ireland and presents detailed information in a useful and insightful format.

We have increased the print run significantly and feel we are getting closer to our goal of ensuring that the book features in the offices of most organisations in Northern Ireland, public, private and voluntary sectors and specifically on the desks of all of Northern Ireland's top decision makers. We are also making the Yearbook available in all libraries, schools and institutions as well as in high street bookshops.

This year most chapters have been expanded in scope and detail and we have added a new lifestyle and leisure chapter. There is also a uniquely detailed and insightful guide to the recent 2003 Northern Ireland Assembly election.

It is entirely right that Northern Ireland should have its own substantial yearbook covering the full political, economic and social spectrum, and we are determined to make this publication a model of its kind. I hope you find this a useful and satisfying addition to your library or office.

Michael McKernan
Editor

Acknowledgments

The authors and publishers owe a debt of gratitude to many people who have contributed their advice and efforts to this substantial publication. Firstly we are indebted to the suppliers of copyright material incorporated into parts of the Yearbook, in particular the Ordnance Survey (OSNI), the Northern Ireland Statistical Research Agency (NISRA), Ulster Business, the Northern Ireland Tourist Board (NITB) and Translink. We have made every effort to ensure that permission has been obtained for all copyrighted material used, and to attribute the source. If there is any lapse in this respect it is entirely accidental.

We are also very appreciative of those whose photographs adorn the Yearbook, particularly the Northern Ireland Tourist Board, Kingdoms of Down and The National Trust and the political parties and those organisations and individuals who supplied their own material. (All photographic sources are acknowledged specifically below).

Thanks are due also to the many individuals who helped with the compilation of Chapter 3 including the listings of Civil Servants and other officials and appointees. The result, while by no means complete, remains the most comprehensive presentation of Northern Ireland's senior Civil Service ever produced. Thanks also to all the communications managers in local councils who helped ensure a high level of accuracy in the Local Government Chapter of the book.

We would like to acknowledge also the many expert individuals who contributed their advice and wisdom to the publication including politicians, leading economists, educationalists and health professionals. Hopefully the book does them justice.

Finally thanks are due to all the 'hands-on' people who worked so hard to actually produce the 2003 Yearbook. The team at Lagan Consulting, Owen, for all the government insight, Sharon and Sandra for research and production, Gareth for all the long hours of design work. Paula and Dan for managing the advertising and the group of checkers and proof readers. Thanks also to Dan, Michael and Nicola at TSO; Peter and Trevor at Northern Whig, Russell at Ulster Business and all other contributors and advertisers.

Photographs

Photographic Sources* (page nos)

Belfast City Council (8,200,502)
Hilda Winter (11)
Northern Ireland Tourist Board (22,234,519,520,522,545,558)
Lisburn City Council (24,525,527,559)
Omagh District Council (25)
Dungannon & South Tyrone Borough Council (25)
Northern Ireland Assembly (48)
Police Service of Northern Ireland (138)
Forest Service (193,566)
Kingdoms of Down (471,561,562,563,568)
Irish News (517)
CCEA (316,331)
The National Trust (532)
Belfast City Airport (535)
Seacat (537)
Translink (537,538,540,541,542,543)
Fermanagh Tourist Information Centre (545)
Hastings Hotels (547,551)
Jury's Inn (548)
Park Avenue Hotel (380, 548)
Hilton Templepatrick (549)
Linen Hall Library (557)
Derry Visitor & Convention Bureau (565)
The Linen Green (566)
Grand Orange Lodge of Ireland (13)
Premier Power (352)
Galen, Portadown (357)
Peter Morrison (448)

* Excludes bmf business services private portfolio

Contents

Chapter

The Place and Its People

Northern Ireland: A Brief History

Northern Ireland is a relatively young political entity, having been created in 1920 by the Government of Ireland Act, which partitioned Ireland into two separate jurisdictions. Each was awarded their own executive and Home Rule parliament; a 26 county Southern Ireland was given relative independence but the remaining six counties of Armagh, Antrim, Down, Fermanagh, Londonderry and Tyrone were retained within the United Kingdom, establishing their own devolved administration. Despite its relative brevity, Northern Ireland's history has been coloured with conflict and controversy, characterised by deep and festering divisions between its people, based largely on issues of religion and nationality. In very general terms the division is thus: the Protestant or unionist community look to Britain for political parentage, whilst the Catholic or nationalist community believe ultimately in a unified Irish Republic independent for Britian.

The debate over the terminology used to refer to Northern Ireland is itself indicative of the difficulties inherent in providing an objective commentary on its past. Because Northern Ireland is composed of only six of the nine counties of the ancient Irish province of Ulster, use of the terms "Ulster", or the "Province" is perceived as inaccurate by nationalists. They tend to prefer "Six Counties" or "the north of Ireland" which in turn often irritates unionists. This example highlights how events, which to an outside observer seem clear-cut and straightforward can be interpreted by different people in different ways. It is generally accepted that no presentation of facts can be considered universally objective. The representation of Northern Ireland's history which follows here may therefore be perceived as too 'orange' or too 'green', depending on the sensitivities of the reader; it has however been intended as neither.

Pre-Christian Era

The early history of Ireland as a whole is shrouded in semi-myth and legend; indeed anything before around 500AD is extremely difficult to prove. Historians estimate that the Celts came to Ireland from the Rhine and Danube areas in Europe, around 400 BC. They introduced the Gaelic language, along with their own culture and beliefs. Only culture and language unified Celtic Ireland at this stage: the country was divided into about 150 small communities (tuatha). A king ruled each tuath, and an overking ruled a group of tuatha. Similarly, a group of overkings would hold allegiance to a provincial king. Ireland was roughly divided into five provinces: Ulster, Munster, Leinster, Connacht and Mide, although the number and precise boundaries of provinces were in a constant state of flux. The rulers of Ireland fought each other frequently, and while individual leaders variously assumed the title of "High King" of Ireland, no one person ruled all of Ireland at this time. According to legend, in 300 BC High King Fiachadh founded the Fianna. This was the military elite of Ireland, charged with guarding the High King, although at first it is said to have been a somewhat undisciplined and incoherent group. This changed with the arrival of Fionn mac Cumhail, more commonly known as Finn MacCool who is celebrated as the Fianna's greatest ever leader. Finn challenged the Fianna to become champions of the people, and implemented a code of honour, chivalry and justice.

There are many legends surrounding Finn MacCool and the Fianna; one of the most famous gives an account of the creation of the "Giant's Causeway", a hexagonal-shaped volcanic rock formation on the north coast of Ireland, which has become Northern Ireland's most popular visitor attraction. A Scottish giant angered Finn by questioning his fighting ability, but was unable to accept the resulting challenge because he could not swim to Ireland. The story says that Finn tore great strips of rock from the coast, and made them into pillars to stretch from Ireland to Scotland. The giant was forced to cross over to Ireland, and Finn chased him back to Scotland, flinging huge chunks of earth at him. The biggest crater caused by this flooded with water and became Lough Neagh, the largest lake in Ireland or Britain, whilst a huge lump of earth fell into the Irish Sea and became the Isle of Man. A similar myth tells how Ulster got its symbol, the Red Hand. Two chiefs, one of whom was of the ancient House of O'Neill, disputed ownership of a piece of land (often claimed to be Ulster). The dispute was to be settled by a race: the chiefs would sail to the shore, and whoever touched it first with his right hand would win the land. O'Neill saw his opponent leading and about to step out of his boat, and so he cut off his right hand with his sword and threw it onto the shore, thus winning the contest.

Perhaps the most famous Ulster hero from the early period is Cu Chulainn, said to have been born around 500 BC. His name was originally Setanta, but as a young man he accidentally killed the guard dog of Culainn, a local warrior, who was distraught at its loss. Setanta took the dog's place to guard Culainn, and was thereafter known as Cu Chulainn, the Hound of Culainn. Cu Chulainn led the so-called "Red Branch" of Ulster warriors, mainly against forces led by Queen Maeve of Connacht.

Early Christian Era

The Celts followed a religion based on natural phenomena and related spiritual beliefs until the introduction of Christianity to Ireland, during the 5th century AD. The establishment of Christianity in Ireland is accredited to St. Patrick, although he was by no means the first Christian in Ireland. St Patrick is believed to have been born in western Britain, possibly Wales; a Romanised Celt who was kidnapped and sold into slavery in Ireland. Patrick eventually escaped to the Continent, where he studied for the priesthood until he decided to return to Ireland, traditionally dated 432 AD.

Armagh, once a site associated with pagan rituals, became the centre of Christianity in Ireland after St Patrick supposedly received a cauldron from a powerful Druid (Celtic priest), but angered the druid by saying just a small word of thanks. When the druid demanded the cauldron back, Patrick said the same word of thanks, which induced the druid to repent, giving Patrick not only the cauldron back, but also a piece of land on

Belfast City Centre

which to build a church. Armagh still remains the ecclesiastical capital of Ireland, with both Catholic and Church of Ireland cathedrals built on two hilltops overlooking the city. Ireland, north and south, has a plethora of churches named after the island's patron saint. Probably one of the best-known legends about St Patrick is his supposed banishment of all snakes from Ireland. This is probably a metaphor for Patrick's having banished the "demons of paganism", as it had arguably been documented two centuries earlier that Ireland had no indigenous snakes. 1500 years later, St Patrick has become a symbol of both inspiration and division within Northern Ireland today. He is Ireland's patron saint, celebrated on his feast day, 17th March, by Irish people across the globe. However, in Northern Ireland St Patrick is viewed in different ways. To the majority of Catholics and nationalists, he is a Catholic saint on account of his having been in Ireland long before the Protestant Reformation. The Protestant and unionist majority in Northern Ireland, however, tend to waver between rejecting the saint, and embracing him as a British preacher who civilised the native Irish. Both communities lay claim to St Patrick's final resting place: either at Saul, near Downpatrick (the Catholic view), or in the grounds of Downpatrick Church of Ireland Cathedral (the Protestant belief).

Saul Monument, Downpatrick

A distinctive feature of the development of early Christianity was the role of monasticism. During the Dark Ages (500-800 AD) religion and scholarship almost disappeared in other European countries, largely as a result of barbarian invasions that did not reach Ireland. Irish monks established communities all over Europe, such as those at St Fursey at Peronne in France and St Columbanus at Bobbio in Italy. In the early centuries AD, missionary success was complemented by Ireland's cultural achievements. Ornate chalices and jewellery were created, while scribes produced magnificently illuminated manuscripts. The Book of Kells is the most famous example, begun around 800 AD. Its name derives from the Abbey of Kells, Co Meath, its home until 1541, although it was probably begun on the island of Iona, between Ireland and Scotland. The Book of Kells marks what many have called the Golden Age of Irish history, the period when Ireland was the "land of saints and scholars". The Book of Kells is now permanently on display at Trinity College, Dublin, where a page is turned every day.

From around 800 AD Ireland was initially attacked and then settled by Vikings, raiders and traders from Northern Europe, who founded Dublin, Limerick, Cork and Waterford. Ireland's disunity made the country vulnerable to attacks, and the southern half was conquered easily, while the relative strength of the O'Neill dynasty of kings enabled the northern half to withstand assault. Towards the end of the 10th century Brian Boru became king of Munster, and engaged the Vikings in a battle, which they were ultimately to lose. At the turn of the century Boru gained control of the whole country and was crowned High King of all Ireland. For the first time the country was united under his leadership. After Brian Boru's death in 1014 other Irish kings sought to follow his example; the trend was towards the development of a strong, centralised monarchy, as seen elsewhere in Europe, until the arrival of Norman forces in 1167-9. Brian Boru's grave may still be visited in Armagh City to this day.

The first Normans in Ireland were effectively mercenaries, invited to assist the King of Leinster in his claim to the High Kingship in 1169. Their leader, Richard de Clare, nicknamed Strongbow, succeeded the Leinster throne, and in 1171 the Normans' overlord, Henry II of England, declared himself overlord of the whole of Ireland. Led by John de Courcy, Normans settled in many parts of Ireland, establishing similar systems of law, parliament and administration as they had in England. Norman influence in Ireland was never as strong as it had been in England following the battle of Hastings in 1066; the Normans tended to assimilate themselves into Irish culture, rather than the other way round. French names gradually evolved into Irish forms, for example de Burgh became Burke, and the prefix Fils became Fitz, as in FitzGerald and FitzWilliam.

Meanwhile, the native Gaelic population remained numerically strong and the people intermarried with the Normans. By 1500 English control (previously Norman) had receded to a small area around Dublin called "the Pale", as Normans in Ireland became increasingly integrated. The modern expression "beyond the pale" refers to this time, when everything outside the Pale area was considered dangerous and uncivilised. It is interesting that, despite colonising Ireland, the Normans eventually came to be described as "more Irish than the Irish".

The Plantation of Ulster

From the 16th century English Tudor monarchs began a further conquest of Ireland. Henry VIII became the first English ruler to declare himself king of Ireland in 1541 but the most significant event in the development of the modern Northern Ireland could be said to be the Plantation of Ulster. This involved the systematic introduction of large numbers of English and Scottish settlers, designed to establish English rule and control the native Irish. Mary I was the first English monarch to attempt plantation, mainly in Ulster, from 1556, but it was left to her successor, Elizabeth I, to secure Ireland. Land was taken from the native population and redistributed to settlers, often as a reward for services rendered in Britain. This process was not transacted without resistance: by 1594 Hugh O'Neill, Earl of Ulster, had united the ruling families of the north of Ireland, and begun a rebellion against the English crown that was to last nine years. O'Neill was strengthened by some assistance from Spain, traditional enemies of England, but the battle of Kinsale in 1601 was decisive in quashing the uprising. This was the first time that England had ever established control over the whole of Ireland, and in 1603 O'Neill and other rebellious Gaelic nobles fled to France (an event known as the "Flight of the Earls").

Having united the English and Scottish thrones, King James I continued with the plantation of Armagh, Derry, Cavan, Donegal, Tyrone and Fermanagh, later adding Down and Antrim. In 1613 James I formed the new county of "Londonderry", renaming the ancient city by royal charter. The Honourable The Irish Society in London paid for defensive walls to be erected around the city, which was to serve as headquarters for many of the society's commercial projects.

The British government invited their people to settle throughout Ulster, and many skilled and industrious people did just that. The skill and motivation of many English and French Huguenots formed the basis of a linen industry that was eventually to become the biggest in the world. From being the poorest province of Ireland, Ulster gradually became the most prosperous. Its place as the most industrialised region of Ireland continued until relatively recent times and it was accepted by many as being largely attributable to the British influence on this part of the country.

The influx into the province of Protestant colonists, primarily Presbyterians from Scotland, meant that Ulster became the only part of Ireland where the Protestant religion was established with any real success. As with the Normans some centuries earlier, the Ulster-Scots settlers brought their own culture, the difference being that, unlike the Normans, Ulster-Scots tended to retain their distinct identity rather than integrate themselves into the native culture. In fact the settlers were emphatic in celebrating their religious freedoms which in the case of Presbyterians and non-conformists had been a right denied to them by the king who was head of the establishment Church of England.

Two separate cultural, political and religious identities began to emerge in the north of Ireland: the vast majority of native Irish people were Catholic, and held their allegiance to their native Ireland, whilst Protestant settlers, including Anglican, Methodist and other denominations, considered themselves loyal to Britain. It is argued by many that the Plantation was the event in which much of today's conflict has its roots.

Seventeenth Century Conflict

The 17th century English civil war between Charles I and Parliament also had far-reaching consequences in Ireland.

King Billy

Oliver Cromwell, leader of the victorious parliamentary forces, maintained the English presence in Ireland and consolidated his success in Britain by quashing ensuing Irish rebellions. Following Cromwell's military success, the 1653 Act of Settlement involved large-scale confiscation of land. Further colonisation ensured that property and political power passed to loyal Protestants: before 1641, Catholics owned about three-fifths of the land; by the 1680s, they owned one-fifth of it. However, many Catholics did not and had never owned land, and were tenants or serfs already. For them, the change was in landlord and in attitude towards them, but they perceived themselves and their people as dispossessed.

The accession of the Catholic James II to the British throne in 1685 sparked a new wave of discord in Ireland. The Protestant aristocracy in Britain vehemently opposed the Catholic king who sought to expand his power at their expense. On being deposed, James fled to Ireland, where he found support everywhere apart from the Protestant community in the north. In what have become famous historical events, the predominantly Protestant towns of Derry and Enniskillen closed their gates against James and defied his authority. In the face of a strong military force the governor of Derry, Robert Lundy, was initially prepared to negotiate with James, but Lundy was overthrown and the gates remained closed. In modern-day loyalist circles the name Lundy has become synonymous with 'traitor', and every year his effigy is ritually burned on loyalist bonfires across Northern Ireland in a celebration of the famous siege. James besieged Derry for three months but failed to breach the city's fortified walls. On account of this, Derry became known as "the Maiden City".

The British throne, meanwhile, had been offered to a Protestant Dutch prince, William of Orange, as part of a pan-European coalition (supported by the Pope) against the dominant, Catholic French king Louis XIV. William followed James to Ireland as part of a Europe-wide conflict, and fought a number of battles, most notably the militarily decisive Battle of Aughrim and the less significant but more famous Battle of the Boyne in 1690. The Catholic population supported James, who had been sympathetic to their situation, while Protestant settlers (some of whose families had lived in Ireland for several generations) sided with William. The war ended in victory for William and subsequently brought the longest peace that Ulster had ever known. Today "Protestant King Billy" is a loyalist hero, and is depicted on many Orange banners and also in street murals across the province. Like the Siege of Derry, the Battle of the Boyne has been celebrated enthusiastically by many within the Ulster Protestant community as part of Orange Order demonstrations. The anthem of Ulster loyalism, "The Sash", refers to an Orange sash (still a symbol of the Orange Order) being worn in "Derry, Aughrim, Enniskillen and the Boyne", although the Orange Order itself was not actually founded until a century later.

Throughout the 18th century Catholics throughout the British Isles were perceived as a potential threat to the Protestant monarchy, and Ireland in particular was considered a platform for the creation of instability in Britain. Despite the Plantation the Protestant establishment remained a minority in Ireland, although Scots Presbyterians in Ulster had risen in strength alongside the established Church of Ireland (Anglican) ascendancy. A series of Penal Laws were passed which kept the bulk of the Catholic population in a state of relative poverty and without many of the most basic civil rights. As the Penal Laws applied to all non-Anglicans, Presbyterians in Ulster were also denied full civil rights, though to a somewhat lesser extent. This meant that members of the Established Church were the chief beneficiaries of Ulster's newfound prosperity.

By 1782, British rule in Ireland was stable enough to allow the Westminster government to grant full legislative independence to the Irish Parliament (Grattan's Parliament), effectively making Ireland a separate kingdom sharing the British monarch as head of state (although the Dublin administration would be directly appointed by the British king).

Towards the end of the eighteenth century the British government also began to relax the Penal Laws and proposed Catholic Emancipation (repeal of some of the anti-Catholic legislation) in 1795.

Late 18th century Co Armagh land skirmishes between Protestant Peep o' Day Boys and Catholic Defenders, which culminated in the Battle of the Diamond in September 1795, led to the formation of the Orange Order in Dan Winter's Cottage in Loughgall. The Order was created primarily as a Protestant defence association in support of the British King and the wider Protestant Ascendancy. It had the aim of galvanising the minority Protestant population against rising Catholic power and confidence. The Order, taking its name from William of Orange two or three generations earlier, was oathbound, making use of passwords and signs and was comprised mainly of Protestant weaver-farmers, with initially very few members from the landed gentry. Apart from economic and other considerations the members of the Orange Order feared the historical authoritarianism of Catholicism, and saw the Order as a vehicle for preserving Protestant liberties.

Dan Winter's Cottage

Orangemen formed associations know as lodges throughout Ireland (although it was predominant in the North) and organised marches to commemorate the Battle of the Boyne and other events; these marches often led to rioting between Catholics and Protestants. By 1836 the British government had banned Orange marches on account of the rioting that followed, but this ban was defied from 1849 onwards. Over the years the Orange Order founded lodges all over the world with the "Twelfth of July", the historical date of the Battle of the Boyne, becoming the focal point for Orange parades.

Act of Union to the Land War

The United Irishmen, formed in 1791, was a revolutionary group of idealists, inspired by the thinking behind the French Revolution, who aimed to unite Catholic, Protestant and Dissenter against British rule. Inspired as much by radical Protestant liberals as by Catholics, and led by Theobald Wolfe Tone and Lord Edward Fitzgerald the United Irishmen attempted a rebellion against Britain in 1798. Despite French assistance the rebellion, which was accompanied by a smaller uprising in Ulster, was easily suppressed. One result of which was to strengthen the case (which had been growing in the minds of British politicians since the early 1770s) for a legislative union between Britain and Ireland, on the grounds that Ireland represented a security threat to Britain. The idea was opposed by many and varied groups throughout the country (including representatives from Dublin commerce, the law, country gentlemen and the Orange Order) however due to the unrepresentative nature of the Irish parliament and the strength of the Unionist position at Westminster, their arguments had little impact. It took just over a year (and the distribution of much political patronage) to persuade the Irish parliament to vote itself out of existence and the Act of Union took effect from 1 January 1801.

Under the terms of the Act of Union, all Irish parliamentary business was conducted at Westminster with Ireland represented in the new united parliament by 100 MPs who were actually more representative of the Irish population than their predecessors in the Irish parliament had been. The Catholic community, however, remained largely excluded from politics, both in terms of the right to vote and the right to stand for parliament. Various Catholic relief bills were rejected by both the House of Commons and the House of Lords in the early 19th century and proponents of the issue remained largely divided until the 1820s and the formation of the Catholic Association under lawyer Daniel O'Connell.

O'Connell made membership of the Association accessible to everyone with associate membership costing just a penny a month. By mobilising those few Catholics who did have the right to vote, along with liberal Protestant sympathisers, O'Connell was successful in getting first his supporters, and then himself, elected to parliament. The government was faced with the fact that O'Connell had been elected, but due to the nature of the constitution was unable to take his seat, a situation they realised could quickly lead to an uprising in Ireland. In response, parliament passed an emancipation bill in 1829, opening the way to Catholic participation in parliament and to public office.

In the late 1840s Ireland suffered enormous hardship due to the "Great Famine", precipitated by successive failures of the potato crop, upon which Ireland's labouring poor were dependent as their staple foodstuff. The Famine devastated many parts of Ireland, causing many of its survivors to emigrate, and the population of the island fell from almost 8 million to around 4 million, a combination of death by starvation and disease, and emigration. The industrialised northeast was less affected by this struggle than the rest of Ireland because tenant farming was not the sole local economy, although the Famine and the failure of government to bring adequate relief was an issue of grievance throughout the island .

The Famine had a profound impact on not just the Irish population but the entire way of life. Death, migration and eviction of the very poorest cottiers and labourers, combined with the financial difficulties experienced by the gentry led to the dominance of the farmer class in Irish agricultural society. This trend was accompanied by a change in farming methods with a move away from tillage towards animal husbandry and pastoral farming. Living standards for those who remained also rose with real wages increasing and housing stock and literacy levels improving. In political terms, the most enduring legacy of the Famine was the way in which it highlighted the problems with the Irish land system and popularised the struggle which became associated with these. It was via the land issue that the issue of Irish nationalism came again to the fore towards the end of the 19th century.

Home Rule

It was out of the struggle for land reform in the 1870s and 1880s that the movement for 'home government', in the form of restoration of an Irish parliament, gained support, firstly under the leadership of Isaac Butt and then Charles Stuart Parnell. Parnell was successful in creating a modern, highly disciplined political party, the Irish Parliamentary Party, which had Home Rule as its first objective. By 1886, the IPP had won enough seats at Westminster to hold the 'balance of power' thereby forcing Gladstone to introduce a Home Rule Bill in order to restore the Liberal party to power.

Although Parnell had won 85 Westminster seats in Ireland, including a majority of those in Ulster, Home Rule enjoyed far from universal support, both within parliamentary circles and outside. A huge number of Gladstone's own party voted with the opposition to defeat the Bill, a move which was applauded loudly in Ulster and which actually led to the worst riots of the 19th century in Belfast, as Protestants asserted their victory over their Catholic neighbours and colleagues.

By the late nineteenth century Belfast had become a prosperous and growing city, and in 1891 bypassed Dublin to become the largest city in Ireland. In terms of industry Belfast had become renowned worldwide for its linen, engineering, aerated waterworks, tobacco works, distilleries and shipyards. In fact Belfast's shipbuilding and engineering prowess captured the imagination of the world in the form of the most famous ship in history, Titanic, which was built at the Belfast shipyard, Harland and Wolff. Although her maiden voyage ended in disaster, Titanic still brings recognition to Belfast, and to a yard that at its peak employed over 30,000 men on site.

Belfast's industrial and commercial success and the prosperity of the north east of Ulster in general, was largely attributable to its strong links with Britain. Coal and raw materials for Belfast's industries came from mainland Britain, and it was Britain and the Empire which were the destination for many of the province's manufactured goods. Increasingly, this prosperous region was unwilling to be subsumed into a larger but poorer, nationalist Ireland. It was widely felt that a Dublin parliament, dominated by the landed interest, would impose heavy taxes on northern industry and introduce protective tariffs to promote southern self-sufficiency. Economic fears and religious and cultural differences combined to ensure that the suggestion of Home Rule for Ireland, or indeed any degree of self-rule by the Irish, was, met with what ranged from vociferous opposition to, at times, civil unrest in Ulster.

It was in opposition to Home Rule that Conservatives in Ireland organised themselves into a coherent Unionist grouping, under the leadership of Ulster landowner Sir Edward Saunderson. This group enjoyed the support of prominent British Conservatives and was successful in seeing Gladstone's Second Home Rule Bill defeated in the House of Lords in 1893.

The Home Rule issue, although in hibernation for almost twenty years re-emerged on the political agenda in 1910, when the Irish Parliamentary Party, under the leadership of John Redmond, was again able to force the Liberals to support Home Rule. The 1911 Parliament Bill reduced the power of the House of Lords to delaying legislation for two years so that when Asquith introduced the Third Home Rule Bill in April 1912 it seemed certain to become law by 1914. Sure in the knowledge that the permanent Conservative majority in the Lords would never accept Home Rule, Unionists had, in 1886 and 1893 been content to confine their objections to Irish self-government to parliamentary means. By 1912, it had become clear that they could only depend on themselves to defend against any Home Rule measure and began to make provisions for less constitutional means of opposition.

Covenant Day, September 1912

Under the leadership of Dublin lawyer Sir Edward Carson and Ulster whiskey millionaire James Craig, Unionist resistance to Home Rule was organised. Preparations were made for a Unionist Provisional Government to come into effect with the passage of any measure of Home Rule; mass demonstrations were organised in Ulster and in Britain; the Solemn League and

Covenant was signed, by some in their own blood; the Ulster Volunter Force (UVF) formed and drilling began; guns were brought into Ulster by night. Unionists were showing themselves to be serious in their opposition to Home Rule.

Nationalists were, at the same time, showing themselves to be just as serious in their pursuit of their long-time political objective. An Irish Volunteer Force was formed in opposition to 'Carson's Army' and guns were brought by night into Howth, just as they had been into Larne several months earlier.

Despite all this sabre-rattling, negotiations were ongoing in the period 1912-14 to try and find a peaceful resolution to the Home Rule crisis. Despite Carson's reluctance as a Southern Unionist, as time went on it became increasingly obvious that Unionists could only, realistically, hope to 'save' Ulster from the fate of Home Rule. Their minority was too small to have any hope of preventing the measure taking effect for the rest of Ireland and they preferred to retain an area that they could easily control. By the spring of 1914 the idea of partition seemed to have been accepted in principle by many of the parties concerned. Divisions did however still exist on the precise nature of any agreement which excluded some Ulster counties from Home Rule and focused on whether exclusion should be permanent and to how many counties it should apply.

Partition

Thus was the situation with the outbreak of World War I in August 1914. Redmond gave his support to the war effort in return for a promise of Home Rule at the end of the war. Although passed on 18 September 1914, Home Rule was suspended for the duration of the war when amending legislation would make special provision for Ulster. Attempts by Lloyd-George to reach a solution during the war came to nothing and when the issue was re-visited at the end of the international conflict the result was the 1920 Government of Ireland Act, which effectively combined the principles of Home Rule with those of Unionism, creating a six-county Northern Ireland and a 26-county Southern Ireland, each with their own executive and parliament. The powers of the two new jurisdictions were initially limited and provision was made, in the shape of the Council of Ireland, for their amalgamation. This body was never to meet, however and Northern Ireland was there to stay. The Irish 'War of Independence' was fought in the south in the period 1919-21 and led to the signing of the Anglo-Irish Treaty in December 1921, whereby the remaining 26 counties were given the name Irish Free State and dominion status within the British Empire.

The 1920 Government of Ireland Act led to the formation of Northern Ireland as a new political entity. The new jurisdiction was made up of the six north-eastern counties of Antrim, Armagh, Down, Fermanagh, Londonderry and Tyrone. Following elections in May 1921, the first parliament of Northern Ireland was opened on 7 June 1921 by King George V in the Council Chamber of Belfast City Hall, where a Unionist Party government, headed by James Craig was sworn in.

The new government (which became known as the Stormont government, after the splendid new building in which it sat after 1932) was from the outset dominated by the Ulster Unionist Party. Its executive comprised seven departments, headed by the Department of the Prime Minister, which maintained a central co-ordinating role with Westminster and across the six other local ministries of Finance, Home Affairs, Labour, Education, Agriculture and Commerce.

The new Northern Ireland Parliament consisted of two chambers. The first, a 52 member House of Commons, the second, a Senate, consisting of 26 members all elected by the lower chamber except for the two ex-officio seats held by the Lord Mayor of Belfast and the Mayor of Londonderry. Although Northern Ireland was given its own devolved government, Section 75 of the Government of Ireland Act 1920 specified that the supreme authority of the UK parliament would continue. In addition, to continue the formal presence of the monarch in the most peripheral region of the United Kingdom, the office of Governor of Northern Ireland was created under the Act.

From the outset the powers of the new government were clearly defined. All powers relating to defence, armed forces and foreign policy were retained by Westminster and the powers of the northern Government were limited in relation to taxation, with Westminster reserving the power to raise income tax and customs and excise duties.

The continuation of political conflict for several years following the 1921 Treaty of Independence in the South (the Irish Civil War) meant that the anticipated reunification of the two administrations, North and South, did not occur. The Institutions established under the first Craig Government continued relatively uninterrupted until the Second World War with Craig's Ulster Unionist party permanently in government.

The First Northern Ireland Government

The new Northern Ireland government had a less than auspicious start, facing threats and difficulties from every direction. Internally, it had to cope with sectarian rioting which in the period 1920-22 killed 455 and wounded 1766 people in Belfast alone. By the end of 1920 7,400 people had been driven from their jobs and nearly 23,000 from their homes. This was a situation the new administration found difficult to contain since although having responsibility, it was largely devoid of power to act.

Craig also felt his new state faced an external threat from the Free State Army, a fear which was in part confirmed in May 1922 when Irish troops occupied a triangle of land at Belleek on the Co Fermanagh border and defeated the local Ulster Special Constabulary garrison.

From the outset, the Stormont government was also beset with financial difficulties. Its allocation of funds from Westminster were based on the boom years of 1920-21 which showed that the Northern Ireland government would have a surplus of £2.5 million but in reality the situation was the opposite and the Finance Minister experienced an almost permanent shortfall. Most of the money allocated to Northern Ireland was actually collected by the London Treasury, and only 'handed over' after the imperial contribution and other levies for legal and customs services were deducted. The result in Northern Ireland was uncertainty as to how much money the government would get each year which made budgeting difficult. This was all at a time when Northern Ireland's unemployment rate averaged 19% as a result of the decline of traditional industries in Belfast.

Despite all this the most immediate threat that the new political entity faced in its first few years came in the shape of the Boundary Commission. In the course of negotiations over the Anglo-Irish Treaty in 1921, which had created the Boundary Commission, Lloyd-George had assured Craig that only minor territorial changes would take place whilst leading the Free State side to believe that huge areas would change hands. It wasn't until 1925 that it was decided that no changes would be made and Northern Ireland would be left as it was.

The situation in Northern Ireland was not made any easier by the lack of experience of government ministers. Only Craig had had previous government experience, most of the rest of the posts were allocated as a reward for political service and not necessarily on any basis of suitability or fitness to perform their job. This was compounded by the fact that there had been no pre-planning for a Home Rule parliament in Northern Ireland.

Sometimes criticism of individual ministers for their uninspired style of government can be harsh, considering the atmosphere in which they tried to function when every policy or initiative was subject to accusations of partisanship or sectarianism. One such example was Lord Londonderry's 1923 Education Act which made provision for the establishment of a non-sectarian, secular system of education. Ironically this came under attack from both the Catholic Church (as it took the education of Catholic children out of exclusively Catholic hands) and the Protestant community because it didn't make compulsory the teaching of a programme of Protestant Bible instruction by teachers. The largely 'segregated' system of primary and secondary education that exists today evolved from Church actions rather than by any design of the state.

Signs of Discontent...

With the Ulster Unionist party in permanent government and firmly in control of all state institutions, nationalists and Catholics took little part in the new Northern Ireland state. Nationalist leaders initially boycotted the new parliament, but did take their seats from 1925 in an attempt to provide the Catholic minority with some representation at Stormont. Their level of representation was, however, significantly reduced by the abolition of proportional representation for parliamentary elections in 1927. Electoral discrimination was to be one of the biggest grievances of the nationalist community under the Stormont government.

Other, more day-to-day grievances were felt in the areas of housing, policing and employment - in both the public and private sectors. In all these areas Catholics felt that they were deliberately discriminated against by Protestants who, from their positions of power, tended to control decision-making in particular the allocation of housing and jobs.

All this contributed to the mentality that Northern Ireland was a 'Protestant state for a Protestant people'. Whilst at the time of partition in 1920, it had been envisaged by some that Northern Ireland and its southern neighbour might, at some time in the future, come together again, in actual fact the two jurisdictions and their people grew further apart. Partition became entrenched in the inter-war years, and was reinforced by the Southern Ireland's constitutional change in 1948, when it became a Republic. Essentially Northern Ireland over time developed and established a unique political identity, and the Republic of Ireland's leaders in practice made little effort to understand or engage it.

Parity

Growing acceptance of the "principle of parity" in terms of the requirement to treat Northern Ireland citizens on the same basis as the Westminster government would treat citizens of Great Britain had developed throughout this period. However, despite the "principle of parity" successive governments held relative freedom in their management of the internal administration of the North and were able, amongst other initiatives, to introduce reforms, effectively reinforcing the government's political control at the expense of nationalists.

The establishment of the post-war Labour government at Westminster under the leadership of Clement Atlee had an agenda for social and economic reform, which unsettled the right-of-centre Unionist administration in Northern Ireland from the outset and brought the principle of parity into sharper focus.

In the post war period the financial relationship underpinning parity was extensively developed between London and Belfast. The establishment of parity in public services and taxation in 1946 consequently meant that the Northern Ireland budget had to be "cleared" in advance by the Treasury in London. Comprehensive National Insurance legislation passed in 1948 consolidated previously separated funds into a single fund for the United Kingdom guaranteeing equal benefits throughout the jurisdiction. This was followed in 1949 by further developments which saw national assistance, family allowances, pensions and health service provisions being put onto an equal footing with the rest of the UK coupled with the guarantee that where the cost of providing these services should be higher in Northern Ireland than in Britain the UK government would fund 80% of the surplus costs. To some extent this was the ancestry of the current system of financial management for Northern Ireland, now administered under the terms of the Barnett Formula.

The passing of the Public Health and Local Government Act of 1946 led to the creation of a new Ministry of Health and Local Government at Stormont with responsibility for rolling out the provisions for the Welfare state as envisaged by the Beveridge Report and originating from Westminster. Greater emphasis was placed on improving the housing stock and social housing was built largely at the expense of the Treasury to be administrated by Northern Ireland's local authorities.

Throughout this period inter-communal relations in Northern Ireland were poor and the arrival of the 'liberal' Unionist leader

Captain Terence O'Neill as Prime Minister in 1963 was to bring matters to a head. On taking office, O'Neill stated that he planned to raise living standards, not just for Catholics, but across the working classes. O'Neill's view was that Catholic discontent and the instability that came with it could be addressed through a series of relatively modest reforms which, by giving Catholics more of a 'stake' in Northern Ireland affairs, would make them 'normal' citizens. This attracted fierce opposition; both from within O'Neill's own party, and from other unionists, in particular, Ian Paisley. Paisley's main aim was to keep Northern Ireland Protestant at all costs and he opposed O'Neill's reforms vigorously and vociferously, particularly those granting equality to Catholics and co-operation with the Republic of Ireland. Despite O'Neill's condemnation, Paisley commanded substantial support among working-class Protestants. His uncompromising politics provided a strong contrast to those of the upper-class patrician O'Neill. O'Neill's promised reforms were acknowledged by the minority community in terms of the resumption of their Stormont seats by the Nationalist Party, who had previously boycotted the Parliament, but many felt that the reforms did not go far enough. Major government decisions continued to be seen as unfair, in particular the siting of a new 'city' (Craigavon, named after James Craig) and a new university (at Coleraine, as opposed to Derry) in predominantly Protestant areas.

Civil Rights to Hunger Strikes

Organisations such as the Campaign for Social Justice and the Northern Ireland Civil Rights Association (NICRA) were formed to demand equal rights for Catholics in housing, employment and voting. A student march, associated with NICRA, from Belfast to Derry in January 1969 broke out into fierce rioting after it passed through predominantly loyalist areas and was attacked by a crowd of loyalists. In the aftermath of the march, widespread rioting broke out across Northern Ireland and the issue started to move away from that of civil rights towards that of religious and national identity.

Free Derry Corner, Derry

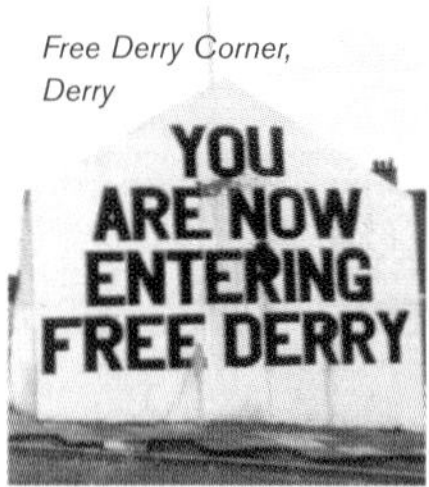

By the time of O'Neill's resignation in April 1969 (he was succeeded by Major Chichester-Clark), limited reforms had been undertaken, but following the unrest, the RUC (Royal Ulster Constabulary) had banned all similar marches. Continued street violence led to the deployment of British troops in Derry and Belfast in August that year, initially to protect Catholic communities from sectarian attacks.

In 1971, amid further escalations of violence, internment (imprisonment without trial) was reintroduced to Northern Ireland by Unionist Prime Minister Brian Faulkner (who had succeeded Chichester-Clark), albeit with little if any success. Though banned, civil rights marches continued, and on 30th January 1972, a civil rights march ended with the British army shooting dead 13 men in controversial circumstances during a march in Derry. The day has become universally known as "Bloody Sunday" and is currently the subject of a major long-running public enquiry. Nationalist political passions reached a new pitch not only in Northern Ireland but in the South as well; the British Embassy in Dublin was burned down in protest at the killings. The security situation continued to deteriorate rapidly beyond the control of the Northern Ireland government to the extent that the Conservative government at Westminster led by Prime Minister Ted Heath was forced to suspend the Stormont parliament to allow political negotiations on institutional reform to proceed. The consequent introduction of Direct Rule, meant that Northern Ireland, for the first time since 1921, was to be governed politically from Westminster.

The 1970s saw an unprecedented resurgence of paramilitary violence, from both republican and loyalist quarters. The chief protagonists were the Provisional IRA, who took their name, following an ideological split, from the old 'official' Irish Republican Army of the Irish Civil War. The IRA saw its support rise dramatically through the 1970s, especially after the British government's re-introduction of internment, and it began a campaign of violence aimed at making the administration of Northern Ireland unprofitable and unmanageable for the British government. They waged war on the economic life of Northern Ireland by bombing numerous commercial and administrative targets, and on the police and army security establishment through direct attacks on personnel.

On the loyalist side, the UVF (the name taken from Carson's 1914 volunteer army, the Ulster Volunteer Force) had become an active armed group intent on defending Ulster from the rising power of Irish nationalism. Following a number of murders and activities the group, led by Gusty Spence was proscribed in 1966. Nonetheless, by the 1970s its membership had risen, along with that of the much larger Ulster Defence Association (UDA). Loyalist paramilitary violence was spontaneous and random, mainly taking the form of indiscriminate shooting of Catholics in retaliation for IRA attacks on police officers, British Army troops and Protestant civilians.

The stakes were raised in 1979 when, amongst many other violent atrocities Lord Mountbatten, a prominent member of the British royal family, and later eighteen British soldiers were murdered in two republican attacks. The subsequent security clampdown brought about the loss of special category (PoW) status in local prisons, which led republican prisoners to go on hunger strike. 10 IRA men starved themselves to death, including the leader of the hunger-strikers, Bobby Sands, who was elected to the Fermanagh/South Tyrone Westminster seat whilst on hunger strike. Their deaths led to further rioting in Northern Ireland and Dublin, symptomatic of continuing polarisation. The long-term significance of the hunger strikes was the stimulus they gave to the development of Sinn Féin and republicanism as a serious mainstream political force.

Bobby Sands Mural, Belfast

Violence and general civil unrest in Northern Ireland continued throughout the 1970s and 1980s, with devastating impact, until the ceasefires in the early 1990s. Throughout this period many attempts at reaching political agreement were made and these are outlined overleaf.

Direct Rule and Political Initiatives 1972 - 2003

Sunningdale

The British government attempted to introduce various initiatives aimed at establishing a devolved administration for Northern Ireland after the prorogation of the Stormont administration. The first of these was the Sunningdale Agreement of 1973, which emerged following historic British and Irish Government negotiations alongside discussions involving the local political parties. A 78-seat assembly to be elected under proportional representation was proposed. This would establish a power-sharing executive, composed of unionist and nationalist parties. Of the many political parties in Northern Ireland, only three accepted: the Ulster Unionist Party (UUP), the Social Democratic and Labour Party (SDLP) and Alliance. Political opposition to 'Sunningdale' was intense and the agreement ultimately failed to capture the support of a majority of Unionists. The Executive was faced with severe pressure from loyalists who opposed power sharing. A general strike, organised by loyalists and supported by most unionists, brought Northern Ireland to a standstill and the Executive collapsed, replaced again by Direct Rule on 30 May 1974. Despite its failure, the Sunningdale Agreement had established the principle of power sharing in Northern Ireland, which would become an important development in the context of future political initiatives.

Despite numerous and varied political initiatives including attempts to create a gradual re-introduction of a local administration (rolling devolution) Direct Rule was to continue unabated for the next 25 years. This however did not stop the process of ongoing institutional reform.

From 1972 onwards Northern Ireland was governed by a Secretary of State, a full member of the British Cabinet who was assisted by several junior ministers, generally MPs from Britain. The Northern Ireland Office took over responsibility for the law and order functions of the Ministry of Home Affairs and reported to the Secretary of State on broad political matters.

In 1976 the Department of the Civil Service was separated out of the Department of Finance but re-attached in the form of the new Department of Finance and Personnel in 1982. Government departments were again re-formed to comprise six new departments. These were:

- Department of Economic Development;
- Department of the Environment;
- Department of Education;
- Department of Social Services;
- Department of Health;
- Department of Agriculture.

In addition there was a radical reform of local government under the Local Government (Northern Ireland) Act of 1972 providing for the replacement of all previous local authorities with 26 new district councils. This reform coincided with the demise of Stormont and the introduction of Direct Rule and councils were given fewer powers than had previously been envisaged. District councils' responsibilities were confined to the relatively minor functions of street cleaning, refuse collection, cemeteries and leisure facilities. The main functions of health and education were operated by area Boards largely comprised of central government appointees. A new centralised housing authority, the Northern Ireland Housing Executive, assumed all previous local authority housing duties.

Rolling Devolution

In the early 1980s, Secretary of State James Prior proposed what became known as 'rolling devolution', the idea being that a Northern Ireland assembly would initially be given limited, consultative powers. These new powers could increase significantly as circumstances permitted, i.e. as a culture of power-sharing and cross-community co-operation evolved. 59 members were elected to a new assembly in October 1982, although the SDLP and Sinn Féin refused to participate in the new institution. The Ulster Unionists boycotted the assembly over security policy, so that the only full participants were the DUP and Alliance. The 'Prior' Assembly offered a limited degree of power-sharing via Committee chairmanships but was doomed to failure when so many of the major parties refused to take part in its precedings.

The Anglo-Irish Agreement

The next major political development was the Anglo-Irish Agreement signed on 15 November 1985 by the British and Irish governments, which in an all-round constitutional package gave the Irish Republic, for the first time, a formal albeit consultative, role in the government of Northern Ireland.

The establishment of an Irish Governmental physical presence in Belfast and the involvement of Dublin ministers in a consultative role across a range of policy areas in Northern Ireland created fierce resentment in the Unionist community. The signing of this Agreement in 1985 proved highly unacceptable to unionists, who resigned their Westminster seats in protest, boycotted district councils and generally made it clear that they would not allow the Republic of Ireland any role as of right in Northern Ireland. Unionist politicians were united in opposition to an Agreement, which they felt had, unjustly, been formulated without their input and imposed without their consent, and employed protests, resignations and other tactics in a major campaign to thwart it. Their use of the ongoing Assembly to criticise the Anglo-Irish Agreement eventually led to its dissolution by the British government.

The Anglo-Irish Agreement established a permanent secretariat at Maryfield, on the eastern outskirts of Belfast. In effect the British government, led by Prime Minister Margaret Thatcher, had acknowledged the right of the Republic of Ireland to consultation over the future of Northern Ireland. The British government also asserted that it had no selfish or strategic interest in Northern Ireland and reaffirmed that Northern Ireland could only rejoin the Republic of Ireland if a majority of its people consented, thus establishing what has become known as the 'principle of consent'. Up untill this time the republican movement had refused to accept that 'consent' was necessary in order to achieve a united Ireland

Despite much pessimism in the early years following the signing of the Anglo-Irish Agreement, the Northern Ireland parties continued in talks to break the political deadlock. Unionists were motivated by a desire to reach an outcome that would create a locally devolved government and shift the trend away from Anglo-Irish joint administration. Unionist leaders increasingly recognised the need to cut a deal with Northern Ireland nationalists to achieve this. Nationalists, buoyed by the backing of the Dublin government, were also looking for a locally based government providing it offered the prospect of power sharing.

The Peace Process

Hume-Adams Talks

Towards the end of the 1980s, SDLP leader John Hume had engaged in exploratory talks with Sinn Féin President Gerry Adams, aimed at identifying the political circumstances in which the IRA could move from their military focused stance into the mainstream political arena. By 1993 the Hume-Adams talks had produced a series of documents and statements which were fed into continuing inter governmental discussions. Hume argued that if London stated it had no selfish desire to hold onto Northern Ireland then the IRA would h
ave no reason to continue to fight its "war". The Hume-Adams dialogue was taken forward by Taoiseach Albert Reynolds and the Irish government into discussions with London.

Downing Street Declaration

The ongoing talks between the British and Irish governments were to culminate in the Downing Street Declaration of December 1993, in which the British government acknowledged and accepted the principle of self-determination of the people in both parts of the island of Ireland, together with the principle of consent for any change being made. The Declaration reaffirmed that Britain had no selfish or strategic interest in Northern Ireland and it was hoped that this affirmation would facilitate an IRA ceasefire. Ceasefires were to follow, the IRA in August 1994, with the UVF and the UDA under the banner of the Combined Loyalist Military Command (CLMC) following in October that year. Although the ceasefires did not do a lot to improve trust between Northern Ireland's warring groups, they improved the climate for political talks and these got underway under the auspices of Prime Minister John Major and Taoiseach Albert Reynolds.

Fresh Talks

The UK general election of 1997 saw the return of a Labour government with a solid parliamentary majority, which enabled the new Prime Minster, Tony Blair, to inject fresh momentum into the peace process. Multi-party talks opened in September, following a three-strand formula. Strand one dealt with the internal administration of Northern Ireland; strand two considered the relationship between North and South, and strand three relations between London and Dublin: the East-West Dimension.

The Belfast (Good Friday) Agreement

Following considerable personal involvement by Prime Minister Tony Blair, Irish Taoiseach Bertie Ahern, American President Bill Clinton, and intensive discussions between the local political parties, the Belfast Agreement (the 'Good Friday Agreement') was signed on Good Friday, 10th April 1998. The majority of political parties supported the Agreement, notable exceptions being Ian Paisley's DUP and the smaller UKUP, both of whom refused to participate in the talks. *(The Good Friday Agreement is reproduced in full in the Reference Section, at the back)*

Essentially the Agreement was a balanced constitutional deal which recognised the need to establish institutions which would give expression to three sets of relationships: the two traditions in Northern Ireland; the two traditions in Ireland North and South; and the two nations Britain and Ireland (East and West). Alongside the Belfast-based institutions there was to be a series of cross-border development bodies with representation from both sides reporting into a North/South Ministerial Council. In addition, there would be a British/Irish Council addressing issues on an East/West basis and a consultative Civic Forum reflective of sectoral and community interests outside of the party political system.

The proposed arrangements, which were voted through the London and Dublin parliaments and put to separate referenda in Northern Ireland and the Republic, created an elected Assembly in Northern Ireland with a power-sharing Executive. There would be an increase in the number of government departments to 10 along with a unique joint central Department of the First and Deputy First Minister (OFMDFM).

Belfast Agreement Referenda Results

Northern Ireland

Electorate: 1,175,403 Turnout: 80.98%

	VOTES	PERCENTAGE
YES	676,966	71.12%
NO	274,879	28.88%

Republic of Ireland

Electorate: 2,753,127 Turnout: 56.1%

	VOTES	PERCENTAGE
YES	1,442,583	94.4%
NO	85,748	5.6%

Following approval by Westminster, parliament passed the Northern Ireland (Elections) Act 1998, which provided for the holding of Assembly elections on 25 June 1998. The Act also provided for the Assembly to meet in 'shadow' mode, pending the coming into effect of the substantive powers of the new institutions provided for in the Northern Ireland Act 1998.

Elections held on 25 June 1998 returned 108 MLAs to the new Assembly. The Assembly met for the first time on 1 July 1998. David Trimble MP Leader of the Ulster Unionist Party was elected as First Minister Designate and Séamus Mallon MP Deputy Leader of the SDLP as Deputy First Minister-designate.

Assembly Results by Party June 1998

Party	% total vote	Seats
SDLP	22.0	24
UUP	21.3	28
DUP	18.1	20
Sinn Fein	17.6	18
Alliance	6.5	6
UKUP	4.5	5
Ind Unionist	2.9	3
PUP	2.6	2
NIWC	1.6	2
Others	2.9	0
Total	**100**	**108**

Review of the Agreement

However, despite the election of an Assembly there remained some significant political obstacles to the formation of a devolved government, most notably surrounding the decommissioning of paramilitary weapons. The Secretary of State Mo Mowlam announced a review of the implementation of the Agreement, facilitated by US Senator George Mitchell, and focused on how to carry forward matters relating to inclusive devolution and decommissioning. Eventually the Review produced consensus on the issues of the formation of an inclusive Executive and the decommissioning of weapons, enabling the necessary actions to trigger devolution.

Devolution

Power was finally devolved to the Assembly and its Executive Committee on 2 December 1999. The Assembly succeeded in electing a cross community 12 strong Executive Committee using the d'Hondt system and assigning Ministers to their new Departments.

Despite the devolution of most of the day to day activities and powers of government to the new power-sharing Assembly, and the establishment of North/South bodies, Northern Ireland continued to operate unambiguously as part of the United Kingdom. Northern Ireland would continue to have representation at Westminster and significant governmental powers (excepted matters) would remain with Westminster for the foreseeable future.

However, once established, the Assembly and Executive were dogged by ongoing political difficulties. The continuing delay in paramilitary decommissioning eroded trust and confidence and meant that Ulster Unionists spent much of their time fending off internal critics. While the DUP occupied its two ministerial offices, it refused to participate in the round table Executive Committee which included Sinn Féin. Sinn Féin refused to take up its positions on the Northern Ireland Policing Board and the Ulster Unionist Party on occasions withdrew co-operation from the all-island bodies created under the Agreement.

At the 'backbencher' level, there was unease at what was perceived to be a relatively 'light' legislative programme in the unusual circumstance where all four main parties were effectively in a coalition and there was no effective opposition.

The continuing tensions led to several suspensions of the operation of the Assembly – the first time between February and May 2000. Again the lack of agreement on decommissioning forced further suspensions in August and September 2001. Finally, following a series of security-related 'breaches' attributed by Unionists to Sinn Féin, the Assembly and its institutions were suspended once again in October 2002. Despite ongoing negotiations the natural life of the Assembly expired in May 2003 before any agreement on restoration could be reached. The lack of agreement on the circumstances under which devolution could be restored, led the British government to postpone the Assembly elections due to be held in May 2003.

Devolved Government in Operation

Despite the general disappointment at the failure to reach agreement – except of course for the minority totally opposed to the Agreement in the first place – the experience of devolution in practice was generally regarded as positive. Some of the local politicians were seen to have risen to the challenge of ministerial office and for the first time in many years Northern Ireland had leaders capable of effecting change.

The new administration had some notable successes – the rapid introduction, as promised, of free transport for citizens of pensionable age; the decisive management of the Foot and Mouth Disease crisis which had bedevilled the UK mainland; the tireless efforts to promote Northern Ireland abroad as an investment location and the creation of innovative and imaginative approaches to public spending, most notably the Reinvestment and Reform Initiative (RRI).

The Assembly Committees worked effectively scrutinising ministerial proposals and evolving in some cases into an 'opposition' advocacy role. At the operational level, Committee members comprising, in many cases, totally opposing parties, who previously had refused to sit together went about their business calmly and effectively. At the level of the citizen, Northern Ireland individuals and groups enjoyed a period of comparatively easy access to ministerial decision-makers and the opportunity to have real influence over government decisions and policies effecting them.

Future Devolution

Efforts to 'do a deal' during the summer of 2003, despite further weapons decommissioning in October, came to nothing and the government finally called the Assembly election for 26 November 2003, in the absence of any agreement on how the institutions could be restored.

The election resulted in a hardening of attitudes in both communities with the anti-Agreement DUP getting the largest single share of the vote and 30 seats. The Ulster Unionist Party held on to 27 seats. On the Nationalist side Sinn Fein emerged as the larger party winning 24 seats against the SDLP's 18. Apart from the Alliance Party, which retained all of its 6 seats despite a greatly reduced vote, the smaller parties were for the most part squeezed out electorally.

The result of the election is effectively a stalemate with a clear anti-Agreement majority elected on the Unionist side – although there is a clear pro-agreement majority overall. It is expected that the negotiations on the way forward will be difficult and prolonged. At the heart of the debate on the way forward was the 'Joint Declaration' paper which the British and Irish governments had prepared to address in one pass all of the outstanding implementation issues associated with the Agreement. The Joint Declaration covered areas such as demilitarisation and normalisation as well as decommissioning and the devolution of authority for security and policing.

However with the DUP success in the Election the political centre of gravity has moved from the Joint Declaration to the proposition that the entire Agreement should be renegotiated.

Looking Forward...

Although inter-communal strife is still going on in many parts of Northern Ireland, for the most part, ordinary people can go about their everyday life without constant fear of terrorist activity and generally, Northern Ireland has prospered during peacetime. New buildings, shops, restaurants and other entertainment venues are appearing all over the province and the numbers of visitors is gradually increasing.

It is clear however that there is still a long way to go towards a 'normalisation' of the political and security situation here, but it is accepted by many that the crucial constitutional issues relating to the status of Northern Ireland itself have been decided, for the short term at least. Nonetheless divisions nurtured over centuries remain deep-rooted and will not disappear easily. Loyalists unclaimed by paramilitary groups and republican splinter groups have not ceased violence; they are seen as a minority by both moderate and extreme parties, nationalist and unionist. Both communities have many issues that they feel are outstanding.

The future, however, is not entirely without hope. Most people recognise that Northern Ireland is now a better place, in which to live, visit or do business, than it was before the ceasefires. Despite short-term setbacks the long term signs indicate a trend towards a more peaceful future.

Northern Ireland: The Place

Geographical Overview

Northern Ireland occupies 5461 square miles in the northeast of the island of Ireland, which itself lies on the extreme northwest of the European continent. Its area takes up around one sixth of the island, approximately the size of Connecticut or Yorkshire. On the east it is separated from Scotland by the North Channel and from England by the Irish Sea; to the west and south it borders the Republic of Ireland. Its greatest distance north-south measures 85 miles, east-west 111 miles.

Northern Ireland's landscape consists mainly of low hill country, although there are two significant mountain ranges: the Mournes, which extend from South Down to Strangford Lough in the east, and the Sperrins, reaching through the northwest boundaries of Northern Ireland. The highest point in Northern Ireland is one of the twelve peaks of the Mournes: Slieve Donard in Co Down, some 2796 ft above sea level. From the top of Slieve Donard the Isle of Man is visible and in favourable conditions, the Scottish coast, Mount Snowdon in Wales and even the Cumbrian Hills of England may be seen. There is also a substantial tract of high land in Co Antrim known as the Antrim Plateau, or more commonly the 'Glens of Antrim'. In contrast, the lowest lying point in Northern Ireland is The Marsh, near Downpatrick, actually 1.3 ft below sea level.

There are also over 60 forests, including 9 forest parks, and a number of wooded areas. The southwest is mainly forested, with a number of small lakes and rivers which drain into Lough Erne. The lake, split into Upper and Lower Lough Erne, is a 50-mile waterway favoured by many for fishing and pleasure boating, particularly following the recent development of the Shannon-Erne waterway.

A basalt plateau extends throughout Northern Ireland, leading to brown earth soil that varies as a result of glacially transported material. This can appear as drumlins, smooth mounds that occur principally in parts of South Down and Armagh. Glaciation also created the area's principal valleys: the River Bann in the north, the Blackwater in the southwest and the Lagan in the east. These valleys have always been vital in providing routes through the heart of the North, and the waterways are still used commercially and for pleasure. Land between the estuary of the River Roe and the city of Derry was reclaimed from the sea in the nineteenth century for flax growing. As the land is below sea level, it is drained artificially and the estuary itself is now a nature reserve.

Lough Neagh is the largest freshwater lake on the whole island; the largest in the British Isles and one of the largest in Europe. It covers an area of 153 square miles out of Northern Ireland's total of 246 square miles of inland water and tideways. As well as providing all kinds of freshwater fish, the Lough is also the centre of a centuries-old eel fishery, which exports hundreds of tonnes of Ulster eels every year. The best view of Lough Neagh is generally available from a plane flying into Belfast International Airport: the surrounding land is very flat, making the Lough, despite its size, a somewhat hidden feature of Northern Ireland.

Farming land in Northern Ireland varies from the fertile arable expanses of North Down and South Antrim to the boggy low lying lands of the Fermanagh lakelands and the stony upland of mid Ulster and the Sperrins.

Nonetheless there is sufficient quality land to support a major agricultural industry with the abundance of pasture giving dairy and livestock industries a competitive advantage. Peat soils, historically the main source of fuel for peasant farmers, are a feature of the island and quite common in the North. Peat and turf are still cut extensively for fuel, although mainly for private domestic use as commercially they are not particularly significant. Few mineral resources are naturally present in Northern Ireland although gravel, clays, chalk and limestone provide the basis for the manufacture of lime, bricks and cement. Most other raw materials, such as oil and coal, are not rich in Northern Ireland and need to be imported. In fact Northern Ireland is at something of a competitive disadvantage in that it is entirely dependent on imported fuels to meet its energy requirements. The town of Coalisland is named after a vein of coal that, although present, has never been successfully mined. There is also a significant deposit of lignite on the western shores of Lough Neagh but this has yet to be proven commercially viable.

Northern Ireland's climate is temperate, although much affected by its maritime location. High winds are common, especially in the north and on the east coast, and south westerly winds tend to drive away clouds from the Atlantic. As a result, the weather in Northern Ireland can be fairly changeable, going from overcast to a blue sky in a short space of time. Rainfall varies from as little as 32.5 inches to 80 inches per year, generally increasing towards eastern areas. Spring is relatively dry; summer and winter are disproportionately wet. Winters are generally long because of Northern Ireland's location north and west, which also leads to shorter days in the winter months. Snow is not uncommon, but rarely settles and is seldom severe. However, summer days are also proportionately longer than

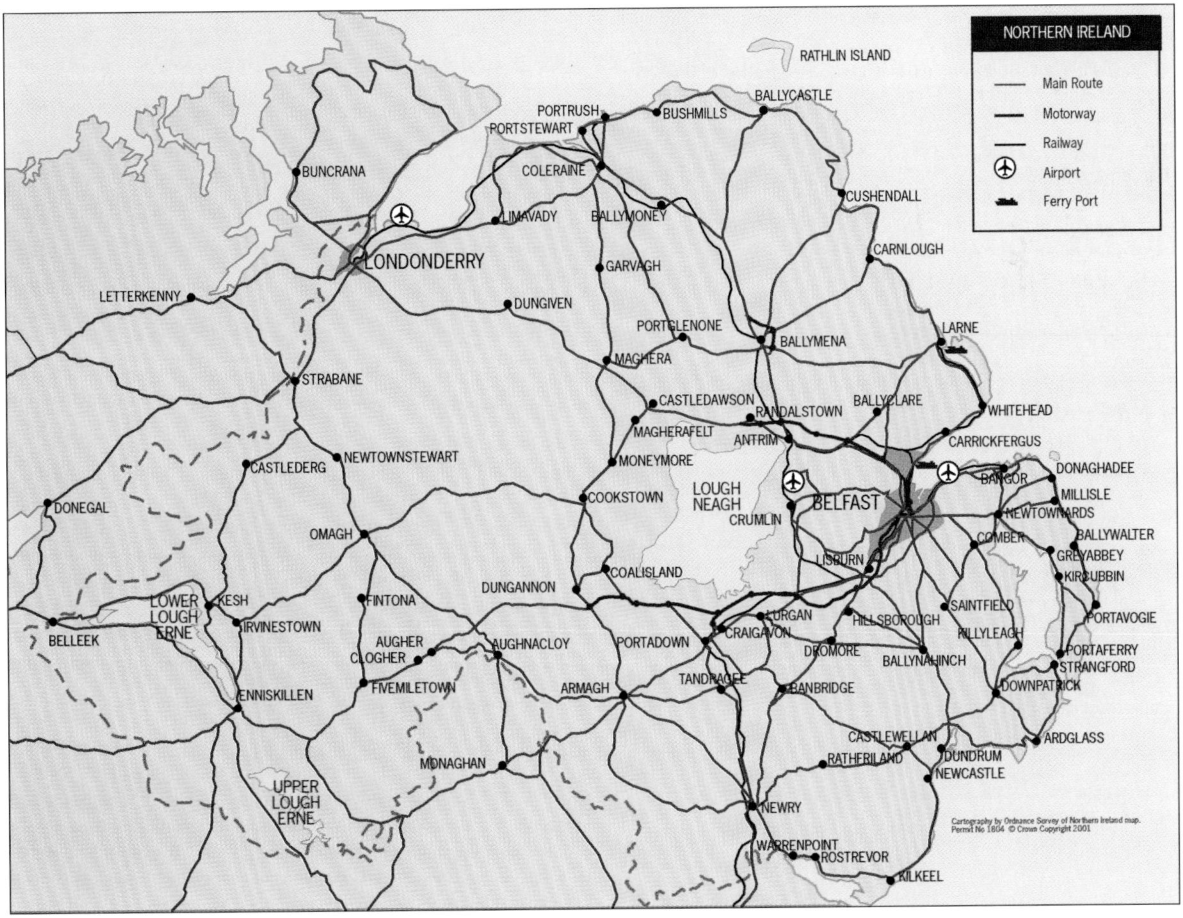

Northern Ireland: Towns and Roads

average. Average temperatures range from 3.3 degrees centigrade in winter to 18 degrees in the summer, indicating few extremes of hot and cold. The mildness and humidity of Northern Ireland's climate, together with slow natural drainage, has given the area a reputation for lush green fields and constant rain, although conditions are generally quite pleasant. Northern Ireland is also widely noted for its breathtaking scenery, including some 330 miles of coastal road. In fact, over 20% of the land has been designated as Areas of Outstanding Natural Beauty. This has been helped by low population density in many areas, leaving the countryside largely unspoilt. The generous natural landscape has also led to the growth of all kinds of outdoor pursuits. There are several championship standard golf courses, as well as opportunities for coarse fishing, as salmon and trout are plentiful in rivers. Watersports such as sailing and windsurfing are also popular, as are climbing, hiking and horse riding.

Northern Ireland: Main Geographical Features

Area of Counties

Antrim	1176 sq miles
Armagh	513 sq miles
Down	982 sq miles
Fermanagh	715 sq miles
Londonderry	814 sq miles
Tyrone	1261 sq miles
Total	5461 sq miles

Mountains

Slieve Donard Co Down	2796 ft
Sawel Co Tyrone / Co Londonderry border	2240 ft
Cuilcagh Co Fermanagh	2188 ft
Slieve Gullion Co Armagh	1894 ft
Trostan Co Antrim	1817 ft

Lakes

Lough Neagh	153 sq miles
Lower Lough Erne	42 sq miles
Upper Lough Erne	13 sq miles

Rivers

Upper Bann: 47 miles from Mourne Mountains to Lough Neagh

Lower Bann: 38 miles from Lough Neagh to the Atlantic Ocean

Lagan: 32 miles from the Mournes to Belfast Lough

The Six Counties...

Northern Ireland is comprised of six of Ireland's 32 counties. Although often thought of as having some ancient tribal or cultural significance, the county divisions were entirely a British administrative creation in the 19th Century. The six counties of Northern Ireland each have their own unique image and characteristics and are described briefly below.

Antrim

Antrim occupies the north-east corner of Northern Ireland, stretching from Belfast in the south to the north coast. To the east is the Irish Sea, and Antrim's western boundary for the most part is Lough Neagh and the River Bann. It is Northern Ireland's second largest county by size. County Antrim is a mixture of urban centres including most of north and west Belfast, the towns of Ballymena, Larne, Carrickfergus, Ballymoney and Antrim town itself, and large rural stretches. Antrim is possibly best known for its picturesque 'Glens', home to traditional rural lifestyles and splendid mountain scenery, and its rugged north coast where Northern Ireland's premier visitor attraction, the Giant's Causeway, is located.

Armagh

Armagh is Northern Ireland's smallest county, characterised by the large towns of Lurgan and Portadown (Craigavon) to the north, the ecclesiastical city of Armagh itself mid-county and drumlin country in the south. Known in Ireland and worldwide as the 'Orchard County', Armagh has a major apple production and processing industry, famous for the local 'Bramley' cooking apple. The cathedral city itself, with its religious significance, is described below under 'cities'. The border areas have witnessed much of the anti-British violence carried out during the Troubles and the area of South Armagh, near the Irish border, earned the unfavourable tag of 'bandit country' during the 1970s and 1980s. However South Armagh offers fine scenery around Slieve Gullion and many interesting attractions.

Londonderry

County Londonderry – the 'Oak Leaf' county - lies to the north west of Northern Ireland, and combines the major population centres of Derry city and Coleraine with numerous small towns and villages becoming ever more rural toward the south of the county. Northern Ireland's second largest mountain range, the Sperrins, runs through the heart of the county and 'Crossing the Sperrins', through the steep 'Glenshane Pass', is a well known feature of any journey between Derry and Belfast. The county is defined geographically by four main river valleys: the Bann, the Roe, the Faughan and the Foyle.

Down

Like Antrim, County Down incorporates a major slice of Belfast – most of the south and east of the city. The other substantial towns in the county are Bangor and Newtownards in the north-east, Lisburn in the north-west, Banbridge and Ballynahinch in mid-county and Newcastle, Downpatrick and Newry in the south. Down is home to the Mountains of Mourne, Northern Ireland's highest mountain range and source of the River Bann. It also encloses Northern Ireland's second largest inland waterway, Strangford Lough, which opens up to the Irish sea. Down incorporates the industrial with the rural and with numerous attractive small towns such as Moira, Hillsborough and Castlewellan. It has a significant tourism industry centred around the popular tourist resorts of Newcastle and Bangor.

Fermanagh

Fermanagh is a predominantly rural county located to the south-west of Northern Ireland. It has by far the smallest population of any of the six counties and its main industries are agriculture and tourism. The tourism industry is largely based around Fermanagh's two major internal waterways: Lower and Upper Lough Erne. These lakes are a major attraction to anglers and a centre for boating holidays. Fermanagh's main centre is the picturesque town of Enniskillen, the regional administrative centre which is built around a series of islands at the mouth of Lower Lough Erne. Other significant towns, providing employment and centres of population are Lisnaskea, in the south of the county and Irvinestown in the north.

Tyrone

Tyrone is Northern Ireland's largest county by size and stretches from Lough Neagh in the East to the border with Donegal in the West. There is no dominant town in the county, the four main ones being Strabane to the north west, Cookstown to the east, Omagh in the centre and Dungannon to the south. The main industry is agriculture although there is a spread of industry throughout the main towns. Tyrone, meaning Eoin's Land, is the ancient home of the O'Neill clan, once the dominant rulers of Ulster. The 'Red Hand' of Ulster remains the symbol of the county to this day. Tyrone's main rivers include the Ballinderry, the Owenreagh and Strule and are known to anglers for the quality of their fishing.

Cities in Northern Ireland

Northern Ireland now has five cities: Belfast, Derry/Londonderry, Armagh, Lisburn and Newry although these are quite different from each other in size and all are very small by global standards. Lisburn and Newry were awarded city status during the 2002 Golden Jubilee celebrations.

Belfast

The capital city of Northern Ireland, Belfast is also its administrative, industrial and commercial centre. It has a population of around 350,000 and enjoys an enviable setting, facing out to sea and cradled on all sides by ranges of hills and mountains. The name Belfast itself is derived from the Irish béal feirste. This literally means 'mouth of the river' and came from Belfast's position at the head of the River Lagan, which becomes Belfast Lough as it joins the Irish Sea. Originally a small town, Belfast saw its population increase significantly with the Industrial Revolution. In 1800 its population was around 20,000 but the enormous growth of the linen industry caused Belfast to expand rapidly. Rows of small terraced housing serve as a reminder of the thousands of mill and factory workers who moved from the countryside and settled in the city. In 1888, Belfast became a city by royal charter and by the end of the 19th century had overtaken Dublin in terms of population. By the beginning of the Second World War, during which Belfast experienced bombing at the hands of German planes targeting its shipyards and engineering works, its population had exceeded 400,000.

The city also suffered heavily in economic and social terms during the 'Troubles', when it became a frequent target of paramilitary bombs. In recent years however it has enjoyed a major revival of cultural activities and a more positive atmosphere, with new hotels, restaurants and entertainment venues springing up all over the city. Belfast is also a district, in local Government terms, covering some 44 square miles (115 square km), taking in several smaller towns and villages around its limits. 2001 Census figures reveal the population of Belfast's electoral district to be 277,391, which demonstrates the importance to Northern Ireland of its capital city.

Derry (Londonderry)

Derry, the 'Maiden City', is located on the river Foyle in the north west of Northern Ireland, and has a population of around 100,000. It is one of the oldest settlements on the island of Ireland, having traditionally been founded in 546 AD by St Columba. The name Derry comes from the Irish word Doire or Daire, meaning oak grove, in particular one surrounded by water or a peat bog. This was the case in Derry, the grove being on an island in the River Foyle. The water beside the island gradually dried out, leaving a boggy area that became known as the 'Bogside'. In the early seventeenth century, King James I gave the City of London responsibility for settling this area of Ireland. Derry was fortified in 1613 and renamed Londonderry by royal charter as part of the Plantation of Ulster. The debate over what the city should be called is a long-standing one with some people now adopting the phrase 'Stroke City' as a humourous and inoffensive option.

Although much smaller than Belfast and no bigger than a typical English town the inhabitants of Derry are very proud of their City status and their rich heritage. The defined area of Derry city itself is relatively small, only 3.4 square miles. Derry has never been a prosperous city, with unemployment continually above the Northern Ireland average. Traditionally it has had a particular problem with male unemployment as its well-established shirtmaking industry has tended to provide more jobs taken up by women. Poverty remains a problem in the city. In recent years, although the shirt factories have been closing there has been an influx of new engineering and high-tech investments in the city, and Derry has developed a new economic self-confidence. It is expected that initiatives such as re-locating public sector jobs to the city will help go some way towards further alleviating unemployment.

Despite its image as a divided city Derry is developing a vibrant cultural life with its new Millennium Forum hosting many famous musicians and theatrical productions. Each October the entire city comes alive for the annual Halloween festival, when houses are decorated and people dress up to enjoy the festivities.

Architecturally the city boasts the famous City Walls and the Guildhall, which are both must-see sights for any visitor. The emergence of new hotels, bars and restaurants have meant that Derry city has become more appealing as a place for people to visit as well as to live and work.

Armagh

Armagh is similarly an historical city, first founded on the hill fort of Ard Mhacha in the 4th century AD. It has a population of less than 20,000 and barely merits inclusion in the top 10 of Northern Ireland's towns (by population). Important in terms of Ulster and Ireland as a whole, it is the ancient city of St Patrick. Both Church of Ireland and Catholic cathedrals in the city are named after the patron saint of Ireland and both churches' archbishops are based in the ecclesiastical city.

Armagh city also boasts an observatory (founded in 1765) and planetarium. Of particular note is the fine Regency and Georgian architecture that is prominent around the City Centre in the area of the Mall. The wider Armagh local Government district covers an area of 261 square miles, and, according to the 2001 Census figures has a population of 54,263 indicating low population density in what is a heavily rural area. The county of Armagh is known as the Orchard County; famous for fruit growing, in particular apples, although there are a number of light industrial centres as well.

Lisburn

Lisburn, some 8 miles southwest of Belfast and increasingly merging with the south western outskirts of the city, was a small village until plantation. The English government invited French Huguenots to settle there, who nurtured the growing linen industry by the introduction of new Dutch looms. Lisburn quickly became a major linen producer, although today this focus has progressed to synthetic fabrics. The River Lagan, runs through the centre of Lisburn and although the linen industry based around the river has declined, Lisburn remains an important centre for commerce and industry in Northern Ireland and is also a popular residential location, acting as a 'commuter town' for Belfast.

Newry

Newry is notable for having the first inland waterway in the British Isles, which contributed greatly to the town's prosperity in the nineteenth century. The canal had 14 locks and provided a means to export mainly linen and stone. By 1840 its importance had declined, however. The name Newry is derived from the Gaelic for a yew tree, which was according to legend planted by St Patrick in the area. Newry has experienced rapid growth in population and economic activity in recent years and today is a busy city benefiting from its close proximity to the border with the Republic of Ireland. The city itself is strategically located some forty miles south of Belfast and only sixty miles north of Dublin.

Major Towns in Northern Ireland

Many of Northern Ireland's towns date from the seventeenth century, when London companies formed the Honourable The Irish Society. They planned and built towns around a central meeting place, known as a diamond. Two streets would intersect the diamond and the town itself would be built on a grid pattern. These towns would usually include fortifications around the town's boundary, a market house and a planter's residence. Limavady and Coleraine in County Londonderry are good examples of 'plantation towns'.

Later, in the nineteenth century, smaller 'mill villages' such as Bessbrook in County Armagh, were planned around greens which may have been used as 'bleach greens' for bleaching linen. These villages and small towns were characterised by terraces of small, neat mill-workers houses, many of which have been modernised but are preserved in their original architectural form.

Other larger market towns tend to have a long, wide main street. For example, Cookstown in County Tyrone is known for its main street, 1.25 miles long and 130 ft wide. Lurgan in County Armagh is another example. Given the rural environment, there are many small market towns throughout the area. Northern Ireland also has an abundance of tiny villages and hamlets, especially in more remote areas. The smallest Irish description of a rural district is a 'townland' which could be as little as 300 acres. In 1846 Ordnance Survey recorded more than 60,000 of these townlands across the island of Ireland. In some parts of Northern Ireland, people are very proud of their townlands and actively try to preserve them by using them in preference to their official road or street name as part of their postal address.

During the seventeenth century plantation, the majority of place names all over Ireland were 'anglicised', from their original Gaelic Irish. Translation meant that many place names are remarkably similar, especially in terms of prefix; the basic difference being a spelling closer to the English phonetics of the original Gaelic name. Common examples include Bally-, from Baile, meaning town; and Drum- or Drom-, from droim, meaning ridge. Knock comes from the Irish word cnoc meaning hill, and carrick from the Irish carraig, meaning rock.

The Bann river is often seen as a political and economic dividing line in Northern Ireland: the more prosperous east and the poorer, less populated west. Derry is unquestionably the major population centre of the West and local businesses often complain that Northern Ireland stops 'left of the Bann'. Most people live east of the Bann and few of the towns to the west have more than 10,000 inhabitants.

Northern Ireland's main towns (in terms of population based on 1991 census figures) are described briefly below:

Bangor (pop 52437)

Third in terms of population after Belfast and Derry, Bangor is a large town located on the affluent North Down coastline, some 16 miles east of Belfast. The town centre is very close to the sea front at the mouth of Belfast Lough. Although it is a commercial and administrative centre in its own right Bangor is also a residential location for many people whose employment is in Belfast. Bangor is a popular seaside tourist resort attracting many visitors, particularly to its splendid marina, during the summer months.

Ballymena (pop 28717)

Ballymena is also one of Northern Ireland's largest and busiest towns, and is the main administrative centre for the north east region of Northern Ireland. The town is home to some major manufacturing industries and also services a large and prosperous rural population, enjoying one of the lowest rates of unemployment in the North. Despite its prosperity, Ballymena's image has been under assault with the town being associated in recent years with acts sectairianism and like many towns in Northern Ireland a growing problem with drugs - related crime. Nonetheless the town is highly regarded in terms of the quality of its shops and its people maintain a reputation for friendliness and warmth.

Craigavon, Including **Lurgan** (pop 21905) and **Portadown** (pop 21299).

Craigavon, Portadown and Lurgan are all part of a south west extension of the Lagan Valley and Belfast's industrial area. The central Craigavon area was originally designated a 'new town' in the late 1960s, hoping to create a new lifestyle in a modern environment with a fully integrated approach to planning. The town, named after unionist Prime Minister James Craig, later Lord Craigavon, was supposed to join together the established towns of Lurgan and Portadown (just 5 miles apart) and provide relief for the overcrowding experienced in Belfast at that time. However, people did not move to Craigavon in the numbers anticipated and, particularly in the 1970s, there was insufficient employment available for those who did.

The result was surplus, unwanted public housing alongside economic deprivation. Its popularity did not reach expectations at the time of its creation, although more recently Craigavon is becoming a preferred location for Belfast-bound commuters.

The Craigavon area with its proximity to Lough Neagh and good communications infrastructure is increasingly developing a very positive lifestyle image built around recreation and leisure.

Coleraine (pop 20721)

Coleraine is in County Londonderry, although it is the main town on the north east coast of Northern Ireland, which mainly falls under County Antrim. The town is centred where Northern Ireland's biggest river, the Bann, joins the Sea. It is a busy industrial centre and market town, as well as being a University town with a major campus located on its northern outskirts. Coleraine is a popular base for touring the north Antrim coast, and is close to two of Northern Ireland's most popular holiday resorts, Portrush and Portstewart.

Larne (pop 17575)

Larne is home to Northern Ireland's second most important port (only Belfast ranks above it), as well as a busy commercial centre. Situated about 20 miles north east of Belfast and sheltered by the Islandmagee headland, Larne is a busy ferryport, taking heavy volumes of passengers and cargo to the Scottish ports of Stranraer and Cairnryan. It is also home to some of Northern Ireland's busiest industries, with a narrow stretch of water separating it from the North's biggest power station, Ballylumford.

Omagh (pop 17280)

Omagh has seen significant growth as a result of increased administration in the western regions of Northern Ireland. In more recent times it experienced the worst single atrocity of the Northern Ireland troubles – a bomb in the town centre in August 1998 which killed 29 people. Omagh is a busy market town and its location in the rural centre of Northern Ireland means that it serves a substantial rural hinterland. Its people have earned extensive recognition for the dignified manner in which the community has rebuilt itself following the 1998 atrocity.

Strabane (pop 11981)

Strabane is situated on the border, some 20 miles south of Derry, and sits to the east of the River Foyle. It is the gateway to North Donegal. Strabane has historically experienced some of the highest levels of unemployment in any of Northern Ireland's large towns. However, its heritage is rich, as Strabane was an important printing and publishing centre in the eighteenth century and the American Declaration of Independence was printed there.

Enniskillen (pop 11436)

Enniskillen is the unofficial capital of the Fermanagh lakelands, as well as being the administrative and commercial centre for the county. It is possibly Northern Ireland's most picturesque large town. With its island location and accompanying attractions Enniskillen is a popular tourist centre, particularly for boating and angling enthusiasts.

Dungannon (pop 9420)

Dungannon town is situated in the south of County Tyrone in the centre of Northern Ireland. Its Irish name is Dún Geanainn, meaning Gannon's fort. Today Dungannon is a market town, also hosting light industries including food processing, crystal and fabrics. Dungannon is the main commercial centre for the largely rural area of South Tyrone. It is well located as the gateway to the West of Northern Ireland, adjacent to the M1 Motorway.

Northern Ireland: The People

Northern Ireland's "Troubles" are rooted in social and cultural differences that go back many hundreds of years and it is impossible to describe the people without reference to history and religion. The area has always had strong links with the western areas of Scotland as a consequence of its close proximity. English and Scottish settlers during the Plantation found that apart from their nationality, their Protestant faith marked them as separate from the native Irish. Unlike the Norman invaders of 1170, the English and Scottish planters of the 16th and 17th centuries resisted any integration of their culture into that of the native population. Over time they came to form the majority of the population in County Antrim, North Down and the Lagan Valley.

The Protestant planters of Ulster contributed greatly to the government's anglicisation of Ireland. They did this by translating place names from Irish, and establishing English over Gaelic as the official language. Scottish influence is especially striking in the regional accents and dialects of Northern Ireland. Areas with stronger Scottish links, such as the county of Antrim and parts of county Down, have discernible Scottish accents; indeed inhabitants of towns like Ballymena are often mistaken for Scots by visitors. Similarly, areas close to the border with the Republic of Ireland show southern characteristics in language, for example people from Derry and Donegal sound quite similar.

There is an uneven distribution of Protestant and Catholic communities throughout Northern Ireland. Protestants are concentrated in large numbers in the east of Northern Ireland, and particularly so in the areas immediately surrounding Belfast. Meanwhile areas such as Newry and Mourne and Derry, in the South and West respectively have overwhelmingly Catholic populations. The broad overall picture is that Northern Ireland is strongly Catholic overall west of the Bann and overwhelmingly Protestant to the east of the river.

Population

Size and Composition

The population of Northern Ireland on 30 June 2002 (estimated) was 1,696,641; a 3% increase on the 1995 figure. Over the period 1997-2002, the population of Banbridge Local Government District increased the most (by almost a tenth). The population of Belfast City Council area decreased by almost 5% over the same period. Banbridge, Carrickfergus and Ards experienced the greatest increases. There is a small (but growing) female majority of 42,000 which translates as a balance in the total population of 51% females to 49% males.

The three key determinants of population size are the birth rate, death rate and net inward or outward migration. Although Northern Ireland's birth rate has always outpaced the death rate, the natural growth in population has tended to be checked by a high degree of net outward migration. Birth rates are generally higher in the West and South of Northern Ireland than in the East and North. These factors impacting population growth are discussed in greater detail later. Population by age and gender is set out in table 1.4

Table 1.4 Northern Ireland Population by gender and age (June 2002)

Age Group	Male	Female	Total
under 16	201,647	191,368	393,015
16 and over	627,209	676,417	1,303,626
16-29	164,895	162,340	327,235
30-44	185,530	192,356	377,886
45-59 Female and 45-64 Male	183,116	149,201	332,317
60+ Female and 65+ Male	93,668	172,520	266,188
16 to 59 Female and 16 to 64 Male	533,541	503,897	1,037,438
75 & over	37,235	65,479	102,714
Total: All Ages	828,856	867,785	1,696,641

Source NISRA

Population Density

The overall population density of Northern Ireland in 2002 was estimated at 125 persons per square kilometre. Population density varies considerably across Northern Ireland tending to be at its lowest in the west (Local Government Districts Fermanagh, Omagh and Strabane) and in the very north of the province (Moyle, which includes the low population on Rathlin Island) and higher in the east and in the hinterlands of the larger towns and cities.

Table 1.5 Population density by Local Government District 1981-2002

District Council	1981	2002
Antrim	109	116
Ards	152	195
Armagh	73	82
Ballymena	87	94
Ballymoney	55	66
Banbridge	67	94
Belfast	2,886	2,501
Carrickfergus	355	472
Castlereagh	717	780
Coleraine	97	116
Cookstown	55	64
Craigavon	261	290
Derry	237	279
Down	83	100
Dungannon	57	62
Fermanagh	31	34
Larne	87	92
Limavady	47	57
Lisburn	191	245
Magherafelt	58	72
Moyle	29	33
Newry & Mourne	86	99
Newtownabbey	481	532
North Down	827	952
Omagh	40	43
Strabane	42	45
Northern Ireland	114	125

Source NISRA

Moyle has the lowest population density in Northern Ireland at just 33 persons per square kilometre, in comparison to the 2,501 in Belfast. High population densities are also recorded in North Down, Newtownabbey and Castlereagh.

Another unusual dimension to the population distribution of Northern Ireland is that it is not overwhelmingly concentrated in cities and towns. Although the Greater Belfast area accounts for almost one third of the total population in Northern Ireland, most of the remaining inhabitants are to be found in numerous small towns, villages, hamlets and relatively remote rural locations. Two thirds of Northern Ireland's land mass is west of the River Bann, and there are virtually no towns of population greater than 15,000 people (excluding the City of Derry).

Life Expectancy and Population Growth

Birth rates in Northern Ireland are generally high by UK standards although the overall birth rate for the region has slowed down significantly in recent years. In 1971 there were 20.6 births per 1,000 population in Northern Ireland, falling to 17.6 in 1981, 16.2 in 1991 and down to 13.0 in 2001. This figured has fallen again in 2002 to 12.6. Birth rates are generally higher in the West and South of Northern Ireland than in the East and North. The highest birth rate in Northern Ireland is in Newry and Mourne (15.5 per 1000 compared to Northern Ireland average of 12.6). The lowest birth rate in Northern Ireland is in North Down at 9.6 births per 1000.

Death rates have also been falling over the same period, albeit more slowly (see Table 1.6), reflecting the general tendency for people to live longer. Indeed life expectancy for children born in the period 1999-2001 is calculated to be 80 (women) and 75 (men); the highest ever. At the turn of the 20th century (1900-02) life expectancy for men and women was just 47. Table 1.2 illustrates recent trends in births, deaths and life expectancy in Northern Ireland over the last 30 years.

Table 1.6 Birth Rate, Death Rate, Life Expectancy in Northern Ireland (2002)

Year	Births*	Deaths*	Life Expectancy**	
			Male	Female
1971	20.6	10.5	67.6	73.7
1981	17.6	10.5	69.2	75.6
1991	16.2	9.4	72.8	78.7
2002	12.6	8.6	74.8	79.8

* per 1000 population
** years

Source NISRA

Marriage rates in Northern Ireland have been falling steadily over the past 30 years. Whilst in 1971 there were 7.9 marriages per 1000 of population, the figure for 2002 has fallen to just 4.5. This is indicative of changing trends in society, whereby it has become increasingly common for people to live together without getting married.

With increasing life expectancy, and death rates which are falling more dramatically than birth rates, it would be expected that the population of Northern Ireland would be increasing rapidly. As it happens, the population is increasing, but at a fairly slow rate (2001 census figures show an increase of around 82,000 people on the 1991 figures). Part of the explanation for this is Northern Ireland's continued high level of outward migration.

In 2001/02 there was a net inward migration of 85, which represented a significant change on the 2000/01 figure when there was a net outward migration of 1,875. It remains to be seen if this is the start of a trend whereby people will begin to come to, rather than leave Northern Ireland. The year 1995/96 also saw a net inward migration of 4,684 which can be partly explained by the newfound 'peace' in Northern Ireland and an ongoing campaign to encourage people to come back to the province to take advantage of new opportunities afforded by peacetime. What is notable about the figures for outward migration is that until relatively recently there has been an overwhelming majority of males choosing to emigrate.

Many of those who choose to leave the province are young people who go to obtain their higher education in Britain or elsewhere and never return. Similarly many graduates and other young people feel obliged to leave Northern Ireland in order to find suitable employment. Another factor relating to migration, which is particularly relevant to Northern Ireland is political stability and in light of current developments, this is something which it will be difficult to predict reliably.

Table 1.7 Northern Ireland Population Projection to 2041 (thousands)

	2001	2006	2011	2016	
Males	824	837	847	856	
Females	865	877	888	898	
Total	1,689	1,714	1,735	1,754	
	2021	**2026**	**2031**	**2036**	**2041**
Males	862	862	857	845	830
Females	907	912	912	905	894
Total	1,769	1,775	1,768	1,750	1,723

Source NISRA

Future projections of population (see table 1.7 above) indicate a steady population increase until 2025 then a slow reduction thereafter. The NISRA long-term forecast shows Northern Ireland's population being only 2.1% higher in 2041 than it is today. Other forecasts have however been more bullish on population growth with Economist Graham Gudgin presenting the 2003 Northern Ireland Economic Conference with a higher increase in the population in the short to medium term.

Population and Religion

One of the key insights into Northern Ireland – from a political perspective – is the changing religious composition of the population. Given that political affiliations correlate significantly with religious divisions, any changes in the relative numbers of the two communities are assumed to have political implications. In most other parts of the western world the religious breakdown of the population would only be of academic interest but in Northern Ireland it attracts much more attention for this reason.

Of considerable political significance is the perception that the birth rate in the Catholic community is traditionally much higher than in the Protestant community, adding weight to the majority community's fear that political power would shift from the declining Protestant majority to the growing Catholic minority. Over recent years both birth rates have slowed down and the gap has narrowed significantly.

Religious Affiliation

Northern Ireland is home to people from a variety of ethnic and religious backgrounds. However, most people in the region describe themselves in terms of the principal Christian denominations found throughout the English-speaking world: the Roman Catholic Church; the Church of Ireland (Anglican); the Presbyterian Church; or other, smaller Protestant denominations. In the 2001 Northern Ireland Census of population, 40% of the population stated directly that they were Roman Catholic, with 46% stating they belonged to other Christian religions, the vast majority of which were Protestant.

Other religions and philosophies were stated by only 0.3% of those responding. In the 2001 census 14% responded as having no religion or not stating it, which represented a significant increase on 4% recorded in 1991. Examining the census results at a Local Government District level it is apparent that there is a much higher incidence of people in urban areas recording no religion (or not stating it). Highest percentages are to be found in North Down (25%), Carrickfergus (23%) and Ards (21%) while the lowest figures are in Strabane and Magherafelt (both 6%) and Cookstown (7%).

The second largest denomination in Northern Ireland after Roman Catholic is the Presbyterian Church followed by the Church of Ireland (Anglican) with Methodists a distant fourth. In addition there are numerous other smaller Protestant denominations often characterised by evangelical zeal and more fundamentalist doctrines. Unlike may Western countries where the Catholic Church would find itself almost done on the right wing of social policy, in Northern Ireland these smaller churches exert a strong conservative influence on social policy being apposed for example to abortion and euthanasia (like Roman Catholics) but also to homosexuality and failure to fully observe the Sabbath Day. As a result many parts of Northern Ireland observe a strict regime on Sundays where working of participation in organised leisure activities is not encouraged.

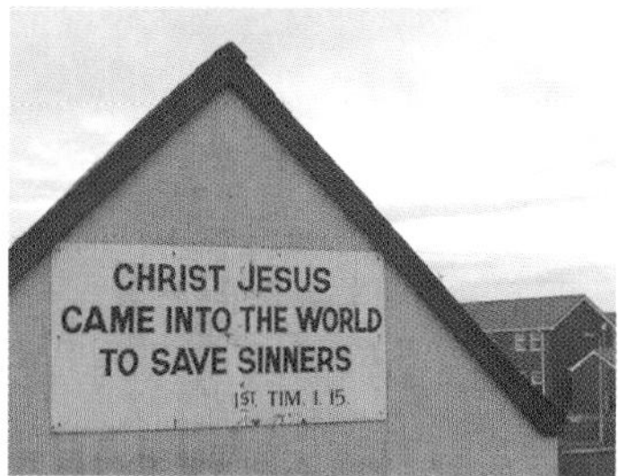

These results are interesting when compared with the figures for community background which includes religion or religion brought up in: just 3% of the population responded as having brought up with no religious or community background. This suggests that around 10% of the population have chosen not to adhere to the traditional religious beliefs in which they were brought up. Again, there is a much higher than average incidence of people having been brought up with no religious or community background in urban areas – figures are highest in North Down, Carrickfergus and Ards and are lowest (under 1%) in Strabane, Newry and Mourne and Dungannon. This all implies that people are more likely to continue to adhere to the beliefs in which they were brought up in rural areas, where there is a higher percentage of the population who are brought up within a religious or community background.

Northern Ireland has higher rates of church attendance than elsewhere in the United Kingdom and religion is, in its own right, important to the life of the area. Even people who have little formal religious commitment often have a social background which is linked to one or other of the two main religious communities. Frequently it is on this basis that they are perceived by others to belong to either the Protestant or Catholic community.

The community to which a person belongs often influences many other aspects of their life: their national identity, language, the area in which they live, the school they or their children attend, the political party they support and even their name. Religious community background (rather than theological belief) as the principal source of social identity in Northern Ireland has been the subject of considerable academic attention.

Segregation

Overall the 2001 census figures show that 44% of respondents were brought up in the Catholic religion/background and 53% were brought up with Protestant and other Christian backgrounds. These are the figures for Northern Ireland as a whole and suggest an increasingly even Catholic/Protestant split. The situation is somewhat different when examined in greater detail.

In the Local Government Districts of Carrickfergus, Ards, North Down, Castlereagh and Newtownabbey over 75% responded as being brought up within the Protestant community. In Newry and Mourne and Derry over 75% responded as being brought up within the Catholic community. This all points to the fact that while, overall Northern Ireland appears a fairly mixed community, when examined in greater detail, many areas remain dominated by one or other of the main religions.

Language and Identity

The Northern Ireland Social Attitudes Survey was first conducted in 1989. Focusing on a range of social and political issues, it collected the opinions of a representative sample of persons aged 18 or over who live in private households. In the 1995 survey, 63% of Catholic respondents described themselves as 'Irish' compared with 5% of Protestants. In contrast, 64% of Protestant respondents described themselves as 'British' compared with 11% of Catholics.

The 2001 Census also contained a question on knowledge of the Irish language, which was to be answered in respect of the population aged three or over. Just over one in ten people (10.35%) had some knowledge of Irish (ie could speak, read or write the language). In 1995-96, 1038 pupils in Northern Ireland, equating to 0.3% of all school enrolments, were taught through the medium of Irish.

Northern Ireland Households

Household size and Type

Households in Northern Ireland tend to be significantly larger than the average for the United Kingdom as a whole. The average Northern Ireland household comprised 3 persons in 2001-02, with people living alone representing a quarter of the region's households.

In 2001-02 30% of Northern Ireland households comprised 4 or more people. Traditionally Northern Ireland's households have been larger than the UK average, partly because of the tendency for Northern Ireland families to have more children, and also the fact that the traditional extended family (including grandparents) has survived to a greater extent in Northern Ireland. Although family sizes are higher in Northern Ireland, they have been coming down steadily in absolute terms. Higher expectations about living standards and changes to the structure of living costs has meant that many families on average incomes would struggle to maintain a desired standard of living for larger household sizes, i.e. with more than 2 or 3 children. Economic forces therefore, combined with social attitudinal change in relation to family planning have put downward pressure on family size. This trend has been apparent in both religious communities.

Table 1.8 Number of Persons in Household 1997-98 to 2001-02

No of persons	Northern Ireland				
	97-98	98-99	99-00	00-01	01-02
1	26	25	25	25	26
2	27	30	30	28	29
3	16	15	15	16	18
4	16	16	16	16	15
5	8	8	8	9	7
>6	6	5	5	5	5
Average Household size	2.74	2.71	2.67	2.72	2.67

Source: NISRA

Looking at the pattern of household size over the period 1997-98 to 2001-02 (Table 1.8), it is apparent that overall, the size of Northern Ireland households is remaining fairly unchanged. Average household size over this time has remained at around 2.7 and there are no dramatic increases or decreases in any of the categories, although it should be noted that the number of larger households is steadily falling.

There is an overwhelming tendency for lone parents to be mothers rather than fathers. Of all families with dependent children, 25% are lone mothers and just 2% are lone fathers. Of the 25% who are lone mothers, 13% of these are single (as opposed to being widowed, divorced or separated), a figure which has risen significantly from the 8% recorded in 1996-97.

A slight increase is discernable in the number of lone parent households with dependent children; from 8% in 1997-98 to 10% in 2001-02 (see Table 1.9 below).

Table 1.9 Type of Household 1997-98 to 2001/02

Type of household	Northern Ireland				
	97-98	98-99	99-00	00-01	01-02
1 person only	26	25	26	26	26
2 or more adults	3	3	3	3	3
Married / Cohabiting couple:					
with dependent children	30	29	29	29	27
with non-dependent children only	7	8	7	8	8
no children	20	21	22	20	22
Lone parent:					
with dependent children	8	9	8	10	10
with non-dependent children only	4	5	4	4	4
Two or more families	1	1	1	1	1

Source: NISRA; General Household Survey, Office for National Statistics

Household Income and Expenditure

In 2001-02 63% of household income in Northern Ireland was derived from wages and salaries, 8% from self-employment and approximately 21% from social security benefits. Northern Ireland households derive almost twice as much of their income from state benefits compared with the UK as a whole. Also , average household income in Northern Ireland is much lower than the UK average. Expenditure in Northern Ireland as a proportion of total income is also significantly higher.

In 2001-02 the highest proportion of Northern Ireland weekly household expenditure was spent on food (20%), transport (13%) and leisure services (12%). The biggest distinguishing factors between Northern Ireland and the UK as a whole was the extent to which a higher proportion of average weekly expenditure in Northern Ireland was on food, reflecting the overall lower average income. It is also notable that Northern Ireland households spend a significantly lower proportion of their income on housing than those in the rest of the UK around 10% compared with 17%. Northern Ireland households on average spend twice as much of their weekly income on fuel, light and power than the UK average, which reflects the higher energy costs in Northern Ireland. In all other areas (alcohol, tobacco, clothing, household goods/services etc), the proportion of weekly expenditure going on these items is broadly in line with the UK average.

Within Northern Ireland levels of household income and expenditure vary significantly with social class, housing classification and household composition. There is little variation in income and expenditure by geographical area, although incomes are slightly lower within Belfast City Council area than the rest of Northern Ireland, but correspondingly, rates of expenditure are also lower. The eastern region of Northern Ireland enjoys a higher than average level of income and expenditure per capita but is still below the UK average.

Overall, although household income and expenditure in Northern Ireland is lower than the UK average it follows a similar pattern when analysed by household composition and tenure.

(Further related socio-economic information is set out in Chapter 7 'The Northern Ireland Economy' with more about household tenure covered in Chapter 5 'Housing in Northern Ireland')

The Government and Politics of Northern Ireland

The Governance of Northern Ireland

The Role of Westminster

As part of the United Kingdom, Northern Ireland is subject to the authority of the Westminster Parliament. There has generally been a consensus both in London and Belfast however, that Northern Ireland should ideally govern itself according to local policy priorities. There is a general view that a devolved administration offers greater policy sensitivity for Northern Ireland as well as greater accessibility to government in terms of influencing the formulation and execution of policy and the final allocation of resources.

Despite the creation of the new state in 1920, and the devolution of powers to the first Northern Ireland administration, Westminster has always retained ultimate sovereignty over Northern Ireland. Northern Ireland has always continued to send its quota of MPs to the Westminster parliament. Exactly how Westminster has impacted upon Northern Ireland, and what powers it has had, has varied considerably, depending on whether or not Northern Ireland has had its own devolved government at any given time.

During the period 1921-1972, Northern Ireland had its own administration, based at Stormont, (from 1932) and legislation for Northern Ireland was made in the form of Acts of Parliament debated and passed through the Northern Ireland parliament, which comprised a 52 member elected House of Commons and a 26 member nominated House of Lords.

From 1972, following the suspension of the Northern Ireland parliament, Northern Ireland was governed directly from Westminster. The government was represented in Northern Ireland by a Secretary of State and the vast bulk of Northern Ireland's primary legislation was carried into effect by means of Orders in Council. From the late seventies certain Acts relating to Great Britain contained clauses known as "parity orders", enabling the same legislation to be issued for Northern Ireland.

Since 1972 there have been three devolved assemblies, 1974, 1982-86 and the most recent assembly established under the terms of the Northern Ireland Act 1998. The Assembly of 1974 and the 1998 Assembly were given legislative powers, transferred from Westminster; the Assembly of 1982-86 had no legislative powers. (The current assembly elected in late 2003 has yet to convene)

The Belfast Agreement 1998

The Belfast Agreement saw the reestablishment of a Northern Ireland Assembly implemented by the Northern Ireland Act 1998. In elections using proportional representation in the existing eighteen Westminster constituencies one hundred and eight members were elected to the new Assembly. When the Assembly first met on 1 July 1998 it held no legislative powers until devolution on 2 December 1999, when a range of legislative powers were transferred from Westminster to the Assembly and executive power to the power-sharing Executive.

Parliament Buildings Stormont

The terms of the Northern Ireland Act 1998 provide for the establishment of a legislative assembly and the creation of an Executive with a First Minister, Deputy First Minister and ten ministers appointed under the d'Hondt voting procedure. The establishment of new institutions such as the North/South Ministerial Council were also provided for under the Act. Areas devolved to the Assembly and Executive include education, social services, the arts and agriculture, broadly corresponding with those areas devolved to the Welsh Assembly and Scottish Parliament. Full details of exactly which areas of responsibility were devolved and which remain under the control of Westminster are set out below.

Excepted and Reserved Matters

Even under devolution the Secretary of State retains certain clearly defined powers. These include constitutional and security matters relating to Northern Ireland, policing and relationships with the European Union which are not devolved matters under the terms of the Northern Ireland Act 1998. Under the terms of the Northern Ireland Act 1998 Westminster continues to legislate in non-devolved or excepted matters in the form of Orders in Council, Acts and Statutory Instruments. Some presently reserved matters including criminal law and civil defence may eventually be transferred to the Northern Ireland legislature. However, excepted matters will remain permanently under the control of Westminster.

The main areas of government which remain "reserved" or "excepted" are set out below.

Reserved	Excepted	Transferred
• Policing • Security • Prisons • Criminal Justice • Income Tax • National Insurance • Regulation of Telecommunications and Broadcasting	• Elections • Europe • Peace and Reconciliation • Foreign Policy	• All matters not excepted or reserved

Northern Ireland Elected Representation at Westminster

Northern Ireland currently returns 18 MPs to Westminster, but in the past it had a disproportionately lower representation. From the enactment of the Government of Ireland Act 1920 until 1983 it had a representation of 12 MPs. However, the Boundary Commission in 1983 revised the level of representation and five extra seats were created. These were contested for the first time in the June 1983 general election. In 1995, the Boundary Commission examined the situation again and created a further seat bringing the total to eighteen for the May 1997 election.

In addition to its MPs, Northern Ireland also has significant representation in the House of Lords. Details of Ulster Unionist Party members of the House of Lords are set out on page 62.

Current Westminster MPs (elected in 2001)

Constituency	Name	Party
Belfast East	Peter Robinson	DUP
Belfast North	Nigel Dodds	DUP
Belfast South	Rev Martin Smyth	UUP
Belfast West	Gerry Adams	SF
East Antrim	Roy Beggs	UUP
East Londonderry	Gregory Campbell	DUP
Fermanagh & South Tyrone	Michelle Gildernew	SF
Foyle	John Hume	SDLP
Lagan Valley	Jeffrey Donaldson	DUP*
Mid Ulster	Martin McGuinness	SF
Newry and Armagh	Séamus Mallon	SDLP
North Antrim	Rev Ian Paisley	DUP
North Down	Sylvia Hermon	UUP
South Antrim	David Burnside	UUP
South Down	Eddie McGrady	SDLP
Strangford	Iris Robinson	DUP
West Tyrone	Pat Doherty	SF
Upper Bann	David Trimble	UUP

By Party

Party	Seats
DUP	6
UUP	5
SDLP	3
SF	4
Total	18

* Jeffrey Donaldson was elected for the UUP but subsequently joined the DUP

Contact Details for Northern Ireland Westminster MPs

Gerry Adams
Constituency: Belfast West
Party: **Sinn Féin**
Contact: 51-55 Falls Road
Belfast, BT12 4PD
Tel: 028 9022 3000 / Fax: 028 9022 5553

Roy Beggs
Constituency: East Antrim
Party: **Ulster Unionist Party**
Contact: East Antrim Constituency Office
41 Station Road
Larne, BT40 3AA
Tel: 028 2827 3258 / Fax: 028 2828 3007

Westminster: Tel: 020 7219 6305 / Fax: 020 7219 3889

David Burnside
Constituency: South Antrim
Party: **Ulster Unionist Party**
Contact: South Antrim Constituency Office
24 Fountain Street
Antrim, BT41 4BB
Tel: 028 9446 1211
Westminster: Tel: 020 7219 8493

Gregory Campbell
Constituency: East Londonderry
Party: **DUP**
Contact: 25 Bushmills Road
Coleraine, BT52 2BP
Tel: 028 7032 7327 / Fax: 028 7032 7328

Nigel Dodds
Constituency: Belfast North
Party: **DUP**
Contact: 210 Shore Road
Belfast, BT15 3QB
Tel: 028 9077 4774 / Fax: 028 9077 7685

Jeffrey Donaldson*
Constituency: Lagan Valley
Party: **DUP**
Contact: Tel: 028 9266 8001 / Fax: 028 9267 1845
Westminster: Tel: 020 7219 3407 / Fax: 020 7219 0696

* Jeffrey Donaldson was elected for the UUP but subsequently joined the DUP

Pat Doherty
Constituency: West Tyrone
Party: **Sinn Féin**
Contact: 1 Melvin Road
Strabane, BT82 9AE
Tel: 028 7188 6464 / Fax: 028 7188 6466

Michelle Gildernew
Constituency: Fermanagh/South Tyrone
Party: **Sinn Féin**
Contact: 60 Irish Street
Dungannon, BT70 1DQ
Tel: 028 8772 2776 / Fax: 028 8772 2776

Sylvia Hermon
Constituency: North Down
Party: **Ulster Unionist Party**
Contact: North Down Unionist Office
77a High Street, Bangor, BT20 5BD
Tel: 028 9147 0300 / Fax: 028 9147 0301
Westminster: Tel: 020 7219 8491

John Hume
Constituency: Foyle
Party: **SDLP**
Contact: 5 Bayview Terrace
Derry, BT48 7EE
Tel: 028 7126 5340 / Fax: 028 7136 3423

Seamus Mallon
Constituency: Newry and Armagh
Party: **SDLP**
Contact: 2 Bridge Street
Newry, BT35 8AE
Tel: 028 3026 7933 / Fax: 028 3026 7828

Eddie McGrady
Constituency: South Down
Party: **SDLP**
Contact: 32 Saul Street
Downpatrick, BT30 6NQ
Tel: 028 4461 2882 / Fax: 028 4461 9574

Martin McGuinness
Constituency: Mid Ulster
Party: **Sinn Féin**
Contact: 32 Burn Road
Cookstown, BT80 8DN
Tel: 028 8676 5850 / Fax: 028 8676 6734

Ian Paisley
Constituency: North Antrim
Party: **DUP**
Contact: 256 Ravenhill Road
Belfast, BT6 8GJ
Tel: 028 9045 8900 / Fax: 028 9045 7783

Iris Robinson
Constituency: Strangford
Party: **DUP**
Contact: 2b James Street
Newtownards, BT23 4DY
Tel: 028 9182 7701 / Fax: 028 9182 7703

Peter Robinson
Constituency: Belfast East
Party: **DUP**
Contact: Strandtown Hall
96 Belmont Avenue
Belfast, BT4 3DE
Tel: 028 9047 3111 / Fax: 028 9047 1797

Martin Smyth
Constituency: South Belfast
Party: **Ulster Unionist Party**
Contact: South Belfast Unionist Office
117 Cregagh Road
Belfast, BT6 0LA
Tel: 028 9045 7009 / Fax: 028 9045 0837
Westminster: Tel: 020 7219 4098 / Fax: 020 7219 2347

David Trimble
Constituency: Upper Bann
Party: **Ulster Unionist Party**
Contact: Upper Bann Unionist Office
2 Queen Street
Lurgan / BT66 8BQ
Tel: 028 3832 8088 / Fax: 028 3832 2343
Westminster: Tel: 020 7219 6987 / Fax: 020 7219 2489

Northern Ireland Business at Westminster

The right to debate matters pertaining to Northern Ireland and legislate in those areas not devolved to the Northern Ireland Assembly is retained by Westminster.

Northern Ireland business in the Commons is conducted in a number of ways:

- For Primary legislation, through the full Westminster legislative process;
- Through the Northern Ireland Grand Committee;
- Through the Northern Ireland Affairs Select Committee;
- Through questions addressed to the Secretary of State for Northern Ireland.

Northern Ireland Affairs Select Committee

The Northern Ireland Affairs Select Committee was first proposed in 1990 and then established in 1994 to examine the expenditure, policy and administration of the Northern Ireland Office and the administration of the Crown Solicitor's Office. It has the power to send for persons, papers and records. The committee has investigated areas such as employment, electricity prices, education, BSE and the security forces in Northern Ireland. It produces detailed reports and recommendations on these matters following an extensive process of "taking of evidence" from interested parties on any given issue. The committee has a maximum of thirteen members with a quorum of four.

During the 2002-03 parliamentary session the Committee produced reports on issues as varied as Cross-Border Fuel Price Differerentials, the Illegal Drugs Trade and the Control of Firearms.

Membership of the Northern Ireland Affairs Select Committee

Member	Party	Constituency
Adrian Bailey	Lab	West Bromwich West
Harry Barnes	Lab	North East Derbyshire
Henry Bellingham	Con	North West Norfolk
Roy Beggs	UUP	East Antrim
Tony Clarke	Lab	Northampton South
Stephen McCabe	Lab	Dundee East
Eddie McGrady	SDLP	South Down
Stephen Pound	Lab	Ealing North
Peter Robinson	DUP	Belfast East
Martin Smyth	UUP	Belfast South
Mark Tami	Lab	Alyn & Deeside
Bill Tynan	Lab	Hamilton South
Michael Mates(Chair)	Con	East Hampshire

Committee Clerk: Elizabeth Hunt
Northern Ireland Affairs Committee
House of Commons, London SW1A 0AA
Tel: 020 7219 2172 / Fax: 020 7219 0300
Email: northircom@parliament.uk
Web: www.parliament.uk/commons/section/niahome.htm

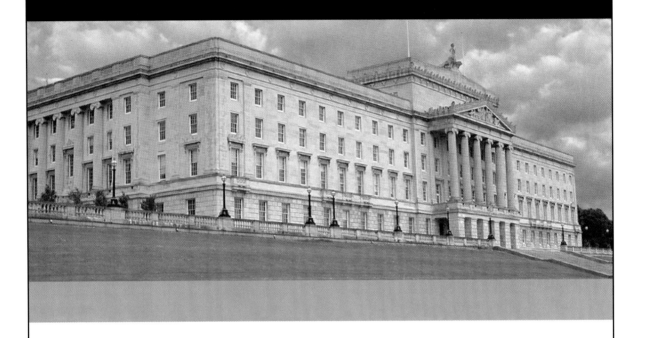

The Northern Ireland Assembly

The Northern Ireland Assembly
Parliament Buildings
Belfast, BT4 3XX
Tel: 028 9052 1862
Fax: 028 9052 1959
Web: www.ni-assembly.gov.uk

Overview

The Northern Ireland Assembly was established as part of the Good Friday Agreement (also referred to as the Belfast Agreement) following its endorsement by simultaneous referenda in Northern Ireland and the Republic of Ireland *(the results of these referenda are set out in Chapter 1 on page 18)*. The Assembly is composed of 108 elected members: 6 elected, using proportional representation, from each of the 18 Westminster constituencies. There are 12 Executive Ministers, including the First Minister and Deputy First Minister who share a unique joint Department, the Office of the First Minister and Deputy First Minister (OFMDFM). The structure of the Assembly and its institutions, including other institutions of the Good Friday Agreement are set out in the following diagram.

The legislative Assembly has full legislative and executive authority to make laws and take decisions on the functions of the 10 departments. Whilst certain functions remain reserved, the Assembly may legislate on these areas with the approval of the Secretary of State for Northern Ireland, under the overall control of the Westminster Parliament.

An individual member, committee or Minister may initiate legislation. Voting is by simple majority unless cross-community support is required. A petition of 30 concerned members can trigger such a voting procedure. In these cases, parallel consent or a weighted majority of 60% of those members present and voting, is required.

Cross Community Decision-Making

Arrangements to ensure decisions are taken on a cross community basis:

(i) Either parallel consent, i.e. a majority of those members present and voting, including a majority of the unionist and nationalist designations present and voting;

(ii) Or a weighted majority (60 per cent) of members present and voting, including at least 40 per cent of each of the nationalist and unionist delegations present and voting.

Key decisions requiring cross-community support will be designated in advance, including election of the Chair of the Assembly, the First Minister and Deputy First Minister, standing orders and budget allocations. In other cases, such decisions could be triggered by a Petition of Concern brought by a minimum of 30 Assembly Members.

Ministerial departments and membership of their respective committees are allocated according to a system of proportional representation ensuring that parties are given ministerial posts, committee chairs and committee seats in proportion to the number of Assembly members returned.

The ministerial posts during the first Assembly were allocated as follows:

Ulster Unionist Party: 4
SDLP: 4
DUP: 2
Sinn Féin: 2

Much of the internal work of the Assembly and its Committees is governed by Standing Orders (produced mainly by the Assembly Procedures Committee).

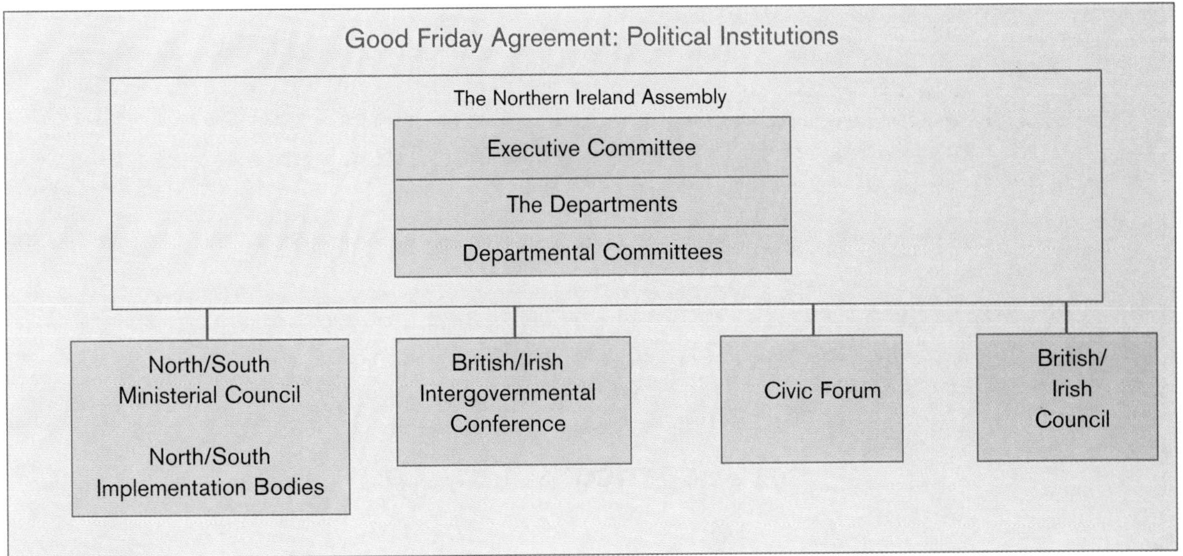

Principal Officers and Officials of the Northern Ireland Assembly

In addition to the Permanent Secretaries, the civil service through the provision of clerical and administrative staff supports the work of the Northern Ireland Assembly. Clerks play a key role in the legislative process within the Assembly including the operation of the Committees and the management of the business of the House.

Clerk to the Assembly/ Chief Executive	Arthur Moir
Deputy Chief Executive	Tom Evans
Deputy Clerk to the Assembly	Joe Reynolds
Private Secretary to the Clerk	Sheila McClelland
Clerk Assistant	Nuala Dunwoody
Editor of Debates	Simon Burrowes
Keeper of the House	Agnes Peacocke
Director of Research and Information	Allan Black
Head of Finance	Fiona Hamill
Head of Personnel	Evan Hobson
Director of Legal Services	Claire McGivern
Principal Clerk Bill Office	Martin Wilson
Principal Clerk Business Office	Alan Rogers
Clerk to the Commission	Tony Logue
Principal Clerks	Alan Patterson
	John Torney
	Debbie Pritchard
Examiner of Statutory Rules	Gordon Nabney
Comptroller and Auditor General	John Dowdall
Assembly Ombudsman	Tom Frawley

The Speaker's Office

Speaker: Lord John Alderdice (pictured)
Speaker's Private Secretary:
Georgina Campbell
Tel: 028 9052 1862
Speaker's Counsel:
Nicolas Hanna QC

The Speaker is the Presiding Officer of the Northern Ireland Assembly. The ruling of the Speaker is final on all questions of matter and procedure in the Assembly.

The function of the Speaker's Office is to provide support to the Speaker in the execution of his duties, which include, amongst others:

- Presiding over plenary sessions of the Assembly;
- Scrutinising legislation at pre introduction and final stages;
- Nomination of members to various bodies, e.g. the Senate of the University of Ulster.

The position of the Speaker was held by Lord John Alderdice, during the lifetime of the first Assembly. Despite the suspension of the Assembly in 2002 and the second Assembly elections of 2003, Lord Alderdice continues to hold this position until such time as a new Speaker is elected. This will be the first item of business to be carried out if and when the Assembly elected in 2003 meets for the first time.

Office of the Clerk and Records of the Assembly

The Clerk notes all proceedings of the Assembly and the minutes of proceedings, having been perused and signed by the Speaker, are printed and constitute the Journal of the Proceedings of the Assembly. The Clerk is the custodian of all Journals of Proceedings, records and other documents belonging to the Assembly.

The Assembly Commission

Tel: 028 9052 1930

The Assembly Commission is responsible for providing and maintaining the property, services and staff required for the purposes of the Assembly.

Its task is to represent the interests of the Assembly and its 108 elected Members. Some of the responsibilities of the Assembly Commission are as follows:

- Agreement of room allocation for individual Assembly Members, Assembly parties, Committee Chairpersons, Ministers and the Assembly's own staff as well as office accommodation, press and visitors' facilities;
- Ensuring that the public has ready access to the public areas within Parliament Buildings;
- Arranging of all the services required to support the work of the Assembly e.g. the Office of the Official Report, Members' Services;
- Determining staffing levels and carrying out recruitment competitions to obtain the complement of staff required to support the Assembly.

An organisation chart for the Assembly Commission is shown on the next page.

The Office of the Clerk to the Northern Ireland Assembly

Tel: 028 9052 1790

The function of the Office of the Clerk to the Northern Ireland Assembly is to provide a central policy and management function and to offer a range of corporate services to the Assembly. The Office also provides support services for the Clerk and Chief Executive, the Deputy Chief Executive, the Deputy Clerk, the Head of Legal Services and the Examiner of Statutory Rules. The Office comprises the following functional areas:

- Private office;
- Internal audit;
- Procurement office;
- Legal services;
- Examiner of statutory rules.

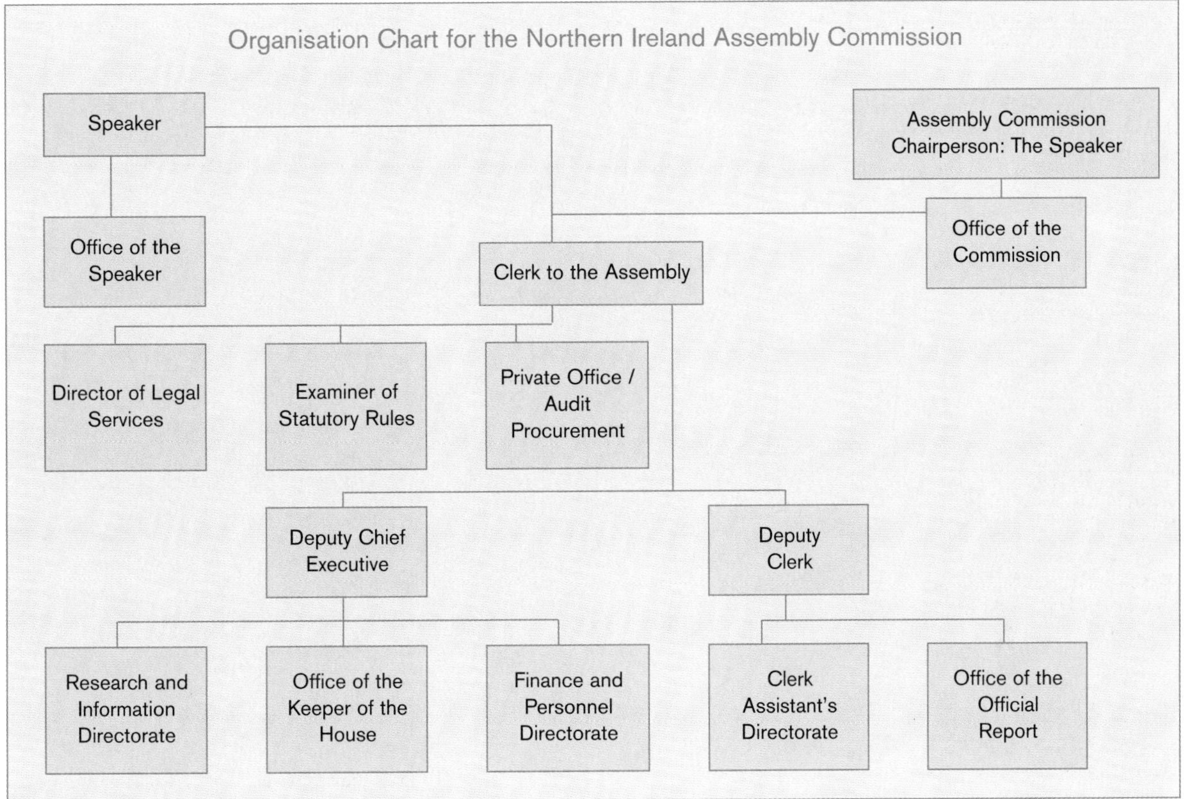

Clerk Assistant's Directorate

The function of the Clerk Assistant's Directorate is to meet the needs of Members and Committees when carrying out Assembly business, to establish a team of trained staff and maintain a programme of continuous staff training and development and to maximise resources within its budget. The Directorate is organised into three offices:

- The Bills Office;
- The Business Office;
- The Committee Office.

Office of the Official Report (Hansard)

The Function of the Office of the Official Report is to produce the Official Report of all sittings of the Assembly, including details of debates, resolutions, questions, votes and appropriate Committee sessions. The Hansard report, which is available to the public, lists the names of all the Members, reports what they say and records all the Assembly's decisions.

Keeper of the House Directorate

The function of the Keeper of the House Directorate is to deliver the best possible service to Members, the public and all those who work in or visit Parliament Buildings. Key areas of work include events, support services, works, health and safety and security.

This is managed by the:

- Events Co-ordination Office;
- Facilities Branch;
- Works Branch;
- Health and Safety Branch;
- Security Branch.

Research and Information Directorate

The function of the Research and Information Directorate is to source, process, transform and communicate information for and within the Assembly and to ensure that its business is open to public interest and scrutiny. The Directorate is comprised of three functional units:

- Research and Library Services;
- Information Office;
- Information Systems Office.

Finance and Personnel Directorate

The function of the Finance and Personnel Directorate is to provide support for Members and the Secretariat ranging from recruitment to pensions and including accounting systems, the provision of stationery, filing systems and reprographic services. The Directorate has four units:

- Personnel Office;
- Finance Office;
- Recruitment Office;
- Registry.

Elected Members of the Assembly (2003)

The table below summarises the outcome of the 2003 Northern Ireland Assembly elections in terms of party strength.

Overall Assembly Election Results by Party November 2003

Party	% 1st pref Votes	Seats
DUP	25.7	30
UUP	22.7	27
Sinn Féin	23.5	24
SDLP	17.0	18
Alliance	3.7	6
UKUP	0.8	1
PUP	1.2	1
Others	5.4	1
Total	**100**	**108**

What follows is a detailed listing of the elected members firstly by party affiliation, then by constituency and then A-Z with contact details.

Assembly Members by Party Affiliation (as elected in November 2003)

Democratic Unionist Party (30)

Paul Berry	Newry and Armagh
Thomas Buchanan	West Tyrone
Gregory Campbell	East Londonderry
Wilson Clyde	South Antrim
George Dawson	East Antrim
Dianne Dodds	Belfast West
Nigel Dodds	Belfast North
Alex Easton	North Down
George Ennis	Strangford
Paul Girvan	South Antrim
William Hay	Foyle
David Hilditch	East Antrim
Nelson McCausland	Belfast North
Rev William McCrea	Mid Ulster
Maurice Morrow	Fermanagh and South Tyrone
Stephen Moutray	Upper Bann
Robin Newton	Belfast East
Rev Ian Paisley	North Antrim
Ian Paisley Jr	North Antrim
Edwin Poots	Lagan Valley
George Robinson	East Londonderry
Iris Robinson	Strangford
Mark Robinson	Belfast South
Peter Robinson	Belfast East
Jim Shannon	Strangford
David Simpson	Upper Bann
Mervyn Storey	North Antrim
Peter Weir	North Down
Jim Wells	South Down
Sammy Wilson	Belfast East

Ulster Unionist Party (27)

Billy Armstrong	Mid Ulster
Norah Beare*	Lagan Valley
Roy Beggs	East Antrim
Billy Bell	Lagan Valley
Dr Esmond Birnie	Belfast South
David Burnside	South Antrim
Fred Cobain	Belfast North
Michael Copeland	Belfast East
Rev Robert Coulter	North Antrim
Leslie Cree	North Down
Jeffrey Donaldson*	Lagan Valley
Tom Elliott	Fermanagh/South Tyrone
Sir Reg Empey	Belfast East
Arlene Foster*	Fermanagh/South Tyrone
Samuel Gardiner	Upper Bann
Norman Hillis	East Londonderry
Derek Hussey	West Tyrone
Danny Kennedy	Newry and Armagh
David McClarty	East Londonderry
Alan McFarland	North Down
Michael McGimpsey	Belfast South
David McNarry	Strangford
Dermot Nesbitt	South Down
Ken Robinson	East Antrim
John Taylor	Strangford
David Trimble	Upper Bann
Jim Wilson	South Antrim

* Jeffrey Donaldson, Arlene Foster and Norah Beare subsequently joined the DUP raising DUP representation to 33 seats and reducing UUP representation to 24.

Sinn Féin (24)

Gerry Adams	Belfast West
Bairbre de Brún	Belfast West
Francis Brolly	East Londonderry
Willie Clarke	South Down
Pat Doherty	West Tyrone
Geraldine Dougan	Mid Ulster
Michael Ferguson	Belfast West
Michelle Gildernew	Fermanagh and South Tyrone
Davy Hyland	Newry and Armagh
Gerry Kelly	Belfast North
Alex Maskey	Belfast South
Fra McCann	Belfast West
Barry McElduff	West Tyrone
Philip McGuigan	North Antrim
Martin McGuinness	Mid Ulster
Mitchel McLaughlin	Foyle
Francie Molloy	Mid Ulster
Conor Murphy	Newry and Armagh
Mary Nelis	Foyle
John O'Dowd	Upper Bann
Pat O'Rawe	Newry and Armagh
Thomas O'Reilly	Fermanagh and South Tyrone
Caitriona Ruane	South Down
Kathy Stanton	Belfast North

Social Democratic and Labour Party (18)

Alex Attwood	Belfast West
Dominic Bradley	Newry and Armagh
PJ Bradley	South Down
Mary Bradley	Foyle
Thomas Burns	South Antrim
John Dallat	East Londonderry
Mark Durkan	Foyle
Dr Sean Farren	North Antrim
Tommy Gallagher	Fermanagh and South Tyrone
Carmel Hanna	Belfast South
Dolores Kelly	Upper Bann
Patricia Lewsley	Lagan Valley
Alban Maginness	Belfast North
Dr Alasdair McDonnell	Belfast South
Patsy McGlone	Mid Ulster
Eugene McMenamin	West Tyrone
Pat Ramsay	Foyle
Margaret Ritchie	South Down

Alliance Party (6)

Eileen Bell	North Down
Seamus Close	Lagan Valley
David Ford	South Antrim
Naomi Long	Belfast East
Kieran McCarthy	Strangford
Sean Neeson	East Antrim

United Kingdom Unionist Party (1)

Robert McCartney	North Down

Progressive Unionist Party (1)

David Ervine	Belfast East

Independent (1)

Kieran Deeny	West Tyrone

Assembly Members by Constituency (as elected in November 2003)

Belfast East

Michael Copeland	UUP
Sir Reg Empey	UUP
David Ervine	PUP
Naomi Long	All
Robin Newton	DUP
Peter Robinson	DUP

Belfast North

Fred Cobain	UUP
Nigel Dodds	DUP
Gerry Kelly	SF
Alban Maginness	SDLP
Nelson McCausland	DUP
Kathy Stanton	SF

Belfast South

Esmond Birnie	UUP
Carmel Hanna	SDLP
Alex Maskey	SF
Alasdair McDonnell	SDLP
Michael McGimpsey	UUP
Mark Robinson	DUP

Belfast West

Gerry Adams	SF
Alex Attwood	SDLP
Bairbre de Brún	SF
Dianne Dodds	DUP
Michael Ferguson	SF
Fra McCann	SF

East Antrim

Roy Beggs Jr	UUP
George Dawson	DUP
David Hilditch	DUP
Sean Neeson	All
Ken Robinson	UUP
Sammy Wilson	DUP

East Londonderry

Francis Brolly	SF
Gregory Campbell	DUP
John Dallat	SDLP
Norman Hillis	UUP
David McClarty	UUP
George Robinson	DUP

Fermanagh and South Tyrone

Tom Elliott	UUP
Arlene Foster*	UUP
Tommy Gallagher	SDLP
Michelle Gildernew	SF
Maurice Morrow	DUP
Thomas O'Reilly	SF

*Arlene Foster subsequently joined the DUP

Foyle

Mary Bradley	SDLP
Mark Durkan	SDLP
William Hay	DUP
Mitchel McLaughlin	SF
Mary Nelis	SF
Pat Ramsay	SDLP

Lagan Valley

Norah Beare*	UUP
Billy Bell	UUP
Seamus Close	All
Jeffrey Donaldson*	UUP
Patricia Lewsley	SDLP
Edwin Poots	DUP

*Norah Beare and Jeffrey Donaldson subsequently joined the DUP

Mid Ulster

Billy Armstrong	UUP
Geraldine Dougan	SF
Rev William McCrea	DUP
Patsy McGlone	SDLP
Martin McGuinness	SF
Francie Molloy	SF

Newry and Armagh

Paul Berry	DUP
Dominic Bradley	SDLP
Davy Hyland	SF
Danny Kennedy	UUP
Conor Murphy	SF
Pat O'Rawe	SF

North Antrim

Rev Robert Coulter	UUP
Sean Farren	SDLP
Philip McGuigan	SF
Rev Ian Paisley	DUP
Ian Paisley Jr	DUP
Mervyn Storey	DUP

North Down

Eileen Bell	All
Leslie Cree	UUP
Alex Easton	DUP
Robert McCartney	UKUP
Alan McFarland	UUP
Peter Weir	DUP

South Antrim

Thomas Burns	SDLP
David Burnside	UUP
Wilson Clyde	DUP
David Ford	All
Paul Girvan	DUP
Jim Wilson	UUP

South Down

PJ Bradley	SDLP
Willie Clarke	SF
Dermot Nesbitt	UUP
Margaret Ritchie	SDLP
Caitriona Ruane	SF
Jim Wells	UUP

Strangford

George Ennis	DUP
Kieran McCarthy	All
David McNarry	UUP
Iris Robinson	DUP
Jim Shannon	DUP
John Taylor	UUP

Upper Bann

Samuel Gardiner	UUP
Dolores Kelly	SDLP
Stephen Moutray	DUP
John O'Dowd	SF
David Simpson	DUP
David Trimble	UUP

West Tyrone

Thomas Buchanan	DUP
Kieran Deeny	Ind
Pat Doherty	SF
Derek Hussey	UUP
Barry McElduff	SF
Eugene McMenamin	SDLP

A-Z of Assembly Members with Contact Details

Due to the ongoing suspension of the Assembly following the 2003 Assembly elections, each *party* was allocated offices at Stormont, rather than each *individual member* as was previously the case. Contact details for parties at Stormont are as follows:

Democratic Unionist Party (DUP)
Room 207, Parliament Buildings
Stormont Estate
Belfast BT4 3XX
Tel: 028 9052 1323

Ulster Unionist Party (UUP)
Room 209, Parliament Buildings
Stormont Estate
Belfast BT4 3XX
Tel: 028 9052 1328

Sinn Féin (SF)
Room 263
Parliament Buildings
Stormont Estate
Belfast BT4 3XX
Tel: 028 9052 1144

Social Democratic & Labour Party (SDLP)
Room 272
Parliament Buildings
Stormont Estate
Belfast BT4 3XX
Tel: 028 9052 1319

The Alliance Party of Northern Ireland (All)
Room 220
Parliament Buildings
Stormont Estate
Belfast BT4 3XX
Tel: 028 9052 1315

United Kingdom Unionist Party (UKUP)
Room 214
Parliament Buildings
Stormont Estate
Belfast BT4 3XX
Tel: 028 9052 1482

Progressive Unionist Party (PUP)
Room 260
Parliament Buildings
Stormont Estate
Belfast BT4 3XX
Tel: 028 9052 1143

Members

Adams, Gerry MP, Sinn Féin
Constituency: Belfast West

Constituency Office:
53 Falls Road
Belfast, BT12 4PD
Tel: 028 9022 3000

Armstrong, Billy, Ulster Unionist
Constituency: Mid Ulster

Constituency Office:
Prospect House
Coagh House
Dungannon, BT71 5JH
Tel: 028 8773 8641

Attwood, Alex, SDLP
Constituency : Belfast West

Constituency Office:
60 Andersonstown Road, Belfast
Tel: 028 9080 7808

***Beare, Norah**, DUP
Constituency: Lagan Valley

Constituency Office:
The Old Town Hall
Castle Street Lisburn, BT27 4XD
Tel: 028 9266 8001

Beggs, Roy MP, Ulster Unionist
Constituency: East Antrim

Constituency Office:
41 Station Road, Larne, BT30 3AA
Tel: 028 2827 3258

Bell, Billy, Ulster Unionist
Constituency: Lagan Valley

Constituency Office:
2 Sackville Street,
Lisburn, BT27 4AB
Tel: 028 9262 9171

Bell, Eileen, Alliance
Constituency: North Down

Constituency Office:
27 Maryville Road
Bangor, BT20 3RH
Tel: 028 9145 2321

Berry, Paul, DUP
Constituency: Newry and Armagh

Constituency Office:
78 Market Street
Tandragee, BT62 2BP
Tel: 028 3884 1668

Birnie, Dr Esmond, Ulster Unionist
Constituency: Belfast South

Constituency Office:
117 Cregagh Road
Belfast, BT6 0LA
Tel: 028 9087 3794

Bradley, Dominic, SDLP
Constituency: Newry and Armagh

Constituency Office:
2 Bridge Street
Newry, BT35 8AE
Tel: 028 3026 7933

Bradley, Mary, SDLP
Constituency: Foyle

Constituency Office:
7B Messines Terrace
Derry, BT48 7QJ
Tel: 028 7136 0700

Bradley, PJ, SDLP
Constituency: South Down

Constituency Office:
2 East Street
Warrenpoint, BT34 3JE
Tel: 028 4177 2228

Brolly, Francis, Sinn Féin
Constituency: East Londonderry

Constituency Office:
Contact Party HQ
53 Falls Road, Belfast, BT12 4PD
Tel: 028 9022 3000

Buchanan, Thomas, DUP
Constituency: West Tyrone

Constituency Office:
c/o 46 Kirlish Road, Drumquin
Omagh
BT78 4PY
Tel: 07803 190157

*Norah Beare was elected for the UUP but subsequently joined the DUP.

Burns, Thomas, SDLP
Constituency: South Antrim

Constituency Office:
25D New Street
Randalstown, BT41 3AF
Tel: 028 9447 8315

Burnside, David, Ulster Unionist
Constituency: South Antrim

Constituency Office:
24 Fountain Street
Antrim, BT41 4BB
Tel: 028 9446 1211

Campbell, Gregory MP, DUP
Constituency: East Londonderry

Constituency Office:
25 Bushmills Road
Coleraine, BT52 2BP
Tel: 028 7032 7327

Clarke, Willie, Sinn Féin
Constituency: South Down

Constituency Office:
Contact Party HQ
53 Falls Road, Belfast, BT12 4PD
Tel: 028 9022 3000

Close, Seamus, Alliance
Constituency: Lagan Valley

Constituency Office:
123 Moira Road
Lisburn, BT28 1RJ
Tel: 028 9267 0639

Clyde, Wilson, DUP
Constituency: South Antrim

Constituency Office:
69 Church Street
Antrim, BT41 4BG
Tel: 028 9446 2280

Cobain, Fred, Ulster Unionist
Constituency: Belfast North

Constituency Office:
23a York Road
Belfast, BT15 3GU
Tel: 028 9059 4801

Copeland, Michael, Ulster Unionist
Constituency: Belfast East

Constituency Office:
4A Belmont Road
Belfast, BT4 2AN
Tel: 028 9065 8217

Coulter, Rev Robert, Ulster Unionist
Constituency: North Antrim

Constituency Office:
30A Ballmoney Street
Ballymena, BT43 6AL
Tel: 028 2564 2262

Cree, Leslie, Ulster Unionist
Constituency: North Down

Constituency Office:
77A High Street
Bangor, BT20 5BD
Tel: 028 9147 0300

Dallat, John, SDLP
Constituency: East Londonderry

Constituency Office:
11 Bridge Street
Kilrea, BT51 5RR
Tel: 028 2954 1880

Dawson, George, DUP
Constituency: East Antrim

Constituency Office:
22A High Street
Carrickfergus, BT38 7AA
Tel: 028 9332 9980

de Brún, Bairbre, Sinn Féin
Constituency: Belfast West

Constituency Office:
53 Falls Road
Belfast, BT12 4PD
Tel: 028 9022 3000

Deeny, Kieran Dr, Ind
Constituency: West Tyrone

Assembly Office:
Room 223 Parliment Buildings
Stormont Estate, Belfast BT4 3XX
Tel: 028 9052 0464

Constituency Office:
c/o Carrickmore Health Centre
4 Termon Road
Carrickmore, BT79 9JR
Tel: 028 8076 1242

Dodds, Nigel MP, DUP
Constituency: Belfast North

Constituency Office:
210 Shore Road
Belfast, BT15 3QB
Tel: 028 9077 4774

Dodds, Dianne, DUP
Constituency: Belfast West

Constituency Office:
210 Shore Road
Belfast, BT15 3QB
Tel: 028 9077 4774

Doherty, Pat MP, Sinn Féin
Constituency: West Tyrone

Constituency Office:
1A Melvin Road
Strabane, BT82 9PP
Tel: 028 7188 1020

***Donaldson, Jeffrey MP**, DUP
Constituency: Lagan Valley

Constituency Office:
The Old Town Hall
Castle Street Lisburn, BT27 4XD
Tel: 028 9266 8001

Dougan, Geraldine, Sinn Féin
Constituency: Mid Ulster

Constituency Office:
32 Burn Road
Cookstown, BT80 8DN
Tel: 028 8676 5850

Durkan, Mark, SDLP
Constituency: Foyle

Constituency Office:
7B Messines Terrace, Racecourse Road
Derry, BT48 7QJ
Tel: 028 7136 0700

*Jeffrey Donaldson was elected for the UUP but subsequently joined the DUP.

Easton, Alex, DUP
Constituency: North Down

Constituency Office:
94 Abbey Street
Bangor, BT20 4JB
Tel: 028 9145 4500

Elliott, Tom, Ulster Unionist
Constituency: Fermanagh/South Tyrone

Constituency Office:
1 Regal Pass
Enniskillen, BT74 7NT
Tel: 028 6634 2846

Empey, Sir Reg, Ulster Unionist
Constituency: Belfast East

Constituency Office:
4A Belmont Road
Belfast, BT4 2AN
Tel: 028 9065 8217

Ennis, George, DUP
Constituency: Strangford

Constituency Office:
34A Frances Street
Newtownards, BT23 7DN
Tel: 028 9182 7990

Ervine, David, PUP
Constituency: Belfast East

Constituency Office:
299 Newtownards Road
Belfast, BT4 1AG
Tel: 028 9022 5040

Farren, Dr Sean, SDLP
Constituency: North Antrim

Constituency Office:
Bryan House, 16-18 Bryan Street
Ballymena, BT43 6DN
Tel: 028 2563 8765

Ferguson, Michael, Sinn Féin
Constituency: Belfast West

Constituency Office:
53 Falls Road
Belfast, BT12 4PD
Tel: 028 9022 3000

Ford, David, Alliance
Constituency: South Antrim

Constituency Office:
9 Carnmoney Road
Newtownabbey, BT36 6HL
Tel: 028 9084 0930

***Foster, Arlene,** DUP
Constituency: Fermanagh/South Tyrone

Constituency Office:
21 Belmore Street
Enniskillen, BT74 6AA
Tel: 028 6632 0722

Gallagher, Tommy, SDLP
Constituency: Fermanagh/South Tyrone

Constituency Office:
39 Darling Street
Enniskillen, BT74 7DP
Tel: 028 6634 2848

Gardiner, Samuel, Ulster Unionist
Constituency: Upper Bann

Constituency Office:
2 Queen Street
Lurgan, BT66 8BQ
Tel: 028 3832 8088

Gildernew, **Michelle MP,** Sinn Féin
Constituency: Fermanagh/South Tyrone

Constituency Office:
60 Irish Street
Dungannon, BT70 1DQ
Tel: 028 8772 2776

Girvan, Paul, DUP
Constituency: South Antrim

Constituency Office:
69 Church Street
Antrim, BT41 4BG
Tel: 028 9446 2280

Hanna, Carmel, SDLP
Constituency: Belfast South

Constituency Office:
102 Lisburn Road
Belfast, BT9 6BD
Tel: 028 9068 3535

*Arlene Foster was elected for the UUP but subsequently joined the DUP.

Hay, William, DUP
Constituency: Foyle

Constituency Office:
9 Ebrington Terrace
Waterside, Londonderry, BT47 1JS
Tel: 028 7134 6271

Hilditch, David, DUP
Constituency: East Antrim

Constituency Office:
22 High Street
Carrickfergus, BT38 7AA
Tel: 028 9332 9980

Hillis, Norman, Ulster Unionist
Constituency: East Londonderry

Constituency Office:
12 Dunmore Street
Coleraine, BT52 1EI
Tel: 028 7032 7294

Hussey, Derek, Ulster Unionist
Constituency: West Tyrone

Constituency Office:
48 Main Street
Castlederg, BT81 7BP
Tel: 028 8167 9299

Davy Hyland, Sinn Féin
Constituency: Newry and Armagh

Constituency Office:
38 Irish Street
Armagh, BT61 7EP
Tel: 028 3751 1797

Kelly, Dolores, Sinn Féin
Constituency: Upper Bann

Constituency Office:
41 North Street Lurgan
Dungannon, BT67 9AG
Tel: 028 3832 2140

Kelly, Gerry, Sinn Féin
Constituency: Belfast North

Constituency Office:
291 Antrim Road
Belfast, BT15 2GZ
Tel: 028 9074 0817

Kennedy, Danny, Ulster Unionist
Constituency: Newry & Armagh

Constituency Office:
3 Mallview Terrace
Armagh, BT61 9AN
Tel: 028 3751 1655

Lewsley, Patricia, SDLP
Constituency: Lagan Valley

Constituency Office:
21B Railway Street
Lisburn, BT28 1XG
Tel: 028 9266 9974

Long, Naomi, Alliance
Constituency: Belfast East

Constituency Office:
44A Newtownards Road
Belfast, BT4
Tel: 028 9073 8703

Maginness, Alban, SDLP
Constituency: Belfast North

Constituency Office:
228 Antrim Road
Belfast, BT15 2AN
Tel: 028 9022 0520

Maskey, Alex, Sinn Féin
Constituency: Belfast South

Constituency Office:
Contact Party HQ
53 Falls Road, Belfast, BT12 4PD
Tel: 028 9022 3000

McCann, Fra, Sinn Féin
Constituency: Belfast West

Constituency Office:
53 Falls Road
Belfast, BT12 4PD
Tel: 028 9022 3000

McCarthy, Kieran, Alliance
Constituency: Strangford

Constituency Office:
13 Court Street,
Newtownards, BT23 7NX
Tel: 028 9183 2004

McCartney, Robert, UKUP
Constituency: North Down

Constituency Office:
10 Central Avenue
Bangor, BT20 3AF
Tel: 028 9147 9860

McCausland, Nelson, DUP
Constituency: Belfast North

Constituency Office:
210 Shore Road
Belfast, BT15 3QB
Tel: 028 9077 4774

McClarty, David, Ulster Unionist
Constituency: East Londonderry

Constituency Office:
12 Dunmore Street
Coleraine, BT52 1EI
Tel: 028 7032 7294

McCrea, Rev William, DUP
Constituency: Mid Ulster

Constituency Office:
10 Highfield Road
Magherafelt, BT45 5JD
Tel: 028 7963 2664

McDonnell, Dr Alasdair, SDLP
Constituency: Belfast South

Constituency Office:
143 Ormeau Road
Belfast, BT7 2EB
Tel: 028 9024 2474

McElduff, Barry, Sinn Féin
Constituency: West Tyrone

Constituency Office:
21 Main Street
Carrickmore, BT79 9NH
Tel: 028 8076 1744

McFarland, Alan, Ulster Unionist
Constituency: North Down

Constituency Office:
77A High Street
Bangor, BT20 5BD
Tel: 028 9147 0300

McGimpsey, Michael, Ulster Unionist
Constituency: Belfast South

Constituency Office:
Unit 2, 127-145 Sandy Row
Belfast, BT12 5ET
Tel: 028 9024 5801

McGlone, Patsy, SDLP
Constituency: Mid Ulster

Constituency Office:
54A William Street
Cookstown, BT80 8NB
Tel: 028 7964 5424

McGuigan, Philip, Sinn Féin
Constituency: North Antrim

Constituency Office:
Contact Party HQ
53 Falls Road, Belfast, BT12 4PD
Tel: 028 9022 3000

McGuinness, Martin MP, Sinn Féin
Constituency: Mid Ulster

Constituency Office:
32 Burn Road
Cookstown, BT80 8DN
Tel: 028 8676 5850

McLaughlin, Mitchel, Sinn Féin
Constituency: Foyle

Constituency Office:
15 Cable Street
Derry, BT48 9HF
Tel: 028 7130 9264

McMenamin, Eugene, SDLP
Constituency: West Tyrone

Constituency Office:
33A Abercorn Square
Strabane, BT82 9AQ
Tel: 028 7188 6633

McNarry, David, Ulster Unionist
Constituency: Strangford

Constituency Office:
6 William Street
Newtownards, BT23 4AE
Tel: 028 9181 4123

Molloy, Francie, Sinn Féin
Constituency: Mid Ulster

Constituency Office:
7-9 The Square
Coalisland, BT71 4LN
Tel: 028 8774 8689

Morrow, Maurice, DUP
Constituency: Fermanagh/South Tyrone

Constituency Office:
62B Scotch Street
Dungannon, BT70 1BJ
Tel: 028 8775 2799

Moutray, Stephen, DUP
Constituency: Upper Bann

Constituency Office:
10 Windsor Avenue
Lurgan, BT67 9BG
Tel: 028 3834 6111

Murphy, Conor, Sinn Féin
Constituency: Newry & Armagh

Constituency Office:
35 Main Street
Camlough, BT35 7JG
Tel: 028 3083 9470

Neeson, Sean, Alliance
Constituency: East Antrim

Constituency Office:
North Street
Carrickfergus, BT38 7AQ
Tel: 028 9335 0286

Nelis, Mary, Sinn Féin
Constituency: Foyle

Constituency Office:
21A Glenbrook Terrace
Derry, BT48 0DY
Tel: 028 7137 7551

Nesbitt, Dermot, Ulster Unionist
Constituency: South Down

Constituency Office:
19 Causeway Road
Newcastle, BT33 0DL
Tel: 028 4372 4400

Newton, Robin, DUP
Constituency: Belfast East

Constituency Office:
13 Castlereagh Road
Belfast, BT5 5FB
Tel: 028 9045 9500

O'Dowd, John, Sinn Féin
Constituency: Upper Bann

Constituency Office:
77 North Street
Lurgan, BT67 9AH
Tel: 028 3834 9675

O'Rawe, Pat, Sinn Féin
Constituency: Newry & Armagh

Constituency Office:
38 Irish Street
Armagh, BT61 7EP
Tel: 028 3751 1797

O'Reilly, Thomas, Sinn Féin
Constituency: Fermanagh/South Tyrone

Constituency Office:
7 Market Street
Enniskillen, BT74 7DS
Tel: 028 6632 8214

Paisley, Dr Rev Ian, DUP
Constituency: North Antrim

Constituency Office:
46 Hill Street
Ballymena, BT43 6BH
Tel: 028 2564 1421

Paisley, Ian Jnr, DUP
Constituency: North Antrim

Constituency Office:
46 Hill Street
Ballymena, BT43 6BH
Tel: 028 2564 1421

Poots, Edwin, DUP
Constituency: Lagan Valley

Constituency Office:
The Old Town Hall
Castle Street Lisburn, BT27 4XD
Tel: 028 9266 8001

Ramsay, Pat, SDLP
Constituency: Foyle

Constituency Office:
7B Messines Terrace, Racecourse Road
Derry, BT48 7QJ
Tel: 028 7136 0700

Ritchie, Margaret, SDLP
Constituency: South Down

Constituency Office:
32 Saul Street
Downpatrick, BT30 6NQ
Tel: 028 4461 2882

Robinson, George, DUP
Constituency: East Londonderry

Constituency Office:
25 Bushmills Road
Coleraine, BT52 2BP
Tel: 028 7032 7327

Robinson, Iris MP, DUP
Constituency: Strangford

Constituency Office:
2B James Street
Newtownards, BT23 4DY
Tel: 028 9182 7701

Robinson, Ken, Ulster Unionist
Constituency: East Antrim

Constituency Office:
32c North Street
Carrickfergus, BT38 7AQ
Tel: 028 9336 2995

Robinson, Mark, DUP
Constituency: Belfast South

Constituency Office:
215A Lisburn Road
Belfast, BT9 7EJ
Tel: 028 9022 5969

Robinson, Peter, DUP
Constituency: Belfast East

Constituency Office:
Strandtown Hall, 96 Belmont Avenue
Belfast, BT4 3DE
Tel: 028 9047 3111

Ruane, Caitriona, Sinn Féin
Constituency: South Down

Constituency Office:
17 Circular Road
Castlewellan, BT31 9ED
Tel: 028 4377 0185

Shannon, Jim, DUP
Constituency: Strangford

Constituency Office:
34A Frances Street
Newtownards, BT23 7DN
Tel: 028 9182 7990

Simpson, David, DUP
Constituency: Upper Bann

Constituency Office:
10 Windsor Avenue
Lurgan, BT67 9BG
Tel: 028 3834 6111

Stanton, Kathy, Sinn Féin
Constituency: Belfast North

Constituency Office:
291 Antrim Road
Belfast, BT15 2GZ
Tel: 028 9074 0817

Storey, Mervyn, DUP
Constituency: North Antrim

Constituency Office:
142A Main Street
Bushmills, BT57 8QE
Tel: 028 2073 1303

Taylor, John, Ulster Unionist
Constituency: Strangford

Constituency Office:
6 William Street
Newtownards, BT23 4AE
Tel: 028 9181 4123

Trimble, David MP, Ulster Unionist
Constituency: Upper Bann

Constituency Office:
2 Queen Street
Lurgan, BT66 8BQ
Tel: 028 3832 8088

Weir, Peter, DUP
Constituency: North Down

Constituency Office:
94 Abbey Street
Bangor, BT20 4JB
Tel: 028 9145 4500

Wells, Jim
Constituency: South Down

Constituency Office:
2 Belfast Road
Ballynahinch, BT24 8DZ
Tel: 028 9056 4200

Wilson, Jim, Ulster Unionist
Constituency: South Antrim

Constituency Office:
3a Rashee Road
Ballyclare, BT39 9HJ
Tel: 028 9332 4461

Wilson, Sammy, DUP
Constituency: East Antrim

Constituency Office:
13 Castlereagh Road
Belfast, BT5 5FB
Tel: 028 9045 9400

*Norah Beare, Jeffrey Donaldson and Arlene Foster were elected for the UUP but subsequently joined the DUP.

The 1998-2003 Assembly in plenary session

The Executive Committee

Strand 2 of the Good Friday Agreement provided for executive authority to be discharged on behalf of the Assembly by an executive committee comprising a First Minister, Deputy First Minister and up to ten Ministers with Departmental responsibilities. The First and Deputy First Minister are elected on a cross community basis and following their election the posts of Ministers allocated to parties on the basis of the d'Hondt system by reference to the number of seats each party has in the Assembly. The Ministers constitute an Executive Committee convened and presided over jointly by the First and Deputy First Minister.

The Executive Committee (effectively Northern Ireland's Cabinet) provides a forum for the discussion of issues which cut across the responsibilities of two or more Ministers, prioritising executive and legislative proposals and recommending a common position where necessary in dealing with external relationships. Ministers hold full executive authority in their respective areas of responsibility within any broad programme agreed by the Executive Committee and endorsed by the Assembly as a whole.

A party may decline the opportunity to nominate a person to serve as a Minister or subsequently change its nominee. All Northern Ireland Departments are headed by a Minister who liaises with his/her respective statutory Committee. As a condition of appointment Ministers must affirm the pledge of office undertaking to discharge effectively and in good faith all the responsibilities attaching to their office.

The Northern Ireland Executive is a body unique in the multi party membership of its composition in contrast to the one party representation in the British Cabinet. Experience of the first Executive established under the Belfast Agreement indicated that the structure could work quite effectively. However experience of the first Assembly demonstrated that the 'whip' system was not as thoroughgoing as in the Westminster model and there were instances where legislative proposals brought by the Executive Committee to the floor of the Assembly could actually be defeated.

The First Minister and Deputy First Minister

The First and Deputy First Minister must stand for election as a pair of candidates, one from each of the two political traditions, and must be elected by the Assembly as a pair. The First Minister and Deputy First Minister must be elected within six weeks following the election of the Assembly, otherwise the procedures operational under the Belfast Agreement launch a period of Review. Together they must have the support of an absolute majority of the Assembly, plus a majority of nationalist and a majority of unionist members. If there is an absence of a viable option for the election of First Minister or Deputy First Minister, another Minister may hold the position as acting First or Deputy First Minister for a period of six weeks.

The duties defined for the First Minister and the Deputy First Minister include dealing with and co-coordinating the work of the Executive Committee and the response of the Northern Ireland Executive to external business.

Junior Ministers

In the first Northern Ireland Executive established under the Belfast Agreement there were two junior ministers appointed to OFMDFM, one from each of the two largest parties.

Programme for Government

It was agreed in the Good Friday Agreement that in order to create effective government for Northern Ireland:

"The Executive Committee will seek to agree each year, and review as necessary a programme incorporating an agreed budget linked to policies and programmes, subject to approval by the Assembly, after scrutiny in Assembly Committees, on a cross-community basis".

The Programme for Government is the administration's core policy document providing a strategic overview of the planned work of the Executive and demonstrating how policies and programmes delivered by different departments and agencies may be combined to achieve agreed priorities. The Programme for Government may be best described as an amalgamation of departmental business plans into the overall corporate plan.

The First Minister and Deputy First Minister hold responsibility for setting the overall priorities for government through the Programme for Government. Ministers are expected to adhere to these priorities.

In the first Assembly 1999-2003, four important areas were identified for greater emphasis within the Programme for Government:

- Investment in infrastructure;
- Improved service delivery;
- Tackling social exclusion, in particular poverty;
- Partnership.

The Barnett Formula

The Barnett Formula is used to determine the resources available for the devolved administrations in Scotland, Wales and Northern Ireland. Subject to the agreement of the Assembly, the Executive has full discretion under the Treasury's Funding Policy in the allocation of resources under the Northern Ireland Executive Departmental Expenditure Limit to meet local requirements.

The first Northern Ireland Executive expressed concerns about the Barnett Formula, which broadly measures spending on a per person basis taking little account of relative need. These concerns have been addressed to the Treasury and may eventually lead to a review of the formula.

The Reinvestment and Reform Initiative

The Reinvestment and Reform Initiative was announced by the First and Deputy First Minister of the First Assembly on the 2 May 2002 as an innovative approach for the provision of substantial investment in the modernisation and improvement of infrastructure, progression of sustainable economic and social improvements and the delivery of better public services.

Under a favourable borrowing environment the Reinvestment and Reform Initiative provides significantly increased funds to meet requirements for capital investment in health, education and transport, far in excess of the resources available under traditional means of funding.

At the heart of the RRI a new entity, the Strategic Investment Board has been established to ensure that infrastructure is planned at a strategic level, resources are maximised and existing programmes complemented. The SIB can use alternative sources of financing and procurement methods including public private partnerships.

The funds available under the Reinvestment and Reform Initiative allow future Executives discretion to vary their spending powers, and by borrowing from the Treasury at advantageous interest rates, set the pace of investment programmes in a manner previously unknown, without the need to operate solely within the confines of the allocations under the Barnett Formula. This new power to raise funds for investment is coupled with the responsibility to raise finance through new income streams.

Assembly Committees

Introduction

The executive structures under the Good Friday Agreement have the effect of creating a strong inclusive government but weakening the possibility of having a strong formal opposition. The architects of the Agreement therefore saw the need to create a strong committee system where elected members would play a robust formal role in interfacing with the Executive.

The Good Friday Agreement sets out the formal powers of the Committees, which include a "scrutiny, policy development, and consultation role with respect to the Department with which each is associated". The Committees also play a role in the "initiation of legislation", a significant and considerable power to vest in a legislative committee. However, based on the experience of the first Assembly, the main focus of Committee work has tended to be driven by the Executive Programme, although in terms of reporting and the breadth of their inquiries they have shown a readiness to take the initiative.

Scrutiny Role of Committees

In effect the Committees act as a democratic check and balance on the power of Ministers and the Executive in the absence of an "opposition" as is traditionally understood within the UK Westminster model.

The ability of Committees to scrutinise effectively and hold the Executive to account is hampered by the inclusive nature of the Executive, and the fact that the majority of seats on each committee are held by the larger parties who also hold the majority of Executive positions.

Statutory Committees (Departmental Committees)

The Good Friday Agreement created an Assembly which had 10 statutory committees, corresponding to the 10 government departments. The allocation of seats on Statutory Committees (which consist of 11 members) reflects the diversity of political parties represented within the Assembly.

The number of seats allocated to each party should be proportionate to its membership of the Assembly. The Chair and Deputy Chair of the committees are elected using the d'Hondt system which allocates positions on the basis of numerical representation. The Business Committee holds responsibility for the allocation of seats to individual members or the parties subject to approval by the Assembly.

There are no co-opted members on to any of the Committees, whether Statutory, Standing or Ad Hoc. However Statutory Committees do appoint specialist advisors where they deem it appropriate to the conduct of their work.

Statutory Committees have the power "to consider and advise on departmental budgets and annual plans in the context of the overall budget allocation". The procedure for processing the budget requires each of the Statutory Committees to examine and scrutinise departmental allocations in line with the current Programme for Government and to submit their views to the Finance and Personnel Committee who interpret and draw together the respective views. These views are then submitted to the Department of Finance and Personnel, enabling the Minister to bring forward a revised budget for consideration.

The quorum for the Statutory Committees is set at five and a member in attendance by video link is deemed to be admissible in meeting the quorum requirement. Simple majority passes votes by a show of hands. The duration of the Committees is the life of the Assembly.

Non-Statutory Committees

Standing Committees and Ad Hoc Committees are the two types of non-statutory committee in the Assembly.

Standing Committees

Standing Committees are permanent Assembly Committees whose chair and deputy chair are filled utilising the same procedures for Statutory Committees as described above and detailed in Standing Order 46. However the process for nomination of chairs and deputies to Statutory and Non Statutory Committees is different.

With respect to other matters such as quorum and nomination of members the same procedures apply as those for Statutory Committees. The first Assembly established a number of standing committees, to take care of the many aspects of running a legislative forum. These are:

- The Business Committee;
- Procedures Committee;
- Committee of the Centre;
- Public Accounts Committee;
- Committee on Standards and Privilege;
- Audit Committee.

Business Committee

The Business Committee chaired by the Speaker discusses forthcoming business and makes arrangements for the business of the Assembly. The Committee consists of thirteen members, with two members appointed to act as Chair in the absence of the Speaker. Each party delegation is entitled to cast the number of votes equivalent to the number of members who adhere to the Whip of that party. The Business Committee also determines the dates of Recess.

Procedures Committee

The Committee on Procedures is a Standing Committee of the Northern Ireland Assembly with 11 members including a Chairperson and Deputy Chairperson and a quorum of five.

The Committee has the power to:

- Consider and review on an ongoing basis the Standing Orders and procedures of the Assembly;
- Initiate enquiries and publish reports;
- Update the Standing Orders of the Assembly for punctuation and grammar;
- Annually republish Standing Orders.

Committee of the Centre

The Committee of the Centre was established to scrutinise the Office of the First Minister and Deputy First Minister, although it is restricted by its remit to only some of the functions of the OFMDFM, including the following:

- Economic Policy Unit (other than the Programme of Government);
- Equality Unit;
- Civic Forum;
- European Affairs and International Matters;
- Community Relations;
- Public Appointments Policy;
- Freedom of Information;
- Victims;
- Nolan Standards;
- Public Service Office;
- Emergency Planning;
- Women's Issues.

The Committee consists of 17 members and has the power to send for persons and papers as required in conjunction with its role in the legislative process. The Committee of the Centre replaces the Standing Committees on Human Rights and Community Relations, European Affairs and Equality.

The Public Accounts Committee

The role of the Public Accounts Committee is "to consider accounts, and reports on accounts laid before the Assembly". It is in effect the "financial watchdog" of the Assembly. The Committee has the power to send for persons, papers and records and neither the Chair nor the Deputy Chairperson of the Committee shall be a member of the same political party as the Minister of Finance and Personnel or of any Junior Minister appointed to the Department of Finance and Personnel.

Committee on Standards and Privileges

The role of the Committee on Standards and Privileges is to:

- Consider specific matters relating to privileges referred to it by the Assembly;
- Oversee the work of the Assembly Clerk on Standards;
- Examine the arrangements for the compilation, maintenance and accessibility of the Register of Members Interests and any other registers of interest established by the Assembly and from time to time the form and content of those registers;
- Consider any matter relating to the conduct of Members, including specific complaints in relation to alleged breaches of any code of conduct to which the Assembly has agreed which have been drawn to the Committee's attention;
- Recommend modifications to the Code of Conduct;
- Make a report to the Assembly on any matter falling within Standing Order 51.

The Committee has the power to send for persons, papers and records that are relevant to its enquiries. An Assembly Commissioner for Standards will carry out an investigation into any matter referred to him by the Assembly Clerk of Standards and will report to the Committee on Standards and Privileges. However, his report may not include any recommendations for any sanction or penalty to be imposed upon any Members of the Assembly.

Whilst exercising his duties in relation to the role of Assembly Commissioner for Standards, he will not be subject to the direction or control of the Assembly.

Audit Committee

The Audit Committee is governed by procedures set out in Standing Order 53. Under the terms of the order no more than one member of the Committee may simultaneously be a member of the Public Accounts Committee. The Audit Committee has a membership of five and quorum of two.

Ad Hoc Committees

Ad Hoc Committees are established to deal with specific time-bounded terms of reference that the Assembly may set. Their role is often to consider a piece of draft legislation and produce a written report on it.

Sub Committees

Each Committee has the authority to establish sub Committees. However, unless approved by the Business Committee, no Committee may have more than one sub Committee in operation at any one time. Sub Committees may be appointed to consider specific, time-bounded matters within the terms of reference set by the parent Committee. Once these matters have been resolved the sub committee will report to the Parent Committee and be dissolved.

Each sub Committee should reflect the party strengths in the Assembly as far as possible and the parent committee will determine the quorum for the sub committee.

Other Institutions of the Belfast Agreement

Introduction

The Good Friday Agreement radically transformed British and Irish government institutional and constitutional relationships with Northern Ireland. Under the terms of the Agreement both governments made significant constitutional and legislative changes altering their expressions of sovereignty over Northern Ireland. Following the agreement of the Republic of Ireland to amend Articles 2 and 3 of the Irish Constitution, the British Government repealed the Government of Ireland Act 1920. These changes became effective with the enactment of the Northern Ireland Act 1998, which became law on 19 September 1998, thereby implementing the Agreement.

New Structures

To reflect the changed expressions of British and Irish sovereignty over Northern Ireland, new institutions were created. These were the: North/South Ministerial Council; North/South Implementation Bodies; British/Irish Council; British/Irish Intergovernmental Conference.

North/South Bodies

The North/South Ministerial Council

The North/South Ministerial Council (NSMC) was established on 2 December 1999, under the terms of the Good Friday Agreement and is the lead institution in developing all aspects of North/South co-operation, bringing together Ministers from Northern Ireland and the Irish Government. The role of the Council is to develop consultation, co-operation and action on all-island and cross-border matters of mutual interest. It also provides leadership and direction for the six North/South implementation bodies.

The North/South Ministerial Council, provided for in Strand Two of the Good Friday Agreement, meets in plenary format twice a year with Northern Ireland represented by the First and Deputy First Minister and other relevant ministers and the Irish government by the Taoiseach and relevant ministers. Smaller groups meet on a "regular and frequent" basis to discuss specific cross-border issues with each side represented by the appropriate minister. The Council may also meet to resolve disagreements and discuss common issues and concerns. Agendas for all meetings are settled by prior agreement.

Both sides must abide by "the rules for democratic authority and accountability in force in the Northern Ireland Assembly and the Oireachtas respectively". The Agreement obliges all relevant government Ministers in the Assembly and Oireachtas to participate in the Council.

Within the NSMC, government ministers have considerable discretion but they remain accountable to their legislatures, the Assembly and the Oireachtas respectively. The First and Deputy First Minister have a duty to ensure "cross-community participation" on the Council. The Council is supported by a Joint Secretariat in Armagh staffed by personnel from OFMDFM and the Irish Civil service.

Responsibility for arranging NSMC meetings in sectoral and plenary formats, arranging papers for the meetings and monitoring the work of the bodies rests with the Joint Secretariat.

NSMC Joint Secretariat
39 Abbey Street, Armagh, BT61 7EB
Northern Ireland Joint Secretary: Peter Smyth
Tel: 028 3751 5002
Irish Joint Secretary: Tim O'Connor / Tel: 028 3751 5001

North/South Implementation Bodies

On 2 December 1999 under the aegis of the North/South Ministerial Council, six North/South Implementation Bodies, established between the British and Irish Governments came into being. These bodies exist to implement policies agreed by Ministers in the North/South Ministerial Council and are expected to develop cross-border co-operation on practical matters of mutual concern.

The bodies operate under the North/South Ministerial Council and are funded from grants made by the relevant government departments, North and South. They are staffed by a combination of civil servants (either transferred or seconded from their parent Departments, North and South) and, increasingly beyond the initial period, directly recruited staff. With the agreement of the Northern Ireland Assembly and the Oireachtas it will be open to the North/South Ministerial Council to set up additional Implementation Bodies in the future. The six North/South Implementation Bodies are: Waterways Ireland; The Food Safety Promotion Board; Inter*Trade*Ireland; The Special EU Programmes Body; The Foyle, Carlingford and Irish Lights Commission; The North/South Language Body (includes twin agencies promoting Irish and Ulster Scots).

The Food Safety Promotion Board

The Food Safety Promotion Board
7 Eastgate Avenue, Eastgate, Little Island, Cork
Tel: 00 353 21 230 4100 / Fax: 00 353 21 230 4111
Web: safefoodonline.com
Chief Executive: Martin Higgins

Members of the Food Safety Promotion Board
Leslie Craig, Past Chairman, NI Agricultural Producers Association
Carmel Foley, Director of Consumer Affairs, Dublin
Ronan Garvey, Lecturer Institute of Technology, Tallaght
Prof Michael Gibney, Chairman of the Food Safety Authority of Ireland
Prof Cecily Kelleher, Professor of Health Promotion, National University of Ireland
Bertie Kerr, Fermanagh District Council
Damien O'Dwyer, Pallasgreen Co Limerick
Danny O'Hare, Chairman of the Food Safety Authority of Ireland
Anne Speed, Trade Union Official SIPTU
Prof Sean Strain, Professor of Human Nutrition University of Ulster
Michael Walker, Public Health Analyst

The Food Safety Promotion Board is principally charged with promoting food safety – through public campaigns, conferences, training and advising professionals and the general public. It is also involved in supporting North/South scientific co-operation, and links between institutions working in the field of food safety – laboratories, food safety enforcement agencies, and international and domestic research bodies.

Waterways Ireland

Headquarters, 5-7 Belmore Street
Enniskillen, Co Fermanagh, BT74 6AA
Tel: + 44 (0)28 6632 3004
Fax: + 44 (0)28 6634 6237
Website: www.waterwaysireland.org
Email: information@waterwaysireland.org

Chief Executive Officer
John Martin

Directors:
Brian D'Arcy (Operations)
Colin Brownsmith (Finance and Personnel)
Martin Dennany (Marketing and Communications)
Nigel Russell (Technical Services)
Brian McTeggart (Corporate Services)

Waterways Ireland is one of six North-South implementation Bodies established under the British-Irish Agreement in 1999 and has responsibility for the management, maintenance, development and restoration of Ireland's inland navigations, principally for recreational purposes.

Inter*Trade*Ireland

Old Gasworks Business Park
Kilmorey Street, Newry, BT34 2DE
Tel: 028 3083 4100 / Fax: 028 3083 4155
Email: info@intertradeireland.com
Web: www.intertradeireland.com
Chief Executive: Liam Nellis

Formerly the Trade and Business Development Body Inter*Trade*Ireland exercises a range of functions in the development of cross border trade and business. It also has a focus on promoting North/South trade and business co-operation by building knowledge enterprise capability and competitiveness.

Board Members of Inter*Trade*Ireland:
Chairman: Dr Martin Naughton
Founder and Chairman of Glen Dimplex Group
Vice Chairman: Barry Fitzsimons
Senior Director, Cunningham Coates Stockbrokers
Liam Nellis, Chief Executive, InterTrade Ireland
Mary Breslin, Chairman, Londonderry Port and Harbour Commissioners
Feargal McCormack
Managing Partner, FPM Chartered Accountants
Jackie Harrison
Director of Social Policy, Irish Business and Employers' Confederation (IBEC)
Carl McCann, Vice-Chairman, Fyffes
Inez McCormack, Northern Ireland Regional Secretary, Unison
Mary Ainscough, Director of Equality, Dublin City University
Robbie Smyth, General Secretary, Sinn Féin
Jack Gilmour, Businessman, Hospitality Trade, Belfast
John Fitzgerald, Dublin City Manager
Dr Trefor Campbell, Managing Director, Moy Park

The Special European Union Programmes Body (SEUPB)

Special EU Programmes Body (SEUPB)
Headquarters: EU House
6 Cromac Place
Belfast, BT7 2JB
Tel: +44 (0) 28 9026 6660
Fax: +44 (0) 28 9026 6661
Email: info@seupb.org
Web: www.seupb.org
Acting Chief Executive: Nuala Kerr

The SEUPB is one of the six cross border Bodies set up under the "Agreement between the Government of Ireland and the Government of the United Kingdom of Great Britain and Northern Ireland establishing implementing bodies".

The SEUPB is the managing authority for the EU Programme for Peace and Reconciliation in Northern Ireland and the Border Region of Ireland and INTERREG IIIA. The Body is also involved in the cross border elements of other Community Initiatives (Leader+, Urban II and Equal) and are responsible for implementing the Common Chapter.

A principal aim of the Special European Union Programmes Body is to promote cross border co-operation through the administration of the cross border element of the Peace II programme and the monitoring and promotion of cross border activities in the context of the National Development Plan 2000-2006 for Ireland and the Structural Funds Plan 2000-2006 for Northern Ireland. *(Further details of the Peace II programme along with relevant contact details are set out in Chapter Nine).*

SEUPB Management Team

Jack O'Connor	Director, Interreg III and other community initiatives
Shaun Henry	Director, Peace II
Gina McIntyre	Corporate Services Director

The North/South Language Body

(Includes Irish Language and Ulster-Scots Agencies)
The Language Body is a single body reporting to the North/South Ministerial Council, but composed of two separate and largely autonomous agencies: the Irish Language Agency, Foras na Gaeilge, and the Ulster-Scots Agency, Tha Boord o Ulster-Scotch. Each of these agencies has a separate board, which together constitutes the Board of the North/South Language Body.

Foras na Gaeilge

Foras na Gaeilge
7 Cearnóg Mhuirfean
Baile Átha Cliath 2
Teil: (00353 1) 639 8400
1850 325 325
Tuaisceart: 0845 309 8142
Facs: (00353 1) 639 8401
Email: Eolas@forasnagaeilge.ie
Web: www.forasnagaeilge.ie

Cathaoirleach
Maighréad Uí Mháirtín

Bunaíodh Foras na Gaeilge ar 2 Nollaig 1999 faoin Acht um Chomhaontú na Breataine - na hÉireann agus is í an príomhaidhm atá ag an bhForas ná an Ghaeilge a chur chun cinn ar fud oileán na hÉireann.

Foras na Gaeilge was established on 2 December 1999 under the terms of the British-Irish Agreement Act, and the main objective of the Foras is to promote the Irish language on the island of Ireland.

The main functions of the Foras are: promotion of the Irish language; facilitating and encouraging its use in speech and writing in public and in private life in the south, and in the context of part III of the European Charter for Regional or Minority Languages, in Northern Ireland where there is appropriate demand; advising both administrations, public bodies and other groups in the private and voluntary sectors; undertaking supportive projects, and grant aiding bodies and groups as considered necessary; undertaking research, promotional campaigns, and public and media relations; developing terminology and dictionaries; supporting Irish medium education and teaching of Irish.

Board Members
Chairperson: Maighread Ní Mhairtin
Anne Craig
Gordon McCoy
Aodán MacPóilín
Liam Corey
Patsy McGlone
Gearoíd MacSiacais
Gearoíd O'hEara
Treasa Ni Ailpin
Brid Uí Néill
Maolsheachlainn O Caollaí
Padraig O Duibhir
Leachlann Ó Catháin
Mairéad Nic Sheaghain
Caitríona Ní Cheallaigh
Diarmuid Ó Murchú

Tha Boord o Ulster Scotch: The Ulster Scots Agency

The Ulster Scots Agency
Franklin House
10-12 Brunswick Street, Belfast, BT2 7GE
Tel: 028 9023 1113 / Fax: 028 9023 1898
Email: info@ulsterscotsagency.org.uk
Web: www.ulsterscotsagency.com
Chairman: Lord Laird of Artigarvan

The Ulster Scots Agency, Tha Boord o Ulster Scotch is the body responsible for the promotion of the Ulster Scots language and culture on the island of Ireland. It is part of the north south language implementation body that was set up under the Belfast Agreement. The Agency is responsible to the North/South Ministerial Council, and in particular to the two ministers, in the Northern Ireland Assembly and Dail Eireann, whose remits include language and culture.

Board Members
Chairman: Lord Laird of Artigarvan
Deputy Chairman: Jim Devenney
Board Members: Bob Stoker
Alistair Simpson
Dr Linde Lunney
Pat Wall
Eddie O'Donnell
Dr Ian Adamson

The Foyle, Carlingford and Irish Lights Commission

The Foyle, Carlingford and Irish Lights Commission - At present one Agency has been established (Loughs Agency). A second Agency (Lights Agency) will be established once the appropriate legislation is in place.

Loughs Agency

Foyle Carlingford and Irish Lights
Commission (FCILC)
Loughs Agency Headquarters
22 Victoria Road
Londonderry
BT47 2AB

Email: general@loughs-agency.org
Tel: 0044 (0)28 7134 2100
Fax: 0044 (0)28 7134 2720

Carlingford Regional Office
Old Quay Lane
Carlingford, Co Louth
Email: Carlingford@loughs-agency.org
Tel/Fax: 00353 (0)42 9383888

Chief Executive
Derick Anderson

Senior Policy Officer: John Pollock
Chief Inspector: Stanley Thorpe
Biologist: Patrick Boylan

FCILC Board
Peter Savage (Chair)
Lord Cooke of Islandreagh (Vice Chair)
Jack Allen
Keith Anderson
Dick Blakiston-Houston
Francis Feely
Pat Griffin
Siobhan Logue
Joseph Martin
Tarlach O Crosain
Jacqui McConville
Andrew Ward

MISSION
The Loughs Agency aims to provide sustainable social, economic and environmental benefits through the effective conservation, management, promotion and development of the fisheries and marine resources of the Foyle and Carlingford Areas.

Lights Agency

British and Irish legislation, when implemented will allow transfer of the Commissioner of Irish Lights functions to the Foyle, Carlingford and Irish Lights Commission, and such functions will be exercised through an agency of the FCILC known as the Lights Agency. FCILC will become the General Lighthouse Authority for the island of Ireland.

Other Areas Identified for North/South Co-operation

In addition to the six Implementation Bodies a further six areas have initially been identified for co-operation between existing government departments and other bodies, North and South. They cover aspects of transport, agriculture, education, health, environment and tourism.

The North/South Ministerial Council is responsible for taking forward:

Transport

Strategic planning and development of cross-border co-operation (while co-operation would primarily arise in respect of road and rail planning, it would take account of issues arising in the port and airport sectors) and road and rail safety;

Agriculture

Discussion of Common Agricultural Policy (CAP) issues, animal and plant health policy and research and rural development, between North and South;

Education

Education for children with special needs (e.g. autism, dyslexia), educational underachievement, teacher qualifications, and school, youth and teacher exchanges on a cross-border basis;

Health

Accident and emergency planning, emergency services, co-operation on high technology equipment, cancer research and health promotion. The Ministerial Council in the health and food safety sector considers matters for co-operation in Health as well as considering matters relating to the Food Safety Promotion Board;

Environment

Research into environmental protection, water quality management and waste management in a cross-border context;

Tourism

North/South co-operation on tourism has led to the creation of the all-island tourism organisation Tourism Ireland Limited.

Tourism Ireland

5th Floor, Bishop's Square
Redmond's Hill, Dublin 2
Tel: +353 (0)1 476 3400
Fax: +353 (0)1 476 3666

Beresford House, 2 Beresford Road
Coleraine, BT52 1GE
Tel: 028 7035 9200
Fax: 028 7032 6932

Chief Executive Officer
Paul O'Toole

Tourism Ireland was established as one of the 'six areas of co-operation' under the Belfast Agreement and is responsible for marketing the island of Ireland overseas as a tourist destination.

To fulfil these roles, the company employs a wide range of marketing tools including an extensive suite of branded literature available in nine languages, direct marketing and advertising (television and press). The company also has an online presence, with local language Tourism Ireland websites. Tourism Ireland acts as an agent for Bord Fáilte and the Northern Ireland Tourist Board in implementing the international element of their product and regional marketing programmes.

North South Consultative Forum

Although it was not established during the lifetime of the first Assembly, the Belfast Agreement specifically provided for the possibility of establishing an equivalent of the Civic Forum, structured on an all island basis.

Supporters of the concept, particularly in the voluntary and community sector, see considerable benefits in such an institution although the Republic does not at present have a direct "mirror" institution to Northern Ireland's Civic Forum from which to draw the southern membership of the new body.

British Irish Institutions

The British Irish Council

The British-Irish Council was established to 'promote the harmonies and mutually beneficial development of relationships among the peoples of the United Kingdom and Ireland'. It is made up of representatives of the British and Irish Governments, of the devolved institutions in Northern Ireland, Scotland, Wales, the Isle of Man and the Channel Islands.

The Council has decided as a priority to examine and develop policies for co-operation on drugs, social exclusion, the environment and transport. Other areas for discussion will include agriculture, tourism, health, education, approaches to EU issues, links between cities, towns and local districts, sporting activity and minority and lesser-used languages.

The British Irish Council Secretariat
UK Joint Secretary: Peter Thompson
Tel: 0207 270 6779
Irish Joint Secretary: Úna Ní Dhubhghaill
Tel: 00 353 1 408 2351

British-Irish Intergovernmental Conference

The British-Irish Intergovernmental Conference was designed to replace the Anglo-Irish Intergovernmental Council and the Intergovernmental Conference established under the 1985 Anglo-Irish Agreement. It comprises primarily representation of the UK Government at Westminster and the Irish Government in Dublin. Its task is to promote bilateral co-operation on matters of mutual interest between the British and Irish Governments, including, in particular, issues in relation to Northern Ireland.

Joint Ministerial Committee on Devolution

A Joint Ministerial Committee on Devolution has been established to enable Ministers from the devolved governments of Scotland, Wales and Northern Ireland to take forward joint action. The role of the Committee is to examine non-devolved matters which may conflict with responsibilities devolved in the regions. Joint Ministerial Committees have been created on the Knowledge Economy, Health and Poverty. Ministers have also engaged in less formal meetings to discuss matters such as Housing, Agriculture and the Environment.

The Prime Minister of the United Kingdom is the Chair of the Joint Ministerial Committee on Devolution. Meetings are attended by the Secretaries of State for Scotland, Wales and Northern Ireland and may be located anywhere in the UK. Whilst the agenda and location are made public the content of these meetings is confidential. A secretariat comprising staff from the UK cabinet office and staff from each of the devolved regions in the UK supports the work of the committee.

The Civic Forum

Civic Forum Secretariat
Tel: 028 9052 8841 / Fax: 028 9052 8833
Email: secretariat@civicforum-ni.org
Web: www.civicforum-ni.org

The Civic Forum is a consultative body, with no formal legislative or governmental powers consisting of 60 members plus a Chairperson. Members are representative of the voluntary, business, agriculture, trade union, education, culture, community relations and fisheries sectors. The Civic Forum was suspended, along with the other devolved institutions, in October 2002.

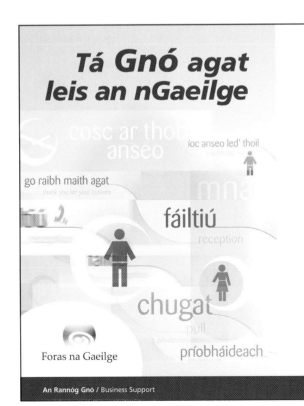

Electoral Systems, Political Parties and Election Results

Electoral Systems

By UK standards Northern Ireland is something of a 'guinea-pig' when it comes to the application of electoral systems. Northern Ireland maintains a consistency with the rest of the UK in terms of how Westminster elections and European elections are conducted, but is radically different in the approach taken to regional assemblies and local government.

At the heart of Northern Ireland's differentiated treatment is the recognition that in a place that is deeply divided it is all the more important that the election results reflect the wishes of the electorate proportionately. The second most important consideration after proportionality is inclusiveness – and in recent years there has been a considerable effort to ensure that the electoral system does not crowd out the smaller parties.

First-past-the-post (Simple Plurality)

The first-past-the-post electoral system is used throughout the UK for local (except in Northern Ireland) and general elections. Each constituency returns a single winner, the candidate with the most votes. The winner does not require a majority of votes cast, merely more votes than the closest rival.

First past the post is particularly disproportionate in its translation of votes into seats and this has a number of highly significant ramifications with regard to the composition and operation of parliament and political leadership.

The first-past-the-post system has generally delivered stability in the UK in that the leading party, even though it achieves less than 50 per cent share of vote, can gain a comfortable majority of seats in parliament. In Northern Ireland this less representative system has occasioned considerable "tactical voting" where people will often vote for a candidate who would not be their first choice in an STV election in order to defeat a candidate to whom they are strongly opposed.

Proportional Representation
Single Transferable Vote (STV)

A number of proportional representation alternatives exist to the first past the post electoral model, which seek to ensure a direct, and close correlation between total votes cast for each party and the number of seats won. The first past the post system, properly referred to as simple plurality, is the one that is least connected to the principle of proportional representation.

The single transferable vote system (STV), used for local, European and Northern Ireland Assembly elections under the Northern Ireland Act 1998, is based on multi member constituencies in which voter preferences for candidates are expressed in numerical order. Voters rank candidates in order of preference (1 for their most preferred candidate, 2 for their second choice, etc). A quota is calculated by dividing the number of votes cast plus one by the number of seats available plus one. If a candidate has enough votes to reach the quota, he or she is elected. If the candidate has more votes than the quota, the surplus votes are taken and redistributed proportionately according to the voter's next choice. The candidate with the least number of votes is eliminated, and their votes redistributed in the same way. The process continues until all available seats have been filled. A candidate can be elected under STV without reaching the quota, in circumstances where further re-distribution of votes would not alter the outcome.

The d'Hondt Mechanism

Proportional representation has a role beyond the election of Members in the Northern Ireland Assembly. The d'Hondt system of proportional representation is the designated method for the appointment of Ministers in the Assembly and the assignment of committee chairmanships. The d'Hondt mechanism has its origins in Belgium where it was first applied in 1889 between the Flemings and Walloons to ensure representation for whichever ethnic group was in a minority
The formulae to allocate seats under the mechanism were also devised by a Belgian, H.R. Droop who produced the procedure for establishing the quota in multi member constituencies. Victor d'Hondt devised what is technically known as the "largest average" formula for allocating seats in an assembly.
The d'Hondt system takes the number of seats obtained by each party and divides them by one, two, three, four, etc. The ministries are then given to the parties with the twelve largest quotients ranked from the largest to the smallest quotient.
Although, the majority party is favoured under d'Hondt the advantage is that minority interests also gain representation, a critical factor for the success of the new Assembly and power sharing in the Northern Ireland Executive. However it does make it unlikely that significantly smaller parties would be able to obtain a ministry under this system.

The Office of the Chief Electoral Officer

The Chief Electoral Officer position is unique to Northern Ireland and is appointed by the Secretary of State for Northern Ireland. He is an independent officer responsible for the conduct of all elections in Northern Ireland. The Chief Electoral Officer has no direct counterpart in Great Britain, where electoral registration and the conduct of all elections are primarily the responsibility of local authorities.

The Chief Electoral Officer is the registration and returning officer for each parliamentary constituency in Northern Ireland, and the returning officer for European parliamentary elections, Assembly elections and district council elections. He is responsible for the preparation of polling station schemes, the maintenance of election equipment and all other administrative matters relating to elections in Northern Ireland.

The Chief Electoral Officer has a small number of Deputy Electoral Officers and Assistant Electoral Officers to assist him, primarily in the compilation of the electoral register and related duties, but they also act as Deputy Returning Officers, except for local government elections where the Clerk of the particular Council is the ex-officio Returning Officer but acts under the control and supervision of the Chief Electoral Officer.

The Chief Electoral Officer is supported by the Electoral Office for Northern Ireland in carrying out his statutory activities.

The Electoral Office Headquarters
15 Church Street, Belfast, BT1 1ER
Tel: 028 9024 5353
Chief Electoral Officer: Denis Stanley
Tel: 028 9033 9955

Area Electoral Offices
Foyle and East Londonderry
20 Queen Street, Londonderry, BT48 7EQ
Tel: 028 7136 2761

North Antrim and Mid Ulster
9A Linenhall Street, Ballymoney, BT53 6DP
Tel: 028 2766 5052

West Tyrone and Fermanagh and South Tyrone
21 Kevlin Avenue, Omagh, BT78 1ER
Tel: 028 8224 3600

Upper Bann, Newry and Armagh, South Down and Lagan Valley
52 Bridge Street, Banbridge, BT32 3JU
Tel: 028 4066 2857

East Antrim and South Antrim
1-3 Portland Avenue, Glengormley, Newtownabbey, BT36 5EY
Tel: 028 9034 2263

Strangford and North Down
2B Regent Street, Newtownards, BT23 4LH
Tel: 028 9181 8576

Belfast East, Belfast North, Belfast South and Belfast West
6-10 William Street, Belfast, BT1 1PR
Tel: 028 9023 1443

Electoral Fraud

Increasingly in recent years, there have been many allegations of various kinds of electoral fraud, the most common being 'vote stealing' by impersonation. Although the electoral authorities have failed to find evidence of systematic or wide ranging electoral fraud taking place, Northern Ireland elections now operate under tight regulations governing identification at the polling station. 2003 saw the compilation of a new electoral register, which required individuals to actively register their right to vote. Failure to do so would result in disenfranchisement.

The Electoral Commission
Seatem House, 28-32 Alfred Street, Belfast, BT2 8EN
Web: www.electoralcommission.org.uk
Head of The Electoral Commission (Northern Ireland):
Seamus Magee

The Electoral Commission is an independent body set up by the UK Parliament in 2000. Its aim is to gain public confidence and encourage people to take part in the democratic process within the United Kingdom by modernising the electoral process. Any group that wishes to become a registered political party must register with the Electoral Commission. The Electoral Commission also has a role in regulating all expenditure incurred by political parties for electoral purposes.

Political Parties

Northern Ireland has around 25 registered political parties although throughout the last 20 years electoral politics have been dominated by 4 or 5 major parties. The minor parties comprise in the main fringe unionist parties and socialist groups, along with a number of sectional interests.

There are two large unionist parties: the Ulster Unionist Party (UUP) and the Democratic Unionist Party (DUP). Two main parties also represent the nationalist community: the Social Democratic and Labour Party (SDLP) and Sinn Féin. In some sense there is symmetry between these alignments, with the UUP and SDLP appealing increasingly to middle-class and middle-ground unionists and nationalists respectively. The more aggressive and uncompromising DUP and Sinn Féin tend to attract more support among the working classes and young voters. The fifth biggest group, the Alliance Party, straddles the two political communities, although its support base has been severely eroded in recent years. The following is a list of all political parties registered in Northern Ireland with the Electoral Commission.

Alliance – The Alliance Party of Northern Ireland
Children's Party (The)
Community Awareness Party/Protecting Children
Community Candidates
Conservative and Unionist Party (The)
Democratic Party (The)
Democratic Unionist Party – D.U.P.
Flauntit.Net Internet Party (The)
Green Party
Labour (Federation of Labour Groups)
Liberal Unionist Party
National Front
Natural Law Party Northern Ireland
New Party (The)
Newtownabbey Ratepayers Association
No Candidate Deserves My Vote!
Northern Ireland Unionist Party
Northern Ireland Women's Coalition
Official Monster Raving Loony Party (The)
People's Progressive Party (The)
Progressive Unionist Party of Northern Ireland
Real Democracy Party
Renaissance Independent Party of Europe (The)
SDLP (Social Democratic & Labour Party)
Sinn Féin
Socialist Environmental Alliance
Socialist Party (Northern Ireland)
UK Anti Party
UK Social and Countryside Party
Ulster Protestant League (The)
Ulster Third Way
Ulster Unionist Party (UUP)
United Kingdom Independence Party
United Kingdom Unionist Party U.K.U.P.
United Unionist Coalition
Vote for Yourself
Workers Party (The)
World

Political Parties Religious/Ethnic Spectrum

As a consequence of historical political divisions it is very difficult to attempt to show Northern Ireland parties on a traditional left-right spectrum. The parties themselves place tremendous emphasis on the constitutional issue of Northern Ireland in their manifestoes, leaving more traditional economic and social issues aside as secondary considerations. Some politicians would contend that their ideologies and policies do exist, but are overshadowed by 'sectarian politics', and that most people in Northern Ireland tend to vote according to religion and nationality, leaving less 'demand' for other policies.

Religious/Ethnic Distribution of Parties

Catholic/Nationalist

- SDLP
- Sinn Féin
- Workers Party

Centre/Other

- Alliance
- Northern Ireland Women's Coalition

Protestant/Unionist

- Ulster Unionist Party
- DUP
- Progressive Unionist Party
- Northern Ireland Unionist Party
- UK Unionist Party

Pro/Anti Agreement Spectrum

The UUP is broadly pro-Agreement, but has a significant anti-Agreement faction, which gained in strength over the lifetime of the first Assembly. All of the nationalist parties represented in the Northern Ireland Assembly are pro-Agreement.

Pro-Agreement

- Ulster Unionist Party
- SDLP
- Sinn Féin
- Northern Ireland Women's Coalition
- Alliance
- Progressive Unionist Party

Anti-Agreement

- DUP
- United Kingdom Unionist Party
- Northern Ireland Unionist Party

Main Political Parties in Northern Ireland

Democratic Unionist Party (DUP)

91 Dundela Avenue, Belfast, BT4 3BU
Tel: 028 9047 1155 / Fax: 028 9047 1797
Email: info@dup.org.uk
Web: www.dup.org.uk

Leader: Rev Ian Paisley MP MEP (pictured)
Deputy: Peter Robinson MP
Secretary: Nigel Dodds MP
Chairperson: Maurice Morrow
President: Jim McClure
Contact: Alison Pickering

The DUP is staunchly anti agreement, in contrast to the Ulster Unionists although sharing their core belief that Northern Ireland should remain within the United Kingdom. Founded in 1971 by the Rev Ian Paisley, replacing his Protestant Unionist Party the party is popularised by its uncompromising stance on the constitutional status of Northern Ireland as part of the UK and resistance towards co-operation with the Irish Republic.

The party currently holds five Westminster seats and won 30 Assembly seats in the 2003 Assembly elections to become the largest Unionist party, overtaking the Ulster Unionist Party. Their position was further enhanced by the decisions of Jeffrey Donaldson, Arlene Foster and Norah Beare to resign from the Ulster Unionist Party and join the DUP. The DUP was the only party to secure representation in all 18 constituencies.

Despite its opposition to the Agreement, and public stance of non-cooperation with Sinn Féin, the DUP accepted its Ministerial positions during the first Assembly and participated in the cross party committees.

After many years of leading the opposition to political change in Northern Ireland, the DUP is now for the first time Northern Ireland's largest political party and has acknowledged that it has a responsibility to table new proposals for political progress.

DUP Leadership

Ian Paisley is the leader of the DUP, MP for North Antrim since 1970 and a popular MEP since 1979, consistently topping the poll in European elections. Unyielding in his opposition to republicanism, he is vociferously critical of the peace process and the involvement of the Ulster Unionist party. As leader of the Free Presbyterian Church Dr Paisley is a staunch opponent of ecumenism and his attitude to the Roman Catholic faith draws much criticism from his opponents.

DUP Elected Representation

European Parliament: Dr Ian Paisley MEP

Westminster: 6 MPs *(see pages 34-35 for details)*

Northern Ireland Assembly:
A full list of all DUP members elected to the Northern Ireland Assembly in the 2003 elections can be found on page 40.

Local Government:
DUP Councillors (A-Z by Council)
Total number of DUP Councillors: 128

Antrim Borough Council (4)
Wilson Clyde; Samuel Dunlop; Brian Graham; John Smyth.

Ards Borough Council (9)
Margaret Craig; Robin Drysdale; George Ennis; David Gilmore
Hamilton Gregory; Hamilton Lawther; William Montgomery
Jim Shannon; Terence Williams.

Armagh City and District Council (4)
Paul Berry; Heather Black; Freda Donnelly; William Irwin.

Ballymena Borough Council (11)
Elizabeth Adger; James Alexander; Martin Clarke;
Samuel Gaston; Roy Gillespie; Samuel Hanna; Maurice Mills;
Thomas Nicholl; Hubert Nicholl; Robin Stirling; David Tweed

Ballymoney Borough Council (8)
Frank Campbell; Cecil Cousley; John Finlay; Robert Halliday
Bill Kennedy; Ian Stevenson; Mervyn Storey; Robert Wilson.

Banbridge District Council (4)
David Herron; Stephen Herron; Jim McElroy;
Wilfred McFadden.

Belfast City Council (10)
Wallace Browne; Ian Crozier; Nigel Dodds;
Nelson McCausland; Elaine McMillen; Robin Newton;
Ruth Patterson; Eric Smyth; Harry Toan; Sammy Wilson

Carrickfergus Borough Council (6)
William Ashe; May Beattie; Terence Clements; David Hilditch
James McClurg; Patricia McKinney.

Castlereagh Borough Council (10)
John Beattie; Joanne Bunting; Claire Ennis; Kim Morton;
John Norris; Iris Robinson; Peter Robinson; Mark Robinson;
Vivienne Stevenson; Jim White.

Coleraine Borough Council (7)
Maurice Bradley; William Creelman; Timothy Deans;
Phyllis Fielding; James McClure; Adrian McQuillan;
Desmond Stewart.

Cookstown District Council (2)
Anne McCrea; Ian McCrea.

Craigavon Borough Council (6)
Jonathan Bell; Alan Carson; Stephen Moutray; David Simpson
Robert Smith; Woolsey Smith.

Derry City Council (4)
Gregory Campbell; Mildred Garfield; William Hay; Joe Miller.

Down District Council (2)
William Dick; Jim Wells

Dungannon and South Tyrone Borough Council (3)
Roger Burton; Johnston McIlwrath; Maurice Morrow.

Fermanagh District Council (2)
Joe Dodds; Bert Johnston

Larne Borough Council (5)
Winston Fulton; Bobby McKee; Jack McKee; Gregg McKeen
Rachel Rea.

Limavady Borough Council (2)
Leslie Cubitt; George Robinson.

Lisburn City Council (5)
Cecil Calvert; David Craig; Edwin Poots; Paul Porter; James Tinsley.

Magherafelt District Council (3)
Thomas Catherwood; Paul McLean; William McCrea.

Moyle District Council (3)
George Hartin; Gardiner Kane; David McAllister.

Newry and Mourne District Council (1)
William Burns.

Newtownabbey Borough Council (7)
William de Courcy; Paul Girvan; Nigel Hamilton; Victor Robinson; Pamela Hunter; John Mann; Arthur Templeton

North Down Borough Council (5)
Ruby Cooling; Gordon Dunne; Alexander Easton; Alan Graham; John Montgomery.

Omagh District Council (2)
Thomas Buchanan; Oliver Gibson.

Strabane District Council (3)
Allan Bresland; John Donnell; Thomas Kerrigan.

Ulster Unionist Party (UUP)

429 Holywood Road, Belfast, BT4 2LN
Tel: 028 9076 5500 / Fax: 028 9076 9419
Email: uup@uup.org
Web: www.uup.org

Westminster:
Office of Rt Hon David Trimble MP (pictured)
House of Commons
Westminster, London, SW1A 0AA
Tel: 020 7219 0505 / Fax: 020 7219 1575
Email: whiteb@parliament.uk

North American Bureau:
Ulster Unionist Party
North American Bureau
1919 Pennsylvania Avenue, NW, Suite 200
Washington, DC 20006, USA
Tel: (202) 828-9866 / Fax: (202) 223-2278
Email: aws.uupna@earthlink.net

Leader: David Trimble MP
Deputy: John Taylor
President: Rev Martyn Smyth MP
Vice-President: Lord Maginnis of Drumglass
Vice-President: Sir Reg Empey
Vice-President: Jim Nicholson MEP
Chairman of Executive Committee: James Cooper
Vice-Chairman of Executive Committee: Donn McConnell OBE
Honorary Secretary: Lord Rogan
Honorary Secretary: Cllr Jim Rodgers
Honorary Secretary: Dermot Nesbitt
Honorary Treasurer: Jack Allen OBE
Honorary Assistant Treasurer: May Steele MBE

The Ulster Unionist Party is the oldest political party in Northern Ireland. Its central cause is the maintenance of Northern Ireland's position within the UK and the legitimacy of Northern Ireland as a distinct political, economic and cultural entity. While supportive of the co-operative relationships with the Irish Republic, the Ulster Unionist party prefers cross border matters to be considered within the economic rather than political arena. Formal links are retained with the Orange Order, which enjoys voting rights within the party.

UUP Leadership

David Trimble, MP for the Upper Bann constituency was elected leader of the Ulster Unionist party in 1995. Throughout his career David Trimble has moved along the spectrum of Unionism from an uncompromising member of the hard-line loyalist Vanguard movement in the 1970s, to a more pragmatic leader supporting the Good Friday Agreement and accepting limited cross border bodies. In 1998 he and John Hume, then leader of the SDLP shared the Noble Peace Prize for their efforts in securing the Agreement. David Trimble has undergone much criticism from Unionists, both within his own party and from outside of it as a result of the number of 'concessions' he has made to political opponents, which it has been argued have weakened the cause of Unionism.

UUP Elected Representation

European Parliament: Jim Nicholson MEP

Westminster: 5 MPs - see pages 34-35 for details

Members of House of Lords
Lord Cooke of Islandreagh
The Rt Hon The Lord Kilclooney of Armagh
Lord Maginnis of Drumglass
The Rt Hon The Lord Molyneaux of Killead KBE
Lord Laird of Artigarvan
Lord Rogan of Lower Iveagh

Westminster: Tel: 020 7219 5679

Northern Ireland Assembly:
A full list of all UUP members elected to the Northern Ireland Assembly in the 2003 elections can be found on page 40.

Local Government:
Ulster Unionist Party Councillors (A-Z by Council)
Total number of UUP Councillors: 153

Antrim Borough Council (7)
Paddy Marks; Paul Michael; Stephen Nicholl; Mervyn Rea; Roy Thompson; Edgar Wallace; Adrian Watson.

Ards Borough Council (8)
Angus Carson; Ronnie Ferguson; Robert Gibson; Tom Hamilton; Jeffrey Magill; John Shields; Philip Smith; David Smyth.

Armagh City and District Council (6)
James Clayton; Evelyn Corry; Sylvia McRoberts; Eric Speers; Jim Speers; Robert Turner.

Ballymena Borough Council (7)
Neil Armstrong; Peter Brown; David Clyde; James Currie; Joseph McKernan; William McNeilly; Lexie Scott.

Ballymoney Borough Council (5)
Joe Gaston; William Logan; Tom McKeown; John Ramsay; James Simpson.

Banbridge District Council (7)
Joan Baird; Norah Beare; Derrick Bell; Ian Burns; John Hanna; John Ingram; William Martin

Belfast City Council (11)
Dr Ian Adamson; David Browne; Jim Clarke; Margaret Clarke; Margaret Crooks; Alan Crowe; Sir Reg Empey; Dr Chris McGimpsey; Michael McGimpsey; Jim Rodgers; Robert Stoker.

Carrickfergus Borough Council (4)
Roy Beggs; Darin Ferguson; Eric Ferguson; Gwen Wilson.

Castlereagh Borough Council (5)
Michael Copeland; David Drysdale; Cecil Hall; Michael Henderson; Barbara McBurney.

Coleraine Borough Council (10)
Pauline Armitage; David Barbour; Toye Black; Olive Church Norman Hillis; Elizabeth Johnston; William A. King; David McClarty; Robert McPherson; Jim Watt.

Cookstown District Council (3)
Sam Glasgow; Walter Greer; Trevor Wilson.

Craigavon Borough Council (8)
Sidney Anderson; Sidney Cairns; Fred Crowe; Meta Crozier; Samuel Gardiner; Arnold Hatch; George Savage; Kenneth Twyble.

Down District Council (6)
Lt Col Harvey Bicker; Robert Burgess; Albert Colmer; Gerald Douglas; Jack McIlheron; Edward Rea.

Dungannon and South Tyrone Borough Council (6)
Norman Badger; Walter Cuddy; Jim Hamilton; Derek Irwin; Lord Maginnis of Drumglass; Robert Mulligan.

Fermanagh District Council (7)
Harold Andrews; Tom Elliott; Wilson Elliott; Raymond Ferguson; Robert Irvine; Bertie Kerr; Cecil Noble.

Larne Borough Council (4)
Roy Beggs; Dr Brian Dunn; Joan Drummond; David Fleck.

Limavady Borough Council (3)
Jackie Dolan; Jack Rankin; Edwin Stevenson.

Lisburn City Council (13)
David Archer; David Archer Jnr; James Baird; William Bell; Ivan Davis; Jim Dillon; Edmund Falloon; W. Gardiner-Watson; Sam Johnston; Harry Lewis; Joseph Lockhart; Lorraine Martin; William Ward.

Derry City Council (2) Andrew Davidson; Mary Hamilton.

Magherafelt District Council (2) John Junkin; George Sheils

Moyle Borough Council (3)
William Graham; Helen Harding; Robert McIlroy

Newry and Mourne District Council (4)
Isaac Hanna; Danny Kennedy; Andrew Mofftt; Henry Reilly.

Newtownabbey Borough Council (9)
Jim Bingham; Janet Crilly; Barbara Gilliland; Ivan Hunter; Vera McWilliam; Ken Robinson; Vi Scott; Edward Turkington; Dineen Walker.

North Down Borough Council (8)
Irene Cree; Leslie Cree; Roy Davies; Roberta Dunlop; Ian Henry; Ellie McKay; Diana Peacocke; Marion Smith

Omagh District Council (3)
Reuben McKelvey; Allan Rainey; Robert Wilson.

Strabane District Council (2)
James Emery; Derek Hussey.

Sinn Féin (SF)

51/55 Falls Road, Belfast, BT12 4PD
Tel: 028 9022 3000 / Fax: 028 9022 3001
Email: sinnfein@iol.ie
Web: www.sinnfein.ie

President: Gerry Adams MP (pictured)
Deputy: Pat Doherty MP
Secretary: Lucilita Bhreatnach
Chairperson: Mitchel McLaughlin

Representing republicanism within the Northern Ireland political spectrum, Sinn Féin's share of the catholic/nationalist vote has continued to rise, attracting more first preference votes than the SDLP, and overtaking that party in the 2003 Assembly elections. Sinn Féin dates its all-island origins from the independence movement that gathered momentum at the end of World War I in 1918. Linked with the Provisional IRA, Sinn Féin followed a policy of abstentionism in politics until the 1980s, and the party continues to abstain from taking its Westminster seats.

A significant shift in party policy occurred in 1998 when members voted to change the party's constitution and allowed elected party representatives to take their seats in a devolved Northern Ireland Assembly. They have not, however, taken their seats on the Policing Board. Whilst Unionist scepticism remains about the durability of Sinn Féin's commitment to the peace process, recent movement on decommissioning by the IRA has helped demonstrate the party's commitment to constitutional politics.

Sinn Féin Leadership
Gerry Adams, President of Sinn Féin since 1990, has been credited with the transformation of Sinn Féin from a political vehicle representing the aims of the IRA to a sophisticated well-organised political party. An MP for West Belfast from 1982 to 1992 and again from 1997, he acknowledged as early as 1980 that Republican aims were unlikely to be satisfied through military means alone.

Sinn Féin Elected Representation

Westminster: 4 MPs - see pages 34-35 for details
Dail Eireann: 5 seats

Northern Ireland Assembly:
A full list of all SF members elected to the Northern Ireland Assembly in the 2003 elections can be found on page 40.

Local Government: Sinn Féin Councillors (A-Z by Council)
Total Number of Sinn Féin Councillors: 108*

Antrim Borough Council (2): Martin McManus; Martin Meehan.

Armagh City and District Council (5)
Paul Corrigan; Brian Cunningham; Pat McNamee; Pat O'Rawe Cathy Rafferty.
**(Also SDLP Coleraine Councillor Billy Leonard has left the SDLP and joined Sinn Féin)*

Ballymoney Borough Council (1) Philip McGuigan.

Belfast City Council (14)
Gerald Brophy; Michael Browne; Máire Cush; Tom Hartley; Danny Lavery; Alex Maskey; Paul Maskey; Chrissie McAuley Fra McCann; Margaret McClenaghan; Marie Moore; Eoin O'Broin; Joseph O'Donnell; Gerard O'Neill.

Cookstown District Council (6)
Seamus Campbell; Dessie Grimes; Pearse McAleer; Michael McIvor; John McNamee; Oliver Molloy.

Craigavon Borough Council (4)
Maurice Magill; Brian McKeown; Francie Murray; John O'Dowd.

Derry City Council (10)
Peter Anderson; Cathal Crumley; Lynn Fleming; Paul Fleming; Tony Hassan; Gerry MacLochlainn; Maeve McLaughlin; Barney O'Hagan; Gearoid O'hEara; William Page.

Down District Council (4) Francis Braniff; Willie Clarke; Eamonn McConvey; Francis McDowell.

Dungannon and South Tyrone Borough Council (8)
Desmond Donnelly; Seamus Flanagan; Phelim Gildernew; Michael Gillespie; Sean McGuigan; Larry McLarnon; Francie Molloy; Barry Monteith.

Fermanagh District Council (9) Joe Cassidy; Pat Cox; Patrick Gilgunn; Stephen Huggett; Ruth Lynch; Robin Martin; Brian McCaffrey; Gerry McHugh, Thomas O'Reilly.

Limavady Borough Council (4)
Anne Brolly; Francis Brolly; Marion Donaghy; Martin McGuigan

Lisburn City Council (4)
Paul Butler; Michael Ferguson; Sue Ramsey; Veronica Willis.

Magherafelt District Council (7)
Patrick Groogan; Oliver Hughes; John Kelly; Sean Kerr; Hugh Mullan; Seamus O'Brien; Seamus O'Neill.

Moyle District Council (1) Monica Digney.

Newry and Mourne District Council (13)
Colman Burns; Charlie Casey; Martin Cunningham; Brendan Curran; Terry Hearty; Davy Hyland; Breandan Lewis; Elena Martin; Jimmy McCreesh; Packie McDonald; Pat McGinn; Mick Murphy; Michael Ruane.

Newtownabbey Borough Council (1) Briege Meehan.

Omagh District Council (8) Sean Begley; Sean Clarke; Damien Curran; Peter Kelly; Barney McAleer; Michael McAnespie; Barry McElduff; Patrick Watters.

Strabane District Council (7)
Ivan Barr; Daniel Breslin; Eamon McGarvey; Claire McGill; Charlie McHugh; Brian McMahon; Jarlath McNulty.

Social Democratic and Labour Party (SDLP)

121 Ormeau Road, Belfast, BT7 1SH
Tel: 028 9024 7700 / Fax: 028 9023 6699
Email: sdlp@indigo.ie
Web: www.sdlp.ie

Leader: Mark Durkan (pictured)
Deputy: Brid Rodgers
Secretary: Gerry Cosgrove
Chairperson: Alex Attwood

For the past 30 years, the SDLP had been recognised as the main nationalist party attracting the majority of the 'Catholic' vote. Recent elections have seen Sinn Féin erode the position of the SDLP, and in the 2003 Assembly elections Sinn Féin comfortably overtook the SDLP as the largest nationalist party.

Founded in 1970 by seven individuals including John Hume and the socialist Gerry Fitt following the civil rights agitation, the SDLP sought to replace the old Nationalist party with a more dynamic version of politics.

The SDLP supports the principle of Irish unity advocating the achievement of this through exclusively constitutional political means and the principle of consent of the majority. The SDLP is supportive of the development of the North/South bodies and co-operation between the East/West bodies as set out in the agreement.

SDLP Leadership
Mark Durkan stood unopposed as leader of the SDLP in succession to John Hume and was subsequently elected Deputy First Minister on 6 November 2001.

Previously Mark Durkan was Chairperson of the SDLP from 1990-1995 and a Member of the Forum for Peace and Reconciliation from 1994 until 1996. Durkan was also one of the SDLP's chief negotiators at the inter-party talks leading to the Good Friday Agreement and was widely regarded as being the principal author of the Good Friday Agreement. He was also Director of the Referendum campaign in 1998.

SDLP Elected Representation

European Parliament: John Hume MEP

Westminster: 3 MPs - see pages 34-35 for details

Northern Ireland Assembly:
A full list of all SDLP members elected to the Northern Ireland Assembly in the 2003 elections can be found on page 41.

Local Government:
SDLP Councillors (A-Z by Council)
Total number of SDLP Councillors: 105*

Antrim Borough Council (4): Thomas Burns; Oran Keenan; Bobby Loughran; Donovan McClelland.

**(Councillor Billy Leonard has left the SDLP and joined Sinn Féin)*

Armagh City and District Council (6)
Pat Brannigan; Anna Brolly; John Campbell; Tom Canavan; Tommy Kavanagh; James McKernan.

Ballymena Borough Council (4)
Margaret Gribben; Seamus Laverty; PJ McAvoy; Declan O'Loan.

Ballymoney Borough Council (2)
Harry Connolly; Malachy McCamphill.

Banbridge District Council (3)
Seamus Doyle; Pat McAleenan; Catherine McDermot.

Belfast City Council (8)
Alex Attwood; Patrick Convery; Carmel Hanna; Alban Maginness; Patrick McCarthy; Catherine Molloy; Martin Morgan; Peter O'Reilly.

Castlereagh Borough Council (2)
Brian Hanvey; Rosaleen Hughes

Coleraine Borough Council (3)
John Dallat; Gerry McLaughlin; Eamon Mullan.

Cookstown District Council (4)
Mary Baker; Peter Cassidy; James McGarvey; Patsy McGlone

Craigavon Borough Council (6)
Ignatius Fox; Dolores Kelly; Patricia Mallon; Mary McAlinden Nuala McAlinden; Tony Elliott.

Derry City Council (12)
Mary Bradley; Sean Carr; Jim Clifford; Thomas Conway; Gerard Diver; Shaun Gallagher; John Kerr; Kathleen McCloskey; Marie McDaid; Jim McKeever; William O'Connell; Helen Quigley; Pat Ramsey.

Down District Council (10)
Peter Craig; Dermot Curran; John Doris; Peter Fitzpatrick; Anne McAleenan; Carmel O'Boyle; Eamonn O'Neill; Margaret Ritchie; Patrick Toman; Anne Trainor.

Dungannon and South Tyrone (4)
Jim Cavanagh; Vincent Currie; Patsy Daly; Anthony McGonnell.

Fermanagh District Council (4)
Frank Britton; Gerry Gallagher; Fergus McQuillan; John O'Kane.

Larne Borough Council (2)
Daniel O'Connor; Martin Wilson.

Limavady Borough Council (4)
Michael Carten; Michael Coyle; Dessie Lowry; Gerard Mullan.

Magherafelt District Council (3)
Kathleen Lagan; Joseph McBride; Patrick McErlean.

Moyle District Council (2)
Madeline Black; Christine Blaney.

Newry and Mourne District Council (10)
PJ Bradley; Paul McKibbin; Michael Carr; Michael Cole; John Fee; John Feehan; Frank Feeley; John McArdle; Pat McElroy; Josephine O'Hare.

Newtownabbey Borough Council (2)
Noreen McClelland; Tommy McTeague.

Omagh District Council (6)
Joe Byrne; Josephine Deehan; Patrick McDonnell; Liam McQuaid; Gerry O'Doherty; Seamus Shields.

Strabane District Council (4)
Ann Bell; Tom McBride; Eugene McMenamin; Bernadette McNamee.

The Alliance Party of Northern Ireland

88 University Street, Belfast, BT7 1HE
Tel: 028 9032 4274 / Fax: 028 9033 3147
Email: alliance@allianceparty.org
Web: www.allianceparty.org

Leader: David Ford (pictured)
Deputy: Eileen Bell
Secretary: Stephen Farry
Chairperson: Tom Ekin

The Alliance Party describes itself as a non-sectarian political group, dedicated to co-operation between all the people of Northern Ireland. The party was formed in 1970 to give political expression to those who felt that nationalist and unionist political parties did not reflect their views. Alliance draws its members from all religious and political perspectives.

6 members in the Assembly and 28 councillors in local government represent the Alliance Party. The 2003 Assembly elections saw Alliance's share of the 1st preference vote decrease significantly to 3.7% from 6.5% in 1998. The party did, however, retain all 6 seats it had held by gaining transfers from other candidates. Despite running candidates in successive Westminster elections, the Alliance Party has never held a Westminster seat.

Alliance Party Leadership

The Alliance Party is led by David Ford, a member of Antrim Borough Council since 1993 and elected Assembly Member for South Antrim. He was elected leader of the Alliance party in October 2001, following roles as Party General Secretary from 1990-1998 and Chief Whip.

Alliance Elected Representation

Northern Ireland Assembly:
A full list of all Alliance members elected to the Northern Ireland Assembly in the 2003 elections can be found on page 41.

Local Government:
Alliance Party Councillors (A-Z by Council)
Total number of Alliance Party Councillors: 28

Ards Borough Council (4)
Linda Cleland; Jim McBriar; Alan McDowell; Kieran McCarthy.

Banbridge District Council (1)
Frank McQuaid.

Belfast City Council (3)
David Alderdice; Thomas Ekin; Naomi Long.

Carrickfergus Borough Council (5)
Robert Cavan; Janet Crampsey; Stewart Dickson; Noreen McIlwrath, Sean Neeson

Castlereagh Borough Council (4)
Sara Duncan; Michael Long; Peter Osborne; Geraldine Rice.

Larne Borough Council (2)
John Mathews; Geraldine Mulvenna.

Lisburn City Council (3)
Elizabeth Campbell; Seamus Close; Trevor Lunn.

Newtownabbey Borough Council (1)
Lynn Frazer.

North Down Borough Council (5)
Stephen Farry; Marsden Fitzsimons; Tony Hill; Susan O'Brien Anne Wilson.

United Kingdom Unionist Party (UKUP)

10 Central Avenue
Bangor, BT20 3AF
Tel: 028 9147 9860

Leader: Robert McCartney (pictured)

Founded by Robert McCartney in 1996 the UKUP campaigned for a No vote in the Referendum, and returned 5 members to the first Assembly in 1998. In January 1999, 4 members left the party, leaving the UKUP with Robert McCartney as its sole representative in the Assembly. He was also the only candidate returned for the party in the 2003 election where overall support for the party collapsed. The party is staunchly unionist believing the maintenance of the union to be "in the best interests of all of the people of Northern Ireland". Its principle objections to the agreement lie in the view that the agreement has "violated the basic principles of democracy by installing the frontmen for terror into Government".

UKUP Elected Representation

Northern Ireland Assembly:
Robert McCartney

Local Government:
Total number of UKUP Councillors: 2

North Down Borough Council (2)
Bill Keery; Valerie Kinghan

Progressive Unionist Party (PUP)

128 Shankill Road, Belfast, BT13 2BH
Tel: 028 9032 6233 / Fax: 028 9024 9602
Email: central@pup-ni.org
Web: www.pup.org

Leader: David Ervine (pictured)
Secretary: William Mitchell
Chairperson: William Smyth

Formed in 1997, the Progressive Unionist Party seeks to represent loyalist working class voters and is linked to the paramilitary UVF. The party has adopted a pro agreement stance believing that there must be "sharing of responsibility" between Unionists and Nationalists, whilst maintaining their firm belief in the Union with Great Britain. The party has one member in the Assembly, the party leader David Ervine and holds five local councillor positions.

While in favour of compromise with nationalists, the PUP remains opposed to a United Ireland and believes the loyalist ceasefire depends on the continued security of Northern Ireland within the UK.

PUP Elected Representation

Northern Ireland Assembly:
David Ervine

Local Government:
PUP Councillors (A-Z by Council)
Total number of PUP Councillors: 5

Belfast City Council (3)
David Ervine; Billy Hutchinson; Hugh Smyth

Castlereagh Borough Council (2)
Cecil Hall; Thomas Sandford

Northern Ireland Women's Coalition (NIWC)

50 University Street, Belfast, BT7 1HB
Tel: 028 9023 3100 / Fax: 028 9024 0021
Email: niwc@iol.ie
Web: www.niwc.org

Leader: Monica McWilliams (pictured)
Chairperson: Helen Crickard
Contact: Elizabeth Byrne McCullough

The Northern Ireland Women's Coalition, which is strongly pro-Agreement, was established in 1996 with the aim of putting forward an agenda of "reconciliation through dialogue, accommodation and inclusion" and ensuring that women were represented in the Forum talks on the future of Northern Ireland. Like Alliance the party seeks to draw members from all religious and political persuasions, but with an emphasis on the involvement of women. Leader Monica McWilliams, along with Jane Morrice represented the Women's Coalition in the first Assembly but both were unsuccessful in the 2003 election campaign meaning the party will have no representation in any new Assembly.

NIWC Elected Representation

Local Government:
Total number of NIWC Councillors: 1

North Down Borough Council (1)
Patricia Wallace

Northern Ireland Unionist Party (NIUP)

c/o 2B Ann Street, Newtownards, BT23 7AB
Tel: 028 9181 0484
Email: info@niup.org
Web: www.niup.org
Leader: Cedric Wilson

Following the resignation of four Assembly members from the UKUP the NIUP was formed on the 5 January 1999. The Northern Ireland Unionist Party is pro union and anti agreement. The party is led by Cedric Wilson. The party unsuccessfully contested the 2003 Assembly elections and will not be represented in any new Assembly.

Green Party

537 Antrim Road, Belfast, BT15 3BU
Tel: 028 9077 6731
Email: vote@greens-in.org
Web: www.greens-in.org

Leader: John Barry

The Green Party has contested Northern Ireland elections since 1990, albeit with very little success. Despite running candidates in most elections, the party remains among the smallest in Northern Ireland, campaigning on ecological and environmental issues.

The Conservative Party

PO Box 537
Belfast, BT16 1YF
Web: www.conservativesni.com

Conservative Party Northern Ireland Chairman:
Julian Robertson

The Conservative Party is the only mainstream political party to contest elections in all four parts of the United Kingdom.

In the 1980s there was pressure within the Conservative Party to stand candidates in Northern Ireland elections. A small number of Conservative Councillors have previously been elected in North Down, but the party was unsuccessful in the 2003 Assembly elections and has currently no elected representation in Northern Ireland.

Workers' Party

6 Springfield Road, Belfast, BT12 7AG
Tel: 028 9032 8663
Fax: 028 9033 3475
Email: info@workers-party.org
Web: www.workers-party.org

Northern Ireland Secretary: Thomas Owens
Chairperson: Gerry Grainger
President: Sean Garland
General Secretary: John Lowry

The Workers' Party has republican origins and is strongly socialist. Formed after a split within Sinn Féin in the 1970s it proceeded to adopt a Marxist ideology. The party suffered a split in 1992. The Workers Party has seen its share of the vote decrease substantially in recent elections, and currently has no political representation at any level.

Natural Law Party

The Natural Law Party has contested many elections since its launch in 1992 but has never been successful, despite fielding many candidates.

Election Results

Northern Ireland is unique within the United Kingdom in that it conducts all its elections, except those to the Westminster Parliament, by proportional representation.

Introduction

The legislative and institutional framework of the electoral system for Northern Ireland is also unique in a number of aspects within the UK. All elections and electoral matters, including the franchise and electoral registration are excepted matters, and therefore remain the responsibility of the Government at Westminster regardless of devolution.
Four types of election are held in Northern Ireland:

- Local government;
- Northern Ireland Assembly;
- Westminster parliament;
- European parliament.

Proportional representation, the single transferable vote (STV), is used for all elections except Westminster where, in keeping with the rest of the UK, simple plurality, the 'first past the post' system is applied. Although arguably less democratic than STV, 'first past the post' has continued to be favoured by successive governments as this electoral approach provides a successful UK government with a substantial majority of seats.

Electoral Results and Analysis

Northern Ireland has had 18 elections during the period 1982-2003, and despite their plentiful nature each has been vigorously contested and generated keen interest in the community. Whilst voting patterns have shown strong adherence to traditional allegiances, the longer-term trend would suggest that nationalist parties are gaining ground on their unionist counterparts and centre parties are finding it difficult to hold their votes against more uncompromising rivals in both communities.

An interesting development within the electoral landscape has been the emerging struggle for dominance not only between, but also within the two religio-political groupings, i.e. between UUP and DUP, SDLP and Sinn Féin. At present, this is a struggle which has resulted in the two more 'extreme' parties coming out strongest - the DUP on the unionist side and Sinn Féin on the nationalist side.

The table below shows each party's electoral results for all major elections since 1982. This includes elections to the various political initiatives such as the Assembly of 1982 and the Forum of 1996. It excludes by-elections, including the multiple by-elections of 1986, as they are not as significant in terms of long-term trends.

Northern Ireland Elections 1982-2003
Parties' share of vote (%)

Year	Election to	UUP	DUP	SDLP	SF	All	PUP	NIWC	UKUP	Other
1982	Assembly	29.7	23.0	18.8	10.1	9.3	-	-	-	9.1
1983	Westminster	34.0	20.0	18.0	13.4	8.0	-	-	-	6.6
1984	European	21.5	33.6	22.1	13.3	5.0	-	-	-	4.5
1985	Local Government	29.5	24.3	17.8	11.8	7.1	-	-	-	9.5
1987	Westminster	37.8	11.7	21.1	11.4	10.0	0.9	-	-	7.1
1989	Local Government	31.3	17.7	21.0	11.2	6.9	-	-	-	11.9
1989	European	22.2	30.0	25.5	9.2	5.2	-	-	-	7.9
1992	Westminster	34.5	13.1	23.5	10.0	8.7	-	-	-	10.3
1993	Local Government	29.4	17.3	22.0	12.4	7.6	-	-	-	11.3
1994	European	23.8	29.2	28.9	9.9	4.1	-	-	-	4.1
1996	NI Forum	24.2	18.8	21.4	15.5	6.5	3.5	1.0	3.6	5.5
1997	Westminster	32.7	13.6	24.1	16.1	8.0	1.4	0.4	1.6	2.1
1997	Local Government	27.9	15.6	20.6	16.9	6.6	2.2	0.5	0.5	9.2
1998	Assembly	21.3	18.1	22.0	17.6	6.5	2.6	1.6	4.5	5.8
1999	European	17.6	28.4	28.1	17.3	2.1	3.3	-	3.0	0.2
2001	Westminster	26.8	22.5	21.0	21.7	3.6	0.6	0.4	1.7	1.7
2001	Local Government	22.9	21.4	19.4	20.6	5.1	1.6	0.4	0.6	8.0
2003	Assembly	22.7	25.7	17.0	23.5	3.7	1.2	0.8	0.8	4.6

Northern Ireland Westminster Elections

In Northern Ireland the law governing Westminster parliamentary elections is the Representation of the People Act 1983 as amended. The number of Westminster constituencies is determined by the Boundary Commission for Northern Ireland. The Commission is an entirely independent body which is required to make periodic reports and to submit these to the Secretary of State not less than 8 or more than 12 years from the submission of the last report. The Boundary Commission announced the Fifth Periodic Review of constituencies in May 2003. They do not intend publishing Provisional Recommendations for public comment before Spring 2004.

Boundary Commission for Northern Ireland

Forestview, Purdy's Lane, Newtownbreda
Belfast, BT8 4AX
Tel: 028 9069 4800 / Fax: 028 9069 4801
Email: bcni@belfast.org.uk
Web: www.boundarycommission.org.uk

Northern Ireland currently returns 18 MPs to Westminster out of a total for the United Kingdom of 635. MPs are elected under the first-past-the-post electoral system. From its conception under the Government of Ireland Act, 1920, until 1983 it had just 12 MPs. In 1983 the number of MPs was reconsidered by the Boundary Commission and five extra seats were created. These were contested for the first time in the June 1983 general election. In 1995, the Boundary Commission examined the situation again and created a further seat for Northern Ireland, bringing the total to eighteen for the election of May 1997.

Northern Ireland's MPs until recently were somewhat of an anomaly within the British political system. During the existence of the Stormont government, Northern Ireland MPs were not allowed to rise in Westminster matters that came under the remit of the Stormont government, a convention that was strongly criticised by many. Legislation passed in Westminster has tended to exclude Northern Ireland, which has had its own customised version of each Westminster Act. This has resulted in Northern Ireland legislation differing from the rest of the UK, perhaps most notably in recent years, the Provision of Abortion Act, which at present is in effect everywhere in the UK except Northern Ireland.

Westminster MPs by Party 2001

UUP	6
DUP	5
SDLP	3
SF	4

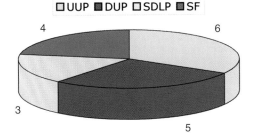

NB: Jeffrey Donaldson subsequently joined the DUP, giving that party 6 MPs to the Ulster Unionists' 5.

Westminster MPs as elected in 2001.

Constituency	Name	Party
Belfast East	Peter Robinson	DUP
Belfast North	Nigel Dodds	DUP
Belfast South	Rev Martin Smyth	UUP
Belfast West	Gerry Adams	SF
East Antrim	Roy Beggs	UUP
East Londonderry	Gregory Campbell	DUP
Fermanagh & South Tyrone	Michelle Gildernew	SF
Foyle	John Hume	SDLP
Lagan Valley	Jeffrey Donaldson*	UUP
Mid Ulster	Martin McGuinness	SF
Newry and Armagh	Séamus Mallon	SDLP
North Antrim	Rev Ian Paisley	DUP
North Down	Sylvia Hermon	UUP
South Antrim	David Burnside	UUP
South Down	Eddie McGrady	SDLP
Strangford	Iris Robinson	DUP
West Tyrone	Pat Doherty	SF
Upper Bann	David Trimble	UUP

*Jeffrey Donaldson subsequently joined the DUP

(Contact details for Westminster MPs can be found earlier in this chapter on page 34-35.)

The performance of the principal parties in Northern Ireland in Westminster elections can be seen in the table overleaf. The Ulster Unionists, the SDLP, the DUP, the Alliance Party and Sinn Féin have tended to dominate Westminster elections. However, the Alliance Party is the only one of the five never to have won a Westminster seat, despite capturing up to 12 per cent of the total vote on occasions.

Northern Ireland Westminster Elections 1979-2001: Parties' Share of Seats

Party	1979	1983	1987	1992	1997	2001
UUP	8	11	9	10	10	6
SDLP	1	1	3	4	3	3
DUP	3	3	3	3	2	5
SF	-	1	1	-	2	4
Other Unionists	2	1	1	1	1	-
Others	1	-	-	-	-	-

The table of seats gained, shown above, reflects the two-party battle within unionism and the similar contest between the two nationalist parties. In 1992 the Ulster Unionists and SDLP enjoyed the majority of votes from their respective communities, but by 2001 the DUP and Sinn Féin had caught up, Sinn Féin overtaking the SDLP for the first time. Smaller parties usually suffer under the first-past-the-post electoral system in Westminster elections, although the figures have previously shown one or two seats going to independents (nationalist or unionist), and unionist breakaway parties such as James Kilfedder's Ulster Popular Unionist Party from 1983 to 1992, and Robert McCartney's UK Unionist Party in 1997.

The influence of 'electoral pacts' between unionist parties is also highly significant. In areas with a large nationalist minority, the UUP and DUP have sometimes agreed that one of their candidates stand down, to allow a straight run for a single unionist candidate and avoid losing the seat to nationalists by splitting the unionist majority. Conversely, the SDLP and Sinn Féin have not entered into such agreements, even where the arithmetic suggested that a single nationalist candidate could comfortably win a seat.

Set out in the table to the right is the historical electoral performance of Northern Ireland's political parties in Westminster elections from 1979-2001 in terms of share of popular vote.

2001 Westminster elections - detailed results

The following tables set out the detailed Westminster 2001 results constituency by constituency.

Northern Ireland Westminster Elections 1979-2001: Parties' % share of vote

Party	1979	1983	1987	1992	1997	2001
UUP	36.6	34.0	37.8	34.5	32.7	26.8
SDLP	18.2	17.9	21.1	23.5	24.1	21.0
DUP	10.2	20.0	11.7	13.1	13.6	22.5
SF	-	13.4	11.4	10.0	16.1	21.7
All	11.9	8.0	10.0	8.7	8.0	3.6
WP	-	2.0	2.6	0.5	0.3	0.3
PUP	-	-	-	-	1.4	0.6
NIWC	-	-	-	-	0.4	0.4
UKUP	-	-		-	1.6	1.7
Others	23.1	4.7	5.4	9.7	1.8	1.4
Turnout %	68.4	73.3	67.4	69.7	67.1	68.0

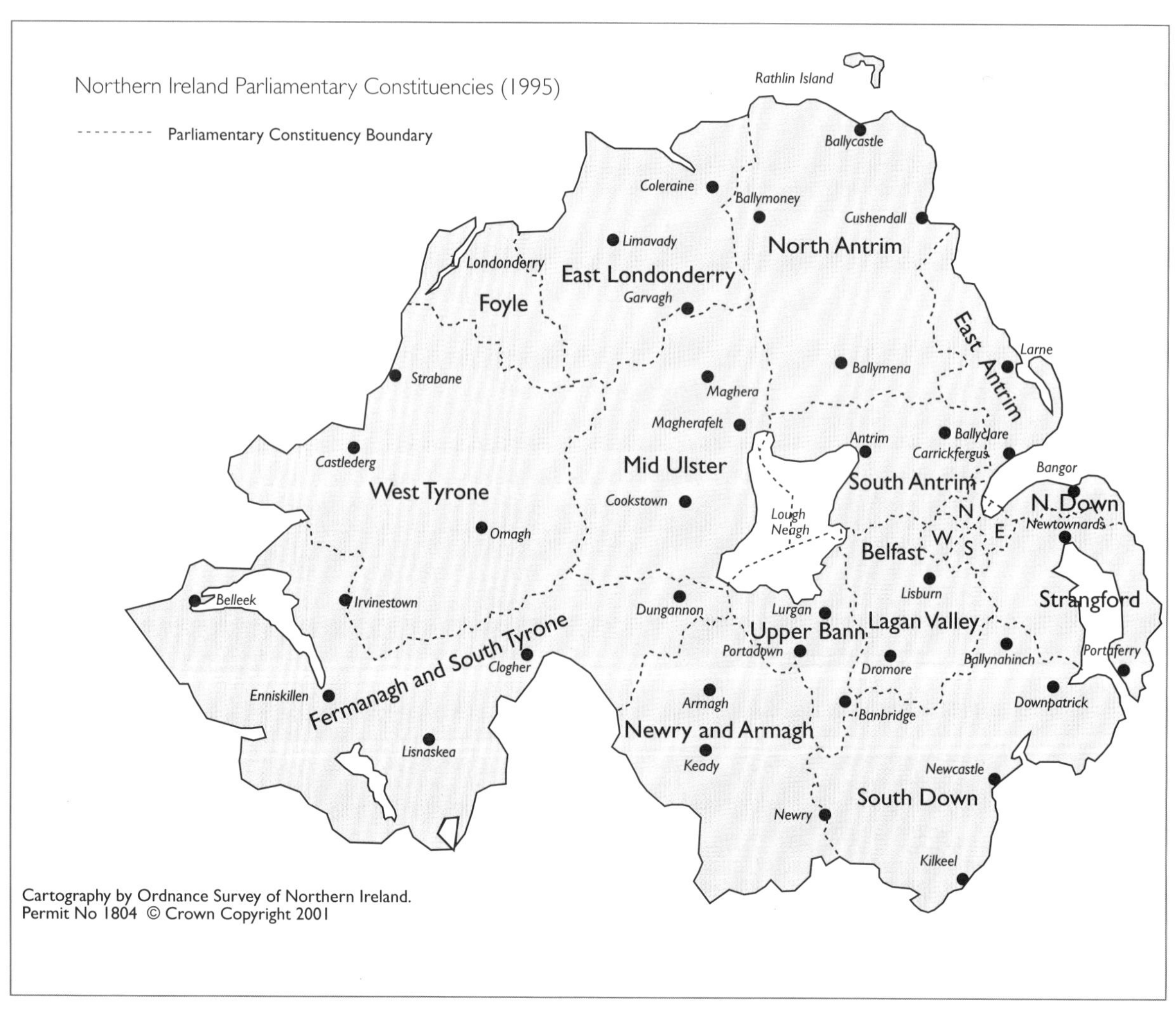

The 2001 UK Westminster Government General Election

Electorate	1,191,070	Total Votes Polled	810,381
Turnout	68.0%	Spoiled Votes	7,074

Results by Constituency

Belfast East

Name	Party	Votes	% Total vote
Peter Robinson*	**DUP**	**15,667**	**42.5**
Tim Lemon	UUP	8,550	23.2
David Alderdice	All	5,832	15.8
David Ervine	PUP	3,669	10.0
Joseph O'Donnell	SF	1,237	3.4
Ciara Farren	SDLP	888	2.4
Terry Dick	Cons	800	2.2
Joseph Bell	WP	123	0.3
Rainbow George Weiss	VFY	71	0.2

**Sitting MP*

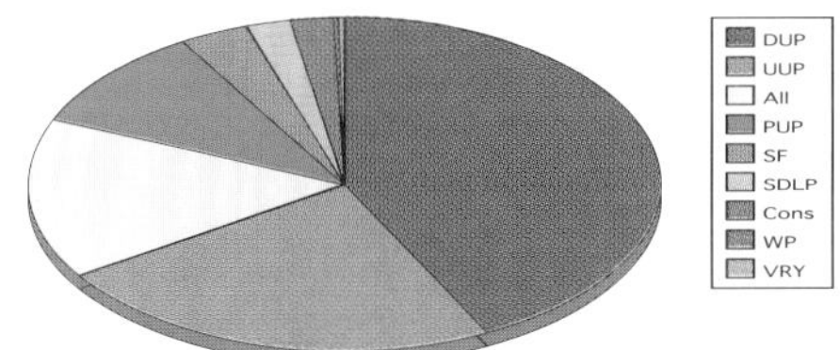

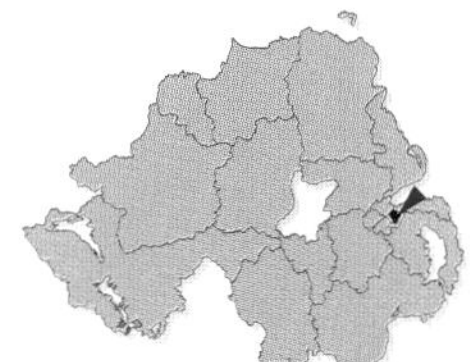

Electorate	58,455
Turnout	63.4%
Total Valid Vote	36,829
DUP Majority	7,117

East Belfast held by Peter Robinson of the DUP since 1979 has a substantial unionist majority. Robinson's nearest rivals were the UUP and Alliance, although the DUP majority was well over seven thousand votes.

Belfast North

Name	Party	Votes	% Total vote
Nigel Dodds	**DUP**	**16,718**	**40.8**
Gerry Kelly	SF	10,331	25.2
Alban Maginness	SDLP	8,592	21.0
Cecil Walker*	UUP	4,904	12.0
Marcella Delaney	WP	253	0.7
Rainbow George Weiss	VFY	134	0.3

**Sitting MP*

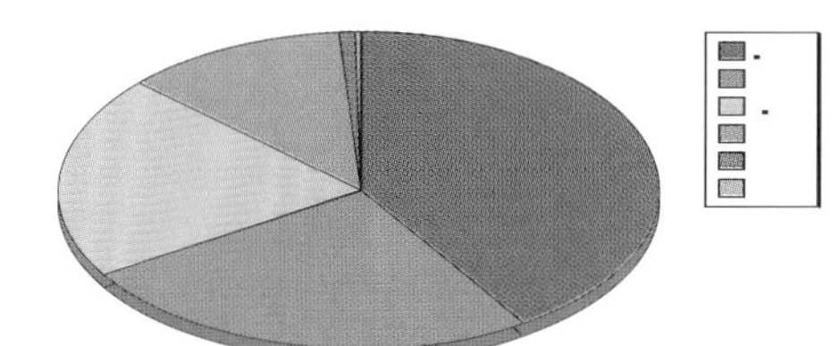

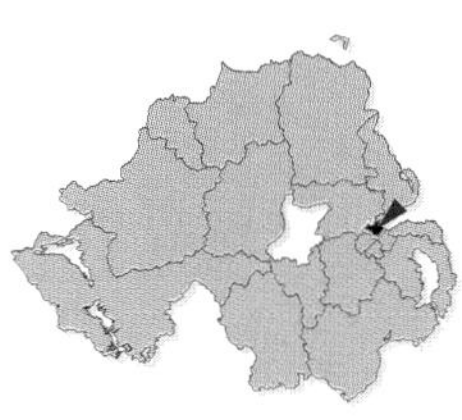

Electorate	60,941
Turnout	67.8%
Total Valid Vote	40,932
DUP Majority	6,387

North Belfast is one of the most deeply divided areas in Northern Ireland, and this is reflected in its elections. Cecil Walker held the seat for the Ulster Unionist Party since 1983, unopposed by candidates from the other Unionist parties until the 2001 election when Nigel Dodds of the DUP ran in direct competition. Nigel Dodds won two fifths of the vote, beating Walker into 4th place, behind SDLP and Sinn Féin.

Belfast South

Name	Party	Votes	% Total vote
Martin Smyth*	**UUP**	**17,008**	**44.8**
Alasdair McDonnell	SDLP	11,609	30.6
Monica McWilliams	NIWC	2,968	7.8
Alex Maskey	SF	2,894	7.6
Geraldine Rice	All	2,042	5.4
Dawn Purvis	PUP	1,112	2.9
Patrick Lynch	WP	204	0.6
Rainbow George Weiss	VFY	115	0.3

**Sitting MP*

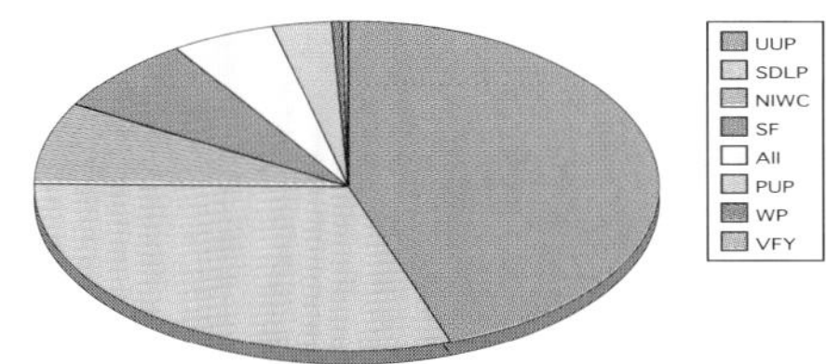

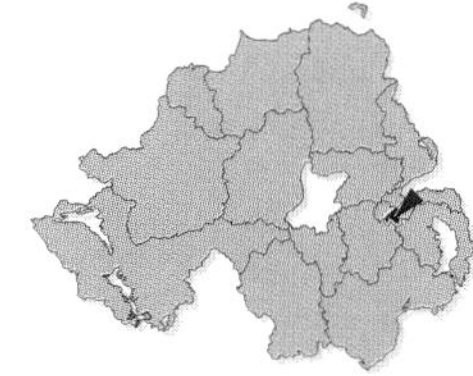

Electorate	59,436
Turnout	64.3%
Total Valid Vote	37,952
UUP majority	5,399

The Ulster Unionist Party candidate Martin Smyth retained South Belfast. Smyth's closest rival was the SDLP's Dr Alasdair McDonnell with Monica McWilliams coming third.

Belfast West

Name	Party	Votes	% Total vote
Gerry Adams*	**SF**	**27,096**	**66.1**
Alex Attwood	SDLP	7,754	18.9
Eric Smyth	DUP	2,641	6.4
Chris McGimpsey	UUP	2,541	6.2
John Lowry	WP	736	1.8
David Kerr	UTW	116	0.3
Rainbow George Weiss	VFY	98	0.2
*Sitting MP			

Electorate	59,617	Turnout	69.9%
Total Valid Vote	40,982	SF Majority	19,342

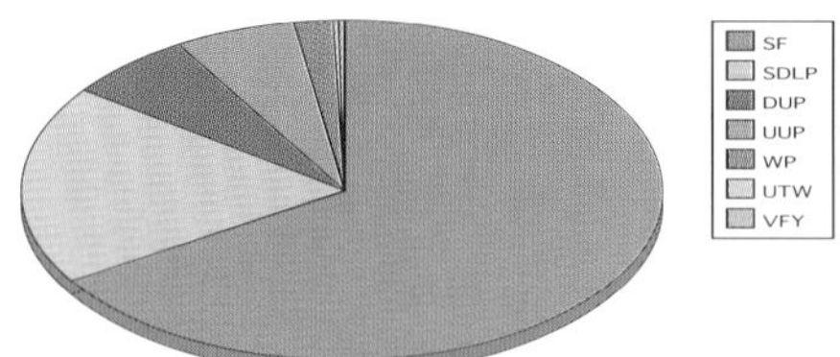

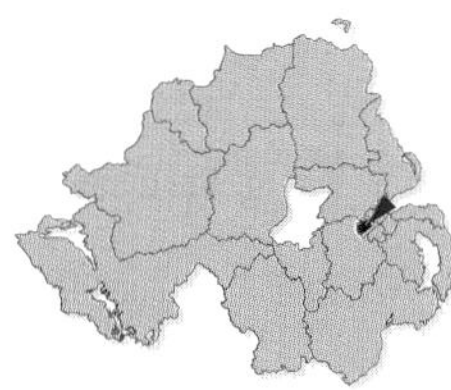

This constituency has a very strong Catholic and nationalist majority, although it includes much of the loyalist Shankill Road within its boundaries. Gerry Fitt, one of the founders and former leader of the SDLP, held Belfast West from 1966 to 1983. By 1983 Fitt had resigned from the SDLP, and Gerry Adams of Sinn Fein won the seat. Although Dr Joe Hendron of the SDLP won the seat back for the SDLP in 1992, Adams was successful in both 1997 and 2001.

East Antrim

Name	Party	Votes	% Total vote
Roy Beggs*	**UUP**	**13,101**	**36.4**
Sammy Wilson	DUP	12,973	36.0
John Matthews	All	4,483	12.5
Danny O'Connor	SDLP	2,641	7.4
Robert Mason	Ind	1,092	3.0
Janette Graffin	SF	903	2.5
Alan Greer	Cons	807	2.2
*Sitting MP			

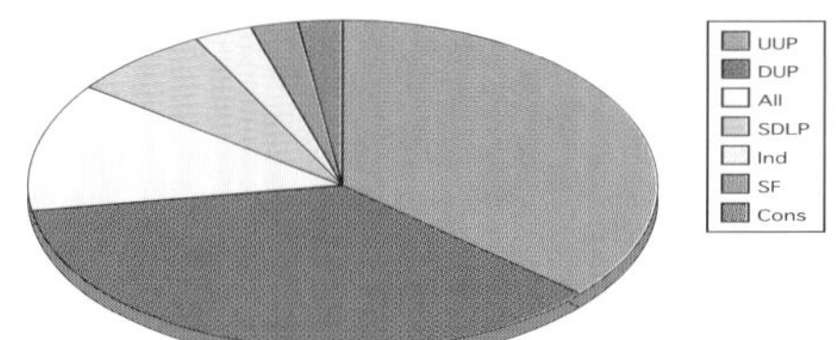

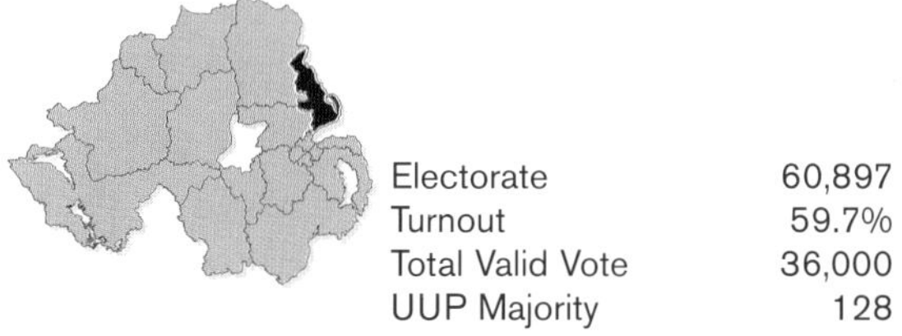

Electorate	60,897
Turnout	59.7%
Total Valid Vote	36,000
UUP Majority	128

East Antrim is one of the smaller constituencies and has an overwhelming unionist majority. Since its establishment by the Boundary Commission in 1983 Roy Beggs of the UUP has held the seat with increasingly strong opposition coming from the DUP.

East Londonderry

Name	Party	Votes	% Total vote
Gregory Campbell	**DUP**	**12,813**	**32.1**
Willie Ross*	UUP	10,912	27.4
John Dallat	SDLP	8,298	20.8
Francie Brolly	SF	6,221	15.6
Yvonne Boyle	All	1,625	4.1
*Sitting MP			

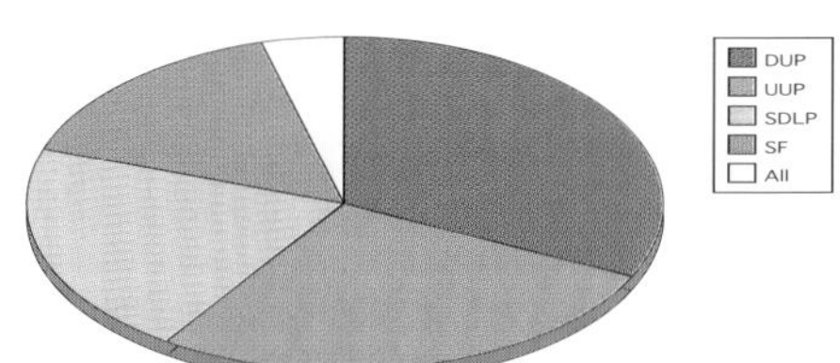

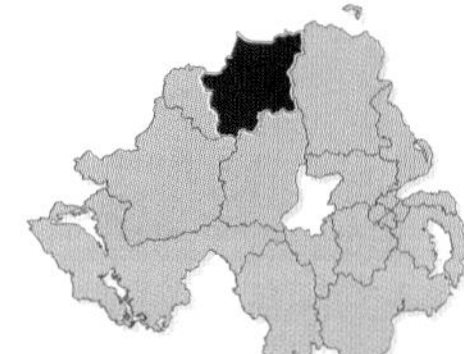

Electorate	60,215
Turnout	66.9%
Total Valid Vote	39,869
DUP majority	1,901

Gregory Campbell of the DUP took the East Londonderry seat from Willie Ross of the UUP who had held it with a majority of 4,000.The loss of this seat for the UUP was unexpected not least because of the hard-line anti-Agreement and anti-Trimble stance of the incumbent MP.

Fermanagh and South Tyrone

Name	Party	Votes	% Total vote
Michelle Gildernew	**SF**	**17,739**	**34.1**
James Cooper	UUP	17,686	34.0
Tommy Gallagher	SDLP	9,706	18.7
Jim Dixon	Ind	6,843	13.2
**Sitting MP*			

Electorate 66,640 Turnout 79.0%

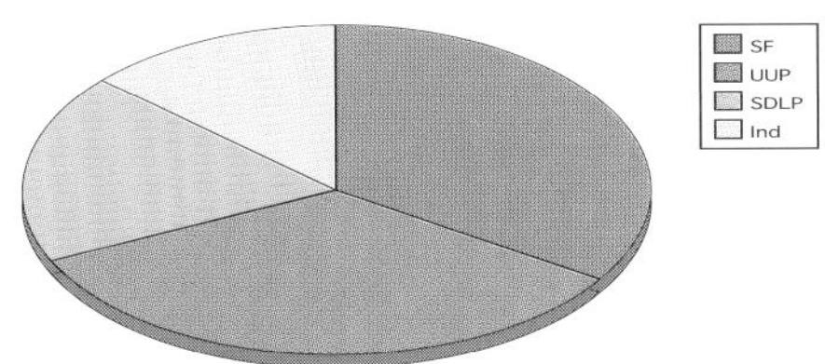

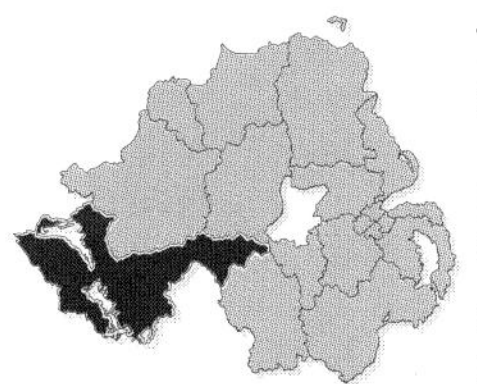

Total Valid Vote 51,974
SF majority 53

Ulster Unionist Ken Maginnis had held Fermanagh South Tyrone since 1983 but his decision not to stand for re-election in 2001 and the entry of independent unionist Jim Dixon enabled Michelle Gildernew of Sinn Féin to win the seat narrowly from the UUP.

Foyle

Name	Party	Votes	% Total vote
John Hume*	**SDLP**	**24,538**	**50.2**
Mitchel McLaughlin	SF	12,988	26.6
William Hay	DUP	7,414	15.2
Andrew Davidson	UUP	3,360	6.9
Colm Cavanagh	All	579	1.1
**Sitting MP*			

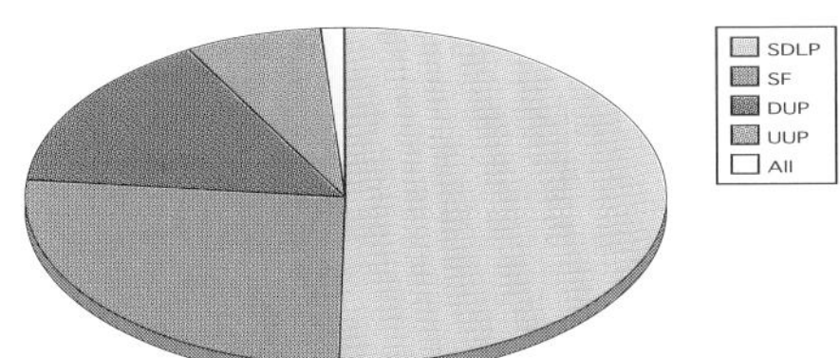

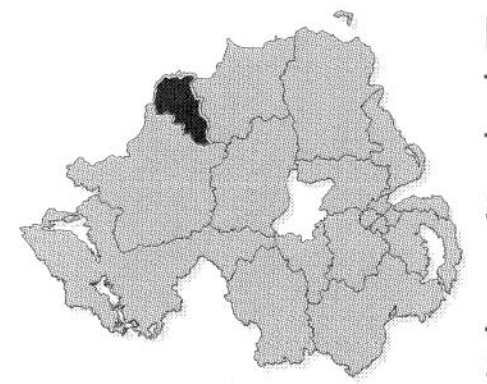

Electorate 70,943
Turnout 69.6%
Total Valid Vote 48,879
SDLP majority 11,550

John Hume, former leader of the SDLP has held the constituency since its creation in 1983. Despite big swings elsewhere from SDLP to Sinn Féin, the seat was retained by the SDLP with a comfortable majority of 11,550. Foyle was possibly the only nationalist constituency where Sinn Féin did not gain significant ground on the SDLP.

Lagan Valley

Name	Party	Votes	% Total vote
Jeffrey Donaldson*	**UUP**	**25,966**	**56.5**
Seamus Close	All	7,624	16.6
Edwin Poots	DUP	6,164	13.4
Patricia Lewsley	SDLP	3,462	7.6
Paul Butler	SF	2,725	5.9
**Sitting MP*			

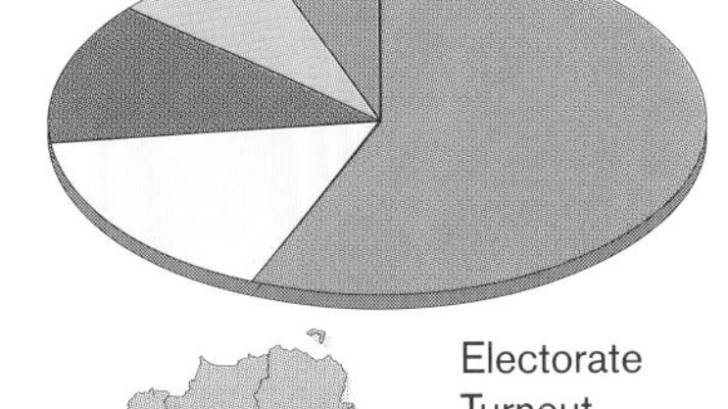

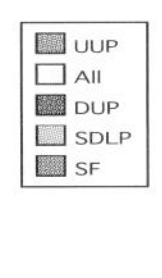

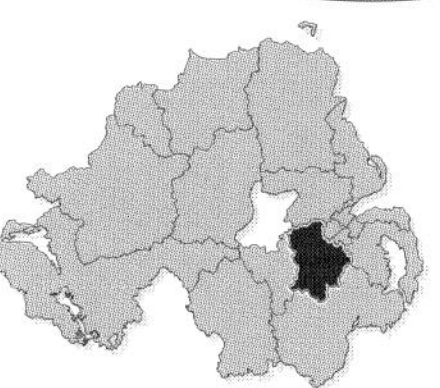

Electorate 72,671
Turnout 63.6%
Total Valid Vote 45,941
UUP majority 18,342

Jeffrey Donaldson has held Lagan Valley since 1997, when he replaced the retiring UUP leader, Jim Molyneaux. Donaldson won over 50 per cent of the vote in 2001, with his nearest rival, Alliance's Seamus Close, 18,000 votes behind. Jeffrey Donaldson has subsequently joined the DUP, taking the Lagan Valley seat out of Ulster Unionist control.

Mid Ulster

Name	Party	Votes	% Total vote
Martin McGuinness*	**SF**	**25,502**	**51.1**
Ian McCrea	DUP	15,549	31.1
Eilish Haughey	SDLP	8,376	16.8
Francie Donnelly	WP	509	1.0

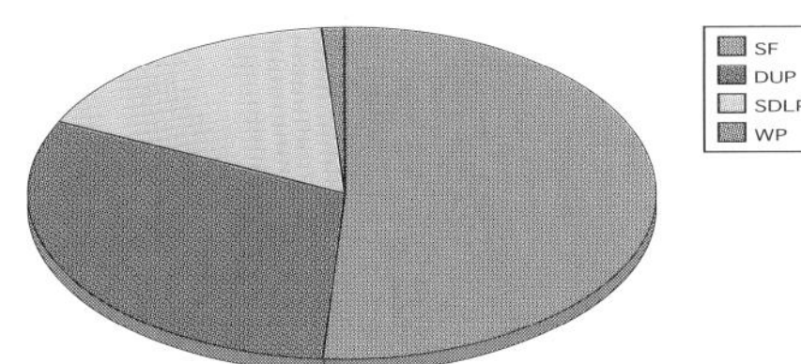

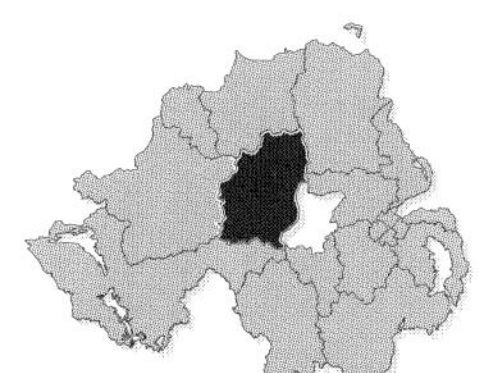

Electorate 61,390
Turnout 82.1%
Total Valid Vote 49,936
SF majority 9,953

Martin McGuinness retained Mid-Ulster for Sinn Féin, increasing his majority from 1,900 to almost 10,000 votes. The SDLP continued to drop behind the two leading parties in an area with very high turnout.

Newry and Armagh

Name	Party	Votes	% Total vote
Séamus Mallon*	SDLP	20,784	37.4
Conor Murphy	SF	17,209	30.9
Paul Berry	DUP	10,795	19.4
Sylvia McRoberts	UUP	6,833	12.3
*Sitting MP			

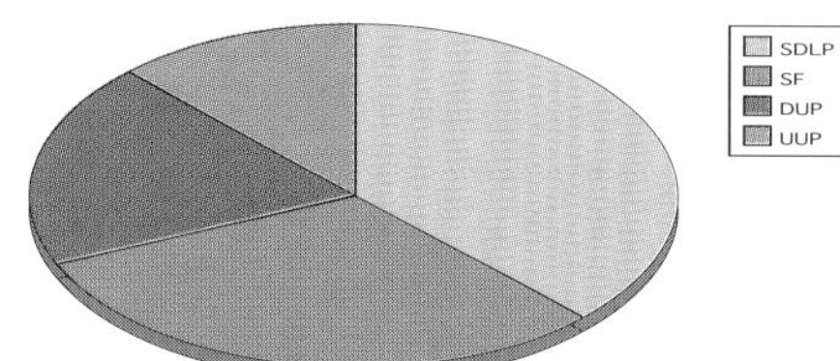

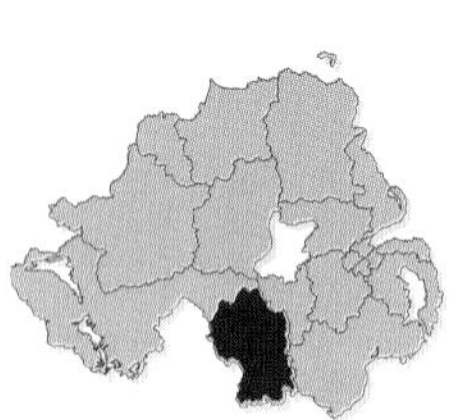

Electorate	72,466
Turnout	77.6%
Total Valid Vote	55,621
SDLP majority	3,575

The SDLP Deputy Leader Seamus Mallon retained Newry and Armagh, with a much-reduced majority of 3,500 votes over Sinn Fein's Conor Murphy. The DUP decided to run a candidate, contrary to their previous tactic of allowing the UUP to present a single unionist. Paul Berry, at 10,795 votes, pushed the UUP's Sylvia McRoberts into 4th place.

North Antrim

Name	Party	Votes	% Total vote
Ian Paisley*	**DUP**	**24,539**	**49.9**
Lexie Scott	UUP	10,315	21.0
Sean Farren	SDLP	8,283	16.8
John Kelly	SF	4,822	9.8
Jayne Dunlop	All	1,258	2.5
*Sitting MP			

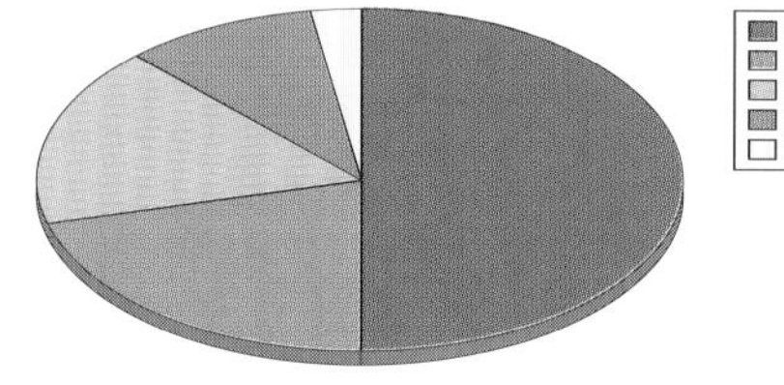

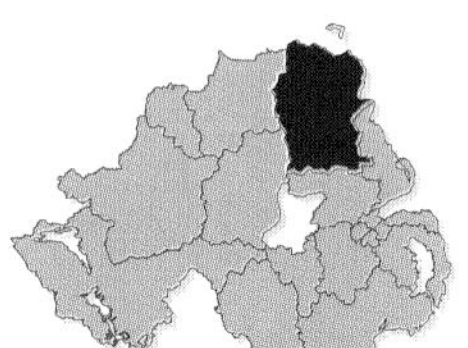

Electorate	74,451
Turnout	66.6%
Total Valid Vote	49,217
DUP Majority	14,224

North Antrim is the stronghold of the DUP leader, Ian Paisley since he first won the seat in 1970 with the UUP coming consistently second. The constituency has a substantial unionist majority.

North Down

Name	Party	Votes	% Total vote
Sylvia Hermon	**UUP**	**20,833**	**56.0**
Robert McCartney*	UKUP	13,509	36.3
Marietta Farrell	SDLP	1,275	3.4
Julian Robertson	Cons	815	2.2
Chris Carter	UIV	444	1.2
Eamon McConvey	SF	313	0.9

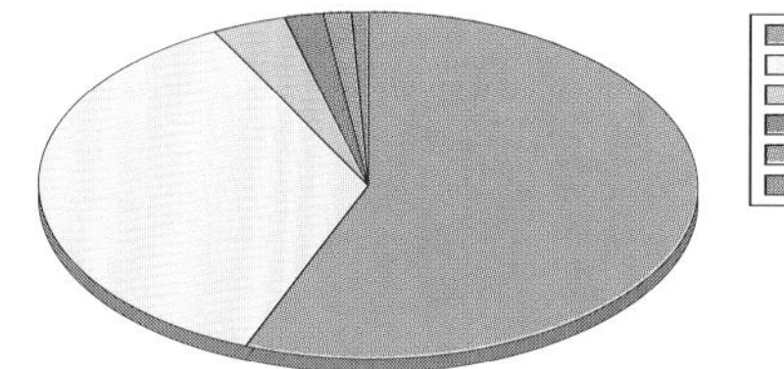

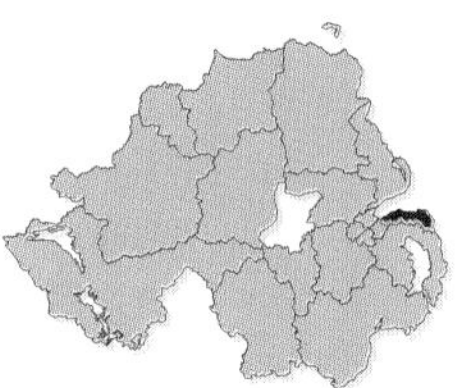

Electorate	63,212
Turnout	59.1%
Total Valid Vote	37,189
UUP Majority	7,324

North Down had not been held by any of the main political parties for over 20 years, Independent Unionist James Kilfedder holding the seat throughout the 70's and 80's succeeded by another Independent Unionist, Robert McCartney in 1995.

McCartney had held the North Down seat since the by-election in 1995. In 2001 the Alliance party withdrew in support of the pro-Agreement UUP candidate, Lady Sylvia Hermon. Its support proved crucial to the UUP. Sylvia Hermon took North Down with a majority of 7,324.

South Antrim

Name	Party	Votes	% Total vote
David Burnside	**UUP**	**16,366**	**37.1**
Willie McCrea*	DUP	15,355	34.8
Sean McKee	SDLP	5,336	12.1
Martin Meehan	SF	4,160	9.4
David Ford	All	1,969	4.4
Norman Boyd	NIUP	972	2.2
*Sitting MP			

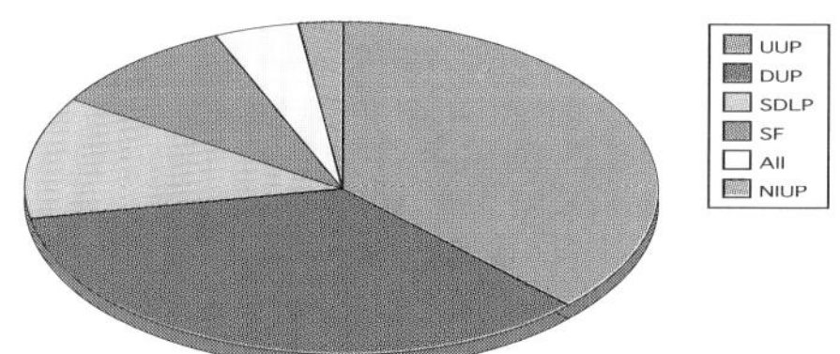

Electorate	70,651
Turnout	62.5%
Total Valid Vote	44,158
UUP Majority	1,011

Clifford Forsythe of the Ulster Unionists held this seat from 1983 until his death in April 2000.

In the 2000 by-election Willie McCrea of the DUP won the seat with a majority of 822 votes. However, the situation was reversed in 2001, when David Burnside won the seat back for the UUP by just over 1,000 votes.

South Down

Name	Party	Votes	% Total vote
Eddie McGrady*	**SDLP**	**24,136**	**46.4**
Mick Murphy	SF	10,278	19.7
Dermot Nesbitt	UUP	9,173	17.6
Jim Wells	DUP	7,802	15.0
Betty Campbell	All	685	1.3

**Sitting MP*

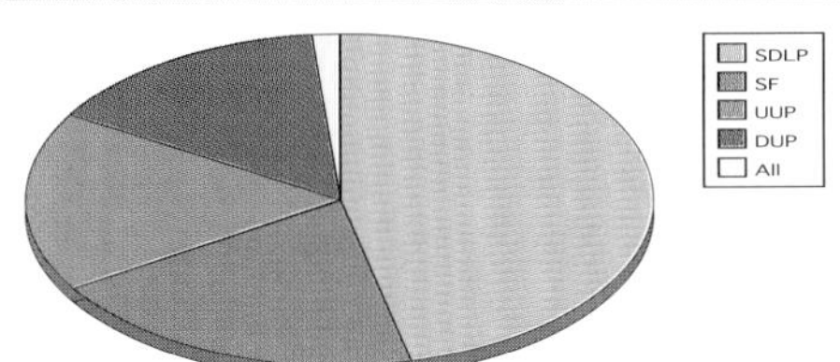

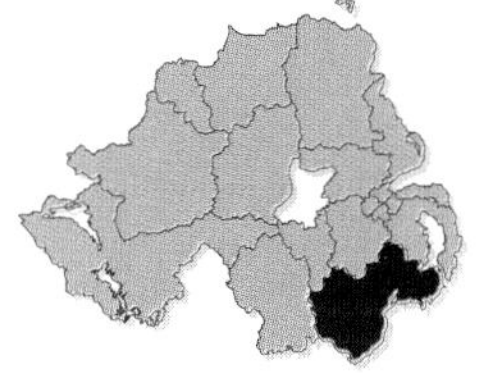

Electorate	73,519
Turnout	71.6%
Total Valid Vote	52,074
SDLP Majority	13,858

Eddie McGrady of the SDLP has held South Down since 1987, when he displaced Enoch Powell of the UUP by just over 700 votes. Since then, McGrady has increased his majority to almost 14,000 votes in 2001.

Strangford

Name	Party	Votes	% Total vote
Iris Robinson	**DUP**	**18,532**	**42.8**
David McNarry	UUP	17,422	40.3
Kieran McCarthy	All	2,902	6.7
Danny McCarthy	SDLP	2,646	6.1
Liam Johnson	SF	930	2.2
Cedric Wilson	NIUP	822	1.9

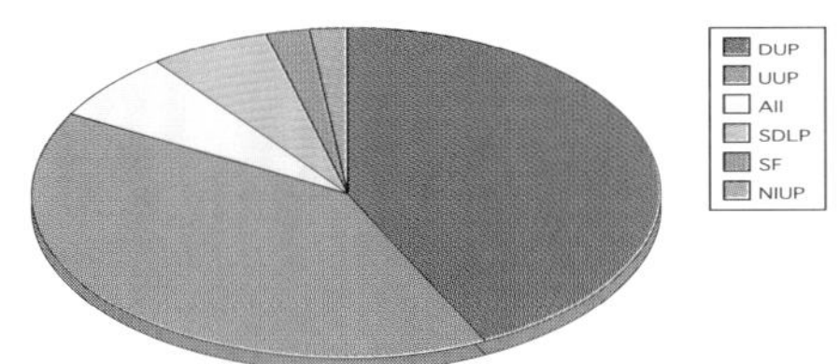

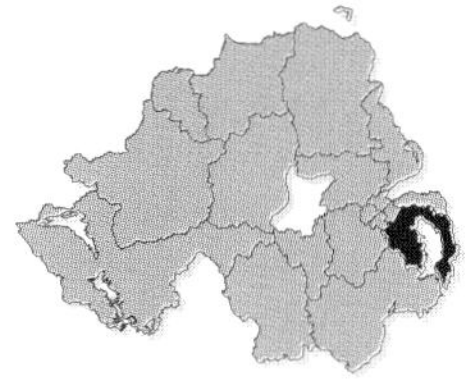

Electorate	72,192
Turnout	60.2%
Total Valid Vote	43,254
DUP majority	1,110

The contest for the Strangford seat, vacated by the UUP's John Taylor was close with David McNarry coming within 1,100 votes of retaining the seat for the UUP. Iris Robinson, DUP, was the eventual winner.

Upper Bann

Name	Party	Votes	% Total vote
David Trimble*	UUP	17,095	33.5
David Simpson	DUP	15,037	29.5
Dara O'Hagan	SF	10,771	21.1
Dolores Kelly	SDLP	7,607	14.9
Tom French	WP	527	1.0

**Sitting MP*

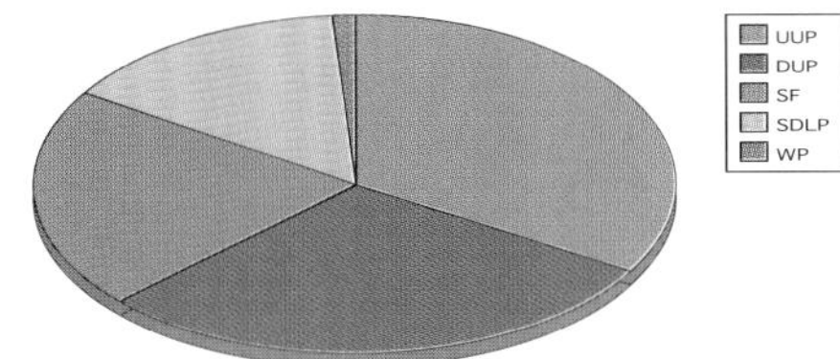

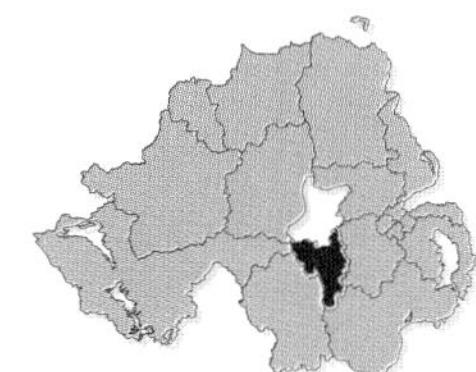

Electorate	72,574
Turnout	70.8%
Total Valid Vote	51,037
UUP majority	2,058

Until 2001 the UUP leader, David Trimble, had comfortably held Upper Bann. In 1997 Trimble enjoyed a majority of over 9,000 votes, with the two nationalist candidates placed between himself and the DUP. In 2001, however, the DUP's David Simpson came within 2,000 votes of winning the seat and causing a major upset.

In the absence of SDLP candidate Bríd Rodgers, the Sinn Féin vote increased significantly, largely at the expense of the SDLP.

West Tyrone

Name	Party	Votes	% Total vote
Pat Doherty	**SF**	**19,814**	**40.8**
Willie Thompson*	UUP	14,774	30.4
Bríd Rodgers	SDLP	13,942	28.8

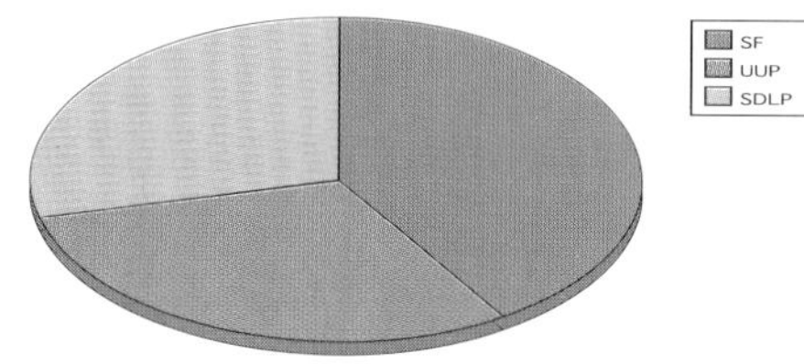

Electorate	60,739	Turnout	80.6%
Total Valid Vote	48,530	SF majority	5,040

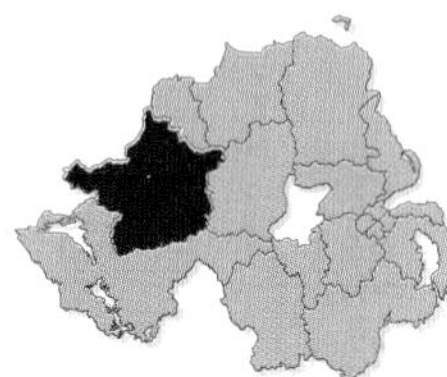

In West Tyrone Pat Doherty of Sinn Féin beat the UUP's Willie Thompson by a majority of over 5,000 votes. The SDLP had hoped to achieve success in this constituency by fielding Bríd Rodgers away from her usual Upper Bann constituency, however this tactic proved unsuccessful.

Northern Ireland Assembly Elections

Over the years, Northern Ireland has elected a number of different local 'assemblies'. Most of these were associated with various initiatives by UK governments to establish a form of devolved administration in Northern Ireland. Given that these initiatives varied in scope and context the results are not readily comparable with the recently elected legislative assembly.

The Secretary of State for Northern Ireland is directly responsible for the law governing elections to the Northern Ireland Assembly, the primary legislation in these cases being the Electoral Law Act (Northern Ireland) 1962 and currently the Northern Ireland (Elections) Act 1998 and the Northern Ireland Act 1998.

Elections were contested for the first Northern Ireland Assembly on Thursday 25 June 1998. The 18 Westminster constituencies were used, each to return 6 Assembly members. The electoral system used was a form of proportional representation, the Single Transferable Vote (STV).

The result suggested a 70% pro-Agreement majority, against a 30% anti-Agreement minority spearheaded by the DUP. In reality however the result was possibly somewhat closer. A number of elected members in David Trimble's ostensibly pro-Agreement Ulster Unionist Party were either actually personally against the Agreement, or had not fallen decisively on either side of the argument. At the outset this did not matter greatly, as there was a pro-Agreement majority within both of the unionist and nationalist camps - as required to make the institutions workable.

However, over time there was undoubtedly an erosion of the pro-Agreement majority within unionism and in particular, within the Ulster Unionist Party.

Northern Ireland Assembly Election 2003

Overview

The 2003 Northern Ireland Assembly election was originally scheduled for May 2003, but was deferred because the previous devolved administration had collapsed and there was no agreement between the pro-agreement parties on how to re-establish the institutions of government. Although there were subsequent attempts to reach agreement, the main point at issue – decommissioning of arms – remained unresolved and agreement over the summer of 2003 proved impossible. The Westminster government finally called an election for 26th November 2003 to go ahead whether there was an agreement to take forward and present to the electorate or not.

The election took place in the absence of a 'deal' between the pro-Agreement parties with the DUP standing on a clear anti-Belfast Agreement platform. The two Nationalist parties maintained the stance that there would be no renegotiations of the Agreement. The Ulster Unionist Party, while overall maintaining its support for the Agreement, had a significant minority of its officially selected candidates (the most prominent being the Lagan Valley MP Jeffrey Donaldson) running on an anti-Agreement ticket.

The election was fought across the 18 Westminster constituencies with 6 seats available in each. A total of 256 candidates contested the 108 seats with a minimum of 11 candidates fielded in Newry and Armagh and a maximum of 19 runners in East Antrim and in North Down.

The campaign was relatively brief and relatively calm and despite attempts to liven up the debate with battle-buses and videos etc and various 'stunts' the media reported that the general public had not been greatly absorbed in the contest.

This observation was reflected in the eventual turnout, which at just under 64% was unusually low for a Northern Ireland election. Some electoral pundits did however attribute the low turnout to the inclement weather as much as to voter indifference.

In what is effectively a 4 party system – two main unionist parties and two main nationalist parties – the election can be seen almost in terms of two different electoral tests – one in each community.

As anticipated in the run-up to the election, the overall result reflected a hardening of attitudes in both the unionist and nationalist communities in Northern Ireland with Ian Paisley's Democratic Unionist Party (DUP) and Gerry Adams' Sinn Féin emerging as the biggest winners.
While Sinn Féin made its gains largely at the expense of its main opponent the SDLP, the DUP gains were not so much at the expense of the rival Ulster Unionist Party but rather gains from a number of smaller unionist parties.

Winners and Losers

There were few major surprises after the votes had been counted. The DUP had been expected to gain seats and Sinn Fein had been expected to open up a gap on the SDLP – although perhaps not by as much as they actually achieved.
One surprise in an election that saw the demise of many smaller parties and independents was the election of a single-issue independent candidate in West Tyrone. A local doctor Kieran Deeny was comfortably elected as a 'hospital' candidate opposed to the closure of Omagh Hospital. He was elected at the expense of the SDLP sitting MLA Joe Byrne.

Northern Ireland Assembly Elections November 2003
Valid Votes, Percentage Poll and Quota

Constituency	Eligible Electorate	Valid Votes	% Poll	Quota
Belfast East	51,937	30,965	60.70	4424
Belfast North	51,353	31,532	62.31	4505
Belfast South	50,707	31,330	62.59	4476
Belfast West	50,861	32,854	65.92	4694
East Antrim	55,473	30,952	56.50	4422
East Londonderry	56,203	34,273	61.75	4897
Fermanagh & S.Tyrone	64,336	46,160	72.86	6595
Foyle	65,303	40,806	63.45	5830
Lagan Valley	67,910	41,254	61.44	5894
Mid Ulster	60,095	44,362	74.92	6338
Newry & Armagh	68,731	47,378	70.18	6769
North Antrim	70,489	44,099	63.32	6300
North Down	57,422	30,835	54.54	4406
South Antrim	63,640	37,421	59.49	5346
South Down	70,149	45,346	65.59	6479
Strangford	66,308	37,250	57.06	5322
Upper Bann	68,814	43,482	64.15	6212
West Tyrone	57,795	41,729	73.24	5962
Total	**1,097,526**	**692,028**	**63.98**	

Northern Ireland Assembly Elections 1998 and 2003

Overall Result by Party Share and Seats

	Votes	% Share of Vote		Number of Seats		
		2003	(1998)	2003	(1998)	+/- since 1998
DUP	177,944	25.7	18.1	30	20	+10
SF	162,758	23.5	17.6	24	18	+6
UUP	156,931	22.7	21.5	27	28	-1
SDLP	117,547	17.0	22.0	18	24	-6
Alliance	25,372	3.7	6.5	6	6	0
UKUP	5,700	0.8	4.5	1	5	-4
PUP/UDP	8,032	1.2	3.6	1	2	-1
NIWC	5,785	0.8	1.6	0	2	-2
Others	31,959	4.6	4.5	1	3	-2
Total	692,028	100	100	108	108	

Other surprises included the DUP capturing a seat in West Belfast where previously there had been no Unionist representation. Dianne Dodds, wife of former DUP Minister Nigel Dodds, took the seat at the expense of long-serving SDLP MLA and former Westminster MP Dr Joe Hendron.

Although David Trimble's pro Agreement UUP performed robustly – and better than many had expected – a number of the anti-Agreement UUP dissidents scored electoral successes. Anti-Agreement UUP Jeffrey Donaldson recorded the top vote of any candidate in the election (securing over 2 quotas) and other prominent dissidents Arlene Foster (Fermanagh/South Tyrone) and David Burnside (South Antrim) were comfortably elected *(see table on page 80, for a list of the top 20 'poll-toppers')*. However in David Trimble's own constituency where he achieved a high personal vote, the dissident UUP candidate and sitting MLA George Savage, was eclipsed by pro-Agreement Samuel Gardiner.

The decision of anti-Agreement unionists Jeffrey Donaldson, Arlene Foster and Norah Beare to join the DUP has left the Ulster Unionist Party with 24 seats to the DUP's 33. This means the DUP have become the largest unionist party as well as the largest overall party in Northern Ireland's political system.

For the SDLP the 2003 election overall was a major disappointment. The 1998 result of the SDLP/Sinn Fein contest 24-18 in favour of the SDLP was completely reversed ie 24 seats for Sinn Fein, 18 for SDLP. In a number of constituencies Sinn Fein took over from the SDLP in share of the vote terms for the first time, while in SDLP strongholds the party made significant inroads. The most disastrous result for the SDLP was possibly Newry and Armagh, an SDLP Westminster seat held by Seamus Mallon, where SDLP was reduced to only 1 seat out of the six. A few hoped-for gains failed to materialise although the party came close to its first ever representation in Strangford.

The election was a major success for the Democratic Unionist Party jumping from 20 seats in 1998 to 30 seats in 2003. The seats were gained primarily from the smaller unionist parties, which, apart from the PUP's leader David Ervine in East Belfast and UKUP leader Robert McCartney in North Down, were effectively obliterated as a force in any new Assembly. The DUP vote share improved in just about every constituency and with better vote management possibly even one or two more seats could have been won by the party.

The rise and rise of Sinn Fein continued in the 2003 election with notable gains in North Antrim, South Belfast, North Belfast, South Down, Newry and Armagh and East Londonderry. There is now no doubt that the largest nationalist party in Northern Ireland is Sinn Fein. Taking account of its elected representation in the Irish Republic some party spokespersons prefer the title of 'third largest party in Ireland'.

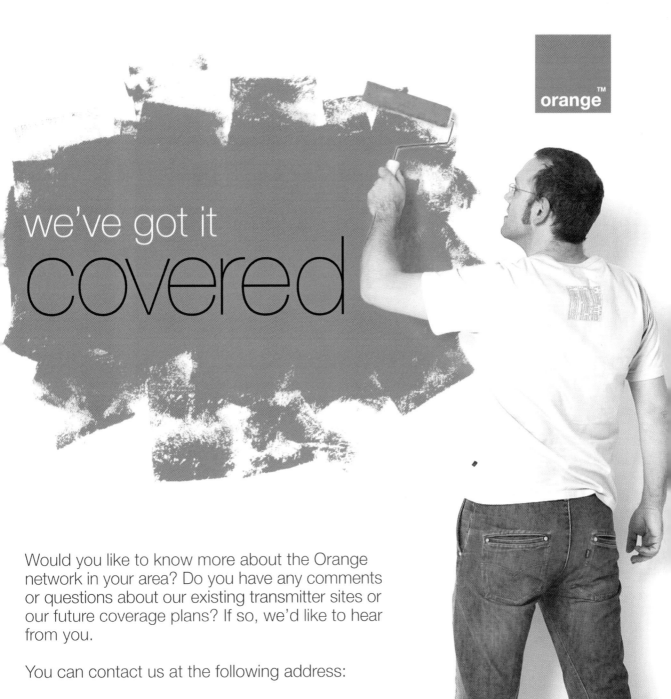

Northern Ireland Assembly Elections 2003
Parties' Percentage Share of the Vote by Constituency

Constituency / Party	DUP	SF	UUP	SDLP	Alliance	Other
Belfast East	39.2	3.8	33.1	3.1	9.0	11.8
Belfast North	34.2	27.0	9.4	16.8	1.0	11.7
Belfast South	20.8	12.6	27.0	22.9	5.9	10.8
Belfast West	7.7	65.0	3.6	19.0	0.2	4.4
East Antrim	34.1	2.5	28.7	7.8	10.9	16.0
East Londonderry	32.4	17.9	22.7	16.3	2.2	8.6
Fermanagh & S.Tyrone	18.7	34.4	28.7	16.3	0.1	1.4
Foyle	15.0	32.4	8.1	36.1	0.1	7.8
Lagan Valley	20.5	7.9	46.2	7.6	10.7	7.1
Mid Ulster	20.8	45.5	14.4	18.3	0.1	0.5
Newry & Armagh	18.1	39.8	15.5	24.6	0.1	1.3
North Antrim	45.9	14.0	21.6	13.6	2.0	2.8
North Down	23.5	0.9	32.1	4.9	8.6	30.0
South Antrim	30.6	11.5	29.8	14.4	9.1	4.6
South Down	15.0	26.5	18.2	35.1	1.1	4.2
Strangford	47.9	3.0	28.9	7.8	7.4	5.0
Upper Bann	28.5	21.8	29.4	15.7	1.3	3.2
West Tyrone	17.5	38.6	13.6	14.6	0.4	15.3

Perhaps the most outstanding performance in terms of seats for votes and in the context of an overall squeeze on centre parties was that of the Alliance Party. The party experienced a 40% drop in its overall first preference vote, yet retained its six seats on the back of a number of robust individual performances and a strong flow of transfers in the later stages of the counts. As mentioned above the smaller parties were largely eclipsed in the 2003 Assembly election. The NI Women's Coalition lost its two seats and prominent representatives of minor Unionist parties or independent Unionists such as Pauline Armitage (UKUP), Billy Hutchinson (PUP), Cedric Wilson (NI Unionist Party) and Fraser Agnew (Independent) failed to retain their seats. The Worker's Party, Green Party and Conservative Party failed to come anywhere near picking up a seat in the election. The tables above and on pages 78 and 81 show the overall results by constituency and by party in terms of percentage share of the vote achieved and seats captured.

Poll-Toppers

Although experts on proportional representation (STV) are clear that in multi-seat constituencies parties need to 'manage' their vote (i.e. spread it out as evenly as possible among its candidates) a number of candidates achieved high individual tallies that can only be attributed to their high personal standing with their electorate. The top-twenty poll-toppers were:

Candidate	No of votes	% 1st pref	No of quotas
Jeffrey Donaldson	14104	34.19	2.39
Peter Robinson	9254	29.89	2.09
Nigel Dodds	9276	29.42	2.06
Iris Robinson	8548	22.95	1.61
David Trimble	9158	21.06	1.47
Sir Reg Empey	6459	20.86	1.46
Dr Ian Paisley	8732	19.8	1.39
David Burnside	7066	18.88	1.32
Gerry Adams	6199	18.87	1.32
William McCrea	8211	18.51	1.3

Candidate	No of votes	% 1st pref	No of quotas
Martin McGuinness	8128	18.32	1.28
Ian Paisley Jnr	7898	17.91	1.25
Gerry Kelly	5524	17.52	1.23
Michael McGimpsey	5389	17.2	1.2
Paul Berry	8125	17.15	1.2
Roy Beggs	5175	16.72	1.17
Mark Durkan	6806	16.68	1.17
Conor Murphy	7595	16.03	1.12
John Taylor	5658	15.19	1.06
Jim Wells	6789	14.97	1.05

Northern Ireland Assembly Elections 2003
Parties' Share of Seats by Constituency

Constituency / Party	DUP	UUP	SDLP	SF	Alliance	Other
Belfast East	2	2	0	0	1	1
Belfast North	2	1	1	2	0	0
Belfast South	1	2	2	1	0	0
Belfast West	1	0	1	4	0	0
East Antrim	3	2	0	0	1	0
East Londonderry	2	2	1	1	0	0
Fermanagh & South Tyrone	1	2	1	2	0	0
Foyle	1	0	3	2	0	0
Lagan Valley	1	3	1	0	1	0
Mid Ulster	1	1	1	3	0	0
Newry & Armagh	1	1	1	3	0	0
North Antrim	3	1	1	1	0	0
North Down	2	2	0	0	1	1
South Antrim	2	2	1	0	1	0
South Down	1	1	2	2	0	0
Strangford	3	2	0	0	1	0
Upper Bann	2	2	1	1	0	0
West Tyrone	1	1	1	2	0	1
Total	**30**	**27**	**18**	**24**	**6**	**3**

The detailed results: analysis constituency by constituency

What follows over the next 36 pages is the detailed results including all the counts from each of the 18 constituencies. Information included for each constituency includes a full list of candidates and their parties and the number of votes they received at each stage of the count, together with the cumulative totals and the number of non-transferable votes. Also shown is a summary table highlighting how the parties performed in terms of share of the vote and seats.

The asterisks indicate those candidates who were members of the 1998 Assembly. In the detailed count information, the numbers highlighted in bold indicate the 'active' votes being re-distributed at that stage of the counting.

The successful candidates are pictured, and their details are colour-coded by party as per the following key:

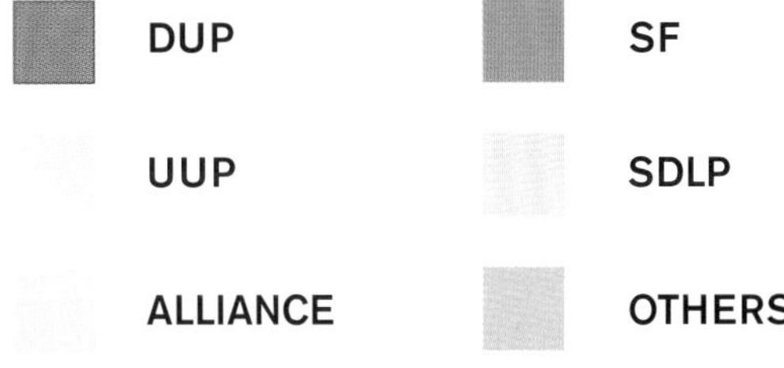

Belfast East

Total Valid Pole 30965 **Quota 4424** **Turnout 60.7%**

Party performance

Party	Seats	1st Pref Vote	%	(1998)%
DUP	2	12132	39.2	30.9
SF	-	1180	3.8	2.3
UUP	2	10252	33.1	24.3
SDLP	-	967	3.1	2.6
Alliance	1	2774	9.0	18.0
Others	1	3660	11.8	21.9

At a glance...

No surprises in this predominantly unionist constituency with the party share out of the six seats remaining unchanged. Local MP Peter Robinson (DUP) topped the poll as expected followed by Sir Reg Empey (UUP). Despite a significant reduction in first preference votes David Ervine (PUP) and Naomi Long (All), the latter running in place of Lord Alderdice, held on to their party seats. Runner-up overall was UUP former Lord Mayor Jim Rodgers. The total nationalist vote was less than half a quota.

		Stage 1	Stage 2
		1st preference votes 30,965	Transfer of Robinson's surplus
Joseph Bell	WP	125	(+3.12) 128.12
Thomas Black	Soc	176	(+5.2) 181.2
*Michael Copeland	UUP	2291	(+63.96) 2354.96
Terry Dick	Cons	232	(+2.08) 234.08
*Reg Empey	UUP	6459	(n/a) 6459
David Ervine	PUP	2990	(+221.52) 3211.52
Naomi Long	All	2774	(+20.28) 2794.28
John McBlain	Ind	72	(+6.76) 78.76
Robin Newton	DUP	1475	(+2943.2) 4418.2
Joseph O'Donnell	SF	1180	(+4.16) 1184.16
*Peter Robinson	DUP	9254	(-4830) 4424
Jim Rodgers	UUP	1502	(+288.6) 1790.6
Harry Toan	DUP	1403	(+1230.32) 2633.32
Leo Van Es	SDLP	967	(2.6) 969.6
George Weiss	VFY	65	(+1.56) 66.56
	Non-transferable		(36.64) 36.64

Candidates Elected	Count
Peter Robinson DUP	1st
Reg Empey UUP	1st
Robin Newton DUP	3rd
David Ervine PUP	6th
Naomi Long All	6th
Michael Copeland UUP	6th

Peter Robinson

Reg Empey

Robin Newton

David Ervine

Naomi Long

Michael Copeland

Stage 3	Stage 4	Stage 5	Stage 6
Transfer of Empey's surplus	Exclusion of Weiss, McBlain, Bell, Black & Dick	Exclusion of Van Es & O'Donnell	Exclusion of Toan
(+0.93) 129.05	**(-129.05)** 0	-	-
(+2.48) 183.68	**(-183.68)** 0	-	-
(+777.79) 3132.75	(+87.76) 3220.51	(+77.41) 3297.92	(+352.57) 3650.49
(+16.43) 250.51	**(-250.51)** 0	-	-
(-2035) 4424	(0) 4424	(0) 4424	(0) 4424
(+165.85) 3377.37	(+132.11) 3509.48	(+151.31) 3660.79	(+602.60) 4263.39
(+83.08) 2877.36	(+133.31) 3010.67	(1001.34) 4012.01	(+44.53) 4056.54
(+2.48) 81.24	**(-81.24)** 0	-	-
(+26.04) 4444.24	(0) 4424.24	(0) 4424.24	(0) 4424.24
(+1.55) 1185.71	(+20) 1205.71	**(-1205.71)** 0	-
(0) 4424	(0) 4424	(0) 4424	(0) 4424
(+891.25) 2681.85	(+100.8) 2782.65	(+56.72) 2839.37	(+457.11) 3296.48
(+9.92) 2643.24	(+73.42) 2716.66	(+11.12) 2727.78	**(-2727.78)** 0
(+16.43) 986.03	(+49.62) 1035.65	**(-986.03)** 0	-
(+0.62) 67.18	**(-67.18)** 0	-	-
(40.15) 76.79	(114.64) 191.43	(943.46) 1134.89	(1270.97) 2405.86

Belfast North

Total Valid Pole 31532 Quota 4505 Turnout 62.3

Party performance

Party	Seats	1st Pref Vote	%	(%1998)
DUP	2	10776	34.2	21.3
SF	2	8514	27.0	21.3
UUP	1	2961	9.4	10.9
SDLP	1	5294	16.8	21.1
Alliance	-	305	1.0	3.1
Others	-	3682	11.7	22.3

At a glance...

DUP MP Nigel Dodds topped the poll (with 2 quotas) followed by Sinn Féin's Gerry Kelly. The main change in North Belfast was the winning of a second seat by Sinn Féin's Kathy Stanton, ultimately that held previously by the PUP's Billy Hutchinson. The poll witnessed a substantial increase in DUP and Sinn Féin vote share mainly at the expense of the SDLP and PUP. The UUP vote slipped to under 3,000 for the first time, although candidate Fred Cobain was comfortably elected, as was Alban Maginness for the SDLP. Overall North Belfast reflected the two main features of the election overall - gains by SF and the DUP and a real squeeze of the smaller parties.

		Stage 1	Stage 2	Stage 3	Stage 4	Stage 5
		1st pref votes 31,532	Transfer of Dodds' surplus	Transfer of Kelly's surplus	Transfer of McCausland's surplus	Exclusion of Gallagher & Delaney
*Fraser Agnew	UUC	802	(+198.39) 1000.39	(0) 1000.39	(+157.05) 1157.44	(+0.09) 1157.53
Elizabeth Byrne-McCullough	NIWC	467	(+11.22) 478.22	(+4.14) 482.36	(+3.24) 485.6)	(+12.6) 498.2
*Fred Cobain	UUP	2961	(+377.91) 3338.91	(+0.36) 3339.27	(+170.19) 3509.46	(+5.18) 3514.64
Pat Convery	SDLP	2108	(+5.61) 2113.61	(+45.18) 2158.79	(+1.71) 2160.5	(+23.18) 2183.68
Marcella Delaney	WP	90	(+1.02) 91.02	(+0.18) 91.2	(+0.72) 91.92	**(-91.92)** 0
*Nigel Dodds	DUP	9276	**(-4771)** 4505	(0) 4505	(0) 4505	(0) 4505
Peter Emerson	Green	261	(+8.16) 269.16	(+2.34) 271.5	(+6.39 277.89	(+21.51) 299.4
John Gallagher	VFY	17	(+2.55) 19.55	(0) 19.55	(+0.36) 19.91	**(-19.91)** 0
Margaret Hawkins	All	305	(+8.67) 313.67	(+1.62) 315.29	(+3.06) 318.35	(+7.51) 325.86
*Billy Hutchinson	PUP	1358	(+329.46) 1687.46	(+0.9) 1688.36	(+122.76) 1811.12	(+7.53) 1818.65
*Gerry Kelly	SF	5524	(n/a) 5524	**(-1019)** 4505	(0) 4505	(0) 4505
*Alban Maginness	SDLP	3186	(+13.26) 3199.26)	(+111.42) 3310.68	(+2.25) 3312.93	(+10) 3322.93
Nelson McCausland	DUP	1500	(+3600.6) 5100.6	(n/a) 5100.6	**(-595.6)** 4505	(0) 4505
Raymond McCord	Ind	218	(+66.81) 284.81	(+1.8) 286.61	(+38.52) 325.13	(+4.69) 329.82
Frank McCoubrey	Ind	469	(+82.62) 551.62	(+0.36) 551.98	(+66.6) 618.58	(+0.18) 618.76
Kathy Stanton	SF	2990	(0) 2990	(+813.78) 3803.87	(+0.09) 3803.78	(+9) 3812.87
	Non-transferable		(64.72) 64.72	(36.92) 101.64	(22.66) 124.3	(10.36) 134.66

Candidates Elected	Count
Nigel Dodds DUP	1st
Gerry Kelly SF	1st
Nelson McCausland DUP	2nd
Fred Cobain UUP	10th
Alban Maginness SDLP	12th
Kathy Stanton SF	12th

Nigel Dodds

Gerry Kelly

Nelson McCausland

Fred Cobain

Alban Maginness

Kathy Stanton

Stage 6	Stage 7	Stage 8	Stage 9	Stage 10	Stage 11	Stage 12
Exclusion of Emerson	Exclusion of McCord	Exclusion of Hawkins	Exclusion of McCoubrey	Exclusion of Byrne-McCullough & Agnew	Transfer of Cobain's surplus	Exclusion of McCoubrey
(+10.74) 1168.27	(+49.37) 1217.64	(+16.98) 1234.62	(+100.6) 1335.22	**(-1335.22)** 0	-	-
(+74.96) 573.16	(+12.41) 585.57	(+107.98) 693.55	(+8.69) 702.24	**(-702.24)** 0	-	-
(+24.34) 3538.98	(+68.79) 3607.77	(+88.52) 3696.29	(+205.21) 3901.50	(654) 4555.5	**(-50.5)** 4505	(0) 4505
(+29.54) 2213.22	(+15.18) 2228.4	(+44.36) 2272.76	(+6.6) 2279.36	(+201.1) 2480.46	(+6.51) 2486.97	**(-2486.97)** 0
-	-	-	-	-	-	-
(0) 4505	(0) 4505	(0) 4505	(0) 4505	(0) 4505	(0) 4505	(0) 4505
(-299.4) 0	-	-	-	-	-	-
-	-	-	-	-	-	-
(+44.29) 370.15	(+13.18) 383.33	**(-383.33)** 0	-	-	-	-
(+17.79) 1836.44	(+37.84) 1874.28	(+13.29) 1887.57	(+199.85) 2087.42	(+404.53) 2491.95	(34.41) 2526.36	(+78.69) 2605.05
(0) 4505	(0) 4505	(0) 4505	(0) 4505	(0) 4505	(0) 4505	(0) 4505
(+27) 3349.93	(+15.87) 3365.8	(+70.74) 3436.54	(+7.54) 3444.08	(+223.02) 3667.1	(+8.37) 3675.47	(+1894) 5569.47
(0) 4505	(0) 4505	(0) 4505	(0) 4505	(0) 4505	(0) 4505	(0) 4505
(10.87) 340.69	**(-340.69)** 0	-	-	-	-	-
(+2.09) 620.85	(+55.68) 676.53	(+6) 682.53	**(-682.53)** 0	-	-	-
(+20.05) 3832.92	(+5.36) 3838.28	(+3.36) 3841.64	(+0.18) 3841.82	(+53.62) 3895.44	(+0.93) 3896.37	(+222.06) 4118.43
(37.73) 172.39	(67.01) 239.4	(32.1) 271.5	(153.86) 425.36	(501.19) 926.55	(0.28) 926.83	(292.22) 1219.05

Belfast South

Total Valid Pole 31330 Quota 4476 Turnout 62.6

Party performance

Party	Seats	1st Pref Vote	%	(%1998)
DUP	1	6529	20.8	13.1
SF	1	3933	12.6	6.4
UUP	2	8469	27.0	23.4
SDLP	2	7176	22.9	21.7
Alliance	-	1849	5.9	10.0
Others	-	3374	10.8	25.4

At a glance...

The headline news from South Belfast was Sinn Féin's Alex Maskey gaining the party's first ever seat – in this case at the expense of outgoing MLA and Northern Ireland Women's Coalition leader Monica McWilliams. Former Arts and Culture Minister Michael McGimpsey topped the poll and was returned with colleague Esmond Birnie. The SDLP, in one of the few constituencies where its vote share actually increased, held on (narrowly) to its two seats. Mark Robinson easily retained the single DUP seat, with the party raising its vote share at the expense of the smaller unionist parties.

		Stage 1	Stage 2	Stage 3	Stage 4	Stage 5
		1st pref Vote 31,330	Transfer of McGimpsey's surplus	Elimination of Steven	Elimination of Lynn	Elimination of Barbour & Lomas
James Barbour	Soc	167	(+1.19) 168.19	(+2) 170.19	(+11) 181.19	**(-181.19)** 0
*Esmond Birnie	UUP	2311	(+551.99) 2862.99	(0) 2862.99	(+3) 2865.99	(+56.19) 2922.18
Tom Ekin	All	664	(+8.5) 672.5	(+1) 673.5	(+5) 678.5	(+19.68) 698.18
*Carmel Hanna	SDLP	3910	(+12.92) 3922.92	(+3) 3925.92	(+10) 3935.92	(+17.17) 3953.09
John Hiddleston	UUP	769	(+199.75) 968.75	(+1) 969.75	(+1.17) 970.92	(+19.68) 990.6
Roger Lomas	Cons	116	(+3.06) 119.06	(+1) 120.06	(0) 120.06	**(-120.06)** 0
Patrick Lynn	WP	96	(+0.17) 96.17	(-1) 97.17	**(-97.17)** 0	-
*^Alex Maskey	SF	3933	(+2.55) 3935.55	(+2) 3937.55	(+10) 3947.55)	(+21) 3968.55
*Alasdair McDonnell	SDLP	3266	(+17) 3283	(+4) 3287	(+20) 3307	(+10.34) 3317.34
*Michael McGimpsey	UUP	5389	**(-913)** 4476	(0) 4476	(0) 4476	(0) 4476
Monica McWilliams	NIWC	2150	(+30.43) 2180.43	(+5) 2185.434	(+18) 2203.43	(+45) 2248.43
Thomas Morrow	PUP	495	(+14.62) 509.62	(0) 509.62	(+2) 511.62	(+9) 520.62
Ruth Patterson	DUP	2538	(+18.7) 2556.7	(0) 2556.7	(0) 2556.7	(+19.34) 2576.04
Geraldine Rice	All	1185	(+13.94) 1198.94	(+3) 1201.94	(+1) 1202.94	(+12) 1214.94
*Mark Robinson	DUP	3991	(+33.32) 4024.32	(0) 4024.32	(+1) 4025.32	(+14.34) 4039.66
Lindsay Steven	VFY	42	(+0.17) 42.17	**(-42.17)** 0	-	-
John Wright	GP	308	(+1.19) 309.19	(+16.17) 325.36	(+5) 330.36	(+37.17) 367.53
^Alex Maskey was previously MLA for Belfast West	Non- transferable		(3.5) 3.5	(3) 6.5	(10) 16.5	(20.34) 36.84

Candidates Elected	Count
Michael McGimpsey UUP	1st
Mark Robinson DUP	11th
Esmond Birnie UUP	11th
Carmel Hanna SDLP	12th
Alex Maskey SF	12th
Alasdair McDonnell	12th

Michael McGimpsey

Mark Robinson

Esmond Birnie

Carmel Hanna

Alex Maskey

Alasdair McDonnell

Stage 6	Stage 7	Stage 8	Stage 9	Stage 10	Stage 11	Stage 12
Elimination of Wright	Elimination of Morrow	Elimination of Ekin	Elimination of Hiddleston	Elimination of Rice	Elimination of Patterson	Transfer of Robinson's surplus
-	-	-	-	-	-	-
(+16.51) 2938.69	(+99.4) 3038.09	(+50.02) 3088.11	(+783.2) 3871.31	(+441.18) 4312.49	(+224) 4536.49	(n/a) 4536.49
(+28.17) 726.35	(+13.51) 739.86	**(-739.86)** 0	-	-	-	-
(+29.17) 3982.26	(+8.51) 3990.77	(+65.53) 4056.3	(+6.38) 4062.68	(+270.02) 4332.7	(+4.85) 4337.55	(+67) 4404.55
(+5) 995.6	(+94.21) 1089.81	(+21.19) 1111	**(-1111)** 0	-	-	-
-	-	-	-	-	-	-
-	-	-	-	-	-	-
(+19) 3987.55	(+2) 3989.55	(+2) 3991.55	(0) 3991.55	(+12) 4003.55	(+8) 4011.55	(+1) 4012.55
(+23) 3340.34	(+10.17) 3350.51	(+30.51) 3381.02	(+8.53) 3389.55	(+199.55) 3589.1	(+10.87) 3599.97	(+50) 3649.97
(0) 4476	(0) 4476	(0) 4476	(0) 4476	(0) 4476	(0) 4476	(0) 4476
(+139.17) 2387.6	(+43.53) 2431.13	(+86.87) 2518	(+24.23) 24542.23	(+626.25) 3168.48	(+40.06) 3208.54)	(+314) 3522.54
(+8) 528.62	**(-528.62)** 0	-	-	-	-	-
(+4) 2580.04	(+100.21) 2680.25	(+3.17) 2683.42	(+135.25) 2818.67	(+20.17) 2838.84	**(-2838.84)** 0	-
(+55) 1269.94	(+14.68) 1284.62	(+462.72) 1747.34	(+15.38) 1762.72	**(-1762.72)** 0	-	-
(+9.17) 4048.83	(+102.04) 4150.87	(+4.34) 4155.21	(+91.61) 4246.82	(+21.34) 4268.16	(+2393) 6661.16	**(-2185.16)** 4476
-	-	-	-	-	-	-
(-367.53) 0	-	-	-	-	-	-
(31.34) 68.18	(40.36) 108.54	(13.51) 122.05	(46.42) 168.47	(172.21) 340.68	(158.06) 498.74	(1753.16) 2251.9

Belfast West

Total Valid Pole 32854 Quota 4694 Turnout 65.9

Party performance

Party	Seats	1st Pref Vote	%	(%1998)
DUP	1	2544	7.7	3.2
SF	4	21368	65.0	59.0
UUP	-	1170	3.6	3.9
SDLP	1	6250	19.0	24.9
Alliance	-	75	0.2	0.3
Others	-	1447	4.4	8.6

At a glance...

Sinn Féin confirmed their complete dominance of nationalist West Belfast, narrowly missing out on taking a fifth seat out of six, despite impressive vote management. Dianne Dodds regained a unionist seat ultimately at the expense of SDLP veteran Dr Joe Hendron. Sinn Féin retained four, although sitting MLA Sue Ramsey lost out to a party colleague. Despite further slippage in SDLP vote share, party policing spokesman Alex Attwood comfortably retained his seat. Sitting MP and Sinn Féin President Gerry Adams topped the poll followed immediately by three Sinn Féin colleagues.

The 65% Sinn Féin share of the vote was the highest recorded by any party in any of the 18 constituencies.

		1st stage	2nd stage
		1st preference votes 32,854	Transfer of Adams' surplus
*Gerry Adams	SF	6199	(-1505) 4694
*Alex Attwood	SDLP	3667	(+129.6) 3796.6
Mary Ayers	All	75	(+3.12) 78.12
*Bairbre de Brun	SF	4069	(+407.58) 4476.52
Dianne Dodds	DUP	2544	(0) 2544
Michael Ferguson	SF	3849	(+63.84 3912.84
*Joe Hendron	SDLP	2583	(+71.28) 2654.28
David Kerr	UTW	16	(0) 16
John Lowry	WP	407	(+3.84) 410.84
John MacVicar	Ind	211	(+0.24) 211.24
Fra McCann	SF	4263	(+74.16) 4337.16
Chris McGimpsey	UUP	1170	(+4.56) 1174.56
*Sue Ramsey	SF	2988	(+685.2) 3673.2
Hugh Smyth	PUP	813	(+1.68) 814.68
	Non-transferable		(59.96) 59.96

Candidates Elected	Count
Gerry Adams SF	1st
Alex Attwood SDLP	5th
Bairbre de Brun SF	6th
Fra McCann SF	6th
Michael Ferguson SF	8th
Dianne Dodds DUP	8th

Gerry Adams

Alex Attwood

Bairbre de Brun

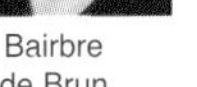
Fra McCann

Michael Ferguson

Dianne Dodds

3rd stage	4th stage	5th stage	6th stage	7th stage	8th stage
Elimination of Kerr, Ayers, MacVicar & Lowry	Elimination of Smyth & McGimpsey	Elimination of Hendron	Transfer of Attwood's surplus	Transfer of de Brun's surplus	Transfer of McCann's surplus
(0) 4694	(0) 4694	(0) 4694	(0) 4694	(0) 4694	(0) 4694
(+104.44) 3901.04	(+55.24) 3956.28	(+2140) 6096.28	**(-1402.28)** 4694	(0) 4694	(0) 4694
(-78.12) 0	-	-	-	-	-
(+18.44) 4494.96	(+9.24) 4504.2	(+161.48) 4665.68	(+564) 5229.68	**(-535.68)** 4694	(0) 4694
(+87) 2631	(+1513.24) 4144.24	(+112) 4256.24	(+16) 4272.24	(+2) 4274.24	(+2.85) 4277.09
(+8.72) 3921.56	(+23.56) 3945.12	(+54.88) 4000	(+117) 4117	(+229) 4346	(+102.6) 4448.6
(+195.44) 2849.72	(+259) 3108.72	**(-3108.72)** 0	-	-	-
(-16) 0	-	-	-	-	-
(-410.84) 0	-	-	-	-	-
(-211.24) 0	-	-	-	-	-
(+23.72) 4360.88	(+2.48) 4363.36	(+161.64) 4525	(+380) 4905	(n/a) 4905	**(-211)** 4694
(+124) 1298.56	**(-1298.56)** 0	-	-	-	-
(+26.48) 3699.68	(+6.24) 3705.92	(+62.92) 3768.84	(+155) 3923.84	(+161) 4084.84	(+105.45) 4190.26
(+48) 862.68	**(-862.68)** 0	-	-	-	-
(79.96) 139.92	(292.24) 432.16	(415.8) 847.96	(170.28) 1018.24	(143.68) 1161.92)	(0.1) 1162.02

East Antrim

Total Valid Pole 30952 **Quota** 4422 **Turnout** 56.5

Party performance

Party	Seats	1st Pref Vote	%	(%1998)
DUP	3	10563	34.1	22.2
SF	-	768	2.5	2.1
UUP	2	8883	28.7	29.6
SDLP	-	2428	7.8	5.9
Alliance	1	3372	10.9	20.1
Others	-	4938	16.0	20.1

At a glance...

A significant increase in DUP vote share in this predominantly unionist constituency resulted in the party gaining a third seat. The UUP vote share held firm and the party retained its two seats. Despite increasing his share of the vote it was SDLP sitting MLA Danny O'Connor who lost out. The Alliance party former leader Sean Neeson held on to his seat despite the Alliance vote almost halving – further evidence of the overall hardening of attitudes across Northern Ireland. Roy Beggs Junior (UUP) topped the poll, closely followed by DUP education spokesman Sammy Wilson, who ran in this constituency instead of his usual Belfast East. As elsewhere the former UKUP MLA now running as an independent - in this case Roger Hutchinson failed to retain his seat.

		1st stage	2nd stage	3rd stage	4th stage	5th stage	6th stage
		1st pref votes 30,952	Transfer of Beggs' surplus	Transfer of Wilson's surplus	Elimination of Frew	Elimination of Greer	Elimination of Monaghan
John Anderson	Ind	348	(+5.18) 353.18)	(+0.32) 353.5	(+10) 363.5	(+8.02) 371.52)	(+17) 388.52
Roy Beggs	UUP	5175	**(-753)** 4422	(0) 4422	(0) 4422	(0) 4422	(0) 4422
George Dawson	DUP	3163	(+34.3) 3197.3	(+21.48) 3218.78	(+5.14) 3223.92	(+14.18) 3238.1	(+6.04) 3244.14
Stewart Dickson	All	1192	(+23.38) 1215.38	(+0.3) 1215.68	(+27) 1242.68	(+24.28) 1266.96	(+62.14) 1329.1
Andrew Frew	Green	165	(+0.7) 165.7	(+0.04) 165.74	**(-165.74)** 0	-	-
Alan Greer	Cons	196	(+5.74) 201.74	(+0.14) 201.88	(+9) 210.88	**(-210.88)** 0	-
*David Hilditch	DUP	2856	(+27.44) 2883.44	(+56.88) 2940.32	(+3.02) 2943.34	(+20.58) 2963.92	(+11.14) 2975.06
Carolyn Howarth	PUP	534	(+5.74) 539.74	(0) 539.74	(+3) 542.74	(+7.42) 550.16	(+16.14) 566.3
*Roger Hutchinson	Ind	1011	(+8.4) 1019.4	(+0.96) 1020.36	(+2.14) 1022.5	(+8.28) 1030.78	(+5) 1035.78
Robert Mason	Ind	354	(+3.78) 367.78	(+0.54) 368.32	(+17.14) 385.46	(+8.14) 393.6	(+15.14) 408.74
Roy McCune	UUP	1646	(+448.28) 2094.28	(+0.98) 2095.26	(+8.14) 2103.4	(+30.24) 2133.64	(+17.28) 2150.92
Jack McKee	Ind	1449	(+17.92) 1466.92	(+3.96) 1470.88	(0) 1470.88	(+2.14) 1473.02	(+2) 1475.02
Jack McMullan	SF	768	(+0.28) 768.28	(0) 768.28	(+1) 769.28	(+1) 770.28	(+5) 775.28
Anne Monaghan	NIWC	307	(+2.38) 309.38	(+0.12) 309.5	(+31) 340.5	(+7) 347.5	**(-347.5)** 0
*Sean Neeson	All	2180	(+28.28) 2208.28	(+0.98) 2209.26	(+26.14) 2235.4	(+22.42) 2257.82	(+110.46) 2368.28
*Daniel O'Connor	SDLP	2428	(+4.62) 2432.62	(+0.12) 2432.74	(+8) 2440.74	(1) 2441.74	(+39.42) 2481.16
*Ken Robinson	UUP	2062	(+94.08) 2156.08	(+1.68) 2157.76	(+6) 2163.76)	(+28.7) 2192.46	(+11.44) 2203.9
Thomas Robinson	UKUP	564	(+9.52) 573.52	(+1.9) 575.42	(0) 575.42	(+16.02) 591.44	(+3.14) 594.58
*^Sammy Wilson	DUP	4544	(n/a) 4544	**(-122)** 4422	(0) 4422	(0) 4422	(0) 4422
^Sammy Wilson was previously MLA for Belfast East	Non- transferable		(32.98) (32.98)	(31.6) 64.58	(9.02) 73.6	(11.46) 85.06	(26.16) 111.22

Candidates Elected	Count
Roy Beggs UUP	1st
Sammy Wilson DUP	1st
Ken Robinson UUP	15th
Sean Neeson All	15th
David Hilditch DUP	15th
George Dawson DUP	15th

Roy Beggs

Sammy Wilson

Ken Robinson

Sean Neeson

David Hilditch

George Dawson

7th stage	8th stage	9th stage	10th stage	11th stage	12th stage	13th stage	14th stage	15th stage
Elimination of Anderson	Elimination of Mason	Elimination of Howarth	Elimination of TD Robinson	Elimination of McMullan	Elimination of Hutchinson	Elimination of Dickson	Elimination of McKee	Elimination of McCune
(-388.52) 0	-	-	-	-	-	-	-	-
(0) 4422	(0) 4422	(0) 4422	(0) 4422	(0) 4422	(0) 4422	(0) 4422	(0) 4422	(0) 4422
(+29.22) 3273.36	(+19.1) 3292.46	(+89.28) 3381.74	(+90.3) 3472.04	(0) 3472.04	(+180.44) 3652.48	(+18.02) 3670.5	(+390.6) 4061.1	(+67.3) 4128.4
(+33.84) 1362.94	(+35) 1397.94	(+12.56) 1410.5	(+20.28) 1430.78	(+9) 1439.78	(+20.42) 1460.2	**(-1460.2)** 0	-	-
-	-	-	-	-	-	-	-	-
-	-	-	-	-	-	-	-	-
(+5.26) 2980.32	(+23.14) 3003.46	(+96.14) 3099.6	(+89.26) 3188.86	(0) 3188.86	(+239.92) 3428.78	(+35.78) 3464.56	(+569.74) 4034.3	(+107.82) 4142.12
(+7.28) 573.58	(+17.16) 590.74	**(-590.74)** 0	-	-	-	-	-	-
(+25.14) 1060.92	(+40.34) 1101.26	(+48.28) 1149.54	(+30) 1179.54	(+2) 1181.54	**(-1181.54)** 0	-	-	-
(+106.22) 514.96	**(-514.96)** 0	-	-	-	-	-	-	-
(+39.12) 2190.04	(+33) 2223.04	(+91.64 2314.68	(+109.82) 2424.5	(+5) 2429.5)	(+62.1) 2491.6	(+61.72) 2533.32	(+166.52) 2719.84	**(-2719.84)** 0
(+31.44) 1506.46	(+95.98) 1602.44	(+25) 1627.44	(+117.1) 1744.54	(+3) 1747.54	(+226.08) 1973.62	(+10.84) 1984.46	**(-1984.46)** 0	-
(+1) 776.28	(+2) 778.28	(0) 778.28	(+1) 779.28	(-779.28) 0	-	-	-	-
-	-	-	-	-	-	-	-	-
(+56.42) 2424.7	(+93.42) 2518.12	(+49.56) 2567.68	(+36.16) 2603.84	(+59.14) 2662.98	(+49.74) 2712.72	(+1207.58) 3920.3	(+105.04) 4025.34	(+239.28) 4264.62
(+13) 2494.16	(+42.14) 2536.3	(+9.14) 2545.44	(+10.14) 2555.58	(+648) 3203.58	(+11.02) 3214.6	(+37.84) 3252.44	(+46.04) 3298.48	(+33.42) 3331.9
(+19.58) 2223.48	(+27.6) 2251.08	(+94.56) 2345.64	(+104.26) 2449.9	(+2.14) 2452.04	(+79.26) 2531.3	(+29) 2560.3	(+226.16) 2786.46	(+2051.56) 4838.02
(+8) 602.58	(+29.04) 631.62	(+20) 651.62	**(-651.62)** **0**	-	-	-	-	-
(0) 4422	(0) 4422	(0) 4422	(0) 4422	(0) 4422	(0) 4422	(0) 4422	(0) 4422	(0) 4422
(13) 124.22	(57.04) 181.26	(54.58) 235.84	(43.3) 279.14	(51) 330.14	(312.56) 642.7	(59.42) 702.12	(480.36) 1182.48	(220.46) 1402.94

East Londonderry

Total Valid Pole 34273 Quota 4897 Turnout 61.8

Party performance

Party	Seats	1st Pref Vote	%	(%1998)
DUP	2	11091	32.4	23.7
SF	1	6121	17.9	9.8
UUP	2	7769	22.7	25.2
SDLP	1	5584	16.3	23.6
Alliance	-	762	2.2	6.1
Others	-	2946	8.6	11.7

At a glance...

Overall in terms of seats this constituency retained its 4-2 unionist/nationalist balance although on the unionist side the DUP collected a second seat from former UKUP MLA Boyd Douglas. Sinn Féin won its first seat in this constituency from the SDLP's Michael Coyle. The Ulster Unionist Party retained its two seats on a smaller share of the vote with Norman Hillis replacing disenchanted former MLA Pauline Armitage who ran unsuccessfully as a UKUP candidate. As elsewhere, the DUP and Sinn Féin increased their vote share significantly, with the Alliance vote collapsing.

		1st stage	2nd stage	3rd stage	4th stage	5th stage
		1st pref votes 34,273	Elimination of Baur & Boyle	Elimination of Armitage	Elimination of Stevenson	Transfer of McClarty's surplus
*Pauline Armitage	UKUP	906	(+31) 937	(-937) 0	-	-
Marion Baur	Soc Env All	137	(-137) 0	-	-	-
Yvonne Boyle	All	762	(-762) 0	-	-	-
Maurice Bradley	DUP	2836	(+12) 2848	(+187) 3035	(+5) 3040	(+3.33) 3043.33
Francis Brolly	SF	4019	(+32) 4051	(+5) 4056	(0) 4056	(+0.37) 4056.37
*Gregory Campbell	DUP	4789	(+14) 4803	(+220) 5023	(n/a) 5023	(n/a) 5023
Michael Coyle	SDLP	2394	(+131) 2525	(+7) 2532	(+14) 2546	(+2.59) 2548.59
*John Dallat	SDLP	3190	(+240) 3430	(+25) 3455	(+13) 3468	(+4.81) 3472.81
*Boyd Douglas	UUC	1903	(+20) 1923	(+126) 2049	(+122) 2171)	(+19.61) 2190.61
Norman Hillis	UUP	2292	(+85) 2377	(+150) 2527	(+432) 2959	(+240.87) 3199.87
*David McClarty	UUP	4069	(+219) 4288	(+126) 4414	(+762) 5176	(-279) 4897
Cliona O'Kane	SF	2102	(+8) 2110	(+1) 2111	(+3) 2114	(0) 2114
George Robinson	DUP	3466	(+8) 3474	(+40) 3514	(+99) 3613	(+4.07) 3617.07
Edwin Stevenson	UUP	1408	(+35) 1443	(+23) 1466	(-1466) 0	-
	Non-transferable		(64) 64	(27) 91	(16) 107	(3.35) 110.35

Candidates Elected	Count
Gregory Campbell DUP	3rd
David McClarty UUP	4th
Francis Brolly SF	7th
George Robinson DUP	10th
Norman Hillis UUP	11th
John Dallat SDLP	12th

Gregory Campbell

David McClarty

Francis Brolly

George Robinson

Norman Hillis

John Dallat

6th stage	7th stage	8th stage	9th stage	10th stage	11th stage	12th stage
Transfer of Campbell's surplus	Elimination of O'Kane	Transfer of Brolly's surplus	Elimination of Douglas	Elimination of Bradley	Transfer of Robinson's surplus	Transfer of Hillis's surplus
-	-	-	-	-	-	-
-	-	-	-	-	-	-
-	-	-	-	-	-	-
(+47.74) 3091.07	(+4) 3095.07	(+1.66) 3096.73	(+276.79) 3373.52	**(-3373.52)** 0	-	-
(+0.62) 4056.99	(+1839) 5895.99	**(-998.99)** 4897	(0) 4897	(0) 4897	(0) 4897	(0) 4897
(-126) 4897	(0) 4897	(0) 4897	(0) 4897	(0) 4897	(0) 4897	(0) 4897
(0) 2548.59	(+152) 2700.59	(+814.23) 3514.82	(+12) 3526.82	(+7.65) 3534.47	(+11) 3545.47	(+107) 3652.47
(+1.24) 3474.05	(+91) 3565.05	(+169.32) 3734.37	(+25.62) 3759.99	(+18.24) 3778.23	(+16) 3794.23	(+76) 3870.23
(+29.14) 2219.75	(1) 2220.75	(+0.83) 2221.58	**(-2221.58)** 0	-	-	-
(+21.08) 3220.95	(+2) 3222.95	(+0.83) 3223.78	(+660.06) 3883.84	(436.08) 4319.92	(+1027) 5346.92	**(-449.92)** 4897
(0) 4897	(0) 4897	(0) 4897	(0) 4897	(0) 4897	(0) 4897	(0) 4897
(0) 2114	**(-2114)** 0	-	-	-	-	-
(+24.8) 3641.87	(+2) 3643.87	(+0.83) 3644.7	(+1097.29) 4741.99	(+2605) 7346.99	**(-2449.99)** 4897	(0) 4897
-	-	-	-	-	-	-
(1.38) 111.73	(23) 134.73	(11.29) 146.02	(149.82) 295.84	(306.55) 602.39	(1395.99) 1998.38	(266.92) 2265.3

Fermanagh & South Tyrone

Total Valid Pole 46160 Quota 6595 Turnout 72.9

Party performance

Party	Seats	1st Pref Vote	%	(%1998)
DUP	1	8630	18.7	13.9
SF	2	15901	34.4	26.9
UUP	2	13229	28.7	24.6
SDLP	1	7507	16.3	21.6
Alliance	-	243	0.5	1.2
Others	-	650	1.4	11.9

At a glance...

No change to party share of seats with an as-you-were result of 2 Sinn Féin, 2 UUP, 1 DUP and 1 SDLP. Sitting MP Michelle Gildernew of Sinn Féin topped the poll followed by Tom Elliott of the UUP. However there were some personnel changes with former UUP Minister Sam Foster (who retired) being replaced by colleague Tom Elliott and Sinn Féin veteran Gerry McHugh surprisingly losing out to newcomer Thomas O'Reilly. UUP and DUP vote share increased at the expense of smaller unionist parties and Sinn Féin widened its advantage over the SDLP quite significantly – although SDLP Education spokesman Tommy Gallagher comfortably held his seat. Turnout at under 73% was relatively low for the traditionally high turnout constituency. Shortly after the election newly-elected MLA Arlene Foster switched allegiance from UUP to DUP.

		1st stage	2nd stage
		1st pref votes 46,160	Elimination of Cleland & McNulty
Frank Britton	SDLP	2772	(+206) 2978
Linda Cleland	All	243	(-243) 0
Tom Elliott	UUP	6181	(+103) 6284
Arlene Foster	UUP	4938	(+66) 5004
*Tommy Gallagher	SDLP	4735	(+249) 4984
*Michelle Gildernew	SF	6489	(+73) 6562
Bert Johnston	DUP	3094	(+19) 3113
*Gerry McHugh	SF	4393	(+39) 4432
Eithne McNulty	NIWC	650	(-650) 0
*Maurice Morrow	DUP	5536	(+10) 5546
Robert Mulligan	UUP	2110	(+39) 2149
Thomas O'Reilly	SF	5019	(+30) 5049
	Non-transferable		(59) 59

Candidates Elected	Count
Tom Elliott UUP	3rd
Thomas Gallagher SDLP	5th
Michelle Gildernew SF	5th
Arlene Foster UUP	5th
Maurice Morrow DUP	6th
Thomas O'Reilly SF	8th

Tom Elliott

Thomas Gallagher

Michelle Gildernew

Arlene Foster

Maurice Morrow

Thomas O'Reilly

3rd stage	4th stage	5th stage	6th stage	7th stage	8th stage
Elimination of Mulligan	Transfer of Elliott's surplus	Elimination of Britton	Elimination of Johnston	Transfer of Morrow's surplus	Transfer of Gallagher's surplus
(+16) 2994	(+17.75) 3011.75	**(-3011.75)** 0	-	-	-
-	-	-	-	-	-
(+1088) 7372	**(-777)** 6595	(0) 6595	(0) 6595	(0) 6595	(0) 6595
(+864) 5868	(+696.51) 6564.51	(+35) 6599.51	(n/a) 6599.51	(n/a) 6599.51	(n/a) 6599.51
(+19) 5003	(+31.95) 5034.95	(+2325) 7359.95	(n/a) 7359.95	(n/a) 7359.95	**(-764.95)** 6595
(+3) 6565	(0) 6565	(+154) 6719	(n/a) 6719	(n/a) 6719	(n/a) 6719
(+20) 3133	(+6.39) 3139.39	(+23.42) 3162.81	**(-3162.81)** 0	-	-
(+4) 4436	(0) 4436	(+158) 4594	(+8.71) 4602.71	(+89) 4691.71	(+519.79) 5211.5
-	-	-	-	-	-
(+124) 5670	(+14.2) 5684.2	(+5.71) 5689.91	(+2980) 8669.91	**(-2074.91)** 6595	(0) 6595
(-2149) 0	-	-	-	-	-
(+2) 5051	(0) 5051	(+92) 5143	(+9) 5152	(+88) 5240	(233.64) 5473.64
(9) 68	(10.2) 78.2	(218.62) 296.82	(165.1) 461.92	(1897.91) 2359.83	(11.52) 2371.35

Foyle

Total Valid Pole 40806 Quota 5830 Turnout 63.5

Party performance

Party	Seats	1st Pref Vote	%	(%1998)
DUP	1	6101	15.0	12.5
SF	2	13214	32.4	26.0
UUP	-	3322	8.1	9.6
SDLP	3	14746	36.1	47.8
Alliance	-	227	0.6	2.2
Others	-	3196	7.8	1.9

At a glance...

This predominantly nationalist constituency registered an as-you-were outcome with SDLP (3), Sinn Féin (2) and DUP (1) retaining their seats. The most striking aspect of the result was how close Sinn Féin came to taking a third seat from the SDLP – a party greatly weakened by the absence from the ticket of former party leader and Westminster MP John Hume. However, current SDLP leader Mark Durkan topped the poll alongside strong performances from Sinn Féin's Mitchel McLaughlin and the DUP's William Hay. Another interesting feature was the impressive vote gathered by veteran socialist journalist Eamon McCann running for the Socialist and Environmental Alliance for the first time.

		1st stage	2nd stage	3rd stage
		1st pref votes 40,806	Transfer of Durkan's surplus	Transfer of Hay's surplus
Mary Bradley	SDLP	3345	(+254.24) 3599.24	(+1.2) 3600.44
Alan Castle	All	227	(+4.62) 231.62	(+1.52) 233.14
*Annie Courtney	Ind	802	(+33.18) 835.18	(+8.08) 843.26
Gerald Diver	SDLP	1769	(+209.3) 1978.3	(+1.64) 1979.94
*Mark Durkan	SDLP	6806	**(-976)** 5830	(0) 5830
Mary Hamilton	UUP	3322	(+10.5) 3332.5	(+204.32) 3536.82
*William Hay	DUP	6101	(n/a) 6101	**(-271)** 5830
Danny McBrearty	Ind	137	(+3.64) 140.64	(+0.52) 141.16
Eamon McCann	Soc Env All	2257	(+31.64) 2288.64	(+1.04) 2289.68
Raymond McCartney	SF	3679	(+22.12) 3701.12	(+0.12) 3701.24
*Mitchel McLaughlin	SF	6036	(n/a) 6036	(n/a) 6036
*Mary Nelis	SF	3499	(+35.7) 3534.7	(+0.24) 3534.94
Pat Ramsey	SDLP	2826	(+340.62) 3166.62	(+2.4) 3169.02
	Non-transferable		(30.44) 30.44	(49.92) 80.36

Candidates Elected	Count
Mark Durkan SDLP	1st
William Hay DUP	1st
Mitchel McLaughlin SF	1st
Mary Bradley SDLP	8th
Pat Ramsey SDLP	9th
Mary Nelis SF	9th

Mark Durkan

William Hay

Mitchel McLaughlin

Mary Bradley

Pat Ramsey

Mary Nelis

4th stage	5th stage	6th stage	7th stage	8th stage	9th stage
Transfer of McLaughlin's surplus	Elimination of McBrearty, Castle & Courtney	Elimination of Diver	Elimination of McCann	Elimination of Hamilton	Transfer of Bradley's surplus
(+2.88) 3603.32	(+227.43) 3830.75	(+928.01) 4758.76	(+497.87) 5256.63	(+674) 5930.63	**(-100.63)** 5830
(+0.12) 233.26	**(-233.26)** 0	-	-	-	-
(+2.31) 845.57	**(-845.57)** 0	-	-	-	-
(+2.49) 1982.43	(+170.12) 2152.55	**(-2152.55)** 0	-	-	-
(0) 5830	(0) 5830	(0) 5830	(0) 5830	(0) 5830	(0) 5830
(+0.12) 3536.94	(+183.38) 3720.32	(+29.9) 3750.22	(+54.79) 3805.01	**(-3805.01)** 0	
(0) 5830	(0) 5830	(0) 5830	(0) 5830	(0) 5830	(0) 5830
(+0.39) 141.55	**(-141.55)** 0	-	-	-	-
(+4.83) 2294.51	(+193.58) 2488.09	(+97.94) 2586.03	**(-2586.03)** 0	-	-
(+53.01) 3754.25	(+64.18) 3818.43	(+64.44) 3882.87	(+441.53) 4324.4	(+17) 4341.4	(+1.4) 4342.8
(-206) 5830	(0) 5830	(0) 5830	(0) 5830	(0) 5830	(0) 5830
(+107.67) 3642.61	(+83.66) 3726.27	(+57.74) 3784.01	(+554.23) 4338.24	(+12.75) 4350.99	(+0.28) 4351.27
(+4.86) 3173.88	(+160.27) 3334.15	(+843.93) 4178.08	(+500.98) 4679.06	(+1018.5) 5697.56	(+66.64) 5764.2
(27.32) 107.68	(137.76 245.44	(130.59) 376.03	(536.63) 912.66	(2082.76) 2995.42	(32.31) 3027.73

Lagan Valley

Total Valid Pole 41254 **Quota 5894** **Turnout 61.4**

Party performance

Party	Seats	1st Pref Vote	%	(%1998)
DUP	1	8475	20.5	18.0
SF	-	3242	7.9	4.3
UUP	3	19069	46.2	30.8
SDLP	1	3133	7.6	8.7
Alliance	1	4408	10.7	14.6
Others	-	2927	7.1	23.6

At a glance...

In a difficult-to-interpret predominantly unionist constituency, the Ulster Unionist Party and to a lesser extent the DUP increased their vote share at the expense of smaller unionist parties. The UUP (driven by a huge personal vote for unsettled sitting MP Jeffrey Donaldson - the highest individual poll in the whole election) took three seats, narrowly squeezing out former Tory spokesman turned DUP candidate Andrew Hunter. The departure of Jeffrey Donaldson and newly elected colleague Norah Beare to the DUP shortly after the election makes it impossible to assess the relative strengths of the two main unionist parties in Lagan Valley. Alliance MLA Seamus Close and the SDLP's Patricia Lewsley held their seats although in Lewsley's case only just, following a strong challenge from Sinn Féin's Paul Butler.

		1st stage	2nd stage	3rd stage	4th stage
		1st pref votes 41,254	Transfer of Donaldson's surplus	Elimination of McCarthy, Park & Johnston	Transfer of Poots' surplus
Norah Beare	UUP	1508	(+1813.66) 3321.66	(+116.04) 3437.7	(+96.96) 3534.66
*Billy Bell	UUP	2782	(+1957.5) 4739.5	(+117.3) 4856.8	(+105.92) 4962.72
Paul Butler	SF	3242	(+9.28) 3251.28	(+10.58) 3261.86	(+1.28) 3263.14
*Seamus Close	All	4408	(+259.84) 4667.84	(+179.34) 4847.18	(+33.6) 4880.78
*Ivan Davis	Ind	2223	(+316.1) 2539.1	(+98.38) 2637.48	(+24.96) 2662.44
Jeffrey Donaldson	UUP	14104	**(-8210)** 5894	(0) 5894	(0) 5894
Andrew Hunter	DUP	3300	(+785.32) 4085.32	(+101.84) 4187.16	(+479.36) 4666.52
Joanne Johnston	Cons	395	(+67.86) 462.86	**(-462.86)** 0	-
Jim Kirkpatrick	UUP	675	(+1282.96) 1957.96	(+65.4) 2023.36	(+70.72) 2094.08
*Patricia Lewsley	SDLP	3133	(+20.88) 3153.88	(+78.74) 3232.62	(+3.84) 3236.46
Frances McCarthy	WP	97	(+6.38) 103.38	**(-103.38)** 0	-
Andrew Park	PUP	212	(+44.66) 256.66	**(-256.66)** 0	-
*Edwin Poots	DUP	5175	(+1539.32) 6714.32	(n/a) 6714.32	**(-820.32)** 5894
	Non-transferable		(106.24) 106.24	(55.28) 161.52	(3.68) 165.2

Candidates Elected	Count
Jeffrey Donaldson UUP	1st
Edwin Poots DUP	2nd
Billy Bell UUP	6th
Seamus Close All	7th
Patricia Lewsley SDLP	9th
Norah Beare UUP	10th

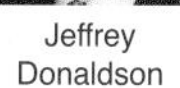
Jeffrey Donaldson

Edwin Poots

Billy Bell

Seamus Close

Patricia Lewsley

Norah Beare

5th stage	6th stage	7th stage	8th stage	9th stage	10th stage
Elimination of Kirkpatrick	Elimination of Davis	Transfer of Bell's surplus	Transfer of Close's surplus	Elimination of Butler	Transfer of Lewsley's surplus
(+840.9) 4375.56	(+391.8) 4767.36	(+428) 5195.36	(+105) 5300.36	(+28.44) 5328.8	(+328.64) 5657.44
(+876.76) 5839.48	(+1094) 6933.48	**(-1039.48)** 5894	(0) 5894	(0) 5894	(0) 5894
(+3.06) 3266.2	(+10.06) 3276.26	(+1) 3277.26	(+1) 3278.26	**(-3278.26)** 0	-
(+74.36) 4955.14	(+870.26) 5825.4	(+470) 6295.4	**(-401.4)** 5894	(0) 5894	(0) 5894
(+72.56) 2735	**(-2735)** 0	-	-	-	-
(0) 5894	(0) 5894	(0) 5894	(0) 5894	(0) 5894	(0) 5894
(+138.42) 4804.94	(+124.76) 4929.7	(+48) 4977.7	(+23) 5000.7	(+13.06) 5013.76	(+30.81) 5044.57
-	-	-	-	-	-
(-2094.08) 0	-	-	-	-	-
(+14.64) 3251.1	(+91.64) 3342.74	(+39) 3381.74	(+154) 3535.74	(+2721) 6256.74	**(-362.74)** 5894
-	-	-	-	-	-
-	-	-	-	-	-
(0) 5894	(0) 5894	(0) 5894	(0) 5894	(0) 5894	(0) 5894
(73.38) 238.58	(152.48) 391.06	(53.48) 444.54	(118.4) 562.94	(515.76) 1078.7	(3.29) 1081.99

Mid Ulster

Total Valid Pole 44362 Quota 6338 Turnout 74.9

Party performance

Party	Seats	1st Pref Vote	%	(%1998)
DUP	1	9240	20.8	21.4
SF	3	20194	45.5	40.8
UUP	1	6394	14.4	13.9
SDLP	1	8138	18.3	22.2
Alliance	-	166	0.4	1.0
Others	-	230	0.5	0.7

At a glance...

Mid Ulster was the only constituency in the election where the DUP vote went down and the UUP vote increased although the movement was small. The result was as-you-were in terms of seats (Sinn Féin 3, DUP 1, UUP and SDLP 1 each) although there were two new faces - Geraldine Dougan of Sinn Féin replacing John Kelly (who didn't run again) Patsy McGlone edging out party colleague and former SDLP junior Minister at OFMDFM Denis Haughey. The poll-topper was DUP veteran Rev. William McCrea followed closely by the MP for the area Martin McGuinness of Sinn Féin. At 74.9% Mid Ulster registered the highest turnout of all 18 constituencies.

		1st stage	2nd stage
		1st pref votes 44,362	Transfer of McCrea's surplus
*Billy Armstrong	UUP	4323	(+138.6) 4461.6
Francis Donnelly	WP	230	(+0.22) 230.22
Geraldine Dougan	SF	5827	(+0.22) 5827.22
Cora Groogan	SF	984	(0) 984
*Denis Haughey	SDLP	3843	(+1.32) 3844.32
James Holmes	All	166	(+1.1) 167.1
*William McCrea	DUP	8211	(-1873) 6338
Patsy McGlone	SDLP	4295	(+5.06) 4300.06
*Martin McGuinness	SF	8128	(n/a) 8128
Alan Millar	DUP	1029	(+1536.7) 2565.7
*Francis Molloy	SF	5255	(+0.44) 5255.44
Trevor Wilson	UUP	2071	(+111.54) 2182.54
	Non-transferable		(77.8) 77.8

Candidates Elected	Count
William McCrea DUP	1st
Martim McGuinness SF	1st
Geraldine Dougan SF	4th
Francis Molloy SF	4th
Billy Armstrong UUP	7th
Patsy McGlone SDLP	8th

William McCrea

Martin McGuinness

Geraldine Dougan

Francis Molloy

Billy Armstrong

Patsy McGlone

3rd stage	4th stage	5th stage	6th stage	7th stage	8th stage
Transfer of McGuinness's surplus	Elimination of Donnelly, Groogan & Holmes	Transfer of Dougan's surplus	Elimination of Wilson	Elimination of Millar	Transfer of Armstrong's surplus
(+0.22) 4461.82	(+47.42) 4509.24	(+5) 4514.24	(+1651.08) 6165.32	(+883) 7048.32	**(-710.32)** 6338
(+7.26) 237.48	**(-237.48)** 0	-	-	-	-
(+171.16) 5998.38	(+918) 6916.38	**(-578.38)** 6338	(0) 6338	(0) 6338	(0) 6338
(+160.16) 1144.16	**(-1144.16)** 0	-	-	-	-
(+96.14) 3940.46	(+170.88) 4111.34	(+101) 4212.34	(+38.1) 4250.44	(+208.24) 4458.68	(+153) 4611.68
(+1.76) 168.86	**(-168.86)** 0	-	-	-	-
(0) 6338	(0) 6338	(0) 6338	(0) 6338	(0) 6338	(0) 6338
(+205.26) 4505.32	(+188.32) 4693.64	(+257) 4950.64	(+34.2) 4984.84	(+155.38) 5140.22	(+106) 5246.22
(-1790) 6338	(0) 6338	(0) 6338	(0) 6338	(0) 6338	(0) 6338
(+5.94) 2571.64	(+8.88) 2580.52	(+1) 2581.52	(+453.8) 3035.32	**(-3035.32)** 0	-
(+1121.78) 6377.22	(n/a) 6377.22	(n/a) 6377.22	(n/a) 6377.22	(n/a) 6377.22	(n/a) 6377.22
(+1.1) 2183.64	(+44.88) 2228.52	(+5) 2233.52	**(-2233.52)** 0	-	-
(19.22) 97.02	(172.12) 269.14	(209.38) 478.52	(56.34) 534.86	(1788.7) 2323.56	(451.32) 2774.88

Newry & Armagh

Total Valid Pole 47378 Quota 6769 Turnout 70.2

Party performance

Party	Seats	1st Pref Vote	%	(%1998)
DUP	1	8599	18.1	13.3
SF	3	18852	39.8	26.0
UUP	1	7347	15.5	18.1
SDLP	1	11637	24.6	35.0
Alliance	-	311	0.7	1.4
Others	-	632	1.3	6.1

At a glance...

No change in the balance between nationalists and unionist (which remained 4-2) with the big change being the surge in support for Sinn Féin at the expense of the SDLP. This was also reflected in terms of seats won with Sinn Féin increasing to 3 and the SDLP slipping down to 1. The SDLP had been weakened by the absence of sitting MP and former Deputy Leader Seamus Mallon from the ticket although the result was still possibly the party's worst of the 18 constituencies. The DUP's Paul Berry topped the poll followed by Sinn Féin's Conor Murphy and UUP's Danny Kennedy – all three returning MLAs. SDLP sitting MLA John Fee lost his seat.

		1st Stage	2nd Stage
		1st Pref Votes 47378	Transfer of Berry's surplus
*Paul Berry	DUP	8125	(-1356) 6769
Dominic Bradley	SDLP	4111	(+8.8) 4119.8
Freda Donnelly	DUP	474	(+1164.64) 1638.64
*John Fee	SDLP	3410	(+1.28) 3411.28
William Frazer	Ind	632	(+111.36) 743.36
Davy Hyland	SF	5779	(+0.48) 5779.48
*Danny Kennedy	UUP	7347	(n/a) 7347
Jim Lennon	SDLP	4116	(+2.88) 4118.88
*Conor Murphy	SF	7595	(n/a) 7595
Pat O'Rawe	SF	5478	(+0.16) 5478.16
Peter Whitcroft	All	311	(+2.72) 313.72
	Non-transferable		(63.68) 63.68

Candidates Elected	Count
Paul Berry DUP	1st
Conor Murphy SF	1st
Danny Kennedy UUP	1st
Dominic Bradley SDLP	5th
Davy Hyland SF	5th
Pat O'Rawe SF	5th

Paul Berry

Conor Murphy

Danny Kennedy

Dominic Bradley

Davy Hyland

Pat O'Rawe

3rd Stage	4th Stage	5th Stage
Transfer of Murphy's surplus	Elimination of Whitcroft, Frazer & Donnelly	Elimination of Fee
(0) 6769	(0) 6769	(0) 6769
(+15.2) 4135	(+265.14) 4400.14	(+2383) 6783.14
(+0.3) 1638.94	**(-1638.94)** 0	-
(+48.1) 3459.38	(+197.58) 3656.96	**(-3656.96)** 0
(+0.7) 744.06	**(-744.06)** 0	-
(+567.9) 6347.38	(+19.62) 6367	(+266.9) 6633.9
(n/a) 7347	(n/a) 7347	(n/a) 7347
(+7.1) 4125.98	(+265) 4390.98	(+721.52) 5112.5
(-826) 6769	(0) 6769	(0) 6769
(+112.5) 5590.66	(+12.66) 5603.32	(+108.68) 5712
(+1) 314.72	**(-314.72)** 0	-
(73.2) 136.88	(1937.72) 2074.6	(176.86) 2251.46

North Antrim

Total Valid Pole 44099 | Quota 6300 | Turnout 63.3

Party performance

Party	Seats	1st Pref Vote	%	(%1998)
DUP	3	20235	45.9	37.6
SF	1	6195	14.0	8.1
UUP	1	9538	21.6	22.3
SDLP	1	6009	13.6	16.9
Alliance	-	867	2.0	4.6
Others	-	1255	2.8	10.5

At a glance...

North Antrim saw a powerful performance by the DUP, which with two Ian Paisleys topping the poll, comfortably held on to its three seats. The big surprise was the election of a Sinn Féin representative Philip McGuigan, eventually taking one of the UUP seats. The remaining UUP seat was held by Robert Coulter while former Finance and Personnel Minister Sean Farren held onto the final seat for the SDLP on a reduced share of the vote. Overall the smaller unionist parties lost ground to the larger two parties.

Candidate	Party	1st stage 1st Pref Votes 44,099	2nd stage Transfer of Paisley (Snr) surplus	3rd stage Transfer of Paisley (Jnr) surplus
*Robert Coulter	UUP	6385	(n/a) 6385	(n/a) 6385
James Currie	UUP	3153	(+94.08) 3247.08	(+73.6) 3320.68
Jayne Dunlop	All	867	(+6.44) 873.44	(+10.2) 883.64
*Sean Farren	SDLP	3648	(+1.68) 3649.68	(+2.4) 3652.08
*Gardiner Kane	Ind	623	(+54.6) 677.6	(+25.6) 703.2
William McCaughey	PUP	230	(+14.84) 244.84	(+9.2) 254.04
Philip McGuigan	SF	6195	(0) 6195	(+0.2) 6195.2
Declan O'Loan	SDLP	2361	(+1.68) 2362.68	(+1) 2363.68
*Ian Paisley Jnr	DUP	7898	(n/a) 7898	**(-1598)** 6300
*Rev Ian Paisley	DUP	8732	**(-2432)** 6300	(0) 6300
Nathaniel Small	UKUP	402	(+42) 444	(+61) 505
Mervyn Storey	DUP	3605	(+2182.6) 5787.6	(+1364.6) 7152.2
	Non-transferable		34.08 (34.08	(50.2) 84.28

Candidates Elected	Count
Rev Ian Paisley DUP	1st
Ian Paisley (Jnr) DUP	1st
Rev Robert Coulter UUP	1st
Mervyn Storey DUP	3rd
Philip McGuigan SF	9th
Sean Farren SDLP	9th

Rev Ian Paisley

Ian Paisley (Jnr)

Robert Coulter

Mervyn Storey

Philip McGuigan

Sean Farren

4th stage	5th stage	6th stage	7th stage	8th stage	9th stage
Transfer of Storey's surplus	Elimination of McCaughey	Transfer of Coulter's surplus	Elimination of Kane	Elimination of Dunlop & Small	Elimination of O'Loan
(n/a) 6385	(n/a) 6385	**(-85)** 6300	(0) 6300	(0) 6300	(0) 6300
(+278) 3598.68	(+77.68) 3676.36	(+59.62) 3735.98	(+305.26) 4041.24	(+933.8) 4975.04	(+74.93) 5049.97
(+13) 896.64	(+17.76) 914.4	(+0.8) 915.2	(+37.94) 953.14	**(-953.14)** 0	-
(+2.8) 3654.88	(+11.4) 3666.28	(+0.33) 3666.61	(+22.99) 3689.6	(+231.22) 3920.82	(+2059.61) 5980.43
(+85) 788.2	(+31.68) 819.88	(+0.86) 820.74	**(-820.74)** 0	-	-
(+43.6) 297.64	**(-297.64)** 0	-	-	-	-
(0) 6195.2	(+3) 6198.2	(+0.06) 6198.26	(+1.2) 6199.46	(+8.48) 6207.94	(+289) 6496.94
(+1.4) 2365.08	(+9.28) 2374.36	(+0.12) 2374.48	(+7.21) 2381.69	(+133.67) 2515.36	**(-2515.36)** 0
(0) 6300	(0) 6300	(0) 6300	(0) 6300	(0) 6300	(0) 6300
(0) 6300	(0) 6300	(0) 6300	(0) 6300	(0) 6300	(0) 6300
(+274.4) 779.4	(+45.56) 824.96	(+0.64) 825.6	(+171.6) 997.2	**(-997.2)** 0	-
(-852.2) 6300	(0) 6300	(0) 6300	(0) 6300	(0) 6300	(0) 6300
(154) 238.28	(101.28) 339.56	(22.57) 362.13	(274.54) 636.67	(643.17) 1279.84	(91.82) 1371.66

North Down

Total Valid Pole 30835 Quota 4406 Turnout 54.5

Party performance

Party	Seats	1st Pref Vote	%	(%1998)
DUP	2	7245	23.5	6.9
SF	-	264	0.9	0.0
UUP	2	9887	32.1	32.6
SDLP	-	1519	4.9	5.5
Alliance	1	2655	8.6	14.4
Others	1	9265	30.0	40.7

At a glance...

The main change in the predominantly unionist North Down constituency was the capture by the DUP of two seats at the expense of Northern Ireland Women's Coalition and also the Ulster Unionist Party, who were reduced from 3 to 2. This was not surprising given the general trend overall and the departure of former UUP MLA Peter Weir to the DUP mid-term. Although known for its 'independent' streak the squeeze on smaller parties also impacted in North Down, where former MP Robert McCartney held on to his UKUP seat (elected sub-quota) and Northern Ireland Women's Coalition MLA Jane Morrice lost out. Alliance Deputy Leader Eileen Bell retained her seat.

		1st stage	2nd stage	3rd stage	4th stage	5th stage
		1st pref votes 30,835	Elimination of Carter	Elimination of Sheridan	Elimination of George	Elimination of Rose
John Barry	Green	730	(+3) 733	(+1) 734	(+14) 748	(+14) 762
*Eileen Bell	All	1951	(+6) 1957	(+5) 1962	(+8) 1970	(+13) 1983
Chris Carter	Ind	109	**(-109)** 0	-	-	-
Alan Chambers	Ind	1077	(+22) 1099	(+3) 1102	(0) 1102	(+17) 1119
Leslie Cree	UUP	3900	(+8) 3908	(+11) 3919	(+1) 3920	(+30) 3950
Alex Easton	DUP	3570	(+9) 3579	(+10) 3589	(0) 3589	(+22) 3611
Stephen Farry	All	704	(+4) 708	(+3) 711	(+11) 722	(+6) 728
Alan Field	Ind	428	(+2) 430	(+2) 432	(0) 432	(+16) 448
Maria George	SF	264	(+1) 265	(0) 265	**(-265)** 0	-
William Logan	SDLP	1519	(+3) 1522	(+1) 1523	(+209) 1732	(+2) 1734
*Robert McCartney	UKUP	3374	(+13) 3387	(+98) 3485	(+3) 3488	(+25) 3513
*Alan McFarland	UUP	3421	(+8) 3429	(+8) 3437	(+2) 3439	(+28) 3467
*Jane Morrice	NIWC	1181	(+7) 1188	(+4) 1192	(+9) 1201	(+18) 1219
Diana Peacocke	UUP	2566	(+2) 2568	(+19) 2587	(+2) 2589	(+34) 2623
Julian Robertson	Cons	491	(+1) 492	(+5) 497	(0) 497	(+4) 501
David Rose	PUP	316	(+1) 317	(+10) 327	(0) 327	**(-327)** 0
Thomas Sheridan	UKUP	209	(+1) 210	**(-210)** 0	-	-
*Peter Weir	DUP	3675	(+6) 3681	(+23) 3704	(0) 3704	(+57) 3761
Brian Wilson	Ind	1350	(+5) 1355	(+2) 1357	(+2) 1359	(+12) 1371
	Non-transferable		(7) 7	(5) 12	(4) 16	(29) 45

Candidates Elected	Count
Leslie Cree UUP	12th
Eileen Bell All	13th
Alan McFarland UUP	14th
Robert McCartney UKUP	14th
Peter Weir DUP	14th
Alex Easton DUP	14th

Leslie Cree

Eileen Bell

Alan McFarland

Robert McCartney

Peter Weir

Alex Easton

6th stage	7th stage	8th stage	9th stage	10th stage	11th stage	12th stage	13th stage	14th stage
Elimination of Field	Elimination of Robertson	Elimination of Farry	Elimination of Barry	Elimination of Chambers	Elimination of Morrice	Elimination of Wilson	Elimination of Logan	Transfer of Bell's surplus
(+6) 768	(+18) 786	(+14) 800	**(-800)** 0	-	-	-	-	-
(+9) 1992	(+16) 2008	(+587) 2595	(+225) 2820	(+126) 2946	(+656) 3602	(+535) 4137	(+1100) 5237	**(-831)** 4406
-	-	-	-	-	-	-	-	-
(+66) 1185	(+21) 1206	(+8) 1214	(+28) 1242	**(-1242)** 0	-	-	-	-
(+39) 3989	(+30) 4019	(+13) 4032	(+41) 4073	(+232) 4305	(+97) 4402	(+80) 4482	(n/a) 4482	(n/a) 4482
(+39) 3650	(+13) 3663	(+4) 3667	(+22) 3689	(+81) 3770	(+13) 3783	(+38) 3821	(+6) 3827	(+12) 3839
(+12) 740	(+11) 751	**(-751)** 0	-	-	-	-	-	-
(-448) 0	-	-	-	-	-	-	-	-
-	-	-	-	-	-	-	-	-
(+4) 1738	(+3) 1741	(+44) 1785	(+66) 1851	(+19) 1870	(+207) 2077	(+81) 2158	**(-2158)** 0	-
(+77) 3590	(+49) 3639	(+9) 3648	(+27) 3675	(+172) 3847	(+65) 3912	(+134) 4046	(+26) 4072	(+30) 4102
(+47) 3514	(+43) 3557	(+13) 3570	(+36) 3606	(+124) 3730	(+103) 3833	(+250) 4083	(+209) 4292	(+210) 4502
(+23) 1242	(+17) 1259	(+28) 1287	(+191) 1478	(+109) 1587	**(-1587)** 0	-	-	-
(+13) 2636	(+41) 2677	(+11) 2688	(+41) 2729	(+66) 2795	(+139) 2934	(+131) 3065	(+193) 3258	(+160) 3418
(+7) 508	**(-508)** 0	-	-	-	-	-	-	-
-	-	-	-	-	-	-	-	-
-	-	-	-	-	-	-	-	-
(+41) 3802	(+20) 3822	(+4) 3826	(+13) 3839	(+67) 3906	(+16) 3922	(+96) 4018	(+8) 4026	(+5) 4031
(+44) 1415	(+14) 1429	(+8) 1437	(+52) 1489	(+109) 1598	(+120) 1718	**(-1718)** 0	-	-
(21) 66	(212) 278	(8) 286	(58) 344	(137) 481	(171) 652	(373) 1025	(616) 1641	(414) 2055

South Antrim

Total Valid Pole 37421 | Quota 5346 | Turnout 59.5

Party performance

Party	Seats	1st Pref Vote	%	(%1998)
DUP	2	11452	30.6	20.1
SF	-	4295	11.5	7.3
UUP	2	11154	29.8	29.9
SDLP	1	5403	14.4	17.7
Alliance	1	3393	9.1	8.6
Others	-	1724	4.6	16.3

At a glance...

The main change in South Antrim was the DUP's picking up Northern Ireland Unionist Party candidate Norman Boyd's former UKUP seat. The UUP held its two seats with local MP and prominent anti-Agreement campaigner David Burnside topping the poll. Alliance Party leader David Ford narrowly held on to his seat actually increasing the Alliance share of the vote and eventually edging out Sinn Féin hopeful Martin Meehan. The SDLP retained its single seat although Tommy Burns took the seat from colleague and former MLA Donovan McClelland. In line with the trend right across Northern Ireland, South Antrim saw a major squeeze of the smaller parties.

		1st stage	2nd stage	3rd stage	4th stage
		1st pref votes 37,421	Transfer of Burnside's surplus	Elimination of Docherty	Elimination of Cosgrove & Wilkinson
*Norman Boyd	NIUP	774	(+52.56) 826.56	(+11.96) 838.52	(+42.48) 881
Thomas Burns	SDLP	2732	(+16.56) 2748.56	(+3) 2751.56	(+65) 2816.56
David Burnside	UUP	7066	**(-1720)** 5346	(0) 5346	(0) 5346
*Wilson Clyde	DUP	5131	(+124.56) 5255.56	(+4.24) 5259.8	(+42.2) 5302
Adrian Cochrane-Watson	UUP	953	(+900.72) 1853.72	(+35.96) 1889.68	(+75.12) 1964.8
Joan Cosgrove	NIWC	465	(+9.36) 474.36	(+10) 484.36	**(-484.36)** 0
Jason Docherty	Cons	174	(+5.52) 179.52	**(-179.52)** 0	-
*David Ford	All	3393	(+63.6) 3456.6	(+47.44) 3504.04	(+250.6) 3754.64
Paul Girvan	DUP	4820	(+80.4) 4900.4	(+13.72) 4914.12	(+62.2) 4976.32
*Donovan McClelland	SDLP	2671	(+6.24) 2677.24	(+1) 2678.24	(+45.48) 2723.72
Martin Meehan	SF	4295	(+1.2) 4296.2	(+2) 4298.2	(+13) 4311.2
John Smyth	DUP	1501	(+29.52) 1530.52	(+2) 1532.52	(+67.96) 1600.48
Kenneth Wilkinson	PUP	311	(+12.24) 323.24	(+4.24) 327.48	**(-327.48)** 0
*Jim Wilson	UUP	3135	(+384.96) 3519.96	(+35.48) 3555.44	(+112.36) 3667.8
	Non-transferable		(32.56) 32.56	(8.48) 41.04	(35.44) 76.48

Candidates Elected	Count
David Burnside UUP	1st
Wilson Clyde DUP	5th
Paul Girvan DUP	6th
Jim Wilson UUP	11th
Thomas Burns SDLP	11th
David Ford All	11th

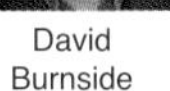
David Burnside

Wilson Clyde

Paul Girvan

Jim Wilson

Thomas Burns

David Ford

5th stage	6th stage	7th stage	8th stage	9th stage	10th stage	11th stage
Elimination of Boyd	Elimination of Smyth	Transfer of Girvan's surplus	Transfer of Clyde's surplus	Elimination of Cochrane-Watson	Transfer of Wilson's surplus	Elimination of McClelland
(-881) 0	-	-	-	-	-	-
(+38.92) 2855.48	(+8.72) 2864.2	(+11) 2875.2	(+1) 2876.2	(+85.16) 2961.36	(+31) 2992.36	(+1986.88) 4979.24
(0) 5346	(0) 5346	(0) 5346	(0) 5346	(0) 5346	(0) 5346	(0) 5346
(+231) 5533	(n/a) 5533	(n/a) 5533	**(-187)** 5346	(0) 5346	(0) 5346	(0) 5346
(+154.68) 2119.48	(+143.68) 2263.16	(+349) 2612.16	(+84) 2696.16	**(-2696.16)** 0	-	-
-	-	-	-	-	-	-
-	-	-	-	-	-	-
(+66.84) 3821.48	(+50.88) 3872.36	(+82) 3954.36	(+15) 3969.36	(+519.48) 4488.84	(+208) 4696.84	(+269.36) 4966.2
(+199.68) 5176	(+1238) 6414	**(-1068)** 5346	(0) 5346	(0) 5346	(0) 5346	(0) 5346
(+3.24) 2726.96	(+5.24) 2732.2	(+6) 2738.2	(+1) 2739.2	(+44.2) 2783.4	(+19) 2802.4	**(-2802.4)** 0
(+1) 4312.2	(+1) 4313.2	(+1) 4314.2	(0) 4314.2	(+3.72) 4317.92	(+1) 4318.92	(+466.72) 4785.64
(+35.36) 1635.84	**(-1635.84)** 0	-	-	-	-	-
-	-	-	-	-	-	-
(+1048.68) 3772.48	(+105.84) 3878.32	(+268) 4146.32	(+68) 4214.32	(+1392) 5606.32	**(-260.32)** 5346	(0) 5346
(45.6) 122.08	(82.48) 204.56	(351) 555.56	(18) 573.56	(651.6) 1225.16	(1.32) 1226.48	(79.44) 1305.92

South Down

Total Valid Pole 46012 Quota 6479 Turnout 65.6

Party performance

Party	Seats	1st Pref Vote	%	(%1998)
DUP	1	6789	15.0	9.4
SF	2	12007	26.5	15.1
UUP	1	8253	18.2	14.4
SDLP	2	15922	35.1	45.3
Alliance	-	489	1.1	2.9
Others	-	1886	4.2	12.8

At a glance...

The big change in South Down was the capture of a second seat by Sinn Féin at the expense of the SDLP who had been expected to hold 3. Again like in Foyle and Newry/Armagh the SDLP ticket had been weakened by the absence of sitting Westminster MP, in this case Eddie McGrady. On the Unionist side it remained one seat apiece with Jim Wells (DUP) who topped the poll, and Dermot Nesbitt (UUP) being reelected. In the end there were three new faces, Caitriona Ruane and Willie Clarke of Sinn Féin and Margaret Ritchie of SDLP. As elsewhere the smaller parties were squeezed out of contention by the 'big 4'. SDLP's Eamonn O'Neill was the one to lose out.

		1st stage	2nd stage	3rd stage
		1st pref votes 46,012	Transfer of Wells's surplus	Elimination of Curran & O'Hagan
Raymond Blaney	Green	799	(+0.76) 799.76	(+52) 851.76
*PJ Bradley	SDLP	5337	(+0.36) 5337.36	(+18) 5355.36
Willie Clarke	SF	4083	(+0.08) 4083.08	(+9) 4092.08
Malachi Curran	Ind	162	(+0.08) 162.08	**(-162.08)** 0
Jim Donaldson	UUP	2885	(+99.52) 2984.52	(+5) 2989.52
Marian Fitzpatrick	SDLP	2382	(+0.44) 2382.44	(+27) 2409.44
Eamonn McConvey	SDLP	2806	(+0.12) 2806.12	(+27) 2833.12
Trudy Miller	NIWC	565	(+0.6) 565.6	(+24) 589.6
*Dermot Nesbitt	UUP	5368	(+43) 5411	(+9) 5420
Desmond O'Hagan	WP	115	(+0.08) 115.08	**(-115.08)** 0
*Eamonn O'Neill	SDLP	3942	(+0.92) 3942.92	(+21) 3963.92
Neil Powell	All	489	(+0.48) 489.48	(+6) 495.48
Margaret Ritchie	SDLP	4261	(+0.76) 4261.76	(+52) 4313.76
Caitriona Ruane	SF	5118	(0) 5118	(+6) 5124
*Jim Wells	DUP	6789	**(-310)** 6479	(0) 6479
Jim Wharton	UKUP	245	(+115.64) 360.64	(+2.08) 362.72
	Non-transferable	666	(47.16) 713.16	(19.08) 732.24

Candidates Elected	Count
Jim Wells DUP	1st
PJ Bradley SDLP	2nd
Dermot Nesbitt UUP	8th
Caitriona Ruane SF	9th
Willie Clarke SF	9th
Margaret Ritchie SDLP	9th

Jim Wells

PJ Bradley

Dermot Nesbitt

Caitriona Ruane

Willie Clarke

Margaret Ritchie

4th stage	5th stage	6th stage	7th stage	8th stage	9th stage
Elimination of Blaney, Powell & Wharton	Elimination of Fitzpatrick	Transfer of Bradley's surplus	Elimination of McConvey	Elimination of Donaldson	Transfer of Nesbitt's surplus
(-851.76) 0	-	-	-	-	-
(+327.6) 5682.96	(+1454) 7136.96	**(-657.96)** 6479	(0) 6479	(0) 6479	(0) 6479
(+93.08) 4185.16	(+83.04) 4268.2	(+10.58) 4278.78	(+1641.96) 5920.74	(+5.7) 5926.44	(+8) 5934.44
-	-	-	-	-	-
(+265.44) 3254.96	(+9.16) 3264.12	(+1.84) 3265.96	(+3.46) 3269.42	**(-3269.42)** 0	-
(+146.2) 2555.64	**(-2555.64)** 0	-	-	-	-
(+128.04) 2961.14	(+25) 2986.16	(+4.14) 2990.3	**(-2990.3)** 0	-	-
(-589.6) 0	-	-	-	-	-
(+339.04) 5759.04	(+38.16) 5797.2	(+5.52) 5802.72	(+20) 5822.72	(+2503) 8325.72	**(-1846.72)** 6479
-	-	-	-	-	-
(+256.32) 4220.24	(+472.08) 4692.32	(+523.02) 5215.34	(+135) 5350.34	(+61.18) 5411.52	(+286) 5697.52
(-495.48) 0	-	-	-	-	-
(+351.56) 4665.32	(+183.04) 4848.36	(+73.14) 4921.5	(+498.46) 5419.96	(+58) 5477.96	(+256) 5733.96
(+87.08) 5211.08	(+204) 5415.08	(+34.96) 5450.04	(+574.38) 6024.42	(+2.12) 6026.54	(+9) 6035.54
(0) 6479	(0) 6479	(0) 6479	(0) 6479	(0) 6479	(0) 6479
(-362.72) 0	-	-	-	-	-
(305.2) 1037.44	(87.16) 1124.6	(4.76) 1129.36	(117.04) 1246.4	(639.42) 1885.82	(1287.72) 3173.54

Strangford

Total Valid Pole 37250 Quota 5322 Turnout 57.1

Party performance

Party	Seats	1st Pref Vote	%	(%1998)
DUP	3	17857	47.9	27.7
SF	-	1105	3.0	1.4
UUP	2	10781	28.9	34.4
SDLP	-	2906	7.8	9.0
Alliance	1	2741	7.4	12.2
Others	-	1860	5.0	15.3

At a glance...

Strangford saw another very strong performance by the DUP, easily increasing its haul of seats from 2 to 3. The loser in this instance and by a distance was NIUP leader Cedric Wilson, elected previously for the UKUP. The UUP held its two seats and despite a sizeable fall in vote share the Alliance MLA Kieran McCarthy held on from SDLP challenger Joe Boyle. Sitting Westminster MP Iris Robinson comfortably topped the poll with former UUP Strangford MP Lord Kilclooney (John Taylor) coming second.

		1st stage	2nd stage	3rd stage	4th stage
		1st pref votes 37,250	Transfer of Robinson's surplus	Transfer of Ennis's surplus	Transfer of Shannon's surplus
Joe Boyle	SDLP	2906	(+3.33) 2909.33	(+0.74) 2910.07	(+5.94) 2916.01
George Ennis	DUP	4606	(+1532.54) 6138.54	**(-816.54)** 5322	(0) 5322
Dermot Kennedy	SF	1105	(+1.11) 1106.11	(+1.48) 1107.59	(+3.3) 1110.89)
*Lord Kilclooney	UUP	5658	(n/a) 5658	(n/a) 5658	(n/a) 5658
Robert Little	UUP	2123	(+49.21) 2172.21	(+199.8) 2372.01	(+222.75) 2594.76
Danny McCarthy	Ind	319	(+1.48) 320.48	(+15.17) 335.65	(+13.86) 349.51
*Kieran McCarthy	All	2741	(+22.57) 2763.57	(+27.75) 2791.32	(+44.55) 2835.87
David McNarry	UUP	3000	(+55.5) 3055.5	(+113.96) 3169.46	(+134.64) 3304.1
Colin Neill	PUP	540	(+18.87) 558.87	(+61.42) 620.29	(+48.51) 668.8
Philip Orr	Green	425	(+12.58) 437.58	(+24.05) 461.63	(+21.12) 482.75
*Iris Robinson	DUP	8548	**(-3226)** 5322	(0) 5322	(0) 5322
*Jim Shannon	DUP	4703	(+1402.67) 6105.67	(n/a) 6105.67	**(-783.67)** 5322
*Cedric Wilson	NIUP	576	(+42.55) 618.55	(+365.19) 983.74	(+282.15) 1265.89
	Non-transferable		(83.59) 83.59	(6.98) 90.57	(6.85) 97.42

Candidates Elected	Count
Iris Robinson DUP	1st
Lord Kilclooney UUP	1st
George Ennis DUP	2nd
Jim Shannon DUP	2nd
David McNarry UUP	10th
Kieran McCarthy All	11th

Iris Robinson

Lord Kilclooney

George Ennis

Jim Shannon

David McNarry

Kieran McCarthy

5th stage	6th stage	7th stage	8th stage	9th stage	10th stage	11th stage
Transfer of Kilclooney's surplus	Elimination of D McCarthy	Elimination of Orr	Elimination of Neill	Elimination of Kennedy & Wilson	Elimination of Little	Transfer of McNarry's surplus
(+4.68) 2920.69	(+69.7) 2990.39	(+56.74) 3047.13	(+24.97) 3072.1	(+878.57) 3950.67	(+143.04) 4093.71	(+66.34) 4160.05
(0) 5322	(0) 5322	(0) 5322	(0) 5322	(0) 5322	(0) 5322	(0) 5322
(+0.72) 1111.61	(+61) 1172.61	(+13.74) 1186.35	(+2.7) 1189.05	**(-1189.05)** 0	-	-
(-336) 5322	(0) 5322	(0) 5322	(0) 5322	(0) 5322	(0) 5322	(0) 5322
(+218.52) 2813.28	(+21.1) 2834.38	(+59.6) 2893.98	(+169.48) 3063.46	(+314.37) 3377.83	**(-3377.83)** 0	-
(+2.1) 351.61	**(-351.61)** 0	-	-	-	-	-
(+11.16) 2847.03	(+121.33) 2968.36	(+178.06) 3146.42	(+64.61) 3211.03	(+401.9) 3612.93	(+619.69) 4232.62	(+218.86) 4451.48
(+90.24) 3394.34	(+19.47) 3413.81	(+35.33) 3449.14	(+139.87) 3589.01	(+295.49) 3884.5	(+1726) 5610.5	**(-288.5)** 5322
(+3.36) 672.16	(+3.85) 676.01	(+21.09) 697.1	**(-607.1)** 0	-	-	-
(+1.02) 483.77	(+18.2) 501.97	**(-501.97)** 0	-	-	-	-
(0) 5322	(0) 5322	(0) 5322	(0) 5322	(0) 5322	(0) 5322	(0) 5322
(0) 5322	(0) 5322	(0) 5322	(0) 5322	(0) 5322	(0) 5322	(0) 5322
(+3.78) 1269.67	(+7.87) 1277.54	(+37.28) 1314.82	(+110.81) 1425.63	**(-1425.63)** 0	-	-
(0.42) 97.84	(29.09) 126.93	(100.13) 227.06	(184.66) 411.72	(724.35) 1136.07	(889.1) 2025.17	(3.3) 2028.47

Upper Bann

Total Valid Pole 43482 Quota 6212 Turnout 64.2

Party performance

Party	Seats	1st Pref Vote	%	(%1998)
DUP	2	12400	28.5	15.5
SF	1	9494	21.8	14.3
UUP	2	12786	29.4	28.9
SDLP	1	6818	15.7	23.7
Alliance	-	571	1.3	3.1
Others	-	1413	3.2	14.5

At a glance...

Although the DUP increased its vote-share significantly and gained a seat at the expense of an independent unionist (although bizarrely the losing MLA in question, Denis Watson actually ran as a DUP candidate this time) the main story was the robust performance of the UUP and under-fire leader David Trimble. In the event the UUP held on comfortably to its two seats with Trimble registering a strong personal poll-topping vote. In addition UUP voters returned his pro-Agreement running-mate Samuel Gardiner (as opposed to outgoing MLA George Savage) a further sign of local solidarity with Trimble. On the nationalist side Sinn Féin overtook the SDLP as the largest nationalist party although both held their seats fairly comfortably with new candidates Dolores Kelly (SDLP) and John O'Dowd (SF).

		1st stage	2nd stage	3rd stage	4th stage
		1st pref votes 43,482	Transfer of Trimble's surplus	Elimination of French	Elimination of Anderson
Sidney Anderson	Ind	581	(+26.24) 607.24	(+0.64) 607.88	**(-607.88)** 0
Kieran Corr	SDLP	3157	(+38.72) 3195.72	(+55.92) 3251.64	(+9) 3260.64
Thomas French	WP	247	(+13.12) 260.12	**(-260.12)** 0	-
Samuel Gardiner	UUP	2359	(+1060.48) 3419.48	(+16.24) 3435.72	(+44.72) 3480.44
David Jones	Ind	585	(+26.56) 611.56	(+1) 612.56	(+403.56) 1016.12
Dolores Kelly	SDLP	3661	(+50.56) 3711.56	(+74.52) 3786.08	(+1) 3787.08
Francis McQuaid	All	571	(+62.08) 633.08	(+37.24) 670.32	(+0.32) 670.64
Stephen Moutray	DUP	4697	(+30.08) 4727.08	(+7) 4734.08	(+18.64) 4752.72
John O'Dowd	SF	5524	(+6.4) 5530.4	(+27) 5557.4	(+2) 5559.4
*Dara O'Hagan	SF	3970	(+13.44) 3983.44	(+21) 4004.44	(0) 4004.44
*George Savage	UUP	1269	(+1423.36) 2692.36	(+4.92) 2697.28	(+29.2) 2726.48
David Simpson	DUP	5933	(+99.52) 6032.52	(+1.64) 6034.16	(+69.12) 6103.32
*David Trimble	UUP	9158	**(-2946)** 6212	(0) 6212	(0) 6212
*Denis Watson	DUP	1770	(+62.08) 1832.08	(+2) 1834.08	(+18.64) 1852.72
	Non-transferable		(33.36) 33.36	(11) 44.36	(11.64) 56

Candidates Elected	Count
David Trimble UUP	1st
David Simpson DUP	5th
Stephen Moutray DUP	6th
Samuel Gardiner UUP	9th
Dolores Kelly SDLP	11th
John O'Dowd SF	11th

David Trimble

David Simpson

Stephen Moutray

Samuel Gardiner

Dolores Kelly

John O'Dowd

5th stage	6th stage	7th stage	8th stage	9th stage	10th stage	11th stage
Elimination of McQuaid & Jones	Elimination of Watson	Transfer of Moutray's surplus	Transfer of Simpson's surplus	Elimination of Savage	Transfer of Gardiner's surplus	Elimination of Corr
-	-	-	-	-	-	-
(+151.32) 3411.96	(+3.32) 3415.28	(+2.61) 3417.89	(+1.64) 3419.53	(+42.66) 3462.99	(206.72) 3668.91	**(-3668.91)** 0
-	-	-	-	-	-	-
(+250.24) 3730.68	(+158.24) 3888.92	(+101.79) 3990.71	(+41.82) 4032.53	(+2840.06) 6872.59	**(-660.59)** 6212	(0) 6212
(-1016.12) 0	-	-	-	-	-	-
(+186.32) 3973.4	(+2.96) 3976.36	(+2.61) 3978.97	(+2.46) 3981.43	(+77.75) 4059.18	(+271.36) 4330.54	(+2648) 6978.54
(-670.64) 0	-	-	-	-	-	-
(+189.88) 4942.6	(+1516) 6458.6	**(-246.6)** 6212	(0) 6212	(0) 6212	(0) 6212	(0) 6212
(+19) 5578.4	(+2.32) 5580.72	(+0.87) 5581.59	(0) 5581.59	(+3.14) 5584.73	(+1.6)) 5586.33	(+326.27) 5912.6
(+21.64) 4026.08	(+1) 4027.08	(0) 4027.08	(0) 4027.08	(+1.96) 4029.04	(+1.92) 4030.96	(+270.16) 4301.12
(+265.12) 2991.6	(+250.24) 3241.84	(+132.24) 3374.08	(+45.1) 3419.18	**(-3419.18)** 0	-	-
(+200) 6303.32	(n/a) 6303.32	(n/a) 6303.32	**(-91.32)** 6212	(0) 6212	(0) 6212	(0) 6212
(0) 6212	(0) 6212	(0) 6212	(0) 6212	(0) 6212	(0) 6212	(0) 6212
(+260.44) 2113.16	**(-2113.16)** 0	-	-	-	-	-
(142.8) 198.8	(179.08) 377.88	(6.48) 384.36	(0.3) 384.66	(453.61) 838.27	(178.99) 1017.26	(424.48) 1441.74

West Tyrone

Total Valid Pole 41729 **Quota 5962** **Turnout 73.2**

Party performance

Party	Seats	1st Pref Vote	%	(%1998)
DUP	1	7286	17.5	17.4
SF	2	16111	38.6	34.1
UUP	1	5667	13.6	15.7
SDLP	1	6110	14.6	25.7
Alliance	-	164	0.4	2.2
Others	1	6391	15.3	4.8

At a glance...

Perhaps the single most surprising result in the entire election was the election at the top of the poll of Independent 'hospital' candidate Carrickmore GP Dr Kieran Deeny. His election at the expense of SDLP MLA Joe Byrne reflected the anger in West Tyrone at the proposed downgrading of Omagh Hospital. Aside from this upset Sinn Féin held its two seats very easily, and sitting MLAs Derek Hussey (UUP) and Eugene McMenamin (SDLP) held on to theirs. The DUP seat formerly held by veteran Oliver Gibson (who did not run for election) passed on to colleague Thomas Buchanan. Sinn Féin MP for the area Pat Doherty was elected on the first count just behind Dr Deeny.

		1st stage	2nd stage
		1st pref votes 41,729	Transfer of Deeny's surplus
Steven Alexander	All	164	(+7.47) 717.47
Thomas Buchanan	DUP	4739	(+4.8) 4743.8
*Joe Byrne	SDLP	2645	(+73.2) 2718.2
Kieran Deeny	Ind	6158	**(-196)** 5962
*Pat Doherty	SF	6019	(n/a) 6019
*Derek Hussey	UUP	3733	(+9.66) 3742.66
*Barry McElduff	SF	5642	(+47.27) 5689.25
Brian McMahon	SF	4450	(+6.99) 4456.99
*Eugene McMenamin	SDLP	3465	(+14.07) 3479.07
Derek Reaney	DUP	2547	(+2.04) 2549.04
Samuel Reid	PUP	233	(+0.57) 233.57
Bert Wilson	UUP	1934	(+6.12) 1940.12
	Non-transferable		(23.83) 23.83

Candidates Elected	Count
Kieran Deeny Ind	1st
Pat Doherty SF	1st
Thomas Buchanan DUP	5th
Derek Hussey UUP	6th
Barry McElduff SF	8th
Eugene McMenamin SDLP	8th

Kieran Deeny

Pat Doherty

Thomas Buchanan

Derek Hussey

Barry McElduff

Eugene McMenamin

3rd stage	4th stage	5th stage	6th stage	7th stage	8th stage
Elimination of Alexander, Reid & Wilson	Transfer of Doherty's surplus	Elimination of Reaney	Transfer of Buchanan's surplus	Transfer of Hussey's surplus	Elimination of Byrne
(-717.47) 0	-	-	-	-	-
(+233.84) 4977.64	(+0.03) 4977.67	(+2245) 7222.67	**(-1260.67)** 5962	(0) 5962	(0) 5962
(+56.72) 2774.92	(+2.95) 2777.87	(+13.12) 2790.99	(+11.25) 2802.24	(+189) 2991.24	**(-2991.24)** 0
(0) 5962	(0) 5962	(0) 5962	(0) 5962	(0) 5962	(0) 5962
(n/a) 6019	**(-57)** 5962	(0) 5962	(0) 5962	(0) 5962	(0) 5962
(+1734.67) 5477.33	(+0.14) 5477.47	(+425.47) 5902.94	(+1235.25) 7138.19	**(-1176.99)** 5962	(0) 5962
(+4.15) 5693.4	(+29.44) 5722.84	(+3.07) 5725.91	(0) 5725.91	(0) 5725.91	(+372) 6097.91
(+7.06) 4464.05	(+19.9) 4483.95	(+1.03) 4484.98	(0) 4484.98	(0) 4484.98	(+73.71) 4558.69
(+38.08) 3517.15	(+1) 3518.15	(+15.09) 3533.24	(+12) 3545.24	(+147.75) 3692.99	(+2282.69) 5975.68
(+225.48) 2774.52	(+0.03) 2774.55	**(-2774.55)** 0	-	-	-
(-233.57) 0	-	-	-	-	-
(-1940.12) 0	-	-	-	-	-
(45.16) 68.99	(3.51) 72.5	(71.77) 144.27	(2.17) 146.44	(839.44) 985.88	(262.84) 1248.72

Local Government Elections

Elections to the twenty-six district councils of Northern Ireland are also conducted by proportional representation using the STV system. Each local government area is divided into a number of wards, which are then grouped together for the purposes of STV into District Electoral Areas. Each District Electoral Area returns a number of councillors. Belfast has 9 District Electoral Areas, but most other councils have between three and five.

The number and boundaries of each local government area (the area controlled by a district council), and ward boundaries, are determined by the Local Government Boundaries Commissioner. The District Electoral Areas Commissioner determines the grouping of wards. Both these Commissioners are entirely independent and submit recommendations to the Government every 10-15 years.

Local government elections are held every four years in Northern Ireland, the last taking place on 7 June 2001, the same day as the general election.

Details of the election results are set out in Chapter Four, Local Government (page 240), but summary results are outlined here. Since Northern Ireland's local government structure was reformed in 1973 there have been 8 local government elections across the 25 Local Government Districts (LGDs). Results for the main parties have tended to correspond with overall performance in other elections although independents have featured more strongly.

Turnout for local elections is generally around 50-60 per cent, which is significantly lower than UK government elections, and also lower than the Assembly elections in 1998. This is probably reflective of the fact that the responsibilities of local authorities include areas such as waste disposal, cemeteries and parks, which although vital in everyday life, go largely unnoticed in comparison with mainstream political issues. Nevertheless the parties and candidates fiercely contest the elections, although issues raised at the hustings are matters over which they actually have little authority.

However, turnout for the 2001 local government election, at 66 per cent, was significantly higher than usual. This was largely due to the fact that Westminster elections were held on the same day. Summary results for all local government elections since 1985 are shown opposite.

2001 Local Government Election Turnout: 66%

	Votes	% votes	seats	% seats
UUP	181336	22.9	154	26.5
DUP	169477	21.4	131	20.1
SDLP	153424	19.4	117	22.5
SF	163269	20.7	108	18.5
All	40443	5.1	28	4.8
PUP	12661	1.6	4	0.7
Others	70247	8.9	40	6.9
Total	790857	100	582	100

1997 Local Government Election Turnout: 53.6%

	Votes	% votes	seats	% seats
UUP	176239	27.9	185	31.9
DUP	98686	15.6	91	15.6
SDLP	130417	20.6	120	20.6
SF	106938	16.9	74	12.7
All	41421	6.6	41	7
PUP	13744	2.2	6	1
UDP	6244	1	4	0.7
Others	58508	9.2	61	10.5
Total	632197	100	582	100

1993 Local Government Election Turnout: 56.6%

	Votes	% votes	seats	% seats
UUP	184608	29.4	197	33.8
DUP	108863	17.3	103	17.7
SDLP	138619	22	127	21.8
SF	78092	12.4	51	8.8
All	47649	7.6	44	7.6
Others	71275	11.3	60	10.3
Total	629106	100	582	100

1989 Local Government Election Turnout 56.1%

	Votes	% votes	seats	% seats
UUP	193028	31.3	194	34.9
DUP	109332	17.7	110	19.8
SDLP	129557	21	121	21.8
SF	69032	11.2	43	7.7
All	42659	6.9	38	6.8
WP	13078	2.1	4	0.7
Others	60523	9.8	46	8.3
Total	617209	100	566	100

1985 Local Government Election

Turnout: 60.1%

	Votes	% votes	seats	% seats
UUP	188497	29.5	190	33.6
DUP	155297	24.3	142	25.1
SDLP	113967	17.8	101	17.8
SF	75686	11.8	59	10.4
All	45394	7.1	34	6
WP	10276	1.6	4	0.7
Others	50505	7.9	36	6.4
Total	639622	100	566	100

European Parliament Elections

Members of the European Parliament

The European Parliament is composed of members from each of the fifteen member states in broad proportion to their population. The Parliament shares legislative and budgetary authority with the European Council and exercises democratic and political supervision over the other institutions.

The UK has an entitlement of 87 European Parliament seats out of a total of 626 members of the European Parliament. Of this, Northern Ireland returns 3 MEPs by an election held every 5 years. In this case Northern Ireland is a single constituency, and the three European MPs are elected by proportional representation, using the Single Transferable Vote (STV) system of voting. The current MEPs, returned in June 1999, are set out below. Full contact details for the three MEPs can be found in Chapter 9.

Name: **Ian Paisley MP MLA**
Party: **DUP**
European Political Group: Non-attached

Name **John Hume MP**
Party **SDLP**
European Political Group Party of European Socialists

Name **Jim Nicholson**
Party **UUP**
European Political Group European People's Party and European Democrats

The European Parliamentary Elections Act 1999, which substantially amended the European Parliamentary Elections Act 1978, governs the electoral provisions for election to the European parliament.

The Treaty of Nice has extended the limit on Members to 732 in consideration of the planned enlargement of the Union. A new distribution of seats in anticipation of the expected growth of the Assembly to as many as 27 member states applicable from the next European elections in 2004 has also been included under the terms of the Treaty. Existing member states will see their share of seats fall from 626 to 535 and in the UK the number of seats will fall from 87 to 72 under the new distribution, effective from the European parliament elections in 2009.

Members of the European parliament attach themselves to ideological political groupings rather than national groupings of which there are eight - see table top right. Nine MEPs, including Northern Ireland's Ian Paisley, have chosen not to align themselves with any of the above groups.

The European parliament elects a President and 14 Vice Presidents who serve two and a half year terms of office and constitute the Bureau of Parliament. The Bureau of Parliament and leaders of each of the political groups constitute the Conference of Presidents. There is further detailed information about the European Union in the context of Northern Ireland in Chapter 9.

European Parliament Political Groupings	Number of MEPs
European Peoples Party (Christian Democrats and European Democrats)	232
European Socialists	180
European Liberal, Democrat and Reform Party	51
Greens/European Free Alliance	48
Confederal Group of the European Left/Nordic Green Left	42
Union for a Europe of Nations	30
Group for a Europe of Democracies and Diversities	16
Technical Group of Independent Members	18

European Parliament Election Results for Northern Ireland

In the European election of June 1999, the Northern Ireland electorate returned the following candidates:

Ian Paisley	DUP	28.4 % of vote	Elected first count
John Hume	SDLP	28.1 % of vote	Elected first count
Jim Nicholson	UUP	17.6 % of vote	Elected third count

Turnout, although higher in 1999 than in the previous election in 1994, was 57.7%, significantly lower than both Westminster and Assembly elections in Northern Ireland. European elections in this area are generally fought hard by the DUP and SDLP who since 1979 have very successfully fielded their party leaders in the election.

The European election in June 1999 was significant in that Ian Paisley called on voters to treat it as a rerun of the Belfast Agreement referendum, in which he claimed that a majority of unionists had actually voted against the Agreement. Once again, Paisley topped the poll, just beating John Hume of the SDLP, although the DUP vote actually decreased from previous European elections. Paisley's vote was broadly in line with the proportion of 'no' votes in the Agreement referendum. The SDLP's vote had been increasing, but was checked by the strength of nationalists voting for Sinn Féin's Mitchel McLaughlin. Sinn Féin's share of the vote nearly doubled, but despite this it failed to displace the UUP as the third winner.

Party % of Total 1st Preference Vote for European Elections

Party	1979	1984	1989	1994	1999
UUP	11.9	21.5	22.2	23.8	17.6
SDLP	24.6	22.1	25.5	28.9	28.1
DUP	29.8	33.6	29.9	29.2	28.4
Sinn Féin	-	13.3	9.1	9.9	17.3
Alliance	6.8	5.0	5.2	4.1	2.1

The table on the previous page clearly demonstrates the dominance of Northern Ireland's (then) three largest political parties in European elections. The DUP candidate, Dr Ian Paisley, has consistently topped the poll since the first election in 1979, with John Hume's SDLP comfortably in second place.

The only battle is for third place, with Sinn Féin chasing the UUP in the most recent election. It should be noted however that turnout is traditionally relatively low in European elections.

Details of the earlier European Parliamentary Elections are set out in the tables below starting with the earliest and finishing with the most recent.

European Election Results 1979-1999

1979 European Election

Electorate 1,029,490 **Total Valid Vote** 572,239
Quota 143,060 **Turnout** 55.6%

Name	Party	1st Pref Votes	Total % Vote	Count Elected
Rev I Paisley	DUP	170,688	29.8	1st
J Hume	SDLP	140,622	24.6	3rd
J Taylor	UUP	68,185	11.9	6th
H West	UUP	56,984	10.0	
O Napier	All	39,026	6.8	
J Kilfedder	Ulster Unionist	38,198	6.7	
B McAliskey	Ind	33,969	5.9	
D Bleakley	Utd. Community	9,383	1.6	
P Devlin	ULP	6,122	1.1	
E Cummings	UPNI	3,712	0.6	
B Brennan	Rep C	3,258	0.6	
F Donnelly	Rep C	1,160	0.2	
J Murray	U. Lib	932	0.2	

ULP: United Labour Party; UPNI: Unionist Party of Northern Ireland; Rep C: Republican Clubs; U. Lib: Ulster Liberal Party

1984 European Election

Electorate 1,065,363 **Total Valid Vote** 685,317
Quota 171,330 **Turnout** 65.4%

Name	Party	1st Pref Votes	Total % Vote	Count Elected
Rev I Paisley	DUP	230,251	33.6	1st
J Hume	SDLP	151,399	22.1	4th
J Taylor	UUP	147,169	21.5	2nd
D Morrison	SF	91,476	13.3	
D Cook	All	34,046	5.0	
J Kilfedder	UPUP	20,092	2.9	
S Lynch	WP	8,712	1.3	
C McGuigan	Ecology	2,172	0.3	

1989 European Election

Electorate 1,106,852 **Total Valid Vote** 534,811
Quota 133,703 **Turnout** 48.3%

Name	Party	1st Pref Votes	Total % Vote	Count Elected
Rev I Paisley	DUP	160,110	29.9	1st
J Hume	SDLP	136,335	25.5	1st
J Nicholson	UUP	118,785	22.2	2nd
D Morrison	SF	48,914	9.1	
J Alderdice	All	27,905	5.2	
A Kennedy	Cons	25,789	4.8	
M Samuel	GP	6,569	1.2	
S Lynch	WP	5,590	1.0	
M Langhammer	LRG	3,540	0.7	
B Caul	Lab '87	1,274	0.2	

GP: Green Party; LRG: Labour Representation Group; Lab '87: Labour '87

1994 European Election

Electorate 1,162,344 **Total Valid Vote** 559,867
Quota 139,967 **Turnout** 49.4%

Name	Party	1st Pref Votes	Total % Vote	Count Elected
Rev I Paisley	DUP	163,246	29.2	1st
J Hume	SDLP	161,992	28.9	1st
J Nicholson	UUP	133,459	23.8	2nd
M Clark-Glass	All	23,157	4.1	
T Hartley	SF	21,273	3.8	
A McGuinness	SF	17,195	3.1	
F Molloy	SF	16,747	3.0	
Rev H Ross	UIM	7,858	1.4	
Myrtle Boal	Cons	5,583	1.0	
J Lowry	WP	2,543	0.5	
N Cusack	Lab	2,464	0.4	
J Anderson	NLP	1,418	0.2	
J Campion	Peace	1,088	0.2	
D Kerr	Ind Ulst.	571	0.1	
S Thompson	NLP	454	0.1	
M Kennedy	NLP	419	0.1	
R Mooney	Con. Ind	400	0.1	

Lab: Labour Party; Peace: Peace Coalition; Ind Ulst: Independent Ulster; Con. Ind: Constitutional Independent

1999 European Election

Electorate 1,190,160 **Total Valid Vote** 678,809
Quota 169,703 **Turnout** 57.7%

Name	Party	1st Pref Votes	Total % Vote	Count Elected
Rev I Paisley	DUP	192,762	28.4	1st
J Hume	SDLP	190,731	28.1	1st
J Nicholson	UUP	119,507	17.6	3rd
M McLaughlin	SF	117,643	17.3	
D Ervine	PUP	22,494	3.3	
R McCartney	UKUP	20,283	3.0	
S Neeson	All	14,391	2.1	
J Anderson	NLP	998	0.2	

Chapter

Guide to Government Departments and Agencies

Castle Buildings, Stormont

The Northern Ireland Office

The Northern Ireland Office (NIO) is a government department, headed by the Secretary of State who is a UK Cabinet Minister, The role of the Northern Ireland Office is to support the Secretary of State and to work closely with UK departments and the Northern Ireland Assembly, to advise, offer guidance and ensure effective consultation between the UK and the Northern Ireland devolved administration.

The Secretary of State

The Role of the Secretary of State under Direct Rule

Under Direct Rule, the Secretary of State, assisted by Direct Rule Ministers, assumes responsibility for all matters relating to the governance of Northern Ireland, including all those matters which would usually be devolved to the local administration.

Secretary of State: Paul Murphy (pictured)

Parliamentary Under Secretary: Ian Pearson

Parliamentary Under Secretary: Angela Smith

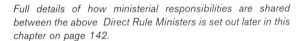

Minister of State: Jane Kennedy

Minister of State: John Spellar

Full details of how ministerial responsibilities are shared between the above Direct Rule Ministers is set out later in this chapter on page 142.

NIO Belfast Office
Castle Buildings
Belfast, BT4 3ST
Tel: 028 9052 0700

NIO London Office
11 Millbank, London, SW1P 4PN
Tel: 020 7210 3000
Web: www.nio.gov.uk

Northern Ireland Secretaries of State 1972-2004

Paul Murphy	Labour	2002 – present
Dr John Reid	Labour	2000 – 2002
Peter Mandelson	Labour	1999 – 2000
Mo Mowlam	Labour	1997 – 1999
Patrick Mayhew	Conservative	1992 – 1997
Peter Brooke	Conservative	1989 – 1992
Tom King	Conservative	1985 – 1989
Douglas Hurd	Conservative	1984 – 1985
James Prior	Conservative	1981 – 1984
Humphrey Atkins	Conservative	1979 – 1981
Roy Mason	Labour	1976 – 1979
Merlyn Rees	Labour	1974 – 1976
Francis Pym	Conservative	1973 – 1974
William Whitelaw	Conservative	1972 – 1973

The Role of the Secretary of State under Devolution

Under devolution the Secretary of State continues to represent Northern Ireland interests within the Cabinet. Provision for consultation, co-operation and exchanges of information in relation to the interests of the devolved administration in the policies of the UK government are provided for by the Memorandum of Understanding and associated system of concordats between the Northern Ireland Office and the Northern Ireland Executive Committee.

Excepted matters as set out in the Northern Ireland Act 1998 cover areas of national responsibility, which it is envisaged, will always remain the responsibility of the UK parliament. Reserved matters set out in the Act are also matters of national policy, although the Assembly may at some stage make provision for dealing with them, subject to the consent of the Secretary of State and parliamentary control. Reserved matters; which currently remain within the responsibility of the Secretary of State; include policing, security, prisions and criminal justice. It is envisaged within the terms of the Good Friday Agreement that these matters will be transferred to the administration in Northern Ireland. Transferred matters – which are all matters that are not excepted or reserved fall within the responsibility of the devolved administration, the Northern Ireland Assembly. For a full list of all those matters which are transferred, excepted and reserved, see Chapter 2, page 33.

A fundamental government power, the power to levy taxation remains a reserved matter. The Northern Ireland Finance Minister is therefore quite constrained in determining the size of the budget of the Northern Ireland government and more involved in the simpler matter of how the public expenditure budget is allocated amongst the various departments.

Under devolution the Secretary of State retains responsibility for a range of excepted and reserved matters including:

- The Criminal Justice System;
- Security and Public Order;
- Prisons;
- Policing;
- Elections.

In addition to representing Northern Ireland interests in all matters in Cabinet, in financial matters the Secretary of State has responsibility for advising the Chancellor, particularly where the Assembly bids for additional funding. There are other excepted and reserved matters, which continue to be the responsibility of the Lord Chancellor in Northern Ireland, such as judicial appointments and matters relating to the courts.

The Secretary of State has statutory responsibility for giving consent to Assembly bills where these impact on reserved matters and for forwarding all Assembly bills for Royal Assent. Should the Secretary of State consider a bill to be incompatible with international obligations, defence, national security or public order he may choose not to submit it for Royal Assent.

In relation to reserved or excepted matters, UK departments have certain responsibilities extending to Northern Ireland; to consider their impact on transferred matters, and also to ensure that UK policies will work effectively in the context of Northern Ireland.

In the conduct of its duties the Northern Ireland Office also operates a number of Executive Agencies across a range of activities. More information on these, together with their contact details are included later in the chapter.

Public Expenditure

The Northern Ireland Office currently employs approximately 4000 staff, over half of whom are prison warders or auxiliaries. It is one of the highest-spending of Northern Ireland's government departments (after health and education). See table below for NIO budgets up to 2005-06.

NIO Budgets 2003-04 to 2005-06

£ Million	2003-04	2004-05	2005-06
Resource Budget	1,088	1,128	1,162
Capital Budget	64	57	72
Total Departmental Expenditure Limit	1,114	1,144	1,190

Source: Northern Ireland Office

It had been hoped that NIO security related expenditure would drop markedly as a result of the peace process, and that the peace 'dividend' would be yielded in terms of extra resources being ploughed into areas of need.

The Administration of Justice in Northern Ireland

The Criminal Justice System

The administration of the Criminal Justice System remains a 'reserved matter' under the Good Friday Agreement so it is currently under the authority of the Northern Ireland Office, but may, at some time in the future become a devolved matter, to be controlled by the Northern Ireland Executive. In addition to the Northern Ireland Office, the main agencies and organisations which make up the Northern Ireland Criminal Justice System are:

- The Northern Ireland Court Service;
- The Department of the Director of Public Prosecutions;
- The Northern Ireland Prison Service;
- The Northern Ireland Probation Board;
- The Police Service of Northern Ireland.

The purpose of the criminal justice system is to support the administration of justice, to promote confidence in the criminal justice system and to contribute to the reduction of crime and the fear of crime.

Ministerial Responsibility for the Criminal Justice System

The Secretary of State for Northern Ireland has responsibility for policing and for criminal justice matters generally. He/she is also responsible for a number of agencies and other bodies: the Northern Ireland Prison Service, Forensic Science Northern Ireland and the Probation Board for Northern Ireland and also funds the Department of the Director of Public Prosecutions.

The Lord Chancellor is responsible for the Northern Ireland Court Service, and has overall responsibility for the effective management of the courts, the appointments of judges and magistrates, policy in respect of legal aid and providing funds to make legal aid payments.

The Attorney General superintends the Director of Public Prosecutions for Northern Ireland.

Review of the Criminal Justice System

The Good Friday Agreement committed the British government to establishing a wide-ranging review of the Northern Ireland criminal justice system. The Agreement indicated that the criminal justice system should be fair and impartial, responsive to the community and encouraging of its involvement, have the confidence of all parts of the community and deliver justice efficiently and effectively.

Terms of Reference

The Review was tasked with addressing the structure, management and resourcing of publicly funded elements of the criminal justice system and to bring forward proposals for future criminal justice arrangements covering issues such as:

- Appointments to the judiciary and magistracy;
- The organisation and supervision of the prosecution process;
- Improving the responsiveness and accountability of, and any lay participation in the criminal justice system;
- Law reform;
- Co-operation between the criminal justice agencies on both parts of the island;
- How criminal justice functions could be devolved to an Assembly, including the possibility of the establishment of a Department of Justice.

Members of the Criminal Justice Review

Chairman: Jim Daniell, Director of Criminal Justice at the NIO; Glenn Thompson, Director of the Northern Ireland Court Service; David Seymour, Legal Secretary to the Law Officer; Brian White, Head of Criminal Justice Policy Division at the NIO; Prof Joanna Shapland, Professor of Criminal Justice at Sheffield University and Director of the Institute for the Study of the Legal Profession; Prof John Jackson, Professor of Public Law and Head of the School of Law at Queen's University; Eugene Grant QC, a barrister in criminal practice in Northern Ireland; Dr Bill Lockhart, Director of Extern and Director of the Centre for Independent Research and Analysis of Crime; His Honour John Gower QC, a retired English circuit judge.

Progress of the Review
June 1998: The Review Group was formally established;

March 2000: publication of Review Group report, containing 294 recommendations. The government conducted a series of consultation processes with interested parties – the recommendations were broadly welcomed by all parts of the community;

November 2001: government publication of preliminary Implementation Plan and draft Justice (Northern Ireland) Bill;

July 2002: Justice (Northern Ireland) Act receives Royal Assent;

June 2003: government publication of updated Implementation Plan providing details of the 294 recommendations – with revised targets and timescales for those which are still in the process of being implemented. The updated Implementation Plan was agreed between the Secretary of State, the Lord Chancellor and the Attorney-General.

Key recommendations in the Criminal Justice Review
Among the 294 recommendations in the Review, significant initiatives, and progress made so far include:

- A new Public Prosecution Service: scheduled for completion by December 2006 – work already underway in restructuring and extending the remit of the DPP(NI);

- Chief Inspector of Criminal Justice: to be responsible for the inspection of all aspects of the criminal justice system, other than the courts, through the Criminal Justice Inspectorate. Kit Chivers appointed to this role in June 2003;

- Community Safety Strategy: strategy document, "Creating a Safer Northern Ireland" published in March 2003 with the aim of creating the conditions to promote an inclusive partnership-based approach in developing community safety initiatives;

- An independent Judicial Appointments Commission: There should be a Judicial Appointments Commission representative of the judiciary, the legal professions and the community, with responsibility for making recommendations on judicial appointments up to the level of High Court judge;

- An independent Northern Ireland Law Commission: A body with responsibilities to include review of both civil and criminal law, including practice and procedure, and making recommendations for change to the government;

- Creation of a Youth Justice Agency: created on 1 April 2003, assuming the range of functions and responsibilities which previously fell to the Juvenile Justice Board. Will focus on the prevention of offending and re-offending and will take forward the major changes recommended by the Review for juvenile justice;

- Youth Conferences: designed to address the needs of victims, to focus on offending behaviour and repairing damaged relationships;

- Victims: The Review recommended that the interests of victims of crime should feature in the codes of practice and plans of all criminal justice organisations that interface with them.

Also in June 2003, the Government appointed The Rt Hon the Lord Clyde as Justice Oversight Commissioner who will provide public assurance about the implementation of the changes in criminal justice arrangements set out in the updated Implementation Plan.

The Northern Ireland Court Service

21st Floor, Windsor House, 9-15 Bedford Street, Belfast BT2 7LT
Tel: 028 9032 8594 / Fax: 028 9032 8494
Web: www.courtsni.gov.uk
Director General: David Lavery

Laganside Court Complex

The Court Service was established by the Judicature (Northern Ireland) Act 1978 as "a unified and distinct Civil Service of the Crown" and is a separate civil service in its own right. The role of the Court Service is to support the administration of justice in Northern Ireland, within the following strategic aims:

- To facilitate the conduct of the business of the Supreme Court, county courts, magistrates courts and coroners, courts and certain tribunals;

- To give effect to judgements to which the Judgements Enforcement (Northern Ireland) Order 1981 applies;

- To discharge such other functions as are conferred on it.

The Northern Ireland Court Service is part of the Department of Constitutional Affairs and is accountable to Parliament at Westminster through the Secretary of State at the Department of Constitutional Affairs. Lord Falconer was appointed first Secretary of State for Constitutional Affairs in June 2003 as part of a continuing government drive to modernise the constitution and public service. The Court Service employs almost 700 staff across court venues throughout Northern Ireland and at its headquarters in Belfast.

Northern Ireland Court Service Contact Details

All offices can be contacted by phone from 9:00am to 5:00pm Monday to Friday, excluding public and bank holidays.

Information Centre
Tel: 028 9032 8594 / Fax: 028 9023 6361
Email: informationcentre@courtsni.gov.uk

Coroner's Office
Tel: 028 9072 8202 / Fax: 028 9072 4559
Email: coronersoffice@courtsni.gov.uk

Court Funds Office
Tel: 028 9032 8594 / Fax: 028 9023 6361
Email: courtfundsoffice@courtsni.gov.uk

Enforcement of Judgments Office
Tel: 028 9024 5081 / Fax: 028 9031 3520
Email: ejo@courtsni.gov.uk

Fixed Penalty Office
Tel: 028 9072 8233 / Fax: 028 9031 0227
Email: fixedpenaltyoffice@courtsni.gov.uk

Office of the Social Security Commissioners and Child Support Commissioners
Tel: 028 9033 2344 / Fax: 028 9031 3510
Email: socialsecuritycommissioners@courtsni.gov.uk

Royal Courts of Justice
Tel: 028 9032 8594 / Fax: 028 9031 3508

Court Offices in Northern Ireland (A-Z)

Antrim Court Office
Tel: 028 9446 2661 / Fax: 028 9446 3301
Email: antrimcourthouse@courtsni.gov.uk

Armagh Court Office
Tel: 028 3752 2816 / Fax: 028 3752 8194
Email: armaghcourthouse@courtsni.gov.uk

Ballymena Court Office
Tel: 028 2564 9416 / Fax: 028 2565 5371
Email: ballymenacourthouse@courtsni.gov.uk

Banbridge Court Office
Tel: 028 4062 3622 / Fax: 028 4062 3059
Email: banbridgecourthouse@courtsni.gov.uk

Bangor Court Office
Tel: 028 9147 2626 / Fax: 028 9127 2667
Email: bangorcourthouse@courtsni.gov.uk

Belfast County Court
Tel: 028 9032 6260 / Fax: 028 9031 3771
Email: belfastcountycourt@courtsni.gov.uk

Belfast Crown Court Jury Line
Tel: 028 9024 2099 (available from 5:00pm to 9:00am)

Belfast Crown Court
Tel: 028 9024 2099 / Fax: 028 9042 2078
Email: belfastcrowncourt@courtsni.gov.uk

Belfast Magistrates' Court
Tel: 028 9023 2721 / Fax: 028 9023 9472
Email: belfastmagistratescourt@courtsni.gov.uk

Coleraine Court Office
Tel: 028 7034 3437 / Fax: 028 7032 0156
Email: colerainecourthouse@courtsni.gov.uk

Craigavon Court Office
Tel: 028 3834 1324 / Fax: 028 3834 1243
Email: craigavoncourthouse@courtsni.gov.uk

Downpatrick Court Office
Tel: 028 4461 4621 / Fax: 028 4461 3969
Email: downpatrickcourthouse@courtsni.gov.uk

Dungannon Court Office
Tel: 028 8772 2992 / Fax: 028 8772 8169
Email: dungannoncourthouse@courtsni.gov.uk

Enniskillen Court Office
Tel: 028 6632 2356 / Fax: 028 6632 3636
Email: enniskillencourthouse@courtsni.gov.uk

Laganside Courts (Customer Service)
Tel: 028 9072 4570 / Fax: 028 9031 0227
Email: csmlaganside@courtsni.gov.uk

Larne Court Office
Tel: 028 2827 2927 / Fax: 028 2827 6414
Email: larnecourthouse@courtsni.gov.uk

Limavady Court Office
Tel: 028 7772 2688 / Fax: 028 7776 8794
Email: limavadycourthouse@courtsni.gov.uk

Lisburn Court Office
Tel: 028 9267 5336 / Fax: 028 9260 4107
Email: lisburncourthouse@courtsni.gov.uk

Londonderry Court Office
Tel: 028 7136 3448 / Fax: 028 7137 2059
Email: londonderrycourthouse@courtsni.gov.uk

Magherafelt Court Office
Tel: 028 7963 2121 / Fax: 028 7966 8794
Email: magherafeltcourthouse@courtsni.gov.uk

Newry Court Office
Tel: 028 3025 2040 / Fax: 028 3026 9830
Email: newrycourthouse@courtsni.gov.uk

Newtownards Court Office
Tel: 028 9181 4343 / Fax: 028 9181 8024
Email: newtownardscourthouse@courtsni.gov.uk

Omagh Court Office
Tel: 028 8224 2056 / Fax: 028 8225 1198
Email: omaghcourthouse@courtsni.gov.uk

Royal Courts of Justice
Tel: 028 9023 5111 / Fax: 028 9031 3508
Email: adminoffice@courtsni.gov.uk

Strabane Court Office
Tel: 028 7138 2544 / Fax: 028 7138 8209
Email: strabanecourthouse@courtsni.gov.uk

The Work of the Different Types of Court

The County Court

Cases dealt with by the County Court

The County Court deals with civil cases which are dealt with by a judge or district judge. A case can be started in any county court but it may be transferred to the defendant's local court. If the case is defended and the claim is for a fixed amount of money, the case will be transferred automatically by the court to the defendant's local court (if the defendant is an individual not a company). In other cases the defendant can request its transfer. All claims arising from regulated credit agreements must be started in the County Court, whatever their value.

Examples of cases dealt with by the County Court

County Courts can deal with a wide range of cases, but the most common ones are:

- landlord and tenant disputes, eg possession (eviction), rent arrears, repairs;
- consumer disputes, eg faulty goods or services;
- personal injury claims (injuries caused by negligence), eg traffic accidents, falling into holes in the pavement, accidents at work;
- undefended divorce cases, but only in some county courts;
- some domestic violence cases, but these may also be heard in the magistrates court;
- race and sex discrimination cases;
- debt problems, eg, a creditor seeking payment;
- employment problems, eg, wages or salary owing or pay in lieu of notice.

Small Claims Cases

In general, a Small Claim is one where the value of the claim is not more than £2,000.

The Magistrates' Court

Magistrates' Courts deal with criminal and some civil cases, and cases are dealt with by paid magistrates. Magistrates' Courts can deal with offences that occur in a number of areas. (For example, where several burglaries have been committed across a number of areas).

Criminal Cases in the Magistrates' Court

Magistrates' Courts deal with criminal offences where the defendant is not entitled to trial by jury. These are known as summary offences and involve a maximum penalty of six months imprisonment and/or a fine of up to £2,000.

Magistrates also deal with offences where the defendant can choose trial by jury but decides to have their case heard in the Magistrates' Court. If the defendant chooses trial by jury, the case will be passed on to the Crown Court.

Civil Cases in the Magistrates' Court

Magistrates can deal with a limited number of civil cases as follows:-

- some civil debts, eg, arrears of income tax, national insurance contributions, VAT arrears, rates;
- licences, eg, granting, renewing or taking away licences for pubs and clubs;
- some matrimonial problems, eg, maintenance and removing a spouse from the matrimonial home;
- welfare of children, eg, local authority care or supervision orders, adoption proceedings and residence orders.

The Youth Court

The Youth Court deals with young people who have committed criminal offences, and who are aged between 10 and 17. The Youth Court is part of the magistrates court and up to three specially-trained magistrates hear the case. If a young person is charged with a very serious offence, which in the case of an adult is punishable with 14 years imprisonment or more, the Youth Court can commit them for trial at the Crown Court.

The Crown Court

The Crown Court deals with the following types of cases:-

- more serious criminal offences which will be tried by judge and jury;
- appeals from the Magistrates' Court which are dealt with by a judge and at least two magistrates;
- convictions in the Magistrates' Court that are referred to the Crown Court for sentencing.

Imprisonment and fines in the Crown Court are more severe than in the Magistrates' Court.

The High Court

The High Court deals with civil cases, hears appeals in criminal cases, and also has the power to review the actions of individuals or organisations to make sure they have acted legally and justly. The High Court has three divisions, as follows:

The Family Division

The Family Division deals with complex defended divorce cases, wardship, adoption, domestic violence etc. It also deals with appeals from magistrates and county courts in matrimonial cases and deals with the affairs of people who are mentally ill and also simple probate matters.

Craigavon Court House

The Queens Bench Division

The Queens Bench Division deals with large and/or complex claims for compensation. It also deals with a limited number of appeals from magistrates' courts or Crown Courts, as well as reviewing the actions of organisations to see whether they have acted legally, and with libel and slander actions.

The Chancery Division

The Chancery Division deals with trusts, contested wills, winding up companies, bankruptcy, mortgages, charities, contested revenue (usually income tax) cases etc.

Non-family Claims

The High Court can be used for a case if the value of the claim is over £15,000. In some circumstances, a case over £15,000 can be remitted to the county court and similarly a case under the value of £15,000 may be transferred from the High Court to the county court.

The Court of Appeal

The Court of Appeal deals with civil and criminal appeals in England and Wales. In Northern Ireland, there can be a rehearing of a county court case in the High Court and an appeal from there if the case is stated to the Court of Appeal.

The House of Lords

The House of Lords deals mainly with appeals from the Court of Appeal, or direct from the High Court, where the case involves a point of law or general public importance. Appeals are mostly about civil cases although the Lords do deal with some criminal appeals.

The Court of First Instance

The Court of First Instance is based in Luxembourg. A case can be taken to this court if European Community law has not been implemented properly by a national government or if there is confusion over its interpretation or if it has been ignored. A case which is lost at the Court of First Instance may be able to be appealed against at the European Court of Justice.

The European Court of Justice

The European Court of Justice advises on interpretation of European Community law and takes action against infringements. It examines the validity of acts of the European Community institutions and clarifies European Community law by making preliminary rulings. It also hears appeals against decisions made by the Court of First Instance.

The European Court of Human Rights

The European Court of Human Rights deals with cases in which a person thinks their human rights have been contravened and there is no legal remedy within the national legal system.

The Lord Chancellor holds responsibility for a wide range of functions affecting the administration of justice in Northern Ireland and has the leading role in appointments to judicial, quasi-judicial offices and Queen's Counsel. He holds ministerial responsibility for legal aid, matters affecting the provision of legal services to the public, and determining the statutory framework for the structure, jurisdiction and operation of the courts in Northern Ireland. The role of the Court Service is to support the Lord Chancellor in the discharge of these responsibilities.

Organisational Structure of the Court Service

The Court Service is led by a Director General, Mr David Lavery, who is Head of Department, Principal Accounting Officer and Accountant General of the Supreme Court of Judicature of Northern Ireland, reporting directly to the Lord Chancellor and supported by three directors, each with responsibility for a division within the Court Service. The three divisions are:

- Operations;
- Policy and Legislation;
- Corporate Services.

Alan Hunter has been appointed as director with responsibility for Legal Aid.

Operations Division

The Operations Division led by Mr George Keatley is responsible for:

- Delivering operational functions associated with the administration of the courts ranging from issuing originating processes to the implementation of court decisions;
- Administering the Fixed Penalty Office;
- Enforcing court judgements under the Judgements Enforcement (Northern Ireland) Order 1981;
- Providing administrative support to the Social Security and Child Support Commissioners, the Pensions Appeals Tribunals and the Tribunal established under section 91 of the Northern Ireland Act 1998;
- Meeting the standards laid down in the Courts Charter for Northern Ireland.

Policy and Legislation Division

The Policy and Legislation Division led by Mrs Laurene McAlpine undertakes central government functions in support of the Lord Chancellor's ministerial responsibilities including:

- Determining the policy and legislative framework within which the courts will operate;
- Carrying out on behalf of the Lord Chancellor the functions of the Central Authority under the European and Hague Conventions on Child Abduction;
- Providing legal advice to the Court Service and HM Coroners on the complete range of executive functions;
- Developing legal aid policy;
- Monitoring expenditure on legal aid and its associated administration;
- Providing the Secretariat to Court Rules Committees, the Judicial Studies Board for Northern Ireland, the Lay Panel Training Committee and the Lord Chancellor's Legal Advisory Committee.

The Court Structure in Northern Ireland (and the UK)

The House of Lords
Final court of Appeal in the UK
Hears appeals on points of law in cases of major importance

The Court of Appeal
Hears appeals on points of law in criminal and civil cases from all courts

The High Court
Hears complex or important civil cases in three divisions and also appeals from County Courts

Queen's Bench Division | **Chancery Division** | **Family Division**

County Courts including Family Care Centres (7 Divisions)
Hear a wide range of civil actions from Magistrates' Courts

Small Claims Courts
Hear consumer claims and minor civil cases

The Crown Court
Hears all serious criminal cases

Magistrates' Courts (including Juvenvile Courts and Family Proceedings Courts)
(21 Petty Sessions Districts)
Conduct preliminary hearings in more serious criminal cases, cases involving juveniles and some civil and domestic cases, including family proceedings

Coroners' Courts
Investigates the circumstances of sudden, violent or unnatural deaths

The Enforcement of Judgements Office
Enforces money and other judgements

Corporate Services Division

Mr Frank Duffy leads the Corporate Services Division. The division has responsibility for:

- Providing a range of services in support of other divisions and the judiciary, including personnel and training, resource management, procurement, including capital projects and information technology;
- Supporting judicial appointments, including advisory committees;
- Providing an internal audit function;
- Managing funds lodged in court on behalf of adults and minors.

A new multi court complex has been completed on Belfast's Laganside. The complex comprises Crown, county and magistrates courts and their administration. A new headquarters for the Bar Council and the Department of the Director of Public Prosecutions has recently been completed on a site adjacent to the Royal Courts of Justice in Belfast.

Policy and Legislative Programme

The Court Service aims to provide policy advice and deliver an agreed programme of legislation including court rules involving the formulation of non executive policy, including civil and criminal policy, advice on such policy to ministers and on the general administration of justice. The Court Service also advises the Chancellor on judicial and public appointments and the operation of recruitment procedures.

The Department of the Director of Public Prosecutions

The aim of the Department is to provide the people of Northern Ireland with an independent, fair and effective prosecution service. The Department of the Director of Public Prosecutions in Northern Ireland was established by the Prosecution of Offences (Northern Ireland) Order 1972. The current Director of Public Prosecutions in Northern Ireland is Sir Alasdair Fraser CB QC.

Functions of the DPP

The main function of the Director is to consider facts or information contained in police investigation files and reach decisions as to a prosecution or no prosecution. Where the decision is for prosecution:

- Prosecute in the Crown Court – this generally occurs for the most serious offences (eg murder, serious assaults); or
- Prosecute certain offences in the Magistrates' Courts – generally these prosecutions are for the more serious offences (eg criminal damage, minor sexual assaults) which can be heard in the Magistrates' Courts including where the prosecution is of a police officer or a member of the security forces.

The Director also considers, with a view to prosecution, investigation files from government departments. Other duties include making representations in bail applications and in cases which go on appeal to the County Court, the Court of Criminal Appeal and the House of Lords.

Relationship with the Attorney General and Others

The Director and Deputy Director of Public Prosecutions are appointed by the Attorney General for Northern Ireland, currently The Right Honourable The Lord Goldsmith QC. The Director and his staff are wholly independent of government and the police.

Attorney General's Office

Legal Secretariat to Law Officers
Attorney General's Chambers
9 Buckingham Gate, London, SWI1 6JP
Tel: 0207 271 2412
Web: www.lslo.gov.uk

The Northern Ireland Judiciary

The role of the Court Service is to ensure the efficient and effective disposal of court business and support the Judiciary. The relationship between the Judiciary and the Courts Service is crucial in the administration of the courts and tribunals. However, whilst close co-operation is required it is imperative that the independence of the judiciary is maintained.

As of 31 March 2003 the full time judicial complement was 62 with 81 deputy or part time. The full time tribunal complement was 10 full time and 274 part time tribunal appointments.

Full and Part Time Judiciary

Supreme Court	
Lord Chief Justice	1
Lord Justices of Appeal	3
High Court Judges	8
Masters of the Supreme Court	7
Principal Secretary and Legal Secretary to the Lord Chief Justice	1
Official Solicitor	1
County Courts	
County Court Judges	15
District Judges	4
Magistrates Courts	
Resident Magistrates	19
Chief Social Security & Child Support Commissioner	1
Social Security and Child Support Commissioner	1
Coroner	1

Lord Chief Justice for Northern Ireland

Royal Courts of Justice
Chichester Street, Belfast, BT1 3JF
Tel: 028 9023 5111
Web: www.courtsni.gov.uk

The Lord Chief Justice for Northern Ireland is currently The Honourable Sir Brian Kerr. Sir Brian took up his position in January 2004 following the elevation of his predecessor Sir Robert Carswell to the House of Lords as a Law Lord.

Appointments to the Judiciary

Recommendations to the Lord Chancellor are made by Advisory Committees on the appointment of Justices of the Peace, Lay Panel Members and General Commissioners of Income Tax. The manager of the Judicial Appointments Branch performs the role of Assistant Secretary of Commissions (Northern Ireland) to each Committee. This system is currently being revised under the Review of the Criminal Justice System, which has recommended the establishment of a Judicial Appointments Commission to recommend on judicial appointments up to the level of High Court Judge.

Courthouse, Armagh

The Legal Profession in Northern Ireland

The legal profession in Northern Ireland is composed of two separate and complementary branches:

- Barristers;
- Solicitors.

Differences in the services each provide are reflected by the differences in their training and organisation. Solicitors provide the first point of contact for those seeking legal advice and in many cases such as conveyancing, making wills or matrimonial matters may be the only contact necessary. However a barrister may be required to advise or represent a client in court. Contact in the first instance is usually through the client's solicitor rather than directly with the client, this is thought to aid the maintenance of impartiality.

Should a case proceed, the solicitor may undertake the preparatory work although barristers with their experience of litigation and knowledge of the procedures of the court and judiciary will focus on the presentation of the matter. The client and solicitor meet as and if required by the nature of the case, which is determined by the likelihood of the case succeeding.

In April 2003 there were 555 barristers in independent practice in Northern Ireland. There are 66 Queen's Counsel, barristers who have earned a high reputation and are appointed by the Queen on the recommendation of the Lord Chancellor as senior advocates and advisers. The title does not imply an association with the State. Barristers who are not Queen's Counsel are called Junior Counsel. This term is misleading since many members of the Junior Bar are experienced barristers with considerable expertise.

The Executive Council and the Bar Council
The General Council of the Bar of Northern Ireland
PO Box 414
Royal Courts of Justice
Chichester Street, Belfast, BT1 3JP
Tel: 028 9056 2349 / Fax: 028 9056 2350
Web: www.barlibrary.com

The Executive Council is involved with Barrister education; fees of students; calling counsel to the Bar (although the call to the Bar is performed by the Lord Chief Justice on the invitation of the Benchers); administration of the Bar Library, (to which all practising members of the Bar belong) and liaising with corresponding bodies in other countries.

The Bar Council is responsible for the maintenance of the standards, honour and independence of the Bar and, through its Professional Conduct Committee, receives and investigates complaints against members of the Bar as professionals.

The Bar Library is the base of all practising barristers in Northern Ireland, providing office and other support and facilities as well as library and information services. The new Bar Library building opened in April 2003.

The Bar Library
91 Chichester Street
Belfast, BT1 3JQ

The Law Society
The Law Society of Northern Ireland
Law Society House
98 Victoria Street
Belfast, BT1 3JZ
Tel: 028 9023 1614 / Fax: 028 9023 2606
Web: www.lawsoc-ni.org

The Law Society is set up by Royal charter, and its powers and duties are to regulate the solicitor's profession in Northern Ireland. It operates through a Council of thirty members, all practicing solicitors who serve on a voluntary basis. Any solicitor whose name is on the Roll of Solicitors in Northern Ireland and who has not been suspended from practising as a solicitor may become a member of the Society on payment of the annual subscription. There are approximately 1850 solicitors currently practising in Northern Ireland.

Legal Aid Administration
The Law Society of Northern Ireland holds statutory responsibility for the civil legal aid scheme and administers criminal legal aid on behalf of the Lord Chancellor. The Legal Aid department is managed by the Legal Aid Committee of the Law Society composed of solicitors and barristers, one of whom is appointed by the Lord Chancellor. Financial memoranda and management statements govern relationships between the Law Society, its Legal Aid committee and department and the Court Service. The Court Service facilitates the administration of legal aid by the Legal Aid department.

The Compensation Agency

Royston House, 34 Upper Queen Street
Belfast, BT1 6FX
Tel: 028 9024 9944
Web: www.compensationni.gov.uk
Chief Executive: Anne McCleary

The Compensation Agency was established in April 1992 to support the victims of violent crime by providing compensation to those who sustain loss as a result of actions taken under emergency provisions legislation. This work is carried out on behalf of the Secretary of State for Northern Ireland.

Elections Administration

The Secretary of State for Northern Ireland also retains overall responsibility for elections in Northern Ireland although day to day-executive responsibility rests with the Electoral Office headed up by the Chief Electoral Officer. The Secretary of State appoints the Chief Electoral Officer.

The Electoral Office Headquarters
15 Church Street
Belfast, BT1 1ER
Tel: 028 9023 9431
Chief Electoral Officer: Denis Stanley

(More detailed information on elections including recent results is included in Chapter 2.)

Security in Northern Ireland

The government's security policy is designed to secure lasting peace in Northern Ireland based on the Good Friday Agreement. The government has expressed its desire to achieve a return to normal security and policing arrangements, with the army assuming a peacetime role within Northern Ireland, the removal of military bases and barriers, a reduction in troop levels and a cessation of emergency legislation.

It remains a priority for the government to maintain security policies for Northern Ireland, supported by a sufficient capability for counter-terrorism. Although progress towards 'normalisation' has been made, the estimated threat of further terrorist attack and concern for public safety determine the rate at which long-term objectives can be achieved.

In September 2000 the army published its long-term vision for its presence in Northern Ireland, which envisaged a "peacetime garrison of around 8,000 full time soldiers based in no more than 20 sites".

Since the reinstatement of the IRA ceasefire on 20 July 1997, a wide range of security measures have been relaxed and reduced:

- Currently under 13,000 troops in Northern Ireland, the lowest level since 1970. Troop levels have decreased year on year since 1992, when there were approximately 18,200;
- Closure, demolition or vacation by the Army of 50 of the 105 military bases and installations occupied in 1997;
- Demolition of almost half of the surveillance sites which were in existence at the time of the ceasefire;
- Castlereagh, Strand Road and Gough Holding Centres now closed;
- 102 cross-border roads re-opened;
- Closure of Ebrington Army Base in December 2003.

The current role of the army in Northern Ireland is to support the PSNI in countering the threat of terrorism and assist in the government's objective of restoring normality to the province.

Northern Ireland's politicians are deeply divided on security with most unionists concerned at the relaxation of security and the reduction in capability, while nationalists want to see more closed bases, fewer troops and a much faster rate of 'normalisation' particularly in border areas.

Prisons Administration in Northern Ireland

Northern Ireland Prison Service
Dundonald House
Upper Newtownards Road
Belfast, BT4 3SU
Tel: 028 9052 2922 / Fax: 028 9052 5160
Email: info@niprisonservice.gov.uk
Web: www.niprisonservice.gov.uk
Director General: Peter Russell

The Northern Ireland Prison Service is an executive agency of the Northern Ireland Office. It is responsible for providing prison services in Northern Ireland and is a major component of the wider criminal justice system. The Secretary of State is the minister responsible for the Prison Service and is accountable to parliament.

The Prison Service currently has three operational establishments and a staff training facility, the Prison Service College.

Hydebank Wood Young Offenders Centre
Hospital Road
Belfast, BT8 8NA
Tel: 028 9025 3666

Maghaberry Prison
Old Road
Ballinderry Upper
Lisburn, BT28 2PT
Tel: 028 9261 1888

Magilligan Prison
Point Road
Limavady, BT49 0LR
Tel: 028 7776 3311

Prison Service College
Woburn House
Millisle, BT22 2HS
Tel: 028 9186 3000

The Prison Population
(December 2003)

	Sentenced	Awaiting Trial	Total
Maghaberry	338	315	653
Magilligan	345	0	345
Hydebank Wood YOC	92	78	170
Total	775	393	1168

The Maghaberry total includes 21 female prisoners (14 sentenced and 7 remand) and 4 male immigration detainees. The bulk of the prison population in Northern Ireland is now made up of people convicted of non-terrorist related offences.

Life Sentence Prisoners

As of 1st February 2002 there were 85 life sentence prisoners including 3 prisoners detained at the Secretary of State's pleasure. Since 1981 special arrangements have been in place for the release on licence of life sentence prisoners and under these arrangements 457 prisoners have been released to date.

The power to release a life sentence prisoner rests with the Secretary of State, after consultation with the Lord Chief Justice of Northern Ireland and the trial judge.

The non-statutory Life Sentence Review Board formally advises the Secretary of State on the release of such prisoners. The average sentence served by a life sentence prisoner is 15 years.

Accelerated Release Prisoners
Under the terms of the Good Friday Agreement, the Northern Ireland (Sentences) Act was introduced in July 1998. Prisoners convicted of such offences and attracting a sentence of five years or more became eligible to apply for early release from the Independent Sentence Review Commission. The first releases under this scheme came on 11th September 1998.

The releases to date are as follows:

Loyalist	194
Republican	241
Non-Aligned	12
Total	447

Staffing Statistics (July 2003)
The Northern Ireland Prison Service employs around 2100 staff. The Prisoner Escort Group – responsible for producing people to and returning them from courts – has staff based at courtrooms throughout Northern Ireland.

Prision Service Staff by Location and Category (July 2003)

Location	Civilian Staff	Prison Staff-Uniformed	Prision Staff Civilian	Total
PSHQ*	204.5	45	9.5	259
Maghaberry	67.5	845.5	31	944
Magilligan	44	393	22	459
Hydebank Wood YOC	31.5	243	8	282.5
Prisoner Escort Group	5	90	1	96
Total	352.5	1616.5	71.5	2040.5

*total for PSHQ includes those employed at the Prison Service College

Civilian staff includes administrative officers as well as psychologists, teachers, special advisors and health and safety officer.

Prison staff (uniform) includes all governor, principal officer, senior officer, officer and auxiliary officer grades including specialists eg dog handlers, hospital officers and physical education instructors. Prison staff (civilian) includes searchers, cooks, drivers, cleaners.

Prison Service Running Costs
The financial resources available to the Prison Service for the next two years are given in the table below and were determined as part of the Spending Review 2000.

Prision Service Running Costs 2002/03 -2003/04

Allocation Category	2002-03 £m	2003-04 £m
Running Costs	90.2	88.2
Non-Running Costs	8.3	8.3
Capital Costs	14.2	12.2
Total	112.7	108.7

The Probation Board for Northern Ireland

80-90 North Street, Belfast, BT1 1LD
Tel: 028 9026 2400 / Fax: 028 9026 2470
Web: www.pbni.org.uk / Email: info@pbni.org.uk
Chairman: Brian Rowntree
Chief Executive: Noel Rooney

Members of The Probation Board for Northern Ireland (from 1 December 2003):
Julian Crozier, Bernadette Grant, Robert Hanna, Janine Hillen Pat Killen, Maura McCann, Francesca Reid, Geraldine Rice, Brian Stuart, Eileen Bell, Mary Clarke-Glass, Denis Moloney, Aidan Sherrard, Mairead Gilheaney
Board Secretary: Peter Moss

The Probation Board is a non-departmental body with the aim of reducing crime and the harm it does. Its mission is to integrate offenders successfully into the community by reducing re-offending.

The Probation Board has a number of functions:

- To carry out assessments and provide reports to courts which are designed to make a contribution to the decisions which Magistrates and Judges make in relation to sentencing;
- To have staff who work in prisons providing a range of social welfare services.

The Probation Board may fund organisations that provide hostels for offenders and run projects in the community, which address the offending behaviour of offenders who are under Probation Board supervision. The Secretary of State for Northern Ireland has responsibility for appointments to the Board.

Victims

Victims Liaison Unit

The Victims Liaison Unit was established in the Northern Ireland Office as a response to the report by Sir Kenneth Bloomfield "We Will Remember Them". Following devolution many of the issues facing victims became the responsibility of the new administration. In response a Victims Unit was set up in the Office of the First Minister and Deputy First Minister. However, it was also necessary to retain the Victims Liaison Unit within the NIO as many victims' issues fell within the reserved and excepted matters, which had not been devolved. The minister with responsibility for victims is Angela Smith.

Responsibilities of the NIO's Victims Liaison Unit

- Support for Ministers in the NIO;
- Provision of core funding to victim's support groups;
- Management and provision of grant aid to the Northern Ireland Memorial Fund;
- Ensuring victims' issues are dealt with in the reserved and excepted fields in Northern Ireland particularly in areas such as compensation, criminal justice, security and dealing with the "disappeared";
- Articulating the case for victims in the reserved and excepted fields.

Responsibilities of the OFMDFM's Victims Unit

- Support for Ministers in the devolved administration;
- Development of a suitable programme under PEACE II to address victims' needs;
- Development of a separate programme of activities designed to meet the strategic needs of victims;
- Ensuring the needs of victims are addressed in the devolved administration including management of an interdepartmental working group on victims' issues;
- Ensuring that the commitments on victims contained in the Programme for Government are met;
- Articulating the case for victims within the devolved assembly.

Victim Support Centre, Lurgan

Both organisations have responsibility for:

- Improving the capacity and professionalism of victims' organisations and introducing core values and standards for groups to adhere to;
- Implementing the findings of the Bloomfield report; Building networks for victims and victims' organisations to share experience and best practice.

To date the government has committed over £18.25 million to support measures for victims of the Troubles, which include the establishment of a regional Family Trauma Centre, an Educational Bursary Scheme, the establishment of the Northern Ireland Memorial Fund, a review of Criminal Injuries Compensation and funding for groups working with victims.

Victim Support Northern Ireland

Regional Office

Annsgate House
70-74 Ann Street
Belfast, BT1 4EH
Tel: 028 9024 4039
Fax: 028 9031 3839
Email: info@victimsupportni.org.uk

Northern Ireland Branches

Ballymena
25 Thomas Street
Tel: 028 2563 0784

Belfast North & West
Annsgate House, 70-74 Ann Street
Tel: 028 9024 3133

Londonderry
7 Bayview Terrace
Tel: 028 7137 0086

Lisburn
5 Railway Street
Tel: 028 9267 5642

Lurgan
12 Windsor Avenue
Tel: 028 3834 7340

Newry
3-5 Railway Street
Tel: 028 3025 1321

Omagh
22 Campsie Road
Tel: 028 9023 2523

Court Witness Service
Laganside
Belfast
Tel: 028 9023 2523

Policing in Northern Ireland

Policing and security have been a source of great political and social division in Northern Ireland. With over 3,000 civilians, including hundreds of security force personnel and members of government killed throughout the thirty years of the "Troubles", policing and the role of the Police Service in Northern Ireland remains an emotive issue within all sections of the community. Recent reforms under Patten, the launch of the PSNI and controversial unresolved matters such as alleged security force collusion in paramilitary crimes have continued to maintain the high priority of policing on the general political agenda.

The Review of Policing in Northern Ireland

The Good Friday Agreement proposed the establishment of an Independent Commission on Policing for Northern Ireland. The Rt Hon Chris Patten was appointed to chair this Commission and it published its plans for the future of policing (known as the 'Patten Report') in September 1999. The process of implementation of the Patten recommendations is already well underway with progress to date including:

- *31 May 2000:* Oversight Commissioner, Tom Constantine appointed to oversee the change process;
- *6 November 2000:* Police (Northern Ireland) Act 2000;
- *1 April 2001:* establishment of police district command units based on council areas;
- *17 August 2001:* revised Implementation Plan published;
- *29 September 2001* – appointment of a new Policing Board (to replace the Police Authority);
- *4 November 2001:* first new recruits enter training;
- *4 November 2001:* Policing Board assumes its powers;
- *4 November 2001:* RUC changes name to Police Service of Northern Ireland (PSNI);
- *14 November 2001:* names of trustees on RUC George Cross Foundation and Northern Ireland Police Fund announced;
- *5 April 2002:* new uniform and emblem comes into service; first recruits under 50:50 graduate; new flag-flying rules introduced;
- *29 April 2002:* intergovernmental agreement signed between the UK and Republic of Ireland on police co-operation;
- *4 March 2003:* public appointments to DPPs;
- *8 April 2003:* Police (Northern Ireland) Act 2003;
- *December 2003:* The new oversight commissioner Al Hutchison succeeds Tom Constantine

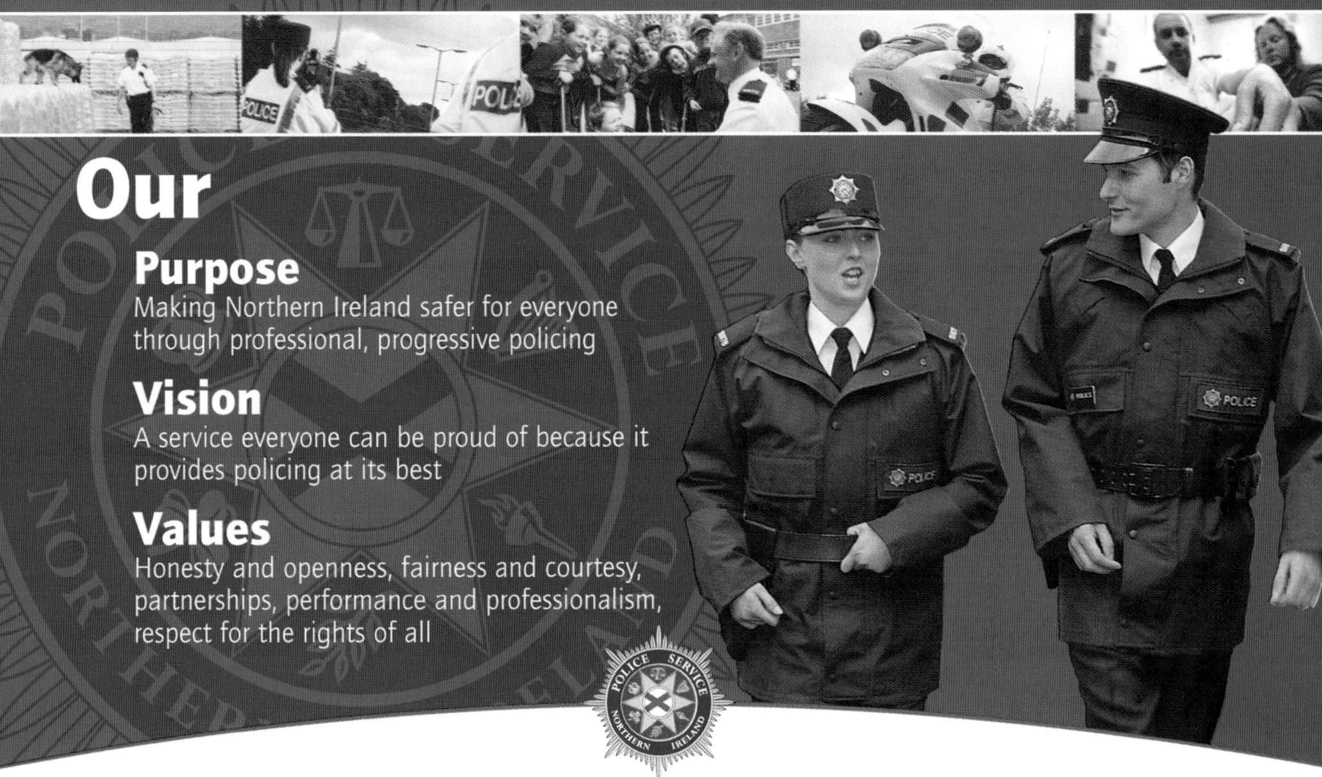

Our
Purpose
Making Northern Ireland safer for everyone through professional, progressive policing
Vision
A service everyone can be proud of because it provides policing at its best
Values
Honesty and openness, fairness and courtesy, partnerships, performance and professionalism, respect for the rights of all
POLICE SERVICE NORTHERN IRELAND
Making Northern Ireland Safer For Everyone Through Professional, Progressive Policing

Oversight Commissioner

Tom Constantine was appointed as Oversight Commissioner on 31 May 2000 and was succeeded by Al Hutchinson in December 2003. He is responsible under the 2000 Act for overseeing the implementation of the changes in policing arrangements and structures recommended in the context of the Patten Report.

Tripartite Policing Responsibilities

Policing in Northern Ireland is governed by the "tripartite structure" involving the Secretary of State for Northern Ireland, the Policing Board and the Chief Constable. The detailed provisions for this arrangement are set out in the Police (NI) Act 2000, as amended by the Police (Northern Ireland) Act 2003, which implements the Patten recommendations.

The Role of the Secretary of State in Policing

The Secretary of State sets the statutory framework for policing, (which as a reserved matter has not yet been devolved to the Northern Ireland Assembly) and is empowered to set long term policing objectives. In addition the Secretary of State obtains and provides the annual police grant and approves the appointment of senior police officers. He makes regulations which set out the terms and conditions of service of police officers and may regulate on the emblems and flags of the police service.

He appoints the independent members of the Policing Board as well as the Oversight Commissioner and is involved in the process of appointing the Police Ombudsman. The Secretary of State may issue codes of practice to the Policing Board and a code on the appointment of independent members to District Policing Partnerships (DPPs). He may also issue guidance on the use of public order equipment. He appoints inspectors of constabulary to inspect the police service and has responsibility for issues concerning national security.

The Chief Constable

The Police Service of Northern Ireland is led by the Chief Constable, currently Hugh Orde, who took up his post on 2 September 2002.

The Chief Constable is responsible for the operational direction and control of the police service with managerial responsibility for the police and other staff of the service and the use of resources.

Under the terms of the Police (NI) Act 2000, as amended by the Police (Northern Ireland) Act 2003, the Chief Constable is required to:

- Produce a draft of the policing plan detailing how he will police Northern Ireland in line with priorities set by the Secretary of State and the Policing Board. The Policing Board approves and publishes this plan before the commencement of each financial year;
- District Commanders are required to produce local policing plans, consistent with the annual plan after consultation with the local District Policing Partnership;
- Bring to the attention of all officers the terms of the new declaration (or oath);
- Draft an action plan for increasing the number of women in the Police Service should the Board require;
- Provide guidance to officers on the registration of notifiable memberships (memberships of an organisation which might be regarded as affecting the ability of an officer to discharge his duties effectively and impartially);
- Ensure officers read and understand the code of ethics;
- Report on any matter connected with policing to the Board. The Chief Constable may "appeal" against such a request to the Secretary of State in specific grounds as set out in the Act;
- Produce and publish an annual report.

The Police Service of Northern Ireland

PSNI Headquarters
65 Knock Road, Belfast, BT5 6LE
Tel: 028 9065 0222
Web: www.psni.police.uk

The Police Service of Northern Ireland (PSNI) came into being on 4 November 2001. The Service is divided into 2 geographical areas – Urban and Rural Regions. Each region is commanded by an Assistant Chief Constable.

The two regions are made up of 29 smaller District Command Units (DCUs). Twenty-five of these match the boundaries of District Council areas outside Belfast. For administrative and logistical reasons Belfast City Council area has been split into four DCUs – North, South, East and West.

The Urban Region covers 12 District Command Units and the Rural Region covers 17 District Command Units.

The development of DCUs is in line with the RUC's own 'Fundamental Review of Policing' published in 1996 and with one of the central recommendations in the Patten Report that policing should be delivered with and for the community. The new structure devolves decision making about resources, personnel, services and budgets to local District Commanders.

The Police Service is accountable to the Northern Ireland Policing Board, which in addition to independent members drawn from the broader Northern Ireland community, has representatives from almost all the main political parties.

Aims of the PSNI:

- To promote safety and reduce disorder;
- To reduce crime and the fear of crime;
- To contribute to delivering justice in a way which secures and maintains public confidence in the rule of law;
- To implement the programme of change.

Police Service of Northern Ireland Organisational Chart*

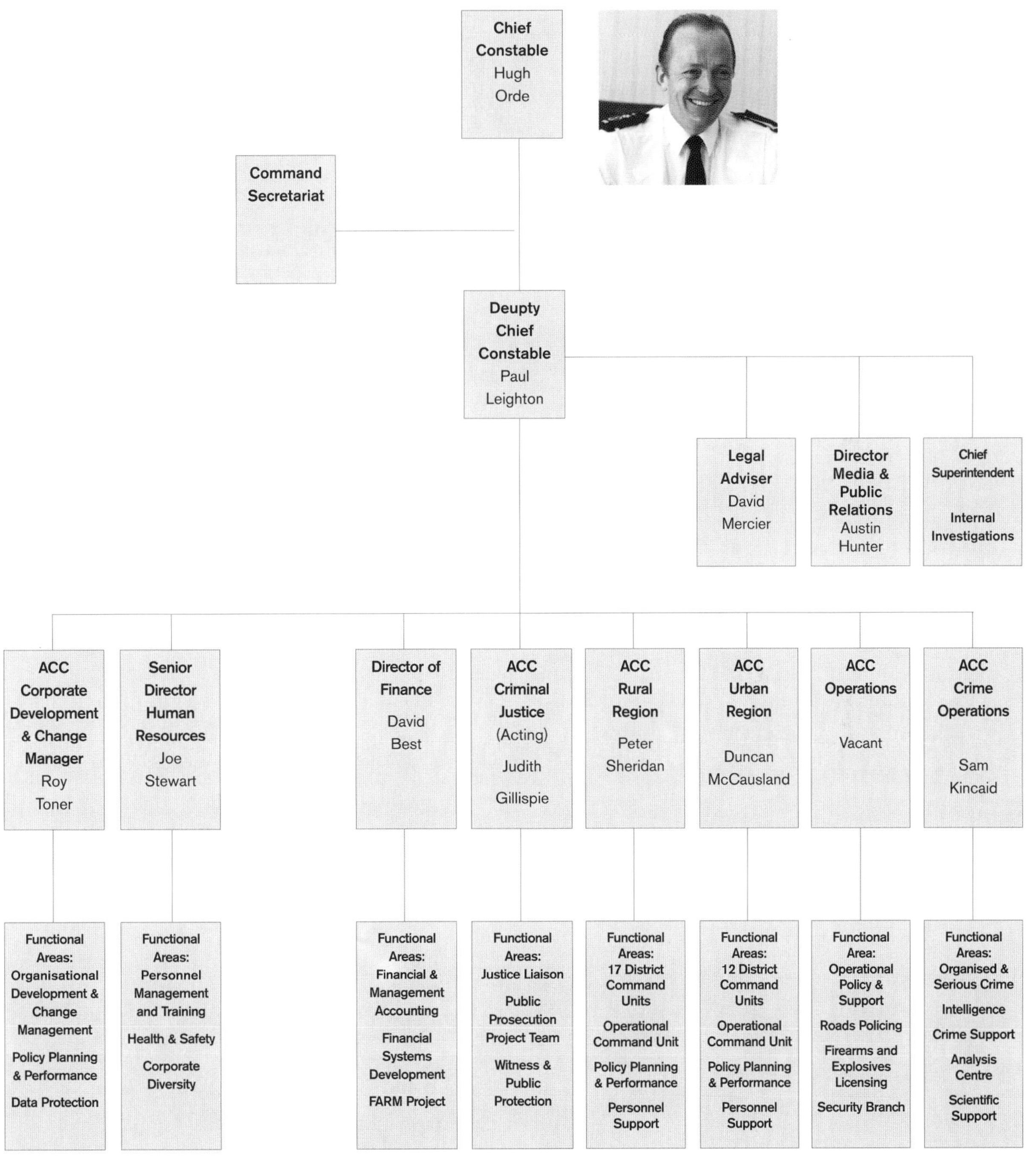
Chief Constable Hugh Orde
Command Secretariat
Deupty Chief Constable Paul Leighton
Legal Adviser David Mercier
Director Media & Public Relations Austin Hunter
Chief Superintendent Internal Investigations
ACC Corporate Development & Change Manager Roy Toner
Senior Director Human Resources Joe Stewart
Director of Finance David Best
ACC Criminal Justice (Acting) Judith Gillispie
ACC Rural Region Peter Sheridan
ACC Urban Region Duncan McCausland
ACC Operations Vacant
ACC Crime Operations Sam Kincaid
Functional Areas: Organisational Development & Change Management
Policy Planning & Performance
Data Protection
Functional Areas: Personnel Management and Training
Health & Safety
Corporate Diversity
Functional Areas: Financial & Management Accounting
Financial Systems Development
FARM Project
Functional Areas: Justice Liaison
Public Prosecution Project Team
Witness & Public Protection
Functional Areas: 17 District Command Units
Operational Command Unit
Policy Planning & Performance
Personnel Support
Functional Areas: 12 District Command Units
Operational Command Unit
Policy Planning & Performance
Personnel Support
Functional Area: Operational Policy & Support
Roads Policing
Firearms and Explosives Licensing
Security Branch
Functional Areas: Organised & Serious Crime
Intelligence
Crime Support
Analysis Centre
Scientific Support

*portfolios of Assistant Chief Constables may change throughout the year

Chief Officers of the PSNI January 2004
Chief Constable: Hugh Orde
Deputy Chief Constable: Paul Leighton
Assistant Chief Constable: Roy Toner, Corporate Development and Change Manager
Assistant Chief Constable: Vacant, Operations
Assistant Chief Constable: Peter Sheridan, Rural Region
Assistant Chief Constable: Duncan McCausland, Urban Region
Assistant Chief Constable: Sam Kinkaid, Crime Operations
Assistant Chief Constable (Acting): Judith Gilliespie, Criminal Justice

Director of Finance: David Best
Senior Director of Human Resources: Joe Stewart
Director of Media and Public Relations: Austin Hunter
Legal Advisor: David Mercier

Policing Resources

The Secretary of State has established a grant for policing at the beginning of the 2003-04 financial year of nearly £708.9 million. Of this some £481 million is required for staff costs and £7.7m has been granted to the Policing Board for its running costs.

The Board has overall financial responsibility for police resources but it delegates the day to day management and control of these (except acquisition of land) to the Chief Constable who is responsible for delivering the policing service.

The following table shows the strength of the police service on 31 August 2003.

PSNI Personnel by Gender (August 2003)

Category	Male	Female	Total
Regulars	5967	1056	7023
Reserve (Full Time)	1565	158	1723
Reserve (Part Time)	569	323	892
Support Staff	1123	2306	3429
Overall total	**9224**	**3843**	**13067**

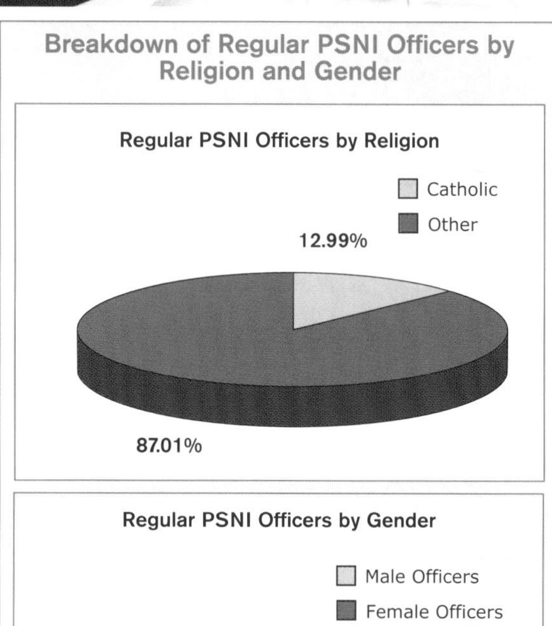

Our vision

To secure for all the people of Northern Ireland an effective, efficient, impartial and accountable police service which will secure the confidence of the whole community.

Our work

The Northern Ireland Policing Board is responsible for ensuring that the Police Service of Northern Ireland is effective, efficient and accountable to the community it seeks to serve. This means holding the Chief Constable to account for all his actions and those of his staff. Independent police oversight is essential for public confidence in the Service and the Board is committed to ensuring that it is open and transparent in how it conducts its business.

For further information on the role, work and membership of the Board contact us at the address below or visit our website at www.nipolicingboard.org.uk

Chairman: Professor Desmond Rea   Vice Chairman: Mr Denis Bradley   Chief Executive: Mr Trevor Reaney

The Policing Board

Northern Ireland Policing Board
Waterside Tower, 31 Clarendon Road
Clarendon Dock, Belfast, BT1 3BG
Tel: 028 9040 8541
Fax: 028 9040 8525
Web: www.policingboard.org.uk
Chairman: Professor Desmond Rea
Chief Executive: Trevor Reaney (pictured)

A key element of the 2000 Act and a central aspect of police reform is the creation of a new Policing Board. It replaced the Police Authority on 4 November 2001 and is made up of 10 democratically elected Assembly members chosen by parties and 9 independents, appointed by the Secretary of State on the basis of their skills and experience.

The DUP, SDLP and Ulster Unionists are all represented on the Board. Sinn Fein did not take up an invitation to nominate members. The full membership was announced by the Secretary of State on 29 September 2001. The Board had its first meeting on 7 November 2001.

The Policing Board has responsibility for the accountability of the police and monitoring and evaluating the service provided. The powers of the Board include:

- Ensuring the efficiency and effectiveness of the service; Setting objectives and performance targets for the annual Policing Plan published by the Board;
- Monitoring the performance of the Chief Constable against the plan;
- Monitoring the human rights performance of the service;
- Maintaining the knowledge of the Board in relation to patterns of recruitment and assessment of the effectiveness of recruitment procedures;
- Assessing the effectiveness of the new police code of ethics;
- Assessing public satisfaction with police and district policing partnerships;
- Requiring the Chief Constable to report on any matter connected with policing and the option to establish an inquiry;
- Determining the policing budget;
- Appointing senior officers subject to approval of the Secretary of State;
- Making arrangements to secure the economy, efficiency and effectiveness of the Board and police service; Production of an annual report.

The Board in fulfilling its function is required to give consideration to the principle that policing should be impartial and to the overall policing plan.

Members of the Policing Board

Professor Desmond Rea
Chairman

Denis Bradley	**Vice-Chairman**
Alex Attwood	SDLP
Viscount Brookeborough	UUP
Joe Byrne	SDLP
Fred Cobain	UUP
Brian Dougherty	Non-Party
Barry Gilligan	Non-Party
William Hay	DUP
Tom Kelly	Non-Party
Lord Kilclooney	UUP
Sam Foster	UUP
Pauline McCabe	Non-Party
Alan McFarland	UUP
Eddie McGrady	SDLP
Rosaleen Moore	Non-Party
Ian Paisley (Junior)	DUP
Suneil Sharma	Non-Party
Sammy Wilson	DUP

(November 2003)

Following the Secretary of State's decision to suspend devolved government with effect from midnight 14 October 2002, he was required to reconstitute the Board. All 19 members of the Board accepted the Secretary of State's invitation to take up appointment and the work of the Board continued without interruption. In September 2002, the Policing Board began a campaign to recruit Independent members to District Policing Partnerships. Following a public appointment process, District Policing Partnerships were launched in March 2003.

For the most part the DPPs have gone about their public business with very little rancour or controversy. There have however been a few instances of paramilitary intimidation of DPP members at local level but very few resignations as a result.

(A comprehensive listing of District Policing Partnerships is set out in the reference section at the back of this book.)

The Police Ombudsman

Police Ombudsman for Northern Ireland
New Cathedral Buildings
St Anne's Square
11 Church Street
Belfast, BT1 1PG
Tel: 028 9082 8600 / 0845 601 2931
Fax: 028 9082 8659
Email: info@policeombudsman.org
Web: www.policeombudsman.org
Police Ombudsman: Mrs Nuala O'Loan (pictured)

The Police Ombudsman's Office deals with complaints from the public about the conduct of police officers on duty in Northern Ireland. You do not have to pay for this service.

The current ombudsman is Nuala O'Loan. The role of the Police Ombudsman includes the following:

- Receives complaints;
- Deals with complaints about how the police behave when they are doing their job. Complaints may involve allegations of criminal behaviour by a police officer, or allegations that the police officer broke the police code of conduct;
- Decides how to deal with complaints;
- Decides the outcome of complaints;
- Monitors trends and patterns in complaints.

The Police Ombudsman may investigate a matter if there reason to think that a police officer may have committed a criminal offence or broken the police code of conduct.

Devolution of Policing

The government remains committed to the position set out in the Good Friday Agreement. Once the devolved institutions are working effectively, the Westminster government intends to devolve responsibility for policing and justice functions, as set out in the Belfast Agreement. Before it can do this, it needs to take some major steps to implement the Criminal Justice Review and to make some more progress on detailed implementation of the Patten Report. A final decision to devolve these functions can only be taken at the time taking account of security and other relevant considerations and must be on a basis that is robust, workable and broadly supported by the parties.

Forensic Science Northern Ireland

151 Belfast Road
Carrickfergus, BT38 8PL
Tel: 028 9036 1888 / Fax: 028 9036 1900
Web: www.fsni.gov.uk Email: forensic.science@fsni.gov.uk
Chief Executive: Brett Hannon

Forensic Science Northern Ireland is an Executive Agency within the Northern Ireland Office. The services it provides include:

- Scientific support for the investigation of crime;
- Scientific advice for the legal profession and objective expert testimony to the Courts;
- Scientific support for the Police Ombudsman (NI);
- Training in the effective and efficient application of forensic science;
- Analytical support for pathologists.

The principal customer for these services is the Police Service of Northern Ireland. The organisation currently employs around 145 staff, approximately 100 of whom are scientists directly involved with casework.

Organised Crime Task Force

The Organised Crime Task Force (OCTF) was created in September 2000 as part of a multi-agency approach to tackling organised crime. Under its Chair, Minister of State Jane Kennedy, the OCTF aims to tackle, amongst other things: extortion, the drugs trade, the smuggling of fuel, tobacco and alcohol, money laundering, counterfeit goods and armed robbery. The OCTF brings together government, law enforcement and a wide range of other agencies including the newly-formed Assets Recovery Agency (ARA).

Assets Recovery Agency

The Assets Recovery Agency (ARA) is an independent government department, which became operational in February 2003 with the aim of reducing crime and recovering the assets of crime by criminal confiscation, civil recovery or taxation. The Assets Recovery Agency's Belfast operation is headed by former PSNI Assistant Chief Constable Alan McQuillan who consults with the Secretary of State with regard to the organisation's strategy for Northern Ireland.

Northern Ireland's Government Departments

Introduction

Although Northern Ireland had its own devolved government from the foundation of the state in 1920 until 1972, for most of the last 30 years the province has been governed directly from Westminster. However, since the passing of the 1998 Northern Ireland Act a devolved government was restored featuring a power sharing Executive and eleven new government departments.

Up until the suspension of the first Assembly in October 2002, local politicians headed the ten government departments (as listed below). An eleventh, joint department, the Office of the First Minister and Deputy First Minister was established to oversee the work of the other departments and before suspension was headed by First Minister David Trimble and Deputy First Minister Mark Durkan.

The eleven government departments during the Assembly were as follows:

Office of the First Minister and Deputy First Minister
Department of Agriculture and Rural Development
Department of Culture, Arts and Leisure
Department of Education
Department for Employment and Learning
Department of Enterprise, Trade and Investment
Department of the Environment
Department of Finance and Personnel
Department of Health, Social Services and Public Safety
Department for Regional Development
Department for Social Development

Following the suspension of the Northern Ireland Assembly ministers from Westminster, who operate under the Northern Ireland Office, replaced local ministers representing the ten departments on the Northern Ireland Executive.

Northern Ireland Office Team

Secretary of State	Paul Murphy MP
Minister of State	Jane Kennedy MP
Minister of State	John Spellar MP
Parliamentary Under Secretary	Ian Pearson MP
Parliamentary Under Secretary	Angela Smith MP

Secretary of State Paul Murphy
Following the introduction of direct rule, the ministerial portfolios were allocated as follows:

Four ministers support the Northern Ireland Office headed by the Secretary of State Paul Murphy and together they are responsible for the governance of Northern Ireland and the management of the ten departments whilst direct rule is in place.

Minister of State Jane Kennedy MP retained her existing NIO responsibilities for security and prisons and assumed responsibility for the Department of Education, and the Department of Employment and Learning. She also has responsibility for the Assets Recovery Agency and Organised Crime Task Force.

Minister of State John Spellar MP has responsibility for political development, criminal justice, human rights and equality. He is also Minister at the Department for Social Development and the Department for Regional Development.

Parliamentary Under Secretary of State Ian Pearson MP has responsibility for Europe and the Review of Public Administration. He is also Minister for the Department of Agriculture and Rural Development, the Department of Finance and Personnel and the Department of Enterprise, Trade and Investment .

Parliamentary Under Secretary of State Angela Smith MP has responsibility for victims and reconciliation as well as the Department of the Environment, Department of Health, Social Services and Public Safety and the Department of Culture, Arts and Leisure.

Details of the Northern Ireland government departments and their senior personnel are set out as follows.

Office of the First Minister and Deputy First Minister (OFMDFM)

Stormont Castle
Stormont, Belfast, BT4 3TT
Tel: 028 9037 8044 / Fax: 028 9037 8224
Web: www.ofmdfmni.gov.uk

Head of the Civil Service:
Nigel Hamilton (pictured)
Tel: 9037 8133
Private Office:
Private Secretary: Debbie Sweeney
Tel: 028 9037 8132

The Office of the First Minister and Deputy First Minister was established as a department on 1 December 1999 following the devolution of power to Northern Ireland.

The work of the department revolves around three interrelated roles:

- To support the work of the Executive during devolution;
- To undertake the departmental functions allocated to the Office of the First Minister and Deputy First Minister;
- To provide a service to the other government departments.

Functions

- Brussels Office;
- Central Emergency Planning Unit;
- Children and Young Peoples Unit;
- Civic Forum Secretariat;
- Community Relations Unit;
- Economic Policy Unit;
- Equality Unit;
- Executive Information Service;
- Executive Secretariat;
- Honours;
- Human Rights;
- Machinery of Government;
- North/South Ministerial Council;
- Northern Ireland Bureau in Washington;
- Public Appointments;
- Public Service Reform Unit;
- Review of Public Administration;
- Secretariat for Commissioner for Public Appointments;
- Victims Unit.

Castle Buildings, Stormont

Legal Services Directorate

Director: Denis McCartney
Tel: 028 9037 8125 / Fax: 028 9037 8037
Email: irena.elliott@ofmdfmni.gov.uk

Contact: Caroline Webb
Tel: 028 9037 8126 / Fax: 028 9037 8037
Email: caroline.webb@ofmdfmni.gov.uk

Executive Information Service

Director: Stephen Grimason
Tel: 028 9037 8101 / Fax: 028 9037 8013
Email: stephen.grimason@ofmdfmni.gov.uk

Deputy Director: John McKervill
Tel: 028 9037 8103 / Fax: 028 9037 8013
Email: john.mckervill@ofmdfmni.gov.uk

The Executive Information Service (EIS), provides the full range of news and public relations services to ministers and their departments. It seeks to present policy and activity of the Northern Ireland Administration. The central unit of EIS is based in Castle Buildings with staff out posted to provide an information service in each department.

Public Relations Unit
Contact: Lorna Armstrong
Tel: 028 9037 8018 / Fax: 028 9037 8112
Email: lorna.armstrong@ofmdfmni.gov.uk

Press Office
Contact: Don McAleer
Tel: 028 9037 8105 / Fax: 028 9037 8016
Email: don.mcaleer@ofmdfmni.gov.uk

Contact: Paul Pringle
Tel: 028 9037 8106 / Fax: 028 9037 8016
Email: paul.pringle@ofmdfmni.gov.uk

Co-ordination and Planning
The Co-ordination and Planning unit co-operates with departments to provide a mechanism to maximise the impact of announcements and reduce the possibility of clashes of events.

Contact: Don McAleer
Tel: 028 9037 8105 / Fax: 028 9037 8016
Email: don.mcaleer@ofmdfmni.gov.uk

Press officers assigned to other Ministers can be contacted at Department headquarters as follows:

Department of Agriculture and Rural Development
Contact: Bernie McCusker
Tel: 028 9052 4619 / Fax: 028 9052 5003
Email: bernadette.mccusker@dardni.gov.uk

Department of Culture, Arts and Leisure
Contact: Jill Heron
Tel: 028 9025 8900 / Fax: 028 9025 8906
Email: jill.heron@dcalni.gov.uk

OFMDFM Organisation Chart

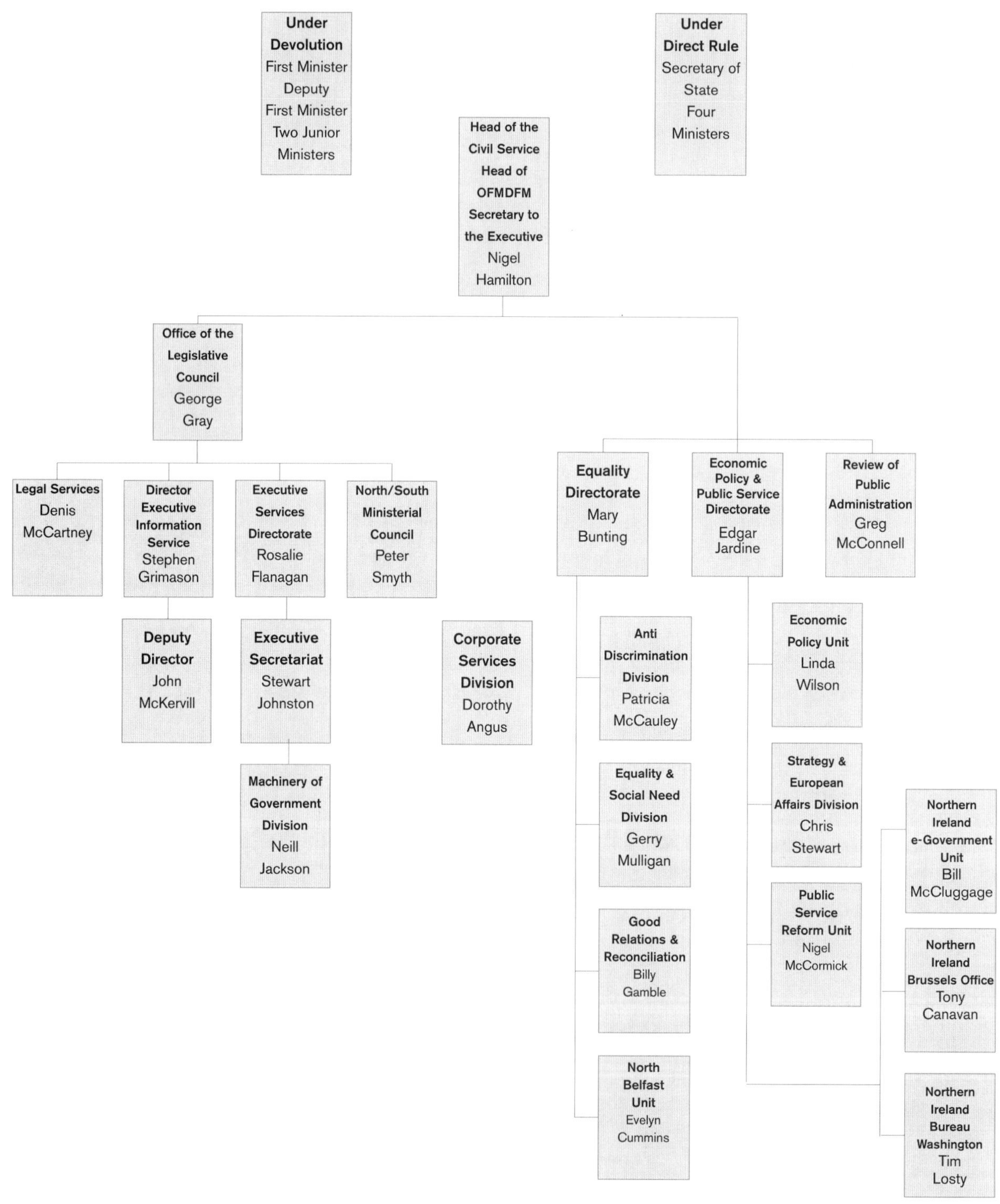

Department of Education
Contact: Jill Garrett
Tel: 028 9127 9356 / Fax: 028 9127 9271
Email: jill.garrett@deni.gov.uk

Department of Enterprise, Trade and Investment
Contact: Philip Maguire
Tel: 028 9052 9353 / Fax: 028 9052 9546
Email: philip.maguire@detni.gov.uk

Department of the Environment
Contact: Brian Kirk
Tel: 028 9054 0013 / Fax: 028 9054 1129
Email: brian.kirk@doeni.gov.uk

Department of Finance and Personnel
Contact: Colin Ross
Tel: 028 9052 7375 / Fax: 028 9052 7149
Email: colin.ross@dfpni.gov.uk

Department of Health, Social Services and Public Safety
Contact: Colm Shannon
Tel: 028 9052 0636 / Fax: 028 9052 0572
Email: colm.shannon@dhsspsni.gov.uk

Department for Employment and Learning
Contact: Gwyn Treharne
Tel: 028 9025 7790
Fax: 028 9025 7795
Email: gwyn.treharne@dhfeteni.gov.uk

Department for Regional Development
Contact: Paddy Cullen
Tel: 028 9054 0817 / Fax: 028 9054 0029
Email: eamon.deeny@drdni.gov.uk

Department for Social Development
Contact: Jim Hamilton
Tel: 028 9056 9211 / Fax: 028 9056 9269
Email: jim.hamilton@dsdni.gov.uk

Executive Services Directorate

Director: Rosalie Flanagan
Tel: 028 9037 8123 / Fax: 028 9037 8035
Email: rosalie.flanagan@ofmdfmni.gov.uk

Executive Secretariat (Including North/South Ministerial Council, British Irish Council)

Head of Division: Stewart Johnston
Tel: 028 9037 8149 / Fax: 028 9037 8035
Email: stewart.johnston@ofmdfmni.gov.uk

Contact: Tom Watson
Tel: 028 9037 8159 / Fax: 028 9037 8035
Email: tom.watson@ofmdfmni.gov.uk

NSMC, BIC and Civic Forum Liaison
Contact: Gail McKibbin
Tel: 028 9037 8033 / Fax: 028 9037 8035
Email: gail.mckibbin@ofmdfmni.gov.uk

Machinery of Government Division

Head of Division: Neill Jackson
Tel: 028 9037 8157 / Fax: 028 9037 8221
Email: neill.jackson@ofmdfmni.gov.uk

Machinery of Government Division essentially performs an internal support function within the Northern Ireland administration. It operates at the interface of the OFMDFM and other government departments and the Northern Ireland Assembly, co-ordinating and monitoring flows of information and providing guidance on a range of activities.

Machinery of Government and Assembly Section
Contact: Dr Deirdre Griffith
Tel: 028 9037 8162 / Fax: 028 9037 8221
Email: deirdre.griffith@ofmdfmni.gov.uk

Contact: Geoff Beattie
Tel: 028 9037 8161 / Fax: 028 9037 8221
Email: geoff.beattie@ofmdfmni.gov.uk

Legislation Progress Unit
Contact: Jim Hamilton
Tel: 028 9037 8158 / Fax: 028 9037 8221
Email: jim.hamilton@ofmdfmni.gov.uk

The functions of the Legislation Progress Unit are to manage, co-ordinate and monitor Northern Ireland legislation from the Northern Ireland Departments.

The North/South Ministerial Council Joint Secretariat

Joint Secretary: North: Dr Peter Smyth
Tel: 028 3751 5004 / Fax: 028 3751 1406
Email: peter.smyth@ofmdfmni.gov.uk

Contact: Pat Donaghy
Tel: 028 3751 5008 / Fax: 028 3751 1406
Email: pat.donaghy@ofmdfmni.gov.uk

Contact: Basil Davidson
Tel: 028 3751 3036 / Fax: 028 3751 1406
Email: basil.davidson@ofmdfmni.gov.uk

North/South Ministerial Council
Joint Secretariat
39 Abbey Street, Armagh, BT61 7EB
Web: www.northsouthministerialcouncil.org

Equality Directorate

Director: Mary Bunting
Tel: 028 9052 2857 / Fax: 028 9052 0761
Email: mary.bunting@ofmdfmni.gov.uk

Anti-Discrimination Division

Head of Division: Patricia McAuley
Tel: 028 9052 3156 / Fax: 028 9052 8300
Email: patricia.mcauley@ofmdfmni.gov.uk

Single Equality Bill

Contact: Ivan Millen
Tel: 028 9052 3365 / Fax: 028 9052 3272
Email: ivan.millen@ofmdfmni.gov.uk

Race, Fair Employment and Disability Discrimination

Contact: Ken Walker
Tel: 028 9052 3158 / Fax: 028 9052 3272
Email: ken.walker@ofmdfmni.gov.uk

Sex and Sexual Orientation Discrimination and Equal Pay

Director: Drew Haire
Tel: 028 9052 0088 / Fax: 028 9052 3272
Email: drew.haire@ofmdfmni.gov.uk

Oversight of Equality Commission

Director: Drew Haire
Tel: 028 9052 0088 / Fax: 028 9052 3272
Email: drew.haire@ofmdfmni.gov.uk

Equality and Social Need Division

Head of Division: Gerry Mulligan
Tel: 028 9052 3148 / Fax: 028 9052 8300
Email: gerry.mulligan@ofmdfmni.gov.uk

New TSN Unit

Contact: Harriet Ferguson
Tel: 028 9052 2048 / Fax: 028 9052 3323
Email: harriet.ferguson@ofmdfmni.gov.uk

Statutory Duty and Human Rights Unit

Contact: Clare Archbold
Tel: 028 9052 3140 / Fax: 028 9052 3272
Email: clare.archbold@ofmdfmni.gov.uk

Gender Equality Unit

Contact: Hilary Harbinson
Tel: 028 9052 8194 / Fax: 028 9052 3323
Email: hilary.harbinson@ofmdfmni.gov.uk

Research Branch

Contact: Dr Stephen Donnelly
Tel: 028 9052 3284 / Fax: 028 9052 3272
Email: stephen.donnelly@ofmdfmni.gov.uk

Good Relations and Reconciliation Division

Head of Division: Billy Gamble
Tel: 028 9052 8351 / Fax: 028 9052 8474
Email: billy.gamble@ofmdfmni.gov.uk

Community Relations Unit

Contact: Denis Ritchie
Tel: 028 9052 3460 / Fax: 028 9052 2229
Email: denis.ritchie@ofmdfmni.gov.uk

Race Equality Unit

Contact: Ken Fraser
Tel: 028 9052 2615 / Fax: 028 9052 3323
Email: ken.fraser@ofmdfmni.gov.uk

Victims Unit

Contact: Caroline Evans
Tel: 028 9052 8353 / Fax: 028 9052 8354
Email: caroline.evans@ofmdfmni.gov.uk

Children and Young People's Unit

Contact: Heather Stevens
Tel: 028 9052 3118 / Fax: 028 9052 8275
Email: heather.stevens@ofmdfmni.gov.uk

North Belfast Community Action Unit

Head of Unit: Evelyn Cummins
Tel: 028 9072 6014 / Fax: 028 9072 6102
Email: evelyn.cummins@ofmdfmni.gov.uk

The North Belfast Community Action Unit is part of the Office of the First Minister and Deputy First Minister but also reports to the Department for Social Development. The Unit is guided by a steering group of officials from both these departments and has responsibility for developing a long term strategic action plan; encouraging partnerships; building community capacity; and addressing interface issues in North Belfast. The Unit is also responsible for the development and regeneration of the Crumlin Road Gaol.

Corporate Services Division

Head of Division: Dorothy Angus
Tel: 028 9052 8153 / Fax: 028 9052 0748
Email: dorothy.angus@ofmdfmni.gov.uk

Finance

Contact: Aubrey Playfair
Tel: 028 9052 3440 / Fax: 028 9052 8135
Email: aubrey.playfair@ofmdfmni.gov.uk

Personnel and Office Services

Contact: Liz Elliott
Tel: 028 9052 2119 / Fax: 028 9052 2339
Email: liz.elliott@ofmdfmni.gov.uk

Information Technology

Contact: Robert Fee
Tel: 028 9052 2670 / Fax: 028 9052 3452
Email: robert.fee@ofmdfmni.gov.uk

Knowledge Network Team

Contact: Robert Fee
Tel: 028 9052 2670 / Fax: 028 9052 3452
Email: robert.fee@ofmdfmni.gov.uk

Central Management Branch

Contact: Geoffrey Simpson
Tel: 028 9052 3245 / Fax: 028 9052 2933
Email: geoffrey.simpson@ofmdfmni.gov.uk

Central Appointments Unit (CAU)
Contact: Geoffrey Simpson
Tel: 028 9052 3245 / Fax: 028 9052 8125
Email:geoffrey.simpson@ofmdfmni.gov.uk

Honours
Contact: Gary Smyth
Tel: 028 9052 8162 / Fax: 028 9052 8200
Email: gary.smyth@ofmdfmni.gov.uk

Central Emergency Planning Unit (CEPU)
Contact: John Hinds
Tel: 028 9052 8860 / Fax: 028 9052 8875
Email: john.hinds@ofmdfmni.gov.uk

Economic Policy Unit and Public Service Directorate

Director: Edgar Jardine
Tel: 028 9052 8505 / Fax: 028 9052 2262
Email: edgar.jardine@ofmdfmni.gov.uk

Economic Policy Unit
Head of Division: Linda Wilson
Tel: 028 9052 3198 / Fax: 028 9052 2262
Email: linda.wilson@ofmdfmni.gov.uk

The role of the Economic Policy Unit is to support the First Minister and Deputy First Minister, and through them the Executive Committee as a whole, in their strategic role and responsibilities for the formulation, co-ordination and management of the policies of the new Administration.

Economic Policy and Effectiveness
Tel: 028 9052 2428 / Fax: 028 9052 2552

Programme for Government and Financial Resources

Programme for Government and PSAs
Contact: Robbie Saulters
Tel: 028 9052 2516 / Fax: 028 9052 2552
Email: robbie.saulters@ofmdfmni.gov.uk

Finance Issues
Contact: John McKenna
Tel: 028 9052 2742 / Fax: 028 9052 2552
Email: john.mckenna@ofmdfmni.gov.uk

Public Private Investment Unit
Contact: Fergus Devitt
Tel: 028 9052 2752 / Fax: 028 9052 2552
Email: fergus.devitt@ofmdfmni.gov.uk

Strategy and European Affairs Division

Head of Division: Chris Stewart
Tel: 028 9052 8389 / Fax: 028 9052 2262
Email: chris.stewart@ofmdfmni.gov.uk

The Division deals with European policy and co-ordination issues and Measure 4.1 of the Peace II Programme. It also deals with a range of important strategic issues likely to come before the Executive.

European Policy and Co-ordination Unit

European Policy Issues
Contact: Julie Mapstone
Tel: 028 9052 3105 / Fax: 028 9052 2552
Email: julie.mapstone@ofmdfmni.gov.uk

Measure 4.1 and Interface with NI EU Interests
Contact: Paul Geddis
Tel: 028 9052 8445 / Fax: 028 9052 2552
Email: paul.geddis@ofmdfmni.gov.uk

Policy Innovation Unit
Contact: Colin Jack
Tel: 028 9052 8439 / Fax: 028 9252 2552
Email: colin.jack@ofmdfmni.gov.uk

Reinvestment and Reform Initiative
Contact: Alan Maitland
Tel: 028 9052 8251 / Fax: 028 9052 2552
Email: alan.maitland@ofmdfmni.gov.uk

Public Service Reform Unit

Head of Division: Nigel McCormick
Tel: 028 9052 6104 / Fax: 028 9052 6103
Email: nigel.mccormick@ofmdfmni.gov.uk

Continuous Improvement of Public Services
Contact: Gerry O'Neill
Tel: 028 9052 6108 / Fax: 028 9052 6107
Email: gerry.oneill@ofmdfmni.gov.uk

Investors in People (IIP) Standard
Contact: Gerry O'Neill
Tel: 028 9052 6108 / Fax: 028 9052 6107
Email: gerry.oneill@ofmdfmni.gov.uk

Policy on Agencies and Non-Departmental Public Bodies
Contact: Angela Duilaghan
Tel: 028 9052 6710 / Fax: 028 9052 6107
Email: angela.duilaghan@ofmdfmni.gov.uk

Central Freedom of Information Unit
Contact: Gordon Bell
Tel: 028 9052 6111 / Fax: 028 9052 6107
Email: gordon.bell@ofmdfmni.gov.uk

Northern Ireland eGovernment Unit
Head of Division: Bill McCluggage
Tel: 028 9052 7426 / Fax: 028 9052 7235
Email: bill.mccluggage@ofmdfmni.gov.uk

The Northern Ireland eGovernment Unit (formerly CITU(NI)) has the remit to drive forward the use of modern technology within the framework of the government's commitment that by 2005 all key public services will be capable of electronic delivery.

eGovernment Policy Strategy and Policy Age
Contact: Ray Wright
Tel: 028 9052 7688 / Fax: 028 9052 7235
Email: ray.wright@ofmdfmni.gov.uk

eGovernment Technology Standards and Architecture
Contact: John McKernan
Tel: 028 9052 7313 / Fax: 028 9052 7235
Email: john.mckernan@ofmdfmni.gov.uk

eGovernment Collaborative Projects
Contact: John Price
Tel: 028 9052 7405 / Fax: 028 9052 7235
Email: john.price@ofmdfmni.gov.uk

Northern Ireland Brussels Office

Head of Division: Tony Canavan
Tel: 00 322 290 1335 / Fax: 00 322 290 1332
Email: tony.canavan@ofmdfmni.gov.uk

Deputy Director: William Dukelow
Tel: 00 322 290 1334 / Fax: 00 322 290 1332
Email: william.dukelow@ofmdfmni.gov.uk

Agriculture Policy Advisor: Eileen Kelly
Tel: 00 322 290 1342 / Fax: 00 322 290 1332
Email: eileen.kelly@ofmdfmni.gov.uk

The Brussels office provides the focal point for developing and progressing the Executive's policy approach to Europe. Its main functions are:

- Monitoring the development of EU policies relevant to NI and providing up to date information to Ministers and Departments;
- Ensuring that NI interests are taken fully into account in the work of the EU institutions and the development of UK policy on EU matters;
- Raising the positive profile of Northern Ireland among European policy makers and opinion formers;
- Pursuing co-operation of practical benefit to NI with other European regions;
- Facilitating improved contacts with the EU by the NI non-governmental and local government sectors.

Northern Ireland Bureau Washington

Contact: Tim Losty, Director/Counsellor
Tel: 001 202 367 0461 / Fax: 001 202 367 0468
Email: tlosty@nibureau.com
Deputy Director/First Secretary: Michael Gould
Tel: 001 202 367 0462 / Fax: 001 202 367 0468
Email: mgould@nibureau.com
Web: www.nibureau.com

The Northern Ireland Bureau acts as a focal point for Northern Ireland affairs in the US and represents the interests of the Government (or Executive and the Northern Ireland Assembly) with the US government in Washington. Beyond that, however, it also has a remit to explore with relevant State governments the possibilities for developing co-operative linkages with organisational counterparts in Northern Ireland

Review of Public Administration
Chief Operating Officer: Greg McConnell
Tel: 028 9027 7688 / Fax: 028 9027 7610
Email: greg.mcconnell@rpani.gov.uk

Deputy Chief Operating Officer: Vacant

Project Officers
Joan Cassells: Tel: 028 9027 7601 / Fax: 028 9027 7633
Email: joan.cassells@rpani.gov.uk

Debbie Donnelly: Tel: 028 9027 7602 / Fax: 028 9027 7633
Email: debbie.donnelly@rpani.gov.uk

Hugh McPoland: Tel: 028 9027 7606 / Fax: 028 9027 7633
Email: hugh.mcpoland@rpani.gov.uk

Office of the Legislative Counsel

Head of Directorate: George Gray
Tel: 028 9052 1307 / Fax: 028 9052 1306
Email: george.gray@ofmdfmni.gov.uk

Agencies, Non Departmental Public Bodies and other organisations within OFMDFM

Community Relations Council

6 Murray Street, Belfast, BT1 6DN
Tel: 028 9022 7500 / Fax: 028 9022 7551
Chief Executive: Dr Duncan Morrow

Equality Commission for Northern Ireland

Equality House, 7-9 Shaftesbury Square, Belfast, BT2 7DP
Tel: 028 9050 0600 / Fax: 028 9033 1544
Web: www.equalityni.org
Email: information@equalityni.org
Chief Executive: Evelyn Collins
Chief Commissioner: Joan Harbison

Northern Ireland Economic Council

Pearl Assurance House
1-3 Donegall Square East, Belfast, BT1 5HB
Tel: 028 9023 2125 / Fax: 028 9033 1250
Web: www.niec.org.uk
Acting Director: Paul Montgomery

Office of the Commissioner for Public Appointments (Northern Ireland)

E5.20, Castle Buildings
Stormont Estate, Upper Newtownards Road, Belfast, BT4 3SR
Tel: 028 9052 8187 / Fax: 028 9052 2522
Web: www.ocpa.gov.uk

Planning Appeals Commission

Park House, 87-91 Great Victoria Street, Belfast, BT2 7AG
Tel: 028 9024 4710 / Fax: 028 9031 2536
Web: www.pacni.gov.uk
Email: info@pacni.gov.uk
Chief Commissioner: John Warke

Water Appeals Commission

Park House, 87-91 Great Victoria Street, Belfast, BT2 7AG
Tel: 028 9024 4710 / Fax: 028 9031 2536
Web: www.pacni.gov.uk
Email: info@pacni.gov.uk

Department of Agriculture and Rural Development

Dundonald House
Upper Newtownards Road, Belfast, BT4 3SB
Tel: 028 9052 4999 / Fax: 028 9052 5003
Web: www.dardni.gov.uk

Direct Rule Minister: Ian Pearson

Permanent Secretary: Pat Toal
Tel: 028 9052 4613
Email: pat.toal@dardni.gov.uk

Press Office
Principal Information Officer: Bernie McCusker
Tel: 028 9052 5619
Email: bernie.mccusker@dardni.gov.uk

The Department of Agriculture and Rural Development (DARD) aims to promote sustainable economic growth and the development of the countryside in Northern Ireland. The department assists the competitive development of the agri-food, fishing and forestry sectors of the Northern Ireland economy having regard for the need of the consumers, the welfare of animals and the conservation and enhancement of the environment.

DARD has responsibility for food, farming and environmental policy, as well as development of the agricultural, forestry and fishing industries in Northern Ireland. It provides a business development service for farmers, and a veterinary service with administration of animal health and welfare. It is responsible to the Department of the Environment, Food and Rural Affairs (DEFRA) in Great Britain, for the administration in Northern Ireland of schemes affecting the whole of the United Kingdom. The department also oversees the application of European Union agricultural policy to Northern Ireland.

Central Policy Group

Deputy Secretary: Tony McCusker
Tel: 028 9052 4628
Email: Tony.McCusker@dardni.gov.uk

Animal Health and Welfare Policy Division

Assistant Secretary: Liam McKibben
Tel: 028 9052 4193
Email: Liam.McKibben@dardni.gov.uk

Animal Welfare & Trade Branch
Principal: C Connor

Disease Control Branch
Principal: C McMaster

TSE Branch
Principal: K Davey

Agri-Environmental Policy Division

Assistant Secretary: David Small
Tel:028 90524479
Email: David.Small@dardni.gov.uk

Environmental Policy Branch: Principal: J B McKee

Food Policy Branch: Principal: P Scott

Farm Policy Branch: Principal: J Cassells

Policy and Economics Division

Assistant Secretary: Tom Stainer
Tel: 028 9052 4655
Email: Tom.Stainer@dardni.gov.uk

Policy, Co-ordination & Central Support Branch
Principal: N Fulton

Policy Development Unit: Principal: Post vacant.

Economics and Statistics Unit: Senior Principal: S McBurney
Principals: I Hunter, A Crawford, S Magee, N Fulton

Fisheries Division

Assistant Secretary: Noel Cornick
Tel: 028 9052 4387
Email: Noel.Cornick@dardni.gov.uk

Aquaculture and Fish Health Branch: Principal: A Dorbie

Sea Fisheries Policy and Grants Branch:
Principal: Eileen Sung

Fisheries Inspectorate Branch: Principal: M McCaughan

Central Services Group

Deputy Secretary: Gerry Lavery
Tel: 028 9052 4628
Email: Gerry.Lavery@dardni.gov.uk

Personnel Division

Assistant Secretary: David Trelford
Tel: 028 9052 4287
Email: David.Trelford@dardni.gov.uk

Personnel Management Branch: Principal: R J Campton

Personnel Services Branch: Principal: E Dickson

Business Development Branch: Principal: G Hill

Corporate Policy Division:

Assistant Secretary;
Gerry McWhinney
Tel: 028 9052 4272
Email: Gerry.McWhinney@dardni.gov.uk

Department of Agriculture and Rural Development Organisation Chart

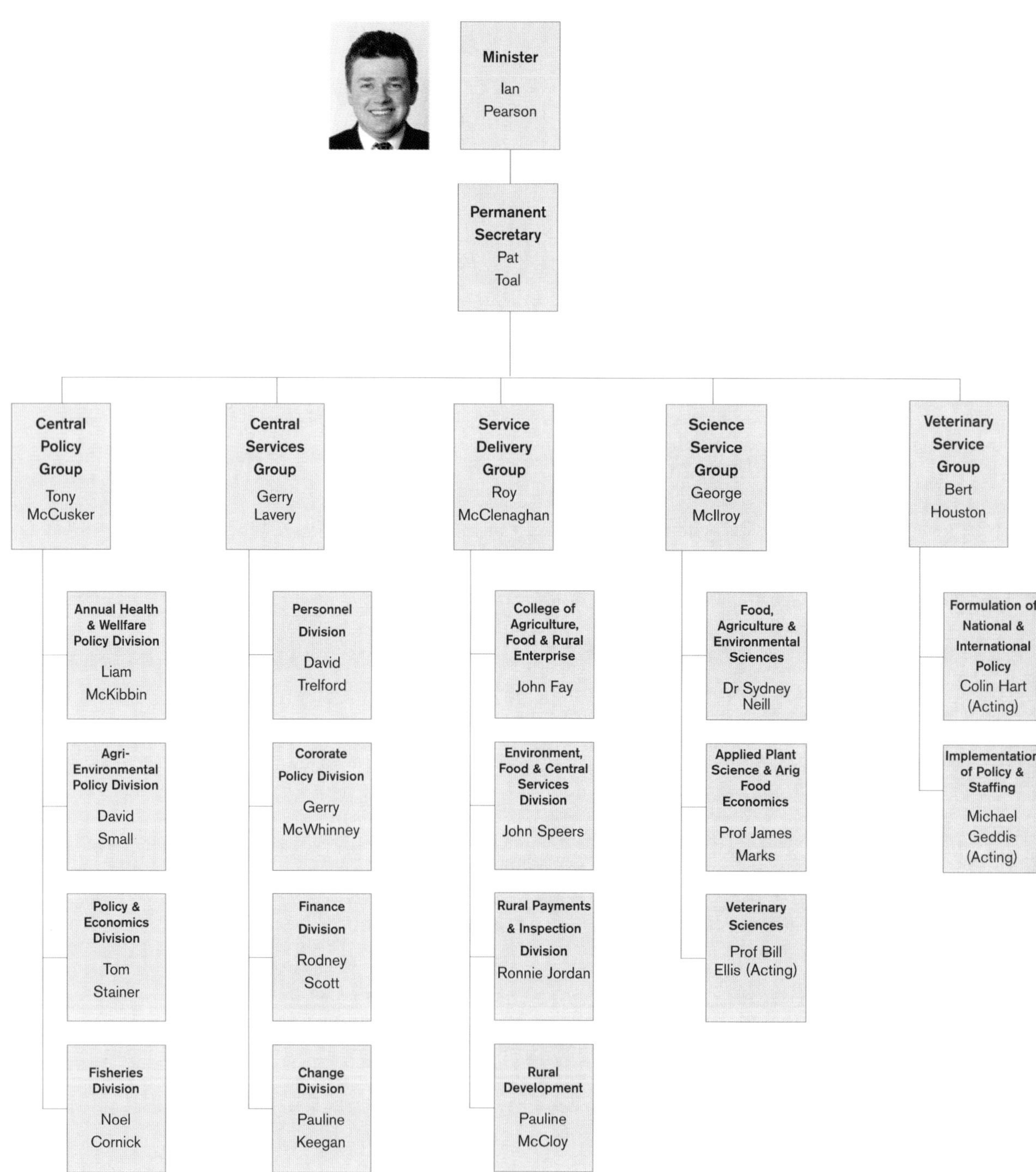
Minister
Ian Pearson
Permanent Secretary
Pat Toal
Central Policy Group
Tony McCusker
Annual Health & Wellfare Policy Division
Liam McKibbin
Agri-Environmental Policy Division
David Small
Policy & Economics Division
Tom Stainer
Fisheries Division
Noel Cornick
Central Services Group
Gerry Lavery
Personnel Division
David Trelford
Cororate Policy Division
Gerry McWhinney
Finance Division
Rodney Scott
Change Division
Pauline Keegan
Service Delivery Group
Roy McClenaghan
College of Agriculture, Food & Rural Enterprise
John Fay
Environment, Food & Central Services Division
John Speers
Rural Payments & Inspection Division
Ronnie Jordan
Rural Development
Pauline McCloy
Science Service Group
George McIlroy
Food, Agriculture & Environmental Sciences
Dr Sydney Neill
Applied Plant Science & Arig Food Economics
Prof James Marks
Veterinary Sciences
Prof Bill Ellis (Acting)
Veterinary Service Group
Bert Houston
Formulation of National & International Policy
Colin Hart (Acting)
Implementation of Policy & Staffing
Michael Geddis (Acting)

Media Services Branch: Principal: B McCusker

Central Management Branch: Principal: E Gallagher

Rural Proofing Branch: Principal: L Hodges

Finance Division

Assistant Secretary: Rodney Scott
Tel: 028 9052 4678
Email: Rodney.Scott@dardni.gov.uk

Financial Systems Branch: Principal: Vacant

Resource Control Branch: Principal: T Rodgers

Internal Audit Branch: Principal: S McGuinness

Financial Reporting Branch: Principal: E Gaw

Financial Policy and Investigations Branch:
Principal: J Ditchfield

Change Division

Assistant Secretary: Pauline Keegan
Tel: 028 9052 4557
Email: Pauline.Keegan@dardni.gov.uk

Modernisation Unit: Principals: B Stuart, H Hagan

Information Systems and Estate Management Unit:
Senior Principal: E Long

Information Management Branch:
Deputy Principal: C Bennett

Service Delivery Group

Deputy Secretary: Roy McClenaghan
Tel: 0289052 4589
Email: Roy.McClenaghen@dardni.gov.uk

College of Agriculture/Food and Rural Enterprise

Director: John Fay
Tel: 028 9442 6600
Email: John.Fay@dardni.gov.uk

Development Service: P McGurnaghan

Beef and Sheep Development Branch: J Herron

Dairy and Pigs Development Branch: I McCluggage

Crops and Horticulture Development Branch: S Millar

Food Technology Development Branch: D Legge

Educational Development Branch: Vacant

Education Service: I Titterington

Higher Education Branch: S Kennedy

Further Education Branch: H Jones

Supply and Packaging Branch: D McDowell

Food Technology Education Branch: M Mullan

Equine and Rural Enterprise Branch: S McAlinney

Environment, Food and Central Services Division

Director: John Speers
Tel: 028 9052 4324
Email: John.Speers@dardni.gov.uk

Countryside Management Branch: H Gracey

Supply Chain Development Branch: J McGaughey

Organisational Improvement Branch: E Long

Technical Promotions Branch: B Niblock

Education and Finance Branch: P Rooney

Rural Connect Branch: J Torney

Rural Payments and Inspection Division

Assistant Secretary: Ronnie Jordan
Tel: 028 9052 4555
Email: Ronnie.Jordan@dardni.gov.uk

Grants and Subsidies Policy Branch: Principal: V Bell

Grants and Subsidies Payments Branch:
Principal; B Glendinning

Grants and Subsidies Inspection Branch: W McWhirter

Quality Assurance Branch: W Weatherup

Rural Development

Assistant Secretary: Pauline McCloy
Tel: 028 9052 4586
Email: Pauline.McCloy@dardni.gov.uk

Rural Development Central Branch: Principal: M McLernon

Rural Development North Branch: Principal: G Evans

Rural Development South Branch: Principal: V McKevitt

Rural Development West Branch: Principal: S Nugent

Rural Development Peace Branch: B Morrison

Science Service Group

Deputy Secretary: Dr George McIlroy
Tel: 028 9052 4635
Email: George.McIlroy@dardni.gov.uk

Administration:
Senior Principal Scientific Officer: Dr R Boyd

Biometrics: Senior Principal Scientific Officer: Dr E Goodall

Food, Agricultural & Environmental Sciences

Deputy Chief Scientific Officer: Dr Sydney Neill
Tel: 028 9025 5349
Email: Sydney.Neill@dardni.gov.uk

Food Science:
Senior Principal Scientific Officers: Prof A Gilmour, Dr L Farmer

Agriculture & Environmental Sciences
Senior Principal Scientific Officers:
Dr S Heaney, Dr R Stevens, Prof C Gibson
Dr S Mayne (Acting)

Applied Plant Service and Agri-food Economics

Deputy Chief Scientific Officer:
Prof James Marks
Tel: 028 9025 5281
Email: James.Marks@dardni.gov.uk

Applied Plant Science: Senior Principal Scientific Officers:
Dr M Camlin, Dr S Sharma

Agri-food Economics Unit: Deputy Chief Agricultural Economist; Dr J Davis

Veterinary Sciences

Deputy Chief Scientific Officer: Prof William Ellis (Acting)
Tel: 028 9052 5062
Email: Bill.Ellis@dardni.gov.uk

Deputy Chief Veterinary Research Officers:
Dr T Bryson, Dr S Kennedy

Veterinary Service Group

Assistant Secretary: Bert Houston
Tel: 028 9052 4643
Email: Robert.Houston@dardni.gov.uk

Formulation of National and International Policy

Deputy Chief Veterinary Officer: Colin Hart (Acting)
Tel: 028 9052 4662
Email: Colin.Hart@dardni.gov.uk

Veterinary Public Health Policy
Senior Principal Veterinary Officer: Robert Huey

Trade, Residues and Medicine
Divisional Veterinary Officer: Paul Pollard

Tranmissible Spongiform Encephalopathy Meat including by-products
Divisional Veterinary Officer: J O'Neill

Meat Hygiene
Divisional Veterinary Officer: J Wells

Zoonoses
Divisional Veterinary Officer: B Cooper

Cattle and Sheep Identification, Registration and Movement
Divisional Veterinary Officer: D Cassells

Epizootic Section
Senior Principal Veterinary Officer: Cyril Rutledge

Scrapie, Northern Ireland Scrapie Plan, Animal Protein
Divisional Veterinary Officer: Sandra Dunbar

BSE, Transmissible Spongiform Encephalopathy
Divisional Veterinary Officer: G Byrne

Epizootic Disease, Artificial Insemination
Divisional Veterinary Officer: Michael Hatch

Welfare/AD including Welfare of Animals, Slaughter or Killing
Divisional Veterinary Officer: Fiona Murdock

Enzootic Section
Senior Principal Vererinary Officer: Owen Denny

Bovine Tuberculosis
Divisional Veterinary Officer: Paddy McGuckian

Brucellosis- Routine
Divisional Veterinary Officer: Roy Watt

Brucellosis- New Initiatives
David Irwin

Epidemiology
Divisional Veterinary Officer: Darrell Abernethy

Enforcement
Divisional Veterinary Officer: Vacant

Implementation of Policy and Staffing

Deputy Chief Veterinary Officer: Michael Geddis (Acting)
Tel: 028 9052 4305
Email: Michael.Geddis@dardni.gov.uk

Northern Region
Senior Principal Veterinary Officer: B McCartan

Ballymena DVO
Divisional Veterinary Officer: M Sherry

Coleraine DVO
Divisional Veterinary Officer: J Breen

Larne DVO
Divisional Veterinary Officer: D Marshall

Omagh DVO
Divisional Veterinary Officer: L Rutlege

Londonderry DVO
Divisional Veterinary Officer: R W Kirke

APHIS Development (Animal and Public Health Information System)
Divisional Veterinary Officer: D Torrens

Southern Region
Senior Principal Veterinary Officer: Divisional Veterinary Officer M Steel

Armagh DVO
Divisional Veterinary Officer: J Gillespie

Dungannon DVO
Divisional Veterinary Officer: I McKeown

Enniskillen DVO
Divisional Veterinary Officer: D Brown

Newry DVO
Divisional Veterinary Officer: R Harwood

Newtownards DVO
Divisional Veterinary Officer: P Price

Veterinary Public Health - Implementation
Senior Principal Veterinary Officer: R O'Flaherty

Meat North
Divisional Veterinary Officer: T Coulter

Meat South
Divisional Veterinary Officer: P Treanor

Portal Inspectorate, Management of College Veterinary Officers
Divisional Veterinary Officer: J Guy

Corporate Services Division
Principal Officer: A Ralston

Agencies, Non Departmental Public Bodies and other organisations within the Department of Argiculture and Rural Development

Agricultural Research Institute of Northern Ireland
Large Park
Hillsborough, BT26 6DR
Tel: 028 9268 2484 / Fax: 028 9268 9594
Web: www.arani.ac.uk

Director: Dr Sinclair Mayne

Agricultural Wages Board
Agricultural Wages Secretariat
Room 910
Dundonald House, Upper Newtownards Road
Belfast, BT4 3SB
Tel: 028 9052 0813

Drainage Council
c/o Alan Morton
The Secretary
Rivers Agency, Hydebank
4 Hospital Road, Belfast, BT8 8JP
Tel: 028 9025 3357

Chairman: Dr Robert Myers

Forest Service
Dundonald House
Upper Newtownards Road, Belfast, BT4 3SB
Tel: 028 9052 4480 / Fax: 028 9052 4570
Web: www.forestserviceni.gov.uk

Chief Executive: Malcolm Beatty
Tel: 028 9052 4434
Email: Malcolm.Beatty@dardni.gov.uk

Corporate Services
Director: Crawford McCully
Tel: 028 9052 4458
E-mail crawford.mccully@dardni.gov.uk

Functions: Corporate Services, Resource Accounting and Finance, Personnel and Industrial Relations, Estates & Technical Services,

Operations
Director: John O'Boyle
Tel: 028 9052 4464
E-mail: John.O'Boyle@dardni.gov.uk

Functions: Management of state forest for: Timber Production, Timber Marketing, Conservation and enhancement of the environment, Recreation and education, Engineering.

Policy and Standards
Director: Pat Hunter Blair
Tel: 028 9052 4465
E-mail: pat.hunter-blair@dardni.gov.uk
Functions: Policy, Practice, Private Woodlands, Plant Health, Research, Safety and Development

Foyle, Carlingford and Irish Lights Commission

The Loughs Agency
22 Victoria Road, Waterside
Londonderry, BT47 2AB
Tel: 028 7134 2100 / Fax: 028 7134 2720
Web: www.loughs-agency.org
Email: general@loughs-agency.org

Livestock and Meat Commission for Northern Ireland

Lissue House
31 Ballinderry Road, Lisburn, BT28 2SL
Tel: 028 9263 3000 / Fax: 028 9263 3001
Web: www.lmcni.com
Email: info@lmcni.com

Chief Executive: David Rutledge

Northern Ireland Fishery Harbour Authority

3 St Patrick's Avenue
Downpatrick, BT30 6DW
Tel: 028 4461 3844 / Fax: 028 4461 7128
Web: www.nifha.fsnet.co.uk
Email: info@nifha.fsnet.co.uk

Chief Executive: Chris Warnock

Pig Production Development Committee

c/o Farm Policy Division
Room 910, Dundonald House
Upper Newtownards Road
Belfast, BT4 3SB
Tel: 028 9052 4873 / Fax: 028 9052 4266

Rivers Agency

Hydebank
4 Hospital Road, Belfast, BT8 8JP
Tel: 028 9025 3355 / Fax: 028 9025 6455

Chief Executive: John Hagan
Tel: 028 9025 3440
Email: John.Hagan@dardni.gov.uk

Corporate Services
Director of Corporate Services: Alan Morton
Tel: 028 9052 4578
E-mail: alan.morton@dardni.gov.uk

Functions: Finance, Personnel, Legislation, Corporate Planning, Annual Reports, Human Resource Development

Operations
Director of Operations: Melvyn Hamilton
Tel: 028 9025 3358
E-mail: melvyn.hamilton@dardni.gov.uk

Functions: Operational Management, Design, Health and Safety, Environment, Plant Unit, Emergency Planning.

Principal Engineers: P Aldridge, A Kirkwood, P McCrudden

Development
Director of Development: Ronald White
Tel: 028 9025 3424
E-mail: ronald.white@dardni.gov.uk

Functions: Capital Works Programme, Construction Procurement, Hydrometrics, Asset Management, Planning Advice, Information Technology, Professional Standards

Principal Engineers: J Clarke, S Dawson, P Mehaffey, J Nicholson

Rural Development Council

17 Loy Street
Cookstown, BT80 8PZ
Tel: 028 8676 6980 / Fax: 028 8676 6922
Web: www.rdc.org.uk
Email: info@rdc.org.uk

Chief Executive: Martin McDonald

Dundonald House, Stormont

Department of Culture, Arts and Leisure

Interpoint
20-24 York Street
Belfast, BT15 1AQ
Tel: 028 9025 8825 / Fax: 028 9025 8906
Web: www.dcalni.gov.uk

Direct Rule Minister: Angela Smith MP
Permanent Secretary: Dr Aideen McGinley OBE
Tel: 028 9025 8814
Deputy Secretary: Carol Moore
Tel: 028 9025 8848

Private Office
Private Secretary: Julie Childs
Tel: 028 9025 8807

Press Office
Principal Information Officer: Jill Heron
Tel: 028 9025 8900

The Department of Culture, Arts and Leisure (DCAL), was formed from an amalgamation of agencies and functions previously associated with DANI, DENI and DoE. Its chief aim is to promote individual, social and economic development. This is to be achieved principally by maximising participation in a wide range of cultural, arts, sports and leisure activities.

DCAL has responsibilities for libraries and museums, with the aim of increasing public interaction in these areas and improving facilities and services available. It also aims to encourage public participation in the areas of sport and the arts, again by increasing opportunities for participation.

DCAL oversees the Public Record Office of Northern Ireland (PRONI) and Ordnance Survey of Northern Ireland (OSNI), both executive agencies established to provide information and other resources to the public. DCAL also funds the Northern Ireland Events Company.

DCAL has direct involvement in two cross-border implementation bodies: the North/South Language body, which incorporates boards for the development of Irish and Ulster-Scots, and Waterways Ireland. Through these the Department seeks to maximise the benefits of cross-border co-operation.

Corporate Services

Director: Damian Price
Tel: 028 9025 8821

Equality & External Relations: Head of Branch: Colin Watson

Press Office: Head of Branch: Jill Heron

Policy Evaluation & Research:
Head of Branch: Dennis McCoy

Central Services: Head of Branch: David Craig

Economics: Head of Branch: Tom Flynn

Finance & Accounts: Heads of Branch: Michelle Estler & Bernadette McGuinness

Human Resources: Head of Branch: Sharon Irwin

Culture

Director: Bryan Davis
Tel: 028 9025 8843

Arts: Head of Branch: Mark Mawhinney

Libraries: Head of Branch: Phillips Wilson

Linguistic Diversity: Heads of Branch: Pat McAlister (Ms) & Victor Douglas

Cultural Diversity: Head of Branch: Wendy Hunter

Sports, Museums & Recreation

Director: Nigel Carson
Tel: 028 9025 8801

Sports: Head of Branch: Jack Palmer

Museums: Head of Branch: Marie Garvey

Inland Waterways & Inland Fisheries:
Head of Branch: Hazel Campbell

Legislation: Head of Branch: Alison McQueen

Agencies, Non Departmental Public Bodies and other organisations within Department of Culture, Arts and Leisure

Arts Council of Northern Ireland

MacNeice House, 77 Malone Road
Belfast, BT9 6AQ
Tel: 028 9038 5200 / Fax: 028 9066 1715
Web: www.artscouncil-ni.org
Email: info@artscouncil-ni.org

Chief Executive: Roisin McDonagh

Fisheries Conservancy Board

1 Mahon Road
Portadown, BT62 3EE
Tel: 028 3833 4666 / Fax: 028 3833 8912
Web: www.fcbni.com

Chief Executive: Karen Simpson

Department of Culture, Arts and Leisure Organisation Chart

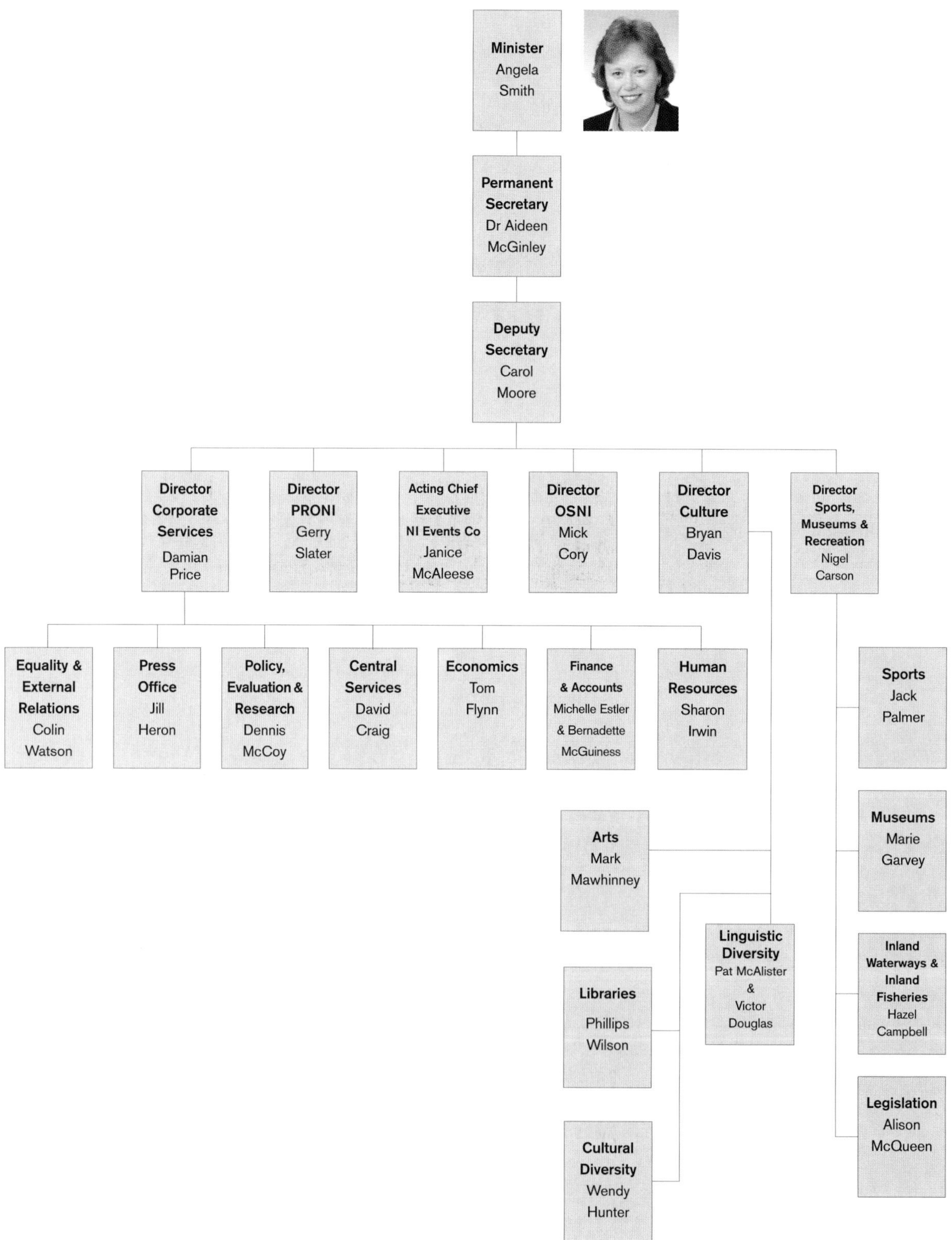

Museums & Galleries of Northern Ireland (MAGNI)
Ulster Museum
Botanic Gardens
Belfast, BT9 5AB
Tel: 028 9038 3000 / Fax: 028 3083 3003
Web: www.magni.org.uk

Chief Executive: Mike Houlihan

Ordnance Survey of Northern Ireland
Colby House
Stranmillis Court
Belfast, BT9 8BJ
Tel: 028 9025 5755 / Fax: 028 9025 5700
Web: www.osni.gov.uk

Chief Executive: Mick Cory

Northern Ireland Museums Council
6 Crescent Gardens
Belfast, BT7 1NS
Tel: 028 9055 0215 / Fax: 028 9055 0216
Web: www.nimc.co.uk
Email: info@nimc.co.uk

Director: Chris Bailey

Northern Ireland Events Company
Redwood House
66 Newforge Lane
Belfast
BT9 5NT
Tel: 028 9066 6661
Fax: 028 9066 8040
Web: www.nievents.co.uk
Email: info@nievents.co.uk

Acting Chief Executive: Janice McAleese

North/South Language Body
The North/South Language Body is a single body composed of two separate and largely autonomous agencies:

Ulster Scots Agency
Franklin House
10-12 Brunswick Street
Belfast
BT2 7GE
Tel: 028 9023 1113
Fax: 028 9023 1898
Web: www.ulsterscotsagency.com
Email: info@ulsterscotsagency.org.uk

Chief Executive: George Patten
Chairman: Lord Laird of Artigarvan

Foras na Gaeilge
7 Merrion Square, Dublin
Tel: 00 353 1 639 8400 / Fax: 00 353 1 639 8401
Web: www.forasnagaeilge.ie
Email: eolas@forasnagaeilge.ie

Chief Executive: Seosamh MacDonncha
Chairperson: Maighread Ní Mhairtin

Public Record Office of Northern Ireland
66 Balmoral Avenue
Belfast, BT9 6NY
Tel: 028 9025 1318 / Fax: 028 9025 5999
Web: www.proni. gov.uk
Email: proni@dcalni.gov.uk

Chief Executive: Dr Gerry Slater

Head of Access: Aileen McClintock
Head of Records Management and Administration: Dr David Lammey
Head of Corporate Services: Tom Robinson
Head of Education, Learning and Outreach: Valerie Adams
Head of Funding and Project Management/Head of Preservation: Patricia Kernaghan
Head of Public Service (Readers): Roger Strong
Head of Information Systems: Hugh Campbell

Department of Education

Rathgael House
Balloo Road
Bangor, BT19 7PR
Tel: 028 9127 9279 / Fax: 028 9127 9100
Web: www.deni.gov.uk

Direct Rule Minister: Jane Kennedy

Permanent Secretary: Gerry McGinn
Tel: 028 9127 9309

Deputy Secretary: Eddie Rooney
Tel: 028 9127 9313

Private Office
Private Secretary: Fiona Barnes
Tel: 028 9027 9303
Email: fiona.barnes@deni.gov.uk

Press Office
Principal Information Officer: Jill Garrett
Tel: 028 9127 9356
Email: jill.garrett@deni.gov.uk

The Department of Education has responsibility for aspects of education relating to schools and the Youth Service. This includes policy, legislation and resource issues for both areas.

As regards the Education Service, the Department of Education has responsibility for strategic planning and accounting for public expenditure. The Department manages the funding and administration of schools. It monitors schools' effectiveness, and oversees school planning and provision. The Department also has an inspectorate, and makes appointments to the five Education and Library Boards.

The Department develops policy regarding schools curriculum, and the assessment of pupils, including examinations. It oversees transfer procedures and school enrolment, and provides special education services and pupil support.

The Department of Education also has responsibility for community relations among young people, which is part of its overall youth services remit. The Department provides a comprehensive youth service, and supports many associated organisations.

(more information about the work of the department is set out in Chapter 6 'Education and Training in Northern Ireland')

Resource Allocation Division

Head of Division: John Caldwell (Acting)
Tel: 028 9127 9321

Teacher Negotiating Committee Branch
Principal: Ted McGuigan
Deputy Principal: John McClure
Functions: Teachers' salaries and conditions of service,

Teachers' Pay and Administration and Teachers' Pensions Branches
Principal: Mervyn Gregg
Deputy Principal: (Acting) Brian Quinn
Functions: Teachers' Pay and Administration

Deputy Principal: Mrs Esterina Large
Functions: Teachers' Pensions

Deputy Principal: Celine Elliott (Acting)
Functions: Computer System Project Manager

Special Funding Initiatives Unit
Deputy Principal: Richard Hodgett
Deputy Principal: Dave Bradley
Functions: Peace II funding, Building Sustainable Prosperity Programme (BSP), Belfast Regeneration Initiative, Londonderry Regeneration Initiative

Development and Infrastructure Division

Head of Division: Eugene Rooney / Tel: 028 9127 9332

Buildings Branch
Principal: Sean Johnston
Deputy Principal: Derek Patterson
Functions: Finance and Energy Efficiency Section

Deputy Principal: Brian Miller
Functions: School Projects Section (including Education Reform)

Development Branch
Principal: Russell Welsh
Deputy Principal: Jacqui Loughrey
Functions: Economic Appraisals, Development Proposals and Capital Priorities in respect of Secondary, Grammar Schools, Pre-school Expansion Programmes SEELB/BELB/WELB

Deputy Principal: Roy Newell
Functions: Economic Appraisals, Development Proposals and Capital Priorities in respect of Primary, Special, Nursery, Pre-school Expansion Prog SELB/NEELB

Deputy Principal: (Acting) Eric Mayne
Function: Estates management project

PPP Unit
Principal: Paddy McNally
Deputy Principal: Pamela McCormick; Michael Stewart
Functions: Policy and Development of PPP in Education; General PPP guidance.

Deputy Principal: John Williamson
Functions: To develop, update and implement strategy in relation to schools estate. Departmental oversight of classroom 2000 issues

School Policy Branch
Principal: Stephen Sandford
Deputy Principal: Bruce Fitzsimmons
Functions: Pre-school Education Expansion Programme

Department of Education Organisation Chart

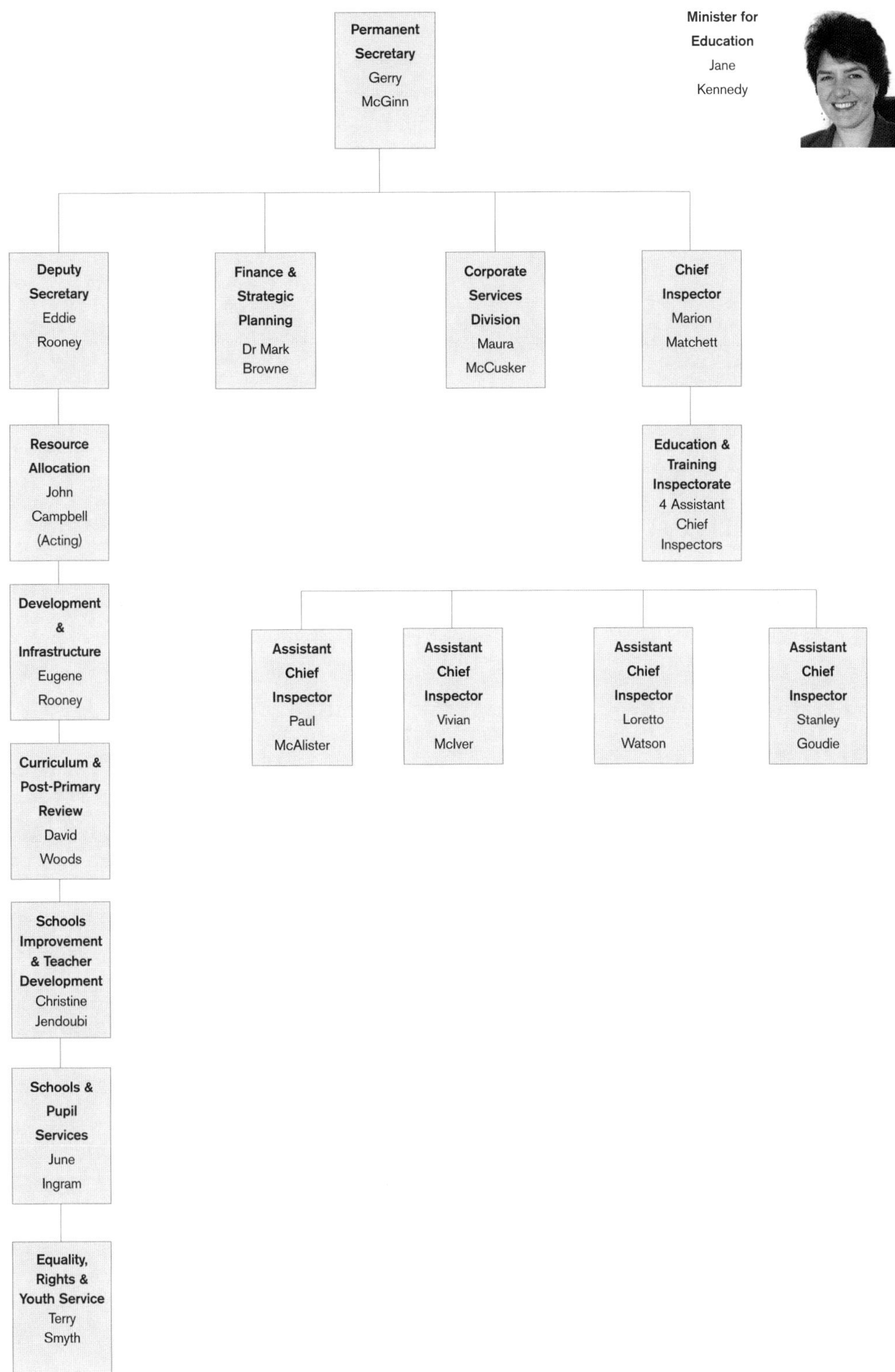
Minister for Education
Jane Kennedy
Permanent Secretary
Gerry McGinn
Deputy Secretary
Eddie Rooney
Finance & Strategic Planning
Dr Mark Browne
Corporate Services Division
Maura McCusker
Chief Inspector
Marion Matchett
Resource Allocation
John Campbell (Acting)
Education & Training Inspectorate
4 Assistant Chief Inspectors
Development & Infrastructure
Eugene Rooney
Assistant Chief Inspector
Paul McAlister
Assistant Chief Inspector
Vivian McIver
Assistant Chief Inspector
Loretto Watson
Assistant Chief Inspector
Stanley Goudie
Curriculum & Post-Primary Review
David Woods
Schools Improvement & Teacher Development
Christine Jendoubi
Schools & Pupil Services
June Ingram
Equality, Rights & Youth Service
Terry Smyth

Deputy Principal: Linda Martin
Functions: Policy on Provision of Integrated Education, Irish Medium Education, Funding of NICIE and Comhairle na Gaelscolaiochta, Registration of Independent schools.

School Finance Branch
Principal: John Caldwell
Deputy Principal: Peter O'Neill
Deputy Principal: Ken Reid
Functions: Recurrent funding of voluntary, grammar and grant maintained integrated schools.

Deputy Principal: Alan Bell
Deputy Principal: Gareth Manderson
Functions: School finance, LMS schemes

Area Board Resource Allocation and Monitoring Branch (ABRAM)
Principal: Eric McCloy
Deputy Principal: Frank Ferguson
Functions: Resource Distribution to ELBs, budgeting control and monitoring, ELB personnel and accountability issues

Curriculum and Post-Primary Review
Head of Division: David Woods
Tel: 028 9127 9332

Principal: Leslie Ashe
Principal: Des Whyte
Deputy Principal: Jacqui McLaughlin
Functions: Review of post primary education including transfer from primary to post primary schools

School Improvement and Teacher Development Division

Head of Division: Christine Jendoubi
Tel: 028 9127 9337

Qualifications and Business/Education Links Branch
Principal: Vacant
Deputy Principal: David Mann
Functions: Examinations/Qualifications, 14-19 Issues, Key Stage 4

Flexibility Pilot Scheme
6th Form Provision/Careers Education, School Information and Prospectus Regulations, School/Industry Links, Northern Ireland Business Education Partnership

Curriculum and Assessment Branch
Principal: Alastair Bradley
Deputy Principal: Ashley Waterworth
Functions: CCEA, Curriculum 4-16, Assessment 4-14, Target-setting

School Improvement Branch

Principal: Peter Lowry
Deputy Principal: David McMullan
Functions: School Improvement and Support Programmes

Teacher Education Branch
Principal: Vacant
Deputy Principal: Ron Armstrong
Functions: General Teaching Council, Initial/In Service Teacher Education, Education Technology

Schools and Pupil Services Division

Head of Division: June Ingram
Tel: 028 9127 9325

School Administration Branch
Principal: Brian Hill
Deputy Principal: Gary Montgomery
Functions: Home to school transport, school meals service, funding and administration of CCMS.

Deputy Principal: Vacant
Functions: General administration and school management issues.

Open Enrolment and Transfer Procedure Branch
Principal: John Leonard
Deputy Principal: Vacant
Functions: Open Enrolment Policy and Legislation Administration, Transfer/Selection Policy and Research Project, Class Sizes (KS1) Policy and Legislation, Implementation.

School Education Branch
Principal: Irene Murphy
Deputy Principal: Susan Carnson
Deputy Principal: Tommy Mitchell
Functions: School Finance
Deputy Principal: Garth Manderson
Functions: Special educational needs policy, legislation, codes of practice

Equality, Rights and Youth Service Division

Head of Division: Terry Smyth
Tel: 028 9127 9312

Equality, Rights and Social Inclusion Branch
Principal: Sharon Lawlor
Deputy Principal: Elaine McFeeters
Function: New TSN, Human Rights, Racial Awareness, Special Education Needs, Disability Legislation; Equality Scheme

Youth Service Branch
Principal: Tom McCready
Deputy Principal: Ivan Houston
Functions: Policy for Youth Service, Youth Council for Northern Ireland, Capital grants to recognised voluntary organisations, Grants for Training of Youth Workers.

Community Relations Branch
Deputy Principal: Phyllis Richardson
Functions: Schools Community Relations Programme, Youth Service Community Relations Support Scheme, Community Relations Core Funding Scheme, Cultural Traditions Programme

Pupil Support Branch
Principal: Mary Potter
Deputy Principal: Jackie Simpson
Deputy Principal: Brian White
Deputy Principal: Philip Melarkey
Function: Issues affecting children and young people at risk of underachievement in education. Promoting social inclusion and tackling disadvantage

Finance and Strategic Planning Division

Head of Division: Mark Browne
Tel: 028 9127 9337

Financial Planning Branch
Principal: Brian Morrow
Deputy Principal: Garth Manderson
Functions: Public Expenditure Planning, Budgeting and Monitoring, Resource Budgeting, Main and Supplementary Estimates.

Accounts Branch
Principal: Ronnie McQuitty
Deputy Principal: Jason Hayes
Functions: Payment Processing, Appropriation Accounts, Resource Accounts, Accountability Issues.

Internal Audit Unit
Principal: Michelle Anderson
Deputy Principal: Alistair McIlroy
Deputy Principal: Brendan McLernon
Functions: Internal Audit and monitoring of systems of Internal control.

Economic Advisory Unit
Principal Economist: Mike Archer
Deputy Economist: Rodney Smith
Function: Economic advice on policy issues, advice of value for money of projects and in relation to specific issues.

Strategy Management Unit
Principal: Vacant
Deputy Principal: Vacant
Function: To promote the arrangements for strategic and business planning both in the department and in relation to the main education partners. To co-ordinate the Programme for Government and Public Service Agreement and Service Delivery Agreement targets.

Corporate Services Division

Head of Division: Maura McCusker
Tel: 028 9127 9325

Business Development Unit
Principal: Mary Cromey
BDU: Deputy Principal: Ken Reid
Functions: Staff development
ISU: SSA: Billy Girvan, Mary Cromey
Functions: Information systems development and support
Freedom of Information
Principal: Tom Orr

Machinery of Government Branch
Principal: Liam Barr
Deputy Principal: Trevor Brant
Functions: Co-ordination of business and development of relations with NI Assembly/Westminster, Legislation, Greening Government, Central Bureau

Personnel Services Branch
Principal: Paul Cartwright
Deputy Principal: Donal Moran
Functions: Accommodation, Support Services, Health and Safety, Equal Opportunities
Deputy Principal: Mary Donnelly
Functions: Personnel and Pay, Staff Welfare Service

Information Services
Principal: Jill Garrett
Deputy Information Officer: Kim Martin
Functions: Organising Press Conference, In-house magazine, Preparing Press Releases and Statements, Media Monitoring, Media Queries.

Statistics and Research Branch
Principal: Dr Ivor Johnston
Deputy Principal: Patricia Wyers, Martin Thompson, Jonathan Crook
Functions: Research, Statistical Series, Analysis.

Education and Training Inspectorate

Chief Inspector: Marion Matchett
Tel: 028 9127 9738

Policy, Planning and Improvement
Assistant Chief Inspector: Stanley Goudie

Special Education, Alternative Provision; Youth and Community; Culture, Arts and Leisure
Assistant Chief Inspector: Paul McAllister

Post-16 Education including Schools, Further Education, Training, Higher Education and Teacher Education
Assistant Chief Inspector: Mr Vivian McIver

Pre-16 Education, including pre-school, primary and post-primary
Assistant Chief Inspector: Loretto Watson

Inspection Services Branch (ISB)
Deputy Principal: Jenny McIlwain

Agencies, Non Departmental Public Bodies and other organisations within Department of Education

Comhairle na Gaelscolaíochta
Teach an Gheata Thiar
4 Stráid na Banríona
Béal Feirste, BT1 6ED
Guthán: 028 9032 1475 / Facs: 028 9032 4475
Web: www.comhairle.org
R-Phost: eolas@comhairle.org

Príomhfheidhmeannach: Seán Ó Coinn

West Gate House
4 Queen Street
Belfast, BT1 6ED
Tel: 028 9032 1475 / Fax: 028 9032 4475
Web: www.comhairle.org
Email: eolas@comhairle.org

Chief Executive: Seán Ó Coinn

Council for Catholic Maintained Schools
160 High Street
Holywood, BT18 9HT
Tel: 028 9042 6972 / Fax: 028 9042 4255

Chief Executive: Donal Flanagan

General Teaching Council for Northern Ireland
4th Floor , Albany House
73-75 Great Victoria Street
Belfast, BT2 7AF
Tel: 028 9033 3390 / Fax: 028 9034 8787
Web: www.gtcni.org.uk
Email: info@gtcni.org.uk

Chairman: Dr Robert Rodgers

Integrated Education Fund
41 University Street
Belfast, ,BT7 1FY
Tel: 028 9033 0031 / Fax: 028 9033 0061
Web: www.ief.org.uk

Director: Tina Merron
Email: tina@ief.org

Iontaobhas na Gaelscolaiochta
199 Bothár na bhFal
Béal Feirste
BT12 6FB
Guthán: 028 9024 1510
Príomhfheidhmeannach: Pilib Ó Runaidh

199 Falls Road
Belfast. BT12 6FB
Tel: 028 9024 1510
Chief Executive: Pilib Ó Runaidh

Northern Ireland Council for Curriculum, Examinations and Assessment
29 Clarendon Road
Clarendon Dock, Belfast, BT1 3BG
Tel: 028 9026 1200 / Fax: 028 9026 1234
Web: www.ccea.org.uk
Email: info@ccea.org.uk

Chief Executive: Gavin Boyd

Northern Ireland Council for Integrated Education
44 University Street
Belfast, BT7 1HB
Tel: 028 9023 6200 / Fax: 028 9023 6237
Web: www.nicie.org.uk
Email: info@nicie.org.uk

Chief Executive Officer: Michael Wardlow

Staff Commission for Education and Library Boards
Forestview
Purdy's Lane, Belfast, BT8 7AR
Tel: 028 9049 1461 / Fax: 028 9049 1744
Web: www.staffcom.org.uk
Email: info@staffcom.org.uk

Chairman: Maurice Moroney

Youth Council for Northern Ireland
Forestview
Purdy's Lane, Belfast, BT8 7AR
Tel: 028 9064 3882 / Fax: 028 9064 3874
Web: www.youthcouncil-ni.org.uk

Chief Executive: David Guilfoyle

Department for Employment and Learning

Adelaide House, Adelaide Street
Belfast, BT2 8FD
Tel: 028 9025 7777 / Fax: 028 9025 7778
Web: www.delni.gov.uk

NIO Minister: Jane Kennedy
Permanent Secretary: Will Haire
Tel: 028 9025 7834
Private Office
Private Secretary: Jill Patton
Tel: 028 9025 7791
Press Office:
Principal Information Officer: Gwyn Treharne
Tel: 028 9025 7790

The Department of Employment and Learning (DEL) is responsible for the development of policy for, and the planning, funding and administration of further and higher education, with advice from the Northern Ireland Higher Education Council and the Further Education Consultative Committee. It is also responsible for policy in respect of student loans and awards (mandatory, discretionary and postgraduate) and for the payment of postgraduate awards.

DEL's key objective is to develop a culture of lifelong learning, and to promote wider access to, and greater participation in, further and higher education, particularly from groups previously underrepresented. It aims to improve quality and performance in the higher and further education sectors, and to enhance the contribution of these sectors to the regional economy.

The department has assumed the responsibilities of the former Training and Employment Agency. In this respect DEL's aim is to assist economic development and help people find sustainable employment through training and employment services. DEL also deals with the processing of Northern Ireland employment and industrial relations legislation, and has responsibility for matters relating to the Labour Relations Agency and the Certification Officer for Northern Ireland.

(Further information on Higher Education and Training in Northern Ireland is set out in chapter 6.)

Skills and Industry Division

Head of Division: Tom Scott
Tel: 028 9025 7807

Management Development
Head of Unit: Tom Hunter

Sectoral Development
Head of Unit: Jim Hanna

Supplier Services: Head of Unit: Tommy McVeigh

Training Programmes/IFI: Head of Unit: Richard Kenny
Training Services: Head of Unit: Francis Creagh (Acting)

Preparation for Work Division

Head of Division: Adrian Arbuthnot Tel: 028 9025 7807

Eastern Region: Regional Manager: Kieran Brazier

Western Region: Regional Manager: Daragh Shields

Employment and Policy: Head of Unit: Jim Wilkinson

New Deal Policy: Head of Unit: Martin Caher

Disablement Advisory Service: Head of Unit: John Campbell

Partnership Team: Head of Unit: Martin Boyd (Acting)

Regional Operations Support: Head of Unit: Peter Poland

Employment Programmes: Head of Unit: Liz Young

Employment Assessment Unit: Head of Unit: Joe Carleton

Business Change Team: Head of Unit: Siobhan Logue

Employment Rights Division

Head of Division: Roy Gamble Tel: 028 9025 7806

Employment Rights (1) Head of Unit: Tim Devine

Employment Rights (2) Head of Unit: Vacant

Bill Team: Head of Unit: William Caldwell

Office of Industrial Tribunals and Fair Employment Tribunals Head of Unit: Ann Loney

Higher and Further Education and Corporate Services

Deputy Secretary: Robson Davison

Finance & European Division

Head of Division: George O'Doherty Tel: 028 9025 7810

Finance (1): Head of Unit: Denis Lowry

Finance (2): Head of Unit: Jim Russell

European Policy Unit: Head of Unit: Raymond Little

European Unit: Head of Unit: John Neill

Higher Education & Student Support Division

Head of Division: David McAuley

Student Support: Head of Unit: Gerry Rogan

Higher Education Finance: Head of Unit: Geoff Harrison

Department for Employment and Learning Organisation Chart

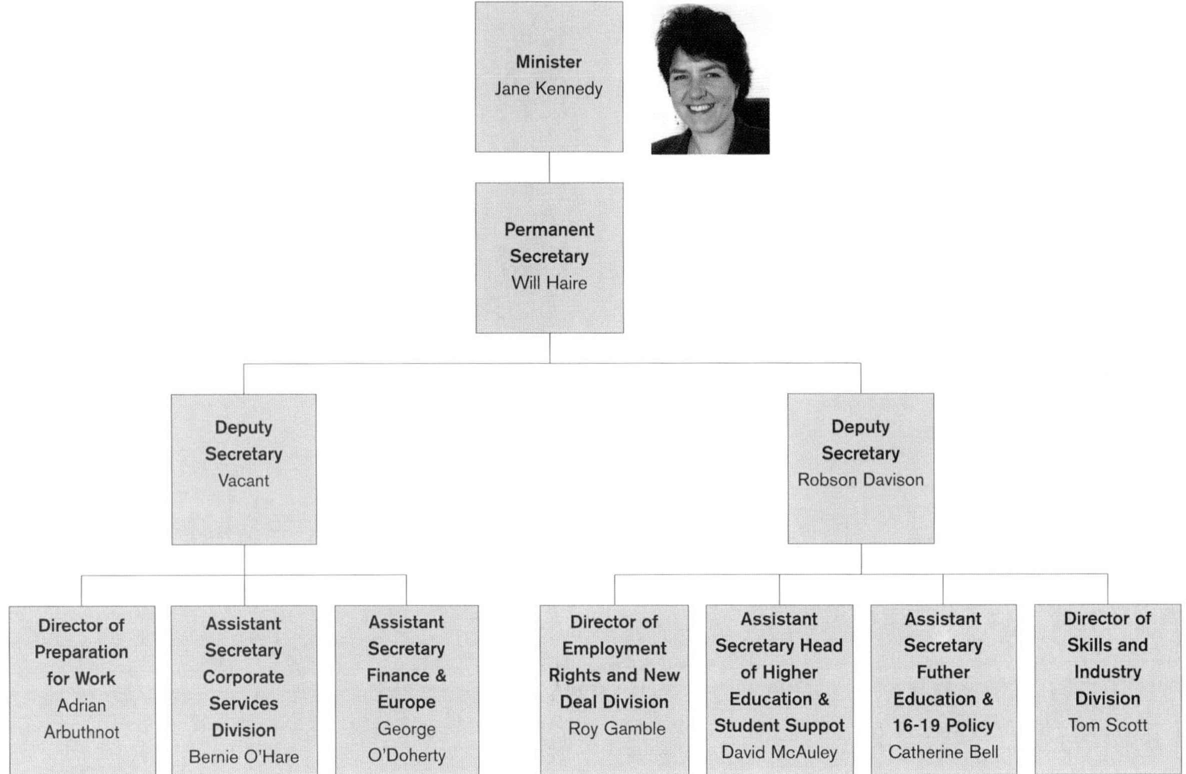

Higher Education Policy: Head of Unit: Sean McGarry

Tertiary Education Economic Unit: Head of Unit: Dr Linda Bradley

Tertiary Education Statistics and Research
Head of Unit: Victor Dukelow

Research and Evaluation: Head of Unit: Terry Morahan

Life Long Learning Division: Head of Division: Catherine Bell
Tel: 028 9025 7856

Further Education Accountability
Deputy Head of Division: Dr Roy Graham

Further Education Finance: Head of Unit: Rose Morrow

Further Education Capital Development
Head of Unit: Tom Redmond

Further Education Policy and Strategic Development
Head of Unit: Sheena Mairs
Learndirect: Head of Unit: Jan Harvey (Acting)

Qualifications and Learning Policy: Head of Unit: Deirdre McGill

Corporate Services Division: Head of Division: Bernie O'Hare
Tel: 028 9052 7769

Personnel: Head of Unit: Judith Shaw

CIS: Head of Unit: Mervyn Langtry

Central Policy and Planning: Head of Unit: Daryl Young

Media and Marketing Unit: Head of Unit: Gwyn Treharne

Agencies, Non Departmental Public Bodies and other organisations within the Department for Employment and Learning

Construction Industry Training Board
Nutts Corner Training Centre
17 Dundrod Road, Crumlin, BT29 4SR
Tel: 028 9082 5466 / Fax: 028 9082 5693
Web: www.citbni.org.uk / Email: info@citbni.org.uk
Chief Executive: Allan McMullen

Enterprise Ulster
The Close
Ravenhill Reach
Belfast, BT6 8RB
Tel: 028 9073 6400 / Fax: 028 9073 6404
Web: www.enterpriseulster.co.uk
Chief Executive: Joe Eagleson

Labour Relations Agency
Head Office
2-8 Gordon Street
Belfast, BT1 2LG
Tel: 028 9032 1442 / Fax: 028 9033 0827
Web: www.lra.org.uk
Email: info@lra.org.uk
Chief Executive: William Patterson

Learning and Skills Advisory Board
c/o Department for Employment and Learning
Adelaide House, Adelaide Street
Belfast, BT2 8FD
Tel: 028 9025 7777 / Fax: 028 9025 7778
Web: www.del.gov.uk
Chairman: Bill McGinnis

Northern Ireland Higher Education Council
Adelaide House
39-49 Adelaide Street
Belfast, BT2 8FD
Tel: 028 9025 7777 / Fax: 028 9025 7778
Chairman: Tony Hopkins

Northern Ireland Industrial Court
Room 203, Adelaide House, 39-49 Adelaide Street
Belfast, BT2 8FD
Tel: 028 9025 7676
Web: www.delni.gov.uk/er
Senior Case Manager: Anne-Marie O'Kane

Ulster Supported Employment Limited
182-188 Cambrai Street, Belfast, BT13 3JH
Tel: 028 9035 6600 / Fax: 028 9035 6611
Web: www.usel.co.uk
Email: info@usel.co.uk
Chief Executive: Mitchell Wylie

Department of Enterprise, Trade and Investment

Netherleigh House, Massey Avenue
Belfast, BT4 2JP
Tel: 028 9052 9900 / Fax: 028 9052 9550
Web: www.detini.gov.uk

Direct Rule Minister: Ian Pearson
Permanent Secretary: Bruce Robinson (pictured)
Tel: 028 9052 9441
Private Office
Private Secretary: Michael Harris
Tel: 028 9052 9208
Press Office
Press Officer: Philip Maguire
Tel: 028 9052 9201

DETI is responsible for economic policy development, energy, tourism, mineral development, health and safety at work, Companies Registry, Insolvency Service, consumer affairs, and labour market and economic statistics services. It also has a role in ensuring the provision of the infrastructure for a modern economy. Economics, financial and personnel management services are provided centrally within the Department.

DETI has four agencies, established as non-departmental public bodies (NDPBs), to assist in strategy implementation.

- Invest Northern Ireland (Invest NI), which supports business growth and inward investment, promotes innovation, research and development and in-company training, encourages exports and supports local economic development and company start up:
- The Northern Ireland Tourist Board (NITB), which is responsible for the development, promotion and marketing of Northern Ireland as a tourist destination:
- The Health and Safety Executive for Northern Ireland (HSENI), which is responsible for health, safety and welfare at work: and
- The General Consumer Council for Northern Ireland (GCCNI), which is responsible for promoting and safeguarding the interests of consumers and campaigning for the best possible standards of service and protection.

Policy Group

Director: Wilfie Hamilton Tel: 028 9052 9203

Strategic Policy: Head of Division: Malcolm Briant

Strategy Unit Principal: Rosemary Crawford

Policy Innovation Unit Principal: Vacant
Contact: Bernard McKeown
Tel: 028 9052 9302

Planning Unit: Principal: Mark Pinkerton

Telecomms: Principal: Anne Conaty

Policy Services

Head of Division: Robin McMinnis

Tourism Policy: Principal: David Carson

Equality/TSN/Euro: Principal: Mike Maxwell

Policy Services Unit/IFI BEP/State Aids
Principal: Ashley Ray

Minerals: Principal: Jim King

Invest NI Support Unit: Principal: Gerry McGeown

Energy

Head of Division: Mike Warnock

Gas Regulation: Principal: Tony Doherty

Electricity Regulation: Principal: Jenny Pyper

Sustainable Energy: Principal: David Stanley

Economics

Head of Division: Victor Hewitt

Economics: Principal: Philip Rodgers

Statistics Research: Principal: James Gillan

Management Services Group

Director: Noel Lavery / Tel: 028 9052 9226

Business Regulation: Head of Division: Mike Bohill

Insolvency: Director: Reg Nesbitt
Principals: Joe Hassan, Lesley Gawley

Consumer Affairs: Principal: David Livingstone

Corporate Regulation: Principal: Rosaleen McMullan

Social Economy: Principal: Anne-Marie Davison

Finance and EU: Head of Division: Vacant

Finance Branch and Accounts Branch:
Principal: Rodney Brown

Resource Accounting: Principal: Rodney Brown

Department of Enterprise, Trade and Investment Organisation Chart

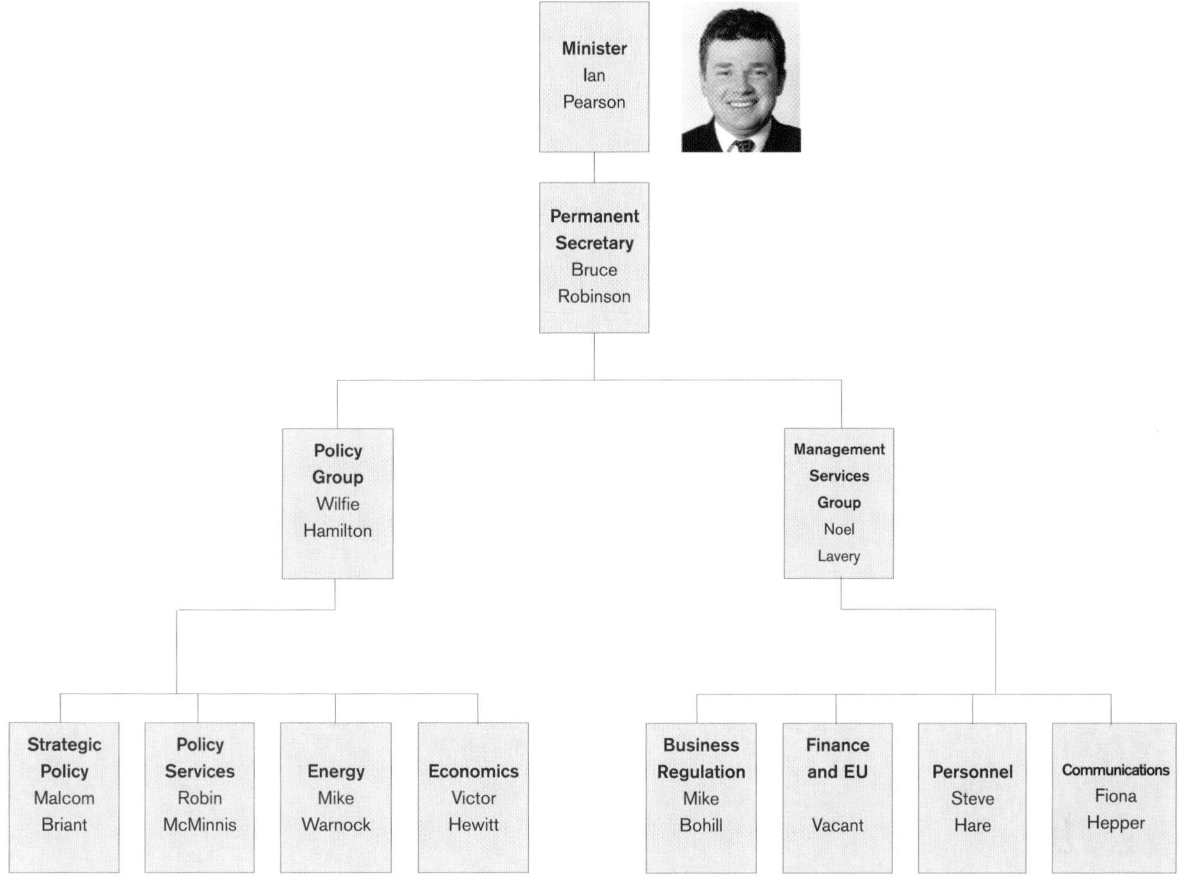

Invest Northern Ireland Accounts Project
Principal: Erroll Crooks

Internal Audit: Principal: Alan Magee

European Programmes
Principal: Howard Keery
Accountability & Invest NI Casework
Principal: Alberta Pauley

Finance: Principal: Bernie Brankin

Personnel

Head of Division: Steve Hare

Personnel/Services/IT: Principal: Alan Lamont

Personnel Development: Principal: Paula McCreary

Corporate Services: Principal: Terry Long
Information Management: Principal: Joe O'Hare

IT: Principal: Pat Cunningham

Communication

Head of Division: Fiona Hepper

Press Office: Principal Information Officer: Philip Maguire

Private Office/Central Management & Public Appointments /Parliamentary Support & Legislative Monitoring
Principal: David McCune

Marketing & Communication
Deputy Principal: Angela Jackson

Agencies, Non Departmental Public Bodies and other organisations within the Department of Enterprise Trade and Investment

General Consumer Council for Northern Ireland
116 Holywood Road, Belfast, BT4 1NY
Tel: 028 9067 2488 / Fax: 028 9065 7701
Web: www.gccni.gov.uk

Chief Executive: Eleanor Gill

Health and Safety Executive for Northern Ireland
83 Ladas Drive
Belfast, BT6 9FR
Tel: 028 9024 3249 / Fax: 028 9023 5383
Web: www.hseni.gov.uk

Chief Executive: Jim Keyes

Inter*Trade*Ireland
Old Gasworks Business Park, Kilmorey Street
Newry, BT34 2DE
Tel: 028 3083 4100 / Fax: 028 3083 4155
Web: www.intertradeireland.com
Email: info@tbdb.org

Chief Executive: Liam Nellis

Invest Northern Ireland
64 Chichester Street, Belfast, BT1 4JX
Tel: 028 9023 9090 / Fax: 028 9054 5000
Web: www.investni.com

Chief Executive: Leslie Morrison
Managing Directors: Chris Buckland, Tracy Meharg, Leslie Ross, Terri Scott
(further information on the structure and work of Invest Northern Ireland can be found in Chapter 8 A Guide to Doing Business in Northern Ireland).

Northern Ireland Tourist Board
St Anne's Quarter, North Street, Belfast, BT1 1NB
Tel: 028 9023 1221 / Fax: 028 9024 0960
Web: www.nitb.com

Chief Executive: Alan Clarke extn: 2212
Director of Corporate Services: Jim Perry extn: 2141
Director of Business Development: Philip Pentland extn: 2240
Director of Marketing: Sue Ward extn: 2256

Tourism Ireland Limited
Beresford House, 2 Beresford Road, Coleraine, BT52 1GE
Tel: 028 7035 9200 / Fax: 028 7032 6932

Chief Executive: Paul O'Toole

Department of the Environment

Clarence Court
10-18 Adelaide Street
Belfast, BT2 8GB
Tel: 028 9054 0540 / Fax: 028 9054 0024
Web: www.doeni.gov.uk

Minister: Angela Smith
Permanent Secretary: Stephen Peover
Tel: 028 9054 0002

Private Office
Acting Private Secretary: Anne Loughran
Tel: 028 9054 1166

Press Office
Principal Information Officer: Brian Kirk
Tel: 028 9054 0013

The Department of the Environment has a number of strategic objectives, relating to the conservation, protection and improvement of the natural and built environment. It is also charged with promoting a system of local government that meets the needs of ratepayers and citizens.

The Department has responsibility for planning policy in Northern Ireland, as well as the promotion of sustainable development. As part of this the Department of the Environment oversees the Driver and Vehicle Testing Agency, which checks the safety and roadworthiness of road vehicles, including their impact on the environment. The Department also oversees the Driver and Vehicle Licensing.

The Department of the Environment has a central role in protecting wildlife and the countryside, including pollution and waste management. The Department's Environment and Heritage Service has an important role in enhancing the natural and built environment.

The Department also has responsibility for the promotion of road safety, both by publicity campaigns and direct action.

Planning and Local Government

Deputy Secretary: Cynthia Smith

Planning Service
Chief Executive: David Ferguson
Tel: 028 9054 0649

Local Government Policy
Director of Local Government: John Ritchie
Tel: 028 9054 0844

Corporate Services

Director: Dr Murray Power

RSVSD, DVTA, DVLNI, Environment and Heritage

Deputy Secretary: Felix Dillon
Tel: 028 9054 1178

Environment and Heritage Service
Chief Executive: Richard Rogers

Environment Policy Division
Director: Judena Goldring
Tel: 028 9025 7360

Driver and Vehicle Testing Agency (DVTA)
Chief Executive: Stanley Duncan

Road Safety Division
Director: Wesley Shannon
Tel: 028 9054 0843

Driver and Vehicle Licensing Northern Ireland (DVLNI)
Chief Executive: Brendan Magee

Agencies, Non Departmental Public Bodies and other organisations within DOE

Council for Nature Conservation and the Countryside

Waterman House, 5-33 Hill Street
Belfast, BT1 2LA
Tel: 028 9054 3076

Chairman: Dr Lucinda Blakiston Houston

Driver and Vehicle Licensing Northern Ireland

County Hall, Castlerock Road, Coleraine, BT51 3TA
Web: www.doeni.gov.uk/dvlni
Email: dvlni@doeni.gov.uk

Chief Executive: Brendan Magee
Tel: 028 7034 1461
Director of Development: Trevor Evans
Director of Drivers and Road Transport Licensing: Colin Campbell
Director of Programmes: Bernie Cosgrove
Director of Vehicle Licensing: Ann McCabe
Director of Corporate Services: Seamus McClean
Director of Finance: Lucia O'Connor

Driver Licensing Division:
Tel: 028 7034 1469 / Fax: 028 7034 1398

Vehicle Licensing Division:
Tel: 028 7034 1461 / Fax: 028 7034 1422

Vehicle Licensing Central Office
Telephone Re-Licensing Section
Tel: 028 7034 1514

Sale of Mark Section
Tel: 028 7034 1244

Commercial Operator Licensing:
148-158 Corporation Street
Belfast, BT1 3DH
Tel: 028 9025 4100 / Fax: 028 9025 4086

Department of the Environment Organisation Chart

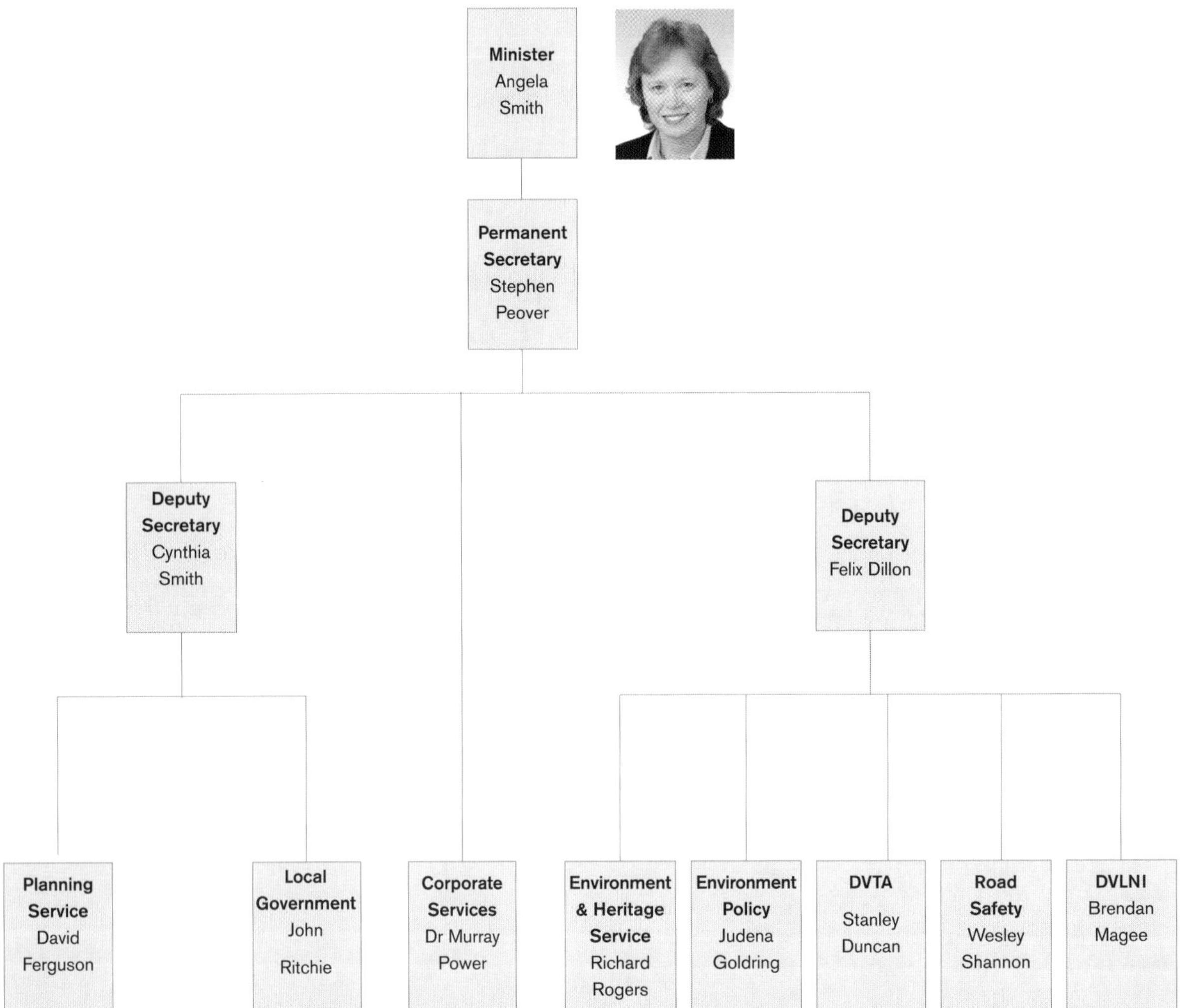

Driver and Vehicle Licensing NI continued...

Local Offices

Opening hours for all local offices: 9.15am – 4.00pm

Armagh
Dobbin Centre
Dobbin Lane, Armagh, BT61 7QP
Tel: 028 3752 7305 / Fax: 028 3752 8721
Contact: Jill Kane

Ballymena
County Hall, Galgorm Road, Ballymena, BT42 1HN
Tel: 028 2565 3333 / Fax: 028 2566 2067
Contact: Ronnie Rowe

Belfast
Royston House, Upper Queen Street, Belfast, BT1 6FA
Tel: 028 9054 2042 / Fax: 028 9054 7379
Contact: Christine Clark

Coleraine
County Hall, Castlerock Road, Coleraine
Tel: 028 7034 1417 / Fax: 028 7034 1418
Contact: Clare Wilson

Downpatrick
Rathkeltair House, Market Street, Downpatrick, BT30 6AJ
Tel: 028 4461 2211 / Fax: 028 4461 8089
Contact: Mary Keenan

Enniskillen
County Buildings
East Bridge Street, Enniskillen, BT74 7BW
Tel: 028 6634 6555 / Tel: 028 6632 2750
Contact: Kate Charity

Londonderry
Orchard House, 40 Foyle Street, Londonderry, BT48 6AT
Tel: 028 7131 9900 / Fax: 028 71319819
Contact: Terence Healey

Omagh
Boaz House, 15 Scarffes Entry
Omagh, BT78 1JE
Tel: 028 8225 4700 / Fax: 028 8225 4711
Contact: Annie Alexander

Driver and Vehicle Testing Agency

Balmoral Road, Belfast, BT12 6QL
Tel: 028 9068 1831 / Fax: 028 9066 5520
Web: www.doeni.gov.uk/dvta
Chief Executive: Stanley Duncan

Director of Finance: Colin Berry
Director of Customer Services: John Crosby
Director of Human Resources: Marianne Fleming
Director of Operations: Trevor Hassin
Director of Technical Policy and Legislation: Alastair Peoples
Director of Corporate Services: David Wilson

Local Offices

Armagh
47 Hamiltonsbawn Road, Armagh, BT60 1HW
Tel: 028 3752 2699

Ballymena
Pennybridge Industrial Estate
Larne Road, Ballymena, BT42 3ER
Tel: 028 2564 6801

Belfast
Balmoral Road, Belfast, BT12 6QL
Tel: 028 9068 1831

Coleraine
2 Loughan Hill Industrial Estate
Gateside Road, Coleraine, BT52 2NJ
Tel: 028 7034 3819

Cookstown
Sandholes Road, Cookstown, BT80 9AR
Tel: 028 8676 4809

Craigavon
3 Diviny Drive
Carn Industrial Estate, Craigavon, BT63 5RY
Tel: 028 3833 6188

Downpatrick
Cloonagh Road
Flying Horse Road, Downpatrick, BT30 6DU
Tel: 028 4461 4565

Enniskillen
Chanterhill, Enniskillen, BT74 6DE
Tel: 028 6632 2871

Larne
Ballyboley Road, Ballyloran, Larne, BT40 2SY
Tel: 028 2827 8808

Lisburn
Ballinderry Industrial Estate
Ballinderry Road, Lisburn, BT28 2SA
Tel: 028 9266 315

Londonderry
New Buildings Industrial Estate, Victoria Road, Londonderry
Tel: 028 7134 3674

Mallusk
Commercial Way, Hydepark Industrial Estate
Newtownabbey, BT36 8YY
Tel: 028 9084 2111

Newry
51 Rathfriland Road, Newry, BT34 1LD
Tel: 028 3026 2853

Newtownards
Jubilee Road, Newtownards, BT23 4XP
Tel: 028 9181 3064

Omagh
Gortrush Industrial Estate, Derry Road, Omagh, BT78 5EJ
Tel: 028 8224 2540

Environment and Heritage Service

Chief Executive: Richard Rogers
Web: www.ehsni.gov.uk

Natural Heritage, Waste Management, Regional Operations, Information and Education
Commonwealth House
35 Castle Street, Belfast, BT1 1GU
Tel: 028 9025 1477 / Fax: 028 9054 6660

Historic Buildings and Monuments
5-33 Hill Street, Belfast, BT1 2LA
Tel: 028 9054 3076

Water Management, Drinking Water, Air and Environmental Quality
Calvert House, 23 Castle Place
Belfast, BT1 1FF
Tel: 028 9025 4754

Air and Environmental Quality
Tel: 028 9054 6425
Email: ep@doeni.gov.uk

Built Heritage General Enquiries
Tel: 028 9054 3034
Email: bh@doeni.gov.uk

Directorate and Corporate Affairs
Tel: 028 9025 1477
Email: ca@doeni.gov.uk

Drinking Water Inspectorate
Tel: 028 9054 6474
Email: ep@doeni.gov.uk

Duty of Care
Tel: 028 9054 6450

EHS Web Manager
Tel: 028 9054 6689
Email: emma.penney@doeni.gov.uk

Environmental Protection
Tel: 028 9025 4754
Email: ep@doeni.gov.uk

General Waste Enquiries
Tel: 028 9054 6725
Email: wakeuptowaste@doeni.gov.uk

Historic Buildings General Enquiries
Tel: 028 9054 3061
Email: hb@doeni.gov.uk

Historic Buildings Grants
Tel: 028 9054 3064 or 028 9054 3073
Email: hbgrants@doeni.gov.uk

Historic Buildings Listing
Tel: 028 9054 3058 or 028 9054 3075
Email: hblisting@doeni.gov.uk

Historic Monuments
Tel: 028 9054 3048
Email: ivan.minnis@doeni.gov.uk

Historic Monuments Enquiries
Tel: 028 9054 3037
Email: hm@doeni.gov.uk

Industrial Pollution
Tel: 028 9025 4773
Email: irpi@doeni.gov.uk

Information and Education
Tel: 028 9054 6533
Email: ehsinfo@doeni.gov.uk

Monuments and Buildings Record
Tel: 028 9054 3004
Email: mbr@doeni.gov.uk

Natural Heritage Conservation Science
Tel: 028 9054 6461
Email: meredith.thompson@doeni.gov.uk

Natural Heritage Grants
Tel: 028 9054 6442
Email: stephen.acheson@doeni.gov.uk

Natural Heritage Protected Landscapes
Tel: 028 9054 6556
Email: ruth.blair@doeni.gov.uk

Natural Heritage Research Database
Tel: 028 9054 6501
Email: alison.burke@doeni.gov.uk

Producer Responsibility and Packaging Waste
Tel: 028 9054 6487

Radioactivity/Radon
Tel: 028 9025 4733
Email: ipri@doeni.gov.uk

Registration of Carriers
Tel: 028 9054 6694

Special/Hazardous Waste
Tel: 028 9054 6463

State Care Monuments Enquiries
Tel: 028 9054 3037
Email: sc@doeni.gov.uk

Wake Up to Waste Campaign
Tel: 028 9064 6725
Email: wakeuptowaste@doeni.gov.uk

Water Management Unit
Tel: 028 9025 4754
Email: ep@doeni.gov.uk

Water Pollution Hotline
Tel: 0800 807060
Email: emergency-pollution@doeni.gov.uk

Historic Buildings Council
Secretariat, 5-33 Hill Street, BT1 2LA
Tel: 028 9054 3076
Email: hb@doeni.gov.uk

Historic Monuments Council
Chairman: Richard Black
Tel: 028 9054 3037
Email: hm@doeni.gov.uk

Local Government Staff Commission
Commission House
18-22 Gordon Street, Belfast, BT1 2LG
Tel: 028 9031 3151
Fax: 028 9031 3200
Web: www.lgsc.org.uk
Email: info@lgsc.org.uk
Chief Executive: Adrian Kerr

Northern Ireland Local Government Officers Superannuation Committee
Templeton House, 411 Holywood Road, Belfast, BT4 2LP
Tel: 028 9076 8025
Fax: 028 9076 8790
Web: www.nilgosc.org.uk
Email: info@nilgosc.org.uk
Chairman: John Galbraith

Planning Service
Clarence Court, 10-18 Adelaide Street, Belfast, BT2 8GB
Tel: 028 9054 0540 / Fax: 028 9054 0665
Web: www.planningni.gov.uk

Chief Executive: David Ferguson
Tel: 028 9054 0649
Director Corporate Services: Ian Maye
Tel: 028 9054 0650
Director Planning Policy: Mr Pat Quinn
Tel: 028 9054 0727
Director Operations: Mr Pat McBride
Tel: 028 9054 0647
Professional Services Manager: Anne Garvey

Regional Offices

Ballymena
County Hall, 182 Galgorm Hall, Ballymena, BT42 1QF
Tel: 028 2565 3333 / Fax: 028 2566 2127
Divisional Planning Manager: Helena O'Toole

Belfast
Bedford House, 16-22 Bedford Street, Belfast, BT2 7FD
Tel: 028 9025 2800 / Fax: 028 9025 2828
Divisional Planning Manager: David Carroll

Coleraine
County Hall, Castlerock Road, Coleraine, BT51 3HS
Tel: 028 7034 1300 / Fax: 028 7034 1434
Divisional Planning Manager: Jim Cavalleros

Craigavon
Marlborough House, Central Way, Craigavon, BT64 1AD
Tel: 028 3834 1144 / Fax: 028 3834 1065
Divisional Planning Manager: Hilary Heslip

Downpatrick
Rathkeltair House, Market Street, Downpatrick, BT30 6EJ
Tel: 028 4461 2211 / Fax: 028 4461 8196
Divisional Planning Manager: Tom Clarke

Enniskillen
County Buildings, 15 East Bridge Street, Enniskillen, BT74 7BW
Tel: 028 6634 6555 / Fax: 028 6634 6550
Divisional Planning Manager: Brian Hughes

Londonderry
Orchard House, 40 Foyle Street, Londonderry, BT48 6AT
Tel: 028 7131 9900 / Fax: 028 7131 9777
Divisional Planning Manager: Jim Cavalleros

Omagh
County Hall, Drumragh Avenue, Omagh, BT79 7AE
Tel: 028 8225 4000 / Fax: 028 8225 4009
Divisional Planning Manager: Brian Hughes

Waste Management Advisory Board for Northern Ireland
Chairman: Professor Deborah Boyd

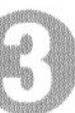

Department of Finance and Personnel

Rathgael House
Balloo Road
Bangor, BT19 7NA
Tel: 028 9127 9279 / Fax: 028 9185 8104
Web: www.dfpni.gov.uk

Direct Rule Minister: Ian Pearson
Permanent Secretary: John Hunter
Tel: 028 9185 8174
Second Permanent Secretary: Andrew McCormick
Tel: 028 9052 7437

Private Office
Private Secretary: David McCreedy
Tel: 028 9052 9140

Press Office
Principal Information Officer: Colin Ross
Tel: 028 9052 7375

The Department of Finance and Personnel, or DFP, has a wide range of functions, many of which are carried out centrally either by the department directly or through an agency on behalf of the Civil Service in Northern Ireland.

DFP is responsible for public expenditure, including the formulation of an annual Budget. It seeks to secure appropriate funding from various sources, including the European Union. It is also responsible for personnel, which translates as the general management of the Civil Service (including the areas of policy, pay, recruitment and security). The Department is also responsible for law reform and the provision of legal services to other Northern Ireland departments.

The Department provides procurement services for goods, services and works to the Northern Ireland government departments and their associated public bodies. It is also responsible for the development of procurement policy for the Civil Service in Northern Ireland and the dissemination of best practice and provides a single point of contact for advice on procurement matters.

It provides a valuation service to the public sector, and through the Rate Collection Agency (RCA), collects rates in Northern Ireland. The Department is also responsible for the Land Registers of Northern Ireland, and also provides a range of design, maintenance and advisory services on construction matters to the Northern Ireland public sector.

DFP oversees the work of NISRA, the Northern Ireland Statistics and Research Agency, which provides a service to support the development, monitoring and evaluation of social and economic policy, as well as providing information to the general public, and organising the Census of Population.

Departmental Solicitor's Office
Head of Legal Services: Robin Cole
Victoria Hall, 12 May Street
Belfast, BT1 4NL
Tel: 028 9025 1221 / Fax: 028 9025 1235

Office of Law Reform
Director: Ethne Harkness
Lancashire House
5 Linenhall Street, Belfast, BT2 8AA
Tel: 028 9054 2901 / Fax: 028 9054 2909

Central Finance Group
Rathgael House, Balloo Road, Bangor, BT19 7NA

Budget Directorate
Budget Director: Leo O'Reilly
Tel: 028 9127 7601 / Fax: 028 9127 7672

Treasury of Accounts & Supply Directorate
Treasury Officer of Accounts: David Thomson
Tel: 028 9185 8150 / Fax: 028 9185 8261

European Union Division
Assistant Secretary: Bill Pauley

Health Estates
Stoney Road, Belfast, BT16 0UP
Tel: 028 9052 3707 / Fax: 028 9052 3949

Central Personnel Group
Director: Linda Brown
Rosepark House, Upper Newtownards Road, Belfast, BT4 3NR
Tel: 028 9052 6166 / Fax: 0289052 6466

Corporate Services Division
Director: Chris Thompson
Rathgael House, Balloo Road, Bangor, BT19 7NA
Tel: 028 9185 8045 / Fax: 028 9185 8048

Central Procurement
Director: John McMillen
Churchill House, 20-34 Victoria Square, Belfast, BT1 4QW
Tel: 028 9025 0250

Agencies, Non Departmental Public Bodies and other organisations within DFP

Business Development Service
Craigantlet Buildings, Stoney Road, Belfast, BT4 3SX
Tel: 028 9052 7406 / Fax: 028 9052 7270
Web: www.nics.gov.uk/bds
Chief Executive: Ray Long

Land Registers of Northern Ireland
Lincoln Building, 27-45 Great Victoria Street
Belfast, BT2 7SL
Tel: 028 9025 1515 / Fax: 028 9025 1550
Web: www.lrni.gov.uk

Chief Executive: Patricia Montgomery

Department of Finance and Personnel Organisation Chart

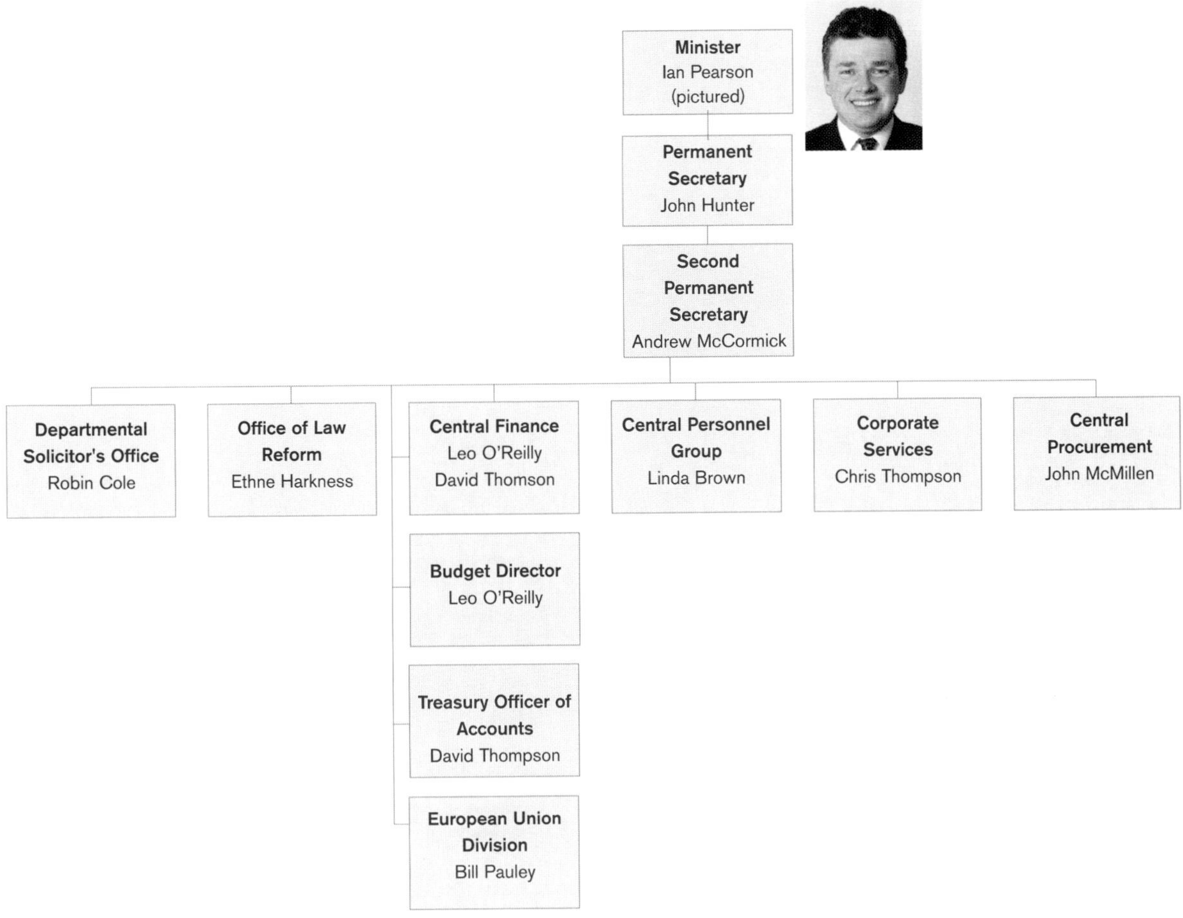

Law Reform Advisory Committe for Northern Ireland

Lancashire House
5 Linenhall Street, Belfast, BT2 8AA
Tel: 028 9054 2900 / Fax: 028 9054 2909
Web: www.olrni.gov.uk

Secretary: Clare Irvine
Email: clare.irvine@dfpni.gov.uk

Northern Ireland Building Regulations Advisory Committee

Building Regulations Unit
Office Estates and Building Standards Division
Department of Finance and Personnel, 3rd Floor
Lancashire House, 3 Linenhall Street, Belfast, BT2 8AA
Tel: 028 9054 2923 / Fax: 028 9054 7866
Secretary: Hugh Murray

Northern Ireland Statistics and Research Agency

McAuley House, 2-14 Castle Street, Belfast, BT1 1SA
Tel: 028 9034 8100 / Fax: 028 9034 8106
Web: www.nisra.gov.uk

Chief Executive: Norman Caven

Rate Collection Agency

Oxford House, 49-55 Chichester Street, Belfast, BT1 4HH
Tel: 028 9052 2252 / Fax: 028 9052 2113
Web: www.ratecollectionagencyni.gov.uk

Chief Executive: Arthur Scott

Valuation and Lands Agency

Queen's Court, 56-66 Upper Queen Street, Belfast, BT1 6FD
Tel: 028 9025 0700 / Fax: 028 9054 3750
Web: www.vla.nics.gov.uk

Chief Executive: Nigel Woods

Department of Health, Social Services and Public Safety

Castle Buildings, Stormont Estate
Upper Newtownards Road, Belfast, BT4 3SQ
Tel: 028 9052 0500 / Fax: 028 9025 0572
Web: www.dhsspsni.gov.uk

Direct Rule Minister: Angela Smith
Permanent Secretary: Clive Gowdy
Tel: 028 9052 0559
Fax: 028 9052 0573

Private Office
Private Secretary: Sharon Lindsay
Tel: 028 9052 0642
Fax: 028 9052 0557

Information Office
Press Officer: Colm Shannon
Tel: 028 9052 0636
Fax: 028 9052 0572

The Department of Health, Social Services and Public Safety (DHSSPS) has three main business responsibilities:

- **Health and Personal Social Services**, which includes policy and legislation for hospitals, family practitioner services and community health and personal social services;
- **Public Health**, which covers policy, legislation and administrative action to promote and protect the health and well-being of the population and emergency planning;
- **Public Safety**, which includes responsibility for the policy and legislation for public safety policies, including Ambulance Services, and Fire Services.

The Department's mission is to improve everyone's health and social well-being. It does so by ensuring the provision of appropriate health and social care services, both in clinical settings, such as hospitals and GPs' surgeries, and in the community, through nursing, social work and other professional services. It also supports programmes of health promotion and education to encourage the community to adopt activities, behaviours and attitudes that will lead to better health and well-being.

Primary, Secondary and Community Care Group
Deputy Secretary: Andrew Hamilton
Tel: 028 9052 3263

This Group deals with the operational issues relating to the commissioning and delivery of services in the Health and Personal Social Services. It maintains a close relationship with the various bodies making up the HPSS and works with them to ensure that they operate within the policy framework set by Ministers.

Primary Care Directorate
Director: Dr Jim Livingstone
Tel: 028 9052 2788

Secondary Care Directorate
Director: Dean Sullivan
Tel: 028 9052 2101

Community Care Directorate
Director: Leslie Frew
Tel: 028 9052 2786

Resources and Performance Management Group

Deputy Secretary: Don Hill
Tel: 028 9052 0560

This Group negotiates and has management of financial resources for the DHSSPS, departmental staffing policy and resources and internal audit arrangements for the Department. It also deals with the collection and provision of information and analysis on HPSS matters and is responsible for monitoring and management of the performance of the HPSS.

Personnel & Corporate Services Directorate
Director: Paul Conliffe
Tel: 028 9052 2825

Finance Directorate
Director: Julie Thompson
Tel: 028 9052 2446

Information & Analysis Directorate
Director: Dr Liz McWhirter
Tel: 028 9052 2522

Planning & Performance Management Directorate
Director: Vacant
Acting Director: Ray Martin
Tel: 028 9052 2795

Strategic Planning and Modernisation Group

Deputy Secretary: Paul Simpson
Tel: 028 9052 2667

This Group has responsibility for strategic management and planning issues for the DHSSPS. It manages the capital development programme and provides strategic direction on HR. It has responsibility for public safety policies (including ambulance services, fire services and regional transport services), the regional strategy for health and social well-being, and overall co-ordination of New TSN, equality and Human Rights.

Support Services Unit
Head: Patricia Blacker
Tel: 028 9052 3184

Department of Health, Social Services and Public Safety Organisation Chart

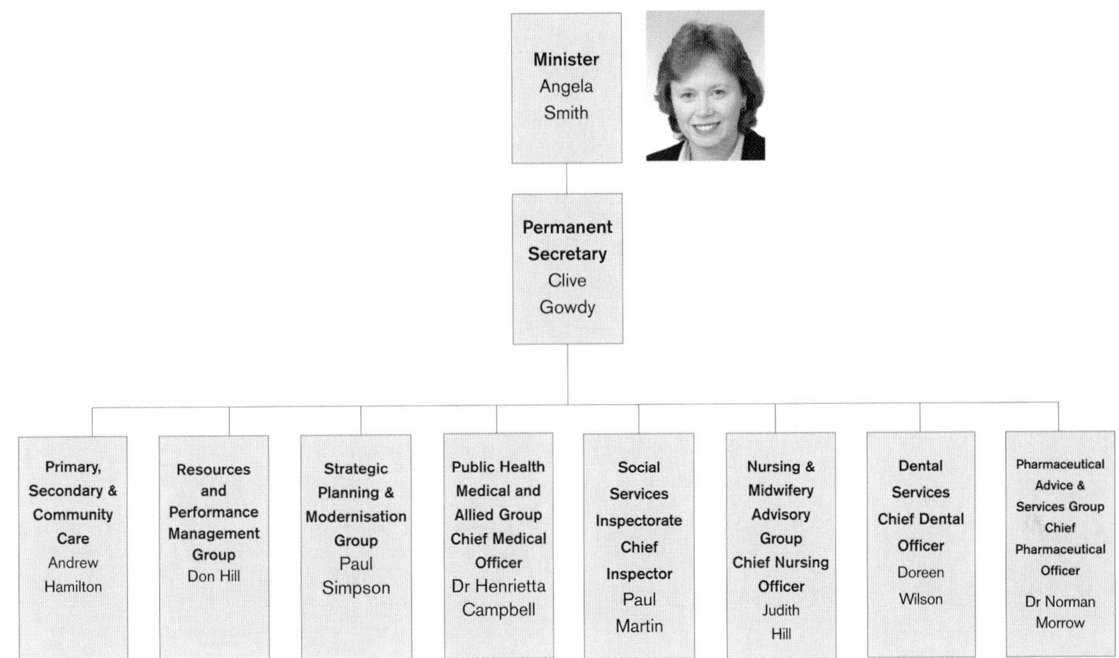

Directorate of Information Systems/ITG
Director: Garry Williams
Tel: 028 9054 2201

Human Resources Directorate
Director: David Bingham
Tel: 028 9052 0781

Modernisation Unit
Director: David Finegan
Tel: 028 9052 2784

Public Safety Directorate
Director: Dr Bill Smith
Tel: 028 9052 0231

Strategy, Inclusion & Development Directorate
Director: Dr Denis McMahon
Tel: 028 9052 0553

Public Health, Medical and Allied Group

Chief Medical Officer
Dr Henrietta Campbell
Tel: 028 9052 0563

The Public Health, Medical and Allied Group, led by the Chief Medical Officer, provides advice and specific medical services for the Department, the wider Northern Ireland Civil Service, and the Prison Service. This Group is also responsible for the public health business area, comprising the Investing for Health initiative; health protection; health promotion; emergency planning and strategies on smoking, drugs and alcohol.

Social Services Inspectorate
Chief Inspector
Paul Martin
Tel: 028 9052 0561

The Social Services Inspectorate, under the leadership of the Chief Inspector, provides advice and support to Ministers, the Department, other Government Departments and agencies in the field of Social Care. An Annual Inspection Programme across a range of services and providers is carried out for the Department and the Northern Ireland Office. The Inspectorate also carries responsibility for policy on social work and social care training and education including the disbursement of postgraduate social work bursaries and other training support funding linked to the PSS Training Strategy.

Nursing and Midwifery Advisory Group
Chief Nursing Officer: Judith Hill / Tel: 028 9052 0562

The Nursing & Midwifery Advisory Group, led by the Chief Nursing Officer, is responsible for advising the Department, the wider Northern Ireland Civil Service and the Prison Service on all aspects of policy which affect nursing, midwifery and health visiting, education and services.

Dental Services Group
Chief Dental Officer: Doreen Wilson / Tel: 028 9052 2940

Dental Services Group, led by the Chief Dental Officer, provides advice on oral health to the Department, the wider Northern Ireland Civil Service and other bodies and agencies. Monitoring of dental treatment provided by general dental practitioners is carried out by the Referral Dental Service. It also delivers direct dental services to the Prisons and Young Offenders Centre.

Pharmaceutical Advice and Services Group
Chief Pharmaceutical Officer: Dr Norman Morrow
Tel: 028 9052 3219

The Pharmaceutical Advice and Services Group, led by the Chief Pharmaceutical Officer, is responsible for the provision of specialist advice in respect of medicines and pharmaceutical services. It also has responsibility for medicines legislation, including inspection and enforcement under that legislation pertaining to both human and veterinary medicines.

Health Estates
The Department of Health, Social Services and Public Safety also operates the Northern Ireland Health and Social Services Estates Agency, known as Health Estates.

Health Estates, established as an Agency in October 1995, determines policy on estate issues in relation to the delivery of health and social care. The Agency's task is to provide professional and technical advice, guidance and support on estate matters, at both strategic and operational levels, to the various bodies charged with responsibility for the Health and Social Services estate. It also provides a range of executive consultancy services, principally in the disciplines of architecture, mechanical and electrical engineering, quantity surveying and site inspection and manages the contract for the treatment and disposal of clinical waste for the whole of Ireland.

Health Estates
Stoney Road, Dundonald, Belfast, BT16 1US
Tel: 028 9052 0025 / Fax: 028 9052 3900
Web: www.dhsspsni.gov.uk/hea

Chief Executive: John Cole / Tel: 028 905 23823
Estates Development

Director: Eddie Brett / Tel: 028 905 23702
Estates Policy / Director: Stan Blayney
Tel: 028 905 23763

Agencies, Non Departmental Public Bodies and other organisations within DHSSPS

Altnagelvin Hospitals HSST
Glenshane Road
Londonderry, BT47 6SB
Tel: 028 7134 5171 / Fax: 028 7161 1222

Chairman: Denis Desmond CBE
Chief Executive: Stella Burnside

Armagh and Dungannon HSST
St Luke's Hospital
Armagh, BT61 7NQ
Tel: 028 3752 2381 / Fax: 028 3752 6302

Chairman: James Shaw
Chief Executive: Pauline Stanley

Belfast City Hospital HSST
51 Lisburn Road
Belfast, BT9 7AB
Tel: 028 9032 9241 / Fax: 028 9032 6614

Chairman: Joan Ruddock OBE
Chief Executive: Quentin Coey

Central Services Agency
25-27 Adelaide Street, Belfast, BT2 8FH
Tel: 028 9032 4431 / Fax: 028 9023 2304
Web: www.centralservicesagency.com
Email: chiefexec@csa.n-i.nhs.uk

Chairperson: Professor John Frances Fulton
Chief Executive: Stephen Hodkinson

Causeway HSST
80 Coleraine Road
Ballymoney, BT53 6BP
Tel: 028 2766 6600 / Fax: 028 2766 1201

Chairman: Jean Jefferson
Chief Executive: Norma Evans

Craigavon and Banbridge Community HSST
Bannvale House
10 Moyallen Road
Gilford, BT63 5JX
Tel: 028 3883 1983 / Fax: 028 3883 1993

Chairman: David Cook
Chief Executive: Denis Preston

Craigavon Area Hospital HSST
68 Lurgan Road
Craigavon, BT63 5QQ
Tel: 028 3833 4444

Chairman: E McClurg
Chief Executive: John Templeton

Distinction and Meritorious Service Awards Committee
Room D.13
Castle Buildings, Stormont
Belfast, BT4 3SJ
Tel: 028 9052 2817 / Fax: 028 9052 2912

Secretary: John Nesbitt

Down Lisburn HSST
Lisburn Health Centre
25 Linenhall Street
Lisburn, BT28 1LU
Tel: 028 9266 5181 / Fax: 028 9267 6206

Chairman: Denise Fitzsimnons
Chief Executive: John Compton

Eastern Health and Social Services Board
Champion House
12-22 Linenhall Street
Belfast, BT2 8BS
Tel: 028 9032 1313 / Fax: 028 9055 3680

Chairman: David Russell
Chief Executive: Paula Kilbane

Eastern Health and Social Services Council
1st Floor McKelvey House
24-27 Wellington Place
Belfast, BT1 6GQ
Tel: 028 9032 1230 / Fax: 028 9032 1750

Chairman: Brian Coulter
Chief Officer: Jane Graham

Fire Authority for Northern Ireland
Brigade Headquarters
1 Seymour Street, Lisburn, BT27 4SX
Tel: 028 9266 4221 / Fax: 028 9267 7402
Web: www.nifb.org.uk

Chairman: William Gillespie
Chief Fire Officer: Colin Lammey

Food Safety Promotion Board
7 Eastgate Avenue
Eastgate, Little Island, Cork
Tel: 00 353 21 230 4100 / Fax: 00 353 21 230 4111
Web: www.safefoodonline.com

Chief Executive: Martin Higgins

Foyle HSST
Riverview House
Abercorn Road
Londonderry, BT48 6FB
Tel: 028 7126 6111

Chairman: Anthony Jackson
Chief Executive: Elaine Way

Green Park Healthcare HSST
20 Stockman's Lane
Belfast, BT9 7JB
Tel: 028 9066 9501 / Fax: 028 9059 1501

Chairman: Ian Doherty
Chief Executive: Hilary Boyd

Health Estates Agency
Stoney Road, Dundonald, Belfast, BT16 1US
Tel: 028 9052 0025 / Fax: 028 9052 3900
Web: www.dhsspsni.gov.uk/hea

Chief Executive: John Cole
Estates Development
Director: Eddie Brett
Tel: 028 9052 3702

Estates Policy
Director: Stan Blayney
Tel: 028 9052 3763

Health Promotion Agency for Northern Ireland
18 Ormeau Avenue, Belfast, BT2 8HS
Tel: 028 9031 1611 / Fax: 028 9031 1711
Web: www.healthpromotionagency.org.uk
Email: info@hpani.org.uk

Chairman: Alice Quinn
Chief Executive: Dr Brian Gaffney

Homefirst HSST
The Cottage, 5 Greenmount Avenue
Ballymena, BT43 6DA
Tel: 028 2563 7000 / Fax: 028 2563 3733

Chairman: William Boyd
Chief Executive: Christie Colhoun

Mater Infirmorum HSST
45-51 Crumlin Road
Belfast, BT14 6AB
Tel: 028 9080 2338 / Fax: 028 9074 9784

Chairman: Lady McCollum
Chief Executive: Patricia Gordon

Mental Health Commission
Elizabeth House
118 Holywood Road, Belfast, BT4 1NY
Tel: 028 9065 1157 / Fax: 028 9047 1180
Email: mhc@dhsspsni.gov.uk

Chairperson: Marian O'Neill
Acting Chief Executive: Stephen Jackson

Mental Health Review Tribunal
Room 11 Annex 6
Castle Buildings, Stormont
Belfast, BT4 3SQ
Tel: 028 9052 3388 / Fax: 028 9052 0683

Chairman: Fraser Elliott QC
Secretary: Esther Clarke/Alison Bray

Newry and Mourne HSST
5 Downshire Place
Downshire Road, Newry, BT34 1DZ
Tel: 028 3026 0505 / Fax: 028 3026 9064

Chairman: Sean Hogan
Chief Executive: Eric Bowyer

North and West Belfast HSST
Glendinning House
6 Murray Street, Belfast, BT1 6DP
Tel: 028 9032 7156 / Fax: 028 9082 1285

Chairman: Patrick McCarten
Chief Executive: Richard Black

Northern Health and Social Services Board
County Hall, 182 Galgorm Road
Ballymena, BT42 1HN
Tel: 028 2565 3333 / Fax: 028 2565 5112

Chairman: Michael Wood
Chief Executive: Stuart Macdonnell

Northern Health and Social Services Council
8 Broadway Avenue, Ballymena, BT43 7AA
Tel: 028 2565 5777 / Fax: 028 2565 5112

Chairman: Joe McFadden
Chief Executive: Noel Graham

Northern Ireland Ambulance Services HSST
Knockbraken Healthcare Park
Saintfield Road, Belfast, BT8 8SG
Tel: 028 9040 0999 / Fax: 028 9040 0900

Chairman: Doug Smyth
Chief Executive: Paul McCormick

Northern Ireland Blood Transfusion Service Agency
Belfast City Hospital Complex
51 Lisburn Road, Belfast, BT9 7TS
Tel: 028 9053 4662 / Fax: 028 9043 9017
Web: www.nibts.org
Email: chiefexec@nibts.n-i.nhs.uk

Chairperson: Stephen Costello
Chief Executive: Morris McClelland

Northern Ireland Council for Postgraduate Medical and Dental Education
5 Annadale Avenue, Belfast, BT7 3JH
Tel: 028 9049 2731 / Fax: 028 9064 2279
Web: www.nicpmde.com
Email: nicpmde@nicpmde.gov.uk

Chairperson: Dr Don Keegan
Chief Executive: Dr JR McCluggage

Northern Ireland Guardian Ad Litem Agency
Centre House
79 Chichester Street, Belfast, BT1 4JE
Tel: 028 9031 6550 / Fax: 028 9031 9811
Web: www.nigala.n-i.nhs.uk
Email: admin@nigala.n-i.nhs.uk

Chairperson: Jim Currie
Chief Executive: Ronnie Williamson

Northern Ireland Practice and Education Council for Nursing and Midwifery
Centre House, 79 Chichester Street
Belfast, BT1 4JE
Tel: 028 9023 8152 / Fax: 028 9023 3298
Web: www.nipec.n-i.nhs.uk
Email: enquiries@ nipec.n-i.nhs.uk

Chairperson: Maureen Griffith
Chief Executive: Ms Paddy Blaney

Northern Ireland Regional Medical Physics Agency
Musgrave and Clarke House
Royal Hospitals Site
Grosvenor Road, BT12 6BA
Tel: 028 9063 4430 / Fax: 028 9031 3040
Web: www.medicalphysics.n-i.nhs.uk
Email: office.administrator@mpa.n-i.nhs.uk

Chairperson: Professor David Walmsley
Chief Executive: Professor Peter Jaritt

Northern Ireland Social Care Council
7th Floor Millennium House
19-25 Great Victoria Street
Belfast, BT2 7AQ
Tel: 028 9041 7600 / Fax: 028 9041 7601
Web: www.niscc.info

Chief Executive: Brendan Johnston
Chairman: Jeremy Harbison

Royal Group of Hospitals and Dental Hospital HSST
Grosvenor Road, Belfast, BT12 6BA
Tel: 028 9024 0503
Fax: 028 90 24 0899

Chairman: Paul McWilliams
Chief Executive: William McKee

South and East Belfast HSST
Knockbracken Healthcare Park
Saintfield Road
Belfast, BT8 8BH
Tel: 028 9056 5656
Fax: 028 9056 5813

Chairman: Robin Harris
Chief Executive: Patricia Gordon

Southern Health and Social Services Board
Tower Hill
Armagh
BT61 9DR
Tel: 028 3741 0041
Fax: 028 3741 4550

Chairman: William Gillespie
Chief Executive: Colm Donaghy

Southern Health and Social Services Council
Quaker Buildings
High Street
Lurgan
BT66 8BB
Tel: 028 3834 9900
Fax: 028 3834 9858

Chairman: Roisin Foster
Chief Executive: Delia van der Lenden

Sperrin Lakeland HSST
Strathdene House
Tyrone and Fermanagh Hospital
Omagh, BT79 0NS
Tel: 028 8283 5285
Fax: 028 8283 5286

Chairman: Richard Scott
Chief Executive: Hugh Mills

Ulster Community and Hospitals HSST
39 Regent Street
Newtownards
BT23 4AD
Tel: 028 9181 6666
Fax: 028 9182 0140

Chairman: Siobhan Grant
Chief Executive: Jim McCall

United Hospital HSST
Bush House
45 Bush Road
Antrim
BT41 2QB
Tel: 028 9442 4673
Fax: 028 9442 4675

Chairman: Dr Harry McGuigan CBE
Chief Executive: Bernard Mitchell

Western Health and Social Services Board
15 Gransha Park
Clooney Road
Londonderry
BT47 6FN
Tel: 028 7186 0086
FAX: 028 7186 0311

Chairman: J Bradley
Chief Executive: S Lindsay

Western Health and Social Services Council
Hilltop
Tyrone and Fermanagh Hospital
Omagh
BT79 0NS
Tel: 028 8225 2555
Fax: 028 8225 2544

Chairman: F Hughes
Chief Executive: Stanley Millar

Department for Regional Development

Clarence Court
10-18 Adelaide Street
Belfast, BT2 8GB
Tel: 028 9054 0540 / Fax: 028 9054 0024
Web: www.drdni.gov.uk

Direct Rule Minister: John Spellar
Permanent Secretary: Stephen Quinn
Tel: 028 9054 1175

Private Office
Private Secretary: Paul Gill
Tel: 028 9054 0105

Principal Information Officer: Paddy Cullen
Tel: 028 9054 0817

The Department for Regional Development (DRD) is charged with strategic and transport planning in Northern Ireland. It is responsible for the provision and maintenance of roads, water and sewage services. The Department also develops policy relating to public transport, including rail, bus, ports and airports. Much of DRD's operational work is carried out by its two executive agencies: the Roads Service and the Water Service.

The department has recently published a ten-year development strategy, which has created considerable interest in future infrastructural development priorities.

Regional Planning and Transportation

Deputy Secretary: Paul Sweeney
Tel: 028 9084 0100

Director of Transport Policy and Support Division:
Richard Aiken
Tel: 028 9025 7320

Director of Regional Planning and Transportation Division:
Mike Thompson

Director of Air and Sea Ports Division: Robin McMinnis
Tel: 028 9054 2989

Resources and Management Services

Deputy Secretary:
Principal Establishment and Finance Officer: David Sterling
Tel: 028 9054 1180

Director of Personnel: Wendy Johnston
Tel: 028 9054 1070

Director of CPMU: Alan McArthur
Tel: 028 9054 1195

Director of Finance: Jack McGibbon
Tel: 028 9054 0847

Director of Infrastructure and Funding Division: Jackie Kerr
Tel: 028 9054 1008

Internal Audit: Ronnie Balfour
CCU: Stephen Murphy

Roads Service

Chief Executive: Malcolm McKibbin
Tel: 028 9054 0191

Director of Corporate Services: Jim Carlisle
Tel: 028 9054 0906

Director of Network Services: David Orr
Tel: 028 9054 0462

Director of Engineering: Geoff Allister
Tel: 028 9054 0471

Director of Finance: John McNeill
Tel: 028 9054 0469

Water Service

Chief Executive: Katharine Bryan
Tel: 028 9024 4711

Director of Finance: David Carson
Tel: 028 9024 4711

Acting Director of Operations: William Gowdy
Tel: 028 9024 4711

Director of Development: Trevor Haslett
Tel: 028 9024 4711

Acting Director of Technology: Raymond Cummings
Tel: 028 9024 4711

Director of Corporate Services: Robin Mussen
Tel: 028 9024 4711

Director of Customer Services: William Duddy
Tel: 028 9024 4711

Reform Coordinator: Peter May
Tel: 028 9024 4711

Agencies, Non Departmental Public Bodies and other organisations within DRD

Coleraine Harbour
Harbour Office, 4 Riversdale Road, Coleraine, BT52 1RY
Tel: 028 7034 2012 / Fax: 028 7035 2000
Web: www.coleraineharbour.f9.co.uk
Email: info@ coleraineharbour.f9.co.uk

Department for Regional Development Organisation Chart

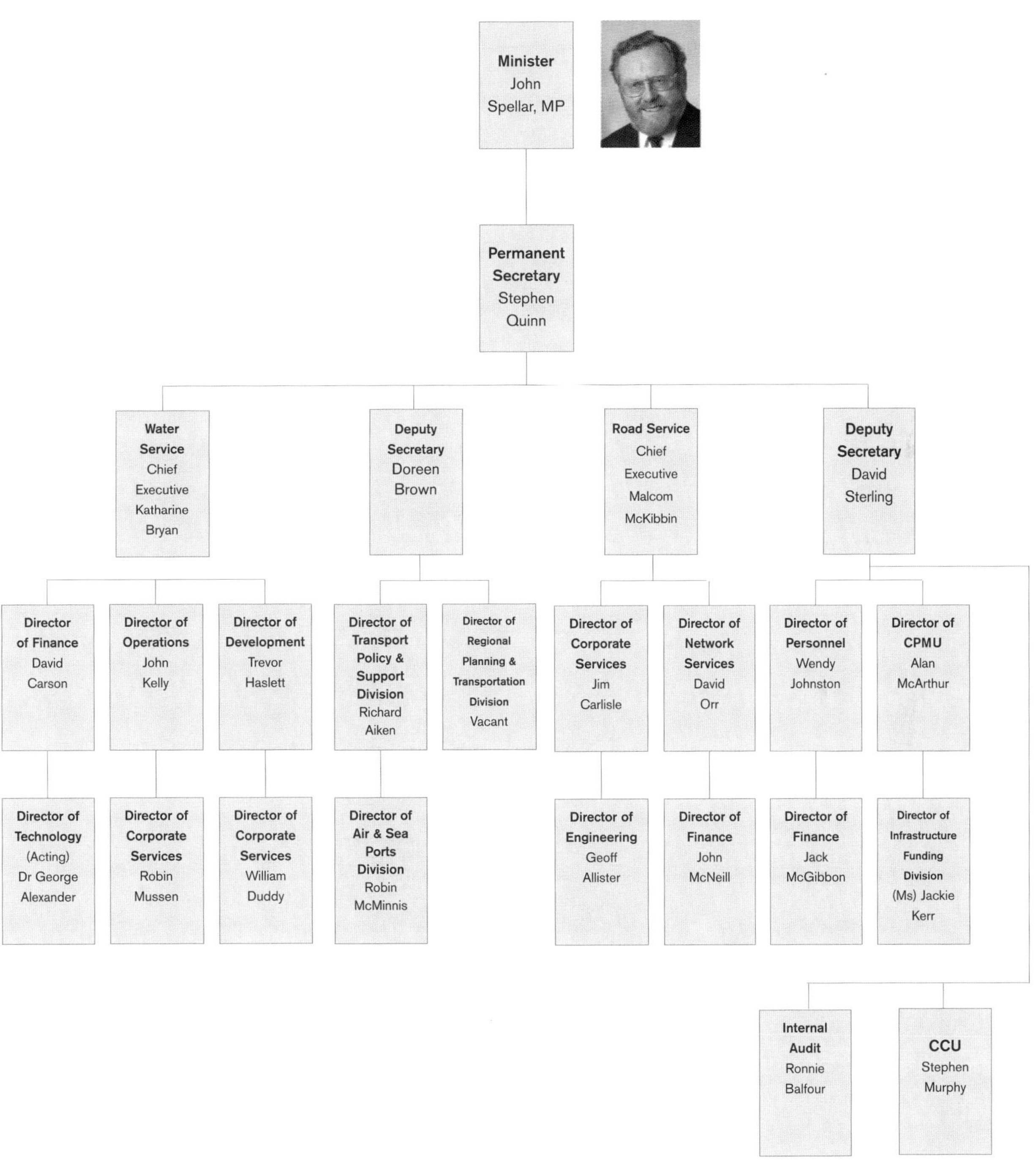

Londonderry Port and Harbour
Harbour Office
Port Road, Lisahally
Londonderry, BT47 6FL
Tel: 028 7186 0555 / Fax: 028 7186 1168
Web: www.londonderryport.com
Email: info@londonderry-port.co.uk

Chief Executive: Brian McGrath

Northern Ireland Transport Holding Company
Chamber of Commerce House
22 Great Victoria Street, Belfast, BT2 7LX
Tel: 028 9024 3456 / Fax: 028 9043 8717
Web: www.translink.co.uk/nithco
Email: nithc@dialstart.net

Chairperson: Dr Joan Smyth
Corporate Director: Jim Aiken

Port of Belfast
Belfast Harbour Commissioners
Belfast, BT1 3AL
Tel: 028 9055 4422 / Fax: 028 9055 4411
Web: www.belfast-harbour.co.uk
Email: info@belfast-harbour.co.uk

Chief Executive: Vacant

Roads Service
Clarence Court
10-18 Adelaide Street, Belfast, BT2 8GB
Tel: 028 9054 0540 / Fax: 028 9054 0024
Web: www.roadsni.gov.uk
Email: roads@drdni.gov.uk

Chief Executive: Dr Malcolm McKibben

Regional Offices

Eastern Division
Hydebank, 4 Hospital Road
Belfast, BT8 8JL
Tel: 028 9025 3000 / Fax: 028 9025 3220

Divisional Manager: Joe Drew

Northern Division
County Hall
Castlerock Road, Coleraine, BT51 3HS
Tel: 028 7034 1300 / Fax: 028 7034 1430

Divisional Manager: Dr Andrew Murray

Southern Division
Marlborough House
Central Way, Craigavon, BT64 1AD
Tel: 028 3834 1144 / Fax: 028 3834 1867

Divisional Manager: John White

Western Division
County Hall
Drumragh Avenue, Omagh, BT79 7AF
Tel: 028 8225 4111 / Fax: 028 8225 4010

Divisional Manager: Pat Doherty

Warrenpoint Harbour
Warrenpoint Harbour Authority
Warrenpoint, BT34 3JR
Tel: 028 4177 3381 / Fax: 028 4175 2875
Web: www.warrenpointharbour.co.uk
Email: info@warrenpointharbour.co.uk

Chief Executive: Quintin Goldie

Water Council
Water Service Strategic Policy Branch
Room 1.08
34 College Street, Belfast, BT1 6DR
Tel: 028 9054 1158 / Fax: 028 9054 1156
Web: www.watercouncilni.gov.uk
Email: secretary@watercouncilni.gov.uk

Water Service
Northland House
3 Frederick Street, Belfast, BT1 2NR
Tel: 028 9024 4711 / Fax: 028 9032 4888
Web: www.waterni.gov.uk
Email: waterline@waterni.gov.uk

Chief Executive: Katharine Bryan

Regional Offices

Eastern Division
34 College Street
Belfast, BT1 6DR
Tel: 028 9032 8161 / Fax: 028 9035 4828

Northern Division
Academy House
121a Broughshane Street
Ballymena, BT43 6BA
Tel: 028 2565 3655 / Fax: 028 2566 3131

Southern Division
Marlborough House
Central Way
Craigavon, BT64 1AD
Tel: 028 3834 1100 / Fax: 028 3832 0555

Western Division
Belt Road
Altnagelvin
Londonderry, BT47 2LL
Tel: 028 7131 2221 / Fax: 028 7131 0330

Department for Social Development

Churchill House, Victoria Square, Belfast, BT1 4SD
Tel: 028 9056 9100 / Fax: 028 9056 9240
Web: www.dsdni.gov.uk

Direct Rule Minister: John Spellar
Permanent Secretary: Alan Shannon
Tel: 028 9056 9203
Private Office
Private Secretary: Allister Macrory
Tel: 028 9056 9216
Press Office
Principal Information Officer: Jim Hamilton
Tel: 028 9056 9211

The Department for Social Development (DSD) brings together areas of work from both the former Department of Health and Social Services and the Department of the Environment. It administers the social security, child support and pension schemes and associated appeals services.

DSD is responsible for housing policy and urban regeneration and community development, along with social and charities legislation and the voluntary and community unit. The department sponsors a number of non-departmental public bodies. These include the Northern Ireland Housing Executive (NIHE), Laganside Corporation and several advisory and tribunal bodies.

The Department for Social Development's mission is to promote individual and community wellbeing through integrated social and economic action. Many of its policies impact on health, particularly housing. It interacts with many of the poorest in society, and has responsibility for improving housing, delivering social security benefits, providing child support services and developing community infrastructure. A key elements of current DSD strategies include providing through the Northern Ireland Housing Executive and Housing Associations high quality affordable social housing for those on low incomes and in greatest need.

Central Policy and Co-ordination Unit

Director: Philip Angus
Tel: 028 9056 9775

Office of the Permanent Secretary
Principal: George Davidson
Tel: 028 9056 9200

Information Office
Principal: Jim Hamilton
Tel: 028 9056 9211

Statistics
Principal: Dr Chris Morris
Tel: 028 9052 2280

Economics
Principal: Noel McNally
Tel: 028 9055 1953

Corporate Policy and Planning Branch
Principal: Robert Breakey
Tel: 028 9056 9161

Corporate Improvement Team
Principal: Karen Robinson
Tel: 028 9056 9171

Departmental Record Office
Principal: Paul McAllister
Tel: 028 9056 9301

Urban Regeneration and Community Development Division

Deputy Secretary: John McGrath
Tel: 028 9056 9204

Victoria Square Project Team
Director: Jackie Johnston
Tel: 028 9027 7678

Belfast Regeneration Office
Director: Frank Duffy
Tel: 028 9025 1973

Urban Regeneration Strategy Directorate
Director: Henry Johnston
Tel: 028 9056 9262

North West Development Office
Director: Declan O'Hare
Tel: 028 7131 9782

Regional Development Office
Director: Eddie Hayes
Tel: 028 9025 1901

Voluntary and Community Unit
Director: Dave Wall
Tel: 028 9056 9304

Resources Housing and Social Security Group

Deputy Secretary: Derek Baker
Tel: 028 9056 9205

Financial Management Directorate

Director: John Deery
Tel: 028 9056 9104

Finance
Principal: Brendan Devlin
Tel: 028 9056 9358

Decision Making & Appeals Service
Deputy Principal: Roisin McRory
Tel: 028 9054 3628

Department for Social Development Organisation Chart

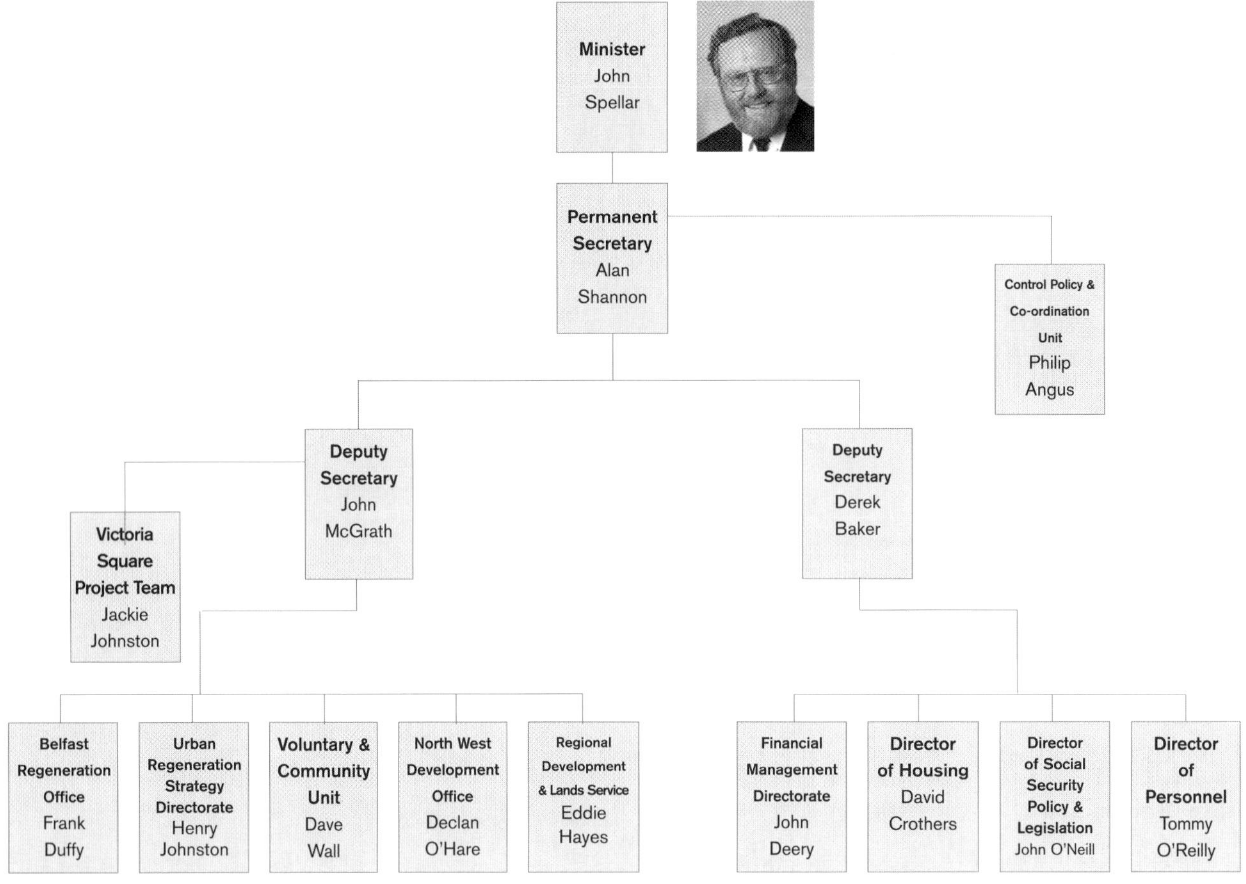

Housing Division

Director David Crothers
Tel: 028 9091 0007

Housing Management
Principal: Scott Carson
Tel: 028 9091 0061

Housing Finance
Principal: Patrick Anderson
Tel: 028 9091 0074

Housing Associations Branch
Principal: Billy Graham
Tel: 028 9091 0382

Housing Policy
Principal: Jerome Burns
Tel: 028 9054 0789

Housing Policy
Principal: Jerome Burns
Tel: 028 9091 0062

Housing Bill
Principal: Scott Carson
Tel: 028 9091 0061

Social Security Policy and Legislation Division

Director: John O'Neill
Tel: 028 9052 2434

Personnel Division

Director: Tommy O'Reilly
Tel: 028 9056 9130

Establishment Officer
Rosaleen Carlin
Tel: 028 9022 4009

Social Security Agency

Chief Executive: Gerry Keenan
Tel: 028 9056 9127

Personnel and Planning Directorate

Personnel Director: Tommy O'Reilly
Tel: 028 9056 9130

Personnel Branch
Senior Manager: Mr Pat Magee
Tel: 028 9056 9457

Support Services
Senior Manager: Noel Walker
Tel:028 9052 2871

Welfare Reforms Accommodation
Senior Manager: Janis Hatchell
Tel: 028 9056 9659

Training and Development Unit
Principal: Andrew Bell
Tel: 028 9054 3649

Chief Executive's Office
Principal: Margaret Boyle
Tel: 028 9056 9166

Communications Unit
Manager: Martin McDermott
Tel: 028 9056 9335

Benefit Security Directorate

Director: David McCurry
Tel: 028 9056 9131

Benefit Investigation Services
Principal: Rene Murray
Tel: 028 9054 4604

Risk Management Unit
Principal: P Crossley
Tel: 028 7036 1085

Monitoring Advice and Guidance
Principal: L Bell
Tel: 028 9056 9198

Welfare Reforms
Principal: J O'Neill
Tel: 028 9037 6088

Business Development Directorate

Director: Tommy O'Reilly
Tel: 028 9056 9130

Service Delivery
Principal: Trevor Moutray
Tel: 028 9056 9656

IS/IT Unit
Principal: Johnny Graham
Tel: 028 9054 4627

Active Modern Service
Principal: Sean Johnston
Tel: 028 9056 9177

Belfast Benefit Centre
Principal: Mervyn Adair
Tel: 028 9023 4920

Finance and Support Unit

Director: Heather Cousins
Tel: 028 9056 9129

Agency Resources Branch
Principal: Damian Prince
Tel: 028 9065 8821

Finance Support Branch
Principal: Alan Harvey
Tel: 028 9052 2007

Agency Audit Unit
Principal: Donald Heaney
Tel: 028 9025 2642

Support Services
Principal: Noel Walker
Tel: 028 9052 2871

Commercial Services Branch
Principal: Michael Bray
Tel: 028 9052 0084

Operations Directorate

Director: Vacant
Network Support Branch
Principal: Tom Quinn
Tel: 028 9056 9538

Family and Disability Benefits
Principal: Colin McRoberts
Tel: 028 9033 6940
Tel: 028 9054 5664

Customer Services Directorate

Director of Disability & Carers and Equality: Anne Flanagan
Tel: 028 9056 9141

Child Support Agency

Chief Executive: Barney McGahan
Tel: 028 9089 6805

Director of Resources: John Canavan
Tel: 028 9089 6840

Director NICSAC Operations: Mary Quinn
Tel: 028 9089 6967

Director EBO Field Operations (GB): Martin Johnston
Tel: 01226 776513

Operations Manager (NI): Michael Donnelly
Tel: 028 9089 6855

Senior Ops Manager: Catherine McCallum
Tel: 028 9047 6240

CSR: David Sales
Tel: 028 903 9200

Personnel Officer: Jayne Forster
Tel: 028 9027 7959

Resourcecs: Stephen Boyd
Tel: 028 9089 6789

Agencies, Non Departmental Public Bodies and other organisations within DSD

Appeals Service

Cleaver House, 3 Donegall Square North, Belfast, BT1 5GA
Tel: 028 9056 8501 / Fax: 028 9051 8516
Web: www.dsdni.gov.uk/appeals-service

Charities Advisory Committee

Treasury and Management Branch, 4th Floor
Churchill House, Victoria Square, Belfast, BT1 4QW
Tel: 028 9056 9650
Secretary: Trevor Campbell

Child Support Agency

Great Northern Tower, 17 Great Victoria Street
Belfast, BT2 7AD
Tel: 028 9089 6666 / Fax: 028 9089 6777
Chief Executive: Barney McGahan

Disability Living Allowance Advisory Board for Northern Ireland

Castle Court, Royal Avenue, Belfast, BT1 1DS
Tel: 028 9033 6916 / Fax: 028 9054 2112

Laganside Corporation

Clarendon Building, 15 Clarendon Road, Belfast, BT1 3BG
Tel: 028 9032 8507 / Fax: 028 9033 2141
Web: www.laganside.com
Email: info@laganside.com
Chief Executive: Kyle Alexander

Northern Ireland Housing Executive

The Housing Centre
2 Adelaide Street, Belfast, BT2 8GA
Tel: 028 9024 0288 / Fax: 028 9043 9803
Web: www.nihe.gov.uk
Chief Executive: Paddy McIntyre

Rent Assessment Panel

Housing Policy Branch
2nd Floor, Andras House
60 Great Victoria Street, Belfast, BT2 7BB
Tel: 028 9091 0050 / Fax: 028 9091 0060

Rent Officer: Joan McCrum

Social Security Agency

Churchill House
Victoria Square, Belfast, BT1 4SS
Tel: 028 9056 9100 / Fax: 028 9056 9178
Web: www.ssa.gov.uk
Email: customerservice.unit@dsdni.gov.uk

Chief Executive: Gerry Keenan

Other Government Organisations

An A-Z Guide to Government Agencies and other Public Bodies

In addition to the 11 government departments, there exists in Northern Ireland a substantial number of other organisations within the public sector with responsibility for delivering public services. These fall into a number of different categories:

Agencies
Agencies tend to be organisations responsible for delivering specific and often customer-facing public services, operating at 'arm's length' from government. Their day-to-day work is involved in delivering that service, the general policy framework under which they operate is set by the relevant department. They are usually run by a Chief Executive and management team, and report to the minister of the relevant department, rather than an appointed Board. Examples of government agencies are Social Security Agency, Health Estates Agency, Business Development Service.

Non-Departmental Public Bodies
Non-Departmental Public Bodies (NDPBs) are attached to a sponsoring government department but are not part of that department. They are, however, the responsibility of the Minister of the department they are attached to. There are three categories of non-departmental public bodies: executive NDPBs, advisory NDPBs and tribunal NDPBs. NDPBs are usually accountable to an appointed Board.

Executive NDPBs
Executive bodies are public organisations whose duties include executive, administrative, regulatory or commercial functions. Operating within broad policy guidelines set by departmental ministers they are to varying degrees independent of government in the execution of their day-to-day responsibilities, employ their own staff and have their own budget. Examples of Executive NDPBs in Northern Ireland include the Northern Ireland Housing Executive, Fire Authority for Northern Ireland or Invest Northern Ireland

Advisory NDPBs
These bodies provide provide an advisory function to government ministers or departments – examples are the Health and Social Services Councils, the Water Council and the Waste Management Advisory Board. Members of these organisations often contribute on a voluntary basis, in addition to their 'day-job'.

Tribunal NDPBs
These organisations have jurisdiction in a specified field of law, for example, Mental Health Review Tribunal, Rent Assessment Panel, Fair Employment Tribunal.

Agricultural Research Institute of Northern Ireland
Large Park
Hillsborough, BT26 6DR
Tel: 028 9268 2484 / Fax: 028 9268 9594
Web: www.arani.ac.uk

Director: Dr Sinclair Mayne
Relevant department: Department of Agriculture and Rural Development

Agricultural Wages Board
Agricultural Wages Secretariat
Room 910, Dundonald House, Upper Newtownards Road
Belfast, BT4 3SB
Tel: 028 9052 0813
Relevant department: Department of Agriculture and Rural Development

Altnagelvin Hospitals HSS Trust
Glenshane Road, Londonderry, BT47 6SB
Tel: 028 7134 5171 / Fax: 028 7161 1222

Chairman: Denis Desmond CBE
Chief Executive: Stella Burnside
Relevant department: Department of Health, Social Services and Public Safety

Appeals Service
Cleaver House
3 Donegall Square North, Belfast, BT1 5GA
Tel: 028 9051 8518 / Fax: 028 9051 8516
Web: www.dsdni.gov.uk/appeals-service
Relevant department: Department for Social Development

Armagh and Dungannon HSS Trust
St Luke's Hospital
Armagh, BT61 7NQ
Tel: 028 3752 2381 / Fax: 028 3752 6302

Chairman: James Shaw
Chief Executive: Pauline Stanley
Relevant department: Department of Health, Social Services and Public Safety

Arts Council of Northern Ireland
MacNeice House
77 Malone Road
Belfast, BT9 6AQ
Tel: 028 9038 5200 / Fax: 028 9066 1715
Web: www.artscouncil-ni.org
Email: info@artscouncil-ni.org

Chief Executive: Roisin McDonagh
Relevant department: Department of Culture, Arts and Leisure

Belfast City Hospital HSS Trust

51 Lisburn Road
Belfast, BT9 7AB
Tel: 028 9032 9241 / Fax: 028 9032 6614

Chairman: Joan Ruddock OBE
Chief Executive: Quentin Coey
Relevant department: Department of Health, Social Services and Public Safety

Belfast Education and Library Board

40 Academy Street
Belfast, BT1 2NQ
Tel: 028 9056 4000 / Fax: 028 9033 1714

Chairperson: Carmel McKinney
Chief Executive: David Cargo
Relevant department: Department of Education

Business Development Service

Craigantlet Buildings, Stoney Road
Belfast, BT4 3SX
Tel: 028 9052 7406 / Fax: 028 9052 7270
Web: www.nics.gov.uk/bds

Chief Executive: Ray Long
Relevant department: Department of Finance and Personnel

Causeway HSS Trust

80 Coleraine Road
Ballymoney, BT53 6BP
Tel: 028 2766 6600 / Fax: 028 2766 1201

Chairman: Jean Jefferson
Chief Executive: Norma Evans
Relevant department: Department of Health, Social Services and Public Safety

Central Services Agency

25-27 Adelaide Street
Belfast, BT2 8FH
Tel: 028 9032 4431 / Fax: 028 9023 2304
Web: www.centralservicesagency.com
Email: chiefexec@csa.n-i.nhs.uk

Chairperson: Professor John Frances Fulton
Chief Executive: Stephen Hodkinson
Relevant department: Department of Health, Social Services and Public Safety

Charities Advisory Committee

Treasury and Management Branch
4th Floor, Churchill House
Victoria Square, Belfast, BT1 4QW
Tel: 028 9056 9650

Secretary: Trevor Campbell
Relevant department: Department for Social Development

Child Support Agency

Great Northern Tower
17 Great Victoria Street, Belfast, BT2 7AD
Tel: 028 9089 6666 / Fax: 028 9089 6777

Chief Executive: Barney McGahan
Relevant department: Department for Social Development

Community Relations Council

6 Murray Street, Belfast, BT1 6DN
Tel: 028 9022 7500 / Fax: 028 9022 7551

Chief Executive: Dr Duncan Morrow
Relevant department: Office of the First Minister and Deputy First Minister

Coleraine Harbour

Harbour Office
4 Riversdale Road, Coleraine, BT52 1RY
Tel: 028 7034 2012 / Fax: 028 7035 2000
Web: www.coleraineharbour.f9.co.uk
Email: info@coleraineharbour.f9.co.uk
Relevant department: Department for Regional Development

Comhairle na Gaelscolaíochta

Teach an Gheata Thiar
4 Stráid na Banríona, Béal Feirste, BT1 6ED
Guthán: 028 9032 1475 / Facs: 028 9032 4475
Web: www.comhairle.org
R-Phost: eolas@comhairle.org

Príomhfheidhmeannach: Seán Ó Coinn

West Gate House
4 Queen Street, Belfast, BT1 6ED
Tel: 028 9032 1475 / Fax: 028 9032 4475
Web: www.comhairle.org
Email: eolas@comhairle.org

Chief Executive: Seán Ó Coinn
Relevant department: Department of Education

Compensation Agency

Royston House, 34 Upper Queen Street
Belfast, BT1 6FX
Tel: 028 9024 9944
Web: www.compensationni.gov.uk

Chief Executive: Anne McCleary
Relevant department: Northern Ireland Office

Construction Industry Training Board

Nutts Corner Training Centre
17 Dundrod Road, Crumlin, BT29 4SR
Tel: 028 9082 5466 / Fax: 028 9082 5693
Web: www.citbni.org.uk
Email: info@citbni.org.uk

Chief Executive: Allan McMullen
Relevant department: Department for Employment and Learning

Council for Catholic Maintained Schools

160 High Street, Holywood, BT18 9HT
Tel: 028 9042 6972 / Fax: 028 9042 4255

Chief Executive: Donal Flanagan
Relevant department: Department of Education

Council for Nature Conservation and the Countryside

Waterman House, 5-33 Hill Street, Belfast, BT1 2LA
Tel: 028 9054 3076 / Fax: 028 9054 3076

Chairman: Dr Lucinda Blakiston Houston
Relevant department: Department of the Environment

Craigavon and Banbridge Community HSS Trust

Bannvale House
10 Moyallen Road, Gilford, BT63 5JX
Tel: 028 3883 1983 / Fax: 028 3883 1993

Chairman: David Cook
Chief Executive: Denis Preston
Relevant department: Department of Health, Social Services and Public Safety

Craigavon Area Hospital HSS Trust

68 Lurgan Road, Craigavon
BT63 5QQ
Tel: 028 3833 4444

Chairman: E McClurg
Chief Executive: J Templeton
Relevant department: Department of Health, Social Services and Public Safety

Disability Living Allowance Advisory Board for Northern Ireland

Castle Court
Royal Avenue, Belfast, BT1 1DS
Tel: 028 9033 6196 / Fax: 028 9054 2112
Relevant department: Department for Social Development

Distinction and Meritorious Service Awards Committee

Room D.13, Castle Buildings, Stormont
Belfast, BT4 3SJ
Tel: 028 9052 2817 / Fax: 028 9052 2912

Secretary: John Nesbitt
Relevant department: Department of Health, Social Services and Public Safety

Down Lisburn HSS Trust

Lisburn Health Centre, 25 Linenhall Street
Lisburn, BT28 1LU
Tel: 028 9266 5181 / Fax: 028 9267 6206

Chairman: D Fitzsimmons
Chief Executive: J Compton
Relevant department: Department of Health, Social Services and Public Safety

Drainage Council

c/o Alan Morton
The Secretary, Rivers Agency
Hydebank, 4 Hospital Road, Belfast, BT8 8JP
Tel: 028 9025 3357

Chairman: Dr Robert Myers
Relevant department: Department of Agriculture and Rural Development

Driver and Vehicle Licensing Northern Ireland

County Hall, Castlerock Road, Coleraine, BT51 3TA
Web: www.doeni.gov.uk/dvlni
Email: dvlni@doeni.gov.uk

Chief Executive: Brendan Magee
Tel: 028 7034 1461
Relevant department: Department of the Environment

Driver Licensing Division:
Tel: 028 7034 1469 / Fax: 028 7034 1398

Vehicle Licensing Division:
Tel: 028 7034 1461 / Fax: 028 7034 1422

Vehicle Licensing Central Office
Telephone Re-Licensing Section
Tel: 028 7034 1514

Sale of Mark Section
Tel: 028 7034 1244

Commercial Operator Licensing:
148-158 Corporation Street, Belfast, BT1 3DH
Tel: 028 9025 4100 / Fax: 028 9025 4086

Local Offices
Opening hours for all local offices: 9.15am – 4.00pm

Armagh
Dobbin Centre, Dobbin Lane, Armagh, BT61 7QP
Tel: 028 3752 7305 / Fax: 028 3752 8721
Contact: Jill Kane

Ballymena
County Hall, Galgorm Road, Ballymena, BT42 1HN
Tel: 028 2565 3333 / Fax: 028 2566 2067
Contact: Ronnie Rowe

Belfast
Royston House, Upper Queen Street, Belfast, BT1 6FA
Tel: 028 9054 2042 / Fax: 028 9054 7379
Contact: Christine Clark

Coleraine
County Hall, Castlerock Road, Coleraine
Tel: 028 7034 1417 / Fax: 028 7034 1418
Contact: Clare Wilson

Downpatrick
Rathkeltair House, Market Street, Downpatrick, BT30 6AJ
Tel: 028 4461 2211 / Fax: 028 4461 8089
Contact: Mary Keenan

Enniskillen
County Buildings, East Bridge Street, Enniskillen, BT74 7BW
Tel: 028 6634 6555 / Tel: 028 6632 2750
Contact: Kate Charity

Londonderry
Orchard House, 40 Foyle Street, Londonderry, BT48 6AT
Tel: 028 7131 9900 / Fax: 028 71319819
Contact: Terence Healey

Omagh
Boaz House, 15 Scarffes Entry, Omagh, BT78 1JE
Tel: 028 8225 4700 / Fax: 028 8225 4711
Contact: Annie Alexander

Driver and Vehicle Testing Agency

Balmoral Road, Belfast, BT12 6QL
Tel: 028 9068 1831 / Fax: 028 9066 5520
Web: www.doeni.gov.uk/dvta
Chief Executive: Stanley Duncan
Relevant department: Department of the Environment

Local Offices

Armagh
47 Hamiltonsbawn Road, Armagh, BT60 1HW
Tel: 028 3752 2699

Ballymena
Pennybridge Industrial Estate, Larne Road
Ballymena, BT42 3ER
Tel: 028 2564 6801

Belfast
Balmoral Road, Belfast, BT12 6QL
Tel: 028 9068 1831

Coleraine
2 Loughan Hill Industrial Estate, Gateside Road
Coleraine, BT52 2NJ
Tel: 028 7034 3819

Cookstown
Sandholes Road, Cookstown, BT80 9AR
Tel: 028 8676 4809

Craigavon
3 Diviny Drive, Carn Industrial Estate, Craigavon, BT63 5RY
Tel: 028 3833 6188

Downpatrick
Cloonagh Road, Flying Horse Road, Downpatrick, BT30 6DU
Tel: 028 4461 4565

Enniskillen
Chanterhill, Enniskillen, BT74 6DE
Tel: 028 6632 2871

Larne
Ballyboley Road, Ballyloran, Larne, BT40 2SY
Tel: 028 2827 8808

Lisburn
Ballinderry Industrial Estate, Ballinderry Road
Lisburn, BT28 2SA
Tel: 028 9266 3151

Londonderry
New Buildings Industrial Estate, Victoria Road, Londonderry
Tel: 028 7134 3674

Mallusk
Commercial Way, Hydepark Industrial Estate
Newtownabbey, BT36 8YY
Tel: 028 9084 2111

Newry
51 Rathfriland Road, Newry, BT34 1LD
Tel: 028 3026 2853

Newtownards
Jubilee Road, Newtownards, BT23 4XP
Tel: 028 9181 3064

Omagh
Gortrush Industrial Estate, Derry Road, Omagh, BT78 5EJ
Tel: 028 8224 2540

Eastern Health and Social Services Board

Champion House, 12-22 Linenhall Street
Belfast, BT2 8BS
Tel: 028 9032 1313 / Fax: 028 9055 3680

Chairman: David Russell
Chief Executive: Paula Kilbane
Relevant department: Department of Health, Social Services and Public Safety

Eastern Health and Social Services Council

1st Floor
McKelvey House, 24-27 Wellington Place, Belfast, BT1 6GQ
Tel: 028 9032 1230 / Fax: 028 9032 1750
Relevant department: Department of Health, Social Services and Public Safety

Enterprise Ulster

The Close
Ravenhill Reach, Belfast, BT6 8RB
Tel: 028 9073 6400 / Fax: 028 9073 6404
Web: www.enterpriseulster.co.uk

Chief Executive: Joe Eagleson
Relevant department: Department for Employment and Learning

Environment and Heritage Service

Chief Executive: Richard Rogers
Web: www.ehsni.gov.uk
Relevant department: Department of the Environment

Natural Heritage, Waste Management, Regional Operations, Information and Education
Commonwealth House, 35 Castle Street, Belfast, BT1 1GU
Tel: 028 9025 1477 / Fax: 028 9054 6660

Historic Buildings and Monuments
5-33 Hill Street, Belfast, BT1 2LA
Tel: 028 9054 3076

Water Management, Drinking Water, Air and Environmental Quality
Calvert House, 23 Castle Place, Belfast, BT1 1FF
Tel: 028 9025 4754

Equality Commission for Northern Ireland

Equality House
7-9 Shaftesbury Square, Belfast, BT2 7DP
Tel: 028 9050 0600 / Fax: 028 9033 1544
Web: www.equalityni.org
Email: information@equalityni.org

Chief Executive: Evelyn Collins
Chief Commissioner: Joan Harbison
Relevant department: Office of the First Minister and Deputy First Minister

Fire Authority for Northern Ireland

Brigade Headquarters, 1 Seymour Street, Lisburn, BT27 4SX
Tel: 028 9266 4221 / Fax: 028 9267 7402
Web: www.nifb.org.uk

Chairman: William Gillespie
Chief Fire Officer: Colin Lammey
Relevant department: Department of Health, Social Services and Public Safety

Fisheries Conservancy Board

1 Mahon Road, Portadown, BT62 3EE
Tel: 028 3833 4666 / Fax: 028 3833 8912
Web: www.fcbni.com

Chief Executive: Karen Simpson
Relevant department: Department of Culture, Arts and Leisure

Food Safety Promotion Board

7 Eastgate Avenue, Eastgate, Little Island, Cork
Tel: 00 353 21 230 4100 / Fax: 00 353 21 230 4111
Web: www.safefoodonline.com

Chief Executive: Martin Higgins
Relevant department: Department of Health, Social Services and Public Safety

Foras na Gaeilge

7 Merrion Square, Dublin
Tel: 00 353 1 639 8400 / Fax: 00 353 1 639 8401
Web: www.forasnagaeilge.ie
Email: eolas@forasnagaeilge.ie

Chief Executive: Seosamh MacDonncha
Chairperson: Maighread Ní Mhairtin
Relevant department: Department of Culture, Arts and Leisure

Forensic Science Northern Ireland

151 Belfast Road, Carrickfergus, BT38 8PL
Tel: 028 9036 1888 / Fax: 028 9036 1900
Web: www.fsni.gov.uk
Email: forensic.science@fsni.gov.uk

Chief Executive: Brett Hannon
Relevant department: Northern Ireland Office

Forest Service

Dundonald House, Upper Newtownards Road
Belfast, BT4 3SB
Tel: 028 9052 4480 / Fax: 028 9052 4570
Web: www.forestserviceni.gov.uk

Chief Executive: Malcolm Beatty
Tel: 028 9052 4434
Email: Malcolm.Beatty@dardni.gov.uk
Relevant department: Department of Agriculture and Rural Development

Foyle HSS Trust

Riverview House, Abercorn Road, Londonderry, BT48 6FB
Tel: 028 7126 6111 /Fax: 028 7126 0806

Chairman: Anthony Jackson
Chief Executive: Elaine Way
Relevant department: Department of Health, Social Services and Public Safety

Foyle, Carlingford and Irish Lights Commission

The Loughs Agency
22 Victoria Road, Waterside, Londonderry, BT47 2AB
Tel: 028 7134 2100 / Fax: 028 7134 2720
Web: www.loughs-agency.org
Email: general@loughs-agency.org

Relevant department: Department of Agriculture and Rural Development

General Consumer Council

Elizabeth House
116 Holywood Road
Belfast, BT4 1NY
Tel: 028 9067 2488
Fax: 028 9065 7701
Web: www.gccni.org.uk

Chief Executive
Eleanor Gill

The Council carries out research, publishes reports, influences decision makers and campaigns for a fair deal for consumers. It deals with complaints about electricity, gas, coal, and passenger transport.

Relevant department: Department of Enterprise, Trade and Investment

General Council of the Bar of Northern Ireland

PO Box 414
Royal Courts of Justice, Chichester Street, Belfast, BT1 3JP
Tel: 028 9056 2349 / Fax: 028 9056 2350
Web: www.barlibrary.com

Relevant department: Northern Ireland Office

General Teaching Council for Northern Ireland

4th Floor, Albany House, 73-75 Great Victoria Street
Belfast, BT2 7AF
Tel: 028 9033 3390 / Fax: 028 9034 8787
Web: www.gtcni.org.uk
Email: info@gtcni.org.uk

Chairman: Dr Robert Rodgers
Relevant department: Department of Education

Green Park Healthcare HSS Trust

20 Stockman's Lane, Belfast, BT9 7JB
Tel: 028 9066 9501 / Fax: 028 9059 1501

Chairman: Ian Doherty
Chief Executive: Hilary Boyd
Relevant department: Department of Education

Health and Safety Executive for Northern Ireland

83 Ladas Drive, Belfast, BT6 9FR
Tel: 028 9024 3249 / Fax: 028 9023 5383
Web: www.hseni.gov.uk

Chief Executive: Jim Keyes
Relevant department: Department of Health, Social Services and Public Safety

Health Estates Agency

Stoney Road, Dundonald, Belfast, BT16 1US
Tel: 028 9052 0025 / Fax: 028 9052 3900
Web: www.dhsspsni.gov.uk/hea

Chief Executive: John Cole
Relevant department: Department of Health, Social Services and Public Safety

Health Promotion Agency for Northern Ireland

18 Ormeau Avenue, Belfast, BT2 8HS
Tel: 028 9031 1611 / Fax: 028 9031 1711
Web: www.healthpromotionagency.org.uk
Email: info@hpani.org.uk

Chairman: Alice Quinn
Chief Executive: Dr Brian Gaffney
Relevant department: Department of Health, Social Services and Public Safety

Historic Buildings Council Secretariat

5-33 Hill Street, BT1 2LA
Tel: 028 9054 3076
Email: hb@doeni.gov.uk
Relevant department: Department of the Environment

Historic Monuments Council

Chairman: Richard Black
Tel: 028 9054 3037
hm@doeni.gov.uk
Relevant department: Department of the Environment

Homefirst HSS Trust

The Cottage, 5 Greenmount Avenue
Ballymena, BT43 6DA
Tel: 028 2563 7000 / Fax: 028 2563 3733

Chairman: William Boyd
Chief Executive: Christy Colhoun
Relevant department: Department of Health, Social Services and Public Safety

Integrated Education Fund

41 University Street, Belfast, BT7 1FY
Tel: 028 9033 0031 / Fax: 028 9033 0061
Web: www.ief.org.uk

Director: Tina Merron
Email: tina@ief.org
Relevant department: Department of Education

Inter*Trade*Ireland

Old Gasworks Business Park, Kilmorey Street
Newry, BT34 2DE
Tel: 028 3083 4100 / Fax: 028 3083 4155
Web: www.intertradeireland.com
Email: info@tbdb.org

Chief Executive: Liam Nellis
Relevant department: Department of Enterprise, Trade and Investment

Invest Northern Ireland

64 Chichester Street, Belfast, BT1 4JX
Tel: 028 9023 9090 / Fax: 028 9054 5000
Web: www.investni.com

Chief Executive: Leslie Morrison

Managing Directors: Chris Buckland
Tracy Meharg, Leslie Ross, Terri Scott

Relevant department: Department of Enterprise, Trade and Investment
(Further information on the structure and work of Invest Northern Ireland can be found in Chapter 8 A Guide to Doing Business in Northern Ireland).

Iontaobhas na Gaelscolaiochta

199 Bothár na bhFal,
Béal Feirste, BT12 6FB
Guthán: 028 9024 1510

Príomhfheidhmeannach: Pilib Ó Runaidh
199 Falls Road, Belfast, BT12 6FB
Tel: 028 9024 1510

Chief Executive: Pilib Ó Runaidh
Relevant department: Department of Education

Labour Relations Agency

Head Office
2-8 Gordon Street
Belfast, BT1 2LG
Tel: 028 9032 1442
Fax: 028 9033 0827

Regional Office
1-3 Guildhall Street
Londonderry, BT48 6BJ
Tel: 028 7126 9638
Fax: 028 7126 7729

Chief Executive
Willam Patterson

The Labour Relations Agency promotes the improvement of employment relations in Northern Ireland by providing impartial and independant services for promoting good employment practices and preventing and resolving disputes.

Relevant department: Department for Employment and Learning

Laganside Corporation

Clarendon Building, 15 Clarendon Road, Belfast, BT1 3BG
Tel: 028 9032 8507 / Fax: 028 9033 2141
Web: www.laganside.com
Email: info@laganside.com

Chief Executive: Kyle Alexander

Relevant department: Department for Social Development

Land Registers of Northern Ireland

Lincoln Building, 27-45 Great Victoria Street
Belfast, BT2 7SL
Tel: 028 9025 1515 / Fax: 028 9025 1550
Web: www.lrni.gov.uk

Chief Executive: Patricia Montgomery

Relevant department: Department of Finance and Personnel

Law Reform Advisory Committee for Northern Ireland

Lancashire House, 5 Linenhall Street, Belfast, BT2 8AA
Tel: 028 9054 2900 / Fax: 028 9054 2909
Web: www.olrni.gov.uk

Secretary: Clare Irvine
Email: clare.irvine@dfpni.gov.uk
Relevant department: Department of Finance and Personnel

Learning and Skills Advisory Board

Chairman: Bill McGinnis
c/o Department for Employment and Learning
Adelaide House, Adelaide Street, Belfast, BT2 8FD
Tel: 028 9025 7777 / Fax: 028 9025 7778
Web: www.del.gov.uk
Relevant department: Department for Employment and Learning

Livestock and Meat Commission for Northern Ireland

Lissue House, 31 Ballinderry Road, Lisburn, BT28 2SL
Tel: 028 9263 3000 / Fax: 028 9263 3001
Web: www.lmcni.com / Email: info@lmcni.com

Chief Executive: David Rutledge
Relevant department: Department of Agriculture and Rural Development

Local Government Staff Commission

Commission House, 18-22 Gordon Street, Belfast, BT1 2LG
Tel: 028 9031 3151 / Fax: 028 9031 3200
Web: www.lgsc.org.uk / Email: info@lgsc.org.uk

Chief Executive: Adrian Kerr
Relevant department: Department of the Environment

Londonderry Port and Harbour

Harbour Office, Port Road, Lisahally, Londonderry, BT47 6FL
Tel: 028 7186 0555 / Fax: 028 7186 1168
Web: www.londonderryport.com
Email: info@londonderry-port.co.uk

Chief Executive: Brian McGrath
Relevant department: Department for Regional Development

Mater Infirmorum HSS Trust

45-51 Crumlin Road, Belfast, BT14 6AB
Tel: 028 9080 2338 / Fax: 028 9074 9784

Chairman: Lady McCollum
Chief Executive: Patricia Gordon
Relevant department: Department of Health, Social Services and Public Safety

Mental Health Commission

Elizabeth House, 118 Holywood Road
Belfast, BT4 1NY
Tel: 028 9065 1157 / Fax: 028 9047 1180
Email: mhc@dhsspsni.gov.uk

Chairperson: Marian O'Neill
Acting Chief Executive: Stephen Jackson
Relevant department: Department of Health, Social Services and Public Safety

Mental Health Review Tribunal

Room 11 Annex 6, Castle Buildings
Stormont, Belfast, BT4 3SQ
Tel: 028 9052 3388 / Fax: 028 9052 0683

Chairman: Fraser Elliott QC
Secretary: Esther Clarke/Alison Bray
Relevant department: Department of Health, Social Services and Public Safety

Museums and Galleries of Northern Ireland (MAGNI)

Ulster Museum
Botanic Gardens, Belfast, BT9 5AB
Tel: 028 9038 3000 / Fax: 028 3083 3003
Web: www.magni.org.uk

Chief Executive: Mike Houlihan
Relevant department: Department of Culture, Arts and Leisure

NI-CO

25-27 Franklin Street
Belfast
BT2 8DS
Tel: 028 90 347 750
Fax: 028 90 249 730
Web: www.nico.org.uk
Chief Executive: Rupert Haydock

NI-CO, the overseas marketing arm of the Northern Ireland public service, is one of the leading technical assistance providers in the UK. Since 1992, the company has delivered over 120 projects in 36 countries worldwide.

Newry and Mourne HSS Trust

5 Downshire Place, Downshire Road, Newry, BT34 1DZ
Tel: 028 3026 0505 / Fax: 028 3026 9064

Chief Executive: Eric Bowyer
Relevant department: Department of Health, Social Services and Public Safety

North and West Belfast HSS Trust

Glendinning House, 6 Murray Street, Belfast, BT1 6DP
Tel: 028 9032 7156 / Fax: 028 9082 1285

Chairperson: Patrick McCartin / Chief Executive: Richard Black
Relevant department: Department of Health, Social Services and Public Safety

North Eastern Education and Library Board

County Hall, 182 Galgorm Road, Ballymena, BT42 1HN
Tel: 028 2565 3333 / Fax: 028 2564 6071

Chairperson: James Currie / Chief Executive: Gordon Topping
Relevant department: Department of Health, Social Services and Public Safety

Northern Health and Social Services Board

County Hall, 182 Galgorm Road, Ballymena, BT42 1HN
Tel: 028 2565 3333 / Fax: 028 2565 2311

Chairman: M Wood / Chief Executive: JS Macdonnell
Relevant department: Department of Health, Social Services and Public Safety

Northern Health and Social Services Council

8 Broadway Avenue, Ballymena, BT43 7AA
Tel: 028 2565 5777 / Fax: 028 2565 5112

Chairman: Joe McFadden / Chief Officer: Noel Graham
Relevant department: Department of Health, Social Services and Public Safety

Northern Ireland Ambulance HSS Trust

Knockbracken Healthcare Park, Saintfield Road, Belfast, BT8 8SG
Tel: 028 9040 0999 /Fax: 028 9040 0900

Chairman: Doug Smyth
Chief Executive: Paul McCormick
Relevant department: Department of Health, Social Services and Public Safety

Northern Ireland Blood Transfusion Service Agency

Belfast City Hospital Complex
51 Lisburn Road, Belfast, BT9 7TS
Tel: 028 9053 4662 / Fax: 028 9043 9017
Web: www.nibts.org
Email: chiefexec@nibts.n-i.nhs.uk

Chairperson: Stephen Costello
Chief Executive: Morris McClelland
Relevant department: Department of Health, Social Services and Public Safety

Northern Ireland Building Regulations Advisory Committee

Building Regulations Unit
Office Estates and Building Standards Division
Department of Finance and Personnel
3rd Floor, Lancashire House, 3 Linenhall Street, Belfast, BT2 8AA
Tel: 028 9054 2933 / Fax: 028 9054 7866
Relevant department: Department of Finance and Personnel

Northern Ireland Council for Curriculum, Examinations and Assessment

29 Clarendon Road, Clarendon Dock, Belfast, BT1 3BG
Tel: 028 9026 1200 / Fax: 028 9026 1234
Web: www.ccea.org.uk
Email: info@ccea.org.uk

Chief Executive: Gavin Boyd
Relevant department: Department of Education

Northern Ireland Council for Integrated Education

44 University Street, Belfast, BT7 1HB
Tel: 028 9023 6200 / Fax: 028 9023 6237
Web: www.nicie.org.uk
Email: info@nicie.org.uk

Chief Executive Officer: Michael Wardlow
Relevant department: Department of Education

Northern Ireland Council for Postgraduate Medical and Dental Education

5 Annadale Avenue, Belfast, BT7 3JH
Tel: 028 9049 2731 / Fax: 028 9064 2279
Web: www.nicpmde.com
Email: nicpmde@nicpmde.gov.uk

Chairperson: Dr Don Keegan
Chief Executive: Dr JR McCluggage
Relevant department: Department of Health, Social Services and Public Safety

Northern Ireland Court Service

21st Floor, Windsor House, 9-15 Bedford Street
Belfast, BT2 7LT
Tel: 028 9032 8594 / Fax: 028 9032 8494
Web: www.courtsni.gov.uk
Relevant department: Northern Ireland Office

Northern Ireland Events Company

Redwood House, 66 Newforge Lane, Belfast, BT9 5NT
Tel: 028 9066 6661 / Fax: 028 9066 8040
Web: www.nievents.co.uk
Email: info@nievents.co.uk

Acting Chief Executive: Janice McAleese
Relevant department: Department of Culture, Arts and Leisure

Northern Ireland Fishery Harbour Authority

3 St Patrick's Avenue, Downpatrick, BT30 6DW
Tel: 028 4461 3844 / Fax: 028 4461 7128
Web: www.nifha.fsnet.co.uk
Email: info@nifha.fsnet.co.uk

Chief Executive: Chris Warnock
Relevant department: Department of Agriculture and Rural Development

Northern Ireland Guardian Ad Litem Agency

Centre House, 79 Chichester Street, Belfast, BT1 4JE
Tel: 028 9031 6550 / Fax: 028 9031 9811
Web: www.nigala.n-i.nhs.uk
Email: admin@nigala.n-i.nhs.uk

Chairperson: Jim Currie
Chief Executive: Ronnie Williamson
Relevant department: Department of Health, Social Services and Public Safety

Northern Ireland Higher Education Council

Adelaide House, 39-49 Adelaide Street, Belfast, BT2 8FD
Tel: 028 9025 7777
Fax: 028 9025 7778

Chairman: Tony Hopkins
Relevant department: Department for Employment and Learning

Northern Ireland Housing Executive

The Housing Centre, 2 Adelaide Street, Belfast, BT2 8GA
Tel: 028 9024 0288 / Fax: 028 9043 9803
Web: www.nihe.gov.uk
Chief Executive: Paddy McIntyre
Relevant department: Department for Social Development

Northern Ireland Industrial Court

Room 203, Adelaide House, 39-49 Adelaide Street
Belfast, BT2 8FD
Tel: 028 9025 7676
Web: www.delni.gov.uk/er

Senior Case Manager: Anne-Marie O'Kane
Relevant department: Department for Employment and Learning

Northern Ireland Local Government Officers Superannuation Committee

Templeton House, 411 Holywood Road, Belfast, BT4 2LP
Tel: 028 9076 8025 / Fax: 028 9076 8790
Web: www.nilgosc.org.uk
Email: info@nilgosc.org.uk

Chairman: John Galbraith
Relevant department: Department of the Environment

Northern Ireland Museums Council

6 Crescent Gardens, Belfast, BT7 1NS
Tel: 028 9055 0215 / Fax: 028 9055 0216
Web: www.nimc.co.uk
Email: info@nimc.co.uk

Director: Chris Bailey
Relevant department: Department of Culture, Arts and Leisure

Northern Ireland Policing Board

Waterside Tower, 31 Clarendon Road
Clarendon Dock, Belfast, BT1 3BG
Tel: 028 9040 8541 / Fax: 028 9040 8525
Web: www.policingboard.org.uk
Chairman: Professor Desmond Rea
Relevant department: Northern Ireland Office

Northern Ireland Practice and Education Council for Nursing and Midwifery

Centre House, 79 Chichester Street, Belfast, BT1 4JE
Tel: 028 9023 8152 / Fax: 028 9023 3298
Web: www.nipec.n-i.nhs.uk
Email: enquiries@ nipec.n-i.nhs.uk

Chairperson: Maureen Griffith / Chief Executive: Ms Paddy Blaney
Relevant department: Department of Health, Social Services and Public Safety

Northern Ireland Prison Service

Dundonald House, Upper Newtownards Road
Belfast, BT4 3SU
Tel: 028 9052 2922 / Fax: 028 9052 5160
Email: info@niprisonservice.gov.uk
Web: www.niprisonservice.gov.uk

Director General: Peter Russell
Relevant department: Northern Ireland Office

Northern Ireland Regional Medical Physics Agency

Musgrave and Clarke House, Royal Hospitals Site
Grosvenor Road, BT12 6BA
Tel: 028 9063 4430 / Fax: 028 9031 3040
Web: www.medicalphysics.n-i.nhs.uk
Email: office.administrator@mpa.n-i.nhs.uk

Chairperson: Professor David Walmsley
Chief Executive: Professor Peter Jaritt
Relevant department: Department of Health, Social Services and Public Safety

Northern Ireland Social Care Council

7th Floor Millennium House, 19-25 Great Victoria Street
Belfast, BT2 7AQ
Tel: 028 9041 7600 / Fax: 028 9041 7601
Web: www.niscc.info

Chief Executive: Brendan Johnston
Chairman: Jeremy Harbison
Relevant department: Department of Health, Social Services and Public Safety

Northern Ireland Statistics and Research Agency

McAuley House, 2-14 Castle Street, Belfast, BT1 1SA
Tel: 028 9034 8100 / Fax: 028 9034 8106
Web: www.nisra.gov.uk

Chief Executive: Norman Caven
Relevant department: Department of Finance and Personnel

Northern Ireland Tourist Board

St Anne's Quarter, North Street, Belfast, BT1 1NB
Tel: 028 9023 1221 / Fax: 028 9024 0960
Web: www.nitb.com

Chief Executive: Alan Clarke
Relevant department: Department of Enterprise, Trade and Investment

Colby House, Stranmillis Court
Malone Lower
Belfast, BT9 5BJ
Tel: 028 9025 5755
Fax: 028 9025 5700

Chief Executive
Mick Cory

MISSION:
"To contribute to the Public Good by supplying the mapping information for Northern Ireland"

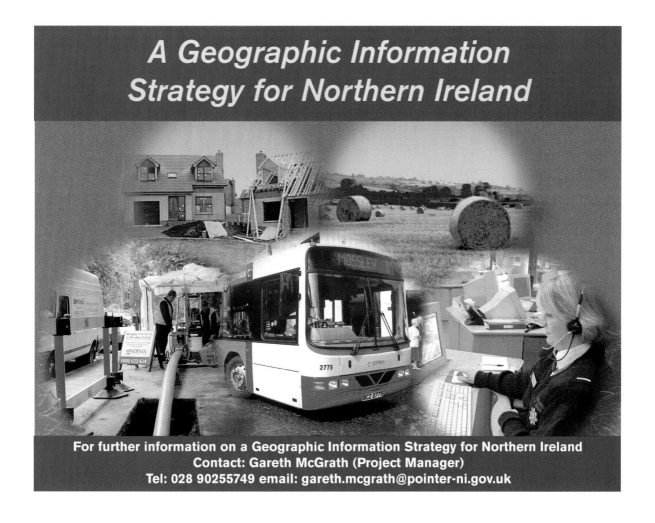

Ordnance Survey of Northern Ireland (OSNI) is the official Government organisation responsible for supplying mapping and Geographic Information for Northern Ireland and for co-ordinating the development of a Geographic Information Strategy for Northern Ireland which includes the development and ongoing maintenance of Pointer - the definitive address database for Northern Ireland. OSNI provides maps in paper and digital form, as well as aerial imagery, geographically referenced address, boundary, road and other mapping related data, underpinning the management and administration of the economy and society. Examples include:

- The efficient administration of Property Rights through Land Registration
- Enabling the Emergency Services to rapidly locate the site of an incident and deploy the nearest resource to deal with the emergency
- Modelling the impact of government policies on the environment to assist analysis and decision-making

OSNI utilises aerial photography with digital stereo photogrammetry as the main method of periodic map update. The continuous revision mapping programme uses traditional land survey techniques, increasingly supported by the use of Pen Computers and Global Positioning Systems technology.

OSNI is organised into 3 Divisions; Business Development, Operations and Corporate Services. The newly established Business Development Division has responsibility for the following functions: Sales, Marketing, Training and Education, Product Management, GIS Application Support and Intellectual Property Rights.

Northern Ireland Transport Holding Company

Chamber of Commerce House
22 Great Victoria Street, Belfast, BT2 7LX
Tel: 028 9024 3456 / Fax: 028 9043 8717
Web: www.translink.co.uk/nithco
Email: nithc@dialstart.net

Chairperson: Dr Joan Smyth / Corporate Director: Jim Aiken
Relevant department: Department for Regional Development

North/South Language Body

The North/South Language Body is a single body composed of two separate and largely autonomous agencies, the Ulster Scots Agency and Foras na Gaeilge – their contact details are listed separately.

Office of the Commissioner for Public Appointments (Northern Ireland)

Room E5.20
Castle Buildings
Stormont Estate
Upper Newtownards Road
Belfast, BT4 3SR
Tel: 028 9052 8187 / Fax: 028 9052 2522
Web: www.ocpa.gov.uk

Relevant department: Office of the First Minister and Deputy First Minister

Pig Production Development Committee

c/o Farm Policy Division
Room 910, Dundonald House
Upper Newtownards Road, Belfast, BT4 3SB
Tel: 028 9052 4873 / Fax: 028 9052 4266

Relevant department: Department of Agriculture and Rural Development

Planning Appeals Commission

Park House, 87-91 Great Victoria Street, Belfast, BT2 7AG
Tel: 028 9024 4710 / Fax: 028 9031 2536
Web: www.pacni.gov.uk
Email: info@pacni.gov.uk

Chief Commissioner: John Warke

Relevant department: Office of the First Minister and Deputy First Minister

Planning Service

Clarence Court, 10-18 Adelaide Street, Belfast, BT2 8GB
Tel: 028 9054 0540 / Fax: 028 9054 0665
Web: www.planningni.gov.uk

Chief Executive: David Ferguson
Tel: 028 9054 0649
Relevant department: Department of the Environment

Regional Offices

Ballymena
County Hall, 182 Galgorm Hall, Ballymena, BT42 1QF
Tel: 028 2565 3333 / Fax: 028 2566 2127

Divisional Planning Manager: Helena O'Toole

Belfast
Bedford House, 16-22 Bedford Street, Belfast, BT2 7FD
Tel: 028 9025 2800 / Fax: 028 9025 2828
Divisional Planning Manager: David Carroll

Coleraine
County Hall, Castlerock Road, Coleraine, BT51 3HS
Tel: 028 7034 1300 / Fax: 028 7034 1434
Divisional Planning Manager: Jim Cavalleros

Craigavon
Marlborough House, Central Way, Craigavon, BT64 1AD
Tel: 028 3834 1144 / Fax: 028 3834 1065
Divisional Planning Manager: Hilary Heslip

Downpatrick
Rathkeltair House, Market Street, Downpatrick, BT30 6EJ
Tel: 028 4461 2211 / Fax: 028 4461 8196
Divisional Planning Manager: Tom Clarke

Enniskillen
County Buildings, 15 East Bridge Street, Enniskillen, BT74 7BW
Tel: 028 6634 6555 / Fax: 028 6634 6550
Divisional Planning Manager: Brian Hughes

Londonderry
Orchard House, 40 Foyle Street, Londonderry, BT48 6AT
Tel: 028 7131 9900 / Fax: 028 7131 9777
Divisional Planning Manager: Jim Cavalleros

Omagh
County Hall, Drumragh Avenue, Omagh, BT79 7AE
Tel: 028 8225 4000 / Fax: 028 8225 4009
Divisional Planning Manager: Brian Hughes

Police Ombudsman

Police Ombudsman for Northern Ireland
New Cathedral Buildings
St Anne's Square
11 Church Street
Belfast, BT1 1PG
Tel: 028 9082 8600 / 0845 601 2931
Fax: 028 9082 8659
Email: info@policeombudsman.org
Web: www.policeombudsman.org
Police Ombudsman: Mrs Nuala O'Loan

The Police Ombudsman's Office deals with complaints from the public about the conduct of police officers on duty in Northern Ireland. You do not have to pay for this service.

Relevant department: Northern Ireland Office

Police Service of Northern Ireland

PSNI Headquarters, 65 Knock Road, Belfast, BT5 6LE
Tel: 028 9065 0222
Web: www.psni.police.uk
Relevant department: Northern Ireland Office

Port of Belfast

Belfast Harbour Commissioners, Belfast, BT1 3AL
Tel: 028 9055 4422 / Fax: 028 9055 4411
Email: info@belfast-harbour.co.uk
Web: www.belfast-harbour.co.uk

Chief Executive: Vacant
Relevant department: Department for Regional Development

Probation Board for Northern Ireland

80-90 North Street, Belfast, BT1 1LD
Tel: 028 9026 2400 / Fax: 028 9026 2470
Email: info@pbni.org.uk
Web: www.pbni.org.uk

Chairman: Brian Rowntree
Chief Executive: Noel Rooney
Relevant department: Northern Ireland Office

Public Record Office of Northern Ireland

66 Balmoral Avenue, Belfast, BT9 6NY
Tel: 028 9025 1318 / Fax: 028 9025 5999
Web: www.proni. gov.uk
Email: proni@dcalni.gov.uk

Chief Executive: Dr Gerry Slater
Relevant department: Department of Culture, Arts and Leisure

Rate Collection Agency

Oxford House, 49-55 Chichester Street, Belfast, BT1 4HH
Tel: 028 9052 2252 / Fax: 028 9052 2113
Web: www.ratecollectionagencyni.gov.uk
Chief Executive: Arthur Scott
Relevant department: Department of Finance and Personnel

Rent Assessment Panel

Housing Policy Branch, 2nd Floor, Andras House
60 Great Victoria Street, Belfast, BT2 7BB
Tel: 028 9091 0050 / Fax: 028 9091 0060

Rent Officer: Joan McCrum
Relevant department: Department for Social Development

Rivers Agency

Hydebank, 4 Hospital Road, Belfast, BT8 8JP
Tel: 028 9025 3355 / Fax: 028 9025 6455
Chief Executive: John Hagan
Tel: 028 9025 3440
Email: John.Hagan@dardni.gov.uk
Relevant department: Department of Agriculture and Rural Development

Roads Service

ROADS Service

Clarence Court
10-18 Adelaide Street
Belfast, BT2 8GB
Tel: 028 9054 0540
Fax: 028 9054 0024
Email: roads@drdni.gov.uk
Web: www.roadsni.gov.uk

Chief Executive
Malcolm McKibbin

Director of Corporate Services: Jim Carlisle
Director of Engineering: Geoff Allister
Director of Network Services: David Orr
Director of Finance: John McNeill

Head of Roads Service Consultancy: Derick McCandless
Head of Roads Service Direct: Ken Hutton
Head of Strategic Planning: Peter McWilliams
Head of Transportation: Denis O'Hagan

Roads Service is responsible for just over 24,800 kilometres of public roads together with about 8,000 kilometres of footways, 6,000 bridges, 240,000 street lights, and 370 public car parks.

Relevant department: Department for Regional Development

Regional Offices

Eastern Division
Hydebank, 4 Hospital Road, Belfast, BT8 8JL
Tel: 028 9025 3000 / Fax: 028 9025 3220
Divisional Manager: Joe Drew

Northern Division
County Hall, Castlerock Road , Coleraine, BT51 3HS
Tel: 028 7034 1300 / Fax: 028 7034 1430
Divisional Manager: Dr Andrew Murray

Southern Division
Marlborough House, Central Way, Craigavon, BT64 1AD
Tel: 028 3834 1144 / Fax: 028 3834 1867
Divisional Manager: John White

Western Division
County Hall, Drumragh Avenue, Omagh, BT79 7AF
Tel: 028 8225 4111 / Fax: 028 8225 4010
Divisional Manager: Pat Doherty

Warrenpoint Harbour
Warrenpoint Harbour Authority, Warrenpoint, BT34 3JR
Tel: 028 4177 3381 / Fax: 028 4175 2875
Web: www.warrenpointharbour.co.uk
Email: info@warrenpointharbour.co.uk
Chief Executive: Quintin Goldie
Relevant department: Department for Regional Development

Royal Group of Hospitals and Dental Hospital HSS Trust
Grosvenor Road, Belfast, BT12 6BA
Tel: 028 9024 0503 / Fax: 028 9024 0899

Chairman: Paul McWilliams
Chief Executive: William McKee
Relevant department: Department of Health, Social Services and Public Safety

Rural Development Council
17 Loy Street, Cookstown, , BT80 8PZ
Tel: 028 8676 6980 / Fax: 028 8676 6922
Web: www.rdc.org.uk
Email: info@rdc.org.uk
Chief Executive: Martin McDonald
Relevant department: Department of Agriculture and Rural Development

Social Security Agency
Churchill House, Victoria Square, Belfast, BT1 4SS
Tel: 028 9056 9100 / Fax: 028 9056 9178
Web: www.ssa.gov.uk
Email: customerservice.unit@dsdni.gov.uk
Chief Executive: Gerry Keenan
Relevant department: Department for Social Development

South and East Belfast HSS Trust
Knockbracken Healthcare Park, Saintfield Road
Belfast, BT8 8BH
Tel: 028 9056 5656 / Fax: 028 9056 5813
Chairman: Robin Harris
Chief Executive: Robert Ferguson
Relevant department: Department of Health, Social Services and Public Safety

South Eastern Education and Library Board
Grahamsbridge Road, Dundonald, Belfast, BT16 2HS
Tel: 028 9056 6200 / Fax: 028 9056 6266
Chairperson: Rev Dr D J Watts
Chief Executive: Mr Jackie Fitzsimons
Relevant department: Department of Education

Southern Education and Library Board
3 Charlemont Place, The Mall, Armagh, BT61 9AX
Tel: 028 3751 2200 / Fax: 0287 3751 2490
Chairman: M Alexander
Chief Executive: Helen McClenaghan
Relevant department: Department of Education

Southern Health and Social Services Board
Tower Hill, Armagh, BT61 9DR
Tel: 028 3741 0041 / Fax: 028 3741 4550
Chairman: William Gillespie
Chief Executive: Brendan Cunningham
Relevant department: Department of Health, Social Services and Public Safety

Southern Health and Social Services Council
Quaker Buildings, High Street, Lurgan, BT66 8BB
Tel: 028 3834 9900 / Fax: 028 3834 9858
Chairman: Roisin Foster
Relevant department: Department of Health, Social Services and Public Safety

Sperrin Lakeland HSS Trust
Strathdene House. Tyrone and Fermanagh Hospital
Omagh, BT79 0NS
Tel: 028 8283 5285 / Fax: 028 8283 5286
Chairman: Richard Scott
Chief Executive: Hugh Mills
Relevant department: Department of Health, Social Services and Public Safety

Staff Commission for Education and Library Boards
Forestview, Purdy's Lane, Belfast, BT8 7AR
Tel: 028 9049 1461 / Fax: 028 9049 1744
Web: www.staffcom.org.uk / Email: info@staffcom.org.uk

Chairman: Maurice Moroney
Relevant department: Department of Education

Tourism Ireland Limited
Beresford House, 2 Beresford Road, Coleraine, BT52 1GE
Tel: 028 7035 9200 / Fax: 028 7032 6932
Chief Executive: Paul O'Toole
Relevant department: Department of Enterprise, Trade and Investment

Ulster Community and Hospitals HSS Trust
39 Regent Street, Newtownards, BT23 4AD
Tel: 028 9181 6666 / Fax: 028 9182 0140
Chairman: Siobhan Grant
Chief Executive: Jim McCall
Relevant department: Department of Health, Social Services and Public Safety

Ulster Scots Agency
Franklin House, 10-12 Brunswick Street, Belfast, BT2 7GE
Tel: 028 9023 1113 / Fax: 028 9023 1898
Email: info@ulsterscotsagency.org.uk
Web: www.ulsterscotsagency.com
Chief Executive: George Patten
Chairman: Lord Laird of Artigarvan
Relevant department: Department of Culture, Arts and Leisure

Ulster Supported Employment Limited
182-188 Cambrai Street, Belfast, BT13 3JH
Tel: 028 9035 6600 / Fax: 028 9035 6611
Web: www.usel.co.uk
Email: info@usel.co.uk
Chief Executive: Mitchell Wylie
Relevant department: Department for Employment and Learning

United Hospitals HSS Trust
Bush House, 45 Bush Road, Antrim, BT41 2QB
Tel: 028 9442 4673 / Fax: 028 9442 4675
Chairman: Dr Harry McGuigan CBE
Chief Executive: Bernard Mitchell
Relevant department: Department of Health, Social Services and Public Safety

Valuation and Lands Agency
Queen's Court, 56-66 Upper Queen Street
Belfast, BT1 6FD
Tel: 028 9025 0700 / Fax: 028 9054 3750
Web: www.vla.nics.gov.uk
Chief Executive: Nigel Woods
Relevant department: Department of Finance and Personnel

Waste Management Advisory Board for Northern Ireland
Chairman: Professor Deborah Boyd
Relevant department: Department of the Environment

Water Appeals Commission
Park House, 87-91 Great Victoria Street, Belfast, BT2 7AG
Tel: 028 9024 4710 / Fax: 028 9031 2536
Web: www.pacni.gov.uk
Relevant department: Office of the First Minister and Deputy First Minister

Water Council
Water Service Strategic Policy Branch
Room 1.08, 34 College Street, Belfast, BT1 6DR
Tel: 028 9054 1158 / Fax: 028 9054 1156
Web: www.watercouncilni.gov.uk
Email: secretary@watercouncilni.gov.uk
Relevant department: Department for Regional Development

Water Service
Northland House, 3 Frederick Street, Belfast, BT1 2NR
Tel: 028 9024 4711 / Fax: 028 9032 4888
Web: www.waterni.gov.uk
Email: waterline@waterni.gov.uk
Chief Executive: Katharine Bryan

Relevant department: Department for Regional Development

Regional Offices

Eastern Division
34 College Street, Belfast, BT1 6DR
Tel: 028 9032 8161 / Fax: 028 9035 4828

Northern Division
Academy House, 121a Broughshane Street
Ballymena, BT43 6BA
Tel: 028 2565 3655 / Fax: 028 2566 3131

Southern Division
Marlborough House, Central Way, Craigavon, BT64 1AD
Tel: 028 3834 1100 / Fax: 028 3832 0555

Western Division
Belt Road, Altnagelvin, Londonderry, BT47 2LL
Tel: 028 7131 2221 / Fax: 028 7131 0330

Western Education and Library Board
1 Hospital Road, Omagh, BT79 0AW
Tel: 028 8241 1411 / Fax: 028 8241 1400
Chairperson: H Faulkner
Chief Executive: Barry Mulholland
Relevant department: Department of Education

Western Health and Social Services Board
15 Gransha Park, Clooney Road, Londonderry, BT47 6FN
Tel: 028 7186 0086 / Fax: 028 7186 0311
Chairman: J Bradley
Chief Executive: S Lindsay
Relevant department: Department of Health, Social Services and Public Safety

Western Health and Social Services Council
Hilltop, Tyrone and Fermanagh Hospital
Omagh, BT79 0NS
Tel: 028 8225 2555 / Fax: 028 8225 2544
Chairman: Raymond Rogan
Chief Officer: Stanley Millar
Relevant department: Department of Health, Social Services and Public Safety

Youth Council for Northern Ireland
Forestview, Purdy's Lane, Belfast, BT8 7AR
Tel: 028 9064 3882 / Fax: 028 9064 3874
Web: www.youthcouncil-ni.org.uk
Chief Executive: David Guilfoyle
Relevant department: Department of Education

Lagan Valley Island, Lisburn

Chapter

Local Government and Administration

COUNCILLOR
L. MARTIN

An Overview of Northern Ireland Local Government

Along with Westminster and the Stormont Executive, Northern Ireland has a third tier of government, in the form of its 26 councils, which are involved in policy and decision-making, and more particularly the direct delivery of a range of services at a local level. These 26 Local Government Districts (LGDs) are subdivided into a number of District Electoral Areas (DEAs), usually between three and five (although Belfast has nine). Each of these DEAs returns a number of councillors who collectively comprise the council and act as a single-tier local authority. Local government elections are held once every four years, with councillors elected by proportional representation. The last local government elections were held on the same day as the last General Election, 7 June 2001. *(Detailed election results are set out later in this chapter, beginning at page 240).*

Recent History

Northern Ireland's present system of local government dates from the 1970s. In the context of the then civil rights movement and continuing general upheaval it was decided to reorganise the administration of key services at local level, and to review the geographical boundaries of local authorities. In response to the Macrory Report, the Local Government (Northern Ireland) Act 1972 sought to address claims of political bias in various areas of service provision. It produced a significant change in the roles and responsibilities of councils, most notably a diminution in their control of education and health care. Housing provision had already been transferred to a newly appointed housing authority, the Northern Ireland Housing Executive, in 1970.

Education, libraries and health were to be administered by area boards of appointed members, not directly accountable to councils. Local authorities retained responsibility for refuse collection, leisure and recreation facilities, building control, cemeteries and tourist amenities while nominating a number of elected members to the appointed health and education and library boards.
Local authorities also retained an important consultative role in matters such as planning, roads and housing, and were encouraged to offer leadership and support to local economic development.

Cities, Boroughs and Districts

A Local Government District may be a borough, city or district council. Belfast, Derry, Armagh, and Lisburn all have city councils (although Armagh is officially a 'City and District' Council); the other 22 are either borough or district councils. Whilst Newry attained city status the council area remains known as Newry and Mourne District Council. A mayor and deputy mayor head city and borough councils, while chairpersons head district councils, the office-bearers in both cases being elected at the council's Annual General Meeting.

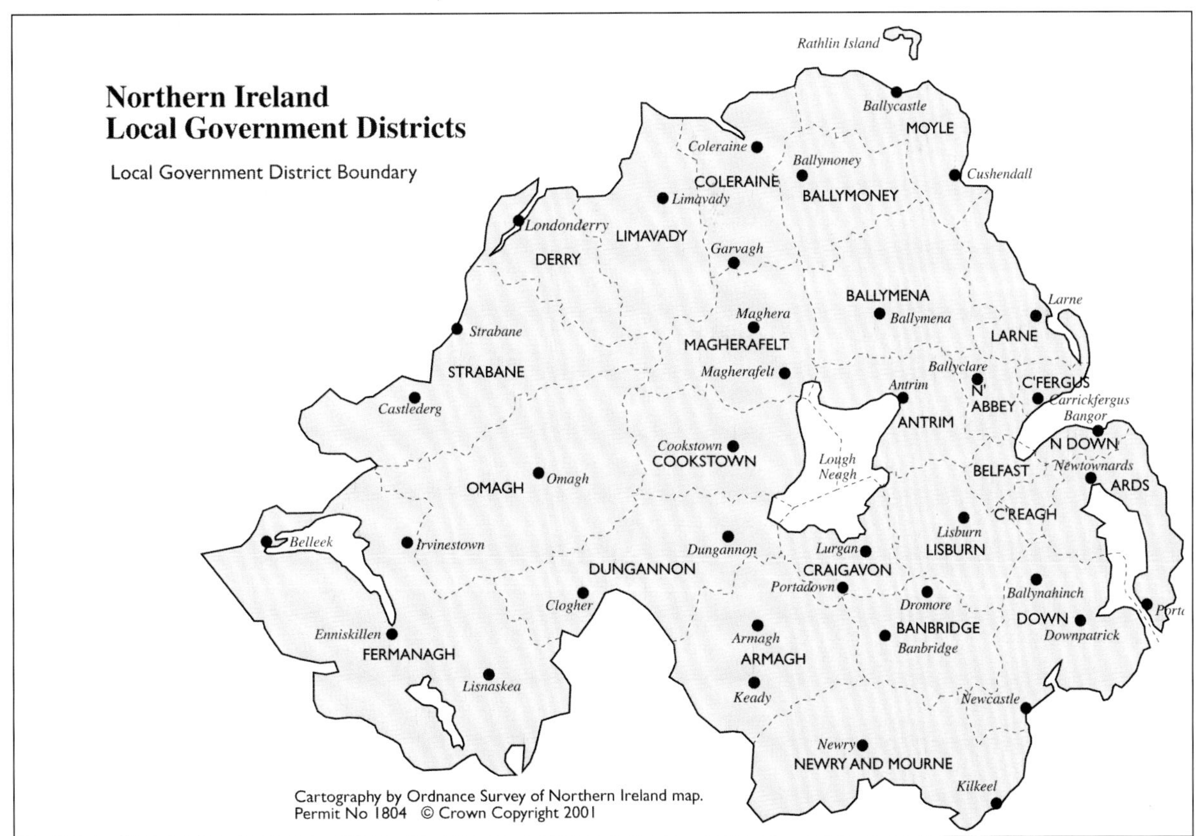

Lisburn City Council Chamber

All Northern Ireland's councils are described in the Local Government Act as District Councils but the following have attained Borough status:

- Antrim
- Ards
- Ballymena
- Ballymoney
- Newtownabbey
- North Down
- Craigavon
- Larne
- Limavady
- Carrickfergus
- Castlereagh
- Coleraine

Each council has to elect a Chairman annually and in the case of the Borough and City councils he or she is known as the Mayor, and in Belfast, as Lord Mayor.

Where a council has a City or Borough status it has two other ceremonial privileges.

It may:

- Designate up to one quarter of its members as aldermen;
- Confer the freedom of the City or Borough on distinguished individuals or groups.

The mayor or chairperson of the council has a high profile within the council area, performing ceremonial duties and often playing a key role in promoting the area and welcoming visiting dignitaries.

Councils vary considerably in size, with Belfast being the largest by far in terms of population, followed by Lisburn, Derry, Craigavon and Newry & Mourne. In contrast, Moyle, Ballymoney and Larne are among the smallest. There is also considerable variation in the geographical area covered by the councils, with Belfast, Castlereagh and North Down among the smallest and Fermanagh the largest followed by Omagh and Strabane. *(Details of the main characteristics of the councils are listed in the table below).*

Principal Characteristics of Local Government in Northern Ireland

Area, Population and Rates Revenue of Local Authorities

Council	Area (Km2)	% of Total	Population	% of Total	Rates Revenue	% of Total
Antrim	576	4.1	48, 366	2.9	7,082,577	2.8
Ards	376	2.7	73, 244	4.3	8,698,274	3.5
Armagh	670	4.7	54, 263	3.2	6,730,026	2.7
Ballymena	632	4.5	58, 610	3.5	7,902,590	3.2
Ballymoney	418	2.9	26, 894	1.6	2,718,770	1.1
Banbridge	452	3.2	41, 392	2.5	4,997,762	2.0
Belfast	114	0.8	277, 391	16.5	65,045,172	26.1
Carrickfergus	81	0.6	37, 659	2.2	5,451,343	2.2
Castlereagh	85	0.6	66, 488	3.9	7,698,484	3.1
Coleraine	485	3.4	56, 315	3.3	8,296,261	3.3
Cookstown	622	4.4	32, 581	1.9	3,300,216	1.3
Craigavon	378	2.7	80, 671	4.7	11,302,591	4.5
Derry	387	2.7	105, 066	6.2	16,830,944	6.7
Down	646	4.6	63, 828	3.8	8,057,339	3.2
Dungannon	783	5.5	47, 735	2.8	4,552,512	1.8
Fermanagh	1875	13.3	57, 527	3.4	5,938,073	2.4
Larne	335	2.4	30, 832	1.8	5,015,743	2.0
Limavady	585	4.1	32, 422	1.9	3,540,049	1.4
Lisburn	446	3.2	108, 694	6.4	13,787,637	5.5
Magherafelt	572	4.1	39, 780	2.4	3,515,675	1.4
Moyle	479	3.4	15, 933	0.9	2,075,711	0.8
Newry and Mourne	902	6.4	87, 058	5.2	11,851,749	4.7
Newtownabbey	150	1.1	79, 995	4.7	13,204,811	5.3
North Down	81	0.6	76, 323	4.5	12,374,235	4.9
Omagh	1130	7.9	47, 952	2.8	6,032,075	2.4
Strabane	861	6.1	38, 248	2.3	3,665,041	1.5
Total:	14135	100	1, 685, 267	100	249,665,673	100

Source: NISRA Northern Ireland 2001 Census Key Statistics

Councils Political Control

Council	Unionist	Nationalist	*Other	Total
Antrim	13	6	-	19
Ards	17	-	6	23
Armagh	11	11	-	22
Ballymena	18	4	2	24
Ballymoney	13	3	-	16
Banbridge	12	3	2	17
Belfast	21	23	7	51
Carrickfergus	10	-	7	17
Castlereagh	15	2	6	23
Coleraine	16	4	2	22
Cookstown	5	10	1	16
Craigavon	13	11	2	26
Derry	6	23	1	30
Down	8	14	1	23
Dungannon	9	12	1	22
Fermanagh	9	13	1	23
Larne	9	2	4	15
Limavady	5	8	2	15
Lisburn	18	7	5	30
Magherafelt	5	10	1	16
Moyle	5	7	3	15
Newry and Mourne	5	23	2	30
Newtownabbey	16	3	6	25
North Down	13	-	12	25
Omagh	5	14	2	21
Strabane	5	11	-	16
Total:	283	226	73	582

*Other includes Independents who may be either unionist or nationalist

Roles and Functions of Local Government

Local councils are responsible for a wide range of functions including a number of key services delivered directly to individual households and workplaces. In addition the council is involved in numerous other roles locally although not always as the central player.

With twenty-six local councils in Northern Ireland, local government is a sizeable employer, with over 9,000 employees. The expansion of local government in recent years has seen its role grow in such areas as economic development, tourism, community development/relations, culture and the arts.

In addition to their established functions, the Northern Ireland Office has in recent times requested councils to develop Community Safety Strategies to enhance the safety of local communities in their area. Under this initiative local councils will work with the police in areas such as drug and alcohol abuse, the provision of youth clubs and other social amenities, with the objective of reducing the potential for crime. Local councils also play a central role in the new police partnership boards, involving a partnership approach with the police at local level.

Local councils also play a key role in dispensing the EU Special Peace and Reconciliation Funds, better known as Peace II. Local Strategy Partnerships (LSPs) were formed with strong representations from the district councils and their role and remit will continue to develop as funding decision makers under the auspices of Peace II. *Full details of the membership of LSPs is included in Chapter 9, beginning at page 439)*

Local councils are also aiming to improve local environmental performance particularly in the area of waste management.
In the context of diminishing landfill capacity and restrictions on construction of new incineration plant local authorities are under unprecedented pressure to reduce the overall volume of waste produced and to recycle as much of this as possible. Ever more stringent environmental legislation will continue to add to these pressures.

The roles and functions conferred on the council by the Local Government Act (N.I.) 1972 and other legislation fall into three types:

- A direct role in which the council is responsible within its own area for the provision and management of certain services;
- A representative role where local authority nominees sit as representatives on a range of statutory bodies;
- A consultative role through which the council reflects the views of the community on the operation of certain regional services.

Representative Role

The representative role relates to the appointment of councillors to a range of statutory bodies such as the Health and Social Services Area Boards and Councils and the Education and Library Boards. The status of the persons so appointed depends upon the legal provisions contained in the appropriate statute. They are in no sense delegates but are entirely free to exercise their own judgement although in practice they tend to represent their Council Area which is part of a wider area covered by the relevant board.

Consultative Role

The consultative role relates to services provided by a government department or other public body in connection with Planning, Roads, Conservation (including water supply and sewerage services) and Housing.

As the locally elected political forum the council is seen as providing a useful consultative sounding board for administrative decisions although local authorities have no rights of decision.

Community concerns or views on proposed administrative decisions are often brought to bear when statutory authorities consult local councils. The consultative role of the local authority is particularly important in the arena of planning where there is no third party right of appeal and in housing where the Northern Ireland Housing Executive - which covers all of Northern Ireland - needs a robust input at the local level.

Roles and Functions of Local Government

Direct Service Provision
- Advice and Information Services
- Arts and Entertainment
- Building Regulations
- Burial Grounds and Crematoria
- Civic Ceremonials
- Community Services
- Dog Control
- Economic Development
- Harbours
- Health Inspection
- Leisure and Community Centres
- Licensing
- Markets and Fairs
- Museums and Art Galleries
- Parks and Open Spaces
- Pollution Control
- Public Conveniences
- Recreation Grounds and Services
- Refuse Collection and Disposal
- Street Cleansing
- Tourism Development

Representative Role
- Education and Library Boards
- Health and Social Services Area Councils
- Health and Social Services Boards

Consultative Role
- Planning
- Roads
- Housing Council
- Infrastructure/Utilities
- Electricity
- Water

The Role of the Department of the Environment

Local Government Division

Although local authorities interact with numerous government departments in the course of carrying out their functions, the Department of the Environment is the central government department responsible for local government issues. Its key objectives in this area are to maintain and strengthen the links between central and local government, and to assist district councils to carry out their functions efficiently and effectively, in the interests of the ratepayer. It has a general supervisory role in relation to the affairs of district councils and exercises a number of statutory controls over certain financial and administrative matters.

Financial Role

The Department provides direct support to the 26 district councils by way of General Exchequer Grant. This grant consists of a "derating element" and a "resources element", and its objectives are twofold:

(1) To compensate all district councils for loss of rate income due to the statutory derating of certain properties; and

(2) To provide additional finance to those councils whose rateable value per head of population falls below a standard determined each year by the Department.

The Department also regulates and determines the rates of allowances payable to councillors and provides guidance on a wide range of issues of interest to councillors and officials.

Audit Function

The Department has statutory powers, under the Local Government Act (NI) 1972, to request information, reports and returns from councils and can order inquiries or investigations into any matter relating to the functions of a council. Where a council fails to discharge any of its functions, the Department can direct it to take specified action. If a council fails to comply with such a direction, the Department can empower its officials to exercise the functions of the council.

The Department of the Environment must also consult with the local council on:

- Applications for planning approval and on the Area Plan which is produced for its area;
- Roads and car parks in the area to ensure that the views of as many local residents are obtained as possible;
- Water and sewerage to ensure the area's requirements are met;
- Environmental issues, listed buildings and Areas of Special Scientific Interest.

Department of the Environment
Local Government Division
Clarence Court
10-18 Adelaide Street
Belfast, BT2 8GB
Tel: 028 9054 0540 / Fax: 028 9054 0025

(More detailed information on the responsibilities of the Department of the Environment is set out in Chapter 3 'Central Government Department and Agencies')

ecos

BALLYMENA
BOROUGH COUNCIL

THE MILLENNIUM COMMISSION
A MILLENNIUM PROJECT
SUPPORTED BY FUNDS
FROM THE NATIONAL LOTTERY

Future Outlook for Local Government

The first Northern Ireland Assembly embarked on a major Review of Public Administration, under the auspices of the Office of the First Minister and Deputy First Minister (OFMDFM) which may change significantly the role of local authorities in the medium term.

Although it will be several years before the Review's findings are implemented, it is widely expected that the result will be fewer local authorities but with enhanced responsibilities. Indeed, the consultation document launched by the Review Team in late 2003 puts forward a number of high-level models for future systems of public administration, the principal differentiator between which is the enhanced role local government may assume.

The Review of Public Administration may also have implications for where local authorities fit into the overall political and governmental framework of Northern Ireland.

A-Z Guide to Northern Ireland's 26 Local Authorities

What follows is a comprehensive profiling of all of Northern Ireland's 26 local authorities.

Each summary profile contains:

- central contact information
- simple diagram of local authority
- socio-economic description
- list of members
- central contact information
- list of senior council officers
- contact details for main council operational locations.

These are listed in an easy-to-use A-Z format.

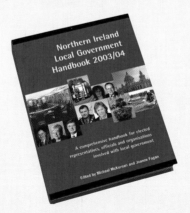

ANTRIM BOROUGH COUNCIL

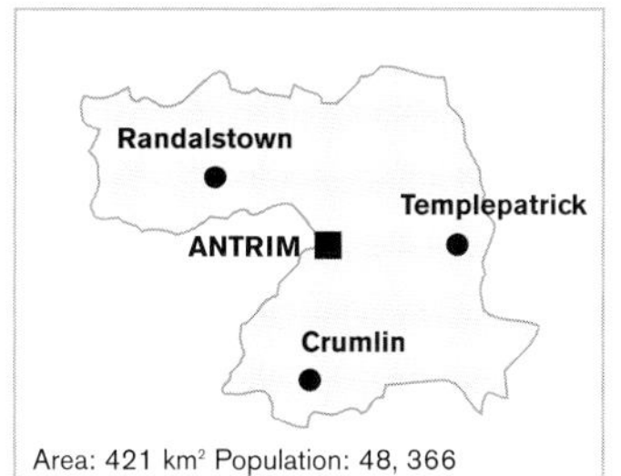

Area: 421 km² Population: 48, 366

The Steeple
Steeple Road
Antrim, BT41 1BJ
Tel: 028 9446 3113
Fax: 028 9446 4469
Email:
admin@antrim.gov.uk
Web: www.antrim.gov.uk

The main population centres in the Borough of Antrim include Antrim town, Crumlin, Randalstown and Templepatrick. The borough is located to the north east of Lough Neagh and enjoys an excellent communications infrastructure, with the M2 motorway running north to Ballymena, and south to Belfast, some 18 miles away. Antrim town is on the railway network and the borough is also home to Northern Ireland's leading airport Belfast International Airport (Aldergrove).

Antrim Borough covers approximately 4.1 per cent of the total area of Northern Ireland and is the third fastest growing local government district, with a population increase of approximately 12 per cent in the last ten years.

It has a relatively low level of deprivation and has only 2.7 per cent of the work force unemployed (source: Corporate Plan 2002-2006), one of the lowest unemployment rates of all 26 District Council areas in Northern Ireland. Antrim's location with its extensive Lough Neagh frontage gives the borough a major opportunity to develop its tourism potential. Antrim Town has a long industrial past and is home to several large indigenous companies, including the internationally renowned company Mivan Construction. The borough also includes the Invest Northern Ireland Technology Park, which is a major 80-acre campus location for high–tech companies, with capacity for further development.

Many major award-winning manufacturing companies such as Randox, Mivan, Fast Engineering and Schrader Electronics have located in the borough. Strong secondary and third level education facilities, as well as industrial training facilities for construction and transport located in Antrim Borough continue to produce a highly trained and qualified workforce. A number of companies including Tesco, Electricworld, Ireland Freight Services and TNT have invested in 'state of the art' warehousing facilities in the area.

Antrim has been identified in the Regional Strategic Framework for Northern Ireland as a major growth area; indicators suggest that Antrim will experience significant additional growth over the next 25 years, both in terms of housing and employment.

Political Composition

The political composition of Antrim Borough Council elected members as elected in June 2001 is: Ulster Unionist Party (UUP) 8, Social Democratic and Labour Party (SDLP) 4, Democratic Unionist Party (DUP) 5, Sinn Féin (SF) 2. The largest party on the council is the UUP with 8 seats. The council has a unionist majority although no single party has overall control.

Elected Members and Council Committees

Mayor: Samuel Dunlop (DUP)
Deputy Mayor: Drew Ritchie (UUP)

Councillor	Party	Development & Leisure Services	Environmental Services	Public Services Liaison	Strategy & Resources
Thomas Burns	SDLP	•	•	VC	•
Wilson Clyde	DUP			•	
Adrian Cochrane-Watson	UUP	•	VC	•	
Samuel Dunlop	DUP	VC	•	•	•
Brian Graham	DUP	•	•	•	
William Harkness	DUP	•	•	•	•
Oran Keenan	SDLP	•	C	•	•
Bobby Loughran	SDLP	•	•	•	•
Paddy Marks	UUP	•	•	•	•
Donovan McClelland	SDLP			•	
Martin McManus	SF	•		•	
Martin Meehan	SF		•	•	•
Paul Michael	UUP	•		•	C
Stephen Nicholl	UUP	C		•	
Mervyn Rea	UUP		•	•	•
Drew Ritchie	UUP	•		•	•
John Smyth	DUP			•	VC
Roy Thompson	UUP		•	C	
Edgar Wallace	UUP		•	•	•

• Member C Chair VC Vice-chair

Senior Officers

Chief Executive: Samuel J Magee, MBE
Director of Development & Leisure Services: Geraldine Girvan
Recreation: Ivor McMullan
Economic Development Officer: Alan Liddle
Director of Environmental Services: John Quinn
Building Services: Reggie Hillen
Environmental Health: Ian Suiter
Director of Corporate Services: Neill Cauwood
Finance: John Balmer

Council Contact Details

Chief Executive's Office	028 9446 3113
Administration	028 9446 3113
Best Value	028 9446 3113
Finance	028 9446 3113
Human Resources	028 9446 3113
Public Relations	028 9448 1303
Registration of Births, Deaths & Marriages	028 9448 1315
Building Control	028 9448 1321
Bulky Waste Collections	028 9448 1308
Civic Amenity Sites	028 9448 1308
Dog Licensing	028 9448 1304
Environmental Health	028 9448 1319
Grounds Maintenance	028 9446 3113
Refuse Collection	028 9448 1308

ARDS BOROUGH COUNCIL

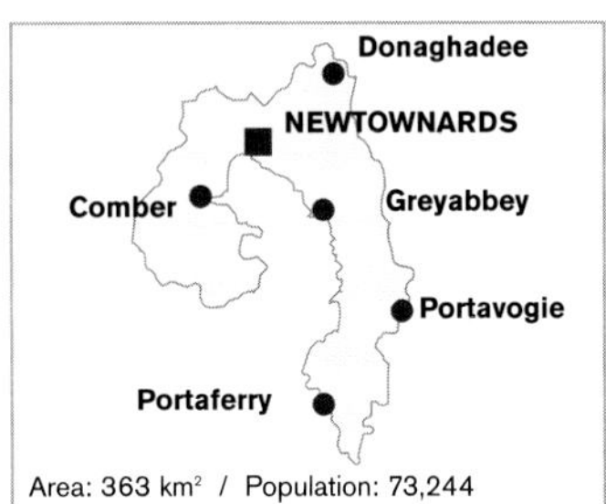

Council Offices
2 Church Street
Newtownards
BT23 4AP
Tel: 028 9182 4000
Fax: 028 9181 9628
Email:
ards@ards-council.gov.uk
Web:
www.ards-council.gov.uk

The Ards Borough, situated southeast of Belfast on the shores of Strangford Lough is designated as an area of outstanding natural beauty and special scientific interest. It is the third fastest growing local government district in Northern Ireland with a population of 73,000.

The area administered by the council covers approximately 140 square miles, with its 90 miles of coastline being one of the longest in local government control. The borough's main town is Newtownards, with Comber and Donaghadee the other main centres of population.

Newtownards' reputation as a prime retailing centre has been enhanced by the presence of national multiples which have established stores in the town as part of their expansion into the Northern Ireland market. Plans are also at an advanced stage to locate a major new shopping complex in the town to include space for a large retailer, retail warehousing, restaurants, a business park and new access roads. Newtownards is only 11 miles from Belfast. Although not on the railway network, the town boasts its own small airfield.

The area has recovered well from the decline in the clothing and textiles sector - traditionally a major employer in the borough - with a diverse economy now being established, particularly in added value food and engineering sectors. The most significant foreign direct investment in recent years has been Humax, the Korean electronics firm. Fishing and agricultural industries continue to provide employment despite the difficulties experienced by both sectors and tourism is a significant contributor to the local economy.

An area plan to the year 2015 is now being finalised which provides a template for the borough's housing, infrastructure and commercial development over the next 12 years.

Political Composition

There are twenty-three elected members, representing four district electoral areas: Newtownards 6 seats, Ards East 6 seats, Ards West 6 seats, Ards Peninsula 5 seats. The political composition of Ards Borough Council elected members as elected in June 2001 is: Ulster Unionist Party (UUP) 8, Democratic Unionist Party (DUP) 9, Alliance 4, Other 2. The largest party on the council is the DUP with 9 seats. The council has a clear unionist majority, but no party has overall control.

The Council meeting is convened on the fourth Wednesday of every month at 7.00pm in the Council offices.

Elected Members and Council Committees

Mayor: Jim McBriar (All)
Deputy Mayor: Hamilton Gregory (DUP)

Councillor	Party	Policy & Resources	Council Services	Economic Development	Health & Social Services	Borough Development
Angus Carson	UUP	•	C	•	•	•
Linda Cleland	All	•	•			•
Margaret Craig	DUP	C	•		•	•
Robin Drysdale	DUP	•	•	•	VC	•
George Ennis	DUP	•	•	•		•
Ronnie Ferguson	UUP	•	•	•		•
Robert Gibson	UUP	•	•	•	•	VC
David Gilmore	DUP	•	•			•
Hamilton Gregory	DUP	•	•	•	•	•
Thomas Hamilton	UUP	•	•	•		•
Hamilton Lawther	DUP	•	•			•
Jeff Magill	UUP	•	•		•	•
Wilbert Magill	Ind	•	•			•
Jim McBriar	All	•	•	•	•	•
Alan McDowell	All	•	•	C	•	•
Danny McCarthy	Ind	•	•		•	•
Kieran McCarthy	All	•	•		•	•
William Montgomery	DUP	•	VC			•
Jim Shannon	DUP	•	•	•	•	•
John Shields	UUP	VC	•	•		•
Philip Smith	UUP	•	•	•		•
David Smyth	UUP	•	•		C	•
Terence Williams	DUP	•	•	•	•	C

• Member C Chair VC Vice-chair

Senior Officers

Chief Executive: David Fallows
Executive Officer: Rachel Nixon
Director of Administration: Ashley Boreland
Director of Corporate Services: David Clarke
Director of Development: Derek McCallan
Director of Environmental Services: John Rea
Director of Leisure Services: Archie Walls
Chief Building Control Officer: Robert Shields
Arts Officer: Eilis O'Baoill
Borough Inspector: Richard Brittain
Community Relations Officer: Paul Killen
Community Safety Co-ordinator: Bob Wilson
District Policing Partnership Manager:Trevor Mawhinney
Economic Development Officer: Karine McGuckin
Equality Officer: Brian Dorrian
Public Relations Officer: Ursula Mezza
Sports Development Officer: Patrick McKibbin
Tourism Development Officer: Sharon Mahaffy

Council Contact Details

Chief Executive's Office	028 9182 4004
Borough Inspector's Office	028 9182 4005
Entertainment Licences	028 9182 4041
Leisure Services	028 9182 4018
Public Relations	028 9182 4021
Registration Services	028 9182 4003
Economic Development	028 9182 4025
Tourism	028 9182 6846
Public Health	028 9182 4057
Building Control	028 9182 4033
Refuse Collection	028 9182 4014
Street Cleaning	028 9182 4015

ARMAGH CITY & DISTRICT COUNCIL

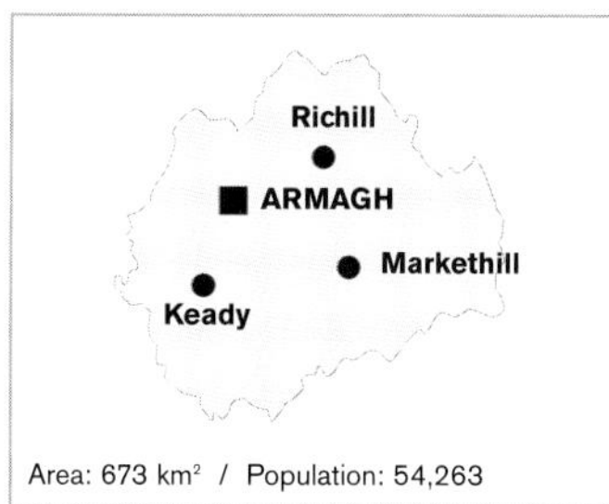

Area: 673 km² / Population: 54,263

Council Offices
The Palace Demesne
Armagh, BT60 4EL
Tel: 028 3752 9600
Fax: 028 3752 9601
Web:
www.armagh.gov.uk

Armagh City and District Council lies in the south east of Northern Ireland 40 miles south of Belfast. It is essentially a rural district, the largest centre of population being Armagh City, the ecclesiastical capital of Ireland which hosts the two impressive hilltop Cathedrals of the Church of Ireland and Roman Catholic Churches. The area is rich in culture and heritage, making it an attractive location for tourism. The public sector is the main source of employment.

Armagh has a diverse light industry and manufacturing base, with the single largest product area being textiles. Agricultural machinery, furniture, plastics and domestic fittings are also produced in the area. The service industries, as well as food processing and tourism have all contributed significantly to economic activity. Armagh City is the commercial and retail centre of the district, offering a mixture of national outlets and local family-run businesses retailing high quality goods.

Cultural, educational and industrial infrastructures are being continuously developed and Armagh's high-speed telecommunications network puts Armagh in touch with commercial and industrial centres around the world. A new council backed 15,000sq ft incubation facility has recently been developed for high-quality ICT start-up businesses. This is linked to a similar facility in Monaghan. The council also has a number of international connections, with strong relationships between Armagh and Eastern Europe and the USA.

Top companies in Armagh include: Fane Valley Co-operative Society Ltd, Tayto, JF McKenna Ltd, Johnston's of Mountnorris, Thomas McLaughlin & Sons, NC Engineering, Redrock Engineering, Rapid International and Wilson's Country Veg. Overseas companies located in the district include: Warner (UK) Ltd (US), Answer Call Direct and E-blana.

Political Composition

Armagh City and District Council is comprised of 22 Councillors elected to four District Electoral Areas (DEA): Armagh City 6 seats, The Orchard 5 seats, Crossmore 5 seats Cusher 6 seats. The political composition of Armagh City and District Council elected members as elected in June 2001 is: Ulster Unionist Party (UUP) 7, Social Democratic and Labour Party (SDLP) 6, Democratic Unionist Party (DUP) 4, Sinn Féin (SF) 5. The largest party on the council is the UUP with 7 seats. No single party has overall control. The council is finely balanced between unionist and nationalist control.

The Council meeting is convened on the 4th Monday of each month at 7.30pm in the Council offices.

Elected Members and Council Committees

Mayor: Pat O'Rawe (SF) Deputy Mayor: No Deputy

Councillor	Party	Enviornment Health & Recreation	Regeneration & Development	Resources	Scrutiny Best Value	Public Services Liason	Executive
Paul Berry	DUP	•				C	•
Heather Black	DUP		•	VC	•	•	
Pat Brannigan	SDLP		•		C	•	•
Anna Brolly	SDLP		•	•		•	
John Campbell	SDLP	•			•	VC	
Tom Canavan	SDLP	VC		•		•	
Jimmy Clayton	UUP		•		•	•	
Paul Corrigan	SF	•			•	•	
Evelyn Corry	UUP			•		•	
Brian Cunningham	SF		VC	•		•	
Freda Donnelly	DUP				•	•	
William Irwin	DUP	•	•	•		•	
Tommy Kavanagh	SDLP		•		•	•	
James McKernan	SDLP	•		•		•	
Pat McNamee	SF	•		C		•	•
Sylvia McRoberts	UUP		•		VC	•	
Pat O'Rawe	SF				•	•	
Cathy Rafferty	SF		•			•	
Charles Rollston	UUP	C			•	•	•
Eric Speers	UUP	•		•		•	
Jim Speers	UUP		C			•	•
Robert Turner	UUP	•		•		•	

• Member C Chair VC Vice-chair

Senior Officers

Chief Executive: Victor Brownlees
Executive Manager and PA: Wendy Geary
Director of Corporate Services: David McCammick
Director of Environment, Health, and Recreation Services: John Briggs
Head of Environmental Health & Protection: Anne Donaghy
Head of Finance: Stephen Hyde
Head of Operational Services: David McKee
Head of Recreation and Leisure: Gerard Houlahan
Head of Regeneration and Development: Sharon O'Gorman
Chief Building Control Officer: Phillip Beattie
Corporate Marketing Officer: Shane Meehan
District Policing Partnership Manager: John Doyle
Economic Development Officer: Diane McConnell
Equality Officer: Dominic McCanny
Urban Regeneration Officer: Anne Doherty
Policy Officer: Nora Winder
Rural Development Officer: Maria Lavery
Registrar of Births, Deaths and Marriages: Jennifer Coulter
Tourism Officer: Sandra Durand
Waste Management Officer: Irene Kempton

Council Contact Details

Corporate Administrative Services	028 3752 9605
Clerk and Chief Executive Secretariat	028 3752 9603
Member Services	028 3752 9649
Registration of Births, Deaths and Marriages	028 3752 9615
Regeneration and Development	028 3752 9642
Environmental Health	028 3752 9626
Building Control	028 3752 9616
Recreation and Leisure	028 3752 9636

BALLYMENA BOROUGH COUNCIL

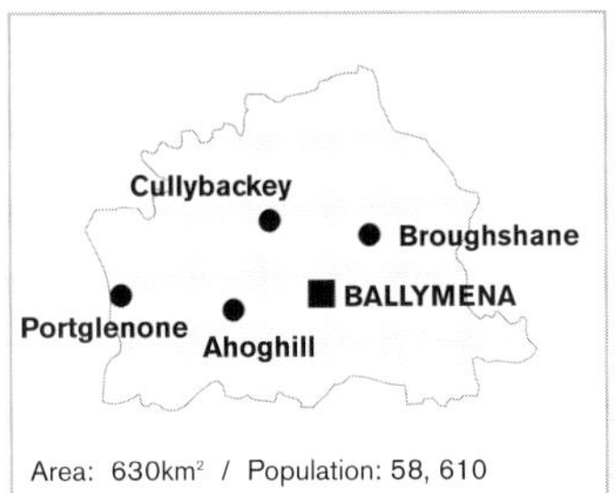

Ardeevin
80 Galgorm Road
Ballymena, BT42 1AB
Tel: 028 2566 0300
Fax: 028 2566 0400
Email:
info@ballymena.gov.uk
Web:
www.ballymena.gov.uk

Ballymena Borough Council is located at the heart of one of Northern Ireland's most fertile and prosperous farming regions. Ballymena town is 27 miles north of Belfast and 22 miles from the Port of Larne. The present borough of Ballymena was created in 1973 and covers 200 square miles. Over half of the borough's total population of 58,610 live in the town of Ballymena, which is the regional administrative centre for many organisations in the north-eastern part of Northern Ireland, including the Health and Social Services Board, Education and Library Board and government departments such as Inland Revenue and Social Security. Other population centres include the smaller towns and villages of Kells, Cullybackey, Portglenone, Broughshane and Ahoghill.

According to the 2001 Census of Employment (DETI), 25,776 people are employed in Ballymena Borough Council Area.

Ballymena town is the foremost retail centre for the region with a good representation of the main high street chains. Farming and agri-food industries play a major role in the borough's economy. The borough is also the home of two of the larger multinationals in Northern Ireland: Gallaher Tobacco Company and Michelin Tyres.

Ballymena Borough Council has placed an increasing emphasis on developing its leisure and environmental facilities. The borough is host to a major environmental project – the £10 million ECOS Centre built on the banks of the River Braid. The centre incorporates numerous interactive features, generates it own power from solar and biomass energy and provides attractive conference and visitor facilities.

Ballymena is recognised in the Regional Development Strategy as one of the major regional growth hubs within Northern Ireland and is expected to generate higher levels of growth reflecting its well established role and strength as a major centre of economic activity.

Political Composition

Ballymena Borough Council is made up of 24 Councillors elected to four District Electoral Areas (DEA), comprising: Ballymena North 7 seats, Ballymena South 7 seats, Bannside 5 seats, Braid 5 seats. The political composition of Ballymena Borough Council elected members as elected in June 2001 is: Ulster Unionist Party (UUP) 7, Social Democratic and Labour Party (SDLP) 4, Democratic Unionist Party (DUP) 11, Other 2. The largest party on the council is the DUP with 11 seats. The council has a clear unionist majority, with no single party having overall control.

Elected Members and Council Committees

Mayor: Joseph McKernan (UUP)
Deputy Mayor: Hubert Nicholl (DUP)

Councillor	Party	Personnel Policy	Development & Leisure	Environmental Services	Finance, Est & Information Comms Technology	Public Sector Liaison
Elizabeth Adger	DUP	•	•	•	•	•
James Alexander	DUP	•	•	•	C	•
Neil Armstrong	UUP	•	•	•	•	•
Peter Brown	UUP	•	•	•	•	C
Martin Clarke	DUP	•	•	•	•	•
James Currie	UUP	•	C	•	•	•
David Clyde	UUP	•	•	•	•	•
Samuel Gaston	DUP	•	•	•	•	•
Roy Gillespie	DUP	•	•	C	•	•
Margaret Gribben	SDLP	•	•	•	•	•
Samuel Hanna	DUP	•	•	•	•	•
James Henry	Ind	•	•	•	•	•
Seamus Laverty	SDLP	•	•	•	•	•
PJ McAvoy	SDLP	•	•	•	•	•
Joseph McKernan	UUP	•	•	•	•	•
William McNeilly	UUP	•	•	•	•	•
Maurice Mills	DUP	C	•	•	•	•
Thomas Nicholl	DUP	•	•	•	•	•
Hubert Nicholl	DUP	•	•	•	•	•
Declan O'Loan	SDLP	•	•	•	•	•
Lexie Scott	UUP	•	•	•	•	•
Robin Stirling	DUP	•	•	•	•	•
David Tweed	DUP	•	•	•	•	•
William Wright	Ind	•	•	•	•	•

• Member C Chair VC Vice-chair

Senior Officers

Town Clerk and Chief Executive: Mervyn Rankin
Executive Manager and PA: Joyce Boal
Director of Building Control Services: Maurice Watterson
Director of Development, Leisure and Cultural Services: Ronnie McBride
Director of Environmental Health Services: Alex Kinghorn
Director of Finance and IT Services: Victor Benson
Director of Personnel, Policy and Operational Services: Rodger McKnight
Cultural Services Manager: Willie Young
Corporate Policy Officer: Greg Dornan
District Policing Partnership Manager: Peter Greenshields
Economic Development Officer: Aidan Donnelly
Equality Officer: Greg Dornan
Leisure Services Manager: Bernie Candlish
Licensing Officer: Clive Kyle
Registrar of Births, Deaths and Marriages: Sheena Booth
Sports Development Officer: Bridget Black
Tourism Officer: Christine Butler
Waste Management Officer: Alex Kinghorn

Council Contact Details

Council Head Office – Ardeevin	028 2566 0300
Arts and Entertainment	028 2563 9853
Births, Deaths and Marriages	028 2566 0352
Building Control	028 2566 0409
Economic Development	028 2563 3930
Environmental Health	028 2566 0372
Ballymena Cemetery	028 2565 6026

BALLYMONEY BOROUGH COUNCIL

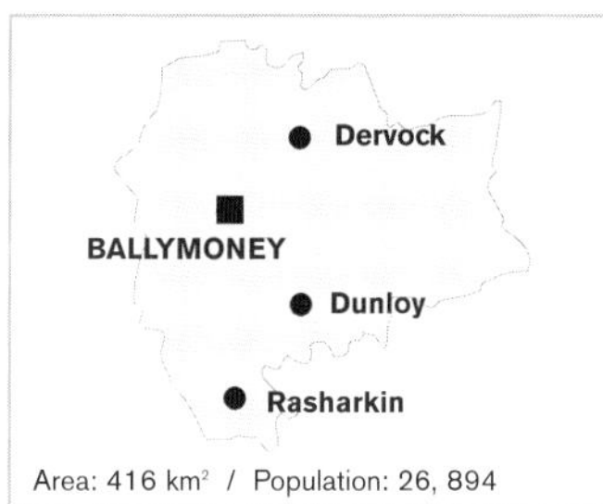

Borough Offices
Riada House
14 Charles Street
Ballymoney, BT53 6DZ
Tel: 028 2766 0200
Fax: 028 2766 5150
Email:
info@ballymoney.gov.uk
Web:
www.ballymoney.gov.uk

Ballymoney Borough Council is one of the smallest local authority areas accounting for 3 per cent of Northern Ireland's land mass. The borough is bordered to the west by the Lower River Bann, to the north and east by Coleraine and Moyle Councils and to the south by Ballymena. Approximately one third of the borough's 26,000 inhabitants live in or near the town of Ballymoney, which is the main administrative, commercial and educational centre for the area. Satellite villages within the borough include: Ballybogey, Cloughmills, Dervock, Dunloy, Loughguile, Rasharkin, and Stranocum.

Ballymoney provides a range of services and employment although it has a relatively small amount of public sector employment. Significant residential growth has occurred within the town over the past number of years, but this has not been matched by growth in the retail, commercial and industrial sectors. The town centre, which is designated a Conservation Area, has benefited greatly from public sector investment in a number of environmental improvement schemes. Recent investment by both the public and private sectors in the refurbishment and redevelopment of town centre commercial properties has also contributed to an improvement in the quality of the town.

Ballymoney Borough is predominantly rural and agriculture is commercially important to the area, with beef and dairy farming being the main activities. Pressure on the farming industry is causing fear of depopulation in the area unless supplementary and alternative sources of land-based income emerge.

A major deposit of lignite is located close to Ballymoney town and there have been plans for the construction of a lignite burning power station. Whilst potentially bringing significant economic benefits for the area the staunch opposition of the local community over the project's possible environmental impact has resulted in the promoters shelving their plans for the present.

Political Composition

Ballymoney Borough Council is made up of 16 Councillors elected to District Electoral Areas (DEA), comprising: Bushvale 5 seats; Ballymoney Town 5 seats; Bann Valley 6 seats. The political composition of Ballymoney Borough Council elected members as elected in June 2001 is: Ulster Unionist Party (UUP) 5, Social Democratic and Labour Party (SDLP) 2, Democratic Unionist Party (DUP) 8, Sinn Féin (SF) 1. The largest party on the council is the DUP with 8 seats. The council has an overwhelming unionist majority, with the DUP close to overall control.

The Council meeting is convened on the 1st Monday of each month at 7.30pm in the Council offices.

Elected Members and Council Committees

Mayor: Frank Campbell (DUP)
Deputy Mayor: Cecil Cousley (DUP)

Councillor	Party	Development	Leisure & Amenities	Finance & General Purposes	Health & Environmental	Best Value
Frank Campbell	DUP	•	•	•	•	•
Harry Connolly	SDLP		•	•		
Cecil Cousley	DUP	•	•	•	•	•
John Finlay	DUP	•	•	•		•
Joseph Gaston	UUP		•		•	
Robert Halliday	DUP		•		•	
Bill Kennedy	DUP	•	•		•	•
William Logan	UUP		•	•	•	•
Malachy McCamphill	SDLP	•	•			•
Philip McGuigan	SF				•	•
Thomas McKeown	UUP	•				
John Ramsay	UUP	•			•	•
James Simpson	UUP	•		•		
Ian Stevenson	DUP	•		•	•	
Mervyn Storey	DUP	•		•		
Robert Wilson	DUP		•	•	•	•

• **Member**

Senior Officers

Chief Executive: John Dempsey
PA: Karen Wilson, Pauline McLaughlin
Director of Financial and Administrative Services: Iris McCleery
Director of Health and Environmental Services: John Michael
Director of Leisure and Amenities: John Paul
Chief Building Control Officer: Joe Martin
Cultural Services Officer: Margaret Edgar
Community Safety Co-ordinator: Julie McStravick
Community Relations Officer: Anne Cummings
Corporate Services Officer: Elizabeth Johnston
District Policing Partnership Manager: Jonny Donaghy
Dog Warden/Enforcement Officer: Karen Mitchell
Economic Development Officer: Lisa O'Kane
Finance and IT Officer: David Wright
Human Resources Manager: Joan Kinnaird
Registrar of Births, Marriages and Deaths: Janet McCaughey
Sports Development Officer: Richard Gormley
Tourism and Amenities Officer: Jim Graham

Council Contact Details

Building Control	028 2766 0220
Ballymoney Town Hall	028 2766 2256
Dog Control	07775 938003
Drumaheglis Marina & Caravan Park	028 2766 6468
Health & Environmental Services	028 2766 0257
Joey Dunlop Leisure Centre	028 2766 0260
Leisure & Amenities	028 2766 0200
Rasharkin Community Centre	028 2957 1990
Registrar of Births, Deaths and Marriages	028 2766 0200
Tourist Information	028 2766 0200
Waste Disposal & Civic Amenity Site	028 2766 5169

BANBRIDGE DISTRICT COUNCIL

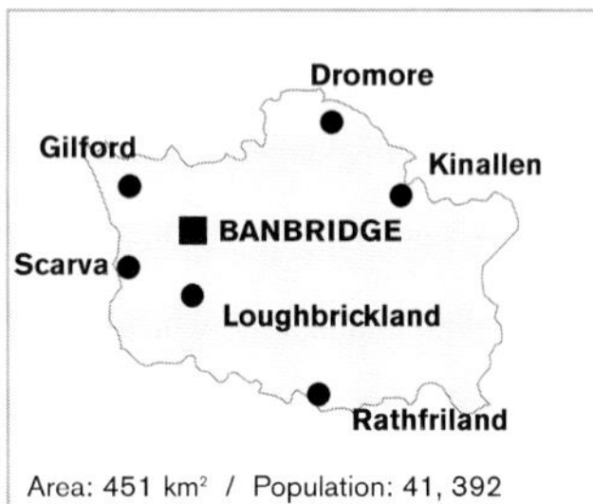

Civic Building
Downshire Road
Banbridge
Co. Down
BT32 3JY
Tel: 028 4066 0600
Fax: 028 4066 0601
Email:
info@banbridgedc.gov.uk
Web:
www.banbridgedc.gov.uk

Banbridge District Council is situated in the north west of County Down adjacent to the main Belfast to Dublin road. It stretches from Dromore in the north to Rathfriland in the south and from Gilford in the west to Ballyward in the east. The district has a population of over 41,000 representing over 2.4 per cent of the population of Northern Ireland. The latest 2001 Census figures show that the Banbridge district is one of the fastest growing areas in Northern Ireland.

The main town is Banbridge, followed by Dromore, Rathfriland and Gilford. Approximately half of the population live in rural areas and small villages and there are around 14,000 private households within the district, some 71 per cent of which are owner occupied.

Banbridge town was established around a major crossing of the River Bann and the town has a unique feature in that its main street is divided into three sections, with an underpass cut out of the middle in order to lower the hill, and a bridge built over the gap.

Banbridge has long been associated with the linen industry. Textiles and agriculture are also important for the local economy. Industry in Banbridge is dominated by the small business sector with 93 per cent of local registered businesses having fewer than 10 employees.

The highest level of employment is accounted for by the services sector (68 per cent), followed by the manufacturing sector (20 per cent), and the construction sector (10 per cent). Major employers include Franklin International, Falmore Industries, Fane Valley Co-Operative and Bowman Windows. Banbridge has the second lowest level of unemployment of all district council areas in Northern Ireland. Banbridge District Council area lies within the Southern Health and Social Services Board and is serviced by the Craigavon and Banbridge HSS Trust.

Political Composition

Banbridge District Council has 17 seats distributed throughout three District Electoral Areas (DEA), comprising: Banbridge town 6 seats; Knockiveagh 6 seats Dromore 5 seats. The political composition of Banbridge District Council elected members as elected in June 2001 is:Ulster Unionist Party (UUP) 7; Social Democratic and Labour Party (SDLP) 3; Democratic Unionist Party (DUP) 5; Other 2

After the council elections in June 2001 the UUP was the largest party on the council with 7 councillors. The Council has a clear unionist majority although no single party has control.

Elected Members and Council Committees

Chairman: Catherine McDermot (SDLP) Vice-Chairman: John Hanna (UUP)

Councillor	Party	Public Services Liaison	Leisure Development	Environmental Services	Policy & Resources	Health Care
Joan Baird	UUP	•		C	•	VC
Norah Beare	UUP	VC	•	•		•
Derick Bell	UUP	•		•	•	
Ian Burns	UUP	•	•	•		•
Seamus Doyle	SDLP	•	•		•	
John Hanna	UUP	•	•		•	
David Herron	DUP	•		•	•	•
Stephen Herron	DUP	C	•	•		
John Ingram	UUP	•	C		•	•
William Martin	UUP	•	•	VC		•
Pat McAleenan	SDLP	•	•	•		•
Malachy McCartan	Ind	•	•	•		
Catherine McDermott	SDLP	•	•	•	•	•
Jim McElroy	DUP	•		•	C	•
Wilfred McFadden	DUP	•	•		•	C
Frank McQuaid	All	•		•	•	•
Paul Rankin	DUP	•	VC		•	

• Member C Chair VC Vice-chair

Senior Officers

Chief Executive: Robert Gilmore
Executive Manager and PA: Eleanor McLoughlin
Director of Corporate Services: Pat Cumiskey
Director of Development: Liam Hannaway
Director of Environmental Services: Ken Forbes
Director of Leisure Services: Mike Reith
District Building Control Officer: William Frazer
Arts and Events Officer: Leah Duncan
Community Relations Officer: Pamela Matthews
Community Safety Officer: Rhonda Abraham
Corporate Marketing Officer: Sharon Harrison
District Policing Partnership Manager: Amanda Scargill
Economic Development Officer: John O'Hare
Environmental Health Manager: Robert Stewart
Finance Manager: Graham Coulter
Leisure Services Manager: Robin McGloughlin
Operations Manager: Eric Morton
Registrar of Births, Deaths and Marriages: Elaine Gilmore
Tourism Officer: John Douglas
Waste Management Officer: Keith Patterson

Council Contact Details

Chief Executive/Member Services	028 4066 0602
Corporate Services Finance Office	028 4066 0607
Human Resource Management	028 4066 0608
Registration of Births,Deaths & Marriages	028 4066 0614
General Office	028 4066 0605
Arts & Events	028 4066 0632
Access to Countryside	028 4066 0617
Community Relations/Development	028 4066 0643
Sports Development	028 4066 0637
Development/General Office	028 4066 0609
Economic Development	028 4066 0635
Heritage & Genealogy	028 4062 6369
The Bridge Partnership	028 4066 0644
Tourism	028 4066 0609
Town Centre Development	028 4066 2668

BELFAST CITY COUNCIL

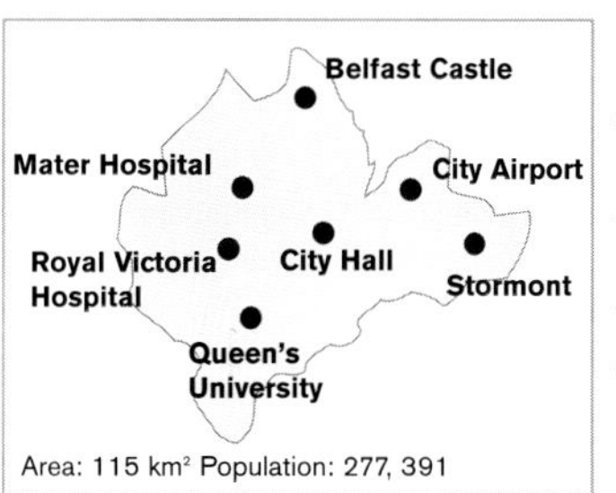

City Hall
Belfast, BT1 5GS
Tel: 028 9032 0202
Fax: 028 9027 0232
Textphone:
028 9027 0405
Web:
www.belfastcity.gov.uk

Belfast City Council has local authority responsibility for Northern Ireland's largest population. Over 700,000 people live in the Greater Belfast Metropolitan area with 277,391 located within the Belfast City Council area.

Belfast City Council is by far the largest of the twenty-six district councils in Northern Ireland. It is responsible for the large scale delivery of key services, refuse collection and disposal, street cleansing, building control and environmental health, community development, indoor and outdoor leisure, parks and recreational facilities, and support for the arts, tourism and economic development. In recent years the council has taken an increasingly proactive role in the development of the city.

The city council has a key role in the life of the city, not only in discharging its statutory duties and functions, but also in representing the public and providing the services and support, which the residents of Belfast have indicated as important.

Although Belfast remains the largest concentrated area of industrial development in Northern Ireland, its traditional manufacturing and engineering sector has been in steady decline. Despite this, Belfast is undergoing a major transformation and there has been rapid growth in new lighter industries such as information technology.

Tourism is a key contributor to the wealth of the city economy. New developments such as the Odyssey arena, the development of the Cathedral Quarter and the planned development of the Titanic Quarter are indicative of the growth and vibrancy of the city. The proposed development at Victoria Square will also bring business growth into Belfast.

Political Composition

The Local Government constituency of Belfast City is made up of nine electoral areas: Balmoral 6 seats, Castle 6 seats, Court 5 seats, Laganbank 5 seats, Lower Falls 5 seats, Oldpark 6 seats, Pottinger 6 seats, Upper Falls 5 seats, Victoria 7 seats. Each Electoral Area comprises between five and six Council Wards, which return 51 elected Members to the Council. The political composition of Belfast City Council elected members as elected in June 2001 is: Ulster Unionist Party (UUP) 11, Social Democratic and Labour Party (SDLP) 9, Democratic Unionist Party (DUP) 10, Sinn Féin (SF), 14, Alliance, 3, Other 4. The largest party on the Council is Sinn Féin with 14 seats. The Council is finely balanced between unionists and nationalists with the Alliance party holding the balance of power.

Elected Members and Council Committees

Lord Mayor: Martin Morgan (SDLP)
Deputy Lord Mayor: Margaret Crooks (UUP)
High Sheriff: Ruth Patterson (DUP)

Councillor	Party	Policy & Resources	Client Services	Contract Services	Development	Health & Environmental Services	Planning
Ian Adamson	UUP				•		C
David Alderdice	All	•				•	
Alex Attwood	SDLP			•			
David Browne	UUP	•		DC			•
Michael Browne	SF	•	•		DC		
Wallace Browne	DUP		DC	•		•	
Jim Clarke	UUP			•		C	
Margaret Clarke	UUP		•	•		•	
Patrick Convery	SDLP		C			•	
Margaret Crooks	UUP	•	•			•	
Alan Crowe	UUP				•	•	
Ian Crozier	DUP	•	•		C		
Máire Cush	SF			•		•	
Nigel Dodds	DUP					•	
Thomas Ekin	All	•		•	•		
Reg Empey	UUP				•		•
David Ervine	PUP		•	•			
Carmel Hanna	SDLP	•				•	
Tom Hartley	SF	C					
Billy Hutchinson	PUP				•		•
Danny Lavery	SF	•					•
Naomi Long	All		•				•
Alban Maginness	SDLP	•		•			•
Alex Maskey	SF	•	•				
Paul Maskey	SF			•			
Chrissie McAuley	SF			•	•	•	
Fra McCann	SF	•	•		•	•	
Patrick McCarthy	SDLP			•	•		•
Nelson McCausland	DUP			•	•		
Margaret McClenaghan	SF		•				•
Frank McCoubrey	Ind		•	•			
Chris McGimpsey	UUP	•		•		•	
Michael McGimpsey	UUP				•		•
Elaine McMillen	DUP	•		•		•	•
Catherine Molloy	SDLP		•		•	•	•
Marie Moore	SF			•		•	•
Martin Morgan	SDLP						
Robin Newton	DUP	•			•		
Caral Ni Chuilin	SF			•	•		
Eoin O'Broin	SF				•	•	
Joseph O'Donnell	SF		•		•		DC
Gerard O'Neill	SF		•	C			•
Peter O'Reilly	SDLP	•			•	DC	
Ruth Patterson	DUP					•	•
Jim Rodgers	UUP	•	•				
Eric Smyth	DUP	DC	•				•
Hugh Smyth	PUP	•				•	•
Robert Stoker	UUP		•		•		
Harry Toan	DUP		•	•			
Margaret Walsh	SDLP	•	•				•
Sammy Wilson	DUP				•		•

• Member C Chair DC Deputy-chair

Senior Officers

Chief Executive: Peter McNaney
Assistant Chief Executive: Robert Wilson
Director of Client Services: Mervyn Elder
Director of Contract Services: Heather Louden
Director of Corporate Services: Trevor Salmon
Director of Development: Marie-Thérèse McGivern
Director of Health and Environmental Services: William Francey
Director of Legal Services: Ciaran Quigley
Head of Corporate Communications: Eamon Deeny
Head of Committee and Members' Services: Liam Steele
Head of Policy Services: David Cartmill
Head of Internal Audit: Andrew Wilson
Head of Human Resources: Stanley Black
Head of Financial Services: Fred Maguire
Head of Civic Buildings and Property Care: Dennis Waring
Head of Business Improvement: John Millar
Head of Information Services Belfast (ISB): Tom Orr
Head of Corporate Systems and Projects: Martin McVitty
Head of Economic Initiatives: Shirley McCay
Head of Urban Development: Gerry Millar
Head of Environmental Health: Andrew Hassard
Head of Waste Management: Tim Walker
Head of Building Control: Trevor Martin
Head of Recreation and Community Development: Philip Lucas
Head of Parks and Amenities: Maurice Parkinson
Belfast Waterfront Hall General Manager: Tim Husbands
Head of Finance & Business Support: Mark McBride
Head of Cleansing: Sam Skimin
Head of Grounds Maintenance: Jim Kennedy
Head of Operational Services: George Wright

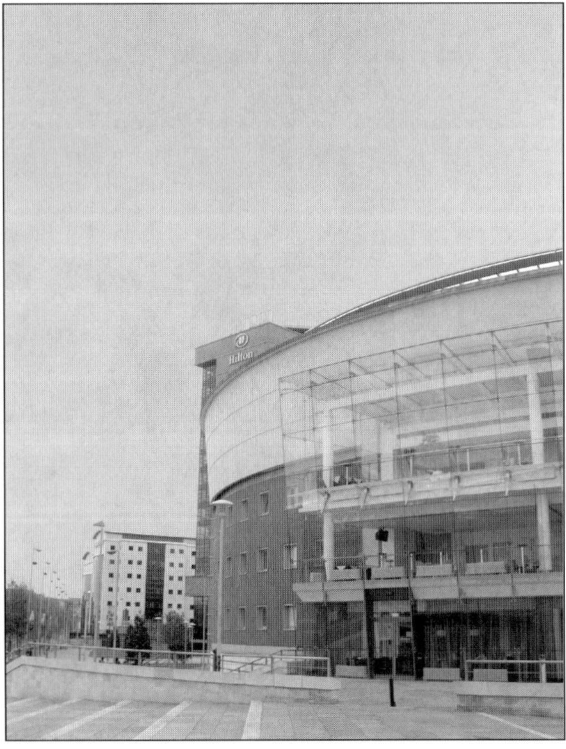

Council Contact Details

Arts and Heritage Unit	028 9027 0461
Belfast Castle	028 9077 6925
Belfast Visitor and Convention Bureau	028 9023 9026
Belfast Welcome Centre	028 9024 6609
Building Control 24 hr line	028 9023 6672
Building Control Technical Helpline	028 9027 0432
Building Control Licensing	028 9027 0287
Bulky Household Waste/Special Collections	028 9027 0230
Business Improvement Section	028 9027 0279
Cemeteries Office	028 9027 0296
Chief Executive's Department	028 9027 0202
City Hall	028 9032 0202
Civic Amenities Sites (Dumps)	028 9027 0656
Client Services Department	028 9032 0202
Committee Services	028 9027 0465
Community Development	028 9027 0417
Complaints Central Helpline	028 9027 0270
Conservation & Education Unit	028 9066 2259
Consumer Advice Centre	028 9032 8260
Contract Services Department	028 9032 0202
Economic Development Unit	028 9027 0482
Equality Officer (Freefone)	0800 0855 412
Events Co-ordinator (Citywide)	028 9027 0222
Financial Services Section	028 9032 0202
First Stop Shop – Business Enquiry Service	028 9027 8399
Food Safety Division	028 9027 0468
Forest of Belfast Officer (Parks & Amenities)	028 9027 0350
Grounds Maintenance Head Office	028 9037 3031
Group Theatre	028 9032 3900
Health & Environmental Services Department	028 9027 0428
Health & Environmental (after hours)	07850499622
Health & Safety at Work	028 9027 0428
Home Safety Division	028 9027 0469
Human Resources Section	028 9032 0202
Information Services Belfast	028 9024 4832
Lord Mayor's Unit	028 9027 0215
Malone House	028 9068 1246
Markets Manager	028 9027 0509
Noise Hotline	028 9037 3006
Pest Control	028 9027 0428
Pollution Control	028 9027 0428
Press and Media	028 9027 0221
Recreation & Community Development	028 9032 0202
Recycling Hotline	0800 0328 100
Refuse Collection (Commercial/Trade Accounts)	028 9027 0298
Refuse Collection (Commercial/ Trade Operations)	028 9032 3190
Refuse Collection Customer Contact Centre	028 9027 0230
Registration of Births, Deaths & Marriages	028 9027 0274
Smoke Hotline	028 9027 0420
St George's Market	028 9043 5704
Tourism Development Unit	028 9027 0426
Ulster Hall	028 9032 3900
Waste Management (Complaints/Enquiries)	028 9027 0297
Waterfront Hall	028 9033 4400
Zoological Gardens	028 9077 4625
Zoological Gardens Information Line	028 9077 6277

Belfast Waterfront Hall

CARRICKFERGUS BOROUGH COUNCIL

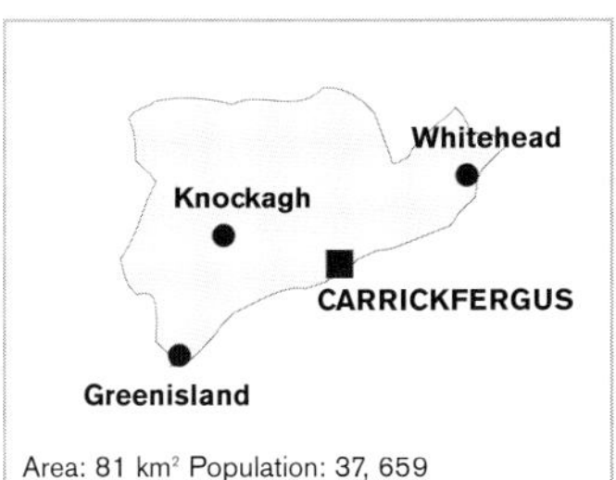

Town Hall
Joymount
Carrickfergus
BT38 7DL
Tel: 028 9335 1604
Fax: 028 9336 6676
Email:
info@carrickfergus.org
Web:
www.carrickfergus.org

In 1973 the original Carrickfergus Borough Council together with the Whitehead Urban District Council and part of Larne Rural District Council were amalgamated to form the present Carrickfergus Borough Council.

Carrickfergus is located along the coast in southeast Antrim with its main settlement, the town of Carrickfergus located on the northern shore of Belfast Lough some 10 miles from Belfast. Other significant settlements in the borough include Greenisland and Whitehead

Carrickfergus has a long history and came to prominence in Norman times. Its harbour area boasts possibly Ireland's best preserved Norman Keep, one of Northern Ireland's main tourist attractions.

With an approximate population of 38,000 Carrickfergus has the second fastest rate of population growth in Northern Ireland, and has a relatively young population with 68 per cent of the population under 44. There is a large graduate population in the borough reflecting the proximity of two universities, and three vocational colleges.

With a long history in manufacturing, Carrickfergus is the chosen base for a number of important international and homegrown manufacturing companies. These include the Japanese Ryobi group, the largest independent die casting company in the world and the first large Northern Ireland Company to convert to newly available natural gas. Korean company Daewoo Electronics Ltd and the Irish Salt Mining Company suppliers to the UK and USA markets with rock salt, primarily for de-icing purposes are all located within the borough. Kilroot power station is also situated within the borough.

Political Composition

Carrickfergus Borough Council has 17 seats distributed throughout three District Electoral Areas (DEA), comprising: Knockagh Monument 6 seats; Carrick Castle 5 seats; Kilroot 6 seats.

The political composition of Carrickfergus Borough Council elected members as elected in June 2001 is: Ulster Unionist Party (UUP) 4; Democratic Unionist Party (DUP) 6; Alliance 5; Other 2

The largest party on the council is the DUP with 6 seats. The council has an overwhelmingly unionist majority although no single party has overall control.

Elected Members and Council Committees

Mayor: May Beattie (DUP) / Deputy Mayor: Eric Ferguson (UUP)

Councillor	Party	Development Services	Chief Executive's Office	Environmental Services	Support Services	Building Services Committee
William Ashe	DUP	C	•	•	•	•
May Beattie	DUP	•	•	•	•	•
Roy Beggs	UUP	VC	•	•	•	•
James Brown	Ind	•	•	•	•	•
Robert Cavan	All	•	•	•	•	•
Terence Clements	DUP	•	•	•	•	VC
Janet Crampsey	All	•	VC	•	•	•
Stewart Dickson	All	•	•	•	•	•
Darin Ferguson	UUP	•	•	•	C	•
Eric Ferguson	UUP	•	•	•	•	•
William Hamilton	Ind	•	•	•	•	•
David Hilditch	DUP	•	•	C	•	•
James McClurg	DUP	•	C	•	•	•
Noreen McIlwrath	All	•	•	•	•	•
Patricia McKinney	DUP	•	•	•	VC	•
Sean Neeson	All	•	•	•	•	C
Gwen Wilson	UUP	•	•	VC	•	•

• Member C Chair VC Vice-chair

Senior Officers

Town Clerk & Chief Executive: Alan C Cardwell
Director of Building Services: Stephen J Johnston
Director of Development Services:John D McCormick
Director of Environmental Services: Alan Barkley
Best Value Officer: Norman Neill
Community Relations Officer: Colin Ellis
Countryside Officer: Neil Luney
District Policing Partnership Manager:Daniel Sweeney
Economic Development Officer: Alan Braithwaite
Enforcement Officer: Alan Reid
Health and Safety Officer: John MacIntyre
Human Resources Manager: Mervyn McDowell
Leisure Centre Manager: Norman Houston
Registrar of Births, Deaths and Marriages:
Sally McDowell, Liz McNeilly
Sports Development Officer: Claire Dorrian
Tourism Officer (Acting): Carol Hall
Waste Management Officer: Jean Stewart

Council Contact Details

Town Hall	028 9335 1604
Administration Department	
Building Regulations	
Dangerous Structures	
Entertainments/Petroleum	
Licensing	
Finance Department	
Noise / Air Pollution	
Property Certificates	
Registration of Births, Deaths and Marriages	
Heritage Centre	028 9336 6455
Carrickfergus Leisure Centre	028 9335 1711
Andrew Jackson Centre	028 9336 6455
Carrickfergus Marina	028 9336 6666
Sullatober Depot	028 9335 1192

CASTLEREAGH BOROUGH COUNCIL

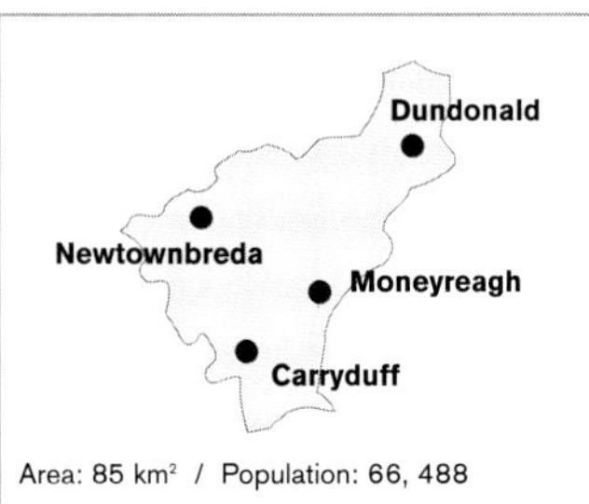

Area: 85 km² / Population: 66, 488

Civic and Administrative Offices, Bradford Court
Upper Galwally
Castlereagh, BT8 6RB
Tel: 028 9049 4500
Fax: 028 9049 4515
Email:
council@castlereagh.gov.uk
Web:
www.castlereagh.gov.uk

Castlereagh Borough Council covers much of the southern and eastern outskirts of Belfast, including the suburbs of Newtownbreda, Knock and Stormont, as well as the satellite town of Carryduff and the villages of Moneyreagh and Crossnacreevy. Covering over 32.6 sq miles, the borough has a rapidly expanding population currently in excess of 67,000.

A number of important industrial firms are located within the borough including Bombardier Aerospace Short Bros Plc and Hughes Christensen Company.

Educational provision within the borough is supplied by eighteen primary schools, seven higher/grammar schools, two special care establishments and one college of further and higher education.

Recreational facilities include Belvoir Park Forest, Lagan Valley Regional Park, Moat Park and the Billy Neill Soccer Centre of Excellence, a 100 acre state of the art football and sports centre. Following on the success of Dundonald International Ice Bowl and the recently established David Lloyd Tennis and Recreation Centre, a new major leisure park development is planned.

The council has long been associated with a record of striking comparatively low rates for its citizens despite the major investment that it has made in the civic and recreational infrastructure.

Political Composition

Castlereagh Borough Council has twenty three seats distributed throughout four District Electoral Areas (DEA), comprising: Castlereagh Central 6 seats; Castlereagh East 7 seats; Castlereagh South 5 seats; Castlereagh West 5 seats

The political composition is: Ulster Unionist Party (UUP) 5; Social Democratic and Labour Party (SDLP) 2; Democratic Unionist Party (DUP) 10; Alliance (All) 4; Other 2

The largest party on the council is the DUP with 10 seats. The council has a clear unionist majority. The Council holds two meetings a month, both of which commence at 7pm in the Council offices.

The council and its individual committees meet on a monthly basis, with sub committee meetings convening as and when required.

Elected Members and Council Committees

Mayor: Michael Henderson (UUP) Deputy Mayor: Mark Robinson (DUP)

Councillor	Party	Planning	Admin & Community Services	Leisure Park Board	Technical Services	Civic	Finance & Leisure Services
John Beattie	DUP	•	•	•	•	•	C
Joanne Bunting	DUP	•	•	•	•	•	•
Michael Copeland	UUP	•	•	•	•	•	VC
David Drysdale	UUP	•	•	•	VC	•	•
Sara Duncan	All	•	•	•	•	•	•
Claire Ennis	DUP	•	•	•	•	•	•
Francis Gallagher	Ind	•	•	•	•	•	•
Cecil Hall	PUP	•	C	•	•	•	•
Brian Hanvey	SDLP	VC	•	•	•	•	•
Michael Henderson	UUP	•	•	•	•	•	•
Rosaleen Hughes	SDLP	•	•	•	•	•	•
Michael Long	All	•	•	•	•	•	•
Barbara McBurney	UUP	•	•	•	•	•	•
Kim Morton	DUP	•	•	•	•	C	•
John Norris	DUP	•	•	•	C	•	•
Peter Osborne	All	•	•	•	•	•	•
Geraldine Rice	All	•	•	•	•	•	•
Iris Robinson	DUP	•	•	•	•	VC	•
Peter Robinson	DUP	•	•	C	•	•	•
Mark Robinson	DUP	•	•	•	•	•	•
Thomas Sandford	PUP	•	•	•	•	•	•
Vivienne Stevenson	DUP	•	VC	•	•	•	•
Jim White	DUP	C	•	VC	•	•	•

• Member C Chair VC Vice-chair

Senior Officers

Chief Executive: Adrian Donaldson
Director of Administration & Community Services: Joan McCoy
Director of Finance and Leisure Services: Edward Patterson
Director of Technical Services: Edwin Campbell
Building Control Manager: Gordon Bratten
Environmental Health Manager: Heather Moore
Leisure Park Manager: Wendy Phillip
Arts Officer: Kim Cobain
Borough Inspector: Tom Duke
Community Relations Officer: Cathy Chambers
Countryside Officer: Michael Lipsett
District Policing Partnership Manager: Karen Collins
Dog Warden/Enforcement Officer: Eileen Logan
Economic Development Officer: Clare Jamison
Finance Manager: Vacant
Health and Safety Officer: Simon Dawson
Human Resources Manager: Joe Simpson
IT Officer: Frank Levi
Public Relations and Corporate Marketing Officer: Jill Simpson
Registrar of Births, Deaths and Marriages: Margaret McVeigh
Tourism Officer: Jill Simpson

Council Contact Details

Headquarters	028 9049 4500
Registrar of Births, Deaths and Marriages	028 9079 8405
Activity Centre, Ballybeen	028 9048 3905
Ballyoran Centre	028 9041 0822
Belvoir Activity Centre	028 9064 2174
Dundonald International Ice Bowl	028 9080 9100
Lough Moss Centre	028 9081 4884
The Robinson Centre	028 9070 3948

COLERAINE BOROUGH COUNCIL

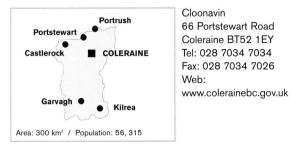

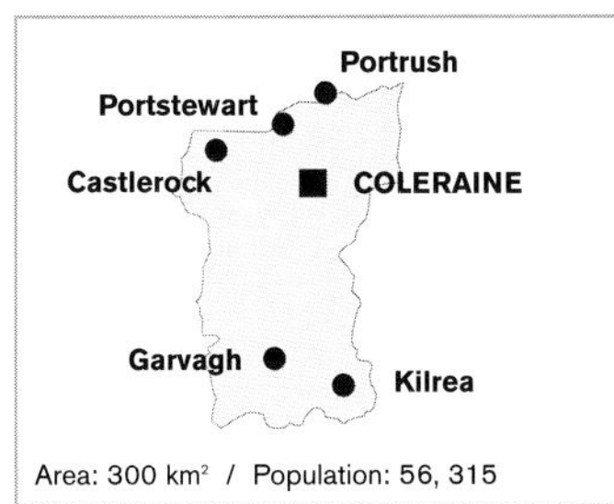

Cloonavin
66 Portstewart Road
Coleraine BT52 1EY
Tel: 028 7034 7034
Fax: 028 7034 7026
Web:
www.colerainebc.gov.uk

Coleraine Borough Council is situated on Northern Ireland's north coast, covering an area of 300 square kilometres. It has a population of 56,400 people, with 23,500 living in Coleraine town. The borough is the most popular tourist destination in Northern Ireland, embracing Portrush and Portstewart, two of Northern Ireland's busiest holiday resorts. The three towns together form an economic and social trio known as the "Coleraine Triangle".

Coleraine is the main retail and service centre within the borough fulfilling commercial, health, educational, employment and administrative functions. The new acute Causeway Hospital opened in 2001. The borough has plentiful education facilities including the headquarters campus of Northern Ireland's largest university, the University of Ulster, a college of Further Education, 3 grammar and 6 secondary schools.

Coleraine is also the chosen centre for the government's Northern Ireland Science Park, with a 50-acre site planned at the University of Ulster's Coleraine campus.

Despite the importance of tourism and agriculture to the borough, Coleraine is a significant location for industry. Leading industrial employers include AVX, Spanboard and DPP Coleraine Cheese Company.

Political Composition

Coleraine Borough Council has 22 seats distributed throughout 4 District Electoral Areas (DEA), comprising: Bann 6; Coleraine Central 6; Coleraine East 5; The Skerries 5

The political composition of Coleraine Borough Council elected members as elected in June 2001 is: Ulster Unionist Party (UUP) 9; Social Democratic and Labour Party (SDLP) 4; Democratic Unionist Party (DUP) 7; Other 2

The largest party on the council is the UUP with 9 seats. The council has a clear unionist majority. Council services are provided by five departments, which report to committees on a monthly basis. These standing committees consider relevant issues before making recommendations for the approval of council.

The Council meeting is convened on the 4th Tuesday of each month at 7.30pm in Council offices.

Elected Members and Council Committees

Mayor: Dessie Stewart (DUP) Deputy Mayor: Eamon Mullan (SDLP)

Councillor	Party	Leisure & Entertainment	Planning	Policy & Development
Christine Alexander	Ind	•	•	•
Pauline Armitage	Ind	•	•	•
David Barbour	UUP	•	•	•
Toye Black	UUP	•	•	•
Maurice Bradley	DUP	•	•	•
Olive Church	UUP	•	•	•
William Creelman	DUP	•	•	•
John Dallat	SDLP	•	•	•
Timothy Deans	DUP	C	•	•
Phyllis Fielding	DUP	•	•	•
Norman Hillis	UUP	•	•	•
Elizabeth Johnston	UUP	•	•	C
William King	UUP	•	•	•
Billy Leonard*	SF	•	•	•
David McClarty	UUP	•	•	•
James McClure	DUP	•	•	•
Gerry McLaughlin	SDLP	•	•	•
Adrian McQuillan	DUP	•	•	•
Robert McPherson	UUP	•	•	•
Eamon Mullan	SDLP	•	•	•
Desmond Stewart	DUP	•	•	•
James Watt	UUP	•	C	•

• Member C Chair VC Vice-chair
* elected for SDLP, now Sinn Féin

Senior Officers

Town Clerk and Chief Executive: Wavell Moore
Director of Corporate Services: David Bell
Director of Environmental Health: George Montgomery
Director of Leisure Services: Jim Curry
Head of Development Services: Moira Mann
Director of Technical Services: Dessie Wreath
Principal Building Control Officer: David Robinson
Environment Officer: Jim Allen
Corporate Marketing Officer: Clair Balmer, Elaine Moore
DPP Manager: Suzanne Crozier
Dog Warden/Enforcement Officer: Nuala Houston
Economic Development Officer: Linda McGuinness
Events Officer: Christine McKee
Registrar of Births, Deaths and Marriages: Gwyneth Kerr
Sports Development Officer: Roger Downey
Waste Management Officer: Tommy Neill

Council Contact Details

Town Clerk & Chief Executive's Dept	028 7034 7034
Administration	028 7034 7034
Registration of Births, Deaths & Marriages	028 7034 7021
Community Relations	028 7034 7044
Corporate Marketing	028 7034 7044
Economic Development	028 7034 7045
Tourism & Marketing	028 7034 7044
Corporate Services	028 7034 7134
Environmental Health Dept	028 7034 7171
Technical Services Dept	028 7034 7272
Buildings Regulations	028 7034 7253
Leisure Services	028 7034 7234
Arts/Events/Entertainment	028 7034 7234

COOKSTOWN DISTRICT COUNCIL

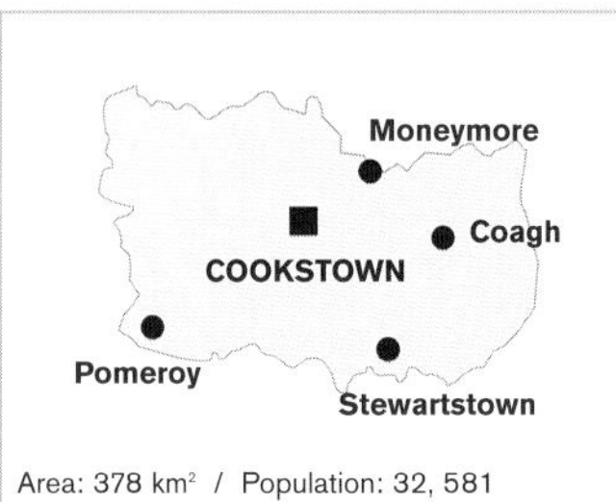

Area: 378 km² / Population: 32, 581

12 Burn Road
Cookstown, BT80 8DT
Tel: 028 8676 2205
Fax: 028 8676 4360
Email:
info@cookstown.gov.uk
Web:
www.cookstown.gov.uk

Cookstown District Council is an area of almost 378 sq. km with an approximate population of 32,000. The main settlement Cookstown, with an population of around 11,000 is the principal administrative and commercial centre for the district. It is noted for its very long and wide main thoroughfare. Other centres include Coagh, Moneymore, Pomeroy and Stewartstown.

Cookstown District has a modest manufacturing base set against an important agriculture sector and an expanding services sector. The main industries are based on the district's natural resources and significant employment is still provided in industries related to food processing and the extraction of minerals and aggregates. Employment growth has been sustained with notable expansion of local firms, Copeland Ltd and Grampian Meats Ltd.

Agriculture is the main land use in the district and the single most important local industry, employing approximately 2,600 people on some 1,430 holdings.

The district also has Northern Ireland's foremost college in the area of food technology and food science based at Loughry. A 12 hectare site has been identified for an Agri-Food Park at Loughry College and high-tech incubation units have been developed

The provision of health and social services care within the district rests with the Northern Health and Social Services Board. The Homefirst Community Health and Social Services Trust is responsible for the provision of most community health and social care services.

Tourism in Cookstown District is based predominantly on the area's natural and built heritage with Lough Neagh and the Sperrins providing the major focal points for a range of recreational and tourism activities.

Political Composition

Cookstown District Council has 16 members distributed throughout 3 District Electoral Areas (DEA), comprising: Ballinderry 6; Cookstown Central 5; Drum Manor 5

The political composition of Cookstown District Council elected members as elected in June 2001 is: Ulster Unionist Party (UUP) 3; Social Democratic and Labour Party (SDLP) 4; Democratic Unionist Party (DUP) 2; Sinn Féin (SF) 6; Other 1. The largest party on the council is Sinn Féin with 6 seats. The council has a nationalist majority.

Elected Members and Council Committees

Chairman: John Fitzgerald McNamee (SF)

Vice-Chairman: Samuel Glasgow (UUP)

Councillor	Party	Policy Resources & Services	Development
Mary Baker	SDLP	•	C
Seamus Campbell	SF	•	•
Peter Cassidy	SDLP	VC	•
Sam Glasgow	UUP	•	•
Walter Greer	UUP	•	•
Dessie Grimes	SF	•	VC
Pearse McAleer	SF	•	•
Anne McCrea	DUP	•	•
Ian McCrea	DUP	•	•
James McGarvey	SDLP	•	•
Patsy McGlone	SDLP	•	•
Michael McIvor	SF	•	•
John McNamee	SF	•	•
Oliver Molloy	SF	C	•
Sam Parke	Ind	•	•
Trevor Wilson	UUP	•	•

• Member C Chair VC Vice-chair

Senior Officers

Chief Executive: Michael McGuckin
Director of Corporate Services: Ivor Paisley
Director of Operational Services: Derek Duncan
Chief Building Control Officer: Trevor McAdoo
Chief Environmental Health Officer: Mark Kelso
Development Manager: Adrian McCreesh
Arts and Cultural Development: Linda McGarvey
Community Relations Officer: Maureen Doyle
Corporate Marketing Officer: John Kerr
District Policing Partnership Manager: Phillip Moffet
Dog Warden/Enforcement Officer: Noel Newell
Economic Development Officer: Fiona McKeown
Health and Safety Officer: Ray Hall
IT Officer: Barry O'Hagan
Operations Officer: Mark McAdoo
Registrar of Births, Marriages and Deaths: Sandra Matchett
Sports Development Officer: Oliver McShane
Tourism Officer: Denise Campbell

Council Contact Details

Services	028 8676 2205
Building Control	
Environmental Health	
Finance / Personnel	
Operational Services	
Registration of Births, Deaths and Marriages	
Cookstown Leisure Centre	028 8676 3853
Dog Warden	028 8676 2205
The Burnavon (Arts Centre)	028 8676 9949
Tourist Information	028 8676 6727
Waste Disposal Site	028 8675 1153

CRAIGAVON BOROUGH COUNCIL

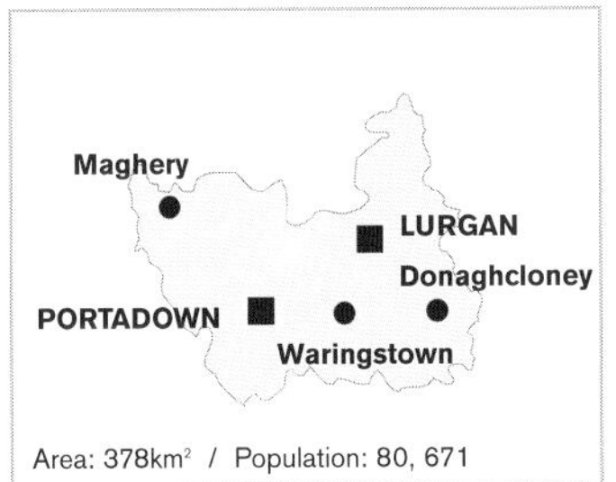

Area: 378km² / Population: 80, 671

Civic Centre
Lakeview Road
Craigavon , BT64 1AL
Tel: 028 3831 2400
Fax: 028 3831 2444
Email:
info@craigavon.gov.uk
Web:
www.craigavon.gov.uk

Craigavon is based largely on the long established towns of Lurgan and Portadown. The third major centre of population is the area of Brownlow, which is situated between the two towns. There is also rural hinterland featuring a number of picturesque villages and hamlets including Waringstown, Magheralin, Donacloney and Derrymacash.

The borough occupies an area of some 25900 hectares (100 sq. miles) and has an estimated population of just over 80,000. This represents a growth of 5.3 per cent since 1991.

Craigavon has a thriving manufacturing base of both indigenous and foreign owned companies. There are over 2000 VAT registered businesses within the borough with manufacturing accounting for over 11 per cent of this. Major employers include NACCO Materials Handling, Moy Park Foods, Smurfit Corrugated Cases and Ulster Carpet Mills.

Craigavon Borough has a wealth of leisure facilities many of which are linked to its location on the shores of Lough Neagh. It has its own urban lakes, Northern Ireland's only artificial ski-slope, leisure centres, an equestrian centre and four golf courses.

Within the last number of years, Craigavon has grown to become the third major growth area in Northern Ireland. With new housing growth of over 600 houses per annum, one of the lowest unemployment rates at 3.8 per cent and high quality recreational infrastructure, Craigavon has enjoyed heightened appeal as a place to live for those who want a modern 'lifestyle'.

Craigavon Borough Council spends around £15 million per year providing over 80 different services for the people who live in Craigavon. As well as providing key services the council also seeks to attract investment for further economic development within the borough. At present there is a focus on exploiting the full potential of tourism in the borough.

Political Composition

Craigavon Borough Council has 26 seats distributed throughout 4 District Electoral Areas (DEA), comprising: Central Electoral Area 7 Seats; Loughside Electoral Area 5 Seats; Lurgan Electoral Area 7 Seats; Portadown Electoral Area 7 Seats

The political composition of Craigavon Borough Council elected members as elected in June 2001 is: Ulster Unionist Party (UUP) 7; Social Democratic and Labour Party (SDLP) 7; Democratic Unionist Party (DUP) 6; Sinn Féin (SF) 4; Independent 2

Elected Members and Council Committees

Mayor: Ignatius Fox (SDLP) Deputy Mayor: David Simpson (DUP)

Councillor	Party	Development	Environmental Services	Leisure Services	Policy & Resources	Public Services Liaison
Sydney Anderson	Ind		C		•	•
Jonathan Bell	DUP	•	•	•	•	C
Sydney Cairns	UUP		•			•
Alan Carson	DUP		•	•		•
Kieran Corr	SDLP		•	•		•
Fred Crowe	UUP	VC			•	•
Meta Crozier	UUP	•		C	•	•
Ignatius Fox	SDLP	•	•	•	C	•
Samuel Gardiner	UUP		•	•		•
Arnold Hatch	UUP	•			•	VC
David Jones	Ind	•		•		•
Dolores Kelly	SDLP	C			•	•
Maurice Magill	SF	•	•		•	•
Patricia Mallon	SDLP	•		•	•	•
Mary McAlinden	SDLP	•	•	VC	•	•
Nuala McAlinden	SDLP					•
Tony Elliott	SDLP		•	•	•	•
Brian McKeown	SF			•		•
Stephen Moutray	DUP	•	VC		•	•
Francie Murray	SF			•		•
John O'Dowd	SF	•	•		•	•
George Savage	UUP	•	•			•
Dvaid Simpson	DUP	•	•	•	VC	•
Robert Smith	DUP	•		•		•
Woolsey Smith	DUP					•
Kenneth Twyble	UUP		•	•	•	•

• Member C Chair VC Vice-chair

Senior Officers

Chief Executive: Francis Rock
Director of Building Control Services: Robert Colvin
Director of Development: Vacant
Director of Environmental Services: Lorraine Crawford
Head of Environmental Services: Colin Kerr
Director of Finance and Corporate Services: David Pepper
Director of Leisure Services: Ross Miller
District Policing Partnership Manager: Alison Clenaghan
Economic Development Officer: Nicola Wilson
Equality Officer: Stephanie Harte
Human Resources Manager: Roger Wilson
Licensing Officer: Maureen Briggs
Marketing Officer: Hugh Carey
PR Officer: Pauline Nixon Black
Registrar of Births, Deaths, Marriages: Linda Steenson
Sports Development Officer: Wanda Rea
Tourism Officer: Brian Johnston
Waste Management Officer: Paul Topley

Council Contact Details

Administration & Finance	028 3831 2400
Building Control, Craigavon	028 3831 2500
Chief Executive	028 3831 2402
Development	028 3831 2581
Environmental Health and Dog Warden	028 3831 2521
Leisure Services	028 3831 2563
Refuse Collection and Street Cleaning	028 3833 9031
Community Halls / Town Halls	028 3831 2584
Playing Fields / All Parks	028 3831 2552

DERRY CITY COUNCIL

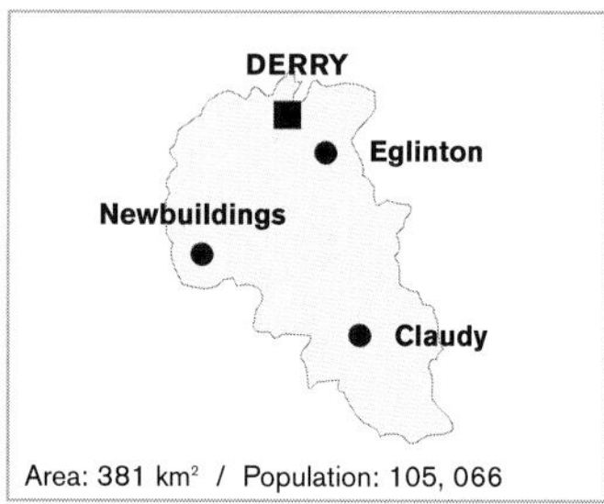

98 Strand Road
Derry, BT48 7NN
Tel: 028 7136 5151
Fax: 028 7126 5448
Email:
townclerk@derrycity.gov.uk
Web:
www.derrycity.gov.uk

Derry City Council is one of the largest District Councils serving a population of 105,066; 85,300 of whom live within the urban area.

Derry City Council's area is located between the Sperrin Mountains and the Donegal Hills with the city straddling the River Foyle. Derry is recognised as the regional city of the north west of Ireland, whose natural hinterland includes the neighbouring districts of Strabane, Limavady and parts of Donegal. The population of this wider region is approximately 300,000.

Derry City Council area was ranked second most deprived Local Authority Area in Northern Ireland. The area has been traditionally dependent upon its manufacturing base with significant emphasis on textiles and clothing. However, in more recent times investment from a number of multi-national firms has resulted in diversification into new areas such as chemicals and computer products. Major employers include: Seagate Technology, DuPont and Stream International. Recent growth in service sector employment reflects the city's increasing vibrancy and general appeal as a strategic employment location.

The recent development of Derry is particularly striking along the riverfront and around the City Centre where significant development has taken place including the addition of a 200m pontoon and numerous new buildings including offices, hotels and shopping centres. There is also considerable further regeneration planned for the City centre with the formation of the ILEX urban regeneration vehicle.
The City of Derry Airport is the main regional airport for the north west of the island, providing scheduled services to Glasgow, Manchester, London and Dublin. The Port of Londonderry is the UK's most westerly port and is of strategic importance to the north west of the island.

Political Composition

Derry City Council has 30 seats, distributed throughout 5 District Electoral Areas (DEA), comprising: Cityside 5 Seats; Northland 7 Seats; Rural 6 Seats; Shantallow 5 Seats; Waterside 7 Seats

The political composition of Derry City Council elected members as elected in June 2001 is: Ulster Unionist Party (UUP) 2; Social Democratic and Labour Party (SDLP) 13; Democratic Unionist Party (DUP) 4; Sinn Féin (SF) 10; Independent 1. The council has a clear nationalist majority with the SDLP being the largest party on the council.

Elected Members and Council Committees

Mayor: Cllr Shaun Gallagher (SDLP)
Deputy Mayor: Alderman Mildred Garfield (DUP)

Councillor	Party	Planning	Recreation & Leisure	Environmental Services	City Marketing	Policy Resources
Peter Anderson	SF	•			•	
Mary Bradley	SDLP	•	•	•		
Gregory Campbell	DUP	•			•	
Sean Carr	SDLP	•	•	•		
Jim Clifford	SDLP	•		•		•
Thomas Conway	SDLP	•	C		•	•
Annie Courtney	Ind	•		•		
Cathal Crumley	SF	C	•		•	•
Gerard Diver	SDLP	•			•	•
Lynn Fleming	SF	•	•			
Paul Fleming	SF	•	•	C		
Shaun Gallagher	SDLP	•	•	•	•	•
Mildred Garfield	DUP	•	•	•	•	•
Ernest Hamilton	UUP	•	•	•		•
Mary Hamilton	UUP	•		•		•
Tony Hassan	SF	•		•		
William Hay	DUP	•	•			
John Kerr	SDLP	•			•	C
Gerry MacLochlainn	SF	•		•	•	•
Kathleen McCloskey	SDLP	•	•	•		
Marie McDaid	SDLP	•	•	•		
Jim McKeever	SDLP	•			•	
Maeve McLaughlin	SF	•	•			•
Joe Miller	DUP	•			•	•
William O'Connell	SDLP	•	•			
Barney O'Hagan	SF	•	•		C	•
Gearoid O'hEara	SF	•			•	
William Page	SF	•		•		
Helen Quigley	SDLP	•		•	•	
Pat Ramsey	SDLP	•			•	

• Member C Chair Committees do not have Vice-chairs

Senior Officers

Town Clerk and Chief Executive: Anthony McGurk
City Treasurer: Joseph Campbell
Chief Environmental Health Officer: John Meehan
Director of City Marketing: Gerard Henry
City Secretary and Solicitor: Damian McMahon
Chief Building Control Officer: Robert White
Director of Recreation and Leisure:James Sanderson
Corporate Marketing Officer: Claire Lundy
Economic Development Officer: Mark Lusby

Council Contact Details

Airport (City of Derry)	028 7181 0784
Building Control	028 7137 6521
Client Services Department	028 7137 6536
Council Offices	028 7136 5151
Economic Development	028 7137 6532
Environmental Health	028 7136 5151
Guildhall	028 7137 7335
Marketing/Communications/PR	028 7137 6504
Millennium Forum	028 7126 4426
Procurement	028 7136 5151
Refuse Collection	028 7137 4107
Registration of Births, Deaths & Marriages	028 7126 8439
Tourist Information	028 7126 7284
Town Clerk & Chief Executive's Department	028 7137 6507

DOWN DISTRICT COUNCIL

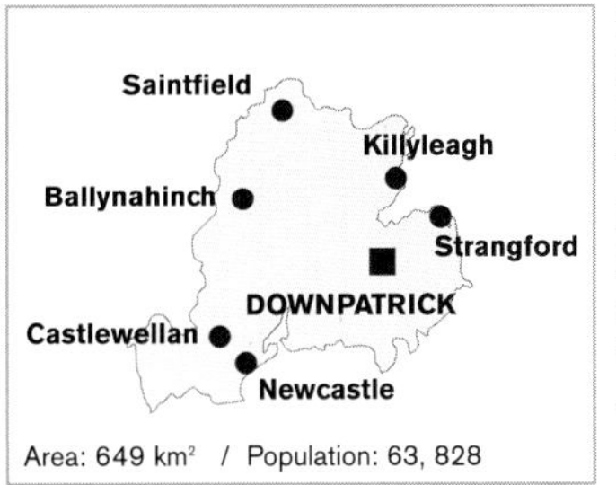

24 Strangford Road
Downpatrick
BT30 6SR
Tel: 028 4461 0800
Fax: 028 4461 0801
Email:
council@downdc.gov.uk
Web:
www.downdc.gov.uk

Down district covers a large geographical area to the south east of the Province, including the Mourne Mountains, Northern Ireland's highest mountain range. The district's main population centres include the historic town of Downpatrick and the popular seaside resort of Newcastle. Downpatrick is well connected through public transport to the district's other main centres of population; Newcastle, Castlewellan, Ballynahinch, Saintfield, Crossgar and Killyleagh, and has traditionally been the administrative and service centre for the South Down region.

Downpatrick as its name suggests has long been associated with Ireland's patron saint, Saint Patrick, and there is a strong cultural link within the district.

Agriculture and tourism contribute significantly to the local economy, with tourism accounting for over 2700 jobs within the district and a £20 million slice of the economic base. Employment in the district is largely provided through the public sector in organisations including: Down Lisburn Trust, South Eastern Education and Library Board and Down District Council. Other notable employers include Walter Watson Ltd (steel), Tesco and Safeway.

Down District has a remarkably high level of artists/crafts producers residing in the district accounting for approximately 75 per cent of total Northern Ireland numbers and there are plans for the development of Down as a centre for the arts as well as developing its appeal generally as a centre of cultural activity.

Political Composition

Down District Council has 23 seats distributed throughout 4 District Electoral Areas (DEA), comprising: Ballynahinch 5 Seats; Downpatrick 7 Seats; Newcastle 6 Seats; Rowallane 5 Seats

The political composition of Down District Council elected members as elected in June 2001 is: Ulster Unionist Party (UUP) 6; Social Democratic and Labour Party (SDLP) 10; Democratic Unionist Party (DUP) 2; Sinn Féin (SF) 4; Other 1

The largest party on the council is the SDLP with 10 seats. The council has a nationalist majority.

The main council meeting is convened on the 3rd Monday of each month at 7.00pm in Council offices.

Elected Members and Council Committees

Chairman: Peter Craig (SDLP) Vice-Chairman: Robert Burgess (UUP)

Councillor	Party	Health	Policy & Resources	Corporate Services	Recreation & Technical Services	Culture & Economic Development
Harvey Bicker	UUP	•				
Raymond Blaney	Ind	•			•	
Francis Braniff	SF	•			•	
Robert Burgess	UUP	•		•		•
Willie Clarke	SF	•			•	VC
Albert Colmer	UUP	VC		•	•	
Peter Craig	SDLP	•			•	
Dermot Curran	SDLP	•		•		•
William Dick	DUP	•	•	•		
John Doris	SDLP	•	•			•
Gerry Douglas	UUP	•	VC			
Peter Fitzpatrick	SDLP	•	•	•		
Anne McAleenan	SDLP	•	•	VC		
Eamonn McConvey	SF	•	•	C		
Francis McDowell	SF	•	•			
John McIlheron	UUP	•	•			•
Carmel O'Boyle	SDLP	•			VC	
Eamonn O'Neill	SDLP	•	C			
Edward Rea	UUP	•			C	•
Margaret Ritchie	SDLP	C			•	•
Patrick Toman	SDLP	•		•	•	C
Anne Trainor	SDLP	•		•		
Jim Wells	DUP	•				•

• Member C Chair VC Vice-chair

Senior Officers

Clerk and Chief Executive: John McGrillen
Director of Corporate Services: Norman Stewart
Director of Cultural and Economic Development: Sharon O'Connor
Director of Recreation and Technical Services: Frank Cunningham
Group Chief Building Control Officer: John Dumigan
Arts Officer: Cathy McKimm
Building Services Manager: Winston Reid
Business Development Officer: Vacant
Business Improvement Officer: Stephen Wright
Community Relations Officer: Damian Brannigan
Countryside Development Officer: Heather Wilson
District Policing Partnership Manager: Liam McLernon
Principal Environmental Health Officer: Tony McCrory
Equality Officer: Gerry McBride
Marketing Manager: Veronica Keegan
Registrar of Births, Deaths and Marriages: Helen Matthews
Sports Development Officer: Pat Power
Towns Development Manager: Eric Tomasini
Tourism Officer: Angela Gilchrist
Waste Management Officer: Laurence McQuoid

Council Contact Details

Recruitment	028 4461 0805
Licensing	028 4461 0808
Food Hygiene, Office Safety	028 4461 0824
District Building Control Offices & Buildings, Entertainment Licences	028 4461 0829
Births, Deaths & Marriages	028 4461 0825
Economic Development	028 4461 0850
Tourism Development	028 4461 0856

DUNGANNON & SOUTH TYRONE BOROUGH COUNCIL

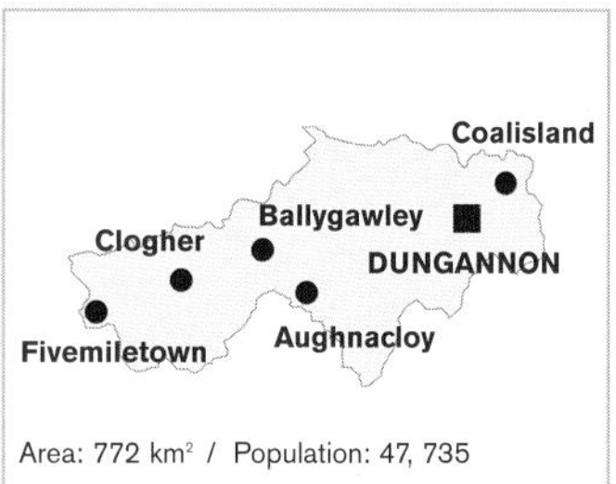

Circular Road
Dungannon
BT71 6DT
Tel: 028 8772 0300
Fax: 028 8772 0368
Web:
www.dungannon.gov.uk

The Borough of Dungannon and South Tyrone covers an area stretching from the shores of Lough Neagh in the east, through the Clogher Valley to Fivemiletown at the Fermanagh border. The Borough touches the border with County Monaghan and reaches up to the foothills of the Sperrins. Some 48,000 inhabitants live in the Borough area, an essentially rural area, but with a strong industrial base. Its central position means that it is an ideal location for industries such as, Tyrone Crystal, Powerscreen, Tyrone Brick and Moy Park.

Development proposals for the Borough have focused on Dungannon, the principal administrative and commercial centre and Coalisland.

Dungannon and South Tyrone Borough has a relatively large manufacturing base set against an important but declining agricultural sector and an expanding services sector. Approximately 3,800 people are employed within the agricultural sector. Over half of farms are involved in cattle and sheep production, while dairy farming also makes a significant contribution to the local economy.

Major industries were traditionally based on the Borough's natural resources and significant employment is still provided in industries related to engineering, mineral extraction and aggregates. The greatest potential for employment growth however is in the services sector.

Tourism in Dungannon and South Tyrone is based around the area's natural and built heritage with Lough Neagh and the Clogher Valley providing the major focal points for a range of recreational and tourism activities.

Political Composition

Dungannon and South Tyrone Borough Council has 22 seats distributed throughout 4 District Electoral Areas (DEA), comprising: Dungannon Town 6 Seats; Clogher Valley 5 Seats; Torrent 6 Seats; Blackwater 5 Seats

The political composition of Dungannon and South Tyrone Borough Council elected members as elected in June 2001 is: Ulster Unionist Party (UUP) 6; Social Democratic and Labour Party (SDLP) 4; Democratic Unionist Party (DUP) 3; Sinn Féin (SF) 8; Other 1

The largest party on the council is Sinn Féin with 8 seats. The council has a nationalist majority.

Elected Members and Council Committees

Mayor: Sean McGuigan (SF) Deputy Mayor: Francie Molloy (SF)

Councillor	Party	Development	Public Services	Corporate Services	Policy & Performance
Norman Badger	UUP	•	VC	•	
Roger Burton	DUP	•	•	•	•
Jim Canning	Ind	•	•	•	•
Jim Cavanagh	SDLP	•	•	•	•
Walter Cuddy	UUP	•	•	VC	
Vincent Currie	SDLP	•	•	•	
Patsy Daly	SDLP	•	C	•	•
Desmond Donnelly	SF	•	•	•	
Seamus Flanagan	SF	•	•	•	
Phelim Gildernew	SF	•	•	•	
Michael Gillespie	SF	VC	•	•	
Jim Hamilton	UUP	•	•	•	•
Derek Irwin	UUP	•	•	•	•
Anthony McGonnell	SDLP	•	•	C	
Sean McGuigan	SF	•	•	•	•
Johnston McIlwrath	DUP	•	•	•	
Larry McLarnon	SF	•	•	•	C
Ken Maginnis	UUP	•	•	•	
Francie Molloy	SF	•	•	•	•
Barry Monteith	SF	C	•	•	
Maurice Morrow	DUP	•	•	•	VC
Robert Mulligan	UUP	•	•	•	

• Member C Chair VC Vice-chair

Senior Officers

Chief Executive: William Beattie
Head of Finance: Paula Kerr
Director of Building Control: Jim McClelland
Director of Development: Iain Frazer
Director of Environmental Health: Alan Burke
Director of Technical Services: Robert McMinn
Arts Officer: Aine Dolan
Borough Inspector: Rodney Gillis
Community Relations Officer: Phillip Clarke
Council Business Manager: Gladys Smith
District Policing Partnership Manager: George Ruddell
Economic Development Officer: Vinny Beggs
Marketing and Events Officer: Emma Cox
Public Relations Officer: Emma Heatherington
Recreation Manager: Ken Barrett
Registrar of Births, Deaths and Marriages: Anne McCourt
Training Development Officer: Leigh Gilmore
Tourism Officers: Libby Mc Clean, Genevieve Bell
Recycling & Education Officer: Nicky Doherty

Council Contact Details

Council Offices	028 8772 0300
Chief Executive's Department	028 8772 0303
Finance and Administration	028 8772 0324
Registrar Births, Deaths and Marriages	028 8772 0329
Building Control	028 8772 0357
Environmental Health	028 8772 0367
Technical Services	028 8772 0390
Refuse Collection	028 8772 0390
Grounds Maintenance	028 8772 0390
Community Relations	028 8772 8613
Economic Development	028 8772 8601

FERMANAGH DISTRICT COUNCIL

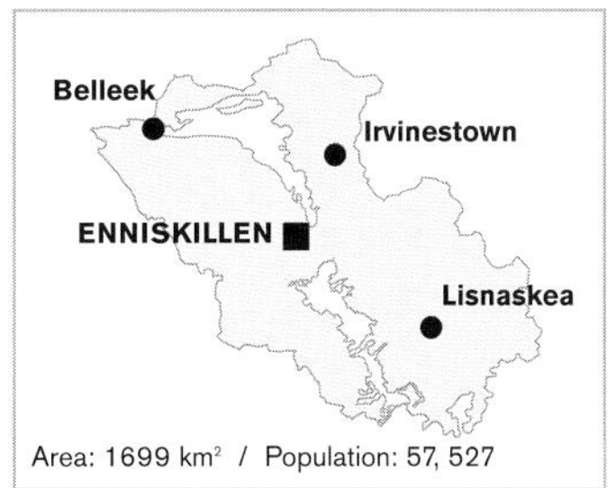

Town Hall
Enniskillen
BT74 7BA
Tel: 028 6632 5050
Fax: 028 6632 2024
Email:
fdc@fermanagh.gov.uk
Web:
www.fermanagh.gov.uk

Located in the south west of Northern Ireland, Fermanagh District Council is unique as a local authority in Northern Ireland as its boundaries are also those of the County of Fermanagh. County Fermanagh makes up an eighth of the province's land mass and represents the largest local government district in geographical terms. Fermanagh is a county renowned for its lakeland scenery and tourism appeal. Often referred to as the lakeland county, tourism spending of almost £20 million per annum is a significant contributor to the local economy.

Enniskillen is the principal town in Fermanagh with a well-developed and thriving town centre, which contains the greatest concentration of shopping and business activity in the district. Other significant settlements include Irvinestown, Lisnaskea and Kesh.

Like many predominantly rural regions Fermanagh faces a number of challenges associated with peripherality. The County has a population density of 31 persons per square km. This low population density is underscored by the natural geography of the area, bisected by Upper and Lower Lough Erne. Fermanagh has higher levels of housing unfitness, long-term unemployment and rural deprivation, than the Northern Ireland average.

Large numbers of people are still employed within agriculture and manufacturing. However, the construction and retail sectors have also become major employers in the county. Large employers include the Quinn Group, Fisher Engineering, Balcas and BT London Customer Services. One of the best known factories in the district is Belleek Pottery.

Most employment in Fermanagh is in the services sector. Such employment is concentrated in the public sector and includes the offices and depots of various government departments, such as the social security agency, the Housing Executive, and the Western Health and Social Services Board.

Political Composition

Fermanagh District Council has 23 seats distributed throughout 4 District Electoral Areas (DEA), comprising: Erne North 5 Seats; Erne East 6 Seats; Erne West 5 Seats; Enniskillen 7 Seats. The political composition of Fermanagh District Council elected members as elected in June 2001 is: Ulster Unionist Party (UUP) 7; Social Democratic and Labour Party (SDLP) 4; Democratic Unionist Party (DUP) 2; Sinn Féin (SF) 9; Other 1

The largest party on the council is Sinn Féin with 9 seats. The council has a nationalist majority.

Elected Members and Council Committees

Chairman: Harold Andrews (UUP) Vice-Chairman: Pat Cox (SF)

Councillor	Party	Environmental Services	Planning	Policy & Resources	Development	Environmental Health
Harold Andrews	UUP	•	•	•	•	•
Frank Britton	SDLP	•	•		•	
Joe Cassidy	SF		•	•	C	•
Pat Cox	SF	•	•	•	•	•
Joe Dodds	DUP		•		•	C
Tom Elliott	UUP	•	•	•	•	
Wilson Elliott	UUP	•	•		•	•
Raymond Ferguson	UUP		•	•	•	
Gerry Gallagher	SDLP		C	•	•	•
Patrick Gilgunn	SF		•		•	
Stephen Huggett	SF	•	•	•	•	
Robert Irvine	UUP		•		•	•
Bert Johnston	DUP	•	•	•	•	
Davy Kettyles	Ind		•		•	•
Bertie Kerr	UUP	•	•	•	•	
Ruth Lynch	SF	•	•		•	
Robin Martin	SF	•	•	•	•	•
Brian McCaffrey	SF		•	•	•	•
Gerry McHugh	SF		•	C	•	
Fergus McQuillan	SDLP	•	•		•	
Cecil Noble	UUP	C	•		•	•
John O'Kane	SDLP		•	•	•	•
Thomas O'Reilly	SF	•	•		•	•

• Member C Chair Committees do not have Vice-chairs

Senior Officers

Chief Executive: Rodney Connor
Director of Building Control: Desmond Reid
Director of Development: Peter Thompson
Director of Environmental Health: Robert Forde
Director of Environmental Services: Robert Gibson
Director of Finance and IT: Brendan Hegarty
Director of Technical Services: Gerry Knox
Head of Administration: David Phair
Arts and Events Officer: Geraldine O'Reilly
Community Development Manager: Ruth Moore
Community Relations Officer: Helen Sheils
District Policing Partnership Manager: David Eames
Economic Development Officer: Anne Quinn
Environmental Services Officer: Brian Hegarty
Policy Development Officer: Margaret McMahon
Registrar of Births, Deaths and Marriages: Lillian Thornton
Sports Development and Recreation Officer: Keith Collen
Tourism Officer: Eddie McGovern

Council Contact Details

Chief Executive	028 6632 5050
Administration	028 6632 5050
Finance	028 6632 5050
Personnel	028 6632 5050
Building Control	028 6632 5050
Community Services	028 6632 5050
Environmental Health	028 6632 5050
Marble Arch Caves	028 6634 8855
Museum – Enniskillen Castle	028 6632 5000
Registrar Births, Deaths, Marriages	028 6632 5050
Technical Services	028 6632 3533

LARNE BOROUGH COUNCIL

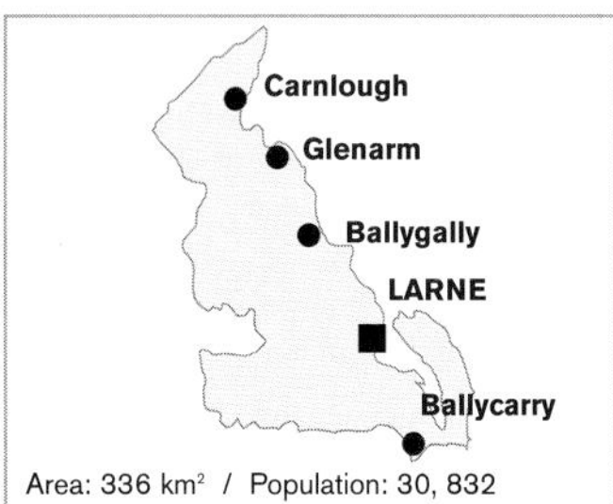

Area: 336 km² / Population: 30, 832

Smiley Buildings
Victoria Road
Larne
BT40 1RU
Tel: 028 2827 2313
Fax: 028 2826 0660
Email:
admin@larne.gov.uk
Web: www.larne.gov.uk

Larne Borough lies on the east coast of Northern Ireland between the Glens of Antrim and the Antrim plateau. Larne is the starting point of the world-famous Antrim Coast Road with its 36 miles of spectacular limestone coastline. Two-thirds of the borough is designated an Area of Outstanding Natural Beauty (AONB), one of the highest percentages of such designation in any of the 26 councils in Northern Ireland. The coastline also includes Garron Tower estate, a former residence of Sir Winston Churchill, which sits on a prominent site overlooking the Irish Sea.

The borough covers an area of approximately 131 sq miles, with a population of over 30,000. This figure includes the nearly 20,000 strong population of Larne town and an employment base of almost 14,000 people. After Larne Town, the next biggest population centres are Ballycarry, Glenarm and Carnlough.

Larne's unemployment rate of 3 per cent (at 30 June 2003) is slightly below the Northern Ireland average. The town is the premier ferry port in Northern Ireland and main gateway to Scotland. Larne has a solid manufacturing and sub-supply base and is host to a number of overseas-owned companies of US and Japanese origin; consequently the town has a relatively lower dependence on public sector employment.

Major employers include FG Wilson (part of the Caterpillar Group), Premier Power and IVEX Pharmaceuticals. In addition, it is estimated that the presence of the port has created over 3,000 indirect jobs.

Political Composition

Larne Borough Council has 15 seats and 3 District Electoral Areas, comprising: Coast Road 5 Seats, Larne Lough 5 Seats, Larne Town 5 Seats.

The political composition of Larne Borough Council elected members as elected in June 2001 is:

Ulster Unionist Party (UUP) 4; Social Democratic and Labour Party (SDLP) 2; Democratic Unionist Party (DUP) 4; Alliance (All) 2; Other 3.

The main council meeting is convened on the 1st Monday of each month at 7.00pm in Council offices and is open to the public.

Elected Members and Council Committees

Mayor: Bobby McKee (DUP) Deputy Mayor: Robert Craig (Ind)

Councillor	Party	Development & Consultative	Finance & General Purposes	Tourism Leisure & Commerical Services	Works & Enironmental Health
Roy Beggs	UUP	•	•	•	•
Roy Craig	Ind	•	•	•	•
Joan Drummond	UUP	VC	•	•	•
Brian Dunn	UUP	•	•	•	•
David Fleck	UUP	•	C	•	•
Winston Fulton	DUP	C	•	•	•
Robert Lyndsay Mason	Ind	•	•	•	•
Bobby McKee	DUP	•	•	•	•
Jack McKee	Ind	•	•	•	•
Gregg McKeen	DUP	•	•	•	•
John Mathews	All	•	•	C	•
Gerardine Mulvenna	All	•	•	•	VC
Daniel O'Connor	SDLP	•	•	•	C
Rachel Rea	DUP	•	•	VC	•
Martin Wilson	SDLP	•	VC	•	•

• Member C Chair VC Vice-chair

Senior Officers

Chief Executive: Colm McGarry
Director of Building Services: Geraldine McGahey
Director of Corporate Services: Trevor Clarke
Director of Environmental Services: Morris Crum
Head of Building Control: Mark Hamill
Head of Environmental Health Unit: Bob Cameron
Community Relations Officer: Catherine Black
Countryside Officer: Linda Foy
DPP Manager: Stephen Burns
Economic Development: Ken Nelson
Financial Controller: Helen Gault
IT Officer: Trevor Clarke
Press Officer: Lorraine Hunter
Technical Services: George Drury

Council Contact Details

Building Control Service	028 2827 2313
Council Depot	028 2826 2307
Larne Leisure Centre	028 2826 0478
Tourist Information Centre	028 2826 0088
Carnfunnock Country Park	028 2827 0541
Browns Bay Caravan Site	028 9338 2497
Larne Museum	028 2827 0824
Redlands Recycling Centre	028 2826 7880

LIMAVADY BOROUGH COUNCIL

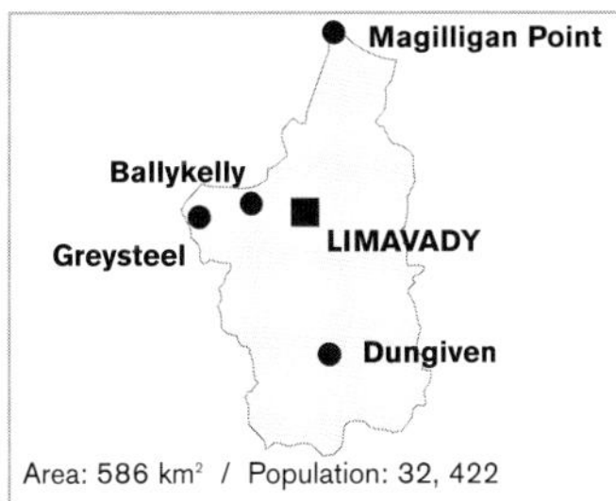

7 Connell Street
Limavady, BT49 0HA
Tel: 028 7772 2226
Fax: 028 7776 5241
Email:
info@limavady.gov.uk
Web:
www.limavady.gov.uk

Limavady Borough Council is one of Northern Ireland's smallest local authorities, located in the picturesque north of County Derry. Limavady town by is far the largest population centre, followed by Ballykelly and Dungiven. The area is well served by an extensive road network and is easily accessible from City of Derry Airport and Lisahally Deep Water port, which are within ten miles. A recent addition to the borough's infrastructure has been the introduction of a car ferry service between Magilligan Point and Greencastle in co. Donegal. The borough stretches from the Sperrin Mountains in the south to Benone beach, a seven-mile strand of golden sand on the Atlantic coast, which was the first beach in Northern Ireland to be awarded a Blue Flag.

Limavady borough's main industries are agriculture, textiles and tourism. The main centre for industry in the borough is the Aghanloo Industrial estate in Limavady town. Manufacturing accounts for nearly a quarter of all employment in the area and has been concentrated traditionally in the textiles sector. Tourism is based around the rural scenery of the Limavady area and has been boosted by continuous investment in quality hotel accommodation and leisure infrastructure.

The borough has a rich cultural and environmental heritage; the world famous 'Londonderry Air' better known as the song "Danny Boy" is historically associated with the area. The rich diverse nature of the local landscape is reflected in the number of protective designations that exist throughout the borough. These designations include five National Nature Reserves, seven Areas of Special Scientific Interest and two Areas of Outstanding Natural Beauty.

Political Composition

Limavady Borough Council has 15 seats distributed throughout District Electoral Areas (DEA), comprising: Bellarena 5 Seats; Benbradagh 5 Seats; Limavady Town 5 Seats. The political composition of Limavady Borough Council elected members as elected in June 2001 is: Ulster Unionist Party (UUP) 3; Social Democratic and Labour Party (SDLP) 4; Democratic Unionist Party (DUP) 2; Sinn Féin (SF) 4; Other 2. The SDLP and Sinn Féin are tied as largest party with 4 seats each. There is a nationalist majority on the council.

The posts of Mayor and Deputy Mayor are generally rotated annually among the political representatives of the two main traditions within the community as part of the partnership process operated by the Council. Similarly, joint chairpersons drawn from each tradition chair each committee.

Elected Members and Council Committees

Mayor: Anne Brolly (SF), Deputy Mayor: Jack Rankin (UUP)

Councillor	Party	Economic Development	Finance & General Purposes	Leisure Services	Planning & Development Services
Anne Brolly	SF	•	•	•	•
Francis Brolly	SF	•	•	CC	•
Brian Brown	Ind	•	•	•	•
Michael Carten	SDLP	•	•	•	•
Michael Coyle	SDLP	•	•	•	CC
Leslie Cubitt	DUP	•	•	•	•
Jack Dolan	UUP	•	CC	•	•
Marion Donaghy	SF	CC	•	•	•
Boyd Douglas	UUAP	•	•	•	CC
Dessie Lowry	SDLP	•	CC	•	•
Martin McGuigan	SF	•	•	•	•
Gerard Mullan	SDLP	•	•	•	•
Jack Rankin	UUP	•	•	CC	•
George Robinson	DUP	CC	•	•	•
Edwin Stevenson	UUP	•	•	•	•

• Member C Co-chair

Senior Officers

Chief Executive: John Stevenson
Chief Environmental Health Officer: Noel Crawford
Chief Finance and Administrative Officer: Eamon McCotter
Chief Recreation/Tourism Officer: Sam McGregor
Chief Technical Services Officer: Victor Wallace
District Chief Building Control Officer: Jim Mullan
Community Relations Officer: Steven Bell
Corporate Policy Officer: Chris Kane
Countryside and Access Officer: Richard Gillen
District Policing Partnership Manager: Linda McKee
Dog Warden/Enforcement Officer: Tom Keogh
Economic Development Officer: Dermot McNally
Equality Officer: Debbie Rogers
Finance Officer: Gerry McCourt
Human Resources Officer: Debbie Rogers
IT Officer: Darren Maynes
Licensing Officer: Jim Mullan
Registrar of Births, Deaths and Marriages: Monica Anderson
Senior Technical and Waste Management Officer: Jonathan Gray
Sports Development Officer: Ollie Mullan
Tourism Development Officer: Clare Quinn

Council Contact Details

Town Clerk & Chief Executive	028 7776 0300
General Enquiries	028 7772 2226
Building Control	028 7776 0301
District Partnership/Leader II	028 7776 0306
Economic Development	028 7776 0311
Environmental Health	028 7776 0302
Finance and Administration	028 7772 2226
Personnel	028 7776 0315
Registration of Births, Deaths & Marriages	028 7772 2226
River Inspector's Office	028 7776 0312
Technical Services Department	028 7776 0305
All Enquiries	028 7776 0304
Benone Tourist Complex	028 7775 0555
Roe Valley Leisure Centre	028 7776 4009
Tourist Information Centre	028 7776 0307

LISBURN CITY COUNCIL

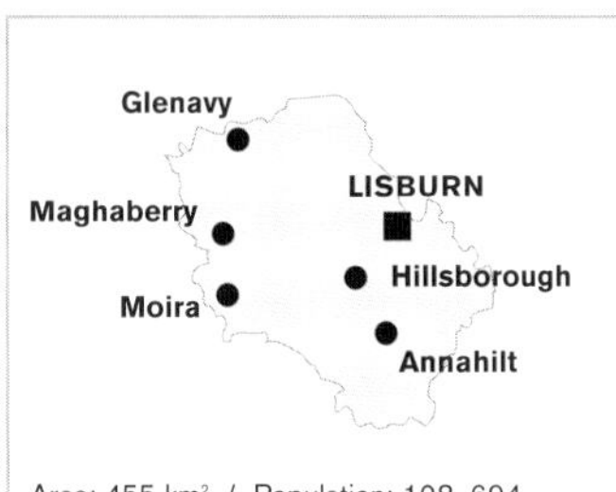

Area: 455 km² / Population: 108, 694

Lagan Valley Island
The Island
Lisburn
BT27 4RL
Tel: 028 9250 9250
Fax: 028 9250 9288
Web:
www.lisburn.gov.uk

Lisburn was awarded City status in the Queen's Golden Jubilee City Status competition in 2002. Lisburn Borough Council subsequently became Lisburn City Council in August 2002.

The City of Lisburn area has a population of 108,694. Lisburn City Council actively promotes the area as an increasingly desirable place to live in, work in, and visit. Lisburn City Council covers 455 square kilometres of southwest Antrim and northwest Down stretching from Glenavy and Dundrod in the north to Dromore and Hillsborough in the south, and from Drumbo in the east to Moira in the west. The City of Lisburn has a significant and growing industrial and commercial base. Major employers include Montupet UK Ltd, Bombardier Aerospace, J&J Haslett, Coca Cola Bottlers and Coates Barbour.

The City of Lisburn is the main residential, industrial and commercial centre and is an important focus for employment and housing. Lisburn has developed as an important retail centre and development of the Bow Street Mall and the Bow Street pedestrianised precinct have consolidated this position. Further recent development at the Sprucefield has will enhanced the range of shopping opportunities in the area.

The year 2002 also saw Lisburn City Council win the Building of the Year Award from the Royal Institute of Chartered Surveyors for Lagan Valley Island, its £25 million flagship headquarters facility, which offers extensive business and conferencing facilities as well as functioning as the administrative centre for the City Council. The River Lagan is a major amenity in the area and tourism has been developed reflecting the linen industry heritage of the Lagan Valley.

The Council's Historic Quarter Initiative is one of the largest heritage projects to be undertaken in Northern Ireland and is a partnership initiative between Lisburn City Council and a number of stakeholders from the private, public and community sectors. One of the biggest projects to have been undertaken on the area is the restoration of Castle Gardens.

Political Composition

Lisburn City Council has 30 seats distributed throughout 5 District Electoral Areas: Killultagh 5 Seats; Dunmurry Cross 7 Seats; Lisburn Town North 7 Seats; Lisburn Town South 6 Seats; Downshire 5 Seats.

The political composition of Lisburn City Council is: Ulster Unionist Party (UUP) 12; Social Democratic and Labour Party (SDLP) 3; Democratic Unionist Party (DUP) 6; Sinn Féin (SF) 4; Other 5

Elected Members and Council Committees

Mayor: William Bell (UUP) Deputy Mayor: Cecil Calvert (DUP

Councillor	Party	Planning	Leisure Services	Economic Development	Environmental Services	Corporate Services
David Archer	UUP	•	•			
T David Archer	UUP	•			•	
James Baird	UUP	•			VC	
William Bell	UUP	•	•		•	•
Paul Butler	SF	•				•
Cecil Calvert	DUP	•	•		•	•
Elizabeth Campbell	All	•	•			
Seamus Close	All	•	•			
David Craig	DUP	•	•			•
Ronnie Crawford	Ind	•		•		•
Ivan Davis	UUP	•	C			
Jim Dillon	UUP	•		VC		C
William Falloon	UUP	VC		•	•	•
Michael Ferguson	SF	•		•	•	
William Gardiner-Watson	UUP	•	•	C		
Samuel Johnston	UUP	•			•	
William Lewis	UUP	•	•	•		
Patricia Lewsley	SDLP	•			•	
Joe Lockhart	UUP	•			•	
Trevor Lunn	All	•		•		•
Billy McDonnell	SDLP	•	•			
Gary McMichael	Ind	•	VC			
Lorraine Martin	UUP	•				
Peter O'Hagan	SDLP	•		•		•
Edwin Poots	DUP	C		•		•
Paul Porter	DUP	•			•	
Sue Ramsey	SF	•	•			
James Tinsley	DUP	•		•	C	
William Ward	UUP	•				VC
Veronica Willis	SF	•				

• Member C Chair VC Vice-chair

Senior Officers

Chief Executive: Norman Davidson
Director of Corporate Services: David Briggs
Director of Environmental Services: Colin McClintock
Director of Leisure Services: Jim Rose
Chief Building Control Officer: Ian Wilson
Community Relations Officer: David Mitchell
District Policing Partnership Manager: Angela McCann
Economic Development Officer: Paul McCormick
Environmental Health Manager: Maurice Woods
Finance Manager: John Gillanders
Lagan Valley Island Manager: Graham Erskine
Purchasing Officer: Margaret McDonald
Tourism Officer: Andrew Kennedy

Council Contact Details

Chief Executive's Department	028 9250 9206
Community Relations	028 9250 9492
Corporate Services Department	028 9250 9270
Financial Services	028 9250 9231
Marketing & Communications	028 9250 9221
Registration Births, Deaths, Marriages	028 9250 9263
Environmental Services	028 9250 9380
Building Control	028 9250 9372
Economic Development	028 9250 9487
Lagan Valley Island	028 9250 9292

MAGHERAFELT DISTRICT COUNCIL

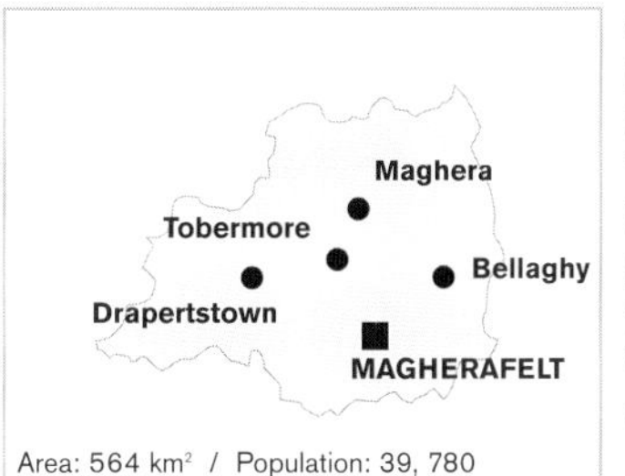

50 Ballyronan Road
Magherafelt
BT45 6EN
Tel: 028 7939 7979
Fax: 028 7939 7980
Email:
info@magherafelt.gov.uk
Web:
www.magherafelt.gov.uk

Magherafelt is one of Northern Ireland's smaller local authorities by population. Magherafelt town is the principal settlement followed by Maghera, and the villages of Bellaghy, Castledawson, Draperstown and Tobermore. The majority of people in the district live outside the towns, in smaller settlements and the open countryside.

The town of Magherafelt is located in the centre of Northern Ireland adjacent to the main Belfast to Derry road, and the north-south route from Coleraine to Cookstown, Dungannon and beyond. The town has an important role as a centre of employment and as a local service hub providing retail, health, educational and community facilities for its own population and an extensive rural hinterland.

Maghera is also a service and employment centre mainly for the northern sector of the District and has developed as an important educational centre in the area.

Agriculture is of vital importance to the local economy and is the major source of income in the district; there is also a significant manufacturing base in engineering and textiles and a thriving construction sector.

In terms of economic development the council is focusing on developing the local tourism infrastructure. Tourism in Magherafelt District is predominantly based on the natural and built heritage, with the Sperrins providing a focus for a range of tourism and recreational activities.

Political Composition

Magherafelt District Council has 16 seats distributed throughout 3 District Electoral Areas (DEA), comprising: Magherafelt Town 6 Seats; Moyola 5 Seats; Sperrin 5 Seats.

The political composition of Magherafelt District Council as elected in June 2001 is:

Ulster Unionist Party (UUP) 2; Social Democratic and Labour Party (SDLP) 3; Democratic Unionist Party (DUP) 3; Sinn Féin (SF) 7; Other 1

The largest party on the council is Sinn Féin with 7 seats. The council has an overall nationalist majority.

Elected Members and Council Committees

Chairman: Kathleen Lagan (SDLP)
Vice-Chairman: Robert Montgomery (Ind)

Councillor	Party	Recreation & Tourism	General Purposes & Finance
Thomas Catherwood	DUP		•
Patrick Groogan	SF		•
Oliver Hughes	SF		•
John Junkin	UUP		•
John Kelly	SF		
Sean Kerr	SF		•
Kathleen Lagan	SDLP		•
Joseph McBride	SDLP	•	
Paul McLean	DUP	•	
Rev William McCrea	DUP		
Patrick McErlean	SDLP		•
Robert Montgomery	Ind	•	
Hugh Mullan	SF	•	
Seamus O'Brien	SF	•	
Seamus O'Neill	SF	•	
George Shiels	UUP	•	

• **Member**

Senior Officers

Chief Executive: John McLoughlin
Director of Finance and Administration: JJ Tohill
Director of Operational Services: Jackie Johnston
Chief Environmental Health Officer: Clifford Burrows
District Chief Building Control Officer: Ian Glendinning
Head of Leisure Services: Lawrence Hastings
Arts and Events Officer: Michael Browne
Community Relations Officer: Sean Henry
Corporate Marketing Officer: Florence Wilson
Economic Development Officer: Michael Brown
Finance Officer: Albert Hogg
Licensing Officer: Anne Boyle
Personnel Officer: Florence Wilson
Registrar of Births, Deaths and Marriages: Margaret Barnes
Tourism Officer: Michael Brown
Sports Development Officer: Nick Hastings
Waste Management Officer: Jackie Johnston

Council Contact Details

Council Offices	028 7939 7979
Greenvale Leisure Centre	028 7963 2796
Magherafelt Area Partnership Ltd	028 7939 7979
Maghera Leisure Centre	028 7954 7400
Meadowbank Centre	028 7963 1680
Sperrins Tourism Ltd	028 8674 7700
Tobermore Driving Range	028 7964 5406
Waste Disposal Site	028 7938 6874
Director of Environment Health (Emergencies)	028 7963 2845

MOYLE DISTRICT COUNCIL

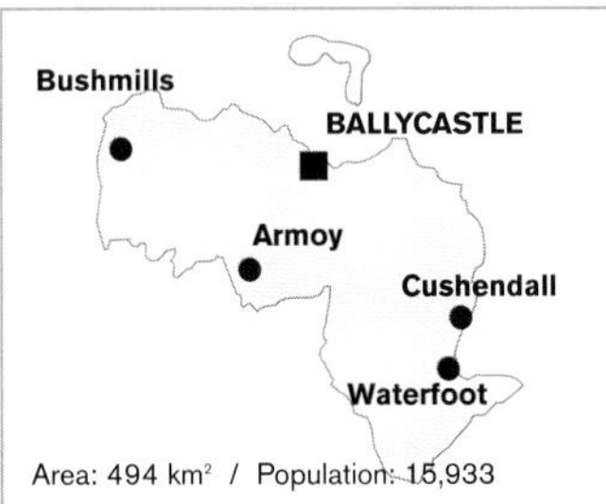

Sheskburn House
7 Mary Street
Ballycastle
BT54 6QH
Tel: 028 2076 2225
Fax: 028 2076 2515
Email:
info@moyle-council.org
Web:
www.moyle-council.org

Moyle District Council is Northern Ireland's smallest local authority covering the north east of County Antrim, embracing the 'Glens of Antrim' and is one of the major tourism destinations in Northern Ireland. It is designated an Area of Outstanding Natural Beauty, and includes the Giant's Causeway, the most visited tourist attraction in Northern Ireland.

In population terms Moyle District Council Area comprises 0.9 per cent of the total Northern Ireland population and is one of the most sparsely populated areas of Northern Ireland.

Moyle's principal town is Ballycastle, with a population of 4,500, and other centres include the villages of Bushmills and Cushendall. In Moyle District most employment is accounted for by the services sector (82.2 per cent), followed by the construction sector (9.3 per cent) and the manufacturing sector (7.4 per cent). The district has a particularly light manufacturing base, largely concentrated in the food sector.

Moyle District lies within the Northern Health and Social Services Board and its services are provided by the Causeway Health and Social Services Trust. There is no locally based acute hospital service provision and there are no institutions of third-level education.

Political Composition

Moyle District Council has 15 seats distributed throughout 3 District Electoral Areas (DEA), comprising: Ballycastle, (5 Seats), Giant's Causeway (5 Seats), The Glens (5 Seats).

The political composition of Moyle District Council as elected in June 2001 is:

Ulster Unionist Party (UUP) 3; Social Democratic and Labour Party (SDLP) 5; Democratic Unionist Party (DUP) 2; Sinn Féin (SF) 2; Other 3

Giants Causeway

Elected Members and Council Committees

Chairman: Catherine McCambridge (SDLP)
Vice-Chairman: Martin (DUP)

Councillor	Party	Councillor	Party
Madeline Black	SDLP	David McAllister	DUP
Christine Blaney	SDLP	Catherine McCambridge	SDLP
Seamus Blaney	Ind	Price McConaghy	Ind
Monica Digney	SF	Randal McDonnell	Ind
William Graham	UUP	Robert McIlroy	UUP
Helen Harding	UUP	Oliver McMullan	Ind
George Hartin	DUP	Michael Molloy	SDLP
Gardiner Kane	DUP		

Moyle District Council does not operate a committee system; all business is conducted at full council meetings

Senior Officers

Chief Executive: Richard Lewis
Director of Administration and Finance: Moira Quinn
Director of District Services: Peter Mawdsley
Chief Building Control Officer: David Kelly
Development Manager: Esther Mulholland
Human Resources Manager: Sandra Kelly
Tourism Development: Recreation Manager: Kevin McGarry
Administration Officer: Kay McCaw
Arts Officer: Pauline Russell
Community Relations Officer: Bridgeen Butler
Countryside Officer: Michael McConaghie
DPP Manager:Adrian Proctor
Economic Development Officer: Colette McMullan
Finance Officer: Anne Dickson
Health and Safety Officer: Rory Donnelly
Registrar of Births, Deaths and Marriages: Imelda McCauley
Senior Environmental Health Officer: Alan Wilson
Sports Development Officer: Damien McAfee
Technical Services Manager: Tony Stuart
Tourism Events Officer: Patricia McMullan
Tourism Officer: Fiona Campbell

Council Contact Details

Bushmills Centre	028 2073 2134
Camping & Caravan Parks	
Cushendall	028 2177 1699
Cushendun	028 2176 1254
Giants Causeway Centre	028 2073 1855
Sheskburn Recreation Centre	028 2076 3300
Tourist Offices	028 2076 2024
Sheskburn House	028 2075 2225

NEWRY & MOURNE DISTRICT COUNCIL

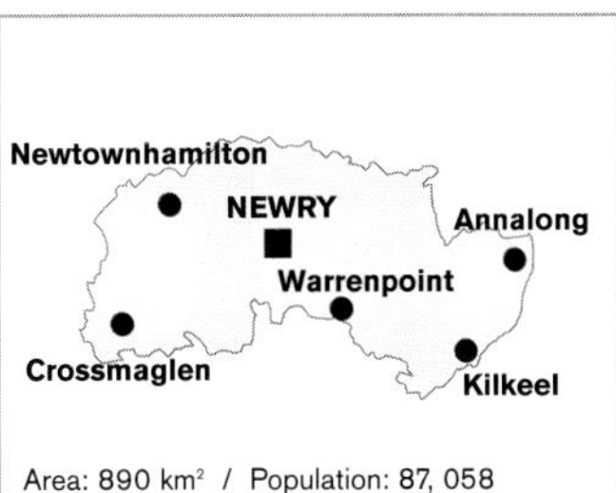

O'Hagan House
Monaghan Row
Newry, BT35 8DJ
Tel: 028 3031 3031
Fax: 028 3031 3077

Newry and Mourne District is situated in the south of Northern Ireland and borders the Republic of Ireland. The main settlements in the area are Newry, the towns of Warrenpoint and Kilkeel, and the villages of Camlough, Newtownhamilton, Annalong, Bessbrook, Crossmaglen, and Rostrevor.

Predominantly rural in character, the district includes the newly designated City of Newry, which lies on the main transport route between Belfast and Dublin.

Cross border trade is vital to the district, with the Irish Republic being the principal market for over 70 per cent of manufacturing companies in the Newry & Mourne area. Major employers in the district include: Glen Dimplex, SCA Packaging, Norbrook, FM Environmental and Haldane Fisher.

The main local administrative centre Newry was designated a city as part of the 2002 Royal Jubilee celebrations. Newry has a vibrant centre, which is characterised by attractive stone buildings, and a pedestrianised shopping area. The canal, which runs through the centre, is an important asset, and there are plans to develop it further as a focal point. Newry has expanded its role as an important shopping centre with the attraction of several major retail investments.

Newry and Mourne is recognised as the strategic gateway between the two jurisdictions on the island of Ireland. The border is more than a political demarcation – it is a currency border and a tax border. This continues to pose significant challenges for businesses seeking to develop trade in what in cultural and geographical terms is an obvious market/hinterland. Nevertheless its strategic location on the Belfast-Dublin corridor offers Newry considerable potential for future economic development.

Newry and Mourne District Council area is already one of the most rapidly developing parts of the regional economy.

Political Composition

Newry and Mourne District Council has 30 seats distributed throughout five district electoral areas: The Mournes 5 Seats; Crotlieve 7 Seats; Newry Town 7 Seats, Slieve Gullion 5 Seats; The Fews 6 Seats

The political composition of Newry and Mourne District Council elected members as elected in June 2001 is set out below

Ulster Unionist Party (UUP)4; Social Democratic and Labour Party (SDLP) 10; Democratic Unionist Party (DUP) 1; Sinn Féin (SF)13; Other 2

Elected Members and Council Committees

Chairman: Jack Patterson (Ind) Vice Chairman: Eleana Martin (SF)

Councillor	Party	Staff & Policy	Building Control	Economic Development	Environmental Control	Technical & Leisure Services	District Development
PJ Bradley	SDLP			•			•
Colman Burns	SF		•				•
William Burns	DUP	•	•		•		•
Paul McKibbin	SDLP						•
Michael Carr	SDLP	•	•	•	•	•	•
Charlie Casey	SF				•	•	C
Michael Cole	SDLP	•	•			•	•
Martin Cunningham	SF		•				•
Brendan Curran	SF	•		•	•		•
John Fee	SDLP						•
John Feehan	SDLP	•	•		•	•	•
Frank Feeley	SDLP	•	•	•	•		•
Isaac Hanna	UUP	•			•		•
Terry Hearty	SF		•			•	•
Davy Hyland	SF	•		•	•	•	•
Danny Kennedy	UUP			•			•
Breandan Lewis	SF	•		•		•	•
Elena Martin	SF	VC	VC	VC	VC	VC	•
John McArdle	SDLP		•		•	•	•
Jimmy McCreesh	SF			•			•
Packie McDonald	SF						•
Pat McElroy	SDLP	•		•			VC
Pat McGinn	SF	•	•		•		•
Andy Moffett	UUP	•	•	•	•	•	•
Mick Murphy	SF	•		•	•		•
Josephine O'Hare	SDLP			•	•	•	•
Jack Patterson	Ind	C	C	C	C	C	•
Henry Reilly	UUP		•	•		•	•
Michael Ruane	SF		•			•	•
Anthony Williamson	Ind						•

• Member C Chair VC Vice-chair

Senior Officers

Chief Executive: Thomas McCall
Director of Administration: Edwin Curtis
Assistant Director of Administration: Eileen McParland
Assistant Director of Administration: Carmel McKenna
Assistant Director of Administration (Equality): Regina Mackin
Equality Officer: Colin Moffett
Director of Finance: Robert Dowey
Purchasing Officer: David Barter
Director of Technical and Leisure Services: Jim McCorry
Director of District Development: Gerard McGivern
Director of Environmental Health: Hugh O'Neill
Director of Building Control: Fulton Somerville
Senior Building Control Surveyor: David Shanks
DPP Manager: Patricia Hamilton
Environmental Liaison Officer: Jennifer Wilson
Licensing Officer: Fintan Quinn

Council Contact Details

Administration/Equality/ Personnel	028 3031 3031
Arts Centre	028 3026 6232
Building Control	028 3031 3000
District Development Dept	028 3031 3233
Technical and Leisure Services Dept	028 3031 3233
Environmental Health Dept	028 3031 3100
Finance Department	028 3031 3031
Disability Liaison Officer	028 3025 6428
Market Clerk's Office	028 3026 3004

NEWTOWNABBEY BOROUGH COUNCIL

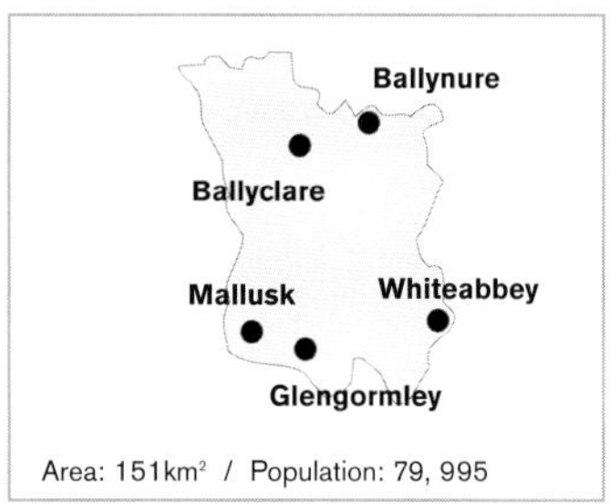

Mossley Mill
Newtownabbey
BT36 5QA
Tel: 028 9034 0000
Fax: 028 9034 0200

Email: info@newtownabbey.gov.uk
Web: www.newtownabbey.gov.uk

Newtownabbey is the fifth largest local authority in Northern Ireland and combines a large urban area with a rural hinterland. Newtownabbey is part of greater North Belfast fringing Belfast Lough, Cave Hill and Carnmoney, but stretches into rural South Antrim and incorporates the busy market town of Ballyclare. Newtownabbey is situated directly north and east of Belfast and has benefited greatly from several large businesses relocating from Belfast city centre. Its close proximity to Northern Ireland's main airports and ports has made it an attractive location for inward investment. The borough hosts the University of Ulster campus at Jordanstown, which has strong links to local industry.

Newtownabbey includes affluent suburbs such as Jordanstown along with relatively deprived areas such as Rathcoole and Monkstown. The borough has a strong industrial base, with high employment in the manufacturing, construction, wholesale and education sectors.

There are a number of large and successful companies that have located in Newtownabbey including: Boxpak Ltd, Leaf Technologies Ltd, Brett Martin, Rotary Group Ltd, Royal Mail, Sx3, Camco, FG Wilson, Nortel Networks, Bombardier Shorts, Freutauf, and Valence Technology Ltd.

Political Composition

Newtownabbey Borough Council has 25 seats distributed throughout four electoral districts of: Antrim Line 7 Seats, Ballyclare 5 Seats, Macedon 6 Seats, University 7 Seats.

The political composition of Newtownabbey Borough Council elected members as elected in June 2001 is:

Ulster Unionist Party (UUP) 9; Social Democratic and Labour Party (SDLP) 2; Democratic Unionist Party (DUP) 7; Sinn Féin (SF) 1; Other 6

The largest party on the council is the UUP with 9 seats. The council has a clear unionist majority.

The main council meeting is convened on the last Monday of each month at 7.30pm in Council offices.

Elected Members and Council Committees

Mayor: Paul Girvan (DUP)
Deputy Mayor: Ted/Edward Turkington (UUP)

Councillor	Party	Environmental & Contract Services	Corporate Services	Development	Policy & Resources	Planning & Consultation
Fraser Agnew	UUAP		•	VC	•	•
James Bingham	UUP	•		•	•	•
Janet Crilly	UUP	•		•	•	VC
William DeCourcy	DUP		VC		•	•
Lynn Frazer	All	•		•	•	•
Barbara Gilliland	UUP	•		•	VC	•
Paul Girvan	DUP	•	•	•	C	•
Nigel Hamilton	DUP	•		•	•	•
Ivan Hunter	UUP	C		•	•	•
Pamela Hunter	DUP	VC	•		•	•
Roger Hutchinson	Ind		•	•	•	C
Tommy Kirkham	Ind		C	•	•	•
Mark Langhammer	Lab			•		•
John Mann	DUP	•	•			•
Briege Meehan	SF	•	•			•
Noreen McClelland	SDLP		•	•		•
Tommy McTeague	SDLP		•	•		•
Vera McWilliam	UUP		•	•		•
Ken Robinson	UUP		•	•	•	•
Victor Robinson	DUP		•	•		•
Vi Scott	UUP	•		•		•
Arthur Templeton	DUP	•		C		•
Edward Turkington	UUP	•		•	•	•
Dineen Walker	UUP		•	•		•
Billy Webb	NRA		•			•

• Member C Chair VC Vice-chair

Senior Officers

Chief Executive: Norman Dunn

Deputy Chief Executive and Head of Development Services: Hilary Brady

Head of Administration and Human Resources: Neal Willis

Head of Building Control: Stephen Montgomery

Head of Contract Services: Hugh Kelly

Acting Head of Environmental Services: Bob Cameron

Head of Financial Services: Peter McCabe

Community Development Manager: Linda McCullough

Community Services Officer: Jonathan Henderson

Corporate Services Manager: Helen McBride

DPP Manager: Campbell Dixon

Economic Development Manager: Jacqui O'Neill

Human Resources Manager: Andrea McCook

Licensing Officer: John Holmes

Marketing Manager: Tracey White

Registrar of Births, Deaths and Marriages: Barbara Blaney

Council Contact Details

Arts Development	028 9034 0063
Births, Deaths & Marriages	028 9034 0180
Building Control	028 9034 0140
Economic Development	028 9034 0072
Environmental Health	028 9034 0160
Marketing & Public Relations	028 9034 0028
Mayor's Office	028 9034 0014
Project Development	028 9034 0078
Recycling Bin Collections	028 9034 0056
Sports Development	028 9034 0067
Street Cleansing	028 9034 0057

NORTH DOWN BOROUGH COUNCIL

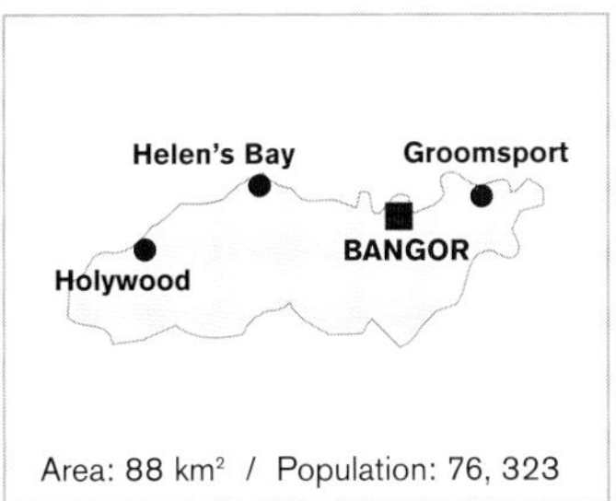

Area: 88 km² / Population: 76, 323

Town Hall
The Castle
Bangor
BT20 4BT
Tel: 028 9127 0371
Fax: 028 9127 1370
Email:
enquiries@northdown.gov.uk
Web:
www.northdown.gov.uk

The Borough of North Down is situated on the southern shores of Belfast Lough. The main town of the Borough, Bangor, which is Northern Ireland's third largest town, functions as a service and administrative centre as well as a market town and seaside resort. There are also several villages, Crawfordsburn, Groomsport, Helen's Bay, Conlig and Seahill. Although North Down is ranked as the least deprived local government district in Northern Ireland sometimes known colloquially as the "gold coast" there are some pockets of high unemployment and relative social deprivation.

Over half the borough's workforce commutes to work, mostly to Belfast, of whom the majority are employed in the service sector. There is a narrow manufacturing base within the borough and this is concentrated in small firms. Light engineering accounts for most of the borough's manufacturing employment; plastics injection moulding, light engineering, IT and multi-media make up the main industry clusters. Major employers include: Denroy/Denman Plastics, the Department of Education at Balloo, Valpar, the Carmichael Hospitality Group and 3M.

The borough is one of the best performing council areas in terms of generating income from tourism. Attractions include the Pickie Family Fun Park which attracts over 300,000 visitors each year, the award winning Bangor Marina, the Ulster Folk and Transport Museum, the Heritage Centre, six golf courses, and new trout fishery in Holywood, Crawfordsburn Country Park and many water based activities.

The retail sector is particularly strong in North Down and represents a high percentage of all registered businesses in the borough. Bloomfield Shopping Centre in Bangor is one of the most successful out of town shopping centres in Northern Ireland.

Political Composition

North Down Borough Council has 25 seats distributed throughout 4 District Electoral Areas (DEAs) of: Abbey 6 Seats; Ballyholme and Groomsport 7 Seats; Bangor West 7 Seats; Holywood 5 Seats;

The political composition of North Down Borough Council elected members as elected in June 2001 is: Ulster Unionist Party (UUP) 8 Seats; Democratic Unionist Party (DUP) 5 Seats; Alliance 5 Seats; Other 7 Seats;

The largest party on the council is the UUP with 8 seats. The council has a clear unionist majority.

Elected Members and Council Committees

Mayor: Anne Wilson (All)

Deputy Mayor: Roberta Dunlop (UUP)

Councillor	Party	Environmental Amenities	Leisure, Tourism Community Development	Planning Public Services Liaison	Corporate	Economic Development
Alan Chambers	Ind		•	•	•	•
Ruby Cooling	DUP	•		•	•	•
Irene Cree	UUP		•	•	•	•
Leslie Cree	UUP	•		•	•	C
Roy Davies	UUP	•		•	•	•
Roberta Dunlop	UUP		•	•	•	•
Gordon Dunne	DUP		•	C	•	•
Alexander Easton	DUP		•	•	•	•
Stephen Farry	All	•		•	•	•
Marsden Fitzsimons	All		C	•	•	•
Alan Graham	DUP	•		•	•	•
Ian Henry	UUP		•	•	•	•
Tony Hill	All	•		•	•	•
Bill Keery	UKUP		•	•	•	•
Valerie Kinghan	UKUP	*C		•	•	•
Austen Lennon	Ind		•	•	•	•
Ellie McKay	UUP	•		•	C	•
John Montgomery	DUP	*C		•	•	•
Susan O'Brien	All		•	•	•	•
Denis Ogborn	Ind	•		•	•	•
Diana Peacock	UUP		•	•	•	•
Marion Smith	UUP		•	•	•	•
Patricia Wallace	NIWC	•		•	•	•
Anne Wilson	All		•	•	•	•
Brian Wilson	Ind	•		•	•	•

• Member C Chair
Committees do not elect Vice-chairs
*Environmental Amenities chair is shared

Senior Officers

Chief Executive: Trevor Polley
Director of Amenities and Technical Services: Jackie Snodden
Head of Policy Unit: John Thompson
Director of Leisure, Tourism and Community Services: Stephen Reid
Director of Environmental Services: Graham Yarr
Director of Corporate Services: Ken Webb
Chief Building Control Officer: Michael McGlennon
Chief Finance Officer: Claire Escott
Borough Inspector: David Brown
Community Cultural Manager: Kevin Thomas
Community Development Manager: Tom Rainey
Community Safety Officer: Suzanne Gowling
Corporate Communications Officer: Lisa Maginnis
District Policing Partnership Manager: Kirsten Mullen
Economic Development Officer: Nick Rogers
Registrar of Births, Deaths and Marriages: Denis Skelton
Tourism and Marketing Officer: Christine Mahon

Council Contact Details

Town Hall, Bangor	028 9127 0371
Borough Inspector	028 9127 0371
Building Control	028 9127 0371
Borough Inspector (after hours)	028 9146 7975
Registration of Births, Deaths Marriages	028 9127 0371
Tower House Tourist Information Centre	028 9127 0069
Bangor Cemetery	028 9127 1909

OMAGH DISTRICT COUNCIL

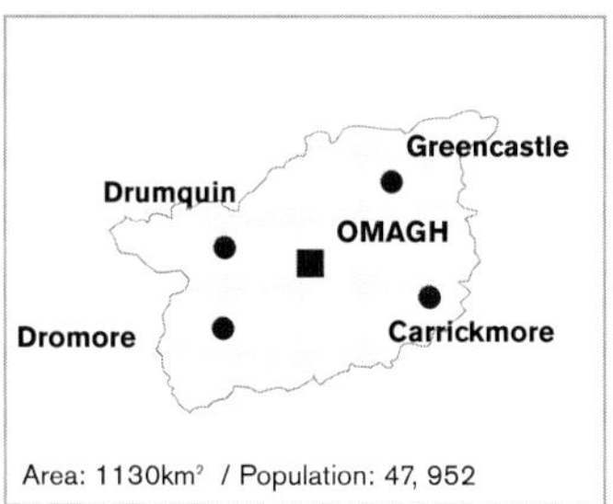

The Grange
Mountjoy Road
Omagh
BT79 7BL
Tel: 028 8224 5321
Fax: 028 8224 3888
Email:
info@omagh.gov.uk
Web:
www.omagh.gov.uk

The district of Omagh covers an area of almost 113,000 hectares (440 sq miles) making it the second largest district council area in Northern Ireland. The market town of Omagh is at the centre of the region with the rest of the Omagh district primarily rural in character. Approximately 20,000 people live in Omagh town. The next largest centres are Fintona and Dromore. Omagh town (with the exception of Derry City) is now the largest in the west of Northern Ireland.

Despite making the international headlines following the Omagh bomb atrocity, in which 29 people were killed, the people of the area have pulled together under the leadership of the local authority and the area is recovering.

The district has a strong services sector accounting for 78 per cent of all people employed. Around two thirds of those are within the public sector. Omagh is the home to regional and area offices of local and central government including the Western Health and Social Services Board, the Western Education and Library Board, Northern Ireland Housing Executive and the Departments of Agriculture and Rural Development, Environment, and Health, Social Services and Public Safety.

Manufacturing accounts for 10 per cent of employment in the district where a number of leading export manufacturers including Naturelle, Leckpatrick and Finlays are located. Rixell, a subsidiary of the Taiwanese Ritek Corporation, has invested £28 million in a facility producing recordable CDs.

Omagh College of Further and Higher Education has an enrolment of over 1,200 full time students and 5,500 part time students. The College has embarked on providing a new purpose built campus costing £15 million on their existing site.

Omagh has been identified as a regional growth town and major service centre by the 'Shaping Our Future' report prepared by the Department for Regional Development as the basis for the overall development of Northern Ireland.

Political Composition

Omagh District Council has 21 Councillors, representing three district electoral areas: Omagh Town 7 Seats; Mid Tyrone 7 Seats; West Tyrone 7 Seats. The main council meeting is convened on the 1st Tuesday of each month at 7.00pm in Council offices. The political composition of Omagh District Council elected members as elected in June 2001 is: Ulster Unionist Party (UUP) 3; Social Democratic and Labour Party (SDLP) 6; Democratic Unionist Party (DUP) 2; Sinn Féin (SF) 8; Other 2.

Elected Members and Council Committees

Chairman: Allan Rainey (UUP)
Vice Chairman: Gerry O'Doherty (SDLP)

Councillor	Party	Policy & Resources	Environmental Services	Planning & Public Services Liaison	Development	Best Value
Sean Begley	SF	•	•	•	•	•
Thomas Buchanon	DUP	•	•	•	•	•
Joe Byrne	SDLP	•	•	•	•	•
Sean Clarke	SF	•	•	•	•	•
Damien Curran	SF	•	•	•	•	•
Josephine Deehan	SDLP	•	•	•	•	•
Oliver Gibson	DUP	•	•	•	•	•
Peter Kelly	SF	•	•	•	•	•
Barney McAleer	SF	•	•	•	•	•
Michael McAnespie	SF	•	•	•	•	•
Patrick McDonnell	SDLP	•	•	•	•	•
Barry McElduff	SF	•	•	•	•	•
Patrick McGowan	Ind	•	•	•	•	•
Reuben McKelvey	UUP	C	•	•	•	C
Johnny McLaughlin	Ind	•	•	•	•	•
Liam McQuaid	SDLP	•	C	•	•	•
Gerry O'Doherty	SDLP	•	•	•	•	•
Allan Rainey	UUP	•	•	•	•	•
Seamus Shields	SDLP	•	•	•	C	•
Patrick Watters	SF	•	•	•	•	•
Robert Wilson	UUP	•	•	C	•	•

• Member C Chair Committees do not elect Vice Chairs

Senior Officers

Chief Executive: Danny McSorley
Chief Client Services Officer: Kevin O'Gara
Chief Environmental Health Officer: Gerry Harte
Chief Finance Officer: Joan McCaffrey
District Chief Building Control Surveyor: Sean Kelly
Head of Arts and Tourism: Frank Sweeney
Head of Corporate Services: Elizabeth McSorley
Head of Development: Vincent Brogan
Head of Personnel/Training: Rosemary Rafferty
Leisure Services Manager: Robert Fitzpatrick
Community Safety Officer: Vacant
Community Relations Officer: Christine Rodgers
District Policing Partnership Manager: Mary Brogan
Enforcement Officer (Dog Control): Anne Marie McCann
Economic Projects Officer: Vacant
Equality Officer: Elizabeth Beattie
IT Officer: Anne Clarke
Licensing Officer: Gerry Donnelly
PR Officer: Elizabeth Harkin
Registrar of Births, Deaths and Marriages: Amy Smyton
Sports Development Officer: Conor McCrory

Council Contact Details

Council Offices	028 8224 5321
Community Centres	
Strathroy	028 8224 3725
Hospital Road	028 8224 4426
CKS Centre	028 8224 7560
Gortin Glen Caravan Park	028 8164 8108
Greenhill Cemetery	028 8224 4918
Omagh Leisure Centre	028 8224 6711

STRABANE DISTRICT COUNCIL

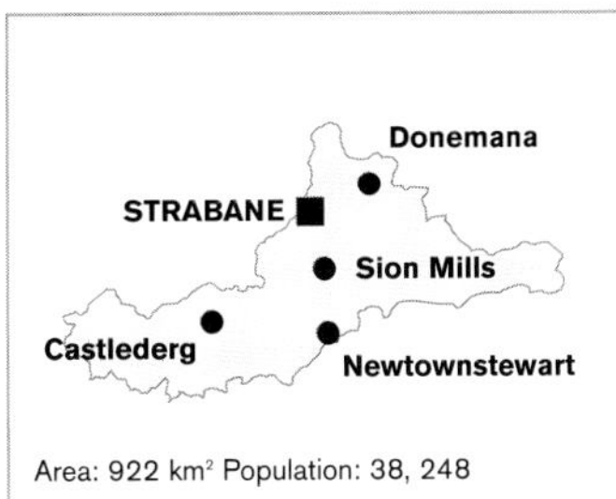

47 Derry Road
Strabane
Co. Tyrone
BT82 8DY
Tel: 028 7138 2204
Fax: 028 7138 1348
Email:
info@strabanedc.com
Web:
www.strabanedc.com

With an area covering some 922 km² of countryside, Strabane District is one of the largest council areas in Northern Ireland. Located on the border between counties Tyrone and Donegal and 20 miles south of Derry, Strabane is at the centre of the North West region of Northern Ireland. Strabane is the district's main town but there are also a substantial number of smaller towns and settlements, including Castlederg, Newtownstewart, Plumbridge and Sion Mills.

Strabane is a mainly rural district, although the town itself is a busy retail and commercial centre, and the wider area includes a growing industrial base. Strabane has a tradition in manufacturing with 35 per cent of its workforce employed in the sector. Amongst the best known of its local companies are: Adria, Leckpatrick, Herdmans, Octupus Sports Wear and Mopack Systems packaging company.

Strabane District offers a wide variety of leisure and sports facilities.

Political Composition

Strabane District Council has 16 Councillors, representing 3 district electoral areas:

Derg 5 Seats; Glenelly 5 Seats; Mourne 6 Seats

The main Council meeting is convened on the 2nd Tuesday of each month at 7.30pm in the Council offices.

The political composition of Strabane District Council elected members as elected in June 2001 is:

Ulster Unionist Party (UUP) 2; Social Democratic and Labour Party (SDLP) 4; Democratic Unionist Party (DUP) 3; Sinn Féin (SF) 7

The largest party on the council is Sinn Féin with 7 seats. The council has a nationalist majority.

Elected Members and Council Committees

Councillor	Party	Culture Arts & Leisure	Environmental	Economic Development	Corporate & Regulatory Services
Ivan Barr	SF	•	•	•	•
Ann Bell	SDLP	•	•	•	•
Allan Bresland	DUP	•	•	•	•
Daniel Breslin	SF	C	•	•	•
John Donnell	DUP	•	•	•	•
James Emery	UUP	•	•	•	•
Derek Hussey	UUP	•	•	•	•
Thomas Kerrigan	DUP	•	C	•	VC
Tom McBride	SDLP	•	•	•	•
Eamon McGarvey	SF	•	•	•	•
Claire McGill	SF	VC	•	•	•
Charlie McHugh	SF	•	VC	•	C
Brian McMahon	SF	•	•	•	•
Eugene McMenamin	SDLP	•	•	C	•
Bernadette McNamee	SDLP	•	•	•	•
Jarlath McNulty	SF	•	•	VC	•

• Member C Chair VC Vice-chair

Chairman: James Emery (UUP)
Vice-Chairman: Brian McMahon (SF)

Senior Officers

Chief Executive: Philip Faithful
Head of Finance: Maureen Henebery
Head of Culture, Arts and Leisure: Karen McFarland
Chief Building Control Officer: John Stewart
Chief Environmental Health Officer: Paddy Cosgrove
Chief Technical Services Officer: Malcolm Scott
Business Manager: Sharon Maxwell
Arts and Events Officer: Lorrie Kyle
Client Services Officer: Liam Donnelly
Community Relations Officer: Clare Mullen
Corporate Policy Officer: Grace Turpin
DPP Manager: Rachelle Harkin
Economic Development Officer: Geraldine Stafford
Human Resources Officer: Paula Donnelly
Leisure Services Manager: Fionnuala O'Kane
Strabane LSP Project Officer: Patrick O'Doherty
Tourism Officer: Phillip McShane

Council Contact Details

Administration	028 7138 2204
Arts and Culture	028 7138 2204
Building Control	028 7138 2204
Cemeteries Administration	028 7138 2204
Community Development	028 7138 2204
Environmental Health	028 7135 1355
Technical Services	028 7138 2771

Local Government Elections

Since Northern Ireland's local government structure was reformed in 1973 there have been 8 local government elections across the 26 Local Government Districts (LGDs). Results for the main parties have tended to correspond with overall performance in other elections although independents have featured more strongly.

Turnout for local elections is generally around 50–60 per cent, which is significantly lower than UK government elections, and also lower than the Assembly elections in 1998. This is probably reflective of the fact that the responsibilities of local authorities include areas such as waste disposal, cemeteries and parks, which although vital in everyday life, go largely unnoticed in comparison with mainstream political issues. Nevertheless the parties and candidates fiercely contest the elections, although issues raised at the hustings are matters over which they actually have little authority.

However, turnout for the 2001 local government election, at 66 per cent, was significantly higher than usual. This was largely due to the fact that Westminster elections were held on the same day.

The tables below show summary results for all local government elections since 1985.

2001 Local Government Election

Turnout: 66%

	Votes	% votes	seats	% seats
UUP	181336	22.9	154	26.5
DUP	169477	21.4	131	20.1
SDLP	153424	19.4	117	22.5
SF	163269	20.7	108	18.5
All	40443	5.1	28	4.8
PUP	12661	1.6	4	0.7
Others	70247	8.9	40	6.9
Total	**790857**	**100**	**582**	**100**

1997 Local Government Election

Turnout: 53.6%

	Votes	% votes	seats	% seats
UUP	176239	27.9	185	31.9
DUP	98686	15.6	91	15.6
SDLP	130417	20.6	120	20.6
SF	106938	16.9	74	12.7
All	41421	6.6	41	7
PUP	13744	2.2	6	1
UDP	6244	1	4	0.7
Others	58508	9.2	61	10.5
Total	**632197**	**100**	**582**	**100**

1993 Local Government Election

Turnout: 56.6%

	Votes	% votes	seats	% seats
UUP	184608	29.4	197	33.8
DUP	108863	17.3	103	17.7
SDLP	138619	22	127	21.8
SF	78092	12.4	51	8.8
All	47649	7.6	44	7.6
Others	71275	11.3	60	10.3
Total	**629106**	**100**	**582**	**100**

1989 Local Government Election

Turnout 56.1%

	Votes	% votes	seats	% seats
UUP	193(028)	31.3	194	34.9
DUP	109332	17.7	110	19.8
SDLP	129557	21	121	21.8
SF	69032	11.2	43	7.7
All	42659	6.9	38	6.8
WP	13078	2.1	4	0.7
Others	60523	9.8	46	8.3
Total	**617209**	**100**	**566**	**100**

1985 Local Government Election

Turnout: 60.1%

	Votes	% votes	seats	% seats
UUP	188497	29.5	190	33.6
DUP	155297	24.3	142	25.1
SDLP	113967	17.8	101	17.8
SF	75686	11.8	59	10.4
All	45394	7.1	34	6
WP	10276	1.6	4	0.7
Others	50505	7.9	36	6.4
Total	**639622**	**100**	**566**	**100**

2001 Local Government Elections: Detailed Results by Council

The Results are arranged by council, and within each council, by DEA. Each DEA lists the electorate, the total number of valid votes cast, and the quota for each DEA and the turnout for each DEA. Every candidate who stood for election is listed, along with his or her party, the number of first-preference votes, and if successful, the count on which they were elected.

Antrim Borough Council

Antrim Borough Council has a total of 19 councillors and 3 wards as follows: Antrim North West 5 seats; Antrim South East 7 seats; Antrim Town 7 seats

Summary of council

Electorate 32430 Valid Vote 20238 Turnout 62.4%

Party	% Vote	Seats
UUP	**33**	**7**
SDLP	**21**	**5**
DUP	**23**	**5**
SF	**13**	**2**
All	**6**	**0**
Others	**4**	**0**
Total	**100**	**19**

Antrim North West (5 seats)

Electorate	8544	Valid Vote	5820
Quota	971	Turnout	69.4%

Party	Candidates	% Vote	Seats
UUP	2	18.2	1
SDLP	2	30.4	2
DUP	1	18.1	1
SF	2	23.9	1
All	1	2.3	
NIUP	1	7.1	
Total	**109**	**100**	**5**

Candidate	Party	1st Pref Votes	Elected
Wilson Clyde	DUP	1053	1st Count
Michael Donoghue	All	133	
Brian Johnston	NIUP	413	
Bobby Loughran	SDLP	1093	1st Count
Joseph McCavana	SF	384	
Donovan McClelland	SDLP	678	5th Count
Martin Meehan	SF	1007	1st Count
Stephen Nicholl	UUP	430	8th Count
Avril Swann	UUP	629	

Antrim South East (7 seats)

Electorate	12770	Valid Vote	8060
Quota	1008	Turnout	64.7%

Party	Candidates	% Vote	Seats
UUP	4	40.4	3
SDLP	2	15.4	1
DUP	2	23.4	2
SF	1	8.7	1
All	1	7.2	
CC	1	4.9	
Total	**11**	**100**	**7**

Candidate	Party	1st Pref Votes	Elected
Thomas Burns	SDLP	1072	1st Count
Samuel Dunlop	DUP	1367	1st Count
William Harkness	DUP	525	9th Count
Sean Mallon	SDLP	168	
Allison McCartney	All	578	
Michael McGivern	Ind	393	
Martin McManus	SF	703	9th Count
Mervyn Rea	UUP	1042	1st Count
Roderick Swann	UUP	213	
Roy Thompson	UUP	1062	1st Count
Edgar Wallace	UUP	937	7th Count

Antrim Town (7 seats)

Electorate	11616	Valid Vote	6358
Quota	795	Turnout	56.4%

Party	Candidates	% Vote	Seats
UUP	4	37.6	3
SDLP	2	19.5	2
DUP	3	25.6	2
SF	1	7.8	
All	1	6.4	
PUP	1	3.1	
Total	**12**	**100**	**7**

Candidate	Party	1st Pref Votes	Elected
Adrian Cochrane-Watson	UUP	632	4th Count
Brian Graham	DUP	516	6th Count
Aine Gribbon	SF	495	
Oran Keenan	SDLP	611	9th Count
Paddy Marks	UUP	1116	1st Count
Jack McClay	DUP	366	
Sean McKee	SDLP	632	9th Count
Paul Michael	UUP	470	6th Count
Drew Ritchie	UUP	268	
John Smyth	DUP	749	3rd Count
Peter Whitcroft	All	406	
Ken Wilkinson	PUP	197	

Ards Borough Council

Ards Borough Council has a total of 23 councillors and 4 DEAs as follows: Ards East 6 seats; Ards Peninsula 5 seats; Ards West 6 seats; Newtownards 6 seats.

Summary of council

Electorate 38416 Valid Vote 21954 Turnout 57.1%

NB: The above figures do not include Ards East Ward because, there only being 6 candidates, no election took place.

Party	% Vote	Seats
UUP	**32**	**8**
SDLP	**4**	**9**
DUP	**37**	**1**
SF	**0**	**0**
All	**17**	**4**
Others	**10**	**1**
Total	**100**	**23**

Newtownards (6 seats)

Electorate	12965	Valid Vote	7050
Quota	1008	Turnout	56.1%

Party	Candidates	% Vote	Seats
UUP	1	33.3	2
DUP	3	37.5	2
All	1	12.2	1
Ind	2	17.0	1
Total	**7**	**100**	**6**

Candidate	Party	1st Pref Votes	Elected
George Ennis	DUP	1608	1st Count
Thomas Hamilton	UUP	1288	1st Count
Hamilton Lawther	DUP	363	5th Count
Wilbert Magill	Ind	889	2nd Count
Bobby McBride	DUP	671	
Alan McDowell	All	859	3rd Count
Nancy Orr	Ind	312	
David Smyth	UUP	1060	1st Count

Ards West (6 seats)

Electorate	13602	Valid Vote	8030
Quota	1148	Turnout	60.7%

Party	Candidates	% Vote	Seats
UUP	3	42.2	2
DUP	3	36.9	3
All	2	18.5	1
Cons	1	2.4	
Total	**9**	**100**	**6**

Candidate	Party	1st Pref Votes	Elected
Christopher Connolly	Cons	190	
Kathleen Coulter	All	732	
Margaret Craig	DUP	1230	1st Count
Robert Gibson	UUP	2454	1st Count
David Gilmore	DUP	693	6th Count
Jim McBriar	All	756	6th Count
William Montgomery	DUP	1039	6th Count
Philip Smith	UUP	625	2nd Count
Arthur Spence	UUP	311	

Ards Peninsula (5 seats)

Electorate	11849	Valid Vote	6874
Quota	1146	Turnout	59.8%

Party	Candidates	% Vote	Seats
UUP	2	17.9	1
SDLP	1	12.5	1
DUP	2	36.8	2
All	2	19.2	1
Ind	3	13.6	
Total	**10**	**100**	**5**

Candidate	Party	1st Pref Votes	Elected
Ronnie Ambrose	Ind	255	
Joseph Boyle	Ind	526	
Angus Carson	UUP	710	8th Count
Paul Carson	UUP	520	
Robert Drysdale	DUP	705	2nd Count
Danny McCarthy	SDLP	860	7th Count
Kieran McCarthy	All	1286	1st Count
James McMullan	Ind	153	
Stephen McSherry	All	35	
Jim Shannon	DUP	1824	1st Count

Ards East

There was no election in Ards East because six candidates stood for the six seats. Therefore, all candidates were automatically re-elected:

Linda Cleland	All	Ronnie Ferguson	UUP
George Gregory	DUP	Jeff Magill	UUP
John Shields	UUP	Terence Williams	DUP

Armagh City and District Council

Armagh City and District Council has a total of 22 councillors and 4 DEAs as follows: Armagh City 6 seats; Crossmore 5 seats; Cusher 6 seats; The Orchard 5 seats.

Summary of council

Electorate 38911 Valid Vote 29962 Turnout 77.0%

Party	% Vote	Seats
UUP	**26**	**7**
SDLP	**24**	**6**
DUP	**26**	**4**
SF	**21**	**5**
All	**0**	**0**
Others	**3**	**0**
Total	**100**	**22**

Armagh City (6 seats)

Electorate	10014	Valid Vote	7438
Quota	1063	Turnout	76.0%

Party	Candidates	% Vote	Seats
UUP	2	18.8	1
SDLP	4	29.1	2
DUP	1	11.6	1
SF	2	29.1	2
Ind	1	8.6	
NIWC	1	2.8	
Total	**11**	**100**	**6**

Candidate	Party	1st Pref Votes	Elected
Pat Brannigan	SDLP	1013	4th Count
Mealla Bratton	SDLP	325	
Anna Brolly	SDLP	370	10th Count
Michael Carson	SDLP	456	
Margaret Connolly	NIWC	209	
Freda Donnelly	DUP	861	8th Count
Gordon Frazer	UUP	528	
Pat McNamee	SF	1261	1st Count
Sylvia McRoberts	UUP	868	7th Count
John Nixon	Ind	646	
Cathy Rafferty	SF	901	3rd Count

Cusher Ward (6 seats)

Electorate	11175	Valid Vote	8588
Quota	1227	Turnout	78.1%

Party	Candidates	% Vote	Seats
UUP	4	34.6	3
SDLP	1	11.6	1
DUP	3	44.7	2
SF	1	6.9	
Ind	1	2.2	
Total	**10**	**100**	**6**

Candidate	Party	1st Pref Votes	Elected
Paul Berry	DUP	3549	1st Count
Heather Black	DUP	185	2nd Count
Tom Canavan	SDLP	1001	7th Count
Jimmy Clayton	UUP	679	7th Count
Derrick Matthews	Ind	186	
Sharon McClelland	UUP	367	
Noel Sheridan	SF	591	
Eric Speers	UUP	1202	2nd Count
Mervyn Spratt	DUP	103	
Robert Turner	UUP	725	7th Count

Crossmore (5 seats)

Electorate	8488	Valid Vote	6758
Quota	1127	Turnout	81.1%

Party	Candidates	% Vote	Seats
UUP	1	13.7	1
SDLP	4	39.9	2
DUP	1	13.8	
SF	2	32.6	2
Total	**8**	**100**	**5**

Candidate	Party	1st Pref Votes	Elected
Noel Berry	DUP	930	
Evelyn Corry	UUP	927	7th Count
Brian Cunningham	SF	1336	1st Count
Tommy Kavanagh	SDLP	989	3rd Count
Jim Lennon	SDLP	554	
Joe McGleenan	SDLP	452	
James McKernan	SDLP	703	5th Count
Pat O'Rawe	SF	867	6th Count

The Orchard (5 seats)

Electorate	9234	Valid Vote	7178
Quota	1197	Turnout	79.0%

Party	Candidates	% Vote	Seats
UUP	3	34.3	2
SDLP	2	20.2	1
DUP	2	28.5	1
SF	1	17.0	1
Total	**8**	**100**	**5**

Candidate	Party	1st Pref Votes	Elected
John Campbell	SDLP	796	5th Count
Paul Corrigan	SF	1221	1st Count
Brian Hutchinson	DUP	1363	1st Count
William Irwin	DUP	686	
Eamon McNeill	SDLP	651	
Charles Rollston	UUP	645	5th Count
Jim Speers	UUP	1324	1st Count
Olive Whitten	UUP	492	

Ballymena Borough Council

Ballymena Borough Council has 24 councillors and 4 DEAs as follows: Ballymena North 7 seats; Ballymena South 7 seats; Bannside 5 seats; Braid 5 seats.

Summary of council

Electorate 43948 Valid Vote 28833 Turnout 65.6%

Party	% Vote	Seats
UUP	**27**	**7**
SDLP	**16**	**4**
DUP	**45**	**11**
SF	**1**	**0**
All	**1**	**0**
Others	**10**	**2**
Total	**100**	**24**

Ballymena North (7 seats)

Electorate	12286	Valid Vote	7742
Quota	968	Turnout	63.0%

Party	Candidates	% Vote	Seats
UUP	4	24.8	2
SDLP	1	13.8	1
DUP	3	27.8	2
SF	1	4.9	
All	1	4.1	
Ind	3	24.2	2
PUP	1	0.4	
Total	**14**	**100**	**7**

Candidate	Party	1st Pref Votes	Elected
James Alexander	DUP	1110	1st Count
James Henry	Ind	1060	1st Count
PJ McAvoy	SDLP	1071	1st Count
James Armstrong	UUP	533	9th Count
Jane Dunlop	All	317	
Simon Hamilton	DUP	411	
Gerard Magee	SF	382	
William McElfatrick	UUP	242	
Joseph McKernan	UUP	613	8th Count
Maurice Mills	DUP	625	9th Count
William Parkhill	PUP	30	
Gillian Scott	UUP	532	
Audrey Wales	Ind	263	
William Wright	Ind	553	9th Count

Ballymena South (7 seats)

Electorate	11772	Valid Vote	7007
Quota	877	Turnout	60.0%

Party	Candidates	% Vote	Seats
UUP	2	22.1	2
SDLP	1	17.3	1
DUP	5	55.8	4
PUP	2	1.4	
Ind	1	3.4	
Total	**11**	**100**	**7**

Candidate	Party	1st Pref Votes	Elected
Elizabeth Adger	DUP	1061	1st Count
Peter Brown	UUP	459	9th Count
Martin Clarke	DUP	793	5th Count
James Currie	UUP	1092	1st Count
William McCaughey	PUP	51	
William Moore	DUP	285	
Hubert Nicholl	DUP	755	6th Count
Declan O'Loan	SDLP	1212	1st Count
Jean Rainey	PUP	43	
David Tweed	DUP	1018	1st Count
David Warwick	Ind	241	

Bannside (5 seats)

Electorate	10493	Valid Vote	7460
Quota	1244	Turnout	72.0%

Party	Candidates	% Vote	Seats
UUP	2	24.0	1
SDLP	2	17.6	1
DUP	4	55.2	3
NIUP	1	2.5	
PUP	1	0.7	
Total	**10**	**100**	**5**

Candidate	Party	1st Pref Votes	Elected
Samuel Gaston	DUP	890	6th Count
Roy Gillespie	DUP	1427	1st Count
Seamus Laverty	SDLP	938	4th Count
Kenneth McCaughey	PUP	53	
Samuel McClean	UUP	727	
William McNeilly	UUP	1060	5th Count
Joseph Montgomery	SDLP	375	
Thomas Nicholl	DUP	962	6th Count
Norman Sloan	NIUP	186	
William Wilkinson	DUP	842	

Braid (5 seats)

Electorate	9397	Valid Vote	6624
Quota	1105	Turnout	71.4%

Party	Candidates	% Vote	Seats
UUP	3	40.3	2
SDLP	1	17.5	1
DUP	3	41.8	2
PUP	1	0.4	
Total	**8**	**100**	**5**

Candidate	Party	1st Pref Votes	Elected
Desmond Armstrong	UUP	815	
David Clyde	UUP	961	6th Count
Margaret Gribben	SDLP	1158	1st Count
Robert Hamilton	PUP	29	
Samuel Hanna	DUP	1242	1st Count
Robert Osborne	DUP	707	
Lexie Scott	UUP	893	6th Count
Robin Stirling	DUP	819	4th Count

Ballymoney Borough Council

Ballymoney Borough Council has a total of 16 councillors and 3 DEAs as follows: Ballymoney Town 5 seats; Bann Valley 6 seats; Bushvale 5 seats

Summary of council

Electorate 19277 Valid Vote 12558 Turnout 65.1%

Party	% Vote	Seats
UUP	**24**	**5**
SDLP	**18**	**2**
DUP	**42**	**8**
SF	**11**	**1**
All	**0**	**0**
Others	**5**	**0**
Total	**100%**	**16**

Ballymoney Town (6 seats)

Electorate	6187	Valid Vote	3733
Quota	623	Turnout	61.5%

Party	Candidates	% Vote	Seats
UUP	3	26.9	2
SDLP	1	12.3	0
DUP	3	44.2	3
Ind	3	16.6	
Total	**10**	**100**	**5**

Candidate	Party	1st Pref Votes	Elected
Jeffrey Balmer	Ind	125	
Cecil Cousley	DUP	788	1st Count
William Johnston	UUP	257	
Anne Logan	Ind	119	
Justin McCamphill	SDLP	459	
Thomas McKeown	UUP	396	3rd Count
James Simpson	UUP	351	5th Count
Ian Stevenson	DUP	433	4th Count
Robert Storey	DUP	429	4th Count
Jim Wright	Ind	376	

Bann Valley (6 seats)

Electorate	7451	Valid Vote	5220
Quota	746	Turnout	71.7%

Party	Candidates	% Vote	Seats
UUP	2	18.6	1
SDLP	2	20.1	1
DUP	3	39.7	3
SF	1	21.5	1
Total	**8**	**100**	**6**

Candidate	Party	1st Pref Votes	Elected
John Finlay	DUP	859	1st Count
Joseph Gaston	UUP	711	3rd Count
Robert Halliday	DUP	675	4th Count
Malachy McCamphill	SDLP	663	2nd Count
Philip McGuigan	SF	1123	1st Count
Paddy O'Kane	SDLP	388	
John Watt	UUP	261	
Robert Wilson	DUP	540	5th Count

Bushvale (5 seats)

Electorate	5706	Valid Vote	3605
Quota	601	Turnout	63.2%

Party	Candidates	% Vote	Seats
UUP	2	27.8	2
SDLP	2	19.4	1
DUP	2	44.0	2
SF	1	8.8	
Total	**7**	**100**	**5**

Candidate	Party	1st Pref Votes	Elected
Frank Campbell	DUP	589	2nd Count
Harry Connolly	SDLP	548	3rd Count
Bill Kennedy	DUP	997	1st Count
William Logan	UUP	457	3rd Count
Francis McCluskey	SDLP	151	
Sean McErlain	SF	318	
John Ramsay	UUP	545	3rd Count

Banbridge District Council

Banbridge District Council has 17 councillors and 3 DEAs as follows: Banbridge Town 6 seats; Dromore 5 seats; Knockiveag 6 seats.

Summary of council

Electorate 30293 Valid Vote 20568 Turnout 67.9%

Party	% Vote	Seats
UUP	**37**	**7**
SDLP	**19**	**3**
DUP	**28**	**5**
SF	**4**	**0**
All	**2**	**1**
Others	**10**	**1**
Total	**100**	**17**

Banbridge Town (6 seats)

Electorate	10939	Valid Vote	7054
Quota	1008	Turnout	65.6%

Party	Candidates	% Vote	Seats
UUP	3	41.4	3
SDLP	1	19.9	1
DUP	2	20.9	1
UKUP	1	5.5	
All	1	6.0	1
Ind	1	6.3	
Total	**9**	**100**	**6**

Candidate	Party	1st Pref Votes	Elected
Joan Baird	UUP	1979	1st Count
Derek Bell	UUP	458	2nd Count
Ian Burns	UUP	485	6th Count
Frank Downey	Ind	448	
Kyle Ferguson	DUP	697	
David Hudson	UKUP	389	
Pat McAleenan	SDLP	1404	1st Count
Jim McElroy	DUP	774	6th Count
Frank McQuaid	All	420	5th Count

Dromore (5 seats)

Electorate	9149	Valid Vote	6129
Quota	1022	Turnout	68.1%

Party	Candidates	% Vote	Seats
UUP	2	29.2	2
SDLP	1	19.6	1
DUP	2	39.3	2
NIUP	1	0.7	
Ind	1	11.2	
Total	**7**	**100**	**5**

Candidate	Party	1st Pref Votes	Elected
Nora Beare	UUP	896	3rd Count
David Herron	DUP	1032	1st Count
Thompson Howe	Ind	685	
William Martin	UUP	894	3rd Count
Cassie McDermott	SDLP	1202	1st Count
Joe McIlwaine	NIUP	45	
Paul Rankin	DUP	1375	1st Count

Knockiveagh (6 seats)

Electorate	9937	Valid Vote	7385
Quota	1056	Turnout	75.4%

Party	Candidates	% Vote	Seats
UUP	3	31.2	2
SDLP	1	18.3	1
DUP	2	24.6	2
SF	1	10.2	
UKUP	1	5.3	
Ind	1	10.4	1
Total	**9**	**100**	**6**

Candidate	Party	1st Pref Votes	Elected
Stephen Briggs	UKUP	387	
Violet Cromie	UUP	486	
Brendan Curran	SF	755	
Seamus Doyle	SDLP	1351	1st Count
John Hanna	UUP	617	5th Count
Stephen Herron	DUP	735	5th Count
John Ingram	UUP	1202	1st Count
Malachy McCartan	Ind	768	5th Count
Wilfred McFadden	DUP	1084	6th Count

Belfast City Council

Belfast City Council has 51 councillors and 9 DEAs as follows: Balmoral 6 seats; Castle 6 seats; Court 5 seats; Lower Falls 5 seats; Upper Falls 5 seats; Laganbank 5 seats; Oldpark 6 seats; Pottinger 6 seats; Victoria 7 seats.

Summary of council

Electorate 167869 Valid Vote 122188 Turnout 72.8%

Party	% Vote	Seats
UUP	**18**	**11**
SDLP	**17**	**9**
DUP	**18**	**10**
SF	**28**	**14**
All	**7**	**3**
Others	**12**	**4**
Total	**100**	**51**

Court (5 seats)

Electorate	15674	Valid Vote	9752
Quota	1626	Turnout	64.3%

Party	Candidates	% Vote	Seats
UUP	2	23.1	1
DUP	2	34.1	2
SF	1	2.7	
UDP	1	17.8	1
UTW	1	0.3	
PUP	2	22.0	1
Total	**9**	**100**	**5**

Candidate	Party	1st Pref Votes	Elected
Fred Cobain	UUP	722	
Mick Conlon	SF	269	
David Kerr	UTW	28	
Frank McCoubrey	UDP	1732	1st Count
Chris McGimpsey	UUP	1527	1st Count
Elaine McMillen	DUP	720	5th Count
William Smyth	PUP	813	
Eric Smyth	DUP	2605	1st Count
Hugh Smyth	PUP	1336	5th Count

Laganbank (5 seats)

Electorate	17799	Valid Vote	10832
Quota	1806	Turnout	62.7%

Party	Candidates	% Vote	Seats
UUP	2	26.2	2
SDLP	2	28.8	2
DUP	1	8.1	
SF	1	16.2	1
All	1	7.6	
PUP	1	2.6	
Ind	2	2.5	
NIWC	1	6.5	
WP	1	1.5	
Total	**12**	**100**	**5**

Candidate	Party	1st Pref Votes	Elected
Jim Clarke	UUP	819	7th Count
Andrew Frew	Ind	141	
Mark Long	All	825	
Patrick Lynn	WP	158	
Patrick McCarthy	SDLP	1511	6th Count
Michael McGimpsey	UUP	2019	1st Count
Alex Maskey	SF	1748	5th Count
Anne Monaghan	NIWC	703	
Barbara Muldoon	Ind	128	
Peter O'Reilly	SDLP	1612	5th Count
Dawn Purvis	PUP	286	
Richard Scott	DUP	882	

Castle (6 seats)

Electorate	21068	Valid Vote	14132
Quota	2019	Turnout	68.8%

Party	Candidates	% Vote	Seats
UUP	1	11.0	1
SDLP	2	27.8	2
DUP	2	33.3	2
SF	1	14.1	1
All	1	6.9	
PUP	1	2.5	
Ind	2	2.0	
WP	1	0.6	
NIWC	1	1.8	
Total	**12**	**100**	**6**

Candidate	Party	1st Pref Votes	Elected
Alexander Blair	Ind	109	
David Browne	UUP	1550	8th Count
Elizabeth Byrne-McCullough	NIWC	253	
Thomas Campbell	All	984	
Janet Carson	PUP	352	
Patrick Convery	SDLP	1403	8th Count
Ian Crozier	DUP	759	2nd Count
Marcella Delaney	WP	84	
Nigel Dodds	DUP	3949	1st Count
Danny Lavery	SF	1991	3rd Count
Alban Maginness	SDLP	2520	1st Count
David Mahood	Ind	178	

Balmoral (6 seats)

Electorate	20958	Valid Vote	13614
Quota	1945	Turnout	66.2%

Party	Candidates	% Vote	Seats
UUP	2	19.7	1
SDLP	2	29.9	2
DUP	2	25.0	2
SF	1	9.9	
All	1	12.4	1
PUP	1	3.1	
Total	**9**	**100**	**6**

Candidate	Party	1st Pref Votes	Elected
Margaret Crooks	UUP	2276	1st Count
Thomas Ekin	All	1684	4th Count
Carmel Hanna	SDLP	3077	1st Count
John Hiddleston	UUP	411	
Stephen Long	SF	1349	
Catherine Molloy	SDLP	987	3rd Count
Thomas Morrow	PUP	421	
Ruth Patterson	DUP	1377	4th Count
Robert Stoker	DUP	2032	1st Count

Upper Falls (5 seats)

Electorate	22107	Valid Vote	15358
Quota	2560	Turnout	72.2%

Party	Candidates	% Vote	Seats
SDLP	2	28.5	1
SF	4	68.3	4
All	1	0.9	
NIWC	1	2.3	
Total	**8**	**100**	**5**

Candidate	Party	1st Pref Votes	Elected
Alex Attwood	SDLP	3260	1st Count
Mary Ayres	All	136	
Michael Browne	SF	2469	3rd Count
Mary Catney	NIWC	365	
Brian Heading	SDLP	1112	
Paul Maskey	SF	3349	1st Count
Chrissie McAuley	SF	1801	4th Count
Gerard O'Neill	SF	2866	1st Count

Lower Falls (5 seats)

Electorate	18349	Valid Vote	12648
Quota	2109	Turnout	72.1%

Party	Candidates	% Vote	Seats
SDLP	1	15.9	1
SF	5	80.2	4
WP	1	3.9	
Total	**7**	**100**	**5**

Candidate	Party	1st Pref Votes	Elected
Marie Cush	SF	2230	1st Count
Tom Hartley	SF	2351	1st Count
John Lowry	WP	488	
Fra McCann	SF	2399	1st Count
Sean McKnight	SF	1247	
Marie Moore	SF	1917	5th Count
Margaret Walsh	SDLP	2016	2nd Count

Oldpark (6 seats)

Electorate	23866	Valid Vote	15975
Quota	2283	Turnout	69.8%

Party	Candidates	% Vote	Seats
UUP	1	7.0	
SDLP	2	19.1	1
DUP	1	14.9	1
SF	4	46.8	3
All	1	1.0	
PUP	1	9.5	1
Ind	2	1.7	
Total	**12**	**100**	**6**

Candidate	Party	1st Pref Votes	Elected
James Bates	Ind	209	
Gerard Brophy	SF	2755	1st Count
Joleen Connolly	SDLP	1114	
Rene Greig	Ind	59	
William Hutchinson	PUP	1516	6th Count
Nelson McCausland	DUP	2392	1st Count
Margaret McClenaghan	SF	2467	1st Count
Thomas McCullough	All	160	
Martin Morgan	SDLP	1932	1st Count
Eoin O'Broin	SF	957	8th Count
Fred Proctor	UUP	1116	
Kathy Stanton	SF	1298	

Victoria (7 seats)

Electorate	28160	Valid Vote	16909
Quota	2114	Turnout	62.0%

Party	Candidates	% Vote	Seats
UUP	3	36.6	3
SDLP	1	1.8	
DUP	3	28.1	2
Cons	1	1.4	
All	2	22.8	2
PUP	1	4.1	
Ind	4	5.2	
Total	**15**	**100**	**7**

Candidate	Party	1st Pref Votes	Elected
Ian Adamson	UUP	3286	1st Count
David Alderdice	All	3119	1st Count
Wallace Browne	DUP	2492	1st Count
Alan Crowe	UUP	582	8th Count
Danny Dow	Ind	746	
Ciara Farren	SDLP	305	
Peter Gray	Cons	239	
Billy Hands	Ind	15	
Lawrence John	Ind	11	
Naomi Long	All	729	9th Count
Margaret McKenzie	DUP	783	
Robert Moorhead	PUP	697	
Robin Newton	DUP	1469	9th Count
Jim Rogers	UUP	2322	1st Count
Sammy Walker	Ind	114	

Pottinger

Electorate	21854	Valid Vote	12968
Quota	1853	Turnout	61.4%

Party	Candidates	% Vote	Seats
UUP	2	28.2	2
SDLP	1	3.5	
DUP	3	36.2	2
SF	1	9.7	1
All	1	5.3	
PUP	2	13.2	1
Ind	1	1.7	
UKUP	1	0.6	
WP	1	1.0	
Cons	1	0.6	
Total	**14**	**100**	**6**

Candidate	Party	1st Pref Votes	Elected
Joseph Bell	WP	129	
John Bushell	Ind	218	
Mary Campbell	DUP	577	
Margaret Clarke	UUP	559	10th Count
Jason Docherty	Cons	66	
Reg Empey	UUP	3097	1st Count
David Ervine	PUP	1582	3rd Count
David Fairfield	UKUP	74	
Mervyn Jones	All	693	
Joseph O'Donnell	SF	1264	10th Count
Robin Stewart	PUP	127	
Harry Toan	DUP	205	10th Count
Leo van Es	SDLP	459	
Sammy Wilson	DUP	3918	1st Count

Carrickfergus Borough Council

Carrickfergus Borough Council has a total of 17 councillors and 3 DEAs as follows: Carrick Castle 5 seats; Kilroot 6 seats; Knockagh Monument 6 seats.

Summary of council

Electorate 27257 Valid Vote 15418 Turnout 56.6%

Party	% Vote	Seats
UUP	24	4
SDLP	0	0
DUP	32	6
SF	0	0
All	24	5
Others	20	2
Total	100%	17

Carrick Castle (5 seats)

Electorate	6542	Valid Vote	3583
Quota	598	Turnout	54.8%

Party	Candidates	% Vote	Seats
UUP	1	12.1	1

DUP	2	31.4	2
PUP	1	7.3	
Ind	3	27.6	1
All	2	21.6	1
Total	**9**	**100**	**5**

Candidate	Party	1st Pref Votes	Elected
David Beck	PUP	259	
William Cameron	Ind	303	
Darin Ferguson	UUP	435	6th Count
William Hamilton	Ind	552	4th Count
Margaret Hawkins	All	112	
David Hilditch	DUP	996	1st Count
Patricia McKinney	DUP	130	6th Count
Sean Neeson	All	662	1st Count
Nicholas Wady	Ind	134	

Kilroot (6 seats)

Electorate	10903	Valid Vote	6184
Quota	884	Turnout	58.1%

Party	Candidates	% Vote	Seats
UUP	1	17.7	1
DUP	2	30.0	2
All	2	24.1	2
Ind	2	28.2	1
Total	**7**	**100**	**6**

Candidate	Party	1st Pref Votes	Elected
William Ashe	DUP	1425	1st Count
James Brown	Ind	1275	1st Count
Robert Cavan	All	684	4th Count
Terence Clements	DUP	430	2nd Count
Janet Crampsey	All	807	3rd Count
Sam Crowe	Ind	470	
Eric Ferguson	UUP	1093	1st Count

Knockagh Monument (6 seats)

Electorate	9812	Valid Vote	5651
Quota	808	Turnout	59.0%

Party	Candidates	% Vote	Seats
UUP	2	38.9	2
DUP	2	34.0	2
PUP	1	2.9	
All	2	24.2	2
Total	**7**	**100**	**6**

Candidate	Party	1st Pref Votes	Elected
May Beattie	DUP	1420	1st Count
Roy Beggs	UUP	1575	1st Count
Stewart Dickson	All	1165	1st Count
Carolyn Howarth	PUP	166	
James McClurg	DUP	501	3rd Count
Noreen McIlwrath	All	199	6th Count
Gwen Wilson	UUP	625	2nd Count

Castlereagh Borough Council

Castlereagh Borough Council has a total of 23 councillors and 4 DEAs as follows: Castlereagh Central 6 seats; Castlereagh East 7 seats; Castlereagh South 5 seats; Castlereagh West 5 seats

Summary of council

Electorate 48943 Valid Vote 30682 Turnout 62.7%

Party	% Vote	Seats
UUP	**22**	**5**
SDLP	**11**	**2**
DUP	**39**	**10**
SF	**2**	**0**
All	**15**	**4**
Others	**11**	**2**
Total	**100**	**23**

Castlereagh East (7 seats)

Electorate	15245	Valid Vote	9159
Quota	1145	Turnout	62.0%

Party	Candidates	% Vote	Seats
UUP	1	20.5	1
DUP	5	50.2	5
PUP	1	5.1	
Ind	2	9.8	
All	2	14.4	1
Total	**11**	**100**	**7**

Candidate	Party	1st Pref Votes	Elected
William Abraham	Ind	245	
David Drysdale	UUP	1879	1st Count
Claire Ennis	DUP	204	7th Count
Francis Gallagher	Ind	650	7th Count
Sandy Geddis	DUP	92	
Gillian Graham	All	400	
Richard Johnston	PUP	466	
Kim Morton	DUP	120	7th Count
Peter Osborne	All	923	3rd Count
Iris Robinson	DUP	4093	1st Count
Jim White	DUP	87	5th Count

Castlereagh South (5 seats)

Electorate	12212	Valid Vote	7992
Quota	1333	Turnout	66.8%

Party	Candidates	% Vote	Seats
UUP	2	27.0	2
SDLP	2	23.6	1
DUP	2	26.3	1
SF	1	5.0	
All	2	17.5	1
Cons	1	0.6	
Total	**10**	**100**	**5**

Candidate	Party	1st Pref Votes	Elected
John Beattie	DUP	1590	1st Count
Christine Copeland	SDLP	949	
Brian Hanvey	SDLP	940	9th Count
Michael Henderson	UUP	1725	1st Count
Roger Lomas	Cons	52	
Sean Hayes	SF	396	
Margaret Marshall	All	381	
Barbara McBurney	UUP	431	7th Count
Andrew Ramsey	DUP	509	
Geraldine Rice	All	1019	6th Count

Castlereagh West (5 seats)

Electorate	10958	Valid Vote	6830
Quota	1139	Turnout	64.0%

Party	Candidates	% Vote	Seats
UUP	1	25.3	1
SDLP	1	17.5	1
DUP	3	29.4	2
SF	1	2.3	
All	1	16.6	1
PUP	1	4.4	
NIWC	1	4.5	
Total	**9**	**100**	**5**

Candidate	Party	1st Pref Votes	Elected
Eileen Cairnduff	NIWC	306	
Sara Duncan	All	1130	2nd Count
Frederick Ferguson	PUP	301	
Cecil Hall	UUP	1728	1st Count
Rosaleen Hughes	SDLP	1196	1st Count
Sean Montgomery	SF	158	
Simon Robinson	DUP	1858	1st Count
Vivienne Stephenson	DUP	61	6th Count
Charles Tosh	DUP	92	

Castlereagh Central (6 seats)

Electorate	10528	Valid Vote	6701
Quota	958	Turnout	65.9%

Party	Candidates	% Vote	Seats
UUP	1	15.4	1
SDLP	1	6.4	
DUP	4	50.4	3
UKUP	1	4.3	
All	1	11.5	1
PUP	1	7.5	1
Ind	1	3.3	
Cons	1	1.2	
Total	**11**	**100**	**6**

Candidate	Party	1st Pref Votes	Elected
Joanne Bunting	DUP	302	2nd Count
Alan Carson	Ind	219	
Michael Copeland	UUP	1032	1st Count
Terence Dick	Cons	82	
Grant Dillon	UKUP	289	
John Dunn	DUP	74	
Michael Long	All	769	2nd Count
Sean Mullan	SDLP	427	
John Norris	DUP	161	2nd Count
Peter Robinson	DUP	2841	1st Count
Thomas Sandford	PUP	505	2nd Count

Coleraine Borough Council

Coleraine Borough Council has a total of 22 councillors and 4 DEAs as follows: Bann 6 seats; Coleraine Central 6 seats; Coleraine East 5 seats; The Skerries 5 seats.

Summary of council

Electorate 39018 Valid Vote 24495 Turnout 62.8%

Party	% Vote	Seats
UUP	**36**	**10**
SDLP	**20**	**4**
DUP	**28**	**7**
SF	**0**	**0**
All	**6**	**0**
Others	**10**	**1**
Total	**100**	**22**

Coleraine East (5 seats)

Electorate	8415	Valid Vote	4753
Quota	793	Turnout	57.8%

Party	Candidates	% Vote	Seats
UUP	2	26.7	2
SDLP	1	7.7	
DUP	3	44.2	3
All	1	5.8	
PUP	1	3.1	
Ind	3	12.5	
Total	**11**	**100**	**5**

Candidate	Party	1st Pref Votes	Elected
Toye Black	UUP	808	1st Count
Maurice Bradley	DUP	1389	1st Count
Alistair Crawford	Ind	149	
William Creelman	DUP	596	2nd Count
Phyllis Fielding	DUP	118	9th Count
David Gilmour	PUP	146	
Thomas Houston	Ind	319	
Martin Hunter	Ind	126	
Paddy McGowan	All	274	
Robert McPherson	UUP	460	8th Count
John Montgomery	SDLP	368	

Bann (6 seats)

Electorate	10232	Valid Vote	7383
Quota	1055	Turnout	73.7%

Party	Candidates	% Vote	Seats
UUP	3	34.0	3
SDLP	2	30.5	2
DUP	2	20.0	1
Ind	2	13.9	
All	1	1.6	
Total	**10**	**100**	**6**

Candidate	Party	1st Pref Votes	Elected
Robert Bolton	Ind	514	
Yvonne Boyle	All	116	
Olive Church	UUP	986	5th Count
John Dallat	SDLP	1714	1st Count
William King	UUP	821	6th Count
Reginald McAuley	Ind	512	
Adrian McQuillan	DUP	1216	1st Count
Eamon Mullan	SDLP	535	2nd Count
Hazel Sommers	DUP	265	
James Watt	UUP	704	6th Count

Coleraine Central (6 seats)

Electorate	11571	Valid Vote	6993
Quota	1000	Turnout	61.6%

Party	Candidates	% Vote	Seats
UUP	3	44.7	3
SDLP	1	17.6	1
DUP	2	30.4	2
All	1	7.3	
Total	**7**	**100**	**6**

Candidate	Party	1st Pref Votes	Elected
David Barbour	UUP	717	3rd Count
Timothy Deans	DUP	699	2nd Count
Elizabeth Johnston	UUP	1016	1st Count
David McClarty	UUP	1395	1st Count
James McClure	DUP	1426	1st Count
Gerry McLaughlin	SDLP	1232	1st Count
Eamon O'Hara	All	508	

The Skerries (5 seats)

Electorate	8800	Valid Vote	5366
Quota	895	Turnout	61.9%

Party	Candidates	% Vote	Seats
UUP	3	35.5	2
SDLP	1	18.4	1
DUP	2	19.3	1
All	1	12.7	
Ind	1	14.1	1
Total	**8**	**100**	**5**

Candidate	Party	1st Pref Votes	Elected
Christine Alexander	Ind	757	5th Count
Pauline Armitage	UUP	729	5th Count
Barbara Dempsey	All	681	
Alexander Gilkinson	DUP	359	
Norman Hillis	UUP	625	4th Count
Samuel Kane	UUP	552	
Billy Leonard	SDLP	988	1st Count
Desmond Stewart	DUP	675	2nd Count

Cookstown District Council

Cookstown District Council has a total of 16 councillors and 3 DEAs as follows: Ballinderry 6 seats; Cookstown Central 5 seats; Drum Manor 5 seats.

Summary of council

Electorate 23065 Valid Vote 18726 Turnout 81.2%

Party	% Vote	Seats
UUP	**21**	**3**
SDLP	**24**	**4**
DUP	**18**	**2**
SF	**33**	**6**
All	**0**	**0**
Others	**4**	**1**
Total	**100**	**16**

Cookstown Central (5 seats)

Electorate	7503	Valid Vote	5656
Quota	943	Turnout	77.0%

Party	Candidates	% Vote	Seats
UUP	2	27.6	1
SDLP	2	19.8	1
DUP	2	20.9	1
SF	2	31.7	2
Total	**8**	**100**	**5**

Candidate	Party	1st Pref Votes	Elected
Seamus Campbell	SF	364	6th Count
Peter Cassidy	SDLP	792	5th Count
Albert Crawford	UUP	238	
Hugh Davidson	DUP	120	
Eddie Espie	SDLP	328	
Ian McCrea	DUP	1064	1st Count
John McNamee	SF	1427	1st Count
Trevor Wilson	UUP	1323	1st Count

Ballinderry (6 seats)

Electorate	8938	Valid Vote	7421
Quota	1061	Turnout	84.8%

Party	Candidates	% Vote	Seats
UUP	2	17.2	1
SDLP	2	32.5	2
DUP	2	20.3	1
SF	2	30.0	2
Total	**8**	**100**	**6**

Candidate	Party	1st Pref Votes	Elected
Mary Baker	SDLP	641	2nd Count
Walter Greer	UUP	946	5th Count
Pearse McAleer	SF	1567	1st Count
Samuel McCartney	DUP	537	
Anne McCrea	DUP	969	5th Count
William McCollum	UUP	334	
Patsy McGlone	SDLP	1771	1st Count
Michael McIvor	SF	656	3rd Count

Drum Manor (5 seats)

Electorate	6624	Valid Vote	5649
Quota	942	Turnout	86.6%

Party	Candidates	% Vote	Seats
UUP	1	19.8	1
SDLP	1	15.6	1
DUP	1	13.4	
SF	2	39.0	2
Ind	1	12.2	1
Total	**6**	**100**	**5**

Candidate	Party	1st Pref Votes	Elected
Sam Glasgow	UUP	1118	1st Count
Dessie Grimes	SF	1233	1st Count
Maureen Lees	DUP	756	
James McGarvey	SDLP	884	2nd Count
Oliver Molloy	SF	969	1st Count
Sam Parke	Ind	689	5th Count

Craigavon Borough Council

Craigavon Borough Council has 26 councillors and 4 DEAs as follows: Central 7 seats; Loughside 5 seats; Lurgan 7 seats; Portadown 7 seats.

Summary of council

Electorate 56717 Valid Vote 39645 Turnout 69.9%

Party	% Vote	Seats
UUP	**28**	**8**
SDLP	**20**	**7**
DUP	**23**	**6**
SF	**21**	**4**
All	**2**	**0**
Others	**6**	**1**
Total	**100**	**26**

Central (7 seats)

Electorate	15747	Valid Vote	10633
Quota	1330	Turnout	67.5%

Party	Candidates	% Vote	Seats
UUP	4	29.5	2
SDLP	2	16.4	2
DUP	3	24.3	1
SF	2	16.9	1
All	1	3.6	
WP	1	1.2	
Ind	2	7.2	
Total	**15**	**100**	**6**

Candidate	Party	1st Pref Votes	Elected
David Calvert	Ind	761	
Kieran Corr	SDLP	745	Elected*
Frederick Crowe	UUP	802	9th Count
Alan Evans	Ind	96	
Tom French	WP	132	
Sean Hagan	All	379	
Audrey Lindsay	UUP	250	
Patricia Mallon	SDLP	996	7th Count
Samuel McCammick	UUP	396	
Francis Murray	SF	1198	6th Count
Robert Smith	DUP	810	Elected*
Woolsey Smith	DUP	1060	10th Count
Peter Toland	SF	602	
Kenneth Twyble	UUP	1694	1st Count
Denis Watson	DUP	712	

* *Elected without reaching quota*

Loughside (5 seats)

Electorate	12545	Valid Vote	8851
Quota	1476	Turnout	72.6%

Party	Candidates	% Vote	Seats
UUP	1	4.9	
SDLP	4	47.2	3
DUP	1	2.9	
SF	3	45.0	2
Total	**9**	**100**	**5**

Candidate	Party	1st Pref Votes	Elected
Alexander Dougan	DUP	261	
Dolores Kelly	SDLP	2022	1st Count
William Lindsay	UUP	433	
Maurice Magill	SF	1131	2nd Count
Mary McAlinden	SDLP	735	2nd Count
Kieran McGeown	SDLP	360	
Sean McKavanagh	SDLP	1055	2nd Count
John O'Dowd	SF	1971	1st Count
Mairead O'Dowd	SF	883	

Lurgan (7 seats)

Electorate	14911	Valid Vote	10510
Quota	1314	Turnout	72.1%

Party	Candidates	% Vote	Seats
UUP	5	47.1	4
SDLP	1	7.6	1
DUP	2	33.3	2
SF	1	6.9	
Ind	1	1.2	
UKUP	1	3.9	
Total	**11**	**100**	**7**

Candidate	Party	1st Pref Votes	Elected
Jonathan Bell	DUP	1942	1st Count
Sydney Cairns	UUP	749	5th Count
Meta Crozier	UUP	965	3rd Count
Samuel Gardiner	UUP	1728	1st Count
William Grafton	Ind	130	
Mary McNally	SDLP	801	5th Count
Stephen Moutray	DUP	1555	1st Count
Matthew Rooney	SF	719	
George Savage	UUP	1237	2nd Count
William Tate	UUP	276	
David Vance	UKUP	408	

Portadown (7 seats)

Electorate	13514	Valid Vote	9651
Quota	1207	Turnout	73.2%

Party	Candidates	% Vote	Seats
UUP	4	26.9	2
SDLP	1	12.8	1
DUP	3	27.3	2
SF	2	20.2	1
All	1	2.8	
Ind	1	10.0	1
Total	**12**	**100**	**7**

Candidate	Party	1st Pref Votes	Elected
Sydney Anderson	UUP	883	8th Count
Alan Carson	DUP	213	9th Count
Ignatius Fox	SDLP	1233	1st Count
George Hatch	UUP	872	8th Count
Davy Jones	Ind	971	8th Count
Brian McKeown	SF	1348	1st Count
Noel Mercer	SF	604	
Mark Neale	UUP	462	
William Ramsey	All	266	
David Simpson	DUP	2352	1st Count
John Tate	DUP	67	
David Thompson	UUP	380	

Derry City Council

Derry City Council has 30 councillors and 5 DEAs as follows: Cityside 5 seats; Northland 7 seats; Rural 6 seats; Shantallow 5 seats; Waterside 7 seats.

Summary of council

Electorate 71476 Valid Vote 48045 Turnout 67.2%

Party	% Vote	Seats
UUP	**6**	**2**
SDLP	**43**	**14**
DUP	**14**	**4**
SF	**30**	**10**
All	**1**	**0**
Others	**6**	**0**
Total	**100**	**30**

Shantallow (5 seats)

Electorate	15381	Valid Vote	10228
Quota	1705	Turnout	68.6%

Party	Candidates	% Vote	Seats
SDLP	4	56.1	3
SF	4	38.6	2
Ind	1	5.3	
Total	**9**	**100**	**5**

Candidate	Party	1st Pref Votes	Elected
Mary Bradley	SDLP	2304	1st Count
Shaun Gallagher	SDLP	1287	3rd Count
Oliver Green	SF	1084	
Tony Hassan	SF	1237	4th Count
Charles McDaid	Ind	542	
Josephine McGinty	SF	384	
William O'Connell	SDLP	1135	5th Count
Ciaran O'Doherty	SDLP	1017	
Gearoid O'hEara	SF	1238	4th Count

Rural (6 seats)

Electorate	14409	Valid Vote	9829
Quota	1405	Turnout	69.0%

Party	Candidates	% Vote	Seats
UUP	2	16.6	1
SDLP	3	39.9	3
DUP	2	24.3	1
SF	2	16.5	1
All	1	1.7	
Total	**10**	**100**	**6**

Candidate	Party	1st Pref Votes	Elected
Thomas Conway	SDLP	1274	4th Count
Annie Courtney	SDLP	1444	1st Count
Andrew Davidson	UUP	1074	6th Count
Paul Fleming	SF	943	7th Count
Ernest Hamilton	UUP	554	
William Hay	DUP	1511	1st Count
Bill Irwin	DUP	879	
Brian Kelly	All	166	
James Kelly	SF	677	
Jim McKeever	SDLP	796	10th Count
Brenda Stevenson	SDLP	511	

City Side (5 seats)

Electorate	9244	Valid Vote	6627
Quota	1105	Turnout	75.0%

Party	Candidates	% Vote	Seats
SDLP	3	45.5	2
SF	4	51.1	3
Ind	1	3.4	
Total	**8**	**100**	**5**

Candidate	Party	1st Pref Votes	Elected
Jim Anderson	SF	989	5th Count
Liam Boyle	SDLP	629	
James Clifford	SDLP	1176	1st Count
Cathal Crumley	SF	1093	1st Count
Seana Deery	Ind	228	
Donncha MacNiallais	SF	618	
Barney O'Hagan	SF	684	6th Count
Pat Ramsey	SDLP	1210	1st Count

Waterside (7 seats)

Electorate	15882	Valid Vote	10354
Quota	1295	Turnout	66.6%

Party	Candidates	% Vote	Seats
UUP	3	13.9	1
SDLP	2	20.7	2
DUP	4	43.3	3
SF	2	12.7	1
All	1	2.6	
PUP	1	1.5	
Ind	2	5.3	
Total	**15**	**100**	**7**

Candidate	Party	1st Pref Votes	Elected
Colm Cavanagh	All	270	
Gregory Campbell	DUP	1887	1st Count
Mildred Garfield	DUP	710	11th Count
Joe Millar	DUP	1218	2nd Count
Drew Thompson	DUP	669	
Jim Guy	Ind	484	
William Webster	Ind	63	
Catherine Cooke	PUP	153	
Gerard Diver	SDLP	1330	1st Count
Anne-Marie McDaid	SDLP	817	11th Count
Lynn Fleming	SF	974	8th Count
Francis O'Deorain	SF	338	
Mary Hamilton	UUP	982	9th Count
Gordon Hill	UUP	98	
James McCorkill	UUP	361	

Northlands (7 seats)

Electorate	16402	Valid Vote	11007
Quota	1376	Turnout	69.1%

Party	Candidates	% Vote	Seats
SDLP	5	54.0	4
SF	4	39.0	3
Ind	4	7.0	
Total	**13**	**100**	**7**

Candidate	Party	1st Pref Votes	Elected
Daniel Bradley	Ind	82	
Colm Bryce	Ind	274	
Catherine Harper	Ind	14	
William Temple	Ind	407	
Sean Carr	SDLP	1157	5th Count
John Kerr	SDLP	1248	3rd Count
Joseph McClintock	SDLP	922	
Kathleen McCloskey	SDLP	1528	1st Count
Helen Quigley	SDLP	1087	5th Count
Maeve McLaughlin	SF	1240	4th Count
Gerry MagLochlainn	SF	938	
Mary Nelis	SF	980	4th Count
William Page	SF	1130	5th Count

Down District Council

Down District Council has 23 councillors and 4 DEAs as follows: Ballynahinch 5 seats; Downpatrick 7 seats; Newcastle 6 seats; Rowallane 5 seats.

Summary of council

Electorate 44909 Valid Vote 29883 Turnout 66.5%

Party	% Vote	Seats
UUP	**22**	**6**
SDLP	**41**	**10**
DUP	**14**	**2**
SF	**17**	**4**
All	**0**	**0**
Others	**6**	**1**
Total	**100**	**23**

Ballynahinch (5 seats)

Electorate	9997	Valid Vote	6868
Quota	1145	Turnout	70.1%

Party	Candidates	% Vote	Seats
UUP	3	24.0	1
SDLP	3	39.4	2
DUP	3	23.0	1
SF	1	13.6	1
Total	**10**	**100**	**5**

Candidate	Party	1st Pref Votes	Elected
William Alexander	DUP	593	
Harvey Bicker	UUP	790	6th Count
Francis Braniff	SF	937	6th Count
Francis Casement	SDLP	592	
John Cochrane	UUP	674	
Ann McAleenan	SDLP	962	3rd Count
Alan McIlroy	DUP	126	
John Reid	UUP	182	
Patrick Toman	SDLP	1150	1st Count
Jim Wells	DUP	862	5th Count

Rowallane (5 seats)

Electorate	10464	Valid Vote	6857
Quota	1143	Turnout	66.9%

Party	Candidates	% Vote	Seats
UUP	3	41.8	3
SDLP	2	25.1	1
DUP	2	26.2	1
SF	1	4.4	
Ind	1	2.5	
Total	**9**	**100**	**5**

Candidate	Party	1st Pref Votes	Elected
Robert Burgess	UUP	1113	3rd Count
Albert Colmer	UUP	1027	5th Count
William Dick	DUP	1198	1st Count
Anthony Lacken	SF	304	
James Marks	Ind	169	
EdDEA Rea	UUP	728	6th Count
Margaret Ritchie	SDLP	1440	1st Count
Kathleen Stockton	SDLP	279	
William Walker	DUP	599	

Downpatrick (7 seats)

Electorate	13109	Valid Vote	8428
Quota	1054	Turnout	66.1%

Party	Candidates	% Vote	Seats
UUP	1	9.3	1
SDLP	6	52.7	4
DUP	1	2.4	
SF	2	21.1	1
Ind	3	13.1	1
WP	1	1.4	
Total	**14**	**100**	**7**

Candidate	Party	1st Pref Votes	Elected
Raymond Blaney	Ind	835	9th Count
Peter Craig	SDLP	1077	1st Count
Dermot Curran	SDLP	1024	1st Count
John Doris	SDLP	852	7th Count
John Foster	DUP	203	
Helen Honeyman	Ind	101	
John Irvine	SDLP	233	
Liam Johnston	SF	633	
Gerry Mahon	SDLP	404	
Eamonn McConvey	SF	1147	1st Count
Jack McIlheron	UUP	782	9th Count
Patrick O'Connor	Ind	173	
Des O'Hagan	WP	115	
Ann Trainor	SDLP	849	7th Count

Newcastle (6 seats)

Electorate	11339	Valid Vote	7730
Quota	1105	Turnout	69.9%

Party	Candidates	% Vote	Seats
UUP	1	15.7	1
SDLP	4	44.6	3
DUP	1	9.0	
SF	2	27.6	2
Ind	1	3.1	
Total	**9**	**100**	**6**

Candidate	Party	1st Pref Votes	Elected
Willie Clarke	SF	1163	1st Count
Gerry Douglas	UUP	1211	1st Count
Peter Fitzpatrick	SDLP	700	3rd Count
David McAllister	Ind	243	
Francis McDowell	SF	972	4th Count
Charles McGrath	SDLP	438	
Carmel O'Boyle	SDLP	1000	3rd Count
Eamonn O'Neill	SDLP	1308	1st Count
Stanley Priestley	DUP	695	

Dungannon and South Tyrone Borough Council

Dungannon and South Tyrone Borough Council has a total of 22 councillors and 3 DEAs as follows: Blackwater 5 seats; Clogher Valley 5 seats; Dungannon Town 6 seats; Torrent 6 seats.

Summary of council

Electorate 34985 Valid Vote 27994 Turnout 80.0%

Party	% Vote	Seats
UUP	23	6
SDLP	17	4
DUP	18	3
SF	36	8
All	0	0
Others	6	1
Total	100	22

Torrent (6 seats)

Electorate	10314	Valid Vote	8390
Quota	1199	Turnout	83.0%

Party	Candidates	% Vote	Seats
UUP	1	10.8	1
SDLP	1	15.2	1
DUP	1	3.6	
SF	4	55.6	3
Ind	1	14.8	1
Total	**8**	**100**	**6**

Candidate	Party	1st Pref Votes	Elected
Norman Badger	UUP	910	5th Count
Jim Canning	Ind	1244	1st Count
Jim Cavanagh	SDLP	1274	1st Count
Desmond Donnelly	SF	944	6th Count
Brendan Doris	SF	985	
Michael Gillespie	SF	1336	1st Count
Robert McFarland	DUP	304	
Francis Molloy	SF	1393	1st Count

Blackwater (5 seats)

Electorate	8102	Valid Vote	6678
Quota	1114	Turnout	83.7%

Party	Candidates	% Vote	Seats
UUP	3	31.6	2
SDLP	1	14.2	1
DUP	2	29.6	1
SF	2	22.6	1
Total	**8**	**100**	**5**

Candidate	Party	1st Pref Votes	Elected
David Brady	UUP	669	
Roger Burton	DUP	991	7th Count
Patsy Daly	SDLP	948	3rd Count
James Ewing	DUP	985	
Phelim Gildernew	SF	1032	2nd Count
William Hamilton	UUP	775	6th Count
Derek Irwin	UUP	801	7th Count
Dominic Molloy	SF	477	

Clogher Valley (5 seats)

Electorate	7827	Valid Vote	6487
Quota	1082	Turnout	84.5%

Party	Candidates	% Vote	Seats
UUP	2	25.1	1
SDLP	2	23.0	1
DUP	2	21.7	1
SF	2	30.2	2
Total	**8**	**100**	**5**

Candidate	Party	1st Pref Votes	Elected
Donald Beatty	UUP	681	
Seamus Flanagan	SF	1159	1st Count
Anthony McGonnell	SDLP	1150	1st Count
Sean McGuigan	SF	799	6th Count
Johnston McIlwrath	DUP	816	4th Count
Robert Mulligan	UUP	951	5th Count
Thomas Murphy	SDLP	342	
David Robinson	DUP	589	

Dungannon Town (6 seats)

Electorate	8742	Valid Vote	6439
Quota	920	Turnout	74.7%

Party	Candidates	% Vote	Seats
UUP	2	24.8	2
SDLP	1	17.2	1
DUP	2	19.2	1
SF	2	30.3	2
Ind	1	8.5	
Total	**8**	**100**	**6**

Candidate	Party	1st Pref Votes	Elected
Walter Cuddy	UUP	853	5th Count
Gerry Cullen	Ind	549	
Vincent Currie	SDLP	1110	1st Count
Derek Greenaway	DUP	363	
John McLarnon	SF	1138	7th Count
Ken Maginnis	UUP	740	1st Count
Barry Monteith	SF	813	2nd Count
Maurice Morrow	DUP	873	4th Count

Fermanagh District Council

Fermanagh District Council has a total of 23 councillors in 4 DEAs as follows: Enniskillen 7 seats; Erne East 6 seats; Erne North 5 seats; Erne West 5 seats.

Summary of council

Electorate 42002 Valid Vote 32187 Turnout 76.6%

Party	% Vote	Seats
UUP	31	7
SDLP	19	4
DUP	12	2
SF	33	9
All	0	0
Others	5	1
Total	100	23

Erne East (6 seats)

Electorate 10700 Valid Vote 8678
Quota 1240 Turnout 82.6%

Party	Candidates	% Vote	Seats
UUP	2	27.0	2
SDLP	1	14.9	1
DUP	1	9.3	
SF	3	42.3	3
Ind	1	6.5	
Total	**8**	**100**	**6**

Candidate	Party	1st Pref Votes	Elected
Harold Andrews	UUP	1348	1st Count
Ruth Lynch	SF	1428	1st Count
Brian McCaffrey	SF	1191	2nd Count
Michael Phillips	Ind	559	
Fergus McQuillan	SDLP	1293	1st Count
Cecil Noble	UUP	998	Elected*
Tomas O'Reilly	SF	1050	4th Count
Paul Robinson	DUP	811	

** Elected without reaching quota*

Enniskillen (7 seats)

Electorate 13326 Valid Vote 9540
Quota 1193 Turnout 73.5%

Party	Candidates	% Vote	Seats
UUP	4	33.4	2
SDLP	2	17.8	1
DUP	2	12.6	1
SF	2	25.3	2
UKUP	1	1.9	
Ind	1	9.0	1
Total	**12**	**100**	**7**

Candidate	Party	1st Pref Votes	Elected
Frank Britton	SDLP	934	6th Count
Joe Dodds	DUP	1096	4th Count
Samuel Dunne	DUP	105	
Raymond Ferguson	UUP	1486	1st Count
Eamonn Flanagan	SDLP	766	
Patrick Gilgunn	SF	1070	3rd Count
Robert Irvine	UUP	709	8th Count
Basil Johnston	UUP	589	
Davy Kettyles	Ind	861	7th Count
Alan Madill	UKUP	182	
Gerry McHugh	SF	1339	1st Count
Barbara Stuart	UUP	403	

Erne West (5 seats)

Electorate 9196 Valid Vote 7299
Quota 1217 Turnout 81.2%

Party	Candidates	% Vote	Seats
UUP	2	24.8	1
SDLP	1	21.6	1
DUP	1	5.4	
SF	3	48.2	3
Total	**7**	**100**	**5**

Candidate	Party	1st Pref Votes	Elected
David Black	DUP	392	
Pat Cox	SF	1266	1st Count
Wilson Elliott	UUP	981	Elected*
Gerry Gallagher	SDLP	1578	1st Count
Stephen Huggett	SF	1111	Elected*
Robin Martin	SF	1139	Elected*
Derrick Nixon	UUP	832	

**Elected without reaching quota*

Erne North (5 seats)

Electorate 8880 Valid Vote 6670
Quota 1112 Turnout 76.6%

Party	Candidates	% Vote	Seats
UUP	3	38.5	2
SDLP	2	21.6	1
DUP	3	22.2	1
SF	1	17.7	1
Total	**9**	**100**	**5**

Candidate	Party	1st Pref Votes	Elected
Joe Cassidy	SF	1181	1st Count
Julie Dervan	SDLP	568	
Tom Elliott	UUP	1030	2nd Count
Billy Gilmore	DUP	277	
Bert Johnston	DUP	1113	1st Count
Bertie Kerr	UUP	854	Elected*
Caldwell McClaughry	UUP	685	
John O'Kane	SDLP	871	3rd Count
Billy Simpson	DUP	91	

**Elected without reaching quota*

Larne Borough Council

Larne Borough Council has a total of 15 councillors and 3 DEAs as follows: Coast Road 5 seats; Larne Lough 5 seats; Larne Town 5 seats.

Summary of council

Electorate 23136 Valid Vote 13819 Turnout 59.7%

Party	% Vote	Seats
UUP	**29**	**4**
SDLP	**10**	**2**
DUP	**29**	**5**
SF	**4**	**0**
All	**14**	**2**
Others	**14**	**2**
Total	**100**	**15**

Larne Lough (5 seats)

Electorate	8552	Valid Vote	5079
Quota	847	Turnout	61.2%

Party	Candidates	% Vote	Seats
UUP	3	38.4	2
DUP	2	35.5	2
All	1	23.1	1
Ind	1	3.0	
Total	**7**	**100**	**5**

Candidate	Party	1st Pref Votes	Elected
Roy Beggs	UUP	1248	1st Count
David Fleck	UUP	374	5th Count
John Hall	UUP	329	
John Mathews	All	1171	1st Count
Bobby McKee	DUP	1341	1st Count
Gregg McKeen	DUP	492	2nd Count
William Small	Ind	151	

Larne Town (5 seats)

Electorate	7463	Valid Vote	4435
Quota	740	Turnout	60.6%

Party	Candidates	% Vote	Seats
UUP	2	22.3	1
SDLP	1	12.9	1
DUP	2	21.2	1
SF	1	4.3	
PUP	1	2.4	
All	1	5.4	
Ind	4	31.5	2
Total	**12**	**100**	**5**

Candidate	Party	1st Pref Votes	Elected
William Adams	Ind	327	
William Adamson	PUP	107	
John Anderson	Ind	292	
Roy Craig	Ind	390	10th Count
James Dunn	UUP	804	2nd Count
Janette Graffin	SF	191	
Alastair Holden	DUP	165	
Robert Lyndsay Mason	Ind	389	10th Count
Jack McKee	DUP	776	2nd Count
Margaret Richmond	All	239	
Andrew Wilson	UUP	185	
Martin Wilson	SDLP	570	8th Count

Coast Road (5 seats)

Electorate	7121	Valid Vote	4305
Quota	718	Turnout	61.8%

Party	Candidates	% Vote	Seats
UUP	2	24.3	1
SDLP	1	17.4	1
DUP	2	28.8	2
SF	1	7.1	
All	1	13.7	1
Ind	1	8.7	
Total	**8**	**100**	**5**

Candidate	Party	1st Pref Votes	Elected
William Cunning	Ind	379	
Joan Drummond	UUP	614	5th Count
Winston Fulton	DUP	753	2nd Count
Martin Graffin	SF	305	
Geraldine Mulvenna	All	589	5th Count
Daniel O'Connor	SDLP	750	2nd Count
Rachel Rea	DUP	485	6th Count
Thomas Robinson	UUP	430	

Limavady Borough Council

Limavady Borough Council has a total of 15 councillors and 3 DEAs as follows: Bellarena 5 seats; Benbradagh 5 seats; Limavady Town 5 seats.

Summary of council

Electorate 21283 Valid Vote 15216 Turnout 71.5%

Party	% Vote	Seats
UUP	**15**	**3**
SDLP	**29**	**4**
DUP	**18**	**2**
SF	**25**	**4**
All	**0**	**0**
Others	**13**	**2**
Total	**100**	**15**

Limavady Town (5 seats)

Electorate	6877	Valid Vote	4720
Quota	787	Turnout	69.5%

Party	Candidates	% Vote	Seats
UUP	3	21.1	2
SDLP	2	22.7	1
DUP	1	30.3	1
SF	1	8.9	
Ind	1	13.6	1
UUAP	1	3.4	
Total	**9**	**100**	**5**

Candidate	Party	1st Pref Votes	Elected
Brian Brown	Ind	642	5th Count
Jack Dolan	UUP	383	4th Count
William Kennedy	UUP	241	
John Kerr	SDLP	530	
Dessie Lowry	SDLP	542	5th Count
Malachy O'Kane	SF	419	
John Rankin	UUP	372	4th Count
George Robinson	DUP	1430	1st Count
Alister Smyth	UUAP	161	

Benbradagh (5 seats)

Electorate	6750	Valid Vote	5037
Quota	840	Turnout	76.3%

Party	Candidates	% Vote	Seats
SDLP	2	21.0	1
SF	3	50.3	3
DUP	1	5.1	
UUAP	2	23.6	1
Total	**8**	**100**	**5**

Candidate	Party	1st Pref Votes	Elected
Anne Brolly	SF	1056	1st Count
Francis Brolly	SF	917	1st Count
Michael Coyle	SDLP	559	6th Count
Marion Donaghy	SF	559	6th Count
Boyd Douglas	UUAP	748	3rd Count
Mark Gibson	UUAP	442	
Gerard Lynch	SDLP	497	
John Murray	DUP	259	

Bellarena (5 seats)

Electorate	7656	Valid Vote	5459
Quota	910	Turnout	72.2%

Party	Candidates	% Vote	Seats
UUP	2	24.7	1
SDLP	3	41.2	2
DUP	1	18.8	1
SF	1	15.3	1
Total	**7**	**100**	**5**

Candidate	Party	1st Pref Votes	Elected
Michael Cartan	SDLP	845	1st Count
Joseph Cubitt	DUP	1027	3rd Count
Martin McGuigan	SF	833	3rd Count
John McKinney	SDLP	685	
Gerard Mullan	SDLP	721	3rd Count
William Smyth	UUP	641	
Edwin Stevenson	UUP	707	5th Count

Lisburn City Council

Lisburn City Council has 30 councillors and 5 DEAs as follows: Downshire 5 seats; Dunmurry Cross 7 seats; Killultagh 5 seats; Lisburn Town North 7 seats; Lisburn Town South 6 seats.

Summary of council

Electorate 75619 Valid Vote 46759 Turnout 61.8%

Party	% Vote	Seats
UUP	**35**	**13**
SDLP	**9**	**3**
DUP	**20**	**5**
SF	**16**	**4**
All	**11**	**3**
Others	**9**	**2**
Total	**100**	**30**

Lisburn Town North (7 seats)

Electorate	17506	Valid Vote	10773
Quota	1347	Turnout	62.5%

Party	Candidates	% Vote	Seats
UUP	3	44.0	4
DUP	2	17.1	1
SF	1	4.2	
All	1	17.7	1
Ind	3	11.7	1
UDP	1	5.3	
Total	**11**	**100**	**7**

Candidate	Party	1st Pref Votes	Elected
David Adams	UDP	577	
David Archer	UUP	1619	1st Count
James Armstrong	SF	451	
William Beattie	Ind	423	
David Craig	DUP	1036	7th Count
Ronnie Crawford	Ind	711	7th Count
Adrian Creighton	Ind	123	
William Watson	UUP	1190	3rd Count
William Leathem	DUP	808	
William Lewis	UUP	1183	4th Count
Trevor Lunn	All	1903	1st Count
Lorraine Martin	UUP	749	7th Count

Lisburn Town South (6 seats)

Electorate	12339	Valid Vote	7053
Quota	1008	Turnout	58.8%

Party	Candidates	% Vote	Seats
UUP	5	47.3	3
DUP	2	19.9	1
SF	1	3.5	
All	1	21.2	1
UDP	1	7.2	1
NIUP	1	0.9	
Total	**11**	**100**	**6**

Candidate	Party	1st Pref Votes	Elected
David Archer	UUP	721	7th Count
Seamus Close	All	1495	1st Count
Ivan David	UUP	1521	1st Count
Francis Kerr	SF	245	
Margaret Little	UUP	253	
Joe Lockhart	UUP	592	8th Count
Tom Mateer	UUP	246	
Gary McMichael	UDP	509	Elected*
Paul Porter	DUP	1061	1st Count
Allen Russell	DUP	346	
Gary Teeney	NIUP	64	

**Elected without reaching quota*

Downshire (5 seats)

Electorate	12983	Valid Vote	8483
Quota	1414	Turnout	66.3%

Party	Candidates	% Vote	Seats
UUP	3	43.7	3
DUP	2	31.1	1
SF	1	1.3	
All	1	14.1	1
Ind	1	7.2	
Cons	1	2.6	
Total	**9**	**100**	**5**

Candidate	Party	1st Pref Votes	Elected
James Baird	UUP	1507	1st Count
William Bleakes	Ind	609	
Elizabeth Campbell	All	1201	4th Count
Allan Ewart	DUP	632	
William Falloon	UUP	1007	Elected*
Joanne Johnston	Cons	217	
Cara McCann	SF	111	
Edwin Poots	DUP	2006	1st Count
William Ward	UUP	1193	4th Count

**Elected without reaching quota*

Dunmurry Cross (7 seats)

Electorate	18673	Valid Vote	11591
Quota	1449	Turnout	64.4%

Party	Candidates	% Vote	Seats
UUP	1	13.4	1
SDLP	2	23.0	2
DUP	1	7.8	
SF	5	53.9	4
Green	1	1.9	
Total	**10**	**100**	**7**

Candidate	Party	1st Pref Votes	Elected
William Bell	UUP	1550	1st Count
Paul Butler	SF	2061	1st Count
Michael Ferguson	SF	1549	1st Count
Paul Flynn	SF	422	
Patricia Lewsley	SDLP	2029	1st Count
Malachy McAnespie	Green	218	
Billy McDonnell	SDLP	640	6th Count
Stephen Moore	DUP	910	
Sue Ramsey	SF	1219	6th Count
Veronica Willis	SF	993	6th Count

Killultagh (5 seats)

Electorate	14118	Valid Vote	8859
Quota	1477	Turnout	63.9%

Party	Candidates	% Vote	Seats
UUP	3	35.2	2
SDLP	1	14.9	1
DUP	2	29.9	2
SF	1	5.2	
All	2	6.4	
Ind	1	3.7	
Cons	1	4.7	
Total	**11**	**100**	**5**

Candidate	Party	1st Pref Votes	Elected
Cecil Calvert	DUP	1382	7th Count
Jim Dillon	UUP	1923	1st Count
Alison Gawith	All	439	
Owen Gawith	All	131	
Ita Gray	SF	457	
Neil Johnston	Cons	419	
Samuel Johnston	UUP	537	Elected*
Peter O'Hagan	SDLP	1318	5th Count
Gordon Ross	Ind	332	
James Tinsey	DUP	1263	Elected*
Ken Watson	UUP	658	

**Elected without reaching quota*

Magherafelt District Council

Magherafelt District Council has 16 councillors and 3 DEAs as follows: Magherafelt Town 6 seats; Moyola 5 seats; Sperrin 5 seats.

Summary of council

Electorate 28033 Valid Vote 22453 Turnout 80.1%

Party	% Vote	Seats
UUP	**10**	**2**
SDLP	**20**	**3**
DUP	**21**	**3**
SF	**44**	**7**
All	**0**	**0**
Others	**5**	**1**
Total	**100**	**16**

Magherafelt Town (6 seats)

Electorate	10509	Valid Vote	8026
Quota	1147	Turnout	77.6%

Party	Candidates	% Vote	Seats
UUP	1	13.7	1
SDLP	2	21.0	1
DUP	2	30.6	2
SF	2	34.7	2
Total	**7**	**100**	**6**

Candidate	Party	1st Pref Votes	Elected
John Kelly	SF	1700	1st Count
Joseph McBride	SDLP	990	4th Count
Rev William McCrea	DUP	2255	1st Count
Paul McClean	DUP	197	2nd Count
Seamus O'Brien	SF	1085	3rd Count
George Shiels	UUP	1103	2nd Count
Frances Symington	SDLP	696	

Sperrin (5 seats)

Electorate	8941	Valid Vote	7478
Quota	1247	Turnout	85.3%

Party	Candidates	% Vote	Seats
SDLP	2	22.5	1
DUP	1	9.7	
SF	3	56.0	3
Ind	1	10.4	1
WP	1	1.4	
Total	**8**	**100**	**5**

Candidate	Party	1st Pref Votes	Elected
Francis Donnelly	WP	104	
Patrick Groogan	SF	1651	1st Count
John Kerr	SF	1206	2nd Count
Kathleen Lagan	SDLP	1136	4th Count
Francis McKendry	SDLP	551	
Rodney Mitchell	DUP	723	
Robert Montgomery	Ind	776	Elected*
Hugh Mullan	SF	1331	1st Count

**Elected without reaching quota*

Moyola (5 seats)

Electorate	8583	Valid Vote	6949
Quota	1159	Turnout	82.8%

Party	Candidates	% Vote	Seats
UUP	1	17.8	1
SDLP	2	15.8	1
DUP	2	20.9	1
SF	2	42.5	2
Ind	1	3.0	
Total	**8**	**100**	**5**

Candidate	Party	1st Pref Votes	Elected
Thomas Catherwood	DUP	1023	4th Count
Elizabeth Forde	DUP	430	
Oliver Hughes	SF	1578	1st Count
Naaman Hutchinson	Ind	210	
John Junkin	UUP	1237	1st Count
Patrick McErlean	SDLP	713	3rd Count
James O'Neill	SF	1375	1st Count
Elizabeth Foster	SDLP	383	

Moyle District Council

Moyle District Council has 15 councillors and 3 DEAs as follows: Ballycastle 5 seats; Giant's Causeway 5 seats; The Glens 5 seats.

Summary of council

Electorate 11272 Valid Vote 7251 Turnout 64.3%

Party	% Vote	Seats
UUP	14	3
SDLP	23	4
DUP	21	3
SF	10	1
All	0	0
Others	32	4
Total	100	15

The Glens (5 seats)

Electorate	4037	Valid Vote	2750
Quota	459	Turnout	69.4%

Party	Candidates	% Vote	Seats
SDLP	3	29.8	2
SF	2	14.4	1
DUP	1	7.0	
Ind	4	48.8	2
Total	**10**	**100**	**5**

Candidate	Party	1st Pref Votes	Elected
Christine Blaney	SDLP	281	Elected *
Monica Digney	SF	216	Elected *
Anne McAuley	SF	178	
James McAuley	Ind	77	
Catherine McCambridge	SDLP	348	6th Count
James McCarry	Ind	279	
Randal McDonnell	Ind	316	6th Count
Archie McIntosh	SDLP	190	
Evelyn Robinson	DUP	194	
Oliver McMullan	Ind	671	1st Count

** Elected without reaching the quota*

Ballycastle (5 seats)

Electorate	4122	Valid Vote	2434
Quota	406	Turnout	61.3%

Party	Candidates	% Vote	Seats
UUP	1	15.6	1
SDLP	2	32.2	2
DUP	1	14.2	1
SF	1	12.2	
Ind	4	25.8	1
Total	**9**	**100**	**5**

Candidate	Party	1st Pref Votes	Elected
Madeline Black	SDLP	429	1st Count
Seamus Blaney	Ind	197	Elected *
Anna EdDEAs	Ind	40	
Helen Harding	UUP	379	4th Count
Gardiner Kane	DUP	345	Elected *
Liam McBride	Ind	202	
Chris McCaughan	Ind	189	
Michael Molloy	SDLP	357	4th Count
Charlie Neill	SF	296	

** Elected without reaching the quota*

Giant's Causeway (5 seats)

Electorate	3123	Valid Vote	2067
Quota	345	Turnout	67.7%

Party	Candidates	% Vote	Seats
UUP	2	30.0	2
SDLP	1	3.7	
DUP	3	47.5	2
Ind	2	18.8	1
Total	**8**	**100**	**5**

Candidate	Party	1st Pref Votes	Elected
Robert Chestnutt	DUP	228	
William Graham	UUP	398	1st Count
George Hartin	DUP	258	5th Count
David McAllister	DUP	495	1st Count
Price McConaghy	Ind	367	1st Count
Moira McGouran	SDLP	76	
Robert McIlroy	UUP	223	5th Count
Thomas Palmer	Ind	22	

Newry and Mourne District Council

Newry and Mourne District Council has 30 councillors and 5 DEAs as follows: Crotlieve 7 seats; The Fews 6 seats; The Mournes 5 seats; Newry Town 7 seats; Slieve Gullion 5 seats.

Summary of council

Electorate 61864 Valid Vote 45566 Turnout 73.7%

Party	% Vote	Seats
UUP	13	4
SDLP	36	10
DUP	6	1
SF	39	13
All	0	0
Others	6	2
Total	**100**	**30**

The Fews (6 seats)

Electorate	11457	Valid Vote	8890
Quota	1271	Turnout	79.6%

Party	Candidates	% Vote	Seats
UUP	2	22.0	2
SDLP	3	28.6	1
DUP	1	7.8	
SF	3	41.6	3
Total	**9**	**100**	**6**

Candidate	Party	1st Pref Votes	Elected
Craig Baxter	DUP	693	
John Feehan	SDLP	1071	2nd Count
Danny Kennedy	UUP	1231	3rd Count
Brendan Lewis	SF	1172	6th Count
Jimmy McCreesh	SF	1279	1st Count
Pat McGinn	SF	1243	2nd Count
Andy Moffett	UUP	727	4th Count
Angela Savage	SDLP	595	
Charlie Smyth	SDLP	879	

The Mournes (5 seats)

Electorate	10440	Valid Vote	7686
Quota	1282	Turnout	75.2%

Party	Candidates	% Vote	Seats
UUP	2	30.7	2
SDLP	2	27.0	1
DUP	2	25.4	1
SF	1	16.9	1
Total	**7**	**100**	**5**

Candidate	Party	1st Pref Votes	Elected
William Burns	DUP	1845	1st Count
Linda Burns	DUP	110	
Michael Cole	SDLP	1205	4th Count
Martin Cunningham	SF	1291	1st Count
Marian Fitzpatrick	SDLP	872	
Isaac Hanna	UUP	1178	2nd Count
Henry Reilly	UUP	1185	2nd Count

Slieve Gullion (5 seats)

Electorate	10524	Valid Vote	8168
Quota	1362	Turnout	80.2%

Party	Candidates	% Vote	Seats
SDLP	3	31.9	2
SF	4	68.1	3
Total	**7**	**100**	**5**

Candidate	Party	1st Pref Votes	Elected
Colman Burns	SF	1431	1st Count
John Fee	SDLP	1195	5th Count
Terry Hearty	SF	1283	3rd Count
Packie McDonald	SF	1415	1st Count
Mary McKeown	SDLP	568	
Elena Martin	SF	1436	1st Count
Pat Toner	SDLP	840	

Crotlieve (7 seats)

Electorate	15786	Valid Vote	11291
Quota	1412	Turnout	73.6%

Party	Candidates	% Vote	Seats
UUP	1	6.2	
SDLP	5	51.0	4
DUP	1	2.4	
SF	3	26.4	2
Ind	2	14.0	1
Total	**12**	**100**	**7**

Candidate	Party	1st Pref Votes	Elected
PJ Bradley	SDLP	2103	1st Count
Hugh Carr	SDLP	1189	2nd Count
Michael Carr	SDLP	714	8th Count
John McConnell	UUP	697	
Ruth McConnell	DUP	274	
Brendan Murney	SDLP	576	
Mick Murphy	SF	1743	1st Count
Ciaran Mussen	Ind	834	
Eamonn O'Connor	SF	428	
Josephine O'Hare	SDLP	1175	3rd Count
Michael Ruane	SF	807	8th Count
Anthony Williamson	Ind	751	8th Count

Newry Town (7 seats)

Electorate	13657	Valid Vote	9531
Quota	1192	Turnout	71.7%

Party	Candidates	% Vote	Seats
UUP	1	7.6	
SDLP	4	33.6	3
SF	4	45.5	3
Ind	2	13.3	1
Total	**11**	**100**	**7**

Candidate	Party	1st Pref Votes	Elected
Charlie Casey	SF	1119	6th Count
Brendan Curran	SF	1025	6th Count
Frank Feeley	SDLP	940	3rd Count
Davy Hyland	SF	1213	1st Count
John McArdle	SDLP	811	6th Count
Billy McCaigue	UUP	727	
Pat McElroy	SDLP	950	3rd Count
Peter McEvoy	SDLP	503	
Conor Murphy	SF	984	
Declan O'Callaghan	Ind	109	
Jack Patterson	Ind	1150	2nd Count

Newtownabbey Borough Council

Newtownabbey Borough Council has 25 councillors and 4 DEAs as follows: Antrim Line 7 seats; Ballyclare 5 seats; Macedon 6 seats; University 7 seats.

Summary of council

Electorate 58535 Valid Vote 35035 Turnout 59.9%

Party	% Vote	Seats
UUP	29	9
SDLP	6	2
DUP	27	8
SF	5	1
All	8	1
Others	25	4
Total	**100**	**25**

Antrim Line (7 seats)

Electorate	16969	Valid Vote	10467
Quota	1309	Turnout	63.2%

Party	Candidates	% Vote	Seats
UUP	3	27.2	2
SDLP	2	19.3	2
DUP	3	22.2	2
SF	2	13.3	1
All	1	5.2	
NIWC	1	2.9	
NIUP	1	4.0	
Ind	2	5.9	
Total	**15**	**100**	**7**

Candidate	Party	1st Pref Votes	Elected
James Beckett	Ind	228	
John Blair	Ind	389	
Norman Boyd	NIUP	418	
Joan Cosgrove	NIWC	299	
Janet Crilly	UUP	1704	1st Count
Nigel Hamilton	DUP	1350	1st Count
Ivan Hunter	UUP	607	8th Count
Arthur Kell	UUP	536	
Noreen McClelland	SDLP	887	10th Count
Tommy McTeague	SDLP	1128	10th Count
Briege Meehan	SF	754	10th Count
Liz Snoddy	DUP	337	
Arthur Templeton	DUP	640	10th Count
Pam Tilson	All	547	
Roisin McGurk	SF	643	

University (7 seats)

Electorate	16785	Valid Vote	9996
Quota	1250	Turnout	60.6%

Party	Candidates	% Vote	Seats
UUP	3	33.6	3
DUP	2	22.7	2
PUP	1	8.1	
NIUP	1	5.0	
CC	1	4.5	
UUAP	2	13.0	1
All	1	13.1	1
Total	**11**	**100**	**7**

Candidate	Party	1st Pref Votes	Elected
Fraser Agnew	UUAP	828	9th Count
Alister Bell	CC	447	
Billy Boyd	NIUP	504	
Lynn Frazer	All	1313	3rd Count
Barbara Gilliland	UUP	1351	3rd Count
Billy Greer	PUP	811	
Roger Hutchinson	DUP	1791	3rd Count
John Mann	DUP	479	9th Count
Ken Robinson	UUP	1535	3rd Count
John Scott	UUAP	469	
Vi Scott	UUP	468	9th Count

Ballyclare (5 seats)

Electorate	12666	Valid Vote	7548
Quota	1259	Turnout	61.1%

Party	Candidates	% Vote	Seats
UUP	4	42.8	3
DUP	2	38.3	2
PUP	1	3.3	
All	1	10.1	
Cons	1	2.2	
CC	1	3.3	
Total	**10**	**100**	**5**

Candidate	Party	1st Pref Votes	Elected
James Bingham	UUP	1192	3rd Count
Paul Girvan	DUP	2583	1st Count
Alan Greer	Cons	169	
Pamela Hunter	DUP	308	2nd Count
Norman Lavery	PUP	249	
Patrick McCudden	All	761	
Vera McWilliams	UUP	1231	2nd Count
Sharon Parkes	CC	247	
EdDEA Turkington	UUP	541	7th Count
Peter Walker	UUP	267	

Macedon (6 seats)

Electorate	12115	Valid Vote	7024
Quota	1004	Turnout	60.1%

Party	Candidates	% Vote	Seats
UUP	1	11.1	1
DUP	2	27.3	2
SF	1	5.0	
PUP	1	5.7	
All	1	2.5	
Ind	4	36.9	2
CC	1	2.3	
NRA	1	9.2	1
Total	**12**	**100**	**6**

Candidate	Party	1st Pref Votes	Elected
Andy Beattie	Ind	276	
Michael Campbell	All	173	
William DeCourcy	DUP	1355	1st Count
Kenneth Hunter	DUP	563	6th Count
Dougie Jamison	PUP	398	
Bob Kidd	Ind	378	
Tommy Kirkham	Ind	611	8th Count
Mark Langhammer	Ind	1326	1st Count
Victor Robinson	CC	160	
Kevin Vernon	SF	350	
Dineen Walker	UUP	784	7th Count
Billy Webb	NRA	650	7th Count

North Down Borough Council

North Down Borough Council has 25 councillors and 4 DEAs as follows: Abbey 6 seats; Ballyholme & Groomsport 7 seats; Bangor West 7 seats; Holywood 5 seats.

Summary of council

Electorate 56614 Valid Vote 32497 Turnout 57.4%

Party	% Vote	Seats
UUP	**27**	**8**
SDLP	**0**	**0**
DUP	**14**	**5**
SF	**0**	**0**
All	**18**	**5**
Others	**41**	**7**
Total	**100**	**25**

Holywood Ward (5 seats)

Electorate	10063	Valid Vote	6125
Quota	1021	Turnout	62.1%

Party	Candidates	% Vote	Seats
UUP	2	30.0	2
DUP	1	15.0	1
PUP	1	2.0	
All	2	24.5	1
NIWC	1	8.3	
Ind	2	17.1	1
Cons	1	3.1	
Total	**10**	**100**	**5**

Candidate	Party	1st Pref Votes	Elected
Lindsay Cumming	Cons	188	
Gordon Dunne	DUP	916	4th Count
Norma Heaton	NIWC	509	
Robert Irvine	Ind	232	
Ellie McKay	UUP	1346	1st Count
Susan O'Brien	All	1070	1st Count
Denis Ogborn	Ind	815	6th Count
Diana Peacock	UUP	491	6th Count
David Rose	PUP	122	
Larry Thompson	All	436	

Ballyholme & Groomsport (7 seats)

Electorate	17348	Valid Vote	1(028)7
Quota	1286	Turnout	60.4%

Party	Candidates	% Vote	Seats
UUP	3	23.7	2
DUP	1	11.3	1
PUP	1	0.9	
UKUP	2	8.1	
NIUP	1	1.4	
NIWC	1	6.4	1
All	2	12.4	1
Ind	3	35.8	2
Total	**14**	**100**	**7**

Candidate	Party	1st Pref Votes	Elected
Alan Chambers	Ind	2099	1st Count
Leslie Cree	UUP	1631	1st Count
Alexander Easton	DUP	1164	4th Count
Marsden Fitzsimons	All	939	8th Count
Arthur Gadd	UUP	202	
Henry Gordon	UKUP	571	
Ian Henry	UUP	601	9th Count
Brian Lacey	PUP	90	
Austen Lennon	Ind	1363	1st Count
Elizabeth Roche	NIUP	140	
Ernest Steele	Ind	218	
Joseph Teggart	UKUP	276	
Gavin Walker	All	336	
Patricia Wallace	NIWC	657	11th Count

Abbey (6 seats)

Electorate	13455	Valid Vote	6975
Quota	997	Turnout	53.7%

Party	Candidates	% Vote	Seats
UUP	2	30.0	2
DUP	2	22.4	2
PUP	1	6.0	
NIUP	1	0.7	
UKUP	1	13.1	1
All	1	17.1	1
Cons	1	2.7	
Ind	3	8.0	
Total	**12**	**100**	**6**

Candidate	Party	1st Pref Votes	Elected
Christopher Carter	Ind	175	
Ruby Cooling	DUP	1263	1st Count
Irene Cree	UUP	1246	1st Count
Stewart Currie	PUP	417	
Colin Dean	NIUP	48	
Roberta Dunlop	UUP	843	3rd Count
Stephen Farry	All	1195	1st Count
Lisa Fleming	Cons	191	
William Gordon	Ind	89	
Valerie Kinghan	UKUP	912	5th Count
Karl McLean	Ind	297	
John Montgomery	DUP	299	10th Count

Bangor West (7 seats)

Electorate	15748	Valid Vote	9110
Quota	1139	Turnout	59.2%

Party	Candidates	% Vote	Seats
UUP	3	27.7	2
DUP	1	10.9	1
PUP	1	5.9	
UKUP	2	14.0	1
Cons	1	1.9	
All	2	19.1	2
Ind	1	20.5	1
Total	**11**	**100**	**7**

Candidate	Party	1st Pref Votes	Elected
Roy Davies	UUP	796	7th Count
Alan Field	UKUP	599	
Alan Graham	DUP	989	6th Count
Tony Hill	All	630	7th Count
Bill Keery	UKUP	676	7th Count
James Rea	PUP	538	
Julian Robertson	Cons	172	
Marion Smith	UUP	1311	1st Count
Evan Ward	UUP	416	
Anne Wilson	All	1112	2nd Count
Brian Wilson	Ind	1871	1st Count

Omagh District Council

Omagh District Council has 21 councillors and 3 DEAs as follows: Mid Tyrone 7 seats; Omagh Town 7 seats; West Tyrone 7 seats

Summary of council

Electorate 33462 Valid Vote 26634 Turnout 79.6%

Party	% Vote	Seats
UUP	16	3
SDLP	22	6
DUP	13	2
SF	40	8
All	0	0
Others	9	2
Total	100	21

Mid Tyrone (7 seats)

Electorate	11421	Valid Vote	9551
Quota	1194	Turnout	85.4%

Party	Candidates	% Vote	Seats
UUP	1	12.4	1
SDLP	2	20.8	2
DUP	1	10.3	4
SF	5	56.5	
Total	**9**	**100**	**7**

Candidate	Party	1st Pref Votes	Elected
John Clarke	SF	1446	1st Count
Damien Curran	SF	1244	1st Count
Barney McAleer	SF	917	2nd Count
Michael McAnespie	SF	995	2nd Count
Cathal McCrory	SF	791	
Samuel McFarland	DUP	984	
Gerry O'Doherty	SDLP	994	4th Count
Seamus Shields	SDLP	989	4th Count
Robert Wilson	UUP	1191	4th Count

Omagh Town (7 seats)

Electorate	11036	Valid Vote	7976
Quota	998	Turnout	74.3%

Party	Candidates	% Vote	Seats
UUP	2	14.6	1
SDLP	3	22.7	2
DUP	2	15.8	1
SF	2	23.6	1
Ind	3	23.2	2
Total	**12**	**100**	**7**

Candidate	Party	1st Pref Votes	Elected
John Anderson	UUP	552	
Sean Begley	SF	1123	1st Count
Joe Byrne	SDLP	1007	1st Count
Vincent Campbell	SDLP	178	
Josephine Deehan	SDLP	629	7th Count
Paddy Gallagher	SF	763	
Oliver Gibson	DUP	1087	1st Count
Thomas McCordick	DUP	171	
Patrick McGowan	Ind	1074	1st Count
Reuben McKelvey	UUP	614	4th Count
Johnny McLaughlin	Ind	759	5th Count
Kevin Taylor	Ind	19	

West Tyrone (7 seats)

Electorate	11005	Valid Vote	9107
Quota	1139	Turnout	84.4%

Party	Candidates	% Vote	Seats
UUP	2	19.8	1
SDLP	2	22.5	2
DUP	2	14.8	1
SF	4	38.4	3
WP	1	2.3	
Ind	1	2.2	
Total	**12**	**100**	**7**

Candidate	Party	1st Pref Votes	Elected
Thomas Buchanon	DUP	1093	4th Count
Stephen Harpur	DUP	257	
Peter Kelly	SF	839	6th Count
Damien McCrossan	SF	614	
Patrick McDonnell	SDLP	1372	1st Count
Barry McElduff	SF	1276	1st Count
Gerry McMenamin	Ind	202	
Liam McQuaid	SDLP	679	7th Count
Tommy Owens	WP	211	
George Rainey	UUP	1135	3rd Count
David Sterritt	UUP	666	
Patrick Watters	SF	763	7th Count

Strabane District Council

Strabane District Council has 16 councillors and 3 DEAs as follows: Derg 5 seats; Glenelly 5 seats; Mourne 6 seats.

Summary of council

Electorate 27312 Valid Vote 24162 Turnout 78.5%

Party	% Vote	Seats
UUP	**17**	**2**
SDLP	**19**	**4**
DUP	**19**	**3**
SF	**40**	**7**
All	**0**	**0**
Others	**5**	**0**
Total	**100**	**16**

Derg (5 seats)

Electorate	8455	Valid Vote	6800
Quota	1134	Turnout	82.0%

Party	Candidates	% Vote	Seats
UUP	2	24.6	1
SDLP	1	11.3	1
DUP	2	21.5	1
SF	3	42.5	2
Total	**8**	**100**	**5**

Candidate	Party	1st Pref Votes	Elected
Kathleen Allison	DUP	672	
Gerard Foley	SF	651	
Derek Hussey	UUP	1110	3rd Count
Thomas Kerrigan	DUP	793	6th Count
Eamonn McGarvey	SF	910	5th Count
Charlie McHugh	SF	1331	1st Count
Bernadette McNamee	SDLP	768	Elected*
Edward Tuner	UUP	565	

**Elected without reaching quota*

Glenelly (5 seats)

Electorate	7867	Valid Vote	6328
Quota	1055	Turnout	82.1%

Party	Candidates	% Vote	Seats
UUP	2	23.1	1
SDLP	1	17.9	1
DUP	2	34.6	2
SF	2	24.4	1
Total	**7**	**100**	**5**

Candidate	Party	1st Pref Votes	Elected
Allan Bresland	DUP	1313	1st Count
Martin Conway	SF	603	
Robert Craig	UUP	585	
John Donnell	DUP	879	2nd Count
James Emery	UUP	876	5th Count
Tom McBride	SDLP	1133	1st Count
Claire McGill	SF	939	6th Count

Mourne (6 seats)

Electorate	10990	Valid Vote	8334
Quota	1191	Turnout	77.6%

Party	Candidates	% Vote	Seats
UUP	1	5.3	
SDLP	3	27.1	2
DUP	1	4.9	
SF	4	50.3	4
Ind	2	12.4	
Total	**11**	**100**	**6**

Candidate	Party	1st Pref Votes	Elected
Ivan Barr	SF	1262	1st Count
Ann Bell	SDLP	438	8th Count
Daniel Breslin	SF	628	8th Count
Kathleen Craig	DUP	408	
Paul Gallagher	Ind	445	
Fred Hanry	SDLP	284	
Sam Martin	UUP	439	
Brian McMahon	SF	977	7th Count
Eugene McMenamin	SDLP	1538	1st Count
Jarlath McNulty	SF	1326	1st Count
James O'Kane	Ind	589	

Local Government Associations & Representative Groups

With the existence of 26 local authorities in Northern Ireland, there are many opportunities for the sector to work collectively across different areas. Some of the main representative local government organisations are listed below.

Best Value Forum
Chairman: John Dempsey
C/o Ballymoney Borough Council
14 Charles Street
Tel: 028 2766 2280
Fax: 028 2766 5150

Emergency Planning Group
Chairman: Mervyn Rankin
C/o Ballymena Borough Council
80 Galgorm Road
Ballymena, BT42 1AB
Tel: 028 2566 0300
Fax: 028 2566 0400

Local Economic Development (Northern Ireland) Forum

Contact: Liam Hannaway
Banbridge District Council
Downshire Road
Banbridge, BT32 3JY
Tel: 028 4066 0600

Local Government Staff Commission for Northern Ireland (LGSC)

Commission House
18-22 Gordon Street
Belfast, BT1 2LG
Tel: 028 9031 3200
Fax: 028 9031 3151
Chief Executive: Adrian Kerr

National Association of Councillors (NAC)

Chairman: Patsy McGlone
C/o Cookstown District Council
12 Burn Road
Cookstown, BT80 8DT
Tel: 028 8676 2205

Northern Ireland Joint Council for Local Government Services (NIJC)

Employers' Secretary: John Adams
Philip House
123 York Street
Belfast, BT15 1AB
Tel: 028 9024 9286
Fax: 028 9023 3328

Northern Ireland Local Government Association (NILGA)

Philip House
123 York Street
Belfast, BT15 1AB
Tel: 028 9024 9286
Fax: 028 9023 3328
Chief Executive: Heather Moorhead
President: Cllr Pat Mallon

Northern Ireland Local Government Officers Superannuation Committee (NILGOSC)

411 Holywood Road
Belfast, BT4 2LP
Tel: 028 9076 8025
Fax: 028 9076 8790
Web: www.nilgosc.org.uk
Email: info@nilgosc.org.uk
Chairman: John Galbraith

Society of Local Authority Chief Executives (SoLACE)

Chairman: Norman Dunn
C/o Newtownabbey Borough Council
Mossley Mill
Newtownabbey, BT36 5QA
Tel: 028 9034 2000
Fax: 028 9034 0200

Chapter

Health, Social Services and Housing in Northern Ireland

Overview of Health in Northern Ireland

The administration and delivery of health services is a hugely challenging undertaking in Northern Ireland as elsewhere. Surveys show it is something the general public cares deeply about and in recent years has become an increasingly important priority for government. In Northern Ireland the Department of Health Social Services and Public Safety is by far the government's biggest spending Department with an allocation in excess of £2.9bn.

Yet long waiting lists, hospital bed shortages, cancelled operations and reports of patients on trolleys in hospital corridors have become a familiar element of daily news coverage not only in the UK but also in Northern Ireland. It is no surprise therefore that, alongside public concern about the state of the health service in Northern Ireland there has been a steady growth in public investment in health with further increases promised.

This chapter sets out the main structures for the provision of healthcare, social services and housing in Northern Ireland, the challenges facing the current system and provides a detailed insight into the government's plans for improvement in the provision of local health care services. It begins with a status-take on health in Northern Ireland and an overview of some of the inequalities and problems.

Life Expectancy

Despite improvements in the last century, in comparison to the rest of Europe Northern Ireland's health record remains consistently poor. Whilst life expectancy rates have improved significantly, Northern Ireland lags behind European life expectancy norms and continues to lead the rankings in international league tables of the major diseases including cancer and coronary heart disease.

Table 5.1 Life Expectancy Rates in Northern Ireland

Expectation of Life

	At Birth		At Age 1 Year		At Age 65 Years	
Period	Male	Female	Male	Female	Male	Female
1900-02	47.1	46.7	-	-	10.5	10.4
1950-52	65.5	68.8	67.5	70.3	12.1	13.5
1975-77	67.5	73.8	67.9	74.1	11.8	15.3
1985-87	70.9	77.1	70.6	76.8	13.2	16.9
1999-01	74.8	79.8	74.3	79.2	15.3	18.5

Source: NISRA

Table 5.1 above shows the long-term improvement in life expectancy in Northern Ireland

The overall gradual improvements in life expectancy conceal a clear pattern of difference that exists between the life expectancy of those in high-income groups against those in lower socio-economic brackets.

Nonetheless life expectancy in Northern Ireland is expected to continue to improve in the period ahead. Life expectancy for a baby boy born in 2010 will be 76.8 and for a baby girl 81.3 according to the latest government projections.

Infant Mortality

Deaths in the first year of life are often regarded as a fair reflection of the overall health status of a population.

As Table 5.2 below indicates, infant mortality rates have fallen gradually for many years and reached on all-time low of 5 per 1000 births in 2000. Although there was an increase to 6 in 2001 the absolute number of deaths was small and year-to-year fluctuations can vary the rate considerably. It is worth noting that multiple births are a risk factor for infant deaths and these have been increasing, mainly due to increased use of fertility treatments. Also the age of the mother is a risk factor and proportionately more babies are now being born to older mothers. The main causes of death in infancy are conditions associated with premature birth, low birth weight and congenital malformations. However Northern Ireland continues to experience levels of infant mortality above the European average.

Table 5.2 Infant Mortality in Northern Ireland 1986-2001

Year	Number	Rate
1986	286	10.2
1990	198	7.5
1994	147	6.1
1998	134	5.6
2001	134	6.0

Source: NISRA (Report of the Chief Medical Officer 2002)

Main Causes of Death and Ill Health

Heart disease, cancer and respiratory disease account for 65 per cent of all adult deaths with suicides, accidents, strokes and other causes accounting for the remaining 35 per cent. Long standing illness is recognised as a measure of poor health in the community. It was found in the 2000/01 Continuous Household Survey that 33 per cent of men and 36 per cent of women in Northern Ireland had a long-standing illness.

Table 5.3 Main Causes of Death and Ill Health in Northern Ireland 2001

Coronary Heart Disease	22%
Respiratory Disease	20%
Stroke	10%
Cancer	24%
Accidents	2%
Suicide	1%
Other	21%

Source: NISRA/DHSSPS

The Royal Victoria Hospital, Belfast

Heart Disease and Cancer

Heart Disease and Cancer continue to be the major causes of death in adults. Heart Disease is the second most frequent cause of death in Northern Ireland. Statistics in relation to cancer show that:

- More than one-third of the population will suffer from a form of cancer during their lifetime;
- Men have a one in six chance and women a one in eight chance of dying from cancer before the age of 75;
- 800 people are killed by lung cancer each year which accounts for one quarter of cancer deaths In the under 75s;
- Breast cancer accounts for one in three cancer cases amongst women.

In the past pneumonia has often been found to be a major cause of death in Northern Ireland. However in many cases pneumonia is a complication of an underlying condition such as cancer, stroke or dementia, which are the real cause of death.

The concept of potential years of life lost (PYLL) is used to measure the contribution made by specific causes of death before age 75. The two main contributors to PYLL are cancer and coronary heart disease. Another significant contributor in Northern Ireland is suicide where although the number of deaths is low relative to the number caused by diseases the contribution to years of life lost is high because suicide often occurs at a young age. Suicide in Northern Ireland is high in comparison to European norms and its incidence is concentrated among males – particularly in younger age groups. Of 502 suicides occurring in Northern Ireland in the period 1998-2001 nearly 30% had been in contact with mental health services in the previous year.

Smoking and Obesity

Smoking is identified as the single greatest cause of premature death and is estimated to cause approximately 3,000 deaths per annum in Northern Ireland. Compared to other members of the European Union Northern Ireland has the second highest percentage of 13 year olds reported to smoke daily and the fourth highest rate of 14 year olds.

Statistics show that although overall smoking rates have fallen over the last fifteen years, this has not occurred to the same extent among the less well off where the levels of smokers remain at their highest.

The figures show that among men in professional and managerial occupations, 15 per cent smoke compared with 42 per cent of those who are unskilled. For women the figures are 16 per cent and 38 per cent respectively. 24 per cent of employed men smoke compared to 49 per cent of unemployed men and 26 per cent of employed women smoke as opposed to 45 per cent who are unemployed.

Obesity is a growing healthcare challenge in Northern Ireland. Surveys show that obesity is an increasing trend with predictions showing that by 2010, 23 per cent of women and 22 per cent of men will be obese. The rate of obesity amongst children is also increasing. It is estimated that over 450 deaths are caused, and 260,000 working days at a cost to the economy of £500 million are lost through the effects of obesity in Northern Ireland each year.

Alcohol and Drugs

Whilst the dangers associated with drugs misuse have a higher profile, the level and effects of alcohol abuse in Northern Ireland is much more significant in terms of the overall wellbeing of the population.

It is estimated that there are over 730 deaths per annum in Northern Ireland attributable to excess alcohol consumption. Statistics show that 82 per cent of men and 72 per cent of women are currently consumers of alcohol in Northern Ireland, and that 25 per cent of men and 14 per cent of women drink in excess of recommended limits.

Drugs misuse is often associated with aspects of deprivation, and lack of educational and employment prospects with their resultant negative social consequences. Drug misuse is also associated with crime, which has high costs for society affecting both victims and the community.

Drug misusers place additional burdens on the health social services and social security system. It is estimated that the costs of enforcement, prevention, treatment and rehabilitation are £8 million per annum whilst it is estimated that drug misuse itself results in additional costs of £300-500 million per annum to society in Northern Ireland.

Accidents and Road Traffic Incidents

Accidents and road traffic incidents are a major cause of death in Northern Ireland. Home accidents account for 41 per cent of the total of all accidents and there is a significant statistical link between the nature of some accidents and socio-economic status. It is estimated that there are over 350 deaths and 150,000 injuries per annum equating to the loss of 180,000 working days and a cost to the economy of £370 million through accidental death and injury costs in Northern Ireland.

Disability

17 per cent of adults in Northern Ireland in comparison to 14 per cent in Britain have a disability. The violence of "the Troubles" resulting in many permanent injuries to victims is a significant factor in Northern Ireland's very high rate of disability. Lower income, social exclusion and limited access to services and transport are some of the additional challenges facing the disproportionately high disabled population.

Mental Health

Overall Northern Ireland's Chief Medical Officer has estimated that up to 300,000 of Northern Ireland's population will at any one-time experience poor mental health.

Increasingly the link between mental health and emotional well-being and chronic physical disease is being accepted. People who are unemployed are twice as likely to experience a mental health problem than those in employment and 60 per cent of women in the lowest social class group are likely to experience a form of neurotic disorder in comparison to those in the professional group.

Statistics from the 2001 Health and Social Well Being Survey indicated that 21 per cent of the population aged 16+ considered themselves to be depressed and a similar percentage had a potential psychiatric disorder

Suicide accounts for 1 per cent of deaths in Northern Ireland, one of the lowest rates in Europe, yet the trend is increasing with 163 registered deaths from suicide in 2000. It is estimated that 150 deaths and over 4,000 hospital admissions equating to 80,000 lost working days and a cost to the economy of £170 million are attributable to the effects of suicides and intentional self harm.

Domestic violence is the most common crime against women in Northern Ireland. It is acknowledged that the actual incidence of such violence is much higher than actually reported.

Children's Health

The differential in health status across social class can be seen in children from birth onwards. Babies in the lower socio-economic groups are more likely to have a low birth weight and die in infancy than the children of more affluent families. Infant mortality rates are nearly 50 per cent higher in the most deprived areas, compared to the least deprived. The proportion of children living in conditions of poverty is significantly higher, and over a quarter of children come from households dependent on Jobseeker's Allowance or Income Support.

Inequalities in health continue to be evident throughout childhood and in young adults. Rates of accidental injury and oral health provide clear examples of this. Accidents are a major cause of death and disability among children and young people. Children from less affluent areas are 15 times more likely to die in a house fire, 7 times more likely to die as a result of a road traffic accident, and 5 times more likely to be injured as pedestrians. These figures are of particular concern as the vast majority of accidents are preventable.

The Westminster Government has placed children at the centre of its anti-poverty strategy and in Northern Ireland a Children's Commissioner has been appointed to help focus policy more tellingly on the interests and needs of children.

Although there has been a gradual improvement in oral health over the past 5 years, the most recent surveys indicate that the general level of oral health in Northern Ireland is still considerably worse than in Britain and the rest of Ireland, particularly amongst children. Oral health demonstrates a stark gradient across social class, with the most deprived children experiencing four times more tooth decay than the most affluent. Children in schools in the North and West of Belfast experience more tooth decay than those in other parts of the greater Belfast area. This is one of the reasons for the proposed introduction of fluoride to the water supply, although there has been strong public opposition to the plan.

Elderly People

People aged 65 and over account for 13 per cent of the population of Northern Ireland; by 2015 this figure is projected to rise to 16 per cent of the population. Smaller families, the growth of the number of women in the workplace and a more mobile population has resulted in an ageing population with rising rates of long-standing illness. It is acknowledged that there is a direct relationship between low income in the elderly and reported levels of disability.

Factors Determining Health in Northern Ireland

The social, cultural, economic and physical environment determines the extent to which a population experiences relatively good or poor health. Many complex and interrelated factors have a role in determining health; these include:

- Disadvantage and social exclusion;
- Poverty;
- Unemployment;
- Low educational achievement;
- Poor social and community environment;
- Living conditions;
- Working conditions;
- The wider environment;
- Individual behaviour and lifestyle.

Disadvantage and Poverty

Disadvantage takes many forms, all tending to concentrate on the same cohort of people, having a long-term detrimental effect on their health. Poverty is acknowledged as the greatest risk factor for health. All the evidence points to quality of health having a strong correlation with levels of income. Recent research shows that 24 per cent of households in Northern Ireland live in poverty, a rise of 3 per cent since 1990. Over 40 per cent of single parents, 19 per cent of single pensioners and 18 per cent of couples with children in Northern Ireland have been defined as living in "absolute" poverty.

Unemployment

Unemployment is often the link between poverty, social exclusion and poor mental and physical health. Whilst levels of unemployment in Northern Ireland have fallen sharply, halving since the early 1990s there are still approximately 300,000 economically inactive people of working age, which is disproportionately high relative to the UK average.

Educational Attainment

There are strong links between levels of educational attainment and deprivation with the most deprived areas showing the lowest rates of educational achievement. According to the Department of Education almost a fifth of the workforce has no formal qualifications and 24% of the population of Northern Ireland has literacy or numeracy problems.

Homelessness

Homelessness is becoming an increasing problem in Northern Ireland and there is a strong link between homelessness and ill health. There were 16,426 homeless households in Northern Ireland in 2002-2003. This figure was a significant increase on the previous year's total of 14,164, and 12,694 the year before that. Northern Ireland has persistently high levels of homelessness running at rates some 50% above the United Kingdom average.
Housing condition is a major contributor to the quality of health.

The most recent survey of housing stock in Northern Ireland by the Housing Executive showed a high level of unfitness including many tenants without central heating. Issues in the wider environment also affect health and well being both directly and indirectly, including air and water quality.

Impact of Gender

The differences in men and women's health are striking, particularly once they reach middle and older age groups. Death rates are much higher in men in middle age and old age than in women in the same age groups, although this gap narrows in the over 80s. However, older women are far more likely than older men to report long-standing sickness and disability. Coronary heart disease is the cause of death in 1 in 3 males and 1 in 4 females, a major cause of mortality.

Geographical Factors

Inequalities are also evident on comparison of geographical locations. About 2000 lives could be saved each year if those living in the council districts with the highest death rates had the health status of those in the districts with the lowest death rates. The electoral wards with the highest death rates are also those with the highest levels of deprivation. This correlation is particularly striking for deaths from coronary heart disease.

Ethnic Minorities

Ethnic groups also suffer from inequalities in health compounded by difficulties accessing services including health and social care, education and language support. Northern Ireland has a number of ethnic minorities, the largest of which is the Chinese community, with approximately 8000 people.

The Travelling Community is recognised as an ethnic group having poorer than average health status. Average life expectancy for a traveller is typically 15 years less than that of a member of the settled community. Only one in 10 of the Traveller population is over 40 years old and only one in 100 over 65. Infant mortality rates in travellers are three times higher than the general population.

Teenage Parenthood

Northern Ireland has one of the highest rates of teenage pregnancy in Western Europe.

Teenage parenthood is recognised as both a cause and a consequence of disadvantage. Evidence demonstrates that levels of teenage pregnancy correlate with those areas of high deprivation.

Department of Health, Social Services and Public Safety

In Northern Ireland responsibility for health policy and provision falls under the Department of Health, Social Services and Public Safety. The stated mission of the department is "to improve people's health and social well-being". 1000 staff are directly employed by the department, 2000 by the Fire Authority and over 40,000 other staff within the health and social services sector. The annual budget for DHSSPS at nearly £3 billion is by far the biggest of any government department in Northern Ireland. The department has three main areas of responsibility:

• Health and Personal Social Services

Including policy and finance legislation for hospitals, family practitioner services and community health and social services;

• Public Health

Including policy, legislation and administrative action to promote and protect the health of the population; and

• Public Safety

Including responsibility for the policy and legislation for the Fire Services, Food Safety and emergency planning.

(For further information about departmental organisation and personnel see Chapter 3 Central Government Departments and Agencies beginning on page 176.)

Health Service Expenditure

Table 5.4 sets out the planned public expenditure on health in Northern Ireland over the next three years.

Table 5.4 Department of Health, Social Services and Public Safety Planned Expenditure 2003/04-2006/07

	2004-05	2005-06	2006-07
Objective A			
Policy Development	35.2	36.5	40.3
Total Objective A	35.2	36.5	40.3
Objective B			
Community Health	2024.1	2182.1	2376.0
Personal Social Services	719.8	772	827.4
Family Health Service	281.4	320.3	359.0
Training Bursaries & Further Education & Research	70.2	74.2	77.5
Other Centrally Financed Services & Welfare Foods	42.9	44.3	45.4
Grants to Voluntary Bodies	7.4	8.0	8.7
N/S Body - Food Safety Promotion	1.7	1.7	1.7
Foods Standards Agency	2.6	2.7	2.8
Total Objective B	**3150.1**	**3405.3**	**3698.5**
Objective C			
Fire Service	62.5	64.1	74.8
Total Objective C	**62.5**	**64.1**	**74.8**
Total DEL*	**3247.8**	**3505.9**	**3813.6**
EU Peace Programme	0.07	0.0	0.0
Total DHSSPS	**3248.5**	**3505.9**	**3813.6**
% Increase	6.8	7.9	8.8

DEL* = Department Expenditure Limit

Structure of the Department

The Department of Health, Social Services and Public Safety is structured into five professional groups each led by a Chief Professional Officer. These are:

Public Health, Medical and Allied Group

The Public Health, Medical and Allied Group led by the Chief Medical Officer Dr Henrietta Campbell is responsible for business relating to public health, including the Investing for Health initiative; health protection; health promotion; and smoking, drugs and alcohol related strategies. The Group also provides medical services for the department, the Northern Ireland Civil Service and the Prison Service.

Social Services Inspectorate

Led by the Chief Inspector, the Social Services Inspectorate advises ministers, departments and government agencies on matters relating to social care. The Inspectorate is responsible for the completion of an annual inspection programme across a range of services and providers on behalf of the Department of Health, Social Services and Public Safety and the Northern Ireland Office. Policy development for social work, social care training and education, including postgraduate social work bursaries and other training support funding linked to the HPSS Training Strategy is the responsibility of the Social Services Inspectorate.

The Social Services Inspectorate is a professional group within the Department of Health, Social Services and Public Safety, which inspects, evaluates and provides professional advice and expertise to the minister, the department and social care and criminal justice agencies.

The Chief Inspector Paul Martin is supported by a team of inspectors and by the Social Services Analysis Branch.

The aim of SSI is to work with others to ensure that social work and social care services are responsive to the needs of the population of Northern Ireland. Their role is to:

- Inspect social services provision and its organisation and management in order to promote quality standards, improve effectiveness and efficiency, and ensure the safety and well-being of service users;
- Provide professional advice and expertise to ministers, government departments and the field on the formulation, implementation and review of social services and related health policies, and the effective and efficient delivery of social services;
- Develop, promote and implement effective strategies for personal social services training and staff development;
- Facilitate the conduct of business between the department and the field.

The Chief Social Services Inspector answers directly to the Minister. He provides advice on the quality of social work and social care services and the need for them. He reports on inspections to the Minister and seeks approval for the publication of inspection reports. The Chief Inspector provides professional advice directly to Ministers where necessary.

The Inspectorate works closely with all Directorates in the Health and Personal Social Services Management Group (HPSS Management Group) and the different Units within the Policy and Strategy Division including the Voluntary Activity Unit. The Inspectorate also provides an inspection and professional advice service to the Northern Ireland Office, which carries responsibility for the criminal justice system.

Inspections are conducted under statutory powers contained in the following enactments:

- Health and Personal Social Services (NI) Order 1972;
- The Adoption (NI) Order 1987;
- The Probation Board (Northern Ireland) Order 1982 as amended by the Criminal Justice (NI) Order 1991;
- The Registered Homes (NI) Order 1992;
- The Children's (NI) Order 1995.

These powers give an effective base for inspecting a whole range of social work and social care services provided by Boards and Trusts, voluntary organisations and other agencies. The Chief Inspector, and each of the Inspectors have the power to inspect social work and social care services.

The Central Personal Social Services Advisory Committee, established under the 1972 Health and Personal Social Services (Northern Ireland) order oversees the inspection programme. This Committee is comprised of representatives from professional, voluntary and educational bodies and its role is to make proposals for inspection and endorse the inspection programme.

Social Services Analysis Branch
(SSAB) is responsible for providing management information, methodological and analytical support to help shape, develop and inform the work of the Social Services Inspectorate. This includes supporting the inspectorate in their inspection work, evaluations and monitoring exercises and other SSI projects including the Annual Report of the Chief Inspector. SSAB publish 'Key Indicators for Personal Social Services' in the form of an annual publication. The branch is also responsible for the development of statistical information to help monitor the delivery of Personal Social Services policy and provides advice and assistance to the wider Department.

SSAB consist of a Principal Statistician (Dr. Eugene Mooney) and two Deputy Principal Statisticians (Manny Fitzpatrick and Patricia McDowell) and Assistant Statistician (Kieran Taggart).

Nursing and Midwifery Advisory Group

The Group led by the Chief Nursing Officer Miss Judith Hill is responsible for advising on all aspects of policy affecting nursing, midwifery, health visiting, education and services.

Dental Services Group

Led by the Chief Dental Officer Doreen Wilson, the Group provides advice on oral health, and delivers direct dental services to the Prisons and Young Offenders Centres. Doreen Wilson advises the Minister and the Department on all aspects of dental policy affecting Northern Ireland. The Referral Dental Service also monitors treatment carried out by general dental practitioners to ensure an adequate overall standard of treatment throughout Northern Ireland. The Chief Dental Officer's primary responsibility is to promote and improve the oral health of the population.

Pharmaceutical Advice and Services Group

The Chief Pharmaceutical Officer Dr Norman Morrow is responsible for advising in regard to medicines and pharmaceutical services and has responsibility for medicines legislation relating to both human and veterinary medicines.

Dr Morrow and his team are responsible for providing specialist advice on Medicines and Pharmaceutical Services to the Minister, Department and wider Health Service.

They also have responsibility for the inspection of premises and the enforcement of human and veterinary medicines under the Medicines Act, Misuse of Drugs Act, Pharmacy (Northern Ireland) Order and Poisons (Northern Ireland) Order.

Inspection and Enforcement

Mr Tom Scott – Principal Pharmaceutical Officer, is primarily responsible for inspections of licensed manufacturers, wholesalers and registered agricultural merchants under the Medicines Act 1968 and respective codes of practice.

Dr Michael Mawhinney – Principal Pharmaceutical Officer, is primarily responsible for inspections under the Medicines Act, Misuse of Drugs Act, and Pharmacy (Northern Ireland) Order. These inspections include community pharmacies, medical, veterinary and dental practitioners, wholesalers, manufacturers, hospitals and private clinics.

Northern Ireland Medicines Governance Project

The Northern Ireland Medicines Governance Projects aims to provide a dedicated medicines risk management function throughout the acute hospital Trusts in Northern Ireland.

The key objectives of the project are as follows;

- To prevent and protect patients from medicine-related adverse events;
- To reduce medicine related morbidity and its associated cost treatment;
- Limit the exposure of HPSS staff to litigation from adverse medication events;
- To ensure that HPSS staff practice with optimal safety

The two other groups are:

Planning and Resources Group

The group negotiates and manages financial resources, departmental staffing policy and resources, information and analysis and ICT support and development for the department and the health and social services bodies.

The Planning and Resources group also has responsibility for public safety policies, these include ambulance services, fire services and emergency planning, publication of the regional strategy for health and social well-being, and overall co-ordination of New TSN, Equality and Human Rights.

Strategic Planning and Modernisation Group

The Group headed up by Mr Paul Simpson is responsible for strategic management and planning issues for the Health and Personal Social Services (HPSS). It provides ICT support and development for the Department and the HPSS, manages the Strategic Capital Development Programme and provides strategic direction on Human Resources, including public appointments to HPSS bodies. It is responsible for policy and strategic development of a range of modernisation issues, including the Review of HPSS organisational structures, and the HPSS Service Improvement Programme.

It is also responsible for the Public Safety policies (including Ambulance Services, Fire Services and Regional Transport Strategy), preparation and publication of the Regional Strategy for Health and Social Well-being, overall co-ordination of New TSN, Equality and Human Rights, and the DHSSPS Information Office.

Health Estates

Stoney Road, Dundonald, Belfast, BT16 1US
Tel: 028 9052 0025 / Fax: 028 9052 3900
Web: www.dhssni.gov.uk/hpss/hea
Chief Executive: Ronnie Brown

The Northern Ireland Health and Social Services Estates Agency, known as Health Estates is the Department's Next Steps Agency. Established in October 1995 the Agency determines policy on estate issues relating to the delivery of health and social care.

The Agency's task is to provide professional and technical advice, guidance and support on estates matters at both a strategic and operational level to the various bodies charged with the responsibility for the Health and Social Services estate in Northern Ireland. With its extensive specialist experience, the Agency is the single body in Northern Ireland with an expertise in health and social estate management, planning and design.

Chief Executive: Ronnie Browne
Estate Policy: Stan Blayney

- Technical Health & Safety Policy
- Medical Equipment
- Telecommunications
- Estate Standards
- Technical Environmental Policy & Monitoring
- Capital Performance
- Fire & Safety in the HPSS
- Trust Development
- Retained Estate
- Estate Policy
- Policy Advice & Briefing
- Health Technical Memorandum Policy
- Estates Professional Support
- Land & Property Transactions
- Specialist Engineering Services
- Authorisation Services
- Northern Ireland Adverse Incident Centre

Estates Development: John Cole

- Approved lists of Contractors & Consultants
- Estate IT Applications
- Land & Property Transactions
- Specialist Architectural, Engineering & Quantity Surveying Consultancy
- Project & Site Inspection Services
- Strategic Estate Control
- Development & Investment Planning
- Business Case Development & Private Finance Initiative
- Project Sponsor Support
- Project Management Services including Scheme Programming
- Definition of User Requirements
- Procurement Strategy
- Appointment of Design Team
- Consultants
- Cost Planning
- Training

Other Health Sector Agencies and Organisations

Associated Bodies of the Department of Health, Social Services and Public Safety

Central Services Agency

Established under the Health and Personal Social Services (Northern Ireland) Order 1972, the Central Services Agency supports HPSS in: Corporate Human Resource and Finance Services, Family Practitioner Services, Legal Services, Procurement, Regional Supplies, Research and Development, Fraud Investigation and NICARE, the health and social services unit working internationally.

25-27 Adelaide Street, Belfast, BT2 8FH
Tel: 028 9032 4431 / Fax: 028 90 23 2304

Chief Executive: Stephen Hodkinson

Director of Finance and Administration: Mr P Gick
Director of Human Resources: Mr H McPoland
Director of Family Practitioner Services: Ms P Shiels
Chairman: Brian Carlin
Non Executive Director: Barry Hession
Non Executive Director: Peter Bloch
Non Executive Director: Alan Cairns
Non Executive Director: Professor Sean Fulton

Main Divisions of the Central Services Agency:

Regional Supplies Service (RSS)
RSS has no direct responsibility for patient care, but indirectly through the purchasing and supply of goods and services provides the infrastructure for the continued ability of the health service to deliver patient care. RSS includes the following divisions:

Regional Contracting Directorate
RSS is charged with the continued negotiation of regional contracts. The total value of regional contracts awarded for the region during 2001 was £33.7million. These contracts include medical and non-medical supplies such as energy, consumables, services and fresh products.

Logistics
Customers of RSS purchased over £23 million from RSS Supplies and Distribution Services during 2001. RSS currently manages over 1.6 million product lines.

Purchasing
In 2001 RSS Purchasing Directorate actioned £133.5 million of Trust procurement activity.

Capital Projects Directorate
The Directorate is directly involved with specific customers in the equipping of major projects such as new theatres, intensive care units and out patient facilities.

Family Practitioner Services
The functions of the Family Practitioner Services Directorate are to pay community practitioners (General Medical Practitioners, General Dentist Practitioners, Chemist Contractors and Community Opthalmic Practitioners) on behalf of the Boards; to provide information derived mainly from the payment processes to Boards, the DHSS&PS and others; and to provide advice and services to practitioners in relation to payments and registration.

FPS also holds information on all payment data for approximately 20% of HPSS expenditure, covering a range of activities from prescription to population data.

Research and Development Office
The remit of the Research and Development Office encompasses the research needs of the Department of Health, Social Services and Public Safety and all elements of health and personal social services.

Directorate of Legal Services
The Directorate of Legal Services is a Business Unit of the Central Services Agency, which provides a range of legal services to the Northern Ireland Health and Social Services and is the largest provider of legal services to the HSS.

Other divisions within the Central Services Agency include:

- **Nicare** which provides a range of health, social care and social security programmes overseas;
- **Human Resources Directorate;**
- **Counter Fraud Unit;**
- **Equality Unit;**
- **Directorate of Finance and Administration.**

Occupational Health Service (OHS)
Musgrave Park Hospital, Stockman's Lane, Belfast, BT9 7JB
Tel: 02890 669501

The service provides comprehensive occupational health and medical advisory services to Northern Ireland Government Departments and Agencies.

The Northern Ireland Health Promotion Agency

18 Ormeau Avenue, Belfast, BT2 8HS
Tel: 028 9031 1611 / Fax: 028 9031 1711
Web: www.healthpromotionagency.org.uk/

Chief Executive: Dr Brian Gaffney

Board Members:

Alice Quinn - Chairperson	Liz Fiddis Carville
Fiona Bagnall	Evelyn Gilroy
Valerie Owens	Anthony Harbinson
Janet Leckey	Dr David Higginson
Gemma Harkin	Una O'Kane

The Health Promotion Agency provides a regional focus for health promotion. Its mission is "To make health a top priority for everyone in Northern Ireland." Its statutory functions include:

- Advising the Department (DHSSPS) on matters relating to health promotion:
- Undertaking health promotion activity;
- Planning and carrying out regional or local actions in co-operation with HSS Boards, District Councils, Education and Library Boards, voluntary organisations and other key interests;
- Sponsoring research and evaluation;
- Assisting the provision of training;
- Providing a regional centre of information and advice on health promotion;
- Making grants to and otherwise supporting voluntary organisations.

The Board meets 4 times per year to discuss strategy and monitor the overall performance of the Agency.

The Northern Ireland Blood Transfusion Service Agency

Belfast City Hospital Complex, Lisburn Road, Belfast, BT9 7TS
Tel: 028 9032 1414 / Fax: 028 9043 9017
Web: www.nibts.org/

Chairman: Mr Steven Costello
Chief Executive/ Medical Director: Dr Morris McClelland

The Northern Ireland Blood Transfusion Service, established in 1946, is a independent, Special Agency of the Health and Personal Social Services. It is responsible for the collection, testing and distribution of over 75,000 blood donation each year. The Service operates three mobile units at around 300 locations throughout the province. Including headquarters, located on the site of Belfast City Hospital, a total of almost 1,000 donation sessions are held each year.

The NIBTS exists to fully supply the needs of all hospitals and clinical units in the province with safe and effective blood and blood products and other related services.

The Northern Ireland Regional Medical Physics Agency

Musgrave and Clarke House, Royal Hospital Site
Grosvenor Road, BT12 6BA
Tel: 028 9034 6488 / Fax: 028 9031 3040

Chairman: Professor D.G Walmsley
Chief Executive: Professor Peter Smith
Business Manager: Mrs P Cassidy

The Agency provides scientific measurement and control of high technology equipment in the application of physics and engineering to health care provided by HPSS bodies. Although most of its work is the provision of services for the health trusts. It also carries out work on behalf of clients outside the HPSS sector. Its main service groupings are:-

- Clinical Engineering and Physiological Sciences;
- Radiation Protection and Imaging;
- Radioisotopes;
- Radiotherapy Physics.

The Northern Ireland Guardian Ad Litem Agency

Centre House, 79 Chichester Street, Belfast, BT1 4JE
Tel: 028 90 9031 6550 / Fax: 028 90 9031 9811
Email: admin@nigala.n-i.nhs.uk

Chief Executive: Ronnie Williamson
Board:
Chairman: Mr Jim Currue
Non-executive Director: Dr Colette McAuley / Jack Corr
Executive Director: Ronnie Williamson

The Northern Ireland Guardian Ad Litem Agency was established under the Health and Personal Social Services (Special Agencies) [NI] Order 1990. The Northern Ireland Guardian Ad Litem (Establishment and Constitution) Order [NI] 1995 commenced on 1 December 1995 making provision for the constitution of the Agency and appointment of the Agency Board.

The Agency established and maintains a panel of guardians appointed by the courts to safeguard the interests of children in proceedings specified under the Children (NI) Order 1987.

The Mental Health Commission for Northern Ireland

Elizabeth House, 118 Holywood Road, Belfast, BT4 1NY
Tel: 028 9065 1157 / Fax: 028 9047 1180

Chairperson: Marian O'Neill
Acting Chief Executive: Stephen Jackson

The Mental Health Commission for Northern Ireland was established under the provisions of Part VI of the Mental Health (Northern Ireland) Order 1986. The Commission is an independent body whose role is to review the care and treatment of persons suffering from mental disorder. The Commission also has a duty to monitor the operation of the Order.

The Commission has a duty to ensure that no patient is either improperly detained or received into guardianship and that patients' rights are not infringed. The Commission visits and interviews patients and relatives in hospital and in the community and has the power to refer cases to the Mental Health Review Tribunal. The Commission has 15 members, including 5 lay people drawn from a cross section of relevant professions.

The Commission is an independent body staffed by members of the legal, medical, nursing, social work and psychology professions, which together with lay members is tasked with the duty to review the care and treatment for those suffering from mental disorder.

The Northern Ireland Training Agency Medical and Dental Education (formerly Northern Ireland Council for Postgraduate Medical and Dental Education)

5 Annadale Avenue, Belfast, BT7 3JH
Tel: 028 9049 2731 / Fax: 028 9064 2279

Chief Executive: Jack McCluggage

The core function of the Agency is the provision and development of postgraduate and continuing medical and dental education within Northern Ireland. The Chief Executive/Postgraduate Dean supported by the Director of General Practice Education holds overall responsibility for this provision. The business of the Agency falls largely into three functional areas: Hospital Medicine, General Practice and Dentistry.

Membership of the Northern Ireland Training Agency Medical and Dental Education

Chairman	Dr Don Keegan
Vice Charman	Dr John Jenkins

Agency Management
Chief Executive: Dr Jack McCluggage
Administrative Director: Ms Margot Roberts
Financial Manager: Mr Tommy Hutchinson
Training Manager: Ms Roisin Campbell
Postgraduate Dental Dean: Mr Ian Saunders
Director of Postgraduate General Practice Education:
Dr Agnes McKnight

The Council oversees the postgraduate and medical education of doctors and dentists and is responsible for the development and delivery of vocational training and continuing medical education for GPs and dentists.

The Northern Ireland Social Care Council (NISCC)

The Social Care Council established in October 2001 replaces the Central Council for Education and Training in Social Work and is responsible for the development, promotion, and regulation of social work and the social care workforce and social care education and training. There are around 30,000 social care workers in Northen Ireland.

7th Floor, Millennium House
19-25 Great Victoria Street, Belfast, BT2 7AQ
Email: info@niscc.ni.nhs.uk
Tel: 028 9041 7600 / Fax: 028 9041 7601

NISCC Council Members
The Council is made up of a Chair and 23 members, appointed by the Minister for Health, Social Services and Public Safety. Membership is split equally between:

- Lay Members – people who have direct experience as users of services, eg care/voluntary worker
- Stakeholder members – people involved In service delivery/commissioning, education/training, professional bodies, or allied professions
- Registrant member – people who are employed as social care workers

Current NISCC members are:
Chairman: Mr Jeremy Harbinson
Mr Richard Black, Mr Mel Byrne, Mrs Jacqueline Carroll, Mr John (Roy) Catney, Mrs Linda Davidson, Mr Jonathan Giles, Mrs Alyson Dunn, Mr Greg Kelly, Mr Kevin Lawrenson, Ms Janeen (Jan) Maconachie, Mr Patrick McAteer, Mrs Lisa McCullough, Mr Lee McDermott, Mrs Gillian McGaughey, Mr Brendan McKeever, Mr Brendan Murphy, Mr John Rafferty, Mr Richard Reid, Mrs Margaret Shevlin, Mr James Smyth, Mrs Eleanor Taggart.

Senior Management
Chief Executive: Brendan Johnstone
Head of Corporate Affairs: Gerard Campbell
Director of Registration: Patricia Higgins
Director of Training: Mary Stuart

The Northern Ireland Practice and Education Council for Nursing and Midwifery

The role of the Council is to support the professional development of the nursing and midwifery professions in areas of best practice, education and performance. So that the public in Northern Ireland can be provided with a high standard of nursing and midwifery care.

Centre House, 75 Chichester Street, Belfast
Tel: 028 90 238 152 / Fax: 028 90 333 298
Chief Executive: Ms Paddie Blaney
Chairman: Mrs Maureen Griffith, Judith Hill CBE, Dr Brendan McCarthy, Dr Sara Magee, Maria O'Hare, Mary Patton, Michael Rea, Professor Jennifer Boore, Thelma Byrne, Dolores McCormick, Iain McGowan, Frances McMurray, Mrs Margaret O'Hagan.

Public Safety

The Fire Authority for Northern Ireland (FANI)

The Authority is responsible for the provision of regional fire services and ensuring their compliance with national fire cover standards and implementing the department's fire safety policy. The Northern Ireland Fire Brigade serves the 1.69million people of Northern Ireland over 5,500 sq. miles.

The Fire Authority is composed of 17 members, appointed by the head of the Department of Health, Social Services and Public Safety.

The role of the Fire Authority is to determine detailed strategic policy for the Fire Brigade and carries out an overseeing role via reports presented at monthly meetings.

The Brigade is divided into four Operational Command Areas, with Brigade Headquarters situated in Lisburn, Co. Antrim. The Brigade is currently structured as follows (October 2002):

- 919 Whole time Fire-fighters;
- 980 Retained Fire-fighters;
- 12 Volunteer Fire-fighters;
- 59 Control Room Staff;
- 208 Support Staff;
- 53 Part time Caretakers.

These in turn serve to maintain 133 front line fire appliances operating from:

- 8 Whole time Fire Stations;
- 6 Whole time/Retained Fire Stations;
- 52 Retained Stations;
- 1 Volunteer Station

Brigade HQ, 1 Seymour Street, Lisburn, BT27 4SX
Tel: 028 9266 4221 / Fax: 028 9267 7402

Chairman: William F Gillespie
Chief Executive: Colin Lamney

Administration and Delivery of Healthcare Services

Structure of Health and Social Services in Northern Ireland

The HSS Boards

Under DHSSPS are the four Health and Social Services Boards, the Western, Northern, Eastern and Southern Health and Social Services Boards, which act as agents of the department. The regional Boards carry out the bulk of all public expenditure on health in Northern Ireland.

Health Boards purchase healthcare services from Northern Ireland's Trusts and at local level from General Practitioner centres. There are 19 trusts of varying sizes the larger of which cover several major hospitals. General Practitioner centres may be large or small practices, which may chose to opt out of the NHS GP fund holder scheme.

Under the new plans announced in the department's Corporate Plan 2002/03-2004/05 and under the Investing for Health strategy Wellbeing Investment Plans (HWIP) are the new arrangements by which the four HSS Boards will secure effective health and social services for their local populations, improve health and social well being and reduce inequalities. These plans, which became effective in 2002, are the key planning and accountability documents for the HPSS and consist of three main elements:

- HSS Boards plans for commissioning services in their local areas;
- HSS Boards plans to deliver on the Investing for Health Strategy of the department and reduce inequalities; and
- HSS Boards plans to deliver on the major underpinning themes of the Programme for Government.

The Health Well Being and Investment Plans will act as the single vehicle for all local HPSS planning. It is expected that health improvement planning will be done on a three year cycle rolling forward annually in the Health Well-Being and Investment Plan.

Under the Investing for Health Strategy launched by the DHSSPS in 2002 the Health Boards will have overarching responsibility for improving health and well being, reducing health inequalities and ensuring effective health and social services and coordinating the Investing for Health Partnerships.

Investing for Health Partnerships

Each Health and Social Services Board will have responsibility for developing an Investing for Health Partnership in their area bringing together different organisations in partnership to ensure that actions to improve health are properly coordinated, and an action plan agreed to improve the health of the local population in line with the Investing for Health Strategy.

The purpose of the Partnerships is to identify opportunities to improve the health of the people in the area by addressing the social, cultural, economic and environmental determinants of health. The Partnerships will also seek to develop long term plans to meet the strategic aims of the department's Investing for Health strategy and will be reflected in the annual Health and Well Being Investment Plans prepared annually by the Boards.

Members of these local partnerships will include representatives from voluntary, community and statutory organisations in the locality, including those from District Councils, the Housing Executive, Education and Library Boards and HSS Trusts. Where applicable, members of the business community will also be invited to participate.

District Councils will have a key role in the Investing for Health Partnerships, presenting concerns particularly relevant to their locality and in respect to many of their statutory functions including environmental health, consumer protection, building control, waste management, community services and local economic development planning which have a direct bearing on health and the determinants of health.

The councils participation in the Investing for Health Partnerships led by the Health Boards will also ensure that health issues are considered in local strategic planning processes and considered by other statutory bodies.

The Investing for Health Partnerships will run in parallel with existing networks such as Health Action Zones, Healthy Cities, Child Care Partnerships and Peace and Reconciliation Partnerships. Funding of £1.5million from Executive Programme Funds has been made available for the establishment of the Partnerships. This funding will be available until March 2004.

The HSS Trusts

HSS Trusts have also been affected by the corporate plan, becoming accountable to the department in relation to the capital, income, workforce, estate and all other resources at their disposal and will be accountable for the effectiveness of their relationships with users, carers and the wider community. Each of the HSS Trusts is now expected to produce a Trust Delivery Plan (TDP) illustrating how the Trust intends to use their resources to deliver in line with planning goals set by the Minister for Health.

The Trusts will work in partnership with the Boards to implement the HWIPs and are required to produce an implementation plan, which will:

- Demonstrate how the HWIP is to be effected within the Trust;
- Identify the consequences and risks to the Trust in relation to current and future clinical support services, funding sources (both capital and revenue) costs, human resources, capital assets and information and management technology.

The Trusts will have a key role in developing the Investing for Health partnerships. Through their links with voluntary and community groups they will facilitate initiatives and maintain existing relationships with Agenda 21, Children's Services Committees, Health Action Zones, and LSPs.

Local Health and Social Care Groups

New primary care arrangements were put in place in April 2002 following consultation on the proposals set out in the paper "Building the Way Forward in Primary Care". Under the new arrangements Local Health and Social Care Groups will be created to provide a framework to help primary care professionals work with others to improve health and well-being.

Health and Social Services Councils

Health Councils were established in 1982 to shadow the areas covered by each of the Health Boards and report independently on the quality of healthcare delivery. The Councils regularly consult with the general public to monitor healthcare from the perspective of the consumer and make recommendations on how services might be improved.
Councils have an important role in representing their local area population and continuing to influence the policies of the Health Boards.

Councils will:

- Contribute to the development of HWIPs and closely monitor their outcomes;
- Report on the practical difference achieved by the HWIP from the perspective of the local population;
- Promote greater participation and involvement of the local community in the Investing for Health strategy.

Health and Social Services Boards (HSSBs)

Northern Ireland is served by 4 Health and Social Services Boards, each representing a geographical area and its population. The Boards were established under the Health and Personal Social Services (Northern Ireland) Order 1972 as amended by the Health and Personal Social Services (Northern Ireland) Order 1991. Originally the Boards had responsibility for all health and social services provided within their area, including hospitals, clinics, social services centres and the like. Towards the end of the 1980s central Government initiated a series of reforms to the National Health Service (NHS), which affected the way services were provided in Britain and in Northern Ireland.

The Health and Social Services Boards work under Government policies and guidelines, overseen by the Department for Health, Social Services and Public Safety. The role of the Boards is primarily to improve the health and wellbeing of the people who live in their area. This involves an assessment of the health and social services needed by local people, and arrangements for the provision of those services. Assessment takes place in consultation with 'stakeholders' in the health sector. Stakeholders include organisations and groups which have an interest in the health sector, and include elected representatives of local councils, professional organisations, voluntary groups, statutory bodies, HSS Trusts, primary healthcare professionals (such as GPs) and representatives of the local community.

From this consultation a plan is devised for the procurement of the services required. This is achieved by purchasing, or 'commissioning' health and social services, principally from 3 sources: Health and Social Services Trusts, voluntary organisations and private sector organisations. Boards negotiate Service Level Agreements with service providers, essentially contracts to provide services to patients.

Health and Social Services Boards are also required to evaluate all services provided, in order to ensure that they are meeting the needs of the population. This includes monitoring services provided in hospitals and in the community.

New primary care arrangements recently introduced by the then Minister for Health, Social Services and Public Safety, meant the abolition of GP fund holding, to be replaced by Local Health and Social Care Groups.

Health and Social Services Boards have responsibilities relating to the areas of family health and childcare. Boards manage the registration, inspection and monitoring of residential and nursing homes, including those for children and the elderly. They also have a role in overseeing arrangements for the delivery of health services to families by GPs, dentists, opticians and pharmacists.

Other services provided by Boards include the control of infectious diseases and the monitoring of the statutory functions delegated to Trusts.

Board Structure

Each Health and Social Services Board is composed of both executive and non-executive directors, and holds a public meeting every month. Geographical divisions between the Boards coincide with local government boundaries, so that each Board covers a number of local government districts. Each local authority nominates at least one representative to sit on the appropriate Board. Other members of the Boards are Government nominees, as well as some senior executives employed by the Boards themselves.

Table 5.5
Northern Ireland: Population by Health Board

	Male	Female	Total
Eastern	319,200	346,530	665,730
Northern	211,310	219,130	430,440
Southern	156,560	159,040	315,600
Western	141,790	143,080	284,880
Total	828,860	867,790	1,696,640

Source NISRA

The Eastern Board is by far the largest in terms of population, with almost two and a half times as many people as the smallest, the Western Board. The Southern Board is slightly bigger, but well behind the Northern Board, which itself is much smaller than the Eastern Board.

Eastern Health and Social Services Board

12-22 Linenhall Street
Belfast, BT2 8BS
Tel: 028 9032 1313
Minicom: 028 9032 4980
(for people who are deaf or
who have hearing problems)

Email: Enquiry@ehssb.n-i.nhs.uk
Web: www.ehssb.n-i.nhs.uk

The Eastern Board 'commissions' or arranges a comprehensive range of health and social services for the 670,000 people who live within its area.

The area served by the Board includes the City Council areas of Belfast and Lisburn, the Borough Council areas of Ards, Castlereagh and North Down, and the Down District Council area.

The Board each year deploys its annual funding from government of around £1 billion to ensure that hospital services, family health services provided by professionals such as GPs and a wide array of community social services are all available to people.

Eastern Health and Social Services Board

Champion House, 12-22 Linenhall Street, Belfast, BT2 8BS
Tel: 028 9032 1313 Ext: 2526 / Fax: 028 9055 3625

Board Structure
The Board consists of non-executive Board members, executive Board members and a senior management team. A team of directors leads the Board:

Non-Executive Directors
Chairman: Mr David Russell
Mr David Beck, Mr Alexander Coleman,
Professor Roderick Hay Mrs Lilian Levers,
Mrs Francesca Reid, Mr Tony McMullan

Executive Directors:
Chief Executive: Dr Paula Kilbane
Tel: 028 9032 1313 / Fax: 028 9055 3625

Medical Director of Primary Care: Dr Stanton Adair
Tel: 028 9055 3782 / Fax: 028 9055 3622

Director of Planning and Contracting: Anne Lynch
Tel: 028 9055 3900 / Fax: 028 9055 3681

Director of Finance: Angela Paisley
Tel: 028 9055 3911 / Fax: 028 9055 3621

Director of Social Services: Hugh Connor
Tel: 028 9055 3964 / Fax: 028 9055 3620

Director of Public Health: Dr David Stewart
Tel: 028 9055 3940 / Fax: 028 9055 3682

Senior Management Team
(Executive Board members are also on the Strategic Management Team).

Head of Corporate Services: Stephen Adams
Tel: 028 9055 3731 / Fax: 028 9055 3680

Director of Pharmaceutical Services: Andreé McCollum
Tel: 028 9055 3793 / Fax: 028 9055 3681

Head of Contracts: Colm McConville
Tel: 028 9055 3907 / Fax: 028 9055 3681

Director of Dental Services: Will Maxwell
Tel: 028 9055 3780 / Fax: 028 9055 3622

Director of Nursing Services: Mary Waddell
Tel: 028 9055 3739 / Fax: 028 9055 3682

The main providers of care within the EHSSB area are:

Acute Hospital Services
Royal Hospitals HSS Trust
Belfast City Hospital HSS Trust
Mater Hospital HSS Trust
Green Park Healthcare HSS Trust

Acute Hospitals and Community Health and Social Services
Down Lisburn HSS Trust
Ulster Community and Hospitals HSS Trust

Community Health and Social Services
North and West Belfast HSS Trust
South and East Belfast HSS Trust

Ambulance Services
Northern Ireland Ambulance Service, Headquarters,
12-22 Linenhall Street, Belfast, BT2 8BS
Tel: 028 90 333 090

Family Health Services
Within the Eastern Health and Social Services Board's area there are currently 146 medical practices, employing approximately 400 doctors. Around 70 per cent of these are fund-holding practices. Chemists, opticians and dentists also provide health services.

Northern Health and Social Services Board

County Hall, 182 Galgorm Road, Ballymena, BT42 1QB
Tel: 028 2566 2081
Fax: 028 2565 2311
Web: www.nhssb.n-i.nhs.co.uk

The Northern Health and Social Services Board serves the district council areas of Antrim, Ballymena, Ballymoney, Carrickfergus, Coleraine, Cookstown, Larne, Magherafelt, Moyle and Newtownabbey, which include around 425,000 people. It is Northern Ireland's second largest health board with an expenditure in 2002/03 of £563.2 million.

Board Structure
The Northern Board meets at 2.00pm on the third Thursday of each month. Mr J C Crutchley is the Board Secretary and Mrs C Reynolds, Corporate Business Manager.

Non-Executive Members
Chairman: Mr Michael Wood
Mrs Molly Mayrs
Mr Tom McKeown
Mr George Owens
Mr Raymond Milnes
Mrs Joan Mulholland

Executive Members
Chief Executive: Stuart MacDonnell
Director of Finance: Wilson Matthews
Director of Nursing & Consumer Services: Elizabeth McNair
Director of Public Health: Professor John Watson
Director of Social Services: Mary Wilmot

Senior Management Team Members
Director, Dental Services: A Millen
Director of Social Services: M Wilmont
Director, Service, Performance and Development: I Deboys
Director, Strategic Planning and Commissioning: E McClean
Director, Pharmaceutical Services: Dr D Morrison
Director of Primary Care: W Boyd
Head of Information Services: M Sloan

Health and Social Services Trusts
The Northern Board covers three Health and Social Services Trusts:

Causeway Health and Social Services Trust
Providing both health and social care services in the local council areas of Ballymoney, Coleraine and Moyle

Homefirst Community Trust
Providing community health, mental health and social care services in the local council areas of Antrim, Ballymena, Carrickfergus, Cookstown, Larne, Magherafelt and Newtownabbey.

United Hospitals Trust
Provides services at Antrim, Braid Valley, Mid Ulster, Moyle and Whiteabbey hospitals.

Southern Health and Social Services Board

Southern Health & Social Services Board

Tower Hill
Armagh
BT61 9DR
Tel: 028 3741 0041
Fax: 028 3741 4550
Web: www.shssb.org

The Southern Health and Social Services Board serves a population of 320,000 in the District Council Areas of Armagh, Banbridge, Craigavon, Dungannon and Newry and Mourne.

Expenditure
In the year ending 31 March 2003, the Southern Board's total revenue expenditure was £421 million on various services.

Health Trusts
Armagh and Dungannon HSS Trust
Craigavon and Banbridge Community HSS Trust
Craigavon Area Hospital Group Trust
Newry and Mourne HSS Trust

Board Members
Chairwoman: Mrs Fionnuala Cook OBE
Chief Executive: Colm Donaghy
Director of Public Health: Dr Anne-Marie Telford
Director of Resources & Contracting: Sean McKeever
Director of Social Services: Brian Dornan
Director of Planning and Performance Management: Mairead McAlinden
Director of Primary Care: Eddie Ritson

Non-Executive Directors
John Brown
Philomena Hagan
Susan Ingram
Paul McCreesh
Eimer Cleland
Roberta Brownlee

Associate Board Members
Edwin Graham - Chair, Craigavon and Banbridge Local Health and Social Care Group

Cathy McPhillips - Chair, Armagh and Dungannon Local Health and Social Care Group

Fergal O'Brien - Chair, Newry and Mourne Local Health and Social Care Group

Western Health and Social Services Board

15 Gransha Park, Clooney Road, Derry, BT47 6FN
Tel: 028 7186 0086 / Fax: 028 7186 0311
Email: foi@whssb.n-i.nhs.uk

The Western Health and Social Services Board covers the District Council areas of Derry, Limavady, Strabane, Omagh and Fermanagh. The Board serves a population of 284,000 over an area of almost 5,000 sq kms from Limavady in the North to the Enniskillen area in the South. It is the smallest of the four Boards in terms of the population it serves and population density is low, at around 58 persons per square kilometre.

Board Structure
Chairman: Ms Karen Meehan

Non-Executive Directors
Mr Edward Turner
Dr Aine Downey
Mrs Bernadette Grant
Mr Vincent Lusby
Mr Ryan Williams

Executive Directors
Chief Executive: Mr Steven Lindsay
Director of Social Care: Mr Dominic Burke
Director of Finance and Information: Mr Peter McLaughlin

Expenditure
In the year up to 31 March 2001, the Board spent approximately £288 million on purchasing services, including £52 million spent on the provision of family health services.

£198.8 million was spent with the HSS Trusts in the Western Board area. This figures includes expenditure on contracts with providers such as the Royal Group of Hospitals, Green Park and Belfast City Hospital.

The Central Services Agency makes payments on behalf of the Board to General Medical Practitioners, General Dental Practitioners and for Ophthalmic Services.

The running costs of the Board attributable to the Board Administration and Commissioning and Registration and Inspection Unit were £4.698m, accounting for 1.6% of the board's expenditure. The ceiling set by the department for administration costs was 1.9%. All savings in administration made by the Board of have been applied directly towards patient and client care.

Health and Social Services Trusts

Details of Northern Ireland's Health and Social Services Trusts (HSS Trusts) are set out below in an A-Z format for ease of reference. The trusts are essentially providers of healthcare operating under contract to the regional Health and Social Services Boards, and are primarily appointed bodies. Each Health and Social Services Trust is required to ensure that income is sufficient to cover expenditure, referred to as the 'break-even' duty.

Altnagelvin Hospitals Trust

Glenshane Road, Derry, BT47 6SB
Tel: 028 7134 5171 / Fax: 028 7161 1222
Chairman: Denis Desmond CBE
Chief Executive: Stella Burnside

The Trust provides a range of acute hospital services; Altnagelvin is the major district general hospital in the north-west and is the largest acute hospital in the north of Ireland, providing a designated cancer unit, and offering the most comprehensive and complex range of services of any hospital outside Belfast. The hospital has an extensive 10-year investment plan to develop the quality of its accommodation and services. The Trust serves a population of over 275,000 people and employs almost 2000 staff. It has an annual turnover of around £70m.

Board Members

Columb Henry	Non Executive Director
Marlene Jefferson	Non Executive Director
Joan Casey	Non Executive Director
Gerard Guckian	Non Executive Director
Neville Orr	Non Executive Director
Irene Duddy	Director of Nursing
Geoff Nesbitt	Medical Director
Raymond McCartney	Director of Business Services

Altnagelvin Hospital, Derry

Acute Hospital Services Main Facilities within the Altnagelvin Hospitals Trust

Altnagelvin Area Hospital
Acute Hospital Services
488 Inpatient Beds
54 Day Case Beds
Ward 5, Waterside Hospital
Slow Stream Rehabilitation
18 Inpatient Rehabilitation Beds for elderly people

Spruce House, Gransha Park
Care of the Young Physically Disabled
17 In patient beds (This facility will be replaced by a new purpose-built facility on the Altnagelvin site.)

Armagh and Dungannon HSS Trust

St Luke's Hospital, Loughgall Road, Armagh, BT61 7NQ
Tel: 028 3752 2381 / Fax: 028 3752 6302

Chairman: Mrs Deirdre Dorman
Chief Executive: Pauline Stanley

Armagh and Dungannon Health and Social Services Trust shares its service boundaries with those of Armagh City and District Council and Dungannon and South Tyrone Borough Council. The combined population of the area is 103,000 and represents 33% of the population in the Southern Health and Social Services Board. The Trust employs a total of 2,651 employees including 892 home helps. Expenditure on the provision of services across the Trust's nine programmes of care for the year ending 31st March 2003 was £72.3m.

Board Members

Eric Hamilton	Director of Social Services
Stephen McNally	Director of Finance
Dr Harold McNeill	Medical Director
James Lennon	Non Executive Director:
Cecilia Woods	Non Executive Director:
Deirdre I Dorman JP	Non Executive Director
W Oliver Ross	Non Executive Director
Patrick McCabe	Director of Planning and Performance Management
Kevin Toal	Director of Mental Health Services
Gordon Wells	Director of Personnel

Table 5.6 Trust Spending By Programme of Care 2002/03

Programme of Care	(£m)	%
Acute Services	1.1	1.5
Physical and Sensory Disability	3.5	4.8
Learning Disability	16.6	23.0
Mental Health	11.1	15.4
Family and Child Care	6.3	8.7
Maternity and Child Health	1.8	2.5
Primary Health and Adult Community	1.2	1.7
Health Promotion and Disease Prevention	1.9	2.6
Elderly Care	28.8	39.8
Total	**72.3**	**100**

Main Facilities within the Armagh and Dungannon HSS Trust

Mullinure Hospital
Armagh Community Hospital
South Tyrone Hospital

Belfast City Hospital HSS Trust

51 Lisburn Road, Belfast, BT9 7AB
Tel: 028 9032 9241 / Fax: 028 9032 6614

Chairman: Joan Ruddock OBE
Chief Executive: Quentin Coey

Belfast City Hospital

Board Members

Mr W F I McKay	Deputy Chairman
Mr V Fiddis	Non ExecutiveMember
Professor J R Hayes	Non Executive Member
Mrs R Fug	Non Executive Member
Ms P Morgan	Non Executive Member
Dr K J Fullerton	Medical Director
Mr J Copeland	Director of Finance
Mrs A McCabe	Director of Nursing
Mr A Brown	Director of Operational Support
Miss PA Haines	Director of Planning
Mr MC Barkley	Director of Personnel

Causeway HSS Trust

8E Coleraine Road, Ballymoney, BT53 6BP
Tel: 028 2766 6600 / Fax: 028 2766 1201

Chairperson: Jean Jefferson
Chief Executive: Norma Evans

The Causeway Trust covers the most Northerly parts of Antrim and East Londonderry. Its main facility is the recently built Causeway Acute Hospital. The Trust has an operating budget of around £88m.

Board Members

Fergus Wheeler	Vice Chairman
Stanley Forsythe	Non Executive Director
Paddy McAteer	Non Executive Director
Brian McMurray	Non Executive Director
Derek Irwin	Non Executive Director
Jim Loughrey	Director of Child and Community Care Services
Neil Guckian	Director of Finance
Alan Braiden	Director of Acute Hospital Services
Mike Ledwith	Director of Medical Services
Linda Marshall	Director of Nursing and Quality
Jacinta Melaugh	Director of Human Resources
Nevin Oliver	Director of Business and Corporate Services
Dr Windsor Murdock	GP Representative

Table 5.7: Trust Spending By Programme of Care 2002-2003

Programme of Care	(£,000)
Acute Services	30,484
Maternity and Child Care	4,301
Family and Child Health	5,362
Elderly	25,118
Mental Health	4,635
Learning Disability	4,923
Physical and Sensory Disabled	2,629
Health Promotion and Disease Prevention	1,604
Primary Care and Adult Community	3,646

Acute Facilities within the Causeway HSS Trust

Causeway Hospital, Coleraine

Craigavon Area Hospital Group HSS Trust

68 Lurgan Road, Craigavon, BT63 5QQ
Tel: 028 3833 4444
Chairman: E McClurg
Chief Executive: J Templeton

The Craigavon Area Hospital Group Trust was established in 1993 and incorporates services across four main locations – Craigavon Area Hospital, Lurgan Hospital, South Tyrone Hospital and Banbridge and Dungannon Polyclinic.

During 2000/1 the Trust provided services to all four of the Northern Ireland Health and Social Services Boards. The SHSSB remains the main purchaser and user of Trust services. The Trust was also contracted to provide services to the patients of the 18 GP practices within the Southern Board area and to 30 GP practices outside the area. The Trust has a major £80m development plan for the Craigavon Hospital Site. The Trust has a annual budget of around £85m.

Board Members

Dr Caroline Humphrey	Director of Medical Services/ Deputy Chief Executive
Dr NN Damani	Pathology and Laboratory Services
Dr SJ Hall Radio	Diagnosis and Imaging
Dr RJE Lee	Medicine
Mr D Lowry	Obstetrics and Gynaecology
Dr I Orr	Anaesthesia and Theatres
Mr WJI Stirling	Surgery
Mr D Herron	Business Planning and Contracts
Mr PC Legge	Estates
Mr John Mone	Nursing and Quality
Mrs M Richardson	Human Resources
Mr LA Stead	Finance

Table 5.8 Craigavon Area Hospital Group HSS Staffing (end March 2003)

Admin and Clerical	397
Works and Maintenance	25
Ancillary and General	94
Nursing and Midwifery	1458
Social Work	11
Professional and Technical	374
Medical and Dental	255
Total	2614

Main Facilities within the Craigavon Area Hospital Group Trust

South Tyrone Hospital
Craigavon Area Hospital
Lurgan Hospital
Banbridge Polyclinic

Craigavon Hospital

Craigavon and Banbridge Community HSS Trust

Bannvale House, 10 Moyallen Road, Gilford, BT63 5JX
Tel: 028 3883 1983 / Fax: 028 3883 1993

Chairman: J Graham Martin
Chief Executive: Dennis Preston

Established in April 1994 the Craigavon and Banbridge Community Health and Social Services Trust is responsible for the management of a range of community health and social care services and also for purchasing similar services from the independent and community/voluntary agencies.

The Trust covers a largely rural area, the principal towns of which are, Banbridge, Lurgan and Portadown. The population of the Trust area is approximately 119, 600 representing 38% of the Southern Board's population.

Almost half of the Trust's annual expenditure relates to services for the elderly with around one quarter dedicated to services relating to mental health and learning disability.

Board Members

John Farleigh	Non Executive Director
Cyril McElhinney	Non Executive Director
Louise Boyle	Director of Child and Family Care
Rosaleen Moore	Director of Mental Health and Disability
Stephen Best	Medical Director – Psychiatry
Mary Mc Parland	Non Executive Director
Michael Morrow	Non Executive Director
Sean Wilson	Medical Director – General Practice
Martin Kelly	Director of Planning and Information
Kieran Donaghy	Director of Human Resources
Ronnie Crozier	Director of Finance
Roisin Burns	Director of Elderly and Primary Care
Roisin McDonagh	Non Executive Director

Down Lisburn HSS Trust

Lisburn Health Centre, 25 Linenhall Street, Lisburn, BT28 1LU
Tel: 028 9266 5181 / Fax: 028 9267 6026

Down Lisburn HSS Trust has recently received the good news that Downpatrick is to get a new hospital with the full range of acute services. This development resulted from a major campaign to keep open a hospital in Downpatrick as the existing 'Downe' hospital in the town had been earmarked for closure.

Chairman:	Mrs Denise Fitzsimmons
Chief Executive:	Mr John Compton
Mr D Gorman	(Vice Chairman) Non Executive Director
Mrs R Lavery	Non Executive Director
Mrs B McErlane	Non Executive Director
Mrs L Tavakoli	Non Executive Director
Mr Donal Flanagan	Non Executive Director
Mr P Simpson	Director of Finance
Mrs Kate Thompson	Executive Director for Social Work
Mr A Finn	Executive Director for Nursing
Dr Harry Beers	Joint Medical Director
Dr Noeleen Devaney	Joint Medical Director

Acute Facilities within the Down Lisburn HSS Trust

Downe Hospital, Lagan Valley Hospital, Downpatrick Maternity Hospital

Foyle HSS Trust

Riverview House, Abercorn Road, Derry, BT48 6FB
Tel: 028 7126 6111 / Fax: 028 7126 0806

Chairman: Anthony Jackson
Chief Executive: Elaine Way

Board Members

Mrs Gay Durnan	Non Executive Director
Mrs E Hogg	Non Executive Director
Ms Anne-Marie Holmes	Non Executive Director
Dr Artie O'Hara	Medical Director
Mr Joseph Doherty	Non Executive Director
Mr Philip Babington	Non Executive Director
Mrs Phil Mahon	Director of Healthcare
Mr John Doherty	Director of Social Care
Mrs Lesley Mitchell	Director of Finance
Mr Joe Lusby	Director of Business Services
Mrs Nuala Sheerin	Director of Personnel

Foyle Trust was established in 1996 and provides a wide range of community health and social care services to cover 160,000 people in the council areas of Derry City, Limavady and Strabane.

The total annual budget of the Trust is around £80 million, including income from Westcare Business Services, legally part of Foyle HSS Trust, which operates as a trading agency providing common support services to the Western Health and Social Services Board and to the Trusts in the Western Board area.

Green Park HSS Trust

20 Stockmans Lane, Belfast, BT9 7JB
Tel: 028 9066 9501 / Fax: 028 9038 2008

Chairman: Ian Doherty
Chief Executive: Hilary Boyd

Board Members

Mr Brian Sore	Director of Corporate Planning and Deputy Chief Executive
Dr Denis Connolly	Medical Director
Mr Jim Cooper	Non Executive Director
Mr Alan Hanna	Non Executive Director
Mr Mike Lewis	Non Executive Director
Ms Jennifer Power	Non Executive Director
Ms Margaret Shevlin	Non Executive Director
Mr Colin Bradley	Director of Finance
Ms Patricia O'Callaghan	Director of Nursing and Clinical Effectiveness

Non-Board Executives

Miss Therese McKernan	Director of Human Resources
Mr Colin Cairns	Director of Support Services

Major Facilities within the Greenpark HSS Trust

Musgrave Park Hospital
Belvoir Park Hospital
Forster Green Hospital

Homefirst Community HSS Trust

Homefirst Community Trust is the largest Community Trust in Northern Ireland employing in excess of 5,000 staff and providing a range of services to the population of around 327,000 people in the local authority areas of Antrim, Ballymena, Carrickfergus, Cookstown, Larne, Magherafelt and Newtownabbey. The Trust had an income of £156m in 2002/03.

The Cottage, 5 Greenmount Avenue
Ballymena, BT43 6DA
Tel: 028 2563 3700 / Fax: 028 2563 3733

Chairman: William Boyd
Chief Executive: Christie Colhoun

Board Members

Ms Mary Jo Higgins	Non Executive Director
Ms Sheelagh Hillan	Non Executive Director
Mr Adam J McKin	Non Executive Director
Mr Ian Rainey	Non Executive Director
Mr Trevor Wilson	Non Executive Director
Mr Harold Sharp	Executive Director, Finance
Mrs Hazel Baird	Executive Director, Nursing, Dental & Governance
Mrs Rosemary Simpson	Director Social Care and Disability Services
Mr Martin Sloan	Director Planning & Information
Mr William Day	Director Personnel
Mr Glenn Houston	Director Mental Health Services
Dr Michael Mannion	Medical Director
Mrs Brenda Smyth	Director Social Work and Child Care
Mrs Joan Stephenson	Acting Director Child Health & Allied Health Services

Mater Infirmorum Hospital HSS Trust

The Mater Trust is an acute hospital providing services to North Belfast and surrounding areas. It employs over 1,000 staff. The Mater Hospital was originally destined under the Hayes Report to lose its acute (accident & emergency) status. However following a campaign to retain acute services health minister Des Browne announced that the Hayes recommendation would not be applied to the Mater.

45-51 Crumlin Road, Belfast, BT14 6AB
Tel: 028 9080 2338
Fax: 028 9074 9784

Chairman: Lady McCollum
Chief Executive: Mr Sean Donaghy

Board Members

Mr B McCaughey	Non Executive Director
Mr Aidan A Canavan	Non Executive Director
Mr Charles Jenkins	Non Executive Director
Ms E Rosemary Dunlop	Non Executive Director
Mr W Odling-Smee	Non Executive Director
Mr Larry O'Neill	Director of Finance and Information
Mr Colm Harvey	Director of Nursing
Ms Joan Pedan	Director of Corporate Development

Acute Facilities within the Mater Infirmorum Hospital HSS Trust
Mater Infirmorum Hospital

Newry and Mourne HSS Trust

5 Downshire Place, Downshire Road, Newry, BT34 1DZ
Tel: 028 3026 0505 / Fax: 028 3026 9064

Chairman: Mr Sean Hogan
Chief Executive: Mr Eric Bowyer

The Newry and Mourne HSS Trust came into being on 1 April 1994 and provides a wide range of hospital community health and social services to the 86,000 population of the Newry and Mourne area.

Over 1700 staff are employed by the Trust.

Board Members

Mr M Dillon	Director of Finance and Planning
Dr P Loughran	Director of Acute Services
Mrs J O'Hagan	Director of Nursing and Community Health
Mr J Flynn	Director of Social Services
Mrs E Cleland	Non Executive Director
Mr L McArdel	Non Executive Director
Mr D Farrell	Non Executive Director
Mrs P McCabe	Non Executive Director
Mr M Ferris	Director of Personal and Operational Services
Dr M Hollinger	Director of Community Medical and Preventative Services
Mrs L Cavan	Director of Professions Allied to Medicine
Dr A Mulholland	General Practitioner Advisor

Acute Facilities within the Newry and Mourne HSS Trust
Daisy Hill Hospital

North and West Belfast HSS Trust

Glendinning House, 6 Murray Street, Belfast, BT1 6DP
Tel: 028 9032 7156 / Fax: 028 9082 1285

Chairperson: Pat McCartan
Chief Executive: Richard Black

The North and West Belfast HSS Trust provides a full range of community based health and social care services to 145,000 people, providing specialist services for people with learning disabilities at Muckamore Abbey Hospital. These services are provided to all four health and social services boards in Northern Ireland.

The Trust also provides the Eastern Board with community

nutrition and dietetic services, the child health information system, family planning services, services for people travelling abroad and services relating to sexual health and AIDS. The Trust operates from 50 locations and employs over 3,500 people.

Board Members

Baroness Mary Blood	Non Executive Director
Sarah Brennan	Non Executive Director
Denis Power	Non Executive Director
Adrian Watson	Non Executive Director
Brenda Connolly	Director of Nursing
Peter Harvey	Director of Finance
Dr Caroline Marriott	Director of Medical Services (Hospitals)
Dr Robin McKee	Director of Medical Services (Community)
Eamonn Molloy	Director of Human Resources & Corporate Affairs
Paul Ryan	Director of Planning
Norma Evans	Director of Hospital Services
Paul Ryan	Director of Planning, Contracts and Information, Deputy Chief Executive
Miriam Somerville	Director of Hospital Community Learning & Disability Services

Main Facilities within the North and West Belfast HSS Trust
Muckamore Abbey

Northern Ireland Ambulance Service HSS Trust

12-22 Linenhall Street
Belfast, BT2 8BS
Tel: 028 9040 0999
Fax: 028 9040 0900

Chairman: Doug Smyth
Chief Executive: Liam McIvor

Royal Group of Hospitals and Dental Hospital HSS Trust

The Royal Group of Hospitals and Dental Hospital HSS Trust is Northern Ireland's biggest and best-known hospital complex on a 70-acre site on the Southern outskirts of Belfast. Many, if not most of Northern Ireland's regional speciality healthcare services are provided by the Trust. The Royal Group of Hospitals comprises the Royal Victoria Hospital; the Royal Jubilee Maternity Services; Royal Belfast Hospital for Sick Children and the Dental Hospital. The Royal Group has over 20% of all acute beds in Northern Ireland and has over 6,000 staff. The Group has a operating budget of around £250m.

Grosvenor Road, Belfast, BT12 6BA
Tel: 028 9024 0503 / Fax: 028 9024 0899
Corporate Affairs: 028 9089 4702

Chairman: Dr Paul McWilliams OBE
Chief Executive: Mr William McKee (pictured)

Royal Victoria Hospital

Board Members

Michael McBride	Medical Director
Deirdre O'Brien	Director of Nursing and Patient Services
Sean Donaghy	Director of Finance
Hugh McCaughey	Director of Organisational Development
De Ben Wilson	Non Executive Director
Anne Balmer	Non Executive Director
Frank Caddy	Non Executive Director
Cllr Tom Hartley	Non Executive Director
James O'Kane	Non Executive Director

Main Facilities within the Royal Group of Hospitals and Dental Hospital HSS Trust

The Royal Victoria Hospital; Royal Jubilee Maternity Hospital; Royal Belfast Hospital for Sick Children; Dental Hospital;

South and East Belfast HSS Trust

Knockbracken Healthcare Park,
Saintfield Road, Belfast, BT8 8BH
Tel: 028 9056 5656 / Fax: 028 9056 5813

Chairman: Robin Harris
Chief Executive: Patricia Gordon
The Trust has an annual budget of around £135m.

Board Members

Dr Paul Bell	Executive Chief of Medicine
Norman Carson	Executive Director of Finance
Stephen O'Brian	Executive Director of Social Work Head of Adult Services
Ray McGee	Executive Director of Nursing
John Veitch	Head of Children's Services
Dr Gillian Rankin	Head of Service Development
Jennifer Thompson	Head of Planning
Eddie Currie	Head of Operational Services
Vivienne Walker	Head of Human Resources
Eamon Hanna	Non Executive Director
Eileen Evason	Non Executive Director
Peter Osborne	Non Executive Director
Patrick Scott	Non Executive Director

Acute Facilities within the South and East Belfast HSS Trust
Acute Psychiatric at the Knockbracken Healthcare Centre Park

Sperrin Lakeland HSS Trust

The Sperrin Lakeland Health and Social Care Trust covers the three District Council Areas of Fermanagh, Omagh and Strabane (part). It provides services to around 178,000 people spread over a wide area including some of Northern Ireland's remotest locations. The Trust has an annual budget of around £115m. The Trust is at the heart of a major struggle in Omagh where a very strong lobby exists against the proposed downgrading of Omagh hospital.

Strathdene House, Tyrone and Fermanagh Hospital,
Omagh, BT79 0NS
Tel: 028 8283 5285 / Fax: 028 8283 5286
Email: hhcc@slt.n-l-nhs.uk

Chairman: Richard Scott
Chief Executive: Hugh Mills

Patrick Grogan	Non Executive Director
Jenny Irvine	Non Executive Director
Kevin Martin	Non Executive Director
Pat O'Kane	Non Executive Director
Dinah Short	Non Executive Director
Dr Jim Kelly	Medical Director
Gabriel Carey	Director of Mental Health & Elderly Services
Eugene Fee	Director of Acute Hospital Services
Colm McCauley	Director of Finance

Main Facilities within the Sperrin Lakeland HSS Trust
Erne Hospital
Tyrone County Hospital

Ulster Community and Hospitals Trust

Ulster Community and Hospitals Trusts provide a comprehensive range of hospital community health and social services. It is one of the largest HSS Trusts in Northern Ireland with an annual budget of around £160m.

39 Regent Street, Newtownards, BT23 4AD
Tel: 028 9181 6666 / Fax: 028 9182 0140

Chairman: Eileen Grant
Chief Executive: Jim McCall

Acute Facilities within the Ulster Community and Hospitals Trust
Ulster Hospital

United Hospitals HSS Trust

Bush House, 45 Bush Road, Antrim, BT41 2QB
Tel: 028 9442 4673 / Fax: 028 9442 4675

Chairman: Mr Raymond Milnes
Chief Executive: Bernard Mitchell

Acute Facilities within the United Hospitals HSS Trust
Antrim Hospital
Whiteabbey Hospital
Mid Ulster Hospital

Health and Social Services Councils

Northern Ireland has four Health and Social Services Councils; one shadowing each of the four Health and Social Services Boards. The Councils were established in 1991 under the provisions of the Health and Personal Social Services (Northern Ireland) Order 1991.

The principal function of each Council is to represent the interests of the general public in all areas of health and social services. This includes providing advice, information and support on a wide range of related issues, and guidance for those considering making a complaint about a service. Councils also work with local groups to monitor services, and to encourage people to put forward their opinions on health and social services, partly by carrying out surveys to gauge opinion. Councils represent the public by participating in consultations about health and social services, and acting to improve services. Finally, Councils visit health and social services facilities, to ensure that the public is being effectively provided for.

A Work Programme for each of the Councils is drawn up in conjunction with the Health Board being shadowed, and an annual report is published. The Councils are funded by their respective Boards but are autonomous. Councils have the right of consultation on developments and changes to services provided by Health and Social Services Boards, as well as the right to have formal meetings with Boards. They are also entitled to visit and inspect health and social service facilities.

Each Health and Social Services Council is composed of representatives from local councils, voluntary organisations and other interested groups. The Eastern Council has 30 members as the Eastern Board represents more people than any other Board. The Northern, Southern and Western Boards each have 24 members. A team of full-time staff support the councils. Membership comprises approximately:

- 40% district councillors;
- 30% voluntary/community nominations;
- 30% individuals with an interest in health and social care.

The Councils have a statutory duty to publish and distribute an annual report giving details of their performance during the preceding year.

The Councils must also adhere to a Code of Practice on Openness in the HPSS. Members must abide by a Code of Conduct, covering issues such as impartiality, financial accountability, confidentiality, non-discriminatory practices, casual gifts, hospitality and declaration of interests.

Each council maintains an up to date register of members' interests, which is open to the public for inspection. The Councils also have a procedure to enable members of the public to make complaints. The Ombudsman can ultimately investigate complaints about the Councils.

Details of each of the four Health and Social Services Councils follow.

Eastern Health and Social Services Council

1st Floor McKelvey House, 25-27 Wellington Park
Belfast, BT1 6GQ
Tel: 028 9032 1230 / Fax: 028 9032 1750
Email: ecouncil@dhssc.n-i.nhs.uk

Chairman: Brian Coulter

Council Members

Eileen Askham	Newtownards
Cllr Elizabeth Campbell	Lisburn City Council
Cllr James Convery	Belfast City Council
Cllr Alan Crowe	Belfast City Council
Cllr Dermot Curran	Down District Council
Cllr Gordon Dunn North	Down Borough Council
Cecil Graham	East Belfast
Elizabeth Hamilton	Comber
Dr Michael Harriott	South Belfast
Ald Michael Henderson	Castlereagh Borough Council
Brian Henning	Bangor
Brendan Henry	North Belfast
James Hutchinson	Comber
Cllr Joseph Lockhart	Lisburn City Council
Cllr Naomi Long	Belfast City Council
Brian Marshall	South Belfast
Sylvia McGarry	Lisburn
Patricia McMillen	Donaghadee
Cllr Elaine McMillen	Belfast City Council
George Monds	South Belfast
Cllr Marie Moore	Belfast City Council
Mary Muldoon	South Belfast
Myrtle Neill	Dundonald
Muriel Patterson	South Belfast

Chief Officer: Jane Graham
Senior Managers: Raymond Newman, Brenda Devine
Research Officer: Geraldine Boyle

The Eastern Health and Social Services Council has 30 members in comparison to the 24 members of the other Councils. 12 members of the Eastern Council are elected representatives of city, district and borough councils. Voluntary and community groups or people in the community with an interest in health and social services nominate the other 18 members.

Northern Health and Social Services Council (NHSSC)

8 Broadway Avenue, Ballymena, BT43 7AA
Tel: 028 2565 5777 / Fax: 028 2565 5112

Chairperson: Mr Tom Creighton
Chief Officer: Noel Graham

Board Members

Rosemary Armstrong	Portstewart
Mary Baker	Magherafelt
Mr Cameron	Ballymena
Tom Creighton	Carrickfergus
Robert Montgomery	Magherafelt

Beth Adger	Ballymena
Maureen Anderson	Ballgally
May Beattie	Carrickfergus
Marina Bigger	Magherafelt
Pearse Boyle	Maghera
Joan Drummond	Larne
Denise Hamill	Ballymena
Nigel Hamilton	Islandmagee
Irene Johnston	Coleraine
Liz Johnston	Coleraine
George Kernohan	Carrickfergus
Catherine McCambridge	Ballycastle
Hugh McKenna	Jordanstown
John Millar	Carrickfergus
Janet Montgomery	Antrim
Rae Morrison	Portstewart
Stephen Nicholl	Antrim
Tommy Nicholl	Cullybackey
Mark Nolan	Islandmagee
Ian Stevenson	Ballymoney

The total expenditure of the Northern Health and Social Services Council amounted to £171, 258 to 31 March 2001. The Northern Health and Social Services Council provides services to 430, 500 people covering ten District and Borough Council areas of:

- Antrim
- Ballymena
- Magherafelt
- Cookstown
- Larne
- Carrickfergus
- Newtownabbey
- Coleraine
- Ballymoney
- Moyle

Southern Health and Social Services Council

Quaker Buildings, High Street
Lurgan, BT66 8BB
Tel: 028 3834 9900 / Fax: 028 3834 9858

Chairperson: Mrs Roisin Foster
Chief Officer: Delia van der Lenden

Board Members

Roisin Foster, Sydney Anderson, Pat Brannigan, Annie Burrell, Lynne Cairns, John Coulter, Brendan Curran, Mary Ferris, Nazy Harris, Clive Henning, Peter Kearns, Pat Mallon, Brendan Montague, Peter Murray, John McArdle, Jim McCart, Wilfred McFadden, Adrian McKinney, Yvonne McKnight, David Simpson, Charles Rollston, Eileen Wright

The Southern Health and Social Services Council was established in 1991 as one of the four Health and Social Services Councils in Northern Ireland. The Council is an independent consumer organisation, which has the legal right to:

- Be consulted by the Southern Health and Social Services Board on any major development in or changes to the service;
- Receive information from the Board about the planning and running of services;
- Visit health and social services facilities in the public sector.

Western Health and Social Services Council

Hilltop, Tyrone and Fermanagh Hospital
Omagh, BT79 0NS
Tel: 028 8225 2555 / Fax: 028 8225 2544

Chairman: F Hughes
Vice-Chairman: M Falls
Chief Officer: Stanley Millar

Board Members

Mr G A Baxter	Omagh District Council
Mr P Brogan	Beragh
Mr G Campbell	Derry City Council
Mr M Coyle	Dungiven (Council Representative)
Mr M Devlin	Londonderry
Mrs H Quigley	Derry City Council
Mr S Gallagher	Derry City Council
Mrs M Harte	Carrickmore
Mr C Mc Claughry	Kesh (District Council Representative)
Mr L McQuaid	Dromore (District Council Representative)
Mr F McQuillan	Newtownbutler (District Council Representative)
Mr W T Monthgomery	Castlederg
Mrs A Moore	Omagh
Mr G MacLochlainn	Derry City Council
Mr J H O'Brien	Londonderry
Mr J O'Kane	Strabane (District Council Representative)
Mr R Rogan	Londonderry
Mrs M Rolston	Garvary
Miss M C Timoney	Garrison
Mrs S White	Omagh

Local Health and Social Care Groups

Local Health and Social Care Groups (LHSCGs), which are committees of Health and Social Services Boards, bring together providers of local primary and community services under a management board whose membership is drawn from representatives of primary care professionals, the community and services users, as well as Health and Social Services Boards and Trusts. While others may be co-opted onto the management boards, the core membership comprise the following:

Table 5.9 Local Health and Social Care Groups Membership Core

Local Community Trusts HSS Boards*	5
Local Acute Trusts	1
GPs	5
Nurses	1
Community/Service Users	2
Social Workers	1
Community Pharmacists	1
Allied Health Professionals	1
LHSCG Manager	1

* (Must include 1 Nurse, 1 Social Worker & 1 Allied Health Professional)

There are 15 LHSCGs based around GP practices and representing natural communities. There are six groups in the Eastern Board area, four in the Northern Board, three in the Southern Board and two in the Western Board area, covering populations ranging between 60,000 to 200,000.

LHSCGs are responsible for the planning and delivery of primary and community care and for contributing to their Health and Social Services Boards' commissioning decisions seeking to reflect the local dimension. Ultimately they will assume greater responsibility for the commissioning of services which will involve delegated budgets. Key tasks for the LHSCGs include:

- Identifying local health and social care needs and setting objectives to meet them;
- Contributing to Heath and Wellbeing Investment Plans;
- Taking steps to promote equality of opportunity and reduce inequalities in health and social care and in access to services, consistent with the existing Targeting Social Need Policy;
- Looking for ways to improve and develop primary care services at local levels while taking account of local and national priorities;
- Contributing to efforts to reduce waiting lists and waiting times for treatment;
- Complying with HPSS quality standards and guidelines for services;
- Working across health and social services boundaries and in partnership with other organisations to meet their communities' needs: and
- Ensuring value for money in the use of resources available.

Table 5.10 Local Health and Social Care Groups Membership Core

LHSCGs	GPs (No of)	Dentists (No of)	Opticians Optometrist practices	Pharmacists Community practices
Ards	40	22	12	20
North Down	37	45	12	19
Down	33	22	9	21
Lisburn	56	38	16	28
North & West Belfast	129	89	14	62
South & East Belfast	132	128	40	71
Antrim/Ballymena	69	44	11	20
Causeway	63	41	15	28
East Antrim	75	57	16	37
Mid Ulster	43	27	9	24
Southern	79	26	16	44
Northern	107	35	14	44
Newry & Mourne	60	38	8	29
Craigavon & Banbridge	79	48	13	31
Armagh & Dungannon	66	61	10	29

North/South, East/West and International Co-operation on Health

North/South

The Belfast Agreement introduced new arrangements for co-operation on health issues. The North/South Ministerial Council provides a structure for Ministers of all departments throughout Ireland to facilitate the exchange of information, discussion and consultation with a view to cooperating on matters of mutual interest. While agreement may be reached on the adoption of common policies in areas where there is a mutual cross-border and all-island benefit, decisions would be taken on implementation separately in each jurisdiction. Where appropriate, decisions on policies and action at an all-island and cross-border level would be implemented by the new cross-border implementation bodies. Six cross-border implementation bodies have been established, including the Food Safety Promotion Board.

The Food Safety Promotion Board

The key function of the Food Safety Promotion Board is to ensure that producers, processors, distributors, caterers and general public take responsibility for the provision of safe food. Other functions include microbiological surveillance of food borne diseases, and promotion of scientific co-operation. The Board also aims to develop a strategy for the island of Ireland for the delivery of specialised laboratory services.

The Board consults widely where appropriate and works closely with the Food Standards Agency in Northern Ireland, and the Food Safety Authority of Ireland (FSAI) in the South. Further information on the Food Safety Promotion Board, including contact details can be found on page 53.

Practical North/South Co-operation under Health

In addition the North/South Ministerial Council (NSMC) identified health as one of the six additional areas for co-operation and collaboration. Five specific areas have been highlighted for co-operation under Health:

- Accident and Emergency services;
- Planning for Major Emergencies;
- Co-operation on High Technology Equipment;
- Cancer Research;
- Health Promotion.

The NSMC agreed to share information and discuss opportunities for co-operation in relation to health promotion on an all Ireland basis, and to collaborate on public information campaigns, particularly major media campaigns. The NSMC also aims to examine the scope for research and public information and education in the areas of heart disease, cancer and smoking.

The Institute of Public Health in Ireland

The Institute of Public Health in Ireland, whose establishment predated the Belfast Agreement, works to promote North/South co-operation on public health in the following areas:

- tackling health inequalities;
- strengthening partnerships for health;
- contributing to public health information and surveillance;
- develop public health capacity and leadership;
- networking internationally and nationally.

Under the remit of the Investing for Health strategy the Institute for Public Health will enhance its capacity to include the comparative monitoring of trends in health, the determinants of health, and health inequalities North and South, and relative to other EU countries, and highlighting new areas of concern as they emerge. The Institute advises on the methodology for health equity impact assessments, and disseminates information from international research and experience throughout Ireland.

There are plans for the department to undertake a study on the potential for, and barriers to, North/South co-operation for public health. This study will be undertaken in conjunction with the health departments North and South, involving community organisations, health service and other public sector organisations and professional groups.

CAWT (Co-operation and Working Together)
A major cross-border health initiative known as CAWT, Co-operation and Working Together, is aimed at improving the health and social well being of people in Border areas.

- CAWT is made up of NWHB (ROI), NEHB (ROI), SHSSB (NI), WHSSB (NI) and 7 Trusts.
- Objective is improvement of health and social well being of border area population.
- Population Health Profile – first time comprehensive health and social care information is available on the border area as a region.

CAWT Objectives
- Improve the health and social well being of its resident population;
- Identify opportunities for co-operation in planning and provision of service;
- Assist border area to overcome their relative isolation within the EU;
- Involve the public sector in initiatives to fulfil common primary aims;
- Exploit opportunities for joint working/sharing of resources for mutual advantage.

European and International Programmes
European and international money has also been used to support cross-border programmes in the voluntary and community sector, for example in the area of early years and family support. It has been anticipated that there will be scope for drawing on the new EU Peace Programme in particular for specified cross-border purposes over the coming five years. Another area to be addressed is the development of common data systems to allow meaningful comparisons to be made on a North/South basis.

East/West Co-operation in Health

The British-Irish Council provides a structure for co-operation between Britain and Ireland. It has identified a range of areas for co-operation, including social exclusion, drug misuse, the environment, transport and other issues in health and education.

A Concordat provides a more specific framework for co-operation between the Department of Health in England and Departments concerned with health and social care in each of the devolved administrations. DHSSPS is also included in discussions, which feed in to the European Health Council.

There are a number of Joint Committees, which advise Health Departments such as the Joint Committee on Vaccination and Immunisation and the National Screening Committee.

Joint Ministerial Committee
There is a joint Ministerial committee on health issues, providing an opportunity for the separate administrations to share information, experience and best practice on a wide range of policy issues. These include developing common measures of performance, learning from each other's experiences and sharing ideas on incentives.

Inter-Departmental Group on Tobacco
An interdepartmental group on tobacco was convened at the time of publication of the White Paper 'Smoking Kills' (December 1998). The membership of this group includes representatives from DHSSPS and the health departments in London, Edinburgh and Dublin. The purpose of the group is to provide strategic direction and share information on action against tobacco.

Anti-Drugs Co-ordination
Strong links exist between the devolved administrations and the Anti Drugs Co-ordination Unit in the Cabinet Office. There is frequent contact on a range of issues relating to drug misuse, including progress with the implementation of strategies for action.

Foods Standards Agency
The Food Standards Agency (FSA), operates in Northern Ireland and in Britain. It provides policy advice to Ministers on food safety, food standards and aspects of nutrition, and assists in the preparation of draft subordinate legislation. The Agency also provides representation in negotiations in the EU, and operates the Food Hazards Warning System. In addition, the Agency commissions research, and sets standards for enforcement of the legislation, monitoring performance of the enforcement authorities against these standards. It has the power to issue, refuse, revoke and suspend licences, approvals and authorisations. The Agency exercises its role in partnership with the Food Safety Promotion Board, so combining an East/West with a North/South dimension.

International Co-operation

Northern Ireland is one of the 51 members of the European Region of the World Health Organisation. The health policy framework for Europe, Health 21, sets 21 targets for health action, including closing the health gap between and with countries and multi Sectoral responsibility for health.

World Health Organisation initiatives in Northern Ireland include:

- Healthy Cities;
- Health Promoting Schools;
- Health Promoting Hospitals.

The Health Promotion Agency has recently been designated as a Collaborating Centre for Training and Research in Communications and Information Technology in Health promotion and disease prevention by the World Health Organisation.

Currently under development is a new EU Public Health Strategy and Action Plan and relationships are being developed with the National Cancer Institute in the United States with the objective of improving research and improving patient care. The Institute of Public Health in Ireland is working with leaders in Public Health in the US to develop a groundbreaking Creative Public Health Leadership course in Ireland.

Public Finance Initiative / Public-Private Partnership

The Public Finance Initiative (PFI), now known as Public-Private Partnership (PPP), was announced as a necessary and desirable way of raising finance for projects, by bringing private sector funding and skills to bear on long-term health infrastructural investment. Since its introduction in 1998, many schemes have been initiated using the PPP approach for funding. These have included management and disposal of clinical waste, equipment leasing and a new renal unit.

There is a considerable amount of public debate about the area of Public-Private Partnerships (PPPs), in no small part due to the perceived problems with privatisation in other areas. Opponents of PPP are concerned that private finance will put undue pressure on services to be profitable, rather than concentrate on serving the health needs of the population, and that services will suffer. A further criticism of PPP is that it is a very complex, drawn-out process which can cost the client more in the long term. However, advocates argue that it is vital to draw in private sector finance, as public money is not available in sufficient quantities. PPP also passes most of a project's risks to the private sector, protecting the public purse from some of the spectacular cost overruns that have occurred on major health projects in the past. Nonetheless, public-private finance is still in relatively early development, and whilst government is confident about the benefits it could bring, it remains to be seen how the policy will ultimately contribute in the long-term to health service provision in Northern Ireland.

Key Issues in Health in Northern Ireland

Health has risen steadily as a priority on the Government and public policy agenda in recent years. There has been growing concern that despite increased investment, the quantity and quality of health service delivery is not meeting public expectations. At its most visible Northern Ireland's health service is struggling in terms of long waiting lists for non-emergency surgery and insufficient hospital beds to accommodate demand, particularly in winter or whenever there is a serious flu epidemic. The Government has responded with a major 'Investing for Health' strategy initiative and is in the final stages of reconfiguring the structure administration and process for delivering healthcare effectively.

Investing for Health Initiative

The Investing for Health Initiative falls under "Working for a Healthier People", one of the Northern Ireland Executive's five overarching priorities in its Programme for Government. Investing for Health has been produced with the involvement of all the Departments in the Executive through the Ministerial Group on Public Health and complements the New Targeting Social Need initiative and Equality Agenda.

The aim of the Investing for Health initiative is the development of a long term plan for the improvement of health care in Northern Ireland and by tackling the causes of poor health to individuals such as poor living conditions and social and economic disadvantage, thus pre empting the need for medical care. The Investing for Health initiative is an attempt by the department to shift the emphasis in healthcare from the treatment of ill health to its prevention by tackling the factors that adversely affect health.

The DHSSPS has the lead responsibility for the Investing in Health framework including coordination at regional level. The main responsibilities of the department include:

- Providing guidance to the HPSS on the Investing for Health strategy and assisting with implementation;
- Co-ordinating the development and implementation of specific inter-agency strategies
- Preparation of public health legislation, including legislation to control tobacco advertising;
- Devising policy on and structural arrangements for health promotion monitoring and overseeing the performance of the Health and Social Services, including changes in the roles of Boards, Trusts and the Health Promotion Agency;
- Developing human resources policies for the HPSS to support Investing for Health;
- Implementing and developing its own Equality Scheme and New TSN Action Plan;
- Arranging for the introduction of new systems required to support the HPSS contribution to Investing for Health;
- Supporting regional voluntary organisations working for health improvement;
- Co-ordination of cross-border and international co-operation for health improvement;

- Devising policy on and structural arrangements for the control of communicable diseases, immunisation and screening.

Under the terms of the Investing for Health strategy the DHSSPS has undertaken a review of Public Health functions in Northern Ireland. The aim of the review is to ensure that the department has all the components in place to respond to the health challenges facing Northern Ireland.

The Hayes Report - Hospital Rationalisation

With severe overcrowding in hospitals and a perceived inability on the part of the NHS to cope, in particular with a winter flu epidemic in 1999/2000, the Health Minister announced a wide-ranging review of the health service in the region with a particular emphasis on acute services.

The issue of rationalisation of hospital services has been debated widely, with many interpreting the terms as simply 'cutting back' on services. In August 2001 the report compiled by Chairman of the Acute Hospitals Review Group, Dr Maurice Hayes, was published, which made some far-reaching and controversial recommendations for change.

As a general finding, Dr Hayes reported that in the process of conducting a major consultation exercise all round Northern Ireland he had experienced considerable public dissatisfaction with the current provision of hospital services. Dr Hayes concluded that maintaining the status quo was therefore 'not an option'. The main recommendations of the report are set out below.

Acute Hospitals

Acute Hospitals are those capable of providing comprehensive accident and emergency services. Prior to devolution the Department of Health had been proposing to close seven of Northern Ireland's existing acute hospitals, centralising acute services to six main hospitals.

The original six to retain acute services under the Hayes recommendations were:

- Royal Victoria Hospital (RVH) Belfast
- City Hospital Belfast
- Ulster Hospital (Dundonald) Belfast
- Antrim Area Hospital Antrim
- Craigavon Area Hospital Craigavon
- Altnagelvin Derry

The Hayes report recommended that three more hospitals retain acute services, in addition to the six mentioned above. They were:

- Causeway Hospital Coleraine
- Daisy Hill Hospital Newry
- A New South West Hospital (to be built) Enniskillen

The hospitals that would lose their existing accident and emergency services would be:

- Mater Hospital Belfast
- Omagh Hospital Omagh
- Lagan Valley Lisburn
- Whiteabbey Newtownabbey
- and South Tyrone hospital, where the earlier decision had already been implemented.

In addition the Downe and Downpatrick hospitals would lose their maternity services. Inevitably, there were strong feelings about the downgrading of hospitals, and many critics argued that residents in areas served by them would be disadvantaged and possibly endangered by the reduction of services. Supporters of South Tyrone Hospital were particularly angry that the proposal was implemented so quickly in their area. In Tyrone public anger at the decision to downgrade Omagh Hospital was reflected in the election of a local GP Kieran Deeny as an independent Omagh Hospital candidate in the recent Assembly elections.

To compensate for the loss of acute services in some hospitals the Hayes report recommended that where possible a greater proportion of treatment should be delivered closer to patients' homes, either in health centres or in new local hospitals. The report did not recommend closing any hospitals, although this was of little compensation to those who perceived the loss of acute services at hospitals as a cost-cutting exercise that could have serious implications for the health of the local population.

Reorganisation of Health Service Structures

The Hayes report also made radical recommendations on the existing NHS structures in Northern Ireland.

It recommended that the four existing Health Boards be unified into one large single Board, and that the hospitals of Northern Ireland be further grouped into 3 'super' trusts, comprised as follows:

- **Greater Belfast,** including: RVH, City Hospital, Musgrave Park, Mater Hospital, Ulster Hospital, Whiteabbey Hospital, Lagan Valley, Downe Hospital
- **Northern,** including: Altnagelvin, Antrim Hospital, Causeway, Coleraine
- **Southern,** including: Craigavon Area Hospital, Daisy Hill, 'New' South-West Hospital (Enniskillen)

Other Findings

Although proposing certain cutbacks as part of the overall package, the Hayes report also called for much higher numbers of professional staff, in particular aiming for an increase of 100% in hospital consultants and a 25% increase in the number of general practitioners.

A rotation system for doctors, between acute and local hospitals, was also recommended, as was a higher level of investment in the ambulance service. If implemented its recommendations could take 15 years to fulfilment.

As something of a "hot potato" politically, there has been limited government action on foot of the recommendations of the Hayes Report. It can be expected however that these recommendations will be engaged more fully if local ministers return in a devolved administration following the recent 2003 Assembly election.

Private Healthcare

The NHS dominates healthcare in Northern Ireland although there is also a private sector presence in what is a growing health 'market'. The main players in the private market include BUPA, PPP, Norwich Union and WPA who all offer a range of different levels of private health insurance to individuals and to groups. For those who can afford it, private medical treatment guarantees immediate access to healthcare and it is this instant access rather than the actual treatment delivered that is often the key selling point. Medical insurance is also available, offering financial protection against illness and injury, although some people with poorer health, who are less affluent, are unable to afford it.

Ulster Independent Clinic

The main private sector hospital in Northern Ireland is the Ulster Independent Clinic in South Belfast, which, in addition to a wide range of healthcare treatment allows individuals (appropriately insured) to undergo operations without waiting and via their choice of surgeon.

NHS Consultants are free to operate a private practice as well as carry out their salaried NHS work. Many such consultants have private consulting rooms in their homes although some operate 'privately' within NHS facilities. A similar practice operates within dentistry; a dentist may offer the same service privately or on the NHS, with waiting times and costs differing greatly. Unlike the problems sometimes experienced in Britain, NHS dental services are widely available in Northern Ireland, although as there are sometimes long waiting times for non-emergency NHS treatment, the private sector is growing.

This system has attracted much criticism on grounds of equity. It is argued that a two-tier health service is evolving with a high-quality instant service for those who can afford it and a lower quality service with long waiting lists for those who cannot. In addition, there are controversial regional disparities, whereby some treatments are available on the NHS (i.e. free) in some regions and not in others, which affects Northern Ireland adversely. An example is IVF (in-vitro fertilisation), a fertility treatment that is available on the NHS in various parts of the UK, but not in Northern Ireland. Northern Ireland tends to suffer from significantly less financial support for some treatments, which are not considered essential.

Ulster Independent Clinic
245 Stranmillis Road, Belfast
Tel: 028 9066 1212 / Fax: 028 9038 1704

BUPA Health Screening Centre
83-85 Great Victoria Street, Belfast
Tel: 028 90 232 723 / Fax:028 90 238 1233

Complementary Medicine

Complementary medicine is a growing sector in Northern Ireland, including reflexology, Chinese medicine, homeopathy, acupuncture, chiropractic and hypnotherapy. These are not widely (if at all) available on the NHS, so patients have to pay for these types of health care.

Health Definitions

Acute Services/Secondary Care
Treatment and health care provided by hospitals. Of particular importance in hospital restructuring is the provision of accident and emergency services.

Acute Trusts
Trusts providing acute hospital care only

Community Care Services
Health or social care provided outside hospital

Community Trusts
Trusts providing Community Health and social services, but not acute hospital services

Primary Care
Health services provided by the GP, dentist, chemist, optician. Includes family and community health services and major components of social care delivered outside of hospitals, which may be accessed by an individual on their own behalf.

Social Care
Social care encompasses services provided to help people to cope with many types of personal hardship including:

- Physical or sensory disability;
- Protection of vulnerable children

Hospitals and Hospices Listing

Hospitals A-Z

Albertbridge Road Day Hospital
225 Albertbridge Road
Belfast, 4DR
Tel: 028 9045 6007
Fax: 028 9045 2638

Alexander Gardens Day Hospital
603 Antrim Road, BT15
Tel: 028 90 802 171
Fax: 028 90 802 176

Antrim Hospital
45 Bush Road
Antrim, BT41 2RL
Tel:028 94 42 4000
Fax: 028 94 42 4654

Ards Community Hospital
Church Street
Newtownards
BT23 4AS
Tel: 028 91 81 2661
Fax: 028 91 51 0113

Bangor Community Hospital
Castle Street
Bangor
BT20 4TA
Tel: 028 91 47 5100
Fax: 028 9147 5112

Belfast City Hospital
Lisburn Road
Belfast, BT9 7AB
Tel: 028 90 32 9241
Fax: 028 90 32 6614

Belvoir Park Hospital
Hospital Road
Belfast, BT8 8JR
Tel: 028 90 69 9069
Fax: 028 90 69 9337

Braid Valley Hospital
Cushendall Road
Ballymena
Tel: 028 2563 5200
Fax: 028 2563 5237

Causeway Hospital
4 Newbridge Road
Coleraine, bt52 1hs
Tel: 028 7032 7032
Fax: 028 7034 6190

Craigavon Area Hospital
68 Lurgan Road
Portadown, BT63 5QQ
Tel: 028 3833 4444
Fax: 028 3861 2471

Daisy Hill Hospital
5 Hospital Road
Newry, BT35 8DR
Tel: 028 3083 5000
Fax: 028 3083 5303

The Dental Hospital (RVH)
Grosvenor Road
Belfast
Tel: 028 90 240 503
Fax: 028 90 438 861

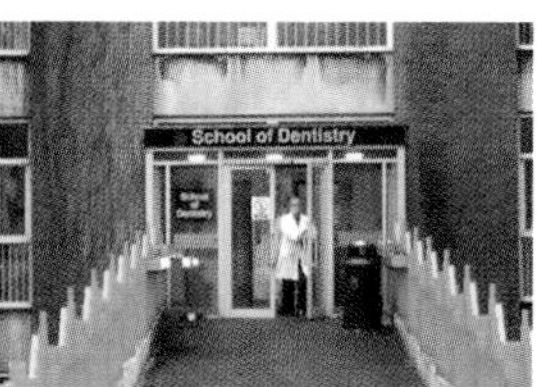

School of Dentistry, RVH

Downshire Hospital
Ardglass Road
Downpatrick
Tel: 028 4461 3311
Fax: 028 4461 2444

Downe Hospital
Pound Lane
Downpatrick, BT30 6JA
Tel: 028 4461 3311
Fax: 028 4461 5551

Erne Hospital
Cornagrade Road
Enniskillen, BT74 6AY
Tel: 028 6632 4711
Fax: 028 6682 6466

Forster Green Hospital
110 Saintfield Road
Belfast, BT8 4HD
Tel: 028 90 79 3681
Fax: 028 90 70 1526

Gransha Hospital
Clooney Road
Campsie, BT47 6TF
Londonderry
Tel: 028 7186 0261
Fax: 028 7186 5185

Holywell Hospital
60 Steeple Road
Antrim, BT41 2RJ
Tel: 028 9446 5211
Fax: 028 9441 3190

Lagan Valley Hospital
Hillsborough Road
Lisburn, BT28 1JP
Tel: 028 9266 5141
Fax: 028 9266 6100

Lurgan Hospital
100 Sloan Street
Lurgan, BT66 8NX
Tel: 028 3832 3262
Fax: 028 3832 9483

Mater Infirmorum Hospital
47-51 Crumlin Road
Belfast, BT14 6AB
Tel: 028 90 741 211
Fax: 028 90 741 342

Mid Ulster Hospital
59 Hospital Road
Magherafelt, BT45 5EX
Tel: 028 7963 1031
Facsimile:028 796 33050

Mourne Hospital
Newry Street
Kilkeel, BT34 4DP
Telephone:028 4176 2235
Fax: 028 4176 9770

Moyle Hospital
Old Glenarm Road
Larne
Tel: 028 2827 5431
Fax: 028 9442 4654

Muckamore Abbey Hospital
1 Abbey Road
Muckamore
Antrim, BT41 4SH
Tel: 028 9446 3333
Fax: 028 9446 7730

Multiple Sclerosis Centre
Dalriada Hospital
1A Coleraine Road
Ballycastle
BT54 6EY
Tel: 028 2076 3793
Fax: 028 2076 1501

Musgrave Park Hospital
Stockman's Lane
Belfast, BT9 7JB
Tel: 028 90 66 9501
Fax: 028 90 38 2008

Northwest Independent Hospital
Churchill House
Ballykelly
Limavady, BTG53 6HB
Tel: 028 7776 3090
Fax: 028 7776 8306

Robinson Memorial Hospital
Newal Road
Ballymoney
Tel: 028 2766 0322
Fax: 028 2766 0326

Royal Belfast Hospital for Sick Children (RVH)
184 Falls Road
Belfast
BT12 6BA
Tel: 028 90 24 0503
Facsimile:028 90 23 5340

Royal Maternity Hospital (RVH)
Grosvenor Road
Belfast
BT12 6BA
Tel: 028 90 24 0503
Fax: 028 90 23 5256

Royal Victoria Hospital (RVH)
Grosvenor Road
Belfast
BT12 6BA
Tel: 028 90 24 0503
Fax: 028 90 23 5256

St Luke's Hospital
Loughall Road
Armagh, BT61 7NQ
Tel: 028 3752 2381
Fax: 028 3752 6302

Shaftesbury Square Hospital
116-120 Great Victoria Street
Belfast, BT2 7BJ
Tel: 028 9032 9808
Fax: 028 90321 2208

South Tyrone Hospital
Carland Road
Dungannon, BT71 4AU
Tel: 028 8772 2821
Fax: 028 8772 7332

Thompson House Hospital
19-21 Magheralave Road
Lisburn, BT28 3BP
Tel: 028 9266 5646
Fax: 028 9266 7681

Whiteabbey Hospital
Doagh Road
Newtownabbey
Whiteabbey, BT37 9RH
Tel: 028 90 865 181
Fax: 028 90 365 083

Hospices

Foyle Hospice
61 Culmore Road, Derry, BT48 8JE
Tel: 028 7135 1010
Fax: 028 7135 1010

Northern Ireland Hospice
74 Somerton Road
Belfast, BT15 3LH
Tel: 028 90 781 836
Fax: 028 90 370 585

Northern Ireland Hospice Children's Service
525 Antrim Road
Belfast, BT36 2WB
Tel: 028 90 777 635
Fax: 028 90 777 144

Southern Area Hospice Services
St John's House
Courtenay Hill
Newry, BT34 2EB
Tel: 028 3026 7711
Fax: 028 3026 2816

Marie Curie Centre
Beaconsfield
Knock Road
Belfast, BT5 6NF
Tel: 028 9088 2000
Fax: 028 9088 2022

Housing in Northern Ireland

Overview

Until the reorganisation of local government in the early 1970s, responsibility for housing in Northern Ireland was held by local councils. In 1971 the Northern Ireland Housing Executive (NIHE) was created to take on this responsibility, under the then Department of the Environment. The NIHE was unique in that it was the UK's first comprehensive housing authority, with a wide range of powers and responsibilities beyond that of managing the public rented housing sector. Since the establishment of a new configuration of Government Departments, under the Belfast Agreement. The Department for Social Development has now, overall control over housing and housing policy, in Northern Ireland.

Table 5.11
The Housing Market in Northern Ireland

	Dec 1990	%	March 2002	%
Owner Occupancy	347, 000	60.9	464,000	70.4
NIHE	160,000	28.1	111,000	16.7
Housing Association	9,000	1.6	19,700	3.0
Private Rented	19,500	3.4	31,000	4.8
Vacant	34,500	6.1	33,600	5.00
Total	570,500		660,200	100

Source: NIHE Market Review and Perspectives 2003/06

Housing Market Analysis

Housing Policy

Responsibility for housing policy falls to the Housing Division within the Department for Social Development (DSD). The Division works closely with the Northern Ireland Housing Executive (NIHE) and the Registered Housing Associations (RHA). The Housing Division holds regulatory powers over these organisations, as well as overseeing that section of the private rented sector, which is controlled by the Rent (Northern Ireland) Order 1978. The Division also appoints the Board of the Northern Ireland Housing Executive and the Rent Assessment Panels.

The draft programme for Government published by the devolved administration in September 2002 gave housing a degree of priority but clearly behind that attached to health, education and infrastructure. The suspension of the devolved administration will not have had a beneficial effect on housing, probably slowing policy development and the legislative process. The period of suspension has also coincided with a marked slow-down in the Northern Ireland housing market following a period of rapid growth.

For the financial year 2002/2003 the overall Housing budget was around £612 million, obtained from rental income, capital receipts and government contribution. Within this total the Housing Executive's budget was £537 million with around £73 million allocated to Housing Associations. An additional £35 million from private finance supplements the social housing new build programme carried out by Housing Associations and the Co-Ownership Housing Association.

New house prices rose throughout 2002 and 2003, although more slowly than in 2000. The vast majority of new dwellings started were commissioned by the private sector, with over a third being detached. Actions for mortgage possession dropped sharply from the previous quarter, and less dramatically, from the same quarter in 2000.

The Northern Ireland Housing Executive

The Housing Centre
2 Adelaide Street, Belfast, BT2 8PB
Tel: 028 9024 0588 / Fax: 028 9043 9803

The Northern Ireland Housing Executive is a non-departmental public body established under the Housing Executive (Northern Ireland) Act, 1971. Since then it has built over 90,000 new homes, housed more than 500,000 people, improved 350,000 homes in the private sector, and sold over 100,000 homes to sitting tenants.

Housing Executive Headquarters

Its primary responsibilities cover a wide range of issues relating to housing and its provision in Northern Ireland. The NIHE assesses housing conditions and requirements, and devises strategies to address them. It also seeks to improve the condition of housing stock where practical, and to demolish unfit housing. The NIHE manages its own housing stock and provides information and advice on housing issues. It works with the Housing Council, and with the 26 local district councils, and acts as the Home Energy Conservation Authority in Northern Ireland to encourage energy efficiency within the residential sector.

The Housing Executive Headquarters is located in central Belfast. Five area offices are located in principal towns around Northern Ireland with a further 37 district offices and 12 grants offices providing a range of housing services at the local level.

During 2001/02 the Housing Executive:

- Invested a net £240m in Northern Ireland;
- Approved over 10,000 grant applications in the private sector;
- Completed 2,495 major adaptations;
- Improved 1,997 Housing Executive homes;
- Carried out major repairs to over 23,000 Housing Executive homes;
- Paid £319m in Housing Benefits to public and private sector tenants.

Housing Board

Responsibility for general policy, management and operation of the Housing Executive lies with the Housing Board. The ten person Board, including Chairman, Sid McDowell, meets every month and decides on all important matters affecting the Housing Executive including expenditure and new or revised policies. Seven members of the Board are appointed by the Minister responsible for housing, ie the Minister for Social Development, and the remaining three are nominated by the Northern Ireland Housing Council. At least one member must be female.

Members of the Board

Sid McDowell	Chairman
Jack Hood	Deputy Chairman
Anne Henderson	
Frank Cushnahan	
Mary McMahon	
Hugh Smyth	
Anne McAleenan	
Sam Gardiner	
Bobby McKee	
Cecil Noble	

Northern Ireland Housing Council

The Housing Council was established by the Housing Executive Act (Northern Ireland) 1971. The Council is consulted by the Housing Executive and the DSD on all matters that affect housing policy in Northern Ireland. The Housing Executive meets once a month with the Housing Council, explaining operations and strategy. The Housing Council is made up of one representative from each of the 26 District Councils in Northern Ireland. There are three Housing Council members on the Board of the Housing Executive who are appointed for a one-year period. The current membership of the Housing Council is set out below.

Local Authority Housing Council Members

Cllr B Loughran	Antrim Borough Council
Ald J Shields	Ards Borough Council
Cllr J Speers	Armagh City & District Council
Cllr J McKernan	Ballymena Borough Council
Cllr B Kenedy	Ballymoney Borough Council
Cllr J Baird	Banbridge District Council
Cllr D Browne	Belfast City Council
Cllr B J Crampsey	Carrickfergus Borough Council
Cllr B McBurney	Castlereagh Borough Counci
Ald P E A Armitage	Coleraine Borough Council
Cllr P McGlone	Cookstown District Council
Ald S Gardiner	Craigavon Borough Council
Cllr T Conway	Derry City Council
Cllr A McAleenan	Down District Council
Cllr B Monteith	Dungannon & South Tyrone BC
Cllr G Gallagher	Fermanagh District Council
Cllr R McKee	Larne Borough Council
Ald M Carten	Limavady Borough Council
Cllr W J Dillon	Lisburn Borough Council
Cllr P McErlean	Magherafelt District Council
Cllr D McAllister	Moyle District Council
Cllr B Curran	Newry & Mourne District Council
Cllr D Walker	Newtownabbey Borough Council
Cllr I Cree	North Down Borough Council
Cllr L McQuaid	Omagh District Council
Cllr T Kerrigan	Strabane District Council

Chief Executive and Central Directors

The Chief Executive, Paddy McIntyre, is the accounting officer and chief officer in the Housing Executive and reports directly to the Board. He is responsible for setting the organisation's strategic direction and objectives and for ensuring performance is maintained.

Chief Executive
Paddy McIntyre

The team of Central Directors report to the Chief Executive and as members of the Chief Executive's Management and Business Committees, decide on operational issues delegated by the Board as well as referring matters to it for approval. They are:

Stuart Cuddy	
John Wilson	
Mike Shanks	Director of Development
Colm McCaughley	Director of Client Services
Maureen Taggart	Director of Personnel and Management Services
Paul Brown	Director of Design Services
Imelda McGrath	Head of Information and Secretariat

The Structure of the Northern Ireland Housing Executive

The current structure of the Housing Executive is based on the following six divisions:

Corporate Services Division

The Director of Corporate Service Division is also the Deputy Chief Executive, presently Stewart Cuddy.

The division retains responsibility for strategic planning and research, information services and audit whilst taking responsibility for strategic relationships with housing associations and other private sector partners.

Housing and Regeneration

The division develops housing policy, landlord activity, commissioning and monitoring of physical projects including all regeneration activity.

Housing and regeneration is responsible for the management, maintenance and improvement of the Executive's 140,000 dwellings. Services are delivered to the public through a network of 37 local offices, including rent collection, maintenance, housing benefit, allocations, transfers and estate management.

District Managers report in turn to one of five Area managers. Schemes for the planned maintenance and improvement of dwellings are project managed by a province wide project services group. Building, maintenance and design standards are set by a technical standards group.

Design and Property Services

The division comprises all technical staff and is responsible for the design and delivery of physical programmes on site, as well as the management and operation of the private sector improvement grants function.

The division provides professional, technical and administrative support for the Housing Executive's programmes through five Practice Groups. Each Group operates as a business and has to compete with private sector consultants for Housing Executive work. The Division also includes the Direct Labour Organisation.

Personnel and Management Services

This Division maintains a range of support services:

- Personnel: covering training and development activities.
- Facilities Services: including purchasing, accommodation, health & safety, office services and security.
- Legal Services: providing legal advice to the Board and Directors.
- Information Technology: involved with the introduction and management of computerised systems across the organisation.

Finance Division

The division provides support in relation to financial planning, financial accounting, management accounting and financial services.

Contact with Community Associations

The Housing Executive maintains regular contact with more than 500 community associations. This contact takes place at a local level with district officers, through local community associations and the District Consumer Panel. Contact at area level is with the Community Advisory Group and at central level, with the Central Community Advisory Group.

Housing Executive Contact Details

Headquarters

Housing Executive
The Housing Centre
2 Adelaide Street, Belfast, BT2 8GA
Tel: 028 9024 0588
Contact name: Mr Paddy McIntyre

Area Offices

Belfast
32-36 Great Victoria Street, Belfast, BT2 7BL
Tel: 028 9031 7000
Contact name: Maurice Johnson

Homeless Advice Centre
32-36 Great Victoria Street, Belfast, BT2 7BL
Tel: 028 9031 7000
Contact name: Des Marky

Private Sector
Housing Benefit, 32-36 Great Victoria Street
Belfast, BT2 7BL
Tel: 028 9031 7000
Contact name: Helen Walkers

North East
Twickenham House
Mount Street, Ballymena, BT43 6BP
Tel: 028 2565 3399
Contact name: Frank O'Connor

South
Marlborough House
Central Way, Craigavon, BT64 1AJ
Tel: 028 3834 1188
Contact name: Eamon McKeown

South East
Strangford House
28 Court Street, Newtownards, BT23 7NX
Tel: 028 9182 0600
Contact name: Jim Jackson

West
Richmond Chambers
The Diamond, Derry, BT48 6QP
Tel: 028 7137 2000
Contact name: Sean Mackie

District Offices

Antrim

48 High Street, Antrim, BT41 4AN
Tel: 028 9442 8142
Contact name: Michael Dallat
Covers: Antrim Town, Crumlin, Randlestown, Templepatrick, Toome

Armagh

48 Dobbin Street, Armagh, BT61 7BR
Tel: 028 3752 3379
Contact name: Mrs Joyce Dobbin
Covers: Armagh, Benburb, Charlemont, Keady, Loughgall, Markethill, Poyntzpass, Richhill, Tandragee

Ballycastle

Fleming House, Coleraine Road
Ballycastle, BT54 6EY
Tel: 028 2076 2014
Contact name: Mr Gerry McCloskey
Covers: Ballycastle, Armoy, Cushendun, Bushmills, Cushendall, Waterfoot

Ballymena

Twickenham House
Mount Street, Ballymena, BT43 6BP
Tel: 028 2564 4211
Contact name: Mr Frank O'Connor
Covers: Ballymena Town, Ahoghill, Broughshane, Cullybackey, Galgorm, Kells, Portglenone, Straid

Ballymoney

50-54 Main Street
Ballymoney, BT53 6AL
Tel: 028 2766 3442
Contact name: Mr Micahel Dallot
Covers: Ballymoney Town, Cloughmills, Dunloy, Rasharkin

Banbridge

56 Bridge Street, Banbridge, BT32 3JU
Tel: 028 4066 2721
Contact name: Mr Paul Major
Covers: Banbridge Town, Dromore, Gilford, Rathfriland

Bangor

2 Alfred Street, Bangor, BT20 5DH
Tel: 028 9127 0761
Contact name: Mr Robert Mahaffy
Covers: Bangor, Conlig, Groomsport, Holywood

Belfast 1

9 Upper Queen Street, Belfast, BT1 6FB
Tel: 028 9032 8282
Contact name: Mr Jan Sweeney
Covers: West Belfast, Hannahstown, Upper Falls

Belfast 2

Laganview House, 95 Ann Street
Belfast, BT1 3HF
Tel: 028 9032 4558
Contact name: Mr Richard Williamson
Covers: East Belfast

Belfast 3

Murray House, Murray Street
Belfast, BT1 6DN
Tel: 028 9032 3642
Contact name: Mr Jim Carlin
Covers: West Belfast, Lower Falls, Clonard, Divis

Belfast 4

10-16 Hill Street, Belfast, BT1 2LA
Tel: 028 9024 1525
District Manager Mr Sean McKenna
Covers: North Belfast, Whitewell, Shore Road

Belfast 5

83-87 Shankill Road, Belfast, BT13 1FD
Tel: 028 9032 9442
Contact name: Mr Gordon Reilly
Covers: West Belfast, Shankill, Woodvale, Glencairn

Belfast 6

1st Floor, Spencer House
71 Royal Avenue, Belfast, BT1 1FE
Tel: 028 9032 6477
Contact name: Mr Ivan Kelly
Covers: North Belfast, Ardoyne, Glenbryn, Oldpark

Belfast 7

90-106 Victoria Street
Belfast, BT1 3GN
Tel: 028 9024 8312
Contact name: Mr Liam Kinney
Covers: South Belfast, Ormeau, Donegall Road, Taughmonagh

Brownlow (Craigavon)

16 Legahory Centre
Craigavon, BT65 5BE
Tel: 028 3832 6417
Contact name: Mr Paul Hughes
Covers: Brownlow, Craigavon Central area, Derrymagh, Derrytrasna

Carrickfergus

19 High Street
Carrickfergus, BT38 7AN
Tel: 028 9335 1115
Contact name: Mr Aisling Marks
Covers: Carrickfergus Town, Greenisland, Whitehead

Castlereagh

30 Church Road, Dundonald, BT16 0LN
Tel: 028 9048 5237
Contact name: Mr Paul Carland
Covers: Castlereagh area, Newtownards, Carryduff, Moneyreagh

Coleraine

19 Abbey Street, Coleraine, BT52 1DU
Tel: 028 7035 8111
Contact name: Ms Joan Baird
Covers: Coleraine Town, Castlerock, Kilrea, Portrush, Portstewart

Cookstown

15 Morgan's Hill Road
Cookstown, BT80 8HA
Tel: 028 8676 2004
Contact name: Mr Bob Smyth
Covers: Cookstown, Moneymore, Pomeroy, Stewartstown

Dairy Farm (Lisburn)

Stewartstown Road, Belfast, BT17 0SB
Tel: 028 9061 1199
Contact name: Mr Danny Cochrane
Covers: Poleglass, Twinbrook

Downpatrick

51 John Street, Downpatrick, BT30 6HS
Tel: 028 4461 3551
Contact name: Mr Ian McCrickard
Covers: Downpatrick, Ardglass, Ballynahinch, Castlewellan, Killyleagh, Newcastle, Saintfield

Dungannon

Ballygawley Road, Dungannon, BT70 1AT
Tel: 028 8772 3000
Contact: Mr John Quigley
Covers: Dungannon Town, Aughnacloy, Ballygawley, Coalisland, Fivemiletown, Moy

Fermanagh

Riverview House, Head Street
Enniskillen, BT74 7O4
Tel: 028 6632 5770
Contact name: Mr Michael Callaghan
Covers: Fermanagh County, Belleek, Irvinestown, Kesh, Lisbellaw

Larne

Sir Thomas Dickson Buildings,
Victoria Road, BT40 1RU
Tel: 028 2827 4426
Contact name: Mrs Phylis Graig

Limavady

33 Catherine Street, Limavady, BT49 9DA
Tel: 028 7176 2711
Contact name: Mr John Donnell
Covers: Limavady Town, Ballykelly, Bellarena, Dungiven

Lisburn
29 Antrim Street, Lisburn, BT28 1AU
Telephone 028 9266 5222
Contact name: Mr Malocky McMahon
Covers: Lisburn City, Aghalee, Drumbo, Glenavy, Hillsborough, Moira

Londonderry 1
Ulster Bank Chambers
Waterloo Place, Derry, BT48 6BT
Tel: 028 7126 6227
Contact name: Mr Sam McPherson
Covers: Bogside, Brandywell, Creggan, Rosemount

Londonderry 2
2 Glendermott Road
Waterside, Derry, BT47 1AU
Tel: 028 7131 1490
Contact name: Ms Avril McAllister
Covers: Waterside, Claudy, Eglinton

Londonderry 3
14 Collon Terrace, Derry, BT48 7QP
Tel: 028 7137 3683
Contact name: Mr Walter Mullan
Covers: Culmore Road, Ballymcgroarty, Shantallow

Lurgan (Craigavon)
122 Hill Street, Lurgan, BT66 6BU
Tel: 028 3832 6417
Contact name: Mr Paul Hughes
Covers: Lurgan Town

Magherafelt
3 Ballyronan Road, Magherafelt
BT45 6BP
Tel: 028 8673 1121
Contact name: Mr Herbert Patterson
Covers: Magherafelt, Bellaghy, Draperstown, Maghera, Tobermore

Newry
35-45 Boat Street, Newry, BT34 2DB
Tel: 028 3026 7331
Contact name: Mr Gervase McGuigan
Covers: Newry City, Bessbrook, Crossmaglen, Hilltown, Rostrevor, Warrenpoint, Annalong, Kilkeel

Newtownabbey 1
Rantalard House, Rathcoole Drive
Rathcoole, Newtownabbey, BT37 9AG
Tel: 028 9036 5911
Contact name: Mr Keery Irvine
Covers: Bawnmore, Rathcoole, Whiteabbey

Newtownabbey 2
2 Ballyearl Drive, New Mossley
Newtownabbey, BT36 5XJ
Tel: 028 9084 3711
Contact name: Mr Brian Newman
Covers: Ballyclare, Glengormley, Monkstown, New Mossley

Newtownards
2-32 Frederick Street
Newtownards, BT23 4LR
Tel: 028 9181 8979
Contact name: Mr Michael Taylor
Covers: Newtownards, Ballygowan, Comber, Portaferry, Portavogie

Omagh
Riverston House, 7 Holmview Terrace
Omagh, BT79 0AH
Tel: 028 8224 7701
Contact name: Mr Ivan Armstrong
Covers: Omagh, Dromore, Fintona, Sixmilecross

Portadown
41 Thomas Street, Portadown, BT62 3AF
Tel: 028 3836 1895
Contact name: Mrs Jill England
Covers: Portadown Estates

Strabane
48 Railway Road, Strabane, BT82 8EH
Tel: 028 7138 2637
Contact name: Mr Seamus Kelly
Covers: Strabane, Donemana, Castlederg, Newtownstewart, Sion Mills

Home Improvement Grant Offices

Ballyclare
141 Mill Road, Ballyclare, BT39 9DZ
Tel: 028 9335 2849

Ballymena
Twickenham House, Mount Street
Ballymena, BT43 6BP
Tel: 028 2565 3399

Belfast
32-36 Great Victoria Street
Belfast, BT2 7BL
Tel: 028 9031 7000

Craigavon
Marlborough House, Central Way
Craigavon, BT64 1AJ
Tel: 028 3834 1188

Fermanagh
Riverview House, 15 Head Street
Enniskillen, BT74 7DA
Tel: 028 6632 5770

Lisburn
46 Graham Gardens, Lisburn, BT28 1XE
Tel: 028 9266 5222

Londonderry
Richmond Chambers
The Diamond, Derry, BT48 6QP
Tel: 028 7137 2000

Newry
35-45 Boat Street, Newry, BT34 2DB
Tel: 028 3026 7331

Newtownards
Strangford House, 28 Court Street
Newtownards, BT23 7NX
Tel: 028 9182 0600

Omagh
McAllister House, Woodside Avenue
Omagh, BT79 7BP
Tel: 028 8224 6111

Housing in Multiple Occupation Units
32-36 Great Victoria Street
Belfast, BT2 7BL
Tel: 028 9031 7000

19 Abbey Street, Coleraine, BT52 1DU
Tel: 028 7035 8111

After Hours Homeless Service

Armagh
Tel: 028 3752 2381
Banbridge
Tel: 028 3833 4444
Belfast Inner & Greater
Tel: 028 9056 5444
Co Antrim
Tel: 028 9446 8833
Co Down (East, Mid & North)
Tel: 028 9056 5444
Coleraine
Tel: 028 9446 8833
Craigavon
Tel: 028 3833 4444
Derry
Tel: 028 7134 5171
Dungannon
Tel: 028 3752 2381
Enniskillen
Tel: 028 6632 4711
Magherafelt
Tel: 028 9446 8833
Newry & Mourne
Tel: 028 3083 5000
Omagh
Tel: 028 8224 5211

Emergency Repairs – After HourS

Belfast
Tel: 028 9024 6111
Derry
Tel: 028 7126 2628

Housing Associations

There are approximately 39 officially registered Housing Associations in Northern Ireland. These are independent not-for-profit organisations, often community-based, which provide good quality affordable housing for people in housing need. Although many of the associations are locally focused serving a particular locality, some of the larger associations operate throughout Northern Ireland. Others specialise in a particular kind of accommodation provision e.g. supported housing for the elderly. All are funded by the Department for Social Development. Housing Associations have around 24,000 social housing units under management. This accounts for around 18% of social housing – the remainder accounted for by the Northern Ireland Housing Executive. These proportions are likely to change significantly going forward as responsibility for social housing new build now rests exclusively with housing associations (no longer the responsibility of NIHE) while at the same time, the Housing Executive social housing stock will continue to decline through house sales to tenants.

One of the challenges facing Housing Associations is to project manage and complete new social housing at the rate targeted to meet priority housing need and to make inroads on existing waiting lists. The table below indicates the main players in the Housing Association sector.

Housing Associations A-Z

Table 5.12 Housing Associations with more than 500 Units of Accommodation, March 2002

	Total Units
BIH	3,363
Fold	3,410
Oaklee	3,121
North and West	2,127
Clanmill	1,389
Habinteg	1,303
SHAC	1,047
South Ulster	637
Presbyterian	612
Ulidia	516
Total	**17,525**
Total Housing Association Stock	**23,563**

Source: DSD, Housing Association Branch

Abbeyfield Housing Association
3 Grand Parade, Belfast, BT5 5HG
Tel: 028 9040 2045 / Fax: 028 9070 3776

Abode Housing Association
2a Wesley Court, Carrickfergus, BT38 8HS
Tel: 028 9336 0973 / Fax: 028 9336 1472

Management Committee

Chairman	Mr W C Balmer
Vice Chair	Mr H McKillen
Hon Secretary	Mr C Stewart
Hon Treasurer	Mr R Smyth

Mr V Scott, Mr J Patterson, Mrs M McCormick

Ark Housing Association
9 Stranmillis Road, Belfast, BT9 5AF
Tel: 028 9068 1808 / Fax: 028 9066 4524

Board of Management

Chairman	Oliver Migill
Secretary	Brian Greene
Treasurer	Jo-Anne McDonald

Sinead McKeag, Oliver Magill, Jack Boyle, Padraig McKeag
Eileen Gilmore, Rory Savage, Dr Gerard McCann

Ballynafeigh Housing Association Ltd
70 Kimberly Street, Belfast, BT7 3DY
Tel: 028 9049 1569 / Fax: 028 9064 3068
Mr Duncan Graham

Belfast Community Housing Association Ltd
131 Ravenhill Road, Belfast, BT6 8DR
Tel: 028 9046 3686 / Fax: 028 9046 0788
Mr Denis Blakely

BIH Housing Association Ltd
Russell Court
Claremont Street, Belfast, BT9 6JX
Tel: 028 9032 0485 / Fax: 028 9033 0402

Board of Management

Raymond Kilgore	Chairman
Mervyn McQuillan	Secretary
Harry Fletcher	Secretary

Martin Downey, Judith Eve, Mavis Hogg, Raymond Kilgore
Peter Murray, Donal McRandal, Clare McVeigh, Ian Nelson
Dr Peter Passmore, Anna Watson

Broadway Housing Association Ltd
Bedeque House, 3 Annesley Street, Belfast, BT14 6AJ
Tel: 028 9074 2984
Dr J. Cooper

Choice Housing Association
95A Finaghy Road South, Belfast, BT10 0BY
Tel: 028 9030 6920 Fax: 028 9030 6929
Chairman Mr Aurther Canning

Clanmil Housing
Waring Street, Belfast, BT1 2DX
Tel: 028 9087 6000 Fax: 028 9087 6001

Management Committee

Chairman	Derek Rankin
Vice Chair	Geraldine Rice
Honorary Treasurer	Mr C T Hogg
Chief Executive and Secretary	Clare McCarty
Director of Housing	Colette Moore
Finance Director	Jonathan Boggs
Corporate Services Manager	Karen Stilges
Director of Property Services	Carol McTaggart

Connswater Housing Association Ltd
2 Severn Street, Belfast, BT4 1FB
Tel: 028 9045 6596 Fax: 028 9045 6539
Chairman: Rev James McAllister

Co-Ownership Housing

Creating ***Homes*** *- Building* ***Communities***

Murray House, Murray Street
Belfast, BT1 6DN
Tel: 028 9032 7276
Fax: 028 9033 0720
Email: nicha@co-ownership.org
Web: www.co-ownership.org

Chief Executive
Alan Crowe

NICHA operates a form of Do It Yourself Shared Ownership (DIYSO) scheme called Co-Ownership throughout Northern Ireland. On an individual level Co-Ownership provides a low cost route into home ownership for people who could not afford to buy a home of their own otherwise. On a regional level it plays an important role in creating balanced and sustainable communities through tenure diversification as well as an active role in urban and rural regeneration initiatives.

Purchasers start with a 50%, 62.5% or 75% share in the property of their choice, and may increase their share at any time.

18,000 homes have been purchased through Co-Ownership to date.

Management Committee

Chairman	Alan Nicol
Vice Chairman	Anne O'Hara
Executive Director	Kevin Butler
Estates Manager	Eileen Heaney
Administration Manager	David McCallum
Finance Manager	Carol Shields

The Covenanter Residential Association Ltd

Cameron House, 98 Lisburn Road
Belfast, BT9 6AG
Tel: 028 9066 4875

Donacloney Housing Association Ltd

38 Main Street
Donaghcloney
Craigavon, BT66 7LR
Tel: 028 3888 1307 / Fax: 028 3888 1307
Contact: Mr George Savage

Dungannon & District Housing Association Ltd

27 Market Square, Dungannon, BT70 1JD
Tel: 028 8772 2121 / Fax: 028 8775 3870
Contact: John Gill

Filor Housing Association Ltd

82-290 Crumlin Road, Belfast, BT14 7AU
Tel: 028 9035 1131 / Fax: 028 9074 1755

Management Committee

Chairperson	Susan Russam
Vice Chairperson	Ms S Nichol
Secretary	Mr W Hutchinson
Treasurer	Mr J Hewitt

Fold Housing Association

3 Redburn Square, Holywood, BT18 9HZ
Tel: 028 9042 8314 / Fax: 028 9042 8167

Management Committee

Chairman	Mr W Cameron
Vice Chairman	Mr G LaveryTreasurer
Chief Executive	Mr B G Coulter
Director of Care Services	Mrs E Askham
Director of Development	Miss A Conway
Director of Finance	Mr T Dillon
Director of Housing	Mr L Flanigan
Director of Human Resources	Mrs M Pickles

Gosford Housing Associations Armagh Ltd

6 Georges Street, Armagh, BT60 1BY
Tel: 028 3752 8272 / Fax: 028 3752 8272
Contact: Grahan Crozier

Grove Housing Association Ltd

139 York Road, Belfast, BT15 3GZ
Tel: 028 9074 0803 / Fax: 028 9074 3520

Management Committee

Hon Treasurer Chairperson	Miss A Gibson
Hon Secretary	Mrs M Gyle

Habinteg Housing Association (Ulster) Ltd

Alex Moira House, 22 Hibernia Street
Holywood, BT18 9JE
Tel: 028 9042 7211 / Fax: 028 9042 8069

Management Committee

Chairman	John Cole
Vice Chairman/Treasurer	George D B Harkeness
Secretary	Martin H Turnbull

Senior Management Team

Director	David Duly
Assistant Director	Mai Moore
Housing Managers	Mary Hollywood Paul Kerr, Frances Magee
Development Manager	John Ferris
Finance Manager	Barry Caruth
PA to Director	Edith Ennis

Hearth Housing Association
66 Donegall Pass, Belfast, BT7 1BU
Tel: 028 9053 0121 / Fax: 028 9053 0122

Committee of Management

Chairman	Mrs K Latimer
Director	M Patton

Larne & District Housing Association
Pound Green Court, St Johns Place, Larne, BT40 1TB
Tel: 028 2827 6431
Chief Executive: Marie Kyle

Millbern Trust
18 Hamel Court, Belfast, BT6 9HX
Tel: 028 9079 5563 / Fax: 028 9070 5758
Chairman: Mr C.T. Hogg

Newington Housing Association (1975) Ltd
300 Limestone Road, Belfast, BT15 3AR
Tel: 028 9074 4055 / Fax: 028 9074 7624

Management Committee

Chairperson	Mr P Privilege
Vice-Chairperson	Mr M Salmon
Secretary	Mr G Walsh
Treasurer	Mr L Mooney

North Belfast Mission Housing Society Ltd
17 Palmerston Road, Belfast, BT4 1QA
Tel: 028 9336 3558 / Fax: 028 9335 5319

Management Committee

Chairman	H S Hughes
Treasurer	W Carson
Chief Executive	L McAdams,
Finance Officer	Ms B Surgenor
Property Officer	T Cooper
Head of Home	Mrs E Hastings

North & West Housing Ltd
18 Magazine Street, Derry, BT48 6HH
Tel: 028 7126 3819 / Fax: 028 7126 3362
Chairman: Joe Cowan

Oaklee Housing Association Ltd
Leslie Morrell House
37-41 May Street, Belfast, BT1 4DN
Tel: 028 9044 1300 / Fax: 028 9044 1346

Management Committee

Chairman	Mr Jim White
Treasurer	Jean Todd
Tenant Representative	Joyce Topley
Alicia Trueman	
Maureen Walker	
Vice Chairman	James White

Open Door Housing Association (NI) Ltd
10-14 Commercial Court, Belfast, BT1 2NB
Tel: 028 9024 3785 / Fax: 028 9023 5336

Management

Chairman	Paddy Gray
Treasurer	John Osborne
Secretary	Adrian McParlan

Presbyterian Housing Association (NI) Ltd
7A Weavers Court, Linfield Road, Belfast, BT12 5GH
Tel: 028 9050 7755 / Fax: 028 9050 7756

Committee of Management

Chairman	Mr Dermot Finnegan
Secretary	Mr R Kerr
Director	Mr John Tinman
Housing Manager	Mrs S Little
Finance Officer	Mr T Glenn
Maintenance Officer	Mrs S Lyons
Housing Officers	Mrs S Murphy

Rural Housing Association Ltd
64A Derry Road, Omagh, BT78 5DY
Tel: 028 8224 6118 / Fax: 028 8224 6120
Web: www.ruralhousing.co.uk/

Board of Management

Chairman	Mr A Kane
Vice Chairperson	Mrs K Burns
Honorary Secretary	Mr M Conway
Honorary Treasurer	Mr P McShane
Chief Executive	Mr Paddy McGurk
Housing Management Executive	Mr Stephen Fisher
Housing Officer	Ms Martina Cranny
Technical Officer	Mr Robert Clements
Administrative Officer	Ms Sharon Shortt

St Matthews Housing Association Ltd
58 Harper Street, Belfast, BT5 4EN
Tel: 028 9045 1070 / Fax: 028 90 45 4205

Chairman	Mr Patrick Devlin
Director	Mr Michael Mc Keever

South Ulster Housing Association Ltd
20 Carleton Street, Portadown, BT62 3EN
Tel: 028 3833 9795 / Fax: 028 3835 0944

Chairman	Mr Brian Castles
Director	Mr Sam Preston

Strathfoyle Tenants Maintenance Ltd
34 Bawnmore Place, Strathfoyle, Derry, BT47 1XP
Tel: 028 7186 0077 / Fax: 028 7186 1444
Chairman: Glis Hastings

Students Housing Association Co-op Ltd (SHAC)
29 Bedford Street
Belfast, BT2 7EJ
Tel: 028 9024 6811
Fax: 028 9033 3724

Chairperson	Mark McClean
Deputy Chairperson	Ciaran Hanna
Secretary	Brian Slevin
Treasurer	Hugh Cox

Triangle Housing Association Ltd
60 Eastermeade Gardens
Ballymoney, BT53 6BD
Tel: 028 2766 6880
Fax: 028 2766 2994

Board of Management

Chairperson	Mrs Oonagh Boyle
Vice Chairperson	Shiela Dwyer
Treasurer	Kathy MacKenzie
Executive Manager	Edna Dunbar
Housing Development Manager	Chris Alexander
Finance/Administration Manager	Alan Crilly
Support Services Manager	Margaret Cameron

Ulidia Housing Association Ltd
20 Derryvolgie Avenue
Belfast, BT9 6FM
Tel: 028 9038 2288
Fax: 028 9038 2738

Management Committee

Chief Executive Officer	John Gartland
Director of Development and Property Services	Seamus Mullan
Finance Officer	Carol Ervine
Director of Housing and Customer Services	Siobhan Lowery
Development Officer	Elaine Greenan

Ulster Provident Housing Association
Carlisle Memorial Centre
88 Clifton Street
Belfast, BT13 1AB
Tel: 028 9031 1156

Woodvale & Shankill Housing Association Ltd
93 Woodvale Road
Belfast, BT13 3BP
Tel: 028 9074 1618
Fax: 028 9074 7407

Chief Executive: Mr Jim Smyth

Northern Ireland Federation of Housing Associations

38 Hill Street, Belfast, BT1 2LB
Tel: 028 9023 0446 / Fax: 028 9023 8057
Chairman: Arnold Hatch
NIFHA is the umbrella organisation for the Housing Association sector providing a range of representational and other services for its members.

Membership of NIHFA Council

Chairperson	Mr Arnold Hatch
Dungannon & District Housing Association	
Vice Chairperson	Ms J Fulton
BIH	
Belfast Community	Mr D Bleakley
Grove	Cllr D Browne
NI Co-Ownership	Mr K Bulter
Choice	Mr A Canning
Fold	Mr B Coulter
Habinteg	Mr D Duly
Triangle	Mrs E Dunbar
Oaklee	Mr I Elliott
Filor	Col C G H Filor
Ark	Ms J Fullerton
South Ulster	Mr A Hatch
Glenall	Mr E Holmes
Flax	Mrs M Kane
Connswater	Rev J McAllister
Rural	Mr P McGurk
Ulster Provident	Mrs M Mitchell
St Matthew's	Mr J O'Donnell
Hearth	Mr M Patton
Clanmil	Mr D Rankin
Ulidia	Mr R Roulston
Presbyterian	Mr T Tinman
Open Door	Ms P Whittley

Education and Training in Northern Ireland

Introduction

Children in Northern Ireland are legally obliged to attend school between the ages of 5 and 16. The system has three learning levels: primary, secondary and tertiary. In addition to this are pre-school/nursery and higher/adult education. Most children in Northern Ireland begin primary school at the age of 4. Primary education is geared toward completion of the UK Government's Key Stages 1 and 2, a curriculum designed to ensure basic standards of literacy and numeracy, as well as some initial science and possibly a foreign language. While in their last year at primary school, many pupils take what is known as the '11 plus' exam. This is a formal examination, the results of which for the most part determine the type of secondary school the child will attend.

According to their performance in the 11 plus, children progress to one of a variety of educational institutions. The most academically able children (according to the examination) for the most part attend a grammar school. These schools are generally focused towards academic results, normally A-levels, traditionally seen as the passport to a university place. The majority of the remainder of children, i.e. those who do not attain a high enough grade in the examination, or those who do not sit it, attend comprehensive or secondary intermediate schools, which tend to be more vocational in their outlook. A smaller proportion of these pupils go on to attain A-levels and move onward to university, although many study for more vocational qualifications such as GNVQs, which are increasingly becoming a route to a university education.

Whilst different types of secondary school each have their own priorities, all are obliged to follow the curriculum formulated by the UK Department of Education. This tries to ensure that pupils leave school with certain basic levels of literacy and numeracy, as well as studying science and at least one foreign language.

A small percentage of children leave school with no qualifications, and some leave directly after taking their GCSE exams. However the majority stay on to undertake further qualifications. As well as secondary schools, many colleges of higher and further education offer both academic and vocational qualifications. Students can resit GCSEs and study for A-levels, BTECs, HNCs (Higher National Certificates) and HNDs (Higher National Diplomas) in a wide range of subjects. This can then lead to university, or alternatively provides a vocational qualification which is useful in the workplace.

As the needs of society change the education system seeks to be flexible and is currently supporting both the desire to increase availability of pre-school provision and encourage life-long learning. Alongside traditional, formal education there is also the Open University, offering part-time university education, and numerous colleges providing nighttime and daytime classes for part-time students. Despite this flexibility, however, there remain a number of perceived inequities in the system of education in Northern Ireland. Many educationalists regard the selection system as being more than unsatisfactory while others see the religious segregation of Northern Ireland's pupil population as being the fundamental weakness in the system. In addition there are concerns about pupil teacher ratios and the level of investment and resources allocated to education. Some of the principal issues facing the sector are discussed later in this chapter.

Structure of the Northern Ireland Education System

The structure of the education system in Northern Ireland is complex, with ten Statutory Bodies involved in the management and administration of the system, including:

- The Department of Education;
- The Education and Library Boards (5);
- The Council for Catholic Maintained Schools;
- The Northern Ireland Council for the Curriculum, Examinations and Assessment (CCEA);
- The Staff Commission for Education and Library Boards;
- The Youth Council for Northern Ireland.

There are also a number of voluntary bodies involved in the administration of the education system, including the Northern Ireland Council for Integrated Education, Comhairle na Gaelscolaiochta, (the council for Irish-medium schools) the Transferor Representatives Council which brings together representatives of the Transferor Churches (Church of Ireland, Presbyterian and Methodist); the Association of Governing Bodies which represents the voluntary grammar schools.

The roles and functions of these bodies are described in detail in the relevant sections below. However, here follows a brief overview of the main responsibilities of the Department, the Education and Library Boards (ELBs) and the Council for Catholic Maintained Schools (CCMS) to provide a context for the later material.

The Department of Education

The Department of Education is responsible for the central administration of education and related services in Northern Ireland. Its primary duties are to promote the education of young people in Northern Ireland and to secure the effective execution of its policy in relation to the provision of the education service. The structure, functions and senior personnel of the Department of Education are set out in detail in Chapter 3, Government Departments and Agencies, beginning on page 158.

Education and Library Boards

There are five Education and Library Boards (ELBs), which are the local education authorities and library authorities for their areas. ELBs have a statutory responsibility to ensure that there are sufficient schools of all kinds to meet the needs of their area; to provide all the finance for the schools under their management; and to equip, maintain and meet other running costs of maintained schools. ELB expenditure is funded at 100 per cent by the Department but the funding arrangements are necessarily complex:

- Expenditure provision for some services is determined centrally by the Department because such expenditure is demand determined or where there are specific initiatives targeted on specific schools across Northern Ireland;
- The bulk of ELB funding is through a Block Grant: ELBs have responsibility for considering the relative priority of different services in their areas and they reflect their views in financial schemes which are subject to Departmental approval;
- The total provision for block grant is distributed by the ELBs by an objective and open methodology (the Assessment of Relative Needs Exercise: ARNE);
- A wide range of need indicators are used in this formula with pupil population being the most important;
- Some 5 per cent of the total is distributed on the basis of the number of pupils in each area entitled to free school meals under Targeting Social Need (TSN).

Enrolments in Educational Institutions

Table 6.1 shows the current levels of educational provision in Northern Ireland in terms of numbers and categories of educational institution, along with associated student numbers.

Table 6.1: Educational Attendance by Type of Institution 2002/03

Education Type	Number	Number of Students
NURSERY	100	6,269
PRE-SCHOOL*	363	5,804
PRIMARY	897	174,151
SECONDARY (Excl Grammar)	164	92,645
GRAMMAR (Years 8-14)	71	63,102
SPECIAL	47	4,879
INDEPENDENT	22	948
HOSPITAL	3	236

Source: NISRA

*Pre-school = Voluntary and private pre-school centres

In addition there are 16 Further Education (FE) Colleges, and 2 Universities: the traditional red-brick Queen's University of Belfast, and the more recent University of Ulster, split between campuses at Jordanstown, Coleraine, Derry and Belfast. The number of students attending Northern Ireland's educational institutions has increased gradually, in most categories, in recent years as illustrated in table 6.2

Although the increases in attendance in the primary and secondary sectors are largely a function of population growth, the recent rapid expansion of third level attendances reflects the policy continued by successive governments, of opening up third level opportunities to as many as possible.

Main Categories of School in Northern Ireland

There are a number of types of school in Northern Ireland, differing in the level of government control, as well as management structures. The main types are detailed below:

Controlled Schools

In terms of the religious divide in Northern Ireland's education system, controlled schools are essentially Protestant in terms of staffing, management and pupil intake. Controlled schools are managed by ELBs, who act as the employer, through Boards of Governors. Primary and secondary school Boards of Governors consist of representatives of transferors (the main Protestant Churches) along with representatives of parents, teachers and ELBs. Nursery, grammar and special school Boards of Governors consist of representatives of the latter three categories.

Maintained Schools

These schools are largely regarded as Catholic schools. Whilst they have a relatively close relationship with their local Education and Library Board, they are also aligned with the Council for Catholic Maintained Schools (CCMS), which is the employing authority for teaching staff. The ELB is the employing authority for non-teaching staff. In all non-Catholic maintained schools, the Board of Governors is the employing authority for all staff members. Maintained schools are able to exercise a greater degree of autonomy than Controlled Schools.

Voluntary Schools

Voluntary schools are quite independent of external control. Most voluntary schools are grammar schools with a total of around 28,000 pupils under Catholic management, and around 20,000 pupils under Protestant management. There is also a large pre-school block of around 3500 children, which operates with considerable autonomy.

Voluntary (Under Catholic Management)

This type of voluntary school is managed by Boards of Governors which consist of members nominated by trustees (mainly Roman Catholic), along with representatives of parents, teachers and ELBs. Voluntary schools vary in the rates of capital grant to which they are entitled, depending on the management structures they have adopted. A majority are entitled to capital grants at 100 per cent.

Voluntary (Under Other Management)

These are mainly voluntary grammar schools, managed by Boards of Governors which consist of persons appointed as provided in each school's scheme of management, along with representatives of parents and teachers and, in most cases, members appointed by the Department or ELBs. Voluntary Grammar schools were previously funded directly by the Department but, under the 1998 Education Order, this responsibility was handed to ELBs.

Table 6.2: Schools - Number of Pupils

	1990/91	1993/94	1996/97	1999/00	2000/01	2001/02
Nursery						
- Full-time	2,702	2,839	2,983	3,277	3,304	3,381
- Part-time	2,224	2,434	2,513	2,675	2,661	2,712
Nursery classes (primary schools)						
- Full-time	1,729	1,747	1,901	2,629	3,225	3,529
- Part-time	838	853	1,125	1,418	2,741	3,483
Primary - Reception	2,084	2,394	2,499	2,318	1,963	1,445
Primary - Years 1-7	181,233	181,852	181,284	172,591	169,700	167,883
Grammar Preparatory - Reception	23	24	45	12	27	29
Grammar Preparatory - Years 1-7	3,641	3,633	3,354	3,011	2,791	2,670
Secondary (excluding Grammar)	86,667	89,167	90,746	92,603	92,979	92,760
Grammar - Years 8-14	54,479	59,097	61,997	62,361	62,574	62,743
Special Schools	3,983	4,392	4,680	4,688	4,674	4,710
Hospital Schools	234	191	178	173	171	246
Independent Schools	1,023	939	925	1,243	1,255	1,072
Total All Schools	**340,880**	**349,562**	**354,230**	**348,999**	**348,065**	**346,663**

Source: Department of Education

Table 6.3: Further Education Colleges

	1990/91	1993/94	1996/97	1999/00	2000/01	2001/02
All Vocational Students						
- Full-time	18,065	23,125	25,033	24,128	24,542	25,163
- Part-time	53,356	58,398	60,069	65,251	66,767	67,253
Students on non-vocational courses	53,505	46,680	59,087	68,988	72,415	N/A

Source: Department of Education

Table 6.4: Higher Education (NI Domiciled Students)

	1990/91	1993/94	1996/97	1999/00	2000/01	2001/02
Full-Time Undergraduates	24,617	31,331	34,940	38,414	39,133	40,288
Part-Time Undergraduates	5,949	7,276	15,079	18,618	19,137	18,704
Full-Time Post Graduates	2,186	2,871	3,382	3,524	3,627	3,652
Part-Time Post Graduates	3,485	4,620	5,650	5,625	5,036	4,561
Total	**36,237**	**46,098**	**59,051**	**66,181**	**66,933**	**67,205**

Source: Department of Education

Grant-Maintained Integrated Schools

In recent years a number of grant-maintained integrated schools have been established at primary and post-primary levels. Such schools have been funded directly by the Department but, under the 1998 Education Order, responsibility was passed to ELBs.

The practical operation of all schools has increasingly become a matter for Boards of Governors. They are responsible for the delivery of the curriculum, admission of pupils, and in the case of schools with delegated budgets, for the management of their own financial affairs, including staff matters.

Controlled Integrated Schools

Within the controlled sector there is a small but growing number of controlled integrated schools. Many of these have made a conscious decision to change over to integrated status.

Pre-School Education

Pre-school education is broken down into nursery and reception classes, provided by the state and by the independent sector. In recent years there has been much debate on the levels and funding of pre-school provision. In 1995/96 there were 10,785 children in funded places. Currently there are 17,878 children in funded places (11,931 in nursery classes, 1,990 in reception classes and 3,957 in voluntary/private pre-school education centres). This is a significant increase but may still leave as many as 7,000 children with no funded provision at all.

Primary Education

Primary education is normally organised on the basis of a delivery period of seven years. Despite its informal appearance primary education is carefully structured against a detailed curriculum. Primary education is dominated by two categories of school: Controlled State Schools and Catholic Maintained Schools. Together they account for 95 per cent of all primary school enrolments. The remainder is accounted for by integrated primary schools.

Primary Curriculum

The Northern Ireland Curriculum, which was established by the Education Reform (Northern Ireland) Order 1989, sets out the minimum educational entitlement for pupils aged 4 to 16 years. The Order was amended in 1993 and in 1996.

The 1989 Order requires schools to provide a curriculum for all pupils which:

- Promotes the spiritual, moral, cultural, intellectual and physical development of pupils at the school and thereby of society; and
- Prepares such pupils for the opportunities and experiences of adult life.

The Northern Ireland Curriculum was introduced on a phased basis from 1990. It was reviewed in 1994 and the revised Northern Ireland Curriculum was introduced in September 1996.

The curriculum is defined in terms of four key stages which cover the 12 years of compulsory schooling. Primary education incorporates Key Stages 1 and 2 as follows:

- Key Stage 1 covers school years 1-4 for pupils aged 4-8;
- Key Stage 2 covers school years 5-7 for pupils aged 8-11.

The Curriculum does not constitute the whole curriculum for schools. Schools can develop additional curriculum elements to express their particular ethos.

Key Stages 1 and 2

The curriculum for Key Stages 1 and 2 includes:

- English;
- Mathematics;
- Science and Technology;
- History and Geography (known as the Environment and Society Area of Study);
- Art and Design, Music and Physical Education (known as the Creative and Expressive Area of Study);
- Religious Education;
- Irish, in Irish speaking schools only; and
- Four educational cross-curricular themes (Education for Mutual Understanding, Cultural Heritage, Health Education and Information Technology). The educational themes are not separate subjects but are woven through the main subjects of the curriculum.

Content

Each subject in the Northern Ireland Curriculum is defined within the Programmes of Study and Attainment Targets. There may be different numbers of Attainment Targets in each subject.

Programmes of Study

The Programmes of Study set out the opportunities which should be offered to all pupils, in terms of the knowledge, skills and understanding at each key stage. Teachers use the programmes of study as a basis for planning schemes of work.

Attainment Targets

Attainment Targets define the expected standards of pupil performance in particular aspects of a subject in terms of Level Descriptions. These provide the basis for making judgements on pupils' attainment at the end of each key stage.

Level Descriptions

There are eight levels in each attainment target. For each level there is a Level Description indicating the type and range of attainment that a pupil working at that level should demonstrate. At the end of Key Stage 1, it is expected that the majority of pupils will be working at Level 2. At the end of Key Stage 2, it is expected that pupils will be working at either Level 3 or 4.

Secondary Education

Northern Ireland Curriculum

The Northern Ireland Curriculum sets out the educational entitlement for pupils aged 11 to 16 years.
Second level education is defined as covering key stages 3 and 4 as follows:

- Key Stage 3, covers school years 8-10 for pupils aged 12-14;
- Key Stage 4, covers school years 11-12 for pupils aged 15-16.

The curricular requirements for Key Stages 3 and 4 are:

Key Stage 3

- English;
- Mathematics;
- Science, Technology and Design;
- History and Geography (known as the Environment and Society Area of Study);
- Art and Design, Music and Physical Education (known as the Creative and Expressive Area of Study);
- French or German or Italian or Spanish or Irish (known as the Modern Languages Area of Study);
- Religious Education;
- Six educational themes (Education for Mutual Understanding, Cultural Heritage, Health Education, Information Technology, Economic Awareness and Careers Education).

Key Stage 4

- English;
- Mathematics;
- Science;
- A course in one of History,Geography, Business Studies, Home Economics, Economics, Politics or an appropriate modular provision;
- Physical Education;
- Religious Education;
- An approved course in a modern language; and
- Six educational themes (Education for Mutual Understanding, Cultural Heritage, Health Education, Information Technology, Economic Awareness and Careers Education).

As with primary education the content of each subject in the Northern Ireland Curriculum at Key Stage 3 and 4 is defined in a Statutory Order and each Order consists of Programmes of Study and Attainment Targets.

At the end of Key Stage 3, it is expected that the majority of pupils will be working at either Level 5 or 6.

Third Level Education

In terms of institutions, tertiary level education in Northern Ireland consists of the two main universities (Queen's University, Belfast and the University of Ulster), two teacher-training colleges (St Mary's and Stranmillis) and 16 Further Education Colleges, including specialist centres for agriculture and catering. Several thousand people in Northern Ireland are also enrolled in the Open University. Participation in third-level education has grown steadily in recent years in Northern Ireland, across both the university and FE sectors, with the number of students approximately doubling over a twenty-year period. Additionally, the number of students availing of full-time undergraduate study opportunities outside Northern Ireland has also doubled.

Details of Northern Ireland's two universities are set out below, including faculty and departmental listings and names of senior university personnel.

Queen's University Belfast

University Road
Belfast
BT7 1NN
Tel: 028 9024 5133
Fax: 028 9024 7895
Web: www.qub.ac.uk

As a top 20 UK university Queen's gives Northern Ireland an international profile through world-class research and teaching, making a major contribution to economic, social and cultural development.

Queen's was founded in 1845 as Queen's College, part of the National University of Ireland. In 1908 it became a university in its own right. It offers a comprehensive range of courses across five faculties. Independent assessment of the teaching and research carried out at the University has placed it in the top 20 out of 170 institutions for research and teaching excellence. Queen's has a total of around 17,500 undergraduates and postgraduate students, plus a further 10,000 enrolled part-time students. Around 7,000 full-time and part-time students enrol each year and the university awards some 3,000 degrees and 1,200 higher degrees annually.

Queen's University is one of Northern Ireland's biggest employers, employing around 3,500 staff including 1,600 teaching and research staff.

Senior Officers of the University

Chancellor:	Senator George Mitchell
Pro-Chancellors:	Brenda McLaughlin Christopher Gibson
President and Vice Chancellor:	Professor Sir George S Bain (to July 2004) Professor Peter Gregson (from August 2004)
Pro-Vice-Chancellors:	Professor Ken Brown (Academic Planning & Resources) Professor Robert J Crawford (Research and Development) Professor K L Bell (Students and Learning) Professor F G McCormac (Community and Communications)
Hon Treasurer:	Teresa Townsley
Registrar:	James P J O'Kane

Table 6.5: Staff Numbers (QUB) 2002/03

Staff 2002/03	Full Time	Part Time
Academic	807	26
Academic Related	450	55
Clerical	449	152
Technical	313	29
Others	870	336
Total	**2889**	**598**

Academic Units

Faculty of Engineering

Schools: Aeronautical Engineering, Architecture, Chemical Engineering, Civil Engineering, Computer Science, Electrical and Electronic Engineering, Environmental Planning, Mechanical and Manufacturing Engineering, Northern Ireland Technology Centre.

Faculty of Medicine and Health Sciences

Schools: Dentistry, Medicine, Nursing and Midwifery, Medicine Research Office.

Faculty of Humanities

Schools: English, History, Languages, Literatures and Arts, Music, Philosophical Studies, Anthropological Studies, Institutes: Irish Studies, Theology, Byzantine Studies.

Faculty of Legal, Social and Educational Sciences

Schools: Law, Management and Economics, Politics and International Studies, Social Work, Sociology and Social Policy

Institutes: European Studies, Governance, Graduate School of Education, University Colleges: Stranmillis, Saint Mary's, Institute of Lifelong Learning, Armagh Outreach Campus.

Faculty of Science and Agriculture

Schools: Agriculture and Food Science, Archaeology and Palaeoecology, Biology and Biochemistry, Chemistry, Geography, Mathematics and Physics, Pharmacy, Psychology. Gibson Institute

Academic Units outside the faculty structure

Centres: Migration Studies, Canadian Studies, Polymer Processing Research, QUESTOR Centre, Institute of Professional Legal Studies

Table 6.6: Student Numbers (QUB) 2001/02

	Undergraduates		Postgraduates		Total
	Full Time	Part Time	Full Time	Part Time	
Faculty of Engineering	2,449	122	463	214	3,248
Faculty of Humanities	1,719	160	169	203	2,251
Faculty of Legal, Social & Educational Sciences	2,672	1,446	782	921	5,821
Faculty of Medicine & Health Sciences	2,811	1,450	158	127	4,546
Faculty of Science & Agriculture	2,447	90	420	618	3,575
Extra Mural Studies	–	2,691	–	–	2,691
Stranmillis University College	911	331	35	128	1,405
St Mary's University College	827	42	16	158	1,043
Total					**24,580**

The Quadrangle, QUB

University of Ulster

The University of Ulster is a major UK university with an international profile for academic and research excellence and is a significant contributor to the region's economic development.

The University of Ulster has four campuses which are listed below with their contact details.

Belfast Campus
York Street, Belfast, BT15 1ED

Coleraine Campus
Cromore Road, Coleraine, BT52 1SA

Jordanstown Campus
Shore Road, Newtownabbey, BT37 0QB

Magee Campus
Northland Road, Londonderry, BT48 7JL

Tel: 08 700 400 700
Web: www.ulster.ac.uk

The University is one of Northern Ireland's largest and most influential institutions with an annual turnover in excess of £130 million and contributes approximately £265 million a year to the local economy through salaries, contracts, visiting students and the hosting of major events. It is a major contributor to the research and development capacity of the region supporting local business and industry.

The course profile covers arts, business and management, engineering, information technology, life and health sciences and social sciences. Courses have a strong vocational element and the majority offer a period of industrial or professional placement. Annually more than 2,800 students undertake periods of placement in the public and private sectors throughout the UK and overseas.

Committed to social inclusion and widening access it is one of the most successful universities in the UK at attracting students with non-traditional backgrounds and qualifications. Nearly 40% of full-time undergraduate entrants are from the three lower social groups, compared to the UK average of 25%.

High standards in teaching and research have been repeatedly achieved. This is demonstrated by the last eleven teaching quality assessments receiving 'excellent' graded scores of 22 or higher and by the awarding of two 5*s together with many other high grades in the most recent Research Assessment Exercise.

Collaboration in exploiting knowledge and technology is promoted by the University's Office of Innovation and Enterprise (http://www.ulster.ac.uk/oie). The Office provides dedicated support to the business community seeking expertise and resources. UUTech Limited, a University-owned company, provides incubation support and consultancy for new spin-out companies in innovation centres and research parks across the campuses and facilitates the commercialisation of intellectual property for existing and new start-up companies.

Senior Officers of the University

President and Vice-Chancellor: Professor P G McKenna DL BSc PhD DSc LLD MRIA CBiol FIBiol FIBMS FRSA

Pro-Vice-Chancellor (Quality Assurance & Enhancement):
Professor D McAlister BSc MSc DipHealthEcon

Pro-Vice-Chancellor (Research):
Professor J G Hughes BSc PhD FBCS

Pro-Vice-Chancellor (Student Support):
Professor J M Allen BSc PhD CBiol FIBiol

Pro-Vice-Chancellor (Teaching and Learning):
Professor R R Barnett BSc PhD

Provost (Jordanstown and Belfast campus):
Professor W Clarke BSc MSc MCIM FCIM

Provost (Coleraine campus):
Professor P Roebuck CBE BA PhD FRHistsS

Provost (Magee campus):
Professor T Fraser MA PhD FRHistsS FRSA

Director of Development: Ms N E R Taggart BA

Director of Finance: Mr P Hope BA MBA FCA

Director of Human Resources:
Mr R Magee BA PGDip MCIPD

Director of Information Services:
Mr N Macartney BA MA DipLib CertEd

Director of Physical Resources:
Mr P P G Donnelly DipQS MRICS MBIFM

Director of Planning and Governance Services:
Ms I I Aston BSc

Director of Public Affairs: Mr B Kelleher BA DipEd

Student Numbers

Tables 6.7 sets out total student population 2001/02 to 2002/03, whilst Table 6.8 shows Total Student Population by Faculty.

Table 6.7: Student Population by Campus (UU)

	2001/02	2002/03
Jordanstown		
Full-time	7,798	8,328
Part-time	4,513	4,697
Campus total	12,311	13,025
Coleraine		
Full-time	3,919	4,144
Part-time	1,012	1,044
Campus total	4,931	5,188
Belfast		
Full-time	908	923
Part-time	146	181
Campus total	1,054	1,104
Magee		
Full-time	2,064	2,559
Part-time	860	836
Campus total	2,924	3,395
Total		
Full-time	14,689	15,954
Part-time	6,531	6,758
University Total	**21,220**	**22,712**

Table 6.8: Total Student Population by Faculty (UU) 2002/03

Faculty	Full Time	Part Time	Total
Arts	2,545	460	3,005
Business & Management	3,102	2,143	5,245
Engineering & Built Environment	2,062	409	2,471
Informatics	1,967	351	2,318
Life & Health Sciences	3,764	1,936	5,700
Social Sciences	2,514	1,459	3,973
Total	**15,954**	**6,758**	**22,712**

Note figures include 587 distance learning students

Faculty and Departments

Faculty of Arts
Academy for Irish Cultural Heritages
Cultural Development
Institute of Ulster Scots Studies
School of Art and Design
School of History and International Affairs
School of Languages and Literature
School of Media and Performing Arts

Faculty of Business and Management
Business Institute
Northern Ireland Centre For Entrepreneurship (Nicent)
School of Accounting
School of Business Organisation and Management
School of Business, Retail and Financial Services
School of Hotel, Leisure and Tourism
School of International Business
School of Marketing, Entrepreneurship and Strategy

Faculty of Engineering
School of the Built Environment
School of Computing and Information Engineering
School of Computing and Intelligent Systems
School of Computing and Mathematics
School of Electrical and Mechanical Engineering

Faculty of Life and Health Sciences
Faculty of Life and Health Sciences, Virtual School
Institute of Postgraduate Medicine and Primary Care
School of Applied Medical Sciences and Sports Studies
School of Biological and Environmental Sciences
School of Biomedical Sciences
School of Nursing
School of Psychology
School of Rehabilitation Sciences

Faculty of Social Sciences
Research Graduate School (Social Sciences)
School of Communication
School of Economics and Politics
School of Education
School of Law
School of Policy Studies
School of Sociology and Applied Social Studies

The Open University

Established in 1971, the Open University is the UK's largest university, with over 200,000 full and part-time students. It is established throughout the UK and Ireland, and is ranked amongst the top UK universities for the quality of its teaching. The Open University is unique within the UK in that it does not require any entry qualifications. Over 30% of students starting courses have qualifications below mainstream university requirements, but 70% of all students pass their courses each year. The majority of Open University students are part time, and although students can enter at the age of 18, two thirds are aged between 25 and 44.

The Open University's regional centre for Ireland is located in Belfast, providing student support and acting as the administrative headquarters for the region. It is led by Dr Rosemary Hamilton, Regional Director.

The Open University in Ireland
40 University Road
Belfast, BT7 1SU
Tel: 028 9024 5025
Fax: 028 9023 0565
Evening Advice: 0870 333 1444

The Centre is open: Monday to Friday 5pm to 9pm, Saturday 9am to 5 pm and Sunday 9 am to 1 pm

University Colleges

Northern Ireland has two major centres for teacher training, St Mary's College and Stranmillis College. Both are University Colleges attached to Queen's University, Belfast.

Stranmillis University College

Stranmillis Road, Belfast, BT9 5DY
Tel: 028 9038 1271 / Fax: 028 9066 4423
Web: www.stran.ac.uk
Principal: Professor Richard McMinn

Stranmillis College was founded in 1922 and has evolved into a multi-professional institution engaged not only in undergraduate and postgraduate teacher education but also the provision of pre-service and in-service training.

The college, which has an enrolment of around 700 full-time students, offers a range of consultancy services to Northern Ireland schools, Education and Library Boards and other education agencies.

Stranmillis University College

St Mary's University College

191 Falls Road, Belfast, BT12 6FE
Tel: 028 9032 7678
Fax: 028 9033 3719
Web: www.stmarys-belfast.ac.uk
Principal: Very Rev Professor Martin O'Callaghan

A Place with a mission

Our purpose is to make a distinctive contribution, in the Catholic tradition, to higher education in Northern Ireland. St Mary's is an academic community committed to the search for meaning and value in the intellectual life, to academic excellence and to individual attention for our students.

We work for the development of the whole person in a Christian, values-sensitive environment in preparation for a lifetime of learning, leadership and service.

We want the college to be a religious, educational, cultural and social resource for the local community and to show concern for the world's poor and powerless.

St Mary's University College

We provide courses for the education of teachers (in English and in Irish) and courses in liberal arts. We offer students on these courses high quality learning, teaching and support.

We aim to increase access to higher education for students from every background.

We emphasize economic regeneration and social development as an important way of facilitating conflict resolution and peace in Ireland. In order to promote our vision we work with a wide range of partners including local communities, particularly those nearest the college in West and North Belfast.

We are committed to a rich international dimension in our teacher education and liberal arts courses.

The college has partnerships with forty Universities in Europe, the United States of America and South Africa. Over one thousand full-time students and three hundred part-time students attend St Mary's University College.

Further Education Sector

Northern Ireland has a network of 16 institutions of Further Education (with approximately 400 out centres) providing a range of courses of a technical or commercial nature as well as a wide range of general educational and recreational classes. Higher education courses have also been franchised from universities to colleges of further education. Part-time courses usually relate to employment and some apprentices are given day release to attend these courses. Colleges also provide courses of training for unemployed young people as part of the New Deal Programme. The Department for Employment and Learning directly funds further education colleges, whilst allowing institutions to become self-standing incorporated bodies.

Details of Northern Ireland's Further Education Colleges are set out below:

Armagh College of Further & Higher Education

College Hill, Armagh, BT617HN
Tel: 028 3752 2205
College Director: Paul Little

Belfast Institute of Further & Higher Education

The Gerald Moag Campus
125-153 Millfield
Belfast, BT1 1HS
Tel: 028 9026 5000
Fax: 028 9026 5451
Email: information@belfastinstitute.ac.uk
Web: www.belfastinstitute.ac.uk

Director
Brian Turtle

Belfast Institute of Further and Higher Education is the largest educational establishment in Northern Ireland. With over 44,000 enrolments, it is one of the largest providers of further and higher education in these islands.

The Institute delivers university degree and equivalent courses to nearly 5,000 students. Courses include Higher National Certificates and Diplomas, degrees, post-graduate qualifications and a range of professional awards.

Almost 20,000 students attend our 1200 further education courses including National Vocational Qualifications, Advanced Vocational Certificates in Education, 'A' Levels and GCSEs, and a wide range of similar qualifications that can be matched to national award standards.

Castlereagh College of Further & Higher Education

16 Montgomery Road
Belfast, BT6 9JD
Tel: 028 9079 7144
Fax: 028 9040 1820
Email: enquiry@castlereagh.ac.uk
Web: www.castlereagh.ac.uk

Principal and
Chief Executive
Muriel W. Shankey

Castlereagh College is a progressive and responsive college of Further and Higher Education offering a wide range of full and part-time programmes. The College has an excellent reputation for academic success, quality education as well as the development and delivery of training programmes for businesses in Northern Ireland.

Causeway Institute of Further & Higher Education

Coleraine Road, Ballymoney BT53 6BT
Tel: 028 2766 0401 / Fax: 028 7035 6377
College Director: Ian Williams

East Antrim Institute of Further & Higher Education

400 Shore Road, Newtownabbey BT37 9RS
Tel: 028 9085 5000 / Fax: 028 9086 2076
College Director: John Blayney

East Down Institute of Further & Higher Education

Market Street, Downpatrick, Co Down, BT30 6ND
Tel: 028 4461 5815 / Fax: 028 4461 5817
College Director: Tom L Place

East Tyrone College of Further & Higher Education

Circular Road, Dungannon, Co Tyrone BT71 6BQ
Tel: 028 8772 2323 / Fax: 028 8775 2018
College Director: Tony Dardis

Fermanagh College

1 Dublin Road, Enniskillen BT74 6AE
Tel: 028 6632 2431 / Fax: 028 6632 6357
College Director: Brian Rouse

Limavady College of Further & Higher Education

Main Street, Limavady BT49 0EX
Tel: 028 7776 2334 / Fax: 028 7776 1018
College Director: Dr A Heaslett

Lisburn Institute of Further & Higher Education

Castle Street, Lisburn BT27 4SU
Tel: 028 9267 7225 / Fax: 028 9267 7291
College Director: A J McReynolds

Newry & Kilkeel Institute of Further & Higher Education
Patrick Street, Newry, BT35 8DN
Tel: 028 3026 1071 / Fax: 028 3025 9679
College Director: Raymond J Mullan

North Down & Ards Institute of Further & Higher Education
Castle Park Road, Bangor, BT20 4TF
Tel: 028 9127 6600 / Fax: 028 9127 6601
College Director: Brian Henry

North East Institute of Further & Higher Education
Magherafelt Site
22 Moneymore Road, Magherafelt, BT45 6AE
Tel: 028 7963 2462 / Fax: 028 7963 3501
College Director: Mr McWilliams

North West Institute of Further & Higher Education
Strand Road, Londonderry, BT48 7AL
Tel: 028 7126 6711 / Fax: 028 7126 0520
College Director: Peter Gallagher

Omagh College of Further Education
2 Mountjoy Road, Omagh, BT79 7AH
Tel: 028 8224 5433 / Fax: 028 8224 1440
College Director: Victor Refausse

Upper Bann College of Further & Higher Education
Lurgan Road, Portadown, BT63 5BL
Tel: 028 3833 7111 / Fax: 028 3839 7751
College Director: Dr Gordon Byrne

Other Colleges

College of Agriculture, Food and Rural Enterprise (CAFRE)

Greenmount Campus
22 Greenmount Road, Antrim BT41 4PU
Tel: 028 9442 6601 / Fax: 028 9442 6606
Email: enquiries@dardni.gov.uk
College Director: John Fay

Enniskillen Campus
Levaghy, Enniskillen, BT74 4GF
Tel: 028 6634 4853 / Fax: 028 6634 4888
Principal: Seamus McAliney

Loughry College
Cookstown, Co Tyrone, BT80 9AA
Tel: 0800 216139 (Freephone) / Fax: 028 8676 1043
Web: www.loughry.ac.uk
College Director: John Fay

Further and Higher Education Organisations

The Association of Northern Ireland Colleges

Unit 3 The Sidings Office Park
Antrim Road
Lisburn, BT28 3AJ
Tel: 028 9262 7512
Fax: 028 9262 7594
Email: info@anic.ac.uk
Web: www.femeansbusiness.com

Chief Executive
John D'Arcy

The Association of Northern Ireland Colleges (ANIC) represents the 16 colleges of further and higher education in Northern Ireland and is the central point of contact for FE and lifelong learning issues in Northern Ireland.

ANIC was set up in 1998 to represent the newly independent F&HE Colleges and provides information about the role and activities of the FE sector in supporting learning, training and economic development in Northern Ireland.

Department for Employment and Learning (DEL)
The Department for Employment and Learning is responsible for the policy, strategic development and financing of the statutory Further Education sector with advice from the Learning and Skills Advisory Board. DEL is also responsible for curriculum and qualification below degree level, with a key focus on the development of adult literacy.

Higher Education
Higher Education Branch is responsible for the formulation, development and oversight of the implementation of higher education policy in accordance with Northern Ireland needs (taking account of developments in the rest of the United kingdom) and for the funding of two universities (Queen's University Belfast and the University of Ulster) and the two university colleges (Stranmillis University College and St Mary's University College).
The main functions of the branch are:

- to promote high standards of teaching;
- to promote high standards of research and encourage enterprise and innovation;

- to promote and support productive interaction between higher education and industry and commerce and encourage the transfer of knowledge;
- to encourage increased access, support lifelong learning, and maximise achievement for all who can benefit from higher education;
- to fund the universities and teacher training colleges and promote the effective financial management, accountability and value for money of public funds in the higher education sector;
- to formulate higher education policy in Northern Ireland and provide advice to Ministers and officials.

Further Education

The Further Education Division of DEL is responsible for the policy, strategic development and financing of the statutory Further Education Sector with advice from the Learning and Skills Advisory Board. It also provides support to a small number of non-statutory further education providers. The Division is also responsible for curriculum and qualification below degree level, with a key focus on the development of adult literacy.

Further Education is defined in legislation as full-time and part-time education (other than Higher Education) for persons over compulsory school age. Key strategic objectives set out for the sector are:

- to support regional economic development and, in particular, to provide the skills necessary for the knowledge-based economy;
- to increase participation and widen access to those previously under-represented in the sector; and,
- to improve the quality of provision and enhance standards of performance.

The Department of Education's Education and Training Inspectorate provides for inspections of FE colleges in relation to the quality of teaching and learning.
The Further Education Division also provides support to and has formal compacts with a small number of non-statutory further education bodies.

- Workers' Education Association (WEA) - provides a range of adult education opportunities throughout Northern Ireland;
- Educational Guidance Service for Adults (EGSA) - provides adults with an independent source of advice and guidance on accessing learning opportunities;
- Ulster People's College - provides community and personal development programmes.

Lifelong Learning
Lifelong Learning Division is responsible for the policy, strategic development and financing of the statutory further education sector as well as supporting a small number of non-statutory further education bodies.

Student Support is divided into two sections with students wishing to undertake either undergraduate or postgraduate study.

Essential Skills
The Essential Skills for Living Strategy marks a radical new approach to literacy and numeracy in Northern Ireland. The Strategy plans the introduction of a regional curriculum, accreditation for adult learners and improved tutor qualifications. It sets targets for building capacity, engaging new learners and suggests ways in which these might be achieved.

Qualifications and National Occupational Standards
The Department collaborates with the other administrations and their respective Regulatory Authorities throughout the UK to support the development of National Occupational Standards as the basis for high quality vocational qualifications and to ensure the establishment of a coherent and well-regulated framework of national qualifications. The Council for the Curriculum, Examinations and Assessment (CCEA) is the main regulatory authority for qualifications in Northern Ireland, however the regulation of National Vocational Qualifications (NVQs) falls within the remit of the Qualifications and Curriculum Authority (QCA).

Portadown Training Centre

Learning and Skills Development Agency
Northern Ireland

Unit 202
20 Adelaide Street
Belfast
BT2 8GB
Tel: 028 9051 7014
Fax: 028 9051 7164

Director: Trevor Carson

The Learning and Skills Development Agency (LSDA) was created in 2003 to create a strategic national resource, supporting the development and policy and assisting in its implementation, across all post 16 education and training in Northern Ireland. The agency has prioritised widening and increasing participation, enhancing quality, making further education relevant to industry and the 16-19 curriculum.

Library Service

The five Education and Library Boards provide library services in Northern Ireland, under the auspices of the Department of Education. As well as fixed libraries in main population centres, library provision includes mobile library services to homes, hospitals and schools. A list of the main public libraries is set out below.

Public Libraries

Andersonstown Library
Slievegallion Drive, Belfast BT11 8JP
Tel: 028 9050 9200

Antrim Library
41 Church Street, Antrim BT41 4BE
Tel: 028 9446 1942

Ardoyne Library
446-450 Crumlin Road
Belfast, BT14 7GH
Tel: 028 9050 9202

Armagh Library
Market Street, Armagh, BT61 7BU
Tel: 028 3752 4072

Armagh Public Library
43 Abbey Street, Armagh, BT61 7DY
Tel: 028 3752 3142

Ballee Library
2 Neighbourhood Centre
Ballee Drive, Ballymena, BT42 2SX
Tel: 028 2564 5761

Ballycastle Library
5 Leyland Road, Ballycastle, BT54 6DP
Tel: 028 2076 2566

Ballyclare Library
School Street, Ballyclare BT39 9BE
Tel: 028 9335 2269

Ballyhackamore Library
1 Eastleigh Drive
Ballyhackamore BT4 3DX
Tel: 028 9050 9204

Ballymacarrett Library
19 Templemore Avenue, Belfast BT5 4FP
Tel: 028 9050 9207

Ballymena Library
25-31 Demesne Avenue
Ballymena, BT43 7BG
Tel: 028 2566 4100

Ballymoney Library
Rodden Foot, Queen Street
Ballymoney, BT53 6JB
Tel: 028 2766 3589

Ballynahinch Library
Main Street, Ballynahinch, BT24 8DN
Tel: 028 9756 6442

Banbridge Library
Scarva Street, Banbridge, BT32 3AD
Tel: 028 4062 3973

Bangor Branch Library
80 Hamilton Road, Bangor, BT20 4LH
Tel: 028 9127 0591

Bellaghy Library
20 Castle Street, Bellaghy
Tel: 028 7938 6627

Belvoir Park Library
Drumart Square, Belfast, BT8 7EY
Tel: 028 9064 4331

Bessbrook Library
12 Church Road, Bessbrook, BT35 7AQ
Tel: 028 3083 0424

Braniel Library
Glen Road, Castlereagh, BT5 7JH
Tel: 028 9079 7420

Broughshane Library
Main Street, Broughshane, BT42 4JW
Tel: 028 2586 1613

Brownlow Library
Brownlow Road, Brownlow
Craigavon, BT65 5DP
Tel: 028 3834 1946

Bushmills Library
44 Main Street, Bushmills, BT57 8QA
Tel: 028 2073 1424

Carnlough Library
Town Hall, Harbour Road
Carnlough, BT44 0EQ
Tel: 028 2888 5552

Carrickfergus Library
2 Joymount Court
Carrickfergus, BT38 7DN
Tel: 028 9336 2261

Carryduff Library
Church Road, Carryduff, BT8 8DT
Tel: 028 9081 3568

Castlederg Library
1A Hospital Road, Castlederg, BT81 7BJ
Tel: 028 8167 1419

Castlerock Library
57 Main Street, Castlerock
Tel: 028 7084 8463

Castlewellan Library
Main Street, Castlewellan, BT31 9DA
Tel: 028 4377 8433

Central Library

Royal Avenue, Belfast, BT1 1EA
Tel: 028 9050 9150

Chichester Library
Salisbury Avenue, Belfast, BT15 5EB
Tel: 028 9050 9210

Cloughfern Library
2a Kings Crescent
Newtownabbey, BT37 0DH
Tel: 028 9085 4789

Coalisland Library
Ground Floor, Lineside
Coalisland, BT71 4LT
Tel: 028 8774 0569

Coleraine Library
Queen Street, Coleraine, BT52 1BE
Tel: 028 7034 2561

Colin Glen Library
Colin Glen Centre, Stewartstown Road
Dunmurry, Belfast, BT17 0AW
Tel: 028 9043 1266

Comber Library
5 Newtownards Road, Comber, BT23 5AV
Tel: 028 9187 2610

Cookstown Library
Burn Road, Cookstown, BT80 8DJ
Tel: 028 8676 3702

Craigavon Divisional Library
24 Church Street,
Portadown, BT62 3DB
Tel: 028 3833 6122

Cregagh Library
409-413 Cregagh Road,
Belfast, BT6 0LF
Tel: 028 9040 1365

Creggan Library
Central Drive, Londonderry, BT48 9QH
Tel: 028 7126 6168

Crossmaglen Library
The Square, Crossmaglen, BT35 9AA
Tel: 028 3086 1951

Crumlin Library
Orchard Road, Crumlin, BT29 4SD
Tel: 028 9442 3066

Cullybackey Branch Library
153 Tobar Park, Cullybackey, BT42 1NW
Tel: 028 2588 1878

Cushendall Library
Mill Street, Cushendall, BT44 0RR
Tel: 028 2177 1297

Derry Central Library
35 Foyle Street, Londonderry, BT48 6AL
Tel: 028 7127 2300

Donaghadee Library
Killaughey Road,
Donaghadee, BT21 0BE
Tel: 028 9188 2507

Downpatrick Library
79 Market Street,
Downpatrick, BT30 6LZ
Tel: 028 4461 2895

Draperstown Library
The Square, High Street
Draperstown, BT45 7AD
Tel: 028 7962 8249

Dromore Library
Town Hall, Market Square
Dromore, BT25 1AW
Tel: 028 9269 2280

Dundonald Library
16 Church Road, Dundonald, BT16 2LN
Tel: 028 9048 3994

Dungannon Library
Market Square, Dungannon, BT70 1JD
Tel: 028 8772 2952

Dungiven Library
74 Main Street, Dungiven, BT70 1JD
Tel: 028 7774 1475

Dunmurry Library
Upper Dunmurry Lane, Dunmurry
Tel: 028 9062 3007

Enniskillen Library
Halls Lane, Enniskillen, BT74 7DR
Tel: 028 6632 2886

Falls Road Library
49 Falls Road, Belfast, BT12 4PD
Tel: 028 9050 9212

Finaghy Library
13 Finaghy Road South
Belfast, BT10 0BW
Tel: 028 9050 9214

Fintona Library
112 Main Street, Fintona, BT78 2AH
Tel: 028 8284 1774

Fivemiletown Library
Main Street, Fivemiletown, BT75 0PG
Tel: 028 8952 1409

Garvagh Library
Bridge Street, Garvagh, BT51 5AF
Tel: 028 2955 8500

Gilford Library
37 Mill Street, Gilford, BT63 6HQ
Tel: 028 3883 1770

Gilnahirk Library
Gilnahirk Rise, Belfast, BT5 7DT
Tel: 028 9079 6573

Glengormley Library
40 Carnmoney Road
Glengormley, BT36 7HP
Tel: 028 9083 3797

Greenisland Library
17 Glassillan Grove
Greenisland, BT38 8TE
Tel: 028 9086 5419

Greystone Library
Greystone Road, Antrim, BT40 1JW
Tel: 028 9446 3891

Heritage Library
12-14 Bishop Street
Londonderry, BT48 6PW
Tel: 028 7126 9792

Holywood Arches Library
4 Holywood Road, Belfast, BT4 1NT
Tel: 028 9047 1309

Holywood Library
86-88 High Street, Holywood, BT18 9AE
Tel: 028 9042 4232

Irvinestown Library
Main Street, Irvinestown, BT95 1GL
Tel: 028 6862 1383

Keady Library
1 Bridge Street, Keady, BT60 3RP
Tel: 028 3753 1365

Kilkeel Library
49 Greencastle Street,
Kilkeel, BT34 4BH
Tel: 028 4176 2278

Killyleagh Library
High Street, Killyleagh, BT30 9QF
Tel: 028 4482 8407

Kilrea Library
27 The Diamond, Kilrea, BT51 5QN
Tel: 028 2954 0630

Larne Library
36 Pound Street, Larne, BT40 1SQ
Tel: 028 2827 7047

Laurelhill Community Library
22 Laurelhill Road, Lisburn, BT28 2UH
Tel: 028 9266 4596

Ligoniel Library
53-55 Ligoniel Road, Belfast, BT14 8BW
Tel: 028 9050 9221

Limavady Library
5 Connell Street, Limavady, BT49 0EA
Tel: 028 7776 2540

Linenhall Library
17 Donegall Square North
Belfast, BT1 5GB
Tel: 028 9032 1707

Lisburn Library
29 Railway Street, Lisburn, BT28 1XP
Tel: 028 9260 1749

Lisburn Road Library
440 Lisburn Road, Belfast, BT9 6GR
Tel: 028 9050 9223

Lisnaskea Library
Drumhaw, Lisnaskea, BT92 0GT
Tel: 028 6772 1222

Lurgan Library
Carnegie Street, Lurgan, BT66 6AS
Tel: 028 3832 3912

Maghera Library
1 Main Street, Maghera, BT66 6AS
Tel: 028 7964 2578

Magherafelt Library
The Bridewell, 6 Church Street
Magherafelt, BT45 6AN
Tel: 028 7963 2278

Moira Library
Backwood Road, Moira, BT67 0LJ
Tel: 028 9261 9330

Moneymore Library
8 Main Street, Moneymore, BT45 7PD
Tel: 028 8674 8380

Monkstown Library
Bridge Road, Monkstown
Tel: 028 9058 3138

Moy Library
The Square, Moy, BT71 7SG
Tel: 028 8778 4661

Newcastle Library
141/143 Main Street
Newcastle, BT33 0AE
Tel: 028 4372 2710

Newry Public Library
79 Hill Street, Newry, BT34 1DG
Tel: 028 3026 4683

Newtownards Library
Regent Street, Newtownards, BT23 4AB
Tel: 028 9181 4732

Newtownbreda Library
Saintfield Road, Belfast, BT8 4HL
Tel: 028 9070 1620

Newtownstewart Library
2 Main Street
Newtownstewart, BT78 9AA
Tel: 028 8166 1245

O'Fiaich Memorial & Archive
15 Moy Road, Armagh, BT61 7LY
Tel: 028 3752 2981

Oldpark Library
46 Oldpark Road, Belfast, BT14 6FF
Tel: 028 9050 9226

Omagh Library
1 Spillars Place, Omagh, BT78 1HL
Tel: 028 8224 4821

Ormeau Library
Ormeau Embankment, Belfast, BT7 3GG
Tel: 028 9050 9228

Poleglass Library
14 Good Shepherd Road
Belfast, BT17 0PP
Tel: 028 9062 9740

Portadown Library
24-26 Church Street
Portadown, BT62 3LQ
Tel: 028 3833 6122

Portaferry Library
47 High Street
Portaferry, BT22 1QT
Tel: 028 4272 8194

Portglenone Library
19 Townhill Road,
Portglenone, BT44 8AD
Tel: 028 2582 2228

Portstewart Library
Town Hall, The Crescent
Portstewart, BT55 7AB
Tel: 028 7083 2712

Randalstown Library
34 New Street, Randalstown, BT41 3AF
Tel: 028 9447 2725

Rathcoole Library
2 Rosslea Way, Rathcoole
Newtownabbey, BT37 9BJ
Tel: 028 9085 1157

Rathfriland Library
John Street, Rathfriland, BT34 5QH
Tel: 028 4063 0661

Richhill Branch Library
1 Maynooth Road, Richhill, BT61 9PE
Tel: 028 3887 0639

Saintfield Library
17 Fairview, Saintfield, BT24 7AD
Tel: 028 9751 0550

Sandy Row Branch Library
127a Sandy Row, Belfast, BT12 5ET
Tel: 028 9050 9230

Shankill Road Library
298 Shankill Road, Belfast, BT13 2BN
Tel: 028 9050 9232

Shantallow Library
92 Racecourse Road, Shantallow
Londonderry, BT48 8DA
Tel: 028 7135 4185

Sion Mills Library
Church Square, Sion Mills, BT82 9HD
Tel: 028 8165 8513

Strabane Library
25 Butcher Street, Strabane, BT82 8AJ
Tel: 028 7188 3686

Strathfoyle Library
22 Temple Road, Strathfoyle
Co Londonderry, BT47 6TJ
Tel: 028 7186 0385

Suffolk Library
57 Stewartstown Road,
Belfast, BT11 9JP
Tel: 028 9050 9234

Tandragee Library
Market Street, Tandragee, BT62 2BP
Tel: 028 3884 0694

Templepatrick Library
23 The Village, Templepatrick, BT39 0AA
Tel: 028 9443 2953

Tullycarnet Library
Kinross Avenue, Belfast, BT5 7GF
Tel: 028 9048 5079

Waringstown Library
Main Street, Waringstown, BT66 7QH
Tel: 028 3888 1077

Warrenpoint Library
Summer Hill, Warrenpoint, BT34 3JB
Tel: 028 4175 3375

Waterside Library
The Workhouse, 23 Glendermott Road
Waterside, Londonderry, BT47 6BG
Tel: 028 7134 2963

Whitehead Library
17b Edward Road
Whitehead, BT38 9RU
Tel: 028 9335 3249

Whiterock Library
195 Whiterock Road
Belfast, BT12 7FW
Tel: 028 9050 9236

Whitewell Library
Ballygolan Primary School
Serpentine Road, Belfast
Tel: 028 9050 9242

Woodstock Road Library
358 Woodstock Road
Belfast BT6 9DG
Tel: 028 9050 9239

Key Issues Facing Northern Ireland Education

This section of the Yearbook addresses five of the key issues facing the education sector in Northern Ireland:

- Integrated education and religion;
- Selection procedure - Post Primary Review Team;
- Pupil Teacher Ratios;
- Investment in Education;
- Student finance/University fees

Integrated Education and Religion

Many commentators agree that Northern Ireland's most fundamental problem is that of sectarian division between Protestants and Catholics. Despite the fact that the divisions date back for centuries, prejudices are passed from generation to generation and preserved by the fact that the two communities are segregated in many areas of everyday life, including education. There is a growing belief that integrated education could be a major contributor to breaking the cycle of prejudice.

The establishment of a set of schools designed specifically to facilitate the education of pupils from Roman Catholic and Protestant backgrounds side by side has been one of the major developments in Northern Ireland education over the last twenty years. There has been steady growth in integrated education during this period.

The first planned integrated school, Lagan College, opened in 1981, the second in 1985, and by 1995, this new sector had grown to have a total enrolment of 5,816 pupils. In the last five years this number has risen to 15,770 pupils, 4.6 per cent of the total primary/post-primary enrolment in Northern Ireland. Table 6.9 lists all of the major existing schools and shows how numbers have grown steadily.

Integrated education is popular, but it is not yet available everywhere due to financial and logistical difficulties, particularly in getting new schools established. It may therefore be some time before the sector realises its full potential. In 2000/01 some 1140 applications for places in integrated education had to be turned away due to lack of places.

Table 6.9 Integrated Schools in Northern Ireland

Opened	Location	Enrolment	School/College
1981	Belfast	967	Lagan College
1985	Belfast	214	Forge CIPS
1985	Belfast	685	Hazelwood College
1985	Belfast	395	Hazelwood IPS
1986	Newcastle	202	All Children's CIPS
1987	Banbridge	394	Bridge IPS
1987	Portrush	241	Mill Strand IPS
1988	Dungannon	185	Windmill IPS
1989	Ballymena	254	Braidside IPS
1989	Enniskillen	207	Enniskillen IPS
1990	Omagh	180	Omagh IPS
1990	Portadown	195	Portadown IPS
1991	Craigavon	362	Brownlow CIC
1991	Garvagh	45	Carhill CIPS
1991	Larne	141	Corran IPS
1991	Derry	394	Oakgrove IPS
1992	Carrickfergus	230	Acorn IPS
1992	Derry	755	Oakgrove IC
1993	Belfast	160	Cranmore IPS
1993	Belfast	213	Loughview IPS
1993	Armagh	193	Saints & Scholars IPS
1994	Enniskillen	376	Erne IC
1994	Newcastle	412	Shimna IC
1995	Dungannon	401	Integrated College Dungannon
1995	Crossgar	156	Cedar IPS
1995	Omagh	547	Drumragh IC
1995	Loughbrickland	387	New-Bridge IC
1995	Portaferry	65	Portaferry CIPS
1996	Lambeg	73	Hilden CIPS
1996	Coleraine	327	North Coast IC
1996	Derriaghy	113	Oakwood IPS
1996	Antrim	106	Rathenraw CIPS
1996	Ballymena	389	Slemish IC
1997	Castlewellan	51	Annsborough CIPS
1997	Whitehead	230	Ulidia IC
1997	Carrowdore	239	Strangford
1997	Belfast	388	Malone IC
1998	Bangor	496	Bangor Central CIPS
1998	Kircubbin	100	Kircubbin CIPS
1998	Rostrevor	63	Kilbroney CIPS
1998	Holywood	392	Priory CIC
1998	Downpatrick	269	Down Academy CIC
1998	Lisburn	813	Forthill CIC
1999	Magherafelt	58	Spires IPS
2000	Saintfield	10	Millennium IPS

Selection Procedure: Post Primary Review

The process of selection (the 11-plus examination) is at the heart of the Northern Ireland education system. Essentially it is the case that all children are placed in either Grammar or Secondary schools based on a test taken during their seventh year at school, when they are ten or eleven years of age. It is widely accepted that this placement, coupled with the educational provision available thereafter, fundamentally affects each child's future prospects and the nature of society as a whole. In September 2000, following a major, wide ranging study, the report titled 'The Effects of the Selective System of Secondary Education in Northern Ireland' was published. It looked at the current system and considered possible alternatives.

Five main models came to the fore:

- A system of delayed selection, perhaps at age 14;
- A system of all-through comprehensive schools, like that currently in operation in Scotland;
- A system using common primary and lower secondary schools, followed by differentiated upper secondary schools, as currently operated in France, Italy and other European countries;
- A system of differentiated post-primary schools with distinctive academic and vocational/technical routes;
- The status quo: selection at 11 years and a system of grammar and secondary schools.

The Current System

Significant strengths in the current selective system in Northern Ireland were identified including:

- The high academic standards achieved in grammar schools;
- The supportive environment provided in secondary schools for pupils who may not succeed in grammar schools;
- Secondary schools tend to draw their enrolment from more localised areas, possibly providing opportunities to strengthen the links between local communities and these schools.

Significant weaknesses in the current selective system in Northern Ireland were identified including:

- The perception that testing is unfair and places undue pressure on young children; this concern is shared by teachers, parents and society more generally;
- Primary teachers in some cases feel obliged to focus curricular attention narrowly on the requirements of the selection test, partly to assist each child in achieving their highest score and also because they feel they are judged in the public mind on the basis of their school's overall transfer test performance;
- Rather than simply identifying all the children suited to grammar schooling the testing procedure enables the grammar schools to admit only the pupils with high scores, possibly leaving many children, who have the academic ability behind. Secondary schools, who then cater for the 'failures' are in turn accorded a lesser status than grammar schools in the eyes of most people. Teachers in secondary schools argue that they have to rebuild the self-confidence and esteem of many pupils who arrive in their schools with a sense of failure;
- In spite of the grading system which is designed so as not to label children as having passed or failed, this is still how results are generally interpreted;
- Increasingly parents feel obliged to pay for out-of-school coaching, and not all parents can afford to do so.

Success and Failure

With regard to the current system, the report concluded that the most important factor for a pupil achieving a high GCSE score is achieving a place in a grammar school.

The original purpose of the transfer test procedure was to identify pupils, from any background, not just those most financially advantaged, deemed able to cope with the academic curriculum provided in grammar schools. However, the current performance patterns may imply that a higher proportion of pupils should have the opportunity to experience a grammar school education or equivalent. Interviews with pupils in both grammar and secondary schools indicated a strong difference in aspirations. The vast majority of those in grammar were planning to enter higher education whereas only a minority of those in secondary schools aspired to do so.

It would appear to be the case that success breeds success and "failure" breeds failure, but in the Northern Ireland selective system the success and the failure seem to be strongly dependent upon one another.

Table 6.10 shows how Northern Ireland compares with Scotland and England/Wales in terms of the spread of exam performance. Proportionately Northern Ireland has more high and low achieving schools, whereas the distribution in England/Wales and, even more so, Scotland shows a more even spread.

Table 6.10: Examination Performance Comparison Across the UK

5+ GCSE grades (A*-C or equivalent)	Northern Ireland	England/Wales	Scotland
0 to 20% of pupils	17%	11%	3%
21 to 40% of pupils	37%	43%	12%
41 to 60% of pupils	13%	31%	38%
61 to 80% of pupils	3%	13%	34%
81 to 100% of pupils	31%	3%	14%
Total	100%	100%	100%

On the government's behalf the Independent Review Body on Post-Primary Education produced a major report called 'Education for the 21st Century'. The Review Body, chaired by Gerry Burns, made four key recommendations, which, if implemented, could mean fundamental reorganisation of Northern Ireland's educational system.
They were:

- Abolition of the transfer test (the 11 plus);
- The ending of selection on academic grounds;
- The development of a 'Pupil Profile' assessment system;
- The creation of a 'collegiate system' of schools across Northern Ireland.

The Burns report called the 11 plus 'divisive' and argued that the exam leads to inequality of opportunity.

Response to the Post Primary Review Group Recommendations

The Review Group report (commonly referred to as the Burns report) published in October 2001 has stirred a major debate including all of the interested players from political parties through all kinds of educational organisations, churches, business groups and trade unions. At a political level, the Minister for Education, Martin McGuinness welcomed the report and indicated his personal support for the abolition of the transfer test. He then embarked on a major consultative exercise, which was completed in September 2002.

The consultative exercise was unprecedented in scale (proposals communicated to every household in Northern Ireland) and yielded over 1300 written responses, including over 500 from schools and 200,000 completed household response forms.

Disappointingly the Northern Ireland Assembly and the Education Committee divided along traditional lines on the issue with the Nationalist parties broadly in support of the Burns proposals and Unionist parties generally opposed.
Overall there was overwhelming support for the objectives of the Burns Report and general acceptance that the 11+ transfer test should be abolished. However, some of the support for abolition was conditional on a suitable alternative means of academic selection being found.

The many educational interests were divided on the broader principle of academic selection. Although there was support from all five Education and Library Boards, two-thirds of schools, CCMS and NICIE, there was opposition from the Governing Bodies Association, voluntary grammar schools and two-thirds of household respondents.

It is difficult to see in what way the government can move on academic selection given the strength of opinion on both sides of the argument. Some kind of academic selection at age 14 as opposed to age 11 may form some part of a compromise. There was broad support for the concept of pupil profiles but uncertainty about the extent to which it would be used for admission purposes. There was widespread opposition to the system of collegiates as proposed in the Burns Report although there was support for greater collaboration and networking between schools.

In April 2003 a Working Group was formed, under the chairmanship of Steve Costello, with the aim to take account of the responses to the consultation on the Burns Report. The details of the report of the consultation group (the Costello Report) were made public in January 2004 and indicated that the 11+ test would not remain beyond 2008, and that any selection on the basis of academic ability would not be allowed from then on. The report did not provide the detailed alternative to academic selection at age 11 but suggested that schools may be able to look at factors such as family connections and limited geography in deciding which pupils to admit. Much of the process will depend on enabling parents to arrive at an 'informed choice' based on pupil profiles. The detailed design of a future scheme has yet to be finalised.

Pupil-Teacher Ratios

Pupil/teacher ratio is an issue close to the hearts of parents and teachers. Parents value lower class sizes. Governments are always keen to show how they have succeeded in reducing the pupil-teacher ratios.
Unfortunately, the ratio figures can be quite misleading. The following table indicates that the ratio in primary schools is about twenty pupils to each teacher. However to reach this figure all teachers will have been included, many of whom have no class duties. 'Floating teachers' such as many principals, vice-principals, supply teachers, reading recovery and special needs teachers give the impression of lower ratios.

Table 6.11 Pupil Teacher Ratios

Education Type	Pupil/Teacher Ratio 2001/02	Pupil/Teacher Ratio 2002/03
Nursery	24.4	24.1
Primary	19.9	19.7
Secondary	13.8	13.8
Grammar	15.3	17.2
Special	5.9	6.0
All Schools	**16.5**	**16.4**

The reality in the classroom is usually higher and in some cases significantly higher than indicated in the table. Nonetheless parents who look around may be surprised to find relatively low pupil-teacher ratios in certain schools or subjects as there can be considerable class-to-class variation against average ratios. However overall, Northern Ireland enjoys pupil-teacher ratios which are significantly below the UK average in both primary and secondary education.

Investment in Education

There is a general consensus that for many years education in Northern Ireland (and perhaps in the UK as a whole) had been an area of under-investment. The Northern Ireland Executive prioritised this area, and planned capital expenditure in 2002/2003 was £108.9 million. However, it is accepted that even these substantial sums will not bring Northern Ireland's ageing educational infrastructure up to modern standards. The problem is particularly acute in terms of outdated school buildings, many in a poor state of repair. A high percentage of Northern Ireland's classrooms are temporary or mobile buildings.

As in other sectors, one possible solution to the infrastructural deficit is PFI, or as it is now known, PPP (Public-Private Partnerships), whereby private sector capital can create the infrastructure and effectively lease it to the Department or Education and Library Board as the client. This approach has both supporters and opponents.

Those in favour of PPP argue that it is the only way of ensuring that necessary investment actually happens and all the construction and operational risks pass to the private sector developer or facilities manager.

Opponents contend that the process is complex and unwieldy, and that in order to give the private sector a good return on their investment, it *must* cost the taxpayer more in the long term. The Treasury has developed public sector comparators which allow the public sector client to judge to some extent how the PPP proposition looks in terms of overall value against the alternative approach.

Nonetheless, while the debate continues, Northern Ireland's educational authorities have been steadily adopting the PPP approach to a number of key projects including:

- Rebuilding of main campus for Belfast Institute of Further & Higher Education (Capital approx. £40 million);
- Secondary schools: Balmoral High School, Wellington College, Drumglass, St Genevieve's.

However, even with this PPP activity Northern Ireland's educational estate will require sustained investment in buildings and equipment in coming years. It is possible that much of the "catching up" that is essential can be achieved under the Reinvestment and Reform Initiative (RRI) which allows the Northern Ireland government to borrow considerable low cost funds for infrastructural development.

Student Finance

The funding of third level education has become a major issue across the UK. A new Higher Education Bill is to be introduced which will see the introduction of 'top-up' fees for university places. Top-up fees, or differential fees, would enable, by law, universities to set their own level of tuition fees. At present all universities charge £1,100 a year to undergraduates, a rate set by government. The new proposals would mean that universities could charge nearer the real cost of studying, which is estimated to be around an average figure of £5,000 in the UK. However, depending on the institution, department and course, it could be higher than this. To meet these higher fee levels the government would make more loans available to help students pay fees up front.

Most universities are in favour of top-up fees as they claim that they are seriously under-funded. In Northern Ireland Queen's University Belfast is in favour of top-up fees and the University of Ulster against their introduction.

Funding of third level education was an issue for the first Northern Ireland Assembly. The then Minster for Employment and Learning Dr Sean Farren announced a £65 million student finance package, which included the restoration of means-tested grants, the application of some fee exemptions and the establishment of a further 1,000 new university places.

Whatever, the outcome of the top-up fees controversy students are increasingly having to work during their education in order to fund their studies. Statistics suggest that in Britain around 80 per cent of students are working part-time. On average a student in Northern Ireland works 17.7 hours per week in addition to studying full-time.

Delivery of Northern Ireland's Education Service

Department of Education

The education system in Northern Ireland is administered by the Department of Education (NI), one of the ten departments devolved under the new arrangements for the government of Northern Ireland.

The Department's stated aim and objective is:

"To provide for the education and development of all our young people to the highest possible standards, with equal access for all."

Key Strategic Aims:
In order to achieve this stated objective, the Department and its public bodies has the following strategic aims:

- Promotion of excellence;
- Provision of choice;
- Ensuring equity and enhancement of accessibility;
- Providing education and personal development for life;
- Doing things better;
- Partnership and joined-up government.

Contact:
Rathgael House
Balloo Road, Bangor, BT19 7PR
Tel: 028 9127 9279 / Fax: 028 9127 9100
Email: deni@nics.gov.uk
Web: www.deni.gov.uk

Statistics and Research Branch
Rathgael House
Balloo Road, Bangor, BT19 7PR
Tel: 028 9127 9311 / Fax: 028 9127 9594
Email: nicola.wilson@deni.gov.uk

Contact: Nicola Wilson

Further detailed information about the Department, including organisational structure and senior officials is set out in Chapter 3, beginning on page 158.

Overview of Education and Library Boards

The Education and Library (NI) Order 1972 took control of the provision of education and library services from local authorities, and placed it under the direction of new Education and Library Boards. Five new Boards were established in 1973 to cover Northern Ireland: Belfast, North Eastern, Western, Southern and South Eastern.

The Constitution of each Board is laid down primarily in the following legislation:

- Education and Libraries (NI) Order 1986;
- Education Reform (NI) Order 1989;
- Education and Libraries (NI) Order 1993;
- Education and Libraries (NI) Order 1997;
- Education and Libraries (NI) Order 1998.

Functions, Duties, Powers and Services
Within the public education system, Education and Library Boards have statutory responsibility for primary and secondary education within their respective areas. The system of education is divided into three stages:

- Primary Education: for pupils aged 5-11 in Key Stages 1 and 2;
- Secondary Education: for pupils aged 11-18 in Key Stages 3 and 4 and post-16 studies;
- Further Education: for people over compulsory school age.

Each Board must also have regard for the need for pre-school education. Boards are responsible for the provision of a youth service and library services to schools and the public.

The principal duties of each Board are:
- To contribute to the spiritual, moral, cultural, intellectual and physical development of the community;
- To ensure that there are sufficient schools for providing primary and secondary education;
- To secure special education provision for those children who have been identified as having special educational needs;
- To provide a comprehensive and efficient library service for people who live, work or undertake courses of study within its area;
- To secure the provision for their respective areas of adequate facilities for recreational, social, physical, cultural and youth service activities and for services ancillary to education.

In support of these main provisions the Board undertakes a range of duties and provides a variety of services including:

- Admission arrangements to schools;
- School transport, meals and milk;
- Music Service;
- Providing a range of services for children with special needs;
- Education welfare services, schools' psychological services and services relating to child protection;
- Provision of boarding and clothing grants;
- Monitoring the employment of school children for compliance with legislative requirements;
- Management and implementation of the transfer procedure;
- Facilitating the provision of student loans and grants;
- Maintenance of controlled and maintained schools, including payment of salaries, provision of a purchasing

service and human resources;

- Appointment of boards of governors; employment of teachers in controlled schools and other staff in controlled and maintained schools;
- Legal and insurance services.

Each Education and Library Board has 32-35 members, appointed by the Minister responsible for the Department of Education in Northern Ireland and representative of the following:

- Each Local Government District in the Board's area;
- Transferors' interests;
- Trustees of maintained schools;
- Those with an interest in the services provided by the Board.

Belfast Education and Library Board

40 Academy Street
Belfast, BT1 2NQ
Tel: 028 9056 4000
Fax: 028 9033 1714

Chairperson: Carmel McKinney
Chief Executive: David Cargo

Belfast Education and Library Board is the local education and library authority for the area served by Belfast City Council, covering, according to the 2001 census figures a population of 277,391. Approximately 65,000 children are enrolled in 178 schools in the Belfast Area. The Board provides 21 libraries, library services to hospitals and homes, a schools' library service, a teachers' reference library and the Northern Ireland Schools' Video Library.

The Board provides music tuition through the School of Music. It also provides a comprehensive youth service through the operation of 53 controlled youth organisations, and support for over 350 voluntary youth organisations. It also maintains two outdoor centres at Delamont and Drumalla, which are used extensively by people from a wide range of schools and youth organisations. Specialist resource and teachers' centres are located in Mountcollyer and Ulidia.

Expenditure

During the financial year 2001-2002, Belfast Education and Library Board spent a total of £230.9 million, the main portion of this going to schools (£154.5 million). A further £12 million went to other education services, bringing the total spent on education to £166.5 million. The remaining £8.4 million was split between Culture, Arts and Leisure, and Further and Higher Education.

Board Membership

Chairperson: Carmel McKinney

Members: Rosemary Rainey, Rev Houston McKelvey, Rev Walter Lewis, Jim Caves, Brian Gibson, Sheelagh Mary O'Prey, James Toner, Finbarr McCallion, Trevor Blayney, Siobhan McIntaggart, Hilary Ann Sloan, Roger Nixon, Brendan Henry, Pauline Leeson, Patricia Diamond, Dr Michael Harriott, Joan MacVicar, Carmel McKinney, Dr Pamela Montgomery, Selina Yu, Edwin Paynter, Cllr Pat Convery, Cllr Pat McCarthy, Cllr Tom Hartley, Cllr Danny Lavery, Cllr Gerard O'Neill, Cllr Catherine Molloy, Cllr Joe O'Donnell, Cllr Nelson McCausland, Cllr David Browne, Cllr Jim Clarke, Cllr Jim Rodgers, Cllr David Alderdice, Cllr Robin Newton, Cllr Rev Eric Smyth.

North Eastern Education and Library Board

County Hall
182 Galgorm Road
Ballymena
BT42 1HN
Tel: 028 2565 3333
Fax: 028 2564 6071
Web: www.neelb.org.uk

Chairperson: Joan Christie
Chief Executive: Gordon Topping

The North Eastern Education and Library Board is the local education and library authority for most of County Antrim and the eastern part of County Londonderry, comprising the Local Government Districts of Antrim, Ballymena, Ballymoney, Carrickfergus, Coleraine, Larne, Magherafelt, Moyle and Newtownabbey.

The population of the Board's area in the 2001 census was 394,384. (The 2001 mid-year population estimate was 395,514). School enrolment figures from 1999/2000 indicate that 74,657 children are enrolled in schools within the Board's area. This includes 1984 children in 17 nursery schools; 37461 in 214 primary schools; 18805 in 35 secondary schools; 947 in 11 special schools and 4572 in 6 grammar schools. There are also 9306 pupils attending 11 voluntary grammar schools and 866 pupils in 5 grant maintained integrated schools, and 716 pupils in 2 grant maintained integrated post-primary schools. There are 36 branch libraries, 9 public service mobile libraries and 4 schools' mobile libraries in the area. There are also 37 controlled youth clubs and 482 voluntary youth organisations.

The Board is the employing authority of approximately 10,745 people in full-time and part-time capacities.

Board Membership

Chairperson: Mrs Joan Christie
Vice-chair: Mr Patsy McShane

D D Barbour, J R Beggs MP, R F Cavan, O M Church, J Convery, J M Crilly, M W Crockett, J K F Currie, M P Devine, U M Duncan, L Frazer, J A Gaston, P A Gillespie, Rev D S Graham, L A Hicklin, Rev J T Jamieson, M J Johnston, M Laverty, J A McBride, K M McCann, A P McConaghy, S A McCrea, P G McShane, N S Macartney, N C Murray, H Nicholl, C M Poots, J C Reid, Rev R B Savage, T Scott, A J Templeton, R Thompson, A D C Watson, C Wegwermer, W T Wright.

South Eastern Education and Library Board

Grahamsbridge Road
Dundonald
Belfast, BT16 2HS
Tel: 028 9056 6200
Fax: 028 9056 6266
Web: www.seelb.org.uk

Library Headquarters
Windmill Hill
Ballynahinch, BT24 8DH
Tel: 028 9756 6400
Fax: 028 9756 5072

Chairperson: Cllr Robert Gibson
Chief Executive: Mr Jackie Fitzsimons

The South Eastern Education and Library Board covers much of County Down, including the Local Government Districts of Ards, Castlereagh, Lisburn and North Down. The population of the Board's area in 2001 was 388,577. School enrolment figures indicate that at October 2001 there were 66,700 children attending schools in the area. The Board is responsible for 18 nursery schools, 29 nursery / pre-school units, 163 primary schools, 29 secondary schools, 10 grammar schools, 11 special schools and 28 special units. The Board also provides or supports 31 public library service points, 3 outdoor education centres, 550 youth organisations, 2 resource centres and a music centre.

Expenditure

During the financial year ending 31 March 2003, the South Eastern Board spent a total of £264.5 million. The majority went on schools, with smaller amounts spent on library and other services.

Structure of the Board
The work of the Board is carried out through a committee structure; the committees being as follows:

- Audit Committee
- Chairmen's Committee
- Committee for the Management of Schools
- Education Committee
- Expulsions Committee
- Finance and Property Services Committee
- General Purposes Committee
- Library and Information Committee
- Teaching Appointments Committee
- Youth Committee

Executive Organisation
Chief Executive: Jackie Fitzsimons
Chief Finance Officer: Ken Brown
Senior Education Officer: Stanton Sloan
Chief Librarian: Beth Porter
Senior Education Officer (Admin): Martin Graham

Board Membership
Chairperson: Cllr R Gibson
Vice Chair: R J McFerran
Rev Dr J P O Barry, Rev C W Bell, Cllr P A Butler, D Cahill, Cllr C Calvert, J Campbell, J L Colgan, Cllr M Craig, S I Davidson, Cllr G N Douglas, Cllr R M Dunlop, Ald G Ennis, M P Flanagan, F A Gault, Rev G N Haire, Ald C Hall, R Jones, R J McFerran, M M McGoran, M M McHenry, A McReynolds, D G Mullan, Cllr J Norris, Cllr C O'Boyle, E M Robinson, Rev Dr R A Russell, Cllr M Smith, J D Uprichard, Cllr W M Ward, Cllr W G Watson, Rev Dr D J Watts, J Williams, Cllr A Wilson

Southern Education and Library Board

3 Charlemont Place, The Mall, Armagh, BT61 9AX
Tel: 028 3751 2200 / Fax: 028 3751 2490
Web: www.selb.org
Chairperson: M Alexander
Chief Executive: Helen McClenaghan

The Southern Education and Library Board is the local authority for education and library services in the Armagh, Banbridge, Cookstown, Craigavon, Dungannon and Newry and Mourne Local Government Districts.

The population of the area, as of April 2001 was 343,700 including 88,600 pupils. To serve this population the Board provides or maintains 18 nursery, 238 primary, 36 secondary, 3 grammar and 6 special schools. It also provides 23 public libraries, 12 youth centres and 3 outdoor education centres. Services are also offered to a further 12 voluntary grammar schools and 8 grant maintained integrated schools in the area, along with 448 voluntary youth clubs. The Board is the employer of 7844 staff. It is required by law to have 2 statutory committees: the Library Committee and the Teaching Appointments Committee. It also has a number of other committees through which much of its detailed work is carried out:

- Education Committee;
- Services Committee;
- Direct Service Committee;
- Committee for Peripatetic Teachers;
- Teachers' Staffing Committee;
- Audit Committee;
- Special Education Committee;
- Consultants' Selection Panel;
- Membership Committee;
- Special Business Committee;
- Policy Committee;
- Best Value Committee;
- Remuneration Committee.

Expenditure

During the financial year 2002/2003, the revenue budget for the Board was £225 million. The majority of this was delegated to schools, with smaller amounts going to various other areas.

Board Membership

Chairperson: Mrs M Alexander
Vice Chair: Very Rev L M McVeigh

P H Aiken, M Alexander, Cllr J F Bell, Cllr P Brannigan, S R Brownlee, Rev J Byrne, M P Campbell, Ald F E Crowe, Dr P Cunningham, M E Donnell, Cllr J Feehan, S M B Fitzpatrick, E Gill, Cllr I E B Hanna, Cllr J Hanna, Ald G A Hatch, Cllr A B Lewis, C Mackin, Cllr W J Martin, W Mayne, P C McAleavey, Cllr P P McAleer, D A McBride, C M McCaul, Rev C D McClure, Cllr P McGinn, Cllr W J McIlwrath, Cllr S McRoberts, Cllr B Monteith, Very Rev S Rice, J W Saunders, A G Sleator, Rev Canon F D Swann, Rev Canon W R Twaddell

Executive Organisation

Chief Executive: Mrs Helen McClenaghan
Head of Corporate Services: Mr T Heron
Head of Educational Services: Mr W Burke
Chief Architect: Mr A McGee
Inter-Board Services Manager: Mr J Curran
Human Resources Manager: Mr Pat Keating

Western Education and Library Board

1 Hospital Road
Omagh, BT79 0AW
Tel: 028 8241 1411
Fax: 028 8241 1400
Web: www.welbni.org

Chairperson: Harry Mullan
Chief Executive: Barry Mulholland

The Western Education and Library Board is the local authority for the provision of education, library and youth services in the District Council areas of Derry, Fermanagh, Limavady, Omagh and Strabane.

The area has a population of 282,000. There are over 63,000 pupils attending schools and over 137,000 registered library users. The Board provides or maintains 10 nursery, 191 primary, 10 special, 35 secondary/high, 4 grammar schools and 16 public libraries. In addition, services are provided to 9 voluntary grammar and 5 grant-maintained integrated schools. The Board also makes extensive provision for youth facilities and over 400 registered youth groups are supported.

The Board has 32 members. The activities of the Board are managed through the Education, Library, Services, Finance and Youth Committees. The Board also has a Teaching Appointments Committee and an Audit Committee. Minutes of the Board and its committees are available for consultation at Headquarters Office, District Offices and Public Libraries.

The Western Board also has a responsibility, on behalf of the five Education and Library Boards, for the Classroom 2000 Project, which has as its purpose the design, development and operation of an ICT infrastructure to support the curricular, management and information needs of the major bodies within the education service in Northern Ireland.

Expenditure

During the financial year ending 31 March 2003, the Western Board's total expenditure was £277.9m. This was largely made up by a departmental grant, as well as funding from other sources. The majority of expenditure was on schools, with smaller amounts spent on library and other services.

Board Members

Chairperson: Mr H Mullan
Vice Chair: Mr H Faulkner

M Bradley, A Brolly, E F Brunt, Dr J Cornyn, M Cunningham, P Donnelly, P Duffy, F G Durkan, H Faulkner, P Fleming, M Garfield, Rev R Herron, D Hussey, R Irvine, J Kerr, N W Lambert, S MacCionnaith, J P Martin, E S McCaffrey, B T Maguire, B McElduff, D N McElholm, C McGill, M McLaughlin, D McNamee, S Morrow, H Mullan, J O'Kane, T O'Reilly, Archdeacon C T Pringle, D Rainey, W D Reilly, S Shields, E Stevenson, E Waterson

Executive Organisation

Chief Executive: Barry Mulholland
Curriculum Head of Department: Sheila McCaul
Finance Head of Department: Owen Harkin
Library Head of Department: Helen Osborne
Services Head of Department: Arthur Rainey

The Board is managed by a Chief Executive through leadership of a team of four Departmental Heads, representing Curriculum, Finance, Library and Services. The Audit Section reports directly to the Chief Executive.

The purpose of the Curriculum Department is to provide a range of advice and support services to schools, youth groups and parents in order to improve the standard of pupils' and young persons' achievements and the quality of their learning experiences.

The purpose of the Finance Department is to secure maximum funding for the services, which the Board provides, and thereafter to allocate resources in accordance with the Board's corporate objectives, and to ensure that proper systems are available to enable financial monitoring and evaluation to take place.

The purpose of the Library Service is to provide access to a comprehensive range of books, information and library facilities in support of the educational, economic and cultural needs of people in the area.

The purpose of the Services Department is to provide the Board with a wide range of services including responsibility for school planning and capital provision, estate management, school administration and recurrent funding, human resources and support services.

Other Agencies and Organisations in Education

Staff Commission for Education and Library Boards

Forestview
Purdy's Lane, Belfast, BT8 7AR
Tel:028 9049 1461
Fax: 028 9049 1744
Email: info@staffcom.org.uk

Chairman: Bernard Collen

The Staff Commission for Education and Library Boards is an Executive Non Departmental Public Body whose aim is to oversee recruitment, promotion, training and terms and conditions of employment for people working in Education and Library Boards in Northern Ireland.

Council for the Curriculum, Examinations and Assessment (CCEA)
Clarendon Dock
29 Clarendon Road
Belfast, BT1 3BG
Tel: 028 9026 1200
Fax: 028 9026 1234

Chairman: Dr Alan Lennon, Former Managing Director, Munster Simms Engineering Limited

Chief Executive: Gavin Boyd
Head of Corporate Services: David Mulholland
Head of Education Services: Dr Alastair Walker

The CCEA was set up by Government to provide advice on and support for what is taught in schools and colleges in Northern Ireland, and how it is assessed. The CCEA is responsible for assessment of pupils at Key Stages 1, 2 and 3, and accreditation of Records of Achievement. The Council conducts public examinations such as GCSE, CES, Certificate of Educational Achievement and Graded Objectives in Modern Languages for students aged 16 to 19 and beyond, and administers the transfer test (known as the 11 plus) on behalf of the Department of Education. The Council is also responsible for the regulation of GNVQs in Northern Ireland.

Council for Catholic Maintained Schools (CCMS)
160 High Street
Holywood , BT18 9HT
Tel: 028 9042 6972
Fax: 028 9042 4255

Chairman: Most Rev J McAreavey DD, Bishop of Dromore
Chief Executive: Donal Flanagan

The Council for Catholic Maintained Schools (CCMS), although entirely independent, has a role in relation to the management of Catholic Schools not unlike the role of an Education and Library Board in relation to controlled schools. It manages, on behalf of the voluntary maintained (Catholic) sector, matters such as staff recruitment and appointments, maintenance and finance. CCMS also has a strong input into the curriculum, where there is an emphasis on maintaining the appropriate ethos in the school environment.

Northern Ireland Higher Education Council
Adelaide House
39-49 Adelaide Street
Belfast, BT2 8FD

Tel: 028 9025 7777
Fax: 028 9025 7778

Chairman: Tony Hopkins CBE

The Northern Ireland Higher Education Council (NIHEC) is a non-executive advisory body established in April 1993. It provides advice to the Department of Employment and Learning on the planning and funding of higher education in Northern Ireland. It is particularly concerned with educational standards, facilities and research.

Employment and Training in Northern Ireland

The Department of Employment and Learning (DEL) manages a range of training and employment measures and programmes in Northern Ireland. These programmes range from a public employment service delivered through a network of 35 JobCentres/Jobs and Benefits Offices through the Investors in People Programme to modern apprenticeship schemes.
The programmes are profiled below and further information is available from:

Department for Employment and Learning
The Information Point
Adelaide House
39-49 Adelaide Street
Belfast, BT2 8FB
Tel: 028 9025 7793
Fax: 028 9025 7795
Web: www.delni.gov.uk

Further detailed information about the Department of Employment and Learning organisation is set out in Chapter 3, beginning on page 163.

Investors In People

The Department for Employment and Learning, through the Northern Ireland Investors in People Quality Centre, is responsible for the delivery of Investors in People in Northern Ireland. The aim of the Northern Ireland Investors in People Quality Centre is to promote awareness of the Investors in People Standard (and its associated models) in Northern Ireland and to encourage and support organisations to achieve and maintain the Standard. The Investors in People Standard is a business improvement tool that helps organisations to compete and succeed through improved people performance.

Management Development

Many of Northern Ireland's business managers and leaders are innovative, creative, visionary and inspirational. Northern Ireland may have some exceptionally successful businesses and organisations, created, led and managed by exceptional people, but, still the need for high quality managers and business leaders here has never been greater.

Too many businesses and organisations continue to fall short of achieving their maximum potential. In many instances, products, services and working methods are not developed with the creativity and speed necessary to meet the ever-present challenges of globalisation, technology and innovation. The skills to cope with these challenges are essential in today's effective manager so that their business remains competitive and positioned to meet increasing customer requirements.

The business case linking high levels of managerial competence with improved performance encourages the business community to take action to strengthen the individual contribution of its managers, at all levels, by investing in their development.

The aim of the Department for Employment and Learning is "to promote a culture of lifelong learning and to equip people for work in a modern economy." The Department's Management Development Branch exists to further this aim through its support measures for Northern Ireland's businesses and organisations.
These support measures include:

A range of entry into management initiatives:
- The Business Education Initiative (BEI);
- The Premiere 2 - Management Development Programme;
- The Rapid Advancement Programme (RAP).

Programmes aimed at developing existing managers:
- Management and Leadership Development Programme;
- Leaders for Tomorrow.

Modern Apprenticeships

Modern Apprenticeships were launched by government in response to employer demand, to enhance the status of apprenticeships and improve the supply into industry of young people with advanced occupational skills and broader key skills. The approach, a further development of the NVQ approach to training, was introduced throughout Great Britain from September 1995 and now covers most skill sectors there. In Northern Ireland, consultation with interested parties showed widespread support for a similar approach. Accordingly, in July 1996, Modern Apprenticeships were introduced here, initially on a pilot basis. The pilots proved successful and there was commitment to the further development and application of Modern Apprenticeships throughout the province, in particular the concept of direct employer involvement in the delivery of training based on the principles of cost sharing between employers, young people and government.

Modern Apprenticeships are now an integral part of the Department's Jobskills programme and have steadily increased in popularity with both young people and employers during recent years. Intake into training has almost doubled over the past two years. Around 5,500 young people in Northern Ireland, ranging in experience from first year to fourth year, are currently following a Modern Apprenticeship and over 2,000 local employers are participating in the programme.

National Training Awards

The National Training Awards (NTA) are the UK's premier accolade for organisations and individuals that have achieved lasting excellence through training. NTA winners are exemplars of training and development in the UK; they are committed to exceptional training that has real benefits for the business, the community and the individual.

New Deal

New Deal is a major element of the government's Welfare to Work strategy. It gives unemployed people aged 18 to 24 and 25+ a chance to develop their potential, gain skills and experience and find work. In addition, the New Deal for Lone Parents and the New Deal for Partners offers assistance to lone parents in receipt of Income Support and partners of

Jobseeker's Allowance (JSA) claimants (and partners of certain other benefit recipients) to find work. New Deal for Musicians is an option available to clients eligible for either New Deal for 18 to 24 year olds or New Deal 25+.

All New Deals start with an interview with a New Deal Personal Adviser who supports the client throughout his or her time on the programme. During this interview the client's skills, experience and job hopes are discussed. Any gaps in skills or knowledge are identified and the New Deal Personal Adviser may suggest extra help to get the client ready for work, such as support to develop self confidence.

The New Deal Personal Adviser helps clients into work by tailoring the support available through New Deal to their individual needs and circumstances. This support can include subsidised employment, work experience with employers, training and help with essential skills. The first phase of New Deal, the "Gateway", provides intensive help to get the client into work. This might include interview practice and help with job applications, or short courses to improve work skills. During this period, clients will have access to a range of services and opportunities to help them prepare for and find work. As people are encouraged to think about what they want to do and are helped to prepare properly, employers get recruits who are motivated and committed to the job. New Deal offers employers a major opportunity to invest in the future of their organisation, tackle skills shortages and help end the waste of unemployment.

Employers, both public and private sector, have a key role within New Deal and can:

- take the opportunity New Deal offers to help make their businesses or organisations more successful by drawing on this key source of potential recruits;
- offer people permanent jobs through New Deal, to give them the chance of showing what they have to offer; and
- possibly obtain a financial subsidy.

Employers have the chance to recruit employees who are motivated, committed and prepared for work and there may be financial help to recruit and train them.

Training Organisations

Abbey Training Services
Lennie House, 314 Antrim Road,
Glengormley
Newtownabbey, BT36 8EH
Contact: Jaraleth McCamphill
Tel: 028 9084 0527

Advance Training & Development
50 Railway Street, Lisburn, BT28 1XP
Contact: Colleen Dalzell
Tel: 028 92 666094

Armagh College
Lonsdale Street
Armagh, BT61 7HN
Contact: Sarah Mallon
Tel: 028 3751 2818

Austins Quality Training Services
The Diamond, Derry, BT48 6HR
Contact: Ann McColgan
Tel: 028 7126 9324

BCW Training Ltd
Unit 18
Leyland Road Industrial Estate,
Ballycastle, BT54 6EZ
Contact: Jacinta Hill
Tel: 028 2076 2902

Belfast Central Training Ltd
98/102 Donegall Street,
Belfast, BT1 2GW
Contact: John Savage
Tel: 028 9032 4973

Belfast Centre of Learning,
H J O'Boyle Belfast
1A Rossmore Avenue, Belfast, BT7 3HB
Contact: Francis Tumelty
Tel: 028 9064 6446

Belfast College of Training &
Education Ltd
Franklin House, 12 Brunswick Street
Belfast, BT2 7GE
Contact: Collette Steele
Tel: 028 9023 2186

Belfast Institute
Millfield Building, Belfast, BT1 1HS
Contact: Christina McCool
Tel: 028 9026 5000

Blackwater House (STC)
Riverpark, Blackwater Road
Mallusk, BT36 4TZ
Contact: Pamela Morgan
Tel: 028 9034 2400

Brookfield Business School
Brookfield Business Centre
333 Crumlin Road
Belfast, BT14 7EA
Contact: Deborah Stewart
Tel: 028 9075 1293

Castlereagh College
Montgomery Road
Belfast, BT6 9JD
Contact: Isobel McClean
Tel: 028 9070 8228

Causeway Institute
2 Coleraine Road
Ballymoney, BT53 6BP
Contact: Carolyn Taggart
Tel: 028 2766 0404

CITB (STC)
17 Dundrod Road
Crumlin, BT29 4SR
Contact: Gary Hindman
Tel: 028 9082 4200/4204

Clanrye Employment & Training Services
The Abbey, Abbey Yard,
Newry, BT34 2EG
Contact: Liam Devine
Tel: 028 3026 7121

Coalisland Training Services Ltd
51 Dungannon Road,
Coalisland, BT71 4HP
Contact: Richard Thornton
Tel: 028 8774 8512

College Training & Employment Centre
72-76 Main Street, Limavady, BT49 0EP
Contact: Ms Sharon Hartin
Tel: 028 77 762745

Conservation Volunteers
Dendron Lodge, Clandeboye Estate,
Bangor, BT19 1RN
Contact: Linda Wilson
Tel: 028 9185 2817

Cookstown Training
New Generation Tech Centre
T5 Cookstown Enterprise Centre
Derryloran Estate, Sandhills Road
Cookstown, BT80 9LU
Contact: Geraldine McIvor
Tel: 028 8676 1145

Craft Recruitment & Training
Mopack Business Complex
Ballycolman Road, Strabane, BT82 9PH
Contact: Marie Nealis
Tel: 028 71 880044

CTRS Community Training
New Hope Centre
Erne Road, Enniskillen, BT74 6NN
Contact: Yvonee Fallis
Tel: 028 66 328073

Customized Training Services
Units 11 & 12, 3-5 Main Street
Strabane, BT82 8AR
Contact: Ms Carmel Boyce
Tel: 028 71 382260

Dairy Farm Training (People 1st)
Unit 18, Dairy Farm Centre,
Stewartstown Road, Belfast, BT17 0AW
Contact: Ronan Heenan
Tel: 028 90 618452

DARD
22 Greenmount Road
Antrim, BT41 4PU
Contact: Marie McAuley
Tel: 028 63674 / 9442 6674

Derry Youth & Community Workshop Ltd
6 Society Street, Derry, BT48 6PJ
Contact: Phyliss Kennedy
Tel: 028 7126 8891

East Antrim Institute
400 Shore Road
Newtownabbey, BT37 9RS
Contact: Mark Sault
Tel: 028 9085 0000

East Down Institute
Market Street
Downpatrick, BT30 6ND
Contact: Jacqueline Doran
Tel: 028 4461 1517

East Tyrone College
Circular Road, Dungannon, BT71 6BQ
Contact: AJ Dardis
Tel: 028 8772 2323

Electrical Training Trust (STC)
Unit 4, Ballymena Business Development,
Fenaghy Road
Ballymena, BT42 1FL
Contact: Claire Alexander
Tel: 028 2565 0750

Engineering Training Council (STC)
Interpoint, 20-24 York Street
Belfast, BT15 1AQ
Contact: Sylvia Law
Tel: 028 9032 9878

Fermanagh College
Fairview, Dublin Road
Enniskillen, BT74 6AE
Contact: Dermot Dolan
Tel: 028 6632 2072

Fermanagh Training Ltd
Skills Centre, Killyhevlin Industrial Estate
Dublin Road, Enniskillen, BT74 4EJ
Contact: Margaret McManus
Tel: 028 6632 4860

Food & Drink Training Council (STC)
4b Weavers' Court, Linfield Road
Belfast, BT12 5GH
Contact: Wendy Kelly
Tel: 028 9032 9269

Graham Training
40-44 Railway Street
Lisburn, BT28 1XP
Contact: Patricia Moley
Tel: 028 9266 5100

H J O'Boyle Training Ltd
15A English Street
Downpatrick, BT30 6AB
Contact: Francis Tumelty
Tel: 028 4461 6438

Hastings Hotel Group (STC)
Midland Building, Whitla Street
Belfast, BT15 1NA
Contact: Patricia Fitzpatrick
Tel: 028 9075 1066

Impact Training (NI) Limited
16 Lanark Way, Belfast, BT13 3BH
Contact: Ms Sarah Cairns
Tel: 028 9033 9910

Jennymount Training Services
Jennymount Industrial Estate, North
Derby Street, Belfast, BT15 3HU
Contact: Eileen Kane
Tel: 028 9043 5414

Joblink Antrim
12 High Street, Antrim, BT41 4AN
Contact: Mr Kane
Tel: 028 9448 7848

Joblink Bangor (Appello)
Market House, 3 Market Street,
Bangor, BT20 4SP
Contact: Karen Bones
Tel: 028 9127 3474

Joblink Belfast
2nd Floor, 1-3 Lombard Street
Belfast, BT1 1RB
Contact: Karen Bones
Tel: 028 9024 6888

Joblink Braid (Ballymena)
48-50 Linenhall Street
Ballymena, BT43 5AL
Contact: Karen Bones
Tel: 028 2563 1800

Joblink Limavady
42 Catherine Street, Limavady, BT49 9DB
Contact: Mr Kane
Tel: 028 7772 174

Joblink Magherafelt
11a Meeting Street
Magherfelt, BT45 6BN
Contact: Mr Kane
Tel: 028 7963 4666

Joblink NE (Coleraine)
Market Court, 57-59 New Row,
Coleraine, BT52 1EJ
Contact: Karen Bones
Tel: 028 7035 2434

Joblink Omagh
2nd Floor, Anderson House,
Market Street, Omagh, BT78 1EE
Contact: Nathan Flatman
Tel: 02882 24 0999

Joblink Strabane
Abercorn House, 2 Railway Street,
Strabane, BT82 9EF
Contact: Karen Bones
Tel: 02870 35 2434

Joblink (Waterloo House)
48 Waterloo Street,
Londonderry, BT48 6HF
Contact: Mr Kane
Tel: 028 7137 0300

JTM Antrim
29-31 Church Street,
Ballymena, BT43 6BD
Contact: Patricia Cathcart
Tel: 028 2565 6567

JTM Carrick (BTE)
29-31 Church Street
Ballymena, BT43 6BD
Contact: Patricia Cathcart
Tel: 028 25 656567
Also covers Antrim, Carrick and Coleraine

Larne Skills Development Ltd
Larne Business Centre, Bank Road
Larne, BT40 3AW
Contact: Ruth Dillon
Tel: 028 2827 3337

Lets Training & Employment Ltd
100 Hill Street
Lurgan, BT66 6BQ
Contact: Myles Haughey
Tel: 028 3832 7307

The Link Works
11 Sugar Island, Newry, BT35 6HT
Contact: Wendy Connor
Tel: 028 3026 2777

Lisburn Institute
39 Castle Street, Lisburn, BT27 4SU
Contact: Mrs Grainne McCartan
Tel: 028 9267 3437

Lisburn YMCA
28 Market Square, Lisburn, BT28 1AG
Contact: Sandra Walsh
Tel: 028 9267 0918

Loughview Training Services
1 Ballyclare Road,
Glengormley, BT36 5EX
Contact: Julie Hughes
Tel: 028 9080 1010

Momentum (STC)
NiSoft House, Ravenhill Business Park,
Ravenhill Road, Belfast, BT6 8AW
Tel: 028 9045 0101

Network Personnel
80-82 Rainey Street
Magherafelt, BT45 5AJ
Contact: Maxine McClean
Tel: 028 7963 1032

Newry & Kilkeel Institute
Patrick Street, Newry, BT35 5DL
Contact: Libby McCreesh
Tel: 028 3026 4721

NIE Powerteam
Nutts Corner, Dundrod Road
Crumlin BT29 4SR
Contact: Helen Gallagher
Tel: 028 9068 8249

North City Training
275 Antrim Road, Belfast, BT15 2GZ
Contact: Richard Henderson
Tel: 028 9074 5408

North Down and Ards
Victoria Avenue, Ards, BT23 7ED
Contact: Jennifer Palmer
Tel: 028 9127 6600

North Down Training
4-6 Conway Square
Newtownards, BT23 4DD
Contact: Nigel Finch
Tel: 028 9182 2880

North East Institute
Jobskills Department
Farm Lodge Building, Ballymena, BT43 7DF
Contact: Ruth Wylie
Tel: 028 2565 6561

Omagh College
Training Office, Woodside Avenue,
Omagh, BT79 7BP
Contact: Jennifer Barton
Tel: 028 8225 4954

Oriel Training Services
Unit 1, 35A Main Street,
Randalstown, BT41 3AB
Contact: Leanne Karney
Tel: 028 9447 8860 / 94 462620

Paragon Services (NI) Ltd
Unit HG2, Twinspires Complex,
North Howard Street, Belfast, BT13 2JS
Contact: Anita Fitzsimons
Tel: 028 9024 2535

Parity Training Ltd
Blackstaff Chamber, 2 Amelia Street,
Belfast, BT2 7GS
Contact: Victoria Allen
Tel: 028 9024 0780

Printing & Packaging (STC)
c/o Graham & Heslip Ltd,
96 Beechill Road, Belfast, BT8 4QM
Contact: Rosie Mitten
Tel: 028 4176 5516

Protocol (Springskills)(Belfast)
Ground Floor, Scottish Legal House
65-67 Chichester Street
Belfast, BT1 4JD
Contact: Ms K Scullion
Tel: 028 9033 0331

Protocol (Springskills) (Derry, Dungannon, Cookstown)
1st Floor, 50-54a Waterloo Street,
Londonderry, BT48 6BU
Contact: Moya McDevitt
Tel: 028 7137 3002

Protocol (Springskills) (Newry)
2 Marcus Street, Newry, BT34 1AZ
Contact: Celine Cunningham
Tel: 028 30 26440

Seven Towers Training Ltd
56 Henry Street, Ballymena, BT42 3AH
Contact: Kim Alexander
Tel: 028 25 644003

Shantallow Training Services
10 Northland Road, Derry, BT48 7GD
Contact: Glen McElwee
Tel: 028 71 351190

Shorts Bombardier
Interpoint, 20-24 York Street
20-24 York Street
Belfast, BT15 1AW
Contact: Helen Savage
Tel: 028 90 468338

Southern Group
Unit 22, Greenbank Industrial Estate,
Warrenpoint, Newry, BT34 2QY
Contact: Mr R Barton
Tel: 028 30 266924

Southern ITEC
52 Armagh Road
Newry, BT35 6DP
Contact: Ms Sharon Toner
Tel: 028 30 268131

Sperrin Lakeland
Tyrone County Hospital, Hospital Road,
Omagh, BT79 0AP
Contact: Ms Esme Hill
Tel: 028 82 245211

Springvale Training Ltd
200 Springfield Road
Belfast, BT12 7GB
Contact: Lorraine Kelly
Tel: 028 90 242362

Strabane Training Services
Ballycolman Industrial Estate
Strabane, BT82 9PH
Contact: Jolene Atkinson
Tel: 028 71 382438

Sureskills

Callender House
58-60 Upper Arthur Street
Belfast, BT1 4GP
Tel: +44 (0) 28 9093 5555
Fax: +44 (0) 28 9093 5566
Email: niinfo@sureskills.com
Web: www.sureskills.com

General Manager
Pauline Thompson

SureSkills is widely recognised as the premier training solutions organisation in Ireland, delivering over 25,000 days of authorised and customised programmes each year to both the private and public sectors. Training is delivered in our state of the art training centres in Belfast and Dublin and where required, on-site at the customer's premises.

Tourism Training Trust (STC)
Caernarvon House, 19 Donegall Pass,
Belfast, BT7 1DQ
Contact: Roisin McKee
Tel: 028 90 320625

Training Direct (North West Institute)
Springtown Industrial Estate,
Londonderry, BT48 0LY
Contact: Susan Currie
Tel: 028 71 276222

Transport Training Services (STC)
15 Dundrod Road, Crumlin, BT29 4SS
Contact:
Tel: 028 90 825653

Tyrone Training Services
38 Gortin Road, Omagh, BT79 7HX
Contact: Colette McCullagh
Tel: 028 82 249999

Ulidia Training Services
165-169 Albertbridge Road
Belfast, BT5 4PS
Contact: Jane Courtney
Tel: 028 90 731030

Upper Bann Institute
Portadown Campus, 36 Lurgan Road,
Portadown, BT63 5BL
Contact: Rosemary Muldrew
Tel: 028 38 397855

Wade Training Ltd, (Armagh & Portadown)
33 Castle Street
Portadown, BT62 1BB
Contact: Orla Waterson
Tel: 028 38 337000

Wholesale & Retail Training Council (STC)
10 Hydepark Road, Mallusk,
Newtownabbey, BT36 4PY
Contact: Zoe Todd
Tel: 028 90 845830

Workforce
90-120 Springfield Road
Belfast, BT12 7AJ
Contact: Tara Toland
Tel: 028 90 247016

Workscene Training Organisation
Curran House, Twin Spires House, 155
Northumberland Street
Belfast, BT13 2JF
Contact: Paul Wilson
Tel: 028 90 311787

Chapter

The Northern Ireland Economy

FUJITSU
northbrook
technology

Overview of The Northern Ireland Economy

Introduction

The Northern Ireland economy is a relatively small regional economy within the United Kingdom and in a European context is a highly peripheral and less favoured economic area.

Although Northern Ireland was traditionally (at least until the 1970s) the most industrialised part of Ireland it has gradually been overtaken economically by the adjacent Republic of Ireland economy, which has enjoyed a sustained boom in recent years.

The Northern Ireland economy has some unique characteristics that present structural challenges for the future. These include:

- An over-dependence on the public sector for employment and health;
- A relatively small industrial and manufacturing base;
- Traditional industries – shipbuilding, engineering, textiles and agriculture, all in crisis or long term decline;
- Difficulty attracting quality international investment and tourism revenue because of political problems.
- Arguably, an introspective culture, which results in low levels of entrepreneurship, export focus and private equity.

However, because these structural difficulties are fully recognised and considerable efforts deployed to counter them, Northern Ireland has an impressively resilient economic long-term performance. It does not collapse in the manner of some other economies in times of international cyclical downturn nor does it enjoy spectacular growth even when all western economies are experiencing a boom.

Although performance has certainly improved over recent years, Northern Ireland is not a major exporter and continues to depend heavily on the rest of the United Kingdom for its key export markets.

The authorities, including the Department of Enterprise, Trade and Investment and its main economic development agency Invest NI have set an ambitious vision for the Northern Ireland economy. The vision is to make Northern Ireland a knowledge-based economy and an exemplar location for starting and growing a successful business.

GDP and Economic Growth

Northern Ireland accounts for around 2.2 per cent of the UK gross domestic product (GDP) and the proportion does not vary greatly around this figure. In recent years Northern Ireland GDP has grown, at rates that have been slightly above the UK average. Table 7.1 below indicates that Northern Ireland not only accounts for a small share of UK GDP but also that per capita GDP in Northern Ireland lags behind the UK average by a considerable margin. Historically Northern Ireland GDP per capita has hovered around 75 per cent of the UK average although this improved noticeably in the later 1990s (possibly but not indisputably coinciding with the "peace process") reaching a peak of 81.5 per cent in 1995.) The latest estimate of Northern Ireland per capita GDP as a proportion of UK is 78.2%.

Remarkably Northern Ireland has continued to have one of the fastest rates of economic growth of any UK region in the past years, although it still has one of the highest rates of unemployment and certainly the highest rate of economic inactivity.

Although GDP per capita is well below the UK average, it is no longer the lowest of the UK regions, with the North East of England now slightly lower.

Table 7.1: GDP and GDP per head in Northern Ireland 1989-19991

	GDP in Northern Ireland		GDP per head in Northern Ireland		
	£m	% of UK GDP	£	Nominal Growth	% of UK average
1989	9,329	2.1	5,893	---	74.7
1990	10,013	2.0	6,300	6.9	73.8
1991	10,890	2.1	6,787	7.7	76.4
1992	11,611	2.2	7,163	5.5	77.6
1993	12,437	2.2	7,610	6.2	78.7
1994	13,344	2.2	8,114	6.6	79.8
1995	14,297	2.3	8,654	6.7	81.5
1996	14,936	2.3	8,964	3.6	80.1
1997p	15,952	2.3	9,507	6.1	80.1
1998p	16,501	2.2	9,754	2.6	77.7
1999p	17,003	2.2	10,050	3.0	77.5

Source: ONS1 GDP at factor cost, current prices UK excludes Extra-Regions

Table 7.2: Gross Domestic Product By Industry

Gross Domestic Product (GDP)

	1990	1992	1994	1996	1998
By industry (£ millions)					
Agriculture, hunting, forestry and fishing	488	641	634	809	653
Mining and quarrying of energy producing materials	10	9	11	9	10
Other Mining and quarrying	30	34	74	65	77
Manufacturing	2,130	2,293	2,628	3,014	3,135
Electricity, gas and water supply	298	372	398	435	354
Construction	652	643	753	868	1,001
Wholesale and retail trade (including motor trade)	1,058	1,266	1,462	1,693	2,085
Hotels and Restaurants	246	281	330	407	505
Transport, storage and communication	540	639	738	812	938
Financial intermediation	312	432	618	558	591
Real estate, renting and business activities	924	1,064	1,347	1,615	2,175
Public administration and defence	1,445	1,883	1,933	1,960	1,966
Education	679	913	953	1,096	1,367
Health & social work	864	1,055	1,295	1,376	1,380
Other services	336	378	538	572	672
FISIM	-243	-293	-367	-355	-406
Gross Domestic Product (£m)		11,611	13,344	14,936	16,501

*FISIM = financial intermediation services indirectly measured

Analysis of Northern Ireland's GDP by sector shows that the economy relies heavily on services, and in particular the public sector.

GDP Comparisons with Republic of Ireland

Although Northern Ireland GDP performance compares favourably with other regions of the UK the comparison with the neighbouring economy of the Irish Republic is quite surprising.

Only 10 years ago Northern Ireland was regarded as being more prosperous as a region than its southern neighbour although both were acknowledged to be Objective 1 regions of the European Union (regions eligible for financial support from Europe where GDP per capita was below 75 per cent of the EU average). At that time Northern Ireland had just under half of the population of the Republic and about half of the Republic's gross domestic product in absolute terms.

With the sustained boom in the Republic and the sluggish growth in Northern Ireland, the province's GDP as a proportion of Republic of Ireland GDP has fallen from approximately 50 per cent in 1992 to 30 per cent in 1999 and this general trend is predicted to continue, although much less dramatically. It is expected therefore that Northern Ireland's share of all-island GDP is currently well under 20 per cent.

Table 7.3 GDP North/South Comparision

	GDP (£m)		% Share of All-Island GDP	
	N Ireland	Republic	N Ireland	Republic
1991	10,890	24,086	31.1	68.9
1993	12,437	27,687	31.0	69.0
1995	14,297	33,126	30.1	69.9
1997	15,952	42,141	27.4	72.6
1999	17,003	56,003	23.2	76.8

ROI GDP converted to Stg £ @ 1 Euro = 0.7 Stg

Although Northern Ireland has lost its Objective 1 status the Republic despite its 'wealth' being recognised as being well over EU average has retained it for its border, midlands and western region.

Labour Force, Employment and Unemployment

At June 2003 there were an estimated 669,110 employee jobs in Northern Ireland – the highest figure on record. Despite this unemployment was among the highest for any UK region.

The dominance of the public sector is reflected in the composition of Northern Ireland's employers. The numbers employed in health, education and public administration combined are over twice the number employed in manufacturing. As with many developed economies the service sector's share of employment has grown steadily.

Table 7.4: Northern Ireland Employees in Employment by Sector (Unadjusted) June 2002

	June 2002
Agriculture	14,640
Mining & Quarrying	1,920
Manufacturing	97,210
Electricity, Gas & Water Supply	3,050
Construction	35,460
Wholesale & Retail Trade; Repairs	111,060
Hotels & Restaurants	39,340
Transport, Storage & Communication	27,010
Financial Intermediation	16,670
Real Estate, Renting & Business Activities	53,220
Public Administration & Defence	60,410
Education	66,970
Health & Social Work	98,460
Other Service Activities	30,360
Services	503,500
Total	**655,770**

Note: Figures rounded. Source: DETI

In contrast the number employed in manufacturing has decreased significantly in recent years. This decrease in manufacturing employment has however not been as dramatic as for the UK as a whole and shows that despite a downturn in many of Northern Ireland's traditional industries the overall manufacturing base although small is proving quite resilient.

Although there has been a stabilising effect from a large public sector it is now recognised by some commentators as being both unsustainable and acting as a barrier to accelerating economic growth.

Unemployment in Northern Ireland is currently running at 5.5%, very low by historical standards and broadly in line with the United Kingdom average. However, some economists have warned that the official unemployment figure for Northern Ireland is misleading and much understated. This is because Northern Ireland – uniquely as a region has a very high level of compulsory early retirement as well as a uniquely high proportion of people of working age in receipt of invalidity benefit.

Public Sector

The public sector employs over 212,000 people in Northern Ireland, which is nearly one third of all employment. In addition to those employed directly by the public sector there is also a large number employed in what one commentator calls the 'pseudo public sector'. That sector comprises many private sector companies relying solely on the public sector for their customer base and therefore by extension dependant on the public sector for their employment. Public sector employment is set to rise further as a proportion of total employment given proposed budgetary increases in the labour-intensive public services sector.

Public Expenditure accounts for a disproportionately high share of value-added. Table 7.5 indicates the planned budget for the next three years. The most substantial increase are in health education and infrastructure and the overall level of spending in 2006-07 is expected to be significantly higher than in 2003/04.

Table 7.5: Public Expenditure Public Expenditure Plans: 2004-05 to 2005-06

Department	2003-04	2004-05	%	2005-06	%
DARD	253.4	264.7		282.1	
DCAL	97.1	103.8		112.2	
DE	1,529.7	1,650.5		1696.0	
DEL	672.7	680.7		721.7	
DETI	248.7	270.6		257.7	
DFP	165.7	138.8		180.8	
DHSSPS	3,009.7	3,227.6		3,497.9	
DOE	133.2	142.9		137.9	
DRD	611.4	752.5		705.8	
DSD	489.7	537.8		555.4	
OFMDFM	49.2	57.1		60.8	
NI Assembly	49.2	49.2		49.2	
Other Departments	10.5	11.8		12.2	
Total Departments **DEL**	**7,320.3**	**7888.0**	**7.8**	**8,269.8**	**4.8**
Prior to Adjustments					
Total DEL*	**6,762.60**	**7,135.70**	**5.5**	**7,571.80**	**6.1**

* After certain adjustments for unallocated capital, overcommittments regional rates, planned borrowing and Peace II

Trade and Exports From Northern Ireland

The recent export performance of the Northern Ireland Economy has been relatively favourable. Between 1996/97 and 2001/02 manufacturing exports from Northern Ireland increased by some 45% in real terms. More recently exports have levelled off with a slight decline in exports to the EU and rest of the World. The Irish Republic has become a growing and increasingly important market for Northern Ireland exports. However Northern Ireland is still heavily dependant on Great Britain as its key export market, still accounting for almost half of all Northern Ireland exports. The equivalent figure for Republic of Ireland exports to Great Britain is 19%.

Although there was growth across a number of sectors, most of the growth in external and export markets has been driven by a small number of large firms in key sectors including transport equipment, food, drink and tobacco, and electrical and optical equipment. The majority of these industrial sectors in Northern Ireland are heavily reliant on external markets for their sales. In seven of the twelve broad industrial sectors, external sales account for more than half of total sales.

There are ongoing difficulties in other key sectors, most notably the textiles and clothing sector and the meat processing and dairy sector, which have been hit by a number of crises in recent years to the detriment of their sectoral export performance.

Northern Ireland Competitiveness and Productivity

Since 1995 manufacturing output rose by 28.9% to 2001, although it fell by 6% in the following year. Although the food, drink and tobacco sub-sector has experienced the most significant growth there have been significant reverses in textiles engineering, the ICT sector and aerospace. Northern Ireland engineering accounts for half of all Northern Ireland's manufacturing exports.

In textiles Northern Ireland's difficulty has been sustaining competitiveness against low-wage mainly Asian economies and there have been significant job losses as a result, particularly in the lower value-added parts of the textiles sector.

Table 7.6: Index of Manufacturing Productivity

Index of Manufacturing Productivity
Annual Averages (Base year 1995 = 100)

	Northern Ireland	United Kingdom
1995	100.0	100.0
1996	101.4	99.1
1197	104.4	100.5
1998	107.8	102.1
1999	117.9	106.5
2000	130.1	113.0
2001	132.9	115.8
2002	132.9	116.4

Source: DETI

A major study by cross-border trade body Inter*Trade*Ireland found that competitiveness in Northern Ireland lagged behind that of the Republic of Ireland significantly in some sectors although was ahead in some also.

Under one key measure 'value added per employee' the Irish Republic registered over twice the real value added for each industrial employee. However the booming economy of Ireland is not 'necessarily' the most reasonable comparator for Northern Ireland. Against the United Kingdom as a whole, Northern Ireland's productivity has been improving much more rapidly. Table 7.6 below shows the improvement in NI and UK productivity as an index (However in absolute numbers UK productivity – indexed from a higher base is still well ahead).

Centre for Competitiveness

Centre for
Competitiveness
www.cforc.org

1st Floor Interpoint
20-24 York Street
Belfast, BT15 1AQ
Tel: 0870 240 6668
Fax: 028 9046 8361
Email: compete@cforc.org
Web: www.cforc.org

Director and Chief Executive
Bob Barbour

Supporting the development of an internationally competitive local economy, the Centre for Competitiveness (CforC) is a not-for-profit membership organisation working to assist local organisations, particularly SMEs, achieve sustainable competitive advantage.

Inward Investment

Northern Ireland continues to attract significant inward investment, which continues to account for a very high proportion of manufacturing and industrial value added and employment.

Table 7.7 shows the number of foreign owned companies operating in Northern Ireland and their home country location. The number of foreign-owned companies operating in Northern Ireland increased by over 60% between 1996 and 2002, to nearly 637. The majority of the companies are from the Republic of Ireland and the US.

Table 7.7 : Number of foreign owned companies operating in Northern Ireland by country of ownership, 1996 to 2002

Country	1996	1998	2000	2002
Republic of Ireland	100	123	165	232
United States of America	71	111	146	160
France	23	23	36	45
Netherlands	17	30	26	34
Germany	17	22	26	36
Denmark	13	12	12	11
Japan	11	15	14	14
Switzerland	10	5	7	12
Canada	8	9	10	11
Australia	7	6	5	8
South Korea	6	8	7	8
Sweden	4	2	3	8
Finland	3	3	5	7
Belgium	3	5	3	4
South Africa	2	2	3	4
Portugal	1	1	4	1
Norway	1	1	9	5
Channel Islands	0	5	5	18
Isle of Man	0	4	3	4
Other Countries	7	2	4	16
All foreign owned companies	**304**	**389**	**497**	**637**

Source: NISRA

Principle responsibility for winning inward direct investment lies with the Government's leading economic development agency Invest NI. In its report on achievements during 2002/03 Invest NI was involved in 135 inward visits of which 98 were first-time visits and 37 were repeat visits. The Agency pointed to prevailing economic circumstances in which investment decisions were being delayed. In the same period 10 new inward investments promising over 800 jobs and £22m investment were secured at a cost of £6m. Although the 800 jobs fell short of Invest NI's target of 1500 new jobs the total achieved represented a respectable 11% of the market share of FDI into the UK and Ireland over the period.

Innovation, Research and Development in Northern Ireland

As might be expected, R&D expenditure in Northern Ireland is concentrated in a small number of large companies. The ten biggest R&D spenders in 1999 accounted for 59 per cent of civil expenditure and five companies have appeared in the top ten in each of the three surveys.

Northern Ireland has relatively low levels of Innovation and Research and Development activity. Research and Development business expenditure per employee is below that for the United Kingdom as a whole.

This shortcoming in the local economy has been recognised by Government, the Economic Development Forum and by Invest NI. As a result the authorities have produced a Regional Innovation Strategy entitled 'think/create/innovate'. The key aim of the strategy is to enhance regional innovation by coordinating the research and education sector with business and government in a new partnership. This is intended to result in a monitor of all R&D activity in Northern Ireland and the wider dissemination of information to all relevant parties.

Improving innovation is one of four priority areas for Invest NI's corporate plan and a number of milestones were reached by the agency in the past – including the leveraging of £23m of private sector investment in R&D (target £20m) through Invest NI's main programme at a cost of £15m. Also the agency established 17 centres of Research Excellence and increased participation in Research and Development programmes by 7.9%. One of the primary purposes of the Centre of Research Excellence is to facilitate collaboration.

Economic Prospects

There are few professional forecasts available in the UK (at a regional level) relating to the future of the Northern Ireland economy. About the best available is produced between the Northern Ireland Economic Research Centre (now part of a new economic research agency ERINI) and Regional Forecast Consultants (Dr Graham Gudgin) who provide an expert forecast for all regions in the United Kingdom.

In recent years the forecast has pointed out that despite its well-publicised difficulties the Northern Ireland economy, taken as a region, has been one of the star performers in the United Kingdom.

Despite its outlying location, Northern Ireland's economic growth has been rapid and close to that of the South-East of England. It has easily outpaced growth in all the northern regions of the UK. Given Northern Ireland's structural disadvantages this is explained by competitive advantages such as low wages and a high level of government subsidies and spending.

The Gudgin forecast sees little medium term change in these fundamentals and therefore concludes that steady growth is set to continue. By UK standards the overall performance projected while continuing to lag the forecast for the Republic of Ireland, is creditable in the context of the United Kingdom.

Sectoral Analysis of The Northern Ireland Economy

Agriculture and Food Sector

Agriculture, forestry and fishing are important elements of the local economy. The sector accounts for around 4.5 per cent of regional Gross Domestic Product (GDP) and 4.8 per cent of total employment. Proportionately, agriculture's contribution to employment in Northern Ireland is the highest of all UK regions and only in East Anglia does it provide a greater share of regional GDP.

There are around 28,500 active, mostly family-run, farm businesses in Northern Ireland, the number of which have been declining at a rate of nearly 2 per cent per year for the past ten years. Although the average size of farms is more than twice the average size of European farms it is half the size of farms in the United Kingdom. In common with other regions in developed countries there has been a long-term downward trend in the number of farms and the average farm size has increased gradually. Three-fifths of farm businesses own the land which they farm and the remainder are a mixture of owned land, and land which is leased on short-term lettings basis.

Table 7.8: Key facts about Agriculture

	NI	UK	ROI
Gross Value Added (GVA) Agriculture as % of total GVA	2.5[1]	0.8[1]	3.2[3]
Employment Agriculture employment	34[2]	390[2]	121[2]
As % of total Civil employment	4.8[2]	1.4[2]	6.9[2]
Land Use As % of total Civil area	78.7[1]	70.4[1]	63.1[2]
Farms Number ('000)	28.5[1]	232[2]	142[2]
Average agricultural area (ha)	37.4[2]	71.6[2]	31.4[2]

Source DARD

1 2002, 2 2001, 3 2000,

There was a sharp fall in farm income in agriculture in 2002. Total income from farming (TIFF), which measures the return to farmers and all members of their families working on farms, declined by 32% per cent to £129 million, from £191 million in 2001. The sharp decline in income was due to two main factors: a fall of 14 per cent in the average producer milk price; and secondly the consequences of adverse weather conditions for much of 2002, which led to reduced volumes of output and increased input costs. Although figures are not yet available for 2003 there are indications that there has been a rise in farm incomes due to the strengthening of the Euro against Sterling.

Agreement was reached in June 2003 on further CAP reform, which requires member states to break the link between agricultural subsidies and production. As reform of the CAP unfolds it should have a significant impact on farm incomes.

There are approximately 400 food processors in Northern Ireland, employing around 19,000 people and generating approximately 20 per cent of the manufacturing sector's total external sales.

Agriculture and Food Agencies

Livestock & Meat Commission for Northern Ireland
31 Ballinderry Road, Lisburn, BT28 2SL
Tel: 028 9263 3000 / Fax: 028 9263 3001
Chief Executive: David Rutledge

Food Standards Agency

10C Clarendon Road
Belfast, BT1 3BG
Tel: 028 9041 7700
Fax: 028 9041 7726
Email: infofsani@foodstandards.gsi.gov.uk
Web: www.food.gov.uk
Director: Morris McAllister

FSANI provides advice to the public and to Government on food safety, nutrition and diet; Protects consumers through effective enforcement and monitoring; Supports consumer choice through accurate and meaningful labelling.

Major Agricultural and Food Companies

Agriculture Dairy Products

Armaghdown Creameries Ltd
30 Rathfriland Road, Banbridge, BT32 4LN
Tel: 028 4066 2742 / Fax: 028 4066 2443
Principal Activity: dairy products
Chief Executive: David Graham

Ballyrashane Co-op Society Ltd
18 Creamery Road, Coleraine, BT52 2NE
Tel: 028 7034 3265 / Fax: 028 7035 1653
Principal Activity: milk and dairy products
Chief Executive: Francis Kerr

Dairy Produce Packers Ltd
Millburn Road, Coleraine, BT52 1QZ
Tel: 028 7035 6231 / Fax: 028 7035 6412
Principal Activity: dairy products
Chief Executive: Alan McMinn

Dale Farm Dairies Ltd
Pennybridge Industrial Estate
Larne Road, Ballymena, BT42 3HB
Tel: 028 2564 5161
Fax: 028 2565 1108
Principal Activity: dairy products
Chief Executive: Neville Cruikshanks

Glanbia Cheese Ltd
35 Steps Road, Magheralin
Craigavon, BT67 0QY
Tel: 028 9261 1274
Fax: 028 9261 2464
Principal Activity: dairy products
Chief Executive: Conor Donovan

Golden Cow Dairies Ltd
25-29 Artabrackagh Road
Portadown, Craigavon, BT62 4HB
Tel: 028 3833 8411
Fax: 028 3835 0292
General Manager: Eamon Rice

Lakeland Dairies (Omagh) Ltd
46 Beltany Road, Omagh, BT78 5NF
Tel: 028 8224 6411
Fax: 028 8225 6496
Chief Executive: Michael Hanley

United Dairy Farmers
456 Antrim Road, Belfast, BT15 5GD
Tel: 028 9037 2237
Fax: 028 9037 2222
Principal Activity: milk collection and sale
Chief Executive: David Dobbin

Meat and Poultry Processing

ABP Newry
Greenbank Industrial Estate
Warrenpoint Road, Newry, BT34 2PD
Tel: 028 3026 3211
Fax: 028 3026 1321
Principal Activity: meat processing
Chief Executive: Colin Duffy

Crossgar Poultry Ltd
11 Kilmore Road
Crossgar, Downpatrick, BT30 9HJ
Tel: 028 4483 0301
Fax: 028 4483 0724
Principal Activity: poultry processing
Chief Executive: Gerald Bell

Dungannon Meats Ltd
Granville Industrial Estate
Dungannon, BT70 1NJ
Tel: 028 8775 3338
Fax: 028 8775 3790
Chief Executive: Jim Dobson

Foyle Meats Ltd
Lisahally, Campsie, Derry, BT47 6TJ
Tel: 028 7186 0691
Fax: 028 7186 0700
Principal Activity: meat processing
Chief Executive: Robert Watson

Henry Denny & Sons Ltd
6 Corcrain Road, Portadown
Craigavon, BT62 3UF
Tel: 028 3833 2411
Fax: 028 3833 4913
Principal Activity: pork processing
Chief Executive: Gareth Fitzgerald

Moy Park Ltd
The Food Park
39 Seagoe Industrial Estate
Craigavon, BT63 5QE
Tel: 028 3835 2233
Fax: 028 3836 8011
Principal Activity: poultry processing
Chief Executive: Trefor Campbell

O'Kane Poultry Ltd
170 Larne Road
Ballymena, BT42 3HA
Tel: 028 2564 1111
Fax: 028 2566 0680
Principal Activity: poultry processing
Chief Executive: Billy O'Kane

Omagh Meats Ltd
52 Doogary Road, Omagh, BT79 0BQ
Tel: 028 8224 3201
Fax: 028 8224 3013
Principal Activity: meat processing
Chief Executive: Wayne Acheson

Drinks Companies

Bass Ireland Ltd
Ulster Brewery, Glen Road
Belfast, BT11 8BY
Tel: 028 9030 1301
Fax: 028 9062 4884
Principal Activity: brewing
Managing Director: Stuart McFarland

Bushmills Distillery Ltd
2 Distillery Road, Bushmills, BT57 8XH
Tel: 028 2073 1521
Fax: 028 2073 1339
Principal Activity: whiskey manufacture
Managing Director: Gill Jefferson

Cantrell & Cochrane Ltd
468-472 Castlereagh Road
Belfast, BT5 6RG
Tel: 028 9079 9335
Fax: 028 9070 7206
Principal Activity: soft drinks manufacturer
Managing Director: Colin Gordon

Coca-Cola HBC Ltd
The Green, Lambeg
Lisburn, BT27 5SS
Tel: 028 9267 4231
Fax: 028 9267 1049
Principal Activity:
drinks bottling and distribution
Executive Director: John Barrett

Diageo Ltd NI
Apollo Road, Adelaide Industrial Estate
Belfast, BT12 6PJ
Tel: 028 9066 1611
Fax: 028 9066 9889
Principal Activity: drinks distribution
Commercial Director: Jude Lynch

Other Food Processing

Cuisine de France
Unit 5
Blaris Industrial Estate, Old Hill Road,
Lisburn, BT27 5QB
Tel: 028 9260 3222
Fax: 028 9260 3072
Principal Activity: bakery products
Managing Director: Hugo Kane

Gallaher Ltd
201 Galgorm Road
Ballymena, BT42 1HS
Tel: 028 2564 6666
Fax: 028 2566 5210
Principal Activity: tobacco products
Chief Executive: Simon Boyle

Irwins Bakery Ltd
5 Diviny Drive
Portadown, Craigavon, BT63 5WE
Tel: 028 3833 2421
Fax: 028 3833 3918
Principal Activity: bakery products
Managing Director: Brian Irwin

Tayto
Tandragee Castle
Tandragee, Craigavon, BT62 2AB
Tel: 028 3884 1466
Fax: 028 3884 0085
Principal Activity: snack food manufacturer
Chief Executive: Paul Allen

Energy and Environment Sector

Energy Policy in Northern Ireland

Northern Ireland has historically faced a number of fundamental challenges in terms of energy supply: lack of indigenous resources has meant over-dependence on fuel imports and coupled with lack of interconnection with adjacent energy grids has lead to comparatively high prices for final energy users. In recent years there has been the development of interconnection with Great Britain (electricity and gas) and the Republic of Ireland (electricity), which has helped negate the inherent disadvantages of a small isolated system.

In 2003 the Department of Enterprise, Trade and Investment produced a draft energy strategy for Northern Ireland. This strategy seeks to set out a strategy to set future priorities for the development of the energy market and infrastructure in Northern Ireland. The responses to DETI's draft strategy covered the key strategic issues facing the energy sector and energy users in Northern Ireland: electricity prices; the all-island energy market; energy efficiency; fuel poverty; renewable energy; and energy and the environment.

In September 2003 the Minister for Enterprise, Trade and Investment announced that there will be £30 million available from economic development funds to offset the high costs of energy. This will help offset increases in the underlying cost base of the sector and should help reduce increases being faced by non-domestic electricity customers.

Energy Market

The electricity market in Northern Ireland has a number of competing suppliers: Viridian Group's marketers, Energia, ESB Independent Energy and renewable energy company, Airtricity. At present 35% of the market is open to competition with around 7,000 customers able to choose their electricity supplier. During 2004 there will be a phased opening of market for non-domestic customers and the market must be fully open to all customers in 2007.

Ballylumford Power Station

Natural gas was introduced to northern Ireland in 1992 and since then Phoenix Natural Gas has invested around £170m in its network in the greater Belfast area. The natural gas market is now partially open with only the very large users of natural able to choose their supplier, although there is no natural gas being supplied by a supplier other than Phoenix Natural Gas. From 1st January 2005 all customers will be able to choose their supplier and by this date their will be an estimated 80,000 natural gas customers in Northern Ireland (7,000 business and 73,000 domestic).

Investment in Energy Infrastructure

Investment in Northern Ireland energy infrastructure has seen two new power stations: a new 600 MW combined cycle gas turbine (CCGT) plant at Ballylumford which came on line in late 2003 and Coolkeeragh power station in the North West, now owned 100% by ESB, is building a new 400 MW CCGT which will come on stream in March 2005. the Coolkeeragh project is also part of the extension of the natural gas network to the North West. Bord Gáis Eireann are building the transmission line to supply the new gas fired power station and are also planning to distribute natural gas to towns along the pipelines route. BGE are also planning to interconnect the gas networks North and South on the Eastern Dublin/Belfast corridor.

Sustainable Energy

DETI's energy strategy, in line with UK energy policy, seeks to put mechanisms in place to support increased renewable energy sources. Overall UK targets seek to double the contribution of renewable sources of electricity to 12%. One important initiative to help achieve this in Northern Ireland is Action Renewables. This is a joint initiative between Viridian Group and DETI to raise awareness of renewable forms of energy and increase the deployment of such technologies in Northern Ireland.

For the foreseeable future, wind is the largest source of renewable energy in Northern Ireland. There are two large scale developers, B9 and Airtricity, and many small scale individual wind farm developments.

In addition to increasing the amount of renewable forms of energy any sustainable energy strategy has also a strong element of using energy more efficiently. In Northern Ireland energy users are supported by the initiatives of Invest NI and the Carbon Trust, a non-profit making company set up by the Government to promote sustainable energy use.

Major Energy Companies

Action Renewables
Woodchester House,
50 Newforge Lane,
Belfast, BT9 5NW
Tel: 028 9068 5061
Fax: 028 9068 5035
Web: www.actionrenewables.org
Director: Dr Andy McCrea MBE

AES Kilroot Power Station
Larne Road Carrickfergus, BT38 7LX
Tel: 028 9335 1644
Fax: 028 9335 1086
Principal Activity: power generation
Managing Director: Shane Lynch

Airtricity Energy Supply Ltd
2nd Floor, 83-85 Great Victoria Street
Belfast, BT2 7AF
Tel: 028 9043 7470
Chief Executive Officer: Mark Ennis

Carbon Trust
17 Antrim Road, Lisburn, BT28 3AL
Tel: 028 9263 3444
Web: www.thecarbontrust.co.uk

Manager,
Northern Ireland
Geoff Smyth

Energia

energia

Energia House
62 Newforge Lane
Belfast, BT9 5NF
Tel: 028 9068 5900
Fax: 028 9068 5902
Email: sales@energia.ie
Website: www.energia.ie
Principal Activity: energy supply

Managing Director
Dr Allister McQuoid

Energia is the largest independent energy supply company operating in the competitive markets in Ireland.

It is a member of the Viridian Group.

Coolkeeragh ESB
Coolkeeragh ESB Ltd, is the joint venture between Coolkeeragh Power and ESB International, constructing the new 400MW natural gas combined cycle power plant at Coolkeeragh in the Northwest. The new plant will offer substantial benefits in terms of providing competitive low cost electricity, which will contribute in the drive to reduce costs to customers

Coolkeeragh ESB Ltd
PO Box 217
2 Electra Road
Maydown
Londonderry BT47 6XU

Tel: 028 7186 4700
Fax: 028 7186 4701
Website: www.coolkeeragh.com
Email: ccgt@coolkeeragh.co.uk

ESB Independent Energy
ESB Independent Energy is a subsidiary company of the ESB Group and one of the largest suppliers in the liberalised electricity market in Northern Ireland. Offering customers a unique combination of competitive price and premium service their offering is based on understanding the business, energy usage patterns and the needs of their customers.

ESB Independent Energy
33 Clarendon Dock
Laganside
Belfast, BT1 3BG

LoCall: 0845 309 8138
Website: www.esbie.co.uk
Email: info@esbie.ie

Invest Northern Ireland
Regional Environment & Energy Unit
17 Antrim Road, Lisburn, BT28 3AL
Tel: 028 9262 3028
Fax: 028 9262 3103

Web: www.investni.com
Energy and Environment
Manager: Dan Sinton

Northern Ireland Electricity
120 Malone Road, Belfast, BT9 5HT
Tel: 028 9066 1100
Fax: 028 9068 9117
Managing Director: Harry McCracken

OFREG
Brookmount Buildings
42 Fountain Street, Belfast, BT1 5EE
Tel: 028 9031 1575
Fax: 028 9031 1740
Principal Activity: gas and electricity regulation
Director General: Douglas McIldoon

Phoenix Natural Gas Limited
197 Airport Road West, Belfast, BT3 9ED
Tel: 028 9055 5555
Fax: 028 9055 5500
Principal Activity: natural gas distribution and supply
Chief Executive: Peter Dixon

Premier Power Limited
Islandmagee, Larne, BT40 3RS
Tel: 028 9338 1100
Fax: 028 9338 1240
Principal Activity: power generation
Chief Executive: Bill Cargo

Energy Efficiency Advice Centres

Belfast Energy Centre
1-11 May Street, Belfast, BT1 4NA
Tel: 028 9024 0664
Fax: 028 9024 6133
Programme Co-ordinator: Orla Ward

Foyle Regional Energy Agency (FREA)
1st Floor Offices, 3-5 London Street
Derry, BT48 6RQ
Tel: 028 7137 3430
Fax: 028 7130 8389
Manager: Lawrence Arbuckle

Western Regional Energy Agency and Network (WREAN)
1 Nugents Entry, Off Townhall Street
Enniskillen, Co Fermanagh, BT74 7DF
Tel: 028 6632 8269
Fax: 028 6632 9771
Manager: Nigel Brady

Neighbourhood Energy Action (NEA)
64-66 Upper Church Lane, BT1 4QL
Tel: 028 9023 9909
Fax: 028 9043 9191
Web: www.northern-ireland.nea.ork.uk
Director: Majella McCloskey

Manufacturing Industry

Manufacturing in Northern Ireland

Following a decade of relative stability in the manufacturing sector in Northern Ireland throughout the 1990s the new millennium saw a decline in manufacturing jobs. In 2003 there were 92,760 people employed in manufacturing compared to nearly 107,000 in 1998. In the year to Q3 2003, manufacturing output dropped by 3 per cent and nearly 5,000 employees lost their jobs. In 2003 a further 4,500 redundancies were announced in manufacturing with just over half of these in the textiles sector.

The continuing strength of the pound has had a huge impact on exports to the eurozone and many manufacturing companies have faced unprecedented pressure on margins, having to absorb price reductions to remain competitive. Many Northern Ireland companies however are overcoming the difficulty of the weak euro by finding new international markets outside the eurozone. Indeed, exports from Northern Ireland manufacturing companies to 'Rest of The World' markets have grown in recent years.

The past decade has also seen a structural change in the make-up of the manufacturing sector. Over the period 1995-2000, NI manufacturing output increased by 29 per cent. The biggest sectoral increase over this period was in engineering and allied industries (an increase of 78 per cent). The largest decrease (approximately 16 per cent) occurred in the leather, textile and textile products industries.

Engineering Sector

Traditionally engineering has been a vital sector of the economy employing over 30,000 people and accounting for a quarter of all manufacturing jobs. There has been strong growth over the last five years with 25,949 employed in 1995, which has risen to 31,050 in March 2000. Large companies dominate, although there are many active small businesses in the sector. Despite a worldwide shift from manufacturing into services the sector continues to perform strongly in Northern Ireland. The key sub-sectors in engineering are aerospace, the automotive sector and shipbuilding.

The aerospace sector was hit hard by the aftermath of the events in New York on 11 September 2001. Shorts, the biggest player in the Northern Ireland aerospace sector, which in buoyant economic conditions employed over 6,000 people in aircraft components manufacture announced the potential for up to 2000 job losses.

A cluster of aerospace-related manufacturing companies has grown around Shorts. Local companies now manufacture aircraft seats, while RFD in Dunmurry are world leaders in the design and production of life rafts and other life-saving equipment for aircrafts. RFD have continually expanded in recent years with acquisitions in the US, Italy and Australia.

In the automotive sector the Visteon plant in Belfast, previously the automotive components division of Ford Motor Company employs 600 people in automotive systems manufacture. The Montupet plant at Dunmurry on the outskirts of Belfast employs a similar number in the production of aluminium and alloy engine blocks and wheels for the major European motor manufacturers. In Craigavon Nacco Materials Handling have over 800 employees producing forklift trucks for worldwide markets.

Extreme difficulties continue for Belfast shipyard Harland and Wolff owned by Norwegian shipping company Fred Olsen Energy. The yard continues to fight for its survival. It recently announced further swingeing job cuts reducing employment at the yard to an all time low of around 150. Many commentators believe it has now gone beyond the point where it can recover its overall ship building capacity. Founded in 1861 Harland & Wolff has dominated the east of Belfast, both physically and economically. It was famed for building the Titanic and at its peak employed 35,000 people.

Chemicals and Plastics

Northern Ireland has been a base for the manufacture of chemicals since the mid 1950s. During the 1960 and 1970s Northern Ireland had a significant chemical sector, which was dominated by the manufacture of man made fibres. ICI, Courtaulds, Monsanto, DuPont and British Enkalon had world scale plants in Northern Ireland. There were also a number of smaller plants supplying process chemicals and services to these plants including a large BOC plant at Maydown. The recession in the man-made fibres sector in the early 1980s saw the closure of all these plants except DuPont who still operate on their Maydown site, although now with only two plants. There are now no upstream polymer companies in Northern Ireland and any plastic and polymers manufacturing is in the extrusion segment of the industry.

Electrical and Electronics

The electrical and electronics sector employs over 11,000 people in Northern Ireland, equivalent to around 10 per cent of manufacturing employment. The average annual turnover in the sector is £829 million. UK and Northern Ireland electronics companies have the lowest operating costs in Europe. Operating costs, particularly labour related costs account on average for approximately 57 per cent of core costs for this sector. Therefore, the Belfast area is particularly attractive to electronics companies seeking a base within the European Union. The information and communications technologies sub sector's share of overall output from the sector is expected to grow by almost 50 per cent over the next ten years.

Northern Ireland is the base for several leading electronics companies including AVX, Seagate Technologies and Nortel Networks. There are also a growing number of local companies operating in specialist niches within the electronics sector. Many of these companies have been spun out of Northern Ireland's two universities, which have internationally renowned electronics research centres. The focus of the centres has been on the information and communication technologies (ICTs) sub-sectors.

The ICT sub-sector is expected to dominate the electronics sector within the next five years, which is in contrast to the consumer electronics sector, which is not expected to grow at the same pace.

Northern Ireland is a world leader in Digital Signal Processing (DSP) with Queen's University renowned for developing this important technology, which powers nearly every sector of the electronics industry. Queen's is one of a few universities in the UK that has its own silicon fabrication facilities, which are based in the university's Northern Ireland Semiconductor Research Centre. DSP chips are being used in an ever-increasing range of electronic products from mobile phones to consumer appliances.

Queen's University has also been at the forefront of innovative microchip technology for compressing digital still video. This technology is being developed by Integrated Silicon Systems which is a local company that started out in the electrical and electronics engineering department at Queen's. This leading edge technology is used in a range of applications from satellite imaging to digital cameras. The University of Ulster has a research centre, which specialises in medical technology. Like the centres at Queen's there have been a number of spin offs from this centre.

Textiles and Clothing

Textiles manufacturing has a 300-year history in Northern Ireland, originating in the world famous Irish linen industry. The industry now comprises businesses in fibres and yarns, threads, fabric (woven, non-woven and knitted), garments, hosiery, carpets, household furnishings and industrial textiles and employs in the region of 11,500 people, contributing approximately £900m to the economy.

The sector has experienced a period of intense competitive pressure over the past five years, and this has changed the landscape of the industry considerably. The drivers for this have been the consumer demand for a wider choice of well-designed clothing and household goods at lower cost – the 'more, better, faster, cheaper' ethos, coupled with the globalisation of the industry.

Manufacturing hubs have developed rapidly in Eastern Europe, Turkey and the Far East, and many of the large publicly owned companies have uprooted to sources of cheaper production. Companies in Northern Ireland servicing the volume high street market have had to re-examine how and where they do business to compete. Excellent design, efficient customer service, IT expertise and balancing home production with offshore sourcing have been the survival tactics of companies such as bedding company Bedeck, which has experienced an average 10% growth year on year over the past decade, and has recently won a major contract to supply designer label French Connection.

Other companies have concentrated on niche markets where products are differentiated either by design, quality and branding or by innovation. Glenaden Shirts, a former Coats Viyella plant manufacturing solely for M&S, underwent a management buyout several years ago. The new company very successfully targeted the luxury market by producing for some of the world's most prestigious brand names and launching its own premium brand - '1,,, like no other'. This has led to great exporting success, particularly in the US where customers include 37 Saks Fifth Avenue stores.

Irish Linen, once seen as the most traditional of fabrics, has also reinvented itself with new treatments and blends to improve performance, including Irish Linen & Lycra®, the result of collaboration between the Irish linen industry, INVISTA (formerly DuPont Textiles & Interiors), University of Ulster and InvestNI.

The Northern Ireland Textiles and Apparel Association (NITA), the industry's representative body in Northern Ireland, has supported its members in refashioning their businesses. It has run a number of programmes in partnership with Invest NI to promote the use of branding, encourage product development and improve business competitiveness. The Technical Textiles Forum provides a focus for innovation and a link to other industries where textiles are increasingly providing a better, more flexible materials solutions e.g. the medical field. NITA has embraced the globalisation of the industry and uses its international network to develop business opportunities for its members.

Life Sciences

The life sciences industry employees almost 4,000 people in some 50 organisations, operating in a range of activities across the industry. There is a growing network of sub contract services ranging from custom synthesis, pharmacology and bio-analytical services to packaging and sterilisation. The sector has also increasing research and development capability in Northern Ireland. There are now several research centres focusing on activities in the sector and these include:

- Cancer Research Centre in Belfast which is a collaboration between Queen's University Belfast, a number of hospital trusts and the Cancer Research Campaign;
- Centre for Molecular Bioscience at the University of Ulster at Coleraine;
- Centre for Endocrine Research at Queen's University;
- The McClay Research Centre for Pharmaceutical Sciences at Queen's University.

Galen Pharmaceuticals, Portadown

Manufacturing Companies: General

Acheson & Glover Ltd
127 Crievehill Roa
Fivemiletown, BT75 0SY
Tel: 028 8952 1275
Fax: 028 8952 1886
Principal Activity: bricks
Managing Director:
Raymond Acheson

John Finlay Ltd
Tullyvannon, Ballygawley
Dungannon, BT70 2HW
Tel: 028 8556 8666
Fax: 028 8556 8447
Principal Activity: concrete products
Managing Director: Stephen Finlay

Quinn Group Ltd
Head Office, Derrylin
Enniskillen, BT92 9AU
Tel: 028 6774 8866
Fax: 028 6774 8800
Principal Activity: concrete products
Managing Director: Sean Quinn

RJ Hall & Sons Ltd
Homebright House
Hillview Industrial Estate
Belfast, BT14 7BT
Tel: 028 9035 1707
Fax: 028 9075 3833
Principal Activity: brushes
Managing Director:
Desmond McClelland

Readymix Northern Ireland
RMC House, Upper Dunmurry Lane
Belfast, BT17 0AJ
Tel: 028 9061 6611
Fax: 028 9061 9969
Principal Activity: concrete Managing Director: Joe Doyle

Wrightbus
Galgorm Industrial Estate
Finaghy Road, Ballymena, BT42 1PY
Tel: 028 2564 1212
Fax: 028 2564 9703
Principal Activity: coaches
Managing Director: Jeff Wright

Rusch Manufacturing (UK) Ltd
Portadown Road, Lurgan
Craigavon, BT66 8RD
Tel: 028 3832 5771
Fax: 028 3832 4306
Principal Activity: medical devices
Managing Director: Gerry McCaffery

Tyrone Crystal Ltd
Killybrackey, Dungannon
BT71 6TT
Tel: 028 8772 5335
Fax: 028 8772 6260
Principal Activity: crystal manufacturing
Managing Director: Peter Nunn

Walter Alexander & Company
Hydepark Industrial Estate
Mallusk
Newtownabbey
BT36 4RP
Tel: 028 9034 2006
Fax: 028 9034 2678
Principal Activity: coach builders
Works Manager: William McMullan

Thales Air Defence Limited

THALES

THALES AIR DEFENCE

Alanbrooke Road
Belfast, BT6 9HB
Tel: +44 (0) 2890 465200
Fax: +44 (0) 2890 465201
Web: www.thales-ad.co.uk

Thales Air Defence, formerly known as Shorts Missile Systems, is a world-class defence company based in Belfast, Northern Ireland.

Thales Air Defence is part of the Thales Group - a key player in the European defence and aerospace electronics markets. Within the Group Thales Air Defence is recognised as the centre of excellence for missile design and manufacture.

Manufacturing Companies: Engineering

Arntz Belting Co Ltd
Pennyburn Pass, Londonderry, BT48 0AE
Tel: 028 7126 1221
Fax: 028 7126 3386
Principal Activity: fan belts
Managing Director: Robert Moore

Bemac EMS Ltd
19a Ballinderry Road, Lisburn, BT28 2SA
Tel: 028 9267 7634
Fax: 028 9266 0258
Principal Activity: sheet metal parts
Managing Director: David Munroe

Bombardier Aerospace
Airport Road, Belfast, BT3 9DZ
Tel: 028 9045 8444
Fax: 028 9073 3396
Principal Activity: aircraft equipment
Vice President: Michael Ryan

BE Aerospace
2 Moor Road, Kilkeel
Newry, BT34 4NG
Tel: 028 4176 2471
Fax: 028 4176 4297
Principal Activity: aircraft seats
Vice President: John Sharkey

Copeland Ltd
Ballyray Industrial Estate
Sandholes Road, Cookstown, BT80 9DG
Tel: 028 8676 0100
Fax: 028 8676 0110
Principal Activity: compressors
Plant Director: Declan Billington

Crane Stockham Valve Ltd
Alexander Road
Belfast, BT6 9HJ
Tel: 028 9070 4222
Fax: 028 9040 1582
Principal Activity: valves
Commercial Director: Paul Clarke

Denroy Plastics & Denman Int
Balloo Industrial Estate
Balloo Drive, Bangor, BT19 2QY
Tel: 028 9127 0936
Fax: 028 9127 7553
Principal Activity: injection moulding
Managing Director: John Rainey

FG Wilson Engineering Ltd
Old Glenarm Road, Larne, BT40 1EJ
Tel: 028 2826 1000
Fax: 028 2826 1111
Principal Activity: generators
Chief Executive Officer: Don Perry

Fisher Engineering Ltd
Main Street, Ballinamallard
Enniskillen, BT94 2FY
Tel: 028 6638 8521
Fax: 028 6638 8706
Principal Activity: steelwork
Managing Director: Ernie Fisher

John Crane UK Ltd
66-96 Queen Street
Ballymena, BT42 2BE
Tel: 028 2565 3569
Fax: 028 2564 1002
Principal Activity: mechanical seals & couplings
General Manager: Hubert Dunlop

Glen Electric Ltd
Greenbank Industrial Estate
Rampart Road, Newry, BT34 2QU
Tel: 028 3026 4621
Fax: 028 3026 6122
Principal Activity: electrical products
Managing Director: Brian McLoran

Harland & Wolff SHI Ltd
Queens Island, Belfast. BT3 9DE
Tel: 028 9045 7040
Fax: 028 9045 8515
Principal Activity: Marine Maintenance
Chief Executive Officer: Mr B Mugaas

Heyn Engineering
1 Corry Place, Belfast Harbour Estate
Belfast, BT3 9AH
Tel: 028 9035 0022
Fax: 028 9035 0012
Principal Activity: engineering
Managing Director: Alec Toland

Langford Lodge Engineering Co
97 Largy Road, Crumlin, BT29 4RT
Tel: 028 9445 2451
Fax: 028 9445 2161
Principal Activity: precision engineering
Managing Director: Denis Burrell

Mivan Ltd
Newpark, Greystone Road
Antrim, BT41 2QN
Tel: 028 9448 1000
Fax: 028 9448 1015
Principal Activity: ship outfitting/fitting
Chief Executive: Ivan McCabrey

Montupet UK Ltd
The Cutts, Dunmurry
Belfast, BT17 9HN
Tel: 028 9030 1049
Fax: 028 9030 3030
Principal Activity: aluminium components
Managing Director: Daniel Cofflard

Morphy Richards (NI) Ltd
Balloo Industrial Estate
16 Balloo Avenue, Bangor, BT19 7QT
Tel: 028 9146 8811
Fax: 028 9146 4009
Principal Activity: household appliances
Managing Director: Ken Ferguson

Munster Simms
Old Belfast Road, Bangor
Tel: 028 9127 0531
Fax: 028 9146 6421
Managing Director: Brian Batchelor

NACCO Materials Handling Ltd
Carn Industrial Estate
Portadown, Craigavon, BT63 5RH
Tel: 028 3835 4499
Fax: 028 3833 9977
Principal Activity: forklift trucks
Managing Director: Alan Little

RFD Ltd
Kingsway
Dunmurry, Belfast, BT17 9AF
Tel: 028 9030 1531
Fax: 028 9062 1765
Principal Activity: life rafts
Managing Director: Uel McChesney

Rotary Group Ltd
5 Trench Road
Mallusk, Newtownabbey, BT36 4XA
Tel: 028 9083 1200
Fax: 028 9083 1201
Principal Activity: electrical mechanical & ventilation engineers
Managing Director: Thomas Jennings

Schlumberger Ltd
Cloughfern Avenue
Doagh Road, Monkstown
Newtownabbey, BT37 0UH
Tel: 028 9036 4444
Fax: 028 9085 2766
Principal Activity: manufacture oil well equipment
Managing Director: Damien Canavan

Ryobi Aluminium Casting (UK) Ltd
5 Meadowbank Road
Troperslane Industrial Estate
Carrickfergus, BT38 8YF
Tel: 028 9335 1043
Fax: 028 9335 5644
Principal Activity: aluminium castings
Managing Director: John Hughes

SDC Trailers Ltd
116 Deerpark Road
Toomebridge, Co Antrim, BT41 3SS
Tel: 028 7965 0765
Fax: 028 7965 0042
Principal Activity: commercial trailers
Managing Director: Darren Donnelly

Seagoe Technology
Church Road, Seagoe, Portadown
Craigavon, BT63 5HU
Tel: 028 3833 3131
Fax: 028 3833 3042
Principal Activity: storage heaters
Managing Director: Neil Stewart

Sperrin Metal Products Ltd
Cahore Road, Draperstown
Magherafelt, BT45 7AP
Tel: 028 7962 8362
Fax: 028 7962 8972
Principal Activity: shelving systems
Director: Patrick Gormley

TK-ECC Ltd
770 Upper Newtownards Road
Dundonald, Belfast, BT16 1UL
Tel: 028 9055 7200
Fax: 028 9055 7300
Principal Activity: car components
Managing Director: Leslie Boyd

Visteon
Belfast Plant
Finaghy Road North, Belfast, BT11 9EF
Tel: 028 9060 8300
Fax: 028 9060 8490
Principal Activity: car parts
Plant Manager: John McLoughlin

Manufacturing Companies: Electronics

AVX Ceramics Ltd
Hillmans Way, Ballycastle Road
Coleraine, BT52 2ED
Tel: 028 7034 4188
Fax: 028 7035 5527
Principal Activity: electrical components
Vice President: Martin McGuigan

Analogue NI Ltd
5 Hannahstown Hill, Belfast, BT17 0LT
Tel: 028 9061 5599
Fax: 028 9061 6788
Principal Activity: electronic equipment
Company Secretary: Celesta Forte

BIA Systems Nitronica Ltd
Antrim Road, Ballynahinch, BT24 8AN
Tel: 028 9756 6200
Fax: 028 9756 6256
Principal Activities: Telecommunications
Managing Director: John Mellon

Contex Ltd
63 Greystone Road, Antrim, BT41 2QN
Tel: 028 9446 3035
Fax: 028 9442 8094
Principal Activity: manufacture electronic components
Managing Director: Mark Macusaka

Elite Electronic Systems Ltd
Lackaboy Industrial Estate
Killyvilly, Enniskillen, BT74 4RL
Tel: 028 6632 7172
Fax: 028 6632 5668
Principal Activity: PCB's electronics manufacturer
Managing Director: Ron Balfour

Fujitsu Telecommunications (Ireland)
10 Antrim Technology Park
Belfast Road, Muckamore, Antrim
BT4 11QS
Tel: 028 9442 8394
Fax: 028 9442 8395
Principal Activity: telecommunications equipment manufacture
General Manager: Peter Bowman

Getty Connections Ltd
Belfast Road, Carrickfergus, BT38 8BG
Tel: 028 9336 4741
Fax: 028 9336 5894
Principal Activity: telephone equipment
Managing Director: Brian Getty

Irlandus Circuits
Annesborough Industrial Estate
Craigavon, BT67 9JJ
Tel: 028 3832 6211
Fax: 028 3832 4037
Principal Activity: printed circuit boards
Joint Managing Directors: Roy Adair, Sean Ritchie

Nortel Networks
Doagh Road, Newtownabbey, BT36 6XA
Tel: 028 9036 5111
Fax: 028 9036 5285
Principal Activity: telecommunications equipment
Managing Director: Chris Conway

Partsnic UK Company Ltd
1 Sloefield Drive
Carrickfergus, BT38 8GD
Tel: 028 9336 0338
Fax: 028 9336 2223
Principal Activity: electronics components
Managing Director: S E Kim

Seagate Technology
1 Disc Drive
Springtown Industrial Estate
Londonderry, BT48 0BF
Tel: 028 7127 4000
Fax: 028 7127 4202
Principal Activity: electronic & computer equipment
Managing Director: John Spangler

Sintec Europe
72 Silverwood Road
Lurgan, Craigavon, BT66 6NB
Tel: 028 3831 4336
Fax: 028 3832 3297
Principal Activity: sub contract manufacturer for electronics

Manufacturing Companies: Textiles and Clothing

3M Industrial Tapes
5-7 Balloo Drive, Bangor, BT19 7PB
Tel: 028 9127 8200
Fax: 028 9145 1072
Principal Activity: industrial tape manufacture
Plant Manager: Phil Ward

Adria Ltd
Beechmount Avenue
Strabane, BT82 9BG
Tel: 028 7138 2568
Fax: 028 7138 2910
Principal Activity: ladies hosiery/socks
Managing Director: David Taylor

Carpets International
7 Saintfield Road, Killinchy
Newtownards, BT23 6RJ
Tel: 028 9754 1441
Fax: 028 9754 1594
Principal Activity: carpet yarns
(Re-opened in late 2003)

Coats Barbour Ltd
Hilden Mill, Hilden, Lisburn, BT27 4RR
Tel: 028 9267 2231
Fax: 028 9267 8048
Principal Activity: thread manufacturer
Managing Director: Mr Shereel Fernando

Desmond & Sons Ltd
Drumahoe, Londonderry, BT47 35D
Tel: 028 7129 5000
Fax: 028 7129 5005
Principal Activity: clothing manufacturer
Managing Director: Denis Desmond

Ferguson Irish Linen
54 Scarva Road, Banbridge, BT32 3AU
Tel: 028 4062 3491
Fax: 028 4062 2453
Principal Activity: textiles
Managing Director: David Neilly

Herdmans Ltd
11 Mill Avenue
Sion Mills, Strabane, BT82 9HE
Tel: 028 8165 8421
Fax: 028 8165 8909
Principal Activity: flax spinning
Managing Director: Neville Orr

Interface Europe
Silverwood Industrial Estate
Lurgan, Craigavon, BT66 6LN
Tel: 028 3831 2600
Fax: 028 3831 2666
Principal Activity: Carpet tiles
General Manager: Richard Nicholson

Magee Clothing Ltd
Milleneum Park, Ballymena, BT42 4QJ
Tel: 028 2564 6211
Fax: 028 2564 5111
Principal Activity: men's clothing

Octopus Sportswear Ltd
Unit 1, Dublin Road Industrial Estate
Strabane, BT82 9EA
Tel: 028 7188 2320
Fax: 028 7188 2902
Principal Activity: sports manufacture
Managing Director: Kieran Kennedy

Regency Spinning Ltd
Comber Road Industrial Estate
Comber, Newtownards, BT23 4RX
Tel: 028 9181 8836
Fax: 028 9182 0569
Principal Activity: textiles manufacture
Manager: Jim Johnson

Ulster Weavers Home Fashions
Maldon Street
Donegall Road, Belfast, BT12 6NZ
Tel: 028 9032 9494
Fax: 028 9032 6612
Principal Activity: textile manufacturers
Managing Director: Ian McMorris

Huhtamaki Lurgan Ltd
Inn Road, Lurgan, Craigavon, BT66 7JW
Tel: 028 3832 7711
Fax: 028 3832 1782
Principal Activity: moulded fibre products
Managing Director: Steve Chapman

William Clark & Sons Ltd
72 Upperlands
Maghera, BT46 5RZ
Tel: 028 7964 2214
Fax: 028 7954 7257
Principal Activity: textile manufacture
Financial Director: Richard Semple

Manufacturing Companies: Chemicals and Plastics

BOC Gases Ltd
Prince Regent Road
Castlereagh, Belfast, BT5 6RW
Tel: 028 9040 1441
Fax: 028 9040 1379
Principal Activity: medical & industrial gases
Operations Manager: Peter Loade

DuPont UK Ltd
PO Box 15, Maydown Works
Londonderry, BT47 6TH
Tel: 028 7186 0860
Fax: 028 7186 4222
Principal Activity: manmade fibres
Site Manager: Pat Carroll

Plastics and Polymers
Creative Composites Ltd
Blaris Industrial Estate
Altona Road, Lisburn, BT27 5QB
Tel: 028 9267 3312
Fax: 028 9260 7381
Principal Activity: reinforced plastic
Chairman: Mr R J Kelly

Brett Martin Ltd
24 Roughfort Road
Mallusk, Newtownabbey, BT36 4RB
Tel: 028 9084 9999
Fax: 028 9083 6666
Principal Activity: PVC plastic sheeting
Managing Director: Lawrence Martin

Dessian Products Ltd
9 Apollo Road
Adelaide Industrial Estate
Belfast, BT12 6HP
Tel: 028 9038 1118
Fax: 028 9066 0741
Principal Activity: uPVC windows
Managing Director: Des Longmore

Glentronics Ltd
64 Mallusk Road
Newtownabbey, BT36 4QE
Tel: 028 9034 2090
Fax: 028 9034 2147
Principal Activity: injection moulding
Managing Directors: Jeremy Brassington

Michelin Tyre plc
Ballymena Factory
190 Raceview Road
Ballymena, BT42 4HZ
Tel: 028 2566 3600
Fax: 028 2566 3628

Polypipe (Ulster) Ltd
Dromore Road
Lurgan, Craigavon
BT66 7HL
Tel: 028 3888 1270
Fax: 028 3888 2344
Principal Activity: plastic pipe fittings
Managing Director: Henry White

Manufacturing Companies: Life Sciences

Galen Holdings plc
22 Seagoe Industrial Estate
Craigavon, BT63 5UA
Tel: 028 3833 4974
Fax: 028 3835 0206
Principal Activity: pharmaceuticals
Chief Executive: John King

Norbrook Laboratories Ltd
Station Works
Camlough Road, Newry, BT35 6JP
Tel: 028 3026 4435
Fax: 028 3026 1721
Principal Activity: veterinary pharmaceutical manufacturer
Managing Director: Dr Edward Haughey

Perfectseal Ltd
Springtown Industrial Estate
Londonderry, BT48 0LY
Tel: 028 7128 7000
Fax: 028 7128 7401
Principal Activity: medical packaging
General Manager: Keith McCracken

Randox Laboratories Ltd
55 Diamond Road
Crumlin, BT29 4QT
Tel: 028 9442 2413
Fax: 028 9445 2912
Principal Activity: clinical diagnostic reagents
Managing Director: Dr Peter Fitzgerald

Tyco Healthcare
20 Garryduff Road
Ballymoney, BT53 7AP
Tel: 028 2766 3234
Fax: 028 2766 4799
Principal Activity: syringes
Plant Manager: Robin Eakin

Information and Communications Technology (ICT) Sector

Northern Ireland has now a sizeable information and communications technology sector (ICT), with several large multi-nationals and a cluster of local IT and software companies.

The sector employs around 7,500 people, which has reduced over recent years from its peak of 10,000 in 2001. Although recent times have seen a fall in employment numbers the current level is still over twice the 1997 level of 3,000 people employed in the sector.

The importance of the sector has been fully recognised by policy makers: in the Government's Strategy 2010 blueprint for Northern Ireland's economic future, specific targets are established for growth in turnover in the various high-tech sub-sectors while an overall target to make high-tech industry account for up to 6 per cent of total employment by 2010 has been established.

With the bursting of the 'dotcom bubble' the excessive valuations seen in this sector have now retreated to more realistic levels. The telecommunications sector has been hit particularly hard, with providers taking on significant levels of debt to pay for third generation network licences. The arrival of real competition has extended customer choice and imposed downward pressure on prices. The mobile market has now reached saturation in Northern Ireland with the main UK mobile operators present.

Although the last two years have been difficult for the technology sector across the globe, the software sector in Northern Ireland remains a key sector for economic growth. The Northern Ireland software and IT sector now consists of over 200 organisations across a wide range of activities including systems development, Internet products and services, financial services applications, telecommunications related products and services, management information systems and manufacturing systems development.

The sector includes inward investors such as Northbrook Technology and several indigenous companies such as B.I.C. Systems. This local 'cluster' of software and IT companies is growing and these companies are exporting a wide range of products and services to markets worldwide. Northern Ireland's universities and technical colleges produce around 1,000 IT graduates each year to meet the growing demands of the sector.

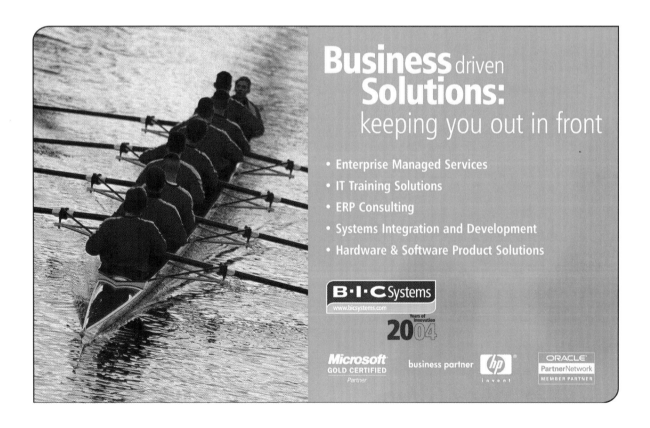

Telecommunications Companies

BT
Riverside Tower, 5 Lanyon Place
Belfast, BT1 3BT
Managing Director: Bill Murphy

Cable & Wireless
Post Quarry Corner
Upper Newtownards Road
Belfast, BT16 1UD
Business Manager: Michelle McGuire

Nevada tele.com
1 Cromac Avenue, Belfast, BT7 2JA
Tel: 028 9072 0400
Web: www.nevadatele.com
Chief Executive: Leslie Harris

ntl Northern Ireland
29 Airport Road West
Belfast, BT3 9EZ
Web: www.ntl.co.uk
Tel: 028 9020 6000
Chief Executive: Ian Jeffers

Opal

Unit 14, Arches Retail Park
East Bread Street
Belfast, BT5 5AP
Tel: 0800 083 2988
Fax: 0845 330 5265
Email: enquiries@opaltelecom.co.uk
Web: www.opaltelecom.co.uk

Sales & Marketing Director
Aiden Dermody

Opal Telecom, the UK's leading business telecoms provider, has arrived in Northern Ireland. A wholly owned subsidiary of The Carphone Warehouse, we are now the new and exciting alternative to current carriers and invite you to enjoy more choice, better value and all the business benefits of working with a company that truly understands your needs.

Orange

Quay Gate House
15 Scrabo Street
Belfast, BT5 4BD
Tel: 028 9073 6600
Fax: 028 9073 6601
Email: media.centre@orange.co.uk
Web: www.orange.co.uk

Eric Carson
General Manager
Orange
in Northern Ireland

Orange is Northern Ireland's best performing mobile network with more transmitters in more places than anyone else and covering more than 99% of the population.

Orange launched in Northern Ireland in 1998 as part of a £200 million investment. Today more than 1 in 5 people in Northern Ireland are Orange customers. The company employs around 90 people locally, mainly through 8 Orange Shops.

Orange has always led the way with value for money and innovative services. With *Your Plan* personal and business customers can build their own service plan with exactly the amount of talk time, messages and services they want - saving them money and giving them better value. They can also rely on Orange's award-winning customer service.

The future's bright, the future's Orange.

Vodafone
16 Wellington Park
Belfast, BT9 6DJ
Tel: 0800 052 5200
Web: www.vodafone.co.uk
Managing Director: Byrom Bramwell

IT and Software Companies

Aepona
Interpoint Building
20-24 York Street, Belfast, B15 1AQ
Tel: 028 9026 9100
Fax: 028 9026 9111
Managing Director: Liam McQuillan

B.I.C. Systems

Sydenham Business Park
201 Airport Road West
Belfast, BT3 9ED
Tel: 028 9053 2200
Fax: 028 9056 0056
Web: www.bicsystems.com
Managing Director: Ed Vernon

B.I.C. Systems is a leading IT Solutions company, delivering business advantage through technology and skills to the public and private sectors in Ireland and the U.K. Founded in 1984, with offices in Belfast and Dublin, key services include; Enterprise Managed Services, IT Training Solutions, ERP Consulting, Systems Integration & Development and Hardware and Software product solutions.

CEM Systems
Unit 4, Ravenhill Business Park
Ravenhill Road, Belfast, BT6 8AW
Tel: 028 9045 6767
Fax: 028 9045 4535
Web: www.cemsys.com
Managing Director: Richard Fulton

Claritas Software
7 Springrowth House, Ballinske Road
Springtown, Derry, BT48 0MA
Tel: 028 7129 1111
Fax: 028 7129 1110
Web: www.claritassoftware.com
Managing Director: Plunkett Devlin

Consilium Technologies
Consilium House, Technology Park
Belfast Road, Antrim, BT41 1QS
Tel: 028 9448 0000
Fax: 028 9448 0001
Web www.task.co.uk
Director: Colin Reid

Fujitsu Telecommunications Software Ireland (FTSI)
Springvale Business Park
Belfast, BT12 7DY
Tel: 028 9031 6300
Fax: 028 9031 0174
Executive Vice-President: M. Fujisaki

Kainos Software
Kainos House
4-6 Upper Crescent Street
Belfast, BT7 1NZ
Tel: 028 9023 6868
Fax: 028 9057 1101
Managing Director: Brendan Mooney

Lagan Technologies
Lagan Court, 20 Wildflower Way
Belfast, BT12 6TA
Tel: 028 9050 9300
Fax: 028 9050 9339
Web: www.lagan.com
Managing Director: Des Speed

Liberty Information Technologies
Clarendon House, 9-21 Adelaide Street
Belfast, BT2 8DJ
Tel: 028 9044 5500
Fax: 028 9044 5511
Web: www.liberty-it.co.uk
Managing Director: Gordon Bell

Northbrook Technology of Northern Ireland
9 Lanyon Place,
Belfast, BT1 3LZ
Tel: 028 9034 6500
Web: www.northbrooktechnology.com
Chief Executive: Bro McFerron

Northland Computer Services
5 Northland Road
Londonderry, BT48 7HX
Tel: 028 7136 3168
Fax: 028 7136 0002
Managing Director: Jim O'Donnell

Parity Solutions Ltd
Unit 1, Technology Park
Belfast Road, Antrim, BT41 1QS
Tel: 028 9446 4901
Fax: 028 9446 0702
Chairman: Paul McWilliams

Singularity

Singularity

100 Patrick Street
Derry, BT48 7EL
Tel : +44 (0)28 7126 7767 - ext:(305)
Fax : +44 (0)28 7126 8085
Email: Adam.Black@Singularity.co.uk
Web: www.Singularity.co.uk
Managing Director: Padraig Canavan

Singularity is a leading provider of process centric solutions, offering the award-winning Singularity Process Platform and a range of professional services. Singularity aims to help customers achieve measurable improvement in their business performance.

SX3 (Service & Systems Solutions) Ltd
Hillview House, 61 Church Road
Newtownabbey, BT36 7SS
Tel: 028 9068 8000
Fax: 028 9066 3579
Managing Director: J Neville

Transport and Distribution Sector

Although a large proportion of the population lives within the greater Belfast area, the rest of Northern Ireland's population is relatively dispersed. Unlike the rest of the UK the population is not concentrated in towns and villages but tends to be scattered throughout the countryside. Therefore road transport is central to most people's daily life. This is reflected in the number of vehicles licensed for use in Northern Ireland's roads which now stands at over 790,000. In the year 2002 there were over 94,000 new registrations for private cars.

Translink is the major provider of public transport services in Northern Ireland, through Citybus, Ulsterbus and Northern Ireland Railways (NIR). At the end of 2002/03 there were nearly 1,200 Ulsterbuses and over 250 Citybuses on the roads. NIR operates a fully integrated rail network covering 211 miles of track services to Derry and Portrush in the north-west; Larne, Belfast and Bangor along the eastern seaboard; Newry in the south and onwards to Dublin, in the Republic of Ireland.

There are three regional main airports in Northern Ireland, the biggest being Belfast International which was the ninth busiest commercial airport in the UK in 2002. During 2002 there were 5.6 million terminal passengers through all three airports, representing a 13% increase on the previous year.

Northern Ireland has four main seaports, which in order of importance are: Belfast, Larne, Warrenpoint and Derry. The Port of Belfast benefits from a safe, accessible, deepwater harbour, which is ideally placed to service middle corridor routes across the Irish Sea Ports in the North-West of England such as Heysham and Liverpool. The designation of Liverpool as channel tunnel rail freight hub with a quayside rail link facilitates access to the European rail network and rapid onward transit of goods to the continent. Heysham and Liverpool also offer links to Great Britain's extensive motorway network and its centres of population and manufacturing. *(For further information on Translink and the Northern Ireland transport system see Chapter 13, 'A Visitors Guide to Northen Ireland')*

Public Road and Rail Transport

Translink Ltd
Central Station, East Bridge Street
Belfast, BT1 3PB
Tel: 028 9089 9400
Fax: 028 9089 9401
Principal Activity: public transport
Managing Director: Keith Moffatt

Sea Transport Companies

Belfast Freight Ferries Ltd
Victoria Terminal 1, Dargan Road
Belfast, BT3 9LJ
Tel: 028 9077 0112
Fax: 028 9078 1217
Principal Activity: shipping/RORO
Secretary: Claire Jenkins

Belfast Harbour Commissioners
Harbour Office, Corporation Square
Belfast, BT1 3PB
Tel: 028 9055 4422
Fax: 028 9055 4411
E-mail: info@belfast-harbour.co.uk
Web: www.belfast-harbour.co.uk
Principal Activity: Harbour Authority
Chief Executive: Frank Cushnahan

Coastal Container Line Ltd
Victoria Terminal 3
West Bank Road, Belfast, BT3 9JL
Tel: 028 9037 3200
Fax: 028 9037 1333
Principal Activity: ship operators
Chief Executive: Ken Wharton

G Heyn & Sons Ltd
1 Corry Place
Belfast Harbour Estate
Belfast, BT3 9AH
Tel: 028 9035 0000
Fax: 028 9035 0011
Principal Activity: shipping agents
Managing Director:
Michael Maclaren

Londonderry Port & Harbour
Harbour Office, Port Road
Lisahally, Londonderry, BT47 6FL
Tel: 028 7186 055
Fax: 028 7186 1168
Principal Activity: pilotage,
storage, cranes

Norse Merchant Ferries
Victoria Terminal 2
Westbank Road, Belfast, BT3 9JN
Tel: 028 9077 9090
Fax: 028 9077 5520
Web: www. norse-irish-ferries.co.uk
Principal Activity: sea transport
General Manager: Philip Shepherd

Port of Larne
9 Olderfleet Road, Larne
Northern Ireland, BT40 1AS
Tel: 028 2887 2100
Fax: 028 2887 2209
Website: www.portoflarne.co.uk
Email: info@portoflarne.co.uk

P&O European Ferries
Larne Harbour, Larne, BT40 1AQ
Tel: 028 2887 2200
Fax: 028 2887 2129
Principal Activity: sea transport
General Manager:
Graham McCullough

Sea-Truck Ferries
Ferry Terminal, The Docks
Warrenpoint, Newry, BT34 3JR
Tel: 028 4175 4400
Fax: 028 4177 3737
Principal Activity: ferry service
Director: Karen Donaldson

Stena Line
Passenger Terminal
Corry Road, Dock Street
Belfast, BT3 9SS
Tel: 028 9088 4089
Fax: 028 2827 5278
Principal Activity:
transport ferry service
Port Service Manger: Billy Wicks

Warrenpoint Harbour Authority
The Docks, Warrenpoint
Newry, BT34 3JR
Tel: 028 4177 3381
Fax: 028 4175 2875
Principal Activity: harbour authority
Chief Executive: Quentin Goldie

Air Transport Companies

Belfast City Airport
Sydenham By-Pass
Belfast, BT3 9JH
Tel: 028 9093 9093
Fax: 028 9093 5007
Principal Activity: airport operator
Airport Director: John Doran

Belfast International Airport
Belfast, BT29 4AB
Tel: 028 9442 2888
Fax: 028 9445 2096
Principal Activity: airport operator
Managing Director: Albert Harrison

British European Airways
City Airport, Belfast, BT3 9JH
Tel: 08705 676 676
Principal Activity: air transport
Manager: Andrea Hayes

bmi - British Midland
Suite 2, Fountain Centre
College Street, Belfast, BT1 6ET
Tel: 028 9024 1188
Fax: 028 9024 1183
Principal Activity: airline
Regional Manager: Valerie Ward

City of Derry Airport
Airport Road, Derry, BT47 3PY
Tel: 028 7181 0784
Fax: 028 7181 1426
Principal Activity: airport
Airport Manager: John Devine

Distribution Companies

Royal Mail Northern Ireland Ltd
20 Donegall Quay
Belfast
BT1 1AA
Tel: 0845 774 0740
Fax: 0870 241 5967
Principal Activity: postal delivery
Managing Director:
Michael Kennedy

Parcel Force Worldwide
Unit 24
2 Westbank Way
The Harbour Industrial Estate
Belfast
BT3 9PF
Tel: 028 9077 7270
Fax: 028 9077 7226
Principal Activity: postal services
General Manager: Rena Sheppard

Montgomery Transport Ltd
607 Antrim Road
Newtownabbey, BT36 4RF
Tel: 028 9084 9321
Fax: 028 9083 2746
Principal Activity:
transport haulage company
Managing Director: H Montgomery

Tradeable Services Sector

Financial Services in Northern Ireland

Employment in the financial services sector in Northern Ireland has grown over the past decade. Most of this growth has been in the non-traditional area of financial services including real estate renting and business activities sub-sector. The traditional side of the financial services sector, financial intermediation which includes mainstream retail banking has seen a decline in employment numbers over the same period.

Some economic commentators suggest that most national economies can only support one physical centre for international financial activity. This is clearly the case for the UK with London being the main centre for international services and the other regional centres, including Belfast, focusing on provides financial services for their own region.

Competition in the financial services sector has increased over the last five years with the introduction of legislation facilitating the deregulation of the sector and many building societies becoming banks. In recent years several of the RoI banks and building societies have entered the Northern Ireland market.

Bank mergers in the 1970s in Northern Ireland and RoI had led to the creation of two Northern-based clearing banks and two clearing banks headquartered in Dublin. In Northern Ireland there are the Ulster Bank (owned by Royal Bank of Scotland) and the Northern Bank (wholly owned by the National Australia Bank) and in RoI there are the Bank of Ireland and Allied Irish Bank (AIB). All the four main banks have operations north and south, with AIB having a Northern Ireland subsidiary called First Trust Bank.

Recent years have seen several large international financial services companies develop operations in Northern Ireland. With the Northern Ireland financial services sector being largely companies headquartered outside Northern Ireland with regional offices, local demand will determine the demand for their services rather than broad international developments. Northern Ireland is the only part of the UK that shares a land border with a Euro participant and the Banking and Financial Services sector in Northern Ireland is already dealing in Euros.

Financial services have grown strongly in recent years, at a time when the rest of the UK is experiencing some concentration in the sector. The major driver of local growth has been call-centres and while there are issues over the long-term value of some call-centre operations, investment from blue-chip companies like Halifax, Abbey National and Prudential has served to position Northern Ireland as a leading call centre location.

Construction and Property

Up to 45, 000 people are employed in the construction industry in Northern Ireland which, although employment levels tend to fluctuate, contributes 8 per cent of GDP. The representative body for the construction industry in Northern Ireland is the Construction Employers Federation. One of the main players is the Construction Industry Training Board (CITB), which ensures that the industry is properly staffed and trained. There has been something of a boom in private house building in recent years (although a slow down in public sector house building) and a number of major development projects including Laganside are underway in Belfast.

Tourism

Northern Ireland's image abroad plays a key role in determining visitor numbers and revenue from tourism. In 2002 there were just over 1.7 million visitors which represented an increase of 3.8 per cent on 2001. For the first half of 2003 visitor numbers were up 15 per cent on the same period for the previous year. The Northern Ireland Tourist Board's 'Tourism Barometer' – a survey of around 200 establishments – found that four out of five hoteliers reported an improvement in business between June and September 2003 compared with the same period in 2002.

The 1.7 million visitors in 2002 earned the industry £395 million (£348 million in 2001), of which £274 million came from staying visitors in Northern Ireland and £121 million from domestic holiday spending. This revenue accounts of around two per cent of Northern Ireland's GDP and supports 19,600 equivalent full-time jobs.

Northern Ireland Tourist Board
Research and Intelligence Department
St Anne's Court,
59 North Street,
Belfast, BT1 1NB
Tel: 028 9023 1221
Fax: 028 9024 0960
Web: www.nitb.com

Financial Services

Allianz

Allianz House
21 Linenhall Street
Belfast, BT2 8AB
Tel: 028 9089 5600
Fax: 028 9043 4222
Web: www.allianz-ni.co.uk

Head of Allianz
Northern Ireland
Adrian Toner

Allianz Northern Ireland is a leading local insurer and part of the Allianz global network. As part of this network, Allianz Northern Ireland enjoys unrivalled access to risk and product knowledge. Working with a network of over one hundred brokers and intermediaries, the company has established itself as market leader in all lines of personal and commercial insurance, providing an efficient and comprehensive service to the local business community.

AXA Insurance

Windsor House
9-15 Bedford Street
Belfast, BT2 7FT
Tel: 028 9033 3222
Fax: 028 9024 2864
Director: Tim Scott

AXA Insurance is one of Northern Ireland's leading personal and commercial motor insurers and is part of the Global AXA Group. The company is a major player in the drive to improve road safety through its involvement in major campaigns such as 'Thump' and 'Damage' with the DOE, and the 'Roadsafe Roadshows' aimed at young drivers.

Bank of Ireland
4-8 High Street, Belfast, BT1 2BA
Tel: 028 9024 4901
Fax: 028 9023 4388
Principal Activity: banking services
Chief Executive: David Magowan
Manager: Bernard Rooney

Bank of Scotland (Ireland) Ltd
10-15 Donegal Square North,
Belfast, BT1 5GB
Tel: 028 9033 0033
Fax: 028 9033 0030
Principal Activity: financial services
Regional Manager: Eugene McGale

Cunningham Coates Ltd
19 Donegall Street, Belfast, BT1 2HA
Tel: 028 9032 3456
Fax: 028 9023 1479
Principal Activity: stockbrokers
Managing Director: Randell Herron

Edward Jones Investments
2 Malone Road
Belfast, BT9 5BN
Tel: 028 9068 7715
Fax: 028 9068 2580
Principal Activity: stockbrokers
Managing Director: Patrick Mahony

First Trust
PO Box 123,
First Trust Centre, 92 Ann Street,
Belfast, BT1 3AY
Web: www.firsttrustbank.co.uk
Tel: 028 9032 5599
Managing Director:
Dennis Licence

Northern Bank Ltd
PO Box 183
14 Donegall Square West
Belfast, BT1 6JS
Tel: 028 9024 5277
Fax: 028 9089 3245
Principal Activity: banking services

HBOS
Donegall Square North
Belfast, BT1 5GL
Tel: 0845 720 3040
Fax: 028 9027 8233
Principal Activity: financial services
Branch Manager: Jim Porter

HFC Bank plc
44-46 High Street
Belfast, BT1 2BF
Tel: 028 9032 4400
Fax: 028 9032 4300
Principal Activity: financial services
Manager: Julie-Anne Burns

HSBC
4th Floor, 5 Donegall Square South
Belfast, BT1 5JP
Tel: 028 9043 4565
Fax: 028 9088 4853
Principal Activity: financial services
Regional Manager: Steve Clayton

Lombard & Ulster Group Ltd
11-16 Donegall Square East
Belfast, BT1 5UD
Tel: 028 9027 6276
Fax: 028 9027 6279
Principal Activity: financial services
Area Director: James Conn

Open+Direct
Royston House, 34 Upper Queens
Street, Belfast, BT1 6FD
Tel: 028 9026 0900
Fax: 028 926 0978
Managing Director: Paul Elliott

Pearl Assurance plc
2 Donegall Square East
Belfast, BT1 5HH
Tel: 028 9032 1938
Fax: 028 9023 7833
Branch Manager: Paul McMullan

Progressive Building Society

Progressive Building Society
12/14 Chichester Street,
Belfast, BT1 4LA
Tel: 028 9032 0573
Fax: 028 9024 2035

33/37 Wellington Place
Belfast, BT1 6HH
Tel: 028 9082 1821
Fax: 028 9043 9421
Chief Executive: William Webb

Your Homegrown Society - with branches and agents across the Province.

Prudential Assurance Co Ltd
Beacon House, 27 Clarendon Road
Belfast, BT1 3PD
Tel: 0845 720 000
Fax: 028 9089 6000
Principal Activity: insurance
Regional Manager: Adrian Clement

Royal Sun Alliance Insurance Plc
Sun Alliance House, 42 Queen Street
Belfast, BT1 6HL
Tel: 028 9024 4433
Fax: 028 9026 2357
Principal Activity: insurance
Chief Executive: Peter Gallagher

Willis
78-86 Dublin Road, Belfast, BT2 7BY
Tel: 028 9024 2131
Fax: 028 9032 1087
Principal Activity: insurance
Managing Director: Jim Halliday

Zurich Insurance
7 Upper Queen Street
Belfast, BT1 6QD
Tel: 028 9024 5222
Fax: 028 9023 2435
Principal Activity: insurance
Area Manager (NI): James Shields

Construction and Property Companies

Ardmac Performance Contracting Ltd
Unit 15 Annesborough Industrial Estate
Craigavon, BT67 9JD
Tel: 028 3834 7093
Fax: 028 3834 1604
Principal Activity: interior
Managing Director: Kevin McAnallen

B Mullan & Sons (Contractors)
Bovally House, 11-13 Anderson Avenue
Limavady, BT49 0TF
Tel: 028 7772 2337
Fax: 028 7776 4780
Principal Activity: stone, asphalt
Managing Director: Sean Mullan

Farrans (Construction) Ltd
99 Kingsway
Dunmurry, Belfast, BT17 9NU
Tel: 028 9061 1122
Fax: 028 9062 9753
Principal Activity: construction
Managing Director: John Gillivray

Felix O'Hare & Co Ltd
88 Chancellors Road
Newry, BT35 8NG
Tel: 028 3026 1134
Fax: 028 3026 1397
Principal Activity: builders
Managing Director: John Parr

Gilbert Ash (NI) Ltd
47 Boucher Road
Belfast, BT12 6HR
Tel: 028 9066 4334
Fax: 028 9066 3634
Principal Activity: building contractors
Managing Director: Eddie O'Neill

Graham Construction
Lagan Mills
Dromore, BT25 1AS
Tel: 028 9269 2291
Fax: 028 9269 3412
Principal Activity: building contractors
Managing Director: Michael Graham

J Kennedy & Co (Contractors) Ltd
1 Letterloan Road
Macosquin, Coleraine, BT51 4PP
Tel: 028 7035 2211
Fax: 028 7035 6308
Principal Activity: builders
Manager: Danny Kennedy
Chief Executive: Chris Kennedy

Lagan Holdings Ltd
19 Clarendon Road
Clarendon Dock, Belfast, BT1 3BG
Tel: 028 9026 1000
Fax: 028 9026 1010
Principal Activity: quarrying civil engineering & construction group
Managing Director: Michael Lagan

Mivan Construction Ltd
Newpark, Greystone Road
Antrim, BT41 2QN
Tel: 028 9448 1000
Fax: 028 9448 1015
Principal Activity: construction
Managing Director: Ivan McCabrey

PJ Conway (Contractors) Ltd
58 Moneymore Road
Magherafelt, BT45 6HG
Tel: 028 7963 2001
Fax: 028 7963 3038
Principal Activity: building contractors
Proprietor: Patrick Conway
Managing Director: Trevor Simpson

Redland Tile & Brick Ltd
61 Largy Road, Crumlin, BT29 4RR
Tel: 028 9442 2791
Fax: 0870 564 2742
Principal Activity: roofing services
Sales Manager: Billy Wright

RJ Maxwell & Son Ltd
209 Bushmills Road
Coleraine, BT52 2BX
Tel: 028 7034 3281
Fax: 028 7035 3346
Principal Activity: civil engineering
Managing Director: Willy McNabb

Ulster Business Top 100

The following tables set out Northern Ireland's top 100 businesses including information relating to their turnover, profit and employment. There is no perfect way to rank businesses by size but the best proxy is turnover. The information below was compiled in August 2003 by Ulster Business Magazine. Obviously there has been some change since then including the closure of Desmonds and Shopelectric and considerable downsizing at Harland and Wolff and Ben Sherman.

Northern Ireland *Top 100 Businesses* 1-20

Top 100 Businesses

RANK	COMPANY	TOWN	ACCOUNTS DATE	TURNOVER (Millions)		PRE-TAX PROFIT (Millions)	
				Current	Previous	Current	Previous
1	Viridian PLC	Belfast	31/03/02	730	647.1	-7.5	85.2
2	Glen Electric Ltd	Newry	31/03/02	578.4	435.6	20.8	22.8
3	Short Bros	Belfast	31/01/02	450.6	500	53	51.8
4	FG Wilson (Eng.) Ltd	Larne	31/12/01	307	274.9	35.6	27.2
5	Charles Hurst Group	Belfast	31/12/02	260.7	-	7.3	-
6	John Henderson (Hldg) Ltd	N'townabbey	31/12/02	255.7	-	6.2	-
7	United Diary Farmers	Belfast	31/03/02	246.7	216.2	1.3	-1
8	Moy Park Ltd	Craigavon	31/12/01	242.2	220.6	3.9	3.1
9	Dunnes Stores Ltd	Newry	31/01/02	217.6	206.7	24.1	18.3
10	J&J Haslett Ltd	Belfast	31/12/01	214.4	203.5	2.3	4.2
11	DCC Energy	Belfast	31/03/02	205.9	102.9	2.4	2.1
12	Galen Group	Craigavon	30/09/02	201.6	182.7	-	16.9
13	SHS Group	N'townabbey	31/12/01	183.1	112.1	17.5	4.9
14	Premier Power Ltd	Larne	31/12/01	177.7	180.5	30.9	-
12.8							
15	Farrans Ltd	Belfast	31/12/01	172.1	181.4	5	6.2
16	Isaac Agnew Hdg Ltd	Belfast	31/12/01	168.4	157.9	4.7	3.1
17	Hilton Food Group	Larne	31/12/01	157.2	152.7	4.9	4.5
18	Coca Cola Bottlers	Lisburn	31/12/02	136.6	124.2	8.8	-
19	Lagan Holdings	Belfast	31/03/02	135.5	135.6	10.6	14.3
20	Sangers NI Ltd	Belfast	30/09/01	130.3	121.2	2	2.6

Northern Ireland *Top 100 Businesses*

1–20

Data compiled by D&B

NET WORTH (Millions)	EMPL.	DATE STARTED	LINE OF BUSINESS	OWNERSHIP	RANK
174.6	3139	1973	Electricity Service	-	1
28.3	5479	1973	Heating Appliance Manufacturers	Glen Dimplex	2
256.1	7356	1936	Aircraft mfrs	Bombardier Inc.	3
88.7	2190	1966	Diesel eng mfrs	Caterpillar Inc.	4
26.9	798	1938	Car Dealers	Lookers PLC	5
26.7	1378	1923	Grocery whlrs	-	6
21.8	600	1995	Milk and Dairy Products	-	7
21	3595	1961	Poultry pdt mfrs	OSI International	8
132.4	132.4	1969	Supermarket props	Dunnes Holding Co	9
-	-	-	-	-	-
3.5	301	1978	Gas & Oil suppliers	Flogas UK Ltd	11
191.5	1580	1991	Pharmaceutical mfrs	-	12
12.7	319	1975	Grocery whlrs	-	13
102.5	244	1992	Electricity supply	BG Group PLC	14
41.6	1056	1941	Construction	CRH PLC	15
21.9	620	1931	Car Dealers	-	16
5.2	427	1998	Fresh Food distributors	Heffer Investments	17
16.5	492	1939	Soft drink mfrs	Molino Holdings	18
61.8	870	1960	Construction	-	19
6.2	211	-	Pharmaceutical mfrs	Alchem PLC	20

Top 100 Businesses

Northern Ireland *Top 100 Businesses*

21-40

Top 100 Businesses

RANK	COMPANY	TOWN	ACCOUNTS DATE	TURNOVER (Millions) Current	TURNOVER (Millions) Previous	PRE-TAX PROFIT (Millions) Current	PRE-TAX PROFIT (Millions) Previous
21	Desmonds & Sons	Londonderry	31/12/01	128.4	126.2	8.9	6.9
22	AES NI Ltd	C'fergus	31/12/01	127.8	117	26.5	11.7
23	Musgrave Supervalu	Belfast	01/01/02	126	113.6	-7.9	-10.1
24	NI Transport Hldg	Belfast	28/03/02	125.8	110	1.4	-13.4
25	Foyle Food Group	L'derry	31/12/01	117.1	86.6	2.9	1.4
26	Fayrefield Foods	Belfast	31/12/01	114.3	107.4	0.2	0.3
27	Diageo Global Supply IBC Ltd	Belfast	30/06/02	111.5	77.3	12.4	10.6
28	Rotary Group	N'townabbey	30/09/02	110	110.3	6.4	6.1
29	Maxol Oil	Belfast	31/12/02	110	107.4	-0.4	-0.6
30	Quinn Group	Enniskillen	31/12/01	101.4	74.4	7.8	7.1
31	David Patton & Sons (NI)	Ballymena	30/11/01	98.9	1.9	-	-
32	Shell NI	Belfast	31/12/01	98	108.7	-1.8	-0.8
33	Thales Air Defence	Belfast	31/12/01	97.5	54.4	14.6	8.9
34	O'Kane Poultry	Ballymena	27/04/02	97.4	87.8	0.1	0.1
35	Lindsay Cars	Lisburn	31/12/01	94.2	68.8	-0.2	-0.9
36	John Kelly Ltd	Belfast	31/03/02	89.5	94.3	1	0.8
37	Humax Electronics	N'townards	31/12/02	83.7	91.8	-0.3	1.3
38	Fane Valley Co-Op	Newry	30/09/01	79.9	67.2	1.2	1.4
39	Donnelly Bros (Gar)	Dungannon	31/03/02	79.2	63.4	1.1	1.5
40	W&R Barnett	Belfast	31/03/02	78.1	72.8	6.7	6.7

Northern Ireland ***Top 100 Businesses***

21-40

NET WORTH (Millions)	EMPL.	DATE STARTED	LINE OF BUSINESS	OWNERSHIP	RANK
48.1	2057	1885	Clothing mfrs	-	21
-56.6	181	1992	Electricity supply	AES Corp	22
-48.3	558	1997	Supermarket props	Musgrave Investments	23
-	3629	1784	Transport Providers	-	24
8.9	750	1975	Food producers	-	25
1.6	24	1992	Dairy Product Wholesalers	Fayrefield Group Ltd	26
53.8	280	1951	Wine & spirit dst	Diageo PLC	27
24.8	1374	1967	Mch/Vent/Elec engrs	Rotary Ltd	28
6.5	124	1918	Petrol/Oil supply	McMullan Bros	29
97.6	801	1973	Quarrymasters+	Quinn Investments	30
11.6	391	1912	Building Contractors	-	31
-2.1	-	1938	Fuel Distributors	Shell Dist (H) Ltd	32
47.7	550	1993	Missile mfrs	Thales Defence	33
10.8	878	1931	Poultry pdt mfrs	-	34
3.6	475	1963	Car Dealers	-	35
10.5	142	1911	Fuel Distributors	Tedcastle holdings	36
2.3	110	1997	Elec Comp Mfrs	-	37
22.7	600	1920	Milk & Diary prdts	-	38
4.6	178	1925	Car Dealers	-	39
74.8	162	1924	Grain & Feed Dstrs	-	40

Top 100 Businesses

Northern Ireland **Top 100 Businesses**

41-60

Top 100 Businesses

RANK	COMPANY	TOWN	ACCOUNTS DATE	TURNOVER (Millions)		PRE-TAX PROFIT (Millions)	
				Current	Previous	Current	Previous
41	McLaughlin & Harvey	Belfast	31/12/02	76.4	83.7	3.1	3.1
42	Brett Martin	Ntownabbey	31/12/01	76.1	72.9	3.7	1.7
43	Musgrave Distribution	Belfast	31/12/01	75.1	65.7	1.9	1.8
44	Leckpatrick Dairies	Strabane	31/12/01	73.5	77.7	-3	3
45	John Hogg & Co	Belfast	30/10/01	73.1	91	0.7	2
46	J P Corry Group	Belfast	31/03/02	71.2	101.9	-0.6	-0.8
47	Ben Sherman Group	Craigavon	30/06/02	71.1	70.5	9.5	6.8
48	Bass Ireland	Belfast	29/12/01	70.5	-	5.6	7.2
49	NI Co-Op Society	Carrickfergus	13/01/02	69.5	70.8	0.5	-0.9
50	BE Aerospace	Kilkeel	23/02/02	67.3	84.5	8.9	7.5
51	Diary Produce Packers	Coleraine	31/12/01	64.2	50.8	1.1	2.5
52	Linden Foods	Dungannon	30/06/01	64.1	61.5	1.4	1.6
53	John Thompson & Sons	Belfast	31/07/01	63.7	58.2	2.1	2
54	Philip Russell	Craigavon	30/06/02	63.2	54.4	0.8	0.4
55	Norbrook Laboratories	Newry	02/08/02	62.7	59.6	0.5	4
56	James E McCabe Ltd	Craigavon	31/12/01	62.4	55.1	3.9	3.2
57	Cantrell & Cochrane (B)	Belfast	31/08/01	59.3	51.1	1.1	0.6
58	Ards Holdings	Warrenpoint	31/12/02	59.2	54.4	1.3	1.4
59	Cuisine de France	Lisburn	31/07/02	58.8	50.6	0.9	0.8
60	Daewoo Electronics	Antrim	31/12/01	56.6	60.6	0	0.7

Northern Ireland ***Top 100 Businesses***

41-60

NET WORTH (Millions)	EMPL.	DATE STARTED	LINE OF BUSINESS	OWNERSHIP	RANK
10.7	215	1993	Building Contractors	-	41
23.6	642	1960	Plastic bldg pdt mfrs	-	42
12.2	154	1983	Wholesale Cash & Carry	Musgrave Group	43
5.7	134	1901	Dairy Produce mfrs	Golden Vale PLC	44
16.6	728	1866	Fuel Distributors	-	45
5.3	504	1814	Bldrs Merchants	-	46
18	446	1993	Clothing mfrs	-	47
30.6	400	1897	Brewers	Coors Holdings Ltd	48
2.7	1200	1899	Supermarket props	Co-operative Wholesale	49
12.2	765	1985	Aircraft seat mfrs	B E Areospace (H)	50
7	311	1944	Cheese Mfrs	Golden Vale PLC	51
7.3	300	1982	Meat processors	Ltd	52
12.3	160	1880	Animal Feedstuff mfrs	BHH Ltd	53
2.5	450	1968	Off Licence & Pub props	-	54
18.9	700	1969	Pharmaceutical pdt mfrs	-	55
19	96	1919	Wine & Spirit Wholesale/Retailers	-	56
4.5	248	1924	Soft drink mfrs	Cantrell & Cochrane (H)	57
7.1	174	1900	Bldg & Civil eng	-	58
4.8	77	1991	Food rtlrs	IAWS Group PLC	59
8.7	770	1989	Video recorder mfrs	Daewoo Electronics Co Ltd	60

Top 100 Businesses

Northern Ireland *Top 100 Businesses*

61-80

Top 100 Businesses

RANK	COMPANY	TOWN	ACCOUNTS DATE	TURNOVER (Millions)		PRE-TAX PROFIT (Millions)	
				Current	Previous	Current	Previous
61	Powerscreen Intl	Dungannon	31/12/01	56.3	56.7	3.6	3.9
62	Belfast Telegraph	Belfast	31/12/01	56	55	21.2	20
63	SDC Trailers	Toomebridge	31/03/02	55.6	47.2	3.3	1.4
64	John Graham (Dromore)	Dromore	31/03/02	54.3	66	-0.7	0.8
65	Ulster Carpet Mills	Craigavon	31/12/02	53.1	46.6	1.4	3.4
66	Readymix (NI)	Belfast	31/12/01	52.9	59.4	3.7	3.5
67	TK-ECC Ltd	Belfast	31/03/02	52.7	39.9	-17.7	-8.7
68	Montupet (UK)	Belfast	31/12/01	52.3	32.5	2.2	1.2
69	W&G Baird	Antrim	31/12/01	51.7	44.5	2.1	2.2
70	Haldane Shiells & Co	Newry	31/12/01	51.5	43.6	1.2	0.7
71	Eason & Son (NI)	Belfast	27/01/02	51	44.6	2.1	2.3
72	Mivan Group	Antrim	31/12/02	50.5	52.4	2	2.7
73	Balcas Ltd	Enniskillen	31/01/02	48.9	44.2	-	2
74	Shop Electric Ltd	Belfast	31/03/02	48.9	57.6	-1.8	-3.9
75	Nicholl (Fuel Oils)	Londonderry	31/05/02	48.1	55.9	1.4	0.3
76	Murdock Group	Newry	31/12/02	47	-	1.1	-
77	Samnina - SCI Enclosures	Lisburn	14/10/01	46	54.7	-9.5	3.5
78	Henry Group (NI)	Magherafelt	31/03/02	45.4	46.9	0.6	0.7
79	Adria Ltd	Strabane	31/12/02	45.2	41	0.1	1.5
80	Harland & Wolff Group	Belfast	31/12/01	45.1	111.1	-84	-32.4

Northern Ireland *Top 100 Businesses*

61-80

NET WORTH (Millions)	EMPL.	DATE STARTED	LINE OF BUSINESS	OWNERSHIP	RANK
7.7	100	1966	Heavy mch mfrs	Powerscreen Ltd	61
25.4	556	1861	Newspaper publishers	Independent News & Media	62
6.6	250	1982	Trialer mfrs	Retlan Mfg Ltd	63
9	473	1955	Bldg & Civil eng	-	64
29.6	1173	1938	Carpet mfrs	-	65
0.9	70	1996	Building merchants	RMC Group PLC	66
0.6	762	1993	Air Bag mfrs	Takata Corp	67
32.2	815	1990	Aluminium Casting mfrs	Montupet SA	68
18.1	750	1882	Printing Group	-	69
13.3	320	1946	Timber & Bldg mchts	-	70
39.1	585	1935	Print whlrs	Eason & Son	71
19.7	600	1981	Construction	-	72
10.8	513	1962	Timber mchts	-	73
19.4	539	1994	Dom appl rtlrs	Lislyn Properties	74
4.5	96	1962	Fuel Distributers	-	75
8.2	251	1991	Builders merchants	-	76
-2.3	350	1969	Sheet metal & elec mfrs	Precismetal	77
7.4	439	1976	Building Contractors	-	78
7.7	1094	1961	Hosiery mfrs	Charnos PLC	79
18.6	600	1861	Ship Builders	Fred Olsen Energy	80

Top 100 Businesses

Northern Ireland *Top 100 Businesses*

81-100

Top 100 Businesses

RANK	COMPANY	TOWN	ACCOUNTS DATE	TURNOVER (Millions)		PRE-TAX PROFIT(Millions)	
				Current	Previous	Current	Previous
81	Clearway Disposals	Craigavon	31/12/02	44.3	37.3	4	1.1
82	Citrus Trading	Dungannon	31/03/01	42	-	0	-
83	Ulster Television	Belfast	31/12/01	39	40.8	11.9	27
84	Brooks Group	Belfast	31/12/02	38.9	52.8	2.4	-1.2
85	Savilles Auto Village	Lisburn	31/12/01	37.9	36.7	0.5	0.5
86	Bettercare Group	Belfast	30/09/01	37.9	30	0.2	0.4
87	Dillon Bass	Belfast	31/12/01	37.2	37.2	0	0
88	Bavarian Garages	Belfast	31/12/01	36.9	-	2.3	1.6
89	Grafton Recruitment	Belfast	31/03/02	36.2	34.7	0.4	1
90	O'Hare & McGovern	Newry	31/12/01	36	33	0.7	0.3
91	Wrightbus Ltd	Craigavon	30/09/01	35.5	39.2	-0.2	2.8
92	Howden Power	Belfast	31/12/01	35.3	33.5	1.1	-3.5
93	Ryobi Aluminium Castings	Antrim	31/12/01	34.9	30.2	4.2	2.8
94	News Speed	Belfast	31/07/02	34.2	-	0.2	0.2
95	Lurgan Chilling	Craigavon	31/03/02	34	27.9	0.7	1.6
96	Phoenix Natural Gas	Belfast	31/12/02	33	24.9	0.7	-2.7
97	L Stanley Ltd	Belfast	29/04/01	32.8	33.9	9.1	7
98	Belfast International Airport	Antrim	31/03/02	32.8	34.6	14	17.4
99	McNaughton Blair	Belfast	31/12/01	32.6	23.5	1.7	0.5
100	WFB Baird	Craigavon	30/04/01	32.2	29.7	-1.4	-4.1

Northern Ireland *Top 100 Businesses*

81–100

NET WORTH (Millions)	EMPL.	DATE STARTED	LINE OF BUSINESS	OWNERSHIP	RANK
8	120	1964	Scrap & Waste dlrs	-	81
0.2	-	1998	Meat whlrs	-	82
-4.4	281	1959	Television Broadcasters	-	83
13.7	64	1996	Timber mchts	Wolseley Centres Ltd	84
1.3	99	1969	Car Dealers	Dutton-Foreshaw Group	85
11.7	2600	1996	Nursery Home props	-	86
0	28	1990	Wine & Spirit whlrs	-	87
1.8	120	1979	Car Dealers	Issac Agnew (H)	88
1	2196	1998	Recruitment Agency	-	89
2.6	150	1971	Building Contractors	Carnbane House Ltd	90
5.5	650	1946	Coach mfrs	-	91
28	258	1881	Ind Fan mfrs	Charter PLC	92
16.4	245	1990	Die Cast product mfrs	Ryobi Ltd	93
1.4	35	1988	News Distributors	-	94
2.1	100	1990	Meat whlrs	Anglo Beef Processors	95
150	83	1992	Gas Distributors	BG Group PLC	96
24.7	165	1958	Licensed Betting Offices	Stanley Leisure PLC	97
88.4	300	1994	Airport operators	TBI PLC	98
-0.2	160	1908	Builders merchants	-	99
0.3	113	1912	Linen mfrs	Electroedit Ltd	100

NORTHERN IRELAND YEARBOOK 2004

Chapter 8: A Guide to Doing Business

SUITE
2
PARK
AVENUE
hotel
SUITE
3

This section of the Northern Ireland Yearbook 2004 is aimed primarily at individuals or groups considering going into business for the first time and people and organisations based outside Northern Ireland who are thinking of developing business opportunities within Northern Ireland. It sets out a detailed description of the environment for business in Northern Ireland as well as the main practical considerations such as company registration, regulations, compliance, employment and taxation.

The Northern Ireland Economic Environment

The population of Northern Ireland as at June 2001 is 1.68m. With an area of 5,240 sq miles it has a population density of 321 persons per square mile. The population of some of Northern Ireland's main towns and cities in 2001 was:
Belfast 350,000; Londonderry 100,000; Bangor 52,500;
Lisburn 42,000; Ballymena 29,000; Newry 23,000;
Armagh 20,000(Source: Northern Ireland Annual Abstract of Statistics 2002)

Northern Ireland is part of the United Kingdom and is governed by the UK tax and business regime. The currency is sterling Northern Ireland is an increasingly attractive location for those seeking to establish a new branch of an existing business or those seeking to build a completely new enterprise. It is characterised by a youthful and well-educated population, a low cost base and one of the most technologically advanced network infrastructures in Europe as the following tables show. Further analysis of the Northern Ireland economy and its key sectors is set out in Chapter 7.

Table 8.1: United Nations Population Comparison

Country	% Aged 0-39
Sweden	50.4
Germany	49.0
United Kingdom	53.2
Northern Ireland	**58.2**

Source: United Nations Statistics Division 2002

Throughout the 1990s, Northern Ireland enjoyed the fastest economic growth of any region of the United Kingdom. In 1999 GDP was £17,003 million ($24,707 million). Between 1989 - 1999, real GDP per head increased by 22.6 per cent in Northern Ireland compared to 18.2 per cent (1.7 per cent per year) increase for the UK as a whole. It can also be seen that the Northern Ireland economy in line with western European economies is increasingly dependant on the services sector. This now accounts for almost 70 per cent of total GDP.

Table 8.2: Origins of GDP by Industrial Sector

Sector	% of total GDP
Services	68.5
Manufacturing	19.0
Construction	6.0
Agriculture	4.0
Electricity, Gas, Water	2.0
Mining and Quarrying	0.5
Total	**100**

Source: Northern Ireland Annual Abstract of Statistics 2001

Over the past five years the performance of Northern Ireland's manufacturing sector has significantly exceeded the UK average. Although manufacturing output contracted during 2001 as the global economy slowed, it has now stabilised.

Table 8.3: Manufacturing Output 1997-2002

Country	% Change
United Kingdom	-4
Northern Ireland	11

Source: DETI "Quarterly Strategic Information Report" June 2002

Output growth has been accompanied by a significant rise in investment by the region's productive industries. Between 1995 and 2000, it increased by 91 per cent compared to a UK rise of 18.5 per cent. The UK is the second largest recipient of Foreign Direct Investment globally and holds 20 per cent of all FDI stock in the EU and 8 per cent worldwide. Northern Ireland has captured a proportional share of this investment.

Table 8.4: Northern Ireland Exports

Exports 2000	Value £ m	% of total
Transport Equipment	603	14.5
Electrical & Optical Equipment	1173	28.5
Chemicals & Man Made Fibres	673	16.0
Food, Drink and Tobacco	648	15.5
Non Metallic Manufacturing Products	315	7.5
Other Machinery & Equipment	339	8.0
Textiles	208	5.0
Basic Metals/Fabricated Metal Products	199	5.0
Total	**4158**	**100.0**

NIERC, DETI "Sales and Exports 00/01" June 2002

Traditionally a very inward looking economy, Northern Ireland has developed an increasing export focus, with exports now accounting for 38 per cent of total sales by Northern Ireland companies – up from 28 per cent in 1991/92. The June 2002 export survey shows that sales to markets outside Europe grew by 25 per cent over the last five years to £1.85 billion. £20m of manufactured goods are exported from Northern Ireland daily to the EU and beyond. These markets now account for almost half of Northern Ireland's total exports.

Northern Ireland Labour Force

Table 8.5: Employment in Northern Ireland

Total at Work	655, 800	% Workforce
Agriculture	14, 640	2.0
Industry	137, 630	21.0
Services	403, 500	77.0

Source: Northern Ireland Annual Abstract of Statistics 2002

Unemployment, which is currently at its lowest level since records began - has fallen steadily from a peak of 17.2 per cent in 1986 to 5.5 per cent in Spring 2003, compared with the current EU average of 7.7 per cent. Between 1998-2003 employee jobs in Northern Ireland increased by 8.9% compared to an increase of 5.7% in the UK as a whole.

The Northern Ireland labour force is well trained and educated and although unemployment is low there are no significant skills shortages.

On average, labour costs are 32 per cent lower in Northern Ireland than in the US. Northern Ireland is unquestionably labour cost competitive with other developed economies.

Table 8.6: Index of Costs for Manufacturing Workers 2001

Country	Index
Germany	116
Japan	111
USA	100
Europe average	93
France	83
Canada	81
United Kingdom	80
Northern Ireland	**68**

Source: US Bureau of Labour Stats September 2001

Industrial Relations

In addition to relatively low cost labour by western standards, Northern Ireland is also a stable environment in terms of its industrial relations, with a lower incidence of industrial disputes than its European neighbours.

Table 8.7: International Comparisons of Labour Disputes 1996-2000

Country	Index
Denmark	296
Spain	182
Finland	56
France	68
Ireland	91
Italy	76
Northern Ireland average	**33**
Europe average	48

Source: UK National Statistics "Labour Market trends" 2003

Levels of staff absenteeism due to sickness in Northern Ireland are the lowest in the United Kingdom.

Productivity

Northern Ireland's manufacturing efficiency in terms of productivity has been increasing at almost twice the rate of the United Kingdom average.

Table 8.8: Manufacturing Productivity 1997-2002

Country	% change
Northern Ireland	27
UK average	14

Source: DETI, "Quarterly Strategic Information Report" June 2003

Education of Labour Force

There are a total of 346,500 pupils in Northern Ireland schools (01/02), with approximately 19,000 schoolteachers and a ratio of 16.5 pupils per teacher.

In the most recent PISA (Programme for International Student Assessment - OECD), which covers the reading, mathematical and scientific abilities of 15 year olds in 32 countries, Northern Ireland significantly exceeds the OECD average in all three areas.

Table 8.9: Public Expenditure on Education as % of total Public Expenditure

Country	%
Northern Ireland	**22.0**
USA	14.4
ROI	13.5
Spain	12.8
UK	12.6
Portugal	12.6
France	11.1
Germany	9.5
Japan	9.8
Netherlands	9.8

OECD, N.I Assembly Public Expenditure Plans 2001-02

On average students in Northern Ireland obtain higher grades on standardised exams than they do elsewhere in the UK. In 2001/02 28.1% of 18 year olds in Northern Ireland sitting their final school exams obtained the highest grade. Northern Ireland's two universities have had major successes in a United Kingdom comparison of research work. The results of the Research Assessment Exercise 2001, demonstrate that 53 per cent of the departments assessed at the University of Ulster and 82 per cent of those at the Queen's University of Belfast are carrying out work of national and international excellence.

Infrastructure and Utilities

Electricity

The electrical power system is 3-phase AC operating at 50Hz with transmission systems of 275kV and 110kV serving a wide distribution network of 33kV and 11kV. Low voltage supplies are 230/400 volts although many large factories take supply at 11kV or 33kV. A range of tariffs is available although most large companies are charged on the basis of an Electricity Purchase Agreement. Rates vary considerably depending on the pattern of usage and voltage of supply. However, as a guide, most large companies pay an average price between 3.3p and 9.2p per kWh.

The Northern Ireland electrical grid has been strengthened considerably in recent years by physical interconnection with both the Republic of Ireland grid and Great Britain, through the North/South and Moyle interconnectors.

Table 8.10: Rate for a Three-Minute Trunk Call at Peak Hours - U.S.$

From	Northern Ireland	Republic of Ireland	France	Germany	Netherlands	Belgium	USA
Northern Ireland (ntl)	0.09	0.23	0.23	0.23	0.23	0.23	0.23
Republic of Ireland	0.38	-	0.94	0.94	0.94	0.94	0.47
France	0.32	0.37	-	0.32	0.32	0.32	0.32
Germany	0.32	0.32	0.32	-	0.32	0.32	0.32
Netherlands	0.26	0.41	0.29	0.26	-	0.29	0.26
Belgium	0.53	0.70	0.53	0.53	0.53	-	0.53
USA	0.24	0.45	0.45	0.45	0.45	0.45	N/A

Source - Tarrifica PBI Media. November 2002

Telecoms

Northern Ireland has an advanced resilient, digital telecommunications network that provides high-speed voice and data connections. It was the first region in the UK to develop a fully fibre-optic infrastructure, and is part of a UK network that supplies greater bandwidth than the rest of Europe combined.

The cost of a typical 3 minute call from Northern Ireland to mainland Europe is on average 48 per cent cheaper than other EU tariffs, whilst contacting the US is nearly 40 per cent less expensive.

Gas

Until relatively recently when a gas pipeline was built across the Irish sea, Northern Ireland had no natural gas network. Phoenix Natural Gas commenced supplying its first major customers in Belfast in January 1997. To date there are over 3,000 industrial and commercial customers using natural gas, saving an estimated £6 million between them on energy costs against their previous fuels. Natural gas is, however, currently only available in the Greater Belfast area although there are plans to extend the network significantly both northwest and south over the next few years. Plans to bring natural gas to the North West are at an advanced stage, and the pipeline should be complete in time to bring gas to the new combined-cycle gas turbine power station currently under construction at Coolkeeragh, Derry and due to come on stream in 2005. The North-West pipeline should also facilitate the extension of natural gas to many towns along its route eg Ballymena. Contract customers, using above 25,000 therms (732,000 kWh) per annum, can expect to pay between 1.1p and 1.4p per kWh depending upon the size of load, load factor, contract duration etc. For large customers with equipment capable of firing on alternative fuels, "interruptible supply" contracts are available at prices below the 1.1p per kWh level.

Water

For industry, metered water costs are made up of two separate charges. The first is a volumetric charge for each cubic metre of water registered on the meter, the second is a yearly standing charge which depends on the internal diameter of the metre supply pipe, (e.g. 41-50mm equates to £289 per annum). Domestic customers are not charged directly for water although there had been growing pressure on Northern Ireland's devolved administration to introduce some kind of charging structure for water in line with the rest of the UK. Opposition to these plans is fierce in many quarters.

Property and Accommodation

New, purpose built and fitted out office space is available throughout Northern Ireland from £12 per square foot in the greater Belfast area. Belfast currently offers the lowest net-rent of any large city in the UK.

Table 8.11: Cost of Office Space per Sq Foot by Location

Region	City	Cost per sq foot (£)
UK and Ireland	Belfast	12.00
	Birmingham	27.50
	Dublin	36.42
	Glasgow	23.00
	London (City)	50.00
	London (West End)	67.50
	Manchester	24.00
USA		
	New York	60.32
	San Francisco	34.76
	Washington	28.77
EU	Amsterdam	22.46
	Madrid	27.79
	Paris	53.81
Asia Pacific	Hong Kong	30.96
	Tokyo (Inner Central)	71.37

Source: Richard Ellis "World Office Rents, February 2003

Specialist incubator units at the Northern Ireland Science Park and the University of Ulster Science and Research Park provide state-of-the-art accommodation and support during the start-up phase for knowledge-based industries.

New business parks such as Invest NI's Global Point International Business Park have flexible leasing at costs that are among the lowest in Europe. Invest Northern Ireland's Speculative Build Initiative will involve the private sector in the provision of property of up to 30,000 sqft (sub divisible into units of 5000 sqft) at a number of locations throughout Northern Ireland. These units are primarily suitable for companies operating in the Information, Communication and Telecoms sectors.

Transport Connections

At the end of 2000-01 there were 24,728 kilometres of public roads in Northern Ireland. Traffic congestion is minimal, compared to main routes in Britain, although larger towns and cities do experience problems during the conventional morning and evening rush hours. The well developed road infrastructure links all major commercial and industrial areas with seaports and airports.

Seaports

Over 80 international shipping lines operate out of Northern Ireland's 5 commercial seaports. 90 per cent of Northern Ireland's total trade, and almost 50 per cent of the Republic of Ireland's freight traffic, leaves through these ports. There are 150 sailings a week to destinations including the United Kingdom, the USA, Continental Europe and the rest of the world. 8,800 ships carrying 17million tonnes of cargo leave Belfast port each year. Over 60 per cent of Northern Ireland's sea borne trade is shipped through the Port of Belfast. The Port of Londonderry at Lisahally is the United Kingdom's most westerly port and has a capacity for 30,000 tonne vessels.

Airports

Serving over 3.7 million passengers a year Belfast International Airport is the principal gateway to the north of Ireland. It is the most technically advanced airport in Ireland and the fifth largest regional air cargo centre in the UK. Airfreight services are currently provided by regular scheduled passenger aircraft and an increasing number of dedicated freighter aircraft. Leading companies operating services from the 24-hour centre at Belfast International Airport are DHL and TNT, while Royal Mail also has a large presence there.

Belfast City Airport has opened a new £21 million terminal as a result of rapidly growing passenger traffic. More than 1.3 million passengers now pass through the terminal each year. The City of Derry airport serves the entire North-West region of Ireland. Located 7 miles from the city of Derry it is within easy reach of Donegal. (Further details of Northern Ireland's sea crossings and connections and airline services are set out in Chapter 13. A Visitors Guide to Northern Ireland.)

Formation and Registration of Companies in Northern Ireland

Forming a company in Northern Ireland is an uncomplicated process, although all companies registered in Northern Ireland are required to register with Companies House, submit accounts and annual returns and follow general procedures relating to registration.

Business entities may be incorporated or unincorporated. Incorporated bodies have a legal status separate from that of their owners and may sue and be sued in their own name. Incorporated bodies include private limited companies, public limited companies and unlimited companies. An unincorporated body may be a sole proprietorship or a partnership.

Registering a Company

There are four main types of company:

- Private company limited by shares - members' liability is limited to the amount unpaid on shares they hold;
- Private company limited by guarantee - members' liability is limited to the amount they have agreed to contribute to the company's assets if it is wound up;
- Private unlimited company - there is no limit to the members' liability;
- Public limited company (PLC) - the company's shares may be offered for sale to the general public and members' liability is limited to the amount unpaid on shares held by them.

A limited company has the fundamental advantage of being a legal entity separate from its members. An unlimited company lacks the advantage: that most people seek from incorporation that of the limited liability of its members.

Limited liability companies have the advantage that the member's liability to contribute to the debts of the company have a fixed limit, which is always clear. The limit is set by issuing shares, (a company limited by shares) or by taking guarantees (a company limited by guarantee) from the members that they will contribute up to a fixed amount to the debts of the company when it is wound up or when it needs money in particular circumstances.

The Companies Act generally allows one or more persons to form a company for any lawful purpose by subscribing to its memorandum of association. However, a public company or an unlimited company must have at least two subscribers.

Company Formation

Those seeking to register a new company must submit the following:

- Form 10: summary of a companies officers, registered company address etc;
- Form 12: declaration of compliance;
- Memorandum of Association;
- Articles of Association;
- Fee of either £20 or £80 (depending on required period of registration).

Form 10 gives details of the first director(s), secretary and the address of the intended registered office. The company's directors must give their date of birth, occupation and details of other directorships they have held within the last five years. Each director appointed and each subscriber (or their agent) must sign and date the form. Form 10 is available from the Companies Office in Belfast or from any of the company registration agents for which details are given below.

The same person can be both a director and company secretary, provided there is another director. A sole director cannot also be the company secretary. Form 12 is a statutory declaration of compliance with all the legal requirements relating to the incorporation of a company. It must be signed by a solicitor who is forming the company, or by one of the people named as director or company secretary on Form 10. It must be signed in the presence of a commissioner for oaths, a public notary, a JP or a solicitor.

Form 12 must be signed and dated after all other documents are signed and dated, as Form 12 confirms that all other documentation is complete. Form 12 is available from the Companies Office in Chichester Street, Belfast, or online. (Full contact details are given below). Provided standard forms of memorandum and Articles of Association are being used documentation may be processed in one working day.

Completed and signed documentation should be forwarded to Companies House who will issue a Certificate of Incorporation. Processing of registration in a standard period of time has a £20 fee; the standard period is three to ten working days. Same day registration has a fee of £80, and is possible provided that Companies House receives all necessary documentation before 3pm.

The Memorandum of Association and Registration

It is essential that a company has a memorandum of association to specify its constitution and objects.
The memorandum of every company must state:

- The name of the company;
- Where the registered office of the company is to be situated;
- The objects of the company; (The object of a company may simply be to carry on business as a general commercial company.);
- That the liability of the members is limited;
- The maximum amount of capital the company may raise and its division into shares of a fixed amount.

The memorandum of a company limited by shares or by guarantee must also state that the liability of its members is limited. The memorandum of a company limited by guarantee must also state that each member undertakes to contribute to the assets of the company if it should be wound up whilst he is a member, or within one year after he ceases to be a member. These assets may then be used for payment of the debts and liabilities of the company contracted before he ceases to be a member, and of the costs, charges and expenses of winding up, and for the adjustment of the rights of the contributories amongst themselves, such amounts as may be required.

Articles of Association

The Articles of Association is a document setting out the rules for the running of the company's internal affairs and contains clauses addressing matters such as the issue and transfer of shares, the appointment and removal of directors, the conduct of shareholders and directors meetings and payment of dividends.

In the case of an unlimited company or a company limited by shares, articles of association signed by the subscribers to the memorandum and prescribing regulations for the company are registered. In the case of an unlimited company having a share capital, the articles must state the amount of share capital with which the company proposes to be registered.

Company Names

The choice of name for a company is of considerable importance and is subject to a number of restrictions.
The name of a public company must end with the words "public limited company". In the case of a company limited by shares or guarantee the company must have "limited" as its last word unless exempted under s.30 of the Companies Act 1986.
It is prohibited to register a company name which is the same as a name appearing in the registrar's index of company names or a name which would in the opinion of the Secretary of State for Northern Ireland constitute a criminal offence or is offensive.
A company may not be registered by any name, unless with the approval of the Secretary of State, which would give the impression that the company is connected in any way with government or the local authority.
If a company goes into insolvent liquidation a person who was acting as a director of the insolvent company is not permitted to act as a director of a new company with the same or a similar name. This restriction lasts for five years and aims to prevent the misuse of limited liability companies by putting one into liquidation, leaving the debts behind and starting another.

Registration and its Consequences

A company's memorandum and articles must be delivered to the Registrar of Companies. Accompanying the memorandum must be a statement in the prescribed form containing the names and details of the director or directors of the company and the person who is or is to be the first secretary or joint secretary of the company. The statement should be signed by all those named as a director or secretary. The statement should specify the intended situation of the company's registered office on incorporation.

The registrar of companies will not register a company's memorandum unless satisfied that all requirements in respect of registration have been complied with. Subject to such compliance the registrar will retain and register the memorandum and articles.

Effect of Registration

Following registration of a company's memorandum, the registrar of companies will give a certificate that the company is incorporated and in the case of a limited company that it is limited. The certificate may be signed by the registrar or authenticated by his official seal. From the date of incorporation contained in the certificate the subscribers of its memorandum shall be a body corporate by the name contained in the memorandum.

Location of Registered Office

A company registered in Northern Ireland is required to have a registered office located in Northern Ireland. Upon formation the proposed registered office of a company and other details should be notified to the Registrar of Companies on Form G21. Any change to the registered address should be notified to Companies House on Form G295. Smaller companies frequently use their accountant's office as their registered address.

Publication of the Company Name

The name and address of a company must be present on company letterheads and other documentation. The name of the company must be displayed outside every place of business including the registered office. Under the terms of the Companies Act 1986 there is a requirement to state the company's name, place of registration, registered number and the address of its registered office on all business letters, notices and official publications, bills of exchange, promissory notes, endorsements, cheques, orders for money or goods, invoices, receipts and letters of credit. Failure to do so may leave the company and officers liable to a fine and may lead to personal liability for a director or agent.

In the case where a company, which is incorporated outside Northern Ireland, wishes to establish a presence within Northern Ireland certain disclosure and registration requirements must be met.

There are two registration regimes applicable in Northern Ireland, where a company has established a place of business in Northern Ireland, or established a branch in Northern Ireland. Once the applicable regime has been determined registration must occur within one month of the date of establishment.
To qualify as a branch the business entity must be part of a company and conduct business in Northern Ireland on behalf of the company. Local decision-making management would also be indicative of branch status. If the activities carried on by the entity are mainly ancillary or incidental to the core business of the organisation then those activities may be insufficient to constitute a branch although they may be sufficient to amount to the establishment of a place of business. To register as a branch the company must deliver prescribed documents to the Register of Companies. These include:

- A completed form BR1 Return Delivered for Registration of a Branch of a Part XXIII company which gives details of its date and country of incorporation, company number, officers and their authority to bind the company and location of branches;
- A certified copy of its charter statutes or Memorandum and Articles;
- Copies of the latest accounting documents;
- A registration fee of £35.00;
- Any amendments to registered details must be delivered within 21 days and special rules apply to the registration of charges or mortgages over assets.

Whilst there is no statutory definition for "establishing" a place of business the establishment of a place of business at a specific location and with a degree of permanency or recognisability as being a location of the business will suffice. To register as having "established" a place of business in Northern Ireland companies must deliver the following documents to the Register of Companies:

- Using the prescribed form 641 a list of the directors and secretary with their details and the names and addresses of those resident in Northern Ireland authorised to accept notices on behalf of the company;
- A certified copy of its charter, statutes or Memorandum and Articles;
- A statutory declaration made by an authorised person stating the date upon which the company's place of business in Northern Ireland was established;
- The registration fee;
- Any alterations in registered details must be delivered within 21 days;
- A company, which has established a place of business in Northern Ireland, does not need to file any accounting documentation at its initial registration. However, for each subsequent financial year it must file accounts and the Director's report as if the company were incorporated under the 1986 Order.

Partnerships

A partnership has many fewer formalities to be complied with than a limited company, however, the members of a partnership are liable for all the debts incurred by the business they run. If large losses are made they must contribute their own money to clear the debts of the business. In practice with small businesses there may be little distinction between partnership and limited status, as banks will not lend money without first securing guarantees from those running the business so that if the company cannot pay its debts, the personal assets of those in charge will meet such debts.

Limited Partnerships

A limited partnership consists of:

- One or more persons called general partners, who are liable for all the debts and obligations of the firm; and
- One or more persons called limited partners, who contribute a sum or sums of money as capital, or property valued at a stated amount. Limited partners are not liable for the debts and obligations of the firm beyond the amount contributed.

A limited partnership must be registered under the Limited Partnership Act. To register as a limited partnership a statement (Form LP5) signed by all the Partners must be delivered to Companies House.

Limited Liability Partnerships

The Limited Liability Partnerships Act, which came into force on 6 April 2001, introduced a new form of association partnerships with limited liability. A limited liability partnership is an alternative corporate vehicle providing the benefits of limited liability but allowing members the flexibility of organising their internal structure as a traditional partnership.
Any new or existing firm of two or more persons will be able to incorporate as a limited liability partnership. Incorporation of a limited liability partnership will be by registration at Companies House through a similar process to registration of a company.
Limited liability partnerships have similar disclosure requirements to a company including the filing of accounts. Limited liability partnerships will also be required to:

- File an annual return;
- Notify any changes to the limited liability partnership's membership;
- Notify any changes to the members names and residential addresses;
- Notify any change to their registered office address.

Joint Ventures

An overseas company may form a base in Northern Ireland by joining an established company. Such joint ventures are usually as a limited company or as a partnership.

Accounts and Audit

Every company has a duty to keep accounting records sufficient to show and explain the company's transactions and should disclose with reasonable accuracy at any time the financial position of the company. Directors must ensure that the balance sheet and profit and loss account is compliant with their obligations under the terms of the Companies Act. Accounting records should contain day to day entries of all sums of money received and expended by the company and the matters in respect of which the receipt and expenditure takes place, and a record of the assets and liabilities of the company.

If a company's business involves dealing in goods, the accounting records should contain statements of stock held by the company at the end of each financial year of the company, all statements of stocktakings from which any statement of stock has been or is to be prepared and except in the case of goods sold by way of ordinary retail trade, statements of all goods sold and purchased, showing the goods and the buyers and sellers in sufficient detail to enable all these to be identified. If a company fails to comply with these provisions every officer of the company who is in default becomes guilty of an offence unless he shows that he acted honestly and that in the circumstances in which the business operated the default was excusable.

A company's accounting records may be held at its registered office or such other place as the directors may think fit, and should be open to inspection by the company's officers at all times. A private company should keep its accounting records for three years from the date upon which they were made.

Annual Accounts

The directors of every company have a duty to prepare a set of accounts for each financial year. These accounts must include a profit and loss account, a balance sheet signed by a director, an auditors report signed by the auditor, notes to the accounts, and if relevant, group accounts.
Small and medium sized enterprises (SMEs) may abbreviate the accounts they submit to Companies House. All limited and public limited companies must submit their accounts to the Registrar. Unlimited companies need only deliver accounts to the Registrar if during the period covered by the accounts, the company was:

- A subsidiary or a parent of a limited undertaking;
- A banking or insurance company;
- A qualifying company within the meaning of the Partnerships and Unlimited Companies (Accounts) Regulations 1993;
- Operating a trading stamp scheme.

A company's first accounts stem from the date of incorporation not the first day of trading. Subsequent accounts start on the day after the previous accounts ended. If a company's first accounts cover a period of more than twelve months they must be delivered to the Registrar within 22 months of the date of incorporation for private companies.

Directors of private limited companies usually have a maximum of ten months from the accounting reference date to deliver accounts to the Registrar. The accounting reference date is the date to which accounts must be prepared. Public limited companies usually have seven months to deliver their accounts from the accounting reference date.

Whilst accountants may prepare the company accounts it is the responsibility of the director to ensure that accounts are filed on time. Late filing penalties are enforced against those companies whose accounts are late. These penalties are shown below:

Table 8.12 Penalties for Late Filing of Company Accounts

Length of Delay	Private Company	Public Company
3 months or less	£100	£500
3 months 1 day to 6 months	£250	£1000
6 months 1 day to 12 months	£500	£2000
More than 12 months	£1000	£5000

Qualification of a Company as Small or Medium Sized

Companies qualifying as small or medium may prepare and deliver abbreviated accounts to the Registrar. Certain small companies with a turnover of less than £1 million, (£250,000 for companies with charitable status) and assets of less that £1.4 million can claim exemption from audit.
Public companies and certain companies in the regulated sectors cannot qualify as small or medium sized. For other

companies, the size of the company (and in the case of a parent company the size of the group headed by it) in terms of its turnover, balance sheet total (meaning the total of the fixed and current assets) and average number of employees determines whether it is classed as small or medium.

To be classified as a small company at least two of the following conditions must be met:

- Annual turnover must be £2,800,000 or less;
- The balance sheet total must be £1,400,000 or less;
- The average number of employees must be 50 or fewer.

To be a medium sized company at least two of the following conditions must be met:

- Annual turnover must be £11,200,000 or less;
- The balance sheet total must be £5,600,000 or less:
- The average number of employees must be 250 or fewer.

If the company is a parent company it cannot qualify as a small or medium sized enterprise unless the group headed by it is also small or medium sized.

The abbreviated accounts of a small company must include:

- The abbreviated balance sheet and notes;
- A special auditor's report unless the company is also claiming audit exemption.

The abbreviated accounts of a medium company must include:

- The abbreviated profit and loss account;
- The full balance sheet;
- A special auditor's report;
- The directors' report;
- Notes to the accounts.

The special auditor's report should state that in the auditor's opinion the company is entitled to deliver abbreviated accounts and that they have been properly prepared in accordance with requirements of the Companies Act.

Company Governance

Company Officers

Every company must have formally appointed company officers at all times.

A private company must have at least:

- One director;
- One secretary - formal qualifications are not required.

A company's sole director cannot also be the company secretary.

A public company must have at least:

- Two directors;
- One secretary - formally qualified.

All company officers have wide responsibilities in law.

After incorporation Companies House must be notified about:

- The appointment of a new officer - use Form 288a;
- An officer's resignation from the company - use Form 288b;
- Changes in an officer's name or address or any of the other details originally registered on Form 10 - use Form 288c.

Company Directors

Anyone of good standing may act as a company director subject to a few exceptions. Every company director has personal responsibility to ensure that statutory documents are delivered to the Registrar of Companies particularly:

- Accounts (only for limited companies);
- Annual returns (Form 363);
- Notice of change of directors or secretaries or their details (Forms 288 a/b/c);
- Notice of change of registered office (Form 287).

Company Secretaries

The company secretary of a public limited company must be qualified. However the company secretary of a private limited company requires no formal qualifications.

Northern Ireland Registrar of Companies
64 Chichester Street, Belfast, BT1 4JX
Tel: 028 9023 4488 / Fax: 028 9054 4888

Off-the-Shelf Companies

Ready-made companies may be acquired from enterprises, which register a number of companies and hold them dormant until they are purchased. This may save time where a company is needed quickly for a particular enterprise.

These ready-made companies are formed with the objects of a general commercial company having the power to carry on any trade or business.

Company Formation Agents

Business World Enterprise Centre Ltd
39 Church Street, Warrenpoint, BT34 3HN
Tel: 028 4177 3542

Company Business Solutions
99 Skegoneill Avenue, Belfast, BT15 3JR
Tel: 028 9059 3810

Company Creations
10 Ravenhill Park Gardens, Belfast, BT6 0DH
Tel: 028 9064 6924

The Company Shop
79 Chichester Street, Belfast, BT1 4JE
Tel: 028 9055 9955

Company Solutions Europe Ltd
4 Lower Crescent, Belfast, BT7 1NR
Tel: 028 9032 9073

Comperia Ltd
26 Donard Avenue, Newtownards, BT23 4NF
Tel: 028 9181 0284

Holdfast
138 University Street, Belfast, BT7 1HH
Tel: 028 9032 9984

Taxation of Businesses in Northern Ireland

Company Taxation

The levels of corporate and personal taxation in Northern Ireland are among the lowest in Europe.

Table 8.13: EU Main CorporateTax Rates 2002 (%)

Country	% Rate
Belgium	40
Italy	37
France	36.5
Netherlands	34
Spain	35.5
Austria	35
Portugal	34
Luxembourg	31
Northern Ireland	**30**
Germany	27.5

Source: UK Key Facts March 2003

The UK has among the lowest corporate tax rates in Europe, making it one of the most competitive and attractive business locations. Since April 2000, a lower "small companies" rate of 10 per cent applies to the income of resident companies in the UK, with marginal relief available to companies with profits from £10,000 to £50,000.

Corporation Tax

Corporation tax is based on the total profits, income and capital gains, arising in an accounting period. The Corporation tax year runs from 1 April to 31 March. Where an organisation has an accounting period not coinciding with the corporation tax year, and the rate of tax varies from one year to the next, the company's profits are distributed pro rata over the two years.

The Corporation Tax Self Assessment (CTSA) regime applies in respect of all accounting periods ending after 30 June 1999. Under CTSA, companies compute their own tax and larger organisations are required to make payments on account.
A company is required to complete a detailed tax return in respect of each accounting period. The return contains a section requiring a computation of corporation tax and a self-assessment of liability. The return must usually be filed within twelve months of the end of the accounting period. Penalties of up to £1000 may be imposed for failure to submit a return and should the failure continue beyond six months, liability may increase to a tax related penalty of up to 20 per cent.

Under the terms of the Corporation Tax Self Assessment scheme a company's self-assessment stands unless amended by the company concerned or by the Inland Revenue. Where a company fails to make a return, the Inland Revenue will determine the tax due.

Payment of Corporation Tax

Corporation tax must be paid no later than nine months and one day from the end of the company's accounting period. This due and payable date predates the date for filing a return. Under self-assessment large companies must operate a quarterly account.

A large company is defined for this purpose as one with taxable profits and UK dividend income exceeding £1.5 million in a particular accounting period. Where a company is a member of a group or has associated companies this limit is divided by the number of associated companies plus one.

Where quarterly payments on account are to be made, they fall due as follows: six months and 14 days from the start of the accounting period; nine months and 14 days from the start of the accounting period; twelve months and 14 days from the start of the accounting period; and three months and 14 days from the end of the accounting period.

Interest on tax paid late runs from the due and payable date with respect to the final liability. The rate of interest on underpaid tax is currently 5 per cent and the interest on overpaid tax 3.75 per cent. During the period leading up to the due date different rates apply. Under CTSA interest on overdue tax is deductible when computing accessible profits and interest on overpaid tax is taxable.

Tax Audits

Under the terms of CTSA, the Inland Revenue has one year from the due filing date to commence an enquiry into a company's return. Where errors are discovered during the period of the enquiry the return may be corrected. However, once the period of the enquiry has expired, the return stands, unless deficiencies emerge of which the Inland Revenue could not reasonably have been made aware on the basis of the information available at the time.

Appeal Procedures

Where disputes arise over a self-assessment, assessment or determination and resolution cannot be achieved with the local tax office, an appeal is heard before the General or Special Commissioners.

Rates of Corporation Tax

The current rate of corporation tax is 30 per cent applicable to all of a company's taxable profits including capital gains, whether retained or distributed.
A reduced rate of 20 per cent applies where taxable profits do not exceed £300,000. The overall rate increases on a sliding scale from 20-30 per cent for profits between £300,00 and £1,500,000. Where taxable profits do not exceed £10,000 a starting rate of 10 per cent applies and a marginal rate applies to taxable profits between £10,000 and £50,000.

Table 8.14: UK Corporation Tax Rates

Band £000	%
0-10	10.0
10-50	22.5
50-300	20.0
300-1.5m	32.5
Over 1.5m	30.0

Capital Gains

Capital gains are computed according to separate rules and once computed are chargeable to corporation tax. Capital gains are computed by deducting from the base cost of the asset and an adjustment for inflation (indexation). The base cost is normally the acquisition price (plus enhancement expenditure), but where the asset was held at 31 March 1982, its market value at that date may normally be substituted for the base cost if greater. The inflation adjustment is restricted where necessary to the amount required to reduce the un-indexed gain to zero. Where a loss is sustained indexation is not available.

Dividends received by UK resident companies from other UK resident companies are exempt from corporation tax. Dividends from abroad are subject to corporation tax, both under domestic legislation and the UK's tax treaties.

Business expenses are deductible but must be incurred wholly and exclusively for the purposes of the taxable activity.

Depreciation and Capital Allowances

Depreciation of capital assets is not an allowable deduction. Deductions in lieu of depreciation are granted in respect of capital expenditure on certain classes of assets. These deductions known as capital allowances apply to the following:

Table 8.15 Assets Eligible for Deductions in lieu of Depreciation

Asset	Deduction
Industrial Buildings (factories & workshops but not commercial or retail premises)	4 per cent per annum straight line
Hotels	4 per cent per annum straight line
Plant and Machinery (including furniture on a reducing balance and office equipment)	25 per cent per annum
Agricultural Buildings and Works	4 per cent per annum straight line
Mineral Extraction	25 per cent or 10 per cent on a reducing balance
Scientific Research	100 per cent in the year of expenditure
Patent Rights	25 per cent per annum on a reducing balance

For expenditure on plant and machinery incurred between 12 May 1998 and 11 May 2002 a "first year allowance" of 100 per cent is available to most small and medium sized enterprises (SMEs) resident in Northern Ireland. The plant and machinery must be used in Northern Ireland by the SME claiming the allowance.

Draft legislation to enable companies to benefit from tax relief on the cost of intellectual property, goodwill and other intangible assets is currently under consideration. No relief is currently available with amortisation of intangible assets included in the statutory accounts being added back in the corporation tax computations as disallowable expenditure.

Research and Development Tax Credits

Research and development tax credits were introduced for small companies with effect from 1 April 2000. Qualifying companies may claim 150 per cent of qualifying revenue research and development expenditure against taxable profits or potentially claim 16 per cent of the 150 per cent as a repayment. The government proposes to extend this type of relief.

Interest and Other Charges on Income

Rules concerning the treatment of corporate debt have been significantly amended since 1996. Under the new rules, the tax treatment is intended to mirror the accounting treatment, provided that the company follows one of the two authorised accounting methods, namely the accruals basis or the mark to market basis.

Under the accruals basis, loan relationships are shown at cost, and payments and receipts are allocated to the accounting period to which they relate, on the assumption that every payable amount is paid when it becomes due. Under the mark to market basis, appropriate mostly for investment dealing, each loan relationship is accounted for in each accounting period at its fair value, and payments and receipts are allocated to the period in which they become due and payable.

Other charges on income, such as patent royalties and donations to charity are deductible from total profits (including capital gains). A deduction is available for a charge on income only when paid. Income tax at a basic rate, 22 per cent must be deducted from charges on income, and the tax must be accounted for on a quarterly basis to the Inland Revenue.

Expenses, which are non-deductible in computing taxable profits, include:

- Depreciation of capital assets;
- Non specific bad debt provisions;
- Entertaining expenses (excluding staff entertainment);
- Corporation tax;
- Capital expenditure;
- Expenditure incurred more than seven years before trading begins;
- Dividends and other distributions.

Personal Taxation

Table 8.16: EU Personal Tax (Higher) Rates 2002

Country	% Rate
Netherlands	52
Belgium	55
France	53
Germany	48
Austria	50
Italy	45
Ireland	42
Spain	48
Portugal	40
Northern Ireland	40

Source: Invest UK "Key Facts" March 2003

The UK has the lowest "top rate" of personal taxation in the EU, and a starting rate of just 10% for most sources of income. In the UK, income becomes liable for taxation if it falls within one of the four schedules listed:

Table 8.17 Income Tax Schedules

Schedule	Description
Schedule A	Rental income from land and property in the UK
Schedule D	
Case I	Income from trade
Case II	Income from a profession or vocation
Case III	Interest, annuities or other annual payments
Case IV	Income from foreign securities
Case V	Income from foreign possessions
Case VI	Miscellaneous income
Schedule E	Income from employment and pensions
Schedule F	Dividends and distributions from other UK companies

Each schedule and case has its own rules for computing income and deductions. The computed income is then aggregated to produce an individual's total income, which is taxable. The tax year commences on the 6 April and ends on the following 5 April. The income assessable in any tax year is the income of that year.

A self-assessment system was introduced on 6 April 1996 for taxpayers whose liability is not satisfied solely by deductions under PAYE. The Inland Revenue sends tax returns to these taxpayers shortly after the end of the tax year. Taxpayers may choose between self-assessments in which case they must complete the return and calculate their own tax payable and file by 31 January and leaving it up to the Inland Revenue to compute tax payable, in which case completed returns must be filed by 30 September. Interest and penalty charges will be incurred if the return is not filed on time.

The Inland Revenue has been trying to move the tax return process on-line but the response from taxpayers has not been as enthusiastic as had been hoped.

PAYE System

Employers on a cumulative basis deduct tax and National Insurance contributions under the PAYE (Pay As You Earn) system. Deductions are made according to a code number (taxcode) for each employee issued by the Inland Revenue.

The taxcode takes into account the employees' allowances, benefits and credits, so that the correct amount of tax should have been deducted by the end of the tax year.

PAYE income tax and primary employee's National Insurance Contributions (NIC) deductions must be applied to virtually all payments of income assessable to Schedule E tax and /or NIC. Deductions cannot be made from payments in kind but a suitable adjustment is made to the employee's PAYE code number to allow for the tax due.

Every employer with a sufficient tax presence in the United Kingdom is obliged to operate PAYE. Special rules apply if the employee is not resident or ordinarily resident in the UK.

Persons operating PAYE are required to account monthly to the Inland Revenue for sums deducted in the previous tax month (from the 6th of one calendar month to the 5th of the next). Employers with small payrolls may apply for quarterly accounting.

At the end of the tax year the employer must provide a certificate of pay and tax deducted to each employee and a return of deductions in respect of all employees to the Inland Revenue, together with the payment of any balance of deductions outstanding. These returns and payments must be submitted to the Inland Revenue by 19 May of the following tax year. Interest is charged on late payment of end of year balances and penalties are imposed for late filing of returns.

Income Tax

For the income tax year 2003-2004 the income tax bands after allowances are as follows:

Table 8.18 Income Tax Bands (after allowances)

First £1,920	Lower Rate 10%
Next £1,921-£29,900	Basic Rate 22%
Balance over £29, 900	Higher Rate 40%

Income tax is computed by aggregating income under the various schedule and cases and subjecting the result (total income) to tax at three progressive rates, after deducting personal and other allowance and deductions.
The names of the various income tax rates used in the United Kingdom are listed below:

Table 8.19 UK Income Tax Rates

Lower Rate	10%
Savings Rate	20%
Basic Rate	22%
Higher Rate on Dividends	32.5%
Discretionary Trusts	34%
Higher Rate	40%

Inland Revenue

www.inlandrevenue.gov.uk

Director
Tina Gallagher
Inland Revenue
Northern Ireland

The Inland Revenue's purpose in Northern Ireland and throughout the UK is to ensure that everyone understands and receives what they are entitled to and understands and pays what they owe.

National Helplines

New Employer: 0845 607 0143
(For registration & advice on PAYE, NI, SSP, SMP)
Open: 8am-8pm Mon-Fri, 8am-4pm Sat/Sun

Existing Employers: 0845 714 3143
(For advice on PAYE, NI, SSP, SMP)
Open: 8am-8pm Mon-Fri, 8am-5pm Sat/Sun

Self Assessment: 0845 900 0444
Open: 8am-8pm Mon-Sun

Self Employed: 0845 915 4655
(Class 2 National Insurance queries)
Open: 8am-5pm Mon-Fri

Newly Self-Employed: 0845 915 4515
(Registration & Advice)
Open: 8am-8pm Mon-Fri, 8am-4pm Sat/Sun

Construction Industry Scheme:
Contractors: 0845 733 5588
8am-8pm Mon-Fri, 8am-5pm Sat/Sun

Sub Contractors: 0845 300 0581
8am-8pm Mon-Sun

Accounts Office Shipley: 01274 530750

Local Enquiry Centres

Offices are open 8.30am – 5pm Monday to Friday unless stated otherwise

Belfast
Beaufort House, 31 Wellington Place, BT1 6GB
Tel: 0845 302 1469

Lisburn
Moira House, 121 Hillsborough Road, BT28 1LA
Tel: 028 9266 5230

For offices listed below please call 0845 302 1481

Antrim
Open 9am - 4.30pm, Mon - Fri
12-14 Castle Street , BT41 4JE

Ballymena
Kilpatrick House, 38-54 High Street, BT43 7DQ

Banbridge
Bridgewater House, 25 Castlewellan Road, BT32 4AX

Coleraine
Fern House, 1A Adelaide Avenue, BT52 1LT

Craigavon
Marlborough House, Central Way, BT64 1AT

Enniskillen
Abbey House, Head Street, BT74 7DB

Londonderry
Foyle House, Duncreggan Road, BT48 0AA

Newry
Downshire House, 22-23 Merchant's Quay, BT35 6AH

Employer Queries
If your reference starts with:-
916 – call 028 2563 3052
925 – call 028 9053 2413
953 – call 028 9260 6072

Other Useful Numbers

Tax Credits/Child Benefit Helpline
0845 603 2000
Open: 8am-8pm Mon-Sun

Enforcement and Insolvency Service
Olivetree House
23 Fountain Street
Belfast, BT1 5EA
Tel: 028 9053 2730

National Insurance Contributions
Tel: 028 9050 5010

Director's Office
Floor 5 Millennium House
17-25 Great Victoria Street,
Belfast
BT2 7AQ
Tel: 028 9093 9700

National Minimum Wage Helpline
0845 650 0207

Capital Taxes Office
Dorchester House
52-58 Great Victoria Street
Belfast
BT2 7BB
Tel: 028 9050 5353

Business Support Team
Tel: 028 9053 2755

Confidential Information
Tel: 028 9053 2706
Open: 9am-5pm Mon-Fri

Stamp Office
Dorchester House
52-58 Great Victoria Street
Belfast
BT2 7BB
Tel: 028 9050 5312
028 9050 5314 / 028 9050 5316

National Insurance

National Insurance is the major labour cost in the United Kingdom and can add up to 10 per cent to salary costs. Social Security Taxes in the form of National Insurance Contributions are payable by individuals and employers. There are six classes of contributions. The greatest share of revenue is raised by Class One contributions, paid by employers and employees. For employees, NICs are payable at a single rate of 10 per cent on the excess of gross earnings (excluding most benefits in kind) over £89 per week (equivalent to £4,615 per year). However, once gross earnings exceed £30,940 per year, the upper earnings limit, a further 1% is payable on the excess. No NICs are payable if earnings do not exceed the lower earnings limit (LEL). For 2003-2004 the LEL is £89 per week or £4615 per year.

Value Added Tax (VAT)

VAT is a tax which VAT registered businesses charge when they supply their goods and services in the UK or the Isle of Man, but there are some exceptions. It is also a tax on goods, and some services, that are imported or acquired from outside the UK. VAT does not apply to certain services. These include loans of money, some property transactions, insurance and certain types of education and training. Supplies, which are exempt from VAT, do not form part of taxable turnover.

There are three rates of VAT in the UK:

- 17.5 per cent (standard rate);
- 5 per cent (reduced rate);
- 0 per cent (zero rate).

Businesses are likely to have to register for and charge VAT if:

- Taxable turnover reaches or is likely to reach a set limit, known as the VAT registration threshold;
- A business has been taken over as a going concern; or
- Goods are acquired from other European Community countries.

The VAT registration threshold was raised to £56,000 in the 2003 Budget. But businesses may opt to register for VAT if taxable turnover is less than this. Turnover is the amount of money going through the business, not just the profit.

The VAT which registered businesses charge and collect from customers is payable to Customs & Excise and is know as 'output tax'. The VAT which businesses are charged by their suppliers is called 'input tax' and can normally be reclaimed from Customs, although there are some exceptions.

Most businesses collect more VAT than they pay to their suppliers, and therefore pay the surplus VAT to Customs. However, if a business's input tax is more than its output tax, the difference will be refunded.

Contact Inland Revenue's Northern Ireland Business Support Team for information on the steps required to register VAT and organise tax and National Insurance payments.

Business Support Team
Tel: 028 9053 2755
Web: www.inlandrevenue.go.uk

Most businesses must fill in a VAT return and pay the surplus VAT to Customs every quarter. Small businesses may opt to make just one return a year, although they may be asked to make interim payments. Businesses, which regularly pay out more, VAT than they collect, may fill in a return every month and obtain a refund.

Customs and Excise

HM Customs and Excise
Custom House, Custom House Square, Belfast BT1 3ET
Tel: 028 9056 2600
Email: ni@hmce.gov.uk
Web: www.hmce.gov.uk

Registration & Deregistration
Tel: 0845 711 2114 / Fax: 028 3026 4165

Debt Management
Tel: 028 9056 2600 / Fax: 028 9056 2975

Belfast International Airport: Tel: 028 9442 3439

Complaints and Suggestions

Tel: 028 9056 2618 / Fax: 028 9056 2970

Customs Confidential: Tel: 0800 59 5000

National Advice Service

Tel: 0845 010 9000
Text-phone for the deaf or hard of hearing: 0845 000 0200

Customs & Excise is the UK Government department responsible for the collection and administration of VAT and excise duties as well as looking after Import & Export formalities. The department provides a range of support services for businesses that may need advice or assistance in operating any of these regimes.

- The National Enquiry Service deals with all general telephone enquiries via a single telephone number - 0845 010 9000. This service is available Monday to Friday from 8am to 8pm;
- If the enquiry is more complex, or a written response is required, the Written Enquiry Service may be contacted at the above address or by e-mail to enquiries.ni@hmce.gsi.gov.uk;
- The local Business Support Team offers support for businesses in Northern Ireland. This support can take the form of a one to one consultation for a single business or a seminar for a group of businesses with a common interest, such as cross border trade. The Business Support Team may be contacted at the above address or by telephone on 028 9056 2600;
- The Customs & Excise Website www.hmce.gov.uk contains further information and visitors to the site may download a wide range of information notices and leaflets.

All Customs & Excise support services are provided free of charge.

Importing and Exporting

If a business involves importing or exporting goods, there are certain requirements, which must be complied with, such as declaration of imports and exports to Customs & Excise and payment of any duties or VAT due.

Some imported goods are also liable to duties; further information on those goods affected is available from Customs and Excise.

With the establishment of the internal market across the European Union import/export procedures have been greatly simplified. However, there are numerous compliance requirements relating to trade with non-EU member states.

Employment of Staff in Northern Ireland

Introduction

The employment of staff for business in Northern Ireland entails much more than the payment of salary and overhead costs. Employers will need to be aware of a plethora of legal employment requirements and regulations across a range of headings. Some of the regulation derives from the Social Chapter of the European Union and is governed by European Directives. The remainder comes from the particular requirements deemed necessary for Northern Ireland in terms of ensuring fairness and equality in the employment sphere.

The table 8.20 sets out the main sources of legislation in relation to employment law in Northern Ireland and provides an overview of the obligations and entitlements of both the employer and the employee.

Unfair Dismissal
Unfair dismissal in Northern Ireland is determined by the Rome Convention on the Law Applicable to Contractual Obligations transposed into UK and Northern Ireland law by the Contracts (Applicable Law) Act, 1990.

Discrimination in Northern Ireland
Equality legislation in Northern Ireland comprises the Fair Employment and Treatment (NI) Order 1998, the Disability Discrimination Act 1995, the Race Relations (NI) Order 1997, the Equal Pay Act (NI) 1970 and the Sex Discrimination (NI) Order 1976. For further details on equality legislation contact:

The Equality Commission for Northern Ireland
Tel: 028 9050 0600
Web: www.equalityni.org

Public Holidays
Public holidays include bank holidays, holidays by Royal Proclamation and "common law holidays". Banks are not allowed to operate on bank holidays.

There is no statutory entitlement to bank or other public holidays, these are days where an employee may receive paid or unpaid leave depending on the terms of their contract. Where employees work on a public holiday to which they are entitled under the terms of their contracts, compensation for doing so is a matter for resolution under the terms of their contract.

Bank holidays in Northern Ireland include the Easter holidays, traditional "12th" holiday of the 12th and 13th July, the August Bank Holiday, 25th and 26th December, 1st January, and May Day.

Table 8.20 Overview of Employment Entitlements and Obligations

Working Time:
Working Time (NI) Regulations 1998. Employees may choose to work in excess of 48 hours per week

Notice:
Employment Rights (NI) Order 1996

Length of Service	Notice
One month	1 week
2-3 year	2 week
3-4 years	3 weeks
12 years or more	up to 12 weeks

Annual Leave and Public Holidays:
Employment Rights (NI) Order 1996

Minimum Wage:
The Minimum Wage (NI) Act 1998
The minimum hourly rate is currently £4.50 per hour (aged 22+) or £3.80 per hour (aged 18-21)

Equality:
The Sex Discrimination (NI) Order 1976, The Equal Pay Act (NI) 1970, the Race Relations (NI) Order 1997, the Disability Discrimination Act 1995, The Fair Employment and Treatment (NI) Order 1998.
Anti-discrimination provisions include:

- 5 discriminatory grounds - sex, race, (includes membership of the travelling community), religious belief, political opinion, disability, sexual orientation
- Discriminatory grounds of family status, marital status and age are not included although laws prohibiting age discrimination are scheduled to be introduced in 2006
- The Part-time Workers (Prevention of Less Favourable Treatment) Regulations (NI) 2000

Unfair Dismissal:
Employment Rights (NI) Order 1996

- Time limit - 3 months from the date of the dismissal or within such further period as the Tribunal considers reasonable
- Compensation: a basic award which would usually equate to the amount an employee would have received had they been made redundant;

Whistle blowers:
The Public Interest Disclosure (NI) Order 1998

Provides protection for workers who are dismissed or victimised as a result of making certain disclosures

Redundancy:
Employment Rights (NI) Order 1996
Service below the age of 18 may not be included in calculating statutory redundancy. Statutory redundancy pay is subject to a ceiling of £240 per week. A collective redundancy arises where 20 or more employees are dismissed as redundant at one establishment within a period of 90 days or less. Where a collective redundancy arises, consultation with employee representatives must begin in good time.

Human Rights:
The Human Rights Act 1998 Article 8 confers the right to respect for family and private life.

Annual Leave

Annual leave is usually accrued over "leave years" from the date of employment or the date of the commencement of the organisation's leave year. If an employee joins an organisation during the course of the leave year their annual leave entitlement is calculated pro rata to the full leave year. Under the terms of the Working Time Regulations (Northern Ireland) 1998 entitlement to statutory leave for part years is proportionate to the amount of leave year that the employee works.

Holidays and Holiday Pay

Entitlement to holidays and holiday pay for most workers is determined by their contract of employment subject to the minimum conditions of the Working Time Regulations (Northern Ireland) 1998. Most employees have the statutory right to receive from their employers a written statement of employment details; although not a contract in itself this statement provides evidence of many of the terms of the contract. These must include provisions relating to holidays, including public holidays and holiday pay.

Restrictions on Taking Holidays

Restrictions on the taking of annual leave may be stated in the contract of employment, implied from custom and practice or incorporated into individual contracts from a collective agreement between the employer and trade unions.

Maternity Leave

Maternity rights are set out in the Employment Relations (Northern Ireland) Order 1996 and the Maternity and Parental Leave Regulations (Northern Ireland) 1999.

- Pregnant employees are entitled to 26 weeks of ordinary maternity leave regardless of length of service:
- Women who have completed 26 weeks service with their employer are entitled to take additional maternity leave commencing at the end of ordinary maternity leave and finishing 29 weeks after the birth.

Fathers are entitled to 2 weeks paid paternity leave, the payments for which can be claimed back from the government.

Parental Leave

Parental leave is a new entitlement to take time off to look after a child or to make arrangements for a child's welfare. Parents may use this entitlement to spend more time with their children and strike a balance between work and family commitments. Employees qualify for this entitlement following one year's service with the employer.

Time Off for Dependants

All employees have the right to take a reasonable period of time off work to deal with an emergency involving a dependant and not be victimised or dismissed for doing so.

Disability Issues

Issues relating to disability are legislated for under the Disability Discrimination Act 1995 which makes it unlawful to discriminate against disabled persons in connection with employment, the provision of goods, facilities and services or the disposal or management of premises. For businesses and organisations it is unlawful to treat disabled people less favourably than other people for a reason related to their disability (December 1996). Organisations are required to make reasonable adjustments for disabled people, such as providing extra help or making changes to the way they provide their services (October 1999) and may have to make reasonable adjustments to the physical features of their premises to overcome physical barriers to access (2004).

European Directives Impacting on Employment in Northern Ireland

Directive Implementing the Principle of Equal Treatment Between Persons Irrespective of Racial or Ethnic Origin (The Race Directive)

The Race Directive was formally adopted on 29 July 2000, to be implemented by member states by 19 July 2003. The Directive prohibits both direct and indirect discrimination on grounds of race or ethnic origin.

Framework Directive on Equal Treatment in Employment and Occupation

The purpose of this Directive is to implement in member states the principle of equal treatment in respect of access to employment of all persons, regardless of their age, sexual orientation, religion, belief or disability.

Draft EU Directive on Information and Consultation at the National Level (the National Works Council Directive)

The purpose of this directive is to set out minimum requirements for the right to information and consultation of employees.

Directive on Fixed Term Work

This directive was introduced with the aim of preventing fixed term employees being treated less favourably than employees on permanent or "continuing" contracts.

Other Regulation of Business in Northern Ireland

Introduction

In addition to the regulation of fundamental business concerns such as employment, taxation and governance, businesses are subject to extensive regulation in many other areas.
Depending on the nature of the business being started it may be affected by legislation and regulations regarding:

- Planning and Building Control;
- Health and safety;
- Fire precautions;
- Environmental protection;
- Intellectual property;
- Fair trading;
- Data protection;
- Licensing;
- Insurance.

Planning Permission, Buildings/Premises

All development activity on a site or premises is subject to planning regulations overseen by the Planning Service. This can include as small a matter as installation of external signage right through to refurbishment and new build. The Planning Service has a network of regional offices (these are listed in Chapter 3).
In addition to planning authorisations all developments require building control approvals. Building control is a function of the Department of the Environment with local offices organised through local councils.
Further information is available from the Building Control department of the relevant local authority.

Health and Safety

Company directors are responsible for the effect their business may have on the health and safety of employees and members of the public and may need to register with the Health & Safety Executive (HSE) or Local Authority. Further information is available from the Health and Safety Executive. Depending on the activities a company is engaged in and the extent of the danger it may present to staff and the public there are exacting procedures, which are legally binding. Larger businesses are required to produce a Health and Safety Policy statement.

Health & Safety Executive for Northern Ireland (HSENI)
83 Ladas Drive, Belfast BT6 9FR
Tel: 028 9024 3249 / Fax: 028 9023 5383
Web: www.hseni.gov.uk

Fire Precautions

All business premises are required to have adequate levels of protection against fire hazard. This includes the installation (and regular checking) of equipment such as fire extinguishers and blankets. Staff should be trained in necessary action to combat fire - a clear fire drill should be established and in larger premises a fire alarm system must be installed. Certain businesses may require a fire certificate, particularly if the business is a guest house, hotel or residential nursing home.

Environmental Protection

There are environmental regulations that may apply to a business if it:

- Uses refrigeration or air-conditioning equipment, fire equipment or solvents for cleaning;
- Produces, imports, exports, stores, transports, treats, disposes of or recovers waste;
- Produces, imports or exports packaging;
- Produces packaging waste.

For more information contact:
Tel: 028 9054 0540
Web: www.ehsni.gov.uk
Email: ehs@doeni.gov.uk

Department of Environment contacts are set out overleaf:

Environmental Protection

Headquarters, Calvert House, 23 Castle Place, Belfast BT1 1FY
Tel: 028 9025 4754

Information and Education

Commonwealth House, 35 Castle Street, Belfast BT1 1GU
Tel: 028 9054 6533

Industrial Pollution & Radiochemical

Inspectorate, Calvert House, 23 Castle Place, Belfast BT1 1FY
Tel: 028 9025 4754

Intellectual Property

'Intellectual property' describes things such as business names, patents and inventions. Businesses should protect their own company name and logo, along with any inventions, product designs or copyrights and must also respect other people's intellectual property rights. The Patent Office can provide useful information and advice.
Tel: 08459 500 505.
Web: www.patent.gov.uk
Web: www.intellectual-property.gov.uk

Fair Trading

The Office of Fair Trading (OFT) is responsible for protecting consumers by promoting effective competition, removing trading malpractice and publishing appropriate guidance. The OFT also issues consumer credit licences. More information is available by contacting The Office of Fair Trading:
Web: www.oft.gov.uk or
Tel: 08457 224499.
Email: enquiries@oft.gsi.gov.uk

Data Protection

Where a business involves keeping detailed information about people, there are regulations governing the type of information which is kept and how it is used or shared under the Data Protection Act 1998. There is a requirement to register if such detailed or private information is held on computer. Further information is available from:
Data Protection Office
Tel: 01625 545745
Web: www.informationcommissioner.gov.uk

Licensing

Most business sectors are specifically regulated and participants are often individually licensed to engage in particular activities. A licence is required for many businesses, not just casinos or public houses. For example, a licence is required to run a hotel, a guesthouse, or a mobile shop. Companies should always check whether the business requires a licence to trade.

Insurance

Employers' Liability Insurance

All employers are required to take out Employers' Liability Insurance to cover the consequences of possible accidents in the workplace. The lower limit for cover is £5m. Depending on the nature of the business directors or staff may also wish to investigate personal indemnity insurance.

A valid certificate of Public Liability Insurance should be displayed at each business premises and should be retained even after it expires. This insurance should cover all employees, including contract staff and casual workers.

Public Liability Insurance

While not a legal requirement, public liability insurance covers damages payments and any legal costs to members of the public for death or injury caused on business premises or as a result of business activities.

Professional Indemnity Insurance

Professional Indemnity Insurance cover protects firms which provide advice in a professional capacity eg as a managment or IT consultanct. If a business is proved to have been negligent in the professional advice it has given, professional indemnity insurance offers cover against damages.

A list of Northern Ireland's leading insurance companies is included in the business services listings, which follow later in this chapter.

Sources of Support for Business

Invest Northern Ireland

In 2002 a new agency, Invest Northern Ireland was established to co-ordinate industrial development efforts. Professor Fabian Monds has been appointed as Chairman and Leslie Morrison is the Chief Executive who is responsible to the board for the day to day management of the organisation.
The agency falls under the auspices of the Department of Enterprise, Trade and Investment, which is the principal department responsible for providing business support for the private sector in Northern Ireland.

Invest Northern Ireland
64 Chichester Street, Belfast BT1 4JX
Tel: 028 9023 9090 / Fax: 028 9054 0490
Email: info@investni.com
Web: www.investni.com

Invest Northern Ireland
Upper Galwally, Belfast, BT8 6TB
Tel: 028 9023 9090 / Fax: 028 9049 0490

Invest Northern Ireland
17 Antrim Road, Lisburn BT28 3AL
Tel: 028 9023 9090 / Fax: 028 9049 0490

Invest Northern Ireland was formed to draw together the activities previously carried out by the Industrial Development Board (IDB), Local Enterprise Development Unit (LEDU), Industrial Research and Technology Unit (IRTU), and certain functions of the Northern Ireland Tourist Board (NITB) and the Business Support Division of the DET&I. It operates under an independant board, the chairman is responsible to the Minister for Enterprise, Trade and Investment . Invest Northern Ireland's mission is "to accelerate the development in Northern Ireland, applying expertise and resources to encourage innovation and achieve business success, increasing opportunity for all within a renewed culture of enterprise".

Invest Northern Ireland Local Offices

North Western Local Office

13 Shipquay Street, Londonderry, BT48 6DJ
Tel: 028 7126 7257 / Fax: 028 7126 6054

Science Innovation Centre
Cromore Road, Coleraine, BT52 1ST
Tel: 028 7028 0055

Email: nwlo@investni.com
Manager: Kevin Helferty

North Eastern Local Office

Clarence House, 86 Mill Street, Ballymena BT43 5AF
Tel: 028 2564 9215 / Fax: 028 2564 8427
Email: nelo@investni.com
Manager: George McKinney

Southern Local Office

6-7 The Mall, Newry BT34 1BX
Tel: 028 3026 2955 / Fax: 028 3026 5358

Upper Bann Institute (Portadown Campus)
36 Lurgan Road, Portadown, BT63 5BL
Tel: 028 3833 5050

Email: slo@investni.com
Regional Manager: Mark Bleakney

Western Local Office

Kelvin Buildings, 47 Kelvin Avenue, Omagh BT78 1ER
Tel: 028 8224 5763 / Fax: 028 8224 4291

The INTEC Centre
36 East Bridge Street, Enniskillen, BT74 7BS
Tel: 028 6634 3942

Email: wlo@investni.com
Manager: Patricia Devine

Organisation Structure of Invest Northern Ireland

Business International

Managing Director: Leslie Ross: Tel: 028 9064 5304

Director of International Sales and Marketing: Colin Lewis
Tel: 028 9054 5330

Director of International Health Technologies and Consumer Products: Ian Murphy: Tel: 028 9054 5322

Director of International Electronics and Industrial Products: Derek Lynn: Tel: 028 90545324

Director of International ICT: Tel: 028 9054 5123

The Business International Directorate is responsible for inward investment and global indigenous companies. Through its network of offices throughout Europe, including Great Britain, North America and Asia Pacific, Invest Northern Ireland works with overseas companies to help identify investment opportunities, source data and set up reconnaissance visits.

Entrepreneurship and Enterprise

Managing Director: Prof Terri Scott: Tel: 028 9082 8092
Director of Local Economic Development Including Property: Graham Davis: Tel: 028 9049 0552
Director of Enterprise Support: Kevin McCann
Tel: 028 9049 0576
Director of Entrepreneurship and Start Up Sector: Vacant

The Entrepreneurship and Enterprise Directorate is responsible for pre-existing LEDU companies, indigenous IDB client companies and NITB client companies.

Innovation and Capability Development Services

Managing Director: Tracy Meharg: Tel: 028 9054 5101
Director of Innovation, Research and Technology:
Diarmuid McClean: Tel: 028 9262 3151
Director of Trade Development Services: Alan Hingston
Tel: 028 9055 9203

Director of Business Improvement Services: Victor Jordan
Tel: 028 9054 4859

Director of Knowledge Management: Tel: 028 9062 3056

The Innovation and Capability Development Services Directorate is responsible for research and development, business development programmes, the former business support division of the T&EA and e-commerce initiatives including the Information Age initiative.

Corporate Services

Managing Director: Chris Buckland: Tel: 028 9064 4873

Director of HR and Internal Communications
Tel: 028 9054 4889

Director of Finance: Alan Neville: Tel: 028 9082 8038

Director of Investment Appraisal: Charles Harding
Tel: 028 9054 5369

Director of Strategic Management and Planning:
Lawson McDonald
Tel: 028 9054 5299

Head of ICT and e-business: Vacant

Corporate Communications: Rosie Clarke
Tel: 028 9054 5194

The Corporate Services Directorate is responsible for corporate affairs and administration.

Business Start Up Assistance, Grant and Funding Opportunities

Support for Start Up Business

As well as providing advice and assistance on every aspect of setting up a business in Northern Ireland, Invest Northern Ireland also maintains a portfolio of land pre-approved for development and a range of property available for immediate leasing.

Also available is a package of financial incentives, recruitment and training support customized to each company's needs. This can include:

- Tax free capital grant of up to 50% on buildings and equipment;
- Employment grant as each new worker is recruited;
- R&D grants up to 50 per cent for innovative market led products and processes;
- Rent grants;
- Access to share capital and loans on commercial terms;
- A total recruitment and selection service at no extra cost;
- Training grants of up to 50% of eligible training costs;
- Free pre-employment training.

A list of business support programmes operated by or through Invest Northern Ireland is available from all Invest NI offices.

Cross Border Business Support Initiatives

As well as support for business development in Northern Ireland there is considerable assistance available to companies wishing to operate on a cross-border basis.

International Fund for Ireland Initiatives

Contact: Rodney Bair
Tel: 028 9076 8832.
Business Enterprise and Technology Programme

The programme aims to promote the development of new products, identify new market opportunities, and encourage partnerships, alliances and joint ventures.

Initiatives include:

- The North American Partnership, which develops linkages between Irish Southern border firms and US companies;
- The American Business Internship Programme (AMBIT);
- The Ron Brown programme of intensive management training in the US;
- The Research and Development between Ireland and North America or Europe (RADIANE).

Peace II

The European Union has allocated substantial funding for the purposes of helping sustain the "peace" in Northern Ireland including a number of economic measures. The funding known as "Peace II" covers a range of initiatives and is administered overall by the Special EU Programmes Body and a number of other intermediary bodies including Co-operation Ireland. Details on the funding available under the Peace II initiative are to be found in Chapter 9.

Inter*Trade*Ireland

The Old Gasworks Business Park
Kilmorey Street
Newry, BT34 2DE
Tel: 028 3083 4100
Fax: 028 3083 4155
Email: info@intertradeireland.com
Web: www.intertradeireland.com

Chief Executive
Liam Nellis

Inter*Trade*Ireland was established in 1999 as part of the Belfast Agreement between the Government of Ireland and the Government of the United Kingdom of Great Britain and Northern Ireland. Inter*Trade*Ireland's mission is to expand cross-border trade and business on the island of Ireland.

Inter*Trade*Ireland provides a range of funding opportunities and business support initiatives on a cross-border basis. Some of the programmes administered by Inter*Trade*Ireland include:

Acumen: Concentrates on stimulating cross-border trade by assisting SMEs North and South by providing tailored consultancy and sales salary support.

Focus: An all-island sales and marketing initiative emphasising the promotion of all-island trade - identifying new market opportunities and delivering cross-border sales.

Go Source (www.Go-Source.com): An online directory aimed at suppliers interested in tackling the all-island €13bn public procurement market.

Supplier Education Programme: Provides guidance to SMEs in Northern Ireland and the Republic in the area of bidding for and servicing public sector contracts.

Other Sources of Support

Belfast First Stop Business Shop Ltd

14 Wellington Place
Belfast, BT1 6GE
Tel: 028 9027 8399
Fax: 028 9027 8398
Email: info@firststopshop.co.uk
Web: www.firststopshop.co.uk

The First Stop Shop provides a free information, advisory and signposting service for potential and existing businesses.

Services Include:

- Business Information
- Advice & Counselling
- Assistance with Market Research
- Health & Safety Advice
- Signposting to further sources of help.

Local Enterprise Agencies

Belfast

Argyle Business Centre Ltd
39 North Howard Street
Belfast BT13 2AP
Tel: 028 90 233777
Fax: 028 90 313446
Email: admin1@abc-ni.co.uk
Web: www.abc-ni.co.uk
Manager: Frank Hamill

Brookfield Business Centre
333 Crumlin Road, Belfast, BT14 7EA
Tel: 028 9074 5241
Fax: 028 9074 8025
Email: bob.mcneill@brookfieldcampus.com
Web: www.flaxtrust.com
Manager: Bob McNeill

Castlereagh Enterprises Ltd
Dundonald Enterprise Park
Enterprise Drive, Carrowreagh Road
Belfast, BT16 1QT
Tel: 028 9055 7557
Fax: 028 9055 7558
Email: enterprise@castlereagh.com
Web: www.castlereagh.com
Manager: Jack McComisky

East Belfast Enterprise
308 Albertbridge Road
Belfast BT5 4GX
Tel: 028 9045 5450
Fax: 028 9073 2600
Email: info@eastbelfast.org
Web: www.eastbelfast.org
Manger: Roisin Boyle

Farset Enterprise Park Ltd
638 Springfield Road, Belfast BT12 7DY
Tel: 028 9024 2373
Fax: 028 9043 8967
Web: www.farset.com
Manager: William Bradley

Glenwood Enterprise Ltd
Glenwood Business Centre
Springbank Industrial Estate, Poleglass
Belfast BT17 0QL
Tel: 028 9061 0311
Fax: 028 9060 0929
Email: office@glenwoodbc.com
Web: www.glenwoodbc.com
Manager: Eamon Foster

Investment Belfast

INVESTMENT
BELFAST

Investment Belfast Ltd
Fifth Floor
40 Linenhall Street
Belfast, BT2 8BA
Tel: +44 (0)28 9033 1136
Fax: +44 (0)28 9033 1137
Website: www.investmentbelfast.com

Belfast's business development and investment company. A partnership between the city's business and political leaders which aims to improve the image of the City, encourage innovation and entrepreneurship and support business growth.

Laganside Corporation
Clarendon Building
15 Clarendon Road
Belfast, BT1 3BG
Tel: 028 90 328507
Fax: 028 90 332141
Email: info@laganside.com
Web: www.laganside.com
Chief Executive: Kyle Alexander

North City Business Centre Ltd
2 Duncairn Gardens, Belfast, BT15 2GG
Tel: 028 9074 7470
Fax: 028 9074 6565
Email: mailbox@north-city.org
Web: www.north-city.co.uk
Centre Manager: Michael McCorry

Ormeau Enterprises Ltd
8 Cromac Avenue, Belfast, BT7 2JA
Tel: 028 9033 9906
Fax: 028 9033 9937
Email: info@ormeaubusinesspark.com
Web: www.ormeaubusinesspark.com
Development Officer: Patricia McNeill

ORTUS:
The West Belfast Enterprise Board
Twin Spires Centre
155 Northumberland Street
Belfast, BT13 2JF
Tel: 028 9031 1002
Fax: 028 9031 1005
Email: hq@ortus.org
Web: www.ortus.org
Manager: Sean Toal

Townsend Enterprise Park Ltd
28 Townsend Street, Belfast, BT13 2ES
Tel: 028 9089 4500
Fax: 028 9089 4502
Email: admin@townsend.co.uk
Web: www.townsend.co.uk
Manager: George Briggs

Westlink Enterprise Limited
Westlink Enterprise Centre
30-50 Distillery Street
Belfast, BT12 5BJ
Tel: 028 90 331549
Fax: 028 90 330803
Email: hq@ortus.org
Web: www.ortus.org
Manager: Sean Toal

Work West Enterprise Agency
Work West, 301 Glen Road
Belfast, BT11 8BU
Tel: 028 9061 0826
Fax: 028 9062 2001
Email: c.ferris@workwest.co.uk
Web: www.workwest.co.uk
Manager: Claire Ferris

Co Antrim

Acorn the Business Centre
2 Riada Avenue, Garryduff Road
Ballymoney, BT53 7LH
Tel: 028 2766 6133
Fax: 028 2766 5019
Email: ballymoney.ec@btinternet.com
Manager: Bobby Farren

Antrim Enterprise Agency
58 Greystone Road, Antrim, BT41 1JZ
Tel: 028 9446 7774
Fax: 028 9446 7292
Email: aea@zetnet.co.uk
Web: www.antrimenterprise.com
Manager: Jennifer McWilliams

Ballymena Business Development Centre Ltd
Galgorm Industrial Estate
62 Fenaghy Road
Ballymena, BT42 1FL
Tel: 028 2565 8616
Fax: 028 630 830
Web: www.bbdc.co.uk
Manager: Melanie Christie

Carrickfergus Enterprise Agency Ltd (CEAL)
8 Meadowbank Road
Carrickfergus, BT38 8YF
Tel: 028 9336 9528
Fax: 028 9336 9979
Email: info@ceal.co.uk
Web: www.ceal.co.uk
Business Development Officer:
Kelli Bagchus

Larne Enterprise Development Co (LEDCOM)
Ledcom Industrial Estate
Bank Road, Larne, BT40 3AW
Tel: 028 2827 0742
Fax: 028 2827 5653
Email: info@ledcom.org
Web: www.ledcom.org
Chief Executive: Ken Nelson

Lisburn Enterprise Organisation Ltd
Enterprise Crescent, Ballinderry Road
Lisburn, BT28 2BP
Tel: 028 9266 1160
Fax: 028 9260 3084
Email: centre@lisburn-enterprise.co.uk
Web: www.lisburn-enterprise.co.uk
Chief Executive: Aisling Owens

Mallusk Enterprise Park Ltd
2 Mallusk Drive
Newtownabbey, BT36 4GN
Tel: 028 9083 8860
Fax: 028 9084 1525
Email: mepark.co.uk
Web: www.mep@btinternet.com
Chief Executive: Melanie Humphrey

Moyle Enterprise Co Ltd
61 Leyland Rd, Ballycastle, BT54 6EZ
Tel: 028 2076 3737
Fax: 028 2076 9690
Email: enquiries@moyle-enterprise.com
Web: www.moyle-enterprise.com
Manager: Vacant

Co Armagh

Armagh Business Centre Ltd
2 Loughgall Road, Armagh, BT61 7NJ
Tel: 028 3752 5050
Fax: 028 3752 6717
Email: info@abcarmagh.com
Web: www.abcarmagh.com
Manager: Tracy Gale

Brownlow Ltd
Office 2, 1st Floor Legahory Centre
Brownlow, Craigavon, BT65 5BE
Tel: 028 3834 4908
Web: www.brownlowltd.co.uk
Manager: Mr Scott

Craigavon Industrial Development Organisation Ltd (CIDO)
Carn Industrial Estate
Craigavon, BT63 5RH
Tel: 028 3833 3393
Fax: 028 3835 0390
Email: mail@cido.co.uk
Chief Executive: Jim Smith

CIDO Business Complex
Charles St, Lurgan, BT66 6HG
Tel: 028 3834 7020
Fax: 028 3834 7052
Chief Executive: Jim Smith

Crossmaglen Community Enterprises Ltd
1 Castleblaney Road, Crossmaglen
Tel: 028 3086 1354

Keady Business Centre Ltd
10 Annvale Road
St Patrick's Street, Keady, BT60 2RP
Tel: 028 3753 9603
Fax: 028 3753 1467
Manager:

Mayfair Business Centre Ltd
193-205 Garvaghy Road
Portadown, BT62 1HA
Tel: 028 3839 1666
Fax: 028 3839 1586
Manager: Michael McCooe

Co Londonderry

Coleraine Enterprise Agency Ltd
Unit 3-5, Loughanhill Industrial Estate
Coleraine, BT52 2NR
Tel: 028 7035 6318
Fax: 028 7035 5464
Email: info@coleraine-enterprise.co.uk
Web: www.coleraine-enterprise.co.uk
Manager: Ray Young

Creggan Enterprises Ltd
Rath More Centre, Blighs Lane
Londonderry, BT48 0LZ
Tel: 028 7137 3170
Fax: 028 7137 3440
Chairperson: Anne Molloy

Dunamanagh & District Community Association Ltd
2a Lisnarragh Road
Dunamanagh, BT82 0QL
Tel: 028 7139 7097
Email: ddca@dunamanagh.freeserve.co.uk
Business Manager: Albert Allen

Enterprise Northwest
Northwest Marketing
16C Queen Street
Londonderry, BT48 7EQ
Tel: 028 7137 1867
Fax: 028 7137 1938
Email: info@north-westmarketing.com
Chief Executive: John McGowan

Eurocentre West Ltd
Unit 25b, Pennyburn Industrial Estate
Buncrana Road
Londonderry, BT48 0LU
Tel: 028 7136 4015
Fax: 028 7126 6032
Email: fdecw@aol.com
Contact: Denis Feeney

Glenshane Business Park
50 Legavallon Rd
Dungiven, BT47 4QL
Tel: 028 7774 2494
Fax: 028 7774 2393
Manager: M Kelly

Glenshane Enterprise Centre
414A Ballyquinn Rd
Dungiven, BT47 4NQ
Tel: 028 7774 2494
Contact: Tony McCall

Limavady Small Business Centre
Aghanloo Industrial Estate
Aghanloo Road, Limavady, BT49 0HE
Tel: 028 7776 5655
Fax: 028 7776 5707
Web: www.lysba.com
Manager: Martin Devlin

Maghera Development Association
10b Coleraine Rd, Maghera, BT46 5BN
Tel: 028 7964 5425
Fax: 028 7964 5425

Noribic Ltd
North West Institute for Further & Higher Education
Strand Road, Londonderry, BT48 7BY
Email: noribic@nwifhe.ac.uk
Web: www.noribic.com
Chief Executive: Barney Toal

Roe Valley Enterprises Ltd
Aghanloo Industrial Estate
Aghanloo Road, Limavady, BT49 0HE
Tel: 028 7776 2323
Fax: 028 7776 5707
Email: info@roevalleyenterprises.com
Manager: Martin Devlin

Workspace (Draperstown) Ltd
The Business Centre, 7 Tobermore Road
Draperstown, BT45 7AG
Tel: 028 7962 8113
Fax: 028 7962 8975
Email: info@workspace.co.uk
Web: www.workspace.org.uk
Chief Executive: Brian Murray

Co Down

Ards Business Centre Ltd
Jubilee Rd, Newtownards, BT23 4YH
Tel: 028 9181 9787
Fax: 028 91 820625
Email: info@ardsbusiness.co.uk
Web: www.ardsbusiness.co.uk
Chief Executive: Margaret Patterson

Banbridge District Enterprises Ltd
Scarva Road Industrial Estate
Banbridge, BT32 3QD
Tel: 028 4066 2260
Fax: 028 4066 2325
Email: info@bdelonline.com
Web: www.bdelonline.com
Manager: Ciaran Cunningham

Banbridge Enterprise Centre

Down Business Centre
46 Belfast Road
Downpatrick, BT30 9UP
Tel: 028 44 616416
Fax: 028 44 616419
Email: business@downbc.co.uk
Web: www.downbc.co.uk
Chief Executive: Joe McCoubrey

Newry and Mourne Enterprise Agency
Enterprise House, Win Business Park
Canal Quay, Newry, BT35 6PH
Tel: 028 3026 7011
Fax: 028 3026 1316
Email: info@nmea.net
Web: www.nmea.net
Chief Executive: Conor Patterson

North Down Development Organisation Ltd
Enterprise House, Balloo Avenue
Balloo Industrial Estate
Bangor, BT19 7QT
Tel: 028 9127 1525
Fax: 028 9127 0080
Email: mail@nddo.u-net.com
Web: www.nndo.u-net.com
Chief Executive: Lynne Vance

Stranney Enterprises
35 Ballylucas Road
Downpatrick, BT30 8AZ
Tel: 028 4461 4445
Manager: Stephen Stranney

Co Fermanagh

Belcoo Enterprise Ltd
Railway Road
Belcoo, BT93 5FJ
Tel: 028 66 386536
Fax: 028 66 386377
Chairman: Harold Johnston

Fermanagh Enterprise Ltd
Enniskillen Business Centre
Lackaghboy Industrial Estate
Tempo Rd, Enniskillen, BT74 4RL
Tel: 028 6632 3117
Fax: 028 6632 7878
Web: www.fermanaghenterprise.com
Manager: John Treacey

(ITEC) Irvinestown Trustee Enterprise Co
Irvinestown Business Park
Market Yard, Mill St
Irvinestown, BT94 1GR
Tel: 028 6862 1977
Fax: 028 6862 8414
Manager: Jenny Irvine

Kesh Development Association
Mantlin Road, Kesh, BT93 1TU
Tel: 028 6863 2158
Fax: 028 6863 2635
Email: dev@kesh.org.uk
Manager: Glenn Moore

Lisnaskea Community Enterprise
Drumbrughas North
Lisnaskea, BT92 0PE
Tel: 028 6772 1081
Fax: 028 6772 1088
Manager: Brian Cosgrove

Rosslea Enterprises Ltd
Rosslea Enterprise Centre
Liskilly
Rosslea, BT92 7FH
Tel: 028 6775 1851
Contact: Jane Collins

South West Fermanagh Development Organisation Ltd
Teemore Business Complex
Teemore, BT92 9BL
Tel: 028 6774 8893
Fax: 028 6774 8493
Email: teemorecomplex@hotmail.com
Web: www.shannon-erne.co.uk
General Manager: James McBarron

Co Tyrone

Castlederg and District Enterprises
Drumquin Road
Castlederg, BT81 7PX
Tel: 028 8167 0414
Fax: 028 8167 0731
Director: Gerald Sproule

Coalisland and District Development Association Ltd
51 Dungannon Rd
Coalisland, BT71 4HP
Tel: 028 8774 7215
Fax: 028 8774 8695
Chief Executive: Pat McGirr

Cookstown Enterprise Centre Ltd
Derryloran Industrial Estate
Sandholes Road
Cookstown, BT80 9LU
Tel: 028 8676 3660
Fax: 028 8676 3160
Web: www.cookstownenterprise.com
Chief Executive: Jim Eastwood

Dungannon Enterprise Centre Ltd
2 Coalisland Road, Dungannon, BT71 6JT
Tel: 028 8772 3489
Fax: 028 8775 2200
Email: brian@dungannonenterprise.com
Web: www.dungannonenterprise.com
Centre Manager: Brian McAuley

Omagh Enterprise Co Ltd
Gortrush Industrial Estate
Great Northern Road
Omagh, BT78 5LB
Tel: 028 8224 9494
Fax: 028 8224 9451
Email: info@oecl.co.uk
Manager: Nicholas O'Shiel

Strabane Industrial Enterprise Agency
Strabane Enterprise Agency
Orchard Road , Strabane, BT82 9FR
Tel: 028 7138 2518
Fax: 028 7188 4531
Email: seagency@aol.com
Chief Executive: Christina Mullen

Other Sources of Business Support

Prince's Trust

Block 5, Jennymount Court
North Derby Street
Belfast, BT15 3HN
Tel: 028 9074 5454
Fax: 028 9074 8416

The Prince's Trust offers support and guidance to young people, aged between 14-30 who may be interested in starting their own business.

Northern Ireland Business Start Programme

The Northern Ireland Business Start Programme provides a package of support to anyone interested in setting up a business. The Programme has three key components:

Business advisory service – provides the services of an expert business advisor on a one-to-one basis.

Training course - comprises 10 modules focused particularly on sales and marketing, financial management, legal and statutory issues, ICT and general business practices.

Financial planning service – explores all potential sources of funding including access to programme grant support and small business loans which are available under the programme.

For further information on the Northern Ireland Business Start Programme contact any Local Enterprise Agency. Full list of Local Enterprise Agencies is included in this chapter, beginning at page 30.

Business Services Listings

What follows below are listings of business services providers. They inlude: Legal Advisors, Economic and Financial Advisors, IT Consultants, Recruitment Agencies and several other categories of service providers.

Legal Advisors

Arthur Cox
Capital House, 3 Upper Queen Street
Belfast, BT1 6PU
Tel: 028 9023 0007

Bernard Campbell & Co Solicitors
91-93 Victoria Street, Belfast, BT1 4PB
Tel: 028 9023 2008

Bigger & Strahane Solicitors
Sinclair House, 89 Royal Avenue
Belfast, BT1 1EX
Tel: 028 9032 5229

C&H Jefferson Solicitors
Norwich Union House
7 Fountain Street
Belfast, BT1 5EA
Tel: 028 9032 9545

Campbell Stafford Solicitors
41 Fitzwilliam Street, University Road
Belfast, BT9 6AW
Tel: 028 9023 0808

Carson Mc Dowell Solicitors
Murray House, Murray Street
Belfast, BT1 6DN
Tel: 028 9024 4951

Cleavar Black
54 Lisburn Road, Belfast, BT9 6AF
Tel: 028 9032 2904

Cleaver Fulton Rankin
50 Bedford Street
Belfast, BT2 7FW
Tel: 028 90243141

Comerton & Hill
8th Floor
14 Great Victoria Street
Belfast, BT2 7BA
Tel: 028 9023 4629

Cooper Wilkinson
Imperial Buildings
38-40 Queen Elizabeth Road
Enniskillen, BT74 7BY
Tel: 028 6632 2615

Culbert & Martin Solicitors
7 Donegall Square West
Belfast, BT1 6JH
Tel: 028 9032 5508

Cunningham & Dickey Solicitors
68 Upper Church Lane
Belfast, BT1 4LG
Tel: 028 9024 5896

Deery McGuinness & Co Solicitors
179-181 Victoria Street
Belfast, BT1 4PE
Tel: 028 9023 3268

Desmond J Doherty & Co
Clarendon Chambers
7 Clarendon Street
Londonderry, BT48 7EP
Tel: 028 7128 8870

Diamond Heron Solicitors
Diamond House
7-19 Royal Avenue
Belfast, BT1 1FB
Tel: 028 9024 3726

Donnelly & Kinder
Claims Exchange Building
11 Victoria Street
Belfast, BT1 3GA
Tel: 028 9024 4999

Donnelly & Wall
58-60 Upper Arthur Street
Belfast, BT1 4GP
Tel: 0289023 3157

Edwards & Co
28 Hill Street
Belfast, BT1 2LA
Tel: 028 9032 1863

EJ Lavery & Co Solicitors
1-3 Hightown Road
Glengormley, BT36 7TZ
Tel: 028 9084 3436

Elliott Duffy Garrett
34 Upper Queen Street
Belfast, BT1 6FD
Tel: 028 9024 5034

Falls & Hanna
123 Main Street
Fivemiletown, BT75 0PG
Tel: 028 8952 1234

Flynn & McGettrick
9 Clarence Street
Belfast, BT2 8DX
Tel: 028 9024 4212

Francis Hanna & Co
75-77 May Street
Belfast, BT1 3JL
Tel: 028 9024 3901

Francis J Irvine & Company Solicitors
86 Great Victoria Street
Belfast, BT2 7BD
Tel: 028 9024 6451

Hewitt & Gilpin
14-16 James Street South
Belfast, BT2 7GA
Tel: 028 9057 3573

IJ Warren & Co
Imperial Buildings
72 High Street
Belfast, BT1 2BE
Tel: 028 9024 9920

James Doran & Co Solicitors
19-21 Cornmarket
Belfast, BT1 4DB
Tel: 028 9024 0440

JG O'Hare & Co Solicitors
St George's Building
37-41 High Street
Belfast, BT1 2AB
Tel: 028 9023 4800

Jones & Company Solicitors
Scottish Provident Building
7 Donegall Square West
Belfast, BT1 6JF
Tel: 028 9024 5471

Keenan Solicitors
54 Knockbreda Road
Belfast, BT6 0JB
Tel: 028 9049 3349

L'Estrange & Brett
Arnott House
12-16 Bridge Street
Belfast, BT1 1LS
Tel: 028 90230426

McCartan & Co Solicitors
83 Victoria Street
Belfast, BT1 4PB
Tel: 028 9033 2303

McCartan Turkington Breen Solicitors
Chancery House
88 Great Victoria Street
Belfast, BT1 3GN
Tel: 028 9032 9801

McCreery Turkington Stockman
Stockman House
39-43 Bedford Street
Belfast, BT2 7EE
Tel: 028 9032 3040

Mills Selig Solicitors
21 Arthur Street
Belfast, BT1 4GA
Tel: 028 9024 3878

Morgan & Murphy Solicitors
1st Floor
42 Castle Street
Belfast, BT1 1HB
Tel: 028 9024 4545

Murphy & O'Rawe Solicitors
Scottish Provident Building
7 Donegall Square West
Belfast, BT1 6JF
Tel: 028 9032 6626

O'Reilly Stewart Solicitors
114-116 Royal Avenue
Belfast, BT1 1DL
Tel: 028 9032 1000

Paschal J O'Hare Solicitors
Donegall House
98-102 Donegall Street
Belfast, BT1 2GW
Tel: 028 9031 3613

Rosemary Connolly Solicitors
2 The Square
Warrenpoint, BT34 3JT
Tel: 028 4175 3121

Tughans Solicitors
30 Victoria Street
Belfast, BT1 3GS
Tel: 028 9055 3300

Wilson-Nesbitt Solicitors
Citylink Business Park
Durham Street
Belfast, BT12 4HB
Tel: 028 9032 3864

Economic & Financial Advisors

Accountants

Adrian Hall & Co.
4th Floor, Franklin House
12 Brunswick Street
Belfast
Tel: 028 9032 4250
Web: www.adrianhallco.co.uk

Arthur Boyd & Company
Franklin House,
12 Brunswick Street
Belfast, BT2 7GE
Tel: 028 9032 9255

ASM Horwath
20 Rosemary Street
Belfast, BT1 1QD
Tel: 028 9024 9222
Web: www.asmhorwath.com
Email: asm@asmhorwath.com

BDO Stoy Hayward
Lindsay House
10 Calender Street
Belfast, BT1 5BN
Tel: 028 9043 9009
Fax: 028 9043 9010
Web: www.bdo.co.uk
Email: belfast@bdo.co.uk

Blythe Grace Chartered Accountants
405 Lisburn Road,
Belfast, BT9 7EW
Tel: 028 9066 3111
Email: info@blythegrace.co.uk

Capita Business Services Ltd
425 Holywood Road
Belfast, BT4 2PL
Tel: 028 9076 3910
Fax: 028 9076 1698
Web: www.capitaconsulting.co.uk

Cooper Hassard McClements
32 East Bridge St
Enniskillen, BT74 7BY
Tel: 028 6632 2002

Crawford Sedgwick & Co.
38 Hill Street
Belfast, BT1 2LB
Tel: 028 9032 1731

Deloitte

Deloitte.

19 Bedford Street
Belfast, BT2 7EJ
Tel: 028 9032 2861
Fax: 028 9023 4786
Web: www.deloitte.co.uk

Senior Partner
Paul Clarke

Deloitte is the UK's fastest growing Big 4 professional services firm with over 10,000 staff nationwide and a fee income of £1,228 million in 2002/2003.

Employing more than 140 people locally, Deloitte Belfast provides fully integrated services that include accounting, business advisory, audit, tax, management consulting, corporate finance and reorganisation services, offering our clients the best possible opportunities and services with access to our global capabilities and extensive network. Our clients include local plcs, subsidiaries of global organisations, locally owned businesses and public sector organisations.

FPM Chartered Accountants

Newry Office:
Drumalane Mill
The Quays
Newry
Co Down BT35 8QF
Tel: 028 3026 1010
Fax: 028 3026 2345

Dundalk Office:
FPM Suite
Excelsior House
3 Jocelyn Place
Dundalk Co Louth
Tel: 00 353 42 938 8898
Fax: 00 353 42 938 8899

Web: www.fpmca.com
E-mail: info@fpmca.com

FPM Chartered Accountants is a client-focused practice with specialist skills in accounts preparation, audit, tax planning, business consultancy, stategic planning, corporate finance, financial management, project management and forensic accounting.

Goldblatt McGuigan
Alfred House
19 Alfred Street, Belfast
Tel: 028 9031 1113
Web: www.goldblattmcguigan.com

Grant Thornton
Waterís Edge, Clarendon Dock
Belfast, BT1 3BH
Tel: 028 9031 5500
Fax: 028 9031 4036

Hanna Thompson & Co.
Century House
Enterprise Crescent, Lisburn
Tel: 028 9260 7355

Helm Corporation Ltd
Commercial House, Demesne Court,
88 Main Street, Moira
Tel: 028 9261 0930
Web: www.helm-corp.com
Email: helm@helm-corp.com

Henry Murray & Company
23 Church Place, Lurgan, BT66 6EY
Tel: 028 3832 7744

Johnston Kennedy
18 Orby Link, Castlereagh Road, Belfast
Tel: 028 9070 5333

KPMG
Stokes House, College Square East
Belfast, BT1 6DH
Tel: 028 9024 3377
Fax: 028 9089 3893

M.B. Grady & Co.
52 St.Patrickís Avenue
Downpatrick, BT30 6DS
Tel: 028 44 616321
Web: www.mbmcgrady.co.uk
Email: nfo@mbmcgrady.co.uk

McClureWatters
Thomas House, 14-16 James St South
Belfast, BT2 7GA
Tel: 028 9023 4343
Fax: 028 9043 9077

McElholm & Company
28 Gortin Road, Omagh, BT79 7HX
Tel: 028 8224 4016

McKeague Morgan & Co
40 University Street, Belfast, BT7 1F2
Tel: 028 9024 2612

Moore Stephens
7 Donegall Square West,
Belfast, BT1 6JH
Tel: 028 9032 9481
Fax: 028 9043 9185

Nichol Donnelly & Partners
222 Ormeau Road
Belfast, BT7 2FY
Tel: 028 9064 6262

O'Hare Chartered Accountants
7 John Mitchel Place
Newry, BT34 2BP
Tel: 028 3026 9933

Paul Hagerty and Co
11 The Square
Rostrevor
Co. Down, BT34 3AX
Tel: 028 4173 9340
Fax: 028 4173 9342
Email: info@paulhagerty.co.uk
Web: www.paulhagerty.co.uk

PricewaterhouseCoopers
8 Laganbank Road, Belfast, BT1 3LR
Tel: 028 9024 5454
Web: www.pwc.com

S D Brown & Company
22 Edward Street
Portadown
Craigavon, BT62 3NE
Tel: 028 3833 8913

Stevenson & Wilson
22-30 Broadway Avenue
Ballymena
Tel: 028 2564 7712

Management Consultants

Abacus Partnership
28 Richmond Court
Lisburn, BT27 4QU
Tel: 028 9267 8582

Amicus Partners Ltd
Amicus House
McLean Road
Eglinton, BT47 3PF
Tel: 028 7181 1888

ASM Horwath
20 Rosemary Street
Belfast, BT1 1QD
Tel: 028 9024 9222

Barklie & Logan Management Consultants
8 Cameron Park
Ballymena, BT42 1QJ
Tel: 028 2564 5447

BDO Stoy Hayward Management Consultants
Lindsay House
10 Callender Street
Belfast, BT1 5BN
Tel: 028 9043 9009
Fax: 028 9043 9010

BearingPoint
Stokes House
17-25 College Square East
Belfast, BT1 6DH
Tel: 028 9089 3888

Benmore Management Consultants Ltd
50 Hydepark Manor
Mallusk
Newtownabbey, BT36 4PA
Tel: 028 9083 9613

Blueprint Development Consultancy
Unit 2 Ormeau Business Park
8 Cromac Avenue
Belfast, BT7 2JA
Tel: 028 9024 4115
Fax: 028 9024 2115

CAM Benchmarking Ltd
9 Wellington Park
Belfast, BT9 6DJ
Tel: 028 9066 7722
Fax: 028 9068 3378

Cap Gemini Ernst & Young
33 Clarendon Dock
Laganside
Belfast, BT1 3BW
Tel: 028 9051 1230

Croner Consulting Ireland
3 Wellington Park
Belfast, BT9 6DJ
Tel: 028 9092 3338

DTZ Pieda Consulting
7 Donegall Square West
Belfast, BT1 6JE
Tel: 028 9024 7623
Fax: 028 9024 7632

EPEC
Floral Buildings
2-14 East Bridge Street
Belfast, BT1 3MQ
Tel: 028 9092 3475

Helm Corporation Limited
Commercial House
Demense Court
88 Main Street
Moira, BT67 0LH
Tel: 028 9261 0930
Fax: 028 9061 0931

Key Consulting Group
144 High Street
Holywood, BT18 9HS
Tel: 028 9042 3635

Level Seven
Curlew Pavilion
Portside Business Park
Airport Road West
Belfast, BT3 9ED
Tel: 028 9092 9777

The Management and Leadership Network
Boxmore Buildings
Enterprise Way
Mallusk, BT36 4EW
Tel: 028 9080 4200
Fax: 028 9080 4301

McCann Consulting
30B East Bridge Street
Enniskillen, BT74 7BT
Tel: 028 6632 0443

Merc Partners
12B Clarendon Road
Clarendon Dock
Belfast, BT1 3BG
Tel: 028 9072 5750
Fax: 028 9072 5751

Penna Consulting
405 Holywood Road
Belfast, BT4 2GU
Tel: 028 9076 4700
Fax: 028 9076 4701

PricewaterhouseCoopers
Waterfront Plaza
8 Laganbank Road
Belfast, BT1 3LR
Tel: 028 9024 5454
Fax; 028 9041 5600

SpenglerFox
3rd Floor
Quay Gate House
15 Scrabo Street
Belfast, BT5 4BD
Tel: 028 9055 6000

Vision Management Services
97E Queen Street
Ballymena, BT42 2BE
Tel: 028 2563 9695

Whitewater Consulting
7/313 Belmont Road
Belfast, BT4 2NE
Tel: 028 9076 9520

Financial Advisers/Investment Consultants

Aegis Insurance Services (NI) Ltd
229-235 Upper Newtownards Road
Belfast, BT4 3JF
Tel: 028 9047 2147

Aiken Kennedy Financial Planning
8-10 Graham Gardens
Lisburn, BT28 1XE
Tel: 028 9260 3175

AMG Financial Services
27 Hill Street
Ballymena
BT43 6BH
Tel: 028 2563 1377

Aon McMillen
31 Bedford Street
Belfast, BT2 7FP
Tel: 028 9024 2771
Fax: 028 9031 3644

Belgravia Associates
6 Belgravia Road
Bangor, BT19 6XJ
Tel: 028 9127 0244

Boyce Financial Services
24 High Street
Portadown, BT62 1HJ
Tel: 028 3833 4141

C&S Associates
14 Cromac Place
Belfast, BT7 2JB
Tel: 028 9072 6500

CRN Financial Advisors
20 Stranmillis Road
Belfast, BT9 5AA
Tel: 0289066 0300

Capital Trust Financial Management
Capital House
28 Lodge Road
Coleraine, BT52 1NB
Tel: 028 7035 8500

Census Financial Planning
437 Lisburn Road
Belfast, BT9 7EY
Tel: 028 9066 8700

Financial Solutions
26 Oldtown Street
Cookstown, BT80 8EF
Tel: 028 8676 5900

Forward Financial Planning
18B Newforge Lane
Belfast, BT9 5NW
Tel: 028 9066 4077

Foundation Financial Consulting
Victoria House
2A Newry Road
Banbridge, BT32 3HF
Tel: 028 4062 9966

Halliday Financial Guidance
32 Hamilton Road
Bangor, BT20 4LE
Tel: 028 9147 2634

Hanna Hillen Financial Services
11 Church Square
Banbridge, BT32 4AS
Tel: 028 4066 2848

Homelink Financial Services
61-63 High Street
Bangor , BT20 5BE
Tel: 028 9127 1771

McClure Watters
Thomas House
14-16 James Street South
Belfast, BT2 7GA
Tel: 028 9023 4343

Medical and Dental Financial Management
41 Malone Road
Belfast, BT9 6RX
Tel: 028 9029 0000

Odyssey Financial Planning (Northern Ireland)
Unit 7 Boucher Plaza
4 Boucher Road
Belfast, BT12 6HR
Tel: 028 9024 3921

Pension & Financial Consultants Ltd
Victoria Buildings
41 Belmore Street
Enniskillen, BT74 6AA
Tel: 028 6632 8080

Professional Insurance Advisers
3 Finaghy Road North
Belfast, BT10 0JA
Tel: 028 9028 8877

Stevenson Financial Planning Centre
73 Main Street
Larne, BT40 1HH
Tel: 028 2827 7357

Stockbrokers

BWD Rensburg Investment Management
St Georges House
99-101 High Street
Belfast, BT1 2AG
Tel: 028 9032 1002

Cunningham Coates
19 Donegall Street
Belfast, BT1 2HA
Tel: 028 9032 3456

Edward Jones Ltd
2 Malone Road
Belfast, BT9 5BN
Tel: 028 9068 7715

Redmayne Bentley Stockbrokers
1st Floor
IPL Building Gasworks Business Park
Belfast, BT7 2DJ
Tel: 028 9023 5555

DM Wright
15 The Diamond
Londonderry, BT48 6HS
Tel: 028 7126 3344

Insurance Brokers

Abbey
10 Governor's Place
Carrickfergus, BT38 7BN
Tel: 028 9335 1525
Fax: 028 9336 2509

Allianz Northern Ireland
Allianz House
21 Linenhall Street
Belfast, BT2 8AB
Tel: 028 9089 5600
Web: www.allianz-ni.gov.uk

Aon McMillen
31 Bedford Street
Belfast, BT2 7FP
Tel: 028 9024 2771
Fax: 028 9031 3644

Bartholomew & James
Metropolitan Building
29-31 Alfred Street
Belfast, BT2 8ED
Tel: 028 9024 1651
Fax: 028 9024 0441
Web: www.bartjames.co.uk

CJ Higgins
22 Mallusk Road
Newtownabbey, BT36 4PP
Tel: 028 9083 0830
Web: www.cjhiggins.co.uk

EPJ Morgan Insurance Brokers
29 Mill Street
Newry, BT34 1EY
Tel: 028 3026 5447
Fax: 028 3026 9738

Hughes & Company
Strangford House
4 Jubilee Road
Newtownards, BT23 4WN
Tel: 028 9181 0081
Fax: 028 9181 8842

Marsh Ltd
Bedford House
Bedford Street
Belfast, BT2 7DX
Tel: 028 9055 6100
Fax: 028 9055 6166

Open + Direct
Arnott House
12-16 Bridge Street
Belfast, BT1 1LU
Tel: 08702 470 470

S Rankin & Co
21-23 Bacheloris Walk
Lisburn, BT28 1XJ
Tel: 028 9267 6235
Fax: 028 9267 1289

Wallace Insurance Brokers
Whitehall Chambers
43 New Row
Coleraine, BT52 1AE
Tel: 028 7032 5999
Fax: 028 7034 3641

Willis & Company
News Letter Building
55-59 Donegall Street
Belfast, BT1 2FH
Tel: 028 9032 9042
Fax: 028 9023 2362

Leasing

Agnew Corporate
45 Mallusk Road
Newtownabbey, BT36 4PS
Tel: 028 9080 4408
Fax: 028 9034 1083

Bank of Scotland (Ireland) Limited
10-15 Donegall Square North
Belfast, BT1 5GB
Tel: 028 9044 2600
Fax: 028 9044 2692

Charles Hurst Business Solutions
62 Boucher Road
Belfast, BT12 6LR
Tel: 028 9038 3426
Fax: 028 9038 3425

CVC Direct
PO Box 30
Ballyclare, BT39 0BQ
Tel: 028 9443 2223
Fax: 028 9443 9220

DFC Ltd
380C Belmont Road
Belfast, BT4 2NF
Tel: 028 9076 1669
Fax: 028 9076 9779

Donnelly Fleet
Mallusk Road
Newtownabbey
BT36 4AA
Tel: 028 9084 2000

Fleet Contracts
2 Apollo Road
Boucher Road
Belfast, BT12 6HP
Tel: 028 9066 2000
Fax: 028 9066 1111

Fleet Financial
7 Mallusk Drive
Belfast, BT36 4GX
Tel: 028 9084 9777
Fax: 028 9084 9555

Hertz Lease
Musgrave Business Centre
45 Stockmanís Way
Belfast, BT9 7ET
Tel: 028 9038 1800
Fax: 028 9038 2001

Lo Lease Options
45 Mallusk Road
Newtownabbey
BT36 4PS
Tel: 028 9034 2200

Market Research

Market Research Northern Ireland Ltd (MRNI)
46 Elmwood Avenue
Belfast, BT9 6AZ
Tel: 028 9066 1037
Fax: 028 9068 2007
Web: www.mrni.co.uk
Email: info@mrni.co.uk

Millward Brown Ulster
115 University Street
Belfast, BT7 1HP
Tel: 028 9023 1060
Fax: 028 9024 3887
Web: www.ums-research.com
Email: enquiries@ums-research.com

Mintel
6 Citylink Business Park
Belfast, BT12 4HB
Tel: 028 9024 1849
Fax: 028 9024 2597
Web: www.reports.mintel.com
Email: irelandinfo@mintel.com

MORI-MRC
92-96 Lisburn Road
Belfast, BT9 6AG
Tel: 028 9050 0800
Fax: 028 9050 0801
Web: www.morimrc.ie
Email: info@morimrc.ie

Quadriga Consulting
99 Hillsborough Road
Lisburn, BT28 1JX
Tel: 028 9266 8968
Fax: 028 9266 8971
Web: www.quadrigaconsulting.com
Email: info@quadrigaconsulting.com

RES (Research and Evaluation Services)
City Link Business Park
Albert Street
Belfast, BT12 4HB
Tel: 028 9050 7777
Fax: 028 9050 7779
Web: www.res.nireland.com
Email: info@res.nireland.com

SMR (Social and Market Research)
3 Wellington Park
Belfast, BT9 6DJ
Tel: 028 9092 3362
Fax: 028 9092 3334
Web: www.smresearch.co.uk
Email: info@smresearch.co.uk

IT Consultants

Advance Systems
80-82 Rainey Street
Magherafelt, BT45 5AJ
Tel: 028 8676 7788
Web: www.advance-systems.co.uk
Email: info@ advance-systems.co.uk

Aerial Networks Ltd
16 Carney Hill
Newry, BT34 1GA
Tel: 028 3083 3458
Web: www.aerial-networks.com
Email: info@aerial-networks.com

Amacis Ltd
Hawthorn House
Wildflower Way
Belfast, BT12 6TA
Tel 028 9087 2000
Web: www.amacis.co.uk

Amt-Sybex (NI) Ltd
Edgewater Office Park
Edgewater Rd
Belfast, BT3 9JQ
Tel 028 9078 1616
Fax 028 9078 1717
Web: www.amt-sybex.com
Email: info@amt-sybex.com

Applied Networks
Building 10
Central Park
Mallusk, BT36 4FS
Tel: 028 9083 0683
Fax: 028 9083 6776
Email: info@applied-networks.com

Armada Solutions
Unit 4 Cookstown Enterprise Centre
Derryloran Industrial Estate
Cookstown, BT80 9LU
Tel: 028 8484 9941
Web: www.armada-solutions.com
Email: info@ armada-solutions.com

B.I.C. Systems Ltd
Enterprise House
201 Airport Road West
Belfast, BT3 9ED
Tel: 028 9053 2200
Fax: 028 9056 0056
Web: www.bicsystems.com
Email: info@bicsystems.com

Biznet
133-137 Lisburn Road
Belfast, BT9 7AG
Tel 028 9022 3224
Fax 028 9022 3223
Web: www.biznet-solutions.com
Email: info@biznet-solutions.com

BT13
Unit 11 Mallusk Enterprise Park
BT36 4GN
Tel: 028 9084 3313
Email: info@bt13.com

Consilium Technologies Ltd
Consilium House
Antrim Technology Pk
Antrim , BT41 1QS
Tel 028 9448 0000
Fax 028 9448 0001
Web: www.ctechs.co.uk
Email: info@ctechs.co.uk

CSM Computer Systems Management
Ards Business Centre
Jubilee Road
Newtownards, BT23 4YH
Tel: 028 9181 4923

Fujitsu
110-112 Holywood Road
Belfast, BT4 1NU
Tel: 028 9047 4200
Web: www.services.fujitsu.com

Gibson Computing & Co
218 Lisburn Enterprise Centre
Enterprise Crescent
Lisburn, BT28 2BP
Tel: 028 9266 9936
Fax: 028 9266 9914
Web: www.gibson-computing.co.uk
Email: sales@:gibson-computing.co.uk

Harbinson Mulholland
IBM House
4 Bruce Street
Belfast, BT2 7JD
Tel: 028 9044 5100
Fax: 028 9044 5101

Hewlett Packard
Rushmere House
46 Cadogan Park
Belfast , BT9 6HH
Tel 028 90381381
Web www.compaq.co.uk

HM Systems
12 Church Avenue
Holywood, BT18 9BJ
Tel: 028 9042 1202
Web: www.hmsystems.ie
Email: info@hmsystems.ie

Horizon Open Systems
The Sidings Office Park
Antrim Road
Lisburn, BT28 3AJ
Tel: 028 9262 9636
Fax: 028 9262 9584
Web: www.hos.horizon.ie
Email: info@hos.horizon.ie

ICC Computers & Support NI Ltd
236 Upper Newtownards Road
Belfast, BT4 3EU
Tel: 028 9065 5788
Fax: 028 9065 3646
Email: sales@iccsupport.co.uk

Ion Technologies
1a Bryson St
Belfast, BT5 4ES
Tel 028 9045 5911
Web: www.iontechnologies.com

IT Works Ltd
46 Lower Quilly Road
Dromore, BT25 1LJ
Tel: 028 9269 8229
Web: www.itworksltd.com

Kainos
4-6 Upper Crescent
Belfast, BT7 1NT
Tel 028 9057 1100
Fax 028 9057 1101
Web: www.kainos.com
Email: info@kainos.com

Lagan Technologies
Falcon Road
Haethorn Business Centre
Belfast, BT12 6SJ
Tel 028 90509300
Web: www.lagan.com
Email: info@lagan.com

Liberty Information Technology Ltd
Clarendon House
9-21 Adelaide Street
Belfast, BT2 8DJ
Tel 028 90445500
Web: www.liberty-it.co.uk

Logic IT Solutions Ltd
19 CIDO Business Complex
Carn Industrial Estate
Craigavon, BT63 5RH
Tel: 028 3833 1070

MCS Micro Computer Solutions Ltd
25 Carn Road
Craigavon, BT63 5WG
Tel: 028 3839 3839
Fax: 028 3839 3838
Web: www.mcsgroup.co.uk
Email: sales@mcsgroup.co.uk

Memsis
Rose House
2A Derryvolgie Avenue
Belfast, BT9 6FL
Tel: 028 9080 6999
Fax: 028 9080 6060
Web: www.memsis.com

Nitec Solutions
Oakmont House
2 Queen's Road
Lisburn, BT27 4TZ
Tel: 028 9262 5000
Fax: 028 9262 5030
Web: www.nitec.com
Email: solutions@nitec.com

Parity Solutions
Address Unit 1
Beecom House
Antrim, BT41 1QS
Tel 028 9446 4901
Fax 028 9446 0702
Web: www.parity.co.uk

Real Time Systems Ltd
Agar House
31 Ballynahinch Road
Carryduff, BT8 8EH
Tel: 028 9081 7171
Web: www.rtsl.com

Sherwood Systems
Ash Grove
Wildflower Way
Boucher Road
Belfast, BT12 6TA
Tel: 028 9066 8585
Fax: 028 9066 5547
Web: www.sherwoodsys.com
Email: info@sherwoodsys.com

Singularity Ltd
100 Patrick Street
Derry, BT48 7EL
Tel 028 7126 7767
Fax 028 7126 8085
Web: www.singularity.co.uk
Email: info@singularity.co.uk

Siemens Business Services
Unit 8 Enterprise House
Boucher Crescent
Belfast, BT12 6HU
Tel:: 028 9066 4331

Sx3
Hillview House
61 Church Road
Newtownabbey, BT36 7SS
Tel: 028 9085 9085
Fax: 028 9085 9086

t.i. solutions
Thomas Andrews House
Queen's Road
Queen's Island, Belfast BT3 9DU
Tel: 028 9053 4570
Fax: 028 9053 4577
Web: www.tisolutions.biz
Email: compass@tisolutions.biz

Xperience
11 Altona Road
Lisburn, BT27 5QB
Tel: 028 9267 7533
Fax: 028 9267 2887
Web: xperience-group.com
Email: info@xperience-group.com

Recruitment Consultants

ABC Recruitment Ltd
40 Frances Street
Newtownards, BT23 7DN
Tel: 028 9182 3333

Adecco
38 Queen's Square
Belfast, BT1 6EJ
Tel: 028 9024 4660

Advance Recruitment Services
80 High Street
Belfast, BT1 2BG
Tel: 028 9027 8278

Apple Recruitment Services
8 Bedford Street
Belfast, BT2 7FB
Tel: 028 9024 9747

Bell Recruitment Services
Shaftesbury House
Shaftesbury Square
1 Donegall Road
Belfast, BT12 5JJ
Tel: 028 9031 1211

Blueprint Appointments
143-147 Great Victoria Street
Belfast, BT1 4PE
Tel: 028 9032 3333

Bond Financial Services
Enterprise House
55-59 Adelaide Street
Belfast, BT2 8FE
Tel: 028 9072 6008

BrightWater Selection (Belfast) Ltd
51-53 Adelaide Street
Belfast, BT2 8FE
Tel: 028 9032 5325

Career Prospects
Park House
87-91 Great Victoria Street
Belfast, BT2 7AG
Tel: 028 9058 9880

Chapter House Financial Recruitment
3 Wellington Park
Belfast, BT9 6DJ
Tel: 028 9092 3340

Contract People (NI) Ltd
2 Crescent Gardens
Belfast, BT7 1NS
Tel: 028 9033 9901

Cornerstone Recruitment
Albany House
73-75 Great Victoria Street
Belfast, BT2 7AF
Tel: 028 9058 0101

Diamond Recruitment
16 Donegall Square South
Belfast, BT1 5JF
Tel: 028 9055 8000

Direct Contract Staff
28 St Julian's Way
Omagh, BT79 7UN
Tel: 028 8224 9248

First Choice Selection Services Ltd
Sinclair House
89 Royal Avenue
Belfast, BT1 1FE
Tel: 028 9031 3693

Flexiskills Recruitment
Washington House
14-16 High Street
Belfast, BT1 2BD
Tel: 028 9032 4249

Forde May Consulting
77 Upper Lisburn Road
Belfast, BT10 0GY
Tel: 028 9062 8877

Grafton Recruitment Ltd
35-37 Queen's Square
Belfast, BT1 3FG
Tel: 028 9024 2824

Hays Montrose
Spencer House
71 Royal Avenue
Belfast, BT1 1FE
Tel: 028 9031 5184

Industrial Temps
Park House
87-91 Great Victoria Street
Belfast, BT2 7AF
Tel: 028 9032 2511

Initial Personnel Services
Magowan Houses
11H West Street
Portadown, BT62 3PL
Tel: 028 3835 1361

Jobfinder
407 Lisburn Road
Belfast, BT9 7EW
Tel: 028 9066 3377

Kennedy Recruitment
31-35 May Street
Belfast, BT1 4NG
Tel: 028 9033 0555

Key Consulting Group
144 High Street
Holywood, BT18 9HS
Tel: 028 9042 2635

Key Staff Recruitment
36 University Street
Belfast, BT7 1FZ
Tel: 028 9024 0340

Lagan Recruitment
3rd Floor
Merrion Business Centre
58 Howard Street
Belfast, BT1 6PL
Tel: 028 9043 7801

Tim Lewis Recruitment
24 Linenhall Street
Belfast, BT2 8BF
Tel: 028 9043 5835

Lynn Recruitment
48-50 Bedford Street
Belfast, BT2 7FG
Tel: 028 9023 4324

Manpower
50-56 Wellington Place
Belfast, BT1 6GF
Tel: 028 9023 6860

Merc Partners
12B Clarendon Road
Belfast, BT1 3BG
Tel: 028 9072 5750

MPA Recruitment
41A Kingsgate Street
Coleraine, BT52 1LD
Tel: 028 7035 7035

MRI Worldwide
163 Upper Newtownards Road
Belfast, BT4 3HZ
Tel: 028 9065 5992

MSL Search & Selection
20 Rosemary Street
Belfast, BT1 1QD
Tel: 028 9023 4444

Mydas Recruitment
1A Information Technology Centre
Balloo Avenue
Bangor, BT19 7QT
Tel: 028 9145 0107

Next Step Recruitment (NI) Ltd
34 Weston Drive
Belfast, BT9 7JF
Tel: 028 9024 3443

Nijobs.com
3rd Floor
Scottish Mutual Building
16 Donegall Square South
Belfast, BT1 5JF
Tel: 028 9043 4477

Oaks Recruitment Services Ltd
12A Market Street
Lurgan, BT66 6AQ
Tel: 028 3834 3311

Optima Recruitment Europe Ltd
134A Great Victoria Street
Belfast, BT2 7BG
Tel: 028 9031 2626

Parity
Blackstaff Chambers
Amelia Street
Belfast, BT2 7GS
Tel: 028 9024 0780

Pertemps Savage Recruitment
Stokes House
17-25 College Square East
Belfast, BT1 6DD
Tel: 028 9023 6999

Precision
28 Campsie Industrial Estate
McLean Road
Londonderry, BT47 3PF
Tel: 028 7186 0135

Premiere People
Hampden House
55 Royal Avenue
Belfast, BT1 1FX
Tel: 028 9023 5777

PSC Management Group
120 Donegall Street
Belfast, BT1 2GX
Tel: 028 9023 4441

Ranstad Employment Bureau Ltd
33-35 Bradbury Place
Belfast, BT7 1RR
Tel: 028 9033 0002

Recruitment Direct
1st Floor
Fanum House
108 Great Victoria Street
Belfast, BT2 7BE
Tel: 028 9058 0888

Reed Accountancy
1 Donegall Square West
Belfast, BT1 6JA
Tel: 028 9033 0604

Reed Employment
10 Ann Street
Belfast
BT1 4EF
Tel: 028 9033 0812

Reed Hospitality
9-11 Castle Lane
Belfast, BT1 5DA
Tel: 028 9031 3453

Riada Recruitment
90 Union Street
Coleraine, BT52 1QB
Tel: 028 7032 6600

Rutledge Recruitment & Training
54 Scotch Street, Armagh, BT61 7DF
Tel: 028 3752 7932

Sales Placement Contract People
2 Crescent Gardens, Belfast, BT7 1NS
Tel: 028 9023 2309

Select Recruitment (NI)
Ground Floor
20 Adelaide Street
Belfast, BT2 8GD
Tel: 028 9023 2328

Supply IT Recruitment
91 Dromalane Road
Newry, BT35 8DE
Tel: 028 3025 6440

TSL IT
58 Greystone Road
Antrim, BT41 1JZ
Tel: 028 9446 7774

Target Recruitment
303A Antrim Road
Glengormley, BT15 2HF
Tel: 028 9084 8897

Task Recruitment
46 Botanic Avenue
Belfast, BT7 1JR
Tel: 028 9033 1020

Tech Trade Recruiting Ltd
13-15 Wilson's Court
Belfast, BT1 4DQ
Tel: 028 9087 7883

Vanrath Financial Selection
6th Floor Lesley Suite
2-12 Montgomery Street
Belfast, BT1 4NX
Tel: 0870 774 1000

Village Industrial Staff Services
Unit 4, 8 Cheston Street
Carrickfergus, BT38 7BH
Tel: 028 9335 9200

WH Recruitment Services
82A Charles Street
Portadown, BT62 1dq
Tel: 028 3839 8550

Worknet
134B Andersonstown Road
BT11 9BY
Tel: 028 9020 8060

www.recruitni.com
135 Albertbridge Road
Belfast, BT5 4BS
Tel: 028 9073 8000

Training Organisations

Abbey Training Services
Lennie House
314 Antrim Road
Newtownabbey, BT36 8EH
Tel: 028 9084 0527

Barklie & Logan
8 Cameron Park
Ballymena, BT42 1QJ
Tel: 028 2564 5447

BIC Systems
Enterprise House
201 Airport Road West
Belfast, BT3 9ED
Tel: 028 9053 2200

CITB - Construction Industry Training Board
17 Dundrod Road
Crumlin, BT29 4SR
Tel: 028 9082 5466

Conexus
16 Montgomery Road
Belfast, BT6 9JD
Tel: 028 9070 8208

DDA Training Services Ltd
21 William Street
Dungannon, BT70 1DX
Tel: 028 8772 6342

Edge Innovative Learning International Ltd
Unit 18
North City Business Centre
Duncairn Gardens
Belfast, BT15 2GG
Tel: 028 9042 6425

Elite Training
Lindsay House
10 Callender Street
Belfast, BT1 5BN
Tel: 028 9031 6840

Envision
Rollo House
6 High Street
Holywood, BT18 9AZ
Tel: 028 9042 7666

FXL Ireland
10 Orpheus Drive
Dungannon, BT71 6DR
Tel: 028 8772 9478

Graham Training
40-44 Railway Street
Lisburn, BT28 1XP
Tel: 028 9266 5100

HMC Communications
18 Shanrod Road
Katesbridge
Banbridge, BT32 5BG
Tel: 028 4067 1246

IMI Northern Ireland Ltd
Interpoint Building
20-24 York Street
Belfast, BT15 1AQ
Tel: 028 9053 0093

ITS (Industry Training Services)
7 Derryneskan Road
Craigavon, BT62 1UH
Tel: 028 3885 2564

Institute of Leadership and Management
7 Hillside Park
Bangor, BT19 6TU
Tel: 028 9146 0720

Job Link
Market Court
57-59 New Row
Coleraine, BT52 1EJ
Tel: 028 7035 2434

Kennedy Training
31-35 May Street
Belfast, BT1 4NG
Tel: 028 9033 0555

Other Business Services Providers

Serviced Office Accommodation Providers

Elmwood House Business Centre
46 Elmwood Avenue, Belfast, BT9 6AY
Tel: 028 9066 4941

Mayfair Business Centre Ltd
193-205 Garvaghy Road
Portadown, BT62 1EH
Tel: 028 3839 1666

Merrion Business Centre
58 Howard Street, Belfast, BT1 6PJ
Tel: 028 9080 0880

The Mount Business and Conference Centre
2 Woodstock Link, Belfast, BT6 8DD
Tel: 028 9073 0188

Premier Business Centres
20 Adelaide Street, Belfast, BT2 8GD
Tel: 028 9051 7000

Regus
33 Clarendon Dock
Laganside, BT1 3BW
Tel: 0845 301 0300

Valley Business Centre
67 Church Road
Newtownabbey, BT36 7LQ
Tel: 028 9055 1600

Weaver's Court Executive Suites
Weaver's Court
Linfield Road
Belfast, BT12 5LA
Tel: 028 9022 4000

Wellington Park Business Centre
3 Wellington Park
Belfast, BT9 6DJ
Tel: 028 9092 3333

Printers

W&G Baird Ltd
Greystone Press
Caulside Drive
Antrim, BT41 2DU
Tel: 028 9446 3911

Dargan Press Ltd
5 Round Tower Centre
Dargan Crescent
Belfast, BT3 9JP
Tel: 028 9077 4478

DMS Digital Printers
34 Waterloo Road
Lisburn, BT27 5NW
Tel: 028 9266 9980
Fax: 028 9266 9981
Web: www.mediasolutionsireland.com
Email: info@mediasolutionsireland.com

Edenderry Print Ltd
Units 6-8 Agnew Street Industrial Estate
Belfast, BT12 1GB
Tel: 028 9074 0192
Fax: 028 9074 6345
Email: edenderryprint@btconnect.com

GPS Colour Graphics Ltd
Alexander Road
Belfast, BT6 9HP
Tel: 028 9070 2020
Fax: 028 9079 8463
Email: sales@gpscolour.co.uk

Graham & Heslip Ltd
96 Beechill Road
Belfast, BT8 6NS
Tel: 028 9049 4949

Graham & Sons Ltd
51 Gortin Road
Omagh, BT79 7HZ
Tel: 028 8224 9222
Fax: 028 8224 9886

Hendersons Print
PO Box 49
Hightown Avenue
Newtownabbey, BT36 4RT
Tel: 028 9033 7826
Fax: 028 9033 7846

Impro Printing
41 Dargan Road
Belfast, BT3 9JU
Tel: 028 9077 7795
Email: sales@impro.co.uk

Impression Print and Design
53 Enterprise Crescent
Ballinderry Road
Lisburn, BT28 2BP
Tel: 028 9260 4432
Fax: 028 9262 9018

Johnston Printing Ltd
Mill Road
Kilrea, BT51 5RJ
Tel: 028 2954 0312
Fax: 028 2954 1070
Web: www.johnston-printing.co.uk

Limavady Printing Co Ltd
26C Catherine Street
Limavady, BT49 9BD
Tel: 028 7776 2051
Fax: 028 7776 2132
Web: www.limprint.com

Minprint Ltd
401 Castlereagh Road
Belfast, BT5 6QP
Tel: 028 9070 5205
Fax: 028 9079 9030
Web: www.minprint.co.uk
Email: sales@minprint.co.uk

Nicholson & Bass Ltd
Michelin Road, Newtownabbey
Tel: 028 9034 2433
Fax: 028 9034 2066

Northern Whig
107 Limestone Road
Belfast, BT15 3AH
Tel: 028 9035 2233
Fax: 028 9035 2181

Peninsula Print & Design
Unit 2
Lansdowne Road
Newtownards, BT23 4NT
Tel: 028 9181 4125
Fax: 028 9181 4864
Web: www.peninsulaprint.co.uk

Universities Press (Belfast) Ltd
6 Alanbrooke Road
Belfast, BT6 9HB
Tel: 028 9070 4464
Fax: 028 9079 3295

Signage

4 Corners
Unit 254 Lisburn Enterprise Centre
Ballinderry Road
Lisburn, BT28 2BP
Tel: 028 9266 4345
Web: www.4corners.org.uk
Email; info@4corners.org.uk

Alexander Boyd Displays
Lambeg Mills
Lambeg
Lisburn, BT27 5SX
Tel: 028 9030 1115

Autosign Graphix
Unit 73 Derriaghy Industrial Park
Dunmurry
Belfast, BT17 9HU
Tel: 028 9061 0282
Web: www.autosign.co.uk

Connswater Graphics
Unit 1 Dargan Court
Dargan Crescent
Belfast, BT3 9JP
Tel: 028 9077 7395
Fax: 028 9077 7065

Delta Sign Systems
Units 2-4 Carn Business Park
Carn Road
Portadown, BT63 5WG
Tel: 028 3835 0698
Fax: 028 3833 4487
Web: www.deltasignsystems.co.uk

The Display Team
6 Greenway Industrial Estate
Conlig
Newtownards, BT23 7SU
Tel: 028 9127 5516
Fax: 028 9127 5612

DMB Graphics
55 Holly Hill
Dollingstown
Craigavon, , BT66 7UB
Tel: 028 3834 9993

Exclaim
2 Ballyoran Lane
Dundonald, BT16 1XJ
Tel: 028 9041 0006
Fax: 028 9041 0044
Web: www.exclaim.co.uk

Gemini Graphics Ltd
21 Derryloran Industrial Estate
Cookstown, BT80 9LU
Tel: 028 8676 1292
Fax: 028 8676 5566
Web: www.thegeminigroup.co.uk

Gilmore Signs
41-45 Middlepath Street
Belfast, BT5 4BG
Tel: 028 9045 5419
Fax: 028 9045 8451

Impact Signs
East Belfast Enterprise Park
Belfast, BT5 4GX
Tel: 028 9073 9402
Fax: 028 9073 8040

Riada Signs
Unit 4D
Ballybrakes Business Park
Ballymoney, BT53 6LW
Tel: 028 2766 2845
Fax: 028 2766 2228
Web: www.riadasigns.biz

Sign D Sign
172A Tate's Avenue
Belfast, BT12 6ND
Tel: 028 9023 6006
Fax: 028 9023 6856
Web: www.signdsign.biz

Fulfilment & Direct Mail

AMA Communication Centre
Newtownards Road
Bangor, BT19 7TA
Tel: 028 9147 2525
Fax: 028 9147 2797
Web: www.andersonmanning.com
Email: info@andersonmanning.com

Community Telegraph
124 Royal Avenue
Belfast, BT1 1EB
Tel: 028 9026 4620
Fax: 028 9055 4582
Web: www.belfasttelegraph.co.uk

Distribution Management NI Ltd
Suite 3 Bank House
133-135 Albertbridge Road
Belfast, BT5 4PS
Tel: 028 9045 9988
Fax: 028 9046 9988
Web: www.dmni.co.uk

Mailroom Ltd
4 Fern Business Park
Blackstaff Road
Belfast, BT11 9DT
Tel: 028 9080 6600
Fax: 028 9080 6699
Email: info@mailroomltd.com

TDS Group
11 Kilbride Road
Doagh
Ballyclare, BT39 0QA
Tel: 028 9332 4405
Fax: 028 9334 1150
Web: www.thetdsgroup.com

Tricord Direct Mail
Trinity House
Lisburn, BT28 2YY
Tel: 028 9260 6966
Fax: 028 9260 6965
Web: www.tricord.co.uk
Email: fulfill@tricord.co.uk

Payroll Services

CJS Payroll Ltd

The Payroll Specialists

240-242 Upper Newtownards Road
Belfast, BT4 3EU
Tel: 028 9047 1754
Fax: 028 9047 1756
E-mail: cjs@cjspayroll.com
Web: www.cjs@cjspayroll.com

Fully Managed Payroll Services (UK & Ireland) that ensure your staff are paid accurately, on time, every time.
Payroll tailored to your business.
We manage your payroll ....
You manage your business

Office Equipment & Supplies

Adelaide Office Supplies
31 Upper Dunmurry Lane
Belfast, BT17 0AA
Tel: 028 9061 8841

Asdon
Systems House
Enterprise Crescent
Lisburn, BT28 2BH
Tel: 028 9267 5114
Fax: 028 9266 0256

Banner
12 Cromac place
Belfast, BT7 2JD
Tel: 0845 712 5926
Fax: 0845 712 5927

Craigavon Office Supplies
1 Moore's Lane
Lurgan, BT66 8DW
Tel: 028 3832 7231

Desk Warehouse
288 Beersbridge Road
Belfast, BT5 5DX
Tel: 028 9046 0055
Fax: 028 9058 0900
Web: www.deskwarehouse.co.uk

ED-CO
Hydepark House
54 Mallusk Road
Newtownabbey, BT36 4WU
Tel: 028 9084 4023
Fax: 028 9084 0705
Web: www.edco.co.uk

Hodge Office Supplies Ltd
4 North Howard Street
Belfast, BT13 2AS
Tel: 028 9024 1812
Fax: 028 9024 6866

Facilities Management

BCC
5 College Court
Belfast, BT1 6BS
Tel: 028 9024 9240
Fax: 028 9023 2834
Web: www.belfastcontractcleaners.co.uk

Maybin Support Services
4 Duncrue Crescent
Belfast, BT3 9BW
Tel: 028 9077 4799
Web: www.maybin.com

Mount Charles
Ascot House
24-31 Shaftesbury Square
Belfast, BT2 7DB
Tel: 028 9032 0070
Fax: 028 9024 5391
Web: www.mountcharles.com

Robinson Cleaning
Unit 5-7 Antrim Enterprise Agency
58 Greystone Road
Antrim , BT41 1JZ
Tel: 028 9442 9717
Web: www.robinson-cleaning.co.uk

Serco
Mallusk Enterprise Park
Mallusk Drive
Newtownabbey, BT36 4GN
Tel: 028 9084 1851
Fax: 028 9083 9251
Web: www.serco.ie

Chapter 9

Northern Ireland and the European Union

Introduction

The European Union was established following World War Two, with the process of European integration launched on 9 May 1950 when France officially proposed to create "the first concrete foundation of a European federation". Six countries Belgium, Germany, France, Italy, Luxembourg and the Netherlands joined. Since then there have been four waves of accessions:

- 1973: Denmark, Ireland and the United Kingdom;
- 1981: Greece;
- 1986: Spain and Portugal;
- 1995: Austria, Finland and Sweden.

The EU currently has 15 member states and is preparing for further enlargement with the accession of 10 new eastern and southern European countries in May 2004. The European Union is built on a unique institutional system and is based on the rule of law and democracy; its member states delegate sovereignty to common institutions representing the interests of the Union as a whole.

EU Enlargement Candidate Countries:

Czech Republic	Hungary
Estonia	Malta
Cyprus	Poland
Latvia	Slovenia
Lithuania	Slovakia

Source: www.europa.eu.int

All decisions and procedures are derived from the basic treaties ratified by the member states. Whilst the role of the Commission is traditionally perceived to be to uphold the interests of the Union as a whole, each national government is represented by the Council of Ministers and individual citizens by the European parliament, which is a directly elected legislature.

Two other institutions, the Court of Justice and the Court of Auditors support the "institutional triangle" of Commission, Council and parliament and are supported by a further five bodies:

- European Central Bank;
- Economic and Social Committee;
- Committee of the Regions;
- European Investment Bank;
- European Ombudsman.

The principal objectives of the Union are to:

- Establish European Citizenship (Fundamental Rights; Freedom of Movement; Civil and Political Rights);
- Ensure freedom, security and justice (Cooperation in the field of Justice and Home Affairs);
- Promote economic and social progress (single market; euro, the common currency; job creation; regional development; environmental protection);
- Assert Europe's role in the world (common foreign and security policy; the European Union in the world).

The Institutions of the European Union

The European Council of Ministers

The Council of Ministers
Rue de la Loi 175
B–1048 Brussels
Tel: +32 2 285 61 11
Fax: +32 2 285 7397
Web: www.ue.eu.int
Email: public.info@consilium.eu.int

The Council of the European Union consists of relevant ministers from all of the member states, and is the European Union's main decision-making body. Its representatives come together regularly at ministerial level. According to the matters on the agenda, the Council meets in different compositions: foreign affairs, finance, education, telecommunications, etc. It co-ordinates the broad economic, foreign and security policies of member states and shares legislative and budgetary authority with the European parliament. The Council generally co-ordinates the activities of member states and adopts measures in the fields of policing and judicial co-operation in criminal matters.

The Council of Ministers is supported by the Committee of the Permanent Representatives (COREPER), which prepares the positions for the ministers prior to their Council meetings. Each country has its own permanent representation team.

The European Commission

200 rue de la Loi
B–1049
Brussels
Tel: +32 2 299 11 11
Web: www.europa.eu.int
Email: sg-info@cec.eu.int
President: Romano Prodi

Windsor House
9–15 Bedford Street
Belfast, BT2 7EG
Tel: 028 9024 0708
Fax: 028 9024 8241
Head of Representation: Eddie McVeigh

The European Commission's members are nominated by the member states. It initiates draft legislation, presents legislative proposals to parliament and the Council and is the executive body of the European Union, implementing legislation, budget and programmes adopted by the European parliament and the Council of the European Union. In addition, the Commission represents the EU internationally, negotiates international agreements (chiefly trade and co-operation) and acts as guardian of the Treaties with the Court of Justice, ensuring that Community law is properly applied.

The Commission consists of 20 Commissioners. A President, assisted by two Vice-Presidents, heads the Commission. Each member state has at least one of its nationals serving on the Commission at any one time, and the larger member states – France, Germany, Italy, Spain and the

United Kingdom – have, at present, two. The members of the Commission are appointed 'by common accord' of the governments of the member states for a renewable term of five years. The seat of the European Commission is in Brussels.

The Commission enjoys wide legislative powers delegated from the Council and certain autonomous legislative powers under the Treaties: but its principal role is setting the general policy agenda for the European Union. Although the Council adopts European legislation, in most cases these institutions may only act on legislative proposals from the Commission itself. In the past, the right of legislative initiative has enabled the Commission to act as the engine of European integration. The Commission also has important investigative, enforcement and quasi-judicial functions, including the power to act against member states believed to be in breach of Community law. It also has powers in relation to the supervision and enforcement of the Community's rules on competition and state aids. The latter can extend to the imposition of extremely heavy fines (subject to rights of appeal) on individuals, undertakings or groups of undertakings found to be breach of the law.

President:	**Romano Prodi**
Vice-Presidents:	
Administrative Reform	Neil Kinnock
Relations with the European Parliament, Transport and Energy	Loyola de Palacio
Members of the Commission:	
Competition	Mario Monti
Agriculture, Rural Development and Fisheries	Franz Fischler
Enterprise and the Information Society	Erkki Liikanen
Internal Market	Frederik Bolkestein
Research	Philippe Busquin
Economic and Monetary Affairs	Pedro Solbes Mira
Development and Humanitarian Aid	Poul Nielson
Enlargement	Günter Verheugen
External Relations	Christopher Patten
Trade	Pascal Lamy
Health and Consumer Protection	David Byrne
Regional Policy and, ad personam, Inter-Governmental Conference	Michel Barnier
Education and Culture	Viviane Reding
Budget	Michaele Schreyer
Environment	Margot Wallström
Justice and Home Affairs	António Vitorino
Employment and Social Affairs	Anna Diamantopoulou
Secretariat General of the Commission:	
Secretary-General:	David O'Sullivan
Deputy Secretary-General:	Bernhard Zepter
Assistant:	François Genisson

The European Commission is not simply an executive body; in particular, it has a key role to play in the management of the European Union's annual budget of over 80 billion euro. Most of this sum represents, running the Community's Common Agricultural Policy.

Directorates-General

Each Directorate-General is headed by a Director-General reporting to the Commissioner who takes overall political and operational responsibility for the work of the Directorate-General. An individual Commissioner's portfolio may well cover the work of more than one Directorate-General. The allocation of portfolios to individual Commissioners is decided collectively, although the President makes initial proposals. The Commissioners meet collectively as the College of Commissioners once a week, act by majority and operate under the political guidance of the President.

European Commission Directorates-General

Legal Services	Michel Petite
Press & Communication Service	Jorge de Oliveira e Sousa
Policy Advisory Group	Ricardo Levi
Economic & Financial Affairs	Klaus Regling
Enterprise	Jean-Paul Mingasson
Competition	Philip Lowe
Employment & Social Affairs	Odile Quintin
Agriculture	José Manuel Silva Rodriguez
Transport & Energy	François Lamoureux
Environment	Catherine Day
Research	Achilleas Mitsos
Joint Research Centre	Finbarr McSweeney
Information Society	Fabio Colasanti
Fisheries	Jörgen Holmquist
Internal Market	Alexander Schaub
Regional Policy	Vacant
Taxation & Custom Unit	Robert Verrue
Education & Culture	Nikolaus Van Der Pas
Health & Consumer Protection	Robert Coleman
Justice & Home Affairs	Jonathan Faull
External Relations	Guy Legras
Trade	Mogens Peter Carl
Development	Jacobus Richelle
Enlargement	Eneko Landaburu
Europe Aid Co-operation Office	Giorgio Bonacci
Humanitarian Aid Office – ECHO	Costanza Adinolfi
Eurostat	Michel Vanden Abeele
Personnel & Administration	Horst Reichenbach
Internal Audit Service	Jules Muis
Budget	Luis Romero Requena
European Anti-Fraud Office	Franz-Hermann Bruener
Joint Interpreting & Conference Service	Marco Benedetti
Translation Service	Vacant
Office for Official Publications	Thomas L Cranfield
Office for Administration & Payment of Individual Entitlements	Edith Kitzmantel
Office for Infrastructure & Logistics	Piet Verleysen Martine Reicharts
European Personnel Selection Office	Erik Halskov

The European Parliament

Strasbourg
Allée du Printemps
B.P. 1024/F
F–67070 Strasbourg Cedev
Tel: +33 03 08 17 40 01
Fax:+33 03 88 25 65 01
Email: civis@europarl.eu.int
Web: www.europarl.eu.int

Brussels
Rue Wiertz
B-1047 Brussels
Tel: +322 284 2111
Fax: +322 284 6974

Elected every five years by individual citizens in each of the member states, the European parliament represents the democratic voice of the 374 million citizens of the European Union.

The European parliament is composed of members from each of the fifteen member states in broad proportion to their population. The parliament shares legislative and budgetary authority with the European Council and exercises democratic and political supervision over the other institutions.

The European parliament has three essential functions:

- Shares with the Council the power to legislate, i.e. to adopt European laws (directives, regulations, decisions), assisting in maintaining the democratic legitimacy of the texts adopted;
- Shares budgetary authority with the Council and can therefore influence spending. At the end of the procedure it adopts the budget in its entirety;
- The parliament exercises democratic supervision over the Commission approving the nomination of Commissioners. It has the right to censure the Commission, and also exercises political supervision over all the institutions.

The UK has an entitlement of 87 European parliament seats. Of this, Northern Ireland returns 3 MEPs by an election held every 5 years. In this case Northern Ireland is a single constituency, and the three European MPs are elected by proportional representation, the Single Transferable Vote (STV).

The next elections to the European Parliament are scheduled to be held in June 2004. Veteran MEP Ian Paisley has recently announced that he will not be running in the election to defend the seat he has held since 1979.

The current Northern Ireland MEPs, returned in June 1999, are:

Ian Paisley MP MLA
DUP

European Political Group: Non-attached
Constituency Contact:
Rhonda Paisley
256 Ravenhill Road
Belfast BT6 8GJ
Tel: 028 9045 4255
Fax: 028 9045 7783

Brussels Contact:
European Parliament
Rue Wiertz
B–1047 Brussels, Belgium
Tel:+ 32 2 284 5410
Fax: + 32 2 284 9410

John Hume MP
SDLP

European Political Group: Party of European Socialists
Constituency Contact:
5 Bayview Terrace
Derry BT48 7EE
Tel: 028 7126 5340 / Fax: 028 7136 3423

Brussels Contact:
Tom Lyne
European Parliament
Rue Wiertz
B–1047 Brussels, Belgium
Tel: + 32 2 284 5190 / Fax: + 32 2 284 9190

Jim Nicholson
UUP

European Political Group: European People's Party and European Democrats
Constituency Contact:
Cunningham House, 429 Holywood Road
Belfast BT4 2LN
Tel: 028 9076 5500 / Fax: 028 9024 6738

Brussels Contact:
European Parliament
Rue Wiertz
B–1047 Brussels, Belgium
Tel: + 32 2 284 5933 / Fax: + 32 2 284 9933

The European Court of Justice

Luxembourg L-2925
Tel: +352 43031 / Fax: +352 4303 2600
Web: www.curia-eu.int

The Court of Justice ensures that Community law is uniformly interpreted and effectively applied. It has jurisdiction in disputes involving member states, EU institutions, businesses and individuals.

The Court of Justice currently consists of 15 Judges and eight Advocates General who are appointed for a renewable term of six years. The task of the Judges and Advocates General is to make reasoned submissions on the cases brought before the European Court of Justice in advance of the Court handing down its final decision.

The European Court of Justice is the highest and sole judicial authority in matters of Community law. Its responsibilities encompass three main areas:

- Monitoring the application of Community law;
- Interpretation of Community law;
- Further shaping of Community law.

The Court of Justice acts as a constitutional court when disputes between Community institutions are before it or legislative instruments are up for review; as an administrative court when reviewing the administrative acts of the Commission or of national authorities applying Community legislation; as a labour court or industrial tribunal when dealing with freedom of movement, social security and equal opportunities; as a fiscal court when dealing with matters concerning the validity and interpretation of directives in the fields of taxation and customs law; as a criminal court when reviewing Commission decisions imposing fines; and as a civil court when hearing claims for damages or interpreting the Brussels convention on the enforcement of judgements in civil and commercial matters.

The European Court of Auditors

12 Rue Alcide De Gasperi
L-1615 Luxembourg
Tel: +352 43981 / Fax: +352 439342

The Court of Auditors checks that all the Union's revenue has been received and all its expenditure incurred in a lawful and regular manner and that financial management of the EU budget has been sound. The Court of Auditors consists of one member from each member state, currently 15.

The duties of the Court of Auditors include:

- Examining the accounts of all revenue and expenditure of the Community;
- Examining the accounts of all revenue and expenditure of all bodies set up by the Community;
- Ascertaining whether all revenue has been received and all expenditure incurred in a 'lawful and regular manner' and whether financial management has been sound;
- Assisting the European parliament and the Council in exercising their powers of control over the implementation of the budget;
- Submitting annual reports at the close of each financial year;
- Submitting observations, opinions or special reports on specific questions.

European Central Bank

Kaiserstrasse 29, D-60311 Frankfurt, Germany
Tel: +49 691 3440 / Fax: +49 691 344 6000
Web: www.ecb.int

The European Central Bank frames and implements European monetary policy; it conducts foreign exchange operations and ensures the smooth operation of payment systems. Its chief tasks are to:

- Maintain the stability of the European currency, the Euro;
- Control the amount of currency in circulation.

In order to carry out its tasks the European Central Bank's independence is guaranteed by numerous legal provisions. The European Central Bank consists of a Governing Council and an Executive Board. The Governing Council comprises the governors of the national central banks and the members of the Executive Board of the European Central Bank. The Executive Board, which is made up of the President, Vice President and four other members, is effectively in charge of running the European Central Bank.

The European Single Currency

Following agreement by EU leaders in 1998 on European and Monetary Union, 1st January 1999 saw the adoption of the single currency by France, Spain, Portugal, Germany, The Netherlands, Austria, Belgium, Finland, Italy, Luxembourg and Ireland. From 1st January 2002 notes and coins became available and the European Single Currency became a reality.

The Euro zone is comparable in size with the United States economy, already including 320 million consumers and accounting for one fifth of the world's GDP. Northern Ireland is the only region of the UK to have a land border with a country operating in the Euro zone and the impact has been substantial.

European Investment Bank

The European Investment Bank exists to assist the Community in its role as financing agency for a 'balanced and steady development' of the common market. It provides loans and guarantees in all economic sectors, especially to promote the development of less-developed regions, to modernise or convert undertakings or create new jobs and to assist projects of common interest to several member states. The 15 member states are all members of the Bank.

European Economic and Social Committee

Rue Ravenstein 2, 1000 Brussels, Belgium
Tel: +32 2 546 9011 / Fax: +32 2 513 4893
Email: info@esc.eu.int

The Economic and Social Committee is a consultative body made up of representatives of Europe's main interest groups: employers' organisations, trade unions, farmers, consumer groups, professional associations, etc. From the 15 member states 222 members of the committee are selected. It is non-political, and exists to advise the European parliament, European Commission and the European Council. It supports the role of civil society organisations in non-EC countries to foster better relations with similar bodies, termed 'institution building'. The Committee is divided into three groups: employers, workers and various interests. They draw up opinions on draft EU legislation and issues affecting European society.

Northern Ireland has two representatives attached to the European Economic and Social Committee:

Claire Whitten

Contact Details: Northern Ireland Centre in Europe
Regus House, 33 Clarendon Dock, Belfast BT1 3BW
Tel: 028 9051 1231 / Fax: 028 9051 1201
Email: cw@ni-centre-in-europe.com
Group III: Various Interests
Committee Membership: Economic and Monetary Union and Social Cohesion; External Relations

John Simpson

Contact Details: 3 Glenmachan Drive, Belfast BT4 2RE
Tel / Fax: 028 9076 9399
Email: johnvsimpson@aol.com
Group III: Various Interests
Committee Membership: Economic and Monetary Union and Social Cohesion; Single Market, Production and Consumption

The European Committee of the Regions

Bertha Von Suttner Building
Rue Montoyer, 92–102
B–1040 Brussels, Belgium
Tel: +32 2 282 2211 / Fax: +32 2 282 2325

The European Committee of the Regions was established under the Maastricht Treaty, to represent local and regional authorities in the European Union. Its aim is to strengthen social and economic cohesion of member states, towards European integration. The Committee meets in plenary session 5 times a year to measure opinions on relevant issues. Like the Economic and Social Committee, the Committee of the Regions consists of 222 representatives of regional and local authorities in the member states. The UK currently has 24 representatives on the Committee. After enlargement the number of members on the Committee will increase to 344, but all current EU member states will retain their present representation.

There are a number of areas in which the Council or the Commission are required to seek the views of the Committee, namely:

- Education
- Culture;
- Public Health;
- Trans-European networks;
- Transport
- Telecommunications and energy infrastructure;
- Economic and Social Cohesion;
- Employment policy;
- Social legislation.

The Council also consults the Committee regularly, but without any legal obligation.

Northern Ireland Members of the Committee of the Regions

Dermot Nesbitt MLA

Political Party: UUP
Contact: 21 Downpatrick Road, Crossgar, BT30 9EQ
Tel: 028 4483 1561 / Fax: 028 4483 1722
Email: dermotnesbitt@hotmail.com
Type of Membership: Full Member
Political Group: European People's Party

Alban Maginness MLA

Political Party: SDLP
Contact: 228 Antrim Road, Belfast, BT15 2AN
Tel: 028 9022 0520 / Fax: 028 9022 0522
Email: a.maginness@sdlp.ie
Type of Membership: Full Member
Political Group: Party of European Socialists

George Savage

Political Party: UUP
Contact: 'Watties Hill'
147 Dromore Road, Donacloney, Craigavon BT66 7NR
Tel: 028 3882 0401 / Fax: 028 3882 0401
Type of Membership: Alternate Member
Political Group: European People's Party

Margaret Ritchie MLA

Political Party: SDLP
Contact: 19 Annacloy Road, Downpatrick, BT30 9AE
Tel: 028 4461 2882 / Fax: 028 4461 9574
Type of Membership: Alternate Member
Political Group: Party of European Socialists

Northern Ireland in Europe

Northern Ireland has a recognised presence in Europe and is no longer seen as a region on the periphery but as a keen participant within the structures of the European Union.

Improvements in infrastructure, the peace dividend (to which the Special Support Programme for Peace and Reconciliation has contributed over £370 million) and further resources from the EU Structural Funds aimed at promoting economic development have heightened awareness of the important role of the EU within the region.

Northern Ireland has faced great social and economic disadvantage and in the recent past the region has focused upon gaining economic parity with other member states of the European Union. The categorisation of Northern Ireland as "lagging behind" in the early 1990s saw the region being eligible for Objective 1 status under the EU's Structural Funds. Nonetheless, even with the economic progress that has been made Northern Ireland as a region has a GDP per capita that is still only 80% of the EU average.

The European Commission has worked to develop relationships with Northern Ireland and the establishment of the Northern Ireland Executive Brussels office operated by the Office of the First Minister and Deputy First Minister reinforces a growing profile for the interests of Northern Ireland government within the Community. This, coupled with the work of the Commission's representation in Belfast ensures that Brussels is au fait with Northern Ireland developments and vice versa.

Local authorities are an increasingly important level of government in European terms and many now have a dedicated European Liaison Officer to keep them informed of developments and co-ordinate their applications for European funding.

The Northern Ireland Government and Legislative Process in a European Context

Northern Ireland has three MEPs with a range of knowledge and experience of working for Northern Ireland; two Northern Ireland representatives on the Committee of the Regions and two representatives on the Economic and Social Committee.

At the UK level, EU policy is a non-transferred matter and the majority of decisions on EU policy are taken at national level. Under devolution, the local role is formalised in the Memorandum of Understanding and the Concordats on Co-ordination of European Union Policy and the Joint Ministerial Council (JMC). Policy is still made through London; the difference under devolution was the ability for the Northern Ireland departments to influence policy on those specific issues which have a clear regional perspective.
The Concordats make specific reference to the involvement of the North/South Ministerial Council.

EU policies and legislation impact on a wide range of matters in Northern Ireland including 80 per cent of policies in the Programme for Government of the first Assembly and up to 60 per cent of all legislation. The degree to which Northern Ireland can influence EU policy depends primarily on its input through London.

Since EU policy decisions are taken at national level it is argued that Northern Ireland should focus on defining areas where there are distinctions in the Northern Ireland position and where returns can be maximised. Due to resource constraints only a limited number of areas may be chosen as priority areas. The experience of other regional parliaments suggests that if there is insufficient planning or co-ordination, the outcome will be volumes of effort with little realisable benefit for Northern Ireland.

During devolution there was some disquiet that Assembly Committees had little opportunity to exert influence on the development and implementation of policy; their first view of European Directive and Commission decisions often occured when the department brought sub-ordinate legislation forward. One plan to address this concern would be for OFMDFM to take a more proactive approach to build capacity within all departments to become engaged with European issues, particularly beyond the remit of implementing legislation. This will be supported by plans to form a Standing Committee on EU Affairs within the next Assembly, should devolution return. Other possibilities under consideration include: the establishment of an Assembly Information Desk in Brussels, possibly in the Office of the Northern Ireland Executive in Brussels, or operating as a shared resource with other regions; appointment of a Junior Minister with responsibility for European Affairs, to manage relationships with the European Parliament and Commission and to support and co-ordinate European matters within any future Assembly.

OFMDFM: European Policy and Co-ordination Unit (EPCU)

The European Policy and Co-ordination Unit comes under OFMDFM's Strategy and European Affairs Division, which is headed by Chris Stewart. The Unit has the lead responsibility among Northern Ireland departments in seeking to make a positive contribution to, and get the most benefit for Northern Ireland from involvement with the European Union. In doing so, it works closely with the Office of the Northern Ireland Executive in Brussels (see below). The Unit seeks to do this through activities in three broad areas:

- Development of a clear strategy on the Northern Ireland Executive's EU Policy priorities;
- Creation of effective mechanisms to ensure Northern Ireland interests are properly championed both in London and Brussels;
- Ensuring that policy-makers in Northern Ireland are up-to-date with all relevant EU policy developments and that Northern Ireland departments comply with EC directives.

European Policy Issues

Contact: Julie Mapstone
Tel: 028 9052 3105
Fax: 028 9052 2552
Emai: julie.mapstone@ofmdfmni.gov.uk

The European Policy and Co-ordination Unit also has a role within the EU Programme for Peace and Reconciliation, as an implementing body for Measure 4.1 (Outward and Forward Looking Region).

Contact: Paul Geddis
Tel: 028 9052 8445
Fax: 028 9052 2552
Emai: paul.geddis@ofmdfmni.gov.uk

Office of the Northern Ireland Executive in Brussels

Rue Wiertz, 50 Wiertzstraat, B-1050 Brussels
Contact: Tony Canavan
Tel: + 322 290 1330
Fax: + 322 2990 1332
Email: tony.canavan@ofmdfmni.gov.uk

The Brussels office, which opened in 2001, provides the focal point for developing and progressing the Northern Ireland Executive's policy approach to Europe. Its main functions are:

- Monitoring the development of EU policies relevant to NI and providing up-to-date information to Ministers and departments;
- Ensuring that Northern Ireland interests are taken fully into account in the work of the EU institutions and the development of UK policy on EU matters;
- Raising the positive profile of Northern Ireland among European policy-makers and opinion-formers;
- Pursuing co-operation of practical benefit to Northern Ireland with other European regions;
- Facilitating improved contacts with the EU by the NI non-governmental and local government sectors.

European Funding and Northern Ireland

European funding falls broadly into the following categories:

- Structural Funds Packages, which are drawn up between the European Commission and regional authorities, to identify the needs and priorities of the particular region. Packages are managed at regional level and projects are based in the region in question.
- Community initiatives which are special forms of assistance, which aim to address problems, identified by the European Commission as being common throughout the EU. They are financed by the Structural Funds and managed at regional level.
- EU funding programmes which are thematic and correspond with EU policy areas. They are managed by the Directorates-General and all projects must be transactional in nature.
- Ad hoc calls for proposals issued by various Directorates-Generals of the European Commission.
- Aid to applicant countries and to other non-member states of the EU in order to support economic restructuring and democratic reforms.

Structural Funds

Four main inter related funds known as the Structural Funds are used to finance EU activities for social and economic development throughout the regions. These are:

The European Regional Development Fund (ERDF)

Provides financial support to regional development programmes in order to reduce socio-economic imbalances.

The European Social Fund (ESF)

The main instrument of community social policy and provides financial assistance for vocational training, retraining and job creation schemes.

The European Agricultural Guidance and Guarantee Fund (EAGGF)

Financial instrument for agriculture and rural development policy and finances development in rural areas throughout the European Union.

The Financial Instrument for Fisheries Guide (FIFG)

Enhances the competitiveness of the fisheries sector and strives to maintain the balance between fishing capacity and resources.

Within the 2000–2006 period the total budget for the Structural Funds Europe wide amounts to 195 billion euro, including 10.44 billion euro for the Community Initiatives representing over one third of the European Union's total budget.

Reform of the Structural Funds

Agenda 2000 was the action programme concluded in 1999 at the Berlin European Council to strengthen Community policies and to give the European Union a new financial framework in consideration of the potential full membership of the EU of 12 countries from Central and Eastern Europe by 2010.
The European Commission has accordingly refined its priority objectives for the classification of the regions. The Structural Funds are then used in different combinations in order to address the three priority objectives.

Objective One

Aims to promote development and structural adjustment of regions whose development are lagging behind. Regions with a GDP per capita of less than 75% of the Community average are eligible for Objective 1 funding.

Objective Two

Aims to support the economic and social conversion of areas experiencing structural problems. For the 2000–2006 period, areas with structural difficulties have been divided into four distinctive categories: industrial, rural, urban and fisheries dependent zones.

Objective Three

Aims to support the adaptation and modernisation of education, training and employment policies and systems. It replaces the former Objectives 3 and 4 and reflects the new Title on Employment in the Treaty of Amsterdam.

Transitional Support

Under the terms of the Agenda 2000 reforms those regions which were eligible for Objective 1 funding during the 1994–1999 period but who have lost this entitlement for 2000–2006 will be given transitional assistance. This system of phasing out support is designed to avoid a sudden cessation of European funding and to consolidate the achievements of structural assistance in the previous period.
Northern Ireland has been classified as an Objective 1 in Transition region for the funding period 2000–2006 as the level of GDP per capita had attained 82 per cent of the EU average; seven per cent above the threshold for Objective 1 status.

The Cohesion Fund

A Cohesion Fund was set up in 1993 to run alongside the Structural Funds. The role of the fund is to finance transport and environment infrastructure in those member states where GDP is less than 90 per cent of the EU average (Greece, Ireland, Spain, Portugal). Eighteen billion euro has been allocated to the Cohesion fund for 2000–2006.

The EU Structural Funds

The Community Support Framework in Northern Ireland (CSF)

The details of the Structural Funds assistance to Northern Ireland are laid down in the Northern Ireland Community Support Framework (CSF) 2000–2006. The CSF for the region was agreed following the submission of the Northern Ireland Structural funds Plan and the subsequent negotiations between the European Commission and the Northern Ireland authorities.
A total of 1.3 billion euro has been allocated to the Northern Ireland Community Support Framework for the period 2000–2006 (The breakdown is 57% ERDF, 33% ESF, 8% EAGGF and 2% FIFG).
The Northern Ireland Community Support Framework 2000–2006 aims to achieve a transition to a more peaceful, stable, prosperous, fair and outward looking society, sustained by a better physical environment. This aim is carried over into five priorities and nine Horizontal Principles, while the CSF itself is divided into two operational programmes.

- Northern Ireland Programme for Building Sustainable Prosperity 2000–2006; 890 million euro (£590 m);
- EU Programme for Peace and Reconciliation in Northern Ireland and the Border Region of Ireland 2000–2004; 425 million euro (£280 m).

For general information on European funding contact:
Department of Finance and Personnel
Block F, Health Estates, Stoney Road,
Dundonald, BT16 1US
Tel: 028 9052 3743 / Fax: 028 9052 3890

Northern Ireland Programme for Building Sustainable Prosperity 2000–2006

(Transitional Objective 1 Programme)
This Transitional Objective 1 operational programme is the largest component of the Community Support Framework, accounting for 68 per cent of the Structural Funds allocated. This programme will therefore be the main instrument for the realisation of the economic and social development identified in the Community Support Framework. The designated priorities under the programme are set out in the table below along with the relevant points of contact in government.

Programme for Building Sustainable Prosperity

Priority 1 Economic Growth and Competitiveness

1.1a Business Support - Enterprise
1.1b Business Support - Competitiveness
Arora Upritchard, Invest NI Tel: 028 9054 5218
arora.upritchard@investni.com
1.1c Business Support - Small Business Network
Maeve Hamilton, Invest NI
maeve.hamilton@detini.gov.uk
1.2 Research and Technology Development
Boyd McDowell, Invest NI
boyd.mcdowell@investni.com
1.3a Tourism - Strategic Marketing
1.3b Tourism - Enhancing the Business of Tourism
Sandra Adair, NITB
Tel: 028 9023 1221 s.adair@nitb.com
1.4 Local Economic Development
Ian Kidd, DETI Tel: 028 9052 9237
ian.kidd@detini.gov.uk
1.5 Information Society
Jenny Pyper, DETI jenny.pyper@detini.gov.uk
1.6a Roads and Transport - Roads
Leslie White, DRD leslie.white@drdni.gov.uk
1.6b Roads and Transport - Transport
Michael Pollock, DRD michael.pollock@drdni.gov.uk
1.7 Telecommunications, Trevor Forsythe, Invest NI
Tel: 028 9262 3138 trevor.forsythe@investni.com
1.8a Energy Infrastructure
1.8b Energy Efficiency, David Stanley, DETI
david.stanley@detini.gov.uk

Priority 2 Employment

2.1 Education and Skills Development
2.2 Tackling the Flows into Long Term Unemployment
2.3 Promoting a Labour Market Open to All
European Unit, DEL
2.4 Improving Opportunities for Lifelong Learning
2.5 Education and Training ICT and
Infrastructure Support
David Bradley, Department of Education
david.bradley@deni.gov.uk
2.6 Developing Entrepreneurship
2.7 Human Resource Development in Companies
2.8 The Advancement of Women
European Unit, DEL bsp@delni.gov.uk

Priority 3 Urban and Social Revitalisation

3.1 Urban Revitalisation
Don Harley, European Unit, DSD
Tel: 028 9056 9307 eugrants@dsdni.gov.uk
3.2 Advice and Information Services
3.3 Community Sustainability
Sinead Crossen, Voluntary & Community Unit, DSD
Tel: 028 9056 9785
3.4 Investing in Early Learning
David Bradley, Department of Education
Tel: 028 9127 9292 david.bradley@deni.gov.uk

Priority 4 Agriculture, Rural Development, Forestry and Fisheries

4.1 Training
Ian Titterington, DARD Agri-Food
Development Service
bsp.afds@dardni.gov.uk
4.2a Improving Processing and Marketing of
Agricultural Products
Gillian Heal, DARD Food Policy Division
gillian.heal@dardni.gov.uk
4.2b Food Processing Development
Ian Titterington, DARD Agri-Food Service
bsp.afds@dardni.gov.uk
4.3 Forestry
Stuart Morwood, DARD Forest Service
grants.forestservice@dardni.gov.uk
4.4 Setting up of Farm Relief and Farm
Management Services
Carol Allen, DARD Rural Development Division
cu.rdd@dardni.gov.uk
4.5 Marketing of Quality Agricultural Products
Cathy Moore, DARD Food Policy Division
cathy.moore@dardni.gov.uk
4.6 Basic Services for the Rural Economy
Rural Development Council bsp@rdc.org.uk
4.7 Renovation and Development of Villages and
Protection and Conservation of the Rural Heritage
4.8 Diversification of Agricultural Activities and
Activities Close to Agriculture to Provide Multiple
Activities or Alternative Incomes
4.9 Development and Improvement of Infrastructure
Connected with the Development of Agriculture
4.10 Encouragement for Tourist and Craft Activities
Carol Allen, DARD Rural Development Division
cu.rdd@dardni.gov.uk
4.11 Protection of the Environment in Connection with
Agriculture, Forestry and Landscape Conservation
and the Improvement of Animal Welfare
Rural Development Council bsp@rdc.org.uk
4.12 Financial Engineering
Carol Allen, DARD Rural Development Division
cu.rdd@dardni.gov.uk
4.13 Fisheries, David Crawford,
DARD Fisheries Division Tel: 028 9052 0042
david.crawford@dardni.gov.uk

Priority 5 The Environment

5.1 Sustainable Management of the Environment and
Promotion of the Natural and Built Heritage
Brian Finlay, DRD Water Service
brian.finlay@waterni.gov.uk
Raymond Anderson, DOE Environment &
Heritage Service bsp5.1@doeni.gov.uk

Priority 6 Technical Assistance

6.1a Management and Implementation of Programme
6.1b Programme Information and Publicity
Ashley Williams, DFP European Division
ashley.williams@dfpni.gov.uk

EU Programme for Peace and Reconciliation in Northern Ireland and the Border Region of Ireland 2000–2004 (PEACE II)

Peace II accounts for 38 per cent of the Structural Funds allocated and complements the Programme for Building Sustainable Prosperity. It also aims to build upon the creative cross-community approaches to funding adopted under the Special Support Programme for Peace and Reconciliation 1994 –1999 (Peace I).

Special EU Programmes Body

EU House
6 Cromac Place
Belfast BT7 2JB
Tel: 028 9026 6660
Email: info@seupb.org
Acting Chief Executive: Nuala Kerr

The full text of the PEACE II Operational Programme can be found at: www.europe-dfpni.gov.uk
Application details can be found at: www.eugrants.org/
Information on Peace I can be found at: www.eu-peace.org/

The Special EU Programmes Body is the key player in managing the overall allocation process relating to Peace II and is the best source of information on the initiative.

The Peace II Programme is designed to address the legacy of "The Troubles" and aims to reinforce progress towards a peaceful and stable society and to promote reconciliation. It also aims to take the opportunities arising from the peace process and contribute to reconciliation by promoting appropriate cross community contacts. Two specific objectives can be identified in relation to the overall aim of the Programme:

- Objective 1 Addressing the legacy of conflict
- Objective 2 Taking opportunities arising from Peace

The Priorities for the PEACE II Programme along with funding allocations are set out in the tables to the right.
The five priorities have been sub divided into an extensive list of measures aimed at achieving the key objectives of the programme. Details of the measures, the bodies appointed to implement them, and contact information are set out in the tables on the next two pages.

The intermediary funding bodies associated with the various measures and relevant abbreviations are set out according to the key (shown right).

Priority 1	**Economic Renewal** This has an allocation of 153.67 million euro in Northern Ireland
Priority 2	**Social Integration, Inclusion and Reconciliation** This has an allocation of 107.04 million euro in Northern Ireland
Priority 3	**Locally Based Regeneration and Development Strategies** This has an allocation of 86.05 million euro in Northern Ireland
Priority 4	**Outward and Forward Looking Region** This has an allocation of 86.05 million euro in Northern Ireland.
Priority 5	**Cross Border Co-operation** This has an allocation of 39.72 million euro in Northern Ireland.

Table Explaining Abbreviations

DETI	Department of Enterprise, Trade and Investment
DRD	Department for Regional Development
EGSA	Educational Guidance Service for Adults
ADM/CPA	Area Development Management/Combat Poverty Agency
TWN	Training for Women Network
DARD	Department of Agriculture and Rural Development
RDC	Rural Development Council
CRC	Community Relations Council
SELB	Southern Education and Library Board
NIPPA	Northern Ireland Pre Schools Playgroup Association
DSD	Department for Social Development
OFMDFM	Office of the First Minister and Deputy First Minister
LSP	Local Strategy Partnership
SEUPB	Special EU Programmes Body
DCAL	Department of Culture, Arts and Leisure
DEL	Department for Employment and Learning
CFNI	Community Foundation for Northern Ireland
RCN	Rural Community Network
DCMNR	Department for Communications, Marine and Natural Resources (ROI)
NITB	Northern Ireland Tourist Board

Measure		Implementing Body	Contact	Telephone
1.	**Economic Renewal**			
1.1	Business Competitiveness and Development			
1.1a	Economic Revitalisation	Invest NI	Elaine Brown	028 9023 9090
1.1b	Trade Development	Invest NI	Arora Upritchard	028 9054 5218
1.1c	Financial Engineering	DETI	Maeve Hamilton	028 9025 7330
1.1d	Business Competitiveness	DRD	Michael Pollock	028 9025 7330
1.1e	Business Competitiveness in the Border Region	ADM/CPA	Ailish Quinn	00353 477 1340
1.2	Sustainable Tourism Development			
1.2a	Water Based Tourism	DCAL	Barry Davidson	028 9025 8870
		DARD	Angela Kelly	028 9052 5435
1.2b	Natural Resource Rural Tourism Initiative	S. Armagh Tourism Initiative	Michelle Boyle	028 3086 8900
		Mourne Heritage Trust	Camilla Fitzpatrick	028 4372 4059
		Causeway Heritage Trust	Peter Harper	028 2075 2100
		Fermanagh LSP	Helen Maguire	028 6632 5050
		Sperrins Tourism Ltd	Kathleen McBride	028 8674 7700
1.3	New Skills and New Opportunities	ADM/CPA	Ailish Quinn	00353 477 1340
		DEL	John Neill	028 9025 7777
		PROTEUS	Pat Donnelly	028 9037 1023
		EGSA	Kevin Donaghy	028 9024 4274
1.4	Promoting Entrepreneurship	TWN	Norma Shearer	028 9077 7199
		Playboard	Hunter Blair	028 9080 3380
		ADM/CPA	Ailish Quinn	00353 477 1340
1.5	Positive Action for Women	DARD	Lesley Fay	028 9054 5893
		ADM/CPA	Ailish Quinn	00353 477 1340
		TWN	Karen Sweeney	028 9077 7199
		Playboard	Caroline Mills	028 9080 3380
		DEL European Unit	Seamus Camplisson	028 9025 7777
1.6	Training for Farmers (NI)	DARD		028 9054 7111
1.7	Diversification of Agricultural Activities (NI)			
1.7a	Obtaining Alternative Employment	DARD		028 9054 7111
1.7b	Part-time Employment	RDC		028 8676 6980
1.8	Technology Support for the Knowledge Based Economy (NI)			
1.8a	Innovation Technology and Networking	Invest NI	Nigel Carr	028 9262 3029
1.8b	Information Age	DETI Information Age Unit		028 9052 9900
1.9	Investment in Agricultural Holdings (NI)	DARD		028 9054 7111
1.10	Basic Services for the Rural Economy and Population			
1.10a	Retail Services	RDC		028 8676 6980
1.10b	ICT	RDC		028 8676 6980
2	**Social Integration, Inclusion and Reconciliation**			
2.1	Reconcilitation for Sustainable Peace	ADM/CPA	Ailish Quinn	00353 477 1340
		CRC	Jim Dennison	028 9022 7500
		OFMDFM	Karen Jardine	028 9052 8400
		Dept of Education	Linda Scott	028 9127 9302
2.2	Developing Children	ADM/CPA	Ailish Quinn	00353 477 1340
2.3	Skilling and Building	CFNI	Felicity McCartney	028 9024 5927
2.4	Reconciliation of Victims			
2.4a	Pathways to Inclusion	CFNI	Felicity McCartney	028 9024 5927
2.4b	Integration and Reconciliation	CFNI	Felicity McCartney	028 9024 5927
2.4c	Inclusion of Target Groups in Border Region	ADM/CPA	Ailish Quinn	00353 477 1340
2.5	Investing in Childcare	NIPPA	Siobhan Fitzpatrick	028 9066 5220
2.6	Promoting Active Citizenship	ADM/CPA	Ailish Quinn	00353 477 1340
2.7	Developing Weak Community	ADM/CPA	Ailish Quinn	00353 477 1340
		CFNI	Felicity McCartney	028 9024 5927

Continued on next page

Measure		Implementing Body	Contact	Telephone
2.8	Accompanying Infrastructure and Equipment Support	SELB	Gregory Butler	028 3751 2200
		ADM/CPA	Ailish Quinn	00353 477 1340
		CFNI	Felicity McCartney	028 9024 5927
		NIPPA	Siobhan Fitzpatrick	028 9066 5220
2.9	Renovation and Development of Villages and Protection and Conservation of Rural Heritage (NI)			
2.9a	Conservation of the Rural Heritage	RCN	Michael Hughes	028 8676 6670
2.9b	Renovation	RDC		028 8676 6980
2.10	Encouragement for Tourism & Craft Activities	RDC		028 8676 6980
2.11	Area Based Regeneration	DSD	Don Harley	028 9056 9307
		Contact Local LSP		
3	**Locally Based Regeneration and Development Strategies**			
3.1	Local Economic Initiatives for Developing the Social Economy	Contact Local LSP		
3.2	Locally Based Human Resource Training and Development Strategies	Contact Local LSP		
3.3	Building Better Communities Border Region	Contact Local Task Force		
3.4	Improving Our Rural Communities	Contact Local Task Force		
4	**Outward and Forward Looking Region**			
4.1	Networking	OFMDFM	Kenny Knox	028 9052 2563
4.2a	Marketing the Region as a Tourism Destination	NITB	Sandra Adair	028 9023 1221
		Cavan Co Council Task Force	Vincent Reynolds	00353 49 433 2427
		Donegal Co Council Task Force	Francis Coyle	00353 74 72433
		Leitrim Co Council Task Force	Sean Kielty	00353 78 50498
		Louth Co Council Task Force	Mary Mulholland	00353 42 935 3150
		Monaghan Co Council Task Force	Adge King	00353 47 38140
		Sligo Co Council Task Force	Padraig Flanaghan	00353 71 56697
4.2b	Enhancing the Region as a Tourism Destination	NITB	Sandra Adair	028 9023 1221
		Cavan Co Council Task Force	Vincent Reynolds	00353 49 433 2427
		Donegal Co Council Task Force	Francis Coyle	00353 74 72433
		Leitrim Co Council Task Force	Sean Kielty	00353 78 50498
		Louth Co Council Task Force	Mary Mulholland	00353 42 935 3150
		Monaghan Co Council Task Force	Adge King	00353 47 38140
		Sligo Co Council Task Force	Padraig Flanaghan	00353 71 56697
5	**Cross Border Co-operation**			
5.1	Increasing Cross Border Development Opportunities	Co-operation Ireland		028 9032 1462
5.2	Improving Cross Border Public Sector Co-operation	SEUPB	Brenda Hegarty	028 8225 5750
5.3	Developing Cross Border Reconciliation and Understanding	ADM/CPA	Ailish Quinn	00353 477 1340
5.4	Promotion of Joint Approaches to Social, Education, Training and Human Resource Devt	ADM/CPA	Ailish Quinn	00353 477 1340
5.5	Education, Cross Border School and Youth Co-operation	Dept of Education (NI)	Linda Scott	028 9127 9302
		Dept of Education (RoI)	Mary O'Driscoll	
5.6	Agriculture and Rural Development Co-operation			
5.6a	Cross Border Community Development	RCN	Tom Kiernan	028 8676 6670
5.6b	Cross Border Diversification	DARD		
5.7	Cross Border Fishing and Aquaculture	DARD	David Crawford	028 9052 0042
		DCMNR	Sean Murray	
6	**Technical Assistance**			
6.1	Programme Information and Publicity	SEUPB		028 9026 6660
6.2a	Management, Monitoring and Evaluation	DSD	Don Harley	028 9056 9307
6.2b	Internal Co-ordination	SEUPB	Brenda Hegarty	028 8225 5750

Other European Union Initiatives

The Community Initiatives

Community Initiatives are special forms of assistance proposed by the Commission to Member states. Implemented throughout the European Union they are financed by Structural Funds aimed at solving specific problems and are additional in financial terms to a region's Community Support Framework.
The Community Initiatives have three defining features:

- Encouraging transactional, cross border and interregional co-operation;
- Increased involvement of people on the ground "bottom up approach";
- Support through a real partnership of those involved in Community initiatives.

Reform of Community Initiatives

The number of Community Initiatives has been reduced with the reform of the Structural Funds under Agenda 2000. There are now 4 Community Initiatives for the period 2000–06 each financed by a Structural Fund; 118 million euro has been allocated to Northern Ireland for this purpose. These are:

- Interreg III
- Leader +
- EQUAL
- Urban II

Details of these initiatives are set out below.

INTERREG III

The main objective is to strengthen economic and social cohesion in the Community through the promotion of cross border, transnational and international co-operation and balanced development of the community territory. This is to be achieved through the promotion of integrated regional development within neighbouring regions.
INTERREG III has 3 strands:

- Strand A: cross-border co-operation
- Strand B: transnational co-operation
- Strand C: interregional co-operation

81 million euro has been allocated to Northern Ireland for INTERREG.

For general information on the Interreg IIIA Initiative, contact:

The Interreg IIIA Secretariat
Special EU Programmes Body
European Union House
Castle Meadow Court
Dublin Road
Monaghan
Tel: 0808 127 5005 (Freephone from Northern Ireland)
1800 80 5005 (Freephone from Republic of Ireland)
Fax: + 353 477 1258
Email: interreg@seupb.ie

The Implementing Bodies for Interreg IIIA are:

Northwest Region Cross Border
Interreg IIIA Partnership
16A The Diamond
Derry, BT48 6HW
Tel: 028 7137 0808
Email: interreg@derrycity.gov.uk
Contact: Eamon Molloy

Irish Central Border Area
Interreg IIIA Partnership
The INTEC Centre
36 Bridge Street
Enniskillen
BT74 7BT
Tel: 028 6632 2556
Email: info@icban.com
Contact: Kate Burns

East Border Region
Interreg IIIA Partnership
Town Hall
Bank Parade
Newry, BT35 6HR
Tel: 028 3025 2684
Email: interreg@eastborderregion.com
Contact: Pamela Arthurs

Business: European Information Centres

Aimed at providing the business community (with emphasis on the SME sector) with information on European developments. The centre has access to EU databases including Tenders Electronic Daily (TED) carrying daily listings for requests for tenders for EU public contracts.

Euro Info Centre

Invest NI, Upper Galwally, Belfast BT8 6TB
Tel: 028 9023 9090
Fax: 028 9049 0490

Northern Ireland Innovation Relay Centre (IRC)

The IRC funded by the EU aims to promote the transfer of innovative technology to and from Northern Ireland.

Innovation Relay Centre

Invest NI, 17 Antrim Road, Lisburn BT28 3AL
Tel: 028 9023 9090
Fax: 028 9049 0490

Leader +

Leader + encourages the design and implementation of innovative development strategies for rural areas. Leader + achieves this by establishing partnerships at a local level.
Leader + comprises three strands:

- Strand 1: support for integrated and innovative development strategies for rural areas
- Strand 2: support for interregional and transnational co-operation
- Strand 3: networking for all EU rural areas

15 million euro has been allocated to Northern Ireland.

Contact:
Rural Development Division, DARD, Dundonald House, Belfast BT4 3SB
Tel: 028 9052 5435/ Fax: 028 9052 4776
Email: leader+.rdd@dardni.gov.uk / Web: www.dardni.gov.uk

The Northern Ireland LEADER+ Programme is being implemented by 12 LEADER+ Groups, each covering a specific geographic area:

Coleraine Local Action Group for Enterprise Ltd
Area covered: Coleraine Borough Council area excluding towns of Coleraine, Portrush and Portstewart
Tel: 028 2955 8066
Email: info@collage.ltd.com

Craigavon & Armagh Rural Development (CARD)
Area covered: Armagh City and District Council Area and Craigavon Borough Council area, excluding the urban localities of Armagh City, Lurgan, Brownlow and Portadown.
Tel: 028 3831 2588
Email: alison.mitchell@craigavon.gov.uk

East Tyrone Rural
Area covered: Cookstown District Council Area and Dungannon & South Tyrone Borough Council excluding the urban areas of Cookstown and Dungannon
Tel: 028 8772 0311
Email: funding.office@dungannon.gov.uk

Fermanagh Local Action Group
Area covered: Co Fermanagh excluding Enniskillen town
Tel: 028 6862 1600
Email: info@fermanaghleader.co.uk

Newry & Mourne Local Action Group
Area covered: Newry & Mourne District Council area excluding the City of Newry and town of Warrenpoint
Tel: 028 3026 3177
Email: micealsdsa@dial.pipex.com

Magherafelt Area Partnership Ltd
Area covered: Magherafelt District Council area excluding the town of Magherafelt
Tel: 028 7939 7979
Email: info@magherafelt.eu.com

North Antrim Leader
Area covered: Moyle District Council area and the Borough Council areas of Ballymena, Ballymoney and Larne, excluding the towns of Ballycastle, Ballymena, Ballymoney and Larne
Tel: 028 2177 2138
Email: north-antrim-leader@antrim.net

REAP South Antrim (Rural Economic Action Partnership)
Area covered: District Council areas of Antrim, Carrickfergus and Newtownabbey excluding the towns of Carrickfergus and Antrim and the urban areas of Newtownabbey
Tel: 028 9446 3113 ext 343
Email: monica.curran@antrim.gov.uk

Roe Valley Rural Development Ltd
Area covered: rural wards of Limavady Borough Council area
Tel: 028 7776 0306
Email: karen.quigley@limavady.gov.uk

Rural Area Partnership in Derry
Area covered: Derry City Council area excluding the urban area of Derry City
Tel: 028 7133 7149
Email: leaderplus@globalnet.co.uk

The Rural Down Partnership
Area covered: Rural areas of Ards, Banbridge and Down Council areas, excluding the towns of Newtownards, Comber, Downpatrick, Ballynahinch and Banbridge
Tel: 028 4066 0609
Email: camilla.fitzpatrick@banbridgedc.gov.uk

West Tyrone Rural Ltd
Area covered: Strabane District Council area and Omagh District Council area excluding the urban areas of Strabane and Omagh towns
Tel: 028 8772 031
Email: info@westtyronerural.com

EQUAL

Equal aims to promote new means to tackle all forms of exclusion, discrimination and inequality in relation to the labour market and leads on from two earlier initiatives: ADAPT and EMPLOYMENT.

The Northern Ireland EQUAL Programme will target two priorities:

- Employability
- Equal opportunities for men and women

12 million euro has been allocated to Northern Ireland for this project.

Contact: Michael Hegarty,
PROTEUS, 8 Edgewater Road, Belfast, BT3 9JQ
Tel: 028 9037 1023 / Fax: 028 9037 1024
Email: equal@proteus-ni.org
Web: www.proteus-ni.org

Urban II

The initiative aims to promote the design and implementation of innovative development models for the economic and social regeneration of urban areas in crisis and aims to strengthen exchanges of information and experience on sustainable urban development in the EU.
Approximately 50 towns with a population of 10,000+ may be eligible for the Urban initiative. The urban areas included may be inside or outside Objective 1 and 2 areas and must fulfil at least three of the following conditions:

- High long term unemployment;
- Low rate of economic activity;
- High level of poverty and exclusion;
- The need for structuring adjustment due to economic and social difficulties;
- High proportion of immigrants, ethnic minorities or refugees;
- Low level of education, major gaps in terms of qualifications and a high rate of pupil failure;
- Unstable demographic environment;
- Particularly poor environmental conditions.

10 million euro has been allocated to Northern Ireland.

Each Urban programme must include measures for strengthening information exchanges and sharing experience on the regeneration of urban areas in crisis.

Contact:
Catherine Taggart, The Urban II Secretariat,
Department for Social Development
Brookmount Buildings, 42 Fountain Street
Belfast BT1 5EE
Tel: 028 9025 1982 / Fax: 028 90 25 1939
Web: www.dsdni.gov.uk

European Documentation Centres

There are two European Documentation Centres based in Northern Ireland. Their role is to provide a resource to students and academics.
The centres have extensive collections of EU information sources and access to EU databases.

European Documentation Centre

The Main Library, Queen's University, Belfast BT7 1NN
Tel: 028 9024 5133 ext 3605
Fax: 028 9033 5040
Web: www.qub.ac.uk/lib/wherelib/
Contact: Marie Griffiths

European Documentation Centre

The Library, University of Ulster, Cromore Road
Coleraine BT52 1SA
Tel: 028 7032 4029
Fax: 028 7032 4928
Email: je.peden@ulst.ac.uk
Web: www.ulst.ac.uk/library

Other Centrally Managed Programmes

SME Development Initiatives

Entrepreneurs or Businesses seeking European business and commercial information and assistance with Community funding should contact:

Euro Info Centre Invest NI
Upper Galwally, Belfast, BT8 6TB
Tel: 028 9023 9090 / Fax: 028 9049 0490

Joint European Venture Programme

The programme aims to stimulate the establishment of joint ventures between European SMEs. JEV has an indicative budget of 85 million euro.

Contact:
Greater London Enterprise Ltd
28 Park Street
London SE1 9EQ
Tel: 0207 403 0300 / Fax: 0207 403 1742

Business Angels Networks

Under the Business Angels programme the Commission finances up to 50% of the costs of feasibility studies for the creation of business networks, as well as a maximum of 50% of the costs of pilot actions aimed at establishing a regional or national network.

European Business Angels Network

Avenue des Arts 12, Bte 7
B–1210 Brussels
Belgium
Tel: 00 32 22 18 43 13 / Fax: 00 32 22 18 45 83
Email: info@eban.org
Web: www.eban.org

Mutual Guarantee Scheme

Mutual Guarantee Schemes involve private groupings of companies, often linked to sector specific interest groups, to provide loan insurance to banks.

Enterprise Directorate General, Access to Finance,
Rue de la Loi 200 (SC-27 04/04), B–1049 Brussels
Tel: 00 322 295 91 86 / Fax: 00 322 295 21 54

I-TEC

I-TEC is part of the Innovation Programme of the European Commission and aims to encourage early stage investments in technologically innovative SMEs.

Enterprise Directorate General
Innovation Policy
Office EUFO 2/2197
L–2920 Luxembourg
Tel: 00 352 4301 39194 / Fax: 00 352 4301 34544

PROTEUS

Proteus is the contact point for the EQUAL initiative and some measures under PEACE II, as well as its role administering training and employment programmes on behalf of the Department for Employment and Learning.

8 Edgewater Office Park, Edgewater Road, Belfast, BT3 9JQ
Tel: 028 9037 1023 / Fax: 028 9077 3543
Email: administrator@proteus-ni.org

The European Employment Service (EURES)

Eures links to a network of over 400 centres throughout Europe providing information on vacancies, recruitment and living and working conditions throughout Europe.

EURES Section, Gloucester House, Chichester Street
Belfast, BT1 4RA
Tel: 028 9025 2270 / Fax: 028 9025 2288
Email: Nicola.mchugh@delni/gov.uk
Web: europa.eu.int/comm./employmentsocial

Rural Carrefours

Carrefours are part of a regional network providing information to all sectors of the agricultural and rural community. They provide regional information and will assist in the search for European partners and help place students seeking work placements in other EU member states.

Carrefour Ulster
Clogher Valley Rural Centre
47 Main Street, Clogher BT76 0AA
Tel:028 8554 8872 / Fax:028 8554 8203
Email: carrefours_Ulster@dnet.co.uk
Web: www.clogher.com/carrefour

Education

The European Resource Centre for Schools and Colleges

Norwich Union House, 7 Fountain Street
Belfast BT1 5EG
Tel: 028 9024 8220 / Fax: 028 9023 7592
Email: Jonathan.Stewart@britishcouncil.org

The British Council

Education and Training Group
Norwich Union House
7 Fountain Street, Belfast BT1 5EG
Tel: 028 9024 8220 /Fax: 028 9023 7592
Email: liz.mcbain@britishcouncil.org

European Bureau

Youth Council for Northern Ireland
Forestview, Purdy's Lane, Belfast BT8 7AR
Tel: 028 9064 3882 /Fax: 028 9064 3874
Email: dguilfoyle@youthcouncil-ni.org.uk
Web: www.youthcouncil-ni.org.uk

Local Strategy Partnerships

The Local Strategy Partnership Boards established to oversee the implementation of Priority 3 Locally Based Regeneration and Development Initiatives will have responsibility for measures relating to the social economy and human resource and development initiatives under Peace II.
Priority 3 accounts for approximately 20 per cent of the EU's Structural Funds allocation to the EU Programme for Peace and Reconciliation in Northern Ireland. The EU allocations will be supplemented by national public and private funds to produce a total of 114.73 million euros.

The Peace II Programme details a vision for the Local Strategy Partnerships building upon the previous structures of District Partnerships, which were established under the EU Programme for Peace and Reconciliation (Peace I). It is intended that the LSPs will be more integrated and sustainable and have greater autonomy in their decision making than the District Partnership Boards. There are two key changes in the new LSPs from the old District Partnership model:

- District Councils are to be involved in the work of local partnerships at a corporate level, not only through the participation of individual district councillors or council officers and
- Statutory agencies at local level are to be actively involved in partnership work, to ensure that the broad strategic direction of Departments and their Agencies take full account of the views and priorities of local communities operating at the local level.

It is envisaged that the role of LSPs will develop into a long-term strategy and that they will establish a remit extending beyond the distribution of EU Structural funds. In furtherance of these aims the central decision making role of the Northern Ireland Partnership Board has not been repeated for Peace II. Responsibility for decision making will rest at local level and the Special EU Programmes Body and the Monitoring Committee will focus upon:

- Ensuring compliance with the Structural Funds Regulations, the Peace II Programme document and the Programme Complement and
- Playing a supportive role for LSPs in association with the new Regional Partnership Board.

The overall strategic aim of Peace II is to "reinforce progress toward a peaceful and stable society and to promote reconciliation". Applications under the programme must contain at least one of two of the specific objectives i.e. they must address the legacy of conflict and/or take the opportunities arising from peace. Peace II Partnerships focus on specific needs in the partnership areas and involve a more structured contribution from the statutory sector which it is hoped will ensure greater sustainability and avoid the criticisms levelled of a lack of sustainability following Peace I.

Local Strategy Partnerships (LSPs) consist of two strands:
- Government (local government and statutory sector);
  The "four pillars" of the:
- Voluntary sector; Business; Agriculture; Trade Unions.

The aim is to achieve a balance of local interests and the development of a structured involvement of the statutory sector in the Partnerships. Partnerships are required to be inclusive and provide equity of standing between the various strands and seek to be open and accountable to their local communities, demonstrate fairness in the allocation of funding in their control and produce structures and mechanisms to enable auditing of all aspects of their work.

Whilst there is no definitive membership quota set for membership of the LSPs it is recommended that a maximum of twenty-eight should not be exceeded. Nominations for members of the LSP occur at a local level and the procedure for processing nominations is determinable at individual local level. However, the process utilised must be documented and submitted to the SEUPB for approval as part of the Global Grant Allocation Agreement.

A listing of Local Strategy Partnerships is set out below (A–Z). The listing includes contact details and membership for each LSP.

A-Z Listing of Local Strategy Partnerships

Membership for each LSP.

Antrim LSP
The Steeple
Antrim, BT41 1BJ
Tel: 028 9446 3113 / Fax: 028 9446 4469
Partnership Manager: Claire Higgins

Members	Nominating Sector
Gilbert Bell	NEELB
Andy Brown	ICTU
John Clarke	UFU
Thomas Burns	Antrim Borough Council
Sam Dunlop	Antrim Borough Council
Alison Flynn	Invest NI
Oliver Frawley	Community/Voluntary
Andrew Little	Chamber of Commerce
Damien Lynch	Chamber of Commerce
Sam Magee	Antrim Borough Council
Brian Mawhinney	Community/Voluntary
John McKee	DARD
Martin McManus	Antrim Borough Council
Stephen Murray	NHSSB
Stephen Nicholl	Antrim Borough Council
Freda Waite	Antrim Enterprise Agency
Adrian Watson	Antrim Borough Council
Robert Chesney	UFU
Kieron Murphy	NIHE
Christine Harper	DEL
Valerie Adams	Citizens Advice Bureau
Brian Johnston	Caddy and District Community Group
Rosemary Magill	Women's Aid

Ards LSP
Council Offices
Crepe Weavers Industrial Estate
20 Comber Road, BT23 4RX
Tel: 028 9182 6913 / Fax: 028 9182 8040
Partnership Manager: Tom Rowley

Members	Nominating Sector
Cllr Angus Carson	Ards Borough Council
Cllr Kieran McCarthy	Ards Borough Council
Cllr Margaret Craig	Ards Borough Council
Cllr Robert Gibson	Ards Borough Council
Cllr Hamilton Lawther	Ards Borough Council
Cllr Alan McDowell	Ards Borough Council
Jackie Brown	Chamber of Commerce
Tony McMullan	NIPSA
Margaret Adair	NIPSA
Harry Liddy	NIPSA
Trevor Kerr	Invest NI
Sam Brown	NDAI
Gordon Orr	PSNI
Eileen Sweeney	Action Mental Health
John Smyth	Rural CommunityNetwork
Valerie Richmond	Ards Community Network
Hilary Forrester	Women's Aid
Carol McNamara	NIPPA
Caroline Mahon	Upper Ards Community Assoc
David Stewart	UFU
Prof Sydney Salmon	UCHT

Armagh LSP

The Palace Demesne
Armagh, BT60 4EL
Tel: 028 3752 9600 / Fax: 028 3752 9601
Partnership Manager: Denise O'Hare/
Sharon O'Gorman

Members	Nominating Sector
Cllr P Brannigan	Armagh City & District Council
Cllr P L Berry	Armagh City & District Council
Cllr P O'Rawe	Armagh City & District Council
Cllr J A Speers	Armagh City & District Council
Cllr R W Turner	Armagh City & District Council
Victor Brownlees	Armagh City & District Council
David McCammick	Armagh City & District Council
A Hamilton	Invest NI
J Dobbin	NIHE
E Hamilton	Armagh and Dungannon HSS
V McKevitt	DARD
C Donaghy	SHSSB
G Butler	SELB
R Jay	Queens University Armagh
Isobel Grimes	ICTU
E Kelly	Crosscurrents
A Rutledge	Rutledge Recruitment
Jacinta Fogarty	ICTU
G Mallon	Keady Community Initiatives
J Doherty	Rutledge Recruitment
T W Johnston	Markethill District Enterprises
K McAnallen	Armagh City Hotel
M Jamison	REACT
T Reddick	Keady Community Initiative
G Mallon	Middletown Development Assoc
JJ Gruggan	Initiative Economic Development
R Cummings	UFU

Ballymena LSP

Ardeevin
80 Galgorm Road
Ballymena, BT42 1AB
Tel: 028 2566 0444 / Fax: 028 2563 9785
Director of the LSP: Majella McAllister

Members	Nominating Sector
Arthur Crowe	NI Housing Executive
Gilly Irwin	NEELB
John Fenton	NHSSB
Claire O'Neill	North East Institute of Further & Higher Education
Cllr R Stirling	Ballymena Borough Council
Cllr Hubert Nicholl	Ballymena Borough Council
Cllr Neill Armstrong	Ballymena Borough Council
Cllr L Scott	Ballymena Borough Council
Cllr Maurice Mills	Ballymena Borough Council
Claire Herron	Invest NI
Michael Scullion	Glenravel Environmental Improvement Association
Deirdre McAuley	Ballymena CAB
James Edmondson	Ulster Farmers Union
John Anderson	Ulster Farmers Union
Gerry Lawn	Ballymena Chamber of Commerce
Roy Bonar	Ballymena Chamber of Commerce
Gerald Bradley	ICTU
Colm Best	Community/Voluntary
Rosemary Magill	Community/Voluntary
Declan O'Loan	Council
Kevin Hayes	Statutory
Richard Totten	Community/Voluntary
Jack Johnston	Community/Voluntary

Ballymoney LSP

Borough Offices
Riada House, 14 Charles Street
Ballymoney, BT53 6DZ
Tel: 028 2766 2280 / Fax: 028 2766 5150
Partnership Manager: Nigel Freeburn

Members	Nominating Sector
Cllr Bill Kennedy	Ballymoney Council
Cllr Mervyn Storey	Ballymoney Council
Cllr Cecil Cousley	Ballymoney Council
Cllr James Simpson	Ballymoney Council
Cllr Malachy McCamphill	Ballymoney Council
John Dempsey	Ballymoney Council
Sam Vallelly	Causeway Trust
Anne Connolly	Education
Geoff Spence	Invest NI
John McKee	DARD
Christine Marks	NIHE
Joe Patton	Rural Development
Vince Boyle	NIAPA
Jonathan Payne	Retail
Heather Hargy	Retail
Michael Fleming	Industrialist
Mac Pollock	Trade Union
Rae Kirk	Community/Voluntary
Pat Crossley	Community/Voluntary
Veronica McKinley	Community/Voluntary
Denis Connelly	Community/Voluntary

Banbridge LSP

Civic Building
Downshire Road
Banbridge, BT32 3JY
Tel: 028 4066 0609 / Fax: 028 4066 0601
Partnership Manager: Joanne Morgan

Members	Nominating Sector
Cllr Ian Burns	Banbridge District Council
Cllr William J Martin	Banbridge District Council
Cllr Frank McQuaid	Banbridge District Council
Cllr Cassie McDemott	Banbridge District Council
Cllr Wilfred McFadden	Banbridge District Council
Robert Gilmore	Banbridge District Council
Nigel Jess	Private Tourism Provider
John Dawson	Banbridge Rotary Club
Patrick Kelly	ROMAL Community Network
Tony Gates	Mourne Heritage Trust
Pamela Johnston	Banbridge & District Gateway Club
Nigel Smith	Banbridge & District Sports Association
Anne Cromie	Banbridge Community Network
Brian Hewitt	ICTU
Sharon Currans	NIPSA
William Cromie	UFU
Esther Ervin	UFU
Aidan McCullough	TADA Rural Network
Kathleen Donnelly	T& EA (Training & Employment Agency)
Dan McCool	SELB

Eamon McKeown	NIHE
Vince McKevitt	DARD
Denis Preston	Craigavon & Banbridge HSS Trust
Eamon Mulvenna	Invest NI
Liam Hannaway	Banbridge District Council
Rhonda Abraham	Banbridge District Council
Mervyn Waddell	Statutory

Belfast LSP

5th Floor
Premier Business Centre
20 Adelaide Street, BT2 8GB
Tel: 028 9032 8532 / Fax: 028 9032 7306
Partnership Manager: Dr Eddie Jackson

Members	Nominating Sector
Cllr David Alderdice	Belfast City Council
Cllr Alan Crowe	Belfast City Council
Cllr Patrick Convery	Belfast City Council
Cllr Ian Crozier	Belfast City Council
Cllr Danny Lavery	Belfast City Council
Cllr Marie Moore	Belfast City Council
Cllr Billy Hutchinson	Belfast City Council
Tim Losty	Invest NI
Dr Paula Kilbane	EHSSB
Billy Gamble	DRD
Declan McKeown	DSD
Kieran Brazier	DEL
Maurice Johnston	NIHE
George Campbell	Belfast Education and Library Board
Sam Burns	Community Voluntary Sector
Marie Cavanagh	Community Voluntary Sector
Sammy Douglas	Community Voluntary Sector
Eileen Howell	Community Voluntary Sector
Liam Maskey	Community Voluntary Sector
Bill Patterson	Community Voluntary Sector
Judith Willoughby	Community Voluntary Sector
Jackie McCoy	Business/Private Sector
Brendan Mackin	Trade Union
Manus Maguire	Trade Union
Anne McVicker	Trade Union
Brian Megahey	Agriculture

Carrickfergus LSP

Town Hall
Joymount
Carrickfergus, BT38 7DL
Tel: 028 9335 1438 / Fax: 028 9336 0868
Partnership Manager: Alan McCay

Members	Nominating Sector
Brenda Leslie	Carrickfergus Women's Forum
Sandra Kelso	NIMBA
Karen Montgomery	Community/Voluntary
Muriel Todd	Trade Union
Beverley Heaney	Trade Union
Sam Crowe	Business
David Mitchell	Business
James Macauley	Business
Edward Adamson	UFU
Ald Roy Beggs	Carrickfergus BC
Cllr Robin Cavan	Carrickfergus BC
Cllr Terry Clements	Carrickfergus BC
Cllr May Beattie	Carrickfergus BC
Cllr Janet Crampsie	Carrickfergus BC
Alan Cardwell	Carrickfergus BC
Dermot Curran	NIHE
Geoffrey McGeagh	NEELB
Stephen Murray	NHSSB
Noel Brown	Invest NI

Castlereagh LSP

Civic and Administrative Offices
Bradford Court, Upper Galwally
Belfast, BT8 6RB
Tel: 028 9048 7997
Partnership Coordinator: Mike Wilson
Assistant Partnership Coordinator: Cecilia Young

Members	Nominating Sector
Cllr Jack Beattie	Castlereagh BC
Cllr Claire Ennis	Castlereagh BC
Cllr Vivienne Stevenson	Castlereagh BC
Cllr Frank Gallagher	Castlereagh BC
Cllr David Drysdale	Castlereagh BC
Cllr Joanne Bunting	Castlereagh BC
Cllr Jim White	Castlereagh BC
Cllr Geraldine Rice	Castlereagh BC
Cllr Cecil Hall	Castlereagh BC
Cllr Brian Hanvey	Castlereagh BC
Fred McKenna	Carryduff Community Forum
Janice Cherry	Gae Lairn
Rosemary Reynolds	Cregagh Community Forum
Richard Mills	Belvoir Players
Elizabeth Walker	Cregagh Community Churches Partnership
Gilmore Andrews	SE Belfast Scout Council
Timothy Morrow	Ulster Farmers Union
Michael Watson	Ulster Farmers Union
Stephen McAuley	M&S Associates
Helen Mathews	Advanced Learning Systems
Jack McComiskey	Castlereagh Enterprises Ltd
Albert Hamilton	Business in the Community
Brenda Smith	Trade Union
Jim Barbour	Trade Union
Karen Bradbury	Statutory
Paul Carland	Statutory
Alan Gregg	Statutory
Andy McInnes	Statutory
Rowan Davison	South & East Belfast Trust
Ray Gilbert	SEELB

Coleraine LSP

Cloonavin
66 Portstewart Road
Coleraine, BT52 1RR
Tel: 028 7034 7050
Partnership Manager: Patricia McCallion

Members	Nominating Sector
Nevin Oliver	Causeway HSS Trust
Joan Baird	NIHE
Nigel Kyle	PSNI
Prof Peter Roebuck	University of Ulster
Wavell Moore	Coleraine BC
Cllr David Barbour	Coleraine BC
Cllr Eamon Mullan	Coleraine BC
Cllr Maurice Bradley	Coleraine BC
Lorna Carson	ICTU
Dr Arthur Williamson	AUT
Liz Baird	Coleraine Rural & Urban Network

Angela Welch	Advice Services in Coleraine
Eddie Clements	Coleraine Enterprise Agency
Ian Donaghey	Coleraine Town Partnership
David Alexander	Causeway Chamber of Commerce
Michael Caulfield	Invest NI
Patsy Bradley	Ulster Farmers Union

Cookstown LSP

Gortalowry House
94 Church Street
Cookstown, BT80 8HX
Tel: 028 8676 4714
Partnership Manager: Maggie Bryson

Members	Nominating Sector
Cllr Trevor Wilson	Cookstown DC
James McGarvey	Cookstown DC
Ian McCrea	Cookstown DC
Oliver Molloy	Cookstown DC
John McNamee	Cookstown DC
Adrian McCreesh	Statutory
Michael McGuckin	Statutory
Michael May	Statutory
David Bradshaw	Statutory
Helen McClenaghan	Statutory
Ursula Marshall	Community/Voluntary
William Wilkinson	Community/Voluntary
May Devlin	Community/Voluntary
Hilary Mallon	Trade Union
Vera McElhone	Trade Union
Raymond McGarvey	Business
Jim Eastwood	Business
Wilbert Mayne	Social Partner

Craigavon LSP

Civic Centre
Lakeview Road
Craigavon, BT64 1AL
Tel: 028 3831 2577
Partnership Manager: Jillian McAreavey

Members	Nominating Sector
Cllr Jonathan Bell	Craigavon BC
Mark Bleakney	Statutory Representative
Ald Frederick Crowe	Craigavon BC
Gerard Devlin	Trade Union Representative
Kathleen Donnelly	Statutory Sector Representative
Jill England	Statutory Sector Representative
Clifford Forbes	Community/Voluntary Sector
Ignatius Fox	Agricultural/Rural Representative
Philomena Horner	Community and voluntary Sector
Cllr Dolores Kelly	Craigavon BC
Teddy Martin	Trade Union Representative
Jim McCammick	Business Sector Representative
Gerard Doran	Statutory Sector Representative
Isabel Murray	Business Sector Representative
Cllr John O'Dowd	Craigavon BC
David Riley	Agricultural/Rural Representative

Derry LSP

98 Strand Road
Derry, BT48 6DQ
Tel: 028 7137 6505
Partnership Manager: Oonagh McGillion

Members	Nominating Sector
Clionagh Boyle	Community/Voluntary
Cllr Mary Bradley	Council
Cllr Thomas Conway	Council
Catherine Cooke	Community/Voluntary
Keith Cradden	Statutory
Eamonn Deane	Community/Voluntary
Edith Dunlop	Community/Voluntary
Gerard Finnegan	Statutory
Cllr Lynn Fleming	Derry City Council
Martin Gallagher	Community/Voluntary
Cllr Joe Millar	Derry City Council
Hugh Hegarty	Private
Tony McGurk	Statutory
Conal McFeely	Community/Voluntary
Cllr Jim McKeever	Derry City Council
Jennifer McLernon	Statutory
Anne Molloy	Trade Union
Eamonn Molloy	Observer
Donald Montgomery	Agriculture/Rural
Declan O'Hare	Statutory
Cllr Gerry O'hEara	Derry City Council
Cllr William O'Connell	Derry City Council
Helen Osborn	Statutory
Des Rainey	Trade Union
Judi McGaffin	Western Health and Social Services Board
Damian McAdams	Jobs and Benefits Office
Terry O'Kane	NIAPA

Down LSP

24 Strangford Road
Downpatrick, BT30 6SR
Tel: 028 4461 7667
Partnership Manager: David Patterson

Members	Nominating Sector
Helen Honeyman	Harmony Community Trust
Sean Garland	St Dymphna's Association
Francis Casement	Racecourse Road Community Association
Marion Flanagan	Ballynahinch Regeneration
Jacquie Richardson	NIPPA, Drumaroad Playgroup
Eamonn King	Down District CAB
Adrian Smyth	Business in the Community
Crosby Clelland	Rural Business
Ian Irwin	Craft Sector/Tourism
Elizabeth Fleming	UFU
Graham Furey	UFU
Lawrence Clarke	Down Lisburn Trust
Vinvent McKevitt	DARD
Ian McCrickard	NIHE
Anne Beggs	Invest NI
James Peel	SEELB
David Smyth	East Down Institute
John McGrillen	Statutory

Peter Craig	Down District Council
Carmel O'Boyle	Down District Council
Dermot Curran	Down District Council
John Doris	Down District Council
Eamon McConvey	Down District Council
Robert Burgess	Down District Council
Eddie Rea	Down District Council

Dungannon and South Tyrone LSP

Bank Buildings
Market Square
Dungannon, BT70 1AB
Tel: 028 8772 0315
Programme Manager: Ursula Quinn

Members	Nominating Sector
Cllr J Canning	Statutory
Cllr J I Cavanagh	Statutory
Cllr S McGuigan	Statutory
Cllr Roger Burton	Statutory
Cllr K Magennis	Statutory
Iain Frazer	Dungannon and South Tyrone Borough Council
Mary Patterson	Armagh and Dungannon HSST
John Quigley	NIHE
Wilfred Mitchell	Community
Monika Donnelly	Community
Jennifer Hamilton	Community
Annette McGahan-McMurray	Community
Mary O'Neil	Community
John Downey	Community
Jean Elliott	UFU
Martin Devlin	ICTU
Roy Wilkins	John Stevenson & Co
Norman Adams	ASM Howarth Accountants
Gregory Butler	Statutory
Shirley Devlin	Statutory
Lorna Thompson	Statutory
Patrick McGirr	Trade

Fermanagh LSP

Town Hall
Enniskillen, BT74 7BA
Tel: 028 6632 6610
Partnership Manager: Helen Maguire

Members	Nominating Sector
John Tracey	Fermanagh Enterprise Ltd
Eamonn Cox	Fermanagh Business Initiative
Tanya Cathcart	Fermanagh Lakeland Tourism
Margaret Gallagher	FLAG
John Sheridan	UFU
Frank Rice	NIAPA
Anne Beattie	NATFHE
Brendan Hueston	TG&WU
Leanne Lyttle	Fermanagh Young Farmers
Jenny Irvine	ITEC
Gerry Maguire	Fermanagh Access Group
Lauri McCusker	Fermanagh Trust
Brenda Whitley	Fermanagh Women's Aid
Jennifer Long	DARD
Henry Robinson	DRD Road Service
Vincent Ryan	Sperrin Lakeland H&SC Trust
Thelma Fitzgerald	Invest Northern Ireland
Seamus Gunn	T&EA
Iris Barker	WELB
Glynis Henry	WH&SSB
Cllr Robin Martin	Fermanagh District Council
Cllr Bertie Kerr	Fermanagh District Council
Cllr Harold Andrews	Fermanagh District Council
Cllr John O'Kane	Fermanagh District Council
Cllr Tom O'Reilly	Fermanagh District Council
June Elliott	Fermanagh Lakeland Tourism
Cllr Paddy McGahan	Fermanagh District Council

Larne Development Partnership

Smiley Buildings
Victoria Road
Larne, BT40 1RU
Tel: 028 2827 0742
Partnership Manager: Patricia Brennan

Members	Nominating Sector
Fred Dodds	Trade Union
William Breen	Trade Union
Jonathan Moore	UFU
Ivan McMullan	UFU
Dermot Murphy	FG Wilson
Norma Shannon	Larne Traders Forum
William Adamson	NIE
Geoffrey Kerr	Larne Community Development Project
Anne Marie McCartan	Barnardos
Karen Moore	Carnlough Community Development Group
Janetta Scott	Ballycarry Community Development Association
Jacqueline Moore	Larne Millennium Initiative
Catherine Lynas	Inter Church Tuesday Group
Cllr Martin Wilson	Larne Borough Council
Cllr Brian Dunn	Larne Borough Council
Cllr Winston Fulton	Larne Borough Council
Geraldine Mulvenna	Larne Borough Council
Trevor Clarke	Larne Borough Council
Morris Crum	Larne Borough Council
Olive Hill	DETI
Pat Davison	NHSSB
Gilvert Bell	NEELB
Phyllis Craig	NIHE
John McKee	DARD
Inspector Noel Rogan	PSNI

Limavady LSP

7 Connell Street
Limavady, BT49 0HA
Tel: 028 7776 0306
Partnership Manager: Paul Beattie

Members	Nominating Sector
Edwin Stevenson	Limavady BC
Leslie Cubitt	Limavady BC
Michael Coyle	Limavady BC
Dessie Lowry	Limavady BC
Marian Donaghy	Limavady BC
Boyd Douglas	Limavady BC
John Stevenson	Limavady BC
Noel Hegarty	Invest NI
Brendan Doherty	NIHE
Bridie Mullin	WELB
Kevin Murphy	DARD
Wayne McCabe	PSNI

Joe O'Kane	T&EA
Damien Corr	Community/Voluntary
Brenda Macqueen	Community/Voluntary
Raymond Wright	Community/Voluntary
Raymond Craig	Community/Voluntary
Dolores O'Kane	Community/Voluntary
Gerard Lynch	Community/Voluntary
Martin Devlin	Business
Alistair Smyth	Business
Sorcha Dunne	Business
Alan Hunter	Agriculture
Nigel McLaughlin	Agriculture
Ian Buchanan	Rural Development
Ian Heaslett	Trade Union
Tony Squires	Trade Union

Lisburn Partnership

Unit 2, The Sidings Office Park
Antrim Road
Lisburn, BT28 3AJ
Tel: 028 9260 5406
Partnership Manager: Alice O'Kane

Members	Nominating Sector
Cllr Jim Dillon	Lisburn City Council
Ald Ivan Davis	Lisburn City Council
Cllr James Baird	Lisburn City Council
Cllr Betty Campbell	Lisburn City Council
Cllr Peter O'Hagan	Lisburn City Council
Cllr Paul Butler	Lisburn City Council
Cllr Gary McMichael	Lisburn City Council
Cllr James Tinsley	Lisburn City Council
Paul McCormick	Economic Development Officer
Sarah Browne	Down Lisburn Trust
Monica Meehan	SEELB
Richard Christie	Invest NI
John Bourke	Probation Board for NI
Danny Cochrane	NIHE
Annie Armstrong	Greater Twinbrook & Poleglass Community Forum
Fiona McCausland	Old Warren Partnership
Gillian Gibson	Footprints Women's Centre
John Lyttle	Voluntary Service Lisburn
Claire Hanna	Lisburn YMCA
Roy Hanna	TADA Rural Network
Joe Vallely	Surestart
Jean McQuitty	Chamber of Commerce
Eamon Foster	Glenwood Business Centre
Aisling Owens	Lisburn Enterprise Organisation
Bumper Graham	NIC ICTU
Jim Quinn	NIC ICTU
Gregg Shannon	UFU
Robert Poots	UFU

Magherafelt LSP

Council Offices
50 Ballyronan Road
Magherafelt, BT45 6EN
Tel: 028 7939 7979
Partnership Manager: Chris McCarney

Members	Nominating Sector
Cllr Sean Kerr	Magherafelt DC
Cllr Thomas Catherwood	Magherafelt DC
Cllr Kathleen Lagan	Magherafelt DC
Cllr Robert Montgomery	Magherafelt DC
John McLaughlin	Magherafelt DC
William McKeown	Yardmaster International
Brendan Clarke	
Brian Murray	Workspace
Kevin Murphy	DARD
Seamus Davey	Magherafelt Disability Forum
Austin Kelly	Bridges Community Group
Gerry Kelly	NEELB
Gerard McGuckin	Rural Development Council
Michael McSorley	DOE Planning Service
Heather McAleese	Ulster Farmers Union
Chris McAleer	Citizens Advice Bureau
Cheryl Chambers	Invest Northern Ireland
Faith Wood	Rural Transport Initiative
William Burke	Bellaghy Dev Assoc
Madeline Heaney	NHSSB
Cherry Dickson	Volunteer Bureau
Bernie Quinn	Volunteer Bureau
Cllr Paul McLean	Magherafelt DC
Donal Mullan	Mid Ulster Properties
Sean Henry	Magherafelt DC
Harold Sinclair	Sixtowns Community Group
Michael Kelly	Moneyneena Dev Assoc
Cllr Pat McErlean	Magherafelt DC
Cllr George Shiels	Magherafelt DC
Cllr John Kelly	Magherafelt DC
Eric Glasgow	Upperlands Dev Group
Mary O'Kane	T&EA
Eugene Corbett	NIHE
Michael McLarnon	McLarnon Shoes
Liam Ward	Ward Design

Moyle LSP

Sheskburn House
7 Mary Street
Ballycastle, BT54 6QH
Tel: 028 2076 2225
LSP Manager: Caitriona McNeill

Members	Nominating Sector
Donnell Black	Agricultural/Rural
Cllr Madeleine Black	Moyle District Council
Anna Burleigh	Trade Union
Marian Cavanagh	Voluntary/Community
Ann Creith	Voluntary/Community
Nigel Flynn	Statutory
Cllr Helen Harding	Moyle District Council
Cllr George Hartin	Moyle District Council
Sharon Kirk	Voluntary/Community
Richard Lewis	Moyle District Council
Eileen McAuley	Voluntary/Community
Gerry McCloskey	Statutory
Seamus McErlean	Agricultural/Rural
John McKee	Statutory
Cllr Oliver McMullan	Moyle District Council
Anne Morrison	Agriculture/Rural Development Sector
Esther Mulholland	Moyle District Council
Mary O'Kane	Statutory
Trevor Robinson	Statutory
Ruth Wilson	Statutory
Tommy McDonald	Private Sector
Victor McFaul	Private Sector
Paddy Burns	Private Sector

Newry and Mourne LSP

O'Hagan House
Monaghan Row
Newry, BT35 8DJ
Tel: 028 3026 6933
Partnership Manager: Deirdre Convery

Members	Nominating Sector
Cllr Martin Cunningham	Newry & Mourne CC
Cllr Michael Carr	Newry & Mourne CC
Cllr Danny Kennedy	Newry & Mourne CC
Cllr Isaac Hanna	Newry & Mourne CC
Cllr Josephine O'Hare	Newry & Mourne CC
Cllr Pat McElroy	Newry & Mourne CC
Cllr Jim McCreesh	Newry & Mourne CC
Cllr Brendan Curran	Newry & Mourne CC
Jim Bagnall	NIHE
Mary Young	Invest NI
Eric Bowyer	Newry & Mourne HSS Trust
Billy Gamble	DRD
Helen McClenaghan	SELB
Vincent McKevitt	DARD
Mairead White	Atticall CA
Betty Moffett	Bessbrook Development
Damian McKevitt	Drumalane/Fathom Development Partnership
Maynard Hanna	Ulster British Forum
Tom McKay	ROSA Ltd
Marian Patterson	ICTU
Gordon Coulter	Toughglass
Jerome Mullen	Newry Chamber of Commerce
Michael Hughes	Vitafresh
Sharon Porter	UFU
Paddy Tiernan	NIAPA
Tom Moore	ICTU
Evelyn Patterson	ICTU

Newtownabbey LSP

Mossley Hill
Newtownabbey, BT36 5QA
Tel: 028 9034 0194 / Fax: 028 9034 0196
Partnership Coordinator: David Hunter

Members	Nominating Sector
Ald W P Girvan	Council/Statutory
Cllr N P Hamilton	Council/Statutory
Cllr J T S Mann	Council/Statutory
Cllr N P McClelland	Council/Statutory
Cllr K W Robinson	Council/Statutory
Cllr E Turkington	Council/Statutory
Cllr D E Walker	Council/Statutory
Veronica Gillen	Council/Statutory
Stella Hewitt	Council/Statutory
Keery Irvine	Council/Statutory
Maureen Wright	Council/Statutory
Sheila McAvoy	Bridge Youth Centre
Sharon Parkes	Ballyclare Community Concerns
John Scott	Ballyduff Community Group
Brian Hunter	Business Representative
Roy Kennedy	UFU
Brian McAvoy	NIC/ICTU
Pat McCudden	Business Representative
John Ross	Business Representative
Sandy Sherrard	UFU
Marjorie Trimble	NIC/ICTU
Shirley Orr	Torrens Hall Management
Mary McKirgan	Melville Residents Assoc

North Down LSP

Town Hall
The Castle
Bangor, BT20 4BT
Tel: 028 9127 8028
Partnership Manager: Jan Nixey

Members	Nominating Sector
David Jackson	Ulster Farmers Union
Janette McNulty	ICTU
Robert Williams	Trade Union
Margaret Ferguson	Holywood Chamber of Trade
Michael Dunlop	Bangor Chamber of Commerce Ltd
Pat Bowen	NITAP
Stephen Dunlop	North Down Community Network
Christine Sloane	Bangor YMCA
James Henderson	Shop mobility Bangor
Ronnie Boyle	Age Concern
Aidan Ferguson	Invest NI
Robert Mahaffy	NIHE
Cecil Worthington	UCHT
John McQuillan	Community/Voluntary
Cllr Alan Chambers	North Down BC
Ald Leslie Cree	North Down BC
Cllr Stephen Farry	North Down BC
Ald Valerie Kingham	North Down BC
Ald Ellie McKay	North Down BC
Cllr Alan Graham	North Down BC
Maura Lavery	Statutory
Graham Shields	Statutory

Omagh LSP

The Grange
Mountjoy Road
Omagh, BT79 7BL
Tel: 028 8225 0202
Partnership Manager: Harry Parkinson

Members	Nominating Sector
Sean Begley	Omagh District Council
Sean Clarke, SF	Omagh District Council
Liam McQuaid, SDLP	Omagh District Council
Gerry O'Doherty, SDLP	Omagh District Council
Oliver Gibson, DUP	Omagh District Council
Reuben McKelvey, UUP	Omagh District Council
Johnny McLaughlin, Ind	Omagh District Council
Danny McSorley	Omagh District Council
Conor McGale	FOCUS/Urban Community
Monica Coyle	FORUM/Rural Community
Brigid McAleer	OWAN
Kieran Downey	Disabled Access Group
Marion Blayney	Early Years/Youth Sector
Paschal McCrumlish	Omagh Traders Association
Nicholas O'Shiel	Omagh Chamber of Commerce and Industry
Vincent Ryan	Sperrin Lakeland Trust
Rosemary Watterson	WELB
Sean Nugent	DARD
Alistair McKane	DOE/DSD
Eileen McFarline	NIPSA
Geraldine Keys	Unison
Gary Hawkes	UFU
Jim Maguire	Leader
Gail Wright	Private Sector

Strabane LSP

47 Derry Road
Strabane, BT82 8DY
Tel: 028 7138 1309 / Fax: 028 7138 1346
Partnership Manager: Patrick O'Doherty

Members	Nominating Sector
Cllr Tom McBride	Strabane District Council
Cllr Ivan Barr	Strabane District Council
Cllr Charlie McHugh	Strabane District Council
Cllr Claire McGill	Strabane District Council
Cllr Derek Hussey	Strabane District Council
Cllr John Donnell	Strabane District Council
Cllr Eugene McMenamin	Strabane District Council
Martin Quigg	DSD
Paddy Mackey	WELB
Paula Falconer	Invest NI
Eamonn McTernan	WELB
Sean Nugent	DARD
Seamus Kelly	NIHE
Mary O'Kane	DEL
Christina Mullen	LEA
Ken Sayers	BITC
Gordon Spear	Castlederg Chamber of Commerce
Brian Forbes	Trade Union Council
Felix McCrossan	Trade Union Council
Anne Bradley	Strabane and District Community Network
Desmond Stewart	St. Vincent de Paul
Jeff Barr	Koram Centre
William Sayers	Ballylaw Regeneration Group
Roy Reid	Millbrook Community Association
Paul Gallagher	Community/Voluntary
Derek Reaney	Derry and Raphoe Action
Howard Pollock	North Tyrone Ulster Farmers Union
Isaac Crilly	Tyrone Quality Livestock

Chapter 10

NORTHERN IRELAND YEARBOOK 2004

The Media and Communications

IRISH NEWS Ltd

The Media in Northern Ireland

Northern Ireland is a veritable hotbed of media and communications activity. Over the period of the last 30 years of political instability the province has attracted highly disproportionate international media attention, which has created a degree of media and communications sophistication normally associated with much larger places.

Northern Ireland has a comparatively high level of newspaper readership despite having a relatively small market. Surveys have shown that almost three quarters of the adult population read at least one paid-for newspaper daily – nearly 900,000 readers a day. There are only four home-produced daily papers in Northern Ireland – one evening, two morning and one Sunday. Of these regional titles only the nationalist Irish News is genuinely local in ownership, being controlled by a local family business. Its unionist counterpart the News Letter was owned by the Trinity Mirror Group since 1996 although along with 6 other regional titles, including the Derry Journal, it has recently been sold to venture capital group 3i in a £46.3 million deal. The main evening newspaper, the Belfast Telegraph, which was formerly owned by the Canadian-based Thomson Regional Newspapers, was sold to the English-based Trinity Holdings in 1995 before being acquired by Tony O'Reilly's Dublin-based Independent Newspaper Group. The Belfast Telegraph has a monopoly on the popular evening paper market and this is reflected in that it is in its own right one of Northern Ireland's most profitable businesses.

In addition to the four local newspapers there are Northern Ireland and Irish editions of many of the British papers. British newspapers, broadsheet and tabloid, are widely read in Northern Ireland. There is also some readership of the leading Southern Irish papers who have been making efforts to increase circulation in Northern Ireland in recent years. Local newspapers are very popular in Northern Ireland with most publishing weekly. A list of the main local newspapers is included later in this chapter, beginning on page 451.

Just fewer than 23m people in the UK hold a television licence. Television is a dynamic industry, which continues to develop at a rapid rate. In addition to the five terrestrial channels, BBC1, BBC2, ITV, Channel 4 (S4C in Wales) and Channel 5, there are now hundreds more available on satellite, cable and digital – and a thriving independent production sector. The BBC is the UK's main public service broadcaster, run by a board of governors and funded by the licence fee. In addition to its two terrestrial channels, the corporation runs several digital services including BBC Knowledge and BBC Choice (both soon to be relaunched) and a news channel, BBC News 24.

ITV was made up originally of 15 regionally based television companies and GMTV, the national breakfast-time service, licensed by the ITC and funded through advertising. However there has been a significant ongoing merger and takeover activity greatly consolidating the independent sector. The ITV Network Centre commissions and schedules programmes and, as with the BBC, 25% of programmes must come from independent producers. There are over 1,500 independent production companies in the UK which generate over £1bn of programming.

Channel 4 and S4C (the fourth channel in Wales) were set up to provide programmes with a distinctive character and which appeal to interests not catered for by ITV and are also funded through advertising. S4C also has to provide a certain amount of Welsh language programming. Channel 4 has two digital services, FilmFour and E4, a youth entertainment channel.

Channel 5 began broadcasting in 1997 and now reaches about 80% of the population. It is advertising-funded and its remit is to show programmes of quality and diversity.

Satellite and cable services are funded mainly through subscriptions. The UK's largest supplier is BSkyB, with over 5m subscribers.

Digital television is expanding rapidly. It has been taken up by about a third of the population and offers the potential to access over 200 channels and other services including interactive TV and the Internet. The government expects all television transmissions to be digital sometime between 2006 and 2010. There are also several teletext services available through both the BBC and commercial TV which carry news, sport, travel, weather and other information and also offer subtitling.

BBC has a regional organisation in Northern Ireland, BBC NI, and in addition to showing network programmes has an autonomous news and current affairs department. The regional independent television company UTV, formerly known as Ulster Television, is the most popular of the two television stations and attracts around 43 per cent of the Northern Ireland television audience against 30 per cent for BBC. The BBC has also a local radio station (Radio Ulster) with bases in both Belfast and the north west (BBC Radio Foyle). Independent radio has also a strong foothold in the local radio market.

An increasing proportion of Northern Ireland households now receive the Southern Irish national broadcaster RTE and there is an estimated subscriber base of 80,000 cable multi-channel services subscribers and a fast rising subscriber base for satellite services.

Northern Ireland is well served by a growing community of communications professionals beyond those operating in the local media. Some of the world's largest communications organisations have Belfast offices in the fields of advertising, public relations and other communications services. A list of PR and advertising agencies is included later in this chapter beginning on page 464.

The Irish News Offices, Belfast

Television and Radio

Associated Press Television

Vision House
56 Donegall Pass
Belfast, BT7 1BU
Tel: 028 9022 1555
Fax: 028 9023 5547

BBC Northern Ireland

Broadcasting House
Ormeau
Belfast, BT2 8HQ
Tel: 028 9033 8000
Fax: 028 9033 8800
News: 028 9033 8806

Press Office
Tel: 028 9033 8226/906
Fax: 028 9033 8279
Web: www.bbc.co.uk

Governor for Northern Ireland:
Professor Fabian Monds

Senior Management Board BBC NI:
Controller: Anna Carragher
Head of Broadcast: Tim Cooke
Head of Public Affairs: Rosemary Kelly
Head of Finance: Crawford MacLean
Head of News & Current Affairs:
Andrew Colman
Head of Marketing & Development:
Peter Johnston
Head of Resources: Stephen Beckett
Head of Entertainment & Events:
Mike Edgar
Head of Factual & Learning:
Bruce Batten
Head of Drama: Robert Cooper
Editor, Foyle: Ana Leddy

Editors BBC NI:
Editor Sport: Edward Smith
Editor Music: Declan McGovern
Editor Specialist Factual: Deirdre Devlin
Editor Entertainment: Alex Johnston
Editor Broadcasting: Fergus Keeling
Editor Learning Unit: Kieran Hegarty
Editor New Media: David Sims
Editor Newsgathering: Michael Cairns
Editor Popular Factual Unit:
Clare McGinn

News Correspondents:
Political Editor: Mark Davenport
Business Editor: James Kerr
Health Correspondent: Dot Kirby
Chief Security Correspondent:
Brian Rowan
Education & Arts Correspondent:
Maggie Taggart
Ireland Correspondents: Denis Murray,
Tom Coulter
Ireland Producer: Kevin Kelly
Sport Producer: Padraig Coyle

Manager, Press Office: Una Carlin
Tel: 028 9033 8014
Fax: 028 9033 8279
Press Officer: Caroline Cooper
Press Officer: Libby Kinney

BBC Radio Foyle

(MW 792, FM 93.1)
8 Northland Road
Londonderry, BT48 7JD
Tel: 028 7137 8600
Fax: 028 7137 8666
Web: www.bbc.co.uk/northernireland
Managing Director: Ana Leddy
Head of News: Eimer O'Callaghan

BBC Radio Ulster

(92.4/95FM)
Broadcasting House
Ormeau Avenue
Belfast, BT2 8HQ
Tel: 028 9033 8000
Fax: 028 9033 8804 (General)
Fax: 028 9033 8806 (News)
Web: www.bbc.co.uk
Head of News and Current Affairs:
Andrew Colman

Belfast Citybeat

(FM 96.7)
46 Stranmillis Embankment
Belfast, BT9 5FN
Tel: 028 9020 5967
Fax: 028 9020 0023
Web: www.citybeat.co.uk
Managing Director: John Rosborough

Channel 9 TV

Springrowth House
Ballinska Road
Springtime
Derry, BT48 0LY
Tel: 028 7128 9900
Fax: 028 7128 9901
Fax: 028 7129 9911 (News)
Web: www.c9tv.tv
Station Manager: Gary Porter
News Editor: Jimmy Cadden

Cool FM

(Greater Belfast FM 97.4)
Kiltonga Industrial Estate
Belfast Road
Newtownards, BT23 4ES
Tel: 028 9181 7181
Fax: 028 9181 4974
Web: www.coolfm.co.uk
Managing Director: David Sloan

Downtown Radio

Kiltonga Industrial Estate
Belfast Road
Newtownards, BT23 4ES
Tel: 028 9181 5555
Fax: 028 9181 8913 (General)
Fax: 028 9181 7878 (News)
Web: www.downtown.co.uk
Chairman: James Donnelly
Managing Director: David Sloan
News/Sports Editor: Harry Castles
Political Correspondent: Eamonn Mailie

All Northern Ireland AM 102.6, Derry FM 102.4, Limavady FM, Enniskillen & Omagh FM 96.6

GMTV Belfast

ITN, Ascot House
24-31 Shaftesbury Square
Belfast, BT2 7DB
Tel: 028 9023 0923
Fax: 028 9043 9395
Ireland Correspondent: Carl Dinnen
Tel: 028 9043 9138
Broadcast Journalists: Siobhan McGarry,
Peter Gregory

ITN (Independent Television News)

Ascot House
24-31 Shaftesbury Square
Belfast, BT2 7DB
Tel: 028 9023 0786
Fax: 028 9043 9395
Web: www.itn.co.uk
Ireland Correspondent: Mark Webster
Tel: 028 9023 0786
Video Journalist: Victoria Hawthorne
Tel: 028 9023 0786

Q97.2FM Causeway Coast Radio

24 Cloyfin Road
Coleraine, Co Derry, BT52 2NU
Tel: 028 7035 9100
Fax: 028 7032 6666
Web: www.q97.2fm
Managing Director: Frank McLaughlin
Station Manager: John Wright
News Editors: Bob McCracken, Caroline Fleck

Q102.9 FM

The Riverside Suite
Old Waterside Railway Station
Duke Street
Waterside
Derry, BT47 6DH
Tel: 028 7134 6666
Fax: 028 7131 177
Managing Director: Frank McLaughlin
Station Manager: David Austin
News Editor: Roger Donnelly

Ulster Television plc

Havelock House
Ormeau Road
Belfast, BT7 1EB
Tel: 028 9032 8122
Fax: 028 9024 605

Newsroom:
Tel: 028 9026 2000
Fax: 028 9023 8381

Press Office:
Tel: 028 9026 2187
Fax: 028 9026 2219
Web: www.utvlive.com
Chairman: John B McGuckian
Managing Director: John McCann
Head of News & Current Affairs: Rob Morrison
Controller of Programming: Alan Bremner
News Producer: Chris Hagan
Political Correspondent: Ken Reid
Sports Editor: Adrian Logan
Producer of 'Kelly': Patricia Moore
Editor of 'Insight': Justin O'Brien
Head of Engineering: Bob McCourt
Head of Press & Public Relations: Orla McKibbin

Northern Ireland Newspapers

Local Daily/Sunday Newspapers

Belfast Telegraph

The Belfast Telegraph

124–144 Royal Avenue
Belfast, BT1 1EB
Tel: 028 9026 4000
Fax: 028 9055 4506
Email: editor@belfasttelegraph.co.uk
Web: www.belfasttelegraph.co.uk
Managing Director: Derek Carvell

The only evening newspaper and the largest selling daily title in Northern Ireland. It provides a unique combination of local, national & international news and sport coupled with extensive information on local events, entertainment and advertising.

Editor: Ed Curran
Tel: 028 9026 4400
Deputy Editor: Jim Flanagan

News Editor: Paul Connolly
Tel: 028 9026 4420
Fax: 028 9055 4540
Email: newseditor@belfasttelegraph.co.uk

Deputy News Editor: Ronan Henry
Features Editor: John Caruth
Political Correspondents: Noel McAdam, Chris Thornton
Business Editor: Nigel Tilson
Business Correspondents: Robin Morton, Maurice Neill

Agriculture Editor: Michael Drake
Education Correspondent: Kathryn Torney
Health Correspondent: Nigel Gould
Sports Editor: John Laverty
Assistant Editors (Sports): Graham Hamilton, John Taylor

Pictures Editor: Gerry FitzGerald
Commercial Director: John Leslie
Tel: 028 9026 4162
Fax: 028 9033 1332

Advertising Director: Simon Mann
Tel: 028 9026 4462
Fax: 028 9033 1332

Marketing Director: Richard McLean
Tel: 028 9026 4138
Fax: 028 9055 4523

Marketing Manager: Ramsey Fawell
Circulation & Resources: Roy Lyttle
Tel: 028 9026 4022

Irish News

113-117 Donegall Street
Belfast, BT1 2GE
Tel: 028 9032 2226
Fax: 028 9033 7505 (News)
Fax: 028 9033 7508 (Advertising)
Email: newsdesk@irishnews.com
Web: www.irishnews.com

Chairman: James Fitzpatrick
Managing Director: Dominic Fitzpatrick
Editor: Noel Doran
Assistant Editor: Stephen O'Reilly
News Editor: Steven McCaffrey
Tel: 028 9033 7544
Features: Joanna Braniff
Head of Content: Fiona McGarry
Business Editor: Gary McDonald
Pictures Editor: Ann McManus
Political Correspondent: William Graham
Health Correspondent: Anne Madden
Travel Editor: James Stinson
Sports Editor: Thomas Hawkins
Derry Correspondent: Seamus McKinney
Tel: 028 7137 4455
Newry Office: Brian Campbell
Tel: 028 3025 7788
Fax: 028 3025 1017
Marketing Manager: John Brolly
Tel: 028 9032 2226
Advertising Manager: Paddy Meehan
Tel: 028 9033 7516
Fax: 028 9033 7508
Deputy Advertising Manager: Sean Higgins
Tel: 028 9033 7509
Fax: 028 9033 7508

News Letter
46-56 Boucher Crescent
Belfast, BT12 6QY
Tel: 028 9068 0000
Fax: 028 9066 4412
Email: newsletter@mgn.co.uk
Web: www.news-letter.co.uk

Editor: Nigel Wareing
Assistant Editor: Helen Greenaway
News Editors: Ric Clarke. Steven Moore
Tel: 028 9068 0005
Political Correspondent:
Ciaran McKeown
Business Correspondent:
Adrienne McGill
Farming Life: David McCoy
Travel & Tourism: Geoff Hill
Women's Editor: Sandra Chapman
Religious Correspondent: Billy Kennedy
Entertainment: Jeff Magill
Sports Editor: Brian Millar
Pictures Editor: Bob Hamilton
Advertising Manager: Shiona Rafferty
Tel: 028 9068 0000
Sales & Marketing Manager:
William Berkeley
Tel: 028 9068 0000
Promotions Manager: Catherine Byrne
Tel: 028 9068 0000

Sunday Life
124-144 Royal Avenue
Belfast, BT1 1EB
Tel: 028 9026 4300
Email: betty.arnold@belfasttelegraph.co.uk
Web: www.sundaylife.co.uk

Editor: Martin Lindsay
Tel: 028 9026 4309
Deputy Editor and News Editor:
Martin Hill
Tel: 028 9026 4305
Women's Editor:
Tel: 028 9026 4315
Pictures Editor: Darren Kidd
Tel: 028 9026 4317
Sports Editor: Jim Gracey
Tel: 028 9026 4308

Local Weekly Newspapers

Andersonstown News
2 Hannahstown Hill
Belfast, BT17 0LT
Tel: 028 9061 9000
Fax: 028 9062 0602
Email: editorial@irelandclick.com
Web: www.irelandclick.com
Editor: Robin Livingstone

Antrim Guardian
5 Railway Street
Antrim, BT41 4AE
Tel: 028 9446 2624
Fax: 028 9446 5551
Email: antrimguardian@macunlimited.net
Editor: Liam Heffron

Antrim Times
22-24 Ballymoney Street
Ballymena, BT43 6AL
Tel: 028 2565 3300
Fax: 028 2564 1517
Web: www.mortonnewspapers.com
Editor: Dessie Blackadder

Armagh Observer/Armagh – Down Observer (Part of Observer Group)
Ann Street
Dungannon, BT70 1ET
Tel: 028 8772 2557
Fax: 028 8772 7334
Email:
editor@observernewspapersni.com
Editor: Desmond Mallon

Ballyclare Gazette
36 The Square
Ballyclare, BT39 9BB
Tel: 028 9335 2967
Fax: 028 9335 2449
Web: www.ulsternet-ni.co.uk

Ballymena Chronicle & Antrim Observer
(Part of the Observer Group)
Ann Street
Dungannon, BT70 1ET
Tel: 028 8772 2557
Fax: 028 8772 7334
Email: editor@observernewspapersni.com
Editor: Desmond Mallon

Ballymena Guardian
83-85 Wellington Street
Ballymena, BT43 6AD
Tel: 028 2564 1221
Fax: 028 2565 3920
Editor: Maurice O'Neill

Ballymena Times
(Part of the Morton Group)
22-24 Ballymoney Street
Ballymena, BT43 6AL
Tel: 028 2565 3300
Fax: 028 2564 1517
Web: www.mortonnewspapers.com
Editor: Dessie Blackadder

Ballymoney Times
(Part of the Morton Group)
6 Church Street
Ballymoney, BT53 6DL
Tel: 028 2766 6216
Fax: 028 2766 7066
Web: www.mortonnewspapers.com
Editor: Lyle McMullen

Banbridge Chronicle
14 Bridge Street
Banbridge, BT32 3JS
Tel: 028 4066 2322
Fax: 028 4062 4397
Editor: Bryan Hooks

The Banbridge Leader
(Part of the Morton Group)
25 Bridge Street
Banbridge, BT32 3JL
Tel: 028 4066 2745
Fax: 028 4062 6378
Web: www.mortonnewspapers.com
Editor: Damien Wilson

Bangor Spectator Group
Spectator Buildings
109 Main Street
Bangor, BT20 4AF
Tel: 028 9127 0270
Fax: 028 9127 1544
Editor: Paul Flowers

Belfast News
46-56 Boucher Crescent
Belfast, BT12 6QY
Tel: 028 9068 0000
Fax: 028 9066 4412
Email: newsletter@mgn.co.uk
Editor: Julie McClay

Carrick Times
(Part of the Morton Group)
19 North Street
Carrickfergus, BT38 7AQ
Tel: 028 9335 1992
Fax: 028 9336 9825
Email: edct@mortonnewspapers.com
Editor: Terence Ferry

Carrickfergus Advertiser
31a High Street
Carrickfergus, BT38 7AN
Tel: 028 9336 3651
Fax: 028 9336 3092
Web: www.ulsternet-ni.co.uk
Editor: Paul Creery

Coleraine Chronicle
20 Railway Road
Coleraine, BT52 1PD
Tel: 028 7034 3344
Fax: 028 7034 3606
Editor: John Fillis

Coleraine Times
(Part of the Morton Group)
71 New Row, Market Court
Coleraine, BT52 1EJ
Tel: 028 7035 5260
Fax: 028 7035 6186
Web: www.mortonnewspapers.com
Editor: Victoria Sloss

Community Telegraph
124-144 Royal Avenue
Belfast, BT1 1EB
Tel: 028 9026 4396
Fax: 028 9055 4585
Editor: Robin Young

County Down Spectator
109 Main Street
Bangor, BT20 4AF
Tel: 028 9127 0270
Fax: 028 9027 1544
Email: editor@spectatornews.co.uk
Editor: Paul Flowers

Craigavon Echo
(Part of Morton Group, distributed free)
14 Church Street
Portadown, BT62 3LQ
Tel: 028 3839 5400
Fax: 028 3835 0203
Editor: David Armstrong

The Democrat
(Part of the Observer Group Newspapers)
Ann Street
Dungannon, BT70 1ET
Tel: 028 8772 2557
Fax: 028 8772 7334
Editor: Desmond Mallon

Derry Journal (Part of Trinity Mirror Group)
22 Buncrana Road
Derry, BT48 8AA
Tel: 028 7127 2200
Fax: 028 7127 2260
Web: www.derryjournal.com
Email: derryj.editorial@mgn.co.uk
Editor-in-Chief: Patrick McArt

Derry News
26 Balliniska Road
Springtown Industrial Estate
Derry, BT48 0LY
Tel: 028 7129 6600
Fax: 028 7129 6611
Email: editorial@derrynews.net
Editor: Garbhan Downey

Down Democrat
74 Market Street
Downpatrick, BT30 6LZ
Tel: 028 4461 6600
Fax: 028 4461 6221
Email: reception@downdemocrat.com
Web: www.downdemocrat.com
Editor: Terry McLaughlin

Down Recorder
2-4 Church Street
Downpatrick, BT30 6EJ
Tel: 028 4461 3711
Fax: 028 4461 4624
Email: downrecorder@ni.com
Web: www.thedownrecorder.com
Editor: Paul Symington

The Dromore Leader
(Part of the Morton Group)
30a Market Square
Dromore, BT25 1AW
Tel: 028 9269 2217
Fax: 028 9269 9260
Email: eddl@mortonnewspapers.com
Editor: Damien Wilson

Dungannon News and Tyrone Courier
58 Scotch Street
Dungannon, BT70 1BD
Tel: 028 8772 2271
Fax: 028 8772 6171
Web: www.ulsternet-ni.co.uk
Editor: Ian Greer

Dungannon Observer
(Part of the Observer Group)
Ann Street
Dungannon, BT70 1ET
Tel: 028 8772 2557
Fax: 028 8772 7334
Editor: Desmond Mallon

East Antrim Advertiser
(Part of Morton Group, free monthly)
8 Dunluce Street
Larne, BT40 1JG
Tel: 028 2826 0605
Fax: 028 2826 0255
Editor: Hugh Vance

East Antrim Gazette
20 Main Street
Larne, BT40 1SS
Tel: 028 2827 7450
Fax: 028 2826 7333
Editor: Stephen Kernohan

East Antrim Guardian
5 Railway Street
Antrim, BT41 4AE
Tel: 028 9446 2624
Fax: 028 9446 5551
Editor: Liam Heffron

East Antrim Times
(Part of Morton Group)
8 Dunluce Street
Larne, BT40 1JG
Tel: 028 2827 2303
Fax: 028 2826 0255
Email: edit@mortonnewspapers.com
Web: www.mortonnewspapers.com
Editor: Hugh Vance

The Examiner
Rathkeeland House
1 Blaney Road
Crossmaglen, BT35 9JJ
Tel: 028 3086 8500
Fax: 028 3086 8580
Email: examiner@btconnect.com
Editor: Gerry Murray

Fermanagh Herald
30 Belmore Street
Enniskillen, BT74 6AA
Tel: 028 6632 2066
Fax: 028 6632 5521
Web: www.fermanaghherald.com
Editor: Pauline Leary

Fermanagh News
(Part of the Observer Group)
Ann Street
Dungannon BT70 1ET
Tel: 028 8772 2557
Fax: 028 8772 7334
Email: editor@observernewspapersni.com
Editor: Desmond Mallon

Impartial Reporter
8-10 East Bridge Street
Enniskillen, BT74 7BT
Tel: 028 6632 4422
Fax: 028 6632 5047
Email: mcdaniel@impartialreporter.com
Web: www.impartialreporter.com
Editor: Denzil McDaniel

Journal Extra
(Part of Derry Journal, distributed free)
22 Buncrana Road
Derry, BT28 8AA
Tel: 028 7127 2200
Fax: 028 7127 2270
Editor: Patrick McArt

LÁ
Teach Basit
2 Cnoc Bhaile Haine
Béal Feirste, BT17 0LT
Tel: 028 9060 5050
Fax: 028 9060 5544
Editor: Ciaran Pronntaigh

The Lakeland Extra
8-10 East Bridge Street
Enniskillen, BT74 7BT
Tel: 028 6632 4422
Fax: 028 6632 5047
Web: www.impartialreporter.com
Editor: Denzil McDaniel

Larne Gazette
20 Main Street
Larne, BT40 1SS
Tel: 028 2827 7450
Fax: 028 2826 0733
Editor: Stephen Kernohan

Larne Times (Part of Morton Group)
8 Dunluce Street
Larne, BT40 1JG
Tel: 028 2827 2303
Fax: 028 2826 0255
Web: www.mortonnewspapers.com
Editor: Hugh Vance

The Leader
20 Railway Road
Coleraine, BT52 1PD
Tel: 028 7034 3344
Fax: 028 7034 3606
Editor: Nicholas Mathers

Lisburn Echo
(Part of Morton Group, distributed free)
12a Bow Street Lisburn, BT28 1BN
Tel: 028 9260 1114
Fax: 028 9260 2904
Web: www.mortonnewspapers.com
Editor: David Fletcher

Londonderry Sentinel
(Part of Morton Group)
Suite 3, Spencer House
Spencer Road, Derry, BT47 1AA
Tel: 028 7134 8889
Fax: 028 7134 1175
Email: edls@mortonnewspapers.com
Web: www.mortonnewspapers.com
Editor: William Allen

Lurgan & Portadown Examiner
(Part of Observer Group)
Ann Street
Dungannon, BT70 1ET
Tel: 028 8772 2557
Fax: 028 8772 7334
Editor: Desmond Mallon

Lurgan Mail (Part of Morton Group)
4a High Street
Lurgan, BT66 8AW
Tel: 028 3832 7777
Fax: 028 3832 5271
Email: edlm@mortonnewspapers.com
Web: www.mortonnewspapers.com
Editor: Richard Elliott

Mid-Ulster Echo (Part of Morton Group)
52 Oldtown Street
Cookstown, BT80 8EF
Tel: 028 8676 1364
Fax: 028 8676 4295
Web: www.mortonnewspapers.com
Editor: John Fillis

Mid-Ulster Mail (Part of Morton Group)
52 Oldtown Street
Cookstown, BT80 8EF
Tel: 028 8676 2288
Fax: 028 8676 4295
Email: edmm@mortonnewspapers.com
Web: www.mortonnewspapers.com
Editor: John Fillis

Mid-Ulster Observer
(Part of Observer Group)
Ann Street, Dungannon, BT70 1ET
Tel: 028 8772 2557
Fax: 028 8772 7334
Editor: Desmond Mallon

Morton Newspapers Limited
2 Esky Drive
Carn Industrial Estate Area
Portadown, BT63 5YY
Tel: 028 3839 3939
Fax: 028 3839 3940
Web: www.mortonnewspaper.com
Group Editor: David Armstrong

Morton is Northern Ireland's largest local newspapers group. Its main titles include: Antrim/Ballymena Times, Ballymoney/Coleraine Times, Carrickfergus/Larne/Newtownabbey Times, Roe Valley/Londonderry Sentinel, Lurgan Mail, Portadown Times, Castlereagh/Dromore/Ulster Star, Banbridge Leader, Tyrone Times, Magherafelt/ Cookstown Mid-Ulster Mail & Echo, Craigavon Echo, Lisburn Echo, North-West-free

Mourne Observer & County Down News
Castlewellan Road
Newcastle, BT33 0JX
Tel: 028 4372 2666
Fax: 028 4372 4566
Email: mobserver@btinternet.com
Editor: Terence Bowman

Newry Democrat
45 Hill Street
Newry, BT34 1UF
Tel: 028 3025 1250
Fax: 028 3025 1017
Email: info@newrydemocrat.com
Web: www.newrydemocrat.com
Editor: Caroline McEvoy

The Newry Reporter
4 Margaret Street
Newry, BT34 1DF
Tel: 028 3026 7633
Fax: 028 3026 3157
Editor: Austin Smyth

Newtownabbey Times
(Part of the Morton Group)
14 Portland Avenue
Glengormley, BT36 8EY
Tel: 028 9084 3621
Fax: 028 9083 7715
Editor: Judith Watson

Newtownards Chronicle & Co Down Observer
25 Frances Street
Newtownards, BT23 3DT
Tel: 028 9181 3333
Fax: 028 9182 0087
Email: news@ardschronicle
Editor: John Savage

Newtownards Spectator
109 Main Street
Bangor, BT20 4AF
Tel: 028 9127 0270
Fax: 028 9127 1544
Email: editor@spectornews.co.uk
Editor: Paul Flowers

North Belfast News
253-255 Antrim Road
Belfast, BT15 2GY
Tel: 028 9058 4444
Fax: 028 9058 4450
Web: www.irelandclick.com
Editor: John Ferris

North West Echo (Part of the Morton Group, distribution free)
Suite 3, Spencer House
Spencer Road
Derry, BT47 1AA
Tel: 028 7134 2226
Fax: 028 7134 1175
Web: www.mortonnewspapers.com
Editor: William McClelland

Northern Constitution
20 Railway Road
Coleraine, BT52 1PD
Tel: 028 7034 3344
Fax: 028 7034 3606
Editor: Maurice McAleese

Northern Newspaper Group
20 Railway Street
Coleraine, BT52 1PD
Tel: 028 7034 3344
Fax: 028 7034 3606
Group Editor: Morris O'Neil

The group's main titles include: Coleraine Chronicle, Ballymena Guardian, Antrim Guardian, Newtownabbey Guardian, The Leader, Northern Constitution

Observer Group
Ann Street
Dungannon, BT70 1ET
Tel: 028 8772 2557
Fax: 028 8772 7334
Group Editor: Desmond Mallon

The group's main titles include: Armagh/Down Observer, Dungannon Observer, Fermanagh News, Lurgan and Portadown Examiner, Mid-Ulster Mail.

The Outlook
Castle Street
Rathfriland
Newry, BT34 5QR
Tel: 028 4063 0781
Fax: 028 4063 1022
Editor: Ruth Rodgers

Portadown Times (Part of the Morton Group)
14A Church Street
Portadown, BT62 3LQ
Tel: 028 3833 6111
Fax: 028 3835 0203
Email: edpt@mortonnewspapers.com
Editor: David Armstrong

Roe Valley Sentinel (Part of the Morton Group)
32A Market Square
Limavady, BT49 0AA
Tel: 028 7772 2234
Fax: 028 7776 4090
Web: www.mortonnewspapers.com
Editor: William Allen

Strabane Chronicle
15 Upper Main Street
Strabane, BT82 8AS
Tel: 028 7188 2100
Fax: 028 7188 3199
Web: www.strabanechronicle.com
Editor: Darach McDonald

Strabane Weekly News
25-27 High Street
Omagh, BT78 1BD
Tel: 028 8224 2721
Fax: 028 8224 3549
Editor: Wesley Atchison

Tyrone Constitution
25-27 High Street
Omagh, BT78 1BD
Tel: 028 8224 2721
Fax: 028 8224 3549
Editor: Wesley Atchison

Tyrone Times (Part of the Morton Group)
Unit B, Butter Market Centre
Thomas Street
Dungannon, BT70 1HN
Tel: 028 8775 2801
Fax: 028 8775 2819
Editor: Clint Aiken

Ulster Farmer (Part of the Observer Group)
Ann Street
Dungannon, BT70 1ET
Tel: 028 8772 3153
Fax: 028 8772 7334
Editor: Desmond Mallon

Ulster Gazette and Armagh Standard
56 Scotch Street
Armagh, BT61 7DQ
Tel: 028 3752 2639
Fax: 028 3752 7029
Editor: Richard Stewart

Ulster Herald Group
10 John Street
Omagh, BT78 1DT
Tel: 028 8224 3444
Fax: 028 8224 2206
Web: www.ulsterherald.com
Editor: Darach McDonald
Deputy Editor: Dominic McClements

Ulster Star
12A Bow Street
Lisburn, BT28 1BN
Tel: 028 9267 9111
Fax: 028 9260 2904
Editor: David Fletcher

National Newspapers (Belfast Offices)

Ireland on Sunday
3rd Floor, Embassy House
Herbert Park Lane, Ballsbridge, Dublin 4
Tel: 003531 637 5800
Email: paul.drury@irelandonsunday.com
Editor: Paul Drury

Irish Examiner
Tel: 0035321 480 2153
Fax: 0035321 427 5477
Email: editor@examiner.ie
Editor: Tim Vaughan

Irish Independent
(Sunday Independent and Evening Herald)
7 North Street
Belfast, BT1 1PA
Tel: 028 9032 9436
Fax: 028 9024 5726
Belfast Correspondent: John Devine

Irish Times
Fanum House
110 Great Victoria Street
Belfast, BT2 7BE
Tel: 028 9032 3324
Fax: 028 9023 1469
Email: gmoriarty@irish-times.ie
Northern Editor: Gerry Moriarty

The Mirror
415 Holywood Road
Belfast, BT4 2GU
Tel: 028 9056 8000
Fax: 028 9056 8005
Editor: Craig McKenzie
News Editor: Joe Gorrod

Sunday Business Post
80 Harcourt Street, Dublin 2
Tel: 003531 602 6000
Fax: 003531 679 6496
Email: sbpost@iol.ie
Editor: Ted Harding

Sunday Independent
90 Middle Abbey Street
Tel: 003531 705 5333
Fax: 003531 705 5779
Email: snews@unison.independent.ie
Editor: Aengus Fanning

The Sunday Mirror
415 Holywood Road
Belfast, BT4 2GU
Tel: 028 9056 8000
Fax: 028 9056 8005
Editor: Chris McCushin

Sunday People
415 Holywood Road
Belfast, BT4 2GU
Tel: 028 9056 8000
Fax: 028 9056 8005
Editor: Greg Harkin

The Sunday Times
72 High Street
Belfast, BT1 2BE
Tel: 028 9043 8208
Fax: 028 9043 8209
Northern Ireland Editor: Liam Clarke
Republic of Ireland Newspapers
(Belfast Offices)

Sunday Tribune
15 Lower Baggot Street, Dublin 2
Tel: 003531 661 5555
Fax: 003531 631 4390
Email: pmurray@tribune.ie
Editor: Paddy Murray

Sunday World
3-5 Commercial Court
Lower Donegall Street
Belfast, BT1 2NB
Tel: 028 9023 8118
Fax: 028 9023 6155
Editor: Jim McDowell

The Times
Queen's Building, Royal Avenue
Belfast, BT1 5AU
Tel: 029 9023 3711
Fax: 028 9023 3588
Chief Ireland Correspondent:
Chris Walker

News Agencies

Press Association
Queen's Building
Royal Avenue, Belfast, BT1 1DB
Tel: 028 9024 5008
Fax: 028 9043 9246
Ireland Editor: Derick Henderson
Political Editor: Dan McGinn

Reuters
2nd Floor
Fanum House, Great Victoria Street
Belfast, BT2 7BE
Tel: 028 9031 5253
Fax: 028 9023 4106
Correspondent: Martin Cowley

Magazines and Periodicals

Northern Ireland has a small but vibrant magazines and periodicals publishing sector covering most areas of economic and social activity. In addition to numerous local offerings available some of the top-selling publications are national products originating in Britain or from the growing Dublin-based industry.

Angling Ireland (Monthly)
124 Low Road
Islandmagee
Larne, BT40 3RF
Tel: 028 9338 2610
Fax: 028 9338 2610
Web: www.anglingireland.com
Editor: Frank Quigley

An Phoblacht (Weekly)
535e Falls Road
Belfast, BT11 9AA
Tel: 028 9060 0279
Fax: 028 9060 0207
Web: www.irlnet.com/aprn
Editor: Martin Spain

Auto Trader (Weekly)
James House
Dargan Crescent
Belfast, BT3 9JP
Tel: 028 9037 0444
Fax: 028 9037 2828

Belfast Magazine (Monthly)
5 Churchill Street
Belfast, BT15 2BP
Tel: 028 9020 2100
Fax: 028 9020 2177
Web: www.glenravel.com
Editor: Joe Baker

BNIL (Bulletin of Northern Ireland Law) (Monthly)
SLS Legal Publications Ltd
School of Law
Queen's University
Belfast, BT7 1NN
Tel: 028 9027 3597
Fax: 028 9032 6308
Editor: Deborah McBride

The Big List (Fortnightly)
Flagship Media Group Ltd
48-50 York Street
Belfast, BT15 1AS
Tel: 028 9031 9008
Fax: 028 9072 7800
Web: www.thebiglist.co.uk
Editor: Gavin Bell

Business Eye (Monthly)
Buckley Publications
20 Kings Road
Belfast, BT5 6JJ
Tel: 028 9073 5859
Fax: 028 9073 5858
Web: www.businesseye.co.uk
Editor: Richard Buckley

Business Ulster
(Bimonthly with Ulster Tatler)
Ulster Journals Ltd
39 Boucher Road, Belfast
Tel: 028 9068 1371
Fax: 028 9038 1915
Email: ulstertatler@aol.com
Editor: Richard Sherry

Carsport Magazine (Monthly)
Greer Publications
5B Edgewater Business Park
Belfast Harbour Estate
Belfast, BT3 9JQ
Tel: 028 9078 3200
Fax: 028 9078 3210
Email: patburns@greerpublications.com
Editor: Patrick Burns

Catering & Licensing Review (Monthly)
Greer Publications
5B Edgewater Business Park
Belfast Harbour Estate
Belfast, BT3 9JQ
Tel: 028 9078 3200
Fax: 028 9078 3210
Email: kathyjensen@greerpublications.com
Editor: Kathy Jensen

Chartered Institute of Transport (Annual Review)
Mainstream Publications Ltd
139-140 Thomas Street
Portadown, BT62 3BE
Tel: 028 3833 4272
Fax: 028 3835 1046
Web: www.mainstreampublishing.co.uk
Managing Editor: Helen Beggs

Cheltenham Racecourse (Annual Review)
Mainstream Publications Ltd
139-140 Thomas Street
Portadown, BT62 3BE
Tel: 028 3833 4272
Fax: 028 3835 1046
Web: www.mainstreampublishing.co.uk
Managing Editor: Helen Beggs

Church of Ireland Gazette (Weekly)
C of I Publishing Co
3 Wallace Avenue
Lisburn, BT27 4AA
Tel: 028 9267 5743
Fax: 028 9266 7580
Web: www.gazette.ireland.anglican.org
Editor: Rev Canon Ian Ellis

Club Review
B101 Portview Trade Centre
Newtownards Road
Belfast, BT4 1RX
Tel: 028 9045 9864
Fax: 028 9045 9034
Email: info@media-marketing.net

Constabulary Gazette (Monthly)
Ulster Journals Ltd
39 Boucher Road
Belfast, BT12 6UT
Tel: 028 9066 3311
Fax: 028 9038 1915
Editor: Bob Catterson

Epsom Derby Annual
Mainstream Publications Ltd
139-140 Thomas Street
Portadown, BT62 3BE
Tel: 028 3833 4272
Fax: 028 3835 1046
Web: mainstreampublishing.co.uk
Managing Editor: Helen Beggs

Equestrian (Bi-monthly)
Mainstream Publications Ltd
139-140 Thomas Street
Portadown, BT62 3BE
Tel: 028 3833 4272
Fax: 028 3835 1046
Web: mainstreampublishing.co.uk
Managing Editor: Fiona Myles

Export & Freight (8 times pa)
Four Square Media
The Mill House, 10 Main Street
Hillisborough, BT 6AE
Tel: 028 9268 8888
Editor: Helen Beggs

Extraction Industry Ireland (Annual Review)
Mainstream Publications Ltd
139-140 Thomas Street
Portadown, BT62 3BE
Tel: 028 3833 4272
Fax: 028 3835 1046
Web: mainstreampublishing.co.uk
Editor: Karen McEvoy

Farmers' Journal (Impartial Reporter) (Weekly)
8-10 East Bridge Street
Enniskillen, BT74 7BT
Tel: 028 6632 4422/425
Fax: 028 6632 5047
Fax: 028 6632 5969 (Advertising)
Web: www.impartialreporter.com
Editor: Denzil McDaniel

Farming Life (Newsletter) (Weekly)
46-56 Boucher Crescent
Belfast, BT12 6QY
Tel: 028 9068 0033
Fax: 028 9066 4432
News Editor: David McCoy

Farm Week (Weekly)
Morton Newspapers Ltd
14 Church Street
Portadown, BT62 3QU
Tel: 028 3833 9421
Fax: 028 3835 0203
Web: www.mortonnewspapers.co.uk
Editor: Hal Crowe

Food Technology & Packaging (Quarterly)
Greer Publications
5B Edgewater Business Park
Belfast Harbour Estate
Belfast, BT3 9JQ
Tel: 028 9078 3200
Fax: 028 9078 3210
Editorial Contact: Peta Bowman

Fortnight (Monthly)
81 Botanic Avenue
Belfast, BT7 1JL
Tel: 028 9023 2353
Fax: 028 9023 2650
Web: www.fortnight.org
Editor: Malachi O'Doherty

Funeral Times (Quarterly)
1 Annagh Drive
Carn Industrial Estate
Portadown, BT63 5RH
Tel: 028 3835 5060
Fax: 028 3833 6959
Editor: Ian Millen

Garage Trader (Quarterly)
Mainstream Publications Ltd
139-140 Thomas Street
Portadown, BT62 3BE
Tel: 028 3833 4272
Fax: 028 3835 1046
Web: www.mainstreampublishing.co.uk
Managing Editor: Janice Uprichard

Getting Married in Northern Ireland
Mainstream Publications Ltd
139-140 Thomas Street
Portadown, BT62 3BE
Tel: 028 3833 4272
Fax: 028 3835 1046
Web: www.mainstreampublishing.co.uk
Editor: Diane Wray

The Gown (Monthly during term)
C/o Students Union
Queen's University
University Road
Belfast, BT7 1PE
Tel: 028 9027 3106
Editor: Peter Cheney

Guide to Industrial Estates (Quarterly)
Mainstream Publications Ltd
139-140 Thomas Street
Portadown, BT62 3BE
Tel: 028 3833 4272
Fax: 028 3835 1046
Web: www.mainstreampublishing.co.uk
Managing Editor: Gerald McAlinden

Home Life Magazine (Monthly)
42a High Street
Lurgan, BT66 8AU
Tel: 028 3832 4006
Fax: 028 3832 5213
Editor: Margaret Kinsella

Horizon Magazine (Monthly)
Unit 11
Broomfield Industrial Estate
333 Crumlin Road
Belfast, BT14 7EA
Tel: 028 9074 5573
Fax: 028 9074 5573
Editor: Eddie McAteer

Industrial & Manufacturing Engineer (Quarterly)
Greer Publications
5B Edgewater Business Park
Belfast Harbour Estate
Belfast, BT3 9JQ
Tel: 028 9078 3200
Fax: 028 9078 3210
Editor: Paul Cairns

Interview (Belfast International Airport Magazine) (Quarterly)
Mainstream Magazines Ltd
139-140 Thomas Street
Portadown, BT62 3BE
Tel: 028 3839 2000
Fax: 028 3835 1071
Web: mainstreampublishing.co.uk
Managing Editor: Karen McAvoy

Ireland's Forecourt & Convenience Retailer
Penton Publications Ltd
Penton House
38 Heron Road
Sydenham Business Park
Belfast, BT3 9LE
Tel: 028 9045 7457
Fax: 028 9045 6611
Editor: Margaret Henderson

Ireland's Homes, Interiors & Living (Monthly)
Unit 65, Dunlop Commercial Park
4 Balloo Drive
Bangor, BT19 7QY
Tel: 028 9147 3979
Fax: 028 9145 7226
Email: mckeenan@ihil.net
Senior Editor: Samantha Blair
Publisher: Mike Keenan

Ireland's Horse Trader (Bi-monthly)
Mainstream Publications Ltd
140 Thomas Street
Portadown, BT62 3BE
Tel: 028 3833 4272
Fax: 028 3835 1046
Web: www.mainstreampublishing.co.uk
Editor: Una McCann

Ireland's Pets (Bi-monthly)
Mainstream Publications Ltd
140 Thomas Street
Portadown, BT62 3BE
Tel: 028 3833 4272
Fax: 028 3835 1046
Web: www.mainstreampublishing.co.uk
Editor: Jackie Harrison

Irish Farmers Journal
Northern Ireland Editorial Office
69 Ballyrainey Road
Newtownards, BT23 5AF
Tel: 028 9181 2054
Fax: 028 9182 0946
Editor: James Campbell

Irish Country Sports and Country Life (Quarterly)
PO Box 62
Portadown, BT62 1XP
Tel: 028 3885 1326/
028 9048 3873
Fax: 028 3885 2237/
028 9048 0195
Editor: Emma Cowan

Keystone (Construction Industry) (Bi-monthly)
Flagship Media Group Ltd
48-50 York Street
Belfast, BT15 1AS
Tel: 028 9031 9008
Fax: 028 9072 7800
Editor: Stephen Preston

LÁ (Irish Language Newspaper) (Weekly)
Teach Basil
2 Cnoc Bhaile hAnnaidh
Béal Feirste, BT17 0LY
Tel: 028 9060 5050
Fax: 028 9060 5544
Web: www.nuacht.com
Eaghatoir: Ciarán Ó Pronntaigh

Licensed Catering News (LCN) (Monthly)
8 Lowes Industrial Estate
31 Ballynahinch Road
Carryduff, BT8 8EH
Tel: 028 9081 5656
Fax: 028 9081 7481
Editor: Brian Phelan

Materials Handling (Annual Review)
Mainstream Publications Ltd
139-140 Thomas Street
Portadown, BT62 3BE
Tel: 028 3833 4272
Fax: 028 3835 1046
Web: www.mainstreampublishing.co.uk
Managing Editor: Helen Beggs

Methodist Newsletter
Edgehill Theological College
9 Lennoxvale, Belfast, BT9 5BY
Tel: 028 9032 0078
Fax: 028 9032 7000
Email: office@egehillcollege.org
Web: www.irishmethodist.org
Manager: Harold Baird

Neighbourhood Retailer & Forecourt Technology (10 issues pa)
Penton Publications Ltd
Penton House
38 Heron Road
Sydenham Business Park
Belfast, BT3 9LE
Tel: 028 9045 7457
Fax: 028 9045 6611
Managing Editor: Margaret Henderson

New Houses in Northern Ireland (Quarterly)
Mainstream Magazines Ltd
139-140 Thomas Street
Portadown, BT62 3BE
Tel: 028 3839 2000
Fax: 028 3835 1071
Web: mainstreampublishing.co.uk
Managing Editor: Karen McAvoy

The Northern Builder Magazine (Quarterly)
Unit 22, Lisburn Enterprise Centre
Ballinderry Road
Lisburn, BT28 2BP
Tel: 028 9266 3390
Fax: 028 9266 6242
Web: www.northernbuilder.co.uk
Editor: Alan Bailie

Northern Farmer (The Irish News) (Weekly)
113-117 Donegall Street
Belfast, BT1 2GE
Tel: 028 9032 2226
Fax: 028 9033 7451
Editor: John Manley

Northern Ireland Legal Quarterly
SLS Legal Publications Ltd
School of Law, Queen's University
Belfast, BT7 1NN
Tel: 028 9027 3597
Fax: 028 9032 6308
Editor: David Capper

Northern Ireland Medicine Today (Monthly)
Penton Publications Ltd
Penton House
38 Heron Road
Sydenham Business Park
Belfast, BT3 9LE
Tel: 028 9045 7457
Fax: 028 9045 6611
Managing Editor: Brian McCalden

Northern Ireland Travel & Leisure News (Monthly)
Unit 1, Windsor Business Park
16-18 Lower Windsor Avenue
Belfast, BT9 7DW
Tel: 028 9066 6151
Fax: 028 9068 3819
Web: www.nitravelnews.com
Editor: Brian Ogle

Northern Ireland Veterinary Today (Quarterly)
Penton Publications Ltd
Penton House
38 Heron Road
Sydenham Business Park
Belfast, BT3 9LE
Tel: 028 9045 7457
Fax: 028 9045 6611
Managing Editor: Brian McCalden

Northern Ireland Visitors' Journal (Annual)
Penton Publications Ltd
Penton House
38 Heron Road
Sydenham Business Park
Belfast, BT3 9LE
Tel: 028 9045 7457
Fax: 028 9045 6611
Managing Editor: Bill Penton

Northern Woman (Monthly)
Greer Publications
5B Edgewater Business Park
Belfast Harbour Estate
Belfast, BT3 9JQ
Tel: 028 9078 3200
Fax: 028 9078 3210
Editor: Lyn Palmer

Perspective (Bi-monthly)
Royal Society of Ulster
Architects Journal, Marlborough House
348 Lisburn Road
Belfast, BT9 6GH
Tel: 028 9066 1666
Fax: 028 9068 1888
Editor: Wendy McCague

Plant & Civil Engineer (6 issues pa)
69 Glen Road
Comber, BT23 5QS
Tel: 028 9187 2656
Editor: Michael McRitchie

Plumbing & Heating (Quarterly)
Mainstream Magazines Ltd
139-140 Thomas Street
Portadown, BT62 3BE
Tel: 028 3839 2000
Fax: 028 3835 1071
Web: www.mainstreampublishing.co.uk
Managing Editor: Jacqueline Farley

The Presbyterian Herald (10 issues pa)
Church House, Fisherwick Place
Belfast, BT1 6DW
Tel: 028 9032 2284
Fax: 028 9024 8377
Web: www.presbyterianireland.org
Editor: Rev Arthur Clarke

Property News (Monthly)
1 Annagh Drive
Carn Industrial Estate
Portadown, BT63 5RH
Tel: 028 3835 5060
Fax: 028 3833 6959
Editor: Graham Brown

Recruitment (Weekly)
48-50 York Street
Belfast, BT15 1AS
Tel: 028 9031 9008
Fax: 028 9072 7800
Web: www.JobsNation.net
Editor: Stephen Preston

Regional Film & Video (Monthly)
Flagship Media Group Ltd
48-50 York Street
Belfast, BT15 1AS
Tel: 028 9031 9008
Fax: 028 9072 7800
Web: www.4rfv.co.uk
Editor: Stephen Preston

Retail Forecourt & Convenience Store (Bi-monthly)
8 Lowes Industrial Estate
31 Ballynahinch Road
Carryduff
Tel: 028 9081 5656
Fax: 028 90281 7481
Editor: Linda Brooks

Retail Grocer (Monthly)
8 Lowes Industrial Estate
31 Ballynahinch Road
Carryduff, BT8 8EH
Tel: 028 9081 5656
Fax: 028 9081 7481
Editor: Brian Phelan

Shelf Building, Extending & Renovations Homes
Corry Home Building Ltd
96 Lisburn Road
Saintfield
Tel: 028 9751 0570
Fax: 028 9751 0576
Editor: Gillian Corry

Specify (Construction Industry) (Bi-monthly)
Greer Publications
5B Edgewater Business Park
Belfast Harbour Estate
Belfast, BT3 9JQ
Tel: 028 9078 3200
Fax: 028 9078 3210
Editor: Emma Cowan

Team Talk (Gaelic Football) (Monthly)
8 Sperrin View
Lough Macrory
Omagh, BT79 9NB
Tel: 028 8076 0769
Fax: 028 8076 0804
Editor: Kenneth Curran

Ulster Architect Magazine (Monthly)
Addemo Press Ltd
182 Ravenhill Road
Belfast, BT6 8EE
Tel: 028 9073 1636
Fax: 028 9073 8927
Editor: Ann Davey Orr

Ulster Bride (Bi-Annual)
Ulster Journals Ltd
39 Boucher Road
Belfast, BT12 6UT
Tel: 028 9068 1371
Fax: 028 9038 1915
Editor: Pauline Roy

Ulster Business (Monthly)

Greer Publications
5B Edgewater Business Park
Belfast Harbour Estate
Belfast, BT3 9JQ
Tel: 028 9078 3200
Fax: 028 9078 3210
Web: www.ulsterbusiness.com

Editor
Russell Campbell

Published monthly, Ulster Business is Northern Ireland's best known business magazine. Highlighting the issues that are dominating the world of business in Northern Ireland, the magazine is very widely read by senior business people and policymakers all over Northern Ireland.

Ulster Farmer (Weekly)
Observer Newspapers
Ann Street
Dungannon, BT70 1ET
Tel: 028 8772 2557
Fax: 028 8772 7334
Editor: Desmond Mallon

Ulster Grocer (Monthly)
Greer Publications
5B Edgewater Business Park
Belfast Harbour Estate
Belfast, BT3 9JQ
Tel: 028 9078 3200
Fax: 028 9078 3210
Editor: Kathy Jensen

Ulster Homes (Quarterly)
Ulster Journals Ltd
39 Boucher Road
Belfast, BT12 6UT
Tel: 028 9068 1371
Fax: 028 9038 1915
Editor: Billy McAllister

Ulster Tatler Series (Monthly)
Ulster Journals Ltd, 39 Boucher Road
Belfast, BT12 6UT
Tel: 028 9068 1371
Fax: 028 9038 1915
Editor: Richard Sherry

Ulster Tatler Wine & Dine Guide (Annual)
Ulster Journals Ltd, 39 Boucher Road
Belfast, BT12 6UT
Tel: 028 9068 1371
Fax: 028 9038 1915
Editor: Walter Love

United News (Farming) (Monthly)
Greer Publications
5B Edgewater Business Park
Belfast Harbour Estate
Belfast, BT3 9JQ
Tel: 028 9078 3200
Fax: 028 9078 3210
Editor: Kathy Jensen

Wedding Journal (Quarterly)
Penton Publications Ltd
38 Heron Road
Sydenham Business Park
Belfast, BT3 9LE
Tel: 028 9045 7457
Fax: 028 9045 6611
Web: www.weddingjournalonline.com
Managing Editor: Tara Craig

Women's News (Monthly)
109-113 Royal Avenue
Belfast, BT1 1FF
Tel: 028 9032 2823
Fax: 028 9043 8788

Publishers

Ambassador
Providence House
Ardenlee Street
Belfast, BT6 8QJ
Tel: 028 9045 0010
Fax: 028 9073 9659
Web: www.ambassador-productions.com
Director: Samuel Lowry

Appletree Press Ltd
14 Howard Street South
Belfast, BT7 1AP
Tel: 028 9024 3074
Fax: 028 9024 6756
Email: reception@appletree.ie
Web: www.appletree.ie

Beyond the Pale Publications
2nd Floor
2-6 Conway Street
Belfast, BT13 2DE
Tel: 028 9043 8630
Fax: 028 9043 9707
Web: www.btpale.com

Blackstaff Press
4C Herron Wharf
Sydenham Business Park
Belfast, BT3 9LE
Tel: 028 9045 5006
Fax: 028 9046 6237
Email: info@blackstaffpress.com
Web: www.blackstaffpress.com

bmf Publishing
Deramore House
76 Main Street
Moira, BT67 0LQ
Tel: 028 9261 9933
Fax: 028 9261 9951
Email: bmf@dnet.co.uk
Web: www.bmfbusinessservices.com

BMG Publishing
5 Ballynahinch Road
Carryduff
Belfast, BT8 8DN
Tel: 028 9081 7333
Fax: 028 9081 744

Colourpoint Books
Colour House, Jubilee Business Park
21 Jubilee Road
Newtownards, BT23 4YH
Tel: 028 9182 0505
Fax: 028 9182 1900
Web: www.colourpoint.co.uk

Cottage Publications
Laurel Cottage
15 Ballyhay Road
Donaghadee, BT21 0NG
Tel: 028 9188 8033
Fax: 028 9188 8063
Email: info@cottage-publications.com

Creagh Media Publications
644 Antrim Road
Belfast, BT15 4EL
Tel: 028 9077 0776
Fax: 028 9077 2577

GCAS Publications
Russell Court
Lisburn Road
Belfast, BT9 6AA
Tel: 028 9055 7700
Fax: 028 9024 5741
Web: www.gcasgroup.com
Managing Director: Robin Hetherington

Greer Publications
5b Edgewater Business Park
Belfast Harbour Estate
Belfast, BT3 9JQ
Tel: 028 9078 3200
Fax: 028 9078 3210

Guildhall Press
Unit 15, Community Service Units
Bligh's Lane
Derry, BT48 0LZ
Tel: 028 7136 4413
Fax: 028 7137 2949
Web: www.ghpress.com

Linenhall Library
17 Donegall Square North
Belfast, BT1 5GB
Tel: 028 9032 1707
Fax: 028 9043 8586
Email: info@linenhall.com
Web: www.linenhall.com

Local Directories
94 University Avenue
Belfast, BT7 1GY
Tel: 028 9095 4651
Fax: 028 9095 4642
Web: www.localdirectories.net
Email: info@localdirectories.net

Locksley Press Ltd
10a Bridge Street
Lisburn, BT28 1XY
Tel/Fax: 028 9260 3195
Freephone: 0800 9178104

Mainstream Publications Ltd
139-140 Thomas Street
Portadown, BT62 3BE
Tel: 028 3833 4272
Fax: 028 3835 1046
Web: www.mainstreampublishing.co.uk

Mathematics Publishing Co
45 Blackstaff Road
Clough
Downpatrick, BT30 8SR
Tel: 028 4485 1211
Fax: 028 4485 1566

Medical Communications Ltd
Ulster Bank Building
142-148 Albertbridge Road
Belfast, BT5 4GS
Tel: 028 9080 9090
Fax: 028 9080 9097

N.I. Media Ltd
Fountain House
41-51 Royal Avenue
Belfast, BT1 1FB
Tel: 028 9058 5000
Fax: 028 9058 5001
Email: info@nimedia.net

Outlook Press
Castle Street
Rathfriland, BT34 5QR
Tel: 028 4176 9995
Fax: 028 4063 1022

Penton Publications Ltd
Penton House
38 Heron Road
Sydenham Business Park
Belfast, BT3 9LE
Tel: 028 9045 7457
Fax: 028 9045 6611
Email: info@pentonpublications.co.uk

Tendering Services Ireland
Coolmaghery
156 Pomeroy Road
Donaghmore, Dungannon, BT7 2TY
Tel: 028 8776 7313
Fax: 028 8776 7030
Email: enquiries@irishtendersdirect.com
Web: www.irishtendersdirect.com

tSO Ireland (The Stationery Office)
16 Arthur Street
Belfast, BT1 4GD
Tel: 028 9023 8451
Fax: 028 9023 5401
Web: www.ukstate.com

Ulster Historical Foundation
Balmoral Buildings
12 College Square East
Belfast, BT1 6DD
Tel: 028 9033 2288
Fax: 028 9023 9885
Email: enquiry@uhf.org.uk
Web: www.ancestryireland.co.uk

Ulster Magazines Ltd
Crescent House
58 Rugby Road
Belfast, BT7 1PT
Tel: 028 9023 0425
Fax: 028 9023 6572

Editoral Solutions
537 Antrim Road
Belfast, BT15 3BU
Tel: 028 9077 2300
Fax: 028 9078 1356
Email: info@editorialsolutions.com
Web: www.editorialsolutions.com

WG Baird
Greystone Press, Caulfield Drive
Antrim, BT41 2RS
Tel: 028 9446 3911
Fax: 028 9446 6250
Email: wgbaird@wgbaird.com
Web: www.wgbaird.com

Communications Services Providers

Advertising Agencies

Anderson Advertising Ltd
Anderson House
409 Hollywood Road
Belfast, BT4 2GU
Tel: 028 9080 2000
Fax: 028 9080 2001
Web: www.asgh.com

Ardmore Advertising & Marketing Ltd
Ardmore House
Pavillions Office Park
Kinnegar Drive
Holywood, BT18 9JQ
Tel: 028 9042 5344
Fax: 028 9042 4823
Email: info@ardmore.co.uk
Web: www.ardmore.co.uk

AV Browne Advertising Ltd
46 Bedford Street
Belfast, BT2 7GH
Tel: 028 9032 0663
Fax: 028 9024 4279
Web: www.avb.co.uk

Coey Advertising & Design
Victoria Lodge
158 Upper Newtownards Road
Belfast, BT4 3EQ
Tel: 028 9047 1221
Fax: 028 9047 1509
Email: info@coeyadvertising.co.uk

Concept Advertising & Marketing
1A Wellington Park, Belfast, BT9 6DJ
Tel: 028 9066 7797
Fax: 028 9066 7745

Condor Community Services Ltd
Site 81, Vico House
Dunmurry Industrial Estate
Dunmurry. Belfast, BT17 9HU
Tel: 028 9060 2168
Fax: 028 9030 7826

Design & Place Recruitment Advertising
409 Holywood Road
Belfast, BT4 2GU
Tel: 028 9080 2010
Fax: 028 9080 2011
Web: www.andersonspratt.com

Fire IMC Ltd
Dargan Crescent
Belfast, BT3 9JP
Tel: 028 9077 4388
Fax: 028 9077 6906
Web: www.fireimc.co.uk

Fox Advertising
1 Union Buildings, Union Place
Dungannon, BT70 1DL
Tel: 028 8772 2962
Fax: 028 8772 9719
Web: www.fox-advertising.com

GCAS Advertising Limited
Russell Court
38-52 Lisburn Road
Belfast, BT9 6AA
Tel: 028 9055 7700
Fax: 028 9024 5741
Web: www.gcasgroup.com

Higher Profile Advertising
74 Ballycrochan Road
Bangor, BT19 6NF
Tel: 028 9127 1016
Fax: 028 9127 1016

KR Graphics
121 University Street
Belfast, BT7 1HP
Tel: 028 9033 3792
Fax: 028 9033 0549
Web: www.krgraphics.co.uk

The Levy McCallum Advertising Agency
10 Arthur Street
Belfast, BT1 4GD
Tel: 028 9031 9220
Fax: 028 9031 9221
Web: www.levymccallum.co.uk

McCann Erickson (Belfast) Ltd
31 Bruce Street
Great Victoria Street
Belfast, BT2 7JD
Tel: 028 9033 1044
Fax: 028 9033 1622
Web: www.mccann-belfast.com

Main Line Marketing
47e Oaks Road
Dungannon, BT71 4AS
Tel: 028 8772 7358
Fax: 028 8772 7358

MRB Creative
24 College Gardens
Belfast, BT9 6BS
Tel: 028 9066 3663
Fax: 028 9066 3600
Web: www.mrbcreative.com

Navigator Blue
The Baths, 18 Ormeau Avenue
Belfast, BT2 8HS
Tel: 028 9024 6722
Fax: 028 9023 1607
Web: www.navigatorblue.com

RLA Northern Ireland Limited
86 Lisburn Road
Belfast, BT9 6AF
Tel: 028 9066 4444
Fax: 028 9068 3497
Web: www.rla.co.uk

TDP Advertising
76 University Street
Belfast, BT7 1HE
Tel: 028 9032 2882
Fax: 028 9033 2727
Web: www.tdpadvertising.co.uk

Walker Communications
The Old Post Office
43 High Street
Holywood, BT18 9AB
Tel: 028 9042 5555
Fax: 028 9042 1222
Web: www.walkercommunications.co.uk

Shandwick Design
425 Holywood Road
Belfast, BT4 2GU
Tel: 028 9076 1007
Fax: 028 9076 1941
Email: 028 9076 3490
Web: www.webershandwickdesign.com

Wyncroft International Communications
Wyncroft House
52 Warren Road
Donaghadee, BT21 0PD
Tel: 028 9188 8808
Fax: 028 9188 4411
Web: www.wyncroft.com

Broadcasting and Studio Services

Associated Press Television
Vision House
56 Donegall Pass
Belfast, BT7 1BU
Tel: 028 9023 5577
Fax: 028 9023 5547

Audio Processing Technology Ltd
Unit 6 , Edgewater Road
Belfast, BT3 9JQ
Tel: 028 9037 1110
Fax: 028 9037 1137
Web: www.aptx.com

BBC Northern Ireland
Broadcasting House
25 Ormeau Avenue
Belfast, BT2 8HD
Tel: 028 9033 8000
Fax: 028 9033 8800
Web: www.bbc.co.uk

BBC Radio Foyle
8 Northland Road
Derry, BT48 7JD
Tel: 028 7137 8600
Fax: 028 7137 8666
Web: www.bbc.co.uk

Belfast Citybeat
46 Stranmillis Embankment
Belfast, BT9 5FN
Tel: 028 9020 5967
Fax: 028 9020 0023
Web: www.citybeat.co.uk

CASP Enterprises
4 Ballycrummy Road
Armagh, BT60 4LB
Tel: 028 3752 3914
Fax: 028 3752 7100

CB Productions
31 Hillsborough Road
Carryduff, Belfast, BT8 8HS
Tel: 028 9081 4477
Fax: 028 9081 5976

Channel 9
1 Crawford Square
Derry, BT48 7HR
Tel: 028 7128 9900
Fax: 028 7129 9911

Cool FM
Kiltonga Industrial Estate
Belfast Road
Newtownards, BT1 1RT
Tel: 028 9181 7181
Fax: 028 9181 4974
Web: www.coolfm.co.uk

CPR Recording Studio
3a Bingham Lane
Bangor, BT20 5DR
Tel: 028 9146 7631
Fax: 028 9146 7631

Downtown Radio Ltd
Kiltonga Industrial Estate
Belfast Road
Newtownards, BT23 4ES
Tel: 028 9181 5555
Fax: 028 9181 8913
Web: www.downtown.co.uk

Duplitape
100 Duncairn Gardens
Belfast, BT15 2GN
Tel: 028 9074 7411
Fax: 028 9029 9001
Email: duplitape@enterprise.net

Elmstree Studio
12 Turmore Road
Newry, BT34 1PJ
Tel: 028 3026 5913
Fax: 028 3026 5913

EMS The Studio
12 Balloo Avenue
Bangor, BT19 7QT
Tel: 028 9127 4411
Fax: 028 9127 4412

Jingle Jangle
The Strand
156 Holywood Road
Belfast, BT4 1NY
Tel: 028 9065 6769
Fax: 028 9067 3771

Komodo Recordings
79 Magheraconluce Road
Hillsborough, BT26 6PR
Tel: 028 9268 8285
Fax: 028 9268 9551

Laganside Studios Ltd
Units 2-3 Ravenhill Business Park
Ravenhill Road
Belfast, BT6 8AW
Tel: 028 9045 0231
Fax: 028 9045 9499

Mach Two
412 Beersbridge Road
Belfast, BT5 5EB
Tel: 08707 300030
Fax: 028 9047 1625

Q97.2FM
24 Cloyfin Road
Coleraine, BT52 2NU
Tel: 028 7035 9100
Fax: 028 7032 6666
Web: www.q97.2fm

Q102.9FM
The Riverside Suite
The Old Waterside Railway Station
Duke Street, Derry, BT47 6DH
Tel: 028 7134 4449
Fax: 028 7131 1177
Web: www.q102.fm

Radio Telefis Eireann
Fanum House
Great Victoria Street
Belfast, BT2 7BE
Tel: 028 9032 6441
Fax: 028 9033 2222

Radio Valley
Lagan Valley Hospital
Hillsborough Road
Lisburn, BT28 1JP
Tel: 028 9267 1151
Fax: 028 9266 6100

Studio 2
69A Whitesides Hill
Craigavon, BT62 3RJ
Tel: 028 3884 1335

TV3 Television Network
46 Bradbury Place
Belfast, BT7 1RU
Tel: 028 9043 5465

UTV plc
Havelock House
Ormeau Road
Belfast, BT7 1EB
Tel: 028 9032 8122
Fax: 028 9024 6695
Web: www.utvlive.com

Television, Film and Video Production

About Face Media
Townsend Enterprise Park
Townsend Street
Belfast, BT13 2ES
Tel: 028 9089 4555
Fax: 028 9089 4502

Acron Film & Video Ltd
13 Fitzwilliam Street
Belfast, BT9 6AW
Tel: 028 9024 0977
Fax: 028 9022 2309

Another World Productions
2nd Floor
11 Lismore House
23 Church Street
Portadown, BT62 3LN
Tel: 028 3833 2933
Fax: 028 3839 6941

Arcom Interactive
157 High Street
Holywood, BT18 9HU
Tel: 028 9042 6334
Fax: 028 9039 7715

Brian Waddell Productions Ltd
Strand Studios
5-7 Shore Road
Holywood, BT18 9HX
Tel: 028 9042 7646
Fax: 028 9042 7922

Christian Communications Networks (Europe) Ltd
646 Shore Road
Whiteabbey, BT37 0PR
Tel: 028 9085 3997
Fax: 028 9036 5536

Extreme Film & TV Productions Ltd
1 Church View
Holywood, BT18 9DP
Tel: 028 9080 9050
Fax: 028 9080 9051

Macmillan Media
729 Lisburn Road
Belfast, BT9 7GU
Tel: 028 9050 2150
Fax: 028 9050 2151

MGTV
Victoria House
1A Victoria Road
Holywood, BT18 9BA
Tel: 028 9020 0060
Fax: 028 9059 2000
Email: info@mgtv.co.uk
Web: www.mgtv.co.uk

Miracles Production
154 Upper Newtownards Road
Belfast, BT4 3EQ
Tel: 028 9047 3838
Fax: 028 9047 3839
Email: info@miriclesproduction.co.uk

Northland Broadcast
30 Chamerlain Street
Derry, BT48 6LR
Tel: 028 7137 2432
Fax: 028 7137 7132

Nosedive Animation Studio
Units 2-3
Laganside Studio
Ravenhill Business Park
Belfast, BT6 8AW
Tel: 028 9022 2410
Fax: 028 9022 2410

The Picturehouse
The Strand
156 Holywood Road
Belfast, BT4 1NY
Tel: 028 9065 1111
Fax: 028 9067 3771

Stirling Productions Ltd
137 University Street
Belfast, BT7 1HP
Tel: 028 9033 3848
Fax: 028 9024 9583

Straight Forward Film & Television Productions Ltd
Ground Floor
Crescent House
17 High Street
Holywood, BT18 9AZ
Tel: 028 9042 6298
Fax: 028 9042 3384

Tyndall PR Productions
58 Edentrillick Road
Hillsborough, BT26 6PG
Tel: 028 9268 9444
Fax: 028 9268 9224

Visionworks Television Ltd
Vision House
56 Dongall Pass
Belfast, BT7 1BU
Tel: 028 9024 1241
Fax: 028 9024 1777
Email: production@visionworks.co.uk

Westway Film Production Ltd
42 Clarendon Street
Londonderry, BT79 4SW
Tel: 028 7130 8383
Fax: 028 7130 9393

Public Relations/Public Affairs Consultancies

Aiken PR
418 Lisburn Road
Belfast, BT9 6GH
Tel: 028 9066 3000
Fax: 028 9068 3030

Anderson Spratt Group Public Relations
Holywood House
Innis Court, High Street
Holywood, BT18 9HT
Tel: 028 9042 3332
Fax: 028 9042 7730

Cactus PR & Communications Ltd
38 Heron Road
Belfast, BT3 9LE
Tel: 028 9045 7700
Fax: 028 9045 6622

Carmah Communications
39a Main Street
Bangor, BT20 5AF
Tel: 028 9127 5965
Fax: 028 9127 5284

Citigate Northern Ireland Ltd
157-159 High Street
Holywood, BT18 9HU
Tel: 028 9039 5500
Fax: 028 9039 5600

Compton Communications
17 Station Road
Holywood, BT18 0BP
Tel: 028 9042 7949
Fax: 028 9042 8459
Email: john@camptoncom.co.uk

Cooper Keaney Communication Ltd
Unit 4, Riversedge
14 Ravenhill Road
Belfast, BT6 8DN
Tel: 028 9020 3992
Fax: 028 9020 0430

Crockard Communications
33A Belmont Road
Belfast, BT4 2AA
Tel: 028 9087 7290
Fax: 028 9065 1400
Email: mail@crockard.co.uk

Davidson Cockcroft Partnership
Bamford House
91-93 Saintfield Road
Belfast, BT8 7HR
Tel: 028 9040 2296
Fax: 028 9040 2291

Doris Leeman Public Relations
27 Berwick View
Moira, BT67 0SX
Tel: 028 9261 1044
Fax: 028 9261 1979

GCAS Public Relations Ltd
Russell Court
38-52 Lisburn Road
Belfast, BT9 6AA
Tel: 028 9055 7777
Fax: 028 9023 0142

Inform Communications
13 University Street
Belfast, BT7 1FY
Tel: 028 9023 3550
Fax: 028 9033 1017
Email: info@informcommunications.com

John Laird Public Relations Ltd
104 Holywood Road
Belfast, BT4 1NU
Tel: 028 9047 1282
Fax: 028 9065 6022

Lagan Consulting (Public Affairs)
TSL House
38 Bachelor's Walk
Lisburn, BT28 1XN
Tel: 028 9261 3216
Fax: 028 9261 9951
Email: info@laganconsulting.com

Life Communications
46 Bedford Street
Belfast, BT2 7FF
Tel: 028 9024 8805
Fax: 028 9024 8806

Morrow Communications Ltd
Hanwood House
Pavillions Office Park
Kinnegar Drive
Holywood, BT18 9JQ
Tel: 028 9039 3837
Fax: 028 9039 3830

The PR Agency
721A Lisburn Road
Belfast, BT9 7GU
Tel: 028 9022 2422
Fax: 028 9022 2423
Email: info@thepragency.co.uk

Event Management Organisations

bmf Business Services
TSL House
38 Bachelor's Walk
Lisburn, BT28 1XN
Tel: 028 9261 9933
Fax: 028 9261 9951
Email: bmf@dnet.com

Class Acts Promotions
39 Wellington Park
Belfast, BT9 6DN
Tel: 028 9068 1041
Fax: 028 9068 7747

Creative Events
1 Dublin Road
Belfast, BT2 7HB
Tel: 028 9023 5001
Fax: 028 9023 5003
Email: info@creativeevents.co.uk

Happening Creative Communications
9 Wellington Park
Belfast, BT9 6DJ
Tel: 028 9066 4020
Fax: 028 9038 1257
Email: happening@happen.oco.uk

Mitchell Kane Associates
The Technology Centre
Townsend Street
Belfast, BT13 2ES
Tel: 028 9089 4504
Fax: 028 9089 4502

Morrow Communications Ltd
Hanwood House
Pavillions Office Park
Kinnegar Drive
Holywood, BT18 9JQ
Tel: 028 9039 3837
Fax: 028 9039 3830

Project Planning International
Montalto Estate
Spa Road
Ballynahinch, BT24 8PT
Tel: 028 9756 1993
Fax: 028 9756 5073

Printers

Dargan Press Ltd
5 Round Tower Centre
Dargan Crescent
Belfast, BT3 9JP
Tel: 028 9077 4478
Fax: 028 9077 4771

Dorman & Sons Ltd
Unit 2, 2A Apollo Road
Boucher Road
Belfast, BT12 6HP
Tel:028 9066 6700
Fax: 028 9066 1881

Graham & Heslip
96 Beechill Road
Belfast, BT8 6NS
Tel: 028 9049 4949

Graham & Sons Ltd
51 Gortin Road
Omagh
BT79 7HZ
Tel: 028 8224 9222
Fax: 028 8224 9886

Impro Printing
41 Dargan Road
Belfast, BT3 9JU
Tel: 028 9077 7795

Johnston Printing Ltd
Mill Road
Kilrea, BT51 5RJ
Tel: 028 2954 0312
Fax: 028 2954 1070
Web: www.johnston-printing.co.uk

LM Press Ltd
47 High Street
Lurgan, BT66 8AH
Tel: 028 3832 2412
Fax: 028 3832 1820

Limavady Printing Co Ltd
26c Catherine Street
Limavady, BT49 9DB
Tel: 028 7776 2051
Fax: 028 7776 2132
Web: www.limprint.com

Northern Whig
107 Limestone Road
Belfast, BT15 3AH
Tel: 028 9035 2233
Fax: 028 9035 2181

Nicholson & Bass Ltd
Michelin Road
Newtownabbey, BT36 4FB
Tel: 028 9034 2433

Graphic Designers

Ardmore Design
Ardmore House
Pavillions
Holywood, BT18 9JQ
Tel: 028 9042 5344
Fax: 028 9042 4823
Web: www.ardmore.co.uk

Darragh Neely Associates
Ama Communication Centre
Newtownards Road
Bangor, BT19 7TA
Tel: 028 9151 6034
Fax: 028 9147 2797
Web: www.daraghneelyassociates.com

GCAS Design
Russell Court
38-52 Lisburn Road
Belfast, BT9 6AA
Tel: 028 9055 7700
Fax: 028 9024 5741
Email: design@gcasgroup.com
Web: www.gcasgroup.com

IPR Communications Group
27 Shore Road
Holywood, BT18 9HX
Tel: 028 9042 7094
Fax: 028 9042 7094
Email: ipr@d-n-a.net

KR Graphics
121 University Street
Belfast, BT7 1HP
Tel: 028 9033 3792
Fax: 028 9033 0549

Leslie Stannage Design
93 Botanic Avenue
Belfast, BT7 1JN
Tel: 028 9023 7377
Fax: 028 9033 0549

Rocket
3 Pavillions Office Park
Kinnegar Drive
Holywood, BT18 9JQ
Tel: 028 9022 7700
www.rocket-design.com

Slater Design
The Old Sorting Office
Strand Avenue
Holywood, BT18 9AA
Tel: 028 9042 1133
Fax: 028 9042 1122

TDP Advertising
75 University Street
Belfast, BT7 1HE
Tel: 028 9032 2882
Fax: 028 9033 2727
Email: mail@tdpadvertising.co.uk
Web: www.tdpadvertising.co.uk

New Media

Internet Access Service Providers (ASPs)

Note: The listing below is for Northern Ireland based Internet access providers who provide access to the Internet. Internet service providers (ISPs) offer access through leased lines and provide hosting and design services.

BT NI
Riverside Tower
5 Lanyon Place
Belfast, BT1 3BT
Tel: 0800 800 800 (Business Enquiries)
Tel: 028 9032 7327 (General Switchboard)
Web: www.bt.com

Energis
1 Cromac Avenue
Belfast, BT7 2JA
Tel: 0808 140 1400
Fax: 028 9095 9401

Firenet Internet
Knockmore Industrial Estate
Moira Road
Lisburn, BT28 2EJ
Tel: 028 9267 0600
Fax: 028 9267 0916
Web: www.fire-net.net

The Internet Business
Holywood House
1 Innis Court
Holywood, BT18 9HF
Tel: 028 9042 4190
Fax: 028 9042 4709
Web: www.tibus.net

Unite Solutions
Edgewater Road
Belfast, BT3 9JQ
Tel: 028 9077 7338
Fax: 028 9077 7313
Web: www.unite.net

UTV Internet Ltd
17 Ormeau Road, Belfast, BT7 1EB
Tel: 0845 2470000
Fax: 028 9020 1203
Web: www.utvinternet.com

Website Hosting and Design

Note: the above ISPs all offer web site development and design services as do most advertising agencies and some PR agencies. The listing below are companies who main business is website design.

Aurion
Laganside Studios
Ravenhill Business Park
Belfast, BT6 8AW
Tel: 028 9045 5244
Fax: 028 9045 3157
Web: www.aurion.co.uk

BizNet Solutions
133-137 Lisburn Road
Belfast
BT9 7AG
Tel: 028 9022 3224
Fax: 028 9022 3223
Web: www.biznet-solutions.com

CV3
22 Ormeau Business Park
Gasworks
Ormeau Road
Belfast
BT7 2JA
Tel: 028 9080 6980
Fax: 028 9080 6880
Web: www.cv3.com

Memsis
Rose House, Derryvolgie Avenue,
Belfast, BT9 6FL
Tel: 028 9080 6999
Fax: 028 9029 0530
Web: www.memsis.com

Net Works
Russell Court
38-52 Lisburn Road
Belfast, BT9 6AA
Tel: 028 9055 7700
Fax: 028 9024 5741
Web: www.networksforyou.co.uk

Parc Computing Limited
Enkalon Business Centre
25 Randalstown Road
Antrim, BT41 4LJ
Tel: 028 9442 9242
Fax: 028 9442 9253
Web: www.parc-computing.co.uk

Revelations Internet.com
27 Shaftesbury Square
Belfast, BT2 7DB
Tel: 028 9032 0337
Fax: 028 9032 0432
Web: www.revelations.co.uk

Sugarcube
1B Castle Street
Carrickfergus, BT38 7BE
Tel: 028 9332 9662
Fax: 028 9335 5507
Web: www.sugarcube.biz

Other Media Organisations

Independent Television Commission
Albany House
75 Great Victoria Street
Belfast, BT2 7AF
Tel: 028 9024 8733
Fax: 028 9032 2828

Institute of Public Relations (IPR)
c/o Happening Creative Communications
9 Wellington Park,
Belfast, BT9 6DJ
Tel: 028 9066 4020
Fax: 028 9038 1257
Web: www.happen.co.uk

Northern Ireland Film Commission
10 Alfred Street,
Belfast, BT2 8ED
Tel: 028 9023 2444
Fax: 028 90239918
Web: www.niftc.co.uk

Northern Ireland Government Affairs Group
C/o Conor McGrath
Lecturer in Political Communication
University of Ulster, Jordanstown
Newtownabbey, BT37 0QB
Tel: 028 9036 6178
Fax: 028 9036 6872

Media and Communications Training

Northern Visions
23 Donegall Street Place
Belfast, BT1 2FF
Tel: 028 9024 5495
Fax: 028 9032 6608
Web: www.northernvisions.org

University of Ulster
School of Design and Communication
York Street
Belfast, BT15 1ED
Tel: 028 9032 8515
Fax: 028 9032 1048

University of Ulster
School of Media and Performing Arts
Cromore Road
Coleraine, BT37 0QB
Tel: 028 7032 4196
Fax: 028 7032 4964

Anderson Spratt Group Public Relations
Holywood House
Innis Court
High Street
Holywood, BT18 9HT
Tel: 028 9042 3332
Fax: 028 9042 7730

Macmillan Media
729 Lisburn Road
Belfast, BT9 7GU
Tel: 028 9050 2150
Fax: 028 9050 2151

Photograph Libraries

Chris Hill Photographic
17 Clarence Street
Belfast, BT2 8DY
Tel: 028 9024 5038
Fax: 028 9023 1942
Web: www.scenic-ireland.com

Pacemaker Press
787 Lisburn Road
Belfast, BT9 7GX
Tel: 028 9066 3191
Fax: 028 9068 2111
Web: www.pacemakerpressintl.com

Esler Crawford Photography
37A Lisburn Road
Belfast, BT9 7AA
Tel: 028 9032 6999
Fax: 028 9033 1542

Roger Kinkead Photo Library
20 Lynden Gate
Portadown, BT63 5YH
Tel: 028 3839 4553

Conference Venues

The conference market in Northern Ireland is worth an estimated £5-6million per annum equating to an approximate spend of £160 per delegate. Whilst the total UK conference market generates income of £6-7 billion, purpose built conference developments such as the Odyssey complex and the Waterfront Hall enable Northern Ireland to compete with other UK conference destinations, heightening the profile of Belfast and Northern Ireland as an attractive conference centre for international events, and generating greater economic revenue for the city.

Some of the major conferences which were held in Belfast in 2003 included:

- European Society for Cystic Fibrosis Congress 1400 delegates
- Federation of Soroptimists International of GB & Ireland Conference 1500 delegates

Below is a listing of some of Belfast and Northern Ireland's major conference venues. Almost all the venues listed offer a full range of audio-visual equipment (such as projectors, sound systems) as well as communications links (telephone and fax points, ISDN connection). Many of the larger venues have a dedicated Business Centre with a range of services, such as photocopying, available. For full details of exactly what facilities are offered by each venue, contact venue directly.

Note: all delegate figures are for theatre style conferences (rows of chairs without tables).

Belfast

Belfast Castle
Antrim Road
Belfast, BT15 5GR
Tel: 028 9077 6925
Fax: 028 9037 0228
Email: bcr@belfastcastle.co.uk
Contact: Brendan Toland, Manager

Max No of Delegates: 200

Part of the Belfast Castle Parks Group, Belfast Castle is situated 400 feet above sea level, on the slopes of Cavehill. Belfast Castle is located 2.5 miles from the City Centre and is in close proximity to both the province's main air and sea ports.

Belfast Waterfront Hall, Conference & Concert Centre
2 Lanyon Place
Belfast, BT1 3WH
Tel: 028 9033 4400
Fax: 028 9033 4467
Contact: Andrew Kyle, Sales & Marketing Manager

Max No of Delegates: 2,000
(Also many smaller venues within the Hall complex)

Belfast Waterfront Hall is a very large venue and offers all the advantages of a City Centre location. Belfast City Airport is a five-minute taxi ride away and Belfast International Airport about 25 minutes. There is a regular Seacat service between Belfast and Scotland and the Belfast to Dublin express train runs six times a day in both directions. Both the Seacat Terminal and Belfast Central Station are five minutes away.

Dukes Hotel
65-67 University Street
Belfast, BT7 1HL
Tel: 028 9023 6666
Fax: 028 9023 7177
Contact: Christine Cardeell, Reception Manager

Max No of Delegates: 150

A converted Victorian building, Dukes is less that a mile from the centre of Belfast and near to both main airports, sea and rail links.

Europa Hotel
Great Victoria Street, Belfast, BT2 7AP
Tel: 028 9027 1066
Fax: 028 9032 7800

Contacts:
Ms Jo-Anne Crossley, Events Manager
Mr Tom Cotter, Events Co-ordinator

Max No of Delegates: 750
(Many smaller rooms also available)
Four-star international hotel situated in the centre of Belfast. Belfast City Airport is five minutes drive away from the Europa, and Belfast International Airport is 16 miles outside the City. The Central Rail Station is located one mile from the Hotel, whilst the Great Victoria Street Railway Station is located next to the Europa. The link road for the M1 and M2 is half a mile from the Hotel and both the Seacat and Ferry Terminals are five minutes away.

Express by Holiday Inn
Inex Conference Centre
106A University Street
Belfast, BT7 1HP
Tel: 028 9020 5000
Fax: 028 9020 5001
Contact: Eleanor Brown, Conference Manager
Max No of Delegates: 200

Fitzwilliam International Hotel
Belfast International Airport
Belfast, BT29 4ZY
Tel: 028 9442 2033
Fax: 028 9442 3500
Contact: Laura Maxwell, Conference & Banqueting Co-ordinator

Max No of Delegates: 590

Three star hotel situated on the Belfast International Airport Complex, 50 metres from the main terminal and 17 miles from Belfast City Centre. The nearest train station is in Antrim (six miles away) and Larne, the nearest port, is 21 miles away.

Hilton Belfast
2 Lanyon Place, Belfast, BT1 3LP
Tel: 028 9027 7000
Fax: 028 9027 7277

Contact: Kelly-Anne Smylie, Conference and Banqueting Sales Manager

Max No of Delegates: 450

The Five-star Hilton hotel is only a few minutes walk from the city centre and close both City and International Airports.

King's Hall Exhibition & Conference Centre
Balmoral, Belfast, BT9 6GW
Tel: 028 9066 5225
Fax: 028 9066 1264
Web: www.kingshall.co.uk
Contact: Lucy Moore, Sales & Marketing Manager

Max No of Delegates: 600

The King's Hall offers a choice of up to five exhibition halls and an adjoining conference centre with a total of up to 10,000 square metres of space available. The conference centre offers a full range of telecommunications technology and audio-visual equipment.

Lansdowne Hotel
657 Antrim Road, Belfast, BT15
Tel: 028 9077 3317
Fax: 028 9037 0125
Contact: Michael Cafolla, General Manager

Max No of Delegates: 200

The Lansdowne Hotel offers a full range of conference facilities for large or small parties. It is within close proximity to Belfast Castle, Fortwilliam Golf Course, Cavehill Country Park and Belfast Zoo, and is only 15 minutes drive from Belfast International Airport.

Odyssey Arena
Queen's Quay, Belfast, BT3 9QQ
Tel: 028 9076 6000
Fax: 028 9076 6111
Web: www.odysseyarean.com
Email: info@smg-sheridan.com
Contact: Colin O'Neill, Marketing Manager

Max No of Delegates: 8400

Odyssey Arena offers the potential to host a huge variety of events due to its large floor area, flexible seating configuration and full range of technical facilities. The venue is suitable for large conferences, with up to 8,500 participants, making it a unique venue within Northern Ireland.

Park Avenue Hotel
158 Holywood Road, Belfast, BT4 1PB
Tel: 028 9065 6520
Fax: 028 9047 1417
Web: www.parkavenuehotel.com
Contact: Angela Reid, Conference Manager

Max No of Delegates: 500

Park Avenue is a family-run hotel, situated in East Belfast within very close proximity to Belfast City Airport, and close to main arterial routes into the city. The hotel offers a full range of conference facilities, along with 250 car parking spaces.

Posthouse Premier Belfast
22 Ormeau Avenue, Belfast, BT2 8HS
Tel: 0870 400 9005
Fax: 028 9062 6546
Web: www.posthouse-hotels.com
Contact: Jenny Carson, Academy Team Manager

Max No of Delegates: 120

The Posthouse Premier, located right in the centre of Belfast, offers a full range of conference facilities from its Academy Conference Centre. The hotel also has a Spirit Health Club with pool and gym.

Queen's University of Belfast
University Road
Belfast, BT7 1NN
Tel: 028 9024 5133
Fax: 028 9024 789
Contact: Conor Browne, Accommodation Manager

Max No of Delegates: 900

Situated in a tree-lined Victorian suburb in the fashionable side of Belfast, this well-established institution is one mile from the City Centre, close to all the mail air, rail and sea links. It offers major conference and residential facilities outside the main University terms. Smaller events can be accommodated all year round.

Ramada Hotel
Shaw's Bridge, Belfast, BT8 7XP
Tel: 028 9092 3500
Fax: 028 9092 3600
Web: www.ramadabelfast.com
Contact: Angela Lennon, Conference & Banqueting Manager

Max No of Delegates: 900

The Ramada Hotel is situated on the southern outskirts of Belfast and is one of the city's newer conference venues. It offers a full range of conference facilities, with The Grand Ballroom accommodating 900 people theatre style of 700 people banquet style.

Spires Conference & Exhibition Centre
Church House, Wellington Street
Belfast, BT1 6DW
Tel: 028 9032 2284
Fax: 028 9023 6609
Contact: Harry Orr, Building Manager

Max No of Delegates: 1150

Spires Conference & Exhibition Centre, built in 1905, is located in Belfast City Centre and is a suitable venue for both small and large events. Full on-site catering facilities are available.

Stormont Hotel
Upper Newtownards Road
Belfast, BT4 3LP
Tel: 028 9065 8621
Fax: 028 9048 0240
Contact: Alwyn Fitzgerald, Sales Manager

Max No of Delegates: 1,240

Stormont Hotel is 4 miles from the City centre. Belfast City Airport is two miles from the Hotel and Belfast International Airport 45 minutes away.

The Wellington Park Hotel
21 Malone Road
Belfast
BT9 6RU
Tel: 028 9038 1111
Fax: 028 9066 5410
Contact: Tracy Wilson, Anne Johnston

Max No of Delegates: 350

Situated in the university area of South Belfast, Wellington Park is five minutes away from the City Centre.

Co Antrim

Ballygally Castle Hotel
Coast Road
Ballygally, BT40 2QR
Tel: 028 2858 1066
Fax: 028 2858 3681
Contact: Stephen Meldrum

Max No of Delegates: 200

Three-star hotel situated 20 miles from Belfast on the Antrim coast road. Ballygally Castle Hotel is also situated 4 miles from Larne, which is serviced by both Northern Ireland Rail and ferry services from Cairnryan in Scotland. The hotel is 30 minutes drive from Belfast City Airport and is 25 minutes from Belfast International Airport.

Dunadry Hotel & Country Club
2 Islandreagh Drive
Dunadry, BT41 2HA
Tel: 028 9443 4343
Fax: 028 9443 3767
Contact: Sheree Davis, Business Development Co-ordinator

Max No of Delegates: 400

Just a short 15 minute drive form Belfast City Centre, 18 miles from Belfast International Airport and 11 miles from Belfast City Airport, the hotel is easily accessible from all major transportation links.

Galgorm Manor
136 Fenaghy Road
Ballymena, BT42 1EA
Tel: 028 2588 1001
Contact: Wendy Dickey, Events Organiser

Max No of Delegates: 500

Galgorm Manor offers a full range of conference and meeting facilities in a tranquil setting. Larger events can be held in The Great Hall, which is located within the grounds of the hotel.

Hilton Templepatrick
Castle Upton Estate
Templepatrick, BT39 ODD
Tel: 028 9443 5500
Fax: 028 9443 5511
Web: www.hilton.co.uk
Contact: Patricia McCusker, Conference & Banqueting Sales Manager

Max No of Delegates: 500

Set in 120 acres of park land within Castle Uptown Estate, Hilton Templepatrick is located 5 minutes from the M2, 20 minutes from Belfast City Airport and City Centre and 10 minutes from Belfast International Airport.

Rosspark Hotel
20 Doagh Road
Kells, Ballymena, BT42 3LZ
Tel: 028 2589 1385
Fax: 028 2589 8178
Email: reception@rossparkhotel.co.uk
Contact: Lesley Ramsey, Conference Manager

Max No of Delegates: 350

The Ross Park Hotel is situated 5 miles from Ballymena town, 21 miles from Belfast and 16 miles from Belfast International Airport. Centrally located in the heart of Co Antrim, the province's major ports are also within easy reach.

Co Armagh

Armagh City Hotel

2 Friary Road, Armagh, BT60 2HE
Tel: 028 3751 8888

Contact: Gary Hynes, Conference & Banqueting Manager

Armagh City Hotel is one of Belfast's newest, and largest, conference venues and offers a full range of conference and banqueting facilities, with its Fisher Suite capable of accommodating 1200 delegates. Full range of audio-visual equipment is available.

Max No of Delegates: 1200

Carngrove Hotel
2 Charlestown Road
Portadown, BT63 5PW
Tel: 028 3833 9222
Fax: 028 3833 2899
Contact: Mrs B Currie, General Manager

Max No of Delegates: 300

Located on the outskirts Portadown town, the two-star Carngrove Hotel is close to all local rail and motorway links, half an hour from Belfast City Airport and only 20 minutes from Belfast International Airport.

Craigavon Civic Centre
PO Box 66, Lakeview Road,
Craigavon, BT64 1AL
Tel: 028 3831 2400
Contact: Ian Bann, Facilities Manager

Max No of Delegates: 320

Market Place Theatre & Arts Centre
Market Street, Armagh, BT61 7AT

Contact: Sharon Kerr/Vincent McCann

Max No of Delegates: 397

Seagoe Hotel
Upper Church Lane
Portadown, BT63 5JE
Tel: 028 3833 3076
Fax: 028 3835 0210
Contact: Catherine McDowell

Max No of Delegates: 300

A three star hotel on the outskirts of Portadown. The hotel is 40 minutes from Belfast International Airport and 5 minutes from Portadown train station, which is on the main Belfast to Dublin line.

Co Down

Canal Court Hotel
Merchant's Quay
Newry, BT35 8HF
Tel: 028 3025 1234
Contact: Aibhinn Rushe, Conference & Banqueting Manager

Max No of Delegates: 300

Clandeboye Lodge Hotel
10 Estate Road
Bangor, BT19 1UR
Tel: 028 9185 2500
Contact: Donna Wilson, Conference & Banqueting Co-ordinator

Max No of Delegates: 350

Culloden Hotel
Holywood, BT18 0EX
Tel: 028 9042 1066
Fax: 028 9042 6777
Contact: Allyson Hastings
Event Co-ordinator

Max No of Delegates: 500

Northern Ireland's first five-star hotel is situated in 12 acres of private parkland on the North Down coast. The Culloden is 6 miles from Belfast City centre where transport links to Belfast City Airport takes only 10 minutes (taxi) and rail links between Cultra and Belfast Central Station are a two minute walk from the hotel. The Culloden is 18 miles away from Belfast International Airport.

Marine Court Hotel
The Marina
Bangor, BT20 5ED
Tel: 028 9145 1100
Fax: 028 9145 1200
Contact: Martha Knapp

Max No of Delegates: 450

The three-star Marine Court Hotel, situated on Bangor's marina, is only 12 miles from Belfast City Centre.

Mourne Country Hotel
52 Belfast Road
Newry, BT34 1TR
Tel: 028 3026 7922
Contact: Donna Quail, Conference & Banqueting Manager

Max No of Delegates: 450

Old Inn
15 Main Street
Crawfordsburn, BT19 1JH
Tel: 028 9185 3255
Contact: Jill Graham, Conference & Events Manager

Max No of Delegates: 120

Slieve Donard Hotel
Newcastle
Co Down, BT33 0AH
Tel: 028 4372 1066
Fax: 028 4372 4830
Contact: Nora Hannah, Business Manager

Max No of Delegates: 825

The four-star Slieve Donard hotel is set in six-acres of Private Grounds. Newcastle is 30 miles from Belfast and approximately 85 miles from Dublin. A bus service, run by Europa Bus Centre, connects Newcastle and Belfast, with Belfast City Airport only a ten-minute drive away.

White Gables Hotel
14 Dromore Road
Hillsborough, BT26 6HS
Tel: 028 9268 2755
Contact: Cheryl Brown

Max No of Delegates: 120

Co Fermanagh

Hotel Carlton
2 Main Street, Belleek, BT93 3FX
Tel: 028 6865 8282
Contact: Sheila McGrath, Conference & Banqueting Manager

Max No of Delegates: 200

Killyhevlin Hotel
Dublin Road
Enniskillen, BT74 76RW
Tel: 028 6632 3481
Fax: 028 6632 4726
Web: www.killyhevlin.com
Contact: David Morrison

Max No of Delegates: 300

Situated on the outskirts of Enniskillen, on the shores of Lough Erne, this four-star hotel is a two hour drive from Belfast International Airport.

Lusty Beg Island
Boa Island, Kesh, BT94 1NY
Tel: 028 6863 2032
Contact: Arthur Cadden, General Manager

This unique venue is situated on an island in Lough Erne and is accessible by boat.

Manor House Country Hotel
Killadeas
Irvinestown, BT94 1NY
Tel: 028 6862 2200
Fax: 028 6862 1545
Contact: Bronagh Donnelly, Functions Manager

Max No of Delegates: 400

Situated on the shores of Lower Lough Erne, four-star Manor House is a two hour drive from Belfast International Airport.

Co Londonderry

Beech Hill Country House Hotel
32 Ardmore Road
Londonderry, BT47 3QP
Tel: 028 7134 9279
Contact: Crawford McIlwaine, General Manager

Max No of Delegates: 100

City Hotel
14-18 Quay's Quay
Derry, BT48 7AS
Tel: 028 7136 5800
Contact: Treasa McGowan, Conference & Banqueting Manager

Max No of Delegates: 145

Everglades Hotel
Prehen Road
Derry, BT47 2NH
Tel: 028 7132 1066
Fax: 028 7134 9200
Contact: Hugh O'Doherty, Conference & Banqueting Manager

Max No of Delegates: 400

The four-star Everglades Hotel is situated in the Southern outskirts of Derry on the banks of the river Foyle.

Inn At The Cross
171 Glenshane Road
Derry, BT47 3EN
Tel: 028 7130 1480
Fax: 028 7130 1394
Contacts: Muriel or Ivan Millar, Hotel Proprietors.

Max No of Delegates: 300

Situated on the main Derry-Belfast Road (A6) in a country setting, the Inn at the Cross is approximately 3 miles from Derry City Centre.

Lodge Hotel & Travelstop
Lodge Road
Coleraine, BT52 1NF
Tel: 028 7034 4848
Fax: 028 7035 4555
Contact: Norma Wilkinson, General Manager

Max No of Delegates: 350

Millennium Forum
Newmarket Street
Londonderry, BT48 6EB
Tel: 028 7126 4426

Max No of Delegates: 1020

Radisson Roe Park
Roe Park
Limavady
Co Londonderry, BT49 9LB
Tel: 028 7772 2222
Fax: 028 7772 2313
Contact: Samantha Ferguson, Event Co-ordinator

Max No of Delegates: 450

4-star hotel with outstanding conference facilities. Situated on the A2 Derry-Limavady Road, the venue is 16 miles from the City of Derry Airport and 45 miles from Belfast International Airport.

Tower Hotel
Butcher Street, Derry, BT48 6HL
Tel: 028 7137 1000
Fax: 028 7137 7123
Contact: Ian Hyland, General Manager

Max No of Delegates: 250

White Horse Hotel
68 Clooney Road
Londonderry, BT47 3PA
Tel: 028 7186 0606
Contact: Ruth Taylor, Conference & Banqueting Manager

Max No of Delegates: 450

Co Tyrone

Fir Trees Hotel
Dublin Road, Strabane, BT82 9EA
Tel: 028 7138 2382
Contact: Christine O'Neill, Manager

Max No of Delegates: 250

Glenavon House Hotel
52 Drum Road, Cookstown, BT80 8JQ
Tel: 028 8676 4949
Fax: 028 8676 4396
Contact: Paula Wilson, Manager

Max No of Delegates: 400

Three-star Glenavon House is located just 30 miles from Belfast International Airport, set in 9 acres of mature grounds on the banks of the Ballinderry River.

Greenvale Hotel
57 Drum Road, Cookstown, BT80 8GS
Tel: 028 8676 2243
Contact: Candice Hughes

Max No of Delegates: 280

Silver Birch Hotel
5 Gortin Road, Omagh, BT79 7DH
Tel: 028 8224 2520
Fax: 028 8224 9061
Contact: Harriet Robinson, Receptionist/Function Co-ordinator.

Max No of Delegates: 230

Situated on the outskirts of Omagh, the Silver Birch Hotel is on the B48 Gorton Road, one and a half hour's drive from both Belfast City and Belfast International Airports.

Representative Groups and Associations

Introduction

Northern Ireland has a vast number of representative groups and associations, large and small, commercial and not-for-profit, covering a wide spectrum of the economic and social life of its people. The main groups are listed A–Z below under appropriate categories. These listings have been extensively researched but they are by no means exhaustive.

Some organisations may fall into more than one categorisation due to the breadth of their activities.

Business, Trade Associations and Representative Groups

Anglo North Irish Fish Producers Organisation Limited
The Harbour, Kilkeel BT34 4AX
Tel: 028 4176 2855
Fax: 028 4176 4904
Chief Executive: Alan McCulla

Arts and Business
53 Malone Road, Belfast BT9 6RY
Tel: 028 9066 4736
Fax: 028 9066 4500
Director: Alice O'Rawe

Association of Landscape Contractors of Ireland
22 Summerhill Park, Bangor, BT20 5QQ
Tel/Fax: 028 9127 2823
Web: www.alci.org.uk
Chairman: Laurence McMinn
Secretary: Mrs Lyn Reaney

Association of Consulting Engineers
C/o Taylor and Fegan, Riversedge, 11 Ravenhill Road, Belfast, BT6 8DN
Tel: 028 9045 4401
Fax: 028 9045 8400
Secretary: Bill Taylor

Association of Municipal Engineers
C/o McAdam Design, 18 Victoria Avenue, Newtownards BT23 7EB
Tel: 028 9181 2831
Fax: 028 9181 1847
Secretary: Mark Oliver

Association of Northern Ireland Colleges
Unit 3, The Sidings Business Park
Antrim Road, Lisburn BT28 3AJ
Tel: 028 9262 7512
Fax: 028 9262 7594
Web: www.anic.ac.uk
Chief Executive: John D'Arcy

Association for Residential Care
43 Marsden Gardens,
Cavehill Road
Belfast BT15 5FL
Tel: 028 9022 9020
Fax: 028 9020 9300
Manager: Siobhan Bogues

Bar Library
Royal Courts of Justice, 91 Chichester Street, Belfast, BT1 3JP
Tel: 028 9024 1523
Web: www.barlibrary.comChief Executive: Brendan Garland

Belfast Naturalists Field Club
78 Kings Road, Belfast BT5 6JN
Tel: 028 90 797 155
Honorary Secretary:
Professor Richard S J Clarke

British Association of Social Workers BASW (NI)
216 Belmont Road, Belfast
BT4 2AT
Tel: 028 9067 2247
Fax: 028 9065 6273
Web: www.basw.co.uk
Professional Officer:
Eileen Ashenhurst

British Cattle Society
22 Ballynahonemore Road,
Armagh BT60 1JD

British Council
2nd Floor, Norwich Union House
7 Fountain Street, Belfast BT1 5EG
Tel: 028 9024 8220
Fax: 028 9023 7592
Web: www.britishcouncil.co.uk
Director: Ms Ann Malamah-Thomas

British Dental Association
The Mount, 2A Woodstock Link,
Belfast, BT6 8DD
Tel: 028 9073 5856
NI Administrative Service:
Alison McMaster

British Medical Association
16 Cromac Place, Ormeau Road,
Belfast, BT7 2JB
Tel: 028 9026 9666
Regional Service Co-ordinator:
Avril Campbell

Chambers of Commerce

Chambers of Commerce represent the business community in Northern Ireland at a local level and are active in dealing with local issues which have implications for the commercial life of a locality. The Northern Ireland Chamber of Commerce and Industry and the regional Chamber of Commerce network currently represents more than 4000 businesses in Northern Ireland.

Members are drawn from every sector of the business community including senior management from major industrial sites, smaller scale retailers and service providers. As well as being an authentic voice for local business and undertaking the representational work, which that entails, local Chambers of Commerce are very active in charitable work in their respective areas

The Northern Ireland Chamber of Commerce and Industry
Chamber of Commerce House
22 Great Victoria Street
Belfast BT2 7BJ
Tel: 028 9024 4113
Fax: 028 9024 7024
Web: www.northernirelandchamber.com
President: Victor Haslett

Antrim Borough Chamber of Commerce
C/o Antrim Enterprise Agency Ltd
58 Greystone Road, Antrim
BT41 1JZ
Tel: 028 9446 7774
Fax: 028 9446 7292
Contact: Mr Douglas Stoddart

Armagh Chamber of Commerce
C/o 19 Russell Street, Armagh
BT61 9BB
Tel: 028 3752 3163
Fax: 028 3741 5111
Contact: Mr Godfrey Abbott

Ballymena Chamber of Commerce
C/o First Trust, 78 Wellington Street, Ballymena, BT43 6AF
Tel: 028 2564 8121
Fax: 028 2564 9799
Contact: Mr William McKean

Ballymoney Chamber of Commerce
C/o Dowds Electrical, 2 Milltown Road, Ballymoney, BT53 6LE
Tel: 028 2766 2789
Fax: 028 2766 5905
Contact: Mr John Dowds

Bangor Chamber of Commerce
C/o 65b Main Street
Bangor BT20 5AF
Tel: 028 9146 0035
Fax: 028 9146 0035
Contact: Mr Evan Ward

Carrickfergus Chamber of Commerce
C/o Wadsworth Estate
Tower House, 33–35 High Street, Carrickfergus BT38 7AN
Tel: 028 9336 0707
Fax: 028 9336 7368
Contact: Mr Peter Wadsworth

Castlederg Chamber of Commerce
24A Main Street, Castlederg, BT81 7AR
Tel: 028 8167 0636
Contact: Mr Gordon Speer

Coleraine Chamber of Commerce
2 Abbey Street, Coleraine
BT52 1DS
Tel: 028 7034 4067
Fax: 028 7032 1416
Contact: Prof. Chris Barnett

Cookstown Chamber of Commerce
PO Box 27, Cookstown
Tel: 028 8676 6023
Contact: Mr John McConnell

Downpatrick Chamber of Commerce
C/o J Laverty & Co,
18 English Street
Downpatrick BT30 6AB
Tel: 028 4461 6413
Contact: Mr John Laverty

Dromore Chamber of Commerce
C/o 21 Princes Street,
Dromore, BT25 1AY
Tel: 028 9269 9628
Contact: Mrs Janice McCructhen

Enniskillen Chamber of Commerce
C/o Fermanagh District Council, Town Hall, Enniskillen, BT74 7BA
Tel: 028 6632 5050
Fax: 028 6634 2878
Contact: Balnaid McKinney

Fivemiletown Chamber of Commerce
Four Ways Hotel, 41 Main Street, Fivemiletown BT75 0PG
Tel: 028 8952 1260
Fax: 028 8952 2061
Contact: Mr Brunt

Holywood Chamber of Trade and Commerce
C/o David Ferguson & Associates
45 Church View, Holywood
BT18 9DP
Tel: 028 9042 7135
Fax: 028 9042 7943
Contact: Ms Margaret Ferguson

Irvinestown Chamber of Commerce
C/o Irvinestown Rectory, Enniskillen Road, Irvinestown BT94 1GL
Tel: 028 6862 1225
Contact: Rev Raymond Thompson

Kilkeel Chamber of Commerce
C/o Dunnes Stores, 18 Greencastle Street, Kilkeel BT34 4BH
Tel: 028 4176 2265
Contact: Mr Tom O'Hanlon

Limavady Chamber of Commerce, Industry & Trade
The Lodge, Main Street, Limavady
BT49 0EY
Tel: 07713 273123
Contact: Mr Douglas Miller

Lisburn Chamber of Commerce
3a Bridge Street, Lisburn
BT28 1XZ
Tel: 028 9266 6297
Contact: Mrs Ellen Hillen

Lisnaskea Chamber of Commerce
C/o Market Yard, Lisnaskea
BT92 0PL
Tel: 028 6772 1081
Fax: 028 6772 1088
Contact: Mr John Mcllwaine

Londonderry Chamber of Commerce
1 St Columbs Court, Bishop Street, Derry BT48 6PT
Tel: 028 7126 2379
Fax: 028 7128 6789
Contact: Mr Niall Birthistle

Magherafelt Chamber of Commerce
37 Rainey Street
Magherafelt BT45 5AB
Tel: 028 7963 2392
Contact: Mr Michael McLarnon

Newcastle Chamber of Commerce
C/o 51 Main Street
Newcastle BT33 0AD
Tel: 028 4372 4903
Fax: 028 4372 4263
Contact: Mr Peter Law

Newry Chamber of Commerce
74 Hill Street, Newry, BT34 1BE
Tel: 028 3025 0303
Contact: Mr Peter Murray

Omagh Chamber of Commerce
2nd Floor, 33 Market Street
Omagh BT78 1EE
Tel: 028 8225 9595
Fax: 028 8225 9596
Contact: Mr Kevin Martin

Portadown Chamber of Commerce
C/o Alexander Gill & Sons Ltd
42 Meadow Lane
Portadown BT62 3NJ
Tel: 028 3833 2875
Contact: Mr Robin Gill

Portrush Chamber of Commerce
C/o 110 Dunluce Road
Portrush BT56 8NB
Tel: 028 7082 2783
Fax: 028 7082 4524
Contact: Mr David Alexander

Portstewart Chamber of Commerce
C/o 17 Ballyleese Park
Portstewart BT55 7QA
Tel: 028 7083 2960
Contact: Mr Peter Bayliss

Strabane Chamber of Commerce
C/o Fir Trees Hotel, Dublin Road, Strabane, BT80 9EA
Tel: 028 7138 2382
Contact: Mr John Kelly

Carrickfergus Gasworks Preservation Society
6 Twinburn Crescent, Monkstown
Newtownabbey BT37 0ER
Tel: 028 9086 2974
Contact: Samuel Gault

CBI (Confederation of British Industry)

Scottish Amicable Building
11 Donegall Square South
Belfast, BT1 5JE
Tel: 028 9032 6658
Fax: 028 9024 5915
Web: www.cbi.org.uk
Chairman: David Dobbin
Vice Chairman: Dr Ian McMorris
Director: Nigel Smyth

CBI is a leading umbrella organisation and representative group for industry and business in Northern Ireland. It coordinates policy positions on behalf of industry for presentation to government on a range of major issues.

CBI / IBEC Joint Business Council

Also based at the address above and at the offices of the CBI counterpart in the Republic of Ireland, IBEC.
Contact: William Poole, Business Development Director

Centre for Competitiveness

Interpoint, 20–24 York Street
Belfast BT15 1AQ
Tel: 028 9046 8362
Fax: 028 9046 8361
Web: www.cforc.org
Chief Executive: Bob Barbour

The Centre for Competitiveness is a private sector, not for profit, membership organisation actively supporting the development of an internationally competitive economy in Northern Ireland.

Chartered Institute of Marketing

22 Great Victoria Street,
Belfast, BT2 7BJ
Tel: 028 9024 4113
Regional Director: Mike Maguire

Construction Employers Federation

143 Malone Road, Belfast BT9 6SU
Tel: 028 9087 7143
Fax: 028 9087 7155
Web: www.cefni.co.uk
Managing Director: Mr W A Doran

Coal Advisory Service (NI)

Unit 18a Lowes Industrial Estate
31 Hillsborough Road
Carryduff, Belfast BT8 8EH
Tel: 0845 7125300
Fax: 028 9081 2145

Construction Industry Training Board

Nutts Corner Training Centre
17 Dundrod Road, Crumlin
BT29 4SR
Tel: 028 9082 5466
Fax: 028 9082 5693
Email: info@citbni.org.uk
Web: www.citbni.org.uk

Chief Executive
Allan McMullen

Northern Ireland's construction industry is unique in having a structure of contractors and sub-contractors, many of whom are self-employed or work in small groups. It is essential that an effective umbrella organisation is responsible for high quality training. The Construction Industry Training Board fulfils this role.

East Belfast Traders Association

Unit 1a, 321 Beersbridge Road
Belfast BT5 5DS
Tel: 028 9022 6464

Electrical Contractors Association

45 Sunningdale Park, Bangor
Tel: 028 9147 9527

Engineering Employers Federation

2 Greenwood Avenue, Belfast
BT4 3JL
Tel: 028 9059 5050
Fax: 028 9059 5059
Web: www.eef.org.uk
Director: Peter Bloch

Federation of Master Builders

42a–44a New Row
Coleraine BT52 1AF
Tel: 028 7034 0999
Fax: 028 7034 0998
Web: www.fmb.org.uk
Administrator: Jim Morrison

Federation of Small Businesses

20 Adelaide Street, Belfast
BT2 8GB
Tel: 028 9051 7024
Fax: 028 9051 7120
Web:www.nireland.policy@fsb.org.uk
NI Press Officer: Glyn Roberts

Federation of the Retail Licensed Trade

91 University Street, Belfast
BT7 1HP
Tel: 028 9032 7578
Fax: 028 9032 7578
Web: www.ulsterpubs.com/
Chief Executive: Nicola Jamison

The Federation represents around 1,100 pubs, hotels and restaurants in Northern Ireland.

Freight Transport Association Ltd

109 Airport Road West,
Belfast, BT3 9ED
Tel: 028 9046 6699
Fax: 028 9046 6690
Web: www.fta.co.uk
Manager: Tom Wilson

Institute of Directors

4 Royal Avenue, Belfast BT1 1DA
Tel: 028 9023 2880
Fax: 028 9023 2881
Web: www.iod.com
Chairman: Denis Rooney
Divisional Director: Linda Brown

Institute of Export (NI Branch)

C/o Denman International Ltd,
Clandeboye Road, Bangor, BT20 7JH
Tel: 028 9146 2141
Fax: 028 9145 1654
E-mail: j.stewart@denmanbrush.com
Chairperson: Mr Jim Stewart

Irish Guild of Master Craftsmen

123–125 Main Street
Bangor BT20 4AE

Irish Linen Guild

5c The Square
Hillsborough BT26 6AG
Tel: 028 9268 9999
Fax: 028 9268 9968
Web: www.irishlinen.co.uk
Director: Linda MacHugh

Founded in 1928, the Irish Linen Guild is a promotion organisation drawing its membership from all sections of the Irish linen industry.

Irish Trade Board

53 Castle St, Belfast BT1 1GH

Knitwear, Footwear & Apparel Trades (KFAT)

The Knitting Centre, 6 London Road,
Kilmarnock KA3 7AD
Tel: 01563 535 888

Livestock & Meat Commission for Northern Ireland

Lissue House, 31 Ballinderry Road
Lisburn BT28 2SL
Tel: 028 9263 3000
Fax: 028 9263 3001
Web: www.lmcni.com
Chief Executive: David Rutledge

Momentum

(Formerly Northern Ireland Software Federation)

Ni-Soft House, Ravenhill Business Park,
Ravenhill Road, Belfast, BT6 8AU
Tel: 028 9045 0101
Fax: 028 9045 2123
Contact: Ruth Walmsley

National Association of Shopkeepers and Self-Employed Business People

338a Beersbridge Road
Belfast BT5 5DT
Tel: 028 9045 9036

National Association for the Self Employed

Tel: 028 9042 7797

National Farmers' Union

72 High Street,
Newtownards BT23 7HZ
Tel: 028 9181 4218
Fax: 028 9181 1574
Group Secretary: Ms J Lyness

National Federation of Retail Newsagents

Yeoman House, 11 Sekforde Street,
London EC1
Tel: 020 7253 4225
Fax: 020 7250 0927

National House Building Council

59 Malone Road, Belfast BT9 6SA
Tel: 028 9068 3131
Fax: 028 9068 3258
Web: www.nhbc.co.uk
Regional Director: Tom Kirk

North Belfast Traders Association

Unit 3, North City Business Centre
Duncairn Gardens, Belfast
BT15 2GF

Northern Ireland Aerospace Consortium

Northern Ireland Technology Centre
Cloreen Park, Malone Road
Belfast BT9 5HN
Tel: 028 9027 4505
Fax: 028 9066 3715
Chairperson: Dr Paul Madden

Northern Ireland Agricultural Producers' Association

15 Molesworth St
Cookstown BT80 8NX
Tel: 028 8676 5700
Fax: 028 8675 8598
Chairman: Sean Clarke

Northern Ireland Amusement Caterers Trade Association

Hydepark Industrial Estate
58 Mallusk Road
Newtownabbey BT36 4PX
Tel: 028 9084 8731
Fax: 028 9083 3104
Secretary: Mr JH Sander

Northern Ireland Bankers' Association

Stokes House
17–25 College Square East
Belfast BT1 6DE
Tel: 028 9032 7551
Fax: 028 9033 1449
Contact: Bill McAlister

Northern Ireland Chamber of Trade

PO Box 444, Belfast BT1 1DY
Tel: 028 9023 0444
Fax: 028 9023 0444
Director: Joan Roberts

Northern Ireland Childminding Association

16–18 Mill St
Newtownards BT23 4LU
Tel: 028 9181 1015
Fax: 028 9182 0921
Web: www.nicma.org
Director: Bridget Nodder

Northern Ireland Council for Ethnic Minorities

Ascot House
24–31 Shaftesbury Square
Belfast BT2 7DB
Tel: 028 9023 8645
Fax: 028 9031 9485

Northern Ireland Dairy Association

Quay Gate House, 15 Scrabo Street
Belfast BT5 4BD
Tel: 028 9045 2292
Fax: 028 9045 3373
Director: Paul Archer

Northern Ireland Dyslexia Association

17a Upper Newtownards Road
Belfast BT4 3HT
Tel: 028 9066 0111
Contact: Jim Clarke

Northern Ireland Fish Producers' Organisation

1 Coastguard Cottages, Harbour Road,
Portavogie
Newtownards BT22 1EA
Tel: 028 4277 1946
Fax: 028 4277 1696
E-mail: nifpo@aol.com
Chief Executive: Mr Richard James

Northern Ireland Food & Drink Association

Quay Gate House, 15 Scrabo Street
Belfast BT5 4BD
Tel: 028 9045 2424
Fax: 028 9045 3373
Web: www.nifda.co.uk
Director: Michael Bell

Northern Ireland Grain Trade Association (NIGTA)

Cuinne an Chaireil, 27 Berwick View,
Moira BT67 0SX
Tel: 028 9261 1044
Fax: 028 9261 1979
E-mail: doris@leemanpr.demon.co.uk
Contact: Doris Leeman

Northern Ireland Heritage Gardens Committee

PO Box 252, Belfast BT9 6GY
Tel: 028 90 668 817
Contact: Belinda Jupp

Northern Ireland Hotels Federation

The Midland Building, Whitla Street
Belfast BT15 1JP
Tel: 028 9035 1110
Fax: 028 9035 1509
Web: www.nihf.co.uk
Director General: Janice Gault

NI Local Government Association

Philip House, 123 York Street, Belfast
BT15 1AB
Tel: 028 9024 9286
Fax: 028 9023 3328
Email: hm@nilga.org.uk
Chief Executive: Heather Moorhead

Northern Ireland Master Butchers' Association
38 Oldstone Hill
Muckamore BT41 4SB
Tel: 028 9446 5180
Fax: 028 9446 5180
Secretary: Mr H Marquess

Northern Ireland Master Plumbers' Association
C/o Mr W Crawford
Crawford Sedgwick & Co
38 Hill Street
Belfast BT1 2LB
Tel: 028 9032 1731
Fax: 028 9024 7521
Secretary: Mr W Crawford

Northern Ireland Meat Exporters Association
24 Ballydown Road
Banbridge BT32 3RP
Tel: 028 4062 6338
Fax: 028 4062 6083
Web: www.nimea.co.uk
Chief Executive: Cecil Mathers

Northern Ireland Museums Council
6 Crescent Gardens, Belfast, BT7 1NS
Tel: 028 9055 0215
Fax: 028 9055 0216
Web: www.nimc.co.uk
Director: Chris Bailey

Northern Ireland Optometric Society
PO Box 20202, Banbridge
Co.Down BT32 4SD
Tel: 028 40 629 978
Fax: 028 90 629 978
General Secretary: Leanora Keating

Northern Ireland Quarry Owners' Association
C/o Mr B Frair, Jackson Andrews,
Andras House, 60 Great Victoria St
Belfast BT2 7ET
Tel: 028 9023 3152
Fax: 028 9033 2757
E-mail: belfast@jackson-andrews.co.uk
Secretary: B Frair

Northern Ireland Seafood Association
Quay Gate House, 15 Scrabo St
Belfast BT5 4BD
Tel: 028 9045 2829
Fax: 028 9045 3373
Web: www.niseafood.co.uk
Chief Executive: Dennis Law

Northern Ireland Textile & Apparel Association
5c The Square
Hillsborough BT26 6AG
Tel: 028 9268 9999
Fax: 028 9268 9968
Web: www.nita.co.uk
Director: Linda MacHugh

Northern Ireland Timber Trade Association
13 Churchhill Drive
Carrickfergus BT38 7LH
Tel: 028 9336 2784
Fax: 028 9332 9011
Secretary: Mr T G Rankin

Pharmaceutical Society
73 University Street, Belfast
BT7 1HL
Tel: 028 9032 6927
Fax: 028 9043 9919
Chief Executive: Sheila Maltby

Professional Craftsmen Association
14 Northland Row
Dungannon BT71 6AP
Tel: 028 8772 5377
Chairman: Paul Devlin

Retail Motor Industry Federation
107a Shore Road, Belfast
BT 15 3BB
Tel: 028 9037 0137
Fax: 028 9037 0706
Regional Manager: Noel Smyth

Royal Life Saving Society
Trinity House, Lisburn, BT28 2YY
Tel: 028 9260 6969
Web: www.rlssdirect.co.uk
Director: Hazel Bradley

Social Economy Agency
45–47 Donegall Street
Belfast BT1 2FG
Tel: 028 9096 1115
Fax: 028 9096 1116
Regional Manager: Eamonn Donnelly

Ulster Archaeological Society
C/o Dept of Archaeology
Queen's University, Belfast BT7 1QF
Tel: 028 9027 3186
Fax: 028 9031 3628
Contact: John O'Neil

Ulster Chemists' Association
73 University Street, Belfast
BT7 1HL
Tel: 028 9032 0787
Fax: 028 9031 3737
President: Paula McDaid

Ulster Farmers' Union
475 Antrim Road, Belfast
BT15 3DA
Tel: 028 9037 0222
Fax: 028 9037 1231
Chief Executive: Clarke Black
President: John Gilliland OBE

Ulster Federation of Credit Unions
218-220 Kingsway, Dunmurry, Belfast,
BT17 9BP
Tel: 028 9023 6301
Co-ordinator: Gladys Copeland

Ulster Launderers' Association
C/o Patrick Bryson, Standard Laundry
213 Donegall Avenue
Belfast BT12 6LU
Tel: 028 9032 7295
Fax: 028 9031 4026
Contact: Patrick Bryson

Ulster GAA Writers Association
20 Stewartstown Park
Belfast BT11 9GL
Tel: 028 9060 0833
Web: www.ulstergaawriters.com
Contact: Tony McGee

YMCA National Council
Memorial House, Waring Street, Belfast,
BT1 2EU
Tel: 028 9032 7757
Fax: 028 9043 8809
Chief Executive: Stephen Turner

Professional Institutes and Associations

Architects Registration Board
8 Weymouth Street,
London W1W 5BU
Tel: 020 7580 5861
Fax: 020 7436 5269
Web: www.arb.org.uk
Chief Executive: Robin Vaughan

Association of Belfast Doctors on Call
The Old Casualty, 64 Crumlin Road
Belfast BT14 6AG
Tel: 028 9074 4447
Fax: 028 9074 9999
Manager: Kerry Cavanan

Association of Chartered Certified Accountants (ACCA)
29 Lincoln's Inn Fields
London WC2A 3EE
Tel: 020 7396 7000
Fax: 020 7396 7070
Email: info@accaglobal.com
Chief Executive: Allen Blewitt

Association of Consulting Engineers (NI Branch)
C/o Taylor and Fagan, Riveredge
11 Ravenhill Road, Belfast
BT6 8DN
Tel: 028 9045 4401
Fax: 028 9045 8400
Secretary: Bill Taylor

Association of Southern Area Doctors on Call
Legahory Green, Craigavon, BT65 5BE
Tel: 028 8778 9713

British Dental Association
The Mount, 2a Woodstock Link
Belfast BT6 8DD
Tel: 028 9073 5856
Fax: 028 9073 5857
NI Administrative Secretary:
Alison McMaster

British Medical Association
16 Cromac Place, Cromac Wood,
Ormeau Road, Belfast BT7 2JB
Tel: 028 9026 9666
Fax: 028 9026 9665
E-mail: info.belfast@bma.org.uk
Regional Service Co-ordinator:
Avril Campbell

Chartered Institute of Building
PO Box 1268, Bangor, BT20 5DY
Tel: 028 9147 9883
Fax: 028 9147 9884
Contact: Trevor Patterson

Chartered Institution of Building Surveyors
c/o The Caldwell Partnership
8 Lorne Street, Belfast BT9 7DU
Tel: 028 9066 9456
Fax: 028 9066 2219
Honorary Secretary: Mark Taylor

Chartered Institute of Housing
Carnmoney House
Edgewater Office Park
Belfast BT3 9JQ
Tel: 028 9077 8222
Fax: 028 9077 8333
E-mail: ni@cih.org
Chief Executive: David Butler

Chartered Institute of Management Accountants (CIMA)
26 Chapter Street
London SW1P 4NP
Tel: 020 7663 5441
Web: www.cimaglobal.com
Tel: 028 9268 3727

Chartered Institute of Marketing
The Mount Business Centre, 2
Woodstock Link, Belfast, BT6 8DD
Tel: 028 9073 5898
Fax: 028 9073 0199
Regional Director: Mike Maguire

Chartered Institute of Public Finance and Accountancy
2nd Floor, Scottish Amicable Building,
11 Donegal Square South,
Belfast, BT1 5JE
Tel: 028 9026 6770
Fax: 028 9026 6771
Contact: David Nicholl
The Accountancy Institute, which represents in the main professional accountants operating in the public sector.

Chartered Institute of Purchasing and Supply
Easton House, Easton on the Hill,
Stamford, Lincolnshire PE9 3NZ
Tel: 01780 756 777
Fax: 01780 751 610
Contact: Sarah Lewithwaite

Chartered Society of Physiotherapy (CSP)
Merrion Business Centre
58 Howard Street, Belfast BT1 6PJ

Chief Executives' Forum
Lancashire House, 5 Linenhall St
Belfast BT2 8AA
Tel: 028 9054 2966
Fax: 028 9054 2970
Web: www.ceforum.org
Director: Alvin McKinley

The Chief Executives' Forum is the association of chief executive officers of public bodies in Northern Ireland. The Forum aims to support the democratic process by promoting excellence in public service and encourage innovation and development of leadership.

The General Council of the Bar in Northern Ireland
Royal Courts of Justice, 91 Chichester Street, Belfast BT1 3JP
Tel: 028 9024 1523
Fax: 028 9023 1850
Chief Executive: Brendan Garland
The Bar Council is responsible for the maintenance of the standards, honour and independence of the bar, and through its Professional Conduct Committee, receives and investigates any complaints against members of the Bar in their professional capacity.

The Law Society of Northern Ireland

Law Society House
98 Victoria Street
Belfast, BT1 3JZ
Tel: 028 9023 1614
Fax: 028 9023 2606
Web: www.lawsoc-ni.org

In 1922 a Royal Charter was granted to solicitors in Northern Ireland to permit the setting up of the Incorporated Law Society of Northern Ireland. Under the Solicitors (Northern Ireland) Order of 1976, the Law Society acts as the regulatory authority governing the education, accounts, discipline and professional conduct of solicitors in order to maintain the independence, ethical standards, professional competence and quality of services offered to the public.

The Society operates through an elected Council which is served by numerous Standing and Special Committees, all comprising practising solicitors. It takes an active interest in all issues connected with law and order and the administration of justice.

The Institute of Chartered Accountants in Ireland
11 Donegall Square South
Belfast BT1 5JE
Tel: 028 9032 1600
Fax: 028 9023 0071
Director: Heather Briars

Institution of Chemical Engineers

(Irish Branch: Northern Section)
School of Chemical Engineering
Queens University Belfast
Tel: 028 9027 4255
Fax: 028 90281753
Contact: Prof. Ronnie Magee

Institution of Civil Engineers
C/o Construction Employers Federation,
143 Malone Road, Belfast, BT9 6SU
Tel: 028 9087 7157
Fax: 028 9087 7155
Regional Secretary: Wendy Blundell

Institution of Electrical Engineers (NI Branch)
1 Glenbrae, Church Road, Holywood, Co Down BT18 9SD
Tel: 028 9042 8281
Web: www.ieeni.com
E-mail: glenbrae@lineone.net
Hon. Secretary: Mr WA Biggerstaff

The Institution of Electrical Engineers is a not-for-profit organisation, registered as a charity in the UK.

Institute of Financial Accountants
Burford House, 44 London Road, Sevenoaks, Kent TN13 1AS
Tel: 01732 458 080
Fax: 01732 455 848
E-mail: mail@ifa.org.uk
Web: www.accountingweb.co.ukifa

Institute of Management
PO Box 34, Newtownards, BT23 6ST
Tel: 028 9754 2451
Tel: 0207 497 0580 (London)
Web: www.inst-mgt.org.uk

Institute of Management Services
Stowe House, Netherstowe, Lichfield Staffordshire WS13 6TJ
Tel: 01543 266 825
Fax: 01543 266 833
E-mail: admin@ims-stowe.fsnet.co.uk
Contact: Vivienne Phillips

The Institute operates through a network of regions throughout the UK and abroad, which work in conjunction with other professional institutes in their region.

Institution of Mechanical Engineers
105 West George Street
Glasgow G2 1QL
Tel: 0141 2217156
Regional Manager: Sandra Mulligan

Institute of Ophthalmology
11–43 Bath Street, London, EC1V 9EL
Tel: 0207 608 6800
Fax: 0207 608 6851
Contact: Colin Bookbinder

Chartered Institute of Personnel and Development
Weavers Court Business Park
Linfield Road, Belfast BT12 5LA
Tel: 028 9022 4005
Web: www.cipd.co.uk
Vice Chairperson: Lynne Stephenson

Institute of Psychiatry
De Crespigny Park, London SE5 8AF
Tel: 0207 848 0140
Fax: 0207 701 9044
Web: www.iop.kcl.ac.uk

Institute of Public Relations
The Old Trading House, 15 Northburgh Street, London EC1V OPR
Tel: 0207 253 5151
Fax: 0207 490 0588
E-mail: info@ipr.org.uk
Contact: Richard George

Royal College of General Practitioners (NI)
44 Elmwood Avenue, Belfast, BT9 6AZ
Tel: 028 9066 7389
Fax: 028 9068 2155
Web: www.rcgp.org
Regional Manager: Valerie Fiddis

Royal College of Midwives
58 Howard St, Belfast BT1 6PJ
Tel: 028 9024 1531
Fax: 028 9024 5889
Web: www.rcm.org.uk
NI Board Secretary:
Ms Bredagh Hughes

Royal College of Nursing
17 Windsor Avenue, Belfast
BT9 6EE
Tel: 028 9066 8236
Fax: 028 9038 2188
Board Secretary: Martin Bradley

Royal Institute of Chartered Surveyors (NI Branch)
9/11 Corporation Square
Belfast BT1 3AJ
Tel: 028 9032 2877
Fax: 028 9023 3465
Director: Ian Murray

Royal Society of Ulster Architects
2 Mount Charles, Belfast BT7 1NZ
Tel: 028 9032 3760
Fax: 028 9023 7313
Web: www.rsua.org.uk
Director: Frank McCloskey

Royal Town Planning Institute (NI Branch)
2 Mount Charles, Belfast BT7 1NZ
Tel: 028 9032 3760
Fax: 028 9023 7313
Chairman: Helen Harrison

Society of Radiographers (SOR)
207 Providence Square
Mill St, London SE1 2EW
Tel: 0207 740 7200

Trades Unions

Northern Ireland has a variety of trades union organisations covering a wide spectrum of economic life. For the most part the unions are regional parts of UK-based national unions, or in quite a number of cases, all-island unions, or unions active throughout the British Isles. There are a few union organisations unique to Northern Ireland.

Generally, Northern Ireland has a reasonably good industrial relations record and relations between management and trades unions across the economic sectors are positive and professional. There has been a long-term decline in individual membership of trades unions but formal union-centred industrial relations procedures still operate in many workplaces.

Irish Congress of Trade Unions (ICTU)
3 Crescent Gardens, Belfast
BT7 1NS
Tel: 028 9024 7940
Fax: 028 9024 6898
Assistant General Secretary:
Peter Bunting

The Irish Congress of Trade Unions is the umbrella organisation of, and provides leadership for, the entire trades union movements in Ireland, North and South. It is organised on a regional basis, which includes a Northern Ireland section.

ICTU negotiates with government directly on national labour issues and carries out research on behalf of the union movement.

Amalgamated Engineering & Electrical Union (AEEU)
Unit 1, City Link Business Park
8 Albert Street
Belfast BT12 4HB
Tel: 028 9024 5785
Fax: 028 9024 5939
Web: www.aeeu.org.uk
Regional Secretary: Peter Williamson

4 Foyle Road, Derry BT48 7FR
Tel: 028 7126 1622
Fax: 028 7136 6025
Regional Secretary:
Peter Williamson

Amalgamated Transport & General Workers Union (ATGWU)
102 High Street, Transport House
Belfast BT1 2DL
Tel: 028 9023 2381
Fax: 028 9032 9904
56–58 Carlisle Road, Derry
BT48 6JW
Tel: 028 7126 4851
Regional Secretary: Brendan Hodges

Association of First Division Civil Servants (AFDCS)
Room 3 Craigantlet Buildings
Stoney Road, Belfast BT4 3SX

Association of Teachers and Lecturers
397a Holywood Road, Belfast
BT4 2LS
Tel: 028 9047 1412
Fax: 028 9047 1535
Office Administrator: Evelyn Rogers

Association of University Teachers (AUT)
C/o Dr S Lowry, Faculty of Science,
University of Ulster
Coleraine BT52 1SA
Tel: 028 7034 4141

Bakers, Food & Allied Workers Union (BFAWU)
80 High Street, Belfast BT1 2BG
Tel: 028 9032 2767

British Actors' Equity Association (EQUITY)
114 Union St, Glasgow G1 3QQ
Tel: 0141 248 2472
Fax: 0141 248 2472
Web: www.equity.org.uk
Secretary: Drew McFarland

Broadcasting, Entertainment, Cinematograph & Theatre Union (BECTU)
373–377 Clapham Road
London SW9 9BT
Tel: 0207 346 0900
Fax: 0207 346 0901
General Secretary: Roger Bolton

Communication Managers' Association (CMA)
Royal Mail House, 20 Donegall Quay
Belfast BT1 1AA
Tel: 028 9089 2288
Secretary: Bobby Smith

Communication Workers' Union (CWU)
8–10 Exchange Place
Belfast BT1 2NA
Tel: 028 9032 1771
Fax: 028 9043 9390
Chairman: John McLoughlin

Connect
C/o Mr A Gibb
BT plc Riverside Tower
5 Lanyon Place, Belfast BT1 3BT

Counteract
2nd Floor Philip House
123–137 York Street
Belfast BT15 1AB
Tel: 028 9023 7023
Fax: 028 9031 3585
Web: www.counteract.org
Director: William Robinson

National Farmers' Union
72 High Street
Newtownards BT23 7HZ
Tel: 028 9181 4218
Fax: 028 9181 1574
Group Secretary: Jane Lyness

Prospect
75–79 York Road, London SE1 7AQ
Tel: 020 7902 6600
Fax: 020 7902 6667
E-mail: enquiries@prospect.org.uk
General Secretary: Paul Noon

Fire Brigades' Union (FBU)
7 Kerrymount Avenue
Belfast BT8 6NL

GMB
3–4 Donegal Quay, Belfast
BT1 3EA
Tel: 028 9031 2111
Fax: 028 90 312 333
Organiser: Bobby Carson

Graphical Paper & Media Union (GMPU)
Unit A First Floor
Loughside Industrial Park
Dargan Crescent, Belfast BT3 9JP
Tel: 028 9077 8550
Fax: 028 9077 8552
Branch Secretary: Davy Edmont

Irish Bank Officials Association (IBOA)
93 St Stephen's Green, Dublin 2
Tel: 01 475 5908
Fax: 01 478 0567
Secretary: Larry Broderick

Irish National Teachers Association (INTO)
23 College Gardens, Belfast
BT9 6BS
Tel: 028 9038 1455
Fax: 028 9066 2803
E-mail: info@ni.into.ie
Northern Secretary:
Mr Frank Bunting

Manufacturing Science & Finance (MSF)
7 Donegall Street, Belfast BT1 2FN
Tel: 028 9032 6688
Fax: 028 9032 6699
Web: www.msf.org.uk
Regional Officer: Kevin McAdam

National Association of Head Teachers
Carnmoney House, Edgewater Office
Park, Belfast, BT3 9JQ
Tel: 028 9077 6633
Fax: 028 9077 4777
E-mail: fernt@naht.org.uk
Regional Officer: Fern Turner

National Association for Probation Officers (NAPO)
C/o Ms E Richardson, PBNI
80/90 Great Patrick St
Belfast BT1 1LD
Tel: 028 9032 6688

National Association of Schoolmasters / Union of Women Teachers (NASUWT)
Ben Madigan House, Edgewater Road
Belfast BT3 9JQ
Tel: 028 9078 4480
Fax: 028 9078 4489
Web: www.teachersunion.org.uk
Regional Officer: Else Margrain

National Association of Teachers in Further & Higher Education (NATFHE)
475 Lisburn Road,
Belfast BT9 7EZ
Tel: 028 9066 5501
Fax: 028 9066 9225
Web: www.natfhe.org.uk
Regional Officer: Jim McKeown

National Union of Journalists (NUJ)
Headland House
308–312 Gray's Inn Road
London WC1X 8DT
Tel: 0207 278 7916

National Union of Rail, Maritime & Transport Workers (RMT)
180 Hope St, Glasgow G2 2UE
Tel: 0141 332 1117
Fax: 0141 333 9583
Regional Organiser: Steve Todd

Northern Ireland Musicians Association (NIMA)

3rd Floor, Unit 4, Fortwilliam Business Park, Dargan Road, Belfast BT3 9JZ
Tel: 028 9037 0037
Fax: 028 9037 0037
NIWA Organiser: Mr Hamilton

NI Public Service Alliance (NIPSA)

Harkin House, 54 Wellington Park
Belfast BT9 6DP
Tel: 028 9066 1831
Fax: 028 9066 5847
Web: www.nipsa.org.uk
General Secretary: John Corey

The National Union of Students (NUS-USI)

NUS-USI, 29 Bedford Street
Belfast BT2 7EJ
Tel: 028 9024 4641
Fax: 028 9043 9659
E-mail: info@nistudents.com
Web: www.nistudents.com
Director: Peter O'Neill
Convenor 2003–2004:
Ben Archibald

Belfast Institute of Further and Higher Education Students Union

Room A24, College Square East
Belfast BT1 6DJ
Union Tel: 028 9024 9040
Union Fax: 028 9026 5101
College Tel: 028 9026 5000

Queen's University of Belfast Students Union

University Road
Belfast BT7 1PE
Union Tel: 028 9097 3106
Union Fax: 028 9023 6900
E-mail: info@qubsu.org
College Tel: 028 9024 5133
Web: www.qubsu.org

University of Ulster Students Union

Cromore Road, Coleraine
BT52 1SA
Union Tel: 028 7032 4319
Union Fax: 028 7032 4915
College Tel: 08700 400 700
E-mail: su.president@uusu.org
Web: www.uusu.org

Jordanstown Site

Shore Road, Co Antrim BT37 0QB
Union Tel: 028 9036 6050
Union Fax: 028 9036 6817
E-mail: su.edwel@uusu.org
E-mail: vp.jordanstown@uusu.org
College Tel: 08700 400 700

Derry Site

Magee College, Northlands Road, Derry
BT48 7JL
Union Tel: 028 7137 5226
Union Fax: 028 7137 5415
College Tel: 08700 400 700
E-mail: vp.magee@uusu.org

Belfast Site

York Street, Belfast BT15 1ED
Union Tel: 028 9026 7302
Union Fax: 028 9026 7351
College Tel: 08700 400 700
E-mail: vp.belfast@uusu.org
E-mail: su.enquiries@uusu.org

Public Commerce Services Union (PCS)

10 Mounthill Court, Cloughmills
Co Antrim BT44 9QU
Tel: 028 2563 3096
Contact: Alastair Donaghy

Royal College of Nursing

17 Windsor Avenue, Belfast
BT9 6EE
Tel: 028 9066 8236
Fax: 028 9038 2188
Board Secretary: Martin Bradley

Services Industrial Professional Technical Union (SIPTU)

3 Antrim Road, Belfast BT15 2BE
Tel: 028 9031 4000
Fax: 028 9031 4044
Regional Secretary: Jack Nash

Ulster Farmers' Union

475 Antrim Road, Belfast
BT15 3DA
Tel: 028 9037 0222
Fax: 028 9037 1231
Web: info@ufunq.com/
Chief Executive: Clarke Black

Ulster Teachers' Union (UTU)

94 Malone Road, Belfast BT9 5HP
Tel: 028 9066 2216
Fax: 028 9066 3055
Web: www.utu.edu/home.html/
Secretary: Ray Calvin

Union of Construction, Allied Trades & Technicians (UCATT)

Rooms 108 / 110, Midland Building,
Whitla Street, Belfast BT15 1JP
Tel: 028 9075 1866
Fax: 028 9075 1867
E-mail: admin@ucatt.org.uk
Regional Secretary: Terry Lally

Union of Shop, Distributive & Allied Workers (USDAW)

40 Wellington Park, Belfast
BT9 6DN
Tel: 028 9066 3773
Fax: 028 9066 2133
Area Organiser: Bob Gourley

UNISON

Unit 4, Fortwilliam Business Park,
Dargan Road, Belfast BT3 9LZ
Tel: 028 9077 0813
Fax: 028 9077 9772
Regional Secretary: Patricia McKeown

Affiliated Councils of Trade Unions

Belfast & District
C/o Transport House
102 High Street, Belfast BT1
Contact: Pearse McKenna

Craigavon & District

47 Cranny Road
Portadown BT63 5SP
Contact: Dr A Evans

Derry

23/25 Shipquay St, Derry
BT48 6DL
Contact: Mr J McCracken

Fermanagh

C/o 5/7 Queen St
Enniskillen BT74 7JR
Contact: Mr D Kettyles

Newry

24 Cherrywood Grove
Newry BT34 1JJ
Contact: Mr J Murphy

North Down

88 Balfour St
Newtownards BT23 4EF
Contact: Mr W Holland

Charitable, Support and Voluntary Organisations

Northern Ireland has an extensive and very active voluntary sector, which includes a wide range of charitable and support organisations. Many of these organisations are affiliated to an umbrella body, the Northern Ireland Council for Voluntary Action (NICVA); an organisation that has been appointed on occasions by the European Commission as an intermediary body to distribute substantial EU funding in Northern Ireland.

It is worth noting that as a region of the UK, Northern Ireland records very high comparative levels of deprivation and it is not surprising therefore that so much voluntary endeavour is required. For example, Northern Ireland has considerably higher levels of homelessness and disability than UK averages and the charities and support groups operating in these areas are necessarily significant players.

Action Cancer
Action Cancer House
1 Marlborough Park,
Belfast BT9 6XS
Tel: 028 9080 3344
Fax: 028 9080 3356
Web: www.actioncancer.org
Chief Executive: Robin McRoberts

Action for Dysphasic Adults NI
Graham House, Knockbracken Healthcare Park
Saintfield Road, Belfast BT8 8BH
Tel: 028 9040 1389
Fax: 028 9050 8025
Web: www.speechmatters.org
Chief Executive: Jackie White

Action Multiple Sclerosis
Knockbracken Healthcare Park
Saintfield Road, Belfast BT8 8BH
Tel: 028 9079 0707
Fax: 028 9040 2010
E-mail: info@actionms.co.uk
Web: www.actionms.co.uk
Director: Anne Walker

ADAPT Fund for Ireland
109 Royal Ave
Belfast BT1 1FF
Tel: 028 9023 1211
Fax: 028 9024 0878
E-mail: info@adaptni.org
Development Manager:
Caroline Shiels

Age Concern NI
3 Lower Crescent, Belfast
BT7 1NR
Tel: 028 9024 5729
Fax: 028 9023 5497
Chief Executive: Chris Common

Aids Helpline NI
7 James Street South
Belfast BT2 8DN
Tel: 028 9024 9268
Free Helpline: 0800 137437
Fax: 028 9032 9845
Web: www.aidshelpline.org.uk
Director: Geraldine Campbell

Alcoholics Anonymous
7 Donegall Street Place
Central Service Office
Belfast BT1 2FN
Tel: 028 9043 4848
Fax: 028 9043 4848
Web: www.alcoholicsanonymous.ie

Alzheimers Disease Society
86 Eglantine Avenue, Belfast
BT9 6EU
Tel: 028 9066 4100
Fax: 028 9066 4440
Regional Manager: Marjorie Magee

Amnesty International NI Region
397 Ormeau Road, Belfast, BT7 3GP
Tel: 028 9064 3000
Fax: 028 9069 0989
Web: www.amnesty.org
NI Programme Manager: Patrick Corrigan

Anti-Poverty Network
61 Duncairn Gardens
Belfast BT15 2GB
Tel: 028 9087 5010
Fax: 028 9087 5011
Development Co-ordinator:
Frances Dowds

Ards Society for Mentally Handicapped Children
203 South Street
Newtownards BT23 4JY
Tel: 028 9181 5363

Armagh Confederation of Voluntary Groups
1 College Street, Armagh
BT61 9BT
Tel: 028 3752 2282
Fax: 028 3752 2262
Web: www.acvg.com
Co-ordinator: Andrea Clark

Arthritis Care NI
Enkalon Business Park, 25 Randalstown Road, Antrim, BT41 4LJ
Tel: 028 9448 1380
Fax: 028 9446 9761
Web: www.arthritiscare.org.uk
Director: Sharon Sinclair

Arthritis Care West
76 Clanabogan Road
Omagh BT78 1SJ
Tel: 028 8225 0380
Fax: 028 8225 0380
E-mail: annettemoore.acni@virgin.net
Contact: Annette Moore

Arthritis Research Campaign
10 Alberta Parade, Belfast, BT5 5EH
Tel: 028 9046 1529
Fax: 028 9046 1529
Area Appeals Manager:
Charlotte Trinder

Arts and Disability Forum
Ground Floor, 109 - 113 Royal Avenue, Belfast, BT1 1FF
Tel: 028 9023 9450
Fax: 028 9024 7770
Web: www.ads.dnet.co.uk
Director: Avril Crawford

ASH
C/o Ulster Cancer Foundation
40–42 Eglantine Avenue
Belfast BT9 6DJ
Tel: 028 9066 3281
Fax: 028 9066 0081
Web: www.ulstercancer.org
Head of Education and Training:
Gerry McElwee

Advice NI
303 Ormeau Road, Belfast
BT7 3GG
Tel: 028 9064 5919
Fax: 028 9049 2313
Web: www.aiac.net/
Director: Bob Strong

Association of Mental Health
80 University Street, Belfast
BT7 1HE
Tel: 028 9032 8474
Fax: 028 9023 4940
Chief Executive: Alan Ferguson

Association for Spina Bifida & Hydrocephalus
Graham House
Knockbracken Healthcare Park
Saintfield Road, Belfast BT8 8BH
Tel: 028 9079 8878
Fax: 028 9079 7071
Regional Manager: Brendan Heaney

Barnardo's
NI Regional Office
542–544 Upper Newtownards Road
Belfast BT4 3HE
Tel: 028 9067 2366
Fax: 028 9067 2399
Web: www.barnardos.org.uk
Senior Director: Linda Wilson

BBC Children in Need
Broadcasting House, Ormeau Ave
Belfast BT2 8HQ
Tel: 028 9033 8221
Fax: 028 9033 8922
National Co-ordinator:
Sheila Jane Malley

Belfast Central Mission
5 Glengall Street, Belfast
BT12 5AD
Tel: 028 9024 1917
Fax: 028 9024 0577
Superintendent: Donald Kerr

The Quayside Project
16 South Street
Newtownards BT23 4YT
Tel: 028 9182 7783
Fax: 028 9182 7784
Team Leader: John Turtle

Belfast and Co Down Railway Trust
9 Abbey Gardens, Millisle, Newtownards
Tel: 0800 980 1242
Contact: Bob Pue

Belfast Common Purpose
Beacon House, 27 Clarendon Road
Belfast BT1 3BG
Tel: 028 9089 2273

Blind Centre for Northern Ireland
70 North Road, Belfast BT5 5NJ
Tel: 028 9050 0999
Fax: 028 9065 0001
Web: www.bcni.co.uk
Chief Executive: Dean Huston

Board for Social Responsibility
Church of Ireland House
61–67 Donegall Street
Belfast BT1 2QH
Tel: 028 9023 3885
Fax: 028 9032 1756
Web: www.cofiadopt.org.uk
Chief Executive: Ian Slane

Brainwaves NI
68 Cable Road, Whitehead
Co Antrim BT38 9PZ
Tel: 028 9337 2505
Fax: 028 9335 3995
Honorary Secretary: Kate Ferguson

British Deaf Association
3rd Floor, Wilton House
5–6 College Street North
Belfast BT1 6AR
Tel: 028 9072 7400
Tel: 028 9072 7407
Web: www.britishdeafassociation.org.uk
Community Development Manager:
Majella McAteer

Diabetics UK
Bridgewood House, Newforge Lane,
Belfast, BT9 5NW
Tel: 028 9066 6646
Fax: 028 9066 6333
E-mail: n.ireland@diabetes.org.uk
Web: www.diabetes.org.uk
National Director: Kate Fleck

British Red Cross
87 University Street, Belfast
BT7 1HP
Tel: 028 9024 6400
Fax: 028 9032 6102
Regional Director: Norman McKinley

British Red Cross Therapeutic Care Service
71 High Street, Bangor, BT20 5BD
Tel: 028 9146 6915
Fax: 028 9146 6915
Regional Service Co-ordinator: Norma Groves

Bryson House
28 Bedford Street, Belfast BT2 7FE
Tel: 028 9032 5835
Fax: 028 9043 9156
Co-Directors: Jo Marley and
John McMullan

Bryson House is a Northern Ireland Charity committed to identifying and developing sustainable responses to existing and emerging social needs. The charity provides a range of services including environmental, family and caring, training and voluntary services.

Bryson House Charity
7a Main St, Ballynahinch
BT24 8DN
Tel: 028 9756 4366
Web: www.brysonhouse.org
Project Manager: Margaret Coffey

C A C D P
5 College Square North,
Belfast, BT1 6AR
Tel: 028 9043 8161
Fax: 028 9043 8161
Minicom: 028 9043 8161
National Development Officer Northern Ireland: Cilla Mullan

Carers Northern Ireland
58 Howard Street, Belfast
BT1 6PJ
Tel: 028 9043 9843
Fax: 028 9032 9299
E-mail: info@carersni.demon.co.uk
Director: Helen Ferguson

Cancer Research Campaign Northern Ireland
Unit 1, Pavilions, 22A Kinnegar Drive,
Holywood Road, Belfast BT18 9JQ
Tel: 028 9042 7766
Fax: 028 9042 1822
E-mail: northernireland@crc.org.uk
Web: www.crc.org.uk
Fundraising Manager: Barbara Blundell

Child Accident Prevention Trust
23A/B Mullacreevie Park,
Killylea Road
Armagh BT60 4BA
Tel: 028 3752 6521
Fax: 028 3752 6521
E-mail: safetycentra@aol.com
Web: www.capt.org.uk
NI Manager: Rosie Mercer

Challenge Work Skills
2 Old Lurgan Road
Portadown BT63 5SG
Tel: 028 3839 2170
Carer Facilitator: Maria McBride

Charles Sheils Charity
Circular Road, Dungannon
BT71 6BJ
Tel: 028 8772 2138
Superintendent: Averill Griffith

Chernobyl Children Appeal
44A Church Street, Ballymena,
BT43 6DF
Tel: 028 2563 2767
Fax: 028 2563 2240

Chest Heart Stroke Association
Chamber Commerce House, 22 Great Victoria Street, Belfast, BT2 7LX
Tel: 028 9032 0184
Fax: 028 9033 3487
Web: www.nicha.com
Chief Executive: Andrew Dougal

Children in NI
216 Belmont Road, Belfast
BT4 2AT
Tel: 028 9065 2713
Fax: 028 9065 0285
Web: www.childcareni.org.uk
Director: Pauline Leeson

Childline
3rd Floor Offices
The War Memorial Building
9–13 Waring Street, Belfast
BT1 2EU
Tel: 028 9032 7773
Fax: 028 90181 8131
Web: www.childline.org.uk
Director: Patrick Shannon

Children in Crossfire
2 St Joseph's Avenue, Derry
BT48 6TH
Tel: 028 7126 9898
Fax: 028 7126 6630
E-mail:
ciara.donnelly@childreincrossfire.org
Director: Richard Moore

Children's Law Centre
3rd Floor, Phillip House
123–137 York Street
Belfast BT15 1AB
Tel: 028 9024 5704
Fax: 028 9024 5679
E-mail: info@childrenslawcentre.org
Director: Paddy Kelly

Cleft Lip & Palate Association
43 Ashley Avenue, Belfast
BT9 7BT
Tel: 028 9066 5115
Web: www.clapa.com

Community Arts Forum
15 Church St, Belfast BT1 1PG
Tel: 028 9024 2910
Fax: 028 9031 2264
Web: www.community-arts-forum.org
Director: Heather Floyd

Community Evaluation NI
295 Ormeau Road, Belfast
BT7 3GG
Tel: 028 9064 6355
Fax: 028 9064 1118
Web: www.ceni.org
E-mail: info@ceni.org
Director: Mr Brendan McDonnell

Community Relations Resource Centre
21 College Square East
Belfast BT1 6DE
Tel: 028 9022 7555
E-mail: info@community-relations.org.uk
Manager: Ellana Tomassa

Community Work Education and Training Network
Phillip House, 123–137 York St
Belfast BT15 1AB
Tel: 028 9023 2618
Fax: 028 9031 2216
E-mail: cwetn@compuserve.com
Co-ordinator: Peggy Flanagan

Conservation Volunteers NI
159 Ravenhill Road, Belfast
BT6 0BP
Tel: 028 9064 5169
Fax: 028 9064 4409
Web: www.cvni.org.uk
E-mail: info@cvni.org.uk
Operations Manager: Ian Humphreys

Community Technical Aid NI Ltd
445 Ormeau Road, Belfast
Tel: 028 9064 2227
Fax: 028 9064 2467
E-mail: info@community technicalaid.org
Director: Colm Bradley

Community Transport Association
Graham House
Knockbracken Health Care Park
Saintfield Road, Belfast BT8 8BH
Tel/Fax: 028 9040 3535
Regional Co-ordinator: Bryan Myles

Concern Worldwide NI
47 Frederick Street, Belfast
BT1 LW
Tel: 028 9033 1100
Fax: 028 9033 1111
E-mail: infobelfast@concern.org.uk
Head of NI Operations: David Gough

Co-operation Ireland
Glendinning House, 6 Murray Street,
Belfast, BT1 6DN
Tel: 028 9032 1462
Fax: 028 9089 1000
Web: www.cooperationireland.org
E-mail: info@cooperationireland.org
Chief Executive: Tony Kennedy
Operations Director:
Anne Anderson Porter

Co-operation Ireland is a leading charitable organisation unique to Northern Ireland. Its central mission is to develop practical cooperation between people North and South of the border with the Irish Republic. It is increasingly expanding its role in reconciling different traditions North and South, to include reconciliation of the different traditions within the North. Co-operation Ireland operates numerous social, economic, youth and community programmes and is an EU-appointed intermediary body for distribution of EU funds for certain programmes in Northern Ireland.

Corrymeela Community Belfast
8 Upper Crescent, Belfast
BT7 1NT
Tel: 028 9050 8080
Fax: 028 9050 8070
E-mail: enquiries@corrymeela.org.uk
Leader of the Community:
Dr David Stevens

Council for the Homeless NI
72 North Street, Belfast, BT1 1LD
Tel: 028 9024 6440
Fax: 028 9024 1266
E-mail: info@chni.org.uk
Director: Ms Ricky Rowledge

Crossroads Caring for Carers
Head Office, 7 Regent Street,
Newtownards BT23 4AB
Tel: 028 9181 4455
Fax: 028 9181 2112
E-mail: mail@crossroadscare.co.uk
Chief Executive: Christine Best

CRUSE Bereavement Care NI
Knockbracken Heathcare Park, Saintfield Road, Belfast BT8 8BH
Tel: 028 9079 2419
Fax: 028 9079 2474
Regional Manager: Ann Townsend
Cruse is the leading bereavement charity in the UK. The organisation currently has 178 branches and over 6,300 volunteers throughout the UK.

Cystic Fibrosis Trust
12 Selshion Manor,
Portadown, BT62 1AF
Tel: 028 3833 4491
Regional Manager: Tom Mallon

Disability Action
Portside Business Park
189 Airport Road West
Belfast BT3 9ED
Tel: 028 9029 7880
Fax: 028 9029 7881
Textphone: 028 9029 7882
E-mail: hq@disabilityaction.org
Chief Executive: Monica Wilson

Downs Syndrome Association NI
Graham House
Knockbracken Healthcare Park
Saintfield Road, Belfast BT7 8BH
Tel: 028 9070 4606
Fax: 028 9070 4075
Web: www.downs-syndrome.org.uk
E-mail: downs-sysdrome@cinni.org
Regional Director: Alan Hanna

Downtown Women's Centre
109–113 Royal Avenue
Belfast BT1 1FF
Tel: 028 9024 3363
Fax: 028 9023 7884
Director: May Desilva

Dungannon & District Women's Centre
43 Thomas Street,
Dungannon, BT70 1HW
Tel: 028 8772 6615
Fax: 028 8722 6615
Co-ordinator: Joanna Donaghey

East Antrim Therapy Centre
100 Shore Road, Magheramorne, Larne
Tel: 028 2827 4670
Fax: 028 2827 4670
E-mail:
info@oxygentherapycentre.co.uk
Centre co-ordinator: Joanne McAuley

East Belfast Independent Advice Centre
85 Castlereagh Street,
Belfast BT5 4NS
Tel: 028 9096 3003
Fax: 028 9096 3004
Manager: Karen McNamee

Family Planning Association NI
113 University Street
Belfast BT7 1HP
Tel: 028 9032 5488
Fax: 028 9031 2212
Director: Dr Audrey Simpson

Federation of Women's Institutes
209–211 Upper Lisburn Road, Belfast
BT10 0LL
Tel: 028 9030 1506
Fax: 028 9043 1127
E-mail: wini@btconnect.com
General Secretary: Irene Sproule

Fibromyalgia Support Group
18 Woodcot Avenue, Bloomfield
Belfast BT5 5JA
Fax: 028 9065 4243
E-mail: msni@fsmsnifreeserve.co.uk
Chairperson: Mrs Romayne Wright

Friedrich's Ataxia Group (NI)
4 Kingsway Close, Cherryvalley
Belfast BT5 7HA
Tel: 028 9048 4046
Web: www.ataxia.org.uk
Contact Member: Ida Walker

Friends in the West
Rathmourne House
143 Central Promenade
Newcastle BT33 0EU
Tel: 028 4372 3300
Fax: 028 4372 6210
Contact: Julian Armstrong

Friends of the Earth
7 Donegall Street, Belfast BT1 2FN
Tel: 028 9023 3488
Fax: 028 9024 7556
Web: www.foe.co.uk/ni
Director (NI): John Woods

Gamblers Anonymous
18 Donegall Street, Belfast
BT1 2GP
Tel: 028 9024 9185
Web: www.gambersanonymous.org

Gay Lesbian Youth Northern Ireland
E-mail: admin@glyni.org.uk
Web: www.glyni.org.uk

Gingerbread
169 University Street
Belfast BT7 1HR
Tel: 028 9023 1417
Fax: 028 9024 0740
E-mail: enquiries:gingerbreadni.org
Director: Marie Cavanagh

Guide Dogs for the Blind
15 Sandown Park South
Belfast BT5 6HE
Tel: 028 9047 1453
Fax: 028 9065 5097
E-mail: Belfast:gdba.org.uk
District Team Manager: Peter Swan

Habitat for Humanity NI
Unit 29, Forset Enterprise Park,
Springfield Road, Belfast BT12 7DY
Tel: 028 9024 3686
Fax: 028 9033 1878
E-mail: belfast@habitat.co.uk
Executive Director:
Peter Farquharson

Hearing Dogs for the Deaf
12 Main St, Crawfordsburn
BT19 1JE
Tel: 028 9185 3669
Contact: Mrs A Jameson

Help the Aged
Ascott House, Shaftesbury Square
Belfast BT2 7DB
Tel: 028 9023 0666
Fax: 028 9024 8183
Advice: 0800 808 7575
Web: www.helptheaged.org.uk
E-mail: helptheagedni@hta.org.uk
Acting NI Executive: Grace Henry

Home Start
533 Antrim Road, Belfast
BT15 3BS
Tel: 028 9077 8999
Fax: 028 9078 1656
Web: www.home-start.org.uk
Scheme Organiser: Patricia Friel

International Fund for Ireland
PO Box 2000, Belfast BT4 1WD
Tel: 028 9076 8832
Fax: 028 9076 3313
Joint Director General:
Mr Sandy Smith

International Voluntary Service
34 Shaftsbury Square,
Belfast, BT2 7DB
Tel: 028 9023 8147
Fax: 028 9024 4356
Co-ordinator: Colin McKinty

Lifestart Family Centre
13 Dunluce Court, Derry BT48 0PA
Tel: 028 7126 9833
Fax: 028 7126 0233
Contact: Margaret McCann

Macmillan Cancer Relief
82 Eglantine Avenue, Belfast
BT9 6EU
Tel: 028 9066 1166
Fax: 028 9066 3661
Fundraising Manager: Paul Sweeney

Make a Wish Foundation UK
Bryson House, 28 Bedford Street,
Belfast, BT2 7FE
Tel: 028 9080 5580
Regional Manager: Stephen Wilkie

Marie Curie Cancer Care
Kensington Road, Belfast
Tel: 028 9067 4200
(Hospice/Nursing Service)
Services Manager: Maeve Hully

Meningitis Research Foundation
71 Botanic Avenue, Belfast
BT7 1JL
Tel: 028 9032 1283
Fax: 028 9032 1284
Freephone: 0800 800 3344
E-mail: info@meningitis-ni.org
NI Manager: Diane McConnell

Mencap
416 Ormeau Road
Belfast BT7 3HY
Tel: 028 9049 2666
Fax: 028 9049 3373
Web: www.mencap.org
Regional Director: Maureen Piggott
Mencap offers a range of services, information and support for children and adults with learning difficulties.

Multiple Sclerosis Society – Northern Ireland
The Resource Centre
34 Annadale Avenue, Belfast
BT7 3JJ
Tel: 028 9080 2802
Web: www.mssocietyni.co.uk
E-mail: providingthestrength@
Director: Kieran Harris

National Deaf Children's Society
Wilton House
5–6 College Square North
Belfast BT1 6AR
Tel: 028 9031 3170
Fax: 028 9027 8205
E-mail: nioffice@ndcsni.co.uk
Director: Pauline Walker

The National Trust
Rowallane House, Saintfield BT24 7LH
Tel: 028 9751 0721
Fax: 028 9751 1242
Web: www.nationaltrust.org.uk
Director: Ruth Laird

The National Trust is a registered charity, which owns and manages a range of historic properties and estates on behalf of the public and for their future preservation. The Trust now cares for over 248,00 hectares of countryside, almost 600 miles of coastline and more than 200 buildings and gardens.

Nexus Institute Belfast
119 University Street
Belfast BT7 1HP
Tel: 028 9032 6803
Fax: 028 9023 7392
E-mail: dominica@nexusinstitute.org
Director: Dominica McGowan

Nexus Institute Derry
38 Clarendon Street, Derry BT48 7ET
Tel: 028 7126 0566
Fax: 028 7130 8399
Web: www.nexusinstitute.org
Project Manager: Helena Bracken

NI Cats Protection
NI Shelter, 270 Belfast Road,
Dundonald BT16 1UE
Tel: 028 9048 0202
Fax: 028 9048 6614

Northern Ireland Children's Holiday Scheme
547 Antrim Road, Belfast
BT15 3BU
Tel: 028 9037 0373
Fax: 028 9078 1161
E-mail: niches@utvinternet.com
Director: Jackie Chalk

Northern Ireland Foster Care Association
216 Belmont Road, Belfast
BT4 2AT
Tel: 028 9067 3441
Fax: 028 9067 3241
E-mail: info.nifca@dnet.co.uk
Director: Kate Lewis

Northern Ireland Gay Rights Association
PO Box 44, Belfast, BT1 1SH
Tel: 028 9066 5257
Fax: 028 9066 4111
E-mail: nigra@dnet.co.uk

Northern Ireland Leukaemia Research Fund
University Floor, Tower Block, Belfast
City Hospital, Lisburn Road
Belfast BT9 7AB
Tel: 028 9032 2603
Fax: 028 9026 3927
Secretary: Frances Parker

NIPPA Childhood Fund
6e Wildflower Way
Apollo Road, Belfast BT12 6TA
Tel: 028 9066 2825
Fax: 028 9038 1270
Web: www.nippa.org

1a Pottinger Street, Culleybackey,
Ballymena, BT42 1BP
Tel: 028 2588 2345
Fax: 028 2588 2338
Chief Executive: Siobhan Fitzpatrick

Northern Ireland Agoraphobia & Anxiety Society
27–31 Lisburn Road, Belfast BT9 7AA
Tel: 028 9023 5170
Fax: 028 9024 5535
Contact: Fiona McFarland

Northern Ireland Association of Citizens Advice Bureaux
11 Upper Crescent, Belfast
BT7 1NT
Tel: 028 9023 1120
Fax: 028 9023 6522
E-mail: info@niacab.org
Chief Executive: Derek Alcorne

The Citizens Advice Bureau originated as an emergency service and now addresses debt and consumer issues, benefits, housing, legal matters, employment and immigration.
Each bureau is affiliated to the National Association of Citizens Advice Bureau (NACAB).

Northern Ireland Cancer Fund For Children
2nd Floor
46 Botanic Avenue, Belfast
BT7 1JR
Tel: 028 9080 5599
Fax: 028 9043 4956
General Manager: Gillian Creevy

Northern Ireland Council For Voluntary Action (NICVA)
61 Duncairn Gardens,
Belfast BT15 2GB
Tel: 028 9087 7777
Fax: 028 9087 7799
E-mail: nicva@nicva.org
Director: Seamus McAleavey

The Northern Ireland Council for Voluntary Action is an umbrella group for Northern Ireland charities, community and voluntary groups.

Northern Ireland Hospice
74 Somerton Road, Belfast
BT15 3LH
Tel: 028 9078 1836
Fax: 028 9037 0585
Web: www.nihospice.com/
E-mail: information@nihospice.com
Acting Chief Executive: Liz Duffin

Northern Ireland Hospice Children's Service
18 O'Neill Road
Newtownabbey BT36 6WB
Tel: 028 9077 7635
Fax: 028 9077 7144
Web: www.nihospice.com
E-mail: children@nihospice.com
Head of Home: Patricia O'Callaghan

Northern Ireland ME Association
Bryson House
28 Bedford Street, Belfast
Tel: 028 9043 9831
Fax: 028 9043 9831

Northern Ireland Mixed Marriage Association
28 Bedford Street, Belfast
Tel: 028 9023 5444
Fax: 028 9043 4544
Web: www.nimma.org.uk
E-mail: nimma@nireland.com
Contact: Nigel Speirs

Northern Ireland Preschool Playgroup Association
1A Pottinger Street, Cullybackey,
Ballymena BT42 1BP
Tel: 028 2588 2345
Fax: 028 2588 2338
Training Co-ordinator:
Jennifer Montgomery

Northern Ireland Transplant Association
51 Circular Road, Belfast BT4 2GA
Tel: 028 9076 1394
Web: www.nita.org.uk
E-mail: nitransplant@email.com
Chairman: David Robinson

Northern Ireland Women's Aid Federation
129 University Street
Belfast BT7 1HP
Tel: 028 9024 9041
Fax: 028 9023 9296
Web: www.niwaf.org
E-mail: niwaf@dnet.co.uk
Director: Hilary Sidwell

NSPCC NI
Jennymount Business Park,
North Derby Street, Belfast
BT15 3HN
Tel: 028 9035 1135
Fax: 028 9035 1100
Web: www.nspcss.org.uk
Divisional Director NI: Ian Elliott

Organisation of the Unemployed NI
14 May Street, Belfast BT1 4NL
Tel: 028 9031 0862
Fax: 028 9031 4975

Oxfam Northern Ireland
52–54 Dublin Road, Belfast
BT2 7HN
Tel: 028 9023 0220
Fax: 028 9023 7771
Web: www.oxfamireland.org
E-mail: oxfam@oxfamni.org.uk
Corporate Services Manager:
Julie McSorley

P A N D A
21 University Street, Belfast BT7 1FY
Tel: 028 9020 7307
Fax: 028 9020 8700
Co-ordinator: Arthur Magill

PAPA (Parents and Professionals and Autism) NI
Knockbracken Health Park, Saintfield
Road, Belfast BT8 8BH
Tel: 028 9040 1729
Fax: 028 9040 3467
Web: www.autismni.org
Director: Arlene Cassidy

Parents Advice Centre
Franklin House, 12 Brunswick Street,
Belfast BT2 7GE
Tel: 028 9040 1729
Fax: 028 9031 2475
Web: www.pachelp.org
E-mail: belfast@pachelp.org
Chief Executive: Pip Jaffa

PHAB
Knockan Road, Broughshane,
Ballymena, BT42 4JY
Tel: 028 2586 1725
Web: www.phabni.org
E-mail: info@phabni.org
Chief Executive: Trevor Boyle

Praxis Care Group
29–31 Lisburn Road, Belfast
BT9 7AA
Tel: 028 9023 4555
Fax: 028 9024 5535
Chief Executive: Nevin Ringland

Praxis Care is a new charity formed out of the amalgamation of four established charities in the mental health area – Praxis Mental Healthcare, Respond, Northern Ireland Agoraphobia and Challenge.

The Princes Trust
5 Jenny Mount Court,
North Derby Street
Belfast BT15 3HN
Tel: 028 9074 5454
Fax: 028 9074 8416
Web: www.princes-trust.org.uk
E-mail: ptnire@princes-trust.org.uk
Director: Tommy Fagan

Prisoners Enterprise Project (South Belfast)
127–145 Sandy Row
Belfast BT12 5ET
Tel: 028 9024 4449
Fax: 028 9024 4471
Co-ordinator: Bill Newman

The Rainbow Project
2-6 Union Street
Belfast BT1 2JF
Tel: 028 9031 9030
Fax: 028 9031 9031
Web: www.rainbow-project.com
E-mail: info@rainbow-project.com
Chairman: Frank Toner

Rape Crisis and Sexual Abuse Centre
29 Donegall Street, Belfast
BT1 2FG
Tel: 028 9024 9696

Reach Across
21 The Diamond, Derry BT48 6HP
Tel: 028 7128 0048
Fax: 028 7128 0058
Web: www.reach-across.co.uk
E-mail: reach-across@hotmail.com
Youth co-ordinator:
Barney McGuigan

Relate NI
74–76 Dublin Road, Belfast
BT2 7HP
Tel: 028 9032 3454
Fax: 028 9031 5298
Web: www.relateni.org
Chief Executive: Gerald Clark

Respond
25–31 Lisburn Road, Belfast
BT9 7AA
Tel: 028 9031 0883
Fax: 028 9024 5535
Director: Irene Sloan

RETHINK
Windhurst
Knockbracken Healthcare Park
Saintfield Road, Belfast BT8 8BH
Tel: 028 9040 2323
Fax: 028 9040 1616
E-mail: info.nireland@rethink.org
Director: Liz Cuddy

Royal National Institute for the Blind
40 Linenhall Street, Belfast
BT2 8BA
Tel: 028 9032 9373
Fax: 028 9027 8119
Web: www.info@rnib.org.uk
Director: Susan Reid

Royal National Institute for the Deaf (RNID)
Wilson House, 5 College Square North,
Belfast BT1 6AR
Tel: 028 9023 9619
Fax: 028 9031 2032
Director: Brian Symmington

Royal National Lifeboat Institution
Unit 1, Lifeboat House
Lesley Office Park
393 Holywood Road
Belfast BT4 2LS
Tel: 028 9047 3665
Fax: 028 9047 3668
Regional Manager: Patricia Mathison

Royal Society for the Prevention of Accidents
Nella House, Dargan Crescent
Belfast BT3 9JP
Tel: 028 9050 1160
Fax: 028 9050 1164
Home Safety Manager: Janice Bisp

Royal Society for the Protection of Birds
Belvoir Park Forest, Belvoir Drive
Belfast BT8 7QT
Tel: 028 9049 1547
Fax: 028 9049 1669
Web: www.rspb.org.uk
Assistant Director: Clive Mellon

Save the Children Fund
15 Richmond Park, Belfast
BT10 0HB
Tel: 028 9062 0000
Fax: 028 9043 1314
Web: www.scfuk.org.uk
Area Manager: Arlene Patterson

Shelter (Northern Ireland)
1–5 Coyles Place, Belfast BT9 1EL
Tel: 028 9024 7752
Fax: 028 9024 7710
Campaign Officer: Laurence Moffat

Simon Community Northern Ireland
57 Fitzroy Avenue, Belfast, BT7 1HT
Tel: 028 9023 2882
Fax: 028 9032 6839
Chief Executive: Carol O'Bryan

Simon Community is one of Northern Ireland's largest charities, with over 200 staff with an annual budget in excess of £4m. Simon Community provides a wide range of services to homeless people including the provision of over 1,000 short-stay accommodation places all across Northern Ireland. In addition to lobbying for more appropriate accommodation for homeless people and better access to public services Simon Community is also focusing on the causes of homelessness and policy changes that could lead to greater prevention of this growing social problem.

Spina Bifida and Hydrocephalus Association (NI) (ASBAH)
Graham House
Knockbracken Healthcare Park
Saintfield Road, Belfast BT8 8BH
Tel: 028 9079 8878
Fax: 028 9079 7071
Web: www.asbah.org
E-mail: margarety@asbah.org
Regional Manager: Margaret Young

St John's Ambulance
35 Knockbracken Healthcare Park
Belfast BT8 8RA
Tel: 028 9079 9393
Fax: 028 9079 3303
Chief Executive: John Hugh

Tara Counselling & Personal Development Centre
11 Holmview Terrace, Omagh
Co Tyrone BT79 0AH
Tel: 028 8225 0024
Fax: 028 8225 0023
Administration Officer: Nuala Quinn

Trocaire
50 King Street, Belfast BT1 6AD
Tel: 028 9080 8030
Fax: 028 9080 8031
Web: www.trocaire.org
Regional Manager: Roisin Shannon

Twins & Multiple Birth Association
Tel: 028 9065 4609
Fax: 028 9065 4609

Ulster Society for the Prevention of Cruelty to Animals
PO Box 103, Belfast, BT6 8US
Tel: 028 9081 4242
Fax: 028 9081 5151
Web: www.planetpets-uspca.co.uk
Manager: Paddy Duffy

Ulster Cancer Foundation
40–42 Eglantine Avenue
Belfast BT9 6DX
Tel: 028 9066 3281
Fax: 028 9066 0081
Web: www.ulstercancer.org
E-mail: info@ulstercancer.org
Chief Executive: Arlene Spiers

North West Regional Office
14–16 The Diamond, Derry
BT47 0HN
Tel: 028 7128 8878
Fax: 028 7128 8879

Ulster Wildlife Trust
Ulster Wildlife Centre
3 New Line, Crossgar
Downpatrick BT30 9EP
Tel: 028 4483 0282
Fax: 028 4483 0888
E-mail: ulsterwt@clx.co.uk
Chief Executive: Dr David Erwin

Victim Support NI
Annsgate House, 70–74 Ann Street
Belfast BT1 4EH
Tel: 028 9024 4039
Fax: 028 9031 3838
E-mail: info@victimsupportni.org.uk

Voluntary Organisations Forum
47 Henderson Avenue
Cavehill Road
Belfast BT15 5FL
Tel: 028 9071 9119
Fax: 028 9020 9300
Director: Siobhan Bogues

Voluntary Service Belfast
34 Shaftsbury Square,
Belfast, BT2 7DB
Tel: 028 9020 0850
Fax: 028 9020 0860
E-mail: info@vsb.org.uk
Director: Bill Osborne

War on Want
1 Rugby Avenue, Belfast BT7 1RD
Tel: 028 9023 2064
Fax: 028 9032 8019
Director: Linda McClelland

The Woodland Trust
1 Dufferin Court, Dufferin Avenue,
Bangor BT20 3BX
Tel: 028 9127 5787
Fax: 028 9127 5942
E-mail: wtni@woodland-trust.org.uk
Operations Director: Patrick Cregg

Women's Aid Belfast
Womens Aid, 49 Malone Road
Belfast BT9 6RY
Tel: 028 9066 6049
Fax: 028 9068 2874
Web: www.belfastwomensaid.co.uk
E-mail: admin@
Web: belfastwomensaid.co.uk
Management co-ordinator:
Margot Hesketh

Women's Aid Coleraine
23 Abbey Street, Coleraine
BT52 1DU
Tel: 028 7032 1263
Administrator: Evelyn Morrow

Women's Aid Craigavon
198 Union Street, Lurgan
Craigavon BT66 8EQ
Tel: 028 3834 3256
Fax: 028 3832 2277
E-mail: info@craigavon
Web: banbridgewomensaid.org.uk

Women's Aid Fermanagh
14A High Street, Enniskillen, BT74 7EH
Tel: 028 6632 8898
Fax: 028 6632 8859
Team Leader: Mary McCann

Women's Aid Newry
7 Downshire Place
Newry, Co Down BT34 1DZ
Tel: 028 3025 0765
Fax: 028 3026 9606
Co-ordinator: Arlene Havern

Women's Forum NI
PO Box 135, Belfast BT5 5WA
Tel: 028 9446 0251
Fax: 028 9446 0251
E-mail: anneking@lineone.net
Vice Chairman: Ms Rosemary Rainey

Youth and Community Organisations

An Crann / The Tree
10 Arthur St, Belfast BT1 4GD
Tel: 028 9024 0209
Fax: 028 9024 0219
E-mail: ancrann1@compuserve.com
Honorary Secretary: Dennis Greig

Ardglass Development Association
19 High Street, Ardglass, BT30 7TU
Tel: 028 4484 2404
Chairperson: Mary McCargoe

Ballymena Community Forum
Glendun Drive
Ballymena BT43 6SR
Tel: 028 2565 1032
Fax: 028 2565 1035
Web: www.ballymenacommunityforum.org
Contact: Corinna Peterson

Ballynafeigh Community Development Association
283 Ormeau Road, Belfast BT7 3GG
Tel: 028 9049 1161
Fax: 028 9049 2393
Web: www.bcda.net
Contact: Katie Hanlon

Ballysillan Community Forum
925–927 Crumlin Road
Belfast BT14 8AB
Tel: 028 9039 1272
Fax: 028 9039 1259
Manager: Dale Harrison

Belfast Community Theatre Workshop
Crescent Arts Centre
2–4 University Road
Belfast BT7 1AH
Tel: 028 9031 0900
Fax: 028 9024 6748
E-mail: bct.comm.arts@ntlworld.com
Contact: Fintan Brady

Belfast Interface Project
Glendinning House, 6 Murray St
Belfast BT1 6DN
Tel: 028 9024 2828
Fax: 028 9024 2828
E-mail: bip@cinni.org
Support Worker: Marnie Kennedy

Belfast Travellers Education & Development Group
13a Glen Road, Belfast BT11 8BA
Tel: 028 9020 3337
Fax: 028 9080 9191
E-mail: info@ b-t-e-d-g@niireland.com/
Director: Paul Noonan

Belfast Traveller Support Group
Unit 12 Blackstaff Complex
77 Springfield Road
Belfast BT12 7AE
Tel: 028 9020 5330
Fax: 028 9020 5331
E-mail: btsp@cinni.org

Belfast Unemployed Resource Centre
45–47 Donegall Street
Belfast BT1 2FG
Tel: 028 9096 1111
Fax: 028 9096 1110
Manager: Joyce Green

Belfast Youth and Community Group
1–5 Donegall Lane, Belfast
BT1 2LZ
Tel: 028 9024 4640
Fax: 028 9031 5629
E-mail: bycg@dial.pipex.com

Belfast Economic Resource Centre
1–5 Coyles Place, Belfast BT7 1EL
Tel: 028 9024 1924
Fax: 028 9024 6985
E-mail:
office@boysandgirlsclub-ni.org.uk
Director of Programmes:
Terry Watson

Business in the Community
770 Upper Newtownards Road,
Dundonald, Belfast BT16 1UL
Tel: 028 9041 0410
E-mail: gillian.mckee@bitcni.org.uk
PR Director: Gillian McKee

Boys Brigade Northern Ireland Headquarters
National Training Centre
Rathmore House
126 Glenarm Road, Larne
BT40 1DZ
Tel: 028 2827 2794
Fax: 028 2827 5150
Director: Alec Hunter

Catholic Guides of Ireland, Northern Region
285 Antrim Road, Belfast
BT15 2G7
Tel: 028 9074 0835
Fax: 028 9074 1311
E-mail:
guides@northern.freeserve.co.uk
Chairperson: Eilish Smyth

Central Community Relations Unit
Block A, Level 5, Room A5.18
Castle Buildings, Stormont
Belfast BT4 3SG
Tel: 028 9052 8258
Fax: 028 9052 8426
Principal Officer: Denis Ritchie

Challenge for Youth
40–46 Edward Street
Belfast BT1 2LP
Tel: 028 9023 6893
Fax: 028 9024 0718
Chief Executive: David Gardiner

Children's Law Centre
Phillip House, York St
Belfast BT15 1AB
Tel: 028 9024 5704
Fax: 028 9024 5679
E-mail: info@childrenslawcentre.org
Director: Ms Paddy Kelly

Children's Project NI
290 Antrim Road, Belfast
BT15 5AN
Tel: 028 9074 1536
Fax: 028 9080 5578
E-mail: cpnibfast@yahoo.co.uk
Director: Gary Rocks

Chinese Welfare Association (NI)
133–135 University Street
Belfast BT7 1HP
Tel: 028 9028 8277
Fax: 028 9028 8278
E-mail: cwa.anna@cinni.org
Chief Executive: Anna Lo

Clogher Valley Rural Centre
Creebought House, 47 Main Street,
Clogher, Co Tyrone BT76 0AA
Tel: 028 8554 8872
Fax: 028 8554 8203
Manager: Sean Kelly

Colin Glen Trust
163 Stewartstown Road
Belfast BT17 0HW
Tel: 028 9061 4115
Fax: 028 9060 1694
E-mail: info@colinglentrust.org
Chief Executive: Tim Duffy

Community Arts Forum
15 Church Street, Belfast BT1 1PG
Tel: 028 9024 2910
Fax: 028 9031 2264
Web: www.cast.ie/
E-mail: admin@cast.ie
Director: Heather Floyd

Community Bridges Programme
16 Donegall Square South, BT1 5JF
Tel: 028 9031 3220
Fax: 028 9031 3180
E-mail: community.bridge@dnet.co.uk
Programme Coordinator: Joe Hinds

Community Change
Philip House, 123 York Street
Belfast BT15 1AB
Tel: 028 9023 2587
Fax: 028 9031 2216
E-mail: info@communitychange-ni.org
Head of Agency: Alison Wightman

Community Development Centre North Belfast
22 Cliftonville Road, Belfast, BT14 6JX
Tel: 028 9028 4400
Fax: 028 9028 4401
E-mail: info.nbcdc@ntlworld.com
Senior Administrator: Heather Stewart

Community Development & Health Network
30A Mill Street, Newry, BT34 1EY
Tel: 028 3026 4606
Fax: 028 3026 4626
E-mail: cdhn@btconnect.com
Director: Ruth Sutherland

Community Dialogue
373 Springfield Road, Belfast, BT12 7DG
Tel: 028 9032 9995
Fax: 028 9033 0482
E-mail: admin@commdial.org
Web: www.commdial.org
Directors: Brian Lennon, David Halloway

Community Empowerment Larne
Stylux Business Park, Lower Waterloo Road, Larne, BT40 1NT
Tel: 028 2826 7552
205a Linn Road, Larne
Tel: 028 2827 3953
Development Officer: Eric Cahoon

Community Evaluation Services (NI)
295 Ormeau Road, Belfast BT7 3GG
Tel: 028 9064 6355
Fax: 028 9064 1118
E-mail: info@ceni.org
Director: Brendan McDonnell

Community Information Technology Unit
45–47 Donegall Street
Belfast BT1 2FG
Tel: 028 9096 1104
Fax: 028 9096 1110
E-mail: citu@burc.org
Director: Brendan Mackin

Community Relations Council

Community Relations Council

6 Murray Street
Belfast, BT1 6DN
Tel: 028 9022 7500
Fax: 028 9022 7551
E-mail: info@community-relations.org.uk
Web: www.community-relations.org.uk
Chief Executive: Dr Duncan Morrow

The Community Relations Council (CRC) was established in 1990 as a registered charity. It aims to help organisations and individuals to create a society free from sectarianism.

CRC is a development agency for peace in Northern Ireland and provides advice and support to community relations initiatives and projects in the voluntary and community sector. Almost 500 grants are awarded each year. CRC also offers advice and guidance to public sector organisations in meeting the section 75 (2) statutory duty under the NI Act (1998) to promote 'Good Relations'.

Community Technical Aid NI
445–449 Ormeau Road
Belfast BT7 3GQ
Tel: 028 9064 2227
Fax: 028 9064 2467
E-mail: info@communitytechnicalaid.org
Director: Colm Bradley

Community Transport Association UK
Graham House, Saintfield Road
Belfast BT7 8BH
Tel/Fax: 028 9040 3535
E-mail: bryan@communitytransport.com
Regional Development Officer:
Bryan Miles

Community Work Education and Training Network
Philip House, York Street
Belfast BT15 1AB
Tel: 028 9023 2618
Fax: 028 9031 2216
Co-ordinator: Peggy Flanagan

Counteract
Phillip House, 123–137 York Street
Belfast BT15 1AB
Tel: 028 9023 7023
Fax: 028 9031 3585
E-mail: counteract@btconnect.com
Director: William Robinson

Devenish Partnership Forum
26 Yoan Road, Kilmacormick,
Enniskillen BT74 6EI
Tel: 028 6632 7808
Fax: 028 6632 7808
Web:
www.devenish.partnership@cinni.org
Manager: John Guthrie

Duke of Edinburgh Award NI
28 Wellington Park, Belfast
BT9 6DL
Tel: 028 9050 9550
Fax: 028 9050 9555
E-mail: nireland@theaward.org
Secretary: Eric Rainey MBE

Dunlewey Substance Advice Centre NI Ltd
226 Stewartstown Road
Belfast BT17 0LB
Tel: 028 9061 1162
Fax: 028 9060 3751
E-mail: dsac@btconnect.com
Director: Annette Goodall

East Belfast Community Development Agency
269 Albertbridge Road
Belfast BT5 4PY
Tel: 028 9045 1512
Fax: 028 9073 8039
E-mail: inf@ebcda.com
Director: Michael Briggs

Enkalon Foundation
25 Randalstown Road
Antrim BT41 4LJ
Tel: 028 9446 3535
Fax: 028 9446 5733
E-mail: enkfoundation@lineone.net
Secretary: John Wallace

Falls Community Council
275–277 Falls Road
Belfast BT12 6FD
Tel: 028 9020 2030
Fax:028 9020 2031
E-mail:
fallscommunitycouncil@yahoo.com
Director: Eileen Howell

Fermanagh Access and Mobility Group
36 Eastbridge Street
Enniskillen BT74 7BT
Tel: 028 6634 0275
E-mail: fermanaghaccess@swiftsoft.net
Chairperson: Gerry Maguire

Fermanagh Rural Community Initiative
8b Queen Elizabeth Road
Enniskillen BT74 7DG
Tel: 028 6632 6478
Fax: 028 6632 5984
E-mail: frci@totalserve.co.uk
Manager: Ciaran Rooney

Fermanagh Volunteer Bureau
12 Belmore Street
Enniskillen BT74 6AA
Tel: 028 6632 8438
Fax: 028 6632 2061
E-mail: info@fermanaghvb.org
Chairperson: Martin Lawson

Girls Brigade Northern Ireland
16 May Street, Belfast BT1 4NL
Tel: 028 9023 1157
Fax: 028 9032 3633
E-mail: info@girlsbrigadeni.com
National Secretary: Doreen Tennis

Greater Shankill Community Council
117 Shankill Road, Belfast
BT13 1FP
Tel: 028 9032 5536
Fax: 028 9024 4469
Manager: Mr Bill Patterson

Greater Shankill Partnership Early Years Project
Alessie Centre, 60 Shankill Road
Belfast BT13 2BB
Tel: 028 9087 4000
Fax: 028 9087 4009
E-mail: irene@earlyyears.org.uk
Project Manager: Irene Cooke

Greater Twinbrook and Poleglass Community Forum
Unit W2, Dairyfarm Centre,
Stewartstown Road, Belfast BT17 0AW
Tel: 028 9060 4004
Fax: 028 9060 4104
Director: Sean Gibson

Greater West Belfast Community Association
76–78 Hamill Street
Belfast BT12 4AA
Tel: 028 9032 8295
Fax: 028 9032 8295
E-mail: gwbcarc@aol.com
Office Admin: Angela Forde

Groundwork NI
Midland Building, Whitla Street
Belfast BT15 1NH
Tel: 028 9074 9494
Fax: 028 9075 2373
E-mail: info@groundworkni.co.uk
Director: Mary McKee

Guide Association
Lorne House, Station Road, Craigavad,
Holywood BT18 0BP
Tel: 028 9042 5212
Fax: 028 9042 6025
E-mail: ulsterhq@guides.org.uk
Ulster Administrator: Claire Bradley

Holywell Trust
10-12 Bishop Street, Derry BT48 6PW
Tel: 028 7126 1941
Fax: 028 7126 9332
Web: www.holywelltrust.com
Director: Eamonn Deane

Housing Rights Service
Middleton Building, 10-12 High Street,
Belfast, BT1 2BA
Tel: 028 9024 5640
Fax: 028 9031 2200
E-mail: hrs@housing-rights.org.uk
Director: Janet Hunter

Horizon Project
234 Upper Lisburn Road
Belfast BT10 0TA
Tel: 028 9060 5424
Fax: 028 9060 5423
E-mail: horizonbel@
admins.freeserve.co.uk
Co-ordinator: George Simms

Initiative on Conflict Resolution and Ethnicity (INCORE)
Aberfoyle House, Northland Road
Derry BT48 7JA
Tel: 028 7137 5500
Fax: 028 7137 5510
E-mail: incore@incore.ulst.ac.uk
Director: Professor Gillian Robinson

Larne Community Development Project
Unit 25, Ledcom Industrial Estate
Larne BT40 3AW
Tel: 028 2826 7976
E-mail: info@larnecdp.org.uk
Chairperson: Geoffrey Kerr

Law Centre NI Belfast
124 Donegall Street, Belfast
BT1 2GY
Tel: 028 9024 4401
Fax: 028 9023 9938
E-mail: admin.belfast@lawcenteni.org
Director: Les Allamby

Leonard Cheshire NI Regional Office
5 Boucher Plaza, 4–6
Boucher Road
Belfast BT12 6HR
Tel: 028 9024 6247
Fax: 028 9024 6395
E-mail: info@ni.leonard-cheshire.org.uk
Regional Director: Roisin Foster

Lifeline
C/o 113 Strandburn Drive, Sydenham,
Belfast BT4 1NB
Tel: 028 9065 8328
Chairperson: Mrs Lindsey

Lifestart Foundation NI
11A Bishops Street, Derry BT48 6PL
Tel: 028 7136 5363
Fax: 028 7136 5334
Director: Dolores McGuinness

Ligoniel Improvement Association
148 Ligoniel Road, Belfast
BT14 8DT
Tel: 028 9039 1225
Fax: 028 9039 1723
E-mail: wolfehill@freeuk.com
Director: Tony Morgan

LINC
33 Castle Lane, Belfast, BT1 5DB
Tel: 028 9027 8163
Fax: 028 907 45983
E-mail: billy.linc@cinni.lorg
Programme Manager: Billy Mitchell
Chairperson: Rev Philip Bell

Link Community Association
7 Avoca Park, Belfast BT11 9BH
Tel: 028 9020 0774
Fax: 028 9020 0774
Chairperson: Barbara Lynn

Lower North Belfast Community Council
The Castleton Centre
30–42 York Road, Belfast
BT15 3HE
Tel: 028 9020 8100
Fax: 028 9020 1103
Programmes Manager: Ian Crozier

Lurgan Council for Voluntary Action
Mount Zion House, Edward Street
Lurgan BT66 6DB
Tel: 028 3832 2066
Fax: 028 3834 8612
E-mail: info@lcva.co.uk
Director: Edwin Graham

Magnet Young Adult Centre
81a Hill Street, Newry BT34 1DG
Tel: 028 3026 9070
Fax: 028 3026 8132
Senior Youth Worker: Eugene Donnelly

Mediation Northern Ireland
10 Upper Crescent, Belfast, BT7 1NT
Tel: 028 9043 8614
Fax: 028 9031 4430
Web: www.mediationni.org
E-mail: info@mediationnorthernireland.org
Director: Brendan McAllister

Mornington Community Project NI
117 Ormeau Road, Belfast
BT7 1SH
Tel: 028 9033 0911
Fax: 028 9023 4730
Director: Ken Humphrey

Multicultural Resource Centre
9 Lower Crescent, Belfast
BT7 1NR
Tel: 028 9024 4639
Fax: 028 9032 9581
Web: www.mcrc-ni.org
Acting Chief Officer: Caroline Coleman

Neighbourhood Energy Action
64–66 Upper Church Lane,
Belfast, BT1 4QL
Tel: 028 9023 9909
Fax: 028 9043 9191
E-mail: northern.ireland@nea.org.uk
Director: Majella McCloskey

Newtownabbey Community Development Agency
Ferbro Buildings, 333 Antrim Road,
Newtownabbey BT36 5DZ
Tel: 028 9083 8088
Fax: 028 9083 0108
Director: Victor Robinson

NIACRO Belfast
169 Ormeau Road, Belfast
BT7 1SQ
Tel: 028 9032 0157
Fax: 028 9023 4084
Chief Executive: Mrs Alwyn Lyner

NIACRO Community Relations Project
16 Russell Street, Armagh BT61 9AA
Tel: 028 3751 5910
Fax: 028 3751 5919
E-mail: jennys.niacro@cinni.org

North Belfast Community Development Centre
22 Cliftonville Road, Belfast
BT14 6JX
Tel: 028 9028 4400
Fax: 028 9028 4401
E-mail: info.nbcdc@ntlworld.com
Chairperson: Brendan Bradley

Northern Ireland Association of Youth Clubs
'Hampton', Glenmachan Park,
Belfast, BT4 2PJ
Tel: 028 9076 0067
Fax: 028 9076 8799
E-mail: info@youthaction.org
Director: June Trimble

Northern Ireland Council for Ethnic Minorities
3rd Floor, Ascot House
24–31 Shaftesbury Square
Belfast BT2 7DB
Tel: 028 9023 8645
Fax: 028 9031 9485
E-mail: nicem@nireland.freeserve.co.uk
Web: www.nicem.org.uk
Executive Director: Patrick Yu

Peace People
Fredheim, 224 Lisburn Road
Belfast BT9 6GE
Tel: 028 9066 3465
Fax: 028 9068 3947
E-mail: peacepeople@gn.apc.org
Chairperson: Gerry Graham

The Phoenix Centre
Mount Zion House, Edward Street,
Lurgan, BT66 6DB
Tel: 028 3832 7614
Fax: 028 3832 7614
Manager: Pearl Snowdon

Poleglass Residents Association
Sallygarden Lane, Belle Steel Road,
Poleglass, Belfast BT17 0PB
Tel: 028 9062 7250
Fax: 028 9062 7250
Chairperson: Sue Ramsay

Quaker House Belfast Joint Project
7 University Avenue, Belfast
BT7 1GY
Tel: 028 9024 9293
E-mail: quaker.house@ntlworld.com
Representative: Mark Chapman

Rural Community Network
38a Oldtown Street
Cookstown BT80 8EF
Tel: 028 8676 6670
Fax: 028 8676 6006
E-mail: info@ruralcommunitynetwork.org
Chairperson: Roy Hanna

Sandy Row Community Forum
C/o Sandy Row Community Centre
63–75 Sandy Row, Belfast
BT12 5ER
Tel: 028 9023 8446
Fax: 028 9023 8446
Chairperson: Ernie Corbett

Scout Association
Old Milltown Road
Belfast, BT8 7SP
Tel: 028 9049 2829
Fax: 028 9049 2830
E-mail: info@scoutsni.com
Executive Commissioner:
Ken Gillespie

Scouting Foundation Northern Ireland (CSI)
12A Lisburn Enterprise Centre
Ballinderry Road, Lisburn, BT28 2BP
Tel: 028 9266 7696
Fax: 028 9266 7897

Shankill Lurgan Community Projects
53 Edward Street BT66 6DB
Tel: 028 3832 4680
Fax: 028 3832 6272
Manager: Mr Hugh Casey

Share Centre
Smiths Strand, Lisnaskea
BT92 0EQ
Tel: 028 6772 2122
Fax: 028 6772 1893
E-mail: celia@sharevillage.org
Director: Oliver Wilkinson

Speedwell Project
Parkanaur Forest Park
Dungannon BT70 3AA
Tel: 028 8776 7392
Fax: 028 8776 1794
E-mail: speedwell.trust@btinternet.com
Director: Jean Kelly

Strabane Community Unemployment Resource Centre
13a Newton Street
Strabane BT82 8DN
Tel: 028 7138 3927
Fax: 028 7138 3927
Manager: Betty Bradley

Training for Women Network Ltd
Unit 9, Edgewater Office Park
Belfast BT3 9JQ
Tel: 028 9077 7199
Fax: 028 9077 0887
E-mail: info@trainingforwomennetwork.org
Chairperson: Alice Higgins

Traveller Movement NI
30 University Street, Belfast
BT7 1FZ
Tel: 028 9020 2727
Fax: 028 9020 2005
E-mail: info@tmni.org

Ulster Community Investment Trust
13–19 Linenhall Street
Belfast BT2 8AA
Tel: 028 9031 5003
Fax: 028 9031 5008
E-mail: info@ucitld.com
Chief Executive: Brian Howe

University for Industry Learndirect
400 Springfield Road, Belfast
Tel: 028 9090 0070
E-mail: info@ufi.com
Head of UFI in Northern Ireland:
Mark Langhammer

WAVE Trauma Centre
5 Chichester Street Park South
Belfast BT15 5DW
Tel: 028 9077 9922
Fax: 028 9078 1165
E-mail: tracey@wavetc.clara.co.uk
Chief Executive: Sandra Peake

West Belfast Economic Forum
148–158 Springfield Road
Belfast BT12 7DR
Tel: 028 9087 4545
Fax: 028 9087 5050
E-mail: info@wbef.org
Contact: Una Gillespie

West Belfast Parent Youth Group
141–143 Falls Road
Belfast BT12 6AF
Tel: 028 9023 6669
Fax: 028 9023 5564
E-mail: marieosbourne@btconnect.co.uk
Centre Manager: Marie Osborne

Women into Politics
109–113 Royal Avenue
Belfast BT1 1FF
Tel: 028 9024 3363
Fax: 028 9023 7884
Director: Max DeSilvia

Women's Resource & Development Agency
6 Mount Charles, Belfast BT7 1NZ
Tel: 028 9023 0212
Fax: 0289024 4363
E-mail: info@wrda.net
Chairperson: Peggy Slanagan

Young Persons Project
2 Old Lurgan Road, Portadown
Tel: 028 3839 1155
Fax: 028 3839 3718
Manager: Peadar White

YMCA National Council
Memorial House, 9–13 Waring Street
Belfast BT1 2EU
Tel: 028 9032 7757
Fax: 028 9043 8809
E-mail: admin@ymca-ireland.org
National Secretary: Stephen Turner

Youth Initiatives
Central Office, 128b Lisburn Road
Belfast BT9 6HA
Tel: 028 9066 3710
Fax: 028 9066 8229
31 Colin Road, Dunmurry
Tel: 028 9030 1174

Youth Link NI
143a University St, Belfast
BT7 1HP
Tel: 028 9032 3217
Fax: 028 9032 3247
E-mail: info@youthlink.org.uk
Director: Rev Patrick White

YouthAction Northern Ireland
Hampton, Glenmachan Park
Belfast BT4 2PJ
Tel: 028 9076 0067
Fax: 028 9076 8799
Director: June Trimble

YouthNet
7 James St South, Belfast
BT2 8DN
Tel: 028 9033 1880
Fax: 028 9033 1977
E-mail: info@youthnet.co.uk
Director: Denis Palmer

Religious, Political and Cultural Organisations

Despite the fact that Northern Ireland has endured many years of conflict it is a deeply religious place by Western European standards.
Church attendances remain the highest of any region in the UK and there is a high ratio of churches to population. The Community is overwhelmingly Christian with the main four churches being Roman Catholic, Presbyterian, Church of Ireland and Methodist, with a strong evangelical tradition within Northern Ireland Protestantism. Most of the other major world religions are represented in Northern Ireland in relatively small numbers. The section below lists the various Churches found in Northern Ireland, with additional contact details for the larger institutions.

Irish Council of Churches
Inter-Church Centre
48 Elmwood Avenue, Belfast BT9 6AZ
Tel: 028 9066 3145
Fax: 028 9066 4160
E-mail: irish.church@btconnect.com
Web: www.irishchurches.org

Bahá'Í Faith
64 Old Dundonald Road
Dundonald BT16 1XS
Tel: 028 9048 0500
Fax: 028 9041 0100

Baptist Union of Ireland
117 Lisburn Road, Belfast BT9 7AF
Tel: 028 9047 1908
Fax: 028 9047 1363

Belfast Islamic Centre
38 Wellington Park, Belfast BT9 6DN
Tel: 028 9066 4465
Fax: 028 9091 3148
Web: www.belfastislamiccentre.com
Contact: Jamal Iweida

Belfast Synagogue
49 Somerton Road, Belfast BT15
Tel: 028 9077 7974

Bethel Temple
95 Main St, Portglenone
Ballymena BT44 8HR
Tel: 028 2582 1167
Contact: David Lamont

Buddhist Centre
409 Donegall Pass, Belfast, BT7 1BS18
Tel: 028 9023 8090
Web: www.potalacentre.org.uk

Roman Catholic Church
The Roman Catholic Church administers Ireland as a single unit, divided into 4 ecclesiastical Provinces. The Province of Armagh comprises of 6 dioceses, which together cover the whole of Northern Ireland and a proportion of the Republic of Ireland.

Catholic Bishops in the Province of Armagh

Most Rev Séan Brady, Archbishop of Armagh
Ara Coeli, Cathedral Road
Armagh BT61 7QY
Tel: 028 3752 2045
Fax: 028 3752 6182

Most Rev Seamus Hegarty, Bishop of Derry
Bishop's House,
St Eugene's Cathedral
Derry BT48 9AP
Tel: 028 7126 2302
Fax: 028 7137 1960

Most Rev Francis Lagan, Auxiliary Bishop of Derry
9 Glen Road, Strabane
Co Tyrone BT82 8BX
Tel: 028 7188 4533
Fax: 028 7188 4551

Most Rev Patrick Walsh, Bishop of Down and Connor
Lisbreen, 73 Somerton Road
Belfast BT15 4DE
Tel: 028 9077 6185
Fax: 028 9077 9377

Most Rev Anthony Farquhar, Auxiliary Bishop of Down and Connor
Lisbreen, 73 Somerton Road
Belfast BT15 4DE
Tel: 028 9077 6185
Fax: 028 9077 9377

Most Rev John McAreavey, Bishop of Dromore
Bishop's House, 44 Armagh Road
Newry BT35 6PN
Tel: 028 3026 2444
Fax: 028 3026 0496

Christian Brothers
The Abbey Monastery, Courtney Hill,
Newry BT34 2EA
Tel: 028 3026 4475

Church of Ireland
Church of Ireland House
61–67 Donegall Street
Belfast BT1 2QH
Tel: 028 9032 2268
Fax: 028 9032 1635

The Church of Ireland divides the island of Ireland into two Provinces, Armagh and Dublin. The majority of its members are in Northern Ireland; this congregation is administered under the province of Armagh.

The General Synod of the Church of Ireland, consisting of the archbishops and bishops, with 216 representatives of the clergy and 432 representatives of the laity, has chief legislative power in the Church.

Church of Ireland Bishops in the Province of Armagh

The Right Honourable the Lord Eames of Armagh
The See House, Cathedral Close,
Armagh BT61 7EE
Tel: 028 3752 7144 (O)
Fax: 028 3752 7823

The Right Rev E Y F Jackson Lord Bishop of Clogher
The See House, Fivemiletown,
Co Tyrone, BT75 0QP
Tel/Fax: 028 8952 2475

The Right Rev Dr James Mehaffey, Lord Bishop of Derry and Raphoe
The See House, 112 Culmore Road
Derry BT48 8JF
Tel: 028 7135 1206 (H)
Tel: 028 7126 2440 (O)
Fax: 028 7135 2554

The Right Rev H C Miller, Lord Bishop of Down and Dromore
The See House
32 Knockdere Park South
Belfast BT5 7AB
Tel: 028 9047 1973
Fax: 028 9065 0584

The Right Rev A E T Harper,
Lord Bishop of Connor
Bishop's House
113 Upper Road, Greenisland
Carrickfergus BT38 8RR
Tel: 028 9086 3165
Fax: 028 9036 4266

Church of Jesus Christ of the Latter Day Saints

403 Holywood Road, Belfast
Tel: 028 9076 9839
President: Eric Noble

Conference of Religious of Ireland

369 Springfield Road
Belfast BT12 7DJ
Tel: 028 9031 3944
Fax: 028 9031 3947
Contact: Sister Brighde Vallely

Elim Pentecostal Church

120a Alexandra Park Avenue
Belfast BT15 3GJ
Tel: 028 9074 4404
Fax: 028 9074 8422
Senior Minister: Brian Madden

Free Presbyterian Church

Martyrs Memorial
356 Ravenhill Road
Belfast
Moderator: Rev I Paisley

International Society for Krishna Consciousness

Inis Rath Island, Geaglum
Derrylin, Enniskillen, Co Fermanagh
Tel: 028 6772 1512
Web: www.iskon.org.uk

Jehovah's Witnesses

9 Belmont Park, Belfast BT4 3DU

Methodist Church in Ireland

Mission House, 13 University Road
Belfast BT7 1NA
Tel: 028 9032 0078
Fax: 028 9043 8700

The Methodist Church divides Ireland into eight district synods, each containing a number of circuits. Each synod is headed by a District Superintendent. The Methodist Conference meets around the island every year, and elects a President as overall head of the Church.

President: Rev James Rea
35 Thomas Street,
Portadown, BT62 3NU
Tel: 028 3833 3030

Secretary: Rev E T I Mawhinney
1 Fountainville Avenue
Belfast BT9 6AN
Tel: 028 9032 4554
Fax: 028 9023 9467

District Superintendents

Belfast District: Rev Dr W B Fletcher
33a Ardenlee Avenue, Belfast BT6 0AA
Tel: 028 9045 5121

Down District: Rev Kenneth Best
46 Seymour Street, Lisburn, BT27 4XG
Tel: 028 9266 2303

Enniskillen and Sligo District:
Rev Alan Ferguson
Tel: 028 6632 2244

North East District: Rev Roy Cooper
1 Glenagherty Drive, Old Galgorm Road, Ballymena, BT42 1AG
Tel: 028 2565 6693

North West District: Rev I D Henderson
Glebe Crest, Donegal
Tel: 00353 73 23588

Portadown District: Rev W James Rea
35 Thomas Street,
Portadown BT62 3NU
Tel: 028 3833 3030

Methodist Administration

Trustees of the Methodist Church in Ireland
1 Fountainville Avenue
Belfast BT9 6AN
Tel: 028 9032 4554
Fax: 028 9023 9467

Presbyterian Church in Ireland

Church House, Fisherwick Place
Belfast BT1 6DW
Tel: 028 9032 2284
Web: www.presbyterianireland.org
General Assembly Moderator:
Rev Dr Alastair Dunlop
Tel: 028 9032 2284
Fax: 028 9024 8366

Clerk of the Assembly:
Very Rev Dr Samuel Hutchinson

The Presbyterian Church in Ireland is divided into congregations or parishes, collectively containing over 280,000 members. The congregations are grouped into 21 district presbyteries. Eighteen of these are in the North, with the majority of Presbyterians in the South of Ireland in Dublin and the border counties. The Church is governed by an annual General Assembly, which is composed of representatives from every congregation. The General Assembly elects a Moderator each June, to act as the chief public representative of Presbyterians in Ireland.

Quakers Religious Society of Friends

Friends Meeting House
Frederick Street, Belfast BT1 2LW
Tel: 028 9082 6708

Salvation Army

12 Station Mews, Sydenham
Belfast BT4 1TL
Tel: 028 9067 5000
Fax: 028 9067 5011
Web: www.salvationarmy.org.uk
Divisional Communications Manager:
Linda Campbell

Seventh Day Adventist Church

9 Newry Road, Banbridge BT32 3HF
Tel: 028 4062 6361
Fax: 028 4062 6361

Sikh Cultural Centre

Simpsons Brae, Derry BT47 6DL
Tel: 028 7134 3523

Ulster Humanist Association

25 Riverside Drive, Lisburn BT27 4HE
Tel: 028 9267 7264

Cultural Organisations

Grand Orange Lodge of Ireland

Schomberg House
368 Cregagh Road, Belfast, BT6 9EY
Tel: 028 9070 1122
Fax: 028 9040 3700

Grand Master: Robert S Saulters
Deputy Grand Master: Roy Kells MBE
Deputy Assistant Grand Masters: Rev, Stephen Dickinson, William Ross
Grand Secretary: Denis J Watson

The Orange Order is possibly Northern Ireland's best-known 'cultural' organisation, with an active membership of over 100,000 men and women. It is a Protestant organisation steeped in the heritage of Protestant struggle for religious freedoms in the seventeenth century. The Order has formal links all over the world with similar institutions and is best known for its colourful militaristic marches during the summer.

Latin American Community and Cultural Association

Tel: 028 9031 9963
E-mail: launida@mcrc.co.uk
Chairperson: Cony Ortiz

Ulster Scots Heritage Council

218 York Street, Belfast BT15 1GY
Tel: 028 9074 6939
Fax: 028 9074 6980
Director: Nelson McCausland

Ulster Scots Historical & Cultural Society

Tel: 028 7133 8457

Political Organisations

Committee on the Administration of Justice

45–47 Donegall St, Belfast BT1 2FG
Tel: 028 9096 1122
Web: www.caj.org.uk
Director: Martin O'Brien

New Ireland Group

C/o 85 Charlotte St
Ballymoney BT53 6AZ
Tel: 028 2766 2235

Political Parties

(Details of Northern Ireland's main political parties are set out in Chapter 2).

Sporting, Leisure and Arts Organisations

Badminton Union of Ireland

House of Sport, Upper Malone Road
Belfast BT9 5LA
Tel: 028 9038 3810
General Secretary: Kathleen Graham

Belfast Giants Ice Hockey Club

Unit 2, Ormeau Business Park
8 Cromac Avenue, Belfast BT7
Tel: 028 9059 1111
Contact: Richard Gowdy

British Association for Shooting and Conservation

The Courtyard Cottage
Galgorm Castle, Ballymena
Tel: 028 2565 2349

British Horse Society (NI Region)

60 Windmill Road
Hillsborough BT26 6LX
Tel: 028 9268 3801
Fax: 028 9268 3801
Web: www.bhsireland.co.uk
Contact: Susan Irwin

Canoeing Association of Northern Ireland (CANI)

C/o House of Sport
Upper Malone Road, Belfast BT9 5LA
Tel: 028 7134 3871
Contact: Dawn Coulter

Disability Sports NI

Unit 10 Ormeau Business Park
8 Cromac Avenue, Belfast BT7 2JA
Tel: 028 9050 8255
Fax: 028 9050 8256
Web: www.dsni.co.uk
E-mail: email@dsdni.co.uk
Contact: Mr Kevin O'Neill

Eventing Ireland

98 Shore Street, Killyleagh BT30 9QJ
Tel: 028 4482 8734
Fax: 028 4482 1166
Secretary: Margaret Spiers

Fitness Northern Ireland

The Robinson Centre, Montgomery Road, Belfast, BT6 9HS
Tel: 028 9070 4080
Contact: Ms I Rea

Gaelic Athletic Association

House of Sport, Upper Malone Road
Belfast BT9 5LA
Tel: 028 9038 3815
Fax: 028 9068 2757
Contact: Seamus McGrattan

The Gaelic Athletic Association is Northern Ireland's leading participant sports organisation. It presides over Gaelic football, hurling, camogie and handball, as well as a range of other cultural activities.

Golfing Unions of Ireland, Ulster Branch

58a High Street, Holywood BT18 9AE
Tel: 028 9042 3708
Fax: 028 9042 6766
Branch Secretary: Mr B Edwards

International Sport Kickboxing Association UK

Dundela Social Club
Wilgar Street, Belfast, BT4 3BL
Tel: 028 9065 6414
Contact: Billy Murray

International Swimming Teachers Association

4 Firfields, Lough Road
Antrim BT41 4DJ
Tel: 028 9448 7050
E-mail: natiinfo@aol.com
Regional Organiser NI: Des Cossum

Irish Amateur Swimming Association

House of Sport
Upper Malone Road, Belfast
Tel: 028 9038 3807
Fax: 028 9068 2757
Development Officer: Clare Hamilton

Irish Bowling Association

78 North Road, Belfast BT5 5NL
Tel: 028 9065 5076
Fax: 028 9065 5076
Honorary Secretary: Mr J Humphreys

Irish Football Association

20 Windsor Avenue, Belfast BT9 6EE
Tel: 028 9066 9458
General Secretary: Mr David Bowen
The IFA presides over soccer in Northern Ireland.

Ulster Branch, Irish Hockey Association

House of Sport, Upper Malone Road
Belfast BT9 5LA
Tel: 028 9038 3819
Fax: 028 9068 2757
E-mail: alan@ulsterhockey.com
Development Officer: Alan McMurray

Irish Indoor Bowling Association
204 Kings Road, Belfast BT5 7HX
Tel: 028 9048 3536
Secretary: Mr D Hunter

Irish Ladies Golf Union, Northern District
12 The Meadows, Strangford Road
Downpatrick BT30 6LN
Tel: 028 4461 2286
Contact: Mrs A Dickson

Irish Rugby Football Union (Ulster Branch)
85 Ravenhill Park, Belfast BT6 0DG
Tel: 028 9064 9141
Fax: 028 9049 1522
Web: www.ulsterrugby.com
E-mail: lyn@ulsterrugby.com
Honorary Secretary: Mr J Eagleson

Irish Table Tennis Association
House of Sport, Upper Malone Road
Belfast
Tel: 028 9038 3811

Irish Water Polo Association, Ulster Branch
78 Wateresk Road
Castlewellan BT31 9EZ
Contact: Ms J Lightbody

Irish Water Skiing Federation, Northern Ireland Sub-Committee
2 Shelling Hill, Lisburn BT27 5NZ
Contact: Mr P Gray

Irish Women's Bowling Association
30 Cromlyn Fold
Hillsborough BT26 6SD
Tel: 028 9268 8254
Fax: 028 9268 8808
Honorary Secretary: Ms J Fleming

Irish Women's Indoor Bowling Association
101 Skyline Drive, Lambeg
Lisburn BT27 4HW
Secretary: Mrs D Miskelly

Karate Association (NIKW)
Oliver Brunton Schools of Karate NI, 35 College Street
Belfast BT1 6BU
Tel: 028 9061 6453
Chairman: Oliver Brunton

Motor Cycle Racing Association
38 Carr Road, Lisburn BT27 6YG
Contact: Mr W McKibbin

Motor Cycle Union of Ireland
23 Kinnegar Rocks
Donaghadee BT21 0EZ
Contact: Mr T Reid

Mountaineering Council of Ireland
Mr R Connell, Concra
Castleblayney, Co Monaghan

Northern Ireland Amateur Fencing Union
58 St Anne's Crescent
Newtownabbey BT36 5JZ
Contact: Mr J Courtney

Northern Ireland Amateur Gymnastics Association
House of Sport, Upper Malone Road
Belfast BT9 5LA
Tel: 028 9038 3813
Contact: Mrs L Phillips

Northern Ireland Weightlifters' Association
130 Brooke Drive, Belfast BT11 9NR
Tel: 028 9080 3876
Secretary: Mr S Dougan

Northern Ireland Area of British Model Flying Association
'Strawberry Hill', 28 Carlston Avenue
Cultra, Holywood BT18 0NF
Tel: 028 9042 4113
E-mail: morrisdoyle@freenet.co.uk
Secretary: Mr M Doyle

Northern Ireland Athletics Federation
Athletics House, Old Coach Road
Belfast BT9 5PR
Tel: 028 9060 2707
Fax: 028 9030 9939
Web: www.niathletics.org
E-mail: info@niathletics.org
Secretary: Mr J Allen

Northern Ireland Boys Football Association
15 Beechgrove Rise, Belfast BT6 0NH
Tel: 028 9079 4677
Contact: Mr J Weir

Northern Ireland Cricket Association
House of Sport, Upper Malone Road
Belfast BT9 5LA
Tel: 028 9038 3805
Fax: 028 9068 2757
E-mail: brian@nica.freeserve.co.uk
Cricket Development Officer:
Brian Walsh

Northern Ireland Federation of Sub Aqua Clubs
56 Ballykeel Road
Moneyreagh BT23 6BW
Contact: Mr R Armstrong

Northern Ireland Ice Hockey Association
25 Channing Street, Belfast BT5 5GP
Contact: Mrs B Carter

Northern Ireland Ice Skating Association
15 Bromcote Street, Bloomfield Road
Belfast BT5 5JL
Tel: 028 9096 6876
Contact: Mr J Passmore

Northern Ireland Ju Jitsu Association
281 Coalisland Road
Dungannon BT71 6ET
Tel: 028 8774 6940
Secretary: Mr J Canning

Northern Ireland Olympic Wrestling Association
312 Stranmillis Road, Belfast BT9 5EB
Contact: Mr P Mooney

Northern Ireland Orienteering Association
62 Wheatfield Crescent,
Belfast BT14 7HT
Contact: Ms V Cordner

Netball Northern Ireland
House of Sport, Upper Malone Road
Belfast BT9 5LA
Tel: 028 9038 3806
Fax: 028 9068 2757
Netball Development Officer: K Harrup

Northern Ireland Schools Football Association
20 Moira Drive, Bangor BT20 4RN
Contact: Mr B Gilliland

Northern Ireland Ski Council
43 Ballymaconnell Road
Bangor BT20 5PS
Tel: 028 9145 0275
Web: www.niweb.com/niid/sport/skiing

Northern Ireland Sports Association for People with Learning Disabilities
1 Clare Hill Road, Moira BT67 0PB
Contact: Mr N Logan

NISSU
29 Rossdowney Road, Derry BT47 1PB
Contact: Mr M Mace

Northern Ireland Ten Pin Bowling Federation
13 Wanstead Road
Dundonald BT16 2EJ
Contact: Ms K Payne

Northern Ireland Trampoline Association
Fir Tree Grove, 40 Monlough Road
Ballygowan BT23 6NH
Contact: Mr T Clifford

Northern Ireland Tug of War Association
22 Annahugh Road
Loughall BT61 8RQ
Contact: Mr C McKeever

Northern Ireland Volleyball Association
21 Broughton Park, Belfast BT6 0BD
Contact: Mr D Orr

Northern Ireland Women's Football Association
11 Ravenhill Gardens, Belfast BT6 8GP
Contact: Ms M Muldoon

Northern Cricket Union of Ireland
33 Dalboyne Park, Lisburn BT28 3BU
Contact: Mr W Carroll

Northern Ireland Alkido Association
57 Glenview Avenue, Belfast BT5 7LZ
Contact: Mr P Bradley

Northern Ireland American Football Association
108 Victoria Rise
Carrickfergus BT38 7UR
Contact: Ms L Sleator

Northern Ireland Archery Society
10 Llewellyn Drive, Lisburn BT27 4AQ
Contact: Mr K Blair

Northern Ireland Billiards and Snooker Association
2 Rockgrove Valley
Ballymena BT43 5HF

Northern Ireland Blind Sports
12 Sandford, Belfast BT5 5NW
Secretary: Ms L Royle

Northern Ireland Cricket Association
20 Pine Street, Waterside
Derry BT47 3QW
Contact: Mr B Dougherty

Northern Ireland Judo Federation
C/o Judo Office, House of Sport
Upper Malone Road, Belfast BT9 5LA
Tel: 028 9038 3814
Contact: Miss L Bradley

Northern Ireland Karate Board
58 Downview Park West
Belfast BT15 5HP
Tel: 028 9028 8609
Contact: Ms N Sleator

Northern Ireland Karting Association
44 Mill Cottage Park
Mallusk, BT22 2FF
Tel: 028 9181 4987
Fax: 028 9182 2190
Contact: Mr K Wilkinson

Northern Ireland Martial Arts Commission
C/o House of Sport
Upper Malone Road, Belfast BT9 5LA
Tel: 028 9267 4758
Web: www.sportsni.org
Contact: Tom Lamont

Northern Ireland Pool Association
8 Birch Drive, Bangor BT19 1RY
Contact: Mr J Humphrey

Northern Ireland Ski Council
43 Ballymaconnell Road
Bangor BT20 5PS
Contact: Mr P White

Northern Ireland Sports Council
House of Sport, Upper Malone Road
Belfast BT9 5LA
Tel: 028 9038 1222
Fax: 028 9068 2757
Chief Executive: Eamonn McCartan

The Sports Council is the leading government agency charged with the development of all sport across Northern Ireland.

Northern Ireland Sports Forum
C/o House of Sport
Upper Malone Road, Belfast BT9 5LA
Tel: 028 9038 3825
Contact: Lynn Greenwood

Northern Women's Cricket Union of Ireland
18 Belvedere Park, Belfast BT9 5GS
Contact: Miss S Owens

Royal Life Saving Society, Ulster Branch
4 Albert Drive, Belfast BT6 9JH
Tel: 028 9070 5644
Web: www.rlssdirect.co.uk
Contact: Mrs K McCurry

Royal Scottish Country Dance Society
1 Rosevale Avenue
Drumbeg, Dunmurry BT17 9LG
Tel: 028 9061 4197
Contact: Mrs M Jordan

Royal Ulster Yacht Club
101 Clifton Road, Bangor BT20 5HY
Tel: 028 9146 5002

Royal Yachting Association (Northern Ireland Council)
House of Sport, Upper Malone Road,
Belfast BT9 5LA
Tel: 028 9038 1222
Contact: Mr H Boyle

Taekwondo Association of Northern Ireland
20 Lester Avenue, Lisburn BT28 3QD
Contact: Mr S Nicholson

Ulster Angling Federation
4 Mill Road, Annalong BT34 4RH
Tel: 028 4376 8531
Contact: Mr A Kilgore

Ulster Aviation Society
16 Ravelston Avenue
Newtownabbey BT36 6PF
Tel: 028 9084 4100

Ulster Basketball Association
2 Ravensdene Crescent
Belfast BT6 0DB
Tel: 028 9064 8000
Contact: Ms M Matthews

Ulster Branch, Badminton Union of Ireland
C/o House of Sport
Upper Malone Road, Belfast BT9 5LA
Contact: Mr T Clarke

Ulster Branch, Irish Amateur Rowing Union
47 Colenso Parade, Belfast BT9 5AN
Contact: Ms C Harrison

Ulster Branch, Irish Hockey Association
Hockey Office, House of Sport
Upper Malone Road, Belfast BT9 5LA
Tel: 028 9038 3826
Contact: Mr W Clarke

Ulster Branch, Irish Table Tennis Association
38 Ballynahinch Road
Carryduff, Belfast BT8 8DL
Tel: 028 9081 3378
Contact: Mr M Guy

Ulster Branch, Irish Triathlon Association
C/o R G Connell and Son, 13 Main Street, Limavady, Derry BT49 0EP
Tel: 028 7772 2617
President: Peter Jack

Ulster Branch, Tennis Ireland
17 Tennyson Avenue
Bangor BT20 3SS
Tel: 028 9146 5155
Contact: Mr G Stevenson

Ulster Camogie Council
10 Stang Road, Cabra
Hilltown BT34 5TG
Contact: Ms H McAleavey

Ulster Coarse Fishing Federation
29 Georgian Villas, Hospital Road,
Omagh BT79 0AT
Contact: Mr R Refausse

Ulster Council, Irish Federation of Sea Anglers
17 Coolshinney Close
Magherafelt BT45 5DR
Tel: 028 7963 3198
Fax: 028 7963 3198
Secretary: Mr P Divito

Ulster Cycling Federation
C/o Mrs Rose Reilly, 18 Belturbet Road
Cornahoule BT92 9AZ
Contact: Mr P N Clarke

Ulster Deaf Sports Council
Wilton House, 5 College Square North
Belfast
Tel: 028 9031 2255

Ulster Federation of Rambling Clubs
40 Clontara Park, Lisburn BT27 4LB
Tel: 028 9260 1030
Honorary Secretary: Mr H Goodman

Ulster Flying Club
Newtownards Airport, Portaferry Road
Newtownards BT23 8SG
Tel: 028 9131 3327
Fax: 028 9131 4575
Chief Flying Instructor:
David Hodgkinson

Ulster Gliding Club
Ballyscullion, Seacoast Road
Bellarena
Tel: 028 7775 0301

Ulster Handball Council
13 Dunmurry Lodge
Belfast BT10 0GR
Contact: Mr R Maguire

Ulster Hang Gliding and Paragliding Club
35 Chester Park, Bangor
Tel: 07801 883524
Secretary: Ian Haslett

Ulster Provincial Council, Irish Amateur Boxing Association
10 Tonagh Heights
Draperstown BT45 7DD
Tel: 028 7962 8450
Fax: 028 7962 8450
Secretary: Mr J Noonan

Ulster Region Swim Ireland
House of Sport, Upper Malone Road
Belfast BT9 5LA
Tel: 028 9038 3807
Fax: 028 9068 2757
Web: www.swim-ulster.com
E-mail: ann@swim-ulster.com
Development Officer: Ruth McQuillan

Ulster Squash
18 Dundela Avenue, Belfast BT4 3BQ
Contact: Mrs R Irvine

Ulster Society of Amateur Dancing
47 Upper Lisburn Road, Finaghy
Belfast BT10 0GX

Ulster Vintage Car Club
11 Ballynahinch Road, Saintfield
Ballynahinch BT24 7AE

Ulster Women's Hockey Union
168 Upper Newtownards Road
Belfast BT4 3ES
Contact: Mrs J Patterson

Yoga Fellowship of Northern Ireland
19 Elsmere Park, Belfast BT5 7QZ
Tel: 028 9079 1213
Contact: Mrs M Harper

Wild Geese Skydiving Club
116 Carrowreagh Road
Garvagh BT51 5LQ
Tel: 028 2955 8609
Fax: 028 2955 7050
Web: www.wildgeese.demon.co.uk
Chief Instructor: Maggie Penny

World Ju-Jitsu Federation Northern Ireland
PO Box 1263
Belfast East Delivery, Belfast
Tel: 028 9079 7041

Arts

Belfast Festival at Queen's
25 College Gardens, Belfast BT9 6BS
Tel: 028 9097 2600
Fax: 028 9097 2630
Web: www.belfastfestival.com
Contact: Anthony McGrath

Cathedral Quarter Arts Festival
20 North Street Arcade
Belfast BT1 1 PB
Tel: 028 9023 2403
Fax: 028 9031 9884
Web: www.cqaf.com
Contact: Sean Kelly

Cinemagic
1st Floor, 49 Botanic Avenue,
Belfast, BT7 1JL
Tel: 028 9031 1900
Fax: 028 9031 9709
E-mail: Ingrid@cinemagic.org.uk
Web: www.cinemagic.org.uk
Contact: Joan Birney

Classical Music Society
Foyle Arts Centre, Lawrence Hill
Derry BT48 7NJ
Tel: 028 7126 1449
Fax: 028 7130 9091
E-mail: info@classicalmusicsociety.com

Community Arts Forum
15 Church Street, Belfast BT1 1PG
Tel: 028 9024 2910
Fax: 028 9031 2264
Web: www.caf.ie
E-mail: admin@caf.ie
Director: Heather Floyd

Community Theatre Association of Belfast
15 Church Street, Belfast BT1 1PG
Tel: 028 9024 2247
Web: www.newbelfaststarts.org

Crescent Arts Centre
2–4 University Road, Belfast BT7 1NH
Tel: 028 9024 2338
Fax: 028 9024 6748
E-mail: info@crescentarts.org
Manager: Liz Donnan

Feile an Phobail
Tel: 028 90 313 440
E-mail: 028 90 313 440

Northern Ireland Film Commission
21 Ormeau Avenue, Belfast BT2 8HD
Tel: 028 9023 2444
Fax: 028 9023 9918
E-mail: info@nifc.co.uk
Chief Executive: Richard Williams

Northern Ireland Media Education Association (NIMEA)
C/o Brooklands Primary School,
Brooklands Avenue,
Dundonald, BT16 2PA
Tel: 028 9048 7589
Contact: David McCartney

NORTHERN IRELAND YEARBOOK 2004

Lifestyle and Leisure in Northern Ireland

SHIP CHANDLERS
SEAFOOD RESTAURANT
SAIL & TENTMAKERS
5 TEDFORD'S RESTAURANT 5

Where to Eat and Drink in Northern Ireland

Northern Ireland has made great progress in recent years in terms of the overall quality and range of offerings to diners. There are an increasing number of genuinely international-class restaurants serving local and international cuisine of the highest standard. Three restaurants in Northern Ireland have been awarded the coveted Michelin Star. They are Dean's, Shanks Restaurant and The Oriel. In addition many of the North's cafes and bars have upgraded their fare with many bars serving good quality local dishes at reasonable prices.

The advent of relative 'peace' in Northern Ireland has encouraged hoteliers and restaurateurs to invest in their industry and many good quality restaurants, bars and brasseries have been opened up.

The same applies to pubs, clubs and nightlife generally. The Dublin Road Great Victoria Street stretch of South Belfast is possibly Northern Ireland's liveliest district in terms of bars clubs and nightlife and is unrecognisable from the quiet area that existed 15 or 20 years ago.

Restaurants

The following is a list of some well known Northern Ireland restaurants and eateries in A-Z format. The list is by no means exhaustive and there is no negative inference in relation to any premises that may have been omitted.

Belfast

Aldens Restaurant
229 Upper Newtownards Road
Belfast, BT4 3JH
Tel: 028 9065 0079
A modern restaurant, Aldens has given east Belfast a taste of the gourmet experience.

ba soba Noodle Bar
38 Hill Street,
Cathedral Quarter, Belfast BT1 2LB
Tel: 028 9058 6868
ba soba is Belfast's first noodle bar modelled on noodle canteens that have been popular in Japan for centuries. Specialising in noodle dishes and curries from across South East Asia, ba soba offers a wide range of exotic flavours, tastes and aromas.

Beatrice Kennedy
44 University Road, BT7
Tel: 028 9020 2290
A gourmet restaurant.

Bokhara Indian Restaurant
143-149 High Street
Holywood
Tel: 028 9042 6767
Quality Indian restaurant.

Café Aero
44 Bedford Street
Belfast BT2 7FF.
Tel: 028 9024 4844
Café Aero is a contemporary fine dining restaurant.

Cafe Paul Rankin
27-29 Fountain Street
Belfast
Tel: 028 9031 5090
Café Paul Rankin offers casual dining.

Cafe Milano
92-94 Lisburn Road,
Belfast BT9 6AG.
Tel: 028 9068 9777
A bustling new Italian restaurant.

Café Vincents
78-80 Botanic Avenue, Belfast
Tel: 028 9024 2020
Eclectic cuisine with a French influence.

Cayenne
7 Lesley House
Shaftesbury Square, Belfast, BT2 7DB
Tel: 028 9033 1532
Cayenne belongs to Paul and Jeanne Rankin of television's 'Gourmet Ireland'.

Chokdee
44 Bedford Street, Belfast, BT2 7FF
Tel: 028 9024 8800
Pan Asian Cuisine in modern surroundings.

Christies Brasserie
7-11 Linenhall Street
Belfast, BT2 8AA
Tel: 028 9031 1150
Web: www.christies-belfast.com
International cuisine and seafood

Connor
11a Stranmillis Road
Belfast
Tel: 028 9066 3266
Bright, modern airy restaurant offering a wide range of dining options from coffee to evening meals.

Tedford's Restaurant, Belfast

Copperfields Bar & Restaurant
9-21 Fountain Street
Belfast, BT1 5EA
Tel: 028 9024 7367

Centrally located in the heart of Belfast, this is a traditional bar and restaurant

Cutters Wharf
Lockview Road,
Stranmillis
Tel: 028 9066 3388

Situated on the banks of the river Lagan, in what was originally an Old Boat House.

Deanes Restaurant & Brasserie

36-40 Howard Street
Belfast, BT1 6PF
Tel: 028 9056 0000

One of Belfast's smartest eateries and home to award-winning chef Michael Deane. One of Northern Ireland's three Michelin Star award-winning restaurants.

Giraffe
54-56 Stranmillis Road, Belfast
Tel: 028 9050 9820

Giraffe situated in the heart of the university area is a well-established eatery with a "bring your own" policy offering casual dining and an extensive menu.

Harry Ramsden's
Yorkgate Complex,
150A York Street, Belfast
Tel: 028 9074 9222

Offering world famous fish and chips in a traditional environment with a fine selection of dishes to choose from.

Hilton Hotel
4 Lanyon Place
Belfast, BT1 3LP
Tel: 028 9027 7000
Fax: 028 9027 7277

The Sonoma Restaurant offers a contemporary menu with a blend of Irish, European and Asian cuisine.

Indie
159 Stranmillis Road
Belfast, BT9 5AJ
Tel: 028 9066 8100
Web: www.indiespice.com

Ink Restaurant
Four Winds, Newton Park, Belfast
Tel: 028 9070 7970

Contemporary European cooking with global influences.

The John Hewitt Bar & Restaurant
51 Donegall Street
Tel: 028 9023 3768

The John Hewitt is very much traditional in style with the emphasis on conversation, traditional music, art displays and "craic".

La Salsa
Odyssey Complex, 2 Queen's Quay
Belfast, BT3 9QQ
Tel: 028 9046 0066

L'etoile
407 Ormeau Road
Belfast, BT7
Tel: 028 9020 1300
French Cuisine in intimate surroundings.

Madison's
59-63 Botanic Avenue
Belfast BT7 1JL
Tel: 028 9050 9800
70 seater 'Award Winning' restaurant.

Malone House Restaurant
Barnett Demesne
Malone Road, Belfast, BT9 5PB
Tel: 028 9068 1246

Period house located in verdant surroundings in Upper Malone, offering highly regarded Irish food.

Malone Lodge Hotel
60 Eglantine Avenue
Belfast, BT9 6DY
Tel: 028 9038 8000
Fax: 028 9038 8088

Located in the leafy Victorian suburbs of the University area of South Belfast contemporary dishes incorporate the best of fresh local produce, organic when available.

McHugh's Bar & Restaurant
29-31 Queen's Square
Belfast, BT1 3FG
Tel: 028 9050 9990

Famous for being the oldest building in Belfast McHugh's offers everything from Oriental cuisine, to traditional pub grub.

Merchants Brasserie
The McCausland Hotel,
34-36 Victoria Street, Belfast.
Tel: 028 9022 0200

The Morning Star
17-19 Pottinger's Entry
Belfast, BT1 4DT
Tel: 028 9023 5986

Halfway down Pottinger's Entry, in the heart of Belfast, the Morning Star is one of the city's most historic pubs. Food is available in both the public bar and upstairs restaurant/lounge, with its discreet booths.

Nick's Warehouse
35-39 Hill Street
Belfast, BT1 2LB
Tel: 028 9043 9690
Fax: 028 9023 0514

Nick's Warehouse is located in the city near to St Anne's Cathedral.

The Northern Whig
2 Bridge Street, Belfast BT1 1LU
Tel: 028 9050 9888

Formerly home to the old Northern Whig printing press, this unique building has been restored with a contemporary eastern European influence.

Olio Restaurant
17 Brunswick Street
Belfast, BT2 7GE
Tel: 028 9024 0239
Fax: 028 9024 2290

Conveniently situated close to Belfast's Grand Opera House. Pasta and main course specialities blend with a selection of traditional favourites. Fresh baked fish is a speciality.

The Oxford Exchange
Grill Bar Restaurant, 1st Floor
St George's Market, Belfast
Tel: 028 9024 0014

Situated on the first floor of St George's Market in the developing Market Quarter of Belfast, Oxford Exchange offers quality dining in stylish surroundings.

Rain City
33-35 Malone Road, Belfast
Tel: 028 9068 2929
Café/Grill owned by Paul and Jeanne Rankin

The Red Panda Chinese Restaurant
60 Great Victoria Street
Tel: 028 9080 8700

Odyssey Pavillion
Tel: 028 9046 6644

Located opposite the Europa Hotel and recently opened in the Odyssey Pavillion, this is the largest of the Chinese restaurants in the city.

Restaurant Porcelain at TEN sq
10 Donegall Square, Belfast
Tel: 028 9024 1001
A fusion of Japanese and European

Ryan's Bar & Grill
116-118 Lisburn Road, Belfast
Tel: 028 9050 9851

This recently refurbished Bar and Grill offers a varied menu adding a touch of European culture with carafes of draught wine.

Shenanagan Rooms
21 Howard Street, Belfast, BT1 6NB
Tel: 028 9023 0603

Downstairs the emphasis is on bar snacks. Upstairs a full Bistro menu operates.

Shu
253 Lisburn Road, Belfast
Tel: 028 9038 1655
AA Sea Food Restaurant of the year.

Speranza
16-19 Shaftesbury Square, Belfast
Tel: 028 9023 0213

The Square
89 Dublin Road, Belfast
Tel: 028 9023 9933

Always busy. Menus change regularly. Booking required.

Suwanna Thai Restaurant
117 Great Victoria Street, Belfast
Tel: 028 9043 9007

Ta Tu Bar & Grill

701 Lisburn Road, Belfast, BT9 7GU
Tel: 028 9038 0818

Winner of the Glen Dimplex Award for Best Bar Interior in Ireland, the restaurant offers gourmet dining.

Tedford's Restaurant
5 Donegal Quay, Belfast, BT1 3EF
Tel: 028 9043 4000

Located in an historic Belfast building, formerly a ship's chandlers dating from 1851, this atmospheric restaurant overlooks the River Lagan.

The Wok
126 Great Victoria Street
Belfast
Tel: 028 9023 3828

The Water Margin
159-161 Donegall Pass, Belfast
Tel: 028 9032 6888

Wrap Works Mexican Cantina
199 Lisburn Road, Belfast
Tel: 028 9022 1141

Co Antrim

Bushmills Inn Hotel
25 Main Street
Bushmills, BT57 8QG
Tel: 028 2073 2339
Fax: 028 2073 2048

Between the Giant's Causeway and Royal Portrush, this atmospheric restored coaching inn with its open turf fires, stripped pine and gas lights offers a selection of traditional dishes prepared from fresh local produce.

Clenaghans
48 Soldierstown Road
Aghalee, BT28 0ES
Tel: 028 9265 2952
Fax: 028 9265 2251

Rural hideaway (near Moira, Co Down) with bar and exclusive restaurant. Serves a range of Irish and international cuisine. Advance booking essential.

Galgorm Manor
136 Fenaghy Road
Ballymena, BT42 1EA
Tel: 028 2588 1001
Fax: 028 2588 0080

Lunch is served Mon-Sat 12.00pm-2.30pm, and in the dining room on Sunday from 12.00-2.30pm. Pub lunches are also available in 'Gillies Bar', a traditional Irish pub with open log fires

The Ginger Tree (Japanese)
29 Ballyrobert Road
Glengormley
Tel: 028 9084 8176

The Harbour Bar
Harbour Road, Portrush
Tel: 028 7082 2430

Londonderry Arms Hotel
20-28 Harbour Road
Carnlough, BT44 0EU
Tel: 028 2888 5255
Fax: 028 2885 5263

This family-owned hotel is a former coaching inn built by the Marchioness of Derry in 1854. The hotel is known for its fresh and simple home style cooking and its smoked salmon from nearby Glenarm.

Lynden Heights
97 Drumnagreagh Road
Ballygally, BT40 2RP
Tel: 028 2858 3560

The Restaurant is situated on the B148 at the southern entrance to the Glens of Antrim.

Marine Hotel
1-3 North Street
Ballycastle, BT54 6BN
Tel: 028 2076 2222
Fax: 028 2076 9507

Rosspark Hotel
20 Doagh Road
Kells, Ballymena, BT42 3LZ
Tel: 028 2589 1663
Fax: 028 2589 1477

'Restaurant at Rosspark' offers locally caught fresh salmon and Northern Irish beef.

The Smuggler's Inn
306 Whitepark Road, Bushmills
Tel: 028 2073 1577

Snappers Restaurant
21 Ballyreagh Road, Portrush
Tel: 028 7082 4945

Tidy Doffer
133 Ravernet Road
Lisburn, BT27 5NF
Tel: 028 9268 9188
Fax: 028 9262 8949

The Tidy Doffer is renowned as the largest thatched roof pub in Ireland. The restaurant offers a range of traditional and international dishes.

Co Armagh

De Averell House
No 3 Seven Houses
47 Upper English Street
Armagh City, BT61 7LA
Tel: 028 3751 1213

Built in the late 18th century, Basement Restaurant offers a range of menus using local and international dishes.

Moneypenny's Restaurant
The Montagu Arms
9-19 Church Street, Tandragee
Tel: 028 3884 0219

The Old Barn Restaurant
7 Mowhan Road, Armagh
Tel: 028 3755 2742

The Oriel
2 Bridge Street Gilford
Tel: 028 3883 1543

The Pot Belly
59 Banbridge Road, Gilford
Tel: 028 3884 1404

The Planters Tavern
4 Banbridge Road
Waringstown, BT66 7QA
Tel: 028 3888 1510

Planters Tavern is a listed 17th century coaching inn. Local beef and poultry are house specialities.

The Seagoe Hotel
22 Upper Church Lane
Portadown, BT63 5JE
Tel: 028 3833 3076

Recently refurbished Avanti Restaurant open for fine dining.

Co Down

The Brass Monkey
16 Trevor Hill
Newry, BT34 1DN
Tel: 028 3026 3176

The Buck's Head
77 Main Street, Dundrum, BT33 0LU
Tel: 028 4375 1868

A country pub dating back to the 18th century which has been completely renovated, adding a conservatory and beer garden

The Burrendale Hotel and Country Club
51 Castlewellan Road
Newcastle, BT33 0JY
Tel: 028 4372 2599

The Burrendale's Vine Restaurant has an a la carte and Table d'Hote menu, a gentle ambience, fresh local food and a fine wine selection. The Cottage Kitchen Restaurant presents a Bistro Menu with an informal atmosphere.

The Cuan
The Square
Stangford, BT30 7ND
Tel: 028 4488 1222

Throughout the day there is a bar snack menu followed in the evening by Table d'Hote and a la Carte. Open 7 days a week, food served all day.

Dufferin Arms Coaching Inn
35 High Street
Killyleagh, BT30 9QF
Tel: 028 4482 8229

The Dufferin Arms Coaching Inn is renowned for its good food, music and atmosphere.

Four Trees Bar & Bistro
61-63 Main Street
Moira, BT67 0LQ
Tel: 028 9261 1437

A traditional public house with a unique stone courtyard leading to its restaurant. The public bar is quaint and charming dating back to the 19th century. The menu uses fresh local produce and incorporates modern trends.

Harry's Bar
7 Dromore Street
Banbridge, BT32 4BS
Tel: 028 4066 2794

The traditional pub serves food and drink in a traditional old world atmosphere.

The Hillside
21 Main Street
Hillsborough, BT26 6AE
Tel: 028 9268 2765
Fax: 028 9268 9888

The bar is housed in a 17th century building over which an antique-filled restaurant is situated. Past winner of both Egon Ronay Bar of the Year 1995 (All Ireland) and Bushmills Bar of the Year Awards.

The Lobster Pot
9-11 The Square, Strangford, BT30 7ND
Tel: 028 4488 1288
Fax: 028 4488 1288

The Lobster Pot retains its old-fashioned charm with comfortable surroundings. Along with traditional Irish dished and classic European cuisine, the Lobster Pot is renowned for its seafood – especially lobster!

Normans Inn
86 Main Street, Moira, BT67 0LH
Tel: 028 9261 1318
Fax: 028 9261 1318

Normans Inn is situated in the picturesque village of Moira and is a traditional bar with a bright, modern lounge. The Lounge Bistro serves food daily, Mon-Sat 12.00-8.00pm.

The Old Inn
11-15 Main Street
Crawfordsburn, BT19 1JH
Tel: 028 9185 3255
Fax: 028 9185 2775

One of Ireland's oldest hostelries, dating back to 1614. Situated in the quiet village of Crawfordsburn, 6 miles from Belfast City Airport en route to Bangor. The highly acclaimed restaurant serving both a la carte and Table d'Hote meals is renowned for its food and extensive wine list.

The Old Schoolhouse Inn
100 Ballydrain Road
Comber, BT23 6EA
Tel: 028 9754 1182
Fax: 028 9754 2583

The School House is a licensed restaurant situated in the country on the Ulster Way near Strangford Lough.

Papa Joes New Orleans Restaurant
7 Hamilton Road, Bangor
Tel: 028 9146 1529

The Portaferry Hotel
10 The Strand
Portaferry, BT22 1PE
Tel: 028 4272 8231

The Portaferry Hotel makes the most of the plentiful supplies of fish and shellfish in the area. Awarded two AA Rosettes, the hotel restaurant is recommended by many international food guides.

Shanks Restaurant
The Blackwood Golf Centre
150 Crawfordsburn Road
Bangor, BT19 1GB
Tel: 028 9185 3313

Table d'Hote Lunch and Dinner menus change monthly. Shanks was awarded a Michelin star in 1996 and again in 2004.

The Slieve Croob Inn
119 Clanvaraghan Road
Castlewellan, BT31 9LA
Tel: 028 4377 1412

Specialities include Dundrum oysters Rockerfeller and Fresh Darne of local Salmon.

Wine & Co.
57 High Street, Holywood
Tel: 028 9042 6083

The unique idea of Wine & Co is to choose your wine from over 400 choices downstairs and bring it upstairs to the Bistro.

Co Fermanagh

Encore Steak House
66 Main Street, Ballinamallard
Tel: 028 6638 8606

Franco's
Queen Elizabeth Road, Enniskillen
Tel: 028 6632 4424

Oscar's Restaurant
29 Belmore Street, Enniskillen
Tel: 028 6632 7037

Picasso's Restaurant
52A Belmore Street, Enniskillen
Tel: 028 6632 2226

Co Derry

Ardtara Country House
8 Gorteade Road
Upperlands, Maghera, BT46 5SA
Tel: 028 7964 4490

A Victorian manor, built in 1856 and set in 8.5 acres of ground. British Airways Tourism Award Winner, 2 AA Rosettes.

Beech Hill Country House Hotel
32 Ardmore Road
Derry, BT47 3QP
Tel: 028 7134 9279

The menu is adventurous with emphasis on local produce in a classical style and attractively presented.

Bohill Hotel & Country Club
69 Cloyfin Road
Coleraine, BT52 2NY
Tel: 028 7034 4406

The Bohill's Gourmet Restaurant – Chapter One, was built in January 1999 in the concept of a 'stand alone' restaurant for both residents and casual diners. It is distinctive in menu and ambience.

Brown Trout Golf & Country Inn
209 Agivey Road
Aghadowey (near Coleraine)
BT51 4AD
Tel: 028 7086 8209

The Inn was first licensed in the last century. The upstairs restaurant is non-smoking, but many customers eat casually around the open peat fires or out on the patio.

Decks Bar & Restaurant
1 Campsie Business Park
McLean Road
Eglinton, BT47 3XX
Tel: 028 7186 0912
Fax: 028 7186 0053

Decks is essentially a Brasserie. The pine panelling in the restaurant dates back to 1902, originally in the Board Room of one of the Maiden City's oldest shirt factories.

Co Tyrone

Ardbeg Lodge
32 Dungannon Road, Ballygawley
Tel: 028 8556 8517

Corick House
20 Corick Road
Clogher, BT76 0BZ
Tel: 028 8554 8216

A licensed Gourmet Restaurant offering a la Carte and Table d'Hote meals. A Grill Bar Restaurant serves Brasserie meals.

The Indigo
10 Gortmerron Link Road, Dungannon
Tel: 028 8772 7121

The Mellon Country Inn
134 Beltany Road
Omagh, BT78 5RA
Tel: 028 8166 1224

A recent winner of the les Routiers Silver Place Award for Best Restaurant, member of the Healthy Eating Circle and Taste of Ulster.

Salley's Restaurant
90 Moore Street
Aughnacloy
Tel: 028 8555 7979

Viscounts Restaurant
10 Northland Row
Dungannon
BT71 6AW
Tel: 028 8775 3800

This 110 year old former church hall, has been converted into a fully licensed restaurant with a unique medieval theme.

Bar Bacca, Belfast

Bars, Pubs and Clubs

Public Houses, known as 'pubs' or 'bars', are at the heart of many people's social lives throughout Northern Ireland, whether as drinking places or just meeting spots. They are also good places to hear live music – folk, traditional, jazz, blues and rock. Several of the pubs listed stay open until 1am or later.

Belfast

Apartment
Donegall Square West, Belfast
Tel: 028 9050 9777

Bar RED TENsq
10 Donegall Square, Belfast
Tel: 028 9024 1001

Bittles Bar
103 Victoria Street, Belfast
Tel: 028 9031 1088

Benedicts of Belfast
7-21 Bradbury Place, Belfast
Tel: 028 9059 1999

The Bodega Bar
4 Callender Street, Belfast
Tel: 028 9024 3177

Culpa
1 Bankmore Square
Dublin Road, Belfast
Tel: 028 9023 3555

Bar 12
13 Lower Crescent, Belfast.
Tel: 028 9032 3349.

An oak panelled, imaginative Gothic style bar. Food served Monday to Saturday 12-3pm.

Bar Bacca
42 Franklin Street, Belfast
Tel: 028 9023 0200
Web: www.barbacca.com

Winner of the Theme Magazine Bar and Restaurant Award for Best Bar in All Ireland in May 2002.
(Pictured left)

The Botanic Inn
23-27 Malone Road
Belfast BT9 6RU
Tel: 028 9050 9740

Popular haunt for Belfast's students and watching major sporting events.

Café Marco Polo
at The McCausland Hotel
34-38 Victoria Street, Belfast
Tel: 028 9022 0200
Continental style café bar.

Chelsea Wine Bar
346 Lisburn Road, Belfast
Tel: 028 9068 7177

The Crown Liquor Saloon
46 Great Victoria Street, Belfast
Tel: 028 9027 9901

Famous traditional Irish bar opposite the Grand Opera House.

Duke of York
7-11 Commercial Court , Belfast
Tel: 028 9024 1062

The Empire
40-42 Botanic Avenue, Belfast
Tel: 028 9032 8110
Music hall and comedy club.

The Fly Bar
5-6 Lower Crescent, Belfast.
Tel: 028 9050 9750

This is one of the more popular venues in Belfast, consisting of three floors, each with their very own characteristic bar.

Irene and Nans
12 Brunswick Street, Belfast
Tel: 028 9023 9123
Fax: 028 9023 0201
E-mail: info@ireneandnans.com
Web: www.ireneandnans.com

Irene and Nans is a haven for cocktail connoisseurs and foodies with kitsch surroundings.

Kitchen Bar
16 Victoria Square, Belfast
Tel: 028 9032 4901

La Lea
43 Franklin Street, Belfast
Tel: 028 9023 0200
Fax: 0285 9023 0201
E-mail: info@lalea.com
Web:www.lalea.com

This trendy nightclub has a sumptuous decorative style.

Lavery's Bar and Gin Palace
12-16 Bradbury Place, Belfast.
Tel: 028 9087 1106

One of Belfast's busiest and most famous pubs with probably the widest diversity of clientele of any bar in Belfast.

M-Club
23-31 Bradbury Place, Belfast
Tel: 028 9023 3131

M-Club has established itself as a student haunt on Thursdays, a 70's party on Fridays and the ultimate Club night on Saturdays.

McHugh's
29-31 Queen's Square, Belfast
Tel: 028 9050 9990

Magennis's
83 May Street, Belfast
Tel: 028 9023 0295

Traditional bar close to St George's Market and the Waterfront Hall offering live music and food.

Mezza(nine)
38-42 Great Victoria Street, Belfast
Tel: 028 9024 7447

Part of the Robinson's Bar Complex

Mercury Bar & Grill
451 Ormeau Road, Belfast
Tel: 028 9064 9017

Milk Bar -Club
10-14 Tomb Street, Belfast
Tel: 028 9027 8876
Trendy nightclub.

The Edge Bar & Restaurant
Mays Meadow
Laganbank Road, Belfast
Tel: 028 9032 2000
Waterfront facility, enjoying spectacular views from balconies.

The Morning Star
17-19 Pottinger's Entry, Belfast
Tel: 028 9032 3976

Morrisons Lounge Bars
21 Bedford Street, Belfast
Tel: 028 9032 0030

The Northern Whig
2 Bridge Street
Belfast
Tel: 028 9050 9880
Fax: 028 9050 9888

The Parlour
2-4 Elmwood Avenue
Belfast
Tel: 028 9068 6970

Robinson's Bars
Great Victoria Street, Belfast
Tel: 028 9024 4774

Several bars in one. One of Belfast's best know public houses.

Shu
253 Lisburn Road, Belfast
Tel: 028 9038 1655

TaTu
Lisburn Road, Belfast
Tel: 028 9038 0818
Trendy new bar and restaurant.

Pat's Bar
Prince's Dock Street, Belfast
Tel: 028 9074 4524

Rotterdam Bar
Pilot Street, off Corporation Street
Belfast, BT3 5HZ
Tel: 028 9074 6021
Fax: 028 9075 3275

Co Armagh

Courthouse Bar
William Street, Lurgan
Tel: 028 3832 9161

McConville Bros
1 Mandeville Street, Portadown
Tel: 028 3833 2070

The Met
109 Drumcairn Road, Armagh
Tel: 028 3751 1360

Co Down

Bar 15
13-15 High Street, Bangor
Tel: 028 9127 1060

The Four Trees
61-63 Main Street, Moira
Tel: 028 9261 1437

Norman's Inn
86 Main Street, Moira
Tel: 028 9261 1318

The Plough Inn
3 The Square, Hillsborough
Tel: 028 9268 2985

Primrose Bar & Restaurant
30 Main Street, Ballynahinch
Tel: 028 9756 3177

Co Fermanagh

Blake's of the Hollow
6 Church Street, Enniskillen
Tel: 028 6632 2143

Mulligan's
33 Darling Street, Enniskillen
Tel: 028 6632 2059

The Necarne Arms
2 Church Street, Irvinestown
Tel: 028 6862 1572

The Mayfly Inn
Main Street, Kesh
Tel: 028 6863 1281

Pat's Bar
1-5 Townhall Street, Enniskillen
Tel: 028 6632 2040

Co Londonderry

Anchor Inn
38 Ferryquay Street, Londonderry
Tel: 028 7136 8601

Castle Bar
Waterloo Street, Derry
Tel: 028 7126 3118

Clarendon Bar
46-48 Strand Road
Tel: 028 7126 3705

Cosmopolitan Bar
29 Strand Road, Derry
Tel: 028 7126 6400

The Metro
3 Bank Place, Londonderry
Tel: 028 7126 7401

Peadar O'Donnell's
Waterloo Street, Derry
Tel: 028 7137 2318

The Strand
35 Strand Road, Derry
Tel: 028 7136 6910

Co Tyrone

The Fort
30 Scotch Street, Dungannon
Tel: 028 8772 2620

Halliday's Bar
9-13 Perry Street, Dungannon
Tel: 028 8772 2198

Sally O'Brien's
35 John Street, Omagh
Tel: 028 8224 2521

Utopia Nightclub & Bar
55-57 Market Street, Omagh
Tel: 028 8225 1192

Cinema, Theatre and the Arts

Cinema

After many years of decline in cinema attendances, Northern Ireland has seen a substantial increase in investment, with new multi-screen cinema complexes in many of the main population centres. Many big screen stars hail from Northern Ireland, such as Kenneth Branagh and Liam Neeson, and the region has produced award winning films and shorts.

Main Cinemas in Northern Ireland

Antrim Cineplex
1 Fountain Street,
Antrim, BT41 1LZ
Tel: 028 9446 1111 (info)
Tel: 028 9446 9500 (booking)

Armagh City Filmhouse
Market Street,
Armagh, BT61 7BU
Tel: 028 3751 1033

Bangor Multiplex
1 Valentines Road
Castle Park
Bangor, BT20 4JH
Tel: 028 9146 5007

Carrickfergus Omniplex Cinema Ltd
Unit 4 Rodger's Quay
Carrickfergus
Tel: 028 9335 1111

Cinema Studio
Gillygooly Road, Omagh
Tel: 028 8224 2034

Enniskillen Omniplex
Factory Road, Enniskillen
Tel: 028 6632 4777

Global Cinema
Oaks Road, Dungannon
Tel: 028 8772 7733

IMC Multiplex Cinema
Larne Road Link
Ballymena, BT42
Tel: 028 2563 1111

Lisburn Omniplex
Lisburn Leisure Park
Governor Road
Lisburn, BT28 1PR
Tel: 028 9266 3664

Movie House Cinemas Ltd
51 St Lurachs Road
Maghera, BT46 5JE
Tel: 028 7964 2936

Movie House Cinemas Ltd
13 Glenwell Road
Glengormley, BT36 7RF
Tel: 028 9083 3424

Movie House Cinemas Ltd
14 Dublin Road
Belfast, BT2 7HN
Tel: 0870 155 5176

Movie House Cinemas Ltd
100-150 York Street, Belfast
Tel: 028 9075 5000

Movieland
Ards Shopping Centre
Circlear Road
Newtownards, BT23 4EU
Tel: 028 9182 0000

Newry Omniplex Cinema
Quays Shopping Centre
Albert Basin, Newry
Tel: 028 3025 2233

Playhouse Cinema
Main Street, Portrush
Tel: 028 7082 3917

Queen's Film Theatre
30 University Square Mews
Belfast, BT7 1JU
Tel: 028 9024 4857

Ritz Multiplex Cinemas
1-2 Burn Road
Cookstown, BT80 8DN
Tel: 028 8676 5182

Sheridan IMAX® Cinema
The Odyssey Pavilion
Queen's Quay
Belfast, BT3 9QQ
Tel: 028 028 9046 7000
www.belfastimax.com

The 380 seat Sheridan IMAX® cinema features a host of 2D and 3D movies.

The Strand Cinema
152-154 Holywood Road
Belfast, BT4 1NY
Tel: 028 9067 3500

Strand Multiplex
Quayside Centre
Strand Road
Derry, BT48
Tel: 028 7137 3900

Warner Village Cinemas
Odyssey Pavilion
2 Queen's Quay
Belfast, BT3 9QQ
Tel: 028 9073 9072

West Belfast Cineplex Ltd
Kennedy Centre
Falls Road, Belfast
Tel: 028 9060 0988

Theatres and Arts Venues

Northern Ireland has a relatively small number of purpose-built theatres and professional theatre companies, but this should not disguise the fact that there is great enthusiasm for the dramatic arts throughout the region. There is a particularly vibrant amateur theatre sector within Northern Ireland. The main theatrical venues are set out below.

Ardhowen Theatre
97 Dublin Road
Enniskillen, BT74 6BR
Tel: 028 6632 3233 (Admin)
Tel: 028 6632 5440 (Box Office)
Fax: 028 6632 7012

Ards Arts Centre
Town Hall
Conway Square, Newtownards
Tel: 028 9181 0803

Ballyearl Arts and Leisure Centre
The Courtyard Theatre
585 Doagh Road, Newtownabbey
Tel: 028 9084 8287

Burnavon Arts & Cultural Centre
Burn Road, Cookstown
Tel: 028 8676 7994 (Admin)
Tel: 028 8676 9949 (Box Office)

Belfast Waterfront Hall & Conference Centre
2 Lanyon Place, Belfast, BT1 3WH
Tel: 028 9033 4455 (Box Office)
Tel: 028 9033 4400 (General Enquiries)
Fax: 028 9024 9862
Web: www.waterfront.co.uk

Clotworthy Arts Centre
Castle Gardens
Randalstown Road, Antrim
Tel: 028 9442 8000

Craigavon Civic Centre
Craigavon
Tel: 028 3834 1618

Crescent Arts Centre
University Road, Belfast
Tel: 028 9024 2338

Converted Victorian school, presenting workshops in all kinds of dance, circus and other skills. Occasional studio performances.

Down Arts Centre
2-6 Irish Street, Downpatrick
Tel: 028 4461 1618

Flax International Arts Centre
Brookfield Mill
333 Crumlin Road, Belfast, BT14 7EA
Tel: 028 9035 2333

Golden Thread Theatre
333 Crumlin Road
Belfast, BT14 7EA
Tel: 028 9074 5241

Grand Opera House
Great Victoria Street, Belfast
Tel: 028 9024 1919 (Box Office)
Tel: 028 9024 0411 (Admin)
Web: ww.goh.co.uk

Island Hall and Studio Theatre
Lagan Valley Island, Lisburn
Tel: 028 9250 9254 (Box Office)

Lyric Theatre
55 Ridgeway Street
Belfast, BT9 5FB
Tel: 028 9038 1081 (Box Office)
Tel: 028 9066 9660 (Admin)

Market Place
Market Street, Armagh, BT61 7BX
Tel: 028 3752 1821

Millennium Forum
Newmarket Street, Derry
Tel: 028 7126 4426 (Admin)
Tel: 028 7126 4455 (Box Office)

Newcastle Centre
Newcastle
Tel: 028 4461 5283

Newry Town Hall
Newry
Tel: 028 3026 6232

Old Museum Arts Centre
7 College Square North, Belfast
Tel: 028 9023 5053

The Playhouse
5-7 Artillery Street, Londonderry
Tel: 028 7126 8027

Portadown Town Hall
15-17 Edward Street
Portadown, BT62 3LX
Tel: 028 3833 5264

Riverside Theatre
University of Ulster, Cromore Road
Coleraine, BT52 1SA
Tel: 028 7035 1388 (Box Office)
Tel: 028 7034 4141 (Admin)
Fax: 028 7032 4924

St Columb's Theatre & Arts Centre
Orchard Street
Derry, BT48 6EG
Tel: 028 7126 2880

Ulster Hall
Bedford Street
Belfast
Tel: 028 9032 3900 (admin)
Fax: 028 9032 1341 (stage door)

King's Hall Exhibition & Conference Centre
Lisburn Road
Belfast
Tel: 028 9066 5225

Ulster Orchestra
Elmwood Hall
University Road
Ticket Hotline: 028 9066 8798

The Ulster Orchestra has established itself as one of the major symphony orchestras in the United Kingdom.

Much loved in Belfast and beyond, successful tours of Europe, Asia and America, and over 50 commercial recordings, broadcasts for BBC television, Radio 3 and Radio Ulster plus regular appearances at the Henry Wood Promenade concerts, have added to the orchestra's growing international reputation.

Art Galleries

Ulster Museum
Botanic Gardens, Belfast
Tel: 028 9038 3000
Fax: 028 9038 3003
Irish artists include Sir John Lavery, Andrew Nicholl and William Conor.

Ormeau Baths Gallery
18A Ormeau Avenue, Belfast
Tel: 028 9032 1402
Bookshop, contemporary art.

Arches Gallery
2 Holywood Road
Belfast
Tel: 028 9045 9031
Irish artists.

Bell Gallery
13 Adelaide Park
Belfast
Tel: 028 9066 2998
Irish artistic, graphics

Elaine Somers Gallery
53a High Street
Holywood
Tel: 028 9042 3337
Contemporary Irish and International art

Nicola Russell Studio and Gallery
2-4 Church Road, Holywood
Tel: 028 9042 7133
Web: www.nicolarussell.com

Tom Caldwell Gallery
04-42 & 56 Bradbury Place, Belfast
Tel: 028 9032 3226
Living Irish artists.

Cavehill Gallery
18 Old Cavehill Road, Belfast
Tel: 028 9077 6784
Irish Artists.

Eakin Gallery
237 Lisburn Road
Belfast
Tel: 028 9066 8522
Irish Artists.

Fenderesky Gallery
2 University Road
Belfast
Tel: 028 9023 5245
Contemporary Art.

Arttank
58 Lisburn Road
Belfast, BT9 6AF
Tel: 028 9023 0500
Irish and international art

McGilloway Gallery
6 Shipquay Street
Derry
Tel: 028 7136 6011
Open 10am-5.30pm Mon-Sat.
Modern Irish paintings.

Orchard Gallery
Orchard Street
Derry, BT48 6EG
Tel: 028 7126 9675
Open 10am-6pm Tues-Sat. Art exhibitions, lectures.

Waring Gallery
87 Main Street Moira
Tel: 028 9261 9100

Festivals: Arts and Music

An Creagán Irish Cultural Festival
September

An Creagán Visitor Centre, Omagh
Traditional music, song and dance festival.
Contact: John Donaghy
Tel: 028 8076 1112

Ards International Guitar Festival
6 – 10 October 2004, Newtownards

Jazz, acoustic, blues and classical guitar concerts, plus tours of the famous Lowden Guitar factory.
Contact: Ards Arts Centre
Tel: 028 9181 0803
Web: www.ardsguitarfestival.com

BBC Music Live Festival
24 April – 1 May 2004

Celebration of live music in all its forms, with performances from world-class musicians. Events throughout Northern Ireland, broadcast locally, nationally and globally.
Contact: Sarah Platt, BBC
Tel: 0207 765 2853
Web: www.bbc.co.uk.musiclive/

Belfast Festival at Queen's
29 October – 14 November 2004, Belfast

Largest arts festival in Ireland with world-class theatre, dance, classical music, jazz and folk music, visual arts and literature. The theme for the 2004 Festival is 'journeys and migrations'.
Tel: 028 9027 2600
Web: www.belfastfestival.com

Belfast Film Festival
25 March – 2 April 2004

Mix of classic, future classic, international and local films screened at venues across the city, plus seminars, discussions and music.
Contact: Anne-Marie at Belfast Film Festival
Tel: 028 9032 5913
Web: www.belfastfilmfestival.org

Between the Lines
March

Between the Lines is Belfast's annual literary festival, which takes place at the Crescent Arts Centre. Features readings and workshops from local, national and international authors.
Contact: Belfast City Council
Tel: 028 9032 0202
Web: www.belfastcity.gov.uk

Blues on the Bay Festival
27 – 31 May 2004, Warrenpoint

Blues and jazz. Three main showcase gigs featuring top-class international artists. Music workshops also on offer.
Contact: Peter Thompson
Tel: 028 4175 2256
Web: www.bluesonthebay.fsnet.co.uk

Castle Ward Opera Season
4 – 26 June 2004, Strangford

Opera in the enchanted setting of Castle Ward. Rigoletto by Verdi and Albert Herring by Benjamin Britten.
Tel: 028 9066 1090
Web: www.castlewardopera.com

Cathedral Quarter Arts Festival
29 April – 9 May 2004

Vibrant arts festival in Belfast's north city centre.
Contact: Sean Kelly
Tel: 028 9023 2403
Web: www.cqaf.com

City of Derry Jazz and Big Band Festival
28 April – 2 May 2004

One of Ireland's top jazz festivals, this year dedicated to big band music. BBC Music Live will offer a fringe programme at the Millennium Forum on 26 and 27 April.
Tel: 028 7137 6545
Web: www.cityofderryjazzfestival.com

Coleraine International Choral Festival
19-20 March 2004, Diamond Hall, University of Ulster, Coleraine

Six Northern Ireland choirs participating along with twenty others from across the UK and further afield.
Contact: Coleraine Borough Council
Tel: 028 7034 7034
Web: www.coleraine.gov.uk

Danny Boy Festival
May, Limavady

Family arts festival with an international flavour, taking place across the borough of Limavady.
Contact: Limavady Borough Council
Tel: 028 7776 0304

Feile an Phobail Community Festival
5 – 15 August 2004, West Belfast

Debates, tours, exhibitions, concerts, drama and street theatre at various venues in West Belfast.

Fiddler's Green International Festival
25 July – 1 August 2004, Rostrevor

Annual celebration of Irish music and culture with an international flavour. The nightly folk club features the best of Irish and international folk performances.
Contact: Festival Office
Tel: 028 4173 9819
Web: www.fiddlersgreenfestival.com

17th Foyle Film Festival
November 2004, Londonderry

Derry's annual Foyle Film Festival since 1987. Combines an international film competition of features, shorts, animation and documentary screenings, with presentations by leading experts.
Tel: 028 7126 7432
Web: www.foylefilmfestival.com

Holywood Jazz and Blues Festival
4 June 2004, Holywood

Holywood's annual jazz and blues festival attracts increasing numbers of top-notch musicians from all over the world.
Tel: 028 9076 8563

International Maiden of the Mourne Festival
August, Warrenpoint, Co Down

Range of events including band concerts, outdoor entertainment, sporting events, parades and children's events.
Contact: Liz Boyle
Tel: 028 4177 3556

Jazz and Blues Festival
3 – 5 June 2004, Ardhowen Theatre, Enniskillen

Three jazz concerts over three evenings.
Contact: Box Office
Tel: 028 6632 3233
Web: www.ardhowentheatre.com

John Hewitt International Summer School
26 – 31 July 2004, Market Place Theatre, Armagh

Talks, debates, discussions and readings by prominent poets and writers on today's literary scene.
Tel: 028 3752 1821
Web: www.themarketplacearmagh.com

On Eagle's Wing
28 – 29 May 2004, Odyssey Arena, Belfast
A celebration in music and dance, this show follows the journey of Scots Irish people from Northern Ireland to America.
Contact: Box Office
Tel: 028 9073 9074
Web: www.odysseyarena.com

6th Open House Festival
3 – 31 October 2004, Belfast

Traditional arts and music festival spread over 5 weekends, based in Belfast's Cathedral Quarter and beyond.
Contact: Kieran Gilmore
Tel: 028 9145 4754
Web: www.openhousefestival.com

Tyrone Fleadh Cheoil
June, Coalisland, Co Tyrone

Irish music, song and dance.
Tel: 028 8224 2777

William Carleton Summer School
2 – 6 August 2004, Co Tyrone

Presents Carleton as a significant figure in 19th century Irish literature and to promote the study of his work.
Tel: 028 8776 7259

11th William Kennedy International Festival of Piping
16 – 21 November 2004, Armagh

Classes, lectures and performances: the world's best pipers celebrate the life of an 18th century piper and pipe maker.
Contact: Brian Vallely
Tel: 028 3751 1249
Web: www.armaghpipers.com

Other Festivals and Events

Banks of the Foyle Halloween Carnival
27 – 31 October 2004, Derry

Fireworks against the backdrop of the River Foyle and huge street party with fancy dress.
Tel: 028 7137 6545
Web: www.derrycity.gov.uk/halloween

Belfast International Rose Trials and Rose Week
19 July 2004, Sir Thomas and Lady Dixon Park, Belfast

Annual rose competition, drawing over 50,000 people every summer.
Tel: 028 9027 0467

Circuit of Ireland Rally
9 April 2004

Ireland's top motor rally with competitors from Ireland and the UK
Contact: Fermanagh Tourist Information Centre
Tel: 028 6632 3110
Web: www.fermanagh-online.com

HERO – Historic Endurance Car Rally
19 – 24 April 2004

This historic rally starts in Dublin with competitors going to Cork, Killarney and Galway and crossing into Northern Ireland with overnight stays in Enniskillen and Limavady, finishing in Belfast on 24 April.
Contact: John Brown
Tel: 01886 833505

Hillsborough International Oyster Festival
2 – 4 September 2004, Hillsborough,

Contact: Hillsborough Tourist Information Centre
Tel: 028 9268 9717
Web: www.hillsboroughoysterfestival.com

Honda F4 Offshore Powerboats
3 – 4 July 2004, Bangor

Power boat series and other thrilling water sports.
Contact: Bangor Tourist Information Centre
Tel: 028 9127 0069

Kingdoms of Down Open Championship
5 – 7 May 2004, Co Down

International golf tournament played on three courses, Scrabo, Clandeboye and Royal County Down.
Contact: Posnett Golf
Tel: 028 4482 8686

Lady of the Lake Festival
July 2004, Irvinestown, Co Fermanagh

10 day annual festival including drama, children's entertainment, fancy dress and a fishing competition.
Contact: Joe Mahon
Tel: 028 6862 1656
Web: www.ladyofthelakefestival.com

Lord Mayor's Show
29 May 2004, Belfast City Centre

A civic festivity of colour makes its way round the city in this annual parade.
Contact: Belfast City Council
Tel: 028 9027 0222
Web: www.belfastcity.gov.uk

Maiden City Festival
1 – 8 August 2004, Derry City

A wide variety of events commemorating the siege of Londonderry.
Contact: Derry Visitor and Convention Bureau
Tel: 028 7137 7577
Web: www.derryvisitor.com

Northern Ireland Game Fair
26 – 27 June 2004, Ballywalter Estate, Co Down

Game and country sports fair with displays, demonstrations & competitions.
Tel: 028 2565 2349
Web: www.irishgamefair.com

North West 200
15 May 2004, Portrush/Causeway Coast

Motorcycle road races on a scenic circuit. International event attracting top riders and thousands of spectators.
Tel: 028 7772 9869

NI D-Day Diamond Anniversary Air Spectacular
5 – 6 June 2004, Portrush

Celebration of the 60th anniversary of the D-Day landings. The programme includes a two-day air spectacular with Red Arrows, Harriers and a collection of WW2 aircraft.
Contact: Alex Carmichael
Tel: 028 7034 7234

Ould Lammas Fair
30 – 31 August 2004, Ballycastle

Ireland's oldest traditional market fair. Horse trading, street entertainment and market stalls.
Contact: Ballycastle Tourist Information Centre
Tel: 028 2076 2024

Stena Line Ulster Rallycross Festival
27 – 28 March 2004, Kirkistown Race Circuit, Co Down & Nutt's Corner

Northern Ireland hosts two rounds of the British Rallycross Championship in 2004.

Contact: Nutt's Corner
Tel: 028 9442 8331

Contact: Kirkistown
Tel: 028 9177 1325

St Patrick's Day Outdoor Celebrations
17 March 2004, Londonderry

City of Derry celebrates Ireland's patron saint with entertainment in Guildhall Square and throughout the city.
Tel: 028 7137 6545
Web: www.derrycity.gov.uk

St Patrick's Festival and Cross Community Parade
13 – 17 March 2004, Downpatrick

St Patrick's Day festival and colourful carnival parade in Downpatrick.
Tel: 028 4461 0800
Web: www.saint-patricksdayfestival.gov.uk

Titanic Made in Belfast
10 – 17 April 2004, Belfast

Celebration incorporating the artisan skills, energy and creativity that helped make Belfast the biggest shipbuilding port in the world.
Contact: Belfast City Council
Tel: 028 9027 0222
Web: www.belfastcity.gov.uk

Ulster Rally
2 – 4 September, Armagh

Ireland's premier motorsport event – supported by the world's top F2 rally teams and promoted by Northern Ireland Motor Club Ltd
Contact: David Gray
Tel: 028 3025 7532
Web: www.ulster-rally.co.uk

Waterways Ireland Classic Fishing Festival
10 – 14 May 2004, Co Fermanagh

One of Europe's premier fishing festivals, with anglers from Ireland and Europe competing on Lower Lough Erne
Contact: Fermanagh Tourist Information Centre
Tel: 028 6632 3110
Web: www.fermanagh.gov.uk

World Irish Dancing Championships
3 – 11 April 2004, Waterfront Hall, Belfast

Belfast's second time to host this event, which until 2000, had traditionally been held in Dublin.

Museums

Armagh County Museum
The Mall East, Armagh
Tel: 028 3752 3070

Ballymena Museum
3 Wellington Court, Ballymena
Tel: 028 2564 2166

Down County Museum
The Mall, Downpatrick
Tel: 028 4461 5218

Fermanagh County Museum
Enniskillen Castle
Castle Barracks, Enniskillen
Tel: 028 6632 5000

Flame – The Gasworks Museum of Ireland
44 Irish Quarter West, Carrickfergus
Tel: 028 9336 9575

Foyle Valley Railway Museum
Foyle Road, Londonderry
Tel: 028 7126 5234

Irish Linen Centre and Lisburn Museum
Market Square, Lisburn
Tel: 028 9266 3377

North Down Heritage Centre
Town Hall, Castle Park, Bangor
Tel: 028 9127 1200

Regimental Museum of the Royal Irish Regiment
St Patrick's Barracks, Meenagh Drive
Ballymena
Tel: 028 2566 1386

Museums & Galleries of NI (MAGNI)

Ulster Folk & Transport Museum
Tel: (028) 9042 8428
Ulster Museum
Tel: (028) 9038 3000
Ulster American Folk Park
Tel: (028) 8224 3292
Armagh County Museum
Tel: (028) 3752 3070

The National Museums and Galleries of Northern Ireland (MAGNI) comprise the Ulster Museum, the Ulster Folk and Transport Museum, the Ulster American Folk Park and the Armagh County Museum. MAGNI's collections promote access to and awareness of the arts, humanities and sciences, the culture, way of life, diversity, migration and settlement of peoples, and to the heritage of Northern Ireland.

Royal Inniskilling Fusiliers Museum
The Castle, Enniskillen
Tel: 028 6632 3142

Royal Irish Fusiliers Museum
Sovereigns House
The Mall, Armagh
Tel: 028 3752 2911

The Tower Museum
Union Hall Place, Londonderry
Tel: 028 7137 2411

Ulster American Folk Park
Mellon Road, Castletown
Omagh
Tel: 028 8224 3292

Ulster Folk & Transport Museum
Cultra, Holywood
Tel: 028 9042 8428

Ulster Museum
Botanic Gardens, Belfast
Tel: 028 9038 3000

Sports and Leisure

Sports

Northern Ireland's main sports are football (soccer, Gaelic and rugby) golf, hockey and cricket. There is also a high level of interest in motorcycling and car rallying. Most other sports are to an extent minority pursuits, but Northern Ireland boasts a strong record in amateur boxing and bowls (with Jeremy Henry and Ian McClure recently claiming the World Indoor Pairs title).

The recently formed ice hockey team, the 'Belfast Giants', has established a regular following of 5,000 enthusiasts.

Soccer

As a small, albeit enthusiastic, footballing country Northern Ireland has limited expectations in terms of international football success, but has performed with credit in the World Cups of 1958 and 1982.

Home of the legendary forward George Best, Northern Ireland has produced many top-class players (although seldom enough at one time to support a good international side). Home internationals are played at Windsor Park in Belfast, the home of Northern Ireland's biggest club, Linfield.

The International team tends to be made up of professional footballers playing in the upper divisions of the English football league, although occasionally a locally based player breaks through to the International side. Much hope has been pinned on new Northern Ireland manager Lawrie Sanchez, who admitted to having three aims for the international side - to score a goal, to win a match and to move up from 124th in the world rankings!

At local level the 'Irish League' constitutes the main attraction. It is primarily part-time football (with a handful of full-time professionals) and comprises a number of teams from Belfast, and a team from most of each of Northern Ireland's largest provincial towns.

The Oval: Home of Glentoran Football Club Irish League Champions 2002/03

The local game suffers from a number of fundamental difficulties. As a spectacle it suffers when compared with the televised glamour of the English 'premiership', and the cream of top young local players tend to leave the local game to play 'across the water'.

Attendance at Irish League games are poor (except for the exciting 'Big-Two' derby clashes between Belfast clubs Linfield and Glentoran) and crowd trouble and sectarianism on the terraces have on occassions made it very difficult for the games' promoters to push up attendances.

Glenavon FC, Lurgan

Like most activities in Northern Ireland soccer does not escape the impact of political divisions. A sizable minority of soccer supporters give their first loyalty to the international team from the Irish Republic. Indeed the top team from Northern Ireland's second City 'Derry City' plays in the Republic of Ireland League rather than the Irish League. This conflict of affiliation also has a negative impact on local attendances at games.

Nonetheless, despite its difficulties most of the different interests in the game came together under the auspices of former Culture Minister Michael McGimpsey to devise a strategy to improve the image and attractiveness of the game and to put Irish League football on a more sustainable financial footing. The Irish Football Association administers the game at all levels.

The Sam Maguire Trophy

Gaelic Sports

There are a number of Gaelic Sports including football, hurling and camogie all administered by the Gaelic Athletic Association (GAA). Gaelic Football has now become the largest participation sport in Northern Ireland.

Again Northern Ireland's political divisions are reflected in this sport which tends to be pursued predominantly although not exclusively by the Catholic, Nationalist community. The GAA has only recently reversed a rule, which excluded participation in Gaelic games by members of the Security Forces, and is currently under pressure to rescind a policy, which prohibits the use of GAA facilities (sports arenas) for other 'foreign games'.

Gaelic Sport is organised on an all-island basis both at club and County level, and its highest prize is the All-Island County Championship (the 'Sam Maguire'). Clubs are organised at a 'parish' level and most would own their own pitches and clubhouses.

Northern Ireland counties have been successful in this prestigious All-Ireland competition in the 1990s notably Armagh, Down, Derry and most recently Tyrone. Most of the 6 counties of Northern Ireland have extensive football leagues at club level.

Despite its high-level of participation and level of spectator attendances as well as TV coverage, Gaelic football remains a completely amateur sport. However pressure is building within the GAA, as it has done in recent years in athletics and rugby, to allow the top players to share in some of the commercial value created.

Hurling

Hurling is played less widely than football, although areas in county Antrim and Down and Derry have a renowned passion for the sport. It is a uniquely Irish game which pre-dates Gaelic football although the Northern counties have traditionally been weak in an all-Ireland context.

Handball

Although in comparison to football and hurling it is something of a minority sport, handball is a popular gaelic sport pursuit. Unlike Olympic handball played between teams this is a sport for individuals or pairs played in an 'alley' similar to a squash court, except there are no racquets!

Rugby Union

Rugby Union has a strong following in Northern Ireland. It tends to be a predominantly, but by no means exclusively, Protestant and middle-class game. Although its organisation is all-island, the sport is based on club and provincial rather than county structures.

Northern Ireland rugby is synonymous with the 'Ulster' team, which showcases Northern Ireland's best players in both the inter-provincial series against the three other Irish provinces and in international competition such as the Celtic Cup and the Heinekein Cup.

In recent times Ulster has won the increasingly important European Cup, a competition featuring the best club and provincial sides from the British Isles, France and Italy.

Ulster were crowned European Champions in 1999 after a Lansdowne Road final at the end of an exciting campaign which re-ignited wider interest in the local game. More recently in 2003 Ulster registered another major success in winning the Celtic Cup.

Northern Ireland players have also contributed prominently to the Irish National Team and to the British Lions with Ballymena's Willie John McBride and North's Mike Gibson ranking among the all-time greats of the game. In more recent times players like David Humphreys, Willie Anderson and Paddy Johns have served the national game with distinction.

Rugby Union is undergoing continuous change. Several years ago the game adopted professional status, and many top-level players departed to play outside Northern Ireland. However, with Ulster's success many of the best local players have largely been retained within Northern Ireland in a thoroughly professional set-up. As well as at the Ireland and Ulster level there is an enthusiastic following for rugby at town and club level.

Cricket

As in Britain, cricket is a popular summer sport in Northern Ireland although it tends to draw very small numbers of spectators.

Much of the cricket activity outside Greater Belfast is based around village sides and villages such as Sion Mills (near Strabane) who once famously humiliated the mighty West Indies and Waringstown (near Lurgan) have become synonymous with the game.

Although a very 'British' game cricket is organised on an all-island basis and there is a National side covering all of Ireland. This team competes with other minor cricketing countries and some of the English County sides but is not competitive at the top international level.

Hockey

Hockey (both men and ladies) is a popular sport right across Northern Ireland although more a participant than a spectator sport.

It is organised in local leagues for clubs – often closely associated with neighbouring rugby and cricket clubs although the international games are organised on an all-island basis. In the men's game Lisnagarvey (near Lisburn) have been the best team in Ireland for long stretches. In the ladies game Pegasus and Portadown have been regularly at the top.

Northern Ireland players can opt to play for Ireland or for Great Britain and many have played with distinction in major international championships including the Olympic Games.

The Belfast Giants

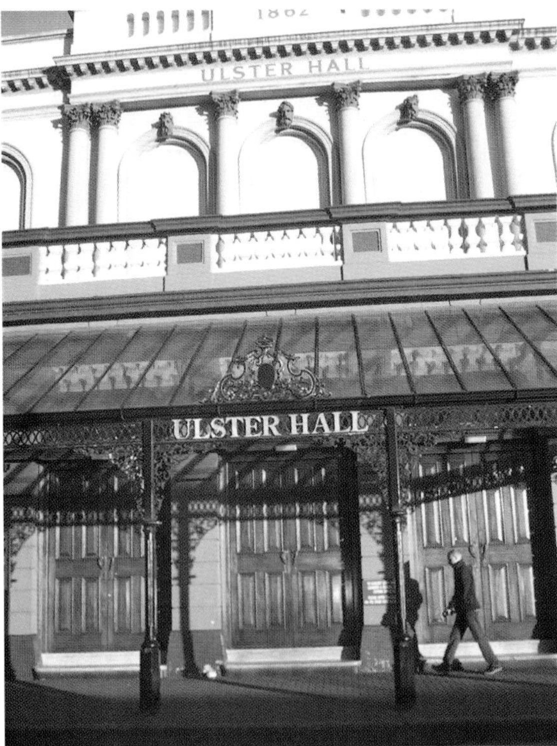

Northern Ireland's 'Home of Boxing'

Boxing
Although it can be seen as affirming certain stereotypical images of the 'fighting Irish', Northern Ireland has regularly produced top quality international boxers both as amateurs and professionals. There is a long history of heroic medal winning performances in Olympic and Commonwealth Championships for amateurs and for such a small place a number of local boxers have made it to World Champion in the professional ring. Names such as Barry McGuigan, Dave McAuley and Wayne McCullough have all held world championship belts. Belfast currently has a world-boxing champion, Brian Magee who holds the IBO super middle-weight title.

Local Soccer Co.Down

Motorsport
Northern Ireland has a large and very enthusiastic following for motor sports, in particular motorcycle road racing and car rallying. Although becoming increasingly expensive and specialist in nature motorsports have major spectator appeal.

A motorcycle race the North West 200, which takes place every year at Portrush is by far the largest spectator event in Northern Ireland's sporting calendar drawing huge crowds and a top quality international field for the racing.

Northern Ireland has always produced motorcyclists of the highest quality, including Isle of Man TT legend and 'King of the Road' Joey Dunlop and circuit racer Jeremy McWilliams.

Car rallying is also hugely popular in Northern Ireland with the highlights being the Circuit of Ireland Rally and the Ulster Rally.

Athletics
Since the era of Mary Peters and Mike Bull in the 1970s, Northern Ireland has rarely made the headlines in international athletics. However there is a strong record over the years of track and field participation in top competition.

Highlights of the local scene are the Belfast Marathon and the major cross-country events at Mallusk and Stormont which usually attract world-class fields. Locally there are 47 clubs in Northern Ireland – affiliated to the IAAF. The Athletics Federation can be contacted at:

The Athletics Federation
Athletics House
Old Coach Road
Belfast, BT9 5PR
Tel: 028 9060 2707
Fax: 028 9030 9939

Golf in Northern Ireland

Northern Ireland is perfect golfing country with an abundance of fine parkland and coastal links courses exploiting the natural contours and features of the land. There are nearly a hundred 18- and 9-hole golf courses (a dozen within 5 miles of the centre of Belfast), including world-famous championship courses such as Royal Portrush and Royal County Down. Northern Ireland continues to produce world-class golfers; in recent years Ronan Rafferty, David Feherty and Darren Clarke have all reached the top international level of the game.

The following listing includes all of Northern Ireland's 18-hole golf courses, along with details of their location, best days to visit and contact information.

Green fees in Northern Ireland are moderate and reductions can be negotiated for groups and visiting golf societies. Caddies can be arranged at some courses and a few have power carts available.

Belfast Area

Balmoral Golf Club
518 Lisburn Road, Belfast, BT9 6GX
Tel: 028 9066 1514
Fax: 028 9066 6759

18 Holes, 6,034 yds, par 69
Parkland course, 3 miles south-west of city centre. Best days for visitors: Monday and Thursday

Belvoir Park Golf Club
73 Church Road, Newtownbreda
Belfast, BT8 7AN
Tel: 028 9049 1693
Fax: 028 9064 6113

18 Holes, 6,516 yds, par 71
Parkland course, 3 miles south of city centre. Best days for visitors: Monday, Tuesday and Thursday

Dunmurry Golf Club
91 Dunmurry Lane
Dunmurry, Belfast, BT17 9JS
Tel: 028 9061 0834

18 Holes, 5,832 yds, par 68
Parkland course, 4 miles south-west of city centre. Best days for visitors: Tuesday and Thursday

Fortwilliam Golf Club
Downview Avenue, Belfast, BT15 4EZ
Tel: 028 9037 0770
Fax: 028 9078 1891

18 Holes, 5,973 yds, par 69
Parkland course, 3 miles north of city centre. Best days for visitors: weekday mornings

Knock Golf Club
Summerfield, Upper Newtownards Road
Dundonald, Belfast, BT16 2QX
Tel: 028 9048 3251
Fax: 028 9048 3251

18 Holes, 6,435 yds, par 71
Parkland course, 4 miles east of city centre. Best days for visitors: Monday, Wednesday and Thursday mornings; Tuesday and Friday afternoons

Malone Golf Club
240 Upper Malone Road
Dunmurry, Belfast, BT17 9LB
Tel: 028 9061 2758

18 Holes, 6,600 yds, par 71
Parkland course, 4 miles south of city centre. Best days for visitors: any day except Tuesday and Saturday

Mount Ober Golf & Country Club
20-24 Ballymaconaghy Road
Newtownbreda, Belfast, BT8 6SB
Tel: 028 9079 5666

18 Holes, 5,182 yds, par 68
Parkland course, 4 miles south-east of city centre. Best days for visitors: any day except Saturday

Rockmount Golf Club
28 Drumalig Road
Carryduff, Belfast, BT8 8EQ
Tel: 028 9081 2279
18 Holes, 6,373 yds, par 72
Parkland course, 2 miles south of Carryduff. Best days for visitors: any day except Wednesday and Saturday

Shandon Park Golf Club
73 Shandon Park
Belfast, BT5 6NY
Tel: 028 9080 5030
Fax: 028 9040 2773

18 Holes, 6,282 yds, par 70
Parkland course, 4 miles east of city centre. Best days for visitors: any day except Tuesday and Saturday

Co Antrim

Aberdelghy Golf Course
Bell's Lane
Lambeg, Lisburn, BT27 4QH
Tel: 028 9266 2738
Fax: 028 9260 3432

18 Holes, 4,526 yds, par 62
Parkland course, 1 mile north of Lisburn. Best days for visitors: any day except Saturday morning

Allen Park Golf Centre
45 Castle Road
Antrim, BT41 4NA
Tel: 028 9442 9001
Fax: 028 9442 9001

18 Holes, 6,683 yds, par 72
Parkland course, 2 miles west of Antrim
Best days for visitors: any day

Ballycastle Golf Club
Cushendall Road
Ballycastle, BT54 6QP
Tel: 028 2076 2536

18 Holes, 5,940 yds, par 70
Links/Parkland course, just south-east of Ballycastle. Best days for visitors: weekdays

Ballyclare Golf Club
25 Springvale Road
Ballyclare, BT39 9JW
Tel: 028 9332 2696
Fax: 028 9332 2696

18 Holes, 5,699 yds, par 71
Parkland course, 2 miles north of town
Best days for visitors: Monday, Tuesday and Wednesday

Ballymena Golf Club
128 Raceview Road
Ballymena, BT42 4HY
Tel: 028 2586 1487
Fax: 028 2586 1487

18 Holes, 5,795 yds, par 67
Parkland course, 2 miles east of Ballymena on A42
Best days for visitors: any day except Tuesday and Saturday

Cairndhu Golf Club
192 Coast Road
Ballygally, Larne, BT40 2QG
Tel: 028 2858 3324
Fax: 028 2858 3324

18 Holes, 6,112 yds, par 69
Parkland course, 4 miles north of Larne
Best days for visitors: weekdays

Carrickfergus Golf Club
35 North Road
Carrickfergus, BT38 8LP
Tel: 028 9336 3713
Fax: 028 9336 3023

18 Holes, 5,759 yds, par 68
Parkland course, west of Carrickfergus
Best days for visitors: any day except Tuesday, Saturday and Sunday afternoon

Galgorm Castle Golf & Country Club
Galgorm Road
Ballymena, BT42 1HL
Tel: 028 2564 6161
Fax: 028 2565 1151

18 Holes, 6,736 yds, par 72
Parkland course, 1 mile south-west of Ballymena. Best days for visitors: any day

Gracehill Golf Club
143 Ballinlea Road
Stranocum, Ballymoney, BT53 8PX
Tel: 028 2075 1209
Fax: 028 2075 1074

18 Holes, 6,600 yds, par 72
Parkland course, 7 miles north-east of Ballymoney
Best days for visitors: weekdays

Greenacres Golf Centre
153 Ballyrobert Road
Ballyclare, BT39 9RT
Tel: 028 9335 4111

18 Holes, 6,020 yds, par 71
Parkland course, 3 miles from Corr's Corner. Best days for visitors: any day except Saturday morning

Hilton Templepatrick Golf Club
Castle Upton Estate
Templepatrick, BT39 0DD
Tel: 028 9443 5542

18 Holes, 7,100 yds, par 71
Parkland course, 5 miles from Belfast International Airport
Best days for visitors: any day

Lisburn Golf Club
68 Eglantine Road, Lisburn, BT27 5RQ
Tel: 028 9267 7216

18 Holes, 6,672 yds, par 72
Parkland course, 2 miles south of Lisburn
Best days for visitors: weekdays

Massereene Golf Club
51 Lough Road, Antrim, BT41 4DQ
Tel: 028 9442 8096

18 Holes, 6,375 yds, par 71
Parkland/sandy course, 1 mile south of Antrim. Best days for visitors: any day except Friday and Saturday

Royal Portrush Golf Club
Bushmills Road, Portrush, BT56 8JQ
Tel: 028 7082 2311

(1) 18 Holes, 6,818 yds, par 73
(2) 18 Holes, 6,273 yds, par 70
Two links courses: (1) Dunluce (2) Valley, 1 mile east or Portrush

Best days for visitors: weekdays except Wednesday and Friday afternoon (Green fees are expensive).

Whitehead Golf Club
McCrea's Brae
Whitehead, BT38 9NZ
Tel: 028 9337 0820
Fax: 028 9337 0825

18 Holes, 6,050 yds, par 68
Parkland course, just north of Whitehead. Best days for visitors: any day except Saturday; members only on Sunday.

Co Armagh

Ashfield Golf Club
Freeduff
Cullyhanna, Newry, BT35 0JJ
Tel: 028 3086 8180
Fax: 028 3086 8611

18 Holes, 5,645 yds, par 67
Parkland course, 4 miles north of Crossmaglen off B30. Best days for visitors: any day

County Armagh Golf Club
7 Newry Road
Armagh, BT60 1EN
Tel: 028 3752 5861
Fax: 028 3752 5861

18 Holes, 6,212 yds, par 70
Parkland course, in palace demesne
Best days for visitors: weekdays and Sunday

Craigavon Silverwood Golf Centre
Turmoyra Lane
Lurgan, BT66 6NG
Tel: 028 3832 6606
Fax: 028 3834 7272

18 Holes, 6,188 yds, par 72
Parkland course, 2 miles north of Lurgan
Best days for visitors: any day

Loughgall Country Park
11 Main Street
Loughgall, BT61 8HZ
Tel: 028 3889 1029
Fax: 028 3889 1029

18 Holes, 5,937 yds, par 69
Parkland course, 100 yards from Loughgall village. Best days for visitors: any day

Lurgan Golf Club
The Demesne
Lurgan, BT67 9BN
Tel: 028 3832 2087
Fax: 028 3831 6166

18 Holes, 5,995 yds, par 70
Parkland course, in Lurgan
Best days for visitors: Monday, Thursday and Friday morning

Portadown Golf Club
192 Gilford Road
Portadown, BT63 5LF
Tel: 028 3835 5356

18 Holes, 6,147 yds, par 70
Parkland course, in Portadown
Best days for visitors: any day except Tuesday and Saturday

Tandragee Golf Club
Markethill Road
Tandragee, Craigavon, BT62 2ER
Tel: 028 3884 1272
Fax: 028 3884 0664

18 Holes, 6,285 yds, par 70
Parkland course, just south of Tandragee
Best days for visitors: any day except Saturday and Thursday

Co Down

Ardglass Golf Club
Castle Place
Ardglass, BT30 7TP
Tel: 028 4484 1219
Fax: 028 4484 1841

18 Holes, 5,776 yds, par 68
Seaside course, in Ardglass
Best days for visitors: weekdays

Banbridge Golf Club
116 Huntly Road
Banbridge, BT32 3UR
Tel: 028 4066 2211
Fax: 028 4066 9400

18 Holes, 5,468 yds, par 67
Parkland course, north-west of Banbridge. Best days for visitors: any day except Tuesday and Saturday

Bangor Golf Club
Broadway, Bangor, BT20 4RH
Tel: 028 9127 0922

18 Holes, 6,410 yds, par 71
Parkland course, in Bangor. Best days for visitors: Monday, Wednesday and Friday

Blackwood Golf Centre
150 Crawfordsburn Road
Clandeboye, Bangor, BT19 1GB
Tel: 028 9185 2706
Fax: 028 9185 3785

18 Holes, 6,500 yds, par 70
Parkland course, 2 miles west of Bangor
Best days for visitors: any day

Bright Castle Golf Club
14 Coniamstown Road
Bright, Downpatrick, BT30 8LU
Tel: 028 4484 1319

18 Holes, 7,143 yds, par 73
Parkland course, 4 miles south of Downpatrick. Best days for visitors: any day

Carnalea Golf Club
Station Road, Bangor, BT19 1EZ
Tel: 028 9127 0368
Fax: 028 9127 3989

18 Holes, 5,548 yds, par 67
Seaside meadowland course, 1 mile west of Bangor. Best days for visitors: any day except Sunday

Clandeboye Golf Club
Tower Road, Conlig
Newtownards, BT23 3PN
Tel: 028 9127 1767
Fax: 028 9147 3711

(1) 18 Holes, 6,559 yds, par 71
(2) 18 Holes, 5,755 yds, par 68
Two parkland/heathland courses (1) Dufferin course (2) Ava Course, 2 miles south of Bangor. Best days for visitors: weekdays, weekend after 2.30pm

Cloverhill Golf Club
Lough Road, Mullaghbawn, Newry
Tel: 028 3088 9374

18 Holes, 6,090 yds, par 70
Parkland course, 7 miles North West of Newry

Donaghadee Golf Club
Warren Road
Donaghadee, BT21 0PQ
Tel: 028 9188 3624
Fax: 028 9188 8891

18 Holes, 6,091 yds, par 69
Seaside course, north side of Donaghadee. Best days for visitors: Monday, Wednesday and Friday

Downpatrick Golf Club
43 Saul Road
Downpatrick, BT30 6PA
Tel: 028 4461 5947

18 Holes, 6,120 yds, par 69
Parkland course, 1 mile from Downpatrick. Best days for visitors: any day, booking is advisable

Down Royal Park Golf Club
Dunygarton Road
Maze, BT27 5RT
Tel: 028 9262 1339

18 Holes, 6,824 yds, par 72
Heathland course, within Down Royal racecourse. Best days for visitors: any day

Edenmore Golf Club
Edenmore House
70 Drumnabreeze Road
Magheralin, Craigavon, BT67 0RH
Tel: 028 9261 1310

18 Holes, 6,244 yds, par 71
Parkland course, 1.5 miles south-east of Magheralin. Best days for visitors: any day except Saturday morning

Holywood Golf Club
Nun's Walk
Demesne Road
Holywood, BT18 9LE
Tel: 028 9042 3135

18 Holes, 5,885 yds, par 67
Parkland course, 1 mile south of Holywood. Best days for visitors: any day except Thursday and Saturday

Kilkeel Golf Club
Mourne Park
Ballyardle, Newry, BT34 4LB
Tel: 028 4176 5095
Fax: 028 4176 5579

18 Holes, 6,625 yds, par 72
Parkland course, 3 miles west of town
Best days for visitors: Monday, Wednesday-Friday

Kirkistown Castle Golf Club
142 Main Road
Cloughey, Newtownards, BT22 1JA
Tel: 028 4277 1233

18 Holes, 6,142 yds, par 70
Links course, 15 miles south-east of Newtownards – A20 and B173. Best days for visitors: any day except Saturday

Ringdufferin Golf Course
36 Ringdufferin Road
Toye, Killyleagh, BT30 9PH
Tel: 028 4482 8812

18 Holes, 5,136 yds, par 66
Drumlin course, 2 miles north of Killyleagh. Best days for visitors: any day

Royal Belfast Golf Club
Station road, Craigavad
Holywood, BT18 0BT
Tel: 028 9042 8165

18 Holes, 5,961 yds, par 69
Parkland course, 7 miles north-east of Belfast. Best days for visitors: by arrangement with Club, visitors require letter of introduction (Green fees are expensive)

Royal County Down Golf Club
36 Golf Links Road
Newcastle, BT33 0AN
Tel: 028 4372 3314

(1) 18 Holes, 7,037 yds, par 74
(2) 18 Holes, 4.681 yds, par 63
Two links courses, (1) Championship (2) Annesley 30 miles south of Belfast
Best days for visitors: (1) Monday, Tuesday, Thursday and Friday (2) any day except Saturday morning

Scrabo Golf Club
233 Scrabo Road
Newtownards, BT23 4SL
Tel: 028 9181 2355
Fax: 028 9182 2919

18 Holes, 6,257 yds, par 71
Undulating course, 1? miles south-west of Newtownards follow Scrabo Country Park signs. Best days for visitors: Monday Tuesday and Thursday, Sunday after 11.30am

Spa Golf Club
20 Grove Road
Ballynahinch, BT24 8PN
Tel: 028 9756 2365
Fax: 028 9756 4158

18 Holes, 6,494 yds, par 72
Parkland course, 1 mile south of town
Best days for visitors: Monday-Thursday

Warrenpoint Golf Club
Lower Dromore Road
Warrenpoint, BT34 3LN
Tel: 028 4175 3695
Fax: 028 4175 2918

18 Holes, 6,200 yds, par 70
Parkland course, 1 mile west of town. Best days for visitors: Monday, Thursday and Friday

Co Fermanagh

Castle Hume Golf Club
Castle Hume, Enniskillen, BT74 6HZ
Tel: 028 6632 7077

18 Holes, 6,900 yds, par 71
Parkland course, 3.5 miles north of Enniskillen
Best days for visitors: any day

Enniskillen Golf Club
Castle Coole, Enniskillen, BT74 6HZ

18 Holes, 6,189 yds, par 69
Parkland course, in Castle Coole estate half a mile east of town. Best days for visitors: any day

Co Derry

Castlerock Golf Club
65 Circular Road
Castlerock, BT51 4TJ
Tel: 028 7084 8314
Fax: 028 7084 9440

18 Holes, 6,687 yds, par 72
Two links courses, 6 miles west of Coleraine. Best days for visitors: Monday-Thursday

City of Derry Golf Club
49 Victoria Road
Prehen, Derry, BT47 2PU
Tel: 028 7134 6369

18 Holes, 6,487 yds, par 71
Parkland course, 2 miles south of city. Best days for visitors: weekdays until 4.30pm

Foyle International Golf Centre
12 Alder Road, Derry, BT48 8DB
Tel: 028 7135 2222

18 Holes, 6,678 yds, par 71
Parkland course, just north of Derry
Best days for visitors: any day

Moyola Park Golf Club
15 Curran Road, Shanemullagh
Castledawson, BT45 8DG
Tel: 028 7946 8468

18 Holes, 6,517 yds, par 71
Parkland course, in Castledawson
Best days for visitors: weekdays except Wednesday

Portstewart Golf Club
117 Strand Road
Portstewart, BT55 7PG
Tel: 028 7083 2015

(1) 18 Holes, 6,779 yds, par 73
(2) 18 Holes, 4,730 yds, par 64
Links course, (1) Strand (2) Old - 1 mile from town centre
Best days for visitors: (1) Monday, Tuesday, Thursday and Friday (2) any day

Radisson Roe Hotel & Golf Resort
Roe Park
Limavady, BT49 9LB
Tel: 028 7776 0105

18 Holes, 6,001 yds, par 70
Parkland course, 1 mile west of Limavady. Best days for visitors: any day

Co Tyrone

Dungannon Golf Club
34 Springfield Lane
Dungannon, BT70 1QX
Tel: 028 8772 7338

18 Holes, 5,861 yds, par 69
Parkland course, 1 mile west of Dungannon. Best days for visitors: Monday, Thursday and Friday morning

Killymoon Golf Club
200 Killymoon Road
Cookstown, BT80 8TW
Tel: 028 8676 3762

18 Holes, 6,149 yds, par 69
Parkland course, south side of Cookstown
Best days for visitors: Monday-Wednesday and Friday, ladies Thursday

Newtownstewart Golf Club
38 Golf Course Road
Newtownstewart, BT78 4HU
Tel: 028 8166 1466

18 Holes, 5,341 yds, par 69
Parkland course, 2 miles south-west of town. Best days for visitors: any day

Omagh Golf Club
83a Dublin Road
Omagh, BT78 1HQ
Tel: 028 8224 3160

18 Holes, 5,885 yds, par 68
Parkland course, just south of town
Best days for visitors: any day except Tuesday and Saturday

Strabane Golf Club
33 Ballycolman Road
Strabane, BT82 9PH
Tel: 028 7138 2271

18 Holes, 6,055 yds, par 69
Parkland course, 1 mile south of town
Best days for visitors: weekdays except Tuesday

Motorsport/Karting

Below is a list of venues in Northern Ireland where groups or individuals can avail of organised karting and motorsport activities.

Alltrak Rallysport
61 Mullantine Road, Portadown
Tel: 028 3833 1919

Bishopscourt Racing Circuit
29 Lismore Road
Downpatrick, BT30 7EY
Tel: 028 4484 2202

Fast Track Karting Club
3 Edergoole Avenue, Omagh
Tel: 028 8225 0170

Gosford Karting
49 Dinnahorra Road
Markethill, Armagh
Tel: 028 3755 1248

Landrover Experience
Clandeboye Courtyard
Bangor, BT19 1RN
Tel: 0870 2644457

Minimotomania
3 Highfields Avenue
Lisburn
Tel: 028 9260 7612

Race School Ireland
92 Bloomfield Road
Belfast, BT5 5LU
Tel: 028 90550 7010

Raceview Indoor Karting
1 Woodside Road East
Ballymena
Tel: 028 2565 1000

Rally School Ireland
Unit 8 Graham Industrial Estate
Dargan Crescent, Belfast
Tel: 028 9077 3777

Superdrive Motorsports Centre
7 Derryneskan Road
Craigavon, BT62 1UH
Tel: 028 3885 2545

Ultimate Karting
11 Kilbride Road
Doagh, Ballyclare
Tel: 028 9334 2777

Riding Schools/ Equestrian Centres

Ballyknock Riding School
38 Ballyknock Road
Hillsborough, BT26 6EF
Tel: 028 9269 2144

Birr House Riding Centre
81 Whinney Hill, Dundonald, BT16 0UA.
Tel: 028 9042 5858.

The Burn Equestrian Club
Knockbracken Healthcare Park,
Saintfield Road, Belfast BT8 8BH
Tel: 028 9040 2384

Danescroft
21 Waterloo Road, Lisburn, BT27 5NW
Tel: 028 9260 2621

Drumgooland House Trekking Centre
29 Dunnanew Road
Seaforde, BT30 8PJ
Tel: 028 4481 1956

East Hope Equestrian Centre
71 Killynure Road West
Carryduff, BT8 8EA
Tel: 028 9081 3186

Enniskillen College of Agriculture
Levaghy, Enniskillen, BT74 4GF
Tel: 028 6634 4853

The Forest Stables
100 Cooneen Road
Fivemiletown, BT75 0NQ,
Tel: 028 8952 1991

Galgorm Parks Riding School
112 Sand Road, Ballymena, BT42 1DN
Tel: 028 2588 0269

Heathview Equestrian
60 Upper Gransha Road
Donaghadee, BT21 0LZ
Tel: 028 9181 3388

Hill Farm Riding Centre
47 Altikeeragh Road
Castlerock, BT51 4SR
Tel: 028 7084 8629

Island Equestrian Centre
49 Ballyrashane Road
Coleraine, BT52 2NL
Tel: 028 7034 2599

Islandmagee Riding Centre
103 Browns Bay Road
Islandmagee, BT40 3TL
Tel: 028 9338 2108

Lagan Valley Equestrian Centre
170 Upper Malone Road, Dunmurry,
Belfast BT17 9JZ
Tel: 028 9061 4853

Lessans Riding Stables
126 Monlough Road, Saintfield
Tel: 028 9751 0141

Maddybenny Stud
Maddybenny Farm, Coleraine, BT52 2PT
Tel: 028 7082 3603

Millbridge Riding Centre Ltd,
Ballystockart, Comber, BT23 5QT
Tel: 028 9187 250

Mossvale Equestrian Centre
18 Church Road, Dromara
Dromore, BT25 2NS.
Tel: 028 9753 2279

Mount Pleasant Trekking Centre
15 Bannonstown Road
Castlewellan, BT31 9BG
Tel: 028 4377 8651

Moy Riding School
131 Derrycaw
Road, Moy, BT71 6NA
Tel: 028 8778 4440

Necarne Castle
The Ulster Lakeland Equestrian Park,
Irvinestown, BT94 1GG
Tel: 028 6862 1919

Newcastle Riding Centre
35 Carnacaville Road
Castlewellan, BT31 9HD
Tel: 028 4372 2694

The Rainbow Equestrian Centre
24 Hollow Road, Islandmagee
Larne, BT40 3RL
Tel: 028 9338 2929

Tullynewbank Stables
25 Tullynewbank Road
Glenavy, BT29 4PQ
Tel: 028 9444 5465

Leisure

Northern Ireland has a proportionately large variety of leisure facilities for an area of its size. The climate and landscape facilitate outdoor pursuits such as hiking, mountain climbing and camping, and many of the lakes and rivers host watersports facilities. There are also many swimming pools, leisure and activity centres equipped with the latest fitness suites, some of which are listed below.

Leisure Centres

Andersonstown Leisure Centre
Andersonstown Road
Belfast, BT11 9BY
Tel: 028 9062 5211

Antrim Forum
Lough Road
Antrim, BT41 4DQ
Tel: 028 9446 4131

Ards Leisure Centre
William Street
Newtownards, BT23 4EJ
Tel: 028 9181 2837
Fax: 028 9182 0807

Avoniel Leisure Centre
Avoniel Road
Belfast, BT5 4SF
Tel: 028 9045 1564

Ballynahinch Community Centre
55 Windmill Street
Ballynahinch, BT24 8HB
Tel: 028 9756 1950
Fax: 028 9756 5606

Ballysillan Leisure Centre
Ballysillan Road
Belfast, BT14 7QQ
Tel: 028 9039 1040

Banbridge Leisure Centre
Victoria Street
Banbridge, BT32 3JY
Tel: 028 4066 2799

Bangor Castle Leisure Centre
Castle Park Avenue
Bangor, BT20 4BN
Tel: 028 9127 0271

Bawnacre Centre
Castle Street
Irvinestown, BT94 1EE
Tel: 028 6862 1177

Beechmount Leisure Centre
Falls Road
Belfast, BT12 6FD
Tel: 028 9032 8631

Belfast Indoor Tennis Arena
Ormeau Embankment
Belfast, BT6 8LT
Tel: 028 9045 8024

Brandywell Sports Centre
Lone Moor Road
Derry, BT48
Tel: 028 7126 3902

Brooke Park Leisure Centre
Rosemount Avenue
Derry, BT48 0HH
Tel: 028 7126 2637

Carrickfergus Leisure Centre
Prince William Way
Carrickfergus, BT38 7HP
Tel: 028 9335 1711

Cascades Leisure Centre
51 Thomas Street
Portadown, BT62 3AF
Tel: 028 3833 2802

Castlepark Recreation Centre
11 Water Road
Lisnaskea, BT92 0LZ
Tel: 028 6772 1299

Comber Leisure Centre
Castle Street
Comber, BT23 5DY
Tel: 028 9187 4350
Fax: 028 9187 0099

Coleraine Leisure Centre
Railway Road
Coleraine, BT52 1PE
Tel: 028 7035 6432

Cookstown Leisure Centre
Fountain Road
Cookstown, BT80 8QF
Tel: 028 8676 3853

Craigavon Leisure Centre
Brownlow Road, Craigavon
Tel: 028 3834 1333

Derg Valley Leisure Centre
6 Strabane Road
Castlederg, BT81 7HZ
Tel: 028 8167 0727

Down Leisure Centre
114 Market Street
Downpatrick, BT30 6LZ
Tel: 028 4461 3426
Fax: 028 4461 6905

Dreamworld Family Entertainment Centre
Glenmachan Place
Boucher Road
Belfast, BT12 6QH
Tel: 028 9020 2300

Dundonald International Ice Bowl
111 Old Dundonald Road
Dundonald, Belfast, BT16 1XT
Tel: 028 9048 2611

Dungannon Leisure Centre
Circular Road
Dungannon, BT71 6BH
Tel: 028 8772 0370

Dungiven Sports Pavilion
3 Chapel Road
Derry, BT47 2AN
Tel: 028 7774 2074

Ecclesville Equestrian Leisure & Community Centre
11 Ecclesville Road
Fintona, BT78 2EF
Tel: 028 824 0591

Falls Swim Centre
Falls Road
Belfast
BT12 4PB
Tel: 028 9032 4906

Fermanagh Lakeland Forum
Broadmeadow, Enniskillen
Tel: 028 6632 4121

Glenmore Activity Centre
43 Glenmore Park, Hilden
Lisburn, BT27 4RT
Tel: 028 9266 2830

Greenvale Leisure Centre
Greenvale Park
Magherafelt, BT45 6DR
Tel: 028 7963 2796

Grove Activity Centre
15 Ballinderry Park, Knockmore
Lisburn, BT28 1ST
Tel: 028 9267 1131

Grove Leisure Centre
York Road
Belfast, BT15 3HF
Tel: 028 9035 1599

Jungle Jim's
Abbey Centre Complex
Longwood Road
Newtownabbey, BT37 9UL
Tel: 028 9036 5533

Kilkeel Recreation & Community Complex
Mourne Esplanade
Kilkeel, BT34 4DB
Tel: 028 4176 4666

Kilmakee Activity Centre
52a Rowan Drive
Seymour Hill, Dunmurry
Belfast, BT17 9QA
Tel: 028 9030 1545

The Kiltonga Leisure Centre
Belfast Road
Newtownards, BT23 4TJ
Tel: 028 9181 8511
Fax: 028 9182 3400

Lagan Valley LeisurePlex
12 Lisburn Leisure Park
Governors Road
Lisburn, BT28 1LP
Tel: 028 9267 2121
Fax: 028 9267 4322
(pictured below left)

Larne Leisure Centre
Tower Road
Larne, BT40 1AB
Tel: 028 2826 0478

Lisnagelvin Leisure Centre
Richill Park, Waterside
Derry, BT47 5QZ
Tel: 028 7134 7695

Longstone Community Association
Community Hall
Longstone Road, Annalong
Tel: 028 4376 8249

Lough Moss Centre
Hillsborough Road
Carryduff
Tel: 028 9081 4884

Loughside Leisure Centre
Shore Road
Belfast, BT15 4HP
Tel: 028 9078 1524

Maghera Recreation Centre
St Lurach's Road
Maghera, BT46 5JE
Tel: 028 7964 4017

Lagan Valley LeisurePlex

Meadowbank Recreation Ground
Ballyronan Road
Magherafelt
Tel: 028 7963 1680

Millburn Community Centre
Linden Avenue
Coleraine, BT52 2AN
Tel: 028 7034 2625

Newcastle Centre
10-14 Central Promenade
Newcastle, BT33
Tel: 028 4372 5034
Fax: 028 4372 2400

Newry Sports Centre
Patrick Street
Newry, BT35 8TR
Tel: 028 3026 7322

Olympia Leisure Centre
Boucher Road
Belfast, BT12 6HR
Tel: 028 9023 3369

Omagh Leisure Centre
Old Mountfield Road
Omagh, BT79
Tel: 028 8224 6711

Orchard Leisure Centre
37-39 Folly Lane
Armagh, BT60 1AT
Tel: 028 3751 5920

The Palladium
10 Quay Street
Bangor, BT20 5ED
Tel: 028 9127 0844

The Queen's Leisure Complex
Sullivan Place
Holywood, BT18 9JF
Tel: 028 9042 1234

Queen's University
(Malone Sports Facilities)
Dub Lane
Belfast, BT9 5NB
Tel: 028 9062 3946

Riada Centre
33 Garryduff Road
Ballymoney, BT53 7DB
Tel: 028 2766 5792

Riversdale Leisure Centre
Lisnafin Park
Strabane
Tel: 028 7138 2672

The Robinson Centre
Montgomery Road
Belfast, BT6 9HS
Tel: 028 9070 3948

St Columb's Park Leisure Centre
Limavady Road
Derry, BT47 6JY
Tel: 028 7134 3941

St Mary's Community Centre
Edenmore
Tempo, BT92 1BN
Tel: 028 8954 1770

Seapark Sports Ground
Ballymenoch Park
Holywood, BT18 0LP
Tel: 028 9042 2894

Sentry Hill Sports Complex
Old Ballymoney Road
Ballymena, BT43 6NE
Tel: 028 2565 6101

Seven Towers Leisure Centre
Trostan Avenue
Ballymena, BT43 7BL
Tel: 028 2564 1427

Shaftesbury Recreation Centre
Ormeau Road, Belfast
Tel: 028 9032 9163

Shankill Leisure Centre
Shankill Road
Belfast, BT13 2BD
Tel: 028 9024 1434

Sheskburn Recreation Centre
7 Mary Street
Ballycastle, BT54 6QH
Tel: 028 2076 3300

Sixmile Leisure Centre
Ballynure Road
Ballyclare, BT39 9YU
Tel: 028 9334 1818
Fax: 028 9335 4357

Station 3000 Ltd
Mega Zone
111a Old Dundonald Road
Belfast, BT16 1XT
Tel: 028 9041 0500

Station 3000 Ltd
Valley Bowling
Valley Leisure Centre
Newtownabbey
Tel: 028 9036 5642

Templemore Complex
Templemore Avenue
Belfast, BT5 4FW
Tel: 028 9045 750

Templemore Sports Complex
Buncrana Road
Derry, BT48 8LQ
Tel: 028 7126 5521

Trillick Enterprise Leisure Centre
Gargadis Road
Trillick, BT78 3
Tel: 028 8956 1333

The Valley Leisure Centre
40 Church Road
Whiteabbey
Newtownabbey, BT36 7LN
Tel: 028 9086 1211
Fax: 028 9085 3211

Waves Leisure Complex
22 Robert Street
Lurgan, BT66 8BE
Tel: 028 3832 2906

Whiterock Leisure Centre
Whiterock Road
Belfast, BT12 7RG
Tel: 028 9023 3239

Private Fitness Clubs

Arena Health and Fitness - Yorkgate
100-150 York Street
Belfast, BT15 1WA
Tel: 028 9074 1235
Fax: 028 9074 1239

Arena Health and Fitness - Finaghy
Tel: 028 9062 9789

Arena Health and Fitness - Ballymena
Unit 20 Larne Road Link
Ballymena
Tel: 028 2563 8833

David Lloyd Leisure
Old Dundonald Road
Belfast, BT16 1DL
Tel: 028 9041 3300
Fax: 028 9041 3339

Elysium Health and Leisure Club
Culloden Hotel, Bangor Road
Craigavad
Tel: 028 9042 5315

Esporta
Mertoun Hall
106 Belfast Road
Holywood, BT18 9QY
Tel: 028 9076 5000
Web: www.esporta.com/belfast
Club Reception Tel: 028 9076 5000
Membership Tel: 028 9076 5000

Fitness First
1 Circular Road
Toscana Retail Park, Bangor
Tel: 028 9147 0000

Ballymena
Unit 3 Pennybridge Industrial Estate
Larne Road, Ballymena
Tel: 028 2563 1333

Belfast
Unit 2 Lesley Retail Centre
Boucher Road, Belfast
Tel: 028 9038 1868

Connswater
Arches Retail Park
Bridge End, Belfast
Tel: 028 9045 0505

Londonderry
Unit 1 Lesley Retail Park
Londonderry
Tel: 028 7127 5500

Newtownabbey
Unit 1 Shore Road Retail Park
Newtownabbey
Tel: 028 9086 9888

LA Fitness
Ramada Hotel, Shaws Bridge
Belfast, BT8 7XT
Tel: 028 90 641 800
Fax: 028 90 641 611

LA Fitness – Belfast
Adelaide Street, Belfast
Tel: 028 9032 8816

LA Fitness – Armagh
Armagh City Hotel
Friary Road, Armagh
Tel: 028 3752 5705

Living Well Health Clubs
Hilton Belfast
Lanyon Place, Belfast
Tel: 028 9027 7490

Hilton Templepatrick
Castle Upton Estate, Templepatrick
Tel: 028 9443 5566

Newforge Leisure & Fitness Club
18B Newforge Lane, Belfast
Tel: 028 9068 5117

Peak Physique
721A Lisburn Road, Belfast
Tel: 028 9066 7887

Lisburn Leisureplex

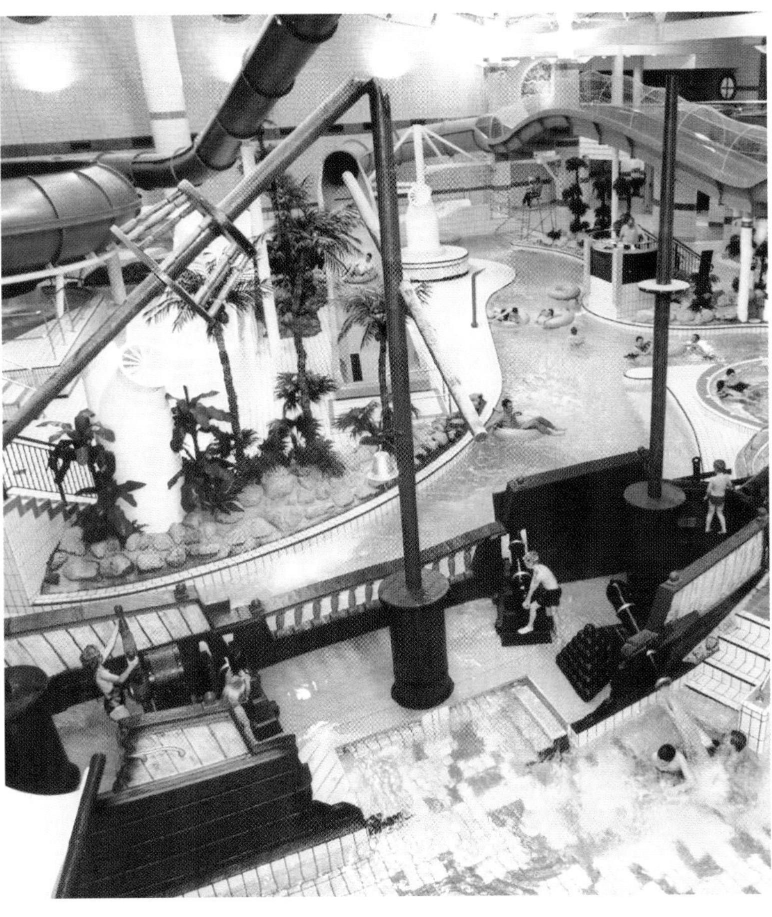

Shopping in Northern Ireland

It would be impossible to take a comprehensive look at lifestyle and leisure in Northern Ireland without taking into consideration one particular leisure activity – shopping!

In recent years, Northern Ireland has begun to attract the large national retail chains, which had, to a large extent previously been absent from Northern Ireland's high streets. Leading this influx has been the large supermarket chains of Sainsbury's and Tesco, both of which now have a significant presence in towns and cities across Northern Ireland. Many of the larger of these supermarkets offer extended opening times, some even opening 24 hours.

British department store Debenham's, which has been the flagship store in Castle Court for many years is also soon to open additional outlets in Northern Ireland, at Craigavon and Newry. Despite the presence of many of the large national and international chains, there are some not yet present in Northern Ireland, such as Scandinavian furniture giant, IKEA, which, despite rumours has yet to find a suitable location in the province. Similarly Dublin department store Brown Thomas has not yet established a presence in the north.

A recent survey has shown Belfast to be in the top 20 retail centres in the UK – coming in at number 17. Belfast's attraction lies in its compact retail centre based, to a large extent, around the Royal Avenue and Donegall Place areas. In the survey the city ranked positively in terms of accessibility and also car-parking, but less well in terms of public transport provision and shopper facilities.

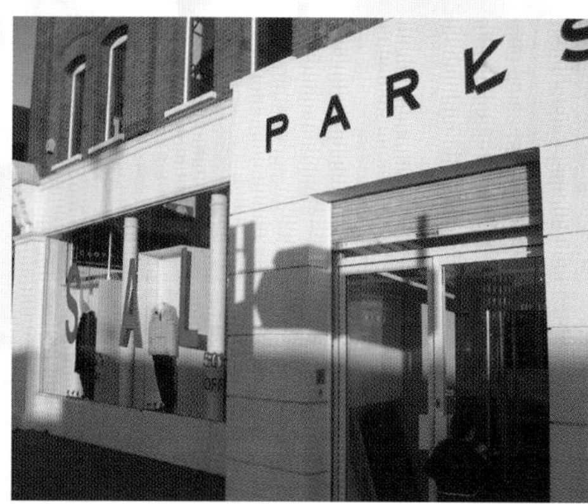

One trend in shopping in Northern Ireland has seen the development of many large 'out-of-town' retail centres which often have the appeal of being less congested than town centres and easily accessible by car. An added benefit is that these retail areas often offer free parking, unlike town centres where parking can cost anything up to £1.50 per hour.

There is concern in some quarters that the development of these large retail parks, with the incoming national chains, will have a detrimental effect on Northern Ireland's family-run businesses, which have in many cases operated in town centres for long numbers of years. Some also fear that by taking shoppers away from town centres, traditional shopping areas will become deserted and run-down and that this will lead to a deterioration in the overall appearance of our towns.

Another trend which is starting to emerge in Northern Ireland is that of 'factory outlet villages' such as The Linen Green in Moygashel, which has been operating for a number of years on the site of a former linen mill near Dungannon. These outlet villages see top, often designer, names (such as Paul Costello or Ramsay) set up outlet or discount stores selling their goods at greatly reduced prices. There are currently plans for the development of further factory outlet villages at Junction One near Antrim and at Gilford in Co Down.

Some of Northern Ireland's most exclusive retail outlets are to be found, not in the largest cities and towns but in provincial villages and small towns such as Holywood, Hillsborough or Moira. It is becoming increasingly common for people to visit these towns to spend time browsing amongst the unique shops selling unusual, often hand-crafted goods or services (such as Scandinavian wood products, luxury food items, upmarket interior design services). Shopping is then combined with a visit to a local coffee bar or delicatessen for refreshment!

The trend for shopping and the 'café lifestyle' is most apparent in Belfast's trendy Lisburn Road area, which offers a host of designer shops along with a wide variety of eateries, perfect for whiling away an idle Saturday afternoon!

Below is a list of Northern Ireland's main shopping centres, arranged in a convenient A-Z format.

Shopping Centres

Abbey Centre
Longwood Road
Newtownabbey
Tel: 028 9086 8018

Ards Shopping Centre
22C Circular Road
Newtownards
Tel: 028 9181 5444

Bloomfield Centre
South Circular Road, Bangor
Tel: 028 9127 0797

Bow Street Mall
Bow Street, Lisburn
Tel: 028 9267 5438

Buttercrane Shopping Centre
Buttercrane Quay, Newry
Tel: 028 3026 4627

Carryduff Shopping Centre
Church Road, Carryduff
Tel: 028 9043 8743

Castle Centre
Market Square, Antrim
Tel: 028 9442 8269

Castle Court
Royal Avenue, Belfast
Tel: 028 9023 4591

Connswater Shopping Centre
Bloomfield Avenue, Belfast
Tel: 028 9045 0111

Diamond Centre
Bridge Street, Coleraine
Tel: 028 7032 1123

Donegall Arcade
5-7 Castle Place, Belfast
Tel: 028 9043 9562

Erneside Shopping Centre
The Point, Enniskillen
Tel: 028 6632 5705

Fairhill Shopping Centre
Fairhill Lane, Ballymena
Tel: 028 2565 1199

The Flagship Centre
Main Street, Bangor
Tel: 028 9145 6700

Flax Centre
Ardoyne Avenue, Belfast
Tel: 028 9059 3366

Forestside Shopping Centre
Upper Galwally, Belfast
Tel: 028 9049 4990

Foyleside Shopping Centre
Orchard Street, Londonderry
Tel: 028 7137 7575

High Street Mall
High Street, Portadown
Tel: 028 3836 2251

Inshops Centres Ltd
Hi Park Centre
High Street, Belfast
Tel: 028 9032 9719

Kennedy Centre
Falls Road, Belfast
Tel: 028 9020 3303

Lisburn Square
3 Lisburn Square, Lisburn
Tel: 028 9264 1384

Lisnagelvin Shopping Centre
Lisnagelvin Road, Londonderry
Tel: 028 7132 9336

The Mall Shopping Centre
The Mall West, Armagh
Tel: 028 3751 8336

Great Victoria Street, Belfast

Rushmere Shopping Centre, Craigavon

Meadow Lane Shopping Centre
Moneymore Road, Magherafelt
Tel: 028 7963 4081

Meadows Shopping Centre
Meadow Lane, Portadown
Tel: 028 3836 3000

Millennium Court
William Street, Portadown
Tel: 028 3835 1710

Northcott Shopping Centre
Ballyclare Road, Glengormley
Tel: 028 9034 2977

Oaks Centre
Oaks Road, Dungannon
Tel: 028 8772 9694

Park Centre
Donegall Road, Belfast
Tel: 028 9032 3451

The Quays
The Quays, Newry
Tel: 028 3025 6000

Richmond Shopping Centre
Richmond Street, Londonderry
Tel: 028 7126 0525

Rushmere Shopping
Central Way, Craigavon
Tel: 028 3834 3350

Springhill Shopping Centre
Killeen Avenue, Bangor
Tel: 028 9127 0185

Tower Centre
Wellington Street, Ballymena
Tel: 028 2564 8921

Westwood Centre
Kennedy Way, Belfast
Tel: 028 9061 1255

Yorkgate Centre
100-150 York Street, Belfast
Tel: 028 9071 0990

Chapter 13

Visitors Guide to Northern Ireland

Mussenden Temple, Castlerock

Introduction

This chapter of the Northern Ireland Yearbook 2004 aims to provide useful information for anyone visiting Northern Ireland. It includes details of how to get here, the public transport system as well as a comprehensive list of where to stay and things to see and do. Further information in relation to places to eat, culture and the arts and other leisure activities is included in Chapter 12. We hope that the practical information, timetables, reservations contacts and general information will be of interest and practical use to those visiting Northern Ireland and also those arranging trips for family, friends and colleagues.

Travelling to and From Northern Ireland

By Air

Northern Ireland has three airports: Belfast International, Belfast City and City of Derry which between them serve a variety of destinations in the UK and the rest of Europe. In addition to the regular year-round services, there are also a large number of flights from Northern Ireland airports to popular holiday destinations during the summer months.

Belfast International Airport

Belfast
BT29 4AB
Tel: 028 9448 4848
Web: www.bial.co.uk
Email: info.desk@bial.co.uk

Belfast International Airport is also known as Aldergrove, and is the largest of the three airports in Northern Ireland. Situated near Templepatrick, 20 miles outside Belfast, it is one of the busiest airports in the United Kingdom, carrying over 3.7 million passengers annually. The airport operates 24 hours a day, 365 days per year as it is not subject to any noise restrictions. During 2003 Concorde paid a visit to Belfast International Airport during its final tour of the UK prior to being withdrawn from service. During his recent visit to Northern Ireland President Bush, with his Airforce One entourage also landed at Belfast International Airport.

Flights from Northern Ireland Airports

Belfast International Airport (Aldergrove)

Flights from Belfast International Airport

Destination	Carrier	Booking Line
Amsterdam	easyJet	0870 6000 000
Bristol	easyJet	0870 6000 000
Liverpool	easyJet	0870 6000 000
London Luton	easyJet	0870 6000 000
London Gatwick	easyJet	0870 6000 000
Newcastle	easyJet	0870 6000 000
Glasgow	easyJet	0870 6000 000
Edinburgh	easyJet	0870 6000 000
London Stansted	easyJet	0870 6000 000
Leeds Bradford	Jet2.com	0870 737 8282
Aberdeen	Eastern Airways	01652 680600
Birmingham	Mytravellite	08701 564564
Manchester	bmibaby	08702 642229
Cardiff	bmibaby	08702 642229
Teesside	bmibaby	08702 642229
East Midlands	bmibaby	08702 642229

Belfast City Airport (Sydenham)

Flights from Belfast City Airport

Destination	Carrier	Booking Line
Birmingham	flybe British European	08705 676676
Glasgow	flybe British European	08705 676676
Edinburgh	flybe British European	08705 676676
Bristol	flybe British European	08705 676676
London Gatwick	flybe British European	08705 676676
Leeds Bradford	flybe British European	08705 676676
London City	flybe British European	08705 676676
Newcastle	flybe British European	08705 676676
Southampton	flybe British European	08705 676676
Blackpool	Flykeen	0800 083 7783
Edinburgh	BA CitiExpress	08457 7333777
Glasgow	BA CitiExpress	08457 7333777
Manchester	BA CitiExpress	08457 7333777
London Heathrow	British Midland Airways Ltd	01332 854000

City of Derry Airport (Eglinton)

Flights from Derry City Airport

Destination	Carrier	Booking Line
London Stansted	ryanair	0871 276 0000
Glasgow	British Airways	0870 850 9850
Manchester	British Airways	0870 850 9850
Dublin	British Airways	0870 850 9850

Flight Information

Airlines currently operating from Belfast International Airport and the destinations to which they fly are as follows:

EasyJet
Amsterdam, Bristol, Liverpool, London Luton, London Gatwick, Newcastle, Glasgow, Edinburgh, London Stansted
To book: Online at www.easyJet.com
Booking line: 0870 6000 000

Note that Check-in for all easyJet flights closes 40 minutes prior to departure.

Jet2.com
Leeds Bradford
To book: Online at www.jet2.com
Booking line: 0870 737 8282

Eastern Airways
Aberdeen
To book: Online at www.easternairways.com
Booking line: 01652 680600

Mytravellite
Birmingham
To book: Online at www.mytravellite.com
Booking line: 08701 564 564

bmibaby

Manchester, Cardiff, Teeside, East Midlands
To book: Online at www.bmibaby.com
Booking line: 0870 264 2229

bmibaby

PO Box 737
Donington Hall
Castle Donnington
Derby DE74 2XP
Sales centre (UK Only):
0870 264 2229
www.bmibaby.com

bmibaby, the award winning airline with tiny fares, currently operates over one hundred flights per week between Belfast (International) airport and its four UK bases at Cardiff, East Midlands, Manchester and Teesside. Flights can be booked online at bmibaby.com from just £12.50 one way including taxes and charges.

Other passenger information

Access
Belfast International Airport is located around 20 miles outside Belfast, near the village of Templepatrick. It is served by the Airbus, which leaves every 30 minutes from Belfast's Great Victoria Street bus centre. Single ticket from Belfast to the Airport is £6.00, with a return costing £9.00. For more information on the Airbus service go to www.translink.co.uk or phone the information line on 028 9066 6630.

Parking
All Belfast International Airport car parks operate a 'pay-on-foot' system and payment machines are located in the exit hall of the terminal and in each of the car parks. Payment is accepted by cash or alternatively ticketless car parking is available through use of a credit card on entry to and exit from the car park.

The short term car park is located close to the terminal building and is ideal for short stays or pick-up. Additional days will be charged at £17 per day or part thereof.
The main car park offers the best value parking for up to 3 days so is suitable for short business trips or weekends.
Additional days will be charged at £6.00 per day or part thereof. The long stay car park is located within easy walking distance of the terminal building, and is regularly patrolled. Pre-booked car parking is available in the long stay car park for passengers parking for 7 days or more. To pre-book contact the booking centre on 0870 013 4747. Additional days will be charged at £3.00 per day or part thereof.

Belfast International Airport Car Parking Rates

Short Term Tariffs		Main Stay Tariffs	
15 mins	£0.50	Up to 1hr	£2.30
up to 30 mins	£1.70	Up to 2hrs	£3.20
30mins – 1hr	£2.70	Up to 1 day	£6.00
1-1.5hrs	£4.00	Up to 2 days	£12.00
1.5hrs – 2hrs	£5.00	Up to 3 days	£17.50
2 – 4hrs	£7.00	Up to 4 days	£23.50
4 – 6hrs	£9.00		
6 – 8hrs	£11.00		
8 – 12hrs	£14.50		
12 – 24hrs	£16.50		
24 – 48hrs	£27.50		

Long Stay Tariffs

Tariffs			
Up to 2hrs	£6.00	Up to 11 days	£33.00
Up to 7 days	£21.00	Up to 12 days	£36.00
Up to 8 days	£24.00	Up to 13 days	£39.00
Up to 9 days	£27.00	Up to 14 days	£42.00
Up to 10 days	£30.00		

Car parking at Belfast International Airport is also provided by:

Boal Car Park
Tel: 028 9445 3812

McCausland Car Park
Tel: 028 9442 2022

Cosmo Car Park
Tel: 028 9445 2565

Car Hire

Car hire from Belfast International Airport is available through:

Avis Rent A Car
Tel: 028 9442 2333

Hertz
Tel: 028 9442 2533

Budget
Tel: 028 9442 3332

National Car Rental
Tel: 0870 191 0605

Europcar
Tel: 028 9442 3444

Thrifty Car Rental
Tel: 028 9442 2777

In addition to passenger services, Belfast International Airport is the fifth largest regional air cargo centre in the UK. Aircraft handling agents at the airport include:

Aer Lingus
Tel: 028 9442 2735 / Fax: 028 6442 2493

BA World Cargo
Tel: 028 9442 2995 / Fax: 028 9445 2570

Servisair
Tel: 028 9442 2474 / Fax: 028 9442 2070

Reed Aviation
Tel: 028 9448 4929

Belfast City Airport

Belfast, BT3 9JH, Tel: 028 9093 9093
Web: www.belfastcityairport.com
Email: info@belfastcityairport.com

Belfast City Airport is located just three miles outside Belfast on the southern shore of Belfast Lough. The Airport is on the site of a former airfield used by Shorts Manufacturing Company. The Airport has recently undergone a major refurbishment and passenger traffic has grown rapidly as the airport serves more and more destinations. There are plans to further develop facilities at the airport to enable the accommodation of larger planes and more frequent flights, however, there is some local opposition to this, especially in relation to late-night flights.

Flight information

Airlines currently operating from Belfast City Airport and the destinations to which they fly are as follows:

flybe British European

Birmingham, Bristol, London Gatwick, Leeds Bradford, London City, Newcastle, Southampton, Glasgow, Edinburgh
To book: Online at www.flybe.com Tel: 08705 676 676

Flykeen: Blackpool
To book: Online at www.flykeen.com Tel: 0800 083 7783

BA CitiExpress: Edinburgh, Glasgow, Manchester
To book: Tel: 0845 77 333 777

British Midland Airways Ltd: London Heathrow
To book: Online at www.flybmi.com Tel: 01332 854000

Other passenger information

Access

Belfast City Airport is located just a couple of miles outside the city. It can be accessed by rail services to Sydenham from both Great Victoria Street and Central Stations. A shuttle bus service operates to bring passengers from the railway station to the terminal building.

It is also served by Belfast City Airlink, a bus service which leaves the airport terminal for Great Victoria Street Bus Station every 40 minutes, at a cost of £2.50 for a single journey. Number 21 Citybus operates every 20 minutes from Sydenham railway station (a 5 minute walk from the terminal building) to the City Hall in the city centre.

The Airporter service operates 6 coaches daily to Londonderry. For booking information contact 028 7136 9996.

Parking

Belfast City Airport Car Parking Rates

Short Stay Tariffs		Main Stay Tariffs	
First 15 mins	£0.50	First 15 mins	£0.50
Up to 30 mins	£1.70	Up to 2hrs	£3.00
30 mins – 1hr	£2.70	2 – 24hrs	£6.00
1 – 1.5hrs	£4.00	1 – 2 days	£12.00
1.5 – 2hrs	£5.00	2 – 3 days	£18.00
2 – 4hrs	£7.00	3 – 4 days	£24.00
4 – 8hrs	£11.00	4 – 5 days	£28.00
8 – 12hrs	£14.00	5 – 6 days	£30.00
12 – 24hrs	£16.00	6 – 7 days	£30.00
		£2.00 per day thereafter	

Car Hire

Car hire from Belfast City Airport is available through:

Avis Rent A Car
Tel: 028 9045 2017

Europcar
Tel: 028 9045 0904

Hertz
Tel: 028 9073 2451

Budget
Tel: 028 9045 1111

National Car Rental
Tel: 028 9073 9400

City of Derry Airport

Airport Road, Eglinton, BT47 3GY
Tel: 028 7181 0784
Web: www.cityofderryairport.com
Email: info@cityofderryairport.com

City of Derry Airport (formerly Eglinton Airport) has undergone significant development in recent years with passenger numbers increasing from 61,461 in 1997 to 204,390 in 2002.

Flight Information

Destinations served from City of Derry Airport are: London Stansted, Manchester, Glasgow, Dublin, Majorca, Lanzarote and Reus (Salou). Detailed timetable information can be accessed at www.cityofderryairport.com.
To book contact airlines directly as follows:

Ryanair

Flights to London Stansted and connecting flights to UK and Europe via Stansted and Dublin.

To book: Online at www.ryanair.com
Booking line: 0871 276 0000

British Airways

Direct flights to Glasgow, Manchester and Dublin with connecting flights via these airports.
To book: Online at www.britishairways.com
Booking line: 0870 850 9850

Other passenger information

Access

The airport is located 7 miles north-east of Derry City on the main A2 Derry to Coleraine road. A typical taxi fare to Derry City Centre from the airport is around £8.00. The airport is served by bus from Derry's Foyle Street bus station.

Derry City Airport Car Parking Rates

Short Stay Tariffs

First 15 mins	Free	1hr – 2hrs	£3.20
Up to 30 mins	£1.70	Over 2hrs	£6.00
30 mins – 1hr	£2.70		

Long Stay Tariffs

Up to 1 day	£6.00	Up to 10 days	£25.00
Up to 2 days	£12.00	Up to 11 days	£28.50
Up to 3 days	£17.50	Up to 12 days	£31.50
Up to 7 days	£19.00	Up to 13 days	£35.00
Up to 8 days	£21.00	Up to 14 days	£38.00
Up to 9 days	£23.00	Subsequent days	£3.50

Car Hire

Abe King: 028 9335 2557
Avis: 028 7181 1708
Europcar: 028 7181 2773
Ford: 028 7136 7137
Hertz: 028 7181 1994

By Sea

Seacat

Seacat Terminal
Donegall Quay
Belfast, BT1 3AL
Operations Manager:
John Burrows

From Belfast, Seacat operates services to both Troon and the Isle of Man. Both are fast craft services carrying cars and passengers but not freight.

For 2004 the Troon service is in operation from 12th March, with 2 services per day in the off-peak season (March-June and September-January) and three services per day in the peak summer season (July and August).

Belfast to the Isle of Man operates twice per week from March until September with a crossing time of 2 hours 45 minutes.

For detailed passenger information or reservations:
Tel: 08705 523 523
www.seacat.co.uk

Stenaline

Stenaline operates services on the Belfast to Stranraer route using both the Stena HSS, which makes the crossing in 1 hour 45 minutes and their Superferry on which the sailing takes 3 hours 15 minutes. Latest check in times for all services is 30 minutes before sailing.

For reservations:
Tel: 028 9074 7747

Ferry check:
Tel: 08705 755 755
www7.stenaline.co.uk

P&O Irish Sea

P&O operates services from Larne to Troon, Cairnryan and Fleetwood.

The Larne to Troon route operates from April to September with the crossing taking 109 minutes on the SuperStar Express ferry.

Larne to Cairnryan operates all year round. During the peak period (April to September) the crossing is 1 hour on the SuperStar Express ferry – at other times the route is serviced by a traditional ferry which takes 1 hour 45 minutes to make the crossing. Latest check-in time for all sailings is 45 minutes before departure for vehicles and 60 minutes for foot passengers.

P&O also operates a service between Larne and Fleetwood, but this is a 'no-frills' service with limited passenger facilities. The crossing takes 8 hours, with check-in 1 hour 30 minutes before sailing.

For detailed passenger information or reservations:
Tel: 0870 2424 777
Web: www.poirishsea.com

Norse Merchant Ferries

In addition to their freight services, Norse Merchant Ferries operates a passenger service between Belfast and Liverpool. There are 12 sailings weekly with the night cruiser service operating from Monday to Sunday and the day breaker service in operation Tuesday to Saturday. The crossing takes 8 hours and latest check in time for all sailings is 1 hour 30 minutes before sailing.

For detailed passenger information or reservations:
Tel: 0870 600 4321 www.norsemerchant.com

By Rail

To and from Dublin

The Enterprise is a direct rail service which runs from Belfast to Dublin 8 times daily (5 times on Sunday). The service departs from Central Station and stops at Portadown and Newry en route to Dublin. The journey takes around 2 hours. For further details on the Enterprise service and for other rail services see information on Translink and NI Railways included later in the chapter on page 18.

Lisburn Station

To and from Great Britain

NIR Travel operates a 'Rail and Sail' service to Great Britain using Stena Line to sail to Stranraer and Seacat to sail to Troon. Passengers make their own way to the port in Belfast, where they travel as a foot passenger on the boat, they then board a train in Scotland for onward travel to destinations throughout Great Britain or onwards to Europe if required. Full details of this service can be obtained from NIR Travel on 028 9024 2420.

By Bus

To and from Dublin

Ulsterbus Service 200 runs from Belfast's Europa Bus Centre to Busaras in Dublin. The service runs 8 times daily Monday – Saturday and 5 times on Sundays and the journey takes approximately 3 hours. For further details on bus services see information on Ulsterbus included later in the chapter.

To and from Great Britain

Ulsterbus Tours operate a service to Great Britain where passengers board their bus at Belfast's Europa Bus Centre, which takes them to the ferry port, where they board the ferry as a foot passenger. On disembarking, they then board a bus for onward travel to destinations throughout Great Britain or onwards to Europe if required. Full details of this service can be obtained from Ulsterbus Tours on 028 9033 7002/3.

Getting Around Northern Ireland

The Public Transport System

The provision of public transport services in Northern Ireland is overseen by the Northern Ireland Transport Holding Company (NITHCo). NITHCo is responsible to the Department for Regional Development for the operation of its subsidiary companies Citybus, Northern Ireland Railways and Ulsterbus. These companies are responsible for the delivery of public transport services. The role of NITHCo is to approve the strategic direction of the operating companies, which each retain their legal status but are marketed under the generic brand-name of Translink. The operations of Citybus, NI Railways and Ulsterbus are managed by a single integrated Executive Team. The following diagram highlights how responsibility for Northern Ireland's public transport system is divided.

Translink - Organisational Structure

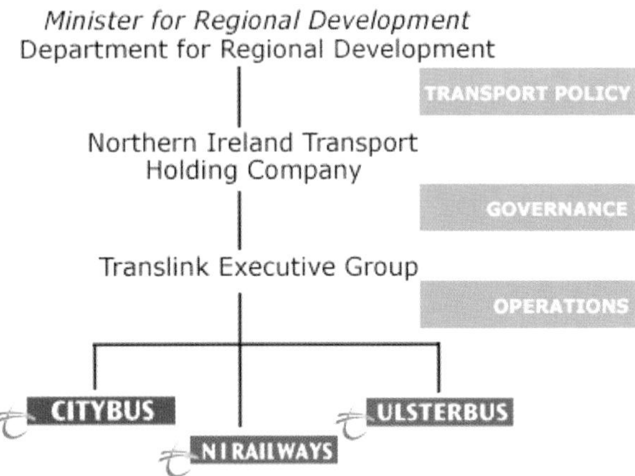

Translink

Translink currently employs approximately 3,500 employees and over 75 million passenger journeys are made on its services each year.

The company is split into 6 divisions:

Operations, Marketing and Human Resources
Central Station
East Bridge Street, Belfast, BT1 3PB
Tel: 028 9089 9400

Finance, Infrastructure and Property
Milewater Road,
Belfast, BT3 9BG
Tel: 028 9035 1201

Mechanical Engineering
York Road, Belfast

Belfast Central Station

Translink Management

Chief Executive: Keith Moffatt (pictured)
Director of Finance: Stephen Armstrong
Director of Operations: Philip O'Neill
Director of Human Resources: Alan Mercer
Head of Marketing: Ciaran Rogan
Infrastructure and Property Executive: Clive Bradberry
Mechanical Engineering Executive: Malachy McGreevy
Head of Projects: David Laird

Detailed passenger information for all Translink services can be obtained from the General Enquiries Line on 028 9066 6630. This is also available as a Textphone service on 028 9038 7505. Alternatively updated information is available online at www.translink.co.uk.

Citybus Services

Bus services within the Greater Belfast area are operated by Citybus. This includes approximately 60 routes in Belfast, serviced by a fleet of over 250 buses. Traditionally Citybuses have been red, but newer buses are being introduced which are green and red in colour. Citybus services depart and terminate in the city centre, but always display the route name and number of their outward journey (even on inward journeys to the city centre).

Bus Lanes

Citybus are gradually introducing a system of Quality Bus Corridors (QBCs) on main arterial routes into the city. With specially designated bus lanes and low floor buses these lead to faster journey times. Currently operating are QBCs from Newtownabbey (City Express) and from the Ormeau Road and Four Winds in the south of the city. These are the first of 15 routes to be introduced in Belfast.

Park and Ride

Park and ride facilities are currently available in East Belfast at Station Street, Bridge Street and Middlepath Street. The park and ride facility serving North Belfast is located at York Street.

Easibus

The Easibus network has been designed to meet local community needs by providing a service to health centres and clinics, local shops, housing for the elderly and a main shopping centre in the area. Easibus services do not follow normal Citybus practice of starting and finishing in the city centre, but instead serve local communities.

The Easibus service in Belfast currently serves the areas around the Connswater, Forestside and Abbey Centre retail areas. There are also Easibus services operating in Bangor and Derry.

For more information on the Easibus service contact a local Translink depot, the general Translink enquiry line on 028 9066 6630 or:

Belfast: Tel: 028 9073 1117
Bangor: Tel: 028 9127 1143 or 028 9147 0111
Derry: Tel: 028 7126 8688

Nightlink
8 Nightlink services provide a late night service from Belfast City Centre to various local towns. All services depart from Donegall Square West on Saturdays only at 0100 and 0200. The fare is £3.50 per person.

Nightlink serves the following destinations:

- Antrim
- Ballynahinch (0100) and Ballynahinch/Downpatrick (0200)
- Bangor
- Carrickfergus
- Comber/Ballygowan
- Lisburn
- Newtownabbey
- Newtownards

Centrelink
Belfast's main bus and rail stations, as well as principal shopping areas and the Waterfront Hall are linked by the Centrelink service (100), which is supported by the Department for Regional Development and Marks and Spencer. Rail and bus users with valid tickets can use the service for free, otherwise a Day Ticket can be purchased which allows passengers to get on and off the bus as often as required over the course of a single day. The service operates every 12 minutes at peak periods.

Citybus Ticketing

Smartlink
In 2003 Translink introduced a new system of ticketing using the Smartlink card. Smartlink is a plastic card which can be loaded with either a certain number of journeys in advance (the Smartlink Multi-Journey Card) or a week or month's worth of unlimited travel (the Smartlink Travel Card).

Smartlink Multi-Journey Card
This card can be loaded with a number of journeys from a minimum of 5 to 40 at any one time. The card holds a maximum of 50 journeys in total, which are valid for 3 months from date of purchase. The card offers a saving of 22% on standard single journey fares

Smartlink Travel Cards
These cards allow unlimited travel across the Citybus network for either 1 week or 1 month (discounted rates are available for children's travel cards). Weekly cards are valid for 7 consecutive days from date of first use (not purchase) and monthly cards are valid for a calendar month from date of first use.

Smartlink Multi-Journey and Travel Cards can be bought or topped up at ticket agents in the Greater Belfast area and at the Citybus kiosk in Donegall Square West.

Day Tickets
Day Tickets offer unlimited travel on all Citybus services including the extended zone. These are available from the driver onboard.

Citybus Contacts
Director of Operations: Philip O'Neill
Tel: 028 9089 9408

Central Area Operations Manager: Billy Gilpin
Tel: 028 9035 4061

Citybus Depots and District Managers
Falls: Damien Bannon Tel: 028 9030 1732

Newtownabbey: Gerry Mullan Tel: 028 9036 5355

Short Strand: Roy Sloan Tel: 028 9045 8345

Citybus Ticket and Information Kiosk:

Donegall Square West
Opening hours: Monday – Saturday 0800 – 1800
Closed Sunday

Translink Information Line

General Travel Enquiries: Open 0700 – 2200, 364 days per year
Tel: 028 9066 6630 / Textphone: 028 9038 7505

Private Hire Enquiries/Tours Enquiries/Credit Card Bookings:
Tel: 028 9045 8484

Lost Property Enquiries: Open 0900 – 1330
Tel: 028 9045 8345 Monday – Friday

Ulsterbus Services

Ulsterbus is responsible for virtually all bus services in Northern Ireland except those in the Greater Belfast area which are operated by Citybus. Ulsterbus currently has 21 main passenger facilities across Northern Ireland, employing 1,250 drivers and operating approximately 1,100 buses.

From Belfast, North and East bound Ulsterbus services depart from the Laganside Buscentre while those going to the South and West depart from the Europa Buscentre in Great Victoria Street.

The Goldline service is a high frequency express service to all main towns Northern Ireland wide. Goldline service 200 runs between Belfast (Europa Buscentre) and Dublin 8 times daily from Monday – Saturday and 5 times on Sundays with a journey time of approximately 3 hours.

Flexibus

Flexibus offers minibus and mini-coach hire (for up to 25 people) in the greater Belfast area and throughout Northern Ireland, and also carries out contract work for schools, churches and industry. Flexibus has a fleet of over 40 vehicles including a replica of a 1930s Charabanc.

For further information or a quotation contact Flexibus:
Tel: 028 9023 3933
Fax: 028 9031 5991

Ulsterbus Ticketing

Return tickets
Offer a saving over the cost of two single tickets.

Ten Journey Tickets
Valid for 10 journeys in either direction between specific points for one month from date of purchase.

40 Journey Commuter Tickets

Valid for 40 single journeys within 3 months from date of purchase. Two or more people can travel together on the same ticket providing the ticket holder travels the further distance. These tickets are transferable so can be passed on to someone else to make the same journey on Ulsterbus.

Monthly Tickets

Valid for unlimited travel between designated points one month from date of purchase.

Sunday Rambler Tickets

Unlimited travel on all scheduled Ulsterbus services within Northern Ireland on Sundays.

Ulsterbus Contacts

General Travel Enquiries:
Open 0700 – 2200, 364 days per year
Tel: 028 9066 6630 / Textphone: 028 9038 7505

Ulsterbus Coach Hire: Contact local bus depot or
Tel: 028 9033 7006

Ulsterbus Tours Travel Centre
Europa Bus Centre, Glengall Street, Belfast
BT12 5AH / Tel: 028 9033 7004

Lost Property Enquiries: Tel: 028 9033 7000

Main Ulsterbus Stations

Belfast Europa Buscentre:	028 9032 0011
Belfast Laganside Buscentre:	028 9032 0011
Antrim:	028 9442 8729
Armagh:	028 3752 2266
Ballyclare:	028 9335 2311
Ballymena:	028 2565 2214
Banbridge:	028 4062 3633
Bangor:	028 9127 1143
Coleraine:	028 7032 5400
Cookstown:	028 8676 6440
Craigavon:	028 3834 2511
Derry City:	028 7126 2261
Downpatrick:	028 4461 2384
Dungannon:	028 8772 2251
Enniskillen:	028 6632 2633
Larne:	028 2827 2345
Limavady:	028 7776 2101
Lisburn:	028 9266 2091
Londonderry County:	028 7126 2261
Magherafelt:	028 7963 2218
Newcastle:	028 4372 2296
Newry:	028 3026 3531
Newtownabbey:	028 9036 5355
Newtownards:	028 9181 2391
Omagh:	028 8224 2711
Strabane:	028 7138 2393

Northern Ireland Railways Services

The present railway system in Northern Ireland comprises approximately 210 route miles, including the Belfast/Dublin main line, a line to Coleraine and Londonderry, with a branch line from Coleraine to Portrush, and suburban routes from Belfast to Portadown, Bangor and Larne. The Antrim/Bleach Green line was re-opened in 2001 as part of a £16.2 million project which is planned to eventually include new stations at Mossley West and Templepatrick. NI Railways currently employs around 700 staff.

NI Railways trains are a mixture of two types of diesel train dating from the 1970s and 1980s but procurement is currently underway to replace 23 train sets to replace the oldest existing trains. This project is expected to be completed by October 2005.

In addition to its passenger services, NI Railways also operate both a parcel and freight service.

Carrickfergus Station

Stations

NI Railways have in recent years undertaken a major building and refurbishment programme to upgrade and replace many of its main stations. Belfast's new Central Station was officially opened by the Minister for Regional Development in March 2003 and includes an extended park and ride scheme as well as a new traffic management system. Major projects have also been completed at Bangor, Coleraine and Carrickfergus

Enterprise Service

The Enterprise is the flagship Belfast to Dublin service which is jointly operated by Iarnród Eireann and NI Railways. 8 services operate in each direction Monday to Saturday and 5 services run in each direction on Sundays. Passengers in possession of a valid Enterprise ticket are entitled to free onward travel on the Centrelink service in Belfast and via the Dart between Connolly Station and Tara Street in Dublin.

The executive 1st Plus service on the Enterprise allows passengers to reserve a seat in advance at no extra cost. 1st Plus passengers can also avail of half price secure parking at Belfast Central Station on presentation of a 1st Plus ticket.

Ticket and Seat Reservations:

Belfast
Tel: 028 9089 9409

Dublin
Tel: 01 703 4070

NIR Travel

NIR Travel provides short break holidays by rail with hotel breaks available in both Dublin and Scotland.

For more information contact: 028 9024 2420

NI Railways Ticketing

Single
Valid on day of issue only, between two stations.

Day Return
Valid on day of issue only, with return journey on the same day.

Monthly Return
Outward journey is valid on day of issue only, return journey is valid up to one month from the date shown on the ticket.

7 Day Weekly Ticket
Seven days' unlimited travel between any two designated stations, valid from Monday to Sunday.

Monthly Moneysavers
Unlimited travel between any two designated stations for a full calendar month plus unrestricted travel over the entire NI Railways network at weekends.

Contract Tickets
Books of 40 single tickets may be purchased for some journeys in Northern Ireland. For details contact Translink's general enquiries line on 028 9066 6630.

Sunday Day Tracker
Unlimited travel on all scheduled train services within Northern Ireland.

Group Travel
Discount of up to 15% for parties of 10 or more passengers on all services. Further details are available from NIR Travel on 028 9024 2420.

Cross Border Rail Tickets

Single
Available for Enterprise Class and 1st Plus travel.

Day Return
Available Monday to Thursday and on Saturday for Enterprise Class only.

Family Day Return
Available for Enterprise Class only and valid for two adults and up to four children.

One Month Return
Available for 1st Plus and Enterprise Class travel. Return journey is valid for up to one month from date shown on ticket.

Family One Month Return
Available for Enterprise Class travel only and valid for two adults and up to four children.

Cross Border Contract Tickets
Books of 20 single journey tickets are available between Belfast/Dublin and Portadown/Dublin. Contact NIR Travel on 028 9024 2420 for further information.

7 Day Weekly Ticket
7 days' unlimited travel between Portadown or Newry to selected cross border stations (valid Monday – Sunday).

NI Railways Contacts
General Travel Enquiries: Open 0700 – 2200,
364 days per year
Tel: 028 9066 6630
Textphone: 028 9038 7505

Lost Property Enquiries:
Tel: 028 9074 1700

Credit/debit card sales
and reservations:
Tel: 028 9089 9409
NI Railways Managers

Rail Services Manager: Seamus Scallon
Stations Manager, Central Station: Hilton Parr
Enterprise Manager: Ken McKnight
Each of the above managers can be contacted at Central Station, Belfast on 028 9089 9400.

Main Northern Ireland Railway Stations

Belfast	
Botanic	028 9089 9400
Central	028 9089 9400
Great Victoria Street	028 9043 4424
Yorkgate	028 9074 1700
Antrim	028 9442 9185
Ballymena	028 2565 2277
Ballymoney	028 7036 3241
Bangor	028 9127 1143
Carrickfergus	028 9335 1286
Coleraine	028 7032 5400
Larne	028 2826 0604
Lisburn	028 9266 2294
Londonderry	028 7134 2228
Lurgan	028 3832 2052
Newry	028 3026 2971
Portadown	028 3835 1422
Portrush	028 7082 2395

Other fare information – bus and rail

Concession Fares

Senior Citizens
Senior citizens (65 years and over) can avail of free travel on bus and rail services throughout Northern Ireland provided they are in possession of a valid Smart Pass.

Blind Persons
Blind Persons are entitled to free travel on all scheduled local and cross-border bus and train services on presentation of a Blind Persons Concession Pass.

Students
Concessions are available on certain tickets to students on presentation of a valid Translink Student Discount Card.

Young People/Children
A 50% reduction is available on all local, cross border and cross channel fares to young persons aged 5-16. Between the ages of 16 and 21 concession fares are available on rail season tickets only.

Jobseekers/Gateway
Reduced bus and rail fares are available to any person who is unemployed and seeking active employment, or any person on the Gateway period of a New Deal Initiative on presentation of an authenticated permit and JS40.

Integrated Bus & Rail Tickets

Freedom of Northern Ireland Tickets
1 day, 3 out of 8 day and 7 day Freedom of Northern Ireland Tickets can be purchased from all main bus and rail stations, offering unlimited travel on all bus and rail services throughout Northern Ireland.

Pupil Tickets
Pupil tickets are available for return travel from home to school. Application forms are available at main bus and rail stations or from:

Pupil Ticket Office, Translink
Milewater Road, Belfast, BT3 9BG Tel: 028 9035 4074

Bangor Station

Translink Commuter Travelcards
Commuter Travelcards are valid for 1 year and offer at least 15% discount compared with the purchase of monthly tickets. They provide unlimited travel between two chosen points (by one mode or a combination of modes of travel) and also provide freedom of Northern Ireland network at weekends.

Bangor Ticketline Tickets
A pilot integrated ticketing scheme operates in the Bangor area. Tickets allow travel on either train or bus between any central zone station and Bangor and outer surrounding areas.

Airport Connections

For detailed passenger information on all airport services call Translink's General Enquiries line on 028 9066 6630 or access online at www.translink.co.uk

Belfast International Airport
The Airbus service No 300 operates between Europa Buscentre and Belfast International Airport. The service operates every 30 minutes from 0630 to 2230 Monday to Saturday and approximately every hour from 0615 to 2130 on Sundays.

Antrim Airlink
The Antrim Airlink service No 309 operates between Antrim bus and rail stations and Belfast International Airport.

Belfast City Airport
Belfast City Airlink service No 600 departs from Europa Buscentre to Belfast City Airport serving Sydenham station. Trains operate to Sydenham station from both Great Victoria Street and Central Stations, and these services connect with the Airlink at Sydenham station.

City of Derry Airport
Ulsterbus Service No 143 from Derry's Foyle Street Bus Station and Service No 234 from Coleraine operate to the City of Derry Airport.

Dublin Airport
Ulsterbus Goldline Service No 200 operates between Europa Buscentre and Dublin Airport. Enterprise train services to Dublin Connolly leave from Central Station.

Car Hire and Taxi Services

Car hire is a popular way of exploring Northern Ireland, especially the more remote rural areas which are not well served by public transport. Cars can be hired from various locations throughout Northern Ireland. Details of car hire firms operating from the 3 airports are detailed earlier in this chapter. (*Other companies across Northern Ireland offering car hire are listed on page 544*).

Driving Information

General rules of the road are the same as in Great Britain, ie drive on the left; overtake on the right. Speed limits are 30 miles per hour in built up areas, 60mph on single carriageways and 70 mph on motorways and dual carriageways. Seatbelts are compulsory for drivers and all passengers; motorcyclists must wear crash helmets. Parking is available on-street or in car parks.

Taxis

Taxis are relatively inexpensive in Northern Ireland. Public taxis, often black 'London' Hackney cabs, can pick up in the street or from taxi ranks. Alternatively, there are many private taxi firms, many of which have waiting rooms. In some buildings (such as airports, shopping centres) there will be a freephone available which automatically connects to a local taxi firm.

Car Hire Companies

A2B Autos
187 Corkey Road, Ballymena, BT44 9JB
Tel: 028 2764 1064

Annagh Motors Car Hire
51 Church Street, Banbridge, BT32 4AA
Tel: 028 4066 2495

Avis Rent a Car
69-71 Great Victoria Street
Belfast, BT2 7AF
Tel: 028 9024 0404

Ballyclare Car Hire
53 Park Street, Ballyclare, BT39 9DQ
Tel: 028 9335 2557

Ballykelly Car & Van Hire
22 Ballykelly Road
Banbridge, BT32 4PS
Tel: 028 4062 4966

Ballymena Car Hire
205 Cullybackey Road
Ballymena, BT43 5JH
Tel: 028 2563 0077

Beatties Car Hire
Quarter Road, Camlough
Bessbrook, BT35 7EY
Tel: 028 3083 9535

Brown & Day
Hilltop Garage, 4 Main Street
Claudy, BT47 4HR
Tel: 028 7133 8102

Budget Rent a Car
Unit 1, 96-102 Great Victoria Street
Belfast, BT2 7BE
Tel: 028 9023 0700

Burnside Vehicle Rentals
Unit 3 Ivan Wilson Complex
277 Dunhill Road
Coleraine, BT51 3QJ
Tel: 0870 444 1471

Carriageway Cars
92 Bloomfield Road, Belfast, BT5 5LU
Tel: 028 9065 2000

Carrick Self Drive
77A Irish Quarter West
Carrickfergus, BT38 8BW
Tel: 028 9335 1113

Charles Hurst Ltd
62 Boucher Road
Belfast BT12 6LR
Tel: 028 9038 3539

Comber Commercial Centre
3C Killinchy Street
Comber, BT23 5AP
Tel: 028 9187 3245

Corrigans Car Hire
72 Old Caulfield Road
Dungannon, BT70 3NG
Tel: 028 8776 1482

Dan Dooley Rent a Car
175B Airport Road, Aldergrove
Crumlin, BT29 4D
Tel: 028 9445 2522

Desmond Motors Ltd
173 Strand Road
Londonderry, BT48 7PN
Tel: 028 7136 7137

Direct Self Drive
57A Kilkeel Road,
Annalong, BT34 4TJ
Tel: 028 4376 8190

Enterprise Rent a Car
Unit 3 Building 10, Mallusk Industrial Estate
Newtownabbey, BT36 4GN
Tel: 028 9084 3749

Europcar
159-161 University Street
Belfast, BT7 1HR
Tel: 028 9031 3500

Gallen Vehicle Hire
96 Drumlegagh Road South
Omagh, BT78 4TW
Tel: 028 8224 6966

Garryduff Car, Van & Minibus Hire
97C Garryduff Road
Ballymoney, BT53 7DH
Tel: 028 2766 7170

Holmes Motors
2-20 Beersbridge Road
Belfast, BT5 4RU
Tel: 028 9045 1850

Independent Car Hire
37 Comber Road
Belfast, BT16 2AA
Tel: 028 9048 2664

Kingdom Car Hire
14 Coolmillish Road
Markethill, BT60 1QA
Tel: 028 3755 1169

Kings Self Drive
96 Oldstone Road
Muckamore, Antrim, BT41 4SP
Tel: 028 9446 6645

Lagan Car & Van Hire
242A Keady Road,
Armagh, BT60 3EW
Tel: 028 3753 1723

Lakeside Self Drive Car Hire Ltd
Ballybrack Road, Sixmilecross
Carrickmore, BT79 9LU
Tel: 028 8076 1060

Lindsay Ford Rental
391 Upper Newtownards Road, Belfast
Tel: 028 9065 4687

Lochside Garages Ltd
Tempo Road
Enniskillen, BT74 6HR
Tel: 028 6632 4366

Low Cost Car & Van Hire
12 Church Street
Bangor, BT20 3HT
Tel: 028 9127 1535

McCausland Car Park
21-31 Grosvenor Road
Belfast, BT12 4GN
Tel: 028 9033 3777

MPC Vehicle Rentals
2 Monaghan Road
Armagh, BT60 4DA
Tel: 028 3752 3775

National Car Rental
90-92 Grosvenor Road
Belfast, BT12 4GN
Tel: 028 9032 5520

National-Alamo
277 Dunhill Road
Coleraine, BT51 3QJ
Tel: 0870 191 0613

Nova Rent a Car Reservations Ltd
1 Castle Street
Portaferry, BT22 1NZ
Tel: 028 4272 8189

SJS Vehicle Hire
Loves Hill
Castledawson, BT45 8DP
Tel: 028 7946 9889

Saville's Vauxhall Rental
70 Belfast Road
Lisburn, BT27 4AU
Tel: 028 9266 3622

Tourism Information for Visitors

Tourism Organisations

Northern Ireland Tourist Board (NITB)
St Anne's Court, 59 North Street, Belfast, BT1 1NB
Tel: 028 9023 1221/Fax: 028 9023 0960
Corporate Website: www.nitb.com
Visitor Information: www.discovernorthernireland.com

16 Nassau Street, Dublin 2
Tel: +353 (0) 1 679 1977/Fax: +353 (0) 1 679 1863

The Northern Ireland Tourist Board is responsible for implementing strategy for the development, promotion and marketing of Northern Ireland as a tourist destination. Detailed visitor information, including places to stay and things to see and do can be accessed on their visitor website www.discovernorthernireland.com.

Tourism Ireland Limited (TIL)
Beresford House,2 Beresford Road, Coleraine, BT52 1GE
Tel: 028 7035 9200/Fax: 028 7032 6932
Web: www.tourismireland.com

TIL was established as one of the six 'areas of co-operation' under the Belfast Agreement. With offices in Coleraine and Dublin, it is responsible for marketing the entire island of Ireland overseas as a tourist destination.

Sperrins Tourism Limited
30 High Street
Moneymore, BT45 7PB
Tel: 028 8674 7700
Web: www.sperrinstourism.com
Email: info@sperrinstourism.com

Regional Tourism Organisations (RTOs)

Northern Ireland's RTOs are responsible primarily for co-ordinating and implementing marketing activity on behalf of and with private sector and local authority members, as well as advising local businesses on tourism opportunities. Together they represent over 1700 private sector businesses and 11 local authorities across Northern Ireland. They are public/private membership companies limited by guarantee.

Belfast Visitor and Convention Bureau
47 Donegall Place
Belfast, BT1 5AD
Tel: 028 9023 9026
Web: www.gotobelfast.com
Email: info@belfastvisitor.com

Causeway Coast & Glens
11 Lodge Road
Coleraine BT52 1LU
Tel: 028 7032 7720
Web: www.causewaycoastandglens.com
Email: mail@causewaycoastandglens.com

Kingdoms of Down
40 West Street
Newtownards, BT23 4EN
Tel: 028 9182 2881
Web: www.kingdomsofdown.com
Email: info@kingdomsofdown.com

Derry Visitor & Convention Bureau
44 Foyle Street
Londonderry, BT48 6AT
Tel: 028 7137 7577
Web: www.derryvisitor.com
Email: info@derryvisitor.com

Fermanagh Lakeland Tourism
Wellington Road
Enniskillen, BT74 7EF
Tel: 028 6634 6736
Web: www.fermanaghlakelands.com
Email: info@fermanaghlakelands.com

Fermanagh Tourist Information Centre

Tourist Information Centres

Antrim
16 High Street, Antrim, BT41 4AN
Tel: 028 9442 8331
Fax: 028 9448 7844

Armagh
Old Bank Building, 40 English Street
Armagh, BT61 7BA
Tel: 028 3752 1800
Fax: 028 3752 8329

Ballycastle
Sheskburn House
7 Mary Street, BT54 6QH
Tel: 028 2076 2024
Fax: 028 2076 2515

Ballymena
76 Church Street, Ballymena, BT43 6DF
Tel: 028 2563 8494
Fax: 028 2563 8495

Banbridge
200 Newry Road, Banbridge, BT32 3NB
Tel: 028 4062 3322
Fax: 028 4062 3114

Bangor
34 Quay Street
Bangor, BT20 5ED
Tel: 028 9127 0069
Fax: 028 9127 4466

Belfast Welcome Centre
34 Donegall Place
Belfast, BT1 5AD
Tel: 028 9024 6609
Fax: 028 9031 2424

Belfast City Airport
Sydenham Bypass
Belfast, BT3 9JH
Tel: 028 9045 7745

Carrickfergus
Heritage Plaza
Antrim Street
Carrickfergus, BT38 7DJ
Tel: 028 9336 6455
Fax: 028 9335 0350

Coleraine
Railway Road
Coleraine, BT52 1PE
Tel: 028 7034 4723
Fax: 028 7035 1756

Cookstown
The Burnavon
Burn Road, Cookstown, BT80 8DN
Tel: 028 8676 6727
Fax: 028 8676 5853

Downpatrick
St Patrick 's Centre, 53A Market Street
Downpatrick, BT30 6LZ
Tel: 028 4461 2233
Fax: 028 4461 2350

Fermanagh
Wellington Road
Enniskillen, BT74 7EF
Tel: 028 6632 3110
Fax: 028 6632 5511

Giant's Causeway
44 Causeway Road
Bushmills, BT57 8SU
Tel: 028 2073 1855
Fax: 028 2073 2537

Hillsborough
The Courthouse, The Square
Hillsborough, BT26 6AG
Tel: 028 9268 9717
Fax: 028 9268 9773

Kilkeel
28 Bridge Street
Kilkeel, BT34 4AF
Tel: 028 4176 2525
Fax: 028 4176 9947

Killymaddy
Ballygawley Road
Dungannon, BT70 1TF
Tel: 028 8776 7259
Fax: 028 8776 7911

Larne
Narrow Gauge Road
Larne, BT40 1XB
Tel: 028 2826 0088
Fax: 028 2826 0088

Limavady
Council Offices
7 Connell Street, BT49 0HA
Tel: 028 7776 0307
Fax: 028 7772 2010

Lisburn
16 Lisburn Square
Lisburn, BT28 1AG
Tel: 028 9266 0038
Fax: 028 9260 7889

Londonderry
44 Foyle Street
Londonderry, BT48 6AT
Tel: 028 7126 7284
Fax: 028 7137 7992

Magherafelt
Bridewell Centre
6 Church Street
Magherafelt, BT46 5EA
Tel: 028 7963 1510

Newcastle
Newcastle Centre
10-14 Central Promenade
Newcastle, BT33 0AA
Tel: 028 4372 2222
Fax: 028 4372 2400

Newry
Town Hall
Newry, BT35 6HR
Tel: 028 3026 8877
Fax: 028 3026 8833

Newtownards
31 Regent Street
Newtownards, BT23 4AD
Tel: 028 9182 6846
Fax: 028 9182 6681

Omagh
1 Market Street
Omagh, BT78 1EE
Tel: 028 8224 7831
Fax: 028 8224 0774

Portaferry (seasonal)
The Stables
Castle Street
Portaferry, BT22 1NZ
Tel: 028 4272 9882
Fax: 028 4272 9822

Portrush (seasonal)
Dunluce Centre
Sandhill Drive
Portrush
BT56 8BF
Tel: 028 7082 3333
Fax: 028 7082 2256

Strabane
Abercorn Square
Strabane
BT82 8AE
Tel: 028 7188 3735
Fax: 028 7138 1348

Where to Stay in Northern Ireland

Hotels

Until relatively recently Northern Ireland has been undersupplied with quality hotel accommodation. In fact, on some occasions when there has been a major international event in the region, hotel accommodation has been insufficient to meet demand. However, over the last few years hoteliers, supported by government tourism policy and the Northern Ireland Tourist Board, have invested heavily in new and improved accommodation. Five years ago Northern Ireland did not have a single 5-star hotel; now it has two. Most of the leading hotels now have well-equipped leisure centres. A number of the big international hotel chains have recently established a presence, including Hilton, Radisson, Ramada and Holiday Inn.

The following is a list of hotels arranged first by county (beginning with those in Belfast), and then in alphabetical order. Where a rating is available, the hotels have been rated according to the Northern Ireland Tourist Board's 'star' system. A description of each category in the system follows below.

(See Chapter 12 for details of places to eat and drink in Northern Ireland).

NITB Star System

Five Star *****
Hotels of an international standard with luxurious and spacious guest accommodation including suites. High quality restaurants with table d'hôte and à la carte and dinner menus.

Four Star ****
Large hotels with a high standard of comfort and service in well appointed premises. All bedrooms ensuite. Cuisine meets exacting standards. Comprehensive room service.

Three Star ***
Good facilities with a wide range of services. All bedrooms ensuite. Food available all day.

Two Star **
Good facilities with a reasonable standard of accommodation, food and services. Most bedrooms are ensuite.

One Star *
Hotels with acceptable standards of accommodation and food. Some bedrooms have ensuite facilities.

Belfast

Balmoral Hotel **
Black's Road, Dunmurry
Belfast, BT10 0NF
Tel: 028 9030 1234
Fax: 028 9060 1455
Web: www.balmoralhotelbelfast.co.uk
43 Rooms

Beechlawn House Hotel ***
4 Dunmurry Lane
Belfast, BT17 9RR
Tel: 028 9060 2010
Fax: 028 9060 2080
Web: www.beechlawnhotel.co.uk
42 Rooms

Belfast City Travelodge**
15 Brunswick Street,
Belfast BT2 7GE
Tel: 028 9033 3555
Fax: 028 9023 2999
Website: www.travelodge.co.uk
Rooms: 90

Benedicts of Belfast ***
7-21 Bradbury Place
Belfast, BT7 1RQ
Tel: 028 9059 1999
Fax: 028 9059 1990
32 Rooms

The Crescent Townhouse**
13 Lower Crescent
Belfast, BT7 1NR
Tel: 028 9032 3349
Fax: 028 9032 0646
Email: info@crescenttownhouse.com
Web: www.belfastpubs-n-clubs.com
11 Rooms

Culloden Hotel *****

Bangor Road
Holywood, BT18 0EX
Tel: 028 9042 1066
Fax: 028 9042 6777
Web: www.hastingshotels.com
79 Rooms

Days Hotel
40 Hope Street
Belfast, BT12 5EE
Tel: 028 9024 2494
Fax: 028 9024 2495
Web: www.dayshotelbelfast.com
244 Rooms

Dukes Hotel ***
65-67 University Street
Belfast, BT7 1HL
Tel: 028 9023 6666
Fax: 028 9023 7177
Web: www.dukes-hotel.com
20 Rooms

Europa Hotel ****
Great Victoria Street
Belfast, BT2 7AP
Tel: 028 9027 1066
Fax: 028 9032 7800
Web: www.hastingshotels.com
240 Rooms

Express Holiday Inn ***
106 University Street
Belfast, BT7 1HP
Tel: 028 9031 1909
Fax: 028 9031 1910
Web: www.holidayinn-ireland.com
114 Rooms

Hilton Belfast *****
4 Lanyon Place
Belfast
BT1 3LP
Tel: 028 9027 7000
Fax: 028 9027 7277
Web: www.hilton.co.uk
195 Rooms

Holiday Inn Belfast ****
22-26 Ormeau Avenue
Belfast
BT2 8HS
Tel: 028 9027 1706
Fax: 028 9062 6546
Web: www.belfast.holiday-inn.com
170 Rooms

Ivanhoe Inn and Hotel
556 Saintfield Road
Belfast
BT8 8EU
Tel: 028 9081 2240
Fax: 028 9081 5516
Web: www.ivanhoeinn.co.uk
21 Rooms

Jurys Belfast Inn ***

Fisherwick Place
Great Victoria Street
Belfast, BT2 7AP
Tel: +44 (0) 28 9053 3500
Fax: +44 (0) 28 9053 3511
Email: jurysinnbelfast@jurysdoyle.com
Web: www.jurysdoyle.com

In the heart of Belfast, within walking distance of the best restaurants and bars; 190 rooms accommodating 3 adults or 2 adults and 2 children; Arches Restaurant serves breakfast and dinner; The Inn Pub serves snacks; Six meeting rooms are available for seminars, training or meetings.

Lansdowne Hotel ***
857 Antrim Road
Belfast, BT15 4EF
Tel: 028 9077 3317
Fax: 028 9023 7177
Web: www.landsdownehotelbelfast.com
25 Rooms

Malone Lodge Hotel ****
60 Eglantine Avenue
Belfast, BT9 6DY
Tel: 028 9038 8000
Fax: 028 9038 8088
E-mail: info@malonelodgehotel.com
Website: www.malonelodgehotel.com
50 Rooms

McCausland Hotel ****
34-38 Victoria Street
Belfast
BT1 3GH
Tel: 028 9022 0200
Fax: 028 9022 0220
E-mail: info@mccauslandhotel.com
Website: www.mccauslandhotel.com
61 Rooms

Park Avenue Hotel ***

158 Holywood Road
Belfast, BT4 1PB
Tel: 028 9065 6520
Fax: 028 9047 1417
Web: www.parkavenuehotel.co.uk
55 Rooms

Ramada Hotel ****
177 Milltown Road
Shaws Bridge
Belfast, BT8 7XP
Tel: 028 9092 3500
Fax: 028 9092 3600
Web: www.ramadabelfast.com
120 Rooms

Stormont Hotel ****
587 Upper Newtownards Road
Belfast, BT4 3LP
Tel: 028 9065 1066
Fax: 028 9048 0240
Web: www.hastingshotels.com
109 Rooms

TENsq Boutique Hotel ****
10 Donegall Square South,
Belfast, BT1 5JD
Tel: 028 9024 1001
Fax: 028 9024 3210
Web: www.tensquare.co.uk
Rooms: 23

Wellington Park Hotel ****
21 Malone Road
Belfast, BT9 6RU
Tel: 028 9038 5050
Fax: 028 9038 5410
Web: www.mooneyhotelgroup.com
75 Rooms

Co Antrim

Adair Arms Hotel ***
Ballymoney Road
Ballymena, BT43 5BF
Tel: 028 2565 3674
Fax: 028 2564 0436
Web: www.adairarms.com
44 Rooms

Ballygally Castle Hotel ***
274 Coast Road
Ballygally
BT40 2QZ
Tel: 028 2858 1066
Fax: 028 2858 368
Web: www.hastingshotels.com
44 Rooms

Bushmills Inn ***
9 Dunluce Road
Bushmills, BT57 8QB
Tel: 028 2073 2339
Fax: 028 2073 2048
Web: www.bushmillsinn.com
32 Rooms

Chimney Corner Hotel **
630 Antrim Road
Newtownabbey, BT36 8RH
Tel: 028 9084 4925
Fax: 028 9084 4352
Web: www.chimneycorner.co.uk
63 Rooms

Comfort Hotel ***
73 Main Street
Portrush, BT56 8BN
Tel: 028 7082 6100
Fax: 028 7082 6160
Web: www.comforthotelportrush.com
50 Rooms

Corr's Corner **
315 Ballyclare Road
Newtownabbey
BT36 4TQ
Tel: 028 9084 9221
Fax: 028 9083 2118
Web: www.corrscorner.co.uk
Email: info@corrscorner.co.uk
30 Rooms

Dobbins Inn Hotel **
6-8 High Street
Carrickfergus
BT38 7AF
Tel: 028 9335 1905
Fax: 028 9335 1905
Web: www.dobbinsinnhotel.co.uk
Email: info@dobbinsinnhotel.co.uk
15 Rooms

Dunadry Hotel & Country Club ****
2 Islandreagh Drive, Dunadry
BT41 2HA
Tel: 028 9443 4343
Fax: 028 9443 3389
Email: reservations@mooneyhotelgroup.com
Web: www.mooneyhotelgroup.com
83 Rooms

Fitzwilliam International ****
Belfast International Airport
BT29 4ZY
Tel: 028 9445 7000
Fax: 028 9442 3500
Web: www.fitzwilliaminternational.com
106 Rooms

Galgorm Manor ****
136 Fenaghy Road
Cullybackey
Ballymena
BT42 1EA
Tel: 028 2588 1001
Fax: 028 2588 0080
Web: www.galgorm.com
25Rooms

Glenavna House Hotel ***
588 Shore Road
Newtownabbey
BT36 6ET
Tel: 028 9086 4461
Fax: 028 9086 2531
Web: www.glenavna.com
32 Rooms

The Golf Links Hotel (Kelly's)
Bushmills Road, Portrush
BT56 8JQ
Tel: 028 7082 3539
Fax: 028 7082 5140
Web: www.kellysportrush.co.uk

Hilton Templepatrick ****
Castle Upton Estate
Templepatrick
BT39 0DD
Tel: 028 9443 5500
Fax: 028 9443 5511
Web: www.hilton.co.uk
Rooms: 130

Leighinmohr House Hotel ***
Leighinmohr Avenue
Ballymena
BT42 2AN
Tel: 028 2565 2313
Fax: 028 2565 6669
20 Rooms

Londonderry Arms Hotel ***
24 Harbour Road
Carnlough
BT44 0EU
Tel: 028 2888 5255
Fax: 028 2885 5263
Web: www.glensofantrim.com
35 Rooms

Magherabuoy House Hotel ***
41 Magheraboy Road
Portrush
BT56 8NX
Tel: 028 7082 3507
Fax: 028 7082 4687
Web: www.magherabuoy.co.uk
38 Rooms

Marine Hotel ***
1 North Street
Ballycastle
BT54 6BN
Tel: 028 2076 222
Fax: 028 2076 9507
Web: www.marinehotel.net
32 Rooms

Peninsula Hotel **
15 Eglinton Street
Portrush
BT56 8DX
Tel: 028 7082 2293
Fax: 028 7082 4315
Web: www.peninsulahotel.co.uk
24 Rooms

The Port Hotel
53-57 Main Street
Portrush
BT56 8BN
Tel: 028 7082 5353
Fax: 028 7082 4862

Quality Hotel ***
75 Belfast Road
Carrickfergus
BT38 8PH
Tel: 028 9336 4556
Fax: 028 9335 1620
Web: www.choicehotels.com
68 Rooms

Rosspark Hotel ***
20 Doagh Road
Kells
Ballymena
BT42 3LZ
Tel: 028 2589 1663
Fax: 028 2589 1477
Web: www.rossparkhotel.com
39 Rooms

Royal Court Hotel ***
233 Ballybogey Road
Portrush
BT56 8NF
Tel: 028 7082 2236
Fax: 028 7082 3176
Web: www.royalcourthotel.co.uk
18 Rooms

The Smugglers Inn
306 Whitepark Road
Bushmills
BT57 8SN
Tel: 028 2073 1577
Fax: 028 2073 1072
Web: www.smugglers-inn.co.uk
12 Rooms

Templeton Hotel ***
882 Antrim Road
Templepatrick
BT39 0AH
Tel: 028 9443 2984
Fax: 028 9443 3406
24 Rooms

Tullyglass Hotel ***
Galgorm Road
Ballymena
BT42 1HJ
Tel: 028 2565 2639
Fax: 028 2564 6938
Web: www.tullyglass.com
35 Rooms

Co Armagh

Ashburn Hotel **
81 William Street
Lurgan
BT66 6JB
Tel: 028 3832 5711
Fax: 028 3834 7194
Web: www.theashburnhotel.com
12 Rooms

Armagh City Hotel ***
2 Friary Road
Armagh
BT60 2HE
Tel: 028 3751 8888
Fax: 028 3751 2777
Web: www.mooneyhotelgroup.com
102 Rooms

Carngrove Hotel **
2 Charlestown Road
Portadown
BT63 5PW
Tel: 028 3833 9222
Fax: 028 3833 2899
35 Rooms

Charlemont Arms Hotel **
57-65 English Street
Armagh
BT61 7LB
Tel: 028 3752 2028
Fax: 028 3752 6979
Web: www.charlemontarmshotel.com
30 Rooms

Drumsill Hotel **
35 Moy Road
Armagh
BT61 8DL
Tel: 028 3752 2009
Fax: 028 3752 5624
10 Rooms

Seagoe Hotel ***
Upper Church Lane
Portadown
BT63 5JE
Tel: 028 3833 3076
Fax: 028 3835 0210
36 Rooms

Co Down

Bannville House Hotel
174 Lurgan Road
Banbridge, BT32 4NR
Tel: 028 4062 8884
Fax: 028 4062 7077

Burrendale Hotel & Country Club ***
51 Castlewellan Road
Newcastle, BT33 0JY
Tel: 028 4372 2599
Fax: 028 4372 2328
Web: www.burrendale.com
69 Rooms

Canal Court Hotel ***
Merchant's Quay, Newry, BT35 3HF
Tel: 028 3025 1234
Fax: 028 3025 1177
Web: www.canalcourthotel.com
51 Rooms

Clandeboye Lodge Hotel ***
10 Estate Road, Bangor, BT19 1NR
Tel: 028 9185 2500
Fax: 028 9185 2772
Email: info@clandeboyelodge.com
Website: www.clandeboyelodge.com
43 Rooms

Downshire Arms Hotel
95 Newry Street
Banbridge, BT32 3EF
Tel: 028 4066 2638
Web: www.downshirearmshotel.com

Kilmorey Arms Hotel **
41-43 Greencastle Street
Kilkeel, BT34 4BH
Tel: 028 4176 2220
Fax: 028 4176 5399
Web: www.kilmoreyarmshotel.co.uk
25 Rooms

La Mon Country House Hotel ***
The Mills, 41 Gransha Road
Castlereagh, BT23 5RF
Tel: 028 9044 8631
Fax: 028 9044 8026
Web: www.lamon.co.uk
71 Rooms

Marine Court Hotel ***
The Marina, Bangor, BT20 5ED
Tel: 028 9145 1100
Fax: 028 9145 1200
Web: www.marinecourthotel.net
52 Rooms

Millbrook Lodge Hotel **
5 Drumaness Road
Ballynahinch, BT24 8LS
Tel: 028 9756 2828
Fax: 028 9756 5405
Web: www.millbrooklodge.co.uk
16 Rooms

Mourne Country Hotel **
52 Belfast Road
Newry, BT34 1TR
Tel: 028 3026 7922
Fax: 028 3026 0896
43 Rooms

The Old Inn ***
15 Main Street, Crawfordsburn,
BT19 1JH
Tel: 028 9185 3255
Fax: 028 9185 2775
Web: www.theoldinn.com
32 Rooms

The Portaferry Hotel ***
10 The Strand, Portaferry, BT22 1PE
Tel: 028 4272 8231
Fax: 028 4272 8999
Web: www.portaferryhotel.com
14 Rooms

Royal Hotel **
26-28 Quay Street, Bangor, BT20 5ED
Tel: 028 9127 1866
Fax: 028 9146 7810
Web: www.the-royal-hotel.com
50 Rooms

Slieve Donard Hotel ****
Downs Road, Newcastle, BT33 0AH
Tel: 028 4372 1066
Fax: 028 4372 1166
Web: www.hastingshotels.com
124 Rooms

Strangford Arms Hotel ***
92 Church Street
Newtownards
BT23 4AL
Tel: 028 9181 4141
Fax: 028 9181 1010
Web: www.strangfordhotel.co.uk
37 Rooms

White Gables Hotel ***
14 Dromore Road
Hillsborough, BT26 6HS
Tel: 028 9268 2755
Fax: 028 9268 9532
31 Rooms

Co Fermanagh

Hotel Carlton **
2 Main Street
Belleek, BT93 3FX
Tel: 028 6865 8282
Fax: 028 6865 9005
Web: www.hotelcarlton.co.uk
19 Rooms

Fort Lodge Hotel **
72 Forthill Street
Enniskillen, BT74 6AJ
Tel: 028 6632 3275
Fax: 028 6632 0275
Web: www.advernet.ie/fortlodge
36 Rooms

Killyhevlin Hotel ****
Dublin Road
Enniskillen, BT74 6RW
Tel: 028 6632 3481
Fax: 028 6632 4726
Web: www.killyhevlin.com
43 Rooms

Lough Erne Hotel **
Main Street
Kesh, BT93 1TF
Tel: 028 6863 1275
Fax: 028 6863 1921
Web: www.loughernehotel.com
16 Rooms

Mahon's Hotel **
Mill Street
Irvinestown, BT94 1GS
Tel: 028 6862 1656
Fax: 028 6862 8344
Web: www.mahonshotel.co.uk
18 Rooms

Manor House Resort Hotel ****
Killadeas
Enniskillen, BT94 1NY
Tel: 028 6862 2211
Fax: 028 6862 1545
Web: www.manorhousehotel.com
81 Rooms

Railway Hotel *
34 Forthill Street
Enniskillen
BT74 6AJ
Tel: 028 6632 2084
Fax: 028 6632 7480
Web: www.railwayhotelenniskillen.com
19 Rooms

Co Londonderry

Beech Hill Country House Hotel ****
32 Ardmore Road
Derry
BT47 3QP
Tel: 028 7134 9279
Fax: 028 7134 5366
Web: www.beech-hill.com
27 Rooms

Bohill Hotel & Country Club ***
69 Cloyfin Road
Coleraine
BT52 2NY
Tel: 028 7034 4406
Fax: 028 7035 2424
37 Rooms

Brown Trout Golf & Country Inn ***
209 Agivey Road
Aghadowey
BT51 4AD
Tel: 028 7086 8209
Fax: 028 7086 8878
Web: www.browntroutinn.com
15 Rooms

Broomhill Hotel ***
Limavady Road
Derry
BT47 6LT
Tel: 028 7134 7995
Fax: 028 7134 9304
42 Rooms

Bushtown House Hotel and Country Club ***
283 Drumcroone Road
Coleraine, BT51 3QT
Tel: 028 7035 8367
Fax: 028 7032 0909
Web: www.bushtownhotel.com
40 Rooms

City Hotel
14-18 Queen's Quay
Derry, BT48 7AS
Tel: 028 7136 5800
Fax: 028 7136 5801
Web: www.greatsouthernhotels.com
145 Rooms

Da Vinci's Hotel Complex***
15 Culmore Road
Derry
BT48 8TB
Tel: 028 7127 9111
Fax: 028 7127 9222
Web: www.davincishotel.co.uk
70 Rooms

Edgewater Hotel **
88 Strand Road
Portstewart
BT55 7LZ
Tel: 028 7083 3314
Fax: 028 7083 2224
Web: www.edgehotel.com
28 Rooms

Everglades Hotel ****

41-53 Prehen Road
Derry
BT47 2NH
Tel: 028 7132 1066
Fax: 028 7134 9200
Web: www.hastingshotels.com
64 Rooms

Inn at the Cross
171 Glenshane Road
Londonderry, BT47 3EN
Tel: 028 7130 1480
Fax: 028 7130 1394
19 Rooms

Lodge Hotel and Travelstop***
Lodge Road
Coleraine, BT52 1NF
Tel: 028 7034 4848
Fax: 028 7035 4555
Web: www.thelodgehotel.com
56 Rooms

Radisson SAS Roe Park Resort ****
Roe Park
Limavady, BT49 9LB
Tel: 028 7772 2212
Fax: 028 7772 2313
Web: www.radissonroepark.com
118 Rooms

Tower Hotel

Tower Hotel Derry ****
(4 Star RAC & NITB)
Butcher Street
Londonderry
BT48 6HL
Tel: 028 7137 1000
Fax: 028 7137 7123
Web: www.towerhotelgroup.com
Email: reservations@thd.ie
General Manager: Ian Hyland

A stylish contemporary 93 bedroom hotel in the heart of Derry City with an award winning restaurant, bar, fitness suite, meeting & conference facilities catering from 14 to 250 people and private underground parking facilities.

Travel Lodge **
22-24 Strand Road
Derry, BT48 7AB
Tel: 028 7127 1271
Fax: 028 7127 1277
Web: www.travelodge.com
39 Rooms

Waterfoot Hotel & Country Club ***
14 Clooney Road
Derry, BT47 1TB
Tel: 028 7134 5500
Fax: 028 7131 1006
Web: www.thewaterfoothotel.co.uk
48 Rooms

White Horse Hotel ***
68 Clooney Road
Derry, BT47 3PA
Tel: 028 7186 0606
Fax: 028 7186 0371
Web: www.whitehorsehotel.biz
57 Rooms

Co Tyrone

Fir Trees Hotel **
Dublin Road
Strabane, BT82 9EA
Tel: 028 7138 2382
Fax: 028 7138 3116
24 Rooms

Four Ways Hotel *
41 Main Street
Fivemiletown, BT75 0PG
Tel: 028 8952 1260
Fax: 028 8952 2061
10 Rooms

Glenavon House Hotel ***
52 Drum Road
Cookstown, BT80 8JQ
Tel: 028 8676 4949
Fax: 028 8676 4396
Web: www.glenavonhotel.co.uk
53 Rooms

Greenvale Hotel **
57 Drum Road
Cookstown, BT80 8GS
Tel: 028 8676 2243
Fax: 028 8676 5539
Web: www.greenvalehotel.com
74 Rooms

Oaklin House Hotel **
Moy Road
Dungannon, BT71 6BS
Tel: 028 8772 5151
Fax: 028 8772 4953
13 Rooms

Silverbirch Hotel ***
5 Gortin Road
Omagh
BT79 7DH
Tel: 028 8224 2520
Fax: 028 8224 9061
Web: www.silverbrichhotel.com
46 Rooms

Tullylagan Country House Hotel **
40B Tullylagan Road
Cookstown
BT80 8UP
Tel: 028 8676 5100
Fax: 028 8676 1715
15 Rooms

Valley Hotel **
60 Main Street
Fivemiletown, BT75 0PW
Tel: 028 8952 1505
Fax: 028 8952 1688
22 Rooms

Camping and Caravanning

Co Antrim

Ballymacrea Caravan and Camping Park
Portrush
Tel: 028 7082 4507

Ballyness Caravan Park
Bushmills
Tel: 028 2073 2393

Bush Caravan Park
Bushmills
Tel: 028 2073 1678

Carnfunnock Country Park and Caravan Park
Larne
Tel: 028 2826 0088

Carrick Dhu Caravan Park
Portrush
Tel: 028 7082 3712

Curran Court Caravan Park
Larne
Tel: 028 2827 3797

Cushendall Caravan Park
Cushendall
Tel: 028 2177 1699

Cushendun Caravan Park
Cushendun
Tel: 028 2176 1254

Drumaheglis Marina and Caravan Park
Ballymoney
Tel: 028 2766 6466

Glenariff Forest and Caravan Park
Glenariff
Tel: 028 2175 8232

Jordanstown Lough Shore Park
Newtownabbey
Tel: 028 9034 0000

Portballintrae Caravan Park
Portballintrae
Tel: 028 2073 1478

Silvercliffs Holiday Village
Ballycastle
Tel: 028 2076 2550

Sixmilewater Marina and Caravan Park
Antrim
Tel: 028 9446 4131

Watertop Farm
Cushendall
Tel: 028 2076 2576

Co Armagh

Gosford Forest Park and Caravan Park
Markethill
Tel: 028 3755 1277

Kinnego Marina Caravan Park
Lurgan
Tel: 028 3832 7573

Co Down

Annalong Caravan Park
Annalong, Newcastle
Tel: 028 4376 8248

The Camping and Caravanning Club Site
Killyleagh
Tel: 028 4482 1883

Castleward Caravan Park
Strangford
Tel: 028 4488 1680

Castlewellan Forest Park and Caravan Park
Castlewellan
Tel: 028 4377 8664

Chestnutt Caravan Park
Kilkeel
Tel: 028 4176 2653

Clogher Valley Country Caravan Park
Clogher
Tel: 028 8554 8932

Cranfield Caravan Park
Kilkeel
Tel: 028 4176 2572

Dundonald Touring Caravan Park
Belfast
Tel: 028 9080 9100

Kilbroney Caravan Park
Rostrevor
Tel: 028 4173 8134

Lakeside View Caravan Park
Hillsborough
Tel: 028 9268 2098

Rathlin Caravan Park
Millisle
Tel: 028 9186 1386

Sandycove Holiday Park
Ballywalter
Tel: 028 4275 8062

Sandilands Caravan Park
Kilkeel
Tel: 028 4176 3634

Tollymore Forest Park Caravan Park
Newcastle
Tel: 028 4372 2428

Windsor Caravan Park
Newcastle
Tel: 028 4372 3367

Co Fermanagh

Blaney Caravan Park
Blaney
Tel: 028 6864 1634

Castle Archdale Caravan Park and Camping Site
Irvinestown
Tel: 028 6862 1333

Lakeland Caravan Park
Kesh,
Tel: 028 6863 1578

Share Holiday Village
Lisnaskea
Tel: 028 6772 2122

Co Londonderry

Castlerock Holiday Park
Castlerock
Tel: 028 7084 8381

Golden Sands Forest Park
Limavady
Tel: 028 7775 0324

Juniper Hill Caravan Park
Portstewart
Tel: 028 7083 2023

Tullans Farm Caravan Park
Coleraine
Tel: 028 7034 2309

Co Tyrone

Ballyronan Marina and Caravan Park
Ballyronan, Cookstown
Tel: 028 8676 2205

Drum Manor Forest Park and Caravan Park
Cookstown
Tel: 028 8676 2774

Dungannon Park and Caravan Park
Dungannon
Tel: 028 8772 7327

Gortin Glen Caravan Park
Gortin, Omagh
Tel: 028 8224 7831

Killymaddy Tourist Amenity Centre
Dungannon
Tel: 028 8776 7259

Round Lake Caravan Park
Fivemiletown, Co Tyrone
Tel: 028 8952 1949

Hostels

Belfast

The Ark
18 University Street
Belfast, BT7 1FZ
Tel: 028 9032 9626
Web: www.arkhostel.com
Email: info@arkhostel.com

Arnie's Backpackers
63 Fitzwilliam Street
Belfast, BT9 6AX
Tel: 028 9024 2867
Web: www.arniesbackpackers.co.uk

Belfast International Youth Hostel
22 Donegall Road
Belfast, BT12 5JN
Tel: 028 9032 4733
Email: info@hini.org.uk

The Linen House Hostel
18 Kent Street
Belfast, 028 9058 6400
Tel: 028 9058 6400
Web: www.belfasthostel.com
Email: bookings@belfasthostel.com

Co Antrim

Ballycastle Backpackers
4 North Street
Ballycastle, BT54 6BN
Tel: 028 2076 3612
Email: am@bcbackpackers.fsnet.co.uk

Castle Hostel
62 Quay Road
Ballycastle, BT54 6BH
Tel: 028 2076 2337
Email: info@castlehostel.com

Colliers Barn
50 Cushendall Road
Ballycastle, BT54 6QR
Tel: 028 2076 2531

Glendun Court
PO Box 14
Glenville Road
Whiteabbey, BT37 0UN
Tel: 028 9085 3005
Web: www.csni.com

Metropole House
70 Eglinton Street
Portrush, BT56 8DY
Tel: 028 7082 3511

Mill Rest
49 Main Street
Bushmills, BT57 8QA
Tel: 028 2073 1222
Email: info@hini.org.uk

Portrush Independent Youth Hostel (Macool's)
35 Causeway Street,
Portrush, BT56 8AB
Tel: 028 7082 4845
Email: scilley@portrush.hostel.fsnet.co.uk

Sheep Island View
42A Main Street
Ballintoy, BT54 6LX
Tel: 028 2076 9391
Email: sheepisland@hotmail.com

Soerneog View Hostel
Ouig
Rathlin Island
Ballycastle, BT54 6RT
Tel: 028 2076 3954

Whitepark Bay Hostel
157 Whitepark Road
Ballintoy, BT54 6NH
Tel: 028 2073 1745
Email: info@hini.org.uk

Co Armagh

Armagh City International Youth Hostel
39 Abbey Street
Armagh, BT61 7EB
Tel: 028 3751 1800
Email: info@hini.org.uk

Waterside Hostel & Activity Centre
Oxford Island
Lurgan, BT66 6NJ
Tel: 028 3832 7573
Email: kinnego.marina@craigavon.gov.uk

Co Down

Ballinran Mourne Centre
42 Ballinran Road
Kilkeel, BT34 4JA
Tel: 028 4176 5727
Email: kenmuir@clara.co.uk

Barholm
11 The Strand
Portaferry, BT22 1PE
Tel: 028 4272 9598
Email: barholm.portaferry@virgin.net

Cnocnafeola Cultural & Activity Centre
Bog Road
Atticall
Kilkeel, BT34 4RZ
Tel: 028 4176 5859
Email: info@cnocnafeolacentre.com

Glenada Holiday & Conference Centre
29 South Promenade
Newcastle, BT33 0EX
Tel: 028 4372 2402
Email: info@glenada-conferences.freeserve.co.uk

Greenhill YMCA – Outdoor Centre
Donard Park
Newcastle, BT33 0GR
Tel: 028 4372 3172
Email: greenhill@ymca-ireland.org

Newcastle Hostel
30 Downs Road
Newcastle, BT33 0AG
Tel: 028 4372 2133
Web: www.hini.org.uk
Email: info@hini.org.uk

Co Fermanagh

The Bridges Youth Hostel
Belmore Street
Enniskillen, BT74 6AA
Tel: 028 6634 0110
Email: info@hini.org.uk

Castle Archdale Youth Hostel
Irvinestown, BT94 1PP
Tel: 028 6862 8118
Email: info@hini.org.uk

Lough Melvin Holiday Centre
Main Street, Garrison, BT93 4ET
Tel: 028 6865 8142
Email:
enquiry@loughmelvinholidaycentre.com

Share Holiday Village
Smith's Strand
Lisnaskea, BT92 0EQ
Tel: 028 6772 2122
Web: www.sharevillage.org
Email: info@sharevillage.org

Field Studies Council Derrygonnelly Centre
Tir Navar
Creamery Street
Derrygonnelly, BT93 6HW
Tel: 028 6864 1673
Email: fsc.derrygonnelly@ukonline.co.uk

Co Londonderry

Derry City Hostel
4-6 Magazine Street
Londonderry, BT48 6HJ
Tel: 028 7128 0280
Email: derrycitytours@aol.com

Derry City Independent Hostel
44 Great James Street,
Londonderry, BT48 7DB
Tel: 028 7137 7989
Web: www.derry-hostel.co.uk
Email: derryhostel@hotmail.com

Downhill Hostel
12 Mussenden Road
Downhill
Coleraine, BT51 4RP
Tel: 028 7084 9077
Web: www.downhillhostel.com
Email: downhillhostel@hotmail.com

Dungiven Castle
Upper Main Street
Dungiven, BT47 4LF
Tel: 028 7774 2428
Email: enquiries@dungivencastle.com

The Flax Mill
Mill Lane
Gortnaghey Road
Dungiven, BT47 4PY
Tel: 028 7774 2655

Hostel 56
56 Rainey Street
Magherafelt, BT45 5AH
Tel: 028 7963 2096
Web: www.hostel.club24.co.uk

Kilcronaghan Activity & Conference Centre
10 Rectory Road
Tobermore
Magherafelt, BT45 5QP
Tel: 028 7962 7826
Email: manager@kilcronaghan.co.uk

Rick's Causeway Independent Hostel
4 Victoria Terrace
Atlantic Circle
Portstewart, BT55 7BA
Tel: 028 7083 3789

Wild Geese Parachute Club
116 Carrowreagh Road
Garvagh, BT51 5LQ
Tle; 028 2955 8609
Email:
parachute@wildgeese.demon.co.uk

Co Tyrone

Gortin Accommodation Suite and Activity Centre
62 Main Street
Gortin
Omagh, BT79 8NH
Tel: 028 8164 8346
Web: www.gortin.net
Email: visit.gortin@virgin.net

Gortin Hostel and Outdoor Centre
198 Glenpark Road
Gortin
Omagh, BT79 8PJ
Tel: 028 8164 8083

Omagh Hostel
9A Waterworks Road
Omagh, BT79 7JS
Tel: 028 8224 1973
Web: www.omaghhostel.co.uk
Email: marella@omaghhostel.co.uk

Things to See and Do

Guided Tours

Belfast City Black Taxi Tours
Tel: 028 9030 1832
Mob: 07712 673178
Web: www.allirelandtours.com
Email: contact@allirelandtours.com

Tour includes famous sites of Belfast and includes the political murals from both traditions. Tours can be arranged to suit.

Belfast City Hall
Tel: 028 9027 0456

Built in 1906 from Portland Stone, Belfast City Hall is a fine example of Classical Renaissance style. Home of Belfast City Council, the tour includes the oak-furnished Council Chamber.

Belfast City Sightseeing
Tel: 028 9062 6888
Web: www.city-sightseeing.com

Tours of the city from open-top bus or luxury coach. Tours depart from Castle Place.

Black Taxi Tours
Tel: 028 9064 2264
Web: www.belfasttours.com
Email: michael@belfasttours.com

Visits some of the well-known sites of Belfast with commentary provided – includes the political wall murals.

Citybus Tours
Tel: 028 9066 6630

Operated by Translink during the months of May - September inclusive. Includes tours of Belfast City, the Belfast Living History Tour and the Titanic Tour.

Due North
Tel: 028 9080 9975
Mob: 07929 823660
Web: www.duenorth-ni.com
Email: info@duenorth-ni.com

Specialists in providing individualised and personalised tours of Northern Ireland.

Historical Pub Walking Tour of Belfast
Tel: 028 9268 3665
Web: www.belfastpubtours.com
Email: judy@belfastpubtours.com

Tour around Belfast's famous and historic pubs. Leaves from Flannigans (above the Crown Liqueur Saloon in Great Victoria Street) on Thursdays at 7pm and Saturdays at 4pm from May until the end of September.
Lasts approximately 2 hours.

Intercomm Tourism
Tel: 028 9035 2165
Web: www.irishhistoricaltours.com

Political, educational and cultural tour package.

KM Tour Guiding Services
Tel: 028 3884 0054
Mob: 07801 541600
Web: www.kmtgs.co.uk
Email: info@kmtgs.co.uk

Complete Blue Badge Guiding Service for Northern Ireland offering tours and visits to Northern Ireland's top tourist attractions.

Lagan Boat Company (NI) Ltd
Tel: 028 9024 6609 for details of scheduled tour bookings
Tel: 028 9033 0844 for private hire and information

Guided Titanic and River Lagan boat tours departing from Donegall Quay.

Leprechaun Tour Guiding Service
Tel: 028 3883 1236
Web: www.leprechauntourguiding.co.uk
Email: ken@leprechauntourguiding.co.uk

Complete Blue Badge Guiding Service for Northern Ireland offering tours and visits to Northern Ireland's top tourist attractions.

Mini Coach Tours
Tel: 028 9032 4733
Web: www.minicoachni.co.uk
Email: info@minicoachni.co.uk

Daily tours of Belfast and The Giant's Causeway also overnight tours including Belfast, The Giant's Causeway and Londonderry. Also provide airport and ferry transfers.

NI Tour Guide Association
Tel: 028 9028 0925

Blue Badge Tour Guides are available to provide tours in all areas of Northern Ireland.

The Original Black Taxi Tours
Tel: UK Freephone 0800 032 2003
Web: www.tobbtt.com
Email: tours@tobbtt.com

Tours of Belfast City including the political wall murals and the peace line. Tailor-made tours on request, operating 7 days a week.

TourUlster
Tel: 028 9065 0866
Mob: 07050 382856
Web: www.tourulster.com
Email: info@tourulster.com

Tours, activities and visitor services for large or small groups and individuals.

Ulsterbus Tours
Tel: 028 9066 6630

Operated by Translink, Ulsterbus tours visit main attractions in Northern and Southern Ireland. Depart daily from the Europa Bus Centre.

Places to Visit

The following list highlights places of interest to visit across Northern Ireland. It is worth noting that opening hours at many of the attractions are limited, especially during winter months so it is worth phoning to check before making a trip to any of the following places. Admission charges may also be payable at some attractions.

In and Around Belfast

Belfast Castle
Antrim Road, Belfast, BT15 5GR
Tel: 028 9077 6925
www.belfastcastle.co.uk

Impressive sandstone building 400ft above sea level on the slopes of Cave Hill.

Belfast Telegraph Newspapers
124 Royal Avenue
Belfast
Tel: 028 9026 4226
www.belfasttelegraph.co.uk

View the printing works and see the next edition being made up for the camera. Admission free.

Belfast Zoo
Antrim Road
Belfast, BT36 7PN
Tel: 028 9077 6277
www.belfastzoo.co.uk

Zoo set in landscaped parkland housing over 160 species of rare/endangered animals.

Botanic Gardens
Stranmillis Road
Belfast
Tel: 028 9032 4902

City park hosting the Ulster Museum and the Victorian Palm House, full of exotic plants. Admission free.

City Hall
Donegall Square
Belfast, BT1 5GS
Tel: 028 9027 0456
www.belfastcity.gov.uk

A magnificent building in Portland stone, the centrally-located City Hall is seat of Belfast City Council. Tours last 1 hour. Admission free.

Colin Glen Forest Park
163 Stewartstown Road
Belfast, BT17 0HW
Tel: 028 9061 4115
www.colinglentrust.org

Wooded river glen consisting of 200 acres of scenic woodland, grassland, waterfalls and ponds.

Crown Liqueur Saloon
46 Great Victoria Street
Belfast
Tel: 028 9027 9901
www.belfasttelegraph.co.uk/crown

Gas-lit Victorian pub with fine tiles, woodwork and glass – now National Trust owned.

Fernhill House: The People's Museum
Glencairn Road
Belfast, BT13 3PT
Tel: 028 9071 5599

Recreated 1930s terraced 'kitchen house' telling history of Shankill districk, Home Rule crisis and both World Wars.

Giant's Ring
Shaw's Bridge
Belfast
www.ntni.org.uk

Prehistoric enclosure over 200m in diameter, with a dolmen in the centre. Admission free.

Grovelands
Stockman's Lane
Belfast
Tel: 028 9032 0202
www.belfastcity.gov.uk
Sunken garden and small ornamental gardens with art deco entrance gates. Admission free.

Lagan Lookout Centre
Donegall Quay
Belfast
Tel: 028 9031 5444
www.laganlookout.com

Background to the River Lagan's weir explained, industrial and folk history of the city. Platform views of river activities.

Lagan Valley Regional Park
Tel: 028 9049 1922

1700 hectares of countryside and 21km of river stretching from Governor's Bridge in Belfast to the former Union Locks in Lisburn. Admission free.

Linen Hall Library
Donegall Square North
Belfast, BT1 5GB
Tel: 028 9032 1707
Web: www.linenhall.com

Belfast's oldest library dating from 1788, internationally recognised as a unique and vital resource for Irish and local studies. Admission free.

Malone House
Barnett Demesne
Upper Malone Road
Belfast
Tel: 028 9068 1246
Web: www.malonehouse.co.uk

Early 19th century house in parkland. Also has restaurant and art gallery. Admission free.

Minnowburn Beeches
Shaw's Bridge
Belfast
Web: www.ntni.org.uk

Woodlands and walks in Lagan Valley.

Odyssey

Queen's Quay, Belfast
BT3 9QQ.
Tel: 028 9045 1055

Main features are an indoor arena, home of Belfast Giants Ice Hockey team, W5 interactive discovery centre, Sheridan IMAX and the Warner Village 12-screen multiplex cinema;

Police Museum
Brooklyn, 65 Knock Road, Belfast
Tel: 028 9065 0222 extn 22499
Web: www.psni.police.uk/museum

Uniforms, photographs and equipment relating to the Irish Constabulary since its formation in 1822 and the Royal Ulster Constabulary since 1922. Admission free.

Public Record Office of Northern Ireland (PRONI)
66 Balmoral Avenue, Belfast, BT9 6NY
Tel: 028 9025 5905
Web: www.proni.gov.uk

PRONI is the official place of deposit for public and private records in Northern Ireland with records dating from 1219.

Queen's Visitors' Centre
Lanyon Building, Queen's University
University Road, Belfast, BT7 1NN
Tel: 028 9033 5252
Web: www.qub.ac.uk/vcentre
Exhibition, information, memorabilia. Admission free.

Royal Ulster Rifles Museum
War Memorial Building
5 Waring Street, Belfast
Tel: 028 9023 2086
Web: www.rurmuseum.tripod.com
Preserves relics of the Royal Ulster Rifles and its predecessor foot regiments.

Sir Thomas and Lady Dixon Park
Upper Malone Road, Belfast
Tel: 028 9032 0202
Web: www.belfastcity.gov.uk

One of the world's best rose gardens which hosts the Belfast International Rose Trials each year. Admission free.

St Anne's Cathedral
Donegall Street, Belfast
Tel: 028 9032 8332
Web: www.belfastcathedral.org

St Anne's Cathedral is built on the site of Belfast's first Church of Ireland parish. Cathedral has excellent glass mosaics and Irish marble and the largest Celtic cross in Ireland. Admission free.

St George's Market
Tel: 028 9043 5704
The last surviving Victorian covered market in Belfast. Market days on Friday and Saturday.

Streamvale Open Dairy Farm
38 Ballyhanwood Road, Belfast
Tel: 028 9048 3244

Chance to see farming at work – pets' corner, milking parlour, animal feeding and rides and nature trail.

Ulster Museum
Stranmillis Road (in Botanic Gardens)
Belfast, BT9 5AB
Tel: 028 9038 3000
Web: www.ulstermuseum.org.uk

Northern Ireland's largest museum, housing major permanent and visiting collections, as well as a permanent exhibition of Irish art. Admission free.

whowhatwherewhenwhy-W5

2 Queen's Quay
Belfast, BT3 9QQ
Tel: 028 9046 7700
Web: www.w5online.co.uk

An amazing place to visit for adults and children alike

W5 is Ireland's first purpose-built interactive discovery centre and is located at the Odyssey complex in the heart of Belfast. The centre has 140 amazing interactive exhibits, which offer fantastic fun for visitors of all ages.

Opening Hours:
Spring/Summer
Mon-Saturday 10.00am-6.00pm.
Sunday 12.00pm-6.00pm.
Last admission 5.00pm.

Autumn/Winter
Mon-Thurs 10.00am-5.00pm
Friday & Sat 10.00am-6.00pm
Sunday 12.00pm-6.00pm

Normal admission times during holidays will be: Monday – Saturdays 10.00am-6.00pm and Sundays 12.00pm-6.00pm.
Last admission at 5.00pm.

World War II Exhibition
9 Waring Street
Belfast
Tel: 028 9032 0392
Web: www.rurmuseum.tripod.com

Co Antrim

Andrew Jackson Centre
Boneybefore
Carrickfergus
Tel: 028 9336 6455
Web: www.carrickfergus.org

Close to site of ancestral home of Andrew Jackson, 7th US President 1829-37, whose parents emigrated in 1765 from Carrickfergus.

Antrim Castle Gardens
Randalstown Road
Antrim
Tel: 028 9442 8000

Restored 17th century Anglo-Dutch water gardens with parterre, ponds, and woodland and riverside walks.

Arthur Ancestral Home
Dreen
Cullybackey
Tel: 028 2563 8494

Restored 18th century farmhouse with open flax-straw thatched roof. Ancestral home of Chester Alan Arthur, 21st US President 1881-85.

Ballance House
118A Lisburn Road
Glenavy
Tel: 028 9264 8492

Birthplace in 1839 of John Ballance, New Zealand Prime Minister 1891-93. Historic house and museum.

Ballycastle Museum
59 Castle Street
Ballycastle
Tel: 028 2076 2942

Folk/social history of the Glens in the town's 18th century courthouse. Admission free.

Ballycastle – Rathlin Island Ferry
14 Bayview Road
Ballycastle
Tel: 028 2076 9299

Ballymena Museum
3 Wellington Court
Ballymena
Tel: 028 2564 2166

Diverse programme of exhibitions, talks, tours and other events exploring the rich heritage of Ballymena borough. Admission free.

Ballymoney Museum
33 Charlotte Street
Ballymoney
Tel: 028 2766 2280

Local history exhibits. Admission free.

Benvarden Garden
Dervock
Ballymoney
Tel: 028 2074 1331

18th century walled garden with herbaceous borders, kitchen garden and Victorian woodland pond. Stable yard with coach and cart houses and mini museum.

Brookhall Historical Farm
2 Horse Park
Ballinderry Road
Lisburn
Tel: 028 9262 1712

Farming museum with duck pond, rare breed animals, gardens, farming implements from a bygone era.

Carnfunnock Country Park
Coast Road, Larne
Tel: 028 2827 0541 or 028 2826 0088

Maze in the shape of Northern Ireland. Walled garden, barbecue/picnic sites, children's activity centre with outdoor adventure playground, forest walks, orienteering, golf activities, miniature railway and modern visitor centre.

Carrick-a-Rede Rope Bridge
Larrybane, Ballintoy, Ballycastle
Tel: 028 2073 1159
Web: www.ntni.org.uk

Swinging rope bridge spans a 60 ft wide chasm, giving access to the salmon fishery. Also 1 mile walk along the cliff path.

Carrickfergus Castle
Marine Highway
Carrickfergus
Tel: 028 9335 1273

Castle started in 1180 by John de Courcy and garrisoned until 1928. Exhibition on the castle's history.

Dunluce Castle
3 miles east of Portrush
Tel: 028 2073 1938

Dramatic ruins on a rocky headland – most of the fortifications date from the 16th and 17th centuries.

Dunluce Family Entertainment Centre
Sandhill Drive
Portrush
Tel: 028 7082 4444

Has soft-play adventure playground, a computerised treasure hunt, motion simulator, restaurant and shops.

East Strand Beach
Causeway Street, Portrush

Beach stretches from Portrush to the White Rocks with views over the Skerries to the Scottish Islands. Backed by an extensive dune system and the famous Royal Portrush golf course.

ECOS Environmental Centre
Kernohans Lane
Broughshane Road
Ballymena
Tel: 028 2566 4400
Web: www.ecoscentre.com

Environmental centre with interactive exhibits highlighting environmental issues; focus on biodiversity, sustainability and alternative energy production from sustainable sources on site in the 150 acre park.

Flame – The Gasworks Museum of Ireland
Irish Quarter West, Carrickfergus
Tel: 028 9336 6455
Web: www.gasworksflames.com

The only Victorian coal-fired gasworks in Ireland built in 1855 to light street lamps, it produced gas until 1964. Site has recently been completely restored.

Ford Farm Park and Museum
8 Low Road
Islandmagee
Tel: 028 9335 3264

Museum, animals, shoreline walks, birdwatching, demonstrations by arrangement – butter-making and spinning.

Giant's Causeway
Bushmills
Tel: 028 2073 1855
Web: www.ntni.org.uk

Ireland's first World Heritage site – over 40,000 stone columns. Various walks and coastal paths.

Glenariff Forest Park
Ballymena/Waterfoot Road
Tel: 028 2955 6000

Spectacular glen walk with three waterfalls. Scenic path and trails to mountain viewpoints.

Hilden Brewery
Hilden House
Hilden, Lisburn
Tel: 028 9266 3863

Guided tour of Ireland's oldest independent brewery in the 19th century courtyard of Hilden House.

Irish Linen Centre and Lisburn Museum
Market Square, Lisburn
Tel: 028 9266 3377

Weaving workshop with hand looms, audio visuals. Exhibitions on local history. Linen/craft shop. Admission free.

Lagan Valley LeisurePlex
12 Lisburn Leisure Park,
Lisburn, BT28 1LP
Tel: 028 9267 2121

Water attractions including a free-form leisure pool, competition and diving pools.

Larne Interpretive Centre
Narrow Gauge Road
Larne
Tel: 028 2826 0088

Story of the building of the Antrim coast road. Admission free.

Larne – Islandmagee Ferry
Tel: 028 2827 4085

Leslie Hill Open Farm
Macfin Road
Ballymoney
Tel: 028 2566 6803

Horse-trap and and pony rides through an 18th century estate. Deer, ornamental fowl, pets, farm animals, walled garden, lakes and trails. Carriages, horse-drawn machines and threshing barn.

Old Bushmills Distillery
Distillery Road
Bushmills
Tel: 028 2073 1521
Web: www.whiskeytours.ie

Oldest licensed whiskey distillery in the world, established in 1608. One hour guided tour and whiskey tasting.

Patterson's Spade Mill
751 Antrim Road, Templepatrick
Tel: 028 9443 3619
Web: www.ntni.org.uk

Last water-powered spade mill in Ireland. All original equipment in working order. Spade-making demonstrations.

Portrush Countryside Centre
Lansdowne Crescent
Bath Road, Portrush
Tel: 028 7082 3600

Countryside centre with seashore exhibition, touch tank and live sea creatures. Opportunities for rock pool rambles, fossil hunts and bird watching. Admission free.

Rathlin Island Boathouse Visitors' Centre
Rathlin Island Harbour
Tel: 028 2076 3951

History, photographs and artefacts.

Royal Irish Regiment Museum
Depot Royal Irish
St Patrick's Barracks
Ballymena
Tel: 028 2566 1383

Regimental history from 1689.

TACT Wildlife Centre
2 Crumlin Road
Crumlin
Tel: 028 9442 2900

200 year old walled garden with bird sanctuary.

Ulster Aviation Heritage Centre
Langford Lodge Airfield
Large Road, Crumlin
Tel: 028 9445 4444
Web: www.ulsteraviationsociety.co.uk

Former US airbase with aircraft on display including a Wildcat, Sea Hawk, Buccaneer, Tucano and the amphibian Sea Hawker. Collection of photographs, documents and artefacts in wartime buildings.

Waterworld
Portrush
Tel: 028 7082 2001

Indoor water centre – giant water flumes, fun pools, water cannon, pirate ships and Jacuzzis.

Whitepark Bay Nature Trail
Ballintoy
Web: www.ntni.org.uk

1 mile trail shows vegetation types developed on sand and chalk. Geological features displayed. Free access always.

Co Armagh

Ardress House
Off M1 Junction 13
Tel: 028 3885 1236
Web: www.ntni.org.uk

17th century famhouse with Adam-style drawing room, fine furniture and paintings. Farmyard with rare breeds. Woodland and riverside walks.

Argory
144 Derrycaw Road, Moy, BT71 6NA
Tel: 028 8778 4753

House dating from 1820 overlooking the Blackwater river and set in wooded countryside. Stable yard and sundial garden.

Armagh Ancestry
38A English Street
Armagh
Tel: 028 3752 1802

Provides a pathway for tracing Armagh ancestors using comprehensive genealogical database.

Armagh County Museum
The Mall East
Armagh
Tel: 028 3752 3070

History of Co Armagh – military, archaeology, railway, costume and local history collections.

Armagh Observatory
College Hill
Armagh
Tel: 028 3752 2928

Modern astronomical research institute with a rich heritage. Grounds include Robinson dome with a 10 inch telescope, Lindsay sundial and the Armagh Astropark. Admission free.

Armagh Planetarium
College Hill
Armagh
Tel:
028 3752 4725

Public telescope, daily audio-visual presentation, exhibition areas.

Armagh Public Library
Abbey Street
Armagh
Tel: 028 3752 3142

Library was established in 1771 and was the first public library outside Dublin. Repository of a fine collection of antiques and ancient manuscripts.

Ballydougan Pottery Visitors' Centre
Bloomvale House
Plantation Road
Craigavon
Tel: 028 3834 2201
Web: www.ballydouganpottery.co.uk

Bloomvale House has been home to generations of crafts people since 1785 and is currently where Ballydougan Pottery is crafted.

Dan Winter's House (Ancestral Home)

The Diamond
Loughgall
Tel: 028 3885 1344

Traditionally thatched, mud-walled farmyard cottage, where decision to form the Orange Order was made by Dan Winter and others following the Battle of the Diamond.

Derrymore House
Newry
Tel: 028 3083 0353

Thatched 18th century mansion was home to Isaac Corry, General-in-Chief of the Irish Volunteers and later Chancellor of the Irish Parliament.

Gosford Forest Park
Markethill
Tel: 028 3755 1277

Estate has associations with Dean Jonathan Swift. Heritage poultry, rare breeds of cattle and sheep in open paddocks, deer-park, walled garden, nature trails and treks.

Keady Heritage Centre
The Old Mill
2 Kinelowen Street, Keady
Tel: 028 3753 9928

The story of local linen production from the 1840s including model of a working mill, weaving loom, local history exhibits, photographs, music recordings.

Loughgall Country Park
11 Main Street
Loughgall
Tel: 028 3889 2900

188 hectare estate of open farmlands and orchards, with 18 hole golf course, 37 acre coarse fishery, bridle path, walks, children's play area and football pitch.

Millworker's House
6 College Square East
Bessbrook
Tel: 028 3083 7143

Restored terrace house built in 1881 depicting the home of a linen millwoker in Bessbrook in the late 19th century.

Moneypenny's Lock
Castle Street
Portadown
Tel: 028 3832 2205

Restored lock-keeper's house, stables and bothy on the Newry canal. Also 2 mile walk along the towpath.

Oxford Island/Lough Neagh Discovery Centre

Oxford Island, Craigavon
Tel: 028 3832 2205
Web: www.oxfordisland.com

4 miles of footpaths, 5 birdwatching hides, woodland, ponds, wildflower meadows, picnic and play areas. Centre houses exhibition about history, culture and wildlife in and around Lough Neagh. Also has craft shop and café with views of the lough.

Palace Stables Heritage Centre
Friary Road
Armagh
Tel: 028 3752 9629
Web: www.visit-armagh.com

Restored Georgian stable block featuring the life of the palace in 1786. Costumed interpreters recreate the grandeur and squalor of the Georgian period.

Peatlands Park
Off Junction 13 M1
Tel: 028 3885 1102

Woods, open bogs, nature reserves and bog garden with 1 mile trip on narrow-gauge railway

Royal Irish Fusiliers Museum
Sovereign's House
The Mall East, Armagh
Tel: 028 3752 2911

Story of the regiment 1793-1968 with large model of the capture of the Imperial French Eagle at the Battle of Barossa 1813. Also contains militaria from the Armagh, Cavan and Monaghan militias.

Slieve Gullion Forest Park
Newry
Tel: 028 3755 1277

8 mile drive up and round this thickly wooded park. Mountain-top trail at 1,880 ft to megalithic cairns and lake with views of Ring of Gullion, Mourne Mountains and Cooley Mountains. Admission free.

St Patrick's Cathedral (Church of Ireland)
Cathedral Close
Armagh
Tel: 028 3752 3142
Web: www.stpatricks-cathedral.org

Present Cathedral dates from the 13th century, built on site where St Patrick established his chief church in 445 AD. Admission free.

St Patrick's Cathedral (Roman Catholic)
Cathedral Road
Armagh
Tel: 028 3752 2802

Building begun in 1840 but suspended during Famine years. Dedicated for worship in 1873 but interior decoration not completed until 20th century. Admission free.

St Patrick's Trian Visitor Complex
40 English Street
Armagh
Tel: 028 3752 1801
Web: www.visitarmagh.co.uk

3 different exhibitions trace Armagh's history, its association with St Patrick and also the adventures of Gulliver, in the 'Land of Lilliput'.

Tayto Factory
Tandragee Castle
Tandragee
Tel: 028 3884 0249
Web: www.tayto.com

Factory inside the grounds of a castle formerly owned by Duke of Manchester. Factory tour demonstrates potato storage techniques and the process of crisp-making.

Co Down

Annalong Corn Mill
Marine Park
Annalong
Tel: 028 4376 8736

Built in around 1830 and powered by a waterwheel, the mill overlooks the harbour in Annalong.

Ark Open Farm
296 Bangor Road
Newtownards
Tel: 028 9182 0445

Over 80 rare species of cattle, pigs, sheep, goats, ponies, ducks, poultry and llamas in 40 acres of countryside.

Ballycopeland Windmill
Millisle
Tel: 028 9054 3033

Late 18th century tower mill in use until 1915 and still in working order. Visitor centre at the miller's house with an electrically operated model of the mill.

Brontë Homeland Interpretive Centre
Drumballyroney
Rathfriland
Tel: 028 4063 1152

Drumballyroney school and church where Patrick Brontë, father of the novelist sisters, taught and preached.

Butterfly House
Seaforde Nursery
Seaforde
Tel: 028 4481 1225

Set in Seaforde Gardens, with large flight area with hundreds of free-flying exotic butterflies. Reptiles and insects behind glass. Parrots, maze, viewing tower, rare plants, nursery garden, play area.

Castle Espie
78 Ballydrain Road
Comber
Tel: 028 9187 4146

Ireland's largest collection of ducks, geese and swans with viewing from hides, waterfowl gardens, woodland walks.

Castle Ward
Strangford
Tel: 028 4488 1204

18th century mansion with facades in different styles – Classical and Gothic. Victorian laundry, restored 1830s cornmill, disused leadmine and sawmill. Exhibition in Strangford Lough Wildlife Centre and guided tours and boat trips.

Castlewellan Forest Park
Main Street
Castlewellan
Tel: 028 4377 8664

Queen Anne style courtyards, tropical birds, hedge maze. Features a national arboretum, initiated in 1740 and also 3 mile trail around the lake with sculptures created from the park's natural materials.

Cranfield Beach
Rostrevor to Kilkeel Road
Tel: 028 4176 2525

South-facing beach at the mouth of Carlingford Lough with Mourne Mountains as its backdrop.

Crawfordsburn Country Park
Helen's Bay
Tel: 028 9185 3621

Beaches, woodland and meadows, coastal and riverside walks. Restored gun site at Grey Pint Fort. Admission free.

Delamont Country Park
Downpatrick to Comber Road
Tel: 028 4482 8333

Strangford stone and Ireland's longest miniature railway. Allows access to, and views over, Strangford Lough.

Down Cathedral and St Patrick's Grave
English Street, Downpatrick
Tel: 028 4461 4922
Web: www.downcathedral.com

Church of Ireland Cathedral built in 1183 as a Benedictine Monastery. St Patrick's grave is reputedly within the graveyard. Church contains magnificent stain glass windows and box pews. Admission free.

Down County Museum
The Mall
Downpatrick
Tel: 028 4461 5218
Web: www.downcountymuseum.com

Restored 18th century gaol containing exhibitions and the history of county Down. Includes restored cell block with life-size figures of prisoners and their jailers.

Downpatrick Railway Museum
Railway Station
Market Street
Downpatrick
Tel: 028 4461 5779

Working engines and steam locomotive on display along with photographic display and model railway.

Exploris Aquarium
The Ropewalk
Castle Street
Portaferry
Tel: 028 4272 8062

Presents marine life on a journey from Strangford Lough to the Irish Sea, with thousands of species on view. New seal sanctuary.

Grey Abbey
Greyabbey
Tel: 028 9054 3037

Ruined Cistercian abbey founded in 1193 by Affreca, wife of John de Courcy. Parkland setting with medieval 'physick' garden.

Hillsborough Castle and Gardens
Main Street
Hillsborough
Tel: 028 9268 1300

18th century mansion, built in 1770s by the first Marquis of Downshire. Formerly the home of the Governor of Northern Ireland the Castle is now the official residence of the Secretary of State. Gardens feature extensive rose garden and lakeside walks.

Hillsborough Courthouse
The Square
Hillsborough
Tel: 028 9054 3034

Exhibition in Georgian courthouse on working of courts through stories, pictures and games. Admission free.

Inch Abbey
Downpatrick

Ruins of Cistercian monastery founded in 1180s by John de Courcy. Situated on island in the Quoile, reached by a causeway.

Mount Stewart House and Gardens
Portaferry Road
Newtownards
Tel: 028 4278 8387

Childhood home of Lord Castlereagh with fine gardens and vistas. Temple of the Winds overlooks Strangford Lough.

Murlough National Nature Reserve
Dundrum
Tel: 028 4375 1467

Sand dune system with heath and woodland surrounded by estuary and sea. Guided walks and nature trail.

Newry Museum
Arts Centre
Bank Parade
Newry
Tel: 028 3026 6232

Demonstrates history of the Gap of the North. Also contains robes of the Order of St Patrick and period furniture in a restored 18th century room, including Nelson's table from HMS Victory. Admission free.

North Down Heritage Centre
Castle Park Avenue
Bangor
Tel: 028 9127 1200

Contains the Ballycroghan Swords dating from 500 BC and a 9th century handbell found near Bangor. Also features toy and railway displays and vintage films. Observation beehive in summer.

Pickie Family Fun Park
The Marina
Bangor
Tel: 028 9127 4430

Swan pedal boats, paddling pools, mini railway, playground, go-karts and superslide.

Portaferry Visitor Centre
Castle Street, Portaferry
Tel: 028 4272 9882

Restored stable featuring exhibitions on the heritage and environment of Portaferry and Strangford Lough.

Quoile Countryside Centre
Downpatrick
Tel: 028 4461 5520

Displays on the wildlife of the Quoile pondage where a barrage has changed the saltwater estuary to fresh water. Includes birdwatching hide.

Rowallane Garden
Saintfield
Tel: 028 9751 0131

Rare trees, shrubs and plants including magnificent rhododendrons and azaleas.

Scarva Visitor Centre
Main Street
Scarva
Tel: 028 3883 2163

History of canals in Ireland, the building of the Newry canal and the history of Scarva. Admission free.

Scrabo Country Park
Newtownards
Tel: 028 9181 1491

Contains Scrabo Tower (with 122 steps to the top), which was built in 1857 as a memorial to the 3rd Marquis of Londonderry.

Silent Valley
Head Road
Kilkeel
Tel: 028 9074 1166

Silent Valley and Ben Crom reservoirs supply 30 million gallons of water per day to Belfast and County Down. Beautiful parkland before the dams.

Somme Heritage Centre
233 Bangor Road
Newtownards
Tel: 028 9182 3202

Highlights Ireland's contribution to the First World War, including reconstructed trenches of the Battle of the Somme.

St Patrick Centre
53A Lower Market Street
Downpatrick, BT30 6LZ
Tel: 028 4461 9000

Exhibition explores the legacy of St Patrick and recalls the story of the saint.

Strangford – Portaferry Ferry
Tel: 028 4488 1637

Tollymore Forest Park
Bryansford Road
Newcastle
Tel: 028 4372 2428

Park has numerous stone follies and bridges and a magnificent Cork Oak in the arboretum. Wildlife and forestry exhibits in barn.

Tyrella Beach
Tel: 028 4482 8333

Miles of flat sandy beach with dune conservation area – car free zone with waymarked walks.

Ulster Folk and Transport Museum
Cultra
Holywood
Tel: 028 9042 8428

Illustrates past Ulster traditions including typical Ulster town of the early 1900s. Transport Museum present's Ireland's most comprehensive transport collection including 'Titanic' and 'Flight Experience' exhibitions.

Ulster Wildlife Centre
3 New Line
Crossgar
Tel: 028 4483 0282

Victorian walled garden providing a sample of the natural heritage of Ulster. Habitats recreated include wild bogland, meadows, woodland and wildlife pond. Admission free.

Co Fermanagh

Belleek China
Belleek, BT93 3FY
Tel: 028 6865 8501

Home of the world-famous porcelain. Tours allow visitors to watch craftsmen at work.

Castle Archdale Country Park
Castle Archdale
Tel: 028 6862 1588

Woodland and loughshore walks, marina, pony trekking, nature trail. Allows access to White Island. Castle Archdale at War exhibition on the Battle of the Atlantic.

Castle Balfour
Main Street
Lisnaskea
Tel: 028 6632 3110

Built around 1618 by Sir James Balfour, a Scottish planter, the castle was in continuous occupation until the early 19th century.

Castle Caldwell Forest Park
Belleek
Tel: 028 6634 3032

RSPB reserve, wildfowl hides, shore walks.

Castle Coole
Dublin Road
Enniskillen
Tel: 028 6634 8249

Designed by James Wyatt for the Earls of Belmore and completed in 1798. Grounds feature mature oak woodland and lake.

Crom Estate
Newtownbutler
Tel: 028 6773 8118

Over 2,000 acres of woodland, farmland and loughs support rare plants and wildlife. Walks around the estate take in the ruins of Crom old castle.

Devenish Island
Famous for its perfect 12th century round tower and ruined Augustinian abbey. Graveyard holds intricately carved 15th century high cross.

Enniskillen Castle and Museum
Castle Barracks, Enniskillen
Tel: 028 6632 5000
Web: www.enniskillencastle.co.uk

Famous castle, once the stronghold of Gaelic Maguire chieftains. History, wildlife and landscape of the area presented in Fermanagh County Museum. Museum of the Royal Inniskilling Fusiliers in the castle keep.

ExploreErne Exhibition
Gateway Centre, Corry, Belleek
Tel: 028 6865 8833

The story of the formation of the lough and its effect on the people who live round its shores.

Fermanagh Crystal
Main Street, Belleek
Tel: 028 6865 8631

Design, marking and cutting of hand-cut lead glass.

Florence Court
Florencecourt
Tel: 028 6634 8249

Built by Earls of Enniskillen in 18th century. Features 1780s walled garden.

Florencecourt Forest Park
Florencecourt
Tel: 028 6634 3032

Walks and walled garden. Grounds boast 200 year old Irish oaks and the original Irish yew tree.

Forthill Park and Cole's Monument
Enniskillen
Tel: 028 6632 5050

Town park on steep hill. Monument built in 1857 commemorating Sir Galbraith Lowry-Cole who was one of Wellington's generals. 108 steps to the top of the monument.

Lough Navar Forest
Derrygonnelly
Tel: 028 6634 3032

7 mile drive through the forest to magnificent panorama over Lower Lough Erne with viewpoints and picnic areas.

Marble Arch Caves and Cuilcagh
Mountain Park, Florencecourt
Tel: 028 6634 8855

Guided tour included walk through ancient ash woodland and boat journey along subterranean river, continuing on foot past a variety of cave formations.

Monea Castle
Monea
Tel: 028 6632 3110

Imposing plantation castle build around 1618 by Malcolm Hamilton. Abandoned in 1750 following a fire.

Roslea Heritage Centre
Monaghan Road
Roslea
Tel: 028 6775 1750

An 1874 schoolhouse with old school desks. Among traditional farming implements on display is a McMahon space, once manufactured locally.

Sheelin Lace Museum
Bellanaleck
Tel: 028 6634 8052

Items of Irish lace dating form 1850 to 1900, including wedding dresses and veils, baby dresses, bonnets and parsols.

Tully Castle
Churchhill

Fortified house and bawn built in 1613 by Sir John Hume and burned by the Maguires in 1641. Formal garden and visitor centre.

Vintage Cycle Museum
64 Main Street, Brookeborough
Tel: 028 8953 1206

Over 100 bicycles including folding army bike, ice-cream tricycle, tandems, 1950s children's cycles and bicycle with levers. Also toys and household memorabilia.

White Island
Kesh
Tel: 028 6862 1333

Main feature of the ruined 12th century church is its Romanesque doorway. The archaic stone figures set into the wall predate the church

Co Londonderry

Bellaghy Bawn
Castle Street, Bellaghy
Tel: 028 7938 6812

Exhibits inside this restored fortified house of 1618 include local history, the Ulster Plantation and the writings of Bellaghy-born Seamus Heaney and other poets.

Benone Strand
Benone
Tel: 028 7775 0555

White beach backed by sand dunes and dramatic cliffs.

Castledawson Open Farm
Leitrim Road, Castledawson
Tel: 028 7946 8207

Rare fowl breeds, goats, rabbits, Jacob and Soya sheep, Dexter cattle, guinea pigs, miniature Shetland ponies, emus.

Derry's Walls
Derry City
Tel: 028 7126 7284

Derry is the only completely walled city in Ireland, its walls have withstood several sieges, the most celebrated 105 days. Fine views from the top of the walls which encircle the old city.

Downhill Castle and Mussenden Temple
Mussenden Road, Castlerock
Tel: 028 7084 8728

Ruins of 18th century palace of the eccentric Earl – Bishop of Derry. Mussenden Temple on the cliff top was built by the Bishop in 1783 as a summer library.

Earhart Centre and Wildlife Sanctuary
Ballyarnet, Londonderry
Tel: 028 7135 4040

Cottage exhibition on Amelia Earhart, the first woman to fly the Atlantic solo who landed in the field here in 1932.

Fifth Province
Calgach Centre, Butcher Street
Tel: 028 7137 3177

Presentation using a variety of dramatic effects and audio-visual techniques which depicts the unique history of the Celtic nation.

Foyle Valley Railway Centre
Foyle Road, Derry
Tel: 028 7126 5234

Built on the site of the Great Northern Railway terminus. Features narrow-gauge networks that carried the Donegal Railway and the Londonderry and Lough Swilly Railway. Diesel railcars of 1932 and 1940 on 6 mile track.

Garvagh Museum and Heritage Centre
Main Street, Garvagh
Tel: 028 2955 7924

Stone Age artefacts from the Bann Valley. Boat from nearby Eel fishery and farming implements.

Guildhall
Guildhall Square, Derry
Tel: 028 7137 7335

The original building, named in honour of the London Guilds, was officially opened in 1890 as the administrative centre of the Londonderry Corporation. The neo-gothic building stands on land reclaimed from the River Foyle; its clock tower is the largest of its kind in Ireland.

Harbour Museum
Harbour Square, Derry
Tel: 028 7137 7331

The maritime history of Derry including a replica of 30 ft Curragh in which St Columba sailed to Iona in 563 AD. Admission free.

Hezlett House
107 Sea Road, Castlerock
Tel: 028 7084 8567

Thatched 17th century former rectory with cruck/truss roof and 19th century furnishings.

Magilligan – Greencastle Ferry
Tel: + (353) 778 1901

Plantation of Ulster Visitor Centre
50 High Street, Draperstown
Tel: 028 7962 7800

The story of the Ulster Plantation, Hugh O'Neil and the 'Flight of the Earls'.

Portstewart Strand
Portstewart
Tel: 028 7083 6396

Two miles of strand and sand dunes with waymarked nature trail.

Roe Valley Country Park
Limavady
Tel: 028 7772 2074

Home to Ulster's first domestic hydro-electric power station opened in 1896 – much of the original equipment is still preserved.

Springhill
20 Springhill Road, Moneymore
Tel: 028 8674 8210

17th century manor house with family belongings and costume museum.

St Columb's Cathedral
London Street, Derry
Tel: 028 7126 7313

Built in 1633 with stained glass depicting heroic scenes from the Great Siege of 1688-89. The keys of the gates which were closed against the Jacobites are displayed in the chapterhouse.

Tower Museum
Union Hall Place, Derry
Tel: 028 7137 2411

History of the city from prehistoric times.

William Clark & Sons Ltd
Upperlands, Maghera
Tel: 028 7954 7200

Linen fabrics for the clothing industry are made here. Beetling machines in operation. Tour passes the dams which used to power the old linen mill and still supply the water for manufacturing processes.

Workhouse Museum
23 Glendermott Road, Derry
Tel: 028 7131 8328
History of the workhouse, Irish famine and city's role during World War II.

Co Tyrone

An Creagán Visitor Centre
Creggan, Omagh
Tel: 028 8076 1112

Archaeological history and stories of the area with interpretive displays and bog walks.

Castle Caulfield
Castlecaulfied

Ruins of mansion built by Sir Toby Caulfield in 1619. Gatehouse with murder holes and Caulfield arms.

Castlederg Visitor Centre
26 Lower Strabane Road, Castlederg
Tel: 028 8167 0795

Local exhibits and displays highlight the area's heritage.

Coach and Carriage Museum
Blessingbourne, Fivemiletown
Tel: 028 8952 1221

Coaches on display including an 1825 London-to-Oxford stagecoach and a 1910 country doctor's buggy.

Drum Manor Forest Park
Cookstown
Tel: 028 8676 2774

Demonstration shrub garden, walled butterfly garden, arboretum. Lakes, heronry, nature trail.

Gortin Glen Forest Park
Gortin, Omagh
Tel: 028 8167 0666

5 mile forest drive with pull-in places for fine views. Trails also lead to viewpoints.

Grant Ancestral Home
Dergina, Ballygawley
Tel: 028 8555 7133

1738 birthplace of John Simpson, great grandfather of Ulysses Simpson Grant, 18th US President 1869-77.

Gray's Printers' Museum
49 Main Street, Strabane
Tel: 028 7188 4094

Associated with famous Ulster-Americans, including John Dunlap, printer of the American Declaration of Independence.

Kinturk Cultural Centre
7 Kinturk Road, Cookstown
Tel: 028 8673 6512

History of the Lough Neagh fishing and eel industry including displays of old traditional boats and equipment.

Sperrin Heritage Centre
274 Glenelly Road
Cranagh, Gortin
Tel: 028 8164 8142

'Treasure of the Sperrins' exhibition unearths the regions rich geological composition and the story of gold.

The Linen Green

Moygashel
Tel: 028 8775 3761

Designer outlet village including visitors' centre depicting the history behind Moygashel linen.

Tyrone Crystal
Killybrackey, Dungannon
Tel: 028 8772 5335

Guided tour of the blowing, marking, cutting and finishing stages of Tyrone Crystal.

Ulster-American Folk Park
Castletown, Omagh
Tel: 028 8224 3292

Outdoor museum of emigration to North America tells the story of people who left Ireland during the 18th and 19th centuries.

Wellbrook Beetling Mill
Cookstown
Tel: 028 8674 8210

Water-powered 18th century linen hammer mill. Linen making demonstrations.

Wilson Ancestral Home
Strabane
Tel: 028 7138 2204
Ancestral home of James Wilson, 28th President of the USA.

Northern Ireland's Forests

Northern Ireland's forests are expanding and the Forest Service encourages this growth and manages its forests in a responsible and environmentally friendly manner. Its forests are open throughout the year, providing facilities and areas for recreational activities such as walking. Forests are listed below by county.

The Forest Service Headquarters
Customer Service Manager
Dundonald House
Upper Newtownards Road
Belfast
BT4 3SB
Tel: 028 9052 4480
Fax: 028 9052 4570

Co Antrim
Ballycastle Forest, Glenarm Forest, Glenariff Forest Park, Tardree Forest, Ballyboley Forest, Ballypatrick Forest, Portglenone Forest, Randalstown Forest, Rea's Wood

Co Armagh
Gosford Forest Park, Slieve Gullion Forest Park

Co Down
Tollymore Forest Park, Castlewellan Forest Park, Donard Forest, Rostrevor Forest, Drumkeeragh Forest, Belvoir Park Forest, Cairn Wood

Co Fermanagh
Florence Court Forest Park, Ely Lodge Forest, Lough Navar Forest, Castle Caldwell Forest, Castle Archdale Forest, Marble Arch Wood, Spring Grove.

Co Derry
Coleraine Woods – Sommerset, Mountsandel, Castleroe, Springwell Forest, Binevenagh

Co Tyrone
Gortin Glen Forest Park, Drum Manor Forest Park, Parkanaur Forest Park, Pomeroy Forest, Seskinore Forest, Knockmany Forest, Fardross Forest

Other Visitor Information

Currency

Northern Ireland uses the Pound Sterling, as in Great Britain. However, the main banks each issue their own banknotes, as well as the more familiar Bank of England and Bank of Scotland. Mastercard/Access and Visa are generally accepted; Diner's Club and American Express less so. Cheques with a bankers' card are also widely accepted.

In towns, most banks have opening hours of 9.30am - 4.30pm, sometimes closing for lunch, or closing early on Friday. A few may open on Saturday mornings, but most do not, and in smaller towns and villages the bank may not be open every day.

Cash dispensers are numerous, and accept most UK bank cards, as well as all types of credit card. Banks such as TSB and Lloyd's do not have branches in Northern Ireland, although cash may be withdrawn via cash dispensers.

For travel to the Republic of Ireland, money must be changed into Euros, the new common currency for most of the European Union. The Euro is commonly accepted in border areas and in larger stores in Belfast and some of the bigger towns.

Shopping

Northern Ireland has most of the high street stores seen in both Great Britain and the Republic of Ireland. Shopping hours are generally 9.00am to 5.30 pm, although in smaller towns shops close for lunch and may close early (or not even open) on one day of the week. In larger towns shops are often open late on Thursday nights, and many open on Sunday from 1pm to 5pm. Some of the larger supermarkets are open 24 hours a day, except Sunday. Most towns also have a market day once a week.

(For a list of shopping centres and more detail on shopping see Chapter 12, page 529).

Northern Ireland Towns 'Closed' Days

Town	Day
Antrim	Wednesday
Armagh	Wednesday
Ballycastle	Wednesday
Ballyclare	Thursday
Ballymena	Wednesday
Ballymoney	Monday
Ballymoney	Monday
Banbridge	Thursday
Bangor	Thursday
Bushmills	Thursday
Carrickfergus	Wednesday
Coleraine	Thursday
Comber	Wednesday
Cookstown	Wednesday
Downpatrick	Wednesday
Dungannon	Wednesday
Enniskillen	Wednesday
Holywood	Wednesday
Larne	Tuesday
Limavady	Thursday
Randalstown	Tuesday & Saturday
Warrenpoint	Wednesday
Lisburn	Wednesday
Londonderry	Thursday
Lurgan	Wednesday
Magherafelt	Tuesday
Newcastle	Thursday
Newry	Wednesday
Newtownards	Thursday
Omagh	Wednesday
Portadown	Thursday
Portstewart	Thursday (except July and August)
Strabane	Thursday

Travelling Distances

Road Distances from Belfast	Miles
Armagh	40
Cork	262
Dublin	103
Enniskillen	83
Larne	23
Derry	73
Newcastle	31
Newry	38
Omagh	68
Portrush	61
Rosslaire	202
Shannon	211
Sligo	125

Weather

Average daytime/night time temperatures, degree C (degrees F)

Average Annual Rainfall: 43 inches

	DAY	NIGHT
January/ February	7 (44)	1 (34)
March/ April	10 (51)	3 (38)
May/June	16 (61)	8 (46)
July/ August	18 (65)	10 (51)
September/ October	15 (59)	8 (46)
November/ December	8 (47)	3 (37)

Emergency Services

To contact the police, fire brigade, ambulance or coastguard in an emergency, dial 999 or 112.

Police Service of Northern Ireland

In non-emergency situations (such as to report lost or stolen property) the police can be contacted at the following local stations.

Main Police Stations

Armagh
Tel: 028 3752 3311

Ballymena
Tel: 028 2565 3355

Belfast
Tel: 028 9065 0222

Coleraine
Tel: 028 7034 4122

Cookstown
Tel: 028 8676 6000

Downpatrick
Tel: 028 4461 5011

Dungannon
Tel: 028 8775 2525

Enniskillen
Tel: 028 6632 2823

Larne
Tel: 028 2827 2266

Londonderry
Tel: 028 7136 7337

Magherafelt
Tel: 028 7963 3701

Newry
Tel: 028 3026 5500

Newtownards
Tel: 028 9181 8080

Omagh
Tel: 028 8224 6177

Portadown
Tel: 028 3833 2424

Medical & Dental Services

Certain hospitals have 24 hour A&E departments which will treat serious injuries and sudden illness. *(See Chapter 5 page 299 for list of hospitals)*

Pharmacies

General hours for pharmacies are 9.00am – 5.30pm Monday to Saturday although some may open late and on Sundays on a rota basis – details can usually be obtained in local press or from pharmacies.

Consulates

American Consulate General
Queen's House, 14 Queen Street, Belfast
Tel: 028 9032 8239

Canadian Consulate
35 The Hill, Groomsport, Bangor
Tel: 028 9127 2060

Consul for the Netherlands
14-16 West Bank Road, Belfast, BT3 9JL
Tel: 028 9037 0223

Denmark, Sweden and Iceland
MWS Maclaran, c/o G Heyn & Sons Ltd
1 Corry Place, Belfast
Tel: 028 9035 0000

Finland
c/o R W Jenkins
11-14 Newry Street
Warrenpoint
Tel: 028 4177 2761

French Honorary Consul
University of Ulster
Shore Road
Newtownabbey
BT37 0QB
Tel: 028 9036 6546

German Consul
M D Getty
c/o AVX Ltd
Hillman's Way
Coleraine
Tel: 028 7034 0403

Italy
O D'Agostino,
7 Richmond Park, Belfast
Tel: 028 9066 8854

New Zealand Consulate
118A Lisburn Road, Glenavy
Tel: 028 9264 8098

Norway, Portugal, Greece
c/o M F Ewings (Shipping) Ltd
15 Corporation Square, Belfast
Tel: 028 9024 2242

Places of Worship

Main Sunday services of major Christian denominations are advertised in the Saturday edition of the Belfast Telegraph. Places of worship for most faith communities are listed in Yellow Pages. The two cathedrals in central Belfast are St. Anne's Cathedral (Anglican/Church of Ireland) on Donegall Street and St. Peter's Cathedral (Roman Catholic) on Derby Street.

Postal Services

Post Offices and red post boxes are all over the city; Main Post Office is at Castle Junction and late mailings are accepted at Tomb Street Sorting Office. Small books of UK stamps are available in most convenience stores and petrol stations.

Cars - Breakdown

Automobile Association Emergency
Tel: 0800 88 77 66

RAC
Tel: 0800 0828 282

Green Flag
Tel: 0800 400 600

Ulster Automobile Club
Tel: 028 9042 6262

Car Parking

Multi-storey and off-street car parks have hourly tariffs dependent on location. On-street pay and display zones are clearly marked. Pay heed to restriction notices drawing attention to morning and evening rush hour clearways and bus lanes when in operation.

Phone Numbers

The Northern Ireland Dialling Code (028) or (28) is used as a prefix when dialling from outside the region, or when making internal calls using a mobile phone. All Belfast numbers are composed of (028) followed by 90 and six digits

Pub Hours

Generally Mon-Sat, 11.30am-11pm, Sundays, 12.30-10pm. Many bars in Belfast have later opening hours on Thurs- Sat nights. Children are not permitted on licensed premises. No alcohol may be served to under 18s

Smoking

No smoking applies on public transport and in most public buildings. Increasingly restaurants are adopting a no-smoking policy; most have a smoke free area.
Travelling

DOE Traffic Watch

Tel: 0345 123 321

Tipping

It is now a generally accepted practice in restaurants to leave a gratuity of 10-15 per cent for good service. Some restaurants may add on an obligatory 10 or 12.5 per cent service charge on large group bookings.

Reference

Reference Section

APPENDIX 1

Northern Ireland Chronology of Events

Event	Date
Government of Ireland Act 1920	23 December 1920
Anglo-Irish War or War of Independence	1920–1922
First Northern Ireland General Election	May 1921
Opening of the first parliament of Northern Ireland; Unionist government led by James Craig sworn in.	7 June 1921
Truce signed between Crown forces and the IRA to allow negotiations between Sinn Fein and the British Government.	July 1921
Face to face negotiations between the British Government and Sinn Féin begin.	September 1921
The Treaty of Independence supersedes the *Government of Ireland Act 1920* and Southern Ireland becomes the Irish Free State with dominion status.	December 1921
Civil Authority (Special Powers) Act introduced in Northern Ireland.	1922
The *Method of Voting and Redistribution of Seats Act (Northern Ireland)* abolishes PR for local government elections.	16 April 1922
Transfer of security powers from Britain to Northern Ireland, the IRA and related organisations proscribed.	22 May 1922
Education Act (Northern Ireland)	1923
House of Commons (Method of Voting and Redistribution of Seats) Act 1929 (Northern Ireland) abolishes PR for parliamentary elections.	1929
Public Health and Local Government Act	1946
Parity extended to include national assistance, family allowances, pensions and health service provisions.	1949
The first civil rights march organised by the Northern Ireland Civil Rights Association (NICRA).	24 August 1968
British Troops sent to Northern Ireland in response to escalating violence.	14 August 1969
Publication of the Cameron Report into disturbances in Northern Ireland.	12 September 1969
Establishment of a Ministry of Community Relations.	October 1969
Publication of the Hunt Report recommending the disbandment of the 'B' Specials and establishment of a locally recruited force under the British Army to be known as the Ulster Defence Regiment.	10 October 1969
The IRA splits into two wings: the provisional and official IRA.	28 December 1969
Macrory Report into local government recommends the abolition of the old structure of local government replaced by 26 new district councils.	29 May 1970
Formation of the Social Democratic and Labour Party.	21 August 1970
Introduction of internment in Northern Ireland.	9 August 1971

Event	Date
Formation of the Democratic Unionist Party.	30 September 1971
13 people shot dead during a civil rights march in Derry – becomes known as Bloody Sunday.	30 January 1972
William Craig launches the Ulster Vanguard movement.	9 February 1972
Devolution suspended. The devolved Executive and legislative powers are taken back to Westminster, and Government is exercised by a Secretary of State, and a Northern Ireland Office (NIO), created by the *NI (Temporary Provisions) Act 1972.*	30 March 1972
Publication of Scarman Report into the causes of violence in summer 1969 and the Widgery Report on Bloody Sunday.	6 April 1972
First district council elections held using PR.	May 1973
Elections held to a new assembly (Sunningdale).	June 1973
NI Constitution Act 1973 passed, bringing about a new system of devolved government with a power sharing Executive.	July 1973
Formation of a power sharing Executive.	November 1973
Sunningdale Agreement agrees Council of Ireland, linking the two administrations on the island and creating a new Northern Ireland Executive.	6 December 1973
Unionist Members of the Executive resign following an Ulster Workers Council political strike. Secretary of State, Merlyn Rees suspends devolution and reintroduces Direct Rule.	19 May 1974
Prevention of Terrorism Act.	29 November 1974
The Northern Ireland Constitutional Convention meets.	1975–76
Prevention of Terrorism Act (1976) takes effect in Northern Ireland.	1976
Fair Employment (NI) Act comes into effect.	5 December 1976
Withdrawal of Special Category status from members of paramilitary organisations.	26 March 1979
Bobby Sands commences hunger strike in protest at the ending of Special Category status for prisoners.	1 March 1981
Bobby Sands dies following 66 days of hunger strike.	5 May 1981
The British Government proposes a 78 member Assembly at Stormont.	5 April 1982
The Northern Ireland Act 1982 establishing the Assembly becomes law.	23 July 1982
Jim Prior, Secretary of State Launches a Programme for Rolling Devolution and elections to the Assembly are held.	October 1982
The Anglo-Irish Agreement is signed by Prime Minister Margaret Thatcher and Taoiseach Garret Fitzgerald.	15 November 1985
The Northern Ireland Assembly is officially dissolved.	23 June 1986
Remembrance Day bomb in Enniskillen.	8 November 1987
John Hume and Gerry Adams meet for the first in a series of discussions (the Hume/Adams talks).	11 January 1988
Brooke Talks commence; bilateral discussions held with the Irish government and main Northern Ireland parties.	January 1990

UUP, DUP, SDLP and Alliance parties agree to talks on the future of Northern Ireland.	25 March 1991
The first talks involving all Northern Ireland political parties since 1976 commence.	17 June 1991
Brooke/Mayhew talks break down following Unionist withdrawal.	10 November 1992
Michael Ancram, Minister for Political Development commences new series of talks with main political parties.	15 September 1993
Conditions for the entry of Sinn Fein to the political arena are disclosed and secret talks between the British government and the IRA are revealed.	15 November 1993
Downing Street Declaration.	15 December 1993
Declaration of IRA ceasefire.	31 August 1994
Loyalist paramilitaries declare ceasefire.	13 October 1994
Establishment of International Body on Decommissioning.	30 November 1995
Canary Wharf bombing in London ends IRA ceasefire.	February 1996
Elections to the all party Forum held.	10 June 1996
UK General Election – Labour elected and Dr. Marjorie Mowlam is appointed as Secretary of State for Northern Ireland	1 May 1997
IRA renew ceasefire and fresh talks begin.	9 September 1997
International Commission on Decommissioning established. General John de Chastelain appointed as Chairman.	24 September 1997
Establishment of a Parades Commission is announced.	17 October 1997
The Good Friday Agreement is signed by the parties in Belfast.	10 April 1998
Northern Ireland (Elections) Act 1998 is passed.	7 May 1998
Referenda held in Northern Ireland and the Republic.	22 May 1998
Membership of Independent Policing Commission is announced by the Secretary of State.	3 June 1998
Elections to the Northern Ireland Assembly held.	25 June 1998
First meeting of the Shadow Northern Ireland Assembly held.	1 July 1998
Enactment of the *Northern Ireland (Sentences) Bill* allowing for the early release of paramilitary prisoners is enacted.	28 July 1998
The Omagh bombing, killing twenty nine people.	15 August 1998
First prisoners released under the prisoner release scheme.	11 September 1998
Northern Ireland Act implementing the Good Friday Agreement, receives Royal Assent.	19 November 1998
Fair Employment and Treatment (Northern Ireland) Order receives Royal Assent and a Human Rights Commission is established.	1 March 1999
The Secretary of State for Northern Ireland and the Irish Foreign Minister sign four treaties establishing the North/South and British/Irish bodies.	8 March 1999
Northern Ireland (Location of Victims Remains) Bill is passed to facilitate the location of the remains of the disappeared.	May 1999

The fifth direct elections to the European Parliament	June 1999
The Mitchell Review of the Good Friday Agreement begins.	6 September 1999
Publication of the Patten Report on Policing	9 September 1999
Peter Mandelson is appointed Secretary of State for Northern Ireland	11 October 1999
Sinn Fein reveal an offer by the IRA to appoint an Official to liaise with the Independent International Decommissioning Commission (IIDC).	8 November 1999
Election of the Northern Ireland Executive.	29 November 1999
NI (Appointed Day) Order to devolve power at Westminster.	1 December 1999
British/Irish Council meets in London for the first time.	7 December 1999
Institutions suspended due to lack of significant developments in decommissioning.	1 February 2002
IRA agrees to put Weapons Beyond Use.	May 2000
The British and Irish governments agree to the restoration of devolution.	22 May 2000
David Trimble resigns as First Minister following failure to make progress on decommissioning.	1 July 2001
The Secretary of State suspends the Northern Ireland Assembly for one day to allow a further six weeks to find agreement and re-elect the First and Deputy First Minister.	10 August 2001
The Northern Ireland Assembly is reinstated.	11 August 2001
The Assembly is suspended by the Secretary of State to allow a further six-week period to find a breakthrough in the outstanding areas of implementing the Good Friday Agreement.	21 September 2001
UUP Ministers resign from the Northern Ireland Executive.	18 October 2001
IRA decommissioning occurs witnessed by the independent arms inspectors.	22 October 2001
The Policing Board replaces the Police Authority.	4 November 2001
Redesignation by some members of the Alliance party enables David Trimble and Mark Durkan to be elected as First and Deputy First Ministers.	6 November 2001
Review of the Legislative Process in Northern Ireland Assembly is published by the Assembly Procedures Committee	16 January 2002
Launch of Review of Public Administration	24 June 2002
Suspension of the Assembly and re-introduction of Direct Rule	15 October 2002
'Assembly' elections take place. The DUP and Sinn Féin emerge as the largest unionist and nationalist parties.	26 November 2003
Jeffrey Donaldson, Arlene Foster and Norah Beare join the DUP from the Ulster Unionist Party.	January 2004
Publication of the Costello report on the future of the 11+ transfer test.	January 2004
Period of review of the Belfast Agreement begins.	3 February 2004

The Belfast Agreement

Signed on 10 April 1998

(Reproduced by kind permission of Northern Ireland Information Service)

TABLE OF CONTENTS

DECLARATION OF SUPPORT

1. We, the participants in the multi-party negotiations, believe that the agreement we have negotiated offers a truly historic opportunity for a new beginning.

2. The tragedies of the past have left a deep and profoundly regrettable legacy of suffering. We must never forget those who have died or been injured, and their families. But we can best honour them through a fresh start, in which we firmly dedicate ourselves to the achievement of reconciliation, tolerance, and mutual trust, and to the protection and vindication of the human rights of all.

3. We are committed to partnership, equality and mutual respect as the basis of relationships within Northern Ireland, between North and South, and between these islands.

4. We reaffirm our total and absolute commitment to exclusively democratic and peaceful means of resolving differences on political issues, and our opposition to any use or threat of force by others for any political purpose, whether in regard to this agreement or otherwise.

5. We acknowledge the substantial differences between our continuing, and equally legitimate, political aspirations. However, we will endeavour to strive in every practical way towards reconciliation and rapprochement within the framework of democratic and agreed arrangements. We pledge that we will, in good faith, work to ensure the success of each and every one of the arrangements to be established under this agreement. It is accepted that all of the institutional and constitutional arrangements - an Assembly in Northern Ireland, a North/South Ministerial Council, implementation bodies, a British-Irish Council and a British-Irish Intergovernmental Conference and any amendments to British Acts of Parliament and the Constitution of Ireland - are interlocking and interdependent and that in particular the functioning of the Assembly and the North/South Council are so closely inter-related that the success of each depends on that of the other.

6. Accordingly, in a spirit of concord, we strongly commend this agreement to the people, North and South, for their approval.

CONSTITUTIONAL ISSUES

1. The participants endorse the commitment made by the British and Irish Governments that, in a new British-Irish Agreement replacing the Anglo-Irish Agreement, they will:

   (i) recognise the legitimacy of whatever choice is freely exercised by a majority of the people of Northern Ireland with regard to its status, whether they prefer to continue to support the Union with Great Britain or a sovereign united Ireland;

   (ii) recognise that it is for the people of the island of Ireland alone, by agreement between the two parts respectively and without external impediment, to exercise their right of self-determination on the basis of consent, freely and concurrently given, North and South, to bring about a united Ireland, if that is their wish, accepting that this right must be achieved and exercised with and subject to the agreement and consent of a majority of the people of Northern Ireland;

   (iii) acknowledge that while a substantial section of the people in Northern Ireland share the legitimate wish of a majority of the people of the island of Ireland for a united Ireland, the present wish of a majority of the people of Northern Ireland, freely exercised and legitimate, is to maintain the Union and, accordingly, that Northern Ireland's status as part of the United Kingdom reflects and relies upon that wish; and that it would be wrong to make any change in the status of Northern Ireland save with the consent of a majority of its people;

   (iv) affirm that if, in the future, the people of the island of Ireland exercise their right of self-determination on the basis set out in sections (i) and (ii) above to bring about a united Ireland, it will be a binding obligation on both Governments to introduce and support in their respective Parliaments legislation to give effect to that wish;

   (v) affirm that whatever choice is freely exercised by a majority of the people of Northern Ireland, the power of the sovereign government with jurisdiction there shall be exercised with rigorous impartiality on behalf of all the people in the diversity of their identities and traditions and shall be founded on the principles of full respect for, and equality of, civil, political, social and cultural rights, of freedom from discrimination for all citizens, and of parity of esteem and of just and equal treatment for the identity, ethos, and aspirations of both communities;

   (vi) recognise the birthright of all the people of Northern Ireland to identify themselves and be accepted as Irish or British, or both, as they may so choose, and accordingly confirm that their right to hold both British and Irish citizenship is accepted by both Governments and would not be affected by any future change in the status of Northern Ireland.

2. The participants also note that the two Governments have accordingly undertaken in the context of this comprehensive political agreement, to propose and support changes in, respectively, the Constitution of Ireland and in British legislation relating to the constitutional status of Northern Ireland.

ANNEX A

DRAFT CLAUSES/SCHEDULES FOR INCORPORATION IN BRITISH LEGISLATION

1. (1) It is hereby declared that Northern Ireland in its entirety remains part of the United Kingdom and shall not cease to be so without the consent of a majority of the people of Northern Ireland voting in a poll held for the purposes of this section in accordance with Schedule 1.

   (2) But if the wish expressed by a majority in such a poll is that Northern Ireland should cease to be part of the United Kingdom and form part of a united Ireland, the Secretary of State shall lay before Parliament such proposals to give effect to that wish as may be agreed between Her Majesty's Government in the United Kingdom and the Government of Ireland.

2. The Government of Ireland Act 1920 is repealed; and this Act shall have effect notwithstanding any other previous enactment.

SCHEDULE 1

POLLS FOR THE PURPOSE OF SECTION 1

1. The Secretary of State may by order direct the holding of a poll for the purposes of section 1 on a date specified in the order.

2. Subject to paragraph 3, the Secretary of State shall exercise the power under paragraph 1 if at any time it appears likely to him that a majority of those voting would express a wish that Northern Ireland should cease to be part of the United Kingdom and form part of a united Ireland.

3. The Secretary of State shall not make an order under paragraph 1 earlier than seven years after the holding of a previous poll under this Schedule.

4. (Remaining paragraphs along the lines of paragraphs 2 and 3 of existing Schedule 1 to 1973 Act.)

ANNEX B

IRISH GOVERNMENT DRAFT LEGISLATION TO AMEND THE CONSTITUTION

Add to Article 29 the following sections:

7. The State may consent to be bound by the British-Irish Agreement done at Belfast on ... the day of ... 1998, hereinafter called the Agreement.
Any institution established by or under the Agreement may exercise the powers and functions thereby conferred on it in respect of all or any part of the island of Ireland notwithstanding any other provision of this Constitution conferring a like power or function on any person or any organ of State appointed under or created or established by or under this Constitution. Any power or function conferred on such an institution in relation to the settlement or resolution of disputes or controversies may be in addition to or in substitution for any like power or function conferred by this Constitution on any such person or organ of State as aforesaid.
If the Government declare that the State has become obliged, pursuant to the Agreement, to give effect to the amendment of this Constitution referred to therein, then, notwithstanding Article 46 hereof, this Constitution shall be amended as follows:
   i. the following Articles shall be substituted for Articles 2 and 3 of the Irish text:
   2. [Irish text to be inserted here]
   3. [Irish text to be inserted here]

   ii. the following Articles shall be substituted for Articles 2 and 3 of the English text:

Article 2

It is the entitlement and birthright of every person born in the island of Ireland, which includes its islands and seas, to be part of the Irish nation. That is also the entitlement of all persons otherwise qualified in accordance with law to be citizens of Ireland. Furthermore, the Irish nation cherishes its special affinity with people of Irish ancestry living abroad who share its cultural identity and heritage.

Article 3

1. It is the firm will of the Irish nation, in harmony and friendship, to unite all the people who share the territory of the island of Ireland, in all the diversity of their identities and traditions, recognising that a united Ireland shall be brought about only by peaceful means with the consent of a majority of the people, democratically expressed, in both jurisdictions in the island. Until then, the laws enacted by the Parliament established by this Constitution shall have the like area and extent of application as the laws enacted by the Parliament that existed immediately before the coming into operation of this Constitution.

2. Institutions with executive powers and functions that are shared between those jurisdictions may be established by their respective responsible authorities for stated purposes and may exercise powers and functions in respect of all or any part of the island.
   iii. the following section shall be added to the Irish text of this Article:
   8. [Irish text to be inserted here]

   and
   iv. the following section shall be added to the English text of this Article:
   8. The State may exercise extra-territorial jurisdiction in accordance with the generally recognised principles of international law.

4. If a declaration under this section is made, this subsection and subsection 3, other than the amendment of this Constitution effected thereby, and subsection 5 of this section shall be omitted from every official text of this Constitution published thereafter, but notwithstanding such omission this section shall continue to have the force of law.

5. If such a declaration is not made within twelve months of this section being added to this Constitution or such longer period as may be provided for by law, this section shall cease to have effect and shall be omitted from every official text of this Constitution published thereafter.

STRAND ONE

DEMOCRATIC INSTITUTIONS IN NORTHERN IRELAND

1. This agreement provides for a democratically elected Assembly in Northern Ireland which is inclusive in its membership, capable of exercising executive and legislative authority, and subject to safeguards to protect the rights and interests of all sides of the community.

The Assembly

2. A 108-member Assembly will be elected by PR(STV) from existing Westminster constituencies.

3. The Assembly will exercise full legislative and executive authority in respect of those matters currently within the responsibility of the six Northern Ireland Government Departments, with the possibility of taking on responsibility for other matters as detailed elsewhere in this agreement.

4. The Assembly - operating where appropriate on a cross-community basis - will be the prime source of authority in respect of all devolved responsibilities.

Safeguards

5. There will be safeguards to ensure that all sections of the community can participate and work together successfully in the operation of these institutions and that all sections of the community are protected, including:
   (a) allocations of Committee Chairs, Ministers and Committee membership in proportion to party strengths;

   (b) the European Convention on Human Rights (ECHR) and any Bill of Rights for Northern Ireland supplementing it, which neither the Assembly nor public bodies can infringe, together with a Human Rights Commission;

   (c) arrangements to provide that key decisions and legislation are proofed to ensure that they do not infringe the ECHR and any Bill of Rights for Northern Ireland;

   (d) arrangements to ensure key decisions are taken on a cross-community basis;
   (i) either parallel consent, i.e. a majority of those members present and voting, including a majority of the unionist and nationalist designations present and voting;

   (ii) or a weighted majority (60%) of members present and voting, including at least 40% of each of the nationalist and unionist designations present and voting.

   Key decisions requiring cross-community support will be designated in advance, including election of the Chair of the Assembly, the First Minister and Deputy First Minister, standing orders and budget allocations. In other cases such decisions could be triggered by a petition of concern brought by a significant minority of Assembly members (30/108).
   (e) an Equality Commission to monitor a statutory obligation to promote equality of opportunity in specified areas and parity of esteem between the two main communities, and to investigate individual complaints against public bodies.

Operation of the Assembly

6. At their first meeting, members of the Assembly will register a designation of identity - nationalist, unionist or other - for the purposes of measuring cross-community support in Assembly votes under the relevant provisions above.

7. The Chair and Deputy Chair of the Assembly will be elected on a cross-community basis, as set out in paragraph 5(d) above.

8. There will be a Committee for each of the main executive functions of the Northern Ireland Administration. The Chairs and Deputy Chairs of the Assembly Committees will be allocated proportionally, using the d'Hondt

system. Membership of the Committees will be in broad proportion to party strengths in the Assembly to ensure that the opportunity of Committee places is available to all members.

9. The Committees will have a scrutiny, policy development and consultation role with respect to the Department with which each is associated, and will have a role in initiation of legislation. They will have the power to:
   - consider and advise on Departmental budgets and Annual Plans in the context of the overall budget allocation;
   - approve relevant secondary legislation and take the Committee stage of relevant primary legislation;
   - call for persons and papers;
   - initiate enquiries and make reports;
   - consider and advise on matters brought to the Committee

   by its Minister.

10. Standing Committees other than Departmental Committees may be established as may be required from time to time.

11. The Assembly may appoint a special Committee to examine and report on whether a measure or proposal for legislation is in conformity with equality requirements, including the ECHR/Bill of Rights. The Committee shall have the power to call people and papers to assist in its consideration of the matter. The Assembly shall then consider the report of the Committee and can determine the matter in accordance with the cross-community consent procedure.

12. The above special procedure shall be followed when requested by the Executive Committee, or by the relevant Departmental Committee, voting on a cross-community basis.

13. When there is a petition of concern as in 5(d) above, the Assembly shall vote to determine whether the measure may proceed without reference to this special procedure. If this fails to achieve support on a cross-community basis, as in 5(d)(i) above, the special procedure shall be followed.
    Executive Authority

14. Executive authority to be discharged on behalf of the Assembly by a First Minister and Deputy First Minister and up to ten Ministers with Departmental responsibilities.

15. The First Minister and Deputy First Minister shall be jointly elected into office by the Assembly voting on a cross-community basis, according to 5(d)(i) above.

16. Following the election of the First Minister and Deputy First Minister, the posts of Ministers will be allocated to parties on the basis of the d'Hondt system by reference to the number of seats each party has in the Assembly.

17. The Ministers will constitute an Executive Committee, which will be convened, and presided over, by the First Minister and Deputy First Minister.

18. The duties of the First Minister and Deputy First Minister will include, inter alia, dealing with and co-ordinating the work of the Executive Committee and the response of the Northern Ireland administration to external relationships.

19. The Executive Committee will provide a forum for the discussion of, and agreement on, issues which cut across the responsibilities of two or more Ministers, for prioritising executive and legislative proposals and for recommending a common position where necessary (e.g. in dealing with external relationships).

20. The Executive Committee will seek to agree each year, and review as necessary, a programme incorporating an agreed budget linked to policies and programmes, subject to approval by the Assembly, after scrutiny in Assembly Committees, on a cross-community basis.

21. A party may decline the opportunity to nominate a person to serve as a Minister or may subsequently change its nominee.

22. All the Northern Ireland Departments will be headed by a Minister. All Ministers will liaise regularly with their respective Committee.

23. As a condition of appointment, Ministers, including the First Minister and Deputy First Minister, will affirm the terms of a Pledge of Office (Annex A) undertaking to discharge effectively and in good faith all the responsibilities attaching to their office.

24. Ministers will have full executive authority in their respective areas of responsibility, within any broad programme agreed by the Executive Committee and endorsed by the Assembly as a whole.

25. An individual may be removed from office following a decision of the Assembly taken on a cross-community basis, if (s)he loses the confidence of the Assembly, voting on a cross-community basis, for failure to meet his or her responsibilities including, inter alia, those set out in the Pledge of Office. Those who hold office should use only democratic, non-violent means, and those who do not should be excluded or removed from office under these provisions.

Legislation

26. The Assembly will have authority to pass primary legislation for Northern Ireland in devolved areas, subject to:
    (a) the ECHR and any Bill of Rights for Northern Ireland supplementing it which, if the courts found to be breached, would render the relevant legislation null and void;

    (b) decisions by simple majority of members voting, except when decision on a cross-community basis is required;

    (c) detailed scrutiny and approval in the relevant Departmental Committee;

    (d) mechanisms, based on arrangements proposed for the Scottish Parliament, to ensure suitable co-ordination, and avoid disputes, between the Assembly and the Westminster Parliament;

    (e) option of the Assembly seeking to include Northern Ireland provisions in United Kingdom-wide legislation in the Westminster Parliament, especially on devolved issues where parity is normally maintained (e.g. social security, company law).

27. The Assembly will have authority to legislate in reserved areas with the approval of the Secretary of State and subject to Parliamentary control.

28. Disputes over legislative competence will be decided by the Courts.

29. Legislation could be initiated by an individual, a Committee or a Minister.
    Relations with other institutions

30. Arrangements to represent the Assembly as a whole, at Summit level and in dealings with other institutions, will be in accordance with paragraph 18, and will be such as to ensure cross-community involvement.

31. Terms will be agreed between appropriate Assembly representatives and the Government of the United Kingdom to ensure effective co-ordination and input by Ministers to national policy-making, including on EU issues.

32. Role of Secretary of State:
    (a) to remain responsible for NIO matters not devolved to the Assembly, subject to regular consultation with the Assembly and Ministers;

    (b) to approve and lay before the Westminster Parliament any Assembly legislation on reserved matters;

    (c) to represent Northern Ireland interests in the United Kingdom Cabinet;

    (d) t o have the right to attend the Assembly at their invitation.

33. The Westminster Parliament (whose power to make legislation for Northern Ireland would remain unaffected) will:
    (a) legislate for non-devolved issues, other than where the Assembly legislates with the approval of the Secretary of State and subject to the control of Parliament;

    (b) to legislate as necessary to ensure the United Kingdom's international obligations are met in respect of Northern Ireland;

    (c) scrutinise, including through the Northern Ireland Grand and Select Committees, the responsibilities of the Secretary of State.

34. A consultative Civic Forum will be established. It will comprise representatives of the business, trade union and voluntary sectors, and such other sectors as agreed by the First Minister and the Deputy First Minister. It will act as a consultative mechanism on social, economic and cultural issues. The First Minister and the Deputy First Minister will by agreement provide administrative support for the Civic Forum and establish guidelines for the selection of representatives to the Civic Forum.

Transitional Arrangements

35. The Assembly will meet first for the purpose of organisation, without legislative or executive powers, to resolve its standing orders and working practices and make preparations for the effective functioning of the Assembly, the British-Irish Council and the North/South Ministerial Council and associated implementation bodies. In this transitional period, those members of the Assembly serving as shadow Ministers shall affirm their commitment to non-violence and exclusively peaceful and democratic means and their opposition to any use or threat of force by others for any political purpose; to work in good faith to bring the new arrangements into being; and to observe the spirit of the Pledge of Office applying to appointed Ministers.

Review

36. After a specified period there will be a review of these arrangements, including the details of electoral arrangements and of the Assembly's procedures, with a view to agreeing any adjustments necessary in the interests of efficiency and fairness.

Annex A

PLEDGE OF OFFICE

To pledge:

(a) to discharge in good faith all the duties of office;
(b) commitment to non-violence and exclusively peaceful and democratic means;
(c) to serve all the people of Northern Ireland equally, and to act in accordance with the general obligations on government to promote equality and prevent discrimination;
(d) to participate with colleagues in the preparation of a programme for government;
(e) to operate within the framework of that programme when agreed within the Executive Committee and endorsed by the Assembly;
(f) to support, and to act in accordance with, all decisions of the Executive Committee and Assembly;
(g) to comply with the Ministerial Code of Conduct.

CODE OF CONDUCT

Ministers must at all times:

- observe the highest standards of propriety and regularity involving impartiality, integrity and objectivity in relationship to the stewardship of public funds;
- be accountable to users of services, the community and, through the Assembly, for the activities within their responsibilities, their stewardship of public funds and the extent to which key performance targets and objectives have been met;
- ensure all reasonable requests for information from the Assembly, users of services and individual citizens are complied with; and that Departments and their staff conduct their dealings with the public in an open and responsible way;
- follow the seven principles of public life set out by the Committee on Standards in Public Life;
- comply with this code and with rules relating to the use of public funds; operate in a way conducive to promoting good community relations and equality of treatment;
- not use information gained in the course of their service for personal gain; nor seek to use the opportunity of public service to promote their private interests;
- ensure they comply with any rules on the acceptance of gifts and hospitality that might be offered;
- declare any personal or business interests which may conflict with their responsibilities. The Assembly will retain a Register of Interests. Individuals must ensure that any direct or indirect pecuniary interests which members of the public might reasonably think could influence their judgement are listed in the Register of Interests;

STRAND TWO

NORTH/SOUTH MINISTERIAL COUNCIL

1. Under a new British/Irish Agreement dealing with the totality of relationships, and related legislation at Westminster and in the Oireachtas, a North/South Ministerial Council to be established to bring together those with executive responsibilities in Northern Ireland and the Irish Government, to develop consultation, co-operation and action within the island of Ireland - including through implementation on an all-island and cross-border basis - on matters of mutual interest within the competence of the Administrations, North and South.

2. All Council decisions to be by agreement between the two sides. Northern Ireland to be represented by the First Minister, Deputy First Minister and any relevant Ministers, the Irish Government by the Taoiseach and relevant Ministers, all operating in accordance with the rules for democratic authority and accountability in force in the Northern Ireland Assembly and the Oireachtas respectively. Participation in the Council to be one of the essential responsibilities attaching to relevant posts in the two Administrations. If a holder of a relevant post will not participate normally in the Council, the Taoiseach in the case of the Irish Government and the First and Deputy First Minister in the case of the Northern Ireland Administration to be able to make alternative arrangements.

3. The Council to meet in different formats:
   (i) in plenary format twice a year, with Northern Ireland representation led by the First Minister and Deputy First Minister and the Irish Government led by the Taoiseach;
   (ii) in specific sectoral formats on a regular and frequent basis with each side represented by the appropriate Minister;
   (iii) in an appropriate format to consider institutional or cross-sectoral matters (including in relation to the EU) and to resolve disagreement.

4. Agendas for all meetings to be settled by prior agreement between the two sides, but it will be open to either to propose any matter for consideration or action.

5. The Council:
   (i) to exchange information, discuss and consult with a view to co-operating on matters of mutual interest within the competence of both Administrations, North and South;
   (ii) to use best endeavours to reach agreement on the adoption of common policies, in areas where there is a mutual cross-border and all-island benefit, and which are within the competence of both Administrations, North and South, making determined efforts to overcome any disagreements;
   (iii) to take decisions by agreement on policies for implementation separately in each jurisdiction, in relevant meaningful areas within the competence of both Administrations, North and South;
   (iv) to take decisions by agreement on policies and action at an all-island and cross-border level to be implemented by the bodies to be established as set out in paragraphs 8 and 9 below.

6. Each side to be in a position to take decisions in the Council within the defined authority of those attending, through the arrangements in place for co-ordination of executive functions within each jurisdiction. Each side to remain accountable to the Assembly and Oireachtas respectively, whose approval, through the arrangements in place on either side, would be required for decisions beyond the defined authority of those attending.

7. As soon as practically possible after elections to the Northern Ireland Assembly, inaugural meetings will take place of the Assembly, the British/Irish Council and the North/South Ministerial Council in their transitional forms. All three institutions will meet regularly and frequently on this basis during the period between the elections to the Assembly, and the transfer of powers to the Assembly, in order to establish their modus operandi.

8. During the transitional period between the elections to the Northern Ireland Assembly and the transfer of power to it, representatives of the Northern Ireland transitional Administration and the Irish Government operating in the North/South Ministerial Council will undertake a work programme, in consultation with the British Government, covering at least 12 subject areas, with a view to identifying and agreeing by 31 October 1998 areas where co-operation and implementation for mutual benefit will take place. Such areas may include matters in the list set out in the Annex.

9. As part of the work programme, the Council will identify and agree at least 6 matters for co-operation and implementation in each of the following categories:
   (i) Matters where existing bodies will be the appropriate mechanisms for co-operation in each separate jurisdiction;
   (ii) Matters where the co-operation will take place through agreed implementation bodies on a cross-border or all-island level.

10. The two Governments will make necessary legislative and other enabling preparations to ensure, as an absolute commitment, that these bodies, which have been agreed as a result of the work programme, function at the time of the inception of the British-Irish Agreement and the transfer of powers, with legislative authority for these bodies transferred to the Assembly as soon as possible thereafter. Other arrangements for the agreed co-operation will also commence contemporaneously with the transfer of powers to the Assembly.

11. The implementation bodies will have a clear operational remit. They will implement on an all-island and cross-border basis policies agreed in the Council.

12. Any further development of these arrangements to be by agreement in the Council and with the specific endorsement of the Northern Ireland Assembly and Oireachtas, subject to the extent of the competences and responsibility of the two Administrations.

13. t is understood that the North/South Ministerial Council and the Northern Ireland Assembly are mutually inter-dependent, and that one cannot successfully function without the other.

14. Disagreements within the Council to be addressed in the format described at paragraph 3(iii) above or in the plenary format. By agreement between the two sides, experts could be appointed to consider a particular matter and report.

15. Funding to be provided by the two Administrations on the basis that the Council and the implementation bodies constitute a necessary public function.

16. The Council to be supported by a standing joint Secretariat, staffed by members of the Northern Ireland Civil Service and the Irish Civil Service.

17. The Council to consider the European Union dimension of relevant matters, including the implementation of EU policies and programmes and proposals under consideration in the EU framework. Arrangements to be made to ensure that the views of the Council are taken into account and represented appropriately at relevant EU meetings.

18. The Northern Ireland Assembly and the Oireachtas to consider developing a joint parliamentary forum, bringing together equal numbers from both institutions for discussion of matters of mutual interest and concern.

19. Consideration to be given to the establishment of an independent consultative forum appointed by the two Administrations, representative of civil society, comprising the social partners and other members with expertise in social, cultural, economic and other issues.

ANNEX

Areas for North-South co-operation and implementation may include the following:

1. Agriculture - animal and plant health.
2. Education - teacher qualifications and exchanges.
3. Transport - strategic transport planning.
4. Environment - environmental protection, pollution, water quality, and waste management.
5. Waterways - inland waterways.
6. Social Security/Social Welfare - entitlements of cross-border workers and fraud control.
7. Tourism - promotion, marketing, research, and product development.
8. Relevant EU Programmes such as SPPR, INTERREG, Leader II and their successors.
9. Inland Fisheries.
10. Aquaculture and marine matters
11. Health: accident and emergency services and other related cross-border issues.
12. Urban and rural development.

Others to be considered by the shadow North/ South Council.

STRAND THREE

BRITISH-IRISH COUNCIL

1. A British-Irish Council (BIC) will be established under a new British-Irish Agreement to promote the harmonious and mutually beneficial development of the totality of relationships among the peoples of these islands.

2. Membership of the BIC will comprise representatives of the British and Irish Governments, devolved institutions in Northern Ireland, Scotland and Wales, when established, and, if appropriate, elsewhere in the United Kingdom, together with representatives of the Isle of Man and the Channel Islands.
3. The BIC will meet in different formats: at summit level, twice per year; in specific sectoral formats on a regular basis, with each side represented by the appropriate Minister; in an appropriate format to consider cross-sectoral matters.

4. Representatives of members will operate in accordance with whatever procedures for democratic authority and accountability are in force in their respective elected institutions.

5. The BIC will exchange information, discuss, consult and use best endeavours to reach agreement on co-operation on matters of mutual interest within the competence of the relevant Administrations. Suitable issues for early discussion in the BIC could include transport links, agricultural issues, environmental issues, cultural issues, health issues, education issues and approaches to EU issues. Suitable arrangements to be made for practical co-operation on agreed policies.

6. It will be open to the BIC to agree common policies or common actions. Individual members may opt not to participate in such common policies and common action.

7. The BIC normally will operate by consensus. In relation to decisions on common policies or common actions, including their means of implementation, it will operate by agreement of all members participating in such policies or actions.

8. The members of the BIC, on a basis to be agreed between them, will provide such financial support as it may require.

9. A secretariat for the BIC will be provided by the British and Irish Governments in co-ordination with officials of each of the other members.

10. In addition to the structures provided for under this agreement, it will be open to two or more members to develop bilateral or multilateral arrangements between them. Such arrangements could include, subject to the agreement of the members concerned, mechanisms to enable consultation, co-operation and joint decision-making on matters of mutual interest; and mechanisms to implement any joint decisions they may reach. These arrangements will not require the prior approval of the BIC as a whole and will operate independently of it.

11. The elected institutions of the members will be encouraged to develop interparliamentary links, perhaps building on the British-Irish Interparliamentary Body.

12. The full membership of the BIC will keep under review the workings of the Council, including a formal published review at an appropriate time after the Agreement comes into effect, and will contribute as appropriate to any review of the overall political agreement arising from the multi-party negotiations.

BRITISH-IRISH INTERGOVERNMENTAL CONFERENCE

1. There will be a new British-Irish Agreement dealing with the totality of relationships. It will establish a standing British-Irish Intergovernmental Conference, which will subsume both the Anglo-Irish Intergovernmental Council and the Intergovernmental Conference established under the 1985 Agreement.

2. The Conference will bring together the British and Irish Governments to promote bilateral co-operation at all levels on all matters of mutual interest within the competence of both Governments.

3. The Conference will meet as required at Summit level (Prime Minister and Taoiseach). Otherwise, Governments will be represented by appropriate Ministers. Advisers, including police and security advisers, will attend as appropriate.

4. All decisions will be by agreement between both Governments. The Governments will make determined efforts to resolve disagreements between them. There will be no derogation from the sovereignty of either Government.

5. In recognition of the Irish Government's special interest in Northern Ireland and of the extent to which issues of mutual concern arise in relation to Northern Ireland, there will be regular and frequent meetings of the Conference concerned with non-devolved Northern Ireland matters, on which the Irish Government may put forward views and proposals. These meetings, to be co-chaired by the Minister for Foreign Affairs and the Secretary of State for Northern Ireland, would also deal with all-island and cross-border co-operation on non-devolved issues.

6. Co-operation within the framework of the Conference will include facilitation of co-operation in security matters. The Conference also will address, in particular, the areas of rights, justice, prisons and policing in Northern Ireland (unless and until responsibility is devolved to a Northern Ireland administration) and will intensify co-operation between the two Governments on the all-island or cross-border aspects of these matters.

7. Relevant executive members of the Northern Ireland Administration will be involved in meetings of the Conference, and in the reviews referred to in paragraph 9 below to discuss non-devolved Northern Ireland matters.

8. The Conference will be supported by officials of the British and Irish Governments, including by a standing joint Secretariat of officials dealing with non-devolved Northern Ireland matters.

9. The Conference will keep under review the workings of the new British-Irish Agreement and the machinery and institutions established under it, including a formal published review three years after the Agreement comes into effect. Representatives of the Northern Ireland Administration will be invited to express views to the Conference in this context. The Conference will contribute as appropriate to any review of the overall political agreement arising from the multi-party negotiations but will have no power to override the democratic arrangements set up by this Agreement.

RIGHTS, SAFEGUARDS AND EQUALITY OF OPPORTUNITY

Human Rights

1. The parties affirm their commitment to the mutual respect, the civil rights and the religious liberties of everyone in the community. Against the background of the recent history of communal conflict, the parties affirm in particular:
   - the right of free political thought;
   - the right to freedom and expression of religion;
   - the right to pursue democratically national and political aspirations;
   - the right to seek constitutional change by peaceful and legitimate means;
   - the right to freely choose one's place of residence;
   - the right to equal opportunity in all social and economic activity, regardless of class, creed, disability, gender or ethnicity;
   - the right to freedom from sectarian harassment; and
   - the right of women to full and equal political participation.

United Kingdom Legislation

2. The British Government will complete incorporation into Northern Ireland law of the European Convention on Human Rights (ECHR), with direct access to the courts, and remedies for breach of the Convention, including power for the courts to overrule Assembly legislation on grounds of inconsistency.

3. Subject to the outcome of public consultation underway, the British Government intends, as a particular priority, to create a statutory obligation on public authorities in Northern Ireland to carry out all their functions with due regard to the need to promote equality of opportunity in relation to religion and political opinion; gender; race; disability; age; marital status; dependants; and sexual orientation. Public bodies would be required to draw up statutory schemes showing how they would implement this obligation. Such schemes would cover arrangements for policy appraisal, including an assessment of impact on relevant categories, public consultation, public access to information and services, monitoring and timetables.

4. The new Northern Ireland Human Rights Commission (see paragraph 5 below) will be invited to consult and to advise on the scope for defining, in Westminster legislation, rights supplementary to those in the European Convention on Human Rights, to reflect the particular circumstances of Northern Ireland, drawing as appropriate on international instruments and experience. These additional rights to reflect the principles of mutual respect for the identity and ethos of both communities and parity of esteem, and - taken together with the ECHR - to constitute a Bill of Rights for Northern Ireland. Among the issues for consideration by the Commission will be:
   - the formulation of a general obligation on government and public bodies fully to respect, on the basis of equality of treatment, the identity and ethos of both communities in Northern Ireland; and
   - a clear formulation of the rights not to be discriminated against and to equality of opportunity in both the public and private sectors.

New Institutions in Northern Ireland

5. A new Northern Ireland Human Rights Commission, with membership from Northern Ireland reflecting the community balance, will be established by Westminster legislation, independent of Government, with an extended and enhanced role beyond that currently exercised by the Standing Advisory Commission on Human Rights, to include keeping under review the adequacy and effectiveness of laws and practices, making recommendations to Government as necessary; providing information and promoting awareness of human rights; considering draft legislation referred to them by the new Assembly; and, in appropriate cases, bringing court proceedings or providing assistance to individuals doing so.

6. Subject to the outcome of public consultation currently underway, the British Government intends a new statutory Equality Commission to replace the Fair Employment Commission, the Equal Opportunities Commission (NI), the Commission for Racial Equality (NI) and the Disability Council. Such a unified Commission will advise on, validate and monitor the statutory obligation and will investigate complaints of default.

7. It would be open to a new Northern Ireland Assembly to consider bringing together its responsibilities for these matters into a dedicated Department of Equality.

8. These improvements will build on existing protections in Westminster legislation in respect of the judiciary, the system of justice and policing. Comparable Steps by the Irish Government

9. The Irish Government will also take steps to further strengthen the protection of human rights in its jurisdiction. The Government will, taking account of the work of the All-Party Oireachtas Committee on the Constitution and the Report of the Constitution Review Group, bring forward measures to strengthen and underpin the constitutional protection of human rights. These proposals will draw on the European Convention on Human Rights and other international legal instruments in the field of human rights and the question of the incorporation of the ECHR will be further examined in this context. The measures brought forward would ensure at least an equivalent level of protection of human rights as will pertain in Northern Ireland. In addition, the Irish Government will:
   establish a Human Rights Commission with a mandate and remit equivalent to that within Northern Ireland;
   - proceed with arrangements as quickly as possible to ratify the Council of Europe Framework Convention on National Minorities (already ratified by the UK);
   - implement enhanced employment equality legislation;
   - introduce equal status legislation; and
   - continue to take further active steps to demonstrate its respect for the different traditions in the island of Ireland.

A Joint Committee

10. It is envisaged that there would be a joint committee of representatives of the two Human Rights Commissions, North and South, as a forum for consideration of human rights issues in the island of Ireland. The joint committee will consider, among other matters, the possibility of establishing a charter, open to signature by all democratic political parties, reflecting and endorsing agreed measures for the protection of the fundamental rights of everyone living in the island of Ireland. Reconciliation and Victims of Violence

11. The participants believe that it is essential to acknowledge and address the suffering of the victims of violence as a necessary element of reconciliation. They look forward to the results of the work of the Northern Ireland Victims Commission.

12. It is recognised that victims have a right to remember as well as to contribute to a changed society. The achievement of a peaceful and just society would be the true memorial to the victims of violence. The participants particularly recognise that young people from areas affected by the troubles face particular difficulties and will support the development of special community-based initiatives based on international best practice. The provision of services that are supportive and sensitive to the needs of victims will also be a critical element and that support will need to be channelled through both statutory and community-based voluntary organisations facilitating locally-based self-help and support networks. This will require the allocation of sufficient resources, including statutory funding as necessary, to meet the needs of victims and to provide for community-based support programmes.

13. The participants recognise and value the work being done by many organisations to develop reconciliation and mutual understanding and respect between and within communities and traditions, in Northern Ireland and between North and South, and they see such work as having a vital role in consolidating peace and political agreement. Accordingly, they pledge their continuing support to such organisations and will positively examine the case for enhanced financial assistance for the work of reconciliation. An essential aspect of the reconciliation process is the promotion of a culture of tolerance at every level of society, including initiatives to facilitate and encourage integrated education and mixed housing.

RIGHTS, SAFEGUARDS AND EQUALITY OF OPPORTUNITY

Economic, Social and Cultural Issues

1. Pending the devolution of powers to a new Northern Ireland Assembly, the British Government will pursue broad policies for sustained economic growth and stability in Northern Ireland and for promoting social inclusion, including in particular community development and the advancement of women in public life.

2. Subject to the public consultation currently under way, the British Government will make rapid progress with:
(i) a new regional development strategy for Northern Ireland, for consideration in due course by the Assembly, tackling the problems of a divided society and social cohesion in urban, rural and border areas, protecting and enhancing the environment, producing new approaches to transport issues, strengthening the physical infrastructure of the region, developing the advantages and resources of rural areas and rejuvenating major urban centres;
(ii) a new economic development strategy for Northern Ireland, for consideration in due course by the Assembly, which would provide for short and medium term economic planning linked as appropriate to the regional development strategy; and
(iii) measures on employment equality included in the recent White Paper (Partnership for Equality) and covering the extension and strengthening of anti-discrimination legislation, a review of the national security aspects of the present fair employment legislation at the earliest possible time, a new more focused Targeting Social Need initiative and a range of measures aimed at combating unemployment and progressively eliminating the differential in unemployment rates between the two communities by targeting objective need.

3. All participants recognise the importance of respect, understanding and tolerance in relation to linguistic diversity, including in Northern Ireland, the Irish language, Ulster-Scots and the languages of the various ethnic communities, all of which are part of the cultural wealth of the island of Ireland.

4. In the context of active consideration currently being given to the UK signing the Council of Europe Charter for Regional or Minority Languages, the British Government will in particular in relation to the Irish language, where appropriate and where people so desire it:
   - take resolute action to promote the language;
   - facilitate and encourage the use of the language in speech and writing in public and private life where there is appropriate demand;
   - seek to remove, where possible, restrictions which would discourage or work against the maintenance or development of the language;
   - make provision for liaising with the Irish language community, representing their views to public authorities and investigating complaints;
   - place a statutory duty on the Department of Education to encourage and facilitate Irish medium education in line with current provision for integrated education;
   - explore urgently with the relevant British authorities, and in co-operation with the Irish broadcasting authorities, the scope for achieving more widespread availability of Teilifis na Gaeilige in Northern Ireland;
   - seek more effective ways to encourage and provide financial support for Irish language film and television production in Northern Ireland; and
   - encourage the parties to secure agreement that this commitment will be sustained by a new Assembly in a way which takes account of the desires and sensitivities of the community.

5. All participants acknowledge the sensitivity of the use of symbols and emblems for public purposes, and the need in particular in creating the new institutions to ensure that such symbols and emblems are used in a manner which promotes mutual respect rather than division. Arrangements will be made to monitor this issue and consider what action might be required.

DECOMMISSIONING

1. Participants recall their agreement in the Procedural Motion adopted on 24 September 1997 that the resolution of the decommissioning issue is an indispensable part of the process of negotiation, and also recall the provisions of paragraph 25 of Strand 1 above.

2. They note the progress made by the Independent International Commission on Decommissioning and the Governments in developing schemes which can represent a workable basis for achieving the decommissioning of illegally-held arms in the possession of paramilitary groups.

3. All participants accordingly reaffirm their commitment to the total disarmament of all paramilitary organisations. They also confirm their intention to continue to work constructively and in good faith with the Independent Commission, and to use any influence they may have, to achieve the decommissioning of all paramilitary arms within two years following endorsement in referendums North and South of the agreement and in the context of the implementation of the overall settlement.

4. The Independent Commission will monitor, review and verify progress on decommissioning of illegal arms, and will report to both Governments at regular intervals.

5. Both Governments will take all necessary steps to facilitate the decommissioning process to include bringing the relevant schemes into force by the end of June.

SECURITY

1. The participants note that the development of a peaceful environment on the basis of this agreement can and should mean a normalisation of security arrangements and practices.

2. The British Government will make progress towards the objective of as early a return as possible to normal security arrangements in Northern Ireland, consistent with the level of threat and with a published overall strategy, dealing with:
   (i) the reduction of the numbers and role of the Armed Forces deployed in Northern Ireland to levels compatible with a normal peaceful society;
   (ii) the removal of security installations;
   (iii) the removal of emergency powers in Northern Ireland; and
   (iv) other measures appropriate to and compatible with a normal peaceful society.

3. The Secretary of State will consult regularly on progress, and the response to any continuing paramilitary activity, with the Irish Government and the political parties, as appropriate.

4. The British Government will continue its consultation on firearms regulation and control on the basis of the document published on 2 April 1998.

5. The Irish Government will initiate a wide-ranging review of the Offences Against the State Acts 1939-85 with a view to both reform and dispensing with those elements no longer required as circumstances permit.

POLICING AND JUSTICE

1. The participants recognise that policing is a central issue in any society. They equally recognise that Northern Ireland's history of deep divisions has made it highly emotive, with great hurt suffered and sacrifices made by many individuals and their families, including those in the RUC and other public servants. They believe that the agreement provides the opportunity for a new

beginning to policing in Northern Ireland with a police service capable of attracting and sustaining support from the community as a whole. They also believe that this agreement offers a unique opportunity to bring about a new political dispensation which will recognise the full and equal legitimacy and worth of the identities, senses of allegiance and ethos of all sections of the community in Northern Ireland. They consider that this opportunity should inform and underpin the development of a police service representative in terms of the make-up of the community as a whole and which, in a peaceful environment, should be routinely unarmed.

2. The participants believe it essential that policing structures and arrangements are such that the police service is professional, effective and efficient, fair and impartial, free from partisan political control; accountable, both under the law for its actions and to the community it serves; representative of the society it polices, and operates within a coherent and co-operative criminal justice system, which conforms with human rights norms. The participants also believe that those structures and arrangements must be capable of maintaining law and order including responding effectively to crime and to any terrorist threat and to public order problems. A police service which cannot do so will fail to win public confidence and acceptance. They believe that any such structures and arrangements should be capable of delivering a policing service, in constructive and inclusive partnerships with the community at all levels, and with the maximum delegation of authority and responsibility, consistent with the foregoing principles. These arrangements should be based on principles of protection of human rights and professional integrity and should be unambiguously accepted and actively supported by the entire community.

3. An independent Commission will be established to make recommendations for future policing arrangements in Northern Ireland including means of encouraging widespread community support for these arrangements within the agreed framework of principles reflected in the paragraphs above and in accordance with the terms of reference at Annex A. The Commission will be broadly representative with expert and international representation among its membership and will be asked to consult widely and to report no later than Summer 1999.

4. The participants believe that the aims of the criminal justice system are to: deliver a fair and impartial system of justice to the community;
   - be responsive to the community's concerns, and encouraging community
   - involvement where appropriate;
   - have the confidence of all parts of the community; and
   - deliver justice efficiently and effectively.

5. There will be a parallel wide-ranging review of criminal justice (other than policing and those aspects of the system relating to the emergency legislation) to be carried out by the British Government through a mechanism with an independent element, in consultation with the political parties and others. The review will commence as soon as possible, will include wide consultation, and a report will be made to the Secretary of State no later than Autumn 1999. Terms of

Reference are attached at Annex B.

6. Implementation of the recommendations arising from both reviews will be discussed with the political parties and with the Irish Government.

7. The participants also note that the British Government remains ready in principle, with the broad support of the political parties, and after consultation, as appropriate, with the Irish Government, in the context of ongoing implementation of the relevant recommendations, to devolve responsibility for policing and justice issues.

ANNEX A

COMMISSION ON POLICING FOR NORTHERN IRELAND

Terms of Reference

Taking account of the principles on policing as set out in the agreement, the Commission will inquire into policing in Northern Ireland and, on the basis of its findings, bring forward proposals for future policing structures and arrangements, including means of encouraging widespread community support for those arrangements.

Its proposals on policing should be designed to ensure that policing arrangements, including composition, recruitment, training, culture, ethos and symbols, are such that in a new approach Northern Ireland has a police service that can enjoy widespread support from, and is seen as an integral part of, the community as a whole.

Its proposals should include recommendations covering any issues such as re-training, job placement and educational and professional development required in the transition to policing in a peaceful society.

Its proposals should also be designed to ensure that:

- the police service is structured, managed and resourced so that it can be effective in discharging its full range of functions (including proposals on any necessary arrangements for the transition to policing in a normal peaceful society);
- the police service is delivered in constructive and inclusive partnerships with the community at all levels with the maximum delegation of authority and responsibility;
- the legislative and constitutional framework requires the impartial discharge of policing functions and conforms with internationally accepted norms in relation to policing standards;
- the police operate within a clear framework of accountability to the law and the community they serve, so:
- they are constrained by, accountable to and act only within the law; their powers and procedures, like the law they enforce, are clearly established and publicly available;
- there are open, accessible and independent means of investigating and adjudicating upon complaints against the police;
- there are clearly established arrangements enabling local people, and their political representatives, to articulate their views and concerns about policing and to establish publicly policing priorities and influence policing policies, subject to safeguards to ensure police impartiality and freedom from partisan political control;
- there are arrangements for accountability and for the effective, efficient and economic use of resources in achieving policing objectives;
- there are means to ensure independent professional scrutiny and inspection of the police service to ensure that proper professional standards are maintained;
- the scope for structured co-operation with the Garda Siochana and other police forces is addressed; and
- the management of public order events which can impose exceptional demands on policing resources is also addressed.

The Commission should focus on policing issues, but if it identifies other aspects of the criminal justice system relevant to its work on policing, including the role of the police in prosecution, then it should draw the attention of the Government to those matters.

The Commission should consult widely, including with non-governmental expert organisations, and through such focus groups as they consider it appropriate to establish.

The Government proposes to establish the Commission as soon as possible, with the aim of it starting work as soon as possible and publishing its final report by Summer 1999.

ANNEX B

REVIEW OF THE CRIMINAL JUSTICE SYSTEM

Terms of Reference

Taking account of the aims of the criminal justice system as set out in the Agreement, the review will address the structure, management and resourcing of publicly funded elements of the criminal justice system and will bring forward proposals for future criminal justice arrangements (other than policing and those aspects of the system relating to emergency legislation, which the Government is considering separately) covering such issues as:

- the arrangements for making appointments to the judiciary and magistracy, and safeguards for protecting their independence;
- the arrangements for the organisation and supervision of the prosecution process, and for safeguarding its independence;
- measures to improve the responsiveness and accountability of, and any lay participation in the criminal justice system;
- mechanisms for addressing law reform;
  the scope for structured co-operation between the criminal justice agencies on both parts of the island; and
- the structure and organisation of criminal justice functions that might be devolved to an Assembly, including the possibility of establishing a

Department of Justice, while safeguarding the essential independence of many of the key functions in this area.

The Government proposes to commence the review as soon as possible, consulting with the political parties and others, including non-governmental expert organisations. The review will be completed by Autumn 1999.

PRISONERS

1. Both Governments will put in place mechanisms to provide for an accelerated programme for the release of prisoners, including transferred prisoners, convicted of scheduled offences in Northern Ireland or, in the case of those sentenced outside Northern Ireland, similar offences (referred to hereafter as qualifying prisoners). Any such arrangements will protect the rights of individual prisoners under national and international law.

2. Prisoners affiliated to organisations which have not established or are not maintaining a complete and unequivocal ceasefire will not benefit from the arrangements. The situation in this regard will be kept under review.

3. Both Governments will complete a review process within a fixed time frame and set prospective release dates for all qualifying prisoners. The review process would provide for the advance of the release dates of qualifying prisoners while allowing account to be taken of the seriousness of the offences for which the person was convicted and the need to protect the community. In addition, the intention would be that should the circumstances allow it, any qualifying prisoners who remained in custody two years after the commencement of the scheme would be released at that point.

4. The Governments will seek to enact the appropriate legislation to give effect to these arrangements by the end of June 1998.

5. The Governments continue to recognise the importance of measures to facilitate the reintegration of prisoners into the community by providing support both prior to and after release, including assistance directed towards availing of employment opportunities, re-training and/or re-skilling, and further education.

VALIDATION, IMPLEMENTATION AND REVIEW

Validation and Implementation

1. The two Governments will as soon as possible sign a new British-Irish Agreement replacing the 1985 Anglo-Irish Agreement, embodying understandings on constitutional issues and affirming their solemn commitment to support and, where appropriate, implement the agreement reached by the participants in the negotiations which shall be annexed to the British-Irish Agreement.

2. Each Government will organise a referendum on 22 May 1998. Subject to Parliamentary approval, a consultative referendum in Northern Ireland, organised under the terms of the Northern Ireland (Entry to Negotiations, etc.) Act 1996, will address the question: Do you support the agreement reached in the multi-party talks on Northern Ireland and set out in Command Paper 3883?. The Irish Government will introduce and support in the Oireachtas a Bill to amend the Constitution as described in paragraph 2 of the section Constitutional Issues and in Annex B, as follows: (a) to amend Articles 2 and 3 as described in paragraph 8.1 in Annex B above and (b) to amend Article 29 to permit the Government to ratify the new British-Irish Agreement. On passage by the Oireachtas, the Bill will be put to referendum.

3. If majorities of those voting in each of the referendums support this agreement, the Governments will then introduce and support, in their respective Parliaments, such legislation as may be necessary to give effect to all aspects of this agreement, and will take whatever ancillary steps as may be required including the holding of elections on 25 June, subject to parliamentary approval, to the Assembly, which would meet initially in a shadow mode. The establishment of the North-South Ministerial Council, implementation bodies, the British-Irish Council and the British-Irish Intergovernmental Conference and the assumption by the Assembly of its legislative and executive powers will take place at the same time on the entry into force of the British-Irish Agreement.

4. In the interim, aspects of the implementation of the multi-party agreement will be reviewed at meetings of those parties relevant in the particular case (taking into account, once Assembly elections have been held, the results of those elections), under the chairmanship of the British Government or the two Governments, as may be appropriate; and representatives of the two Governments and all relevant parties may meet under independent chairmanship to review implementation of the agreement as a whole.

Review procedures following implementation

5. Each institution may, at any time, review any problems that may arise in its operation and, where no other institution is affected, take remedial action in consultation as necessary with the relevant Government or Governments. It will be for each institution to determine its own procedures for review.

6. If there are difficulties in the operation of a particular institution, which have implications for another institution, they may review their operations separately and jointly and agree on remedial action to be taken under their respective authorities.

7. If difficulties arise which require remedial action across the range of institutions, or otherwise require amendment of the British-Irish Agreement or relevant legislation, the process of review will fall to the two Governments in consultation with the parties in the Assembly. Each Government will be responsible for action in its own jurisdiction.

8. Notwithstanding the above, each institution will publish an annual report on its operations. In addition, the two Governments and the parties in the Assembly will convene a conference 4 years after the agreement comes into effect, to review and report on its operation.

AGREEMENT BETWEEN THE GOVERNMENT OF THE UNITED KINGDOM OF GREAT BRITAIN AND NORTHERN IRELAND AND THE GOVERNMENT OF IRELAND

The British and Irish Governments:

Welcoming the strong commitment to the Agreement reached on 10th April 1998 by themselves and other participants in the multi-party talks and set out in Annex 1 to this Agreement (hereinafter the Multi-Party Agreement);
Considering that the Multi-Party Agreement offers an opportunity for a new beginning in relationships within Northern Ireland, within the island of Ireland and between the peoples of these islands;

Wishing to develop still further the unique relationship between their peoples and the close co-operation between their countries as friendly neighbours and as partners in the European Union;

Reaffirming their total commitment to the principles of democracy and non-violence which have been fundamental to the multi-party talks;

Reaffirming their commitment to the principles of partnership, equality and mutual respect and to the protection of civil, political, social, economic and cultural rights in their respective jurisdictions;

Have agreed as follows:

ARTICLE 1

The two Governments:

(i) recognise the legitimacy of whatever choice is freely exercised by a majority of the people of Northern Ireland with regard to its status, whether they prefer to continue to support the Union with Great Britain or a sovereign united Ireland;

(ii) recognise that it is for the people of the island of Ireland alone, by agreement between the two parts respectively and without external impediment, to exercise their right of self-determination on the basis of consent, freely and concurrently given, North and South, to bring about a united Ireland, if that is their wish, accepting that this right must be achieved and exercised with and subject to the agreement and consent of a majority of the people of Northern Ireland;

(iii) acknowledge that while a substantial section of the people in Northern Ireland share the legitimate wish of a majority of the people of the island of Ireland for a united Ireland, the present wish of a majority of the people of Northern Ireland, freely exercised and legitimate, is to maintain the Union and accordingly, that Northern Ireland's status as part of the United Kingdom reflects and relies upon that wish; and that it would be wrong to make any change in the status of Northern Ireland save with the consent of a majority of its people;

(iv) affirm that, if in the future, the people of the island of Ireland exercise their right of self-determination on the basis set out in sections (i) and (ii) above to bring about a united Ireland, it will be a binding obligation on both Governments to introduce and support in their respective Parliaments legislation to give effect to that wish;

(v) affirm that whatever choice is freely exercised by a majority of the people of Northern Ireland, the power of the sovereign government with jurisdiction there shall be exercised with rigorous impartiality on behalf of all the people in the diversity of their identities and traditions and shall be founded on the principles of full respect for, and equality of, civil, political, social and cultural rights, of freedom from discrimination for all citizens, and of parity of esteem and of just and equal treatment for the identity, ethos and aspirations of both communities;

(vi) recognise the birthright of all the people of Northern Ireland to identify themselves and be accepted as Irish or British, or both, as they may so choose, and accordingly confirm that their right to hold both British and Irish citizenship is accepted by both Governments and would not be affected by any future change in the status of Northern Ireland.

ARTICLE 2

The two Governments affirm their solemn commitment to support, and where appropriate implement, the provisions of the Multi-Party Agreement. In particular there shall be established in accordance with the provisions of the Multi-Party Agreement immediately on the entry into force of this Agreement, the following institutions:

(i) a North/South Ministerial Council;
(ii) the implementation bodies referred to in paragraph 9 (ii) of the section entitled Strand Two of the Multi-Party Agreement;
(iii) a British-Irish Council;
(iv) a British-Irish Intergovernmental Conference.

ARTICLE 3

(1) This Agreement shall replace the Agreement between the British and Irish Governments done at Hillsborough on 15th November 1985 which shall cease to have effect on entry into force of this Agreement.

(2) The Intergovernmental Conference established by Article 2 of the aforementioned Agreement done on 15th November 1985 shall cease to exist on entry into force of this Agreement.

ARTICLE 4

(1) It shall be a requirement for entry into force of this Agreement that:
(a) British legislation shall have been enacted for the purpose of implementing the provisions of Annex A to the section entitled Constitutional Issues of the Multi-Party Agreement;

(b) the amendments to the Constitution of Ireland set out in Annex B to the section entitled Constitutional Issues of the Multi-Party Agreement shall have been approved by Referendum;

(c) such legislation shall have been enacted as may be required to establish the institutions referred to in Article 2 of this Agreement.

(2) Each Government shall notify the other in writing of the completion, so far as it is concerned, of the requirements for entry into force of this Agreement. This Agreement shall enter into force on the date of the receipt of the later of the two notifications.

(3) Immediately on entry into force of this Agreement, the Irish Government shall ensure that the amendments to the Constitution of Ireland set out in Annex B to the section entitled Constitutional Issues of the Multi-Party Agreement take effect.

In witness thereof the undersigned, being duly authorised thereto by the respective Governments, have signed this Agreement.
Done in two originals at Belfast on the 10th day of April 1998.

For the Government
of the United Kingdom of
Great Britain and Northern Ireland

For the Government
Of Ireland

ANNEX 1

The Agreement Reached in the Multi-Party Talks

ANNEX 2

Declaration on the Provisions of Paragraph (vi) of Article 1
In Relationship to Citizenship
The British and Irish Governments declare that it is their joint understanding that the term the people of Northern Ireland in paragraph (vi) of Article 1 of this Agreement means, for the purposes of giving effect to this provision, all persons born in Northern Ireland and having, at the time of their birth, at least one parent who is a British citizen, an Irish citizen or is otherwise entitled to reside in Northern Ireland without any restriction on their period of residence.

DISTRICT POLICING PARTNERSHIPS

The following section sets out the political and independent members of each of the District Policing Partnerships by local authority area.

DPPs are autonomous bodies within local councils working to communicate the views of the community on policing, contribute to the formulation of policing plans, monitor local police performance and the prevention of crime.

The Policing Board appointed 207 people to serve as Independent Members alongside the DPPs 241 elected members.

DPP Political Representation

Party	DPP Members
Alliance Party	9
Democratic Unionist Party	69
Independent Councillors	12
Independent Unionists	1
Progressive Unionist Party	1
Sinn Fein	0
Social Democratic and Labour Party	68
Ulster Unionist Party	80
United Kingdom Unionist Party	1

Sinn Fein declined to make appointments to DPPs.

DPP Allowances

The standard allowances (per annum) for all DPP members – excluding Belfast DPP are:

Chairman	£4,800
Deputy Chairman	£3,600
Member	£2,400

Belfast District Policing Partnership

The Belfast DPP has four sub groups covering Belfast's four policing districts, North, South, East and West. The standard allowances (per annum) for members are:

Belfast DPP Chairman	£8,400
Belfast DPP Deputy Chairman	£6,300
Chairman of a Sub Group	£4,700
Deputy Chairman of a Sub Group	£4,500
Belfast DPP Member	£4,200

Antrim District Policing Partnership

DPP Manager: Mairead Smith
Tel: 9446 3113 / Fax: 9446 4469
Email: mairead.smith@antrim.gov.uk

Political Members

Cllr Mervyn Rea (UUP)	DPP Chairperson
Cllr Donovan McClelland (SDLP)	DPP Vice Chairperson

Cllr Paul Michael (UUP), Cllr Adrian Cochrane-Watson(UUP), Cllr Stephen Nicholl (UUP), Cllr Bobby Loughran (SDLP), Cllr Thomas Burns (SDLP), Cllr Sam Dunlop (DUP), Cllr Brian Graham (DUP),
Cllr John Smith (DUP)

Independent Members

Mairead Burke, Daniel Doherty, Christine Ferrin
Oliver Frawley, Christine Keenan, Andrew Little
Amal Ma ani-Hessari, Pamela Surphilis, Heather Watson

Ards District Policing Partnership

DPP Manager: Trevor Mawhinney
Tel: 9182 4000 / Fax: 9181 9628
Email: trevor.mawhinney@ards-council.gov.uk

Political Members

Ald John Shields (UUP)	DPP Chairperson
Ald Jim Shannon (DUP)	DPP Vice Chairperson

Cllr Phillip Smith (UUP), Cllr Robert Gibson (UUP), Cllr Ronald Ferguson (UUP), Cllr Margaret Craig (DUP), Ald George Ennis (DUP), Cllr Hamilton Gregory (DUP), Cllr Alan McDowell (Alliance), Cllr Daniel McCarthy (Ind) Nationalist)

Independent Members

Margaret Adair, Florence Ambrose, Irene Boyd
Anne Drysdale, Donna Hamilton, Lisa Harvey
Elaine McVeigh, Nancy Orr, Roberta Patty-Coffey

Armagh City and District Council District Policing Partnership

DPP Manager: John Doyle
Tel: 3752 9600 / Fax: 3752 9604
Email: j.doyle@armagh.gov.uk

Political Members

Cllr Jim Speers ((UUP))	DPP Chairperson
Cllr Pat Brannigan (SDLP)	DPP Vice Chairperson

Cllr James Clayton (UUP), Cllr Sylvia McRoberts (UUP), Cllr Charles Rolston (UUP), Cllr Anna Brolly (SDLP), Cllr Tom Canavan (SDLP), Cllr John Campbell (SDLP), Cllr Paul Berry (DUP), Cllr Heather Black (DUP)

Independent Members
Carol Burnett, Cathy Donnelly, Diane Hynds, Marion Jamison, Lillian Jennet, Kathy Magee, James Reavey, Brian Rowntree, Mary Wright

Ballymena District Council Policing Partnership

DPP Manager: Peter Greenshields
Tel: 2566 0441 / Fax: 2566 0400
Email: peter.greenshields@ballymena.gov.uk

Political Members

Cllr Maurice Mills(DUP)	DPP Chairperson
Ald James Currie(UUP)	DPP Vice Chairperson

Cllr Peter Brown (UUP), Cllr Lexi Scott (UPP), Ald P J McAvoy (SDLP), Cllr Declan O'Loan (SDLP), Ald Sam Hanna (DUP), Cllr Sam Gaston (DUP), Cllr Hubert Nicholl (DUP), Cllr Tommy Nicholl (DUP)

Independent Members
Delia Close, Liam Corey, Jayne Dunlop, Tracey Gregg, Jane Lamont, Mary McFetridge, Colette Rodgers, Cathy Trenier, Audrey Wales

Ballymoney District Council Policing Partnership

DPP Manager: Jonny Donaghy
Tel: 2766 2280 / Fax: 2766 3852
Email: jonny.donaghy@ballymoney.gov.uk

Political Members

Cllr John Finlay (DUP)	DPP Chairperson
Cllr William Logan (UUP)	DPP Vice Chairperson

Cllr James Simpson (UUP), Ald Joseph Gaston (UUP), Cllr Malachy Campbell (SDLP), Cllr Mervyn Storey (DUP), Cllr Cecil Cousley (DUP), Cllr Frank Campbell (DUP), Ald Robert Halliday (DUP), Cllr Bill Kennedy (DUP)

Independent Members
John Bannon, Joan Christie, Joseph Donaghy, Michael Fleming, Liz Henry, Elizabeth Lindsay, Linda McKendry, Helen McKeown, Brendan Smyth

Banbridge District Council Policing Partnership

DPP Manager: Amanda Scargill
Tel: 4066 0609 / Fax: 4066 0601
Email: dpp@banbridgedc.gov.uk

Political Members

Cllr William John Martin (UUP)	DPP Chairperson
Cllr Winifred McFadden (DUP)	DPP Vice Chairperson

Cllr Joan Baird (UUP), Cllr Ian Burns (UUP), Cllr John Ingram (UUP), Cllr Seamus Doyle (SDLP), Cllr Cathy McDermott (SDLP), Cllr David Herron (DUP), Cllr Jim McElroy (DUP)

Independent Members
Patrick Downey, Deirdre Gordon, David Griffin, Conor McArdle, Justin McNeill, Chris Nelmes, George Patton, Carol Power

Belfast City Council District Policing Partnership

DPP Manager: Stephen McCrory
Tel: 9027 0382 / Fax: 9027 0421
Email: mccrorys@belfastcity.gov.uk

Political Members

Cllr Jim Rogers(UUP)	DPP Chairperson
Cllr Pat Convery(SDLP)	DPP Vice Chairperson

Cllr David Brown (UUP), Cllr Peter O'Reilly (SDLP), Cllr Ruth Patterson (DUP), Cllr Robin Newton (DUP), Cllr Elaine McMillan (DUP), Cllr Naomi Long (Alliance), Cllr Hugh Smyth (PUP), Cllr Frank McCoubry (Ind)

Independent Members
Valerie Allen, Marie Kane, Seamus Lynch, Chris Lyttle, Deirdre MacBride, Caroline McAuley, Thomas McCullough, Anne Monaghan, Harry Smith
Belfast is different from the other District Policing Partnerships in that it has 4 Sub Groups, North, South, East and West, each with a Chairman and Deputy Chairman.

Cllr Hugh Smyth (PUP)	West Belfast DPP Chairperson
Cllr Robin Newton (DUP)	East Belfast DPP Chairperson
Harry Smith (Ind)	South Belfast DPP Chairperson
Seamus Lynch (Ind)	North Belfast DPP Chairperson

Carrickfergus District Council Policing Partnership

DPP Manager: Daniel Sweeney
Tel: 9335 1604 / Fax: 9336 2134
Email: dsweeney.admin@carrickfergus.org

Political Members

Ald David Hilditch(DUP)	DPP Chairperson
Cllr Stewart Dickson(Alliance)DPP	Vice Chairperson

Ald Eric Ferguson (UUP), Ald Roy Beggs Jnr (UUP), Ald Billy Ashe (DUP), Cllr May Beattie (DUP), Cllr Janet Crampsey (Alliance), Cllr Billy Hamilton (Ind)
Independent Members
Anetta Crawford, Marjorie Hawkins, Caroline Howarth, Peter Luney, Elizabeth Maxwell, Alma Melville, Valerie Reynolds

Castlereagh District Policing Partnership

DPP Manager: Karen Collins
Tel: 9049 4500 / Fax: 9049 4577
Email: karencollins@castlereagh.gov.uk

Political Members

Cllr Michael Copeland (UUP)	DPP Chairperson
Cllr Jim White (DUP)	DPP Vice Chairperson

Ald Michael Henderson (UUP), Cllr Brian Hanvey, (SDLP), Cllr Joanne Bunting (DUP), Cllr Clare Ennis (DUP), Cllr Vivienne Stevenson (DUP), Cllr Geraldine Rice (Alliance), Cllr Frankie Gallagher (Ind)

Independent Members
Ian Brush, Leslie Drew, Gretta Falloon, Carolyn Foster, Maimie Ireland, Phillip McBride, Helen McGowan, Derek Simpson

Coleraine Borough Council District Policing Partnership

DPP Manager: Suzanne Crozier
Tel: 7034 7034 / Fax: 7034 7026
Email: suzanne.crozier@colerainebc.gov.uk

Political Members

Cllr William Watt (UUP)	DPP Chairperson
Ald William McClure (DUP)	DPP Vice Chairperson

Cllr William King (UUP), Cllr Robert McPherson (UUP), Cllr Norman Hillis (UUP), Cllr Elizabeth Johnston (UUP), Ald Billy Leonard (SDLP), Cllr Eamon Mullan (SDLP), Cllr Timothy Deans (DUP), Cllr Adrian McQuillan (DUP)

Independent Members
Joan Baird, Trevor Clarke, Heather Lyons, Patricia McQuillan, Angela McLaughlin, Wyona Madden, Rae Morrison, Vinny Robinson, Teresa Young

Cookstown District Council Policing Partnership

DPP Manager: Philip Moffett
Tel: 8676 2205 / Fax: 90 8676 4360
Email: philip.moffett@cookstown.gov.uk

Political Members

Cllr Patsy McGlone (SDLP)	DPP Chairperson
Cllr Trevor Wilson (UUP)	DPP Vice Chairperson

Cllr Samuel Glasgow (UUP), Cllr Mary Baker (SDLP), Cllr James McGarvey (SDLP), Cllr Peter Cassidy (SDLP), Cllr Ian McCrea (DUP), Cllr Samuel Parke (Ind)

Independent Members
Elizabeth Baxter, Eoin Doyle, Samuel Laughlin, Ursula Marshall, Ita Pickering, Tony Quinn, Teresa Rooney

Craigavon Borough Council District Policing Partnership

DPP Manager: Alison Clenaghan
Tel: 3831 2400 / Fax: 3831 2488
Email: alison.clenaghan@craigavon.gov.uk

Political Members

Cllr Kenneth Twyble (UUP)	DPP Chairperson
Cllr Jonathan Bell (DUP)	DPP Vice Chairperson

Ald Samuel Gardiner (UUP), Ald Arnold Hatch (UUP), Cllr Dolores Kelly (SDLP), Cllr Patricia Mallon (SDLP), Cllr Ignatius Fox (SDLP), Cllr Stephen Moutray (DUP), Ald David Simpson (DUP), Cllr Sidney Anderson (Ind)

Independent Members
Grace Black, Hugh Casey, Thomas Flemming, Thomas French, Sean Hughes, Julie Lynn McNally, Lillian Percival, Jenni Power, Margaret Tinsle

Derry City Council District Policing Partnership

DPP Manager: Lorna Somers
Tel: 7136 5151 / Fax: 7136 8536
Email: lorna.somers@derrycity.gov.uk

Political Members

Cllr John Kerr (SDLP)	DPP Chairperson
Cllr Joe Miller (DUP)	DPP Vice Chairperson

Cllr Ernie Hamilton (UUP), Cllr Helen Quigley (SDLP), Cllr Sean Gallagher (SDLP), Cllr Gerard Diver (SDLP), Cllr Jim McKeever (SDLP), Cllr Mary Bradley (SDLP), Cllr Thomas Conwa (SDLP), Cllr Mildred Garfield (DUP)

Independent Members
Marie Brown, Colleen Heaney, Marjorie Keating, Terry Moyne, Eamonn P O'Kane, Marian Quinn, Diana Rudd, Andrew Thompson, Alison Wallace

Down District Council District Policing Partnership

DPP Manager: Liam McLernon
Tel: 4461 0857 / Fax: 4461 0860
Email: liam.mclernon@downdc.gov.uk

Political Members

Cllr Harvey Bicker (UUP)	DPP Chairperson
Cllr Eamonn O'Neill (SDLP)	DPP Vice Chairperson

Cllr Gerry Douglas (UUP), Cllr Albert Colmer (UUP), Cllr Margaret Ritchie (SDLP), Cllr Patsy Toman (SDLP), Cllr John Doris (SDLP), Cllr Dermot Curran (SDLP), Cllr William Dick (DUP)

Independent Members
Audrey Byrne, Una Kelly, Sally McAdam, Dan McEvoy, Tori McKillen, Kay Nellis, Kathleen Stockton

Dungannon and South Tyrone Borough Council DPP

DPP Manager: George Ruddell
Tel: 8772 0300 / Fax: 8772 0333
Email: george.ruddell@dungannon.gov.uk

A District Policing Partnership has yet to be established in the Dungannon and South Tyrone Borough Council area.

Fermanagh District Council Policing Partnership

DPP Manager: David Eames
Tel: 6632 5050 / Fax: 6632 2024
Email: david.eames@fermanagh.gov.uk

Political Members

Cllr Tom Elliott (UUP)	DPP Chairperson
Cllr John O'Kane (SDLP)	DPP Vice Chairperson

Cllr Harold Andrews (UUP), Cllr Wilson Elliott (UUP), Cllr Bertie Kerr (UUP), Cllr Cecil Noble (UUP), Cllr Bert Johnston (DUP), Cllr Gerry Gallagher (SDLP), Cllr Fergus McQuillan (SDLP), Cllr David Kettyles (Ind)

Independent Members

Oliver Breen, Keith Burns, Mandy Egerton, Maeve Ferguson, Hazel Hicks, Seamus McCusker, Mary McHugh, Mannix Magee

Larne Borough Council District Policing Partnership

DPP Manager: Stephen Burns
Tel: 2827 2313 / Fax: 2826 0660
Email: burnss@larne.gov.uk

Political Members

Ald Jack McKee (DUP)	DPP Chairperson
Cllr Danny O'Connor (SDLP)	DPP Vice Chairperson

Cllr Joan Drummond (UUP), Cllr David Fleck (UUP), Cllr Winston Fulton (DUP), Cllr Gregg McKeen (DUP), Cllr Geraldine Mulvenna (Alliance), Cllr Roy Craig (Ind)

Independent Members

Wilson Crawford, Louise Marsden, Charles Massey, Terence McCaughan, Margaret McQuitty, Tom Robinson, Dympna Thornton

Limavady District Council District Policing Partnership

DPP Manager: L(Ind)a McKee
Tel: 7772 2226 / Fax: 7772 2010
Email: l(Ind)a.mckee@limavady.gov.uk

Political Members

Ald Jack Dolan (UUP)	DPP Chairperson
Cllr Desmond Lowry (SDLP)	DPP Vice Chairperson

Cllr Jack Rankin (UUP), Ald Michael Cartin (SDLP), Cllr Michael Coyle (SDLP), Cllr Gerry Mullan (SDLP), Ald George Robinson (DUP)

Independent Members

Damian Corr, Jim Herron, Maureen Hudson, Marie Keown, Mary McCrea, Nigel McLaughlin, Rosemary Savage

Lisburn City Council District Policing Partnership

DPP Manager: Angela McCann
Tel: 9250 9250 / Fax: 9250 9279
Email: angela.mccann@lisburn.gov.uk

Political Members

Cllr William Gardiner-Watson (UUP)	DPP Chairperson
Cllr D Jonathan Craig (DUP)	DPP Vice Chairperson

Cllr David Archer Jnr (UUP), Cllr Sam W Johnston (UUP), Councillor Joseph H Lockhart (UUP), Cllr William M Ward (UUP), Cllr Peter O'Hagan (SDLP), Cllr Paul Porter (DUP), Cllr Seamus A Close (Alliance), Cllr J Gary McMichael (Ind)

Independent Members

David Adams, Christopher Annon, Sandra Irvine, Fiona McCausland, Dympna McGlade, Stephen McGowan, Heather Morrow, Thomas Stewart, Kieran Walsh

Magherafelt District Council District Policing Partnership

DPP Manager: N/A
**John McLoughlin, Chief Executive of Magherafelt District Council is acting District Policing Partnership Manager.
Tel: 7939 7979 / Fax: 7939 7080
Email: chief.executive@magherafelt.gov.uk

Political Members

Cllr Paul McClean (DUP)	DPP Chairperson
Cllr Catherine Lagan (SDLP)	DPP Vice Chairperson

Cllr John Junkin (UUP), Cllr George Shiels (UUP), Cllr Pat McErlean (SDLP), Cllr Joe McBride (SDLP), Cllr Tommy Catherwood (DUP), Cllr Rev John McCrea (DUP), Cllr Bertie Montgomery (Ind)

Independent Members

James Campbell, Stephen Catherwood, John Conlon, Marian Donnelly, Marie McCormack, Alison Scott, Denis Shortall, Francis Symington

Moyle District Council District Policing Partnership

DPP Manager: Adrian Proctor
Tel: 2076 2225 / Fax: 2076 2525
Email: moyledpp@moyle-council.org

Political Members

Cllr Michael Molloy (SDLP)	DPP Chairperson
Cllr William Graham (UUP)	DPP Vice Chairperson

Cllr Helen Harding (UUP), Cllr Madeleine Black (SDLP), Cllr George Hartin (DUP), Cllr David McAllister (DUP), Cllr Price McConaghy (Ind), Cllr Randal McDonnell (Ind)

Independent Members

Philip Christie, Christopher Craig, Kathleen Elliott, Eddie Ferguson, Eamon McIlroy, David McIlwaine, Edward Molloy

Newry & Mourne District Council District Policing Partnership

DPP Manager: Patricia Hamilton
Tel: 3031 3031 / Fax: 3031 3077
Email: patricia.hamilton@newryandmourne.gov.uk

Political Members

Cllr Michael Carr (SDLP)	DPP Chairperson
Cllr Andy Moffett (UUP)	DPP Vice Chairperson

Cllr Henry Reilly (UUP), Cllr Danny Kennedy (UUP), Cllr Josephine O'Hare (SDLP), Cllr John McArdle (SDLP), Cllr John Feehan (SDLP), Cllr Pat McElroy (SDLP), Cllr William Burns (DUP), Cllr Tony Williamson (Ind)

Independent Members

Lorraine Cole, Noel Doherty, Theresa Doran, Catherine Fegan, Peter McEvoy, Val Murphy, Helen Scott, Gary Strokes, Mairead White

Newtownabbey Borough Council District Policing Partnership

DPP Manager: Campbell Dixon
Tel: 34 0011 / Fax: 34 0004
Email: cdixon@newtownabbey.gov.uk

Political Members

Cllr Nigel Hamilton (DUP)	DPP Chairperson
Cllr Jim Bingham (UUP)	DPP Vice Chairperson

Ald Janet Crilly (UUP), Cllr VI Scott (UUP), Cllr Dineen Walker (UUP), Cllr Tommy McTeague (SDLP), Ald Paul Girvan (DUP), Cllr John Mann (DUP), Cllr Arthur John Templeton (DUP), Cllr Billy Webb NRA

Independent Members

Carolyn Arnold, John Blair, Gerry Mullan, Michael McBrien, Carol O'Malley, Connie Thompson, Anita Watson, Patricia Webb, Kathy Wolff

North Down Borough Council District Policing Partnership

DPP Manager: Kirsten Mullen
Tel: 9127 8054 / Fax: 9127 5178
Email: dpp@northdown.gov.uk

Political Members

Ald Leslie Cree (UUP)	DPP Chairperson
Cllr Tony Hill (Alliance)	DPP Vice Chairperson

Ald Ellie McKay (UUP), Cllr Irene Cree (UUP), Cllr Alex Easton (DUP), Cllr Alan Graham (DUP), Cllr Stephen Farry (Alliance), Ald Valerie Kingham (UKUP), Cllr Austin Lennon (Ind), Cllr Brian Wilson (Ind) Community

Independent Members

Ann Adams, Lorna Anderson, Margaret Ferguson, Patrick Fox, Lynn Johnston, Robert McCullough, Renee McKinty, Phillip McMullan, Valerie Miskimmon

Omagh District Council District Policing Partnership

DPP Manager: Mary Brogan
Tel: 8224 5321 / Fax: 8224 3888
Email: mary.brogan@omagh.gov.uk

Political Members

Cllr Gerry O'Doherty (SDLP)	DPP Chairperson
Cllr Alan Rainey (UUP)	DPP Vice Chairperson

Cllr Bert Wilson (UUP), Cllr Jo Deehan (SDLP), Cllr Liam McQuaid (SDLP), Cllr Pat McDonnell (SDLP), Cllr Paddy MacGowan (SDLP), Cllr Tom Buchanan (DUP)

Independent Members

Margaret Geelan, Paddy Hunter, Rozella Kelly, Vida Lake, Breige McClean, Paddy-Joe McClean, Elaine Watterson

Strabane District Council District Policing Partnership

DPP Manager: Rachael Harkin
Tel: 7138 2204 / Fax: 7138 1348
Email: rharkin@strabanedc.gov.uk

Political Members

Cllr Thomas McBride (SDLP)	DPP Chairperson
Cllr Thomas Kerrigan (DUP)	DPP Vice Chairperson

Cllr James Emery (UUP), Cllr Ann Bell (SDLP), Cllr Eugene McMenamim (SDLP), Cllr Bernadette McNamee (SDLP), Cllr John Donnell (DUP), Cllr Allan Bresland (DUP)

Independent Members

Liam Curran, Sean Crawford, Noelle Donnelly, Patrick McCourt, Mary McCrea, Arthur McGarrigle, Lynn Patterson

Index

Mileage Chart

	Antrim	Armagh	Ballycastle	Ballymena	Bangor	Belfast	Belfast Int Airport	Belleek	Carnlough	Coleraine	Cookstown	Craigavad	Cushendall	Downhill	Downpatrick	Dungannon	Enniskillen	Giant's Causeway	Hillsborough	Larne	Limavady	Lisnaskea	Londonderry	Lurgan	Maghera	Newcastle	Newry	Omagh	Portaferry	Portrush
Antrim																														
Armagh	42																													
Ballycastle	41	84																												
Ballymena	11	54	28																											
Bangor	32	54	72	42																										
Belfast	19	41	58	28	14																									
Belfast Int Airport	6	40	46	17	33	19																								
Belleek	91	75	114	92	122	109	97																							
Carnlough	27	70	26	16	53	39	33	108																						
Coleraine	40	61	19	28	71	58	46	95	42																					
Cookstown	28	24	57	28	60	46	33	63	45	37																				
Craigavad	25	49	63	36	5	8	26	108	44	63	53																			
Cushendall	30	73	16	19	61	48	35	110	10	35	47	35																		
Downhill	47	68	26	35	78	65	53	92	49	7	43	71	41																	
Downpatrick	38	52	85	55	27	22	35	119	64	85	60	30	74	91																
Dungannon	45	13	67	39	56	42	42	68	55	47	11	51	58	54	53															
Enniskillen	86	50	110	82	97	84	83	25	98	91	54	101	101	88	95	43														
Giant's Causeway	45	76	13	32	76	63	50	110	40	15	52	69	29	22	82	62	106													
Hillsborough	22	31	59	32	24	12	19	106	49	61	45	20	53	67	18	36	82	85												
Larne	21	65	41	21	38	25	22	111	14	49	48	29	25	56	52	66	108	54	35											
Limavady	45	62	33	42	77	63	50	82	56	14	38	71	48	11	82	48	78	29	65	63										
Lisnaskea	84	42	125	95	96	82	82	37	111	103	59	91	114	101	93	49	12	118	77	104	90									
Londonderry	55	71	51	52	87	73	61	62	68	32	48	81	67	29	93	63	61	47	79	76	18	73								
Lurgan	26	16	66	36	37	23	23	89	52	66	30	34	55	72	34	22	64	70	13	46	70	58	81							
Maghera	23	40	40	18	55	41	29	79	34	21	16	47	37	28	61	27	69	36	45	44	23	75	34	48						
Newcastle	43	40	91	61	38	33	41	115	70	90	55	44	80	97	13	48	90	95	24	56	88	82	99	30	66					
Newry	47	19	88	58	52	38	45	93	75	88	44	46	77	94	30	32	69	92	27	60	81	60	89	23	60	21				
Omagh	54	36	83	55	82	69	60	37	71	64	27	85	74	61	80	28	27	79	66	75	51	39	34	49	42	75	55			
Portaferry	48	60	87	57	24	29	44	128	66	87	69	30	76	93	9	62	103	91	24	52	92	102	102	43	70	21	39	88		
Portrush	46	67	19	34	78	64	52	102	49	6	43	68	34	13	84	54	98	9	65	55	20	92	38	72	27	90	94	71	93	
Strabane	62	56	64	58	93	80	67	51	74	45	46	89	77	42	99	48	47	60	86	82	31	59	15	69	40	94	75	20	108	51

Courtesy of Northern Ireland Tourist Board

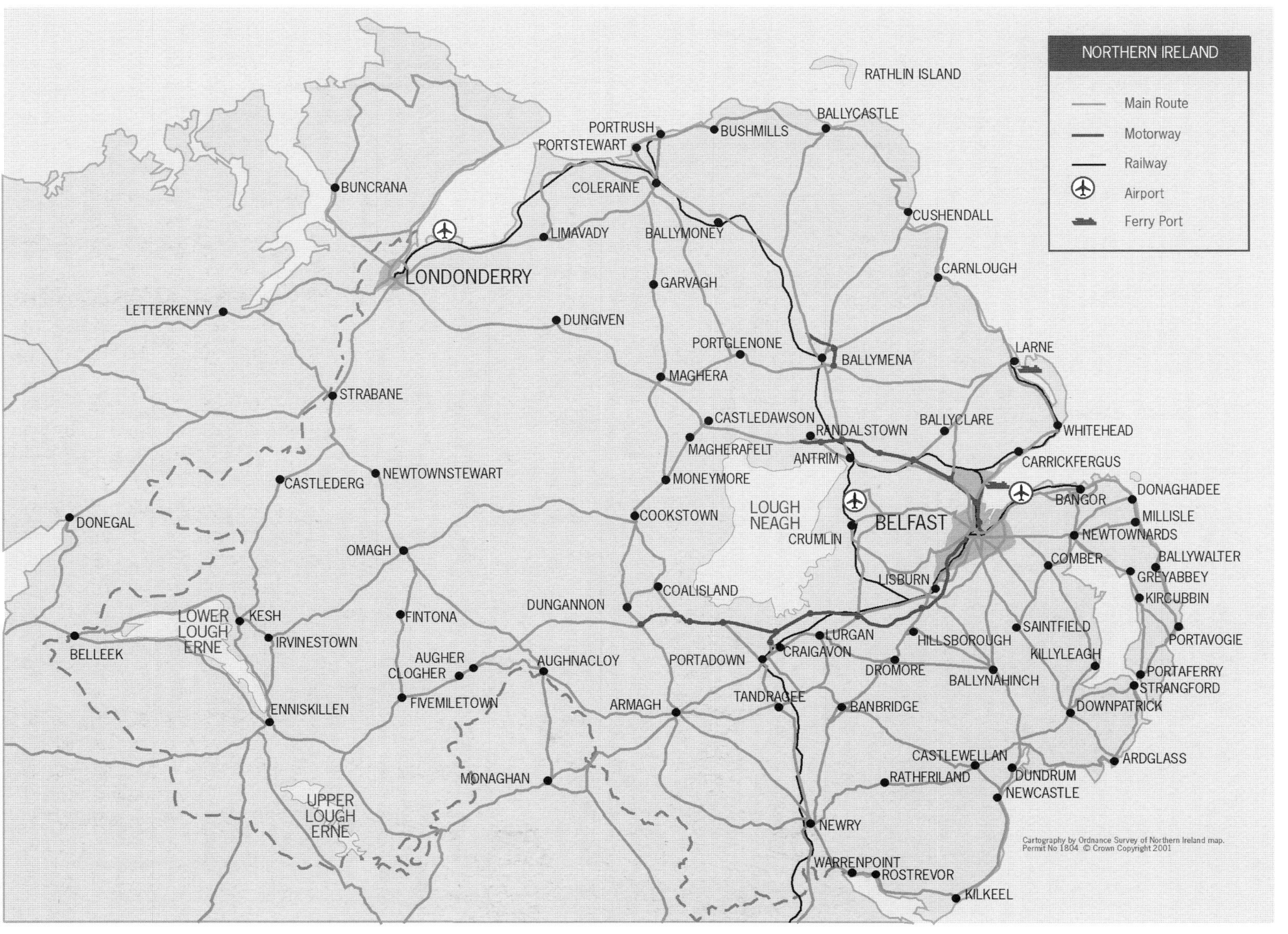
NORTHERN IRELAND
Main Route
Motorway
Railway
Airport
Ferry Port
RATHLIN ISLAND
BALLYCASTLE
PORTRUSH
PORTSTEWART
BUSHMILLS
BUNCRANA
COLERAINE
LIMAVADY
BALLYMONEY
CUSHENDALL
LONDONDERRY
CARNLOUGH
GARVAGH
LETTERKENNY
DUNGIVEN
PORTGLENONE
LARNE
BALLYMENA
MAGHERA
STRABANE
CASTLEDAWSON
RANDALSTOWN
BALLYCLARE
WHITEHEAD
MAGHERAFELT
ANTRIM
CARRICKFERGUS
NEWTOWNSTEWART
CASTLEDERG
MONEYMORE
DONAGHADEE
BANGOR
LOUGH NEAGH
MILLISLE
DONEGAL
COOKSTOWN
BELFAST
NEWTOWNARDS
CRUMLIN
OMAGH
COMBER
BALLYWALTER
GREYABBEY
LISBURN
COALISLAND
KIRCUBBIN
DUNGANNON
LOWER LOUGH ERNE
KESH
FINTONA
SAINTFIELD
PORTAVOGIE
BELLEEK
IRVINESTOWN
LURGAN
HILLSBOROUGH
CRAIGAVON
KILLYLEAGH
AUGHER
CLOGHER
AUGHNACLOY
PORTADOWN
DROMORE
PORTAFERRY
BALLYNAHINCH
STRANGFORD
FIVEMILETOWN
TANDRAGEE
ENNISKILLEN
ARMAGH
BANBRIDGE
DOWNPATRICK
CASTLEWELLAN
ARDGLASS
MONAGHAN
RATHFRILAND
DUNDRUM
NEWCASTLE
UPPER LOUGH ERNE
NEWRY
Cartography by Ordnance Survey of Northern Ireland map.
Permit No 1804 © Crown Copyright 2001
WARRENPOINT
ROSTREVOR
KILKEEL

2003

	January	February	March	April	May	June
Mon	6 13 20 27	3 10 17 24	3 10 17 24 31	7 14 21 28	5 12 19 26	2 9 16 23 30
Tue	7 14 21 28	4 11 18 25	4 11 18 25	1 8 15 22 29	6 13 20 27	3 10 17 24
Wed	1 8 15 22 29	5 12 19 26	5 12 19 26	2 9 16 23 30	7 14 21 28	4 11 18 25
Thu	2 9 16 23 30	6 13 20 27	6 13 20 27	3 10 17 24	1 8 15 22 29	5 12 19 26
Fri	3 10 17 24 31	7 14 21 28	7 14 21 28	4 11 18 25	2 9 16 23 30	6 13 20 27
Sat	4 11 18 25	1 8 15 22	1 8 15 22 29	5 12 19 26	3 10 17 24 31	7 14 21 28
Sun	5 12 19 26	2 9 16 23	2 9 16 23 30	6 13 20 27	4 11 18 25	1 8 15 22 29

	July	August	September	October	November	December
Mon	7 14 21 28	4 11 18 25	1 8 15 22 29	6 13 20 27	3 10 17 24	1 8 15 22 29
Tue	1 8 15 22 29	5 12 19 26	2 9 16 23 30	7 14 21 28	4 11 18 25	2 9 16 23 30
Wed	2 9 16 23 30	6 13 20 27	3 10 17 24	1 8 15 22 29	5 12 19 26	3 10 17 24 31
Thu	3 10 17 24 31	7 14 21 28	4 11 18 25	2 9 16 23 30	6 13 20 27	4 11 18 25
Fri	4 11 18 25	1 8 15 22 29	5 12 19 26	3 10 17 24 31	7 14 21 28	5 12 19 26
Sat	5 12 19 26	2 9 16 23 30	6 13 20 27	4 11 18 25	1 8 15 22 29	6 13 20 27
Sun	6 13 20 27	3 10 17 24 31	7 14 21 28	5 12 19 26	2 9 16 23 30	7 14 21 28

2004

	January	February	March	April	May	June
Mon	5 12 19 26	2 9 16 23	1 8 15 22 29	5 12 19 26	3 10 17 24 31	7 14 21 28
Tue	6 13 20 27	3 10 17 24	2 9 16 23 30	6 13 20 27	4 11 18 25	1 8 15 22 29
Wed	7 14 21 28	4 11 18 25	3 10 17 24 31	7 14 21 28	5 12 19 26	2 9 16 23 30
Thu	1 8 15 22 29	5 12 19 26	4 11 18 25	1 8 15 22 29	6 13 20 27	3 10 17 24
Fri	2 9 16 23 30	6 13 20 27	5 12 19 26	2 9 16 23 30	7 14 21 28	4 11 18 25
Sat	3 10 17 24 31	7 14 21 28	6 13 20 27	3 10 17 24	1 8 15 22 29	5 12 19 26
Sun	4 11 18 25	1 8 15 22 29	7 14 21 28	4 11 18 25	2 9 16 23 30	6 13 20 27

	July	August	September	October	November	December
Mon	5 12 19 26	2 9 16 23 30	6 13 20 27	4 11 18 25	1 8 15 22 29	6 13 20 27
Tue	6 13 20 27	3 10 17 24 31	7 14 21 28	5 12 19 26	2 9 16 23 30	7 14 21 28
Wed	7 14 21 28	4 11 18 25	1 8 15 22 29	6 13 20 27	3 10 17 24	1 8 15 22 29
Thu	1 8 15 22 29	5 12 19 26	2 9 16 23 30	7 14 21 28	4 11 18 25	2 9 16 23 30
Fri	2 9 16 23 30	6 13 20 27	3 10 17 24	1 8 15 22 29	5 12 19 26	3 10 17 24 31
Sat	3 10 17 24 31	7 14 21 28	4 11 18 25	2 9 16 23 30	6 13 20 27	4 11 18 25
Sun	4 11 18 25	1 8 15 22 29	5 12 19 26	3 10 17 24 31	7 14 21 28	5 12 19 26

2005

	January	February	March	April	May	June
Mon	3 10 17 24 31	7 14 21 28	7 14 21 28	4 11 18 25	2 9 16 23 30	6 13 20 27
Tue	4 11 18 25	1 8 15 22	1 8 15 22 29	5 12 19 26	3 10 17 24 31	7 14 21 28
Wed	5 12 19 26	2 9 16 23	2 9 16 23 30	6 13 20 27	4 11 18 25	1 8 15 22 29
Thu	6 13 20 27	3 10 17 24	3 10 17 24 31	7 14 21 28	5 12 19 26	2 9 16 23 30
Fri	7 14 21 28	4 11 18 25	4 11 18 25	1 8 15 22 29	6 13 20 27	3 10 17 24
Sat	1 8 15 22 29	5 12 19 26	5 12 19 26	2 9 16 23 30	7 14 21 28	4 11 18 25
Sun	2 9 16 23 30	6 13 20 27	6 13 20 27	3 10 17 24	1 8 15 22 29	5 12 19 26

	July	August	September	October	November	December
Mon	4 11 18 25	1 8 15 22 29	5 12 19 26	3 10 17 24 31	7 14 21 28	5 12 19 26
Tue	5 12 19 26	2 9 16 23 30	6 13 20 27	4 11 18 25	1 8 15 22 29	6 13 20 27
Wed	6 13 20 27	3 10 17 24 31	7 14 21 28	5 12 19 26	2 9 16 23 30	7 14 21 28
Thu	7 14 21 28	4 11 18 25	1 8 15 22 29	6 13 20 27	3 10 17 24	1 8 15 22 29
Fri	1 8 15 22 29	5 12 19 26	2 9 16 23 30	7 14 21 28	4 11 18 25	2 9 16 23 30
Sat	2 9 16 23 30	6 13 20 27	3 10 17 24	1 8 15 22 29	5 12 19 26	3 10 17 24 31
Sun	3 10 17 24 31	7 14 21 28	4 11 18 25	2 9 16 23 30	6 13 20 27	4 11 18 25

Northern Ireland Year Planner 2004

	January	February	March	April	May	June
Tue						1
Wed						2
Thu	1 New Year's Day			1		3
Fri	2			2		4
Sat	3			3	1	5
Sun	4	1		4	2	6
Mon	5	2	1	5	3 Bank Holiday	7
Tue	6	3	2	6	4	8
Wed	7	4	3	7	5	9
Thu	8	5	4	8	6	10
Fri	9	6	5	9 Good Friday	7	11
Sat	10	7	6	10	8	12
Sun	11	8	7	11	9	13
Mon	12	9	8	12 Easter Monday	10	14
Tue	13	10	9	13	11	15
Wed	14	11	10	14	12	16
Thu	15	12	11	15	13	17
Fri	16	13	12	16	14	18
Sat	17	14	13	17	15	19
Sun	18	15	14	18	16	20
Mon	19	16	15	19	17	21
Tue	20	17	16	20	18	22
Wed	21	18	17 St. Patrick's Day	21	19	23
Thu	22	19	18	22	20	24
Fri	23	20	19	23	21	25
Sat	24	21	20	24	22	26
Sun	25	22	21	25	23	27
Mon	26	23	22	26	24	28
Tue	27	24	23	27	25	29
Wed	28	25	24	28	26	30
Thu	29	26	25	29	27	
Fri	30	27	26	30	28	
Sat	31	28	27		29	
Sun		29	28		30	
Mon			29		31 Bank Holiday	
Tue			30			
Wed			31			